P9-BJR-477

FOR REFERENCE

Do Not Take From This Room

Twentieth-Century Literary Criticism

Topics Volume

Guide to Gale Literary Criticism Series

For criticism on	Consult these Gale series
Authors now living or who died after December 31, 1959	*CONTEMPORARY LITERARY CRITICISM (CLC)*
Authors who died between 1900 and 1959	*TWENTIETH-CENTURY LITERARY CRITICISM (TCLC)*
Authors who died between 1800 and 1899	*NINETEENTH-CENTURY LITERATURE CRITICISM (NCLC)*
Authors who died between 1400 and 1799	*LITERATURE CRITICISM FROM 1400 TO 1800 (LC)* *SHAKESPEAREAN CRITICISM (SC)*
Authors who died before 1400	*CLASSICAL AND MEDIEVAL LITERATURE CRITICISM (CMLC)*
Black writers of the past two hundred years	*BLACK LITERATURE CRITICISM (BLC)*
Authors of books for children and young adults	*CHILDREN'S LITERATURE REVIEW (CLR)*
Dramatists	*DRAMA CRITICISM (DC)*
Hispanic writers of the late nineteenth and twentieth centuries	*HISPANIC LITERATURE CRITICISM (HLC)*
Poets	*POETRY CRITICISM (PC)*
Short story writers	*SHORT STORY CRITICISM (SSC)*
Major authors from the Renaissance to the present	*WORLD LITERATURE CRITICISM, 1500 TO THE PRESENT (WLC)*

ISSN • 0276-8178

R

Volume 54

Twentieth-Century Literary Criticism

Topics Volume

**Excerpts from Criticism of Various Topics
in Twentieth-Century Literature, including Literary
and Critical Movements, Prominent Themes and
Genres, Anniversary Celebrations, and Surveys
of National Literatures**

Laurie Di Mauro
Marie Lazzari
Editors

Joann Cerrito
Nancy Dziedzic
Jennifer Gariepy
Margaret Haerens
Thomas Ligotti
Brigham Narins
David Segal
Associate Editors

Gale Research Inc. • DETROIT • WASHINGTON, D.C. • LONDON

Riverside Community College
Library
DEC '98   4800 Magnolia Avenue
Riverside, California 92506

Ref
PN
771
T9
V. 54

STAFF

Laurie Di Mauro, Marie Lazzari, *Editors*

Joann Cerrito, Nancy Dziedzic, Jennifer Gariepy, Margaret A. Haerens, Thomas Ligotti, Brigham Narins, David Segal, *Associate Editors*

Pamela Willwerth Aue, Christine Bichler, Martha Bommarito, Matthew McDonough, *Assistant Editors*

Jeanne A. Gough, *Permissions & Production Manager*
Linda M. Pugliese, *Production Supervisor*
Donna Craft, Paul Lewon, Maureen A. Puhl, Camille P. Robinson, Sheila Walencewicz, *Editorial Associates*

Sandra C. Davis, *Permissions Supervisor (Text)*
Maria L. Franklin, Josephine M. Keene, Michele Lonoconus, Shalice Shah, Kimberly F. Smilay, *Permissions Associates*
Jennifer A. Arnold, Brandy C. Merritt, *Permissions Assistants*

Margaret A. Chamberlain, *Permissions Supervisor (Pictures)*
Pamela A. Hayes, Arlene Johnson, Keith Reed, Barbara A. Wallace, *Permissions Associates*
Susan Brohman, *Permissions Assistant*

Victoria B. Cariappa, *Research Manager*
Maureen Richards, *Research Supervisor*
Mary Beth McElmeel, Donna Melnychenko, Tamara C. Nott, Jaema Paradowski, *Editorial Associates*
Maria E. Bryson, *Editorial Assistant*

Mary Beth Trimper, *Production Director*
Catherine Kemp, *Production Assistant*

Cynthia Baldwin, *Production Design Manager*
Barbara J. Yarrow, *Graphic Services Supervisor*
Sherrell Hobbs, *Macintosh Artist*
Willie F. Mathis, *Camera Operator*

Since this page cannot legibly accommodate all copyright notices, the acknowledgments constitute an extension of the copyright notice.

While every effort has been made to ensure the reliability of the information presented in this publication, Gale Research Inc. neither guarantees the accuracy of the data contained herein nor assumes any responsibility for errors, omissions or discrepancies. Gale accepts no payment for listing, and inclusion in the publication of any organization, agency, institution, publication, service, or individual does not imply endorsement of the editors or publisher. Errors brought to the attention of the publisher and verified to the satisfaction of the publisher will be corrected in future editions.

The paper used in this publication meets the minimum requirements of American National Standard for Information Sciences—Permanence Paper for Printed Library Materials, ANSI Z39.48-1984. ∞™

This publication is a creative work fully protected by all applicable copyright laws, as well as by misappropriation, trade secret, unfair competition, and other applicable laws. The authors and editors of this work have added value to the underlying factual material herein through one or more of the following: unique and original selection, coordination, expression, arrangement, and classification of the information.

All rights to this publication will be vigorously defended.

Copyright © 1994
Gale Research Inc.
835 Penobscot Building
Detroit, MI 48226-4094

All rights reserved including the right of reproduction in whole or in part in any form.

Library of Congress Catalog Card Number 76-46132
ISBN 0-8103-2432-6
ISSN 0276-8178

Printed in the United States of America
Published simultaneously in the United Kingdom
by Gale Research International Limited
(An affiliated company of Gale Research Inc.)
10 9 8 7 6 5 4 3 2 1

The trademark **ITP** is used under license.

Contents

Preface   ix

Acknowledgments   xiii

American Black Humor Fiction

American Proletarian Literature

Art and Literature

Crime in Literature

Indian Literature in English

Preface

Since its inception more than fifteen years ago, *Twentieth-Century Literary Criticism* has been purchased and used by nearly 10,000 school, public, and college or university libraries. *TCLC* has covered more than 500 authors, representing 58 nationalities, and over 25,000 titles. No other reference source has surveyed the critical response to twentieth-century authors and literature as thoroughly as *TCLC*. In the words of one reviewer, "there is nothing comparable available." *TCLC* "is a gold mine of information—dates, pseudonyms, biographical information, and criticism from books and periodicals—which many libraries would have difficulty assembling on their own."

Scope of the Series

TCLC is designed to serve as an introduction to authors who died between 1900 and 1960 and to the most significant interpretations of these author's works. The great poets, novelists, short story writers, playwrights, and philosophers of this period are frequently studied in high school and college literature courses. In organizing and excerpting the vast amount of critical material written on these authors, *TCLC* helps students develop valuable insight into literary history, promotes a better understanding of the texts, and sparks ideas for papers and assignments. Each entry in *TCLC* presents a comprehensive survey of an author's career or an individual work of literature and provides the user with a multiplicity of interpretations and assessments. Such variety allows students to pursue their own interests; furthermore, it fosters an awareness that literature is dynamic and responsive to many different opinions.

Every fourth volume of *TCLC* is devoted to literary topics that cannot be covered under the author approach used in the rest of the series. Such topics include literary movements, prominent themes in twentieth-century literature, literary reaction to political and historical events, significant eras in literary history, prominent literary anniversaries, and the literatures of cultures that are often overlooked by English-speaking readers.

TCLC is designed as a companion series to Gale's *Contemporary Literary Criticism,* which reprints commentary on authors now living or who have died since 1960. Because of the different periods under consideration, there is no duplication of material between *CLC* and *TCLC*. For additional information about *CLC* and Gale's other criticism titles, users should consult the Guide to Gale Literary Criticism Series preceding the title page in this volume.

Coverage

Each volume of *TCLC* is carefully compiled to present:

- criticism of authors, or literary topics, representing a variety of genres and nationalities

- both major and lesser-known writers and literary works of the period

- 10-15 authors or 4-6 topics per volume

- individual entries that survey critical response to each author's work or each topic in literary history, including early criticism to reflect initial reactions; later criticism to represent any rise or decline in reputation; and current retrospective analyses.

Organization of This Book

An author entry consists of the following elements: author heading, biographical and critical introduction, list of principal works, excerpts of criticism (each preceded by an annotation and followed by a bibliographic citation), and a bibliography of further reading.

- The **Author Heading** consists of the name under which the author most commonly wrote, followed by birth and death dates. If an author wrote consistently under a pseudonym, the pseudonym will be listed in the author heading and the real name given in parentheses on the first line of the biographical and critical introduction. Also located at the beginning of the introduction to the author entry are any name variations under which an author wrote, including transliterated forms for authors whose languages use nonroman alphabets.

- The **Biographical and Critical Introduction** outlines the author's life and career, as well as the critical issues surrounding his or her work. References to past volumes of *TCLC* are provided at the beginning of the introduction. Additional sources of information in other biographical and critical reference series published by Gale, including *Short Story Criticism, Children's Literature Review, Contemporary Authors, Dictionary of Literary Biography,* and *Something about the Author,* are listed in a box at the end of the entry.

- Most *TCLC* entries include **Portraits** of the author. Many entries also contain reproductions of materials pertinent to an author's career, including manuscript pages, title pages, dust jackets, letters, and drawings, as well as photographs of important people, places, and events in an author's life.

- The **List of Principal Works** is chronological by date of first book publication and identifies the genre of each work. In the case of foreign authors with both foreign-language publications and English translations, the title and date of the first English-language edition are given in brackets. Unless otherwise indicated, dramas are dated by first performance, not first publication.

- Critical excerpts are prefaced by **Annotations** providing the reader with information about both the critic and the criticism that follows. Included are the critic's reputation, individual approach to literary criticism, and particular expertise in an author's works. Also noted are the relative importance of a work of criticism, the scope of the excerpt, and the growth of critical controversy or changes in critical trends regarding an author. In some cases, these annotations cross-reference excerpts by critics who discuss each other's commentary.

- **Criticism** is arranged chronologically in each author entry to provide a perspective on changes in critical evaluation over the years. All titles of works by the author featured in the entry are printed in boldface type to enable the user to easily locate discussion of particular works. Also for purposes of easier identification, the critic's name and the publication date of the essay are given at the beginning of each piece of criticism. Unsigned criticism is preceded by the title of the journal in which it appeared. Some of the excerpts in *TCLC* also contain translated material. Unless otherwise noted, translations in brackets are by the editors; translations in parentheses or continuous with the text are by the critic. Publication information (such as footnotes or page and line references to specific editions of works) have been deleted at the editor's discretion to provide smoother reading of the text.

- A complete **Bibliographic Citation** designed to facilitate location of the original essay or book follows each piece of criticism.

- An annotated list of **Further Reading** appearing at the end of each author entry suggests secondary sources on the author. In some cases it includes essays for which the editors could not obtain reprint rights.

Cumulative Indexes

- Each volume of *TCLC* contains a cumulative **Author Index** listing all authors who have appeared in Gale's Literary Criticism Series, along with cross references to such biographical series as *Contemporary Authors* and *Dictionary of Literary Biography*. For readers' convenience, a complete list of Gale titles included appears on the first page of the author index. Useful for locating authors within the various series, this index is particularly valuable for those authors who are identified by a certain period but who, because of their death dates, are placed in another, or for those authors whose careers span two periods. For example, F. Scott Fitzgerald is found in *TCLC*, yet a writer often associated with him, Ernest Hemingway, is found in *CLC*.

- Each *TCLC* volume includes a cumulative **Nationality Index** which lists all authors who have appeared in *TCLC* volumes, arranged alphabetically under their respective nationalities, as well as Topics volume entries devoted to particular national literatures.

- Each new volume in Gale's Literary Criticism Series includes a cumulative **Topic Index,** which lists all literary topics treated in *NCLC, TCLC, LC 1400-1800,* and the *CLC* yearbook.

- Each new volume of *TCLC*, with the exception of the Topics volumes, includes a **Title Index** listing the titles of all literary works discussed in the volume. In response to numerous suggestions from librarians, Gale has also produced a **Special Paperbound Edition** of the *TCLC* title index. This annual cumulation lists all titles discussed in the series since its inception and is issued with the first volume of *TCLC* published each year. Additional copies of the index are available on request. Librarians and patrons will welcome this separate index; it saves shelf space, is easy to use, and is recyclable upon receipt of the following year's cumulation. Titles discussed in the Topics volume entries are not included *TCLC* cumulative index.

Citing *Twentieth-Century Literary Criticism*

When writing papers, students who quote directly from any volume in Gale's literary Criticism Series may use the following general forms to footnote reprinted criticism. The first example pertains to materials drawn from periodicals, the second to material reprinted from books.

[1]T. S. Eliot, "John Donne," *The Nation and the Athenaeum,* 33 (9 June 1923), 321-32; excerpted and reprinted in *Literature Criticism from 1400 to 1800,* Vol. 10, ed. James E. Person, Jr. (Detroit: Gale Research, 1989), pp. 28-9.

[2]Clara G. Stillman, *Samuel Butler: A Mid-Victorian Modern* (Viking Press, 1932); excerpted and reprinted in *Twentieth-Century Literary Criticism,* Vol. 33, ed. Paula Kepos (Detroit: Gale Research, 1989), pp. 43-5.

Suggestions Are Welcome

In response to suggestions, several features have been added to *TCLC* since the series began, including annotations to excerpted criticism, a cumulative index to authors in all Gale literary criticism series, entries devoted to criticism on a single work by a major author, more extensive illustrations, and a title index listing all literary works discussed in the series since its inception.

Readers who wish to suggest authors or topics to appear in future volumes, or who have other suggestions, are cordially invited to write the editors.

Acknowledgments

The editors wish to thank the copyright holders of the excerpted criticism included in this volume, the permissions managers of many book and magazine publishing companies for assisting us in securing reprint rights, and Anthony Bogucki for assistance with copyright research. We are also grateful to the staffs of the Detroit Public Library, the Library of Congress, the University of Detroit Mercy Library, Wayne State University Purdy/Kresge Library Complex, and the University of Michigan Libraries for making their resources available to us. Following is a list of the copyright holders who have granted us permission to reprint material in this volume of *TCLC*. Every effort has been made to trace copyright, but if omissions have been made, please let us know.

COPYRIGHTED EXCERPTS IN *TCLC*, VOLUME 54, WERE REPRINTED FROM THE FOLLOWING PERIODICALS:

The American Scholar, v. 33, Autumn, 1964 for "Laughter in the Dark: The New Voice in American Fiction" by Ihab Hassan. Copyright © 1964, renewed 1992 by the author. Reprinted by permission of the author./ v. 26, Summer, 1957. Copyright © 1957, renewed 1985 by the United Chapters of the Phi Beta Kappa Society. Reprinted by permission of the publishers.—*The Annals of the American Academy of Political and Social Science,* v. 423, January, 1976 for "The Heritage of Cain: Crime in American Fiction" by M. E. Grenander. © 1976, by The American Academy of Political and Social Science. Reprinted by permission of the publisher and the author.—*The Antioch Review,* v. 1, December, 1941. Copyright 1941, renewed 1969 by the Antioch Review Inc. Reprinted by permission of the editors.—*Arizona Quarterly,* v. 30, Winter, 1974. Copyright © 1974 by *Arizona Quarterly.* Reprinted by permission of the publisher.—*Canadian Review of Comparative Literature,* v. X, June, 1983. © Canadian Comparative Literature Association. Reprinted by permission of the publisher.—*The Cimarron Review,* v. 20, July, 1972. Copyright © 1972 by the Board of Regents for Oklahoma State University. Reprinted by permission of the publisher.—*Contemporary Literature,* v. 15, Spring, 1974. © 1974 by the Regents of the University of Wisconsin. Reprinted by permission of The University of Wisconsin Press.—*Critique: Studies in Modern Fiction,* v. XXV, Winter, 1984. Copyright © 1984 Helen Dwight Reid Educational Foundation. Reprinted with permission of the Helen Dwight Reid Educational Foundation, published by Heldref Publications, 1319 18th Street, N.W., Washington, D.C. 20036-1802.—*Dissent,* v. XV, March-April, 1968 for "Anatomy of Black Humor" by Burton Feldman. © 1968, by Dissent Publishing Corporation. Reprinted by permission of the publisher and the author.—*English Institute Annual,* 1941 for "The Parallelism between Literature and the Arts" by René Wellek. Copyright 1942, renewed 1970, Columbia University Press, New York. Reprinted with permission of the publisher and the author.—*Humor,* v. 4, 1991 for "The Schlemiezel: Black Humor and the Shtetl Tradition" by Jay Boyer. © 1991 Mouton de Gruyter. Reprinted by permission of the publisher and the author.—*Indian Express,* for "India's Glorious New Chapter" by Binoo K. John. Reprinted by permission of the publisher and the author.—*Journal of the Karnataka University,* v. XVI, 1972.—*Midwestern Miscellany,* v. 17, 1989. Copyright 1989 by The Society for the Study of Midwestern Literature. All rights reserved. Reprinted by permission of the publisher.—*The Minnesota Review,* v. 24, Spring, 1985 for "Proletarian Literature and Feminism: The Gastonia Novels and Feminist Protest" by Joseph R. Urgo. © 1985 *The Minnesota Review.* Reprinted by permission of the author.—*The New York Times Book Review,* September 27, 1964. Copyright © 1964, renewed 1992 by The New York Times Company. Reprinted by permission of the publisher.—*Partisan Review,* v. XLIII, 1976 for "Black Humor and History: Fiction in the Sixties" by Morris Dickstein. Copyright © 1977 by the author. Reprinted by permission of the author.—*Renascence,* v. XXXII, Winter, 1980. © copyright, 1980, Marquette University Press. Reprinted by permission of the publisher.—*The Saturday Review,* New York, v. XLVIII, June 6, 1964. © 1964, renewed 1992 *Saturday Review* magazine.—*The Sewanee Review,* v. LIII, Spring, 1945 for "Poetry and Painting" by John Peale Bishop. Copyright 1945, renewed 1973 by The University of the South. Reprinted with the permission of the editor of *The Sewanee Review./* v. LIII, Spring, 1945. Copyright 1945, renewed 1973 by The University of the South.

Reprinted with the permission of the editor of *The Sewanee Review.—The Southern Review,* Louisiana State University, v. XVI, Autumn, 1980 for " 'Folded in a Single Party': Agrarians and Proletarians" by Joel D. Wingard. Copyright, 1980, by Louisiana State University. Reprinted by permission of the author.—*Theatre Journal,* v. 34, May, 1982. © 1982, University and College Theatre Association of the American Theatre Association. Reprinted by permission of the publisher.—*The Yale Review,* v. XXVIII, December, 1938. Copyright 1938, renewed 1966, by Yale University. Reprinted by permission of the editors.—*Zeit schrift für Anglistik und Amerikanistik,* v. 33, January, 1985. Reprinted by permission of the publisher.

COPYRIGHTED EXCERPTS IN *TCLC,* VOLUME 54, WERE REPRINTED FROM THE FOLLOWING BOOKS:

Alphonso-Karkala, John B. From *Indo-English Literature in the Nineteenth Century.* University of Mysore, 1970. Copyright © 1970, John B. Alphonso-Karkala.—Barth, John. From *The Floating Opera.* Appleton, Century Crofts, Inc., 1956. Copyright © 1956, 1967, 1988 by John Barth. All rights reserved.—Borowitz, Albert. From *A Gallery of Sinister Perspectives: Ten Crimes and a Scandal.* The Kent State University Press, 1982. Copyright © 1982 by The Kent State University Press, Kent, Ohio 44242. All rights reserved. Reprinted by permission of the author.—Breton, André. From "Preface, 'Anthologie de L'humour noir'," in *Black Humor: Critical Essays.* Edited by Alan R. Pratt. Garland Publishing, Inc., 1993. © 1993 Alan R. Pratt. All rights reserved. Reprinted by permission of the publisher.—Cook, Sylvia Jenkins. From *From Tobacco Road to Route 66: The Southern Poor White in Fiction.* University of North Carolina Press, 1976. Copyright © 1976 by The University of North Carolina Press. All rights reserved. Reprinted by permission of the publisher and the author.—DeVoto, Bernard. From *Forays and Rebuttals.* Little, Brown, and Company, 1936. Copyright, 1936, by Bernard DeVoto. Renewed 1964 by Avis M. DeVoto. All rights reserved. Reprinted by permission of Little, Brown and Company.—Farrell, James T. From "The Categories of 'Bourgeois' and 'Proletarian'," in *A Note on Literary Criticism.* Vanguard Press, 1936. Copyright, 1936, by Vanguard Press, Inc. Renewed 1963 by James T. Farrell. Reprinted by permission of the Literary Estate of James T. Farrell.—Ferrari, Arthur C. From "Proletarian Literature: A Case of Convergence of Political and Literary Radicalism," in *Culture Politics: Radical Movements in Modern History.* Edited by Jerold M. Starr. Praeger, 1985. © 1985 by Praeger Publishers. All rights reserved. Reprinted by permission of Greenwood Publishing Group, Inc., Westport, CT.—Franklin, H. Bruce. From *Prison Literature in America: The Victim as Criminal and Artist.* Revised edition. Oxford University Press, 1989. Copyright © 1978, 1989 by Oxford University Press, Inc. All rights reserved. Reprinted by permission of the publisher.—Freeman, Joseph. From an introduction to *Proletarian Literature in the United States: An Anthology.* Edited by Granville Hicks and others. International Publishers, 1935. Copyright, 1935, renewed 1963, by International Publishers Co., Inc. Reprinted by permission of the publisher.—Friedman, Bruce Jay. From a foreword to *Black Humor.* Edited by Bruce Jay Friedman. Corgi Books, 1965. Reprinted by permission of the author.—Frye, Northrop. From *Myth and Metaphor: Selected Essays, 1974-1988.* Edited by Robert D. Denham. University Press of Virginia, 1990. Copyright © 1990 by the Rector and Visitors of the University of Virginia. Reprinted by permission of the publisher.—Gemmill, Janet P. From "The City as Jungle in the Indo-English Novel," in *India: Cultural Patterns and Processes.* Edited by Allen G. Noble and Ashok K. Dutt. Westview Press, 1982. Copyright © 1982 by Westview Press, Inc. All rights reserved. Reprinted by permission of the editors.—Heller, Joseph. From *Catch-22.* Simon and Schuster, 1961. Copyright © 1955, 1961 by Joseph Heller. All rights reserved.—Iyengar, K. R. Srinivasa. From "India," in *The Commonwealth Pen: An Introduction to the Literature of the British Commonwealth.* Edited by A. L. McLeod. Cornell, 1961. © 1961 by Cornell University. Renewed 1984 by A. L. McLeod. Used by permission of the publisher, Cornell University Press.—Jussawalla, Feroza F. From *Family Quarrels: Towards a Criticism of Indian Writing in English.* Lang, 1985. © Peter Lang Publishing, Inc., New York, 1985. All rights reserved. Reprinted by permission of the publisher.—Kalikoff, Beth. From *Murder and Moral Decay in Victorian Popular Literature.* UMI Research Press, 1986. Copyright © 1986 Rita Beth Kalikoff. All rights reserved. Reprinted by permission of the author.—Kunitz, Stanley. From *A Kind of Order, A Kind of Folly.* Atlantic-Little Brown, 1975. Copyright © 1965 by Stanley Kunitz. Reprinted by permission of the author.—Markandaya, Kamala. From "One Pair of Eyes: Some Random Reflections," in *The Commonwealth Writer Overseas: Themes of Exile and Expatriation.* Edited by

Alastair Niven. M. Didier, 1976. © Librairie Marcel Didier S. A., Bruxelles, 1976. Reprinted by permission of the author.—Meyers, Jeffrey. From *Painting and the Novel.* Manchester University Press, 1975. © 1975 Jeffrey Meyers. Reprinted by permission of the publisher.—Mitchell, W. J. T. From "Going too Far with the Sister Arts," in *Space, Time, Image, Sign: Essays on Literature and the Visual Arts.* Edited by James A. W. Heffernan. Lang, 1987. © Peter Lang Publishing, Inc., New York, 1987. All rights reserved. Reprinted by permission of the publisher.—Mukařofský, Jan. From *The World and Verbal Art.* Edited and translated by John Burbank and Peter Steiner. Yale University Press, 1977. Copyright © 1977 by Yale University. All rights reserved. Reprinted by permission of the author.—Mukherjee, Meenakshi. From *The Twice Born Fiction: Themes and Techniques of the Indian Novel in English.* Second edition. Heinemann Educational Books, New Delhi, 1971. © Meenakshi Mukherjee 1971. Reprinted by permission of the author.—Naik, M. K. From "The Achievement of Indian Drama in English," in *Perspectives on Indian Drama in English.* Edited by M. K. Naik and S. Mokashi-Punekar. Oxford University Press, 1977. © Karnatak University, Dharwar 1977.—Nandakumar, Prema. From "English," in *Indian Literature Since Independence.* Edited by K. R. Srinivasa Iyengar. Sahitya Akademi, 1973. © Sahitya Akademi, 1973. Reprinted by permission of the publisher.—Narayan, R. K. From "English in India," in *Commonwealth Literature: Unity and Diversity in a Common Culture.* Edited by John Press. Heinemann, 1965. © University of Leeds 1965. Reprinted by permission of Wallace Literary Agency, Inc.—Nemerov, Howard. From *Figures of Thought: Speculations on the Meaning of Poetry & Other Essays.* Godine, 1978. Copyright © 1978 by Howard Nemerov. Reprinted by permission of David R. Godine, Publisher, Inc.—Parameswaran, Uma. From *A Study of Representative Indo-English Novelists.* Vikas Publishing House Pvt Ltd., 1976. Copyright © Uma Parameswaran, 1976. Reprinted by permission of the publisher.—Parthasarathy, R. From "Indian English Verse: The Making of a Tradition," in *Alien Voice: Perspectives on Commonwealth Literature.* Edited by Avadhesh K. Srivastava. Print House (India), 1981. © 1981 A. K. Srivastava. All rights reserved. Reprinted by permission of Print House (India), 5T.B. Sapru Marg, Lucknow-1.—Pratt, Alan R. From " 'People Are Equally Wretched Everywhere': 'Candide', Black Humor and the Existential Absurd," in *Black Humor: Critical Essays.* Edited by Alan R. Pratt. Garland Publishing, Inc., 1993. © 1993 Alan R. Pratt. All rights reserved. Reprinted by permission of the publisher.—Praz, Mario. From *Mnemosyne: The Parallel Between Literature and the Visual Arts.* Bollingen Series XXXV. Princeton University Press, 1970. Copyright © 1970 by the Trustees of the National Gallery of Art, Washington, DC. Reprinted with permission of the National Gallery of Art.—Rajan, Balachandra. From "Identity and Nationality," in *Commonwealth Literature: Unity and Diversity in a Common Culture.* Edited by John Press. Heinemann, 1965. © University of Leeds 1965. Reprinted by permission of the author.—Rao, A. V. Krishna. From *The Indo-Anglian Novel and the Changing Tradition: A Study of the Novels of Mulk Raj Anand, Kamala Markandaya, R. K. Narayan and Raja Rao, 1930-64.* Rao and Raghavan, 1972. Copyright © 1972, by A. V. Krishna Rao. Reprinted by permission of the author.—Renza, Louis A. From "Response to W. J. T. Mitchell," in *Space, Time, Image, Sign: Essays on Literature and the Visual Arts.* Edited by James A. W. Heffernan. Lang, 1987. © Peter Lang Publishing, Inc., New York 1987. All rights reserved. Reprinted by permission of the publisher.—Rideout, Walter B. From *The Radical Novel in the United States, 1900-1954: Some Interrelations of Literature and Society.* Cambridge, Mass.: Harvard University Press, 1956. Copyright © 1956 by the President and Fellows of Harvard College. Renewed 1984 by Walter Bates Rideout. Reprinted by permission of the author.—Sagarin, Edward. From *Raskolnikov and Others: Literary Images of Crime, Punishment, Redemption, and Atonement.* St. Martin's Press, 1981. Copyright © 1981 by St. Martin's Press, Inc. All rights reserved. Reprinted with permission of the publisher.—Scholes, Robert. From *The Fabulators.* Oxford University Press, 1967. Copyright © 1963, 1966, 1967 by Robert Scholes. Reprinted by permission of the author.—Schulz, Max F. From *Black Humor Fiction of the Sixties: A Puralistic Definition of Man and His World.* Ohio University Press, 1973. © 1973 by Max F. Schulz. All rights reserved. Reprinted by permission of the author.—Sypher, Wylie. From *Rococo to Cubism in Art and Literature.* Random House, 1960. © copyright, 1960, by Wylie Sypher. Renewed 1988 by Gail S. Jacob and Lucy J. Sypher. All rights reserved. Reprinted by permission of Random House, Inc.—Thurber, James. From "Voices of Revolution," in *The Critic as Artist: Essays on Books 1920-1970.* Edited by Gilbert A. Harrison. Liveright, 1972. Copyright © 1936 James Thurber. Copyright © 1984 Helen Thurber and Rosemary Thurber. Copyright © 1972 by Liveright Publishing. All rights reserved. Reprinted by permission of the Literary Estate of James Thurber.—Verghese, C. Paul. From *Problems of the Indian Creative Writer in English.* Somaiya Publications PVT LTD, 1971. © 1971 by C. Paul Verghese. Reprinted by permission of the publisher.—Walsh, William. From "Fiction: The Founding Fathers-Mulk Raj Anand, Raja Rao and R. K. Narayan," in *Indian Literature in English.* Longman, 1990. © Longman Group UK Limited 1990. All rights reserved. Published in the United States in *R. K. Narayan: A Critical Appreciation.* University of Chicago Press, 1982. © 1982 William Walsh. All rights reserved. Reprinted by permission of William Heinemann Ltd. In the United States and Canada by the University of Chicago Press.—Weber, Brom. From "The Mode of 'Black Humor'," in *The Comic Imagination in American Literature.* Edited by Louis D. Rubin, Jr. Rutgers University Press, 1973. Copyright © 1973 by Rutgers University, the State University of New Jersey. All rights reserved. Reprinted by permission of the author.—Williams, Adelia V. From *The Double Cipher: Encounter Between Word and Image in Bonnefoy, Tardieu and Michaux.* Lang, 1990. © Peter Lang Publishing, Inc., New York 1990. All rights reserved. Reprinted by permission of the publisher.—Ziolkowski, Theodore. From *Dimensions of the Modern Novel: German Texts and European Contexts.* Princeton University Press, 1969. Copyright © 1969 by Princeton University Press. © 1979 assigned to Theodore Ziolkowski. All rights reserved. Excerpts reprinted by permission of the author.

PHOTOGRAPHS AND ILLUSTRATIONS APPEARING IN *TCLC*, VOLUME 54, WERE RECEIVED FROM THE FOLLOWING SOURCES:

©Jerry Bauer: **pp. 5, 11, 22, 43, 49, 70;** The Estate of Alexander Gotfryd: **p. 15;** Photograph by Gerard Malanga: **p. 36;** Photograph by Joel Rubiner: **p. 60;** Photograph by Lynn Sweigart: **p. 76;** Josephson Collection, Kansas College, University of Kansas Libraries: **p. 140;** The New Theatre League Collection, Special Collectiions, The New York Public Library: **p. 153;** ©1994 Artists Rights Society, NY/ADAGP, Paris: **p. 204;** ©1994 Demart Pro Arte/Artist Rights Society, NY: **p. 208;** ©1994 Artists Rights Society, NY/SPADEM, Paris: **pp. 223, 227;** Violette Leduc Collection: **p. 255;** Jacket of *Native Son,* by Richard Wright. Harper, 1941. Reprinted by permission of HarperCollins Publishers, Inc.: **p. 267.**

American Black Humor Fiction

INTRODUCTION

In American literature the term "black humor" is associated with a group of novelists, including John Barth, Thomas Pynchon, Joseph Heller, Ken Kesey, Bruce Jay Friedman, William S. Burroughs, Kurt Vonnegut, and Vladimir Nabokov, whose works combined a frenetic comic exuberance with a profound sense of alienation, despair, and absurdity. Countering the optimism that is often thought to characterize the Eisenhower and Kennedy eras, black humorists trained a cynical eye on America's sense of euphoria and omnipotence following its victory in World War II, ridiculing the ascendancy of complacent idealism and a consumer culture. Their criticism, however, did not take the form of traditional satire. In black humor novels, the comic depiction of human folly and absurdity is not redeemed by a grounding in traditional moral codes. Commentators observe that these works are characterized in large measure by nihilism and an absurdist conception of the world as ultimately meaningless. Most critics agree that the seminal black humor novel in American fiction is Joseph Heller's *Catch-22* (1961), a wildly comic and misanthropic portrayal of the American military in World War II. Other black humor novels which garnered critical praise—and generated considerable controversy—include Nabokov's *Lolita* (1955), Burroughs's *The Naked Lunch* (1959), and Kesey's *One Flew over the Cuckoo's Nest* (1963). The subject matter of these novels was offensive to mainstream readers and some were published only after censorship battles in court. While the aggressively experimental spirit of these novels tended to limit their popular appeal, black humor achieved a wider diffusion in American culture through such film adaptations as *Lonelyhearts* (1958), *The Magic Christian* (1969), and *One Flew over the Cuckoo's Nest* (1975). In spite of the widespread dissemination of black humor in contemporary American culture, critics disagree strongly about its authenticity as a literary genre, with many arguing that it is too easily conflated with Existentialism and the Theater of the Absurd, which share black humor's pessimism and anxiety about the value and meaning of modern existence. Others assert that black humor is generically distinct from satire and other forms of humor and represents a uniquely American conception of the absurd.

REPRESENTATIVE WORKS

Albee, Edward
The Zoo Story (drama) 1959
The American Dream (drama) 1961
Who's Afraid of Virginia Woolf? (drama) 1962
Tiny Alice (drama) 1964

Barth, John
The Floating Opera (novel) 1956
The End of the Road (novel) 1958
The Sot-Weed Factor (novel) 1960
Giles Goat-Boy; or, The Revised New Syllabus (novel) 1966
Lost in the Funhouse: Fiction for Print, Tape, Live Voice (short stories) 1968

Barthelme, Donald
Come Back, Dr. Caligari (short stories) 1964
Unspeakable Practices, Unnatural Acts (short stories) 1968
City Life (short stories) 1971
Sadness (short stories) 1972

Burroughs, William S.
Junky (novel) 1953
The Naked Lunch (novel) 1959
The Soft Machine (novel) 1961
The Ticket That Exploded (novel) 1962
Nova Express (novel) 1964

Coover, Robert
The Origin of the Brunists (novel) 1966
The Universal Baseball Association, Inc., J. Henry Waugh, Prop. (novel) 1968
Pricksongs and Descants (short stories) 1969
The Public Burning (novel) 1977
Gerald's Party (novel) 1985

Donleavy, J. P.
The Ginger Man (novel) 1955
A Singular Man (novel) 1963
The Beastly Beatitudes of Balthazar B (novel) 1968
A Fairy Tale of New York (novel) 1973

Friedman, Bruce J.
Stern (novel) 1962
A Mother's Kisses (novel) 1964
The Dick (novel) 1970
About Harry Towns (novel) 1974
Tokyo Woes (novel) 1985

Gaddis, William
The Recognitions (novel) 1955
JR (novel) 1975
Carpenter's Gothic (novel) 1985

Hawkes, John
The Cannibal (novel) 1949
The Beetle Leg (novel) 1951
The Lime Twig (novel) 1961
Second Skin (novel) 1964
The Blood Oranges (novel) 1971

Heller, Joseph
Catch-22 (novel) 1961
Something Happened (novel) 1974
Good as Gold (novel) 1979

    No Laughing Matter (novel) 1986

Kesey, Ken
    One Flew over the Cuckoo's Nest (novel) 1962
    Sometimes a Great Notion (novel) 1964

Nabokov, Vladimir
    Lolita (novel) 1955
    Pnin (novel) 1957
    Ada; or, Ardor: A Family Chronicle (novel) 1969
    Transparent Things (novel) 1972

Purdy, James
    Malcolm (novel) 1959
    The Nephew (novel) 1960
    Cabot Wright Begins (novel) 1964
    Eustace Chisholm and the Works (novel) 1967

Pynchon, Thomas
    V. (novel) 1963
    The Crying of Lot 49 (novel) 1966
    Gravity's Rainbow (novel) 1973
    Vineland (novel) 1990

Roth, Philip
    Portnoy's Complaint (novel) 1969
    Our Gang (novel) 1971
    The Breast (novel) 1972
    The Great American Novel (novel) 1973

Southern, Terry
    Candy (novel) 1958
    The Magic Christian (novel) 1959
    Red-Dirt Marijuana and Other Tastes (novel) 1967

Vonnegut, Kurt
    Mother Night (novel) 1962
    Cat's Cradle (novel) 1963
    Slaughterhouse-Five (novel) 1969
    Breakfast of Champions; or, Goodbye, Blue Monday!
      (novel) 1973
    Slapstick; or, Lonesome No More! (novel) 1976

West, Nathanael
    The Dream Life of Balso Snell (novel) 1931
    Miss Lonelyhearts (novel) 1933
    A Cool Million (novel) 1934
    The Day of the Locust (novel) 1939

CHARACTERISTICS OF BLACK HUMOR

André Breton

[Breton was a French poet, prose writer, and critic. Best known as the founder of the Surrealist movement, he was strongly influenced by the psychoanalytic theories of Sigmund Freud, the poetry of Arthur Rimbaud, and the post-World War I movement of Dada. He considered reason and logic as merely repressive functions of the mind, and advocated the use of "automatic writing," a method related to the psychoanalytical technique of free association. In 1939 Breton published Anthologie de L'humour noir (Anthology of Black Humor), *and is frequently cited as the first critic to employ the term "black humor" to refer to a literary movement. In the*

following excerpt, his preface to that volume, Breton defines black humor as a gesture of revolt, bolstering his explanation with citations of Baudelaire, Rimbaud, Hegel, and Freud.]

> "In order to have the comic, that is, the emanation, explosion, unloosing of the comic," says Baudelaire, "it is necessary. . . ."

EMANATION, EXPLOSION: It is striking to find these same two words associated in Rimbaud and in the heart of a poem which could not be more lavish with black humor. (Indeed, it is a question of the last poem we have from him, in which "farcical, thoroughly deranged expression" reappears, condensed in the extreme, supreme, from efforts whose purpose has been its affirmation, then its negation):

> "Dream"
> We are hungry in the barracks;
> It's true. . . .
> Emanations, explosions,
> A genius: I am Gruyère.

Chance combination, involuntary memory, citation? To decide, one would have to have carried out a fairly extensive exegesis of this poem, the most difficult in the French language, but this exegesis has not even been undertaken. As it is, such a verbal coincidence is nonetheless significant. It reveals, in both poets, the same preoccupation with conditions which are atmospheric, so to speak, in which the mysterious exchange of humorous pleasure can take place among men. To this exchange has been attached, for a century and a half, a growing price which tends to make it today the source of the only deluxe intellectual commerce. It is less and less certain, given the specific requirements of modern sensitivities, that those poetic, artistic, and scientific works, as well as those philosophical and social systems which are devoid of this sort of humor do not leave a great deal to be desired, and are not condemned to perish more or less rapidly. The issue here is of securities not only rising against all others, but also capable of out-performing all the others to the point that a good number of them cease to be quoted anywhere. We touch here on a burning subject; we advance in a land all in flame; we have all the wind of passion alternately for and against us as soon as we think of raising the veil from this humor whose obvious products, however, we succeed in isolating in literature, in art, in life, with unique satisfaction. Indeed, more or less obscurely, we have the sense of a hierarchy whose highest degree would be assured to the man with an integral possession of humor. It is in this very sense that any global definition of humor escapes us and will escape us probably for a long time, by virtue of the principle that "man tends naturally to defy that which is at the limit of his understanding" [Armand Petitjean, *Imagination and Realization,* 1936]. In the same way that "upper initiation, which only a few elite souls attain, as the ultimate postulate of High Knowledge, scarcely manages to make understood how Divinity can explain itself" (the High Cabala, reduction of High Knowledge to the terrestrial plane, is held jealously secret by the upper initiates), it cannot be a matter of explicating humor and making it serve didactic ends. One might just as well try to draw an ethics for life from suicide. "There is nothing," [stated

Pierre Piobb in *The Mysteries of the Gods,* 1909], "that intelligent humor cannot resolve in bursts of laughter, not even nothingness . . . , laughter, considered as one of man's most extravagant prodigalities all the way to debauchery, is on the edge of nothingness, gives us nothingness as collateral security." One can imagine the advantage humor would be likely to take, among others, from its very definition, and especially from this one.

One should not be astonished under these circumstances if the various inquiries undertaken up until today on the subject have produced the most paltry results. To one of them, very badly conducted, moreover, in the review *Adventure,* in November 1921, M. Paul Valéry replied:

> The word *humor* is not translatable. If it were, the French would not use it. But they use it precisely because of the indeterminacy they grant it, which makes it a very suitable word for the dispute over tastes and colors. Each sentence containing it changes its sense, so much so that this sense itself is, strictly speaking, only the statistical entirety of all the sentences which contain it and which will contain it.

This obstinant position of absolute reticence is still, in the last analysis, preferable to the prolixity which M. Aragon displayed when, in his *Treatise on Style,* he seemed to have assigned himself the task of exhausting the subject (as one drowns a fish). Humor, however, has not forgiven him and there has been no one since whom humor has more radically abandoned:

> You would like the other anatomical parts of humor? Well, Sir, take a finger raised to ask for permission to speak—you will have a head of hair. Eyes—cones for ice cream. Ears—hunting lodges. The right arm, called symmetry, represents the law courts; the left is the arm of a man who has lost his right arm. . . . It is what is missing in soups, in chickens, in symphony orchestras. On the other hand, it is not missing in pavement-workers, in elevators or in cocked hats. It has been pointed out in kitchen equipment; it has made its appearance in bad taste; it has its winter quarters in fashion. . . . What are its haunts? In optical effects. Its home? Little Saint-Thomas. Its favorite authors? A certain Binet-Valmer. Its weakness? Twilights when they are really a fried egg. It does not scorn the serious note. It resembles a great deal, to sum up, the aiming device of a gun.

A good exercise by the best student in the senior class who set for himself this theme like any other and who has only an exterior view of humor. All this juggling is only, once again, avoidance. It is rare that the subject has been squeezed so closely other than by M. Leon Pierre-Quint, who, in his work, *Le Comte de Lautréamont and God,* presents humor as a way of affirming, beyond "the absolute revolt of adolescence and the interior revolt of adulthood," *a superior revolt of the mind.*

In order to have humor . . . the question remains unanswered. However, one can consider that Hegel pushed humor into a decisive step in the domain of knowledge when it was raised to the concept of *objective humor.* "Romantic art," he said,

> had as a fundamental principle the concentration of the soul in itself, which, finding that the real world did not correspond perfectly to its inmost nature, remained indifferent toward it. This opposition developed in the period of romantic art, to the point that we have seen interest settle sometimes on accidents of the exterior world, sometimes on caprices of personality. But, now, if this interest goes so far as to cause the mind to be absorbed in exterior contemplation and at the same time to cause humor, while conserving its subjective and thoughtful character, to be captivated by the object and its real form, we obtain in this intimate penetration a *humor* in some way *objective.*

We have stated [in *Political Position of Surrealism*] that the black sphinx of objective humor could not fail to encounter along that road smothered in dust, the road of the future, the white sphinx of *objective chance,* and that all ulterior human creation would be the fruit of their embrace.

Let us observe in passing that the positions assigned by Hegel to the various arts (poetry, considered as the only *universal art,* commands them, regulating their proceedings by its own in so far as it alone is able to represent the *successive situations* of life) suffice to explain that the form of humor which interests us made its appearance in poetry much earlier than, for example, in painting. A satirical, moralizing intent exerts a degrading influence on almost all the works of the past which, in some respect, could derive from this humor and exposes them as leaning toward caricature. At the most would one be tempted to make exception for some of Hogarth's, of Goya's, and to reserve judgment on some others where humor is rather hinted at, and can only be mentioned as hypothetical, such as almost the whole of Seurat's painted work. It appears that the triumph of humor in its pure and manifest state on the plastic plane must be located in a time much closer to us and must recognize for its first inspired master the Mexican artist Jose Guadalupe Posada who, in his admirable woodcuts of a popular nature, renders us sensitive to the movements of the revolution of 1910. (The shades of Villa and de Fierro should be interrogated concurrently with these compositions on what may well be the passage of humor from speculation to action. Mexico, with its splendid funeral toys, asserts itself, moreover, as the preferred land of black humor). Since then, this humor has behaved in painting as in a conquered land. Its black grass has not stopped crackling everywhere that Max Ernst's horse, "The Bride of the Wind," has passed. Within the limits of the book, there is nothing in this respect more perfect, more exemplary, than his three novels in "collages": *The Headless Woman, Dream of a Little Girl Who Wanted to Become a Carmelite, A Week of Goodness* or *The Seven Deadly Elements.*

The cinema, to the extent that not only like poetry it represents the successive situations of life, but, further, that it claims to account for their sequence, and, to the extent that, to stir the audience, it is condemned to lean toward

> **To take part in the black tournament of humor, it is indeed necessary to have passed through numerous qualifying trials. Black humor is bounded by too many things, such as stupidity, skeptical irony, joking without seriousness . . . (the enumeration would be long), but it is pre-eminently the mortal enemy of sentimentality. . . .**
>
> *—André Breton*

extreme solutions, had to encounter humor almost at the first attempt. The first comedies of Mack Sennett, certain films of Chaplin (*Charlie Escapes, The Pilgrim*), the unforgettable Fatty and Picratt, led a line which necessarily had to end up in the midnight bright and flimsy *Million Dollar Legs* and *Animal Crackers* and in those excursions deep into the mental cave, Fingal's as well as Pouzzoles', *The Andalousian Dog* and *The Age of Gold* of Buñuel and Dali, passing through the *Entr'acte* of Picabia. "It is probably time," said Freud, "to become familiar with certain characteristics of humor."

> Humor has not only something liberating, analogous to that of wit and of the comic, but also something sublime and elevated, traits which are not found in those other two orders of the acquisition of pleasure through intellectual activity. The sublime evidently derives from the triumph of narcissism, from the invulnerability of the ego which affirms itself victoriously. The ego refuses to let itself be broken into, to let suffering impose exterior reality on it. It refuses to admit that the shocks of the exterior world can touch it; much more, it shows that they can even become for it the sources of pleasure.

Freud gives a coarse but sufficient example of this: the condemned man led to the scaffold on a Monday calls out: "Here is a week that is beginning well!" We know that at the end of Freud's analysis of humor, he declares he sees in it a way of thinking which tends toward reducing *the expense necessitated by sorrow.* "We attribute to this rather weak pleasure—without knowing very well why—a character of *high value;* we feel it as particularly apt to free us and to exalt us." According to him, the secret of the humoristic attitude would lie in the extreme ability some beings have, in the case of a serious threat, of displacing the psychic accent from their ego to their superego, the latter conceived of genetically as the heir of parental pressures ("it often holds the ego under a severe tutelage, continuing to treat it as formerly the parents—or the father—treated the child"). It has seemed interesting to us to confront with this thesis a certain number of particular attitudes which are dependent on humor, and on texts where this humor is found carried in literature to its highest degree of expression. With a view to their reduction to a common, fundamental principle, we believed we could use the Freudian vocabulary for greater convenience in our ex-

pose, without prejudice to the reservations which the necessarily artificial distinction between the id, ego, and superego requires in Freud.

We do not deny that we have brought great bias to our choice, so true is it that such a propensity appears to us the only one appropriate for such a subject. The greatest fear, the only cause for regret could be, as it happens, of not having shown ourselves particular enough. To take part in the black tournament of humor, it is indeed necessary to have passed through numerous qualifying trials. Black humor is bounded by too many things, such as stupidity, skeptical irony, joking without seriousness . . . (the enumeration would be long), but it is pre-eminently the mortal enemy of sentimentality with its air of being perpetually at bay—sentimentality always with a blue background—and of a certain short-term fantasy, which is presented too often as poetry, and which persists, very much in vain, in trying to submit the mind to its transitory artifices, and which probably will not for much longer have to hold up against the sun its crowned slut's head among the other poppy seeds.

> *André Breton, "Preface, 'Anthologie de L'humour noir'," in* Black Humor: Critical Essays, *edited by Alan R. Pratt, Garland Publishing, Inc., 1993, pp. 11-18.*

Bruce Jay Friedman

[Friedman is an American novelist, short story writer, scriptwriter, dramatist, editor, and critic whose work is frequently associated with black humor. After the publication in 1965 of his Black Humor, *an anthology of American novelists such as Thomas Pynchon, Joseph Heller, J. P. Donleavy, and John Barth, the term "black humor" gained currency among critics and was recognized as a major trend in American literature of the 1950s and 1960s. In the following preface to that anthology, Friedman identifies some central characteristics of black humor, such as a perception of the absurdity of contemporary American society.]*

It is called "Black Humor" and I think I would have more luck defining an elbow or a corned-beef sandwich. I am not, for one thing, even sure it is black. It might be fuchsia or eggshell and now that I look at the table of contents [of *Black Humor*] I think some of it is in brown polka dots. My story, for example, is a brilliant midnight blue with matching ruffles around the edges. I certainly know what color it is since I did the coloring on this one myself and did not bring in a decorator as is my usual custom.

I am not sure of very much and I think it is true of the writers in this volume that they are not sure of very much either. They have some pretty strong notions, however, and one of mine is that the work under discussion, if not black, is some fairly dark-hued color. The humor part of the definition is probably accurate although I doubt that the writers here are bluff and hearty joke-tellers who spend a lot of time at discotheques. Invite them all to a party and you would probably find a great deal of brooding and sulking. At no time during the evening would they circle round the piano to sing hit tunes from Jerome Kern musicals. I think there would be many furtive glances about the room, each writer eyeing his neighbor suspiciously. One might suddenly fly through an open window, but only after carefully checking to see that the drop was shallow. For all I know one might seize another and cane him soundly about the shoulders as George Washington did to irreverent newspaper editors. They might all begin to cry, although I don't think so, for if there is a despair in this work, it is a tough, resilient brand and might very well end up in a Faulknerian horselaugh.

There would, in other words, be a certain resistance to the idea of lumping together thirteen writers with thirteen separate, completely private and unique visions, who in so many ways have nothing at all to do with one another and would not know or perhaps even understand one another's work if they tripped over it. And it is true that when you read through the work, it is, on the one hand, the separateness that strikes you as much as the similarity. You have storytellers in the old tradition here and you have others who will tell you to take your plot machinery and stick it in your ear. You have writers who know exactly what they are doing and others who do not have the faintest idea and are finding out in rather brilliant fashion as they go along. You have John Barth coming at you out of the late seventeenth century, J. P. Donleavy working his way through some insanely beautiful Irish song and Nabokov demoniacally using muscles no one else is blessed with. There is Thomas Pynchon appearing out of nowhere with a vision so contemporary it makes your nose bleed and there is Celine who reminds you that he thought all your thoughts, worked the same beat, was dumbfounded as many times a day as you are, long before you were born.

So you have thirteen separate writers who could not care less about one another and are certainly not going to attend any bi-monthly meetings to discuss policy and blackball new members. But there are some similarities, some stubborn echoes bouncing from one to the other, and I had better hurry up and outline them or else the anthology is over and everyone has to go home and nobody gets to make a buck.

You hear an awful lot about the "fading line between fantasy and reality" in the modern world and I had better put that in fast or else I am not going to get to do any more Forewords. So here it comes. I agree. There *is* a fading line between fantasy and reality, a very fading line, a goddamned, almost invisible line and you will find that notion riding through all of the selections in this volume. Then, too, if you are alive today, and stick your head out of doors now and then, you know that there is a nervousness, a tempo, a near-hysterical new beat in the air, a punishing isolation and loneliness of a strange, frenzied new kind. It is in the music and the talk and the films and the theater and it is in the prose style of Joe Heller and Terry Southern. You can find it in Gogol and Isaac Babel, too, and perhaps they saw it all coming. But that is another anthology.

These are fairly tangential considerations and what it really comes down to is *The New York Times,* which is the source and fountain and bible of black humor. The Secretary of State, solemnly reviewing the Vietnam crisis, sud-

Joseph Heller.

denly begins to strangle on a wild gastronomical metaphor. Hanoi's support of the rebels, that's the "meat and potatoes issues." When we get to the root of that, then we can consider the salt and pepper issues. The bombing raids? Secondary stuff, just a lot of garlic and oregano talk, really, just a bunch of diversionary sweet basil and East Indian nutmeg baloney.

A ninety-year-old Negro sharecropper lady watches Ladybird Johnson—on a poverty-inspection tour—sweep up to her shack in a presidential limousine and says, "Ain't it wonderful." Fun-loving Tennessee students pelt each other with snowballs and suddenly scores are dead of heart attacks and gunshot wounds. A mid-flight heart-attack victim is removed from an airliner, suddenly slides from the stretcher and cracks her head on the runway. We bomb North Vietnam and nervously await the reaction of Red China, scourge of the Free World. Red China breaks her silence. The Imperialist dogs have behaved like vermin and Communist China is not going to sit idly by. With all the fury and power of a frenzied 900-million populace behind her, Red China speaks.

"We are going," says Radio China, "to return you tit for tat."

You guess that it has always been this way, that Tolstoi must have had this unreal sensation when Napoleon came east. But then the police Urinary Squad swoops down and

> **It is called "Black Humor" and I think I would have more luck defining an elbow or a corned-beef sandwich. I am not, for one thing, even sure it is black. It might be fuchsia or eggshell and I think some of it is in brown polka dots.**
>
> —*Bruce Jay Friedman*

spears a high governmental official at the Y.M.C.A. trough; five hundred captured Congo rebels are ushered into a stadium before their Free World captors. The ones who are booed have their heads blown off. Those with good acts who draw applause go free; Nehru sends troops rushing up to the India-China border "with orders to shout if necessary."

"How does it feel?" the TV boys ask Mrs. Malcolm X when her husband is assassinated. We send our planes off for nice, easygoing, not-too-tough bombing raids on North Vietnam. Sixteen U.S. officers in Germany fly through the night in Klansmen robes burning fiery crosses and are hauled before their commanding officer to be reprimanded for "poor judgment." It confirms your belief that a new, Jack Rubyesque chord of absurdity has been struck in the land, that there is a new mutative style of behavior afoot, one that can only be dealt with by a new, one-foot-in-the-asylum style of fiction.

If you are fond of pinning labels on generations, I wonder whether this one could not be called the surprise-proof generation. What might possibly surprise America? Another presidential assassination. Kidstuff. A thousand Red Chinese landing on the Lever Brothers building and marching toward Times Square. Hardly worth a yawn. Mike Todd suddenly showing up on the Johnny Carson show, not dead after all, involved in Broadway's greatest hoax. It's sort of expected.

What has happened is that the satirist has had his ground usurped by the newspaper reporter. The journalist, who, in the year 1964, must cover the ecumenical debate on whether Jews, on the one hand, are still to be known as Christ-killers, or, on the other hand are to be let off the hook, is certainly today's satirist. The novelist-satirist, with no real territory of his own to roam, has had to discover new land, invent a new currency, a new set of filters, has had to sail into darker waters somewhere out beyond satire and I think this is what is meant by black humor.

So you have Mrs. Liuzzo dead with a bullet in her brain, the federal government swinging into action because her "civil rights have been violated." The New York Police Department steps forth with a plan to keep Puerto Ricans from committing suicide in their cells: guards are to watch them like hawks now, running in to cut them down before they get their nooses rigged up. A news magazine says what's all the fuss about anyhow and describes one of our Vietnam gases as "fragrant-smelling," the implication being that if the little Red bastards weren't so sneaky, hid-

ing in caves, we would not have to use gas in the first place. In one of our states, the penalty for fornication is six-to-seven years in prison while fellatio people (with only one pair of genitals involved) are imprisoned for life. It may be said that the Black Humorist is a kind of literary Paul Revere, a fellow who unfreezes his mind, if only for a moment and says, "For Christ's sake, what in hell is going on here? What do you mean, 35,000 Vietnam *advisers?*"

They say it is a critic's phrase, Black Humor, and that whatever it is, you can count on it to fizzle after a bit. And besides, don't these fellows just write about outcasts? Fags, junkies, hunchbacks, "preverts," Negroes, Jews, other assorted losers? What's that got to do with anything anyway? I think they may be wrong on that first count. I have a hunch Black Humor has probably always been around, always will be around, under some name or other, as long as there are disguises to be peeled back, as long as there are thoughts no one else cares to think. And as to the idea that these writers do not deal with "representative" types—it may be that you can govern by consensus, but you can't write anything distinctive by consensus. And it may be that if you are doing anything as high-minded as examining society, the very best way to go about it is by examining first its throwaways, the ones who can't or won't keep in step (in step with what?). And who knows? Perhaps "bad" behavior of a certain kind is better than "good" behavior. The American Health Society claims that only 5% of syphilis is spread by prostitutes.

So there is a Black Humor, after all, although you wish they would call it something else or perhaps call it nothing and just know it is in the air. Especially since there is no single perfect example of it, the way you can produce a perfect Uppman cigar. What is true is that the serious and effective social critics—the novelists, film makers, playwrights, the Feiffer-Krassner-Bruce axis—are working through humor; there is also an awful lot of questioning these days, some of it despairing, bleary-eyed, bedazzled, some of it young, vigorous, outrageous. And a group of novelists, very often working obliquely, coming at you from somewhere in left field, throwing you some laughs to get you to lower your guard, have decided that the novel is the proper place to open every door, to follow every labyrinthian corridor to its source, to ask the final questions, turn over the last rock, to take a preposterous world by the throat and say okay, be preposterous, but also make damned sure you explain yourself.

It is a good time to be around, to ask some of the questions, to watch the action.

Bruce Jay Friedman, in a foreword to Black Humor, *edited by Bruce Jay Friedman, Corgi Books, 1965, pp. vii-xi.*

Keith Huckabay

[*Huckabay is an American educator and critic. In the following essay he demonstrates that American black humor fiction and the Theater of the Absurd represent an intensification of Existentialism's sense of "ontological insecurity"—anxiety about the stability of self and identity.*]

An excerpt from *Catch-22*

It was a horrible joke, but Doc Daneeka didn't laugh until Yossarian came to him one mission later and pleaded again, without any real expectation of success, to be grounded. Doc Daneeka snickered once and was soon immersed in problems of his own, which included Chief White Halfoat, who had been challenging him all that morning to Indian wrestle, and Yossarian, who decided right then and there to go crazy.

"You're wasting your time," Doc Daneeka was forced to tell him.

"Can't you ground someone who's crazy?"

"Oh, sure. I have to. There's a rule saying I have to ground anyone who's crazy."

"Then why don't you ground me? I'm crazy. Ask Clevinger."

"Clevinger? Where *is* Clevinger? You find Clevinger and I'll ask him."

"Then ask any of the others. They'll tell you how crazy I am."

"They're crazy."

"Then why don't you ground them?"

"Why don't they ask me to ground them?"

"Because they're crazy, that's why."

"Of course they're crazy," Doc Daneeka replied. "I just told you they're crazy, didn't I? And you can't let crazy people decide whether you're crazy or not, can you?"

Yossarian looked at him soberly and tried another approach. "Is Orr crazy?"

"He sure is," Doc Daneeka said.

"Can you ground him?"

"I sure can. But first he has to ask me to. That's part of the rule."

"Then why doesn't he ask you to?"

"Because he's crazy," Doc Daneeka said. "He has to be crazy to keep flying combat missions after all the close calls he's had. Sure, I can ground Orr. But first he has to ask me to."

"That's all he has to do to be grounded?"

"That's all. Let him ask me."

"And then you can ground him?" Yossarian asked.

"No. Then I can't ground him."

"You mean there's a catch?"

"Sure there's a catch," Doc Daneeka replied. "Catch-22. Anyone who wants to get out of combat duty isn't really crazy."

There was only one catch and that was Catch-22, which specified that a concern for one's own safety in the face of dangers that were real and immediate was the process of a rational mind. Orr was crazy and could be grounded. All he had to do was ask; and as soon as he did, he would no longer be crazy and would have to fly more missions. Orr would be crazy to fly more missions and sane if he didn't, but if he was sane he had to fly them. If he flew them he was crazy and didn't have to; but if he didn't want to he was sane and had to. Yossarian was moved very deeply by the absolute simplicity of this clause of Catch-22 and let out a respectful whistle.

"That's some catch, that Catch-22," he observed.

"It's the best there is," Doc Daneeka agreed.

Joseph Heller, in his Catch-22, *Dell, 1955.*

Early in the 1950's two distinctly new literary genres appeared and suddenly became quite important. Their recognition and acceptance continued to grow through the decade of the sixties. Although both genres are poorly defined as yet, they have acquired labels—the new dramatic genre has been given the name *Theatre of the Absurd,* and the new form in the novel has come to be called *Black Humor.* Thus far there seems to have been very little comparison of the two new forms, but the two have significant parallels that invite comment. Primary to both genres is the assumption that existence is absurd. Both depict a world gone completely insane, a world where only the illogical is logical, where madness is the standard condition. The subject matter for both is usually the most hideous or pathetic imaginable—for example, a mutilated old couple live in garbage cans and only come out occasionally for food or conversation. Another example—a man is cut in half by a low-flying airplane. Yet, paradoxically, the new genre treatment of this subject matter produces comedy; audiences and readers laugh, sometimes uproariously.

Looking at these two new genres together in this way raises a difficult but inescapable question. Why should a rather large segment of recent literature suddenly go Absurd? Or to approach the matter from another direction, why have the absurd works achieved such success—what is there that is so satisfying to contemporary audiences in these "anti" forms which deny all traditions of structure and characterization and which make comedy out of their presentation of the horrifying chaos of the modern world? It hardly seems adequate to describe the absurdity of the works and conclude that this is "the only appropriate literary mode for the world the artist lives in." This appears to be the usual critical approach, but it does little toward explaining why the works are so satisfying to the reader or audience.

Certainly these works are pleasurable for many reasons, and it would be impossible to make an exhaustive analysis. They *are* in most cases witty and well written; they are "good art," in spite of their defiance of tradition. But a more significant appeal in these genres lies in their deeper psychological impact—they work very effectively on the lower levels of the mind, releasing hidden and repressed fears and anxieties. This accomplished through a process of confronting the audience with its worst fears and then alleviating the fears by rendering them comic. Martin Esslin, in *The Theatre of the Absurd* (1961), has described the process in this way: an "unease" is "caused by the presence of illusions that are obviously out of tune with reality" and then "dissolved and discharged through liberating laughter." This is obviously very nearly an Aristotelian catharsis, but in a form Aristotle could not anticipate. For it is achieved not through identification but through confronting one's fears in a concrete or personified form: a confrontation which is both frightening and comical at the same time. The reader or audience meets its deepest unconscious anxieties face to face and finds relief in being able to laugh at them.

However, simply to describe this process in this way does not give a completely satisfactory answer to the question raised about the appeal of the Absurd forms. Instead, a new question takes shape: *Why* has so much of contemporary literature turned to this *new type of catharsis?* Why is the new catharsis not only workable but particularly gratifying to the contemporary audience? In my opinion, the strong appeal of the Absurd works—the success of their new catharsis—lies in their singularly effective "cleansing" of an extremely serious and distinctively modern anxiety: man's "ontological insecurity." Very prominent in most of the Absurd works are images or symbols of the ontological ("Being") insecurity of twentieth-century man: throughout the works are representations of the dehumanization or loss of self of modern man. H. M. Ruitenbeek, a sociologist and psychotherapist, has made the significant statement in *Psychoanalysis and Existential Philosophy* (a collection of articles of which he is the editor) that ontological insecurity "has become one of the major distresses of man in modern society." The British psychologist R. D. Laing (whose article "Ontological Insecurity" appears in Ruitenbeek's *Psychoanalysis*) similarly states that Non-being or Selfishness is a widespread "fever" and that "we are all only two or three degrees Fahrenheit from deficiencies of this order." It is no small merit of Absurd literature that it faces and deals effectively with these critical problems to a greater extent, perhaps, than is possible for traditional literary forms. The deepest level of satisfaction in Absurd plays and novels, it seems to me, is their objectification and subsequent relieving of one of the chief anxieties of contemporary man—his ontological insecurity.

Laing's discussion of ontological insecurity includes the following statement concerning the symptoms of the sufferer of this affliction:

> The individual in the ordinary circumstances of living may feel more unreal than real; in a literal sense, more dead than alive; precariously differentiated from the rest of the world, so that his *identity* and *autonomy* [my italics] are always in question. He may lack the experience of his continuity. He may not possess an overriding sense of his own personal consistency or cohesiveness. He may feel more insubstantial, and unable to

assume that the stuff he is made of is genuine, good, valuable.

Laing here provides a very accurate description of modern man in distress. The problem is that there is no longer the firm sense of self that man possessed in former ages which could counteract the perception of chaos or evil in existence. Quite appropriately for the present discussion, Laing quotes from *Waiting for Godot* to illustrate his point:

> ESTRAGON: We always find something, eh, Didi, to give us the impression that we exist?
>
> VLADIMIR (*impatiently*): Yes, yes, we're magicians. But let us persevere in what we have resolved, before we forget.

Empty of meaning, the individual must prove his existence to himself. And as the existentialists have long been saying, the depersonalizing technological society contributes to the individual's anxiety by treating him as a *thing,* perhaps even a *"no-thing."* In the technological society the person becomes an alienated, detached, and unrelated Nothing. He experiences "non-being"—he suffers ontological insecurity.

Three types of anxiety, according to Laing, are encountered by the ontologically insecure person: *engulfment, implosion,* and *petrification. Engulfment* is experienced when the individual is not sure of his autonomous identity and every relationship threatens to engulf him, to enclose and destroy his identity. Images often associated with this anxiety by Laing's patients are such things as being buried, being drowned, being caught and dragged down into quicksand. *Implosion* is similar: it is a feeling of emptiness, as if the person were a vacuum. Reality threatens to rush in and fill the vacuum, destroying all identity the person may yet have. Third, the fear of *petrification* is defined as "the dread of . . . the possibility of turning, or being turned, from a live person into a dead thing, into a stone, into a robot, an automaton, without personal autonomy of action, an *it* without subjectivity."

Dreams expressing one or more of these types of anxieties are frequent in persons suffering from ontological insecurity. Most commonly, the dreams employ the defensive method of turning the threat-figure into a thing. The more potentially dangerous a matter is to the self, the more need there is to transform it into an *it*. For example, one patient dreamed repeatedly of a small black triangle which first appeared in the corner of his room and grew larger and larger until it almost engulfed him. In a similar dream, a patient prepared a meal and then looked through her home for her family. Finding them in various parts of the house, she was horrified to see that each one had been turned into a stone statue. Upon being touched, the statues crumbled into sand.

The kind of defense mechanism illustrated particularly well in the second dream—the petrification of others—functions, according to Laing, both 1) in the dream-state and 2) at an unconscious level in waking life. The person is always afraid of being depersonalized or taken as a thing in his relationships with others. To protect himself, he unconsciously destroys the other's power to do damage by depersonalizing him into an *it*. The other person is turned into a piece of machinery that will no longer be able to engulf or petrify by having personal aliveness.

Before continuing with [this] line of development . . . , before showing, in other words, the relevance of Laing's categories of engulfment, implosion, and petrification to the Absurd genres—it will first be necessary to examine briefly several matters concerning the nature and history of the Absurd literary forms. The first point to be observed is that absurdity is by no means a recent phenomenon in literature: it has informed existential literature since late in the nineteenth century. Novels like Sartre's *Nausea* and Camus' *The Stranger* and dramas like *Caligula, No Exit, Lucifer and the Lord* all postulate absurdity. But absurdity in these works, unlike that in the newer Absurd forms, is a statement—their characters discover absurdity, and the works then discuss it for us, making a "moral" point. The usual result of the meeting with absurdity in this older existential literature is the development of some way to revolt and achieve "authentic existence" in spite of the Nothingness: reactions such as a "leap of faith" or "stoic resistance" are customarily presented as a thesis.

As James Feibleman has observed, this type of existentialism came to full maturity in France during the early decades of this century largely as a reaction to the severe national despair induced by war. Viewed in this way, the first wave of existential literature was, in psychological terms, a "task-oriented" reaction to stress or tension. In other words, faced with a high level of cultural and environmental stress, artists and philosophers—if not all the French people—sought a defense of sorts in a philosophy which recognized Nothingness but revolted against it, asserted the freedom to rebel, and, in effect, determined to do something about Nothingness.

However, much of existential literature made a radical shift in direction around 1950. It began to *demonstrate* absurdity through form, not just tell about it in a calm, naturalistic style. It ceased to protest or revolt against Nothingness and was content merely to *show* it through stress on incommunicability, destruction of the psychology of characterization, and abandonment of orderly structure. Perhaps this shift in direction can be partly explained, at least in a general way, by a statement by James C. Coleman in *Abnormal Psychology and Modern Life*. He states that when stress increases to an extremely high level, behavior or response is no longer task-oriented but becomes ego defense-oriented. When threat to the self becomes sufficiently great, when feelings of worth or adequacy are strongly questioned, response becomes "aimed primarily at protecting ourselves from devaluation and relieving painful tension and anxiety." This seems to be roughly what happened in existential literature. Just as a national despair gave rise to existentialism, the even greater level of despair caused by World War II, Hitler and especially the atomic bomb brought about a marked change in existentialism. When external reality became unbearably harsh, the existentialist artist could no longer be concerned with revolt—with the "leap of faith" or "authentic existence" (task-oriented reactions): very predictably, the artist could be concerned now only with *survival* (or defense of ego). Existentialism—reflecting cultural changes—entered a stage analogous to the ego-protective stage in the individual. And the defense mechanisms of the individual—repression, denial, fantasy, dream—are analogous to the dream world which much of existential literature turned to. The various dream forms of Strindberg, Kafka, Breton and others finally came to fruition and wide acceptance as the new Absurdists began to depict the chaos of the world through something of a combination of expressionism and surrealism. The new artists instinctively fled from the horrifying post-war world into the inner, subjective world in a search for reality. They escaped to a dream world summoned up from the depths of the unconscious; and it was this that was depicted as reality in their work. Martin Esslin remarks that " . . . the reality with which the Theatre of the Absurd is concerned is a psychological reality expressed in images that are the outward projection of states of mind, fears, dreams, nightmares, and conflicts within the personality of the author. . . ."

The theatre of Ionesco—a strong influence on many of the other new artists—helps to illustrate what has been said. In his theatre, showing the split between "realism" and inner reality is a primary concern. He remarks that

> I have always thought that the truth of fiction is more profound, more charged with meaning than everyday reality. Realism, whether it be socialist or not, falls short of reality. It shrinks it, attenuates it, falsifies it; it does not take into account our basic truths and our fundamental obsessions: love, death, astonishment. It presents man in a reduced and estranged perspective. Truth is in our dreams, in the imagination. . . .

Realistic or naturalistic fiction is an imitation of the external world, but for Ionesco as for many recent artists, that external world is not the real world. The real world is "in our dreams, in the imagination," and it takes a special type of dream-like or surrealistic fiction to express it—the type of fiction that has come to be called Absurd.

This new type of fiction has obviously been shaped by such various influences as Strindberg's expressionism, Jarry's 'Pataphysics,' surrealism, and Kafkaesque writings; but no one label precisely fits it. It does not contain the transitions from reality into the dream world that expressionism employs; instead it presents *as reality* a "dream-sequence," an ordering of events "from which the arbitrary restraint of causality has been removed" [Robert S. Brustein, *The Theatre of Revolt,* 1964]. Though the absurd form may or may not be anti-logical, it certainly follows the *"non-sequitur*-order" of the dream. And although there are frequently affinities with the nightmare distortion of surrealism, there is not here a free release of the unconscious as there is in surrealism: the Absurd places greater control and direction on the material. Perhaps the best that can be said is that the Absurd combines all these elements and others into a form that is highly distinctive but difficult to define. The important point to be made here about this form is that the Absurd dream-fiction is an ideal language for communicating the truths of the anxiety-ridden unconscious of the contemporary artist. As will be shown, the nightmare "logic" and distorted images of the

Absurd are a highly successful form for dealing with the anxieties and fears peculiar to mid-century man.

At this point, several lines of thought which have been introduced must be drawn together. First of all, in turning to the subjective, inner world for his reality, the artist has developed the Absurd dream-sequence. This dream-sequence is an excellent background for the projection of the distorted nightmare figures dredged up from the artist's unconscious. Secondly, given this freedom to create wild, surrealistic characters and action on a non-Aristotelian stage or in a non-narrative novel, the artist has in fact created images that not only represent his own fears and obsessions, but that validly objectify some of the deepest anxieties of mid-century man.

Scattered profusely through most of the Absurd works are nightmare images of the depersonalization of man. Images of engulfment, images of petrification, images of persons transformed into *things* by an insane world—these run wild in Absurd literature. In fact, such images become a trademark for the Absurd: inasmuch as Absurd literature is "about" anything, it is about Selfless people. The mad world depicted is one in which people are merely *victims* of reality. There are few humans in these plays and novels; the characters are primarily empty hulls that obey mechanically any and all dictates of an insane society. Most are simply robot figures. Even the few characters who attempt to resist depersonalization and are treated sympathetically are still primarily victims of reality; they can never relax their guard against the forces constantly at work on all sides to dehumanize them.

Joseph Heller's *Catch-22* provides a useful example of the Absurd novel's use of grotesque images of dehumanization. The book is throughout a struggle to avoid precisely what we have referred to as petrification, transformation into a *thing*, an *it*. The book—which Paul Levine describes as a nightmare from which Yossarian, the main character, is trying to awake—is ostensibly about warfare. But as J. L. McDonald has observed, *Catch-22* is not so much concerned with war itself or even death as with the question of human identity.

Heller places two worlds in opposition to each other, the world of the authorities and the world of the victims. Yossarian's struggle against victimization by the authorities links together the otherwise wild disorder of the book. Those in power are given the right to victimize by the notorious "Catch-22," which states that "they" have the right to do anything the victim can't stop them from doing. So it is a vague "they" which Yossarian fears most of the time as being intent on destroying him.

Yossarian can at least recognize his commanding officers to be a part of the threatening "they." These men have obtained power because of their willingness to adhere to the system of ethics of "Catch-22" which "reduces human beings to abstractions, statistics" [McDonald, "I See Everything Twice!: The Structure of Joseph Heller's *Catch-22*," *The University Review*, Spring 1968]. Colonel Cathcart, Yossarian's commanding officer, well displays the dehumanizing official attitude as he writes a letter of "sympathy" to the families of dead airmen: it begins, "Dear Mrs.,

Mr., Miss, or Mr. and Mrs. ————." Just check the correct label and fill in the blank. The attitude is even better expressed by the doctor who persuades Yossarian to play the part of a wounded and dying son for a couple about to visit the hospital:

> "They [the parents] didn't come to see me," Yossarian objected. "They came to see their son."
>
> "They'll have to take what they can get. As far as we're concerned, one dying boy is just as good as any other or just as bad. To a scientist, all dying boys are equal."

Thirdly, Gus and Wes, the medical "officers," work by this same rule; they treat all patients alike, giving everyone laxatives and painting gums and toes purple, whatever the ailment. Such men as these are the true enemies in *Catch-22,* for they destroy quietly and subtly by making men into mechanical things.

Identities are manipulated throughout Heller's book as if they were randomly assigned and re-assigned by computers. Mudd is a dead man who still has a place in Yossarian's tent because he cannot be officially removed from the rolls. Doc Daneeka is a live man who is ignored because he is officially listed as dead. Yossarian himself is constantly in and out of new identities. While in the hospital with a leg injury, he trades beds with A. Fortiori, another patient, and is for some time known as A. Fortiori and treated as a mental patient. During another stay at the hospital, Yossarian censors letters and signs his name as "Washington Irving," "Irving Washington," etc. in order to escape punishment by the officers. Perhaps Yossarian's most interesting identity change comes, though, when he temporarily agrees to become an ally of Colonel Cathcart: during this time he is called "Yo-Yo," a quite appropriate label for what he had become.

One of the most grotesque symbols of the loss of identity in the book is the soldier in white. The soldier in white lies in the hospital completely covered in white gauze and plaster. The only openings are for his eyes, nose, and the two tubes that enter and leave the mummy-like figure. The soldier becomes horrifying to the other men because they begin to wonder who *if anyone* actually is inside the mummy. Yossarian complains that " 'For all we know, it might even be Mudd' " (Mudd is the dead man who supposedly lives in Yossarian's tent).

Quite obviously, retaining a sense of self is the major battle being fought in *Catch-22.* Most of the airmen in the novel are not as lucky as Yossarian; most are either destroyed physically or—even worse, we are led to believe—they lose self by becoming robots or Yo-Yo's.

Very similar robots perform on the stage of Edward Albee's *The American Dream,* a representative work from the Theatre of the Absurd. Albee's characters are overgrown puppets or marionettes of much the same type as those used by Heller (both artists, incidentally, seem to have been influenced by the puppet figures and various techniques of Ionesco's theatre). The characters of *The American Dream* are automatons completely lacking spirit and possessing very little brain.

John Hawkes.

Albee's characters—with the exception of Mrs. Barker—do not even have names to distinguish them; they are labeled according to their functions—Mommy, Daddy, Grandma, and the youth who turns out to be the American Dream. The characters' only identities are these family or social roles, but even these proofs of existence are meaningless. As Henry Goodman states ("The New Dramatists: 4—Edward Albee," *Drama Survey,* II, I [June 1962]), the characters wear the "masks of social conformity," but these "are masks that do not hide faces, for there are no faces to hide; only the masks are real." He continues, "There is nothing to hide. Behind the agreeable smile and the bell-like voice there lurk not so much disagreeable, harsh thoughts and feelings as no thoughts and feelings at all. We see only the pleasant face of the vacuum."

These vacuum characters are rather harshly drawn, especially Mommy. She has emasculated Daddy, mutilated the child they adopted, and tormented Grandma until she fled from the house. Daddy is docile and passive, making no effort to defy Mommy's authority. His time is passed with pleasant little dreams of becoming a senator, winning a Fulbright scholarship, and leaving Mommy's apartment. Grandma alone is somewhat sympathetically portrayed in that she is given the courage to stand up to Mommy. She

becomes a parallel with Yossarian in her resistance against dehumanization; she too is forced to flee or perish.

The young man whom Grandpa discovers to be the American dream could serve as an archetypal symbol for the dehumanized man in Absurd literature. He is a grotesque surrealistic figure who has undergone a hideous form of depersonalization. He is, as he describes himself, a "clean-cut, midwest farm boy type, almost insultingly good-looking in a typically American way. Good profile, straight nose, honest eyes, wonderful smile. . . ." He is a strong and handsome young American idol who could easily have come from the football field or Hollywood; and in fact he has plans for a movie career. As he confesses, though, he has nothing but a magnificent physique and good looks. He is a spiritual vacuum, devoid of emotion or humanity. He is the identical twin of the child which Mommy had mutilated and allowed to die. During the course of the play, this grown twin tells Grandma what has happened to him over the years, and it becomes obvious that the castration and mutilation practiced on the dead twin has affected this one as well: all feelings have slowly been destroyed in him. He tells Grandma:

> . . . I no longer have the capacity to feel anything. I have no emotions, I have been drained; torn asunder . . . disemboweled. I have, now, only my person . . . my body . . . my face. I use what I have. . . . I let people love me. . . . I accept the syntax around me, for while I know I cannot relate . . . I must be related *to.* I let people touch me. . . . I let them draw pleasure from my groin . . . from my presence . . . from the fact of me . . . I can feel nothing. I can feel nothing.

The youthful American Dream is in reality less a dream than a nightmare—he is Albee's nightmare of the loss of self.

The interchangeability of identity pointed out earlier in *Catch-22* is also important in *The American Dream.* First of all, the matured twin is looked upon as a replacement for the one that died. Mommy had been worried that the money invested in the first child would be lost, but the appearance of the American Dream solves the problem. People can be replaced as easily as machines. Grandma provides a similar example of this interchangeability. As stated above, characters are distinguished and labeled only by family function. Grandma loses even this when she forgets whose mother she is: she thinks she is Daddy's mother but is disappointed to find she is Mommy's. Probably the best illustration of the interchangeability of these characters can be seen, however, in what Albee did with them when he later wrote *The Sandbox.* There the same characters are used, but they play different roles. For instance, the youth who had been the American Dream there becomes just a young man lolling on the beach.

At least one other aspect of *The American Dream* deserves notice here. As the play begins Grandma is carrying large numbers of boxes onto the stage. During the progress of the play she continues to bring these in, to stack and restack them. Albee here utilizes a technique very similar to Ionesco's in *The Chairs;* in both cases there is a proliferation of objects on the stage. Ionesco has commented about his use of objects that "The obtrusive presence of objects expresses spiritual absence" (quoted in Nelvin Vos, *Eugene Ionesco and Edward Albee*). This apparently holds true for Albee's theatre as well. The characters demand objects to fill a spiritual vacuum; they gain a sense of identity by the objects. Finally, however, the objects begin to multiply and cover the stage. This is true only to a limited extent in *The American Dream,* but in *The Chairs* objects crowd man out and take over the stage. What happens here is clearly very close to what we have termed engulfment. The same thing can be seen in Ionesco's *Amédée* in which a corpse begins to grow on stage and ultimately crowds a middle-aged couple right out of their home. Similarly, at the end of Hildesheimer's play *The Clocks,* a salesman sells a couple so many clocks that they cover the stage; the couple submissively get inside the clocks and begin to imitate their sounds.

The importance of the characteristics of Absurd literature which have been discussed above can perhaps begin to be seen in this statement by Simon Lesser (in *Fiction and the Unconscious,* 1957):

> Among stories whose artistic authenticity cannot be questioned we give the highest place precisely to those works which ignore no aspect of man's nature, which confront the most disagreeable aspects of life deliberately and unflinchingly—to Greek and Shakespearean tragedy, for example, and to such serious comedies as *Candide, Don Quixote* and *Gulliver's Travels.*

Of course, great fiction or drama appeals on many levels. It must satisfy aesthetically, for one thing, through use of language, suitable structure, etc. But the greatest art, as Lesser says, is that which supplies all this and also confronts life head-on. As he puts it, "The greatest fiction poses [our most urgent] problems in their most essential forms."

Though fiction is an "unreal" world, it can be of great help to the individual in dealing with the "real" world. Lesser comments on this:

> While fiction alters the facts of experience, a fundamental purpose of those alterations, as the first and greatest asthetician, Aristotle, realized, is the achievement of an imaginary world more lifelike than life itself, more directly and honestly concerned with essential problems, more supple in its expression of every aspect of man's nature, less burdened by distracting irrelevancies.

The fictional world actually provides one of the most effective ways to deal with deep, hidden fears in that it lets us dwell consciously on what might otherwise remain repressed in the unconscious.

Traditional theatre and realistic, narrative fiction have accomplished this confrontation with inner emotions and the subsequent gratification through identification with the characters. In the Aristotelian theatre the audience enters the world of the characters, suffers their emotions, and experiences catharsis. Roughly the same thing happens in narrative fiction, according to Lesser. The new Absurdists, however, in turning inward to a dream world are at two removes from reality and have left behind the technique of identification. The Absurd's anti-characters are too exaggerated to allow identification: they are too grotesque—too far from "reality"—to allow the reader to seek the parallels to his life that he finds in other fiction. The reader does not, in other words, join in the protagonist's struggles and victories; he does not enjoy vicariously the experiences of the lover; he does not have his guilt assuaged by identifying with the punished evil-doer. The catharsis in the Absurd form is therefore of a new type which is brought about by two means: first by confronting the reader with his fears and anxieties in personified form. Generally, the characters of Absurd literature are not characters at all; the psychology of traditional characterization has been destroyed in these genres. The characters are, instead, analogous to images from an imagistic poem, flashing before us as representations of states of being or qualities. These characters are, in short, *personified fears.* The second part of the Absurd catharsis lies, then, in *laughing* at these fears. The hideous or pathetic characters of the Absurd are at the same time comic because of the fact that, as just stated, they are too grotesque for us to identify with them. Their situations are comic—just as the painful kicks, falls, etc. of the clown and slapstick comedian are comic—because we are not invited to experience the pain vicariously. The horrible antics and the sufferings of the Absurd characters are so unrealistically distorted that we do not respond empathetically. Instead, we laugh. As Martin Esslin observes, "If . . . our tendency to identify has been inhibited by making such a character grotesque, we laugh at his predicament. We see what happens to him from the outside, rather than from his own point of view." And not only has the Absurd artist exaggerated these characters, allowing us to see them from such a detached viewpoint, he has *distanced* them from us by 1) placing them in a dream world twice removed from reality and 2) by making the overall work highly stylized. The results of all this are, in short, characters that are at the same time grotesquely ugly and comic.

The fears thus relieved in the Absurd genres are predominantly, as has been shown, fears of dehumanization. Though it has been possible to examine only a very limited number of works in this article, many Absurd novels and dramas employ grotesque images of the loss of identity similar to those discussed. In some works, the victim tries to preserve or at least to find an identity—John Barth's *The Sot-Weed Factor* is like *Catch-22* in this respect. In others, there is one dominant symbol for the mechanical man *without* identity; Thomas Pynchon's *V.* shares this characteristic with *The American Dream.* In still other works, there is a manipulation of puppets by an omnipotent "they"; Pinter's *The Dumbwaiter* parallels *Catch-22* on this point, and almost all of Ionesco's plays depict victims of a vague but powerful "Duty." Significantly, two of the dominant images appearing in all these works are images of engulfment and petrification. In most of these novels and dramas the artists have succeeded, whether consciously or unconsciously, in creating grotesque characters that objectify modern man's deep fear of loss of self. Time after time in these works, grotesques which are very much like the dreams of the ontologically insecure person destroy man, either by engulfing him or making him into a puppet.

The Absurd genres quite obviously fit Lesser's criterion for great works—they "confront the most disagreeable aspects of life deliberately and unflinchingly." In fact, they confront one of the most severe anxieties of the twentieth century. As has been stated, a significant part of the appeal of these Absurd genres comes from this confrontation and the relief provided. The Absurd form and the catharsis peculiar to it seem particularly well suited to objectify and laugh at the fear of dehumanization. The comic-grotesques of the Absurd bring this obsessive modern fear into the open and subdue it in a way that seems beyond traditional forms of the novel and drama. The relief afforded is extremely gratifying to the modern audience, and that gratification is no less real if it is largely unconscious. That gratification, on whatever level it occurs, is the foundation for the enjoyment of Absurd literature. One of the deepest satisfactions obtained from this literature arises from one's having met the mechanical man and having found that he was, after all, Absurdly funny.

> Keith Huckabay, "Black Humor and Theatre of the Absurd: Ontological Insecurity Confronted," in The Cimarron Review, Vol. 20, July, 1972, pp. 20-32.

ORIGINS AND DEVELOPMENT

Alan R. Pratt

[*In the following excerpt, Pratt identifies Voltaire's* Candide *(1752) as an important progenitor of the black humor novel.*]

Andre Breton named Jonathan Swift the originator of black humor, but few critics have examined the relationship between contemporary works of black humor and "A Modest Proposal" or *Gulliver's Travels*. Instead, essays about black humor which include the past often refer to Voltaire's *Candide* (1752), and one can find it referenced in discussions of works by Céline, Heller, Barth, Pynchon, Vonnegut and Southern, to name but a few. *Candide* is quite different from Voltaire's other philosophical tales because though the work focuses on metaphysical concerns, rather than social or psychological matters, it ends with a pessimistic assessment of the human condition. It seems clear that Voltaire was wrestling with the same philosophical/existential quandaries that are addressed in the twentieth century literature of the absurd. And that black humorists have been influenced by *Candide* is not surprising because Voltaire worked with a combination of elements which have come to be identified with the modern black humor novel.

Candide has generally been identified as traditional satire attacking a variety of subjects but focusing on Leibniz's notion of "pre-established harmony." To attack what he

perceived as absurd, Voltaire used absurdity, relying on the tools, character types and stylistic flourishes that constitute traditional satiric strategies. But to categorize *Candide* as satire overlooks the fact that while Voltaire's comic invective is value destructive, it is not ameliorative. And modern literary black humor is differentiated from satire for precisely this reason—it relies on the tools of satirical prose to create an apocalyptic reality, but it neither attempts to distinguish between the ideal and reality nor advocates an alternative ordering.

The plot of *Candide* is simple: Candide loses his love Cunegonde, and in search of her he travels around the world. On much of the journey, he is accompanied by the unflappable Dr. Pangloss who can demonstrate, *reductio ad absurdum*, that "things cannot be otherwise. . . . noses were made to wear spectacles. . . . Legs were clearly devised for breeches. . . ." The doctor's best-of-all-possible-worlds view is entirely convincing to Candide who admires Pangloss, seeing him as one of the world's most profound savants.

Critics have commented on the obvious similarities of Candide's relationship with Pangloss and the relationship between Ebenezer Cook, the naive protagonist of John Barth's *The Sot-Weed Factor*, and his teacher, Henry Burlingame. That Barth might emulate features of *Candide* is not surprising. In a number of contexts, Barth has explained that he creates something new by using something old, of using exhausted forms in new ways. In his later novels, this manifests itself as a genius for parody. Not just Barth, though, employs parody; other black humorists have also recognized its liberating possibilities. Terry Southern, to cite one example, created an elaborate parody with *Candy*, a risque version of Voltaire's masterpiece. Parody is, in fact, a favorite strategy of black humorists as it undermines the authority of the parodied genre. Although the literary pedigree of *Candide* can be traced to the picaresque (also a favorite form of black humorists), Voltaire burlesqued the literature of his day as his tale parodies the eighteenth century romance with its precocious "hero gallant" and distressed damsel.

That *Candide* and the modern black humor novel share a similar comic technique is not much in itself. But there are other similarities. Voltaire's *conte*, for instance, begins with a mock-historic title page: "translated from the German of doctor Ralph with additions which were found in the Doctor's pocket when he died at Minden in the Year of Our Lord 1759." In his later novels Barth distracts readers with similar tricks in addition to creating complex pseudo-histories. Raymond Olderman calls attention to the same ploy adopted by many other black humorists to add "authenticity," blurring the line between reality and fantasy.

In addition to the outright fabrication of histories, the black humor novel frequently weaves actual events, albeit exaggerated, into the narrative. [In the "Foreword" to *Black Humor*, 1963] Bruce Jay Friedman said that *The New York Times* was "the source and fountain and bible of black humor." And Barth's *Sot-Weed Factor* and Tom Berger's *Little Big Man*, to name just two, depend on a loose interpretation of actual events. Voltaire does precisely the same thing. The Lisbon earthquake, the Jesuit dictatorship of Peru, slavery in Surinam, the execution of Admiral John Byng, the inquisition, and the Seven Years War between Prussia and the French alliance were all very real catastrophes, though filtered though the artist's mind and transformed in his art.

The Seven Years War, for instance, is used as a setting in an early episode. Shortly after Candide begins his sojourn, he is shanghaied by two recruiters and forced into the war. The battlefield then becomes a source of macabre humor: "First the cannons laid low about six thousand men on each side, then rifle fire removed from the best of worlds about nine or ten thousand scoundrels who had been infesting its surface." This sardonic description is followed by scenes which occasion not laughter but revulsion:

> Old men with wounds all over their bodies were watching the death throes of butchered women who clutched their children to their bloody breasts; girls who had been disemboweled after satisfying the natural needs of several heroes were breathing their last sighs; others, mortally burned, were shrieking for someone to hasten their death; the ground was strewn with brains and severed arms and legs.

By juxtaposing—or integrating—comic understatement with gut-wrenching realism, Voltaire anticipates the same strategy cultivated and refined by the black humorists. In *Journey to the End of Night,* for example, Louis-Ferdinand Céline initiates Bardamu's misadventures with the experience of war. Thomas Pynchon uses a fantasy of war as an image of death in *Gravity's Rainbow.* In *Slaughterhouse Five* Kurt Vonnegut flippantly references the fire-bombing of Dresden where "135,000 Hansels and Gretels . . . baked like gingerbread men." And in *Catch-22* Heller regularly connects comical moments with combat horrors.

Throughout *Candide,* Voltaire juxtaposes the comic and the tragic. Likewise, contemporary uses of the technique are not limited to the context of war, but are found in every conceivable circumstance—startling juxtapositions between subjects or between subject and form is, in fact, the hallmark of black humor. And in the rapidly progressing episodes of *Candide,* Voltaire finds opportunity to lampoon the human condition using many of the topics that are regularly identified with modern black humor, including social, religious and philosophical systems, natural as well as man-made disasters, senseless violence, pestilence, death, mutilation, and even sexually transmitted disease.

After escaping from war, Candide finds himself in Holland where he is fortuitously reunited with the now syphilitic Dr. Pangloss who is toothless, almost blind, and whose nose and ear have been eaten away. Does syphilis come from the devil, then? No, explains Pangloss; rather, "it was an indispensable element in the best of worlds, a necessary ingredient" without which Europeans would not have chocolate. Pangloss' preposterous rationalization allows him to come to terms with the senselessness of human suffering and the inscrutable relationship between cause and effect. Two centuries later, the consequences of sexual activity will once again spark a similar line of questioning when characters from *Catch-22* are faced with the same absurd ordering of events. But rather than Pangloss' cheerful acceptance of *non sequiturs,* they are bewildered:

> There just doesn't seem to be any logic to this system of rewards and punishment. Look what happened to me. If I had gotten syphilis or a dose of clap for my five minutes of passion on the beach instead of this damned mosquito bite, I could see some justice. But malaria? *Malaria?* Who can explain malaria as a consequence of fornication? . . . Just for once I'd like to see all these things sort of straightened out, with each person getting exactly what he deserves. It might give me some confidence in this universe.

While Voltaire's Pangloss links events illogically, in Heller's dark comedy, characters contemplate illogical events. In both examples, though, the message is the same: human beings are helpless when confronting an absurd reality.

The terrors which Candide and Pangloss face continue to grow in intensity; both are whipped, tortured, robbed, beaten and forced into slavery—and for the reader, the laughter seldom abates. At one point Candide is miraculously reunited with Cunegonde. Given its episodic structure, *Candide* contains many inconceivable events (like Candide's meeting with Pangloss above). These preposterous coincidences serve as transitions between episodes, but more importantly the chance escapes, separations, and meetings emphasize Voltaire's impression that contingency, not necessity, orders events. It is an impression that is similarly amplified in the literature of modern black humor.

Cosmic contingency and the relativity of experience are further underscored in *Candide* with the harrowing tale of the old woman. The crippled hag was once the beautiful, virginal daughter of a pope, destined to marry a handsome prince and live happily ever after. But for nothing more than bad luck, the woman's ship is attacked in route to her wedding, and she is repeatedly violated by the pirate crew. Later, she is rescued from a pile of bleeding corpses by a eunuch who admires her voluptuous body (and bemoans the loss of his testicles) only to be sold into slavery where she will lose one of her appetizing buttocks, and the balance of her life will be exhausted through years of abominable slavery. While the old woman's story is a litany of human barbarity, Voltaire weaves a kind of ludicrous eroticism through it. This synthesis of prurient sensuality and savage violence resembles the disturbing incongruencies which are a characteristic of contemporary black humor.

Many times the old woman has wanted to kill herself, and with her extensive experience she has ascertained that vast numbers of people also loathe their lives, though few choose suicide.

> I've wanted to kill myself a hundred times, but I still love life. That ridiculous weakness is perhaps one of our most pernicious inclinations. What could be more stupid than to persist in carrying a burden that we constantly want to cast off, to hold our existence in horror, yet cling to it nonetheless, to fondle the serpent that devours us, until it has eaten our heart.

Black humorists treat the issue of self-destruction in a senseless world with typical impertinence. In Barth's *Floating Opera,* for instance, Todd Andrews concludes, "*There's no final reason for living (or for suicide).*" After further reflection, he adds:

> To realize that nothing makes any final difference is overwhelming; but if one goes not farther and becomes a saint, a cynic, or a suicide on principle, one hasn't reasoned completely.

In contrast to Todd Andrews' rationalized apathy, Voltaire's old woman is unconcerned with the philosophical issue of suicide in an absurd world. Instead, she would like to annihilate herself, but is prohibited from self-destruction by a mysterious force which is beyond her ability to control.

Voltaire returns to the theme of relativism and moral anarchy in the Oreillon episode. Lost in a South American jungle, Candide sees two naked, screaming women being chased by monkeys. To save them, he shoots the offensive beasts only to discover that the dead animals were the women's lovers. In this instance Voltaire couples sexual activity with the grotesque to accentuate another failed attempt to impose order on a mysterious and multi-faceted reality. What is abhorrent in one context is proper pleasure in another. Black humorists are fond of illustrating similar situations, and critics have called attention to the

John Barth.

chaotic plurality that figures prominently in the contemporary black humor. [In *Black Humor Fiction of the Sixties,* 1973] Max Schulz refers to the phenomenon as the "metaphysics of multiplicity," and considers it a principal feature of the black humor novel. Within this frame of reference, "all versions of reality are mental constructs. . . . No one is aprioristically truer than another."

At the end of Candide's and his companions' adventures, the survivors find themselves on an alien shore, exhausted and annoyed by the outcome of events: Candide has discovered that even love is an illusion. The pessimist Martin is more convinced than ever that "people are equally wretched everywhere." Cacambo, working to support the whole group, is "worn out by his work" and curses his fate. Cunegonde is "growing uglier everyday." The old woman is infirm, and even the imperturbable Pangloss despairs because he cannot "shine in some German university." Underlying their irritation is a growing sense of boredom, causing the old woman to reflect,

> I'd like to know which is worse: to be raped a hundred times by Negro pirates, to have one buttock cut off, to run the gauntlet in the Bulgar army, to be whipped and hanged in an auto-da-fé, to be dissected, to be a galley slave—in short, to suffer all the miseries we've all gone through—or to stay here doing nothing.

Martin voices similar thoughts, concluding that mankind is "born to live in either the convulsions of anxiety or the lethargy of boredom."

The problem of boredom is another recurring theme in *Candide.* Even in Eldorado, where there is happiness, peace and plenty, the novelty of perfection quickly fades, replaced by a gnawing sense of insignificance and futility. To alleviate their existential malaise, Candide's group consults the most astute philosopher in Asia Minor. The dervish's response echoes the experience of the biblical Job: "Is it any of your business?" The best one can do, he tells them, is "Keep quiet." This is not Voltaire's last word on meaninglessness, however.

"Let's work without theorizing," Martin says, "it's the only way to make life bearable." And in the end we see Candide intently cultivating his garden, an automaton immersed in mind-numbing labor. "In effect," Robert Adams writes, "the machine of the world has succeeded in grinding down the characters till they too are nothing but mechanisms" ["Candide on Work and Candide as Outsider," in *Candide,* edited by Robert Adams, 1966]. Black humorists feel comfortable with the perception that the pressures of a disintegrating world reduce human beings to the functional. In *V,* for example, Pynchon's characters discover that life can be tolerable only when they learn to emulate the indifference of a machine. And Slothrop's chaotic misadventures in *Gravity's Rainbow,* in many ways comparable to Candide's, end in a kind of defensive resignation.

Without oversimplifying, it's fair to say that *Candide* resembles its distant modern progeny in a number of ways. To depict an absurd world, Voltaire incorporated the subjects and utilized the devices that modern black humorists have embraced to evoke tenebrous laughter. And like the black humor novel, Voltaire's comic masterpiece features a picaresque antihero buffeted by events which conspicuously accent frightful and lurid realities. By the conclusion of the conte, Voltaire has stripped the world of mollifying illusions, offered nothing to replace them, and leaves readers with a vision of the world as a grim place governed by senseless cosmic forces. It is an outlook which is surprisingly similar to those found in books of contemporary black humorists. Where Voltaire's masterpiece differs from its modern counterparts, however, is in the conclusion.

In *Candide* the human situation is a black affair where the best one can do is adopt a kind of stoic resignation. Although the human situation is also bleak in the black humor novel, it most often endeavors "to face the void without flinching," as Ronald Wallace maintains [in *The Last Laugh,* 1979], "to endure the absurd, and by viewing life from a comic perspective, to enjoy the endurance." The contrast between Voltaire's response to cosmic absurdity and that of modern black humorists is underscored by comparing the final scenes of *Candide* with those of Kurt Vonnegut's *Cat's Cradle.* Both works create a comic yet disturbing vision of puny human beings lost in a chaotic labyrinth. Both works end unhappily for the exhausted protagonists; there is no last moment *deus ex machina* that would order or explain. And both works decline into nihilism. Yet, their responses to it are quite different.

In *Cat's Cradle,* the earth has been frozen over by the accidental release of "ice-nine." For the few survivors of the catastrophe, the situation is entirely hopeless. Rather than suggesting "we must cultivate our garden," Bokonon, the outlaw prophet, recommends this course of action:

> If I were a younger man, I would write a history of human stupidity; and I would climb to the top of Mount McCabe and lie down on my back with my history for a pillow; and I would take from the ground some of the blue-white poison that makes statues of men; and I would make a statue of myself, lying on my back, grinning horribly, and thumbing my nose at You Know Who.

Vonnegut's attitude is characteristic of black humorists whose works typically make no plans for living in an absurd universe. The best one can do is ridicule with mocking laughter a cosmos that condemns mankind to an absurd fate. Accordingly, to the bitter end Vonnegut unflinchingly preserves his acerbic whimsicality.

At the conclusion of *Candide* hope is also dead. Voltaire has earlier ruled out suicide, leaving his audience in a metaphysical void with the tedium of work as the only solace. Instead of the zany, albeit, black merriment which characterizes previous episodes, we are left with a mood of somber abdication, a mood altogether different from Vonnegut's ridiculousness. This tonal change in Voltaire's conclusion is in the spirit of existential literature rather than the literature of black humor. Both grapple with an absurd human condition, and both are concerned with how one perseveres. But whereas the existentialist is earnest in delineating the implications of the absurd, the black humorist sees the absurd world as an outrageous joke with laughter as the only viable solution. In the end, Voltaire is not satisfied with laughing into the void. Instead, he grits his teeth.

Alan R. Pratt, " 'People Are Equally Wretched Everywhere': 'Candide', Black Humor and the Existential Absurd," in Black Humor: Critical Essays, *edited by Alan R. Pratt, Garland Publishing, Inc., 1993, pp. 181-93.*

Ultimately, black humor cannot be described as being pessimistic or simply lacking an affirmative moral voice. Rather, it lives outside these limits in a terrain of terrifying candor concerning the most extreme situations. Furthermore, the black humorist cannot be accused of being totally nihilistic, since he refuses to negate the legitimacy of his art and continues to write.

—Bruce Janoff, in his "Black Humor: Beyond Satire," in The Ohio Review, *Fall,* **1972.**

Jay Boyer

[*In the following essay, Boyer suggests that the hapless protagonists of black humor novels may derive largely from the archetypal fools—the schlemiel and the schlimazl—of the Eastern European Jewish humor tradition.*]

In *A Glossary of Literary Terms,* M. H. Abrahams aligns black humor with the theater of the absurd. In the *Concise Dictionary of Literary Terms,* Harry Shaw defines it as humor which is perverted or morbid, a literary elaboration on our sick joke or an American brand of gallows humor. In "Anatomy of black humor," scholar Burton Feldman describes it as the American correlative for French existentialism, with a commitment most of all to "detachment." Scholar Ihab Hassan puts it in an American tradition of the grotesque. John W. Aldridge places it in an American romantic tradition, one heading "away from the fictional treatment of actual events toward the creation of metaphoric and fabulative impressions of the kind of derangement that may be responsible for these events."

Author Bruce Jay Friedman is not so willing to commit himself, and not nearly so trusting of the scholarly method. Struggle as he might, he could not come up with a satisfying definition. As he explained in his introduction to *Black Humor,* "I think I would have more luck defining an elbow or a corned beef sandwich." Friedman continued, "I am not, for one thing, even sure it is black. It might be fuchsia or eggshell." Friedman threw up his hands in the end: he defined "black humor" as that which can't be defined.

That's a joke, of course, but one much in keeping with the absurdist spirit of black humor. It is the kind of joke Richard Kostelanetz, writing in 1967, was finding central to this new, strange subgenre of American fiction. Wrote Kostelanetz [in his introduction to *Twelve from the 60s*]

> In recent American fiction, both long and short, many of the best works express one of two complementary themes: the absurdity of society and the madness of the self. In contrast to the European absurd novel of, say, Sartre and Albert Camus, which discovers through description of rather normal activities a disjunction between values and behavior, intention and effect, belief and reality, so broad and irrefutable that the world is meaningless, the American absurd novel . . . [is] an exuberant, nonrealistic portrait of thoroughly ridiculous events which, *in toto,* suggests that the world is ultimately senseless. In the novel form, the absurd writer can take on history itself, as Thomas Pynchon, John Barth, and Joseph Heller do, and show in a sprawling, diffuse narrative that history, both in its single events and on the whole, is absurd . . . but American [short] story writers confine their absurd vision to more modest, mundane activities. To Donald Barthelme, in many of his stories, the capacity to spend large amounts of money renders life absurd. To Kenneth Koch . . . the absurd activity is the vain attempt to define in declarative sentences the ambiguous experience of art; for Bernard Malamud, it is the artist's irrational and indestructible devotion to his own work; and to Jack Ludwig, it is all situations that reveal the nonsensical discrepancy between social demands and imagines and individual desires and identifies.

Reading what has been written about black humor since the 1960s, one is apt to be impressed with how little specific agreement there is about what the phrase "black humor" really means. Too, one is apt to be impressed with the tendency of scholars of American literature to acknowledge its debt to European letters only in passing. Review the body of scholarship, and one finds that black humor is agreed to be somehow American. Perhaps that is most impressive as one reviews this scholarship: in fact, "black humor" is agreed to be a literature of the absurd which, by degree if not kind, stands distinctly apart from any European writing.

I want to suggest an alternative line of thought. I'm going to propose that "black humor," coming to the American canon of letters after World War II, has some of its deepest roots not in our literary traditions but rather in a tradition we think of as Eastern European. I have in mind the tradition of the fool-as-protagonist, and more precisely, that *shtetl* tradition of the *schlemiel* and the *schlimazl.* For the purpose of this article, I am going to call the notion of this peculiarly modern, American protagonist the *schlemiezel.* In broadest terms, I mean by "schlemiezel" a protagonist who has only lately come to our novels, one who is a loser, a failure, a man out of control, a city dweller living most often on the East coast and, matters of proper geography aside, an "immigrant" who feels he lives among "natives." This is a protagonist who emerges in his most

pristine form, I believe, not in the novels of such widely accepted American black humorists as Pynchon and Barth and Heller but rather in the novels of writers we think of as being pronouncedly Jewish-American writers, Bellow, Malamud, and Roth to be counted among them. This is a protagonist who by his very presence violates some of our most basic suppositions about this country and the literature it has produced.

To be sure, a full exploration of the matters I intend to raise is well beyond the scope of an article such as this; a reader must stand warned. Rather than define "black humor" once and for all, or find the place of *the fool* within it, all I hope to do is to offer a line of thought which might be worth pursuing, one that may lead to some greater agreement about what "black humor" is and how it came to be.

. . . . .

Traditionally, ours has been a literature of accommodation at one extreme and of rebellions at the other. Black humor holds that neither choice is viable any longer, and it is often from the protagonist's failure to recognize this that the comedy originates. We see, even if he does not, that choosing is out of the question. If not by an act of God, then at least by an act of cultural fate, he is doomed to live the life he lives—helpless, without alternatives, no better off than he is at the moment.

Such a point of view is virtually un-American. It suggests a spirit more often associated with the European immigrant than with the native, a sense of an America close at hand and yet nevertheless out of reach. And that may be telling. For our black humor may owe a greater debt to European influence than we have fully recognized. In fact, a literature we associate with Barth, Burroughs, Pynchon, Purdy, a rather WASPish group, really, may owe a significant debt to *the fool* of Eastern European shtetl tradition, particularly those standard figures of Yiddish tales, the *schlemiel* and the *schlimazl.*

The simplest definition of these terms is probably the best, to begin with. The cliché would have it that the *schlemiel* is the poor soul who spills his bowl of soup, while the *schlimazl* is the poor soul he spills it on. That is not a bad distinction. But the matter is slightly more complicated.

The *schlemiel* is a "loser," I would argue. He's a failure. He was born that way. There is nothing he can do to change this, for he was born without the resources necessary to become more than he already is.

To be a *schlimazl,* though—that's a different matter. The schlimazl is a combination of strengths and weaknesses. He's just a man, to be sure, but a man with the potential for better.

The *schlemiel* tries to understand his world using what we quickly recognize as oversimplified beliefs. It is not just that he believes in magic, superstition, and more of the same. Logic, facts, the assimilation of information—such things are virtually beyond him.

Rather than allowing facts to alter his beliefs, the *schlemiel* interprets events to fit what he already believes. This is just the opposite of what the *schlimazl* will do. Possessing a keener, more rational mind, the *schlimazl* tries to integrate more information than he should. Try as he might to hold one set of beliefs fixed in his mind, try as he might to maintain one logical superstructure, new information bombards him. He cannot revise quickly enough to keep up with events.

Unlike the *schlemiel,* the *schlimazl* takes it all in—that is not his problem. His problem is rather that he does not know what to do with the information once he has it. And as a consequence, he is constantly modifying his system of beliefs, trying fruitlessly to find a place for everything, then trying to put everything in its place.

The *schlemiel* is the butt of the joke. Lacking the skills and resources the society embraces, he becomes the outsider. He is incapable of fitting in, for he is incapable of the sort of accommodation the culture demands. But that is not true of the *schlimazl.* Often, he has these skills. Too, he often occupies what might otherwise be a respected position in the community, if only someone else were to occupy it. He learns all the rules, obeys all the laws, lives by all the orders . . . and yet, somehow, for some reason, he never quite prospers. He does all the things the culture says he must do in order to succeed and fails nevertheless.

The *schlemiel* does not develop very much as a character from beginning to end of the story. He is already who he is going to be at the moment we meet him: a dim-witted fellow, most often, someone without the skills of self-preservation his culture demands, someone ruled more by the heart than by the head.

He is also someone more likely to *react* to situations as they occur than someone who acts on his own behalf. It does not really occur to him to try to have his own way with the world.

This last point is particularly significant, for it speaks to why we tend to embrace the fool of the *shtetl* tradition. Without fully recognizing it, the fool stands in opposition to what his culture holds up as a model for manhood. And when we compare him with that model, it is the model, not the *schlemiel* that we are most likely to question. We recognize through the process of comparison that the *schlemiel* is too good for this world—too sweet, too kind, too *human* to fit in.

This is less true of the *schlimazl,* though the function he serves in the narrative is closely related. He embraces his culture, accommodates it, makes its rules and regulations his own, compromises his wishes and dreams, bends over to accommodate his culture until he finds himself in the shape of a paper clip—and for what? Everything he touches turns to dung. Nothing his culture has taught helps him get what he wants.

These distinctions may help us understand and appreciate the protagonists of that form of fiction we have come to call "black humor." I identify "black humor" with particular post-World War II American novelists and their work. I'm thinking of the novels of writers as otherwise diverse as John Barth, William Burroughs, Thomas Pynchon, James Purdy, J. P. Donleavy, Terry Southern,

and John Hawkes. Joseph Heller is occasionally placed in their midst as well, but of late he is just as likely to be grouped with Bernard Malamud, Saul Bellow, Bruce Jay Friedman, Philip Roth, and Herb Gold—that is, as more a Jewish humorist, whatever that means, than a black humorist. And, as I will discuss later, we may be able to account for this cross-over and be guided by it, perhaps.

By the phrase "black humor," I mean much what the gifted American scholar Donald Greiner has in mind in the introduction to *Comic Terror,* his study of the works of John Hawkes, one of the darkest of our black humorists. Like Greiner, I use the phrase "black humor" with three things in mind. The first of these has to do with authorial vision, one which is comic—and then again not.

> The comparable blackness of a particular writer's humor is indeed secondary—all are black, but some are blacker, and funnier, than others. More important is the attempt to decide what the presence of so many modern American comic novelists means. Taken together, the novels of Hawkes, Vonnegut, Heller, John Barth, Donleavy, Friedman, Thomas Pynchon, Ken Kesey, James Purdy and others suggest a type of fiction so refreshingly different from the conventional novel that one suspects the prophets of the novel's death to be wrong. What these authors do have in common is a vision of their world as chaotic and fractured. How can one affirm order in a world which is fragmented? (Greiner)

In addition to this fragmented, disjunctive sense of lived reality in the modern world, the novels themselves seem fragmented, disjointed, often out of whack, and comically illogical. Conventions of plot, character, setting, and theme are often called into question. And why not? None of these writers is certain that an inherent moral order can be found, he suggests, nor do they believe that we can be ordered by individual will in order to approximate it. Writes Greiner, "At the risk of oversimplification, I suggest that these authors refuse to verify a moral code because verification would allude to order and sanity in a world which they see as fractured and absurd."

Satirists have long pointed out the absurdity of human experience, of course, and much of the humor in literature is dark to the point of being gallows humor. Yet the black humorist is neither a satirist as such, nor is his humor a gallows humor precisely. For

> . . . black humorists reject the satirist's faith in the ability of satirical laughter to reform man's follies. Even the most elaborate definition of satire must emphasize the author's use of laughter not so much to tear down as to encourage rebuilding. The black humorist dismisses reformational and ethical certainties. . . . (Greiner)

I agree with Greiner on all of these points, but I want to try to go beyond them. If black humor is not what we normally think of as literary satire, neither is it what we normally think of as American literature. That is a sweeping statement, I realize, and it calls for a bit of background and explanation.

To begin with, ours is a literature more agrarian than urban, more Western than Eastern. As Leslie Fiedler, Richard Chase, and countless other scholars have demonstrated, the American novel has its deepest roots in a romantic, frontier mentality, one evident in this country well before we had a printed literature of our own. You have only to consider our oral traditions to see what they mean. As a country, we are somewhat unique insofar as our richest oral traditions are divisible by gender. On the one hand, there are what we call *fairytales.* These were known as "old wives' tales" in the last century, and in either case they are stories and storylines brought to this country from Europe and handed down from the "old wife," that is, the *grandmother* of the family, to the children for whom she was caring.

That in the extended family the task of raising infants was left generally to the husband's mother is reflected in the fairytales we read to our children today. You will notice that the most positive image of an adult woman in our fairytales is the fairy godmother, the white-haired, apple-cheeked matron who makes your wishes come true with the wave of her wand. You will notice, in other words, that the grandmother cast herself in the most favorable adult female role, leaving her daughter-in-law to fend for herself.

Daughters-in-law, *mothers,* in other words, do not fare very well in our fairytales. This is true even in their Disneyfied, twentieth-century variations, in which the wicked mother becomes the wicked *step*-mother. She is more often the cause of the young protagonist's dilemma—think of the mother-daughter sexual rivalry in *Snow White,* to name but one instance—than the source of the protagonist's salvation.

That the grandmother should have cast her daughter-in-law in such an unfavorable light suggests that certain family tensions have been common down through the ages; and this suggestion is complemented, perhaps, by her depiction of her son. Only the *adolescent* male, the handsome young prince, the *unmarried* son, is sure to have our storyteller's blessing. Positive images of adult males are virtually as hard to come by in our fairytales as positive images of women, for the men in our fairytales are alternately ineffectual (that is, dominated by a scheming woman), evil, or downright stupid.

Such sexual prejudices are small potatoes, however, when you compare them with those of our second oral tradition—the tall tale, the "fish" story. These are male stories with a capital MALE. They emerged on the frontiers of America as men sought to entertain one another at the end of the day, and, perhaps as a consequence, they are about male exploits in the absence of women, told with just the flair for exaggeration that one might expect.

List the legendary figures to emerge in this American oral tradition—Paul Bunyan, John Henry, and so forth—and you will note that they share certain things in common. Size, for one thing. They're bigger than life. Whether they are figures cut from whole cloth, like Paul Bunyan, or vast exaggerations of men who actually lived, like John Henry or Johnny Appleseed, they are sure to be either men of giant size and capabilities or men with some special natural talent which allows them to impose their will on the frontier landscape.

This imposition of will is central to the heroes we have honored through our legends. If you seek to be an American folk hero, the subject of stories passed along from one generation to the next, you are wasting your time in investment banking. Choose instead to live on the frontier, that is, to the west of city life, and choose to work with your body. For frontier, physical skills, and the prowess they entail, are requisite to the image of maleness that these folk tales project.

And requisite too is the need to perform as a male in the absence of women. In American folklore, you must head for the sea or the nearest frontier if you want to be *a man's man*—the water, the wilderness, any place a woman might be unlikely to go. Women played a significant role in the settling of this country, but there is little evidence to that effect in our folktales. Our folk heroes, you see, not only do their best male work independent of women, they do so far away from city life, from domesticity and churches and schools, away from all the institutions where a woman would be expected to leave her mark.

To be a MAN in our folktales is to be most of all *in control* of things, and traditionally, this was to be found as well in our print literature. In its simplest form, this has meant to impose one's will on the landscape, cutting down timber at an impossible pace, say, or laying railroad ties due westward, but it has also meant imposing one's will on other people without a woman there to call a halt. In literature both "highbrow" and "lowbrow" we find such things. Take the Western, the most American of all American genres.

A nation too young to have an *Odyssey* or an *Iliad* or an *Aeneid,* we have in their place the American cowboy and tales of his exploits and journeys. The cowboy's physical courage, his stoic dignity, his self-sufficiency, his penchant for moving beyond the latest civilized settlement are more the stuff of legend and penny-dreadful novels than they are the stuff of American historical fact. Yet the cowboy occupies a larger place in our mythology than he could ever have occupied as a historical figure. To much of the world he is an icon of this country—for better or worse. He is the physical embodiment of American personhood (a euphemism for American *manhood*), the corporal reification of our obsession with independence and remaining in control of our own fate and living by a code of honor having less to do with the letter of the law than with a fiercely independent sense of right and wrong.

It does not take much to see why the *schlemiezel* might be a rather new addition to our literature, coming as it does with the rise of black humor and a particular sort of postwar, Jewish-American writing as well.

Whether it is physical sexual prowess, as in Mailer, the prowess of the seaman, as in Melville, the prowess of the frontiersman, as in Cooper, the prowess of economics, as in Fitzgerald, or the prowess to be had through a private codification of American maleness, as in Hemingway, it is a prowess our literature has honored traditionally. Perhaps that has been its single greatest concern. From its very beginnings, ours has been a literature filled with protagonists determined to gain control of a situation, to take charge of their own destinies, to *light out for the territory ahead,* as Twain puts it at the end of *Huckleberry Finn,* and fend for ourselves.

We have not suffered victims very gladly in such a tradition. Beginning in this country before print literature itself, the victim has been alternately an enigma and an embarrassment. Or at least we have not suffered victims until lately, for black humor is just filled with them.

The protagonist called to mind by the phrase, "black humor" is, as my students might say, "a loser." He is not simply the *naif,* the *picaro* figure, a Huck Finn—the outsider. We have always liked to honor "outsiders." He is different. He is inept.

Too, he is a weakling. And worse, he is out of control. I do not mean to say merely that he cannot gain control of his own fate, though that is the case as well, often; I mean rather that he himself is out of control. He is everything the stoic cowboy would despise. Women torment him, bullies kick sand in his face, parents nag him, and in response, he whines, he bitches, he moans.

This new sort of American protagonist is more Eastern than Western, more likely to be city-bound than he is to be at home on the range. As he is portrayed by our black humorists, he is defined by all the things which limit him. He is the embodiment of that great American male fear, *impotence.* Figuratively, and sometimes literally, he cannot get it up.

He cannot even flee when he wants to. He is city-bound, overcome by the landscape in which he finds himself. He may try to flee the city in which he finds himself, of course; but this will not come to much—we know that. It is one of the great lessons of these novels that all American highways lead back to where they began.

This same sense of circularity is to be found on yet another level. Traditionally in our literature our protagonists have followed one of two paths. The most satisfying has been the first of these, but it has almost always been the most risky: to create a system of values and live true to them, recognizing all the while that to live true to oneself must come at a price.

The second, and often the more practical, path has been to find one's place in the culture, to adopt a role, if you will, one replete with customs and values, and then accommodate that role as well as you can. This is what it has often meant to live one's life as a man: to choose between rebellion, on the one hand, and accommodation on the other. But to *choose*—that is the thing!

Not now, however, at least not in black humor. What sense is there in making a choice when neither alternative can satisfy? Why choose at all, then? Why *light out* when there is no territory ahead?

Both the *schlemiel* and the *schlimazl* serve to point us toward some higher order, toward some greater scheme of things than the values of their own culture, and it is here

that black humor and the *shtetl* tradition of *the fool* meet and then part company. Black humor denies this greater scheme of things. It envisions neither gods nor devil. It has faith in neither grace nor transgression. Nor, for that matter, does it embrace the *shtetl*'s *schlemiel* or *schlimazl* as such.

What we find instead are protagonists midway between these two points on a continuum, as it were, characters embodying the failings of both extremes, moving first toward the right, then back toward the left, forever betwixt and between.

This is a new notion of American manhood, American man as *homo incapacitus,* one might say, where man is defined by his incapacities—a notion offering us in place of *the fool* and his goodness only the sense of man's loss. At one moment rebelling, at another trying to accommodate, at one moment trying to fit the information to a closed set of beliefs, at the next moment furiously trying to rearrange these beliefs to fit the latest information, they are hybrids, one and all classic *fools,* and then again not: *schlemiezels.*

> *Jay Boyer, "The Schlemiezel: Black Humor and the Shtetl Tradition," in* Humor, *Vol. 4, No. 2, 1991, pp. 165-75.*

Donald J. Greiner on the affirmative qualities of black humor:

The comparable blackness of a particular writer's humor is indeed secondary—all are black, but some are blacker, and funnier, than others. More important is the attempt to decide what the presence of so many modern American comic novelists means. Taken together, the novels of Hawkes, Vonnegut, Heller, John Barth, Donleavy, Friedman, Thomas Pynchon, Ken Kesey, James Purdy, and others suggest a type of fiction so refreshingly different from the conventional novel that one suspects the prophets of the novel's death to be wrong. What these authors do have in common is a vision of their world as chaotic and fractured. How can one affirm order in a world which is fragmented—and violently so? But though the disoriented quality of modern life prevents the black humorist from celebrating order, it does not propel him to nihilism. The fact that *Catch-22, Giles Goat-Boy,* and *Second Skin* have been written, published, and read suggests the authors' hope for meaningful communication at the very least. Thus a modern comic novelist like John Barth can insist that art is "exhausted" and yet show how alive the "literature of exhaustion" is.

Donald J. Greiner, Comic Terror: The Novels of John Hawkes, *Memphis State University Press, 1973.*

Robert Scholes

[*Robert Scholes is an American educator and critic who has written a number of influential books on contemporary fiction and critical theory, including* Structuralism and Literature *(1974) and* The Nature of Narrative *(1966). In his study* The Fabulators, *Scholes discusses the relation of black humor to the satirical and picaresque literary traditions.*]

One of the most obvious and permanent qualities of the fable proper—the little brother of the full-scale fabulations we are considering—is that it has a moral. It is didactic. Or so it seems until we look into the matter. In practice we find that many collections of fables include some tales without morals, and that in many other cases, well-meaning souls have tacked morals onto tales for which they are absurd or grossly inadequate. For instance, consider this gem from a collection called *A C. Mery Talys (A Hundred Merry Tales,* 1526—this is Paul Zall's modernized version from his Bison paperback edition):

> A young man of the age of 20 years, rude, and unlearned, in the time of Lent came to his curate to be confessed—which, when he was of his life searched and examined, could not say his Pater Noster. Wherefore his confessor exhorted him to learn his Pater Noster and showed him what an holy and goodly prayer it was and the effect thereof and the seven petitions therein contained:

> "The first petition beginneth, Pater Noster, etc., that is to say—'O Father hallowed by Thy name among men in earth as among angels in heaven.' The second, Adveniat, etc., 'Let Thy kingdom come and reign Thou among us men in earth as among angels in heaven.' The third, Fiat, etc., 'Make us to fulfill Thy will here in earth as Thy angels in heaven.' The fourth, Panem nostrum, etc., 'Give us our daily sustenance always and help us as we give and help them that have need of us.' The fifth, Dimitte, etc., 'Forgive us our sins done to Thee as we forgive them that trespass against us.' The sixth, Et ne nos, 'Let us not be overcome with evil temptation.' The seventh, Sed libera, etc., 'But deliver us from all evil—Amen.'"

> And then his confessor after this exposition to him made, enjoined him in penance to fast every Friday on bread and water till he had his Pater Noster well and sufficiently learned.

> This young man meekly accepting his penance so departed and came home to one of his companions and said to his fellow: "So it is that my ghostly father hath given me in penance to fast every Friday on bread and water till I can say my Pater Noster. Therefore I pray ye teach me my Pater Noster and, by my troth, I shall therefore teach thee a song of Robin Hood that shall be worth 20 of it."

> By this tale ye may learn to know the effect of the holy prayer of the Pater Noster.

This propensity in the fable to point a moral at all costs has been parodied beautifully by Thurber in such tales as "The Unicorn in the Garden," with its splendid moral of "Don't count your boobies until they are hatched." But as readers of fables we can draw, if not a moral, at least a conclusion, from the existence of these two kinds of little fables—that is, the Aesopian kind where the moral really works, and those such as the one I quoted, which are essentially amoral and resist violently any attempt to assimilate them as exempla of an orderly moral world. The moral fable is kind to the larger satire; the amoral fable

to the picaresque tale, which can grow very long indeed. And both of these large forms have something to do with that movement in modern fiction—in modern life, really, because it is not exclusively literary—which is often called Black Humor. Most of this country's exciting young writers are connected in some way with this literary movement. Albee, Barth, Donleavy, Friedman, Hawkes, Heller, Purdy, Pynchon, Southern and Vonnegut have all been stamped with this dark label at one time or another, and, various as the writings of these men actually are, their works differ from those of the previous generation in a manner special enough to justify some common terminology and some consideration of what their work, collectively, implies about the current literary situation. The term Black Humor is probably too clumsy to be of much use to criticism, but before discarding it we should do well to milk it of such value as it may have in helping us to understand this new fiction and to adjust to it. We can begin with a view from the inside:

> They say it is a critic's phrase, Black Humor, and that whatever it is, you can count on it to fizzle after a bit. . . . I think they may be wrong on that . . . count. I have a hunch Black Humor has probably always been around, always will. . . .

The quotation is from Bruce Jay Friedman's shrewd and engaging foreword to an anthology, *Black Humor,* that he edited for Bantam Books in 1965. The anthology itself is worth looking at, as it includes work by a number of exciting writers, including Mr. Friedman himself. But it is not a really successful book, this anthology, mainly because some of the best Black Humorists tend to use larger forms than the short story, building effects over many pages. Selections from Barth's *Sot-Weed Factor* and Heller's *Catch-22,* for example, hardly begin to work in this format.

But I don't mean to discuss Mr. Friedman's anthology here. I mention it because I want to use his definition as a point of departure for some theorizing of my own. Friedman suggests that we have a kind of Black Humor movement in contemporary writing because events "Out There" in the contemporary world are so absurd that the response of the Black Humorist is the most appropriate one possible. But he also suggests, in the lines just quoted, that Black Humor is not merely a modern fad but a continuing mode of literary activity. He doesn't say how this apparent contradiction is to be resolved, however, and this is where I want to begin. I think he is right on both counts. Black Humor is a modern movement but also a development in a continuing tradition.

Most of the literary kinds and modes are with us all the time, but in every era some are very alive and others quite dormant. If we consider literature as a way of looking at the world, for every age certain modes serve better than others to bring things into focus, to align the ideals of the age with actuality. In a historical perspective Black Humor seems allied with those periodic waves of rationality which have rolled through Western culture with continually increasing vigor for over two thousand years. The intellectual comedy of Aristophanes, the flourishing satire of imperial Rome, the humanistic allegories and anatomies of the later Middle Ages, the picaresque narratives of the Renaissance, the metaphysical poems and satires of the seventeenth century, and the great satiric fictions of the Age of Reason—all these are ancestors of modern Black Humor. Of course, an illustrious pedigree does not guarantee the worth of an offspring. Nevertheless, since understanding and evaluating depend so completely on our sense of genre, pedigree is where we must begin. This is especially important in the case of the so-called Black Humorists: first, because their immediate point of departure has been the novel, a form which we view with certain realistic expectations; and second, because nearly two centuries of literature dominated by romantic notions of value lie between the modern Black Humorists and such immediate ancestors as Swift and Voltaire.

Developments in current fiction are very closely analogous to the poetic revolution of a generation or so back, when the rediscovery of the metaphysical poets helped spark a revival of witty, cerebral verse. Current interest in Rabelais, Cervantes, Aleman, Grimmelshausen, Swift, Smollett, and Voltaire is part of the general drift of fiction into more violent and more intellectual channels. The sensibility and compassion which characterized the great novels of the nineteenth century are being modified by the wit and cruelty of Black Humor. Horace Walpole's epigram about life's being tragic for those who feel and comic for those who think is a gross oversimplification, no doubt, but it is useful to us in describing such a massive change in literary climate as the one we are considering here. Such changes, like variations in the weather, are not things one can do much to alter. The question is how to adjust to them.

For us, the question—like most literary questions—becomes one of how to read. What expectations should we bring to this new writing? What benefit can we hope to derive from it? To put it crudely, what's in it for us? I think there is a lot in it for us—it is our literature, speaking to us most immediately. If it seems out of focus, perhaps we must change our lenses to see it clearly. First of all, we must discard the notion that these works are "novels" as novels have been written. They are different from their immediate predecessors. Here the pedigree of Black Humor will help, for it is surely better to think of Voltaire and Swift when reading Vonnegut and Barth than to think of Hemingway and Fitzgerald. But we must not take the pedigree in too simple-minded a fashion either. If we say, "O yes, satire" we may go just as wrong as if we were to expect another realistic novel. Though these works are offshoots of a family tree we recognize, they are a new mutation, a separate branch with its own special characteristics and qualities. To define the special attributes of this new branch is surely the critic's business. But it is a hard business because the writers are a mixed group, differing in temperament, intellect, and experience; and because they themselves are experimenting with this new uncrystallized mode of writing, often trying new things from book to book. A writer like John Hawkes seems almost to obliterate his humor with his blackness, while Bruce Jay Friedman makes a nearly opposite emphasis. How can we unite such disparity other than by mere verbal trickery or sleight-of-word?

Kurt Vonnegut.

I am hedging here, warning the reader to take my attempt to define a revolution in progress as necessarily a tentative formulation. But despite the difficulty, I think enough can be said to justify the project. I see Black Humor as crucially different from its satiric and picaresque ancestors, but also as clearly relatable to these two traditional kinds of fiction. In this chapter and the following one I intend to explore certain aspects of these relationships. First, the relationship of Kurt Vonnegut's kind of Black Humor to the satirical tradition. Then, the relationship of Terry Southern and John Hawkes to the picaresque tradition. This arrangement is not intended to be a neat pigeonholing affair: for, first of all, in practice satire and picaresque are often very hard to distinguish from one another, and second, all three of these writers are clearly inheritors of both traditions. I have divided the genres in this manner mainly for convenience—but not arbitrarily, as I hope to demonstrate.

The satirical kind of Black Humor is qualified by the modern fabulator's tendency to be more playful and more artful in construction than his predecessors: his tendency to fabulate. Fabulative satire is less certain ethically but more certain esthetically than traditional satire. This causes the special tone that the phrase Black Humor so inadequately attempts to capture. The spirit of playfulness and the care for form characteristic of the modern fabulators operate so as to turn the materials of satire and protest into comedy. And this is not a mere modern trick, a wayward eccentricity. These writers reflect quite properly their heritage from the esthetic movement of the nineteenth century and the ethical relativism of the twentieth. They have some faith in art but they reject all ethical absolutes. Especially, they reject the traditional satirist's faith in the efficacy of satire as a reforming instrument. They have a more subtle faith in the humanizing value of laughter. Whatever changes they hope to work in their readers are the admittedly evanescent changes inspired by art, which need to be continually renewed, rather than the dramatic renunciations of vice and folly postulated by traditional satire.

The special tone of Black Humor, often derived from presenting the materials of satire in a comic perspective, is perfectly illustrated in a passage from Vonnegut's *Cat's Cradle.* The narrator in this passage is interviewing the son of a Schweitzer-type jungle doctor on a small Caribbean island:

> "Well, aren't you at all tempted to do with your life what your father's done with his?"
>
> Young Castle smiled wanly, avoiding a direct answer. "He's a funny person, Father is," he said, "I think you'll like him."
>
> "I expect to. There aren't many people who've been as unselfish as he has."
>
> "One time," said Castle, "when I was about fifteen, there was a mutiny near here on a Greek ship bound from Hong Kong to Havana with a load of wicker furniture. The mutineers got control of the ship, didn't know how to run her, and smashed her up on the rocks near 'Papa' Monzano's castle. Everybody drowned but the rats. The rats and the wicker furniture came ashore."
>
> That seemed to be the end of the story, but I couldn't be sure. "So?"
>
> "So some people got free furniture and some people got bubonic plague. At Father's hospital, we had fourteen hundred deaths inside of ten days. Have you ever seen anyone die of bubonic plague?"
>
> "That unhappiness has not been mine."
>
> "The lymph glands in the groin and the armpits swell to the size of grapefruit."
>
> "I can well believe it."
>
> "After death, the body turns black—coals to Newcastle in the case of San Lorenzo. When the plague was having everything its own way, the House of Hope and Mercy in the Jungle looked like Auschwitz or Buchenwald. We had stacks of dead so deep and wide that a bulldozer actually stalled trying to shove them toward a common grave. Father worked without sleep for days, worked not only without sleep but without saving many lives, either."
>
> [*After an interruption*]
>
> "Well, finish your story anyway."
>
> "Where was I?"
>
> "The bubonic plague. The bulldozer was stalled by corpses."
>
> "Oh, yes. Anyway, one sleepless night I stayed up with Father while he worked. It was all we could do to find a live patient to treat. In bed after bed after bed we found dead people.
>
> "And Father started giggling," Castle continued.
>
> "He couldn't stop. He walked out into the night with his flashlight. He was still giggling. He was making the flashlight beam dance over all the dead people stacked outside. He put his hand on my head, and do you know what that marvelous man said to me?" asked Castle.
>
> "Nope."
>
> " 'Son,' my father said to me, 'someday this will all be yours.' "

In the passage an excess of the horrible is faced and defeated by the only friend reason can rely on in such cases: laughter. The whole episode is a comic parable of our times. Progress, that favorite prey of satirists from Swift and Voltaire onward, means that some people get free furniture and some get the plague. Some get Biarritz and some get Auschwitz. Some get cured of cancer by radiation; others get radiation sickness. But the spuriousness of progress is not seen here with the *saeva indignatio* of the satirist. Progress is seen not as a conspiracy but as a joke. The Black Humorist is not concerned with what to do about life but with how to take it. In this respect Black Humor has certain affinities with some existentialist attitudes, roughly distinguishable in terms of the difference between seeing the universe as absurd and seeing it as ridiculous—a joke. The absurd universe is a pretty dismal affair. The best, in fact, that Camus found to offer humanity as a response to the human condition was "scorn." In "The Myth of Sisyphus" he told us that "there is no fate that cannot be surmounted by scorn." The Black Humorists offer us something better than scorn. They offer us laughter. The scorn of Sisyphus leads finally to resignation—"He, too, concludes that all is well." Beneath the hide of this scornful hero beats the heart of Dr. Pangloss after all. Vonnegut's fictional prophet Bokonon suggests a better posture for man on the mountain top than that of Camus's Sisyphus, who simply starts down again to pick up his burden. At the end of *Cat's Cradle,* with the world nearly all frozen, Bokonon gives one of his last disciples a bit of advice:

> If I were a younger man, I would write a history of human stupidity; and I would climb to the top of Mount McCabe and lie down on my back with my history for a pillow; and I would take from the ground some of the blue-white poison that makes statues of men; and I would make a statue of myself, lying on my back, grinning horribly, and thumbing my nose at You Know Who.

What man must learn is neither scorn nor resignation, say the Black Humorists, but how to take a joke. How should one take a joke? The best response is neither acquiescence nor bitterness. It is first of all a matter of perception. One must "get" the joke. Then one must demonstrate this awareness by playing one's role in the joke in such a way as to turn the humor back on the joker or cause it to diffuse itself harmlessly on the whole group which has participated in the process of the joke. Even at the punch line of apocalypse, feeble man can respond with the gesture prescribed by Bokonon, suggesting an amused, tolerant defiance. Of course, a joke implies a Joker, as Gloucester observed amid the cosmic tomfoolery of *King Lear:* "They kill us for their sport." But I do not think the Black Humorists mean to present us with a new deity, crowned with a cap and bells in place of thorns. No more than Paul Tillich do they wish to "bring in God as a *deus ex machina*" to fill the great hole in the modern cosmos. To see the human situation as a cosmic joke, one need not assume a Joker.

Some accidents are so like jokes that the two are indistinguishable. Moreover, it is possible to conceive of all human history as part of a master plan without thinking of the Planner in quite the traditional way. In an early science fiction novel, now re-released in paperback, Kurt Vonnegut developed such a view. In *Sirens of Titan* he presented a cosmos in which the whole of human history has been arranged by intervention from outer space in order to provide a traveler from a distant galaxy with a small spare part necessary for his craft to continue its voyage to the other side of the universe. Such purposefulness to entirely extra-human ends is indeed a cosmic joke, but is not intended as such by those superior beings who have manipulated earthly life for their own ends. This novel suggests that the joke is on us every time we attribute purpose or meaning that suits us to things which are either accidental, or possessed of purpose and meaning quite different from those we would supply. And it doesn't matter which of these mistakes we make.

Samuel Johnson, whose *Rasselas* is a rather solemn ancestor of *Cat's Cradle,* picked on just this aspect of the vanity of human wishes in one of his finest works—an *Idler* paper so black and humorous that Johnson later suppressed it. In this essay Johnson presented a dialogue between a mother vulture and her children, in which the wise old bird, looking down at a scene of human carnage from a recent European battle, tells her young that men do this at regular intervals as part of a divine plan which has shaped the best of all possible worlds—for vultures. In presenting this view of life as a joke on all those who think this is the best of all possible worlds for men, Johnson is very close to his modern descendants. For the joke is one key to the fabulative impulse, especially to the impulse behind Black Humor. To present life as a joke is a way of both acknowledging its absurdity and showing how that very absurdity can be encompassed by the human desire for form. A joke like Dr. Johnson's acknowledges and counteracts the pain of human existence. In the best of all possible worlds there would be no jokes.

Robert Scholes, "Fabulation and Satire," in his The Fabulators, *Oxford University Press, Inc., 1967, pp. 33-56.*

Brom Weber

[Weber is an American critic and educator who specializes in American literature. In the following excerpt, he traces the history of black humor from the eighteenth century to the early 1970s.]

The late Edmund Wilson was one of the most influential of American literary critics. Though generally sympathetic to humor and the unconventional in art, in 1954 he bitterly charged that the humorous writings of a virtually unknown nineteenth-century American writer were unadulterated poison. The occasion was the publication of a collection of George Washington Harris's Sut Lovingood sketches in a volume edited by me. Wilson's *New Yorker* review granted that Harris had "real literary merit." Nevertheless, it condemned Harris for his allegedly "crude and brutal humor." Without mentioning black humor by name, Wilson was denouncing Harris for being one of this nation's early black humorists.

By 1964, ten years after Wilson's outburst, the seriocomic tradition of George Washington Harris had reappeared vigorously in a pack of important novels. Vladimir Nabokov's *Lolita,* William Gaddis's *The Recognitions,* Thomas Berger's *Crazy in Berlin,* James Purdy's *Malcolm,* William Burroughs' *The Naked Lunch,* J. P. Donleavy's *The Ginger Man,* and Terry Southern's *The Magic Christian* were published before the 1950's were over. In their grimly comic wake followed even more powerful works of black humor which startled yet pleased the American public in the early 1960's: Joseph Heller's *Catch-22,* Ken Kesey's *One Flew Over the Cuckoo's Nest,* Thomas Pynchon's *V.,* Walker Percy's *The Moviegoer,* John Barth's *The Sot-Weed Factor,* John Hawkes's *The Lime-Twig,* and Bruce Jay Friedman's *Stern.* Some of these black humorists are now regarded as among the leading American novelists of our time, successors to the previously dominant generation of Sherwood Anderson, Ernest Hemingway, William Faulkner, and F. Scott Fitzgerald.

When Edmund Wilson attacked black humor, he applied a perspective which others also may believe appropriate. Black humor disturbs because it is not necessarily nor always light-hearted, funny, amusing, laughter-arousing. Furthermore, black humor seems to have little respect for the values and patterns of thought, feeling, and behavior that have kept Anglo-American culture stable and effective, have provided a basis of equilibrium for society and the individual. Black humor violates sacred and secular taboos alike without restraint or compunction. It discovers cause for laughter in what has generally been regarded as too serious for frivolity: the death of men, the disintegration of social institutions, mental and physical disease, deformity, suffering, anguish, privation, and terror. For anyone steeped in the dominant tradition of Anglo-American culture, which since the eighteenth century has believed that humor is intrinsically good-natured, trivial, and kindly, the unpredictable, topsy-turvy, often hostile and sadistic character of black humor may well appear to be perverse and intolerable.

As we shall see later when considering the background of black humor in American literature, especially since World War I, neither in its general temper nor in many of its particulars is black humor a newcomer on the American scene. Admittedly, it has played a subordinate role and frequently been neglected, but its practitioners have been among our greatest writers. Before exploring these matters in greater detail, however, one must cope with an issue that has tended to raise confusion about the subject of literary black humor and its continued right to its traditional name.

Ever since the late 1960's, sociopolitical developments in American life have made it difficult for us to continue using the term "black humor" without a sense of confusion. We are not always certain to what the term refers. This was not always the case. In American culture, as in many other cultures, the color white has tended to represent the sacred, the innocent, the pure and the good. On the other hand, an antithetical set of associations has clustered around the color black: the diabolic, the unknown, the irrational, the inhuman, the corrupt and the bad. There is no denying that black humor as a categorical term entered the literary idiom in order to designate, and often strongly to depreciate, a literature which resembled traditional humor yet seemed alien to the latter's spirit and almost to subvert it. Viewed objectively, then, whatever racism is implicit in the use of blackness to denote unpalatability or unwholesomeness may well be implicit in the traditional term "black humor" itself.

Certainly an impressive argument can be made for the abandonment of the literary term. Indeed, those Americans who were once given the appellation "Negro" have made a start toward that end. Their mounting ethnic pride and search for identity has led them to invest blackness with many of the positive elements that once were exclusively properties assigned to whiteness. Thus, by an accelerated evolutionary process, black humor is for some people an ethnic designation that coexists as a phrase alongside such new linguistic coinages as "Black Power," "Black Studies," "Black Politics," and "Black Is Beautiful."

Let me illustrate briefly the tendency to claim for a particular ethnic phenomenon the name of that which had begun as a general literary phenomenon participated in freely by Americans of all ethnic backgrounds and skin colors. Two collections of writings identified as traditional black humor appeared in the 1960's: *Black Humor* in 1965 and *The World of Black Humor* in 1967, edited by Bruce Jay Friedman and Douglas M. Davis respectively. Only two among the contributors to these volumes were known Afro-Americans or Blacks. On the other hand, an anthology entitled *Black Humor,* published in 1972, features works by black writers only. This new collection, with few exceptions, contains no writing that warrants assignment to the category of literary black humor as the term had been conceived of less than ten years ago by editors Friedman and Davis.

The future of the ethnically centered phrase "black humor" in the world of politics and society is uncertain. It already may have served its practical purpose in that arena and thus soon be abandoned like so many other political slogans. In the world of literature, one may hope, the phrase will not disappear at all. Sensitive to language

as they are, many writers might well believe that political censorship of the literary phrase foreshadowed social censorship of the old-time black humor and they would hesitate to express it. One may be sure that some writers will persist. For example, Philip Roth, originally deeply rooted in the Henry James school of psychological analysis and aesthetic formalism, became a forthright black humorist with *Portnoy's Complaint* in 1969 and *Our Gang* in 1972. Established black humorists such as Walker Percy, Thomas Berger, John Barth, Kurt Vonnegut, and William Burroughs seem unable to create in any other mode of vision. In any case, the responsibility of critics is to be sympathetically aware of the impulses animating writers as well as to evaluate them scrupulously. For that reason, accordingly, and also because black humor under that very title has had a lengthy and significant record of achievement in American and other cultures, it seems proper now and in the future to use the term "black humor" with its traditional literary references intact.

The term "black humor" should not be subject to revision of meaning by Americans, furthermore, because it happens not to have originated in the United States, and neither does it describe a mode of vision and expression uniquely limited to American culture. Black humor is a linguistic importation from France which, despite its colonialism, has long provided a hospitable, nonracist environment for those of African ancestry, one in which sensitive, frustrated black Americans such as Richard Wright and James Baldwin have lived with satisfaction. *L'humour noir,* which in English translation becomes black humor, functioned as a central doctrine of French surrealism almost from its inception in the 1920's. Surrealism recognized that black humor transcends race and nation. When André Breton, theorist and leader of French surrealism, compiled his *Anthologie de l'humour noir* in 1940, he included therefore not only such French exemplars as the Marquis de Sade, Count de Lautréamont, Arthur Rimbaud, Alfred Jarry, and Jacques Vaché, but also such prototypical English black humorists as Jonathan Swift, Thomas De Quincey, and Lewis Carroll.

The heterogeneity of the writers whom André Breton dubbed black humorists strongly indicates the extraordinary variability of black humor's form and content. Sade, who extolled sexual and psychological brutality . . . Rimbaud, who sought to abandon logic and language . . . Lautréamont, who revelled in nightmare . . . Jarry, who scatologically mocked and parodied middle-class culture while drinking himself to death . . . Swift, who relentlessly scorned most of mankind . . . Carroll, who wove intricate patterns of fantasy and nonsense . . . Vaché, the Dadaist who asserted that humor was "a sense of the theatrical and joyless futility of everything" and proved it with his blackly humorous suicide that involved the concurrent murder of a friend—Breton linked these conglomerate writers under the generic title of black humorist by profoundly fusing and expanding concepts of humor developed in Hegel's philosophy and Freud's psychoanalytic theories.

Breton's surrealist theory of humor rationalized the disgust with established society and its stabilizing culture, as well as the consequent individualistic breaches of sociocultural taboo, which to a considerable extent are prominent in black humor. Humor, he believed, was a means whereby one defended the inner self against the constraints of the human condition, physical and psychological as well as social. Humor enabled one to transcend the trivial reality in which man is imprisoned by logic, reason, and subjective emotion, freeing him to achieve union with the objective metaphysical Absolute. Detached by humor from the determinism of the material world and from the culturally determined self, man's dark unconscious could express its metaphysical yearnings and intuitions in the form of untrammelled dream, fantasy, and non-sense. Hence black humor.

The indignant laughter of the black humorist, Breton went on to say, animated more men and resounded most vibrantly in periods of great stress engendered by crises such as war or the demoralization of Europe in the 1920's. But it was manifest always, even though minimally, for a few men heard constantly the grinding noises of a crumbling world, were subject to numerous fears, doubted the reality of fact and object. Black humor's blackness, then, derives from its rejection of morality and other human codes ensuring earthly pattern and order, from its readiness to joke about the horror, violence, injustice, and death that rouses its indignation, from its avoidance of sentimentality by means of emotional coolness, and from its predilection for surprise and shock.

André Breton's theoretical system, though probably unknown to most contemporary American black humorists and not applicable without modification to each of them in particular, is nevertheless a generally illuminating key to the motivations, attitudes, and direction of black humor in the 1960's. Breton lived in New York City from 1941 to 1946, a refugee from World War II and fascism. However, it is dubious that his presence did much to advance the understanding and progress of black humor in the United States. Indeed, surrealism, and the dadaism from which it stemmed, had reached the country well before Breton's arrival. The surrealist magazine *View,* for example, had been founded by 1940, the same year in which the annual *New Directions* devoted several hundred pages to European surrealist writing in English translation. Much earlier yet, in 1913, Francis Picabia and Marcel Duchamp had acquainted avant-garde artists in the New York area with the nihilistic rudiments of what a few years later would be known as dadaism in Europe. Many young American writers thereafter became directly familiar with dadaism and surrealism by virtue of residence in France, Germany, and Switzerland in the 1920's. Those who did not cross the Atlantic read dadaist and surrealist literature in little magazines such as *Little Review, Broom,* and *transition,* some of which had been founded by Americans and were published in Europe.

Of all the young American avant-garde writers influenced by the dadaist-surrealist ferment in the 1920's, only one—Nathanael West—managed the feat of creating an extended work of black humor. His extraordinarily good first novel, *The Dream Life of Balso Snell,* appeared in a limited edition in 1931. Despite its stylistic and intellectual brilliance, little attention was given it until the 1950's. Only three hundred copies were made available for sale in the United States, yet I still was able to purchase a copy at list price in the mid-1940's at the bookstore of Moss and Kamin, West's publishers: a whole shelf of unsold copies of the elegantly printed work reposed in neglect in the shop. Despite the great depression and World War II, not all Americans were ready for West's kind of sardonic, scatological, mocking, parodistic assault upon the elements of American civilization, of Western civilization as a whole. His anti-hero Balso Snell undertakes a fantastic journey through the steamy bowels of the Trojan horse. During its course, West questioned and turned upside-down not only the cultural values and patterns of tradition, but also those of the intellectual and artistic vanguard which opposed them. The satire, cool detachment, joking, grotesque characters, wild situations, paradox, morbidity, and wit of *The Dream Life of Balso Snell* were whipped up into a sardonic dark comedy which West admirably sustained in three other novels—*Miss Lonelyhearts, A Cool Million,* and *The Day of the Locust*—completed before his untimely death in 1941.

That West was proud of his membership in the clan of black humorists is evident in an anonymous third-person advertisement he wrote for the publishers of *Balso Snell.* "English humor has always prided itself on being good-natured and in the best of taste," he observed. "This fact makes it difficult to compare N. W. West with other comic writers, as he is vicious, mean, ugly, obscene and insane." Though he acknowledged the similarity of *Balso Snell* to Lewis Carroll's tales of Alice's fantastic adventures, West emphasized more strongly his affinity with French black humorists: "In his use of the violently disassociated, the dehumanized marvelous, the deliberately criminal and imbecilic, he [West] is much like Guillaume Apollinaire, Jarry, Ribemont-Dessaignes, Raymond Roussel, and certain of the surréalistes."

Like most of his American contemporaries in the literary avant-garde of the 1920's and 1930's, Nathanael West consciously sought new artistic and intellectual stimulus from European rather than American sources. A few Americans did not. William Carlos Williams praised the pessimistic, pre-Spenglerian poetry of Edgar Allan Poe. Hart Crane embraced the dark psychophysical mysteries of the sea which Herman Melville had delineated. But they were part of a tiny minority. On the whole, young writers regarded the American literary record as one dominated by superficiality and emptiness, by a vapid contentment with things as they were that discouraged probe and experiment.

William Dean Howells, the novelist-critic who had begun his career in the 1860's and was still alive in 1920, symbolized for them the fossilized state of the American arts. Forgotten were his successful championship of literary realism, his laudable introduction to the United States of nineteenth-century masters from Russia, Italy, and France. American literature from its start, the avant-gardists angrily insisted, had been heading for the dead end epitomized by Howell's famous advice that the American writer should portray the smiling aspects of the national life instead of those which writhed hidden away on its dark underside.

Howell's penchant for happy comedy that softened trage-dy represents the profound streak of optimism in the American character. It has been one of the sustaining fac-tors in the national experience ever since English Puritans and other refugees from European reality first landed on this continent. However, high hopes of creating a spiritual and material paradise on earth have often been frustrated. So it was in the American beginning. Aspiration clashed with the uncontrollable, dream with fact. The Puritan temper was compelled to reconcile incompatibles. Its zeal-ous religious faith was balanced with gloomy foreboding. By 1676, the Puritan poet-satirist Benjamin Tompson typ-ically mourned the moral and social decline of a culture merely fifty years old, satirizing church, government, and men alike for failing to uphold the norms and patterns that had made life free and happy in the past. It was equally in order for Tompson to poke fun at Boston women and Harvard academics, intermingling his gayety with lines and scenes of deeply somber tone. A more toughly humor-ous mood than Howells displayed had been part of the American scene long before the twentieth century.

Puritan culture merits special attention because many contemporary black humorists believe that Puritanism banished love, life, and laughter from North America. It would be more accurate to say that Puritans did their best to come to realistic grips with the limitations inherent in the human condition. Furthermore, they actually cher-ished humor and applied its liberating, restorative spirit to aspects of daily existence that, like war and death, were embittering. The Reverend Richard Bernard declared in 1626, for example, that "there is a kind of smiling and joy-ful laughter, for anything I know, which may stand with sober gravity, and with the best man's piety." In 1707, the Reverend Benjamin Colman devoted three sermons to the improvement of humor, eager to reveal that in the eyes of nature, God, and Christianity humor was beautiful and es-sential.

> Mirth [he wrote] "is some loose or relaxation to the labouring Mind or Body. . . . 'Tis design'd by nature to chear and revive us thro' all the toils and troubles of life. . . . That by no means must they [Puritans] seem to place any thing of Reli-gion in being *Dull and heavy, sad and disconso-late, sour and morose.* Not only does religion *Allow* but *Obliges* unto chearfulness with Sobri-ety: It gives the most reason for it, and is serv'd by it: None have that *License,* and in none is it so Decent and Comely as in them that are good.

Puritan dominance of American culture ended long before the eighteenth century was over. Some elements of its lega-cy have not been satisfactory. But it did provide a model for emulation in its blending of grim experience and disap-pointment with idealistic hope in an amalgam permeated by humor. The model was not always emulated. Indeed, in the United States as in other nations, black humor—at least until the 1960's—has been an underground murmur surfacing only upon occasion. But these occasions have been impressive in a qualitative sense, as we have come in-

creasingly to understand during the past thirty or so years of careful re-examination of American literary culture.

Profuse historical evidence of black humor's long presence can be found in an anthology of American humor that I edited in 1962, the first collection of its kind to encompass the whole body of American humorous literature from the seventeenth century through the 1950's. Two guidelines established to facilitate editorial selection of entries in the book are pertinent, for they were derived from an objective reading and rereading of fiction, poetry, and nonfictional prose without concern for prior categorization of the liter-ature as either humorous or nonhumorous. First, many se-rious, post-Puritan writers not customarily considered hu-morous were in fact darkly seriocomic in intention and re-sult. Second, the view that humor focuses only upon trivia and merely provides frivolous amusement is contradicted by the writings of numerous distinguished American au-thors.

Some outstanding examples of the literature upon which the guidelines were based are the macabre chapter from Nathaniel Hawthorne's *The House of the Seven Gables,* that brutally ridicules Judge Pyncheon's corpse and laughs at the doom of his materialistic values and plans; the cold-blooded, satirical account of a young sailor's le-galized surgical murder by a dehumanized, bureaucratic naval doctor in Herman Melville's *White-Jacket;* and Am-brose Bierce's hilariously ghoulish "Oil of Dog," in which an upholder of bourgeois ideals calmly relates how com-mercial enterprise led his parents first to boil dogs, then children and adults, and finally themselves in order to manufacture oil for medicinal preparations. This brief list-ing of black humor can be expanded with selections from Benjamin Franklin, Washington Irving, Edgar Allan Poe, Mark Twain, Stephan Crane, Edith Wharton, Sherwood Anderson, Robert Frost, F. Scott Fitzgerald, William Faulkner, and Ernest Hemingway, to name only a few of the better-known writers who preceded Nathanael West as deliberate practitioners of black humor.

Black humor leaped into prominence in the ten years be-tween 1955 and 1965, as if it never before had existed in American literature. Indeed, it not only capitalized upon historical ignorance, but often—as in Thomas Pynchon's *V.* and John Barth's *The Sot-Weed Factor*—repudiated the notion that history was relevant to the present. Black humor proved extraordinarily congenial to our now-centered culture. At its best, black humor helped some readers to cope with the omnipresence of potential nuclear destruction, with the massive bureaucratization of social institutions and relations, with the individual's helpless-ness under the power of material objects and invisible forces, with the nerve-racking manner in which all things ceaselessly and rapidly changed, with the terror and death of hot and cold wars that seemed to have fastened them-selves like parasites upon human existence. The saving therapy of laughter was highly beneficial as always.

Despite its initial astonishing success, however, black humor soon experienced a precipitate decline in quality and prestige from which only a few of its writers—Walker Percy and Thomas Berger pre-eminently—have escaped. Some—William Gaddis, Joseph Heller, Terry Southern—

have not been published for several years and may have stopped writing altogether. The recent fiction of Bruce Jay Friedman, J. P. Donleavy, and William Burroughs has been repetitious and uninspired, truly dull. Kurt Vonnegut's apparent upward flight from the juvenile realm of science fiction ironically returned him full-circle in *Slaughterhouse-Five* to the exhausted sentimentality and moral-intellectual banality of the countercultural adolescent. Dark laughter's coolness had been institutionalized into a mechanized, totalitarian disregard of the mundane but important concerns of existential human experience. Culture-fatigue had been succeeded by nihilistic emptiness in which even the creation of black humor had no meaning, so that John Barth devoted himself to demonstrating that writing has no function and silence is preferable. The suicidal example of nightclub comic Lenny Bruce hovered ghost-like over the once promising scene.

Not all black humorists, fortunately, underwent the self-destruction which their apocalyptic spirits had wished in vain upon the rest of the world. Thomas Berger's *Vital Parts* and Walker Percy's *Love in the Ruins,* novels published in 1970 and 1971 respectively, are works in the great black humor tradition of Hawthorne, Melville, Faulkner. Both Berger and Percy have managed to extricate themselves from the morass of intellectual and moral void into which their lesser brethren sank. With the complexity of minds directly attuned to the disintegrating powers of nightmare and chaos, they search for positive alternatives that will provide a rallying center. Berger and Percy have avoided the temptation inherent in black humor to imitate disorder, to parody the incoherence of reality by slipping unself-consciously into literary incoherence. It is a pleasure to note that Thomas Berger and Walker Percy are as hilariously comic and laughter-evoking in their works as black humor traditionally has been. These writers reassure us that black humor will not disappear from American literature.

> Brom Weber, "The Mode of 'Black Humor',"
> *in* The Comic Imagination in American Literature, *edited by Louis D. Rubin, Jr., Rutgers University Press, 1973, pp. 361-71.*

Ihab Hassan

[*An Egyptian-born American educator and critic, Hassan has written extensively about twentieth-century avant-garde literature. His publications include* Radical Innocence: The Contemporary American Novel *(1961),* The Literature of Silence: Henry Miller and Samuel Beckett *(1968), and* The Dismemberment of Orpheus: Toward a Postmodern Literature *(1971). In the following essay, published a year before Bruce Jay Friedman's anthology made "black humor" a commonly accepted label for absurdist fiction, Hassan discusses the "absurd laughter" which permeated fiction of the early 1960s.*]

The sound of absurd laughter crackles in the theaters Off Broadway, and the sick joke or Addamsy cartoon has rippled across the American prairie. In movie houses, *Dr. Strangelove* packs the audiences in. Everywhere, the spirit of gallows humor dances crazily on the wind. Even fiction

now booms or howls as the stately voice of Henry James would never have permitted itself. The booms and howls of fiction, however, are themselves of manifold register; when the imagination breaks forth in laughter, laughter assumes many voices. Let us not presume, therefore, to discover unity where none exists. And yet consider this selection of novels: Bellow's *Henderson the Rain King,* Ellison's *Invisible Man,* Capote's *Breakfast at Tiffany's,* Cheever's *The Wapshot Chronicle,* Purdy's *Malcolm,* and Salinger's *The Catcher in the Rye.* Does not slapstick sometimes echo in them as a scream heard in a nightmare? Better still, consider the cruel japes and gags of some younger novelists: Joseph Heller, Thomas Berger, J. P. Donleavy and Thomas Pynchon. There is dark laughter in their fiction, a good deal of bitterness, and some madness too. Is it the death, then, or the rebirth of comedy that is at hand?

It is, I believe, the birth of a new sense of reality, a new knowledge of error and of incongruity, an affirmation of life under the aspect of comedy. For comedy, broadly conceived, may be understood as a *way of making life possible in this world, despite evil or death.* Comedy recognizes human limitations, neither in broken pride nor yet in saintly humility but in the spirit of ironic acceptance. It is, therefore, the antic child of realism.

Danger, which has made us tightrope walkers to the future, may also make clowns of us all. Yet clowns can have skill and vision too. They can unite horror and slapstick and make men laugh in order to live. This is something that novelists know well, although their critics do not always say so.

The contemporary world does not offer occasions for authentic tragedy—or so the rumor runs. The hero of Miller's *Death of a Salesman* is a sad and broken man, probably more pathetic than tragic. The heroes of our fiction, likewise, are not larger than life. At best, they are rogues with a heart or winsome adolescents—like Holden Caulfield or Holly Golightly. At worst, they are victims with a purpose—like most of us. Bemused by incongruities, besieged in their private as in their social life, they do not stand tall with the dignity of Achilles or Odysseus. Their conflicts seldom allow for final resolutions. This is the way our world strikes the novelist, and no other is yet known to him.

It is no great wonder that younger novelists are now more anxious to respond to the incoherence of life, to its openness. They are relearning the old art of improvisation in fiction; they cultivate the picaresque or fantastic modes; they are repelled by the neat formulations of style or structure that formalist critics once pressed too hard. Their sense of order admits of potential disorder. In short, they have acquired a tolerance for the mixed, causeless quality of experience: its loose ends, its broken links, its surprises and reversals. Knowing how outrageous facts can be, they do not pretend to subdue them with a flourish and a symbol.

The effects of this new comic realism in American fiction are already apparent. Realism, in fact, seems to be introduced through the back door, cloaked in the surrealism of slapstick or nightmare. Bawdiness and even obscenity abound, recalling our attention to the corporeality of man, to his instinctual being. Chance and improvisation are accepted, not simply as a source of humor but also as a critique of social goals, values and traditions. Chance, which defies the rigid predictability of contemporary life, restores a measure of individual freedom. This is sometimes carried so far, in the works of Mailer or Kerouac, as to betray an anarchic impulse masked in tomfoolery. The new comic spirit, we see, is a mixture of boisterousness and bitterness, hope and despair. It is quite simply a reaction to the concrete situation of modern man. Despite its grim, absurd or surreal contortions, the reaction, I believe, is a positive one. The new comedy may find a way of restoring sanity through madness or buffoonery. And by restoring our faith in the surface of life, the simple and tangible things of this world from which tragedy removes itself finally, it may find a way of tightening the bonds of love. Who knows but behind the leering mask of the jester may be concealed the old face of American innocence, vulnerable and responsive?

There are, of course, precedents in modern literature to this development of comedy. Dostoevski's *Notes from Underground* and *The Possessed,* two books that I have always considered a kind of manifesto of the modern disorderly sensibility, resound with grotesque or demonic laughter. The works of Joyce, Kafka and Gide are full of comedy both clownish and satanic. And the fiction of Sartre, Malraux and Camus shows how comedy vanishes behind the mask of irony, revealing the latter as an intellectual grimace, its true emblem a grinning skull. Modern European literature, which is largely existential, is really a raucous record of absurd laughter.

In America, the comic spirit has taken both parallel and divergent forms. The gothic or supernatural strain in classic American fiction, black with laughter, has been brilliantly noted by Leslie Fiedler. Faulkner extends this strain well into the twentieth century. Stories like "A Rose for Emily"—the proud woman who kills her lover and lies in bed by his putrefying corpse for forty years—and novels like *Sanctuary* and *As I Lay Dying* make capital use of macabre humor. Even in his jaunty series of books about the acquisitive Snopes family, *The Hamlet, The Town* and *The Mansion,* Faulkner shows that burlesque, whether in horse or wife trading, may serve as a thin disguise for chilling malevolence. (In *The Reivers,* however, comedy becomes once again a little more broad and good-humored; a boy, a Negro, and a brawny simpleton bounce down the road in a stolen car, board in a brothel, and try to make a fortune on horse betting.) But Faulkner is not alone in exploiting this particular strain of comedy in our time. Sherwood Anderson, that woeful master of the grotesque, focused on the poetry of deviation and infirmity and on their humor. A satirist and surrealist both, Nathanael West revealed in his stories about Hollywood or Manhattan freaks a unique gift for torture-house parody. And Henry Miller, a more sanguine surrealist, seems often at his best when translating acute pain into impish or ribald pleasure. In all this, however, I would not claim that the comic spirits of Europe and America show identical developments; nor would I say that the comic strain I have isolated subsumes the varieties of comedy on both continents.

My purpose, rather, is simply to observe a common and powerful event of the modern imagination: the deflection of laughter toward anguish.

The sound of absurd laughter crackles in the theaters Off Broadway. In movie houses, *Dr. Strangelove* packs the audiences in. Everywhere, the spirit of gallows humor dances crazily on the wind. Even fiction now booms or howls as the stately voice of Henry James would never have permitted itself.

—*Ihab Hassan*

A rapid glance at more recent American fiction shows a wide variety of comic attitudes, all reflecting the intricacies of the new laughter. The gamut of these attitudes runs from nightmare to sheer slapstick. And yet the twisted shape of humor betokens in every case the will to criticize life and still to confirm it.

The obsessive humor of the horror story is familiar to anyone who has seen Poe or Hitchcock in action: it is very much akin to the mournful frolic of nightmare. Its aim, however, is not only sensational. In the hands of such writers as John Hawkes or William Burroughs, it underscores the fact that insanity or evil often puts on an antic disposition. Comedy moves into the midnight terrain where Macbeth met the witches, and there it reckons with the surreal forces of human desires. But the witches' heath may also lie in the heart of a modern city. There guilt and atonement—witness the Jew and Gentile who haunt one another in Bellow's *The Victim*—stage a comedy of errors, at times both ludicrous and horrible.

If there is much warping in nightmare, there is only a little less in the grotesque figures who populate the fiction of Eudora Welty, Flannery O'Connor, Carson McCullers and James Purdy. The aim of these writers is to describe spiritual distortion in our time; in so doing they focus on physical distortion. The one incarnates the other. They create freaks of love or loneliness, or monsters of holiness. (Hazel Motes, for instance, in Miss O'Connor's *Wise Blood,* is a preacher in the "Church Without Christ," an ascetic who blinds himself with quicklime and wears barbed wire next to his skin, yet who is a murderer too.) But freaks and monsters are the subject of veiled mockery; their abnormality shocks and shames us into ironic laughter. This is why the comedy of the grotesque often seems acerb. Only children can laugh at hunchbacks or fanatics with glee. Adults learn to transform their discomfort into irony, which serves to domesticate the monsters roaming the inner landscapes of the soul.

The ironic attitude lies close to the satiric. In the latter, the object of attention is not the monstrous, which is irremediable, but rather the follies or vices of man, things merely reprehensible. There is a combination of both attitudes in the comedy of Nabokov's *Lolita;* its hero still thinks of himself as a grotesque monster. But when satire appears in more pure forms, as it does in the fiction of Mary McCarthy, we are already moving toward the sunnier reaches of comedy. The scalpel is still sharp, but the caricatures of artists or academics to which it is applied are not altogether beyond hope. Their foibles are ours, and in our heart of hearts few of us consider ourselves beyond redemption.

It is this possibility of regeneration that we sense in diverse characters, rogues and innocents abroad, who masquerade as the descendants of gaunt Don Quixote. There is, to be sure, something quixotic and whimsical about them, an idea or illusion raised to the condition of truth. But there is also a good deal of bitter passion, as in Ellison's *Invisible Man,* about the Negro whom everyone manages not to see; or moral disgust, as in Donleavy's *The Ginger Man,* about the bawdy heel who boozes on the milk money of his children until they develop rickets. Comedy in these books can still have a rasping noise. Even in such zany and genuinely humorous "picaresques" as Salinger's *The Catcher in the Rye* and Capote's *Breakfast at Tiffany's,* which move us farther from bitter comedy, laughter trails into a wistful tremor. It is, of course, nostalgia, not nightmare, that in their case qualifies our joy. The smile on our lips

Slim Pickens in Dr. Strangelove.

is sad. Perhaps it is only Saul Bellow who carries comedy over the barrier of human loss, surmounting the bitterness and the doubt. Augie March, that "Columbus of the near-at-hand," and Henderson, too, know pain and error; but they also know the *animal ridens* and they refuse to lead "a disappointed life."

The unrelieved exuberance of life comes through in a number of novels that make large use of fantasy and burlesque. Cheever's *The Wapshot Chronicle,* about a daft and indestructible Yankee family, attests to the continuities of human existence under the aspect of whimsy. Berger's *Reinhart In Love* employs farce and madcap humor to convey the abundance of love. And the buffoonery of Heller's *Catch-22* settles for nothing less than sanity and freedom. The sense of release, of possibility, is very large in these novelists. But we should be doing their spirit violence were we to ignore their undertone of individual and even anarchic protest. The last two novels hold society, its norms, pieties and organizations, in suspicion: neither Reinhart nor Yossarian will accept anything but the Self as sacred. It is as if comedy, finally freed from the dark constraints of the modern world, had suddenly overreached itself to the borders of chaos. But even chaos is sometimes apt.

There are, of course, many other novelists—John Updike, Philip Roth, Herbert Gold, Norman Mailer, Jack Kerouac, *et cetera*—who make their own singular contributions to comedy. But my aim was not to be inclusive. It was rather to convey some sense of the richness of the comic spirit in our time, and to observe the spectrum of attitudes that it has assumed. For, in a sense, the two works by Burroughs and Heller that I have named do not stand far apart: our path through comic attitudes has brought us from nightmare to slapstick and back again.

And this is precisely the point. Nightmare and slapstick do meet in that surreal, comic vision that, recognizing the discrepancies in human life, expresses and mediates them. The new comic spirit, I have already said, deflects humor toward anguish. But like the tragedies of yore the new comedy also purges and cleanses. Its purgation is achieved through a comic recognition of the absurd. The Fool of tradition, as everyone knows, was a mischievous and holy man, and pain was imprinted on his funny face. The rituals of which he was a part are even more ancient. As a Scapegoat, he carried away evil and death. As Reviler and Confuser, he forced the community to defend its most cherished beliefs with force or wit. We could not recapture his wisdom or jollity without experiencing the ambiguous range of his agony.

One is finally led to ask why it is that contemporary fiction still subsists in a twilit region of the public scene. Faulkner and Hemingway are now dead—in my admiration of them, I conceded to no one. It seems that the end of an era of American fiction has been marked. But what of the next? The vital theater of Albee and Gelber has begun to catch our eye. What of the novel? Recent fiction has not lacked astute and sympathetic critics. Some of them, like R. W. B. Lewis, are justly well known; others, like Earl Rovit or Paul Levine, may become better known soon. It may be that the new spirit of comedy in our fiction will

MAJOR MEDIA ADAPTATIONS: Motion Pictures

Lonelyhearts, 1958. United Artists. [Adaptation of *Miss Lonelyhearts* by Nathanael West] Director: Vincent J. Donahue. Cast: Montgomery Clift, Robert Ryan, Myrna Loy, Dolores Hart.

Lolita, 1962. MGM. [Adaptation of the novel by Vladimir Nabokov] Director: Stanley Kubrick. Cast: James Mason, Sue Lyon, Shelley Winters, Peter Sellers.

Dr. Strangelove: or, How I Learned to Stop Worrying and Love the Bomb, 1964. Columbia. [Adapted by Terry Southern from *Red Alert* by Peter George] Director: Stanley Kubrick. Cast: Peter Sellers, George C. Scott, Sterling Hayden, Slim Pickens, James Earl Jones.

Fellini Satyricon, 1969. United Artists. [Adaption of *The Satyricon* by Petronius] Director: Federico Fellini. Cast: Martin Potter, Hiram Keller, Max Born, Salvo Randone, Capucine.

The Magic Christian, 1969. Grand/Commonwealth. [Adaptation of the novel by Terry Southern] Director: Joseph McGrath. Cast: Peter Sellers, Ringo Starr, Isabel Jeans, Graham Chapman, John Cleese.

Catch-22, 1970. Paramount. [Adaptation of the novel by Joseph Heller] Director: Mike Nichols. Cast: Alan Arkin, Martin Balsam, Buck Henry, Martin Sheen, Orson Welles.

M*A*S*H, 1970. Fox. [Adaptation of the novel by Richard Hooker] Director: Robert Altman. Cast: Donald Sutherland, Elliott Gould, Tom Skerritt, Sally Kellerman, Robert Duvall.

A Clockwork Orange, 1971. Warner Brothers. [Adaptation of the novel by Anthony Burgess] Director: Stanley Kubrick. Cast: Malcolm McDowell, Patrick Magee, Adrienne Corri, David Prowse.

Slaughterhouse Five, 1972. Universal. [Adaptation of the novel by Kurt Vonnegut] Director: George Roy Hill. Cast: Michael Sacks, Valerie Perrine, Ron Leibman, Eugene Roche, Perry King.

The Day of the Locust, 1975. Paramount. [Adaptation of the novel by Nathanael West] Director: John Schlesinger. Cast: Donald Sutherland, Karen Black, Burgess Meredith, William Atherton, Billy Barty.

One Flew Over the Cuckoo's Nest, 1975. United Artists. [Adaptation of the novel by Ken Kesey] Directors: Vincent Schiavelli, Milos Forman. Cast: Jack Nicholson, Brad Dourif, Louise Fletcher, Will Sampson, Danny DeVito.

That Obscure Object of Desire, 1977. Greenwich-Galaxie-Incine/First Artists. [Adaptation of *La Femme et la Pantin* by Pierre Louys] Director: Luis Buñuel. Cast: Fernando Rey, Carol Bouquet, Angela Molina.

Naked Lunch, 1991. Naked Lunch Productions; Recorded Picture Co./Fox. [Adaptation of the novel by William S. Burroughs] Director: David Cronenberg. Cast: Peter Weller, Judy Davis, Ian Holm, Julian Sands, Roy Scheider.

serve to heal some rifts between the author and his audience, proving to the latter that all is not dearth or despondency in literature. The serious writer—he is not so rare as he is rumored to be—who can also be affirmative these days faces a grave task. The great temptation he must resist is this: that dark laughter may freeze on his face, may turn into a sophisticated leer or a knowing grimace. That way decadence lies. There are still no substitutes for a passionate sense of life.

> *Ihab Hassan, "Laughter in the Dark: The New Voice in American Fiction," in* The American Scholar, *Vol. 33, No. 4, Autumn, 1964, pp. 636-38, 640.*

R. B. Gill

[*In the following essay, Gill cites the 1970s works of Kurt Vonnegut, Günter Grass, and Milan Kundera as evidence of a shift in black humor novels towards a more traditional pattern of comic resolution, even as an underlying tone of pathos and alienation is retained.*]

Since World War II, comedy has often been a somber affair. Writers like Beckett, Ionesco, Pynchon, and Pinter, even the more popular comics like Lenny Bruce and Monty Python, have found their material in the bleak absurdities and shocking incongruities of modern life. At times this "comedy of the absurd," "comedy of menace," and black humor have seemed closer to the metaphysics of existentialism and the pathos of naturalism than to the imaginative green worlds and happy endings of traditional comedy. Many of the darker works belong to the decades of the fifties and sixties, but if more recent comedy has seemed less self-conscious in its discouraging metaphysics, it is because alienation has become an accepted fact rather than a new fashion. When we examine contemporary comedy, we see plainly how far it has traveled from traditional concepts of the genre. Kurt Vonnegut, Günter Grass, and Milan Kundera, three novelists of widely different backgrounds, but all heirs to the viewpoints of postwar comedy, have recently written works which move closer to traditional comedy but which remain too faithful to their dark heritage to develop a truely comic outlook. Open-eyed and without illusions, they do not suggest that their comic imaginations can transform reality; nevertheless, they attempt to salvage what they can from their worlds, to accommodate themselves to what must be in any case. Their novels, then, record a comic impulse compromised by an unillusioned realism.

Our idea of comedy as a genre has been complicated by the peculiarities of absurd and black humor, which seem comic merely because they create laughter, but, traditionally, comedy has belonged to a world view that thinks justice is possible. In comedy good people have gotten what they deserve in the end and social rituals like dances, meals, and marriages have celebrated the re-establishment of a properly functioning society. Comedy's hopeful attitude has created new ways, new structures, even new worlds, to make its ideals possible. Shakespeare fashioned a green world where love, imagination, poetry, and the magic of a midsummer night's dream change reality; Moliére contrived a *deus ex machina* to set straight the troubled world of *Tartuffe.* In contrast, Ionesco's black humor comes closer to a tragic account of reality than a comic transformation of it. "My characters . . . drift through incoherence, having nothing of their own apart from their anguish, their remorse, their failures, the vacuity of their lives. Human beings saturated in meaninglessness cannot be anything but grotesque, their sufferings cannot be anything but derisively tragic." His mute Orator exits into the darkness of pathos at the end of *The Chairs.*

Such "comedy" shares a basic world view with pathos and tragedy; with traditional comedy it shares only laughter, a physiological response to psychological tension. It is not surprising that comedy and laughter should be confused, even though laughter is certainly neither limited to comedy nor necessarily characteristic of it. They both arouse tension and release it with a resulting sense of superiority or triumph; they both depend on situations of a playful or gamelike nature; they both bring pleasure; and, of course, laughter often occurs in a comedy. Regardless of these similarities, a work filled with laughter may distrust the happy endings of traditional comedy. Certainly, that is so in the recent novels of Vonnegut, Grass, and Kundera, where laughter abounds. It is true that the three lack Ionesco's insistent display of shock that there should be metaphysical unhappiness, but neither do they believe that good people get what they deserve from life. Their laughter is more a sign of their healthy adjustment to a sad world than a result of their confidence in a comic redemption of it.

Vonnegut's *Slapstick* and *Jailbird* share with earlier dark humor a distinctly uncomic belief in the bleakness of life. In *Slapstick* a phone call to the afterlife sounds "like nothing so much as the other end of a telephone call on a rainy autumn day—to a badly run turkey farm." Civilization crumbles into absurdities that are bizarre even for a Vonnegut novel. The most we can do, Vonnegut feels, is to reduce the high quotient of sham in this sad world. Over his door Dr. Swain chisels Hippocrates' words, "If you can do no good, at least do no harm." Yet, there is in his attitude a laughing resilience that goes beyond black humor. He hurls some vigorous obscenities at the pathos of humanity but avoids the pretension of a tragic pose. In spite of the turkey farm, Vonnegut's message is more how to cope than the impossibility of coping. In *Slapstick* the absurdity of life fosters social neuroses, which one can at least begin to treat, rather than metaphysical alienation, which is beyond all cure. The dehumanization in Ionesco's *Rhinoceros* promises little hope for the human condition, but if Vonnegut is not exactly hopeful neither does he completely abandon reform of injustice. *Slapstick* is dedicated to Laurel and Hardy because "they never failed to bargain in good faith with their destinies." Good faith at least, a neutral ineffectuality that refuses to do harm, the rejection of pretense, and a wistful feeling that somehow humans might achieve happiness and fruitful union— these are not heroic attributes, but they are an attempt at accommodation with life.

[In "The Divine Stupidity of Kurt Vonnegut," *Esquire,* September 1970] Leslie Fiedler has suggested that Vonnegut sees "a meaningless universe redeemed by love." That is probably a bit too histrionic for Vonnegut; certainly "redemption" would be too strong a word for love in *Slapstick.* What redemption is possible comes in an entirely different manner. Dr. Swain believes "that life can be painless, provided there is sufficient peacefulness for a dozen or so rituals to be repeated simply endlessly." Humans must fill the void with creations of their own simple actions that offer respite from pain even if they do not offer meaningfulness. Although such rituals do not change reality, they do not surrender to it. Swain suggests that one might serve his fellow humans "by watering their houseplants while they were away; by taking care of their babies so they could get out of the house for an hour or two; by telling them the name of a truly painless dentist; . . . by visiting them in a jail or hospital." His suggestions end with a faint echo of the Gospel of Matthew, a diluted social gospel, but more than Ionesco can find.

God, the inept turkey farmer, gets a toast in *Jailbird* as "the laziest man in town." Strong stuff, notes the narrator. And nature is just as uncaring; life goes on with a whimsical brutality. Everywhere an amazing variety of atrocities backs up the judgment of Ruth Starbuck, survivor of a Nazi concentration camp: "We were a disease, she said, which had evolved on one tiny cinder in the universe, but could spread and spread." The world of *Jailbird* is peopled with poor souls who do not have the ability to counteract their ill fate. Walter F. Starbuck himself, the main character, passively falls into disasters, inadvertently betraying a friend to the McCarthy hearings, inadvertently participating in the Nixon Watergate crimes, naively (and illegally) concealing a will, all in an inept attempt to be helpful. Mary Kathleen O'Looney, owner of RAMJAC, the megacorporation that controlled everything from McDonald's to Saul Bellow, tries to accomplish economic revolution by leaving her vast wealth to the people of the U. S., but, of course, only criminals, lawyers, consultants, a new bureaucracy, and other conglomerates profited from her futile scheme. The book is filled with such lost souls, including in the Prologue Vonnegut's own parents. As Ruth Starbuck notes, humans "could only create meaningless tragedies . . . since they weren't nearly intelligent enough to accomplish all the good they meant to do."

Yet, Vonnegut's black humor is lightened in *Jailbird* more than in *Slapstick* by comic dreams of a just world. Walter Starbuck dreams of a new age of responsibility after the Nuremberg trials: "It's the most important turning point in history." Mary Kathleen O'Looney dreams of a peaceful economic revolution, and woven throughout the novel is a dream that the story of Sacco and Vanzetti's martyrdom "would cause an irresistible mania for justice to the common people to spread throughout the world." In the Prologue Vonnegut notes that he had always been enchanted by brave veterans

> who were still eager for information of what was really going on, who were still full of ideas of how victory might yet be snatched from the jaws of defeat. "If I am going to go on living," I have thought, "I had better follow them."

The answers to life's miseries in *Jailbird* are extensions of those found in *Slapstick.* First, there are the little games that fill up time—smoking, eating chocolates, repeating banal expressions, continuously playing chess, continuously playing Edith Piaf records. These games range from the neuroses that replace angst in Vonnegut's world to the peaceful rituals that Dr. Swain recommended repeating endlessly to prevent pain. Another answer to life's miseries is on the order of the thoughtfulness and companionship that *Slapstick* recommends. Vonnegut repeats approvingly a high-school student's summary of his work, "Love may fail, but courtesy will prevail."

The final antidote to life's miseries in *Jailbird* carries simple courtesies a step further. It is a mixture of that diluted social gospel in *Slapstick,* though a bit stronger here, together with the dream of social justice that Vonnegut thought he "had better follow." When Starbuck was President Nixon's special advisor on youth affairs, he turned out "two hundred or more weekly reports on the sayings and doings of youth" all of which, he notes, could have been reduced to the same telegram: "YOUNG PEOPLE STILL REFUSE TO SEE THE OBVIOUS IMPOSSIBILITY OF WORLD DISARMAMENT AND ECONOMIC EQUALITY. COULD BE FAULT OF NEW TESTAMENT (QUOD VIDE)." The martyrdom of Sacco and Vanzetti, the unifying motif of the novel, is explicitly compared to the Crucifixion. Between the Prologue and Chapter One, Vonnegut quotes Sacco's last letter to his son: "Help the weak ones that cry for me, help the prosecuted and the victim," a plea that echoes throughout the book and finds its main form in the reply of Powers Hapgood to a judge's question why a man from a good background should concern himself with the working class. "Why?" he replied. "Because of the Sermon on the Mount, sir." That also is the answer Starbuck gives to Congressman Nixon during the McCarthy hearings.

Vonnegut almost closes the novel with that thought, but in the last two sentences he shies away from its idealism. When the tape of Starbuck's answer to Nixon is played back at a farewell party for him, it is given merely polite applause by friends who do not understand its profundity. Honest Vonnegut cannot bring himself to end with a comic transformation. He understands the sad facts. What has been learned? Who remembers Sacco and Vanzetti? What difference has Nuremberg made? People are indifferent; they lack seriousness; they say, "It's allright"; time passes and they forget. Starbuck's idealism is lost in the inanity of polite applause. Vonnegut bears witness to the ideal but cannot promise it. With Starbuck, he says in ambivalent but realistic words, "I still believe that peace and plenty and happiness can be worked out some way. I am a fool."

It is in laughter rather than in traditional comedy that Vonnegut's comic urge to create finds its outlet. That laughter issues from the tensions between comic inventiveness and honest bargaining. Few writers toss off stray ideas, themes, and rejected plots with such abandon. In *Slapstick* and *Jailbird* an exuberantly creative self manipulates the absurd at will, short of ending with the false promises of traditional comic transformations. Laughter in Vonnegut's novels is self-conscious and wistful, certainly never boisterous. Such laughter is the wry reaction of a healthy, knowing psyche adjusting itself to facts. It is the self's small moment of triumph as it observes the ignorance and incongruities of others, as it feels its own superiority to an absurd world. This is the laughter that liberates the self from the unnecessary bonds and unthinking rigidities that less adaptable people allow themselves to fall into. That healthful, liberating laughter has been the cause of Vonnegut's popularity as a writer. We admire him precisely because he can laugh at the irrationalities of our world without attempting to substitute the morals of satire or the solutions of comedy. Such laughter, we feel, is full of intelligence and common sense, in touch with ideals and realities at the same time.

Günter Grass also finds an acutely self-conscious position between pathos and comedy. At home in neither, he is not constrained by one viewpoint but, rather, wanders between these positions to explore just where truth lies or meaning can be found. More than Vonnegut's novels, whose Midwestern American naturalism emphasizes the lonely, isolated individual, Grass's *The Flounder, The Meeting at Telgte,* and *Headbirths* search through history and society as if they no longer trust a private and partisan view. The basic situations and metaphors of *The Flounder* are social. There is the pregnancy that divides the novel into nine sections, each with its wife and cook, and issues in the new birth at the close of the book. Cooking and foods from neolithic sorrel to the final, triumphant flounder dinner also give the novel a social bias. In addition, the trial of the Flounder and the Grimms' tale of "The Fisherman and His Wife" are central social themes. *The Flounder,* then, is essentially a social history, an examination not so much of the events as of the universal patterns of meaning that underlie the history of Pomerania from prehistory to present, of its foods, and especially of the relationships between the sexes.

Although Grass is exuberant in his survey of food and sex through history, he also feels the pathos of the human condition. He summarizes a trip to Calcutta in the word "shame." His tale of Amanda Woyke's trip to Heaven reveals starvation there as well as on earth, and no God at all. The Flounder in his guise as *Weltgeist* volunteers to operate in place of the Lord, creating Maoist farm kitchens to dole out potato soup, but even that sort of progress is limited to Heaven. For Grass the problems presented by the "categories of masculine thinking," which have until now guided history, are all but overwhelming. Ready solutions are not to be found. He distrusts revolutions, upheavals, and Great Leaps Forward of all kinds. The Flounder notes, "Every revolutionary process known to us has served up orgiastic rites of death, massacres drawing their justification from some masculine purity-principle or other." Like Vonnegut, Grass cannot find within himself allegiance to transcending causes.

In his last speech to the Women's Tribunal, which is trying him for fostering the atrocities of male-dominated history, the Flounder recounts what had been his hopes. Interestingly, his words are those of a person who seeks a final consummation rather than an accommodation with life. Under his guidance, men have pursued an "ultimate goal" with uncompromising "single-mindedness" and a "cold passion sprung from faith," exalting "death as the essence of life." Dissatisfied with the female principle of "being," the Flounder has engendered a male principle of "becoming," of activity, progress, honor, victory, and death—in short, the tragic principles that have created human history. The Flounder seeks to justify himself by insisting he had hoped that after the wars men would come to their senses, that they would "transvalue all their values." The hope for "transvalues" beyond history has been the energizing soul of tragedy and the despair of pathos. Ironically, the Flounder has encouraged tragic values with the hope that they will lead to a comic solution. That generic mix-up may be considered a major point of the novel. Perhaps, the end of the novel tells us, women will transcend the values of male-dominated history. We could then speculate that the female principle is comic and life affirming, but, unfortunately, the women end up battling each other in a most masculine manner. Grass rejects easy dichotomies.

For Grass, then, as for Vonnegut, the solutions are the smaller, peaceful actions. First, there is humor. There was, he notes, "something dry and theoretical about the demand for justice" of nineteenth-century socialists. They lacked the flesh and blood that "robust humor" can provide. Next, there is food, not *haute cuisine* but hearty food of the people—grains and potatoes, the garden herbs, sausages, and fish soups in plenty. Third, in contrast to the lonely Vonnegut, is sex. The novel begins with Awa, a neolithic ur-mother with three breasts. Awa's capacity for satisfying her whole tribe with sex and mothering prevented the male dissatisfaction needed to motivate the beginning of history. The novel ends on the narrator's union with Maria Kuczorra, a survivor of the strife and shooting in the Gdansk shipyard strikes of 1970 and now a symbol of the new forces of history. The fairy tale of "The Fisherman and His Wife," Grass tells us, exists in two versions, one favorable to men and the other to women. Although the Grimms suppressed the latter, Grass would not have us favor one sex over the other, for, whatever we may hope, in the end the certainties are the simple, accommodating rituals of laughter, eating, and the union of the sexes.

To these rituals, *The Meeting at Telgte* adds art. The book, a short tribute to "Group 47," an association of authors, critics, and publishers instigated by Hans Werner Richter after World War II, portrays a similar gathering of German authors at the close of the Thirty Years War. As in *The Flounder,* Grass's attitude is measured and tentative, exploring history to find sources and parallels for his ideas. He has a point to make but will not push it without acknowledging his reservations. Those old writers, whom Grass so clearly admires, are quarrelsome, prejudiced, ineffectual. They wish to issue a manifesto demanding a just peace, but their conflicting views make the effort all but impossible. Eager to assume moral poses, they nevertheless write "poems in praise of princes to whom murder and arson came as naturally as their daily prayers," as Christoffel Gelnhausen (Grimmelshausen), certainly no innocent himself, reminds them.

Yet, their art offers a means—weak and compromised, but

real—of rising above their limitations. Heinrich Schütz, then the revered master of German music, reminds them that art has the power "to wrest from helplessness—he knew it well—a faint 'and yet.' " It is art that brings them together, art that prompts Paul Gerhardt, the hymnologist and uncompromising Lutheran pastor, to pray that even the Catholic Gelnhausen be endowed with "right words," art alone that they can agree on. "No prince could equal them," Grass writes. "Their riches could not be bought or sold. And even if they should be stoned and buried in hatred, a hand with a pen would rise out of the stone pile. They alone had the power to preserve for all time whatever truly deserved the name of German."

Having reached a final, simple version of their appeal for peace, the writers celebrate concord with a meal, a fish feast reminiscent of the flounder dinner, but their tavern burns, destroying the text of the appeal: "And so, what would in any case not have been heard, remained unsaid." Thus, like Vonnegut, Grass has it both ways. Bargaining in good faith, he realistically refuses a comic transformation of events, but he keeps alive that faint "and yet" of idealism. Rather than traditional comedy, Grass creates the mature laughter that indicates a secure sense of superiority to the restrictions of life. He acknowledges human limitations and refuses to indulge in unrealistic expectations. His lusty acceptance of the peaceful activities of humor, food, and sex, and his respect for even the weak hopefulness of art give him a stability that makes possible his liberating laughter.

In *Headbirths* laughter again signals the free mind's self-aware and balanced reaction to problems. The record of a trip to Southeast Asia, the book is a tortuous examination of personal responsibility in a deeply troubled world. The problems are not only those of the masses in Bangkok and Bali but also those of an enlightened German, or any Westerner, trying to make conscientious decisions about the major issues of the 1980's. Grass takes stands on some of these issues, fails to resolve others, but the book is remarkable for its acute sensitivity to difficulties without surrendering commitment to responsible action. This dilemma all but paralyzes Harm and Dörte Peters, Grass's traveling couple. It is also Grass's own dilemma, leaving him on the border between conflicting claims that are to him serious but amusing at the same time.

Take the lightly smoked liver sausage for instance. Homemade in Itzehoe, West Germany, and vacuum sealed in plastic, it is to be Harm Peters' gift to an old school friend who now lives in Bali, but Peters is not decisive enough to deliver the sausage, and it becomes over and again the laughable occasion for intentions compromised by second thoughts. In the end, Peters carries it in his luggage back to Germany, "another unsolved problem." For Grass, the sausage is a possible plot element, repeatedly considered and rejected, his own counterpart to the Peterses' equivocations. He amuses himself with detailing the possible problems that a liver sausage could pose; it is his headbirth, one more febrile speculation of a brain that will not stop working. While Peters and Grass fret, the sausage spoils, even in its plastic, would-be insulation from the processes of the real world. The liver sausage, then, is

Grass's self-aware and amused commentary on the consequences of his own vacillations.

As the sausage saga indicates, Grass employs a complex narrative technique. *Headbirths,* like *The Flounder,* weaves its history and fiction together. The unidentified narrative voice of *The Meeting at Telgte* here is openly Grass's own, and he is himself as prominent in the book as Harm and Dörte Peters are; his own travels with his wife to China are a subject of *Headbirths.* In addition, he maintains a continuing commentary on his characters, plot variations, a possible movie version, his political views, and so on. The work clearly is another of his headbirths, the product of a brain that cannot resist scrutinizing every aspect of a subject. As the Peterses fly home, watching a John Wayne movie, silent because they have declined earphones, each reads personal fantasies into the silent action. Here Grass playfully heaps layer upon layer of varying degrees of fiction and history: he gives us a novel-essay in which he discusses himself deciding what actions in his book could be made into a film about the Peterses watching a film on which they project the action of a novel they have been reading, which is itself a vehicle for fantasized versions of their experiences in Bali, the subject of *Headbirths,* though of which level it is difficult to say. All the while, the liver sausage grows smelly or remains fresh, depending on which layer of the fiction it happens to be embedded in.

The purposeful confusion is like Pirandello, but the point is not so much that we are uncertain of what is real as that art and life are inextricably mixed. The feeling conveyed by the complex narration is that the issues confronting the 80's are too involved and ambiguous to be relegated to fiction alone; Grass must speak out in his own voice, often dropping the mask of fiction, not in Swift's righteous indignation but rather in an attempt both to express personal responsibility and to reflect faithfully the complexity of the situation. In *Headbirths,* fiction is an enhancement, a means of shaping and illustrating ideas, rather than a replacement, a sufficient world in itself. "To be present again, I often have to take a running start from remote centuries." Not comic transformation but history and social commitment are the defining factors in Grass's fiction.

"It's time for the film to stop," Grass observes as he ends his book. The last page wanders through references to the Soviet invasion of Afghanistan, the German elections, the flounder dinner that Grass and his wife will eat on New Year's Eve, and poor Harm and Dörte Peters, surrounded by street urchins but still undecided after debating the book through whether or not to have a child. Here is the same distrust of comic resolution that we have seen end Grass's other novels and Vonnegut's, too. History cannot be escaped; the sausage illustrates that. Grass can laugh, but like many other contemporary writers he finds the traditional comic resolution alien to his sensibility.

Easy solutions, Grass claims, lead us one step closer to George Orwell's 80's. He has given up on the Christian-Marxist hope, on great leaders of all kinds, and he still rejects the Flounder's masculine principle of progress. What is left? First, art itself, as in *The Meeting at Telgte.* Grass tells of meetings and friendships among authors of the di-

vided Germanys; he hopes for German cultural unity where political unity is impossible. Also left for Grass is an enlightened and engaged liberalism. Harm Peters compares the ethic of democratic socialism to the labor of Sisyphus:

> We put some reform through and, hey, we think, that's not bad, but before we know it the next little reform is due. It never stops. Never, I tell you, it will never stop. The stone is always down at the bottom, waiting.

What is my stone, Grass asks: art, freedom, love, justice? These are his answers, but characteristically he expresses them as questions. No dogmatism, no chance of utopia here:

> I scoff at any promise that my stone will reach the top and rest there once and for all. But I also laugh at the stone, which wants to make me the hero of its overandoveragain. "Look, stone," I say. "See how lightly I take you. You are so absurd and so used to me that you've become my trademark."

His ability to laugh at the stone marks the dominant attitude of the three Grass books we have been discussing. Laughter allows him the detachment that he (as well as Vonnegut and Kundera) feels is the necessary attitude for intelligent choice in the complexities of the modern world. If taking the stone lightly allows him an amused, ironic awareness of the disparity between the pretentious equivocations or headbirths of Western liberals and the massive world problems they face, it also saves him from the easy solutions and monomanias of twentieth-century great men. That light laughter leaves room for a simultaneous awareness that thoughtful though hesitant attempts at reason are better than barbarism and fascism. Thus, all told, Grass likes his equivocating couple, Harm and Dörte Peters. He leaves them childless, "not knowing what to say in German" as a crowd of Third-World children swarm over them. Scarcely a comic ending, for the problems remain, even the ironic failure of language that also ends *The Meeting at Telgte;* and the Peterses' aloneness lacks the mitigation of the new birth in the last section of *The Flounder.*

Laughter itself becomes a theme in Milan Kundera's wonderfully constructed *The Book of Laughter and Forgetting.* Breaking through artificial limits of all kinds, his liberating laughter arises from humane individualism in a sad world of constrictions. Like Vonnegut and Grass, he rejects cant, imposed solutions, and utopias without rejecting a hope for justice. Exiled by the Communist government of Czechoslovakia, Kundera has a unique set of specific concerns, but the sensibility informing them is similar in basic ways to that of the other two novelists. Kundera's book, in fact, works as an explicit commentary on the implications of that sensibility.

"Initially," Kundera writes, "laughter is the province of the Devil. It has a certain malice to it (things have turned out differently from the way they tried to seem), but a certain beneficent relief as well (things are looser than they seemed, we have greater latitude in living with them, their gravity does not oppress us)." An angel, feeling threatened

Ken Kesey.

by the Devil's laughter, invented the opposite type: "whereas the Devil's laughter pointed up the meaninglessness of things, the angel's shout rejoiced in how rationally organized, well conceived, beautiful, good, and sensible everything on earth was." The angel's laughter is "an expression of being rejoicing at being"; it is "serious laughter, laughter beyond joking," but that is the laughter of people who have been able to avoid all unhappiness. They live in exclusive circles, Kundera notes, groups of people dancing in closed rings, forming "a single body and a single soul," utopias excluding the different, the unhappy, the imperfect. Such circles, naturally, appeal to the Communist Party and the angels. As for Kundera, the exile and bargainer in good faith, his narrator tells us, "from the day they excluded me from the circle, I have not stopped falling . . . into the void of a world resounding with the terrifying laughter of the angels that covers my every word with its din." In a world frighteningly full of people with certain answers and ideologies and of people willing to sell their individuality in order to gain the acceptance of utopian circles, Kundera prefers the "beneficent relief" of demonic laughter, that unsettling denier of self-assurance and breaker of rigidities.

In Part One, Mirek, a writer who had welcomed the Communists in Czechoslovakia when he was young, has fallen afoul of the totalitarian, dehumanizing attempt to provide "an idyll for all." His desire to "obliterate his hated youth" takes the form of trying to recover lost love letters to his Communist mistress. Variations of this dilemma

echo throughout the novel. Mistakes of the past can cripple the present, yet attempts to destroy that past create frustration and isolation. In Part Four, which like Part One is titled "Lost Letters," Tamina, a young widow, also tries to recover lost love letters, but for the opposite reason. Instead of wishing to forget, she wishes to remember her dead husband through his letters, but she is surrounded by graphomaniacs, as Kundera calls them, writers self-centered and deaf to others, who affirm their existence in an indifferent universe by forcing themselves on the people around them. Tamina's memory of the past is drowned in her revulsion at them, and like Mirek she becomes another isolated soul, both of them exiled from the constricting circles that oppressive governments and individuals create for themselves.

Part Six, "The Angels," combines Kundera's angels with the story of Tamina, who in this part tries to escape the burden of her past by following an angel into the utopia of childhood. Freed from demonic ties to the "constant tension, fear, agitation" of adult love, Tamina experiences the "angelic simplicity" of physical sexuality, but this child's utopia turns her into a body without a soul. Like progressive states and graphomaniacs, Tamina's utopia absorbs the individual into itself, and her attempt to escape the past leads her only to obliteration of her mind, her soul, and ultimately of herself. She "disappeared beneath the surface" of a Styx-like river of forgetfulness, dying, as Kundera notes in an interview with Philip Roth, "amid the laughter of angels."

One of the wittiest and most ironic sections of the novel, Part Five describes a gathering of Czech writers, Kundera's equivalent of the meeting at Telgte. Some of the writers are angelic in nature; others are more demonic. All of them are caught up in their special identities, busy converting everything to their own views. Kundera is not as reverent as Grass in his attitude towards writers, for many of them are graphomaniacs like those who accosted Tamina. A young student attending the meeting comes to admire romantic love that idolizes its object, but such an essentially dehumanizing attempt at perfection leads only to frustration. In a chapter entitled "The Angels Hover over the Student's Couch," the young man vainly tries to make love to his mistress. His reaction when he learns that she was afraid of getting pregnant rather than "frightened by the boundless horizons of love" is *litost,* the Czech word for the frustration that follows a person's unsuccessful attempt to force others to identify with him. Selfish love and graphomania alike can lead to *litost.* Demonic laughter, of course, is its healthful antidote. "A joke," says the self-absorbed writer who had unfortunately influenced the student, "is the enemy of love and poetry. . . . Love has nothing in common with laughter." What he instinctively fears is the ability of the Devil's laughter to undermine his attempts to impose himself on others. In laughter Kundera, Grass, and Vonnegut all find liberation from unreflecting self-assurance and cant.

The novel also defines *litost* as "a state of torment caused by a sudden insight into one's own miserable self." When the student comes to understand the nonsense of his romantic beliefs, *litost* sweeps over him: "Peering deep into the abyss of his stupidity, he felt like screaming with laughter—tearful, hysterical laughter." Like a Joycean epiphany, it is a moment of intense and crippling insight. *The Book of Laughter and Forgetting* has, in fact, a number of similarities with *Dubliners*. Rather than a novel in the usual sense, it is a series of parts, one could call them stories, each thematically related to the others, a series of variations on a theme. Both books are the work of an exile trying to make sense of his lost country and of his reasons for leaving it. Both are realistic appraisals of the paralysis that has afflicted their homelands. Those paralyzing epiphanies in *Dubliners,* though, stem from conditions of church, society, home, and personality essentially out of the individual's control. Joyce's symbols link the paralysis to impersonal sources. "Araby" ends "gazing up into the darkness"; "Eveline" ends "passive, like a helpless animal"; "The Dead," of course, ends with "snow falling faintly through the universe . . . upon all the living and the dead." And the narrator's attitude is painful, humiliating condescension. Pathos is the mode of *Dubliners.*

Pathos flits through *The Book of Laughter and Forgetting* but never becomes the dominant mode. Certainly there are forces beyond individual control—the modern police state, for one—but Kundera's attitude lacks Joyce's condescension and dramatic irony. His characters are not driven creatures but struggling humans. As in Vonnegut's novels, the constrictions of their lives often produce neurotic symptoms, a torment of others and the self. Such a condition is unfortunate but approachable in a sense that Joycean darkness is not. Joyce's is a self-imposed exile, a rebellion against church and country. Kundera obviously has great affection for Czechoslovakia; his exile has been forced on him. Whereas Joyce must write in "scrupulous meanness," Kundera can write with affirmative laughter.

For Kundera, being human is difficult because it means to be alive to complexity, to ask questions rather than to assert answers, to escape the mechanizations and repetitions of existence, to avoid the totalitarian utopianism, the problem solvers and theorists, the soulless advocates of a new physical freedom. To be human is to live on the border between pessimism and optimism, between the question and the answer, pathos and hope, demonic and angelic laughter. Kundera is life-affirming but in an open-eyed way that does not lose sight of evils or get caught in affirmation for its own sake. He is affirmative but, like the other two novelists, wise and realistic at the same time.

Through a disorderly world all three novelists wander, not so much finding causes to espouse as ideas to experience, embracing little, questioning much. Not at all limited to traditional society and art, they create forms that reflect their own tentative probings. Their fragmented narratives do not propound theories of the Real as, let us say, the older Surreal work of André Breton does, or theories of artifice as the Möbius strip narratives of John Barth do. Their hesitancy does not grow from a settled view of human experience such as we find in Thomas Pynchon's *The Crying of Lot 49,* a book with some interesting parallels to Vonnegut's novels. We must be careful in labeling our three authors because they lack the radical alienation that frequently underlies black humor and comedy of the

absurd, and they purposely withhold from their pronouncements the sense of certainty that usually validates satiric judgments. Perhaps their work is Menippean satire, a disorderly fullness reflecting world views that have no desire to restrict into a tight focus.

They neither despair nor unduly affirm. They have their beliefs but are aware of the complex whole. Their reference points are historical and social rather than philosophical and religious; they are more comfortable with the complexities of experience than with the search for a unified truth. It is for this reason that even Vonnegut's woebegone loners do not end up paralyzed like Beckett's Lucky and Pozzo; the absence of a final answer becomes a condition of life that must be worked within, not a crippling limitation. They do not so much lack the modern sensibility of pathos and alienation as they hesitate to assert it too vigorously. As members of the late stages of artistic and intellectual movements often do, they have acquired the doctrine without the fervor of its first advocates. One must admit, there was inconsistency between alienation and the committed advocacy of alienation by some earlier modern writers, but the gropings of Vonnegut, Grass, and Kundera towards ways of living with the sad facts of reality are as logical an outcome of an absurd vision as existentialism was. Perhaps they differ from earlier probers of the absurd in the way that Epicurean accommodation differs from Stoic defiance. It is a matter of different modes of response to a similar world view. Neither school is sanguine about life.

These sons of the border bargain in good faith with us, and that ultimately may limit their appeal. We may prefer that an author give us visions rather than the messy equivocations of the real world. The finality of silence in Ionesco's *Chairs,* the psychological semiotics and Christian hope of Walker Percy's *Second Coming,* the dance of life and traditional comic affirmation concluding Fellini's *8 1/2*—there is something gratifying in their confidence that they have truth to tell us. But Vonnegut, Grass, and Kundera are disconcertingly hesitant to give us answers. Kundera speaks for the three at the end of his interview with Philip Roth:

> A novel does not assert anything; a novel searches and poses questions. . . . The totalitarian world, whether founded on Marx, Islam, or anything else, is a world of answers rather than questions. There, the novel has no place. In any case, it seems to me that all over the world people nowadays prefer to judge rather than to understand, to answer rather than ask, so that the voice of the novel can hardly be heard over the noisy foolishness of human certainties.

Confident answers are more popular and easier to assert than bargaining in good faith.

Although Vonnegut, Grass, and Kundera certainly demonstrate the creative impulse of comedy in their tumbling wealth of ideas, poetry, music, abundance of characters, multiplication of themes and plots, intricate variations on one theme, and so on, in a real sense this Menippean fullness and creativity is a way of avoiding the traditional comic creation of a transformed world. They move in and out of history, mixing fact and fiction, never letting the creation belie the reality, hesitant to commit themselves completely to a fictional plot. There are no green worlds, magic, or romance. They substitute the Menippean fullness for the distrusted comic vision. That is why laughter seems better than comedy to characterize their work; for laughter is the means by which an individual adjusts his psyche to an aberration in his world rather than attempts to change that world. In laughter, the individual asserts his superiority, affirms his own meaningfulness in the face of absurdity, or congratulates himself on seeing through the incongruity of others. That laughter is a moment of liberation, an individual adjustment, not a metaphysical statement. Comedy, we might say, is the hopeful psyche projecting its desires on reality; laughter is the healthy psyche adjusting itself to that reality.

The laughter of these novelists is more demonic than angelic. Rather than the angel's "expression of being rejoicing at being," it provides that "certain beneficent relief" from the gravity and restrictions of life. Their demonic laughter may be distantly descended from Baudelaire's diabolical laughter, but it is much too healthful and realistic to participate in the pride and delusion that Baudelaire attributes to it. Each of the three authors has the balance to remain on the border, leaning towards the demonic without falling into nihilism. Their demonic laughter has affinities with Freud's humor (not his wit), which "emphasizes the invincibility of [the ego] by the real world, victoriously maintains the pleasure principle . . . without overstepping the bounds of mental health." But here, too, there are some important differences, for Freud's humor "insists that it cannot be affected by the traumas of the external world." It is a mark of the healthfulness of Vonnegut, Grass, and Kundera that they have indeed been hurt by those traumas and their demonic laughter is tinged with sadness. They bargain in good faith with us, hide no problems, promise no comic transformations. They are sensible of the anguish and absurdity that have shaped modern literature. Their strength lies in their ability to respond to that demonic anguish with demonic laughter.

> *R. B. Gill, "Bargaining in Good Faith: The Laughter of Vonnegut, Grass, and Kundera," in* Critique: Studies in Modern Fiction, *Vol. XXV, No. 2, Winter, 1984, pp. 77-91.*

BLACK HUMOR DISTINGUISHED FROM RELATED LITERARY TRENDS

Louis Hasley

[*Hasley is an American educator, poet, humorist, and critic. In the following essay he distinguishes black humor from earlier trends in American humor and complains that its relentless impulsion towards pessimism and misanthropy upset the balanced sensibility which traditional humor requires for its effect.*]

One of the often slighted yet most distinctive features of the American character and temperament, as expressed in its literature, has been its humor. In leading up to its most prominent contemporary manifestation, it may be well to note briefly the stages through which literary humor in America has passed. Of course, to put something briefly, as G. K. Chesterton once remarked, is to put it brutally. Hence the outline that follows will carry some overlappings and some oversimplifications.

The period from the founding of the republic in the late eighteenth century to about 1830 reflects principally the styles of wit and humor found in the established literature of the mother country, England. Only scattered bits begin to hint of a distinctively American flavor. This first period may be called Derivative, as it is almost exclusively so.

In many ways the second period, 1830-1860, is the most notable. The racy vernacular comes into its own. Three important character types, as pointed out by Constance Rourke (*American Humor,* 1930) suddenly emerge in the literature of these years: the "down-East" Yankee, marked by shrewd and rambling understatement, often in dialect; the backwoodsman, or frontiersman, marked by loud exaggeration, ritual brags, practical jokes, and masculine, often bawdy exploits; and the Negro minstrel (a platform rather than a literary manifestation), a forerunner of jazz and swing music and marked by artfully rhythmic, lyric simplicity.

The third period, running from 1860 to 1900, may be called Second-Growth American Humor. It plays prominently with the tricks of language distortion, intentionally bad spelling and grammar, puns, dialect, feigned naïveté, cracker-barrel philosophy. Walter Blair, the outstanding authority, calls this period that of the Literary Comedians. It includes Josh Billings, Artemus Ward, Bill Nye, and even Mark Twain; but Twain, at his best, avoids the trickery, or else refines and deepens it, becoming an unmistakable figure of world literature. Local colorists often contribute significantly to this period as well.

The fourth period, 1900-1925, is one of Incipient Sophistication, focusing on the expanding cities and diminishing ruralism. Here we meet, among others, George Ade, Booth Tarkington, O. Henry, Don Marquis, and Ring Lardner. Satire appears in Ade, Marquis, and outstandingly in Lardner. Intellectual criticism and witty iconoclasm appear in H. L. Mencken.

The fifth period, it seems clear, must be called the *New Yorker* Era (1925-1960). It is a varied time, but with a sophisticated, urban, suburban, cosmopolitan, intellectual bent, little attention being given to rural characters and experience. Nearly every one of the prominent American humor writers of the time was a regular contributor to the *New Yorker* magazine (founded 1925): James Thurber, E. B. White, Robert Benchley, Ogden Nash, S. J. Perelman, and many others. Life becomes art, glamor (in sophisticated low key), entertainment ("show biz"), standard of living. The writing style often tends to homogeneity: it is disciplined, slightly sterile, somewhat esoteric, unemotional. Thurber's statement that "the humor of the *New Yorker* represents the decline of humor in America" is borne out in the stage that follows.

The sixth and current stage, that of Black Humor, may be arbitrarily dated from about 1960. The key is disillusion, pessimism, nihilism. The reader may even want to question whether it is humor at all.

The two world wars of this century have each been followed by deep moods of disillusionment. The Lost Generation of the twenties has its parallel, though a more pronounced one, in the Black Humorists, who have appeared during and since the late 1950s. The difference may well be seen as one of degree. Yet the degree of difference occurs at the crucial point where it becomes a difference in kind.

It is characteristic of Black Humor that it is not strictly satire. It has, in fact, gone beyond satire. Its direction is metaphysical, not social. It has no traffic with the correction of evil, nor does it aim for the enlightenment of those who are less sensitive, less perceptive.

Black Humor has the purpose of easing the private misery of the writers themselves. In its most pronounced form, it shocks by the presentation of life as outrage.

Though Black Humorists often employ discontinuity, it is not out of disbelief in the continuity, or stream, of life and literature. It is rather a device reflecting disbelief in the *intelligence* that controls, or fails to control, the ongoing conditions of life. For it is clear even to the Black Humorists, I feel sure, that the widespread crisis of belief in our time found a gathering momentum in the mid-nineteenth century, Darwin's *Origin of Species* (1859) providing strong impetus. The history of ideas from that time to the present provides the context of Black Humor.

In American literature before World War II, shades of blackness are already found, among others, in Poe, in Hawthorne, in Melville, most unmistakably in the later Twain, concurrently in Ambrose Bierce, later a scattering in Lardner, and then notably in Nathanael West. Probably the most pervasive influence toward blackness in the subsequent forties, fifties, and sixties has been the existentialism of Jean-Paul Sartre.

The earlier American writers just mentioned, however, differ from contemporary Black Humorists. They relieved the gloom of their vision by a lambent play of light and of humor that has no need of special definition. In them there was a searching that never quite concluded that life is meaningless. Counterbalancing the deep gloom of *The Mysterious Stranger,* the most impressive fiction of his last decade, Twain could record in his notebook two years before his death at seventy-five in 1910 that he was inclined to expect a life after death. In him and in Poe, Hawthorne, Melville, and probably in Bierce, Lardner, and Nathanael West, one sees confusion, anxiety, and moods of depression that never quite reject the whole of life's experiences as finally meaningless. With the swelling of a wave of Black Humorists in the late fifties and early sixties, we see a group of writers, not constituting a unity or a school, who have looked at life and decided that, without qualification, it *is* meaningless. Instance *The Floating Opera,* written by

John Barth at age twenty-five. Todd Andrews, its non-hero, decides to commit suicide (and mass murder) by blowing up a showboat with seven hundred persons aboard. When the attempt fails, sheer inertia dictates that he not bother to make a second suicide attempt. His conclusion: *"There's no final reason for living (or for suicide)."* He then adds:

> To realize that nothing makes any final difference is overwhelming; but if one goes no farther and becomes a saint, a cynic, or a suicide on principle, one hasn't reasoned completely. The truth is that nothing makes any difference, including that truth. Hamlet's question is, absolutely, meaningless.

In a great variety of ways, the other Black Humorists testify that they exist in the same metaphysical void.

There are perhaps some fifteen or twenty American contemporary writers who are, with acceptable authority, labeled Black Humorists. Among them are John Barth, Joseph Heller, Bruce Jay Friedman, J. P. Donleavy, Kurt Vonnegut, Jr., James Purdy, and the dramatist Edward Albee. The last named is the most prominent American writer associated with the avant-garde Theater of the Absurd, which represents the Black Humor of the theater. These are the ones who, in my judgment based on reading some forty or fifty of their books, deserve the most critical attention. Older contemporary writers like Saul Bellow and Peter De Vries, despite some depressing tendencies in their work, do not, I believe, warrant pigeonholing as Black Humorists.

Two problems in particular interest me in relation to the Black Humorists. One is the degree of pertinence, or lack of it, that the idea of humor has in their work—that is, what justification, if any, is there for the use of the term *humor* as characterizing their work? Is the term *Black Humor* a paradox or a real contradiction in terms? To answer this involves some attempt at definition and then of application, both operations being fraught with difficulty in a semantically charged area. The other problem, largely speculative and interpretive, is the psychological climate from which their work emanates.

Most critics have adopted a conclusion that humor in any form is indefinable. I disagree. In fact I believe that I have provided a sound definition, as it pertains to the special area called literature, in my essay, "Humor in Literature: A Definition" (*The CEA Critic,* February 1970). The greater problem occurs, not in definition, but in applying the definition to examples, where judgment tends to be guided, not by whether it *is* humor, but by whether it reaches a certain level of quality. I cannot give here the entire rationale of my definition except to say that it boils down to this: *Humor in literature is a departure from a recognized norm viewed by the author with detachment and playfulness.* Anyone familiar with the theories of humor, laughter, and the comic may recognize my indebtedness (apart from some variation) to Max Eastman's *Enjoyment of Laughter.*

Regarding Black Humor, let me now offer a formulation: *Black Humor combines humor and pessimism, employs in-*

congruities ranging from the ridiculous to the grotesque, and carries an overall sense of metaphysical disillusion and nihilism. The need to clarify such a formulation will be readily seen. The difficulty lies in the word *humor* itself, and that takes us to the definition given above. The operative words are *detachment* and *playfulness.*

We may begin with one matter that critics are well agreed on, namely, that comedy, humor, and the like are basically intellectual rather than emotion-involving, that is, they reveal a detached attitude on the part of the author (and hence of the reader). What strikes one in many of the works of Black Humor is the absence, or the relatively slight degree, of detachment they show. And without detachment there cannot be that playfulness that is also an essential of humor. How detached are the authors (despite the frequent use of a third-person point of view character) in such works as John Barth's *Giles Goat-Boy* and *The Floating Opera,* J. P. Donleavy's *The Ginger Man* and *The Saddest Summer of Samuel S,* Joseph Heller's *Catch-22* (more about this one later), James Purdy's *Malcolm* and *Cabot Wright Begins,* Kurt Vonnegut's *Slaughterhouse Five*? The intense gloom and horrifying emptiness which these novels convey indicate the heavy emotional investment of the writer—indicate a merely superficial detachment permitting scarcely more than a hollow playfulness that thwarts any real tendency toward lighthearted amusement.

The most effective humor, strictly as humor, involves incongruity, which is a decisive departure from a norm. The error, I submit, that often occurs in applying the label Black Humor is the failure to see that, however outrageous, incongruity is not enough. The attitude of the writer (which is of course transmitted to the reader) must be one of detachment and playfulness. For life and literature are marked by innumerable everyday incongruities that are not humorous. It cannot be too strongly emphasized that nothing is humorous per se, that humor is an attitude, and that a thing is humorous, ridiculous, or laughable only because and when someone considers it so.

There is no lack of incongruity in the works of the Black Humorists. In their work incongruities abound. But it seems to me that a great deal of the so-called laughter that these works inspire in some readers derives from a sophisticated cynicism toward mere irony and not from detached amusement emanating from the author's attitude toward his work. A reader predisposed to laugh at any irony can fail to see that laughter is not always based on humor.

Having stressed what I consider the dangers and pitfalls involved in seeing humor in Black Humor when no humorous reaction is intended or warranted, I would like to turn the coin over to look at the positive, humorous side. We readily understand that the complexity of literature in its reflection of life is such that humor may exist on one page while grim irony appears on the next. Or, more appropriately, the two contrary qualities may actually be fused. Of all the works of fiction by the Black Humorists mentioned above, perhaps none is at once so humorous and at the same time so grimly tragic as *Catch-22.* Comic scenes and comic detail occur in chapter after chapter, al-most always couched in rampant unrealism. But the unrealism, the incongruities, do not obscure Heller's insistence on the unrelenting truth of the irrationality, the inhumanity, of war. And Heller, in a book that is not *primarily* humorous, reveals the genius that only the greatest humorous writers have shown—the mind-dividing capacity to see and render simultaneously the comic and the tragic—that which in common reaction makes one want to laugh and cry at the same time.

So, to a lesser extent, there is humor in other works by these same Black Humorists. Barth's *The Sot-Weed Factor* is a rollicking parody of older picaresque, intrigue laden, cloak-and-dagger mystery-adventure stories, a remote descendant of *Don Quixote, Tom Jones,* and *Great Expectations.* Donleavy's *The Ginger Man* has moments of humor, though its antihero, Sebastian Dangerfield, is a scapegrace who has almost nothing to recommend him but an artful tongue. Friedman's *A Mother's Kisses* is one of the most accomplished of modern novels, focusing on a provocative character who delightfully misses stock portraiture, that of an alluringly vulgar, possessive, aggressive Jewish mother. James Purdy, whose writing falls almost wholly outside the concept of recognizable humor, is nevertheless one of the most distinguished of the novelists usually classified with the Black Humorists; for Black he is, with inventive incongruities handled with superb artistry, but humorous hardly at all. As a popular author Terry Southern may be mentioned for the humor in *Candy* and *The Magic Christian,* but it is humor diluted to an inferior level in the guise of satire. Of Vonnegut's half-dozen books, I give highest rank to *Cat's Cradle,* principally because it has the same kind of simultaneously operative humor and tragedy found in *Catch-22.*

In this section of my essay I have attempted no detailed analysis of the books mentioned. My main intention has been to show the requirements for the proper application of the term Black Humor and only incidentally to give some relatively unsupported judgment of their literary quality. I now turn to my second focus of interest in the Black Humorists, their psychological motivations, many of which, I venture to suggest, may be unconscious.

I shall not pretend that my analysis will fit any given work with satisfying completeness. It is intended to suggest explanations that appeal to me as plausible in instances more or less typical and that may be accepted as the reader finds them useful. They will reflect, I hope, an understanding of human nature both apart from time and affected by our time.

The need of any individual for identification with others, for links—if only imagined ones—with other persons or groups of persons, is well recognized by psychologists and psychiatrists. So too is a person's need for individuality, a trait or complex of traits that enables him to achieve an identity distinct from others. These opposing psychological instincts exist in all normal persons and even in most abnormal ones. They have been given expert treatment in *Identification and Individuality* by psychiatrist John T. Flynn. I acknowledge a measure of indebtedness herein to that work.

The intelligent artist, aiming to produce works of art that will be enduring and that will attract the rewards of achievement, knows that originality in some form is urgently desirable if not an absolute prerequisite. He may, finding true originality inaccessible to him, settle for novelty. He will have, as Walter J. Ong has pointed out, an "extreme aversion to clichés," for clichés tend to a reflection of the mass mind and to an absence of individuality. Originality is never of course total; so he may seek it in limited areas or movements that have a certain vogue despite necessary if minor elements of identification. An important danger here is that, for the sake of doing something new, something different, the artist, starting with truth, may be lured over the boundary into untruth in order to achieve the individuality so prized by the true artist.

Let me raise a few questions that may be suggestive rather than assertive. Does the Black Humorist always fully believe the philosophy that goes into his book? or is he often betrayed into extremes by his desire for individuality—that is, mere difference—or by his desire to assume an intellectual position that mocks widely held values? Is it true that in a mass culture the only way the artist can achieve individuality is by rebellion? Does today's intellectual climate dictate that if you wish to be "in" as an artist you must be a rebel?

Since I have mentioned that a person's tendency is not merely toward individuality but also toward identification, an opposing quality, does not therefore the need for identification cancel out the drive for individuality?

The two qualities of identification and individuality are, as I have indicated, opposites, but the instinct for both in a given person may not have equal force. In the artist the impulse to demonstrate his individual worth may be considerably greater than the need for identification that might diminish his selfhood. Thus he may identify with another artist or hero (perhaps one long dead or from another culture) or with a small group that paradoxically also serves his need for individuality, that particular group being widely known more for its differences from society at large than for its identification with it. This is a phenomenon that readily occurs among members of small nonconformist groups, where an artist or writer, in his drive for fame, may be drawn to construct a startling, even shocking, view of reality that will realize at least one element of artistic renown, individuality.

A democracy such as ours encourages a special manifestation of individuality that prizes freedom. As a people we give a good deal more of attention to extolling freedom than we do to defining its proper limits. We may be thankful that the artist is one of the most effective voices in the cause of freedom. Without freedom his individuality is bottled up, frustrated. Thus whenever he finds his desires checked he is inclined to set up a cry that often amounts to a demand for a freedom that would violate rights of others.

The ideal of unlimited freedom is recognized as unjust by any normally intelligent person. But with a lax public ethic and a permissive private code the individual is unre- alistically coddled or even "spoiled." Before he has fully matured he has found that his vaunted freedom is to some acute extent illusory. So he may turn against the values by which society in its stabler forms operates and do either of two things: he may defiantly accuse everyone but himself of hypocrisy; or giving in to self-pity he may sulkingly present a view of all mankind as bestial in the total sense of the word.

One philosophical shortcoming that I observe among some of the Black Humorists is a failure to accept man as universally flawed, *the artist himself included.* He sees himself as holier than thou. Here the utopian artist, martyr-like, tells us how things should be, but can't be, because everybody else is depraved: a failure to reconcile the deterministic facts of man's at-large direction with his individual freewill responsibility; a failure to acknowledge that his own shortcomings may not be markedly different from those of the rest of mankind.

Can there be convincingly found in Donleavy's *The Ginger Man,* in Barth's *Giles Goat-Boy* and *The Floating Opera,* in Purdy's *Malcolm, Cabot Wright Begins,* and *Eustace Chisolm and the Works,* in Vonnegut's *Slaughterhouse Five* and *Player Piano*—to mention only a few—the idea that man is anything higher than an unredeemed and unredeemable animal? Are not these works, and many others like them, confessions of insufficiently disciplined wills pitying themselves because it is much easier to be an animal than to be a man? Since man is by definition a moral being, are not we faced with the problem that literature, which reflects man, must reflect his moral nature? If it doesn't, do we have a nonhuman "literature" wherein the reader must furnish, in order to gain a meaningful experience, the ethical dimension which the writer himself has not given?

The Black Humorists, declared *Time* magazine (February 12, 1965), "are as well aware as any conventional moralizer that the times are out of joint, but they choose to greet the dislocation with a jeer rather than a jeremiad." In setting themselves up as telling it like it is (in the nauseating phrase of the day), one may wonder whether, in their common dependence with other mortals on government and society, they opt for the most disillusioned leaders as representing the view of man which their works embody. It is not my judgment alone that assesses their work as showing life to be philosophically meaningless—critic after critic has done so. Let us not descend to the maudlin and speculate that future critics may find, with the sliding scale of relativistic moral and social values, that the Black Humorists represent, not a night, but a dawn!

In Black Humor we are given a view of life that is a monochrome—if darkness can be said to have color. One characteristic complaint that we hear is directed against the universe: man isn't at fault; the universe is. The complaint is of *rational man* in an irrational universe—one of the most mischievous of man's present-day errors. A little reflection should tell us that most of what is called the irrationality of the universe is the irrationality of man. I think it only has to be said to be self-evident: man is both rational and irrational; he is even non-rational. And doesn't that include us all?

The view that is taken of humor by today's generation admittedly allows wider playfulness about a variety of matters than was true in the past. Today's generation more easily joins amused laughter to grotesquerie, to debasement of life (especially of sex), to nose-thumbing mockery, to scatology, to shrill absurdities, to wild irrationality, to extreme eccentricity, to sardonic surrealism. Yet the playfulness, the laughter, when based on the portrayal of life as fundamentally ridiculous, has the constrained air of defensiveness that sees, deep down, in a hopeless dream of ideality, the world and their fellow man as threats to what they would have life to be if only it could be other than it is.

Walter Kerr, eminent drama critic of the *New York Times,* in calling attention to the relationship of black comedy to conventional comedy, has by easy implication done the same for Black Humor and conventional humor in his essay, "Comedy Now" (*The Critic,* April-May 1967):

> The danger that black comedy poses for comedy is that it may succeed all too well in persuading the audience that its vision is a complete one and that no contrast need be set beside it, in persuading the audience to suppress or to forget the counterpoint which is stored in its head and which alone guarantees the light-dark relationship upon which laughter depends.

> *Louis Hasley, "Black Humor and Gray," in* Arizona Quarterly, *Vol. 30, No. 4, Winter, 1974, pp. 317-28.*

Black humor literature is similar to the literature of existentialism in that it begins with the same assumption—that the world is absurd. But, because we now live in an age when the notion of absurdity is more or less taken for granted, writers have had to keep pace, and the aim of the black humorist is significantly different from the existentialist.

—*Alan R. Pratt, in his introduction to* Black Humor: Critical Essays, *1993.*

Patrick O'Neill

[*In the following essay, O'Neill analyzes subgenres of comedy and satire in an attempt to define black humor. In addition to his own definition of the term as the "comedy of entropy," O'Neill asserts that black humor occupies one extreme on a broad spectrum of literary forms which also includes satire, irony, and "benign humor."*]

Though 'black humour' is a phrase which nowadays crops up fairly frequently in casual conversation as well as in literary criticism, there is no general agreement as to what exactly black humour is. This is, of course, hardly surprising, since there is no general agreement either as to what

humour is, though most people are convinced that they know it when they meet with it. Since Plato's day, and doubtless before, there have been theories of humour, laughter, and the comic at first from the poets and philosophers, then, from the beginning of this century, from the sociologists and psychologists, neurophysiologists and semioticians. A recent international conference on humour—held in Wales in 1976—drew almost one hundred separate papers, mostly from psychologists; a bibliography printed with the proceedings, covering only selected material in English, ran to 1500 items, and all concerned were agreed that research into the nature of humour, after a full two millennia, was still in its infancy. Perhaps the most striking symptom of this infancy is the continued lack of any generally accepted taxonomy of humour—though there are those psychologists and literary critics, of course, who argue that the whole area is essentially unclassifiable.

The concept of 'black' humour is an area in which there has been an upsurge of interest, especially in North America, in the last two decades or so, and here too the lack of an agreed terminology has been apparent. Different writers use the term to mean humour which is variously grotesque, gallows, macabre, sick, pornographic, scatological, cosmic, ironic, satirical, absurd, or any combination of these. There are those who would limit its application as a literary term to a particular decade in a particular country; there are those who would use it typologically as an inherent trait of human nature; there are those who claim that in its highest form it is not a species of humour at all; and there are those who would suggest that all humour is at bottom black. Standard dictionaries and encyclopedias offer little help: most of them simply do not include the term 'black humour.' The 1975 edition of the *New Columbia Encyclopedia,* one of the very few exceptions, defines it as 'grotesque or morbid humour used to express the absurdity, insensitivity, paradox, and cruelty of the modern world' and refers the reader for examples to the work of Stanley Kubrick and Jules Feiffer, Kurt Vonnegut, Thomas Pynchon, John Barth, Joseph Heller, and Philip Roth—all of them, we notice, writing in the sixties, and all Americans, as if the phenomenon were of local and recent vintage. Ungar's *Encyclopedia of World Literature in the 20th Century,* in the same year, confirms this impression by using the term exclusively as a label for the work of certain American writers of fiction during the sixties.

Turning to French, where the phrase 'humour noir,' as we shall see, has a longer ancestry than its English equivalent. We find in the *Grand Larousse de la langue française* that 'humour noir' is that form of humour which, using cruelty, bitterness, and sometimes despair, underlines the absurdity of the world—neither necessarily modern nor American, we notice. The 1972 edition of Harrap's *New Standard French and English Dictionary,* incidentally, translates 'humour noir' more laconically, giving the primary meaning as 'sick humour' and only a secondary meaning as 'bitter, sardonic humour.' None of the standard Spanish, Italian, or German works consulted yielded anything at all, with the one exception of the 1969 edition of Gero von Wilpert's *Sachwörterbuch der Literatur,* which explains 'schwarzer Humor' as a new name for what it calls a completely traditional form of 'humorloser Scherz,' a joke without humour, characterized by 'absurd terror, horrible comicry, macabre ridiculousness, dark grotesquerie, and crass cynicism, achieving its comic (but not humorous) effect primarily through exaggeration.'

Of our four definitions, then, the American is specific as to time and place. The French and German on the other hand regard the phenomenon as typological, although the German definition differs in denying the humour-content of the concept and in a definitely censorious approach, which is perhaps echoed in the British Harrap's definition of 'humour noir' as 'sick,' an equivalence which seems to correspond to the most general usage of the term in the English-speaking world. To add an historical dimension at this point, the *OED* records seventeenth- and eighteenth-century occurrences of the phrase 'black humour' as referring to 'black choler' or melancholy, also known as 'black bile' in the medieval theory of physiological humours. Even ignoring the obvious possibility of linguistic confusion between black humour and 'ethnically' black literature, we thus have a range of meanings from the medical and psychological to the dual application in literary criticism as either a period label or a stylistic device.

In North America black humour as a literary concept first attracted widespread attention as the result of the publication in 1965 of a mass-market paperback entitled, simply, *Black Humor.* The volume comprised a collection of thirteen heterogeneous pieces of fiction from writers as different as J. P. Donleavy, Edward Albee, Joseph Heller, Thomas Pynchon, John Barth, Vladimir Nabokov, Bruce Jay Friedman, who was also the editor, and—a final odd bedfellow—Céline. Friedman is reluctant to define his conception of black humour, but suggests that what holds the collection together is a feeling of insecurity, of a 'fading line between fantasy and reality,' a sense of 'isolation and loneliness of a strange, frenzied new kind,' and above all the element of social satire in a world gone mad. A new 'chord of absurdity has been struck' in the sixties, wrote Friedman, and a 'new style of mutative behavior afoot, one that can only be dealt with by a new, one-foot-in-the-asylum style of fiction,' since the normal reaction of the satirist had of necessity been preempted by the daily newspapers. These writers of the new sensibility, says Friedman, move in 'darker waters somewhere out beyond satire.'

Friedman, though he obviously sees black humour as a predominantly contemporary North American phenomenon, manages to have his cake and eat it too by including Céline and by suggesting that black humour 'has probably always been around, always will be around, under some name or other, as long as there are disguises to be peeled back, as long as there are thoughts no one else cares to think.' The usefulness of this attitude is contested, however, in what is to date the fullest critical treatment of modern American black humour fiction, Max F. Schulz's *Black Humor Fiction of the Sixties* (1973), which insists that as a literary term 'black humour' should be restricted to a particular body of fiction produced in North America in the 1960s. Schulz, however, is not primarily interested

in the concept of black humour; rather he is interested in those American writers of the sixties who for good reasons or bad have at one time or another been dubbed black humorists. He is unhappy with the term, avoids almost entirely the whole question of humour, and seems in fact rather to disapprove of his authors for having a 'somewhat limited vision capable of the specific aberrations of comedy, rather than the universal condition of tragedy.'

The literary black humorist, for Schulz, is a post-existentialist for whom the condition of universal absurdity no longer needs to be demonstrated. All versions of reality are only mental constructs; no principle is necessarily truer than any other, morally or intellectually, and nothing has any intrinsic value. Life is a labyrinth, multiple, meaningless, and endless, and the black humorist reacts variously with such all-embracing encyclopedic endgames as John Barth's *Sot-Weed Factor* or *Giles Goat-boy,* with the programmatic skepticism of a Kurt Vonnegut, or with the parody of all systems, as in Thomas Pynchon—or Jorge Luis Borges, who is allowed to join Friedman's resident aliens Nabokov and Céline as honorary members of the club.

But other non-American names immediately suggest themselves on the basis of Schulz's list of characteristics, and quickly explode any American claim to exclusive rights to the territory: what of Gabriel García Márquez and Julio Cortázar in Spanish, Günter Grass and Thomas Bernhard in German, Italo Calvino in Italian, Raymond Queneau in French, and, above all perhaps, what about

Vladimir Nabokov.

Beckett? All share the same detachment, the same irony, the same mocking apocalyptic tone, the same parodic undercutting of all system, the same one-dimensional characters, wasteland settings, disjunctive structure, and self-conscious delight in artistry—and above all they share one central characteristic: a refusal to treat what one might regard as tragic materials tragically, and this not as a cheap method of shocking or evoking irreverent laughter, but because the comic approach is for them clearly the only remaining approach that is artistically acceptable.

Both our American authors, then, regard literary black humour as essentially a post-existentialist, post-modernist, and almost exclusively American phenomenon. A very different approach is adopted by two European anthologists, separated by almost three decades, one French and one German: André Breton's *Anthologie de l'humour noir* of 1939 and, almost simultaneously with the Americans, Gerd Henniger's *Brevier des schwarzen Humors* of 1966. In a preface to a new edition (also in 1966) of his 600-page anthology, Breton claims to have been the first to employ the term 'humour noir,' which, he says, did not exist before his coinage. He casts a very wide net over the whole of European literature since 1700 to include forty-five different authors in all, including Swift, the Marquis de Sade, de Quincey, Grabbe, Poe, Baudelaire, Lewis Carroll, Nietzsche, Rimbaud, Gide, Synge, Jarry, Apollinaire, Picasso, Kafka, Hans Arp, and Salvador Dalí. The list, he implies, could be very much longer. The phenomenon of black humour, Breton further claims, has been growing in importance since 1800 to such a degree that, given the nature of modern sensibility, it is doubtful whether *any* contemporary work of poetry or art or even scientific, philosophical, or social theory can be completely valid without some hint of it, that is to say, of a humour that is in almost all cases primarily subversive, a 'révolte supérieure de l'esprit,' as he calls it, disruptive of accepted values and systems, an aggressive weapon in most cases, in others more clearly a defensive strategy, in almost all cases containing a strongly satirical element, and in most cases having a subject matter which would normally be considered taboo. In terms of reader response—which, as a result of the nature of humour, is admittedly a highly unreliable guide here—the humour in some cases is of a type which would 'normally' give rise to bitter or ironic or sardonic laughter or amusement, in other cases it is of a more extreme type which produces less amusement than horror or disgust, and which I would like to examine more closely for a few moments.

A good example is Swift's *Modest Proposal* of 1729, which Breton, naming Swift the father of black humour, sets at the beginning of his collection and thus, to some extent, establishes the tone of what follows. The *Proposal* begins as an urbane and enlightened essay on the alleviation of the distress of the Catholic Irish poor, and without change of tone metamorphoses into the appallingly rational suggestion that serving the better nourished of the infants, properly cooked and seasoned, on the tables of the better classes would simultaneously provide an interesting change of fare for the latter and a source of honest income for the overreproductive and destitute peasantry—many of whom, Swift adds, suddenly abandoning the urbane

tone for one of slashing attack, would consider themselves better off if they too had been quickly cannibalized as children rather than slowly throughout their miserable lives. The enormous power of these seven or eight pages, however, does not depend primarily on any didactic satirical moral, but rather on the comic incongruity of blending the rationality of satire and the understatement of irony on the one hand with the irrationality and exaggeration of the grotesque on the other, the reformer's care for suffering humanity on the one hand with the guilty and perverse glee of savagely debasing that same humanity on the other.

Very much the same is true of many of the writings of the Marquis de Sade, which also owe their effect far less to their satire on Enlightenment belief in rationality and the innate goodness of man than they do to the grotesque energy and almost insane exaggeration and cumulation of sexual enormities and perversions. But to what degree, if at all, can this be seen as humorous? Is it not simply horrifying? Breton uses the 'Ogre of the Appenines' sequence from *Juliette* (1796), for example, where the Russian giant Minski eats cooked babies and has them served up to him on hot chafing dishes which burn into the naked haunches of the crouching young women who are constrained to serve as human tables. Distressingly, there is undoubtedly an element of the comic here, though any incipient comic reaction is immediately challenged and cancelled by a simultaneous feeling of revulsion such as is typically evoked by that form of the grotesque which stresses functional perversions of the human body. Such 'humour' as may be present for 'normal' readers is one of horrified incredulity and protest at the cruelty and debasement of the world portrayed, a world which belongs far more to the tragic than the comic realm—and yet has a deeply disturbing suggestion of the comic about it. Many of Kafka's stories too, one may add, such as 'In der Strafkolonie,' belong to this realm.

Misanthropy, contempt, and loathing, perversely yoked with the comic, become the very yardstick of black humour in its highest manifestation for our German anthologist, Gerd Henniger. Developing and systematizing Breton's conception, Henniger claims that in its highest order black humour obliterates laughter altogether, or rather transmutes it into despair, and he cites as examples passages from the works of Swift and de Sade, Büchner and Poe, the *Nachtwachen des Bonaventura* and the visions of Lautréamont. Henniger has a greater theoretical interest in black humour than had Breton. Following the latter's introduction, he too uses the Freudian model of humour, which Freud had developed in 1905 in *Der Witz und seine Beziehung zum Unbewussten.* Freud had suggested that all humour is a defence mechanism against the deficiencies of life, a self-protective rechannelling by the superego of feelings of guilt, anxiety, fear, or terror into pleasure-producing form, analogous to dream-work or indeed artwork. Following Freud, Henniger sees black humour as a defence against horror, 'das Grauen,' and accounts for its psychological causes and effects in terms of the comic simultaneity of continued repression and playful revelation of guilt-producing aggression; this in turn produces feelings both of pleasure and renewed guilt; and this combination, says Henniger [in his *Brevier des schwarzen Humors,* 1966], constitutes what we call black humour.

This is certainly plausible as far as it goes, especially for Henniger's archetypal black humorists, de Sade and Lautréamont. However, we notice that from the thematic point of view Henniger's definition rests squarely on the element of taboo, and is of extremely limited use, for example, when we come to those writers of the American sixties whom Schulz calls black humorists; Barth, Vonnegut, Pynchon, and so on, or those other writers whom we might add to his grouping: Beckett, Grass, García Márquez, and so on. Moreover, while these later writers are universally agreed to be comic writers, funny, mirth-provoking, those writers whom both Breton and Henniger regard as classical black humorists tend to evoke horror rather than mirth. Is the term 'black humour' then, we may ask, simply not elastic enough to include writers as diverse as Swift and Nabokov, de Sade and Borges, Lewis Carroll and Kafka? Is it indeed too clumsy to be of any real use to criticism, as has been variously suggested? Can we even distinguish when humour is black and when otherwise? Henniger's definition of black humour, after all, is different from Freud's definition of all humour only in degree, not in kind. To attempt an answer to these questions, and to suggest a foundation for our synthetic model of black humour, let us turn briefly to some of the better-known theories of humour.

There are some very few theorists who regard humour and laughter as being a benign instinct of human beings, primarily amiable and genial in nature. The majority view, however, as is well known, contests this, and regards laughter as primarily derisive, a vestige of snarling attack and the whoop of victory—I believe it was Darwin who said that the smile is simply a socially acceptable way of showing our teeth. Biblical laughter is predominantly born of scorn and mockery. The earliest recorded reference to laughter in the Classics appears to be that of the Olympians mocking the hobbling gait of the lame Hephaestus. In early medieval Ireland a good satire could raise blisters on the face of its victim and shame him into suicide or exile. Plato held humour to arise from delight in the suffering of others; Aristotle felt that the humorous is to be found in some defect, deformity, or ugliness in another; Cicero thought mental affliction to be a prime source of laughter. Sixteen centuries later Hobbes in his *Leviathan* of 1651 still defined laughter as a kind of 'sudden glory' at the misfortune of another, and even in our own century Bergson's *Le Rire* of 1900 sees humour essentially as a punishment inflicted on the unsocial or at least as a castigation of stupidity. Even when laughter is seen to be primarily a defensive rather than an aggressive attitude its origins are often felt to lie in suffering and sorrow rather than joy. 'Man alone suffers so excruciatingly in the world that he was compelled to invent laughter,' says Nietzsche; 'And if I laugh at any mortal thing, 'tis that I may not weep,' says Byron; 'The secret source of humour is not joy but sorrow,' says Mark Twain. Not for nothing does Freud, as we have seen, lay primary stress on the deeply disturbing dynamics behind humour.

One might object here that the humour of the English-speaking world, at least, frequently tends rather towards the genial and amiable, gently tolerant of the foibles of others, recognizing ourselves in those we mock, affirming things as they are in spite of everything. But it is easy to forget that this benign type of humour seems by all accounts to be a very modern phenomenon. Some theorists cannot find it before 1789, few can find it before 1700: the dominant mode of the comic until the end of the seventeenth century at least was that of satire and abrasive wit—aggressive, derisive, and frequently savage. Such a lovable fool as Don Quijote, such a lovable rogue as Falstaff appear to have acquired their amiability mainly in the course of the nineteenth century: to seventeenth-century audiences they seem to have been merely a fool and merely a rogue, butts of comic ridicule as were the 'humorists' of Ben Jonson or Molière. Stuart Tave first coined the phrase 'amiable humour' in 1960, demonstrating that the concept of humour underwent a radical revision in England during the eighteenth and early nineteenth centuries: the ridicule, raillery, and punitive satirical wit of the Restoration gradually lost place to good-natured and good-humoured portrayals of amiable 'originals,' whose peculiarities are no longer satirically instructive, but rather the objects of sympathy, delight, and love. The re-evaluation of Falstaff and Don Quijote was part of this general trend; so was the creation of such figures as Fielding's Parson Adams, Sterne's Uncle Toby, Goldsmith's Vicar of Wakefield, and Dickens's Mr. Pickwick.

The battle between the proponents of Hobbesian superiority and aggressive wit on the one hand and those who associated humour with philanthropy, sympathy, and pathos on the other raged throughout the eighteenth century, and by the beginning of the nineteenth century the new amiable, benign humour was regarded as the norm in England—and had spread to Germany too, mainly through Jean Paul Richter, who, as a disciple of Sterne, declared enthusiastically that benign humour was the Romantic form of the comic as opposed to the cold derision of Classical satire. Whether or not we agree with Tave that humour in this sense was an historical event beginning around 1710 and ending around 1914, there seems little doubt that derisive humour was the original stock, of which benign humour was merely a specialized offshoot, perhaps even a perversion, as argued by Ronald Knox in a classic paper ["On Humour and Satire," in *Essays in Satire* (1928), edited by Ronald Paulson]. Modern psychologists would concur here: Freud provided in his system for a rather grey area of benign or genial or 'harmless' humour, but, as a recent survey of humour theories points out, most subsequent psychoanalytic writers have either ignored or renounced a benign type of humour. Is there something 'black' then after all, something darkly equivocal at the very root of all humour, however much we may have overlaid that fact with the patina of modern democratic and enlightened tolerance? Should we simply conclude that all humour is black humour?

As a philosophical and psychological problem such a suggestion is perhaps not without interest. As practical literary critics, however, we shall hardly be much further forward by simply diffusing the concept to its vanishing point. Nor do we achieve too much by taking the more cautious step of deciding with robust common sense that black humour is quite simply that type of humour which laughs at the 'blacker' sides of life only, at grief, despair, evil, or death, or at subjects protected by more specific taboo, such as rape, murder, suicide, mutilation, or insanity. Certainly such humour very frequently *is* 'black,' of course, in its comic treatment of serious or even tragic material, but it does not always strike us as being *equally* black, since the gamut may range from the cheerful mayhem of a television cartoon through the playful and often silly grotesquerie of Monty Python to the nightmare world of Kafka—which Kafka himself reportedly found hilarious—or the appalling but still largely cartoon-like world of de Sade. Black humour in short cannot be defined in terms of its subject matter alone; it must be defined in terms of its mode of being, and here the existence of a gamut of what might popularly be thought of as black humour ranging from the frivolous to the terrifying provides us with a starting point for a contrastive definition, opposing black humour to other modes of humour, be they benignly understanding or derisively aggressive.

Both the benign and the derisive forms of humour are essentially self-congratulatory, self-reassuring, and spring from an ordered world of unimperilled values—the humour of those inside and safe rather than outside and lost. The world may indeed be threatening, but once the threat has been passed through the protective filter of humour we feel capable once again—even if only momentarily—of handling it and soldiering on. Both the benign and the derisive modes of humour essentially see the self optimistically as a controlling agent in an orderly world. They differ in their mode of expression in that benign humour is warm, tolerant, sympathetic, the humour of sensibility and sentiment, the humour, in a word, of unthreatened norms, while derisive humour is cold, intolerant, unsympathetic, the humour of rejection or correction, the humour of defended norms. They are alike however in that they are both expressions of the humour of certainty, the humour of cosmos. Black humour on the other hand contrasts with both of these in that it is the humour of lost norms, lost confidence, the humour of disorientation. Physicists express the tendency of closed systems to move from a state of order into one of total disorder in terms of the system's entropy: black humour, to coin a phrase, is the comedy of entropy.

Both Breton and Henniger, the only critics so far who have looked in any detail at the historical development of black humour as a literary form, see the eighteenth century as marking its emergence as a force in literature. One could quibble about this and set the date back to at least 1554 and the publication of *Lazarillo de Tormes,* which began the long-lasting tradition of the Spanish and then European picaresque novel. Nonetheless, the very fact that Swift and de Sade could write as they did in the age of Enlightenment, rationality, tolerance, and confidence is startling. It has been variously suggested that modern humour derives ultimately from the breakdown of the medieval world-picture and the consequent intensification of the sense of discrepancy between the real and the ideal. The sense of pessimism thus engendered, combined with the contrary thrust of Renaissance optimism, led, the argument runs, to the new psychological phenomenon of a sense of humour which was conceptual rather than physical, and which we find in varying tinctures in Rabelais, Cervantes, and Shakespeare. Only when the gap between the real and the ideal began to be perceived as extreme, Henniger suggests, when humour began to be self-consciously aware of the futility of its own gestures towards the reconciliation of opposites, did black humour emerge, not any longer as a force of reconciliation, but as one of subversion, of defiance. This 'crisis of humour,' according to Henniger, though prefigured throughout literature in the case of individual writers, reached its fullest development during the eighteenth century, and black humour as a distinguishable literary current was born, as a fundamental criticism of human affairs, sprung from the new, exhilarating, and terrifying freedom of rational thought.

The 'crisis of humour' can be seen as one expression of the larger crisis of the European consciousness in the early years of the eighteenth century as documented by Paul Hazard [in *La Crise de la conscience européenne, 1680-1715*]. If Swift is the father of black humour, his contemporary Shaftesbury, by virtue of the seminal reevaluation of humour in his 'Essay on the freedom of wit and humour' of 1709, has claim to being the father of benign humour. That is to say that black humour and benign humour reached the surface of consciousness, so to speak, virtually simultaneously—Shaftesbury, by the way, detested Swift, whom he considered obscene, profane, and a false wit. We can thus incorporate Henniger's theory of the emergence of black humour as a literary form into a more general theory by seeing it as only one aspect of a polarization of humour which was in its final stages by the eighteenth century: the literary emergence of black humour, tending towards the pornographic horrors of a de Sade, is counterbalanced by the emergence of benign humour, tending towards the joyous affirmation of the virtuous way by such bumbling but lovable characters as Uncle Toby or the Vicar of Wakefield. Both the benign and the black were thus latent in the humour whose dominant expression was derisive until the end of the seventeenth century, infrared and ultraviolent regions just beyond the edges of the narrow visible spectrum. Louis Cazamian has argued persuasively that the self-awareness of benign humour in the eighteenth century, and the subsequent flowering of consciousness of humour as a distinct instrument, came only with the finding of an individual name for the 'new' psychological phenomenon. Black humour had to wait another two centuries before Breton, by assigning it an individual name, incorporated it in the known spectrum.

The next step towards a comprehensive definition of literary black humour, the comedy of entropy, is to attempt a conceptual model in terms of its range of expressive capability, proceeding from the position that entropic humour is based firstly on an essential incongruity—the comic treatment of material which resists comic treatment—and secondly on the evocation of a particular response, namely the reader's perception that this incongruity is the expression of a sense of disorientation rather than a frivolous desire to shock. Both aspects will remain crucial through the various phases of our model, though the response will vary in nature and intensity as the rendering of the central moves from the predominantly thematic towards the predominantly formal. Since humour of any sort is as much a question of perception as it is of expression, the role of the reader here is obviously crucial: the reevaluation of Falstaff and Don Quijote during the eighteenth and nineteenth centuries may serve as illustration.

If the reader will bear for the moment with some apparent mixing on the terminological level, we may say that the basic modes of articulation of entropic or black humour are five in number and we may call them the satiric, the ironic, the grotesque, the absurd, and the parodic. Samuel Beckett's novel *Watt* (1953) contains one strikingly appropriate definition of their interaction, although to my knowledge Beckett has never made use of the phrase 'black humour.' As Watt enters Mr. Knott's house he encounters the departing Arsène, who comments on 'the laughs that strictly speaking are not laughs, but modes of ululation. . . . I mean the bitter, the hollow, and the mirthless.' These correspond, Arsène goes on, to

> successive excoriations of the understanding, and the passage from the one to the other is the passage from the lesser to the greater, from the lower to the higher, from the outer to the inner, from the matter to the form. The laugh that now is mirthless once was hollow, the laugh that once was hollow once was bitter. And the laugh that once was bitter? Eyewater, Mr. Watt, eyewater. . . . The bitter laugh laughs at that which is not good, it is the ethical laugh. The hollow laugh laughs at that which is not true, it is the intellectual laugh. . . . But the mirthless laugh is the dianoetic laugh. . . . It is the laugh of laughs, the *risus purus,* the laugh laughing at the laugh, the beholding, the saluting of the highest joke, in a word the laugh that laughs—silence please—at that which is unhappy.

Black humour of varying degrees of intensity may arise, as we have seen, from the employment of the grotesque as a stylistic device or of taboo materials as subject matter, but as a coherent literary form satire is the soil in which black humour takes root. Satire, though primarily an expression of derisive humour, reflects the spectrum of humour in its own spectrum, which extends from what we might call benign satire, firmly and tolerantly anchored in its own value-system, through derisive satire in the narrower sense, where the emphasis begins to shift from the didactic to the punitive, until finally we reach black or entropic satire, where disorder is seen to triumph over order. At the benign end of the spectrum satire is characterized by a firm belief in its own moral efficacy, by a confidence that the real can indeed be brought closer to the distant ideal. At the entropic end of the spectrum, however, we find an emphatic lack of belief in its own efficacy as an agent of moral education, and didactic confidence gives way to a fascinated vision of maximum entropy, total disorder. Here we have the gradations of Beckett's ethical laugh, directed against that which is not good, and at the black end of the scale we find, for example, Swift and de Sade. The submodes of the comic shade indistinguishably into each other, however, and both of these authors of

course also employ the next and more intense of Arsène's 'modes of ululations,' the intellectual laugh, aimed at that which is not true, and characterized primarily by an ironic rather than a satiric vision, that is to say by a vision where moral militancy has given way to detached observation. Moreover, and to considerable effect, in both of these modes there is also a substantial interaction of what I am designating as the third mode of entropic comedy, namely the grotesque. While the grotesque and the satiric, however, both aggressive modes, work together compatibly, the unstable compound of the ironic and the grotesque is a model conjunction whose volatility provides a formal generator of much of the sense of disjunction characteristic of entropic comedy.

Irony is a constant catalyst of black humour in that it regularly functions as a bridge between the comic and the tragic. Irony, like humour, is variously a literary device, a literary mode, and an existential mode, a way of looking at life. Like humour too it focuses on the discrepancy between the real and the ideal, and like humour it has traditionally been one of the chief devices of satire for this reason. Bergson schematically suggested that, while humour emphasizes the real, irony emphasizes the ideal, and satire attempts to bring them together. While humour points to the real, that is, and laughs, benignly or derisively, at its deficiencies, irony points to the gap separating the real from the ideal, and embodies that disjunction in the inauthentic discourse of ambiguity. As the gap widens, to the point where the real is perceived as no longer being true in Beckett's sense, that is to say no longer reconcilable to the ideal, irony responds less and less to the magnetic attraction of satire, more and more to that of the grotesque, and becomes in the process the dominant mode of entropic comedy in its own right—Frye [in *Anatomy of Criticism,* 1957], characterizes irony as the dominant mode of western literature over the last century. In the process too, irony, so to speak, subverts itself in that it parallels the development of satire already suggested and becomes entropic in its turn, the disjunction of irony proper shading into the disjunction of the grotesque.

Genetically irony is the weapon of the wily underdog, the eirōn of Greek comedy who counters the exaggerations of the boastful alazōn by the inverse strategy of sly understatement. Irony thus tends to be a finely honed instrument, a rapier rather than a bludgeon. The grotesque, on the other hand, operates precisely by exaggeration rather than understatement, by surprise rather than insinuation. Irony is intellectual and rational; the grotesque is emotional and irrational. Irony is genetically self-confident; the grotesque, to quote Wolfgang Kayser, whose book on the grotesque [*Das Groteske,* 1957] established its status as an aesthetic category in its own right, rather is 'the artistic expression of that estrangement and alienation which grips mankind when belief in a perfect and protective natural order is weakened or destroyed.' Like the ironic, and like humour in general, the grotesque too is based on incongruity, but while the more self-assured forms of irony and humour emphasize the possible resolution of conflict and only gradually become entropic, the grotesque always emphasizes the unresolved clash of incompatibles, and it is this primary incongruity in the very nature of the grotesque compounded by the secondary incongruity of combining the exaggeration of the grotesque and the understatement of irony which causes our simultaneous horror and exhilaration when we read Swift's *Modest Proposal* or Kafka's *Verwandlung* or Beckett's hilarious accounts of human misery.

The grotesque functions as our third mode of entropic comedy rather than as a group of formal devices primarily because it is always associated with some form of threat to the perceived autonomy of the individual self vis-à-vis the world. I believe that Philip Thomson is right [in *The Grotesque,* 1972] when he says that it is precisely the element of *balanced* horror and comedy that defines the grotesque. Lacking it, the grotesque shades off into either broad and harmless comedy or unadulterated horror. Whether the comedy or the horror prevails, however, is once again largely a matter of reader response. The grotesque, like irony, is a sort of no man's land between comedy and tragedy, as it is in a deeper sense between both of them and the absurd. Tragedy represents a world of order, where any infraction is summarily judged; comedy, in both its benign and derisive forms, also asserts the primacy of order; the grotesque represents the incursion of disorder, typically associated with physical abnormalities, deformations, and perversions. Though the grotesque may thus be used in a harmless or playful sense for ornamental purposes, as Rabelais and Sterne frequently do, for example, it is essentially a major mode of entropic comedy, an expression—like irony, however different they otherwise may be—of Beckett's intellectual laugh, aimed at that which is not true. To quote Kayser once again, the grotesque is the opposite of the sublime in that the sublime guides our view towards the true and the good, while the grotesque points to the inhuman and the abyss. Henniger, as we have noted, sees black humour as reaching its highest and most appropriate expression as it approaches ever closer to that abyss. I would argue, however, as Thomson does for the grotesque, that once the comic element disappears we have left the realm of black humour. One of the decisive factors in maintaining the element of comedy is precisely the interaction of the grotesque and the ironic modes that we find, for example, in the placid reasonableness of Swift's advocacy of cannibalism, or the detached interest with which Kafka observes Gregor Samsa's desperate attempts to roll out of bed. The sense of disorientation generated by the stylistic misalliance in such cases produces an exhilaration dependent upon the diametrically opposed nature of its two constituent principles.

The satiric mode of entropic comedy, as we have seen, unsuccessfully urges the necessity of reconciling the real and the ideal, while the ironic mode watches the gap become unbridgeable. The grotesque mode goes further in that it undermines the autonomy of the real, and by extension the validity of the guarantee implied by the notion of a linkage between real and ideal. The absurd mode, in turn, registers the disappearance of the ideal altogether, an event commemorated in modern times by Zarathustra's advertisement of the death of God, which simultaneously marks the achievement of self-awareness on the part of entropic humour. 'Wer auf den höchsten Berg steigt, der lacht über alle Trauer-Spiele und Trauer-Ernste,' proclaims Zara-

thustra. 'Das Lachen sprach ich heilig; ihr höheren Menschen, lernt mir—lachen.' The absurd laugh is the '*risus purus . . .* the saluting of the highest joke,' the dianoetic laugh, as Beckett calls it, and in spite of its venerable pedigree reaching back to Ecclesiastes and Democritus of Abdera, it has never been as widely laughed as in the last half-century, and the humour of disorientation, though by no means peculiar to the last century, has never before been as widespread. Satire and irony cross the line dividing self-confident humour from black humour only *in extremis;* the grotesque is usually a form of black humour; the absurd finally, insofar as it is a comic rather than a tragic mode, is always an expression of black humour, and even in its tragic emphasis remains a fertile source of latent entropic humour. All the forms of black humour discussed so far, in short, tend ultimately towards the absurd, towards the dianoetic laugh. All that is left of our play of real and ideal is the gap in the centre, the yawn, the hiatus—the common root of these three variations on emptiness also informs a fourth: 'chaos.'

The dianoetic laugh has two registers, however, one transcending the other, though Beckett does not specifically distinguish them. These two registers are not mutually exclusive; indeed one always implies the other, and by differentiating between them we are able to extend our spectrum of humour a further step to the point where we can begin to see the spectrum curving back on itself. Our spectrum so far contains three varieties of humour, subdivided into two groups: on the one hand benign and derisive humour, on the other black or entropic humour. Benign and derisive humour combine to form a higher class in that they express together the humour of cosmos, benign humour characterized by unthreatened values and the celebration of order, derisive humour characterized by the sense of threatened values and the aggressive rejection of potential disorder. They are, in fact, the passive and active sides respectively of the comedy of cosmos. The comedy of entropy, of black humour, may usefully be seen in similar terms. On the passive side we have black humour in all its modes of expression discussed so far, characterized implicitly by the sense of values lost and the apparent acceptance of total disorder. On the active side we have a form of entropic humour which we may call 'metahumour,' characterized by the sense of values parodied and the transvaluation of 'modes of ululation' into the parodic and paradoxical celebration of entropy.

The term 'metahumour' is appropriate in this context not least in that it is usefully suggestive of a range of meaning corresponding to the gradations of Beckett's dianoetic laugh, 'the laugh laughing at the laugh,' a range which in terms of our model includes not only the absurd mode but also its deconstructive counterpart, the mode of entropic parody. In a broader sense, indeed, all black humour contains the seeds of metahumour in that by its nature it includes its own critique, but in the fullest sense metahumour finds expression in that form of entropic comedy which is highly self-conscious, self-reflexive, and essentially marked by parody, as in, for example, Borges' *Ficciones,* Nabokov's *Pale Fire,* Robbe-Grillet's *Maison de rendezvous,* Calvino's *Cosmicomiche,* Handke's *Die Hornissen.* All of these, in their various ways, laugh the dianoetic laugh, but in each case it is not the passive laughter of simply acknowledging the existence of the 'highest joke,' it is an active laughter of connivance, of keeping up the joke, marked by an essential inauthenticity. This is the humour of parodic norms, flaunted fictivity, gratuitous constructs. Here, in the realm of the game, as satire gives way to parody, is Breton's 'révolte supérieure de l'esprit,' worked into iridescent counterworlds beyond the dianoetic laugh. Metahumour in its full parodic sense is a play with paradox, self-deconstructive in that it is joyously affirmative though what it affirms is nothingness: for in these structurations of uncertainty we discover that the spectrum of humour is inscribed on a Möbius strip, circling back on itself until the celebration of entropy becomes a paradoxical celebration of order, cosmos regained, but through the looking glass.

The dissonance and schizophrenia of entropic humour have traditionally centered on borderland areas of the imagination: taboo and insanity, dream and fantasy, mirror-worlds at the lip of the abyss, realms of the hypothetical, the ostentatiously fictive or surrealist. Metahumour teases disorder into parodic order in its own borderland, in the play of re-creative fictivity. Parody and paradox are the mode of being of these narcissistic antiworlds, and in their play with chaos they emphasize precisely form, shapeliness, structuration in an exhilarated, euphoric flaunting of artifice. Black humour is the humour of disorientation: metahumour is the humour of parodic re-orientation. Metahumour, one may add, finds pervasive expression in modern narrative fiction, and coming to the latter by a different route Robert Scholes classifies it as metafiction. The echo is appropriate, for this is both self-parodic fiction and self-parodic humour, fiction about fiction, humour about humour. Or, to put it in Alfred Jarry's terms, metahumour is applied pataphysics.

Is there any critical advantage in using an integrated concept of black humour in the approach to appropriate texts? I believe there is, and for corroboration one could point once again to the re-evaluation of Shakespeare's humour or Cervantes' humour that took after the theoretical recognition of benign humour in the eighteenth century. The whole area of literary humour is still in need of comprehensive mapping, and false signposts abound. In spite of the fact, for example, that comedy has largely taken over the traditional role of tragedy in our time, the tenacious view that tragedy is somehow a 'higher' genre than comedy has by no means disappeared, and black humorists are regularly attacked on the basis of this and similar arguments. Our model provides a useful tool in such a discussion in that it suggests a tradition and a context against which approaches as apparently different as the satire of de Sade or Swift on the one hand and the parody of Borges or Nabokov on the other may be seen to be correlative.

Some interesting large questions suggest themselves concerning the extent and frontiers of the tradition of entropic comedy. One of the largest would concern the degree to which twentieth-century experimentalism is the product of an attitude which is best classifiable as entropic humour. Breton forecast the growing importance of black humour as an attitude, and one only has to turn to our dominant modern faith, science, to see something of what he meant: the terrifying and exhilarating world of subatomic particle physics, antiworlds, time warps, black holes, cloning, microtechnology, and so on is a world of pure black humour, as if invented by Flann O'Brien's mad philosopher De Selby. For the modern writer, to quote Robbe-Grillet, there is every reason to suppose that 'the "probable" and the "true-to-type" are no longer remotely capable of serving as criteria. Indeed, it is very much as if the *false*—that is to say the possible, the impossible, the hypothesis, the lie, etc.—had become one of the privileged themes' of modern writing. Not all twentieth-century experimentation, of course, is fueled by black humour, but one could argue that large tracts of it certainly are.

In the lyric, for example, one could point to the development of the long tradition of nonsense verse. Nonsense, of course, is not always primarily an expression of the absurd: it can in fact reinforce our sense of superiority over the contingencies of logic and quotidian reality. There is always a latent suggestion of the absurd, however, and as the suggestion becomes stronger we find absurd forms evolving to mirror thematic absurdity, as we see in the contrast of, say, Lewis Carroll or Edward Lear or Christian Morgenstern on the one hand and Dada or the Surrealism of the twenties on the other. In the theatre, what Martin Esslin dubbed the Theatre of the Absurd is clearly enough the major expression of black humour. There were antecedents, of course, notably in the *commedia dell'arte*,

Philip Roth.

in some Shakespearean scenes, especially in *King Lear* and *Hamlet,* for example, and in the grotesque piling up of corpses in the final scenes of certain Jacobean dramas. But while we are frequently jolted by thematic incongruities in such earlier 'dark comedies,' it is only in the Theatre of the Absurd, as Esslin has shown, that we find the refusal to treat tragic materials tragically adequately reflected by formal devices which show us absurdity rather than telling us about it. In fiction the situation is similar. Robert Scholes sees modern black humour fiction as deriving ultimately from the satirical fantasies of the eighteenth century and the picaresque fiction of the sixteenth and seventeenth centuries, and one could push its origins further back to medieval and Renaissance jestbooks and the Classical tradition of what Frye calls Menippean satire. Black humour, however, is only one of many strands, and frequently a relatively unimportant one, in these antecedents; as in the lyric and the theatre the formal consequences of the increasing sway of black humour become most apparent in the twentieth century. As the Theatre of the Absurd of the fifties drew on the formal resources of Surrealism, so it contributes in turn to the major emergence of black humour fiction in the sixties, though the way had already been paved as early as the thirties by Beckett and Raymond Queneau, Flann O'Brien and Alfred Döblin.

We can take modern fiction as a more specific test of the applicability of the model, bearing in mind, of course, that not all texts classified as black humour fiction necessarily demonstrate their blackness or their humour in every sentence, any more than one would expect every phrase of a stage comedy to be relentlessly comic. In one text black humour will flare episodically, while in another it will smoulder pervasively. Thus Lautréamont's *Chants de Maldoror* is black from start to finish; so is Grass's *Blechtrommel* though in an entirely different register; García Márquez's *Cien años de soledad* is so in large part; Nabokov's *Pale Fire* thematically hardly at all at first blush but essentially so in that its essence is disorientation and its expression the perfect mirror. The mirror is a highly polished one here, as it is also in Robbe-Grillet's *Maison de rendez-vous,* for example; but less brilliant reflections can be equally effective, as in Heller's *Catch-22* or even the Alice books.

Central disorientation finds expression in such thematic areas as the portrayal of the existential labyrinth (Borges, Grass), with such submotifs as solitude (Beckett, García Márquez), circularity and stasis (Beckett, Queneau's *Le Chiendent*), entropy (Pynchon). The present is a waste land (*Catch-22*), a technetronic desert (Pynchon); the past is an historical nightmare (Grass, García Márquez, Queneau, Döblin's *Babylonische Wandrung*); the future appears in terms of comic dystopia (Burgess's *Clockwork Orange*) or of comic apocalypse (Vonnegut's *Cat's Cradle*). Central to the vision of the black humorist is the epistemological dilemma of the impotent, imploded self: Beckett's *Murphy,* Cortázar's *Rayuela,* Thomas Bernhard's *Das Kalkwerk.* Formally the self-consuming metahumorous construct is probably the most striking example of modern fictional black humour; others would include the devaluation of plot and character, and the whole area of parodic linguistic experiment, whether as the polyvalent

nonsense of the Jabberwocky or *Finnegan's Wake* or Arno Schmidt's *Zettels Traum* or as the linguistic 'baffle' deliberately obstructing the reader in *Le Chiendent* or *Clockwork Orange.*

In terms of our articulatory model one finds such works as *Catch-22, Die Blechtrommel,* and *Clockwork Orange* marked predominantly by black humour in the form of satire; the works of Borges and Pynchon are marked rather by irony; Döblin's *Babylonische Wandrung* as well as most of Kafka's works are marked by the grotesque; those of Beckett and Cortázar by the absurd; those of Nabokov, Robbe-Grillet, and Calvino by parody. These pedantic distinctions refer, of course, only to predominant emphases: literature rarely sleeps in such Procrustean beds. Awareness of a coherent tradition of black humour and its modal articulation, however, *can* suggest useful and interesting class relationships, and even on the level of the individual text this awareness can lead to fresh angles of vision, as when, for example, we look at Kafka's *Verwandlung* as one of a class that also includes not only *Murphy* and *Rayuela* but also *Pale Fire.*

One concluding point needs to be made. The scholarly analysis of humour smacks all too much of academic humourlessness, and we must not lose sight of what in the final analysis is the most important aspect of black humour as it is of all humour: it allows us to envisage the facelessness of the void and yet be able to laugh rather than despair. Entropic humour, which in the end is seen to be simply an intensification of the disturbing dynamics common to all humour, comes in many shapes and forms, and our laughter may contain many degrees of bitterness and hollowness, mirthlessness and parody and pain, but in the end—we do laugh, and while we laugh there's hope. The last century has seen the loss of belief in our selves, in our societies, and in our gods. The comedy of entropy accepts the absurd as its birth-right, and we are invited to share its descent to a no longer believed-in hell as well as its resurrection towards a non-existent heaven. Laughing at oneself, indeed, may not necessarily be a sign of psychic good health—but we should not forget either that comedy, like tragedy, began its career as part of a fertility rite. The element of joy, of delight in language and design and structure, is everywhere apparent in modern literary black humour, born though it may be of despair and formlessness and silence. 'To become conscious of what is horrifying and to laugh at it,' wrote Ionesco [in 'La démystification par l'humour noir,' *Avante-Scène,* February 1959], echoing Zarathustra, 'is to become master of that which is horrifying.' Or to put it another way, as Valéry is reported to have said once, Sisyphus goes on rolling his stone, but at least he ends up with a remarkable set of muscles. All humour, like all art and all literature, is Janus-faced, looking in one direction towards cosmos and in the other towards chaos. All humour, and *a fortiori* all literary humour, black or otherwise, must ultimately be affirmative of life and a celebration of the victory of the embattled spirit over the void. This is hardly a modern discovery: the Hindu sage knew it about twenty-two centuries ago when he wrote in the *Rāmāyana* that 'there are three things which are real: God, human folly, and laughter. Since the first two pass our comprehension, we must do what we can with the third.'

Patrick O'Neill, "The Comedy of Entropy: The Contexts of Black Humour," in Canadian Review of Comparative Literature, *Vol. X, No. 2, June, 1983, pp. 145-66.*

Alan R. Pratt on the literary origins of black humor:

Considerable controversy centers on black humor's place in literary history. Is it new, a uniquely modern literary reaction to World Wars, the threat of nuclear annihilation, and the violence and chaos of modern life in general? Or, is it as old as writing itself, a fundamental, albeit sporadic, aspect of the Western literary canon?

Although the term "black humor" may be useful and relevant for labeling a new mood in American humor, there are those who suggest that such a definition overlooks the contributions of Europeans. After all, the French surrealist poet and critic André Breton first coined the phrase *humor noir* in the late 1930s. He used this phrase to describe what he perceived as an age-old sensibility, iconoclastic and rebellious, which has served to question and undermine societal norms.

Others argue that black humor is unique to neither America nor Europe—or even the twentieth century. Treating the absurd sensibility with amused horror is the continuation of an ancient tradition, a sometimes waxing and sometimes waning undercurrent in Western letters. Indeed, the nervous laughter elicited by Aristophanes, Juvenal, Petronius, Erasmus, Shakespeare, Cervantes, Rabelais, de Sade, Swift, and Voltaire is the kind of laughter that is familiar to readers of contemporary black humor.

Alan R. Pratt, in his introduction to Black Humor: Critical Essays, *1993.*

Max F. Schulz

[*Schulz is an American educator and critic. In the following excerpt from his* Black Humor Fiction of the Sixties: A Pluralistic Definition of Man and His World, *Schulz attempts to define black humor, distinguishing it from related literary trends such as Existentialism, Theater of the Absurd, and Surrealism.*]

Conrad Knickerbocker is its theoretician, Bruce Jay Friedman its field commander. Yet neither they nor their fellow partisans can agree on a common article of faith or theatre of operations. Black Humor is a movement without unity, a group of guerrillas who huddle around the same campfire only because they know that they are in Indian territory. Even though they grudgingly concur about the enemy, they anarchistically refuse to coordinate their attack. Desperate men, they have abandoned not only the safety of received opinions but have also left to the news media the advance positions of satirical shock treatment, charging instead the exposed flanks of undiscovered lands "somewhere out beyond satire," which require "a new set

of filters" to be seen [according to Friedman in his Foreword to *Black Humor*, 1965].

The irony is that Friedman inadvertently gave literary respectability and philosophical cohesion to the group, when he patched together thirteen pieces (short stories and excerpts from novels, including one of his own, "Black Angels") for Bantam Books in 1965 and nonchalantly entitled them *Black Humor*. The other twelve writers on whom he had perpetrated this travesty were Terry Southern, John Rechy, J. P. Donleavy, Edward Albee, Charles Simmons, Louis-Ferdinand Céline, James Purdy, Joseph Heller, Thomas Pynchon, Vladimir Nabokov, Conrad Knickerbocker, and John Barth. The venture was an exercise in book making. Friedman's novels had had good critical reception but modest sales; he had a living to earn, a family to support. Much to his surprise he found himself tarred with his own black label. Dumbfounded, like one of his fictional characters, to learn that someone was indeed listening, he now regrets his part in this bit of carpentry for the trade. The tag has been applied to his own fiction until he winces when he hears the words. "What I ended up with was 13 separate writers with completely private and unique visions," he admitted with ingratiating candor as early as his foreword to the collection, "who in so many ways have nothing at all to do with one another and would not know or perhaps even understand one another's work if they tripped over it."

Despite Friedman's protestations and a recent effort to describe his play *Scuba Duba* with the more critically usable phrase "tense comedy," the Black Humor tag seems to have stuck. If, however, the term is to have any critical usefulness, aside from an opaque impressionistic meaning, it must be more clearly defined than hitherto. For as a term Black Humor *is* vague. It fails to distinguish among the genres. It fails to differentiate the contemporary movement from the many instances in the past of similar literary reactions to human experience. It fails to focus the means (plot, character, thought, and diction) and the end (effect on reader: laughter, tears, etc.) of literary expression, as Friedman's alternative "tense comedy" attempts more successfully to do. Indeed, Black Humor needs a definition that will be not only inclusive but exclusive.

Although several attempts have been made to define Black Humor, the results have been elusive and chimerical. Despairing of any substantive formula, Friedman opts for a mystery that has been around as long as the human mind has had an iconoclastic itch to peel back disguises and to probe "thoughts no one else cares to think." [In *The Fabulators*, 1967] Robert Scholes tries to channel Friedman's all-out purchase on history by shifting to formalist concerns and identifying Black Humor with the recurrent intellectual reaction of artists to the limitations of realism. As with the painterly aims of some modern artists, Black Humorists, he believes, are absorbed by the possibilities of playful and artful construction. They are master fabulators in the tradition of the Romance and its baroque configurations. Like Plato's "all-in-one," unfortunately, Scholes' "fabulation" becomes in practice a non-discriminating standard, subsuming in its alembic all "artful contrivance," for is not the artist by nature a maker of patterns? Are not the stark fables of Isaac Bashevis Singer as contrived as the mannered convolutions of Vladimir Nabokov? Surely Scholes' already disparate group of fabulators, ranging from Lawrence Durrell to John Hawkes, could not deny membership to the master fabulator—and ironist—Henry James. *Hic reductio ad absurdum!* If, on the other hand, Scholes sees this fabulation as a game to be enjoyed in part for its own sake, a decadence appreciated by a developed taste for the sophisticated, the artful—as his emphasis on Nabokov and Barth as arch-fabulators would suggest—then the moral position of a Henry James or the social gesture of a Bruce Jay Friedman, a Louis-Ferdinand Céline, a Terry Southern, or a Kurt Vonnegut becomes an important distinction. This is not to deny that Nabokov and Barth have their serious themes, or that Friedman has his aestheticism, but to suggest that the ways Nabokov and Barth handle their subjects loom larger in their calculations than the stylisms of Friedman loom in his. The verbal conundrums of Nabokov and Barth in any final analysis would appear more the stance of the aesthete than the verbal uniqueness of Friedman. And Scholes' definition would seem inevitably to polarize the practitioners of Black Humor into at least two groups distinguishable by the formalist means they employ. Conrad Knickerbocker in his groundbreaking essay ["Humor with a Mortal Sting," *New York Times Book Review,* 27 September 1964] diminishes the Black Humorist to *poète maudit,* a scorpion to the status quo, so full of the poison of self-loathing for the "specially tailored, ready-to-wear identities" given to us by TV, movies, the press, universities, the government, the military, medicine, and business, that he mortally stings himself, pricking the surrogate skin of society.

We unnecessarily compound the problem of determining what Black Humor is when we try, like Scholes, to see it as a universal attitude of mind, periodically emerging in the history of literature. Such a *via media* leads to an impasse not unlike that reached by those critics who make romanticism and classicism out to be constant modes of apprehending human experience. More limiting, certainly, but more useful in the long run is to recognize that Black Humor is a phenomenon of the 1960's, comprising a group of writers who share a viewpoint and an aesthetics for pacing off the boundaries of a nuclear-technological world intrinsically without confinement. Equally useful is to discriminate Black Humor from the oral techniques of sick humor and from the dramatic conventions of the theater of the absurd, even though it shares with these modes of expression some of the same assumptions about our century. In this respect, Hamlin Hill's essay ["Black Humor: Its Causes and Cure," *Colorado Quarterly* XVII (1968)], whose subject is the confrontation of humorist and audience, analyzes the technique of such stand-up comedians as Mort Sahl, Mike Nichols, and Lennie Bruce, and the sick humor of Jules Feiffer and Paul Krassner, rather than the literary form of Black Humor; hence it somewhat unwittingly is of help in discriminating sick humor from Black Humor but not in defining Black Humor which was purportedly its intention. And *Catch-22,* widely heralded as a Black Humor novel, actually derives as much from absurdist theater as from Black Humor fictional strategies. Written in the late forties and

early fifties (and published in 1955), its disregard of time and space, repetitiveness of speeches, stichomythia of commonplaces, and exercises in disproportion (that is, the substitution of the trivial as vehicle for and purveyor of the serious), link it more to the plays of Ionesco and Beckett, which cry out against a complex world, than to the elegant fictional structures of Barth, Borges, Grass, Nabokov, and Pynchon. A similar transitional work is Donleavy's *The Ginger Man* (also published in 1955), which displays its Angry Young Man genesis as much as anticipates the Black Humor stance.

The possibility that Black Humor differs in its view of man from existentialism is less easy to determine. Yet I think that an effort to discriminate between the two should be made. Basically, both posit an absurd world devoid of intrinsic values, with a resultant tension between individual and universe. The existentialist, however, retains implicitly a respect for the self. Although existence precedes being, to exist is to act (even for Beckett's almost immobile characters) and to act is to assert the self. The negation of many possibilities in favor of one choice of action thus becomes an heroic primal assent to life, as in Camus' portrait of Sisyphus. More often than not with the French existentialists action leads to cosmic despair rather than to joyous wholeness of being. Nevertheless the realization of self, as with Meursault in Camus' *The Stranger,* Moses in Bellow's *Herzog,* and Rojack in Mailer's *An American Dream,* is potentially present in the act of overcoming the negation of life by way of the assertion of self. Thus, while one finds in existentialism a rejection of suprapersonal law, dogma, and social order, one finds retained a confidence in the dignity and ordering capacity of the individual.

With Black Humor, choice poses the primary difficulty. This is the consequence of a shift in perspective from the self and its ability to create a moral ambience through an act to emphasis on all the moving forces of life which converge collectively upon the individual. But to affirm all possible forces in the likelihood that an act can be self creating is to deliver oneself up to skepticism that the self is anything but chimerical. Such is the plight of Barth's heroes. Yet this refusal to confirm either a suprapersonal or a personal order does not leave the Black Humorist despairing. He remains dissociated, hanging loose (or as has been suggested about Friedman "hanging by his thumbs" [Josh Greenfield, "Bruce Jay Friedman Is Hanging by His Thumbs," *New York Times Magazine* 14 January 1968]), cooly presenting individual efforts to realize oneself in relation to the outer world, with the focus less on the individual than on the world of experiences, less on the agony of struggle to realize self than on the bewildering trackless choices that face the individual.

Nor are its grotesqueries heirs to those of Surrealism. The latter assumes the validity of the human consciousness in its reliance on the processes of dreaming for its substance. If the subconscious mind includes a certain amount of internal disorder, this is realized aesthetically in the techniques of Surrealism, as well as in those of expressionism and stream-of-consciousness. Contrariwise, external disorder, meaningless social disorder, is codified as "absurdity" in existentialist fiction. And here Black Humor finds its logical home.

Divergence from traditional comedy and satire further characterizes Black Humor. New Comedy, according to Northrop Frye's "The Argument of Comedy" [*English Institute Essays 1948*], always worked toward a reconciliation of the individual with society. Either the normal individual was freed from the bonds of an arbitrary humor society, or a normal society was rescued from the whims imposed by humor individuals. As might be suspected, Frye finds lurking beneath this realignment of social forces the yearly triumph of spring over winter. He sees the victory of normality over abnormality as a formalized celebration of the archetypal pattern of death and resurrection. In the marriage of the young hero, in his triumph over the old lecher (*senex*), in the freeing of the slave, New Comedy rehearsed the victory of life over death.

Black Humor stops short of any such victory. It enacts no individual release or social reconciliation; it often moves toward, but ordinarily fails to reach, that goal. Like Shakespeare's dark comedies, Black Humor condemns man to a dying world; it never envisions, as do Shakespeare's early and late comedies, the possibilities of human escape from an aberrant environment into a forest milieu, as a ritual of the triumph of the green world over the waste land. Thus, at the conclusion of Bruce Jay Friedman's *Stern,* the protagonist is as alienated from "the kike man" and the suburban neighborhood he lives in as he was at the outset. Despite his efforts at *rapprochement,* he and society persist in the bonds of abnormality separating each other. The same comic divisiveness holds true for Benny Profane in Thomas Pynchon's *V.,* for Lester in Charles Wright's *The Wig,* for Oskar in Günter Grass's *The Tin Drum,* and for the narrator in Leonard Cohen's *Beautiful Losers,* to name a few of the many instances to be found in this fiction.

Black Humor's denial of social reconciliation or individual release is epitomized in the vision of Louis-Ferdinand Céline, who "worked the same beat" (Friedman admiringly acknowledges), "thought all your thoughts . . . was dumbfounded as many times a day as you are, long before you were born." In *Journey to the End of the Night* the best that Bardamu can offer as a summation of his "aimless pilgrimage" through this "truly appalling, awful world" is that "life leaves you high and dry long before you're really through." With numbness of heart, Bardamu acknowledges that neither person nor house can speak to him, that no one can find another in the darkness through which each is condemned to travel a long way by himself alone. Céline heralds the dead end of the eighteenth-century social and political ideal of the *philosophes,* memorably epitomized in William Godwin's boast that society is a collection of individuals. And the many Black Humorists today who look on him as ur-progenitor continue to push farther into the Célinesque darkness—incredible as that seems—in determined exploration of the permutability of urban existence and the paralysis of human indifference.

The divisiveness of society is certainly one consequence of the individualizing bent of Protestant humanism of the past 500 years. But other causes peculiar to our century are equally discernible. One need only to contrast the Rome of Plautus and the London of Shakespeare to the New York of Friedman and the Los Angeles of Pynchon to see the change in social cohesion that has taken place. Whereas the Plautean Romans and the Shakespearean Londoners were members of cities whose districts added up to coherent and whole communities with identifiable classes and cultures, Friedman's New Yorkers and Pynchon's Angelenos live in cities no longer with centers, connected to each other by subways and freeways. Although they live elbow to elbow, they are separated by vast distances from the places of personal relationships: work, church, parental homes, recreation. Friedman's Everyman, Stern, daily faces a harrowing multi-houred trip to the office, among indifferent, or outright hostile, fellow commuters. Angelenos spend equal numbers of hours speeding down ribbons of concrete, each encased in his metal cocoon of an automobile, cut off from the intimate sounds and smells of human voices and bodies, permitted only the occasional blurred glimpse of a face through two panes of window glass as they whisk past one another. Benny Profane—Pynchon's man profaned—yo-yoing on the Times Square-Grand Central Station subway shuttle embodies the ultimate directionlessness of life in the modern city. In constant motion he lacks destination. Like Bardamu's restless movements from France to Africa to America back to France, life describes a pointless journey with death as the only true destination. It is this disjunctive world that moves the Black Humorist, in part, to arrest the traditional comic reconciliation of individual and society.

Black Humor differs also from current existentialist views of man in refusing to treat his isolation as an ethical situation. Friedman slyly ribs Stern's effort to offset his fearful solitariness. In the last scene of the novel, for example, Stern's self-conscious embrace of wife and child in the nursery becomes a parodic tableau of the holy family, mistimed and miscued:

> Now Stern walked around the room, touching the rugs to make sure they wouldn't fall on his son's face. Then he said, "I feel like doing some hugging," and knelt beside the sleeping boy, inhaling his pajamas and putting his arm over him. His wife was at the door and Stern said, "I want you in here, too." She came over, and it occurred to him that he would like to try something a little theatrical, just kneel there quietly with his arms protectively draped around his wife and child. He tried it and wound up holding them a fraction longer than he'd intended.

Céline's dry tone and Parisian argot are similarly scornful of any mask other than the comic. With a matter-of-factness that suggests the laconic air of boredom (incongruously belied by the precipitous torrent of words), Bardamu recounts his indifference to life:

> Whatever people may care to make out, life leaves you high and dry long before you're really through.
>
> The things you used to set most store by, you one fine day decide to take less and less notice of, and it's an effort when you absolutely have to.

You're sick of always hearing yourself talk. . . . You abbreviate. You renounce. Thirty years you've been at it, talking, talking . . . You don't mind now about being right. You lose even the desire to hang on to the little place you've reserved for yourself among the pleasures of life. . . . You're fed up. From now on, it's enough just to eat a little, to get a bit of warmth, and to sleep as much as you can on the road to nothing at all. . . . The only things that still mean anything very much to you are the little regrets, like never having found time to get round and see your old uncle at Bois-Colombes, whose little song died away forever one February evening. That's all one's retained of life, this little very horrible regret; the rest one has more or less successfully vomited up along the road, with a good many retchings and a great deal of unhappiness. One's come to be nothing but an aged lamppost of fitful memories at the corner of a street along which almost no one passes now.

"If you're to be bored," Bardamu concludes, "the least wearisome way is to keep absolutely regular habits." Not suicide! that would be a nonsensical gesture of metaphysical despair or of archaic heroics. Todd Andrews reaches the same decision at the end of Barth's *The Floating Opera* when he recognizes that if there is no good reason why he should go on living, there is also no reason why he should die. This conception of its protagonist as the common man *manqué* is what makes Black Humor a somewhat limited vision capable of the specific aberrations of comedy, rather than the universal condition of tragedy.

We can gauge the degree of detachment practised by Black Humor if we compare these examples with the contrary moral renunciation of human kind that fires Schrella's decision at the conclusion of Heinrich Böll's *Billiards at Half-Past Nine.* A fugitive from Nazi Germany, Schrella has returned to his native city after an exile of more than twenty years. But he does not plan to stay. Unlike the rest of his countrymen and such Black Humor figures as Stern, he resolutely resists accommodation with the destructive powers of the past which persevere in the continuing forces of the present. As a continuing moral protest he persists in his rooming-house and hotel existence.

> "I'm afraid of houses you move into, then let yourself be convinced of the banal fact that life goes on and that you get used to anything in time. Ferdi would be only a memory, and my father only a dream. And yet they killed Ferdi, and his father vanished from here without a trace. They're not even remembered in the lists of any political organization, since they never belonged to any. They aren't even remembered in the Jewish memorial services, since they weren't Jewish . . . I can't live in this city because it isn't alien enough for me . . . my hotel room's exactly right. Once I shut the door behind me, this city becomes as foreign as all the others."

Billiards at Half-Past Nine is black enough in its vision of man; but its fervid crusade to alter human nature, and its desperate rejection of society until such moral regenera-

tion takes place, give it a tragic rather than comic mask. When he wishes, of course, Böll can write what passes for Black Humor. In *The Clown* he depicts the deterioration of Hans Schnier, a social misfit who cannot adjust to the hypocrisy of post-war Germany. Whereas Dostoevsky's Idiot spirals tragically heavenward, Böll's Clown winds down through Biedermeier instances of insult to a beggar's cushion in the Bonn train station. Like the irreverently treated heroes of *God Bless You, Mr. Rosewater* and *The Sot-Weed Factor,* Schnier the "wise fool" proves to be more foolish than wise. But even at this ebb tide of his life, Schnier unlike Schrella continues to seek out human company.

Like Böll's Clown the protagonist of Black Humor does not despair with the savage bitterness of Nathanael West's Miss Lonelyhearts. Nor does he remain aloof, dismissing society with cold imperviousness, like Evelyn Waugh's Dennis Barlow. Rather, he worries about his place in it. Only after repeated rebuffs in his search for a relationship with others does he accept his empty existence with an angry shrug like Ferdinand Bardamu. He may be a booby like Friedman's Stern, a *naïf* like his Joseph, an anti-hero like Céline's Bardamu, a silly like Vonnegut's Eliot Rosewater, a pervert like Nabokov's Humbert Humbert, a clown like Heller's Yossarian, a fool like Barth's Ebenezer Cooke, a rogue like Berger's Jack Crabb, a drop-out like Grass's Oskar, a dupe like Pynchon's Herbert Stencil— but he is never an untouched innocent like Waugh's Paul Pennyfeather, nor a dismembered scapegoat like West's Lemuel Pitkin, nor an unwitting gull like Swift's Gulliver. At the end of *Decline and Fall* Paul Pennyfeather returns to college unchanged by his scarifying mishaps. At the end of *A Cool Million* Lemuel Pitkin is without thumb, leg, eye, teeth, scalp, indeed his very existence; yet is ironically a heroic witness to the American dream of success. The Black Humor protagonist is not, like these satiric foils, an authorial lens for analyzing the real, corrupt object of the satire. Nor does detachment mean for him withdrawal from the world, as it does for Gulliver, Candide, or Dennis Barlow. He is at once observer of, and participant in, the drama of dissidence, detached from and yet affected by what happens around him. Extremely conscious of his situation, he is radically different from the satiric puppets of Waugh and West, who bounce back like Krazy Kat from every cruel flattening as smooth and round as before, their minds unviolated by experience. His—and the author's— gaze is more often than not concentrated on what Conrad Knickerbocker has called the terrors and possibilities of the world we have brought into being in this century, and of the self-knowledge that this leads us toward. His prison-house loneliness, forced upon him by existence, becomes a Célinesque journey to the end of the night.

The moral quality of society—the aim of satire—is not, according to Northrop Frye [in "The Argument of Comedy," in *Theories of Comedy*], the point of the comic resolution of an individual and a group. Nor is it the objective of Black Humor, which resists any final accommodation. As Scholes notes, the Black Humorist is not concerned with what to do about life but with how to take it. This is not to say that he has no moral position, but only to suggest that this position is *implicit.* He may challenge the trances and hysterias of society, as Conrad Knickerbocker suggests, but he does not ordinarily urge choice on us. He seeks rather a comic perspective on both tragic fact and moralistic certitude. In extreme instances, for example some of Kurt Vonnegut's writings, this attitude of mind will lead to the novel's refusal to take its implied moral position seriously. *The Sot-Weed Factor* has been faulted for its abdication of responsibility to answer the questions it raises about intrinsic values, and *Catch-22* for its central evasiveness as regards war, for its not having a point of view, an awareness of what things should or should not be. Such is the ultimate ethical and aesthetic chaos that these novels risk in their rage for an inclusive purchase on reality.

The skepticism of the Black Humorist suggests an explanation for the distinctly metaphysical bent and American identity of this fiction. Can a writer convinced of the truth of a closed ethical, philosophical, or religious system conceptualize human experience in the terms of Black Humor? I think not. Undeviating acceptance of Christianity would surely make it impossible to produce an anti-God novel like Robert Coover's *The Universal Baseball Association, Inc.—J. Henry Waugh Prop.* other than as an unconvincing pastiche. It is his ardent Catholicism that prompts Heinrich Böll to castigate his bourgeois characters for giving their allegiance to the German economic miracle rather than to the Catholic religious values they nominally profess, and accounts for *The Clown*'s suffering from artistic and philosophical confusion and ultimately for not corresponding to the Black Humor novels considered here. Günter Grass also professes to be a Catholic. His social skepticism, however, qualifies his religious dogmatism. In *The Tin Drum* he contains the two perspectives of Catholicism and Black Humor, content with a simple balance of contraries, especially the dichotomies of guilt and innocence, tempter and tempted, the Christlike and the Satanical, the Dionysian (Oskar's fascination for Rasputin) and the Apollonian (Oskar's attraction to Goethe), without compulsion to reconcile them. His concentration on the outward oriented world of objects—the tin drum, fizz powder, the smells of the women in Oskar's life, the cartridge case, the skat playing of Oskar's parents, his grandmother's petticoats—contributes to this intellectual neutrality, since objects are basically inimical to ideas, or to the resolution of ideas. Consequently Grass's novels observe the frame of reference of Black Humor despite his commitment to traditional beliefs.

The literary tradition of the German and English novels also militates against the inconclusive version of life presented in the Black Humor novel. The German *Bildungsroman*, or *Entwicklungsroman*, presupposes a set of social, as well as moral and ethical, values, a substantive goal toward which the protagonist progresses in preparation for his adult role in the community. *The Tin Drum* conforms to this genre but parodies its fixed principles in its conception of Oskar's being born with awareness, of his being as cognizant of his world at three as at thirty, and in its uncertainty (and plurality) of point of view. The English novel of manners similarly assumes a collective relevance, established social classes and codes of conduct—a context within which narrative conflict is developed. The Ameri-

can novel, short on *Entwicklung* and manners, is more receptive to the inconclusive exploration of ontological and epistemological questions of being, growth, and knowledge. In this respect, the Black Humor novel continues the quest of the *Pequod,* its route updated and its procedure modernized.

It is not accidental probably that the two European writers, other than Grass and Céline, identified with Black Humor—Vladimir Nabokov and Jorge Luis Borges—exhibit a disillusioned cosmopolitanism acquired by the accidents of choice and of history that transcends the literary and cultural suppositions of their Russian and Argentinian heritages. To them has been "given bad times in which to live" in greater measure than is man's normal lot; and their excruciating sense of the instability of life pervades the texture and substance of their fiction. "We are creatures of chance in an absolute void" "the *true* Present . . . an instant of zero duration," Nabokov has Van Veen exclaim in *Ada,* "—unless we be artists ourselves." Only in "the act of artistic correction" is "the pang of the Present" given durability. Heirs of this century's national tensions and philosophical uncertainties, their stories are parodies of man's mistaken faith historically and philosophically in cultural continuity and ideational permanence. Nor is it accidental that Kurt Vonne-

---

An excerpt from *The Floating Opera*

Light step! I wanted to dance across the hall! My opinion? My opinion? SUICIDE! Oh, light step, reader! Let me tell you: my whole life, at least a great part of it, has been directed toward the solution of a problem, or mastery of a fact. It is a matter of attitudes, of stances—of masks, if you wish, though the term has a pejorativeness that I won't accept. During my life I've assumed four or five such stances, based on certain conclusions, for I tend, I'm afraid, to attribute to abstract ideas a life-or-death significance. Each stance, it seemed to me at the time, represented the answer to my dilemma, the mastery of my fact; but always something would happen to demonstrate its inadequacy, or else the stance would simply lose its persuasiveness, imperceptibly, until suddenly it didn't work—quantitative change, as Marx has it, suddenly becoming qualitative change—and then I had the job to face again of changing masks: a slow and, for me, painful process, if often an involuntary one. Be content, if you please, with understanding that during several years prior to 1937 I had employed a stance that, I thought, represented a real and permanent solution to my problem; that during the first half of 1937 that stance had been losing its effectiveness; that during the night of June 20, the night before the day of my story, I became totally and forcibly aware of its inadequacy—I was, in fact, back where I'd started in 1919; and that, finally and miraculously, after no more than an hour's predawn sleep, I awoke, splashed cold water on my face, and realized that I had the real, the final, the unassailable answer; the last possible word; the stance to end all stances. If it hadn't been necessary to tiptoe and whisper, I'd have danced a *trepak* and sung a *come-all-ye!* Didn't I tell you I'd pull no punches? That my answers were yours? *Suicide!*

John Barth, in his The Floating Opera, *Doubleday, 1988.*

gut has waited longest of the Black Humorists for recognition. His novels are not organized according to one fictional kind but follow multiple modes, at once novel of manners, confessional journal, science fiction, social satire, detective story, soap opera, and slick magazine tale. The resultant farrago of literary syntaxes has bewildered and offended both British and American readers, whose expectations are never consistently satisfied. At any rate, Black Humor has remained, with the exception of the few European writers mentioned, a predominantly American phenomenon of the sixties, whose anxieties proceeding from pluralism, conformity, and an irresolute value system give it both its method and its subject.

> Max F. Schulz, "Towards a Definition of Black Humor," in his Black Humor Fiction of the Sixties: A Pluralistic Definition of Man and His World, 1973. Reprint by Ohio State University, 1975, pp. 3-16.

Bruce Janoff

[*In the following essay, Janoff distinguishes between Existentialism and black humor as literary genres, characterizing the latter as a more profoundly nihilistic and comic reaction to absurdity.*]

To the dismay of purists, the generically messy term "black humor" is here to stay. Of course not even the most naïve graduate student would claim that black humor is a deliberate, coordinated literary movement any more than is Martin Esslin's Theater of the Absurd or realism or naturalism or, for that matter, most any other literary ism. Obviously there are dangers inherent in generalizing about the work of an indeterminate group of novelists whose interests are as varied as their number. It is equally obvious, however, that enlightened critical evaluation depends heavily on a sense of genre, and on this score the terminological confusion has grown severe.

For example, it has become common critical practice to use the term black humor interchangeably with more scholarly designations such as "the existential novel," "novel of the absurd," and "the anti-novel," or with more colorful labels like "Yankee existentialism," "nightmare fiction," or "the comic apocalyptic writers." In the first book-length study on the subject, *Black Humor Fiction of the Sixties* (1973), Professor Max Schulz adds the most grandiose term yet in attempting to explain the nature of the beast: The Metaphysics of Multiplicity.

It seems to me that this ongoing confusion in terminology stems in large measure from a fundamental generic confusion, i.e., the critical inability to distinguish between black humorists as a novelistic school and the popular existential novelists, most prominently Jean-Paul Sartre and Albert Camus. Some of the older critics, when referring to novels they feel belong to the literary movement (or movements) loosely circumscribed by these terms, make no distinctions at all. They simply lump together novels of genuine black humor with classically existential works such as Sartre's *Nausea* (1938) or Camus's *The Plague* (1948). More recent critics who scrupulously avoid patently exis-

tential interpretations because they are overused or outmoded, nevertheless make the same tacit assumptions.

Clearly, the existential novel demonstrates a despairing world view which has strong affinities with the grim vision of the black humorists. Perhaps not so clearly, it differs generically from black humor in two significant areas. First, although the typical existential novel is often heavily ironic, it does not contain the consistently wry, comic perspective from which the black humorists view the human condition. Their obvious literary merits notwithstanding, Sartre and Camus write somber, conventional novels that are essentially devoid of humor. Their existential sense of loss and alienation is expressed in terms of serious, technically controlled prose which is rarely played for laughs.

In sharp contrast, the black humorists, regarding the meaninglessness of existence with fascinated horror, present their even darker vision through a unique mixture of comedy and despair. In equal measure with the two Frenchmen, American novelists of the sixties like John Barth and Joseph Heller are by turns enraged and frustrated in coming to terms with their existential loneliness. The metaphysical vision that they share with Sartre and Camus, though, is manifested artistically in distinctly different ways.

For example, instead of becoming literally nauseated as Sartre's Antoine Roquentin does in his confrontation with the existential "void," or like Camus's Dr. Rieux, fighting the invincible forces of the plague with tight-lipped determination, in Heller's *Catch-22* (1961) Yossarian protests the brutality of war by sitting naked in a tree, and in Barth's *The Floating Opera* (1956) Todd Andrews works out a wild legal puzzle involving three million dollars and 129 pickle jars filled with excrement at the same time that he dispassionately contemplates his own suicide. Most blackly humorous of all, at the behest of something he calls "The Absolute Genital," in Barth's *The End of the Road* (1958) Jacob Horner forms a "perfect equilateral triangle" with his best friend and the latter's wife while simultaneously struggling against the sickening realization that in a very real spiritual sense he does not exist.

Horner, compared with Sartre's Roquentin, is especially illustrative of the difference in approach between the two pairs of writers. The metaphysical quandary is essentially the same for Horner and Roquentin: each is overcome by the realization that his physical existence is qualitatively no different from that of the lower animals or even nonhuman matter. Both are aware of the self-delusion inherent in attributing satisfying meanings to aspects of reality which are either unintelligible or so threatening psychologically that they become unacceptable. Given the coincidentally similar situations that Sartre and Barth have constructed, the difference between the two troubled protagonists lies in their individual reactions to the common existential condition. Roquentin faces his perception of the dilemma with deadly seriousness—he grows so involved both intellectually and emotionally that in his famous confrontation with the chestnut tree he becomes physically ill:

> The chestnut tree pressed itself against my eyes. Green rust covered it half-way up; the bark, black and swollen, looked like boiled leather.

The sound of the water in the Masqueret Fountain sounded in my ears, made a nest there, filled them with signs; my nostrils overflowed with a green, putrid odour. . . . Trees, night-blue pillars, the happy bubbling of a fountain, vital smells, little heat-mists floating in the cold air, a red-haired man digesting on a bench: all this somnolence, all these meals digested together, had its comic side. . . . Comic . . . no: it didn't go as far as that, nothing that exists can be comic; it was like a floating analogy, almost entirely elusive, with certain aspects of vaudeville. We were a heap of living creatures, irritated, embarrassed at ourselves, we hadn't the slightest reason to be there, none of us, each one, confused, vaguely alarmed, felt in the way in relation to the others.

Because the scene is rendered with so little appeal to humor, Sartre's reader can react only with a seriousness equal to Roquentin's.

In contrast to Roquentin's intensity, Horner retains a curious emotional detachment from his existential circumstance all the while that he wrestles with it intellectually. Interestingly enough, he too becomes physically ill as a result of his morbid introspection over the question of being or nonbeing. Unlike the Sartrean nausea, however, Horner develops a mysterious paralysis (the etiology of which is ominously undefined) while sitting in a railroad station trying to decide on a destination. The scene is rendered with a subtle comic edge which distinguishes it unmistakably from Sartre's:

There was no reason to go to Cincinnati, Ohio. There was no reason to go to Crestline, Ohio. Or Dayton, Ohio; or Lima, Ohio. There was no reason, either, to go back to the apartment hotel, or for that matter to go anywhere. There was no reason to do anything. My eyes as Wincklemann said inaccurately of the eyes of the Greek statues, were sightless, gazing on eternity, fixed on ultimacy, and when that is the case there is no reason to do anything—even to change the focus of one's eyes. Which is perhaps why the statues stand still. It is the malady *cosmopsis,* the cosmic view, that afflicted me. When one has it, one is frozen like the bullfrog when the hunter's light strikes him full in the eyes, only with cosmopsis there is no hunter, and no quick hand to terminate the moment—there's only the light. . . . After a while Cincinnati, Crestline, Dayton, and Lima dropped from my mind, and their place was taken by that test pattern of my consciousness, *Pepsi-Cola hits the spot,* intoned with silent oracularity. But it, too, petered away into the void, and nothing appeared in its stead.

By normal clinical standards Horner is obviously a sick man. Relatively, he is much more disturbed than Roquentin. Nonetheless, his cheery stoical attitude allows the reader to smile incongruously even as he emphathizes with Horner's emotional, moral, and spiritual vacuity. In the passage just quoted, Horner's wry deduction as to why statues stand still and his reference to the existential concept of nothingness as the "test pattern of his consciousness" help cushion the impact of the void as it ominously takes control over his psyche. Through it all Barth's hero

emerges as an engaging, complex fictional creation rather than a two-dimensional dramatization of a philosophical system as, perhaps, Roquentin does. Both Sartre and early Barth are essentially philosophical novelists whose works stand, largely, as exempla for their respective philosophical systems. Often Sartre's work is so transparent that his philosophizing tends to obstruct the movement and credibility of his plot. It is to Barth's credit that he can make his abstruse philosophical points in economical, entertaining novels that throb with life and with life-sustaining humor.

The second, related generic difference between the two sets of novelists deals directly with philosophy. As nearly all their writing indicates, Sartre and Camus are concerned with the same fundamental problem which has engaged existential thinkers from the Preacher in Ecclesiastes to Rollo May and R. D. Laing: the senselessness of the human situation. Sartre's expression "existence precedes essence" is probably the most famous dictum on the subject, but Camus summarizes the condition most clearly in *The Myth of Sisyphus* with his definition of the absurd:

Man stands face to face with the irrational. He feels within him his longing for happiness and for reason. The absurd is born of this confrontation between the human need and the unreasonable silence of the world.

The black humorists would no doubt accept Camus's statement as an accurate account of the general existential situation. But if the existentialists see the universe as absurd, the black humorists see it "as ridiculous—a joke" [Robert Scholes, *The Fabulators,* 1967]. Both groups are obviously aware of the dismal realities of aging, human suffering, and the inevitability of death. It is their manifestly dissimilar reactions to this common vision which distinguishes them philosophically—and by extension, artistically.

Camus austerely advised struggling, suicidal man to live with defiant persistence in spite of the odds; Sisyphus' eternal labor with the rock symbolizes this attitude. The black humorists, no less cognizant of the absolute hopelessness inherent in an absurd universe, react differently. Insofar as they can be categorized philosophically, the black humorists subscribe to an irrationalist metaphysic that borders on nihilism in contradistinction to the French existential system which is characterized by human involvement and the ideal of service. In Camus's *The Plague,* for instance, Dr. Rieux reaches ecstatic heights of personal gratification when fighting the insuperable forces of the bubonic plague precisely because he continues to fight, knowing that the odds in favor of winning are nil. Only when Camusian man resigns himself to the inevitability of suffering and death does the prospect of living in a plague-ridden world take on a paradoxical aura of hopefulness. Only when he is painfully conscious of the absence of meaning outside this world and the chaos inherent in it, and yet shoulder to shoulder with his fellow man continues the struggle, can he hope to endure. In short, existentialism is a marginally optimistic system which posits that limited meaning, and therefore reason to go on living, may be found through the relationship of self and the external world (which includes other men).

In marked contrast to this existential ethic, the black humorists will not even allow the temporary respite of the "hopeless hope" paradox. They see everything external to the individual mind as irrational, i.e., they find no positive correspondence between reasoning man and an indifferent world (which, again, includes other men). It is the *relationship* that is lethal: man always loses. His only chance for a modicum of dignity lies in his ability to lose gracefully, grudgingly, and comically—and even then, black humorists forlornly intone, the chance is ridiculously slim (possibly one reason why such undignified subjects as scatology and gross sexual perversion find their way into so many black humor novels). These writers derive little joy from the humanistic knowledge that their fellow men are sometimes willing to help ease the pain. Because their irrationalist posture includes the comic element (an obvious attempt to assuage the psychic pain), it is not to be equated with sheer pessimism and misanthropy, but it is hardly a cause for optimism either.

This philosophical aspect of black humor is significant, and is graphically illustrated in the character of Heller's John Yossarian, perhaps the closest the movement comes to producing a definitive central figure. Prior to the last four chapters of *Catch-22*, Yossarian's sole and unwavering compulsion is for personal survival in a preposterously hostile world. Much of the book's comedy is generated by Yossarian's acrobatic maneuvers to keep himself alive, in accordance with his grimly accurate assessment that people in *both* armies are trying to kill him. Until chapter 39 ("The Eternal City"), Yossarian operates from an irrationalist perspective: his frantic need to disengage himself from a host of threatening forces is made convincing because it is private. After he witnesses the depravity and the human degradation of modern Rome, however, Yossarian's attitude changes abruptly. He suddenly learns that there is something more important than total ego involvement aimed at self-preservation: he discovers social involvement—in effect, the existential ideal of service. This attitudinal change is dramatized by Yossarian's altruistic interest in Nately's whore's kid sister and in his desire to escape to Sweden where he believes, naïvely, that the world will be significantly less absurd, a logical impossibility since suffering and death (which know no national boundary) are the ultimate absurdity.

The suddenness of Yossarian's shift in outlook has been much commented upon. Vance Ramsay, for one, notes:

> In his all-absorbing involvement in the threat to his own existence, Yossarian has been so little aware of the threat to others that the sudden change to an awareness of them and dedication to trying to help them does not have the same force.

While the artistic problems peculiar to the ending of *Catch-22* are not to the point here, further consideration of the ending is relevant insofar as it demonstrates the difference in philosophy between black humor and existential fiction.

For the best part of *Catch-22*, Heller writes from an irrationalist perspective. This point of view is indicated by the author's concentrated focus on Yossarian's personal feelings of despair, most of which are caused by Yossarian's consciousness of the absurd (effectively symbolized by catch-22 itself). After chapter 39, however, Heller apparently felt the need for a relatively optimistic (existential) ending; this authorial decision is evidenced by his radical shift in tone, allowing his hero to compromise his spirit of total rebellion against the pernicious forces of catch-22 and move, hesitatingly, back into the system. In this tonal sense, *Catch-22* is a curious mixture of philosophical attitudes: if the book is divided into two at chapter 39, the 400-odd pages that precede this division attest to brilliant stretches of black humor where Yossarian acts consistently as an irrationalist. Similarly isolated, the last four chapters offer a vaguely reconciliatory Yossarian who maintains an existential posture. Fused to the first eight-ninths of the novel, these last fifty pages disrupt the book's rhythm and severely impede its thematic momentum. Clearly, Heller is more comfortable—and probably more successful—when writing as a black humorist from an irrationalist perspective than when imposing a hopeful ending by trying to reconstruct the fictional world he has shattered.

Furthermore, in this tonal context both of Barth's novels are more consistent, if less comically spectacular, than *Catch-22*. This consistency is especially evident in *The End of the Road* where from the beginning Jacob Horner is controlled by irrational forces which only his mysterious Black psychiatrist-spiritual advisor seems able to fathom. Horner's psychological condition deteriorates throughout the novel, reaching its nadir on the final page. There, in a near paralytic state, he climbs into a taxi and gives the driver the ominous instruction, "Terminal!"

Likewise, throughout his narration of the events of June 23 (or 24), 1937, in *The Floating Opera* Todd Andrews is entirely consistent in his decision to kill himself—even to the point of making a deadly serious attempt which fails at the last moment only because a crewmember of the showboat *Floating Opera* discovers Andrews and ventilates the gas-filled galley which he has chosen as a death chamber. Moreover, the curious final chapter called, with some tongue in cheek, "A parenthesis, a happy ending, a Floating Opera," is in line with Andrews's irrationalist philosophy. In this chapter, Andrews manages to subdue his suicidal impulse at least temporarily: by further rationalizing he convinces himself of the existence of relative meaning in the world outside his own mind. While this tentative change of heart (brought about by Andrews's sudden emotion for the delightful three-year-old Jeannie Mack) is mildly suggestive of the philosophical shift in *Catch-22*, the change is not nearly so abrupt or far-reaching as Yossarian's. For the ratiocinative Andrews, even Jeannie's life "had no more absolute, objective value than did anything else." Furthermore, Andrews's very decision to go on living is phrased most equivocally: "I would never, I resolved at that moment, kill myself in confusion!" The novel ends in the paragraph following this resolution without any indication whether Andrews would kill himself at some propitious time when he was *not* confused.

At its best, black humor shows few traces of the enlightened humanism that marks the existential ethic. Despite the philosophical roots it shares with existentialism, black humor, by turns coolly humorous and murderously farcical, is not primarily satirical and seldom leaves any didactic residue. What social institution is Barth satirizing in *The End of the Road,* for example, with his frightening description of Jacob Horner's dread paralysis or Rennie Morgan's hideous accidental death? And what person or group is Heller attacking in *Catch-22* when he shows Yossarian in terrible anguish over the "fertile red meadows of epithelial tissue to catch and coddle a cancer cell . . . lymph glands that might do him in . . . tumors of the brain . . . Hodgkin's disease, leukemia, amyotrophic lateral sclerosis . . . and billions of conscientious body cells oxidating away day and night like dumb animals at their complicated job of keeping him alive and healthy, and every one was a potential traitor and foe."

For Barth, the sinister force that induces Horner's immobility is nothing less than the perplexing multiplicity of life itself which offers an array of choice so vast that it drives Horner into a state of incipient psychosis; and Rennie Morgan's faceless executioner may be identified as the utterly arbitrary state of man's position in the world (by chance, on the night of her abortion she ate a heavy meal of hot dogs and sauerkraut which she regurgitated and strangled on after being given ether). For Heller, it is the horrifying tenuousness of man's physical nature that precipitates Yossarian's moment of helpless anguish. It is Snowden's tragic secret that "man is matter" which triggers Yossarian's despondency. Heller himself puts it best in the "Snowden" chapter:

> Drop . . . [a man] out a window and he'll fall. Set fire to him and he'll burn. Bury him and he'll rot, like other kinds of garbage. The spirit gone, man is garbage.

In 1964 Ihab Hassan was able to describe the new direction of American fiction perfectly in one phrase: "The deflection of laughter toward anguish" ["Laughter in the Dark: The New Voice in American Fiction," *American Scholar,* Autumn 1964]. He then stated that his observation indicates a less enthusiastic but still optimistic and ultimately affirmative American literary voice. Such a view is no doubt accurate when referring to the work of popular, well-established contemporary novelists like J. D. Salinger or Saul Bellow who deflect their style of humor toward anguish in relatively conservative ways.

Affirmation and optimism are decidedly relative terms, however, and when applied to the black humorist they must be considered in a different light. Indeed, the tone of the black humorist's laughter is often deflected more sharply toward anguish than Hassan would like to admit; so sharply, in fact, that in the blackest of the black humor novels affirmation simply means continuing to live rather than committing suicide, and optimism is nothing more

than laughing darkly at a tragically insensitive environment.

Ultimately, black humor cannot be described as being pessimistic or simply lacking an affirmative moral voice. Rather, it lives outside these limits in a terrain of terrifying candor concerning the most extreme situations. Yet the black humorist cannot be accused of being totally nihilistic since he refuses to negate the legitimacy of his art and continues to write. The best conclusion, perhaps, is that within the artistic framework the black humorist is the artist closest to giving it all up. Like his existential forebearers, he is obviously enraged by the cul de sac of the absurdist metaphysic, but unlike them he is on the verge of acknowledging that he is beaten in his feeble literary attempts to combat it. Still, he continues to write. Why? John Barth may have the answer.

In keeping with the nature of the narrative impulse itself, perhaps the most significant lines Barth has written come from his 1967 story, "Title." In it the narrator, nearly exhausted, is struggling within himself to recount the rationalizations for continuing to write:

> The final possibility is to turn ultimacy, exhaustion, paralyzing self-consciousness and the adjective weight of accumulated history . . . against itself to make something new and valid. . . . There's only one direction to go in. Ugh. We must make something out of nothing. Impossible. Mystics do. Not only turn contradiction into paradox, but *employ* it, to go on living and working. . . . There's no hope. This isn't working. But the alternative is to supply an alternative. . . . Just try; quit talking about it, quit talking, quit!

At the nadir of his creative despair, the narrator "ends" the story with these lines:

> The blank of our lives. It's about over. Let the *denouement* be soon and unexpected, painless if possible, quick at least, above all soon. Now, now! How in the world will it ever

The narrator is obviously appalled at the thought of continuing to write, but he is even more appalled at the thought of uttering the word "end."

Convinced of the failure of words, of feeling, of art and of the efficacy of action in life or art, Barth—and perhaps by extension, the black humor movement in general—is also convinced of the failure of failure. The horror of being inwardly blank is to the black humorist even more a cause for despair than struggling to write about the absurdity that surrounds him. In the end, black humor is aimed not so much at the affirmation of art and life as to the negation of silence and lifelessness.

Bruce Janoff, "Black Humor, Existentialism, and Absurdity: A Generic Confusion," in Arizona Quarterly, *Vol. 30, No. 4, Winter, 1974, pp. 293-304.*

BLACK HUMOR AND SOCIETY

Conrad Knickerbocker

[*In the following essay, Knickerbocker asserts that black humor employs the resources of traditional satire to criticize the vulgar, fraudulent excesses and vacuous platitudes of contemporary mainstream American society.*]

Something terrible (to many people) and marvelous (to others) has happened to the national sense of humor since World War II. Not only is more serious American fiction funnier, but our comic writers, like medieval magicians, have divided into two camps, white and black. "White" humorists such as Max Shulman and William Brinkley are as harmless as Lucille Ball or the Flintstones. They chuckle at our foibles, but when the chips are down, they support the familiar comforts of the status quo. Their adherents are many, for everyone agrees that a good laugh—moderate of course—is a wonderful tonic in this careworn world of ours.

Everyone, that is, except an immoderate new breed of American writers, who have wrenched the status quo until it begins to emit tormented laughter. Bitter, perverse, sadistic and *sick*—as the righteous defenders of a sick society aver—the new humor is black in its pessimism, its refusal of compromise and its mortal sting. Its adherents are few as yet but increasing. Bored beyond tears by solemnity and pap, an increasing audience finds in black humor no tonic, but the gall of truth. There are no more happy endings. A cheery wave and a fast shuffle no longer leave them laughing. New for us, black humor has been part of the response of wiser peoples in other times. Its appearance in American fiction may signal the end of certain innocences.

The list of American talents who have opted for a Bronx cheer instead of a handshake has been growing for 10 years. Terry Southern unmasks fraud in its slickest guises. J. P. Donleavy demolishes matrimony. William Burroughs hoots at our ideas of criminal behavior. Warren Miller conjures new saviors and the free state of Harlem. Bruce Jay Friedman aborts motherhood. Charles Simmons unsmuts smut. Thomas Pynchon, Hughes Rudd, William Gaddis, John Barth, Joseph Heller, Donald Barthelme, Elliott Baker, Ivan Gold and Richard G. Stern, all in their various ways are stampeding the vast herd of American sacred cows.

These writers belong to no round table. The mass book audience has not heard of most of them. They work independently in Mexico City, Chicago or Connecticut. Their views which have in common the savagery of their conclusions, signal a major new, and perhaps the only new, development in American fiction since the war.

Incapable of a *détente,* the black humorists torment the American mind by taking nothing at face value. They hate preconceptions, stereotypes and spiritual fat. They laugh in tune with the man on the gallows who asked, "Are you sure this thing is safe?" because their social realities seem just as precarious. They are afraid not so much of the cliché of the Bomb as the more awful prospect that we will

William Burroughs.

survive after all only to win the space race and eliminate washday blues.

We have always had satirists, but *A Connecticut Yankee* and *Main Street* are gentle nudges in the ribs compared to the neo-Swiftian assaults of Mr. Southern's *The Magic Christian* or Mr. Burroughs's *Naked Lunch*. Petronius Arbiter, his barbs incurring the wrath of Nero, opened his veins and recited frivolous verses to his friends as he died. Certain modern humorists may instead shoot heroin into their veins, but the message is the same. As societies convulse, art turns emetic. Whether the new humor ominously resembles the Latin satire that flourished while the totalitarian power of the Empire grew, or the glittering harpoons of Dr. Johnson's age that drew their aim on stupendous social arrogance, indifference and misery, depends on who has the last laugh. One thing is certain: the new humorists bear witness to convulsions.

"I am in the position of liking the roots, somehow, of America and loathing everything it stands for today," James Purdy, one of the grimmest of the grim humorists, wrote a friend recently. "We live in the stupidest cultural era of American history. It is so stupid it inspires me."

Only disappointment—an irremediable sense of expectations betrayed—can account for the violent and amusing shapes that fill his novel *Malcolm* and stories like "Daddy Wolf." "The theme of my work is the estrangement of the human being in America," he has said, an America "based on money and competition, inhuman, terrified of love, sexual and other, obsessed with homosexuality (Hemingway,

O'Hara, etc.) and brutality . . . opposing anything that opposes money."

With a kind of glossolalia of imagery, the new humorists testify to a world filled with discontinuities too huge for normal expression. Benny Profane, the "human yo-yo" who is the hero of Mr. Pynchon's novel *V,* finds solace in New York sewers shooting the gift alligators children have flushed down toilets. The First Church of Christ, Astronaut, calls its followers to the desert to await the arrival of saviors from outer space in Mr. Miller's *Waiting for the General.* But then, after attempting suicide, Lee Harvey Oswald complained about the chow in the Russian hospital where he was recovering: black humor is well acquainted with the incredible facts of the day. Starting from scratch and with an evangelical momentum, these shaggy anchorites in a desert avoid the amenities, the little courtesies to reader and reviewer that have enervated many of our more "normal" writers. Their freedom gives them the elbow room for onslaught, the vigor to deal directly, as the traditional novel seems less and less able to do.

"Normal" novelists prefer to seduce the reader with clever mixtures of the probable and the derived; this kind of fiction waits coyly to be consumed and explained in the normal fashion. The black humorists prefer rape. They ambush the reader and savage his convictions that war, success, big cars, families and fancy restaurants are worth living for.

It was more than 15 years after V-J Day before any American author raised the point that a war of noble purpose could also be a boondoggle not dissimilar to some gigantic used-car auction. Mr. Heller did it in *Catch-22.* Thousands of ex-G.I.'s winced but also winked. Stanley Elkin's *Boswell* concerns a wrestler who worships the ideal of strength, but muscles grown too large bind into immobility. Mr. Gaddis's *The Recognitions,* one of the most serious, most memorable novels of the 1950's, has long stretches of black humor that amplify its themes of spiritual and artistic forgery. In *The Revelations of Dr. Modesto,* Alan Harrington's young man receives a mail-order course on the art of living that actually brings results. Then he discovers that his mentor has been a long-term patient in a psychiatric hospital. These novels bear one message, forceful, repetitive, almost repetitious: in the midst of progress, as we photograph moon craters, as wars continue, and as power structures proliferate, we regress.

Of course this kind of conceptualization is self-defeating, and particularly in relation to the new humorists, with their antagonism toward abstract analysis. The minute one says, "I'm cool," one has lost one's cool. The minute one says, "I laughed. Here's why," one has lost some humor. In a review of Mr. Southern's *Candy* in the *New Republic,* Albert Goldman smacked his lips and attempted the last word on the "liberal, intellectual audience of readers and critics who are forever trying to understand and explain everything, and who seem constitutionally incapable of enjoying fantasy or humor without indulging in the cant of 'redeeming social value.' "

But his statement itself demonstrates the paradox deplored by black humor. Liberal, intellectual readers look to agencies of articulation for their vocabulary. The trouble is that these agencies, with their conflicting presentations, only add to the confusion.

The press, the movies, television, advertising, the universities, business, the government, the military, medicine—every vested social interest that claims the right to articulate the national identity contributes to the national psychosis. Our failure is that we tell ourselves too well who we are. The experts and exegetes each provide specially tailored, ready-to-wear identities. Black humor explodes these articulations as contradictory and irrational. The American psyche, like putty, awaits any imprint, even the *New Republic*'s.

Guy Grand, the eccentric billionaire who spends millions "making it hot for them" in *The Magic Christian,* torments the blank American with infinite jests, exaggerations, switcheroos, and put-ons. Richard G. Stern's *Golk,* a television producer, manipulates the cameras to convince his audience that they are witnessing humorous real-life vignettes. Everybody roars; the program wins national acclaim. Actually all that he has shown is people wounding each other. Grand's and Golk's hoaxes confirm hoggishness. We have not only lost dignity, but like all fat men, we are funny.

It began to show in the 1930's, even as various new orders seemed to promise solutions. Nathanael West in America and Louis-Ferdinand Celine in France used black humor to warn against dream merchants. The French bought Celine's *Death on the Installment Plan* by the thousands. Later the panzers of the greatest dream merchant of them all rolled into Paris. Nobody here paid a great deal of attention to West. We were busy with a new order of our own, rebuilding prosperity, bolstering our souls with De Mille.

The enemy, according to the black humorists, is made up of men of gesture, manipulators of acceptable ideas, wise in the incantation of popular brainstorms. The new humor is anti-intellectual in the conventional sense. The idea, the concept logically advanced by critics, professors, senators and psychiatrists, has been tried and found wanting. John Barth's *The Sot-Weed Factor,* a novel of great learning, has as its target the edifice of the intellect, particularly as guarded by its chief articulator, the university. Purportedly a ribald account of colonial American life, the book squares off at the Ph. D. candidate, with his view that history is somehow redemptive and that progress is the natural order of things. Our early national aspirations were just as squalid as those of the next nation's. The only difference is that we prefer delusions to illusions, Mr. Barth tells us, and he uses the techniques of a doctoral dissertation to give the coup-de-grace.

Most national styles of humor contain elements of social criticism, but the target usually lies without, unless there are worms within. Englishmen used to prefer jokes about the French and Irish; now the English physic themselves continually. In earlier days on the American stage, Uncle Sam and the Yankee trader told jokes about the English; now Mort Sahl tells jokes about the liberal intellectual; the liberal intellectual explains why, and Mr. Barth calls a plague on both houses. The new humor is self-directed. Underneath lie spasms of self-loathing.

Why has satire appealed to so many exceptional talents in the last dozen years, when a generation ago, the more "normal" forms of social commentary—the essay, the social novel—were the accepted channels of protest? One reason is reaction: traditional forms cannot accommodate a reality which now includes Jack Ruby. More, we have begun to lose our accustomed responses to the event. The excesses of civilization have stupefied us. Brutalized, we scream "Jump!" to the man on the ledge.

A number of writers no longer use ideas to explain events, for events have become too mysterious. The black humorists recount events in their natural—which is to say non-logical—sequence. Events can, after all, be found in similar sequence on the front page of any newspaper, equally incomprehensible. *Naked Lunch* consists of a series of dispatches from America and abroad interlaced with a treatise on narcotics addiction. Never mind that the geography is hallucinated. Our laughter is the sad delight of recognition, not to be found in pamphlets on the national purpose.

A collection of short stories by Donald Barthelme, *Come Back, Dr. Caligari,* is a testament to the non-sequiturs of the contemporary event. The stories become prose pop art, spilling past the hitherto agreed-on limits of fiction into realms as mysterious as daily life. Ideally, one should read them while drinking beer, reading *Time,* watching television, and listening to Dizzy Gillespie. More than stories, they are literary "happenings." In "A Shower of Gold," the hero is selected as a contestant on a television program called "Who Am I?" The master of ceremonies asks the hero if he loves his mother. "Yes," he replies, but a bell rings, the tote board flashes, and the announcer screams, "He's lying!" Shortly before this, he has been visited by the player of a cat-piano, a sinister device encasing eight live cats. His mother, furthermore, had always paid for his karate lessons. He is confused.

"Turn off your television sets," he finally rages in the pandemonium of the studio. "Cash in your life insurance, indulge in a mindless optimism. Visit girls at dusk. Play the guitar . . . Think back and remember how it was." The audience shrieks and howls.

More literal, less given to flights, but just as antidotal is Hughes Rudd's short story, "Miss Euayla is the Sweetest *Thang*!" winner of *The Paris Review* prize for humor in 1961. Rudd demonstrates how ordinary aspirations have transcended the absurd to reach, at last, the purely stupid. Lafond T. Cunningham, the hero, is a would-be Texas radio personality who describes himself as no taller than a shotgun, just as Truman Capote once did. In a few pages, Lafond stumbles through the entire range of Southern irrelevancies, capped by the explosion of a mail-order diamond ring. In ways beyond the scope of traditional fiction, Rudd's distortion of regional posturing reveals the emptiness behind the false fronts of our social landscape.

Certain critics may tell us the spirit of alienation—a vitalizing force in much of our best literature—is dying, and that American fiction is moving into a period of accommo-

dation with things-as-they-are. This idea may have been suggested by the present self-satisfaction of our traditional novelists. As always, trying to hear what has already sounded, critics tend to ignore new thunder on the horizon.

Traditional art forms, in which the surfaces of life fit neatly together, cope less and less. Black humor more and more expertly points out the inconstancies of modern experience, the fragmented zaniness of a day at any office. Laughter itself may be a form of accommodation, as the critic Webster Schott has suggested, but if so, it is the only point of juncture between the black humorists and the times in which they live. They are irreconcilable.

So, indeed, are more of us than the image-packagers would care to admit. Black humor has infiltrated middle culture in movies such as *Dr. Strangelove* and the upcoming *Goldstein,* in theater with *Who's Afraid of Virginia Woolf?* and *Oh What a Lovely War,* in the nightclub dementia of Lenny Bruce and Jonathan Winters, in the pop-art put-ons of Roy Lichtenstein and Andy Warhol. The *Ginger Man* might not speak for all of us, but his mockery prophesies a time when life will be lived exactly as blue-printed in the beer commercials, unless we hoot loud enough.

By default, the black humorists have become keepers of conscience. Strident, apt, they challenge the hypnotists and the hysterics. They urge choices on us. Amid the banality, the emptiness and excess, they offer the terrors and possibilities of self-knowledge. "There ought to be no barriers," Terry Southern recently told a *Life* magazine interviewer in an enigmatic put-on. Stop kidding yourself and recover joy, he may have meant. Has the age of hollow laughter dawned? Soon, perhaps, we will move forward to the sound of exploding windbags all around.

> *Conrad Knickerbocker, "Humor with a Mortal Sting," in* The New York Times Book Review, *September 27, 1964, pp. 3, 60-1.*

> There is a built-in contradiction to being a literary nihilist. After all, if you really believe in Nothing, if you finally despair of God, love, and society, if you think nothing matters either ultimately or now, you don't create a work of art to say so; you do, like Kirilov in *The Possessed,* shoot yourself.
>
> —*George P. Elliott, in his "Destroyers, Defilers, and Confusers of Men," in* The Atlantic, *December 1968.*

Morris Dickstein

[An American educator and critic who began his career specializing in English Romantic poetry, Dickstein has

generated vigorous critical debate with his writings on the 1960s in America, including Gates of Eden: American Culture in the Sixties *(1977). In the following essay, he argues that while 1960s black humorists appear to ignore contemporary politics and social issues in their works, their conception of history and the narrative structure of their novels bear a remarkable correspondence to the major sociopolitical upheavals of the decade.*]

It was axiomatic a few years ago to assert that the electronic media had entirely displaced the printed word, that young people in the sixties didn't read, let alone write; that all the most talented of them went into film, or politics, or rock; that those who did write novels simply turned away from the gaudy carnival of contemporary life (as Tom Wolfe said in *The New Journalism*), "gave up by default," leaving the way clear for the hip new journalists and rhetoricians. According to Wolfe, novelists became "Neo-Fabulists" who were entranced by myth and parable understandable only to themselves and lost interest in reality.

Today the enthusiasts of fiction are far less likely to be on the defensive, for the creative impulses in the novel have proved more durable than facile McLuhanite explanations of cultural change. But there is more than a grain of truth in Tom Wolfe's simplistic account. The sixties were a moribund period for the realistic novel, and perhaps in consequence the commercial market for fiction declined precipitously. Novelists who did sustain a realist method, such as Updike, Bellow, and Malamud, were weakest on the topical subjects where Wolfe's journalists were strongest—when they dragged in blacks or hippies, or worried about the war, or unisex, or the future of the moon. Yet the journalists themselves, not only Wolfe but Capote and Mailer, insistently invoked the prestige of the novel to validate their work, much as the early novelists of the eighteenth century had coyly rejected the idea of fiction and masked their work as journals or case histories. The eighteenth-century novelist had to insist that he was artless; the sixties journalist had to prove he was an Artist. In each case the rationale was a relic of an outworn cast of mind, that the work itself would help to superannuate. What died in the sixties was not the novel but the mystique of the novel, its critical prestige, its wide and loyal audience, its status as the royal road to cultural success. The dream of the Great American Novel disintegrated, as did the line between high art and other kinds of cultural performance, but the novels that continued to be written were some of the most staggeringly ambitious that America had produced. The second coming of modernism in American fiction, which Tom Wolfe deplores and misunderstands, may have narrowed the audience for the novel and limited its ability to deal with the immediate carnival aspect of contemporary fashion, but it gave the dream of the novelist a new kind of grandiosity and range. In a topsy-turvy age that often turned trash into art and art into trash, that gaily pursued topical fascinations and ephemeral performances and showed a real genius for self-consuming artifacts—an age that sometimes valued art too little because it loved raw life too much—novels were written that are among the handful of artworks, few enough in any age,

that are likely to endure. The sixties are as likely to be remembered through novels as through anything else they left behind, a bizarre prospect that need not make us shudder.

Yet Tom Wolfe is right in one respect. The future readers who look to the novels of the sixties to learn about society are sure to go awry. The kaleidoscope of fashion, the spectacular changes in morals and manners, which Wolfe claimed as rich new territory for the journalists, evoked scant interest in writers of fiction. There was little good sociology in sixties novels, even among the realists like Updike and early Roth, and there was even less in the more central and innovative strain of sixties fiction, the so-called "comic-apocalyptic" writers or black humorists. Sometimes these writers do illuminate a contemporary setting, providing news of the world that you can't get from the News. I don't know of a better account of the pre-Beat New York under-culture of the mid-fifties—the bars, the floaters and drifters, the artists and would-be artists, the talents and the hangers-on, and everywhere the jazz—than we get in Pynchon's *V.,* just as he does the L.A. scene very brilliantly in his next book, *The Crying of Lot 49.* But Pynchon's imagination goes far afield from these realistic bases, which themselves have been subtly transformed into Pynchonesque metaphors for certain states of mind, peculiar world-historical anxieties. Nor is Heller's *Catch-22* really "about" World War II, though it does contain a good deal of amusing (but marginal) satire on the McCarthy period (such as the Great Loyalty Oath Crusade and the scandal of "Who promoted Major Major? Who promoted Major Major?"); the book's imaginative center is elsewhere.

The imaginative ambitions of these novelists keep them from any sustained social commentary; they illuminate society less through their content than through their experiments in form, by which I mean not simply technique but the pressure of individual vision from which new technique must flow. Critics who use literature as social evidence tend to treat its content as documentation, ignoring the subtle ironies and modifications to which raw life is subjected within an imaginative work. Instead we should be looking for analogies between social change and changes in the *forms* of the arts. Form can be seen as a structure of perception, a deep-seated rhythm of experience and sensibility, by which the individual work (like the individual self) partakes of the social whole willy-nilly, without having to allude to it directly. The conservative form of the novel in the 1950s, which is reflected in Saul Bellow's comment that "realism is still the great literary breakthrough," mirrors the conserving and inward-turning character of the age. Likewise the surge of modernist and experimental fiction in the early sixties is subtly related to the new feelings of social malaise and reformist zeal that set in during the late fifties, gained impetus from the urgent, high-spirited tone of Kennedy's campaign for the presidency, and burst forth during his administration with precious little concrete progress to keep it going. In those early years of the sixties there was a scent of change in the air, a sense of things opening up, of new possibilities. This was not without its dangerous side, for, by the iron law of rising expectations, forces were aroused in society that soon overshot their prescribed bounds. The New Left and the civil rights movement did not develop under Eisenhower, when things were at their worst, but under Kennedy, when inchoate promises and possibilities were in the air. And they died under Nixon, who recreated an atmosphere of utter futility and himself embodied the vengeful spirit of middle-American backlash (as if the election of 1960 were at last undone, the sixties rolled back).

To try to relate the social atmosphere of the early sixties to the key novels of the period would seem to be a thankless task. We all know that there is no easy correspondence between the arts and society, and that all due allowance must be made for individual genius working out its own salvation. Moreover, since books like *The Sot-Weed Factor, Catch-22,* and *V.* are long and complex books, they were also long in gestating; it's difficult to say in what sense they belong to their moment of publication. But the cultural climate of the period was also long in gestating, and the solitary labors of these very writers were surely among the points of gestation. The new sensibility of the sixties was unusually pervasive; in retrospect we can see how it touched every corner of our culture, any one of which, examined closely, helps illuminate the general ferment, the movement of change. Without abridging the distinctive claims of individual genius we can't help but notice a similarity of purpose and form, a common breakthrough, in many of the new novels. This in turn was followed by a loss of verve and force among several of the older writers, as the cultural center seemed to make one of its periodic (and rather cruel) shifts.

Our problem is complicated by the fact that there's no easy symmetry between the older and the newer novel, as some would like to claim. If the Jewish novel, with its beleaguered humanism and weighty moral seriousness, is characteristic of the earlier period, the black humorists of the early sixties offer no easy contrast. It's not simply that several were as Jewish and as morally obsessed as Malamud or Bellow, but because their fascination with the ironies and absurdities of existence flows directly out of the Jewish novel, though it gets expressed in a different way. The opposite of the Jewish novel is not black humor but Camp, which is a form of aestheticism and brittle wit directed against whatever becomes too solemnly moral and humanistic. Camp is decorative, flip, gay, and insouciant, while black humor is pitched at the breaking point where moral anguish explodes into a mixture of comedy and terror, where things are so bad you might as well laugh. This helps explain why even some of the black humorists who are not Jewish, such as Berger and Pynchon, adapt the schlemiel-figure out of Jewish fiction (Berger's Reinhart, Pynchon's Benny Profane); the schlemiel inhabits the shadowy margin between the comedy of errors and a comedy of terrors. As a chronic loser he is indestructible, the kind of man no society can do without: he'll go on losing forever. And as a figure of fun he's a threat to no one; he's low down on the scale of Hobbesian competition, cut off from the rarefied zone of great fortunes and great falls.

Similar things are true of the other main figure at the center of sixties novels, a cousin of the schlemiel, the picaresque anti-hero. One striking difference between novels of the fifties and those of the sixties is that the former, which tend to be more psychological and to focus on the complexities of individual character, preserve a belief—inherited from nineteenth-century realism—in the possibilities of personal growth, a Freudian faith in the maturation of self through the formation of adult relationships. In picaresque fiction, however, the hero, who is often an indestructible naïf or innocent, gets propelled not into familiar human interaction but through a series of external events which are often random, bizarre, even surreal or apocalyptic. Voltaire's Candide is too much of an Everyman to grow or change; he cannot learn from his experience, he can only be inundated. Instead of novelistic development we find a structure of repetition and intensification: the same thing always happens, but no one will ever *learn* anything. Instead of fully rounded real-life characters we find cartoonlike puppets, manipulated according to the author's moral purpose.

Not all the black humor novels of the sixties approximate the *Candide* pattern. Kurt Vonnegut's novels come closest, especially *Slaughterhouse-Five,* whose befuddled, childlike hero, allegorically named Billy Pilgrim, is set down in a world that kills and maims in the most casual and summary way. What complicates this air of shell-shocked simplicity are the bizarre "time warps" which layer the action, so that all the disasters of crazy Billy's life seem to be happening to him simultaneously. To express what he sees as the insanity of contemporary history, Vonnegut does a pop adaptation of modernist experiments with time. Billy is a holy fool who "has come unstuck in time," who keeps uncontrollably enacting different moments of his life. As such he is a kind of novelist whose control has slipped, who remembers too much of modern history and his own private sorrow, so that the pressure has become too great, the ache to tell must somehow be relieved. This is why *Slaughterhouse-Five* is not one of Vonnegut's best books. As a writer he works best when he can be most playful and inventive, ripping off public events in inspired burlesque, making up Borgesian religions, cultures, whole literary *oeuvres,* and writing down their texts. But faced with the firebombing of Dresden, where he himself had been a helpless bystander, a stunned survivor, he lets the intensity of his feelings overshadow the fable that tries to express them. The brilliant first chapter, which tells the story straight, overwhelms the fictional version which follows.

Compared to the moving personal presence of the author in the opening chapter, there's a thinness and insubstantiality, a puppetlike quality, to Billy Pilgrim and his fellow "characters" as they jerk through the time warps laid down for them by the author. The other side of the inventiveness of sixties fiction is the high degree of manipulation and authorial presence we encounter, which entails a depletion of life in the thing made, the story told, the character caricatured. A writer like Barth pays for his Brechtian honesty about what he's making up by a loss of vitality, until the "story" is pared down to his own witty and self-conscious voice soliloquizing about the act of creation. This imbalance between creator and artifact is an ambiguous development. Where fictional characters in the fifties can still subject life to a degree of personal control, can grow and change within the limits of their personality, the zany, two-dimensional characters in Vonnegut, Barth, Pynchon, and Heller declare not simply their authors' departure from realism but their brooding sense that life is increasingly controlled by impersonal forces. For the realist of the fifties, character is destiny; for the comic-apocalyptic writer, destiny turns character into a joke. For the fifties writer, history is remote and irrelevant compared to what Updike calls "private people and their minute concerns"; for the sixties writer, history is absurd but it can kill you. Books like *Slaughterhouse-Five* and *Catch-22* do not slowly gravitate towards death like straightforward novels with unhappy endings. Because of their peculiar structure—in which everything is foreshadowed, everything happens at once—they are drenched in death on all sides, like an epidemic that breaks out everywhere at the same time. Thanks to the time-scheme of Heller's book characters seem perpetually a-dying and reappearing—quite a joke—so that we're shocked when they finally do disappear, one by one, each with his own mock individuality, each to his utterly depersonalizing fate. And the Army stands for fate or necessity itself; it's a machine not for fighting or killing but solely for devouring its own.

Contradicting this pessimism, however, which sees individual life as manipulated and controlled from without, is the high degree of artistic power and license that goes into achieving this effect. If the sense of impotence and fatality in these novels expresses one side of the sensibility of the sixties, their creative exuberance and originality points to another: something crucial to the radicalism of the period, the belief that old molds can be broken and recast, a sense that reality can be reshaped by the creative will. In their inventiveness and plasticity these books are the fictional equivalent of utopian thinking. This is why we must distinguish between verbal black humorists, such as Terry Southern, Bruce Jay Friedman, and even Philip Roth, whose basic unit is the sick joke or the stand-up monologue, and what I would call "structural" black humorists, such as Heller, Pynchon, and Vonnegut. The former take apart the well-made novel and substitute nothing but the absurdist joke, the formless tirade, the cry in the dark; the latter tend toward overarticulated forms, insanely comprehensive plots (the paradox that is more than verbal, that seems inherent in the nature of things). Both kinds of black humorists are making an intense assertion of self—the former directly, the latter in vast structures of self-projection—in the face of the prevailing forces of depersonalization and external control.

All black humor involves the unseemly, the forbidden, the exotic, or the bizarre. Céline shatters the class-bound complacencies of accepted literary language with argot and street-slang, bringing the novel away from high-cultural norms and closer to living speech. His fulminations express the native cynicism of the common man, especially the marginal man of the lower middle class, who knows in his gut that all ideals are a crock of shit. He speaks for the prickly, impossible individual with all his prejudices intact, whom mass society and monopoly capitalism are always threatening to grind under, but who somehow manages to look out for Number One. Black humor al-

ways plays Falstaff to the conventional novel's Hotspur or Prince Hal. Whether it stresses the nether functions of the body, as in Henry Miller, or simply the nether side of all sentimentalities and idealizations, as in Nathanael West, or even the perverse, as with Nabokov's *Lolita,* or *Portnoy's Complaint,* black humor is always affronting taboos, giving offense, recalling people to their gut functions and gut reactions. (That such cynicism conceals its own sentimentalities, that it's the obvious mark of the disappointed sentimentalist, we hardly need emphasize.) Thus black humor became an aspect of the libertarian, idol-shattering side of the sixties. Books like *Portnoy's Complaint* and Mailer's *Why Are We In Vietnam?* could never have been published before the sixties; two decades earlier the language of Mailer's first novel had to be censored for publication, despite its army milieu. Both Mailer and Roth, like all young writers, had been taught to imitate their literary betters; like so many others, both seized on the sixties as a moment for letting go, with predictably mixed results—breakthroughs don't allow for guarantees.

Eventually things reached the point, in serious writing as in pornography, where scarcely any taboos were left to be assaulted. This revealed the intrinsic limitation of the "breakthrough" conceived entirely in terms of subject matter and *épatisme,* without benefit of new discoveries about life or new departures in form. As Susan Sontag once wrote, apropos of a play by Edward Albee:

> What is wrong with Albee's work—or Tennessee Williams', for that matter, is not the emphasis on freakishness, sexual perversion, or the like. It is the insincere, shallow use of this material. The perverse situations are not really probed. They are used, rather, as a conventional device for shocking an audience. . . . [T]he only real shocks in art are those that pertain to form. The real shocks, which the American theater lacks, are those of a bold image carried to the point of a genuine sensuous assault upon the audience.

With few taboos left, the older mold of the novel broken but not recast, the verbal black humorists fell quickly into decadence and self-imitating excess. *Lolita* was followed by *Pale Fire* and *Ada, Portnoy's Complaint* by *Our Gang, The Breast* and *The Great American Novel.* The last of these books is especially indicative of one of the weakest tendencies of black humor. Tossed into its negligible plot is an amazing assortment of dwarfs, cripples, freaks, and grotesques—with a few women thrown in as "slits"—far beyond the ripest excesses of Southern Gothic. Many of these "characters" are casually assigned to monstrous kinds of deformity and death in the course of the book, and by the end their whole world, a baseball league, collapses apocalyptically in ruins. We have a duty to inquire, as Mark Schechner does in a recent essay on Roth (*Partisan Review* 3, 1974), what unexamined impulses of aggression and sadistic cruelty have gone into the making of this type of "humor." By contrast, the earlier breakthrough book, *Portnoy's Complaint,* really does use black humor, psychoanalysis, fantasy, and even lyricism to explore a real novelistic subject, which combines sex, Jewishness, growing up, morality, and the "family romance." After *Portnoy* Roth seems to have imagined that he had found

Sue Lyon and James Mason in Stanley Kubrick's Lolita.

a quite different formula, that a stand-up routine of bad taste and exaggeration were enough in themselves, without any deep personal engagement or formal effort.

The black humorists are generally strong in fantasy, and Roth is unusual among them—much closer to the writers of the fifties—in his inability to fantasticate materials from outside his own experience. But Roth's post-*Portnoy* books do have a typical end-of-the-sixties quality in their gratuitous violence and desperate, but unearned, extremity. They belong to what we might call the Weatherman phase of recent literature, when the utopian hopes of an earlier moment turned sour, when some of the would-be free spirits were driven to such a pitch of frustration and intense desperation that they lost touch with reality. There had been such a thread, though minor, in the politics of the period from the beginning, and even more so in the literature. As Blake made clear in his "Proverbs of Hell," liberation finds its necessary limits only through excess, not by way of caution and prudent restraint. But the verbal black humorists test the limits of exaggeration as a useful literary strategy. Thus the later stories in Malamud's *Pictures of Fidelman* push the schlemiel character into a masochistic comedy of humiliation that is genuinely unpleasant to read. A writer like Terry Southern is often

crass and trivial, except in rare moments like the last pages of *The Magic Christian,* where his imagination brings off an apocalyptic fantasy of large comic proportions. At the bottom of the barrel are novels like Bruce Jay Friedman's *The Dick,* where there is no imagination at all, where instead of imagination the novelist offers up his most rancid prejudices and adolescent twitches, from a repulsive racism to a sophomoric back-alley lechery, all in the name of shock and bad taste. Even a fine writer's writer like Stanley Elkin, who can be terribly subtle in the rhythms of his language, tends to be gross in his emotional tone— hysterical and overwrought in a way that's unbearable because it's so unmodulated. The Dostoevskian extremism and desperation of Jewish black humor is hard to keep under control, even when it's deeply felt; sincerity is not enough. It's a rare book like Bellow's *Herzog* or *Humboldt's Gift* where this frantic quality justifies and fulfills itself, by serving its subject and allowing for emotional nuance. Herzog's letters especially enable Bellow to move from a merely private and psychological case to the redefinition of a whole cultural period (an ambition that boomerangs disastrously in the rank, embittered pages of *Mr. Sammler's Planet*).

Failure to make such connections is what defeats a great

deal of the verbal black humor of the sixties, which makes only a marginal advance on the personal novel of the previous decade. It alters the tone of the fifties novel without expanding its horizons. It brilliantly exploits vulgar, "pop" material, often with sexual audacity, and sometimes achieves a rollicking, exuberant comic tone. But with the exception of a few books like *Portnoy's Complaint* it rarely stakes out new social or fictional territory. It partakes of the liberated spirit of the sixties but rarely does much that's constructive with its new-found freedom. Quite the opposite is true of the writers I've called "structural" in their black humor. Construction is their strong point, mazes of plot, astoundingly complex fictional textures reminiscent of Joyce, Kafka, Borges, and Beckett—though sometimes we may wonder to what point all the energy of formal invention. These writers make a much sharper break with the private world of the fifties novel. Characteristically, like Pynchon, they reinvent an older literary form, the historical novel, which had descended into a moribund popular genre (the costume novel), or, like Vonnegut, they do devious and inspired take-offs on topical materials, such as the Eichmann and Abel cases in *Mother Night,* right-wing lunatic groups in *Mother Night* and *The Crying of Lot 49,* Caribbean dictatorships, the Bomb, and the end of the world in *Cat's Cradle,* the politics and philanthropy of the Rockefeller family in *God Bless You, Mr. Rosewater,* all sorts of politics in the stories in Donald Barthelme's *Unspeakable Practices, Unnatural Acts,* and so on. In other words, these writers of the sixties rediscover the historical world, the public world—even as they are deeply skeptical of it—just as the sixties in general rediscover the joys and horrors of politics, even as many feel poisoned by it.

Like many of the activists of the sixties, the key writers, whatever their feeling for politics, held a profoundly ironic and adversary view of the historical process. Typically, "progressive" literature is muckraking literature: a ferreting out of abuses so that the system can function according to its original ideals. Sixties literature, on the contrary, has an anxious, dead-end feeling about history, a paranoid fear about how it all holds together, a restless bafflement before the puzzle and complexity of it all. One way this attitude gets expressed is in the mock-historical novel, such as Barth's *Sot-Weed Factor,* Berger's *Little Big Man,* and one or two of the historical sections of Pynchon's *V.,* chapters which read like pure Camp. Rather than finding a form of their own to express this sense of historical irony, these books or sections settle for pastiche or anti-novel, for tongue-in-cheek imitation of an earlier genre, such as the eighteenth-century picaresque novel, the Wild West novel, or the international spy novel. Without developing their own sense of history, they merely parrot or parody the historical sense of the books they attach themselves to. Though they are loving recreations, the Barth and Berger books especially miss the robust spirit of the forms they imitate and settle for an easy if not dismissive irony. Though highly indicative of the new feeling for history that followed the private concerns of the fifties, and full of a kind of imagination alien to the fifties, they are basically a literature of latecomers to the feast of the muses, what Barth himself once called a "literature of exhaustion," of self-consciousness: "novels which imitate the

form of the Novel, by an author who imitates the role of Author."

In the pages that follow I'd like to look more closely at the work of Heller, Pynchon, and Vonnegut, and especially at two representative black-humor novels of the early sixties, *Catch-22* and *The Crying of Lot 49.* These books are neither antiquarian nor excessively literary; in a complex way they develop a striking and unusual sense of history that in the end tells us less about history than about the cultural tone of the period when they were written. Vonnegut and Heller return to World War II not for purposes of historical recreation, not simply because it was their own great formative experience, and certainly not to provide the vicarious thrills of the conventional war novel. Rather, it's because the unsolved moral enigma of that period and that experience most closely expresses the conundrum of contemporary life fifteen years later. Earlier writers had been able to approach World War II with a certain moral simplicity; here after all was a "just war" if there ever was one. But after fifteen more years of continuous cold war and the shadow of thermonuclear war, all war seemed morally ambiguous if not outright insane; in the prolonged state of siege the whole culture seemed edged with insanity. With that special prescience that novelists sometimes have, *Catch-22,* though published in 1961, anticipates the moral nausea of the Vietnam war, even famously anticipates the flight of deserters to neutral Sweden. Similarly Vonnegut in *Mother Night* chooses a morally ambiguous double-agent as his "hero," just as he writes about the problematic Allied bombing of Dresden rather than a Nazi atrocity in *Slaughterhouse-Five.*

Like Pynchon, but in a different way, both Vonnegut and Heller are interested in international intrigue; they marvel at the zany and unpredictable personal element at work or play within the lumbering forces of history. Heller's Milo Minderbinder is a satire not simply on the American capitalist entrepreneur but also on the international wheeler-dealer, whose amoral machinations, so hilarious at first, become increasingly sombre, ugly and deadly—like so much else in the book—so that we readers become implicated in our own earlier laughter. Yet Milo is particularly close to the book's hero Yossarian: the two understand each other. They share an ethic of self-interest which in Yossarian comes close to providing the book's moral. As in Céline, it's all a crock: look out for Number One. In the figure of Milo the book and its protagonist confront their seamy underside, a hideous caricature of their own values.

This doubling effect is typical of works of structural black humor. In the historical plot of *V.* the central character is called Stencil, and one key structural element is the pairing of fathers and sons—Hugh Godolphin and Evan Godolphin, Sidney Stencil and Herbert Stencil. The younger Stencil's quest for V., which is also a search for parents and identity, is an attempt to decipher a history whose meaning is encoded in the fragmentary remains of previous histories and earlier generations. Hence the striking resemblance between *V.* and the Oedipal detective novels that Ross Macdonald has been writing since *The Galton Case* in 1959. In Macdonald the mysteries of the present are always solved by decoding the past; there's an abundance of missing parents, traumatized children, and buried corpses that have been mouldering for a generation. In late novels like *The Underground Man* these Oedipal tangles are doubled and redoubled into a plot of appalling complexity, even repetitiveness, so that individual identity pales—it becomes hard to keep track of the characters or to separate them, and the solution comes to interest the author far less than the obsessive mesh of parallel relationships. In *V.* the detective Herbert Stencil is himself a cipher (as his name implies), who merely organizes an immense range of partial perspectives into one large diagram, a pattern of possible coherence and meaning. But where detective novels really do deliver a final secret that solves and abolishes all puzzles—Edmund Wilson objected that "this secret is nothing at all" compared to the preceding mystery—Pynchon is a modernist who leaves open the possibility that this final solution may be a mirage . . . a mirage or a shocking confirmation of a plot-ridden and mysteriously overorganized world.

The doubling and proliferation in the plot of these novels—which approaches a point of surfeit, even nausea, in the dense, choked pages of *Gravity's Rainbow*—always points to an ambiguity of identity, to mysterious correspondences behind the plenitude of the world's surfaces. In Pynchon the ambiguity is historical, ontological: who am I, where do I come from, who's pulling my strings, how can I wrench some meaning from my hieroglyphic surroundings? In Vonnegut the ambiguity is moral: what's the relation within Howard W. Campbell, Jr., the double agent who is the protagonist in *Mother Night,* between the writer, the lover, the Nazi propagandist and the American spy? Vonnegut himself tells us that the moral of the story ("the only story of mine whose moral I know") is that "we are what we pretend to be, so we must be careful what we pretend to be."

What makes Vonnegut appeal so much to adolescents is probably a certain adolescent pessimism and moral absolutism, a modern Weltschmerz, which often threatens to reduce complex human problems to simple dichotomies, easy formulas. This is especially true when he speaks in his own person, in essays, prefaces, and interviews, where the mask of the wise simpleton quickly becomes cloying. But in the novels something else happens. Simplicity of statement begins to have a quite different function. The manner becomes flat and factual, the chapters very brief, like the précis of an action rather than a full-scale novelization. Descriptive and psychological texture are reduced to mere notation, the action to pure plot, and the plot proliferates to a high degree of complexity, taking amazing twists and turns which double back on each other. Like most writers attracted to science fiction, Vonnegut has a precise, logical turn of mind; he loves to scatter the action in twenty separate strands, some of them quite fantastic, only to loop them all neatly together at the end. In this he resembles the genre-writer or the traditional writer of well-made plots more than a modernist addicted to problematic and open-ended forms. But Vonnegut crowds the three-decker story into a book the length of a novella, so that the emphasis on plot and incident, on Aristotelian changes of fortune, becomes overwhelming. (This is espe-

cially true of *Mother Night* and *Cat's Cradle,* his strongest books, which both belong to the early sixties.)

The overall effect of this is to alter subtly our sense of reality, at least as we read the book. Despite the promiscuous mixture of fact and fantasy, the effect of the flat, declarative manner and the simple-man persona is to give the narrator a sort of man-to-man reliability in the mind of the reader. Also, it puts everything in the story on the same plane: the most bizarre events seem more matter-of-fact, while flat-out realities take on a slight glow of lunacy that they would genuinely have if we weren't so inured to them. The Jewish writers of the fifties were drawn to extreme emotional states; they saw life's problems and glories as located in the self. A writer like Vonnegut is drawn to extreme conditions of reality, so extreme as to have addled our minds or dulled our capacity for *any* emotional response. Perhaps under the influence of the deathcamps or the Bomb, Vonnegut and Heller are drawn to situations in which the arbitrary, the terrible, and the irrational have been *routinized.* They find it maniacally comic that men should learn to adjust to insane conditions, cultivate their private lives, go about their business.

Much of the comedy of *Catch-22* comes from the effort to maintain business-as-usual under "insane" conditions. The painstaking records the Nazis kept were perhaps rooted in the same impulse. No wonder Vonnegut and Heller became classics of the anti-Vietnam generation, curious comic bibles of protest, so different from the protest literature of the thirties, while writers like Malamud, who took the fifties posture of stoicism and endurance, or else Jamesian renunciation, gradually lost favor. Vonnegut's zany, cartoonlike plot, his distaste for violence and heroic posturing, and his affinity for a few simple human verities help make his work the moral equivalent of the New Politics of the early sixties, which substituted communitarian good will, anarchic individualism and ethical fervor for the old staples of ideology. But at his best the ingenious reversals of Vonnegut's plots go well beyond the simple verities of his own moralizing, provide indeed as full a helping of moral ambiguity as any modernist could want.

I said earlier that characters in black humor novels tend to be cartoonlike and two-dimensional, without the capacity to grow or change. To this we must add the qualification that the protagonist is usually different: he doesn't completely belong to this mode of reality or system of representation. As Richard Poirier has suggested apropos of Pynchon, the central character of these novels moves often on a different plane: he shows at least the capacity to become a fuller, more sentient human being, a character in a realistic novel. In the first part of the book the "hero" is typically enmeshed in a system of comic repetition: tics of speech and behavior, entanglements of plot, all the "routines" of verbal black humor, life imitating vaudeville. Heller, for example, like Dickens, knows how to make his own comic technique approximate poignant human realities. And, as the comedy in *Catch-22* darkens, the system of dehumanization becomes clearer, and the central character becomes increasingly isolated in his impulse to challenge and step outside it.

In Yossarian, Heller introduces a new figure into postwar

American fiction, descended from the schlemiel of the Jewish novel but finally an inversion of that passive and unhappy figure. Heller tells us he's an Assyrian, but only because (as he said to an interviewer) "I wanted to get an extinct culture . . . My purpose in doing so was to get an outsider, a man who was intrinsically an outsider." The typical schlemiel is certainly no hero, but like Yossarian has a real instinct for survival. In earlier days Yossarian had really tried to bomb the targets, as he was supposed to do. Now his only goal is to avoid flak, to keep alive. "Yossarian was the best man in the group at evasive action." This Yossarian is concerned only with saving his skin, obsessed by the things that threaten his life. "There were too many dangers for Yossarian to keep track of." And Heller gives us a wonderful catalogue of them, from Hitler, Mussolini and Tojo ("they all wanted him dead"), to all the insane and fanatical people in his own army ("they wanted to kill him, too"), to all the organs of his body, with their arsenal of fatal diseases:

> There were diseases of the skin, diseases of the bone, diseases of the lung, diseases of the stomach, diseases of the heart, blood and arteries. There were diseases of the head, diseases of the neck, diseases of the chest, diseases of the intestines, diseases of the crotch. There were even diseases of the feet. There were billions of conscientious body cells oxidating away day and night like dumb animals at their complicated job of keeping him alive and healthy, and every one was a potential traitor and foe. There were so many diseases that it took a truly diseased mind to even think about them as often as he and Hungry Joe did.

Yossarian seems perilously close to the Sterling Hayden character in *Dr. Strangelove,* the general who fears that women are sapping his vital bodily fluids. The insanity of the system, in this case the army, breeds a defensive counter-insanity, a mentality of organized survival that mirrors the whole system of rationalized human waste and devaluation. The self itself becomes an army, a totalitarian body politic, demanding total vigilance against the threat of betrayal and insurrection. Each individual organ, each cell, becomes an object of paranoid anxiety.

The pattern of *Catch-22* is similar to that of *Mother Night:* a world gone mad, a protagonist caught up in the madness, who eventually steps outside it in a slightly mad way. The Sweden to which Yossarian flees at the end of the book is something of a pipe dream, a pure elsewhere. Yossarian's friend Orr has made it there—from the Mediterranean in a rowboat!—but Orr is Yossarian's opposite, utterly at home in the world, as idiotically free of anxiety as Yossarian is dominated by it. Orr is the unkillable imp, the irrepressible innocent, a "likable dwarf with a smutty mind and a thousand valuable skills that would keep him in a low income group all his life." Orr is the gentile Crusoe to Yossarian's Jewish neurotic; along with the diabolical Milo they form a spectrum of the possibilities of survival in extreme situations, which includes not only wartime but just about all of modern life, indeed the whole human condition, for which the war is ultimately a metaphor. But Yossarian goes through a second change before the book ends: he becomes a troublemaker, and worse still,

the unwilling keeper of the book's conscience, just as Nately's whore becomes the figure of Nemesis, the haunting, surreal spirit of female revenge for the callous inhumanity of a man-made world. The earlier Yossarian saw through the no-win bind of Catch-22 and set out monomaniacally to survive. But as each of the others goes separately, uncomplainingly, to his predictable fate, Yossarian becomes more and more the sombre registrar of their deaths and exits:

> Nately's whore was on his mind, as were Kraft and Orr and Nately and Dunbar, and Kid Sampson and McWatt, and all the poor and stupid and diseased people he had seen in Italy, Egypt and North Africa and knew about in other areas of the world, and Snowden and Nately's whore's kid sister were on his conscience, too.

Yossarian has come willy-nilly to brood about more than his own inner organs. Other people have become a desperate reality to him, and with it a sense of their common fate, their mutual essence. The secret of Snowden, who spills his guts in the tail of a plane, is revealed to Yossarian alone:

> His teeth were chattering in horror. He forced himself to look again. Here was God's plenty, all right, he thought bitterly as he stared—liver, lungs, kidneys, ribs, stomach and bits of the stewed tomatoes Snowden had eaten that day for lunch. Yossarian hated stewed tomatoes. . . . He wondered how in the world to begin to save him.
>
> "I'm cold," Snowden whispered. "I'm cold."
>
> "There, there," Yossarian mumbled in a voice too low to be heard. "There, there."
>
> Yossarian was cold, too, and shivering uncontrollably. . . . It was easy to read the message in his entrails. Man was matter, that was Snowden's secret. Drop him out a window and he'll fall. Set fire to him and he'll burn. Bury him and he'll rot, like other kinds of garbage. The spirit gone, man is garbage. That was Snowden's secret. Ripeness was all.

Impelled perhaps by the unconscious Jewish identification, Heller paraphrases the famous "humanizing" speech of Shylock. ("If you prick us, do we not bleed? if you tickle us, do we not laugh? if you poison us, do we not die?") But the final allusion to *Lear* is breathtaking: an impertinence to do it, the height of *chutzpah* to bring it off. The scene must be read as a whole to see how well it works—it's the penultimate moment of the book—but even the delicate texture of these pages of prose would be nothing had not the "secret" of Snowden been such an important leitmotif throughout the book. (Snowden's death had taken place before the book opened, but it's fully remembered and decoded as he lies on an operating table in the next-to-last chapter, as if its meaning, which underlies the whole book, had taken that long to be reduced to its terrifying simplicity and finality.) The sombre tone of this passage—despite the necessary farcical touch of Yossarian's dislike of stewed tomatoes—is something that's not available to verbal black humor, which aims for wild incongruities at every turn, which is more at home with disgust and humiliation and absurdity than with the simple terror of the world as it is; such a poignant effect requires a more fully human respondent, which Yossarian has by now become. Heller's "structural" use of the secret of Snowden makes it a time bomb of ineluctable tragic fact ticking away beneath the book's surface of farce and rollicking insanity; except that the secret unfolds its revelations gradually, alongside the story, until it finally *becomes* the story.

When I first read *Catch-22* I felt strongly that except for the Snowden chapter the book's final shift in tone in the last seventy-five pages didn't work, that after doing an amazing *comic* adaptation of Kafka and Dostoevsky most of the way, Heller unaccountably switched to imitating them directly in the finale, a contest he couldn't win. Rereading the book I can see why I felt that way—we miss the sheer gratuitous pleasure of the comedy—but I also see how much the sombre and even ugly side was present from the beginning, and how gradually the book modulates into it: for such laughter we have the devil to pay. The *Mr. Roberts* element won't do all the way through. I'm now sure the last section works, and makes the whole book work; up against a wall, I'd have to call *Catch-22* the best novel of the sixties.

But what can we learn about the sixties from *Catch-22*? I think the popular success of the book can be attributed to the widespread spiritual revulsion in the sixties against

Donald Barthelme.

many of our most sacrosanct institutions, including the army; to which our leaders replied by heightening just those things which had caused the disgust in the first place, especially the quality of fraud, illusion, and manipulation in our public life. Just as the response to war-protest was escalation and the solution to the failures of the bombing was more bombing, so the push for more honesty in public debate was met by more public relations and bigger lies. The Johnson administration's unshakeable insistence that black was white, that escalation was really the search for peace, and that the war was being won, was a perfect realization of the structure of unreality and insanity that runs as a theme through both *Mother Night* and *Catch-22*. "We're all in this business of illusion together," says Doc Daneeka, who himself later suffers from the general illusion that he is dead, which, morally speaking, he is. Daneeka, whose merely physical presence is powerless to contradict his "official" demise, is destroyed as much by his own insane ethic as by the structure of unreality that is the army. When another doctor asks Yossarian to substitute for a dead soldier whose parents are coming to see him die, he says: "As far as we're concerned, one dying boy is just as good as any other, or just as bad. . . . All you've got to do is lie there a few minutes and die a little." Surprisingly, when Yossarian does it, the parents go along:

> "Giuseppe."
>
> "It's not Giuseppe, Ma. It's Yossarian."
>
> "What difference does it make?" the mother answered in the same mourning tone, without looking up. "He's dying."

When the whole family starts crying Yossarian cries too. It's not a show anymore. Somehow they're right, the doctor's right, they *are* all dying; in some sense it *doesn't* matter. A piece of ghoulish humor has turned into something exceptionally moving. The same point is made with the Soldier in White, a mummy in bandages whose only sign of life is an interchange of fluids. What *is* a man, anyway, when things have come to this extremity? The ground is being readied for revealing Snowden's secret. The *Lear* theme is at the heart of the book, no mere device for concluding it.

Unlike the realistic novelists of the fifties, the black humorists suggest that besides our personal dilemmas, which often loom so large in our imagination, we all share features of a common fate, enforced by society and the general human condition. Though the quest for identity must inevitably be personal, in some sense we *are* interchangeable. Furthermore, the quest will surely be thwarted if society becomes a vast structure of illusion and duplicity, and hence treats us as even more interchangeable and manipulable than we necessarily are. One effect of Vietnam and Watergate was that the official organs of our society lost much of the respect and credence they had commanded. Even middle Americans began to live with less of a mystified and paternalistic sense of Authority. The disillusionment and ruthless skepticism—really, spoiled idealism—of *Catch-22,* outlived the sixties to become the ever more pervasive mood. With Célinean cynics and paranoids installed in the White House, people at large became that much more cynical and paranoid themselves. And the paranoia had some base in fact, for in a highly polarized society, where the self-imposed limitations of tradition and civility have been cast away, it's likely that somebody really is out to get you, by any means fair or foul.

Yet black humor began its great efflorescence during the Kennedy years, in apparent contradiction to the idealism, optimism and high style that we like to attribute to that period. Mailer's *An American Dream* can be read as a testament about the Kennedy years, better than all the tendentious memoirs and eulogies that were published after the assassination. When I first came upon the references to Kennedy in the opening pages I thought them meretricious: one more piece of megalomania for Mailer to associate his all-too-Mailerian hero with the dashing, fallen President. But Mailer's identification with Kennedy had come much earlier and ran much deeper. His first major piece of journalism had been about Kennedy's nomination. A would-be courtier and counselor, he'd addressed a whole book of essays to Kennedy as President. Sexually rivalrous, he'd written an open letter to Jackie, half-scolding her but implicitly trying to woo her away. Like others, Mailer saw Kennedy as some kind of union of style and power—both Irish and Harvard, moneyed and macho—whose classy imperial court had a use for the arts. But in the novel his hero Rojack complains that

> The real difference between the President and myself may be that I ended with too large an appreciation of the moon, for I looked down the abyss on the first night I killed: four men, four very separate Germans, dead under a full moon—whereas Jack, for all I know, never saw the abyss.

Recall the premise that Kennedy and Rojack are alter egos, both war heroes, both elected to Congress in the same year. But Rojack has explored the nether side of violence and power, explores it in the whole book, coming out only "something like sane again" in the last line. The book's plot can be seen as an enactment of his fantasies, his irrationalities, his madness. Walking along the parapet of a skyscraper to prove his courage and manhood, he hears voices that tell him he can fly. The whole book is steeped in magic and dread, the dark underside of a too-purely Apollonian Kennedy vision of power without price or penalty. Rojack is not Mailer but rather Mailer's ambiguous self-portrait as an archetype of the age. Only the best writers have the gift of using the accidents of their own experience, the stuff of their fantasy life, in that significant way, and we can hardly blame the book's first readers, myself included, who were still under the sway of Camelot's idealized Apollonian self-image, for seeing bad taste and confessional self-aggrandizement in its allusions to both Kennedy and the author's own recent bad-boy history.

Today time allows us quite another perspective on that period and its literature. From *Catch-22, Mother Night* and *V.* to *Cat's Cradle, Little Big Man* and *An American Dream,* the black humor novels of the first half of the sixties, even when conceived earlier, are like a secret history of the Kennedy years, when the terrifying specter of thermonuclear war flared garishly one last time before beginning to dim, when fond hopes for building a better society were repeatedly mocked by our inability to deal with the society we have, when a President's civilized, cosmopolitan vision helped conceal the expansion of our imperial role. Pynchon and Heller, like Mailer and Berger, are the first novelists of a new imperial America, even when they write about World War II, that just war, or about German Southwest Africa, or the Fashoda crisis of the 1880's (which neatly foreshadows the Suez crisis of the 1950's), or about the political machinations of Argentine exiles in Florence in 1902. *V.* especially is a novel whose wide-ranging imagination, strongly influenced by European novelists of imperialism like Conrad and Graham Greene, peculiarly parallels America's new world role. Just as *An American Dream* is ambivalent towards power—sexual power, political power, American power—*V.* is ambivalent toward history, seeing it on the one hand as having an exhilarating if frighteningly comprehensive shape and design, but seeing it also as perhaps a fraud, an illusion, the ultimate unreality compared to the individual's humblest private need.

The early sixties was itself an ambiguous period, for like these novels it did really have an exuberant and expansive side that was not mere Camelot rhetoric. A nascent civil rights movement, then still in its hand-in-hand, "We Shall Overcome" mood, was translating the stirrings of the Court into direct action. A nascent New Left, humanistic in its values, spontaneous and American in its methods, but potentially radical in its goals, seemed determined to avoid the ideological rigidity and conspiratorial mentality of the Old. In Beat poetry and the new vogue of folk music these social movements found their artistic accompaniments, as poets and folksingers reached past the academic insularity and pop commercialism of the fifties, towards the cultural side of the left-wing heritage of the thirties, the populism of the Popular Front.

But the opening up of the novel was a deeper, more ambiguous development, and I think it revealed more about the changing sensibility of the early sixties. Grandiose and experimental in form, these books partook of the imperial buoyancy of the Kennedy years. But their vision sometimes had a bleak, dead-end character that belied any official optimism. *Catch-22* had a plastic creative freedom and energy hardly present in the novels of the fifties, but it imagines a world wholly unredeemed by rational purpose or humanistic uplight. A similar ambiguity attaches to the theme of paranoia and the vision of history in Pynchon's novels. On one hand his form and language, his historical range and complexity of plot match Heller in creative exuberance, and many in his endless cast of cartoonish characters are pure products of the comic or satiric spirit. Even his paranoid theme has its exhilarating side: it enables him to make astonishing connections and fantasize breathtaking possibilities, to subvert and intimidate our pedestrian sense of reality and causation, "to bring the estate into pulsing stelliferous Meaning" (as Oedipa Maas muses). *"Shall I project a world?"* Oedipa asks herself in *The Crying of Lot 49,* situating herself neatly somewhere between the novelist and the psychotic. She is neither, but the elaborate plot that her sleuthing gradually intuits makes for a novel that's both impressively somber in tone and yet amazingly conditional and tentative in substance. For those who entirely associate black humor with apocalyptic farce and a tone of raucous extremity *The Crying of Lot 49* should come as a revelation. *V.* embodies more of the positive side of the paranoid vision, with its immense assortment of characters, plots, historical periods, and narrative modes, all spun together into a dazzling web of possible meanings—which still don't measure up to the pleasure of the telling, the joy of imaginative construction, where the paranoid and the novelist *do* come together. But in the spare, perfectly controlled novella that Pynchon wrote next, Oedipa, the heroine, imagines a vast plot that the author mostly doesn't care to enact. *Lot 49* is *about* plotting, and Oedipa is less the projector than the object, the possible victim. Herbert Stencil, the sleuth of *V.*, is an eccentric bird in search of his own identity, who in the process happens to construct an immense historical mosaic. Himself nothing, Stencil could only become; but since the cartoon of history is enough for him, he probably won't. But Oedipa Maas, despite her piquant Pynchonesque name, has the pulse of a full-blooded woman. The California cartoon-world that surrounds her can't possibly satisfy her, but the richer baroque underworld she glimpses won't necessarily do so either. It might be a way out, but not to anything better. The ambiguity of history in *V.*—does it have no meaning or too much meaning? Is it a chaos of random hints or a tightly organized totalitarian web?—becomes the more direct subject of *The Crying of Lot 49.* In trying to sort out the estate of the late Pierce Inverarity, Oedipa gets in a classic double-bind, which eventually comes to represent reality itself, particularly the American reality. Either Oedipa has stumbled onto an immense plot—or into an immense hoax—which has the "secret richness and concealed density of dream" but also a dreamlike pointlessness and ineffectuality. Or else there is nothing, no "real alternative to the exitlessness, to the absence of surprise in life, that harrows the head of everybody American you know," nothing but the official surfaces of life, the "lies, recitations of routine, arid betrayals of spiritual poverty." Oedipa hopes none of these things is true. "She didn't like any of them, but hoped she was mentally ill; that that's all it was." Either no exit, or an exit into rich but unhinging, even appalling realities, or perhaps an exit into madness, clinical paranoia, inner space.

It's astonishing how well the book locates itself on this narrow shelf of ambiguity, this edge of contingency, beautifully epitomized in a small moment when Oedipa comes upon what looks like an ordinary trash can, hand-painted with the initials W.A.S.T.E. "She had to look closely to see the periods between the letters." It's a witty touch, for those tiny periods flickering near the vanishing-point could mean nothing at all, but might also make all the difference between a simple trash can and a system of secret communication going back centuries; she may have stumbled into the dense underbrush of a hidden reality, something she might have uncovered "anywhere in her Republic, through any of a hundred lightly concealed entranceways, a hundred alienations, if she'd only looked." "Behind the hieroglyphic streets there would either be a transcendent meaning, or only the earth."

It should be clear why Pynchon's paranoid myth makes some claim on us, without demanding that we be paranoid ourselves, or give any credence to the reality of V. or the Tristero System. Pynchon's paranoia is neither a clinical paranoia nor a literal paranoid view of history, but instead a metaphor for something the novelist shares with the mystic, the drug-taker, the philosopher, and the scientist: a desperate appetite for meaning, a sense at once joyful and threatening that things are not what they seem, that reality is mysteriously overorganized and can be decoded if only we attend to the hundred innocent hints and byways that beckon to us, that life is tasteless and insipid without this hidden order of meaning but perhaps appalling *with* it.

Without farce or violence, Pynchon's paranoia reveals an alienation from American life greater than that of Heller or any other comic-apocalyptic writer. Society commands no loyalty in *Lot 49,* though the freaked-out scene of California in the sixties evokes an anthropological fascination; the rest is a tissue of falsehood and spiritual deadness. The drifter ambience of *V.,* which Pynchon himself has evidently continued to live out, has ripened in good sixties fashion into a complete rejection of official cant and the square world. Pynchon's sensibility, like that of some of the earlier Beat figures (whom he resembles in many ways, not including his highly structured style of writing, and his aversion to personal publicity), foreshadowed strikingly the mood of young people in the late sixties. For them, paranoia, like radicalism, drug-taking, and communal life, was both a rejection of the official culture and a form of group solidarity, promising a more fully authentic life-possibility.

For Pynchon the paranoid imagination is a special way of rebelling or dropping out, but it's also more than that. He compares it to a hallucinogenic drug. For him it rends the veil of life's banal and numbing surfaces, putting him in touch with something more deep and rich, which may also unfortunately be quite unreal. Above all it makes him feel more fully alive, with a more intense and absolute self than the official rational culture dares allow. It's "a delirium tremens, a trembling unfurrowing of the mind's plowshares." It's also analogous to the powerful sentiment of being that marks certain religious experiences: "the saint whose water can light lamps, the clairvoyant whose lapse in recall is the breath of God, the true paranoid for whom all is organized in spheres joyful or threatening about the central pulse of himself. . . ." It's important that Oedipa herself does not really have such an experience, only a glimmering and conditional intimation of it. Her mind trembles and is unfurrowed, but down to the end she passively receives these intimations and continues to weigh and judge them, caught in her double bind:

> Another mode of meaning behind the obvious, or none. Either Oedipa in the orbiting ecstasy of a true paranoia, or a real Tristero. For there either was some Tristero beyond the appearance of the legacy America, or there was just America and if there was just America then it seemed the only way she could continue, and manage to be at all relevant to it, was as an alien, unfurrowed, assumed full circle into some paranoia.

Evidently Pynchon is tempted to romanticize Oedipa into a figure of rebellion, just as he briefly inflates Pierce Inverarity's "legacy" into an allegory of America; but this is not where the book is really impressive. In the final scene Oedipa, "with the courage you find you have when there is nothing more to lose," prepares to make a final gesture to expose the Tristero secret. But she's far from a heroic figure, only—like Yossarian, like most of Vonnegut's heroes—a modest center of value in a world where human values have been misplaced or forgotten; she's caught between two worlds, the conventional and the paranoid, that have each gone amok in their own way. Oedipa is not simply the drifter and the bumbling amateur sleuth on loan from *V.* She grows more real and human as the book proceeds, trying to make connections but more impressive in her quiet despair and sexual *dis*-connection, a mood that heightens gradually into a sense of apocalyptic foreboding. What really moves us in *Lot 49* is not the paranoid myth itself—we care almost as little about the Tristero System as about the plot of the impossibly elaborate Jacobean play Pynchon parodies—but rather the state of mind, the rhythm of perception it makes possible. The big novels of the early sixties really do belong to the expansive, world-projecting mood of that period. *The Crying of Lot 49,* published in 1966, already anticipates the more sombre expectations of the late sixties, when paranoia gradually ceased to be an ecstatic enlargement of the possibilities of meaning and being, a positive subversion of ordinary reality; instead it darkened into an apocalyptic and pervasive anxiety. The paranoid became the victim of the plot or the helpless onlooker waiting to be engulfed, not the imaginative projector. If *Catch-22* foreshadows the soul-destroying madness of the Vietnam war, *The Crying of Lot 49* foreshadows the darkening green of the end of the sixties, when a government of lawless desperadoes and a half-crazed remnant of young radicals would pair off in unequal contest of mutual paranoia, helping to destroy each other and confirming also Delmore Schwartz's much-quoted adage that "even paranoids have enemies."

The black humor novels of the sixties are not only deeply interested in history but create amazing parallels to the history of their own times, less in their actual subjects than in their whole mode of imagination. The sense of incongruity and absurdity, the mixture of farce, violence, and hysteria that we find in these books, we can also find in the wars, riots, movements, assassinations, conspiracies, as well as in much subtler and less spectacular manifestations of the spirit of the sixties. The black humor novel of the sixties, like the radicalism of the sixties, and, indeed, like the American government and the architects of social policy in the sixties, began with elaborate efforts to assimilate history, to comprehend and shape it along the lines of private mythology, public planning, the enlightened will. By the end of the sixties—in both fiction and reality—this was displaced by a sense that history was out of control, or that the Others had their hands on the wheel, and were preparing to do us in completely. By the end of the sixties paranoia was the last fuel for direct action, the last gasp of a coherent world-view, which soon itself collapsed into fragments. "Fragments are the only forms I trust," wrote Donald Barthelme, as the influence of the more titanic modernists like Joyce gave way to such in-

spired miniaturists as Kafka and Borges, negative visionaries whose work undercut all mythic inclusiveness. In late-sixties writers like Barthelme or Wurlitzer the sense of disconnection is complete, as it is in the Weatherman phase of sixties radicalism, where futility and frustration spawn random violence. Barthelme and Wurlitzer write as if they were surrounded by the curious artifacts of an extinct culture, which they plunder like collectors, or stroll past vacantly like sleepwalkers.

Morris Dickstein, "Black Humor and History: Fiction in the Sixties," in Partisan Review, *Vol. XLIII, No. 2, 1976, pp. 185-211.*

Burton Feldman

[*Feldman is an American educator and critic. In the following essay, he depicts black humorists as academic writers whose detachment compromises the impact of their attacks on American culture.*]

If some critics are right, Black Humor may be the only new or important development in American fiction since World War II. The important writers are John Barth, William Burroughs, and Thomas Pynchon—but also James Purdy, Joseph Heller, J. P. Donleavy, Bruce Friedman, John Hawkes, and Terry Southern (according to really ambitious critics, there is even a Grand Tradition which includes everybody good from Andy Warhol and Voltaire back to Aristophanes).

The label fits some of these writers poorly, but generally they do share a new mood and manner. Their view of life is audaciously "black"—subversive, enraged, even apocalyptic. The stage groans with the wreckage of bewildered innocents and sinister megalomaniacs, cannibals, and intellectual rapists. But the Black Humor manner short-circuits any strong response to this. The novels stay coolly "humorous," murderously farcical, coldly zany, cosmically slapsticky. Black Humor likes nutty plots, mischievous messages, and an acrobatic style. Barth invents a wondrous echo-chamber that no longer needs a human voice; Purdy portrays the most intense events with a calculated deadness that stalemates his subject; and Burroughs gets more detached as his prose gets more chaotic.

What results from this hot-and-cold douche is an enigma. Instead of much blackness or humor, there is a nightmarish neutrality and grotesque deadpan, an elaborate novelistic impasse to feeling and judgment. But the strangest result is this: the effect of all this savage gesture and cold comedy is disappointingly mild, even harmlessly "literary."

This is odd because Black Humor scarcely wishes to be so mild or merely "literary." On the contrary; this writing would like to disavow and destroy any moral or sympathetic bond between itself and the reader. It wants to be utterly remorseless toward all the pieties and proprieties. Reading the perfect Black Humor novel would be like driving on ice. And the Black Humorist hopes to be that passenger beside you who helpfully fondles an ice pick while telling unnerving stories. In short, Black Humor would like to be a pitiless comedy. But something seems to be going wrong.

Such a complaint about Black Humor springs neither from outraged liberal idealism nor from an old-fashioned preference for uplifting literature. The truth is that Black Humor disappoints because it is not as pitilessly black or comic as it pretends to be. Given the wretchedness and folly of our century, a genuinely scathing black-comic view would be a welcome purgative. If we can't have tragic poets, we could certainly use some Swifts. Far from being too audacious, Black Humor isn't audacious enough for a world like ours. So the reader may be pardoned if he casts aside literary gentility and gets a little remorseless himself. The ordinary reader will find that he can trump the nihilism or apocalypse of these novels in a twinkling. There is always Auschwitz, or King Leopold in the Congo, or Hiroshima. Such a reader can only be agreed with if he concludes that the world is surely worse than Black Humor is telling him.

But it may be as irrelevant to talk about Black Humor in terms of Auschwitz as to compare Barth or Pynchon to a Russian satirist like Sinyavsky. Auschwitz is after all an unmistakable horror; Sinyavsky satirizes an unmistakably powerful and dangerous political regime. These issues are clear. Black Humor instead seems to be wrestling with something subtler, more insidiously shapeless—American culture in all its permissive restrictions and glossy emptiness. Indeed, the grand theme of Black Humor is nothing else than fraud. The iciest novel in American literature, Melville's *The Confidence Man,* is itself a "comically" uncanny and savage assault on national and cosmic fraud. But to mention Melville is only to emphasize how tame Black Humor seems. Melville's later and bitter obscurity may provide a clue here, as may Sinyavsky's recent imprisonment for "subversion." Neither Melville nor Sinyavsky demeans his themes. The power of their work springs in part from their ability to make us feel the really formidable stature of the enemy. They convince us that to oppose cosmic fraud or political repression will cost heavily—and that such opposition can thus ennoble and even give joy. By contrast, the saddest side of Black Humor is that it can find no compliments to pay its enemy. For all the violence of its assault on American culture, Black Humor gives no sense that this enemy is worth attacking. It is only there, a vast middle-class moonscape; and then Black Humor slips off into fantasy and parody.

As its reliance on parody shows, Black Humor does not unmask the illness hidden under our bland surface; it merely mimics the violence in front of the scene. Melville's ferocity could convey awesome energy because it was an active force. But Black Humor's violence, though tiresomely inflated, is passive. It is violence stylized, theatricalized, overblown—but static.

This does not mean that Black Humor intends its violence to be decorative. There is something of the terrorist in the Black Humorist. Like the classic terrorist, he nurses contempt for the middle class, and seeks a shortcut solution to the problems of complacency and hypocrisy. Disdainful and ruthless, from his impregnable aesthetic fortress, he strikes out at fraud. But Black Humor has one great advantage over the real terrorist—as over a Melville or Sinyavsky: it risks nothing.

For Black Humor's Literary Terrorism is mated to affluence. Perhaps "Black Humor" never was a good coinage—this kind of writing might better be called "Affluent Terrorism." It wishes to reform but also to indulge us; to scourge us and yet leave us comfortably what we were, neutralized. This ambivalence shows up again in Black Humor's obsession with violence. It is only playing, one knows that. No one will get hurt. If there seem to be pain or degradation or death on the page, the effect will be made incongruous with the fact, sidetracked into a gag, hammed up, parodied away.

The real terrorist was often a man of resentment, dispossessed and declassed; feeling cheated, he could turn into a deadly enemy of his society. Black Humor however springs from affluence, not deprivation. It foments no revolutions, but only literary disdain for its perplexed and perplexing culture. Needless to say, any American novel of worth has resisted the same cultural corruptions. Black Humor does not differ in its rejection of affluence, but only in rejecting it affluently. It can afford to be zany or inhumanly aloof, out of it, punitive with impunity.

For the first time, we may have an intelligentsia at work in the American novel. Rigid European parallels are again misleading: a better comparison is with the "older" American novel. Black Humor novelists are "educated" as American novelists never were before. The point is not sheer learning, but the attitude held toward learning. Melville was genuinely erudite, and the rest were scarcely ignoramuses. But the older American novelist typically is self-educated; his independence of insight as well as parochialism of judgment rise from this. Black Humor is our most knowing and sophisticated novel. But no new age of American urbanity is predicted. Talking plain American, it is more like a shift from buying to spending. One might say that the older American novelist—so self-educated, so distrustful of the Academy—got used to earning what he had to know and wanted to know. He did this painfully, stubbornly, badly, and often went broke (no second acts in American literature). The Black Humorist spends learning, rather than earning it. Black Humor novels burn knowledge with abandon, as gaily and irresponsibly as the millionaire lighting his cigar with a $1000 bill. Nothing personal is intended. It is a generation of college graduates, with higher education assumed at birth. The older American novelist is often described as anti-intellectual, when in fact he is usually anti-academic. The Black Humorist is sometimes said to be a new intellectual, when in fact he is merely academic.

One can call Black Humor a literature of the academy even while admitting that it takes up the American novel's homely themes of sex, money, loneliness, and the rat-race. To all these temptations, however, Black Humor stays cool. The old-fashioned novelist is rarely indifferent to sex or power: they pull at him ferociously. Sometimes, as in Fitzgerald or Mailer, he even has the imagination and nerve to want to conquer and enjoy them. It may seem paradoxical that Black Humor is at once so detached and yet so existentially drenched in these American realities.

It is no paradox. Black Humor is existential in an academic way.

All these novels are inconceivable without the hoary themes behind them of absurdity, alienation, nihilism, and the exhaustion of an age. Black Humor stands to existentialism as the American social novel of the thirties stood to European left-wing thought and revolution. In Hemingway and Dos Passos, European Marxism got transmuted into a peculiarly American kind of compassionate anarchism. In turn, Black Humor Americanizes existentialism into a merciless anarchism. For Black Humor has little or nothing to do with what lies behind existentialism as nourishing and steadying forces—Kierkegaard's Christianity, Nietzsche's aspiration to greatness, or Sartre's and Camus' experience during the Resistance. Black Humor exploits the existential style without the substance. Nihilism becomes a mere literary convention. It has no kinship with the novels of Sartre or Camus, where absurdity earned its right to speak amid the painful actualities of politics and history.

Existentialism has always spoken for commitment. By comparison, Black Humor makes such commitment—unspecific as it is—seem like the Ten Commandments. Committed only to detachment, Black Humor can never be betrayed or duped or ever be wrong. That would be an enviable position, but the suspicion grows that such detachment connives with the middle-class rather than opposes it. In this joyless literary burlesque house, the strip-teasers and blue comedians will do anything but really enrage or satisfy the customers; make them a little excited and then frustrated, yes. It becomes clear that one genuinely new aspect of Black Humor is its appearance in the novel. One suddenly realizes how the American-English novel, like Anglo-American philosophy and political thinking, has always been a moral agent as well as a realistic image. It may be goodbye to all that. The novel used to teach us to resist social pressures. We may now have to learn sobriety and plainness so we can resist at least some of our novels.

Burton Feldman, "Anatomy of Black Humor," in Dissent, *Vol. XV, No. 2, March-April, 1968, pp. 158-60.*

BLACK HUMOR RECONSIDERED

Jerome Klinkowitz

[*An American educator and critic who has written extensively on avant-garde American fiction and narrative theory, Klinkowitz is the author of* Innovative Fiction *(1972),* Literary Disruptions *(1975), and studies of Kurt Vonnegut and Donald Barthelme, among other works. In the following essay, he cites Max Schulz's* Black Humor Fiction of the Sixties *(1973) in his assertion that the classification "black humor" fails to ac-*

knowledge the diversity and originality of the writers to which it is applied.]

"I know you'll ask it," Kurt Vonnegut, Jr., began a question-and-answer session at the Iowa Writers Workshop a few years ago, so Joe David Bellamy did the honors: "Are you a Black Humorist?" he asked. After describing how Bruce Jay Friedman had lowered this bell jar over him and several other unwilling and quite unalike authors, Vonnegut dismissed it as a "label useless except for merchandisers" and got on to more serious and substantial commentary about his works.

Although it was all the rage ten years ago, some time has passed since any critic has mentioned the term "Black Humor." The writers it once described—Vonnegut, Terry Southern, Joseph Heller, J. P. Donleavy, Vladimir Nabokov, John Rechy, John Barth, James Purdy, and Thomas Pynchon—have veered off in a variety of directions which makes Friedman's 1965 anthology of their "work" seem senselessly diverse today. There is a history to be written of the movement, but it is a sad and depressing story. The only such writers to develop into major talents did so by violating the traditions of Black Humor, which included an accommodation by laughter to the world's insanity and a deliberate refusal to find any new forms in fiction appropriate to the strange new worlds they described. Vonnegut grew by daring structural innovation combined with a sharper-edged, yet more complex, vision; Barth and Pynchon agreed that the old forms were exhausted, but despaired of creating new ones, and instead took refuge in parody and ironic comment. Those authors who stayed within the original Black Humor mold, including Southern and Friedman himself, deteriorated as fictionists and are little more than casual entertainers today, authors of film scripts and of casual pieces for *Esquire, Playboy,* and *Penthouse.*

The larger literary history of America has much to do with the failure of Black Humor to develop into a substantial movement in fiction. For one thing, it hit too early: the most seriously inventive works of this sort were still tied up in court, and not until the mid-sixties did the victories won by William S. Burroughs and Henry Miller clear the way for thematic innovations by Donald Barthelme, Jerzy Kosinski, Ronald Sukenick, and others. In the meantime books that were published suffered a debilitating imaginative castration. Vonnegut made it through untouched because his fiction from this period was seeing first light as unnoticed paperbacks; but for anyone trying to make it big, the result was disastrous. Terry Southern began his Black Humor career abroad, with *Candy* published in Paris (1958) and *The Magic Christian* in London (1959). The former novel entered the country as an under-the-counter paperback and survived intact, promising a great disruptive career for Southern.

The Magic Christian was to be his major work, launching Black Humor on a course sure to change the traditions of fiction in the United States. In the English text published by Andre Deutsch, Southern described Guy Grand, the magic Christian who with his millions shows the absurdity of the American people. He plays an accelerating series of jokes, catching Americans in their gullibility and greed.

These pranks grow in scope and in effectiveness until chapter 13, where in the original edition we learn that "Grand received the greatest setback of his career in 1953 when he was undone through a combination of madness and treachery by a key employee in his big project of that year." Challenged by the assertion that "Nobody Ever Went Broke Underestimating The Intelligence Of The American Public," Grand discovers a politician who has parlayed the meaningless slogan, "The threat of American Communism," into a winning election campaign. Grand's crowning touch to this silliness is to hire the man, have him accuse the most unlikely people of being Communists, and see how far the American public will fall for the whole joke. The people, however, accept it entirely. Grand pays the man to act like a lunatic, "But the men with the jacket never came. And, in fact, no one raised a finger—a finger to topple the rotten egg from the wall; *no one.*" This chapter is missing from the Random House edition of *The Magic Christian* published in February, 1960. There we read instead that "Grand had a bit of fun when he engaged a man to smash crackers with a sledgehammer in Times Square." Rewritten as filler, it is one of the weakest sections in the book and is particularly vulnerable because it comes just at the point of a carefully drawn climax. That Terry Southern never developed into a major fictionist, and that Black Humor never rose above its own sick jokes, may be linked to this unwillingness of American publishers to print these texts as the authors conceived them.

Although much of it was written in the sixties, Black Humor fiction is in fact a product of the American 1950s, an attempt to find artistic terms for the decade's bizarre personalities—Roy Marcus Cohn, G. David Schine—and the surreal rhetoric and absurdist non sequiturs in the President's rambling sentences. Philip Roth complained that "The American writer in the middle of the 20th century has his hands full in trying to understand, and then describe, and then make *credible* much of the American reality," that the crazy events of the time were "a kind of embarrassment to one's own meager imagination"; but with a decade's hindsight it now becomes clear that he was judging not just the quality of events, but also the dull and prosaic nature of fictional ideas at the same time. The Black Humorists either were incapable of or despaired of finding innovative forms for their fiction, and only in the seventies, with Black Humor dead and gone, are younger novelists closing successfully with this same material.

Robert Coover is writing about it now, including a chapter on "The public burning of Julius and Ethel Rosenberg—an historical romance." Older Black Humorists saw the fading line between fact and fantasy and panicked; Coover adopts it as a formal strategy for his work. He sets the Rosenbergs' execution for June 18, 1953 (their fourteenth wedding anniversary), in Times Square, New York, using a reconstructed set of an electrocution from an old production of *The Valiants* which had starred Ethel Greenglass [Rosenberg]; an orchestra will play the theme from "High Noon," and at the request of President Eisenhower, Gene Autry will sing, *concert grosso,* "Tumblin' Tumbleweeds" and "Twilight on the Trail"; the sentencing judge, echoed by the President, claims that the Rosenbergs have caused the Korean War and will be responsible for the deaths of "countless millions" in the future; and the key evidence against them (like the "list of Communists" Guy Grand's Senator waves in *The Magic Christian*) is such dynamite that it cannot even be revealed in court; three days before the execution workers in East Berlin rebel, seize the Red flag from atop the Brandenburg Gate, and send it to America, to be sewn into a set of red long johns for the guilty couple to wear at their electrocution. One-third of the details listed are Coover's fantasy; but two-thirds are historical fact, and one must return to the record to find out which is which.

Knowing Coover had this novel in progress, John Leonard of the *New York Times Book Review* asked him to review Louis Nizer's book on the same subject, *The Implosion Conspiracy;* in his commentary (February 11, 1973), Coover adds that fantastic, myth-conscious staging was a real interest at the time, that Eisenhower's "only concern," as voiced to Attorney General Brownell the morning of the execution, "is in the area of statecraft—the *effect* of the action." Coover and his contemporaries are able to keep pace with such realities; the Black Humorists, for all their flurry, were not, and that is why theirs is not a living tradition today, nor even much to be reckoned with in the development of American fiction.

If it were a solid history of "Black Humor Fiction in the Sixties," Max Schulz's book would be a valuable contribu-

Robert Coover.

tion to criticism; but of all the central events and considerations detailed above, Schulz mentions not a single one. His subtitle is "A Pluralistic Definition of Man and His World," and the major thrust of his study is to establish this thesis of the world view behind the early works of Barth, Vonnegut, Pynchon, Coover, Friedman, Jorge Luis Borges, Thomas Berger, and Charles Wright. "Black Humor is a phenomenon of the 1960's," Schulz argues, "comprising a group of writers who share a viewpoint and an aesthetics for pacing off the boundaries of a nuclear-technological world intrinsically without confinement." These authors are non-existential, since they see no self to be created by choice; neither are they accommodationists (as the more mainstream Bellow, Updike, and Malamud might be), since the powers of the world are too destructive to be reconciled. The Black Humorists seek "rather a comic perspective on both tragic fact and moral certitude." To do this some will make parodies (Barth), while others "hold a limited number of viewpoints in equipose, as literary counterparts of a world devoid of a discursive value system" (Vonnegut). Hence a novel such as *God Bless You, Mr. Rosewater* refuses to resolve or confirm any of its premises, leaving the author looking like a befuddled para-intellectual, while the works of Thomas Pynchon end suspended in mid-air, where "Assent is withheld from otherwise untenable and normative intellectual positions, including outright dissent." Schulz agrees with other critics of this fiction that "all versions of reality are mental constructs," but does not investigate further into the ideal and even transcendental implications of such a world view. Instead, because many of the characters in Black Humor fiction lack "inward complexity and self-consciousness," Schulz assumes their authors do too—which leads to a gross misinterpretation of Kurt Vonnegut and Charles Wright, whose own Black Humor visions include a rigorous exercise of self-reflective imaginative powers, in novels which Schulz places at the core of the sixties movement: *Rosewater* in 1965, *The Wig* in 1966. "In a world in which logical cause and effect is absent, the only way of arriving at the 'truth' of experience is to know *all* the possible causes of an occurrence," Schulz realizes. But for the next step, "the reluctance to confirm any one observer as authoritative," he does not look further to see what may be the formal product of such an approach in fiction. The books are inconclusive, Schulz argues, because they are just "one more thing added to the world"; he does not consider that, in the cases of Vonnegut, Wright, Coover, and Borges, this may be their intent, to create not a reordered presentation of reality but instead a piece of art which stands for nothing but itself.

Aside from the limitations of Schulz's thesis, there are serious problems with this book. For the most part an assemblage of previously published articles and convention papers, Schulz has done no updating of his criticism beyond the late 1960s when the separate chapters were first written. His bibliography is especially inaccurate: for half of Vonnegut's novels he lists the wrong date and publisher and credits Joseph Heller's seminal *Catch-22* as being published in 1955 instead of 1961. Borges is described as a "European," and even as a South American is radically out of place in this study otherwise restricted to American works (certainly Cortazar, Céline, Grombrowicz, and sev-

eral others are as appropriate as Borges if we are to go international). Of less importance, but even more annoying, is the author's habit of identifying quotes by chapter instead of by page (except, for some unknown reason, in the section on Bruce Friedman and for part of the chapter on Vonnegut), misspelling several characters' names and occasionally giving them nicknames they don't have in the text, and referring to Shakespeare's play as "the Hamlet caper." These problems, plus the failure to consider seriously the implications of its own thesis, make *Black Humor Fiction of the Sixties* a poor example of contemporary criticism. Contemporary studies will not come into its own unless its critics practice the same rigorous bibliography and full analysis required of other scholars. In his preface Schulz mentions the "healthy skepticism about Black Humor" with which his students of the past five years continually confronted him; these same students are in better touch with Vonnegut, Pynchon, Berger, and the other fictionists Schulz considers here, and he might do better by listening to their objections rather than rehearsing simplifications which the authors themselves resent, and which were outdated half a decade ago.

Jerome Klinkowitz, "A Final Word for Black Humor," in Contemporary Literature, *Vol. 15, No. 2, Spring, 1974, pp. 271-76.*

Black Humor was less a School than a Sensibility and more Protean than both. . . . The lens of Black Humor had a habit of stretching the world into grotesque shapes, of letting us in on the absurdity that was always there. No matter—scratch the surface of nearly any writer in the 1960's and there was sure to be a Black Humorist lurking around the edges somewhere.

—*Sanford Pinsker, in his* Between Two Worlds: The American Novel in the 1960's, *1980.*

Elaine B. Safer

[*Safer is an American educator and critic who specializes in Milton studies. In the following excerpt, she denies that black humor novels are absolutely committed to nihilism and disorder, arguing that John Barth's* Giles Goat-Boy *(1966) and Thomas Pynchon's* Gravity's Rainbow *(1973) achieve their effects through a nostalgia for unity and order.*]

The absurdist vision, as Albert Camus asserts [in *The Myth of Sisyphus*], grows out of man's desire to find meaning in an unreasonable universe. The absurd, explains Camus, is "that divorce between the mind that desires and the world that disappoints, my nostalgia for unity, this fragmented universe, and the contradiction that binds them together." Those who mask the evidence and exclude either the nostalgia for unity or the fragmented universe are "suppressing the absurd by denying one of the terms of its equation."

It is commonplace to speak of John Barth and Thomas Pynchon as novelists of the absurd and black humor without handling both terms of the absurdist equation, that is, to discuss their depiction of a chaotic universe but not their desire for unity. It is the purpose of this essay to show how Barth and Pynchon develop a nostalgia for unity, for a commonly accepted set of values—such as existed in great Renaissance works like the King James Bible and the epic—and utilize this nostalgia and its contradiction in a fragmented universe to create the absurd. The powerful impact of novels of the absurd, ranging from Melville's *The Confidence-Man* to novels of the sixties and seventies, attests to the fact that man cannot divest himself of the desire for a traditional sense of clarity and meaning. Novelists of black humor and the absurd have an eager audience in our post-World War II society because people continue to want unifying principles in a chaotic world.

[In *After the Tradition,* 1969] Robert Alter has presented the following description of the fiction of black humorists Pynchon, Barth, and Heller: the "sharp-edged laughter gives the appearance of cutting to the core of our culture's moral abscesses and so communicates a sense of pain inflicted to work a cure. At the same time, the picaresque exuberance of the comedy offers a welcome release for our deepest feelings of anxiety about the mad state of things in which we live." Alter criticizes such writers of the absurd and black humor for appearing to show a tough-minded honesty, a desire to look things squarely in the face, when in fact they use laughter to inure themselves to painful concerns. He feels that their avoidance of seriousness blocks out crucial, moral issues that are part of the writer's responsibility to face. But actually, it seems to me that black humor novelists such as Barth and Pynchon wish to cause the reader to participate in a serious exploration of the irrationality of the post-World War II society. These novelists are motivated by a frustrated desire to experience a sense of unity and order, and underlying their laughter is a nostalgia for the clarity and cohesion of the past, a nostalgia for "a lost home or the hope of a promised land" (Camus). The longing is not sentimental but rather a tough-minded yearning for shaping principles in a world that seems irrational.

In response, it would appear, to a public hardening to details of horror, black humorists try to uncover laughter in life in order to get a reader off his guard for a moment so as to shock him with painful details of a disintegrating world. Such humor bypasses the reader's defenses and allows him to be touched. It forces the reader to have a heightened consciousness, not a weakened one, as Alter declares. Scholars like Alter who criticize the novels of the absurd and black humor underestimate the impassioned seriousness of these writers, their need to appeal to values of the past, in an effort to show the lack of purpose, the emptiness, in contemporary life. *Giles Goat-Boy,* a "souped-up Bible" in the author's own words, abounds in clear-cut theological allusions that have comic-apocalyptic or absurd effects in Barth's world. *Gravity's Rainbow,* Pynchon's rendering of a contemporary vision of hell, invites comparison to famous traditional descriptions of hell, like Milton's in *Paradise Lost,* which continually present hell in relation to heaven. By forming and then collapsing allusions to a rationally ordered universe, Barth and Pynchon cause the reader to experience the absurd.

Giles Goat-Boy or *The Revised New Syllabus* is divided into two volumes, like the Bible; as in the Bible, the numbers three and seven are prevalent: three calling to mind the doctrine of the Trinity, and seven such details as the Sabbath, the seven Sacraments, the seven visions of the Apocalypse and their subdivision into a sevenfold representation of elements. Barth divides each volume of *Goat-Boy* into three reels and seven subdivisions or visions or chapters. Giles attempts three interpretations of his seven assignments, descends into the belly of WESCAC three times, and completes the revision of the New Syllabus at the age of thirty-three and a third. Giles is a Barthian adaptation of a Christ figure. Born of a virgin mother impregnated by a computer, Giles spends his childhood, or unknown years, among the goats, later reinterprets the New Syllabus, and inspires his followers to set up a Gilesian kingdom.

Giles's first appearance at New Tammany's Spring Carnival reveals how Barth constructs and then collapses allusions that would suggest a meaningfully ordered universe. The buildup and destruction of such details develops the absurd. The scene is described as a Mardi gras, which—for the orthodox Christian—would culminate in the joyous Easter dawn commemoration of Christ's triumph over death and His opening of heaven's gates for the baptized. Barth explains that the tradition originated "in ancient agronomical ceremonies and [was] modified by the Enochist Fraternity to celebrate the Expulsion of Enos Enoch, His promotion of the Old-Syllabus Emeritus Profs from the Nether-Campus, and His triumphal Reinstatement." The scene points toward apocalypse as the Fiend Stoker takes his position before the Turnstile that leads to "the tiny gate somewhere beyond it . . . [and] to the Final Examination."

Giles comes to campus, collects a small following for a new religion, creates a new Bible, but is unable to use reason to handle the complexities of his experience. His striving for perfection reminds us of the quest of Joe Morgan, in *The End of the Road,* who wants to be the super rationalist, and of Ebenezer Cooke, in *The Sot-Weed Factor,* who tries to be the super poet and himself a true poem. Barth wishes to show the hopelessness of such striving in an absurd universe, peopled not by great heroes like Odysseus, Aeneas, or Adam, but by anti-heroes like Ebenezer Cooke, Joe Morgan, and Giles. Giles's repeated failures are not as devastating as those of the inflexible Joe Morgan in Barth's earlier novel. They are more in line with those of Ebenezer, whose expectations are continually thwarted.

Giles's quest is set into comic confrontation with that of the Christian epic hero. The pattern is depicted in the quadrated circle from Barth's "Bellerophoniad" novella in *Chimera.* The diagram shows the multi-leveled structure that underlies heroic literature. Our nostalgia for meaning and order causes us to chart correspondences between *Goat-Boy* and traditional literature: note Giles's extraordinary conception by Virginia Hector and WESCAC, his attempted murder by Reginald Hector in the tape lift, his Summons to Adventure by the mystical sound of the shofar—Tekiah—causing him to leave the goat farm for New Tammany College, his Trials and Helpers as he fulfills the seven assignments of his Pat-card with its PASS ALL/FAIL ALL mystery, his sacred marriage to Anastasia in the belly of WESCAC, and his extraordinary death on Founder's Hill amidst peals of thunder: "It will be finished" he declares, reminiscent of Christ's "It is finished."

Barth encourages us to explore numerous patterns that are basic to the Bible and the epic as well. We grasp what seems to be a master plan of structures, get caught up in its intricacies, and long for the revelation of fundamental truths. However, we repeatedly become aware that the allegorical subjects never move toward an anagogical level. After Giles's three trials, he concludes that there are no final answers: "none was the Answer." At the close of *Goat-Boy* it still is not clear whether Giles indeed is a Grand Tutor, a Christ figure.

The gimping Giles, who views the world from the innocent perspective of a goat, is a subject of laughter, similar in many respects to Barth's earlier hero Ebenezer Cooke, who holds the extremely naïve and rigid perspective of virgin and poet. For Giles and Ebenezer the journey from innocence to experience is fraught with mishaps that obliquely illuminate man's continual attempts to use reason to unravel the complexities operating in a universe that is beyond our comprehension and control. The heroic quests of Giles and Ebenezer lead to awareness of the irrational rather than knowledge of heroic truths. Reason tends to recoil upon itself and become the subject of laughter for Barth. It is a laughter born of the confrontation of "the aspirations of the human mind and the world's incapacity to satisfy them" [Alain Robbe-Grillet, *For a New Novel*].

Goat-Boy is structured to move from an initially chaotic state (Giles with the goats) to a frustrating attempt at order or affirmation of values (Giles's three trials) to a cyclical affirmation of the chaotic or absurd state: "Passage *was* Failure, and Failure Passage; yet Passage was Passage, Failure Failure! Equally true, none was the Answer; . . . my eyes were opened; I was delivered." Such "deliverance" concludes the quest in Barth's novel. This black humor novel shows the inversion of traditional comedy as disorder, not order, emerges at the end of the quest.

The frame of *Goat-Boy* compounds the dissolution of reader expectation. The certainty of the fictional world itself is brought into question by reports on the spurious nature of the comments of Giles, who recorded the tale, and J. B., who typed and sent it to the publisher. The "professor and *quondam* novelist," J. B., believes that the Posttape supposedly recorded by Giles is spurious. The Footnote to the Postscript to the Posttape further eliminates certainties by pointing out that J. B.'s Postscript itself may be spurious because "the type of the typescript pages . . . is not the same as that of the 'Cover-Letter to the Editors

and Publisher.' " This novel of the absurd develops and then collapses hope for any truth whatsoever.

Gravity's Rainbow starts with a rocket screaming across the sky during the last months of World War II and ends with a rocket about to destroy the observers in the theater. The rocket's parabolic course calls to mind the arc of a rainbow. In the Bible and other theistic works, the rainbow symbolizes God's Covenant with man for peace; in *Gravity's Rainbow* it is an ironic allusion to the notion of God's justice in an irrational World War II society that seems to be a hell on earth.

In *Gravity's Rainbow,* Pynchon divides society into the elect and preterite and thus makes explicit Puritan connections to play off against the chaos in our contemporary world. Pynchon shows the absurdist's desire for an ordered past as he alludes to the Puritan elect, God's ordained, and contrasts them with their ironic counterpart in twentieth-century society: those who mysteriously control the system that results in World War II and the Holocaust. A similar collapse of tradition is manifested in the New England Puritan protagonist, Tyrone Slothrop, the "last of his line, and how far fallen," an absurd hero who "hangs at the bottom of his blood's avalanche, 300 years of western swamp-Yankees."

Pynchon uses Puritan themes as a contrast to the randomness in contemporary society even though he himself is critical of a tradition that presupposes the elect and preterition. Tyrone Slothrop's ancestor William wrote a heretical tract, *On Preterition,* which "is among the first books to've been not only banned but also ceremonially burned in Boston. Nobody wanted to hear about all the Preterite, the many God passes over when he chooses a few for salvation, . . . these 'second Sheep,' without whom there'd be no elect." Pynchon indicates that characters like Slothrop (in *Gravity's Rainbow*), Oedipa Maas (in *The Crying of Lot 49*), and Stencil (in *V.*) desire some form of order (no matter what kind) for what they consider to be self-preservation in the face of absurdity. The Puritan past in *Gravity's Rainbow* presents a sense of unity in contrast to the confusion of the present.

Pynchon, in using Puritan themes, is in the tradition of American writers from colonial times to the present; Benjamin Franklin, Hawthorne, Melville, and Barth as well are obvious examples. Pynchon may well have been influenced by his own personal Puritan heritage. Hawthorne described his early New England forebears in *The House of the Seven Gables.* Judge William Pyncheon (1723-1798), a resident of Salem, was among his more prominent ancestors; and another, William Pynchon, published (in 1650) *The Meritorious Price of Our Redemption,* which aimed to correct "errors" in New England Puritan belief, and—like the tract of William Slothrop—was burned in Boston. That the decline of Puritanism and its consequences "are central concerns in *Gravity's Rainbow*" has been cogently argued by John Krafft [in " 'And How Far-Fallen': Puritan Themes in *Gravity's Rainbow,*" *Critique* 18, No. 3 (1977)]. How Pynchon calls upon our longing for the clarity and meaning of a lost Puritan past—in order to develop his absurd world view—is a subject I wish to explore.

In *Gravity's Rainbow* the repeatedly ravaged terrain is a painful symbol of man's fall from grace in a land torn apart by World War II, a shattered abyss that is strongly reminiscent of hell. *Paradise Lost* is the premier example of a Puritan world view to which Pynchon, as an absurdist, is posing a dark contrast in his novel about an irrational and disordered hell on earth: the horrors of World War II and the Holocaust. Pynchon's terms and images bring to mind Milton's. The fallen in *Gravity's Rainbow* experience problems similar to those of Milton's fallen angels. But the unity and reason in Milton's Puritan heaven-hell gestalt is sorely absent in Pynchon's absurd vision of hell.

The opening scene in *Gravity's Rainbow* conveys the feeling of a hell on earth, a dusky atmosphere like the habitation of the fallen in Milton's *Paradise Lost:* "A Universe of death . . . / . . . Where all life dies, death lives, and Nature breeds, / Perverse." Ravaged by war, London is a darkened habitat, fit "to accommodate the rush of souls, . . . where all the rats have died, only their ghosts, still as cave-painting, fixed stubborn and luminous in the walls." There is "no light anywhere," yet the horror seems fixed luminous. It is, in Miltonic terms, a "darkness visible" (*Paradise Lost*). The streets are filled with stench and smoke from recent bombing; there are odors of blackened wood. There is a "smell . . . of old wood, of remote wings empty all this time just reopened to accommodate the rush of souls." There is the constant emission of smoke from the rockets that scream across the sky. And, never fully developed, but always acting as background for all other fire imagery, is the burning in the death camps, seen by the prison children as "a huge refuse dump that always smoldered, day and night."

The opening passages of *Gravity's Rainbow,* like those of *Paradise Lost,* set the tone for a "region of sorrow" where hope and rest never dwell, where confused creatures roam "in wand'ring mazes lost" (*Paradise Lost*). In *Gravity's Rainbow,* the evacuees of darkened, bombed-out London streets move along "blind curves," down streets that get narrower and more broken, eventually finding that "there is no way out." The movement "is not a disentanglement from, but a progressive knotting into." Their movement recapitulates the futile roving of the fallen in Milton's hell. As Pynchon explains: "You didn't really believe you'd be saved. Come, we all know who we are by now. No one was ever going to take the trouble to save you, old fellow."

The condition of the fallen in Milton and Pynchon is physical as well as spiritual. Satan's original brightness dims as he deteriorates from the angel Lucifer to the Archfiend. This changed state is more acutely felt in *Gravity's Rainbow,* where people from all levels of society have been metamorphosed because of the war. The recent evacuees in the carriage early in the novel are recognizable only as "half-silvered images in a view finder." Tyrone Slothrop, the protagonist in this absurd hell, gradually disintegrates before our eyes. And Blicero, Enzian comments, "was changing. Terribly. . . . toad to prince, prince to fabulous monster."

The World War II victims in *Gravity's Rainbow* differ, however, from Milton's fallen angels in a crucial way.

Pynchon's evacuees are helpless victims; Milton's are not. Satan and his followers were "sufficient to have stood, though free to fall." It was "Pride and worse Ambition" that threw Satan down. In *Gravity's Rainbow* we constantly search for reasons for the atrocities perpetuated during World War II. Pynchon gives us no answers. He makes no affirmations about man or God. Pynchon's aim seems to be to trouble the reader repeatedly with the contrast between man's desire for understanding and the lack of all possibility of understanding in our absurd world. We cannot fathom—despite numerous clues—the motivation behind those who contribute to the atrocities: those in power like Blicero/Weissman, the Nazi Captain who is probably the most psychologically frightening creation of Pynchon because he, like Satan, seems inexorably bent on destroying. Whereas Satan destroys because he wants revenge on God, Blicero's reasons for destroying are unknown. He is a devil or a witch who feeds on the innocent—like Katje and Gottfried (or Hansel and Gretel)—in the charmed house in the forest: "he wears a false cunt and merkin of sable both handcrafted in Berlin by the notorious Mme. Ophir, . . . tiny blades of stainless steel bristle from life-like pink humidity, hundreds of them, against which Katje, kneeling, is obliged to cut her lips and tongue."

No matter how much he engages in activity, Blicero, like Satan, finds no relief for his despair. Whether Blicero is making Gottfield dress in women's clothes and Katje in men's before engaging in brutal sexual activities with both of them; whether this commander of a V-2 base is cavorting before the men with his big African lover, Enzian—all of these machinations for Blicero are merely "foreplay": "He only wants now to be out of the winter, inside the Oven's warmth, darkness, steel shelter . . . gonging shut, forever." He is a creature of darkness, with hell fires that draw him onward. We are surprised when we finally see his lineaments: "balding, scholarly, peering up at the African through eyeglass lenses thick as bottles." We are taken aback by the normalcy of his appearance because the associative allusions to a devil figure have created a phantasmagoric creature in our mind's eye.

Blicero's movement toward destruction and also his agony and despair are mirrored in Katje, who recapitulates her teacher's actions. She inflicts pain on others, like Captain Brigadier Pudding who kneels before her, submissive to her every whim. There is a hell burning within Katje. For her, all movement is toward death. She feels she is "corruption and ashes." Like Satan, her dark soul seems to have bottomless depths that threaten to devour her. She, like Blicero (and like Satan), tries to evade her despair, whether it be by dancing naked in groves and thickets or before sailors ashore, or whether it be inflicting pain on Brigadier Pudding or making love to Slothrop. Whatever she does, Katje always is plagued by the fact that she is a decayed creature, belonging to the darkness of the Oven, to *"Der Kinderofen,"* to a "darkness in which flows go in all directions, and nothing begins, and nothing ends." For Katje, as for Satan and his followers, life offers no rest.

We get involved in Katje's ache; we expect clarification of her psychological state and a culmination of her relationships. The narrator responds to our nostalgia for meaning by observing: "You will want cause and effect. All right." Then he sets up more clues—more horizontal patterns—for us to examine and we encounter the meaninglessness of the absurd.

In *Paradise Lost* motives are continually presented, secrets revealed to the reader, relationships developed. There is a movement toward self-knowledge on the part of the reader as he appreciates the evil in Satan and the goodness in God, the despair of the fallen versus the promise of salvation for Adam and Eve. In *Paradise Lost* hell is always observed in relation to heaven, disorder in relation to order, darkness in relation to light. In *Gravity's Rainbow*, on the other hand, the hellish land devastated by World War II never is set into relief with heaven; no epic voice guides the reader or refines his vision. We see all from the vantage point of the fallen alone. There is no sense of God's justice or light in this contemporary novel that depicts a tormented universe. Pynchon's world is a hell that offers the reader no harmony, peace, or joy as respite. It is a hell inhabited by victims, a hell of the absurd.

Pynchon's protagonist of the absurd, Lieutenant Tyrone Slothrop, like Giles Goat-Boy, vainly tries to create order from the clues that he finds in his epic journey through the Zone. The reader, in turn, follows clues as a means to comprehend how Dr. Jamf's conditioning of Slothrop in infancy could result in the strange connection between his sex acts and the rocket falls. As Slothrop searches for answers about the V-2 rocket, about Imipolex G, about the Forbidden Wing in his past, he travels through London, Nice, Zurich, Berlin, and other parts of the Zone. At the end of his epic journey this hero of the absurd achieves not fulfillment but disintegration. He becomes "broken down . . . and scattered." Seaman Bodine observes him before the deterioration is complete: "He's looking straight at Slothrop (being one of the few who can still see Slothrop as any sort of integral creature any more. Most of the others gave up long ago trying to hold him together, even as a concept—'It's just got too remote' 's what they usually say)." We are left to ponder this transformation and also the following:

> "There never was a Dr. Jamf," opines world-renowned analyst Mickey Wuxtry-Wuxtry— "Jamf was only a fiction, to help him explain what he felt so terribly, so immediately in his genitals for those rockets each time exploding in the sky . . . to help him deny what he could not possibly admit: that he might be in love, in sexual love, with his, and his race's, death."

Slothrop's quest, his strange conditioning (if we can call it that), and his deterioration cause us to use our reason to try to understand the unreasonable. We try to find meaning in an irrational universe and we face the absurd.

In *Gravity's Rainbow,* the pain never totally blots out the humor. Slothrop's futile quest, his endless journey, is burlesqued in the meanderings, chance experiences, anger and frustration that we observe in the tale of Byron the immortal light Bulb. We laugh at the *reductio ad absurdum* of Byron the Bulb's journey from Osram, in Berlin, to an opium den in Charlottenburgh, to Hamburg, to Nürenberg, to various homes and factories and streets. The pica-

resque journey amuses us and eases our anxiety over the topsy-turvy quality of Pynchon's world and ours. Then we learn that Byron the Bulb is controlled by an international light bulb organization and that all may be controlled by IG Farben: the company, we realize, that supplied the death camps with poison gas, the company that worked prisoners to death, the company that contributed to the deaths of multitudes in Auschwitz. Pynchon thus pains us while we are laughing and off our guard. He then eases us back to the picaresque description of Byron the Bulb, who—we are informed—"is condemned to go on forever, . . . powerless to change anything." Eventually, he, like the human beings that people *Gravity's Rainbow,* "will find himself, poor perverse bulb, enjoying it."

In an absurd World War II situation, Slothrop continually quests for answers about "Them," the controlling agents, though the obsession leads him in circles; the mathematician Franz Pökler desperately searches for his daughter, Ilse, who, he is told, is at a Nazi "reeducation" camp; Tchitcherine searches for his soul brother Enzian and observes that "what might have been a village apocalypse has gone on now into comic cooperation, as between a pair of vaudeville comedians." These characters recapitulate the desperate wandering of the evacuees in the opening pages of the novel. These tortured people are ceaselessly wandering, like the fallen angels in Milton's hell.

As the characters in *Gravity's Rainbow* quest for answers, go on geographical and psychological journeys, attempt to discover secrets or develop relationships or reveal motives, we—because of our desire for correspondences—expect a movement that will culminate in successful action. There is, however, a negative quality throughout. The helpless position of characters is exemplified early in the novel by Captain Geoffrey (Pirate) Prentice's remarks, as he wakes up, and the narrator's comments that follow: "How awful. How bloody awful." He leaps off his cot, makes his way to an outside ladder to his roof garden, observes "gnarled emissions of steam and smoke" in the distance and then—with casual normalcy—fixes one of his famous Banana Breakfasts. The narrator indicates: "This well-scrubbed day ought to be no worse than any—."

In the world of black humor, Roger Mexico attends an Advent Service in a country church with his girl friend Jessica, even though he senses the service is an ironic celebration of redemption through Christ amidst all the pressures of war. The evensong becomes a call to "leave your war awhile" for the refuge, the safer place, of the church service. Those who sing the evensong are a "pickup group" of people, instead of a choir representative of angels who sing God's praises. For these people there is nothing in the church that can serve even as a physical focus for inspiration: "no counterfeit baby, no announcement of the Kingdom, not even a try at warming or lighting this terrible night." The church service offers no solace for those who are "alone in the dark." There are no answers here for the randomness of the World War II situation.

At the close of *Gravity's Rainbow,* the ironically named Gottfried (God's peace) ascends in a rocket. He holds the mystical belief that this is a transcendent experience as he carries out the will of his lover, Blicero/Weissman, and commits suicide. From Gottfried's point of view there is a sense of ease and affection, a sense that death is a purification process, "a whitening, a carrying of whiteness to ultrawhite." We react to the mystical sense of "whitening," only to find our longing abruptly collapses: "what is it but bleaches, detergents, oxidizers, abrasives." In *Gravity's Rainbow,* "the real movement is not from death to any rebirth. It is from death to death-transfigured," that is, to a death-in-life. This movement stresses the conflict between teleological implications and a barren world. As the rocket descends, there is a sense of anesthetized time, different by far from the eternal glory of God. "It is," as Pynchon points out, "a judgment from which there is no appeal." There is no Covenant between man and God to which to appeal. There can be no dialogue between questioning man—an Abraham or a Moses—and a just God. There are no answers; reason leads only to absurdity.

Giles Goat-Boy and *Gravity's Rainbow* develop their absurd or black humor by inverting the spiritual progression of the allusive mode, as they build and then collapse suggested references. Dante's analysis of four levels of meaning can be seen as a paradigm of the traditional allusive mode that progresses vertically from the literal or referential meaning to the anagogical or mystical meaning that points to the eternal truth of God's glory. For Dante, the opening verses from Psalm 114, depicting Moses's leading the Israelites out of Egypt, convey the following: the literal departure of the sons of Israel, the allegorical significance of man's redemption through Christ, the moral emphasis on the conversion of the soul from sin to the state of grace, and the ultimate spiritual or anagogical sense that the sanctified soul, free from corruption and servitude, aspires to eternal glory and freedom. Christian epics like the *Divine Comedy* and *Paradise Lost* have mystical levels which are seen as being vertically linked to Divine Providence. Such works assume correspondences between this world and a New Jerusalem on earth. They depend on a hierarchical mode of thought that has as its basis faith.

Black humorists like Barth and Pynchon depend on the reader's nostalgia for the allusive mode. They set up patterns of allusions—like the Biblical ones in *Goat-Boy*—collapse them, and laugh at the reader's disappointment. George Levine and David Leverenz comment on Thomas Pynchon's success in trapping the reader who looks for correspondences: "The temptation, clearly, has been irresistible to take his allusions, his dropped clues, his metaphors, and run, right into the ordering patterns that welcome us" (Introduction to *Mindful Pleasures*). Black humorists mock the twentieth-century reader's desire for a hierarchical progression of allusions that culminate in eternal truths. These writers laugh at man's helplessness in an alien universe and in a societal complex that has grown way beyond his control. They speak of entropy with casualness. They encourage the reader to work out endless quests for order that conclude in collapse of expectation, causing the reader to respond with existential anxiety or bitter laughter rather than happiness.

The buildup and collapse of expectation in black humor relates not only to the allusive mode but also to the pattern of comedy. Comedy usually moves toward reconciliation. As Dante observes, comedy "introduces a situation of adversity, but ends its matter in prosperity." If the comedy has a theological base, repentance and forgiveness are at the completion of the pattern toward order; if comedy has a social base, it unmasks our weaknesses and "cures folly by folly" [Wylie Sypher, "The Meanings of Comedy," in *Comedy,* edited by Wylie Sypher] as it progresses from disorder to an ordering in accordance with the customary moral norms of society. "Comedy," as Northrop Frye points out [in *Anatomy of Criticism,* 1957], "usually moves toward a happy ending," a sense that "this should be." "Its opposite," continues Frye, "is not the villainous but the absurd" or irrational. The comedic movement is from illusion to reality. "Hence," as Frye explains, "the importance of the theme of creating and dispelling illusion in comedy: the illusions caused by disguise, obsession, hypocrisy, or unknown parentage." This pattern is found in Chaucer's *The Canterbury Tales,* in Shakespeare's plays, in the plays of Ben Jonson and Molière, to cite a few examples. Works of the absurd and black humor, on the other hand, move toward the conclusion that a firm reality is an illusion or a fiction, that the reasonable or what "should be" always gives way to the irrational.

At the end of "The Miller's Tale," disorderly elements are brought into harmony and characters get what they deserve as the older husband, John the foolish carpenter, is ridiculed and Alison's lover, *hende* Nicholas, is scalded appropriately. In Shakespearean comedy, fallible laws of society, such as the mandate for executing Syracusans in the *Comedy of Errors* and the law of compulsory marriage in *A Midsummer Night's Dream,* are eventually disregarded or clarified. Similarly, correctives are employed to change foolish or misdirected characters like Claudio, in *Much Ado about Nothing,* and Angelo, in *Measure for Measure.* The curative progression also is seen in the plays of Ben Jonson and Molière, e.g., *Volpone* and *The Misanthrope,* for Volpone and Alceste get what they deserve as the dramas advance toward endings which reflect the norms of society.

In theologically based works like *Paradise Lost,* comedy has an eternal perspective which underlies the movement from disorder to order, as repentance and forgiveness are achieved. There is a continual contrast between "chaos worse confounded" of Hell and the harmonious peace of Heaven. There is a progression from the disorder of the fall of Adam and Eve to man's repentance and forgiveness. This culminates in hope for the everlasting future when mankind will be redeemed; when all will be purged and refined: "New Heav'ns, new Earth, . . . / To bring forth fruits Joy and eternal Bliss." Black humor inverts the customary structure of comedy. In black humor comedy, norms are rejected and a sense of chaos is affirmed as in Giles's exclamation, "None was the Answer," or in Slothrop's eventual disintegration at the close of his quest.

An inversion of usual patterns of quest literature causes contemporary protagonists, like Giles in Barth's novel and Slothrop in Pynchon's, to take on the black humor of the absurd. The typical hero of quest literature was described as the protector of mankind, destroyer of evil, epitome of temperance, wisdom, and altruism. His aim was to restore a kingdom for his people. The protagonist left the known—the homeland, was tested by a series of adventures, and returned to the known where his perfection was rewarded. Writers of the absurd and black humor do not wish to show quests of great heroes, but instead desire to have protagonists who are deformed, like the gimping Giles, who was brought up with the goats (not the sheep), and Slothrop, whose actions were programmed from infancy by Dr. Jamf.

Black humor would seem to inhere in the practice of exaggerating deformities till they are grotesque, and of using the grotesque for humorous effects. Deformities may be physical (like the misshapen body of the hunchback in Southern's *Candy* with whom the heroine engages in a bizarre form of sexual behavior) or psychological (like the frightened characters in Kesey's *One Flew Over the Cuckoo's Nest*) or societal (like Bruce Jay Friedman's self-conscious caricature of Jews who laugh at the phrases "orange Jews," "grapefruit Jews," and "prune Jews" in *Stern*). The characters are at the *schlemiel* end of the continuum rather than the heroic; they fail to restore order to a universe characterized by randomness, and their experiences never culminate in reward. They follow vague clues that are never clarified either for them or for the reader. They receive answers that are incomprehensible. And the conclusion of their adventures leaves them very much where they began: in a state of ignorance, lost in wandering mazes instead of progressing toward the light.

Barth and Pynchon encourage the reader to work out numerous possibilities that would reach culmination if they were in traditional works like the Bible and *Paradise Lost,* but in *Giles Goat-Boy* and *Gravity's Rainbow* never do. As a consequence, the reader finds himself in a position similar to that of Jake Horner in *The End of the Road:* "held static like the rope marker in a tug-o'-war where the opposing teams are perfectly matched." The reader's difficulty also is similar to Ebenezer Cooke's in *The Sot-Weed Factor:* "Ebenezer felt bereft of orientation. He could no longer think of up and down: the stars were simply *out there . . .* and the wind appeared to howl not from the Bay but from the firmament itself, the endless corridors of space."

Barth and Pynchon reveal that writers of absurdist literature are motivated by a frustrated desire for order and value. Without a longing for correspondences between man and nature, there would be no literature of the absurd. It is this yearning that makes absurd the grim secret revealed in Joseph Heller's *Catch-22:* "Man was matter. . . . Drop him out a window and he'll fall. Set fire to him and he'll burn. Bury him and he'll rot like other kinds of garbage." [In *Stern*] Bruce Jay Friedman has Stern reveal a yearning for order when he fantasizes that the Kike man will treat him as a fellow human being: "Stern saw himself writing and producing a show about fair play, getting it shown one night on every channel, and forcing the man to watch it since the networks would be bare of Westerns." [In *One Flew Over the Cuckoo's Nest*] Ken Kesey reveals a nostalgia for meaning when he has Bromden ecstatically envision returning to the land of his youth: "I

ran across the grounds in the direction I remembered seeing the dog go, toward the highway. . . . I felt like I was flying. Free."

Kesey juxtaposes the Indian's exultation with our foreboding that Bromden, like the dog he had watched loping in the breeze, will be destroyed. This is the pattern found in literature of black humor and the absurd: a continual buildup and destruction; a longing for unity confronted with fragmentation. This longing provides a painful thrust to works of black humor and contributes to their importance as serious revelations of the human predicament.

> *Elaine B. Safer, "The Allusive Mode and Black Humor in Barth's 'Giles Goat-Boy' and Pynchon's 'Gravity's Rainbow'," in* Renascence, *Vol. XXXII, No. 2, Winter, 1980, pp. 89-104.*

FURTHER READING

Anthologies

Davis, Douglas M. *The World of Black Humor: An Introductory Anthology of Selections and Criticism.* New York: E. P. Dutton & Co., 1967, 350 p.
> The second American anthology of black humor, composed of critical essays and excerpts from novels.

Friedman, Bruce Jay, ed. *Black Humor.* London: Transworld Publishers, 1965, 174 p.
> A frequently cited anthology of black humor fiction. The collection includes excerpts from the works of such authors as Thomas Pynchon, Joseph Heller, John Barth, and Terry Southern.

Criticism

Boskin, Joseph. "The Giant and the Child: 'Cruel' Humor in American Culture." *The Lion and the Unicorn* 13, No. 2 (December 1989): 141-47.
> Examines American jokes which focus on tragic or cruel subject matter, asserting that they function as Freud theorized—as an unconscious means for the conscious mind to assimilate and cope with painful realities.

Brackman, Jacob. "The Put-On." *The New Yorker* XLIII, No. 18 (24 June 1967): 34-73.
> Explains a brand of humor which is linked by some critics with black humor. According to Brackman, the "put-on" is ironic humor which makes the reader or spectator the dupe or butt of the joke. Unlike the practical joke, in which the dupe is let in on the humor, the victim of the put-on is indefinitely confused and disoriented, unable to discover any stable context for the joke.

Charney, Maurice. "Stanley Elkin and Jewish Black Humor." In *Jewish Wry: Essays on Jewish Humor,* edited by Sarah Blacher Cohen, pp. 178-95. Bloomington: Indiana University Press, 1987, 244 p.
> Asserts that Stanley Elkin, despite his denial that he writes from a strictly Jewish and black humorist stance,

draws his material and perspective from a "constructed folklore" of Jewish outsider mythology, which accounts for his affinities with other Jewish black humorists such as Bruce Jay Friedman and Joseph Heller.

Elliott, George P. "Destroyers, Defilers, and Confusers of Men." *The Atlantic* 222, No. 6 (December 1968): 74-80.
Offers a scathing critique of "literary nihilism" as exemplified by the works of William S. Burroughs, John Barth, Edward Albee, the Marquis de Sade, and others.

Erickson, John D. "Surrealist Black Humor as Oppositional Discourse." *Symposium* XLII, No. 3 (Fall 1988): 198-215.
Discusses André Breton's conception of black humor as a form of revolt against the dominant discourse of mainstream Western society. Citing Freudian theories of humor, Erickson interprets Breton's surrealist humor as a means of bringing to light those elements of discourse which are repressed by reason and logic.

Greenberg, Alvin. "The Novel of Disintegration: Paradoxical Impossibility in Contemporary Fiction." *Wisconsin Studies in Contemporary Literature* 7, No. 1 (Winter-Spring 1966): 103-24.
Asserts that such writers as Samuel Beckett, Louis-Ferdinand Céline, and William S. Burroughs are masters of "the novel of disintegration," a tragicomic dramatization of the forces of entropy which thwart the human impulse towards longevity, stability, and order.

Greiner, Donald J. *Comic Terror: The Novels of John Hawkes.* Memphis: Memphis State University Press, 1973, 260 p.
Appreciation of John Hawkes as one of the most accomplished and original black humorists.

Harris, Charles B. *Contemporary American Novelists of the Absurd.* New Haven, Conn.: College and University Press, 1971, 159 p.
Asserts that the absurdist view of modern life is the dominant perspective of American writers of the 1950s and 1960s and contends that their primary techniques are parody and irony, rather than the radical experimentation of the "anti-novel," which would imply a rejection of all prior conventions of the novel.

Hauck, Richard Boyd. *A Cheerful Nihilism: Confidence and "The Absurd" in American Humorous Fiction.* Bloomington and London: Indiana University Press, 1971, 269 p.
Identifies comic absurdity in the works of Herman Melville, Mark Twain, William Faulkner, John Barth, Native American and frontier humorists, and others, supporting his thesis that American black humor confronts nihilism by relying on a resilient cheerfulness.

Janoff, Bruce. "Black Humor: Beyond Satire." *The Ohio Review* XIV, No. 1 (Fall 1972): 5-20.
Compares black humor with satire on the basis of a shared tendency to ridicule the absurdity and hypocrisy of contemporary society. Janoff concludes that black humor moves "beyond" satire in its amorality, nihilism, and preoccupation with aesthetic form.

Kayser, Wolfgang. *The Grotesque in Art and Literature.* Translated by Ulrich Weisstein. New York: Columbia University Press, 1981, 224 p.
Proceeding from an etymological and generic definition of "the grotesque" as a tragicomic view of humanity, Kayser asserts that expression of this ancient perspective

reached its zenith in twentieth-century art and literature.

Kerr, Walter. "Comedy Now." *The Critic* XXV, No. 5 (April-May 1967): 38-43, 46-51.
Asserts that black humor expresses a fundamental interdependence of comedy and tragedy, and that contemporary black humorists have moved beyond passive angst in their vigorous embrace of nihilism.

Lindberg, Stanley W. "One Alternative to Black Humor: The Satire of Jack Matthews." *Studies in Contemporary Satire* 1, No. 1 (Spring 1974): 17-26.
Citing the novels of Jack Matthews, Lindberg suggests that it is possible to write contemporary satire which does not veer into the absurdist nihilism of black humor.

Olderman, Raymond M. *Beyond the Wasteland: A Study of the American Novel in the Nineteen-Sixties.* New Haven and London: Yale University Press, 1972, 258 p.
Explains black humor as the consequence of a revolution in our way of perceiving reality. Confronted with a bureaucratized, frenetic, and valueless society, black humorists document the blurring of the separation between the ordinary and the fantastic and between fact and fiction in contemporary America.

Pinsker, Sanford. "The Graying of Black Humor." In his *Between Two Worlds: The American Novel in the 1960's*, pp. 11-27. Troy, N.Y.: Whitston Publishing Co., 1980, 139 p.
Contends that 1960s black humor fiction was situated uneasily between traditional satire and modernist angst and that the subsequent works of such authors as Bruce J. Friedman, Joseph Heller, and Ken Kesey have lapsed into comic schtick and conventional novelistic devices.

Pratt, Alan R., ed. *Black Humor: Critical Essays.* New York and London: Garland Publishing, 1993, 375 p.
Includes the first essays in which the term "black humor" appears, as well as a wide range of analysis by theoretically-oriented commentators. Appendices include brief profiles of major black humorists and an annotated bibliography of black humor criticism.

Safer, Elaine B. "The Allusive Mode and Black Humor in Barth's *Sot-Weed Factor.*" *Studies in the Novel* XIII, No. 4 (Winter 1981): 424-38.
Suggests that Barth's techniques for generating black humor in *The Sot-Weed Factor* constitute an inversion of the allusive mode deployed in traditional epics such as Dante's *Divine Comedy*. Whereas allusion in classical literature bolsters meaning or truth through reference to authoritative texts, Barth employs parody to deliberately frustrate the reader's desire for a unifying theme or vision, in keeping with the absurdist outlook presented in his works.

——. "The Tall Tale, the Absurd, and Black Humor in Thomas Pynchon's *V.* and *Gravity's Rainbow.*" In her *The Contemporary American Comic Epic: The Novels of Barth, Pynchon, Gaddis, and Kesey*, pp. 79-110. Detroit: Wayne State University Press, 1988.
Cites parallels between the exaggerated descriptions and slapstick humor in American tall tales and the absurdist adventure heroes of Thomas Pynchon's novels.

——. "The Absurd Quest and Black Humor in Ken Kesey's *Sometimes a Great Notion.*" In her *The Contempo-*

rary American Comic Epic: The Novels of Barth, Pynchon, Gaddis, and Kesey, pp. 138-155. Detroit: Wayne State University Press, 1988.

> Contends that Kesey's novel is an exemplary black humor fiction in its persistent coupling of horrifying and humorous elements, in its vision of an absurd universe impervious to moral or rational concerns, and in its use of nihilistic comedy to parody conventional epic-heroic themes.

Schulz, Max F. *Black Humor Fiction of the Sixties.* Athens: Ohio University Press, 1973, 156 p.

> Defines black humor as a distinctively American vision of the absurdity and futility of human existence and examines the fiction of such authors as John Barth, Kurt Vonnegut, Thomas Pynchon, and Robert Coover.

Wallace, Ronald. *The Last Laugh: Form and Affirmation in the Contemporary American Comic Novel.* Columbia and London: University of Missouri Press, 1979, 159 p.

> Situates black humor in a tradition of "comic seriousness," viewing it as a vital and necessary strategy for assimilating the horror and atrocity which characterize so much of the twentieth century.

Widmer, Kingsley. "Twisting American Comedy: Henry Miller and Nathanael West, Among Others." *Arizona Quarterly* 43, No. 4 (Autumn 1987): 218-30.

> Cites Henry Miller and Nathanael West as exemplary practitioners of comic nihilism.

Zolten, Jerome J. "Joking in the Face of Tragedy." *Et Cetera* 45, No. 4 (Winter 1988): 345-50.

> Discusses joke-telling and black humor in the context of psychological theories.

American Proletarian Literature

INTRODUCTION

The "proletarian period" of American literature spans roughly one decade, from the founding of the *New Masses* literary journal in 1926 through the early World War II years of the late 1930s. The writers of proletarian fiction, poetry, drama, and journalism generally embraced Marxian social theory, rejected "bourgeois literature"—which encompassed virtually all traditional and mainstream works—and sought to initiate radical social change through the power of the pen and the press. A typical theme was the call for American workers to repudiate the vagaries of capitalism by organizing themselves into proletarian labor unions. Specific guidelines which supported the political aims of the Communist Party in the United States governed the style, format, and content of critically acceptable proletarian literature; left-wing writers who strayed from the formula were accused by their peers of being unduly influenced by the bourgeois culture. In spite of its favor with intellectual supporters of the political left, proletarian literature was never embraced by the true proletariat, the "masses" of American workers for and about and, in some cases, by whom it was written. Contemporary critical opinion suggests that the works themselves are more remarkable for their inimitable reflection of the political and social turmoil of Depression-era America than for any inherent literary value.

REPRESENTATIVE WORKS

Agee, James
   Let Us Now Praise Famous Men   (journalism)   1941
Anderson, Sherwood
   Beyond Desire   (novel)   1932
   Puzzled America   (essays)   1935
Burke, Fielding [pseudonym of Olive Tilford Dargan]
   Call Home the Heart   (novel)   1932
   A Stone Came Rolling   (novel)   1934
Burke, Kenneth
   Towards a Better Life   (novel)   1932
Cantwell, Robert
   The Land of Plenty   (novel)   1934
Colman, Louis
   Lumber   (novel)   1932
Conrad, Lawrence H.
   Temper   (novel)   1924
Conroy, Jack
   The Disinherited   (novel)   1933
   A World to Win   (novel)   1935

Cunningham, William
   The Green Corn Rebellion   (novel)   1935
   Pretty Boy   (novel)   1936
Dahlberg, Edward
   Bottom Dogs   (novel)   1930
   From Flushing to Calvary   (novel)   1932
   Those Who Perish   (novel)   1934
Davidman, Joy
   Letter to a Comrade   (poetry)   1938
Farrell, James T.
   Young Lonigan: A Boyhood in Chicago Streets (novel)   1932
   The Young Manhood of Studs Lonigan   (novel) 1934
   Judgment Day   (novel)   1935
   A World I Never Made   (novel)   1936
   No Star Is Lost   (novel)   1938
Fearing, Kenneth
   Angel Arms   (poetry)   1929
   Poems   (poetry)   1935
Federal Writers Project
   These Are Our Lives   (journalism)   1939
Funaroff, Sol
   The Spider and the Clock   (poetry)   1938
   Exile from a Future Time   (poetry)   1942
Gilfallen, Lauren
   I Went to Pit College   (journalism)   1934
Gold, Michael
   "Towards Proletarian Art"   (essay)   1921
   Jews without Money   (novel)   1930
Halper, Albert
   The Foundry   (novel)   1934
Herbst, Josephine
   Pity Is Not Enough   (novel)   1933
   The Executioner Waits   (novel)   1934
   Rope of Gold   (novel)   1939
Hicks, Granville [editor]
   Proletarian Literature in the United States: An Anthology   (fiction, poetry, drama, journalism) 1935
Lumpkin, Grace
   To Make My Bread   (novel)   1932
   A Sign for Cain   (novel)   1935
Newhouse, Edward
   You Can't Sleep Here   (novel)   1934
   This Is Your Day   (novel)   1937
Odets, Clifford
   Waiting for Lefty   (drama)   1935
Page, Dorothy Myra
   Gathering Storm: A Story of the Black Belt   (novel) 1932
Patchen, Kenneth
   First Will and Testament   (poetry)   1939
Rolfe, Edwin
   To My Contemporaries   (poetry)   1936

Rollins, William, Jr.
  The Shadow Before (novel) 1934
Rukeyser, Muriel
  Theory of Flight (poetry) 1935
Seaver, Edwin
  The Company (novel) 1930
  Between the Hammer and the Anvil (novel) 1937
Sifton, Claire, and Sifton, Paul
  1931—A Play (drama) 1931
Smedley, Agnes
  Daughter of Earth (novel) 1929
Spector, Herman, and Kalar, Joseph [editors]
  We Gather Strength (poetry) 1933
Steele, James [pseudonym of Robert Cruden]
  Conveyor (novel) 1935
Trumbo, Dalton
  Johnny Got His Gun (novel) 1939
Vorse, Mary Heaton
  Strike! (novel) 1930
  Labor's New Millions (journalism) 1938
Weatherwax, Clara
  Marching! Marching! (novel) 1935
Wilson, Edmund
  The American Jitters (essays) 1932

OVERVIEWS

Malcolm Cowley

[*Cowley was a prominent American critic. He is re-nowned for his editions of American authors Nathaniel Hawthorne, Walt Whitman, F. Scott Fitzgerald, Ernest Hemingway, and William Faulkner, his writings for the* New Republic, *and for his commentary on modern American literature. In the following essay, Cowley offers an assessment of American proletarian literature and its place in American culture, and provides an overview of characteristic proletarian fiction, poetry, and drama.*]

Just thirty years ago, when we were halfway through the Great Depression, the literary world was divided by arguments about proletarian literature. Critics bitterly differed about its nature, about who was qualified to write it, and about whether it would help to usher in a new society. Today, if we hear the almost forgotten term, it suggests a different sort of question. What was it after all, in theory and practice? Did it include many books that can still be read? What sort of place does it deserve in the panorama of American poetry and fiction?

To start with theory, proletarian literature was based on a notion accepted at the time by all the left-wing critics, but disputed by their opponents. The notion was that bourgeois literature—meaning almost all the books we were used to reading—belonged to the past and had entered a period of violent decay. Even the strictly bourgeois writers were turning against it, although their revolt had

assumed the corrupt forms of bohemianism, estheticism, and withdrawal into ivory towers. The result in any case was an art that fed the pride of the leisure classes. But once again a new class was rising, so the critics proclaimed. It was the soon-to-be-victorious army of workers, and they were demanding a new art to express their revolutionary ideals. Proletarian literature was taking shape among the earthquake-shattered ruins of bourgeois literature and the relics of feudalism.

But exactly what shape would it assume? The left-wing critics found it easy to agree among themselves when they were explaining the past or attacking their present enemies, but they each had different notions about the writing of the future. It raised a dozen questions to which they found conflicting answers. Should the term "proletarian literature" be confined to works by certified proletarians? Or might college graduates, even those from the Ivy League, be proletarians, too, if they wrote about the workers or specifically for the workers? Or again, might their books deal with and be intended for their own class, the petty bourgeoisie, yet still have a special attitude that earned them the right to be called proletarian novels?

This last was what Edwin Seaver, a Harvard man, strongly asserted at the first American Writers' Congress, in 1935. "It is not style," he said, "not form, not plot, not even the class portrayed that are fundamental in differentiating the proletarian from the bourgeois novel. . . . It is the present class loyalty of the author that is the determining factor." But Martin Russak, a labor organizer who had gone to work in a textile mill when he was thirteen, and who in 1935 was writing a never-to-be-published novel about the New Jersey silk weavers, held just as strongly to the opposite position. He said, "The proletarian novel has got to be, and is already becoming, a novel that deals with the working class. . . . If we completely understood the nature of class division, we would not say that all people are the same. In the working class we have a distinct kind of human being, a new type of human being, with an emotional life and psychology that is different, and distinct." Seaver and his ilk would never get past the membership committee of Russak's working-class club.

Another question was whether proletarian writers could profit from the technical experiments of bourgeois writers like Joyce and Eliot, for example, and even Henry James, or whether they should confine themselves to straightforward narrative, clear political messages, folksong, mass chants, and other forms of writing that would stir the workers to action. There was a continued bitter argument between *Partisan Review,* then an organ of the John Reed Club, and the *New Masses,* which was more directly controlled by the Communist Party. It was *Partisan Review* that advised its readers to study the new bourgeois writers as examples of technique. The *New Masses* spoke in several voices, but usually it said, in effect, "Down with technique and hurrah for writing that follows the party line." One of its editors, Mike Gold, was applauded when he said in a public debate, "There is no 'style'—there is only clarity, force, truth in writing. If a man has something new to say, as all proletarian writers have, he will learn to say it clearly in time: if he writes long enough."

Most of the left-wing writers must have agreed with *Partisan Review,* at least in their hearts. In public meetings, however, they often became so dizzy with religious enthusiasm, so eager to lead the other neophytes, that they offered to renounce their patiently acquired skill, together with everything they had learned about middle-class life, if only the sacrifice would bring them into communion with the workers. They made me think of the Florentine burghers in 1497, when hundreds of them cast their wicked books and paintings into Savonarola's bonfire. A few of the new enthusiasts, including two or three promising story writers, had abandoned any thought of a literary career in order to become party organizers among the Alabama sharecroppers and the coal diggers of Harlan County, Kentucky.

Not many were tempted so far. The usual sacrifice was to walk in a local picket line, to be carried off in a paddy wagon, to sing "The International" with the other jailed pickets—Mike Gold would carry the bass—to be tried before a judge who obviously wanted to acquit the prisoners, while the Communist attorney for the defense was doing his best to get them convicted, and then, after the judge had overruled the attorney, to rush home and write a turgid account of the strike as the first red glow of a revolutionary dawn. There were other writers, however, who played a part in serious strikes like the big ones in Minneapolis and San Francisco, where pickets were likely to be slugged and given stiff sentences. At the first American Writers' Congress, Robert Gessner, usually a sensible man, advised his fellow poets to go farther: he wanted them to submerge themselves in the mass of workers, lead the lives of workers, and learn about the workers' problems at first hand. "Leave your technique on the fence," he said. "It will come trotting after you with its tail between its legs."

This eagerness on the part of some to renounce the art of making patterns out of words for the easier task of writing cautionary tales and artless sermons might possibly be explained by a parallel that was seldom mentioned, although it must have been present in many minds. Communism was antireligious, true, but even party members often pictured it as the new scientific faith that would take the place of Christianity. Hence the two might bear the same resemblance as the opposite poles of a magnet. The millions who had already died for Communism would be like the early Christian martyrs, while the works of the first proletarian writers would be like the Christian art of the catacombs. Still more, they would resemble the writings of the first church fathers, which seemed graceless, stiff, even barbarous by the standards of a classical style, but which were redeemed by their power and fanaticism.

"Like all new art," Joseph Freeman said in his introduction to a big anthology, *Proletarian Literature in the United States,* "revolutionary art is bound to start crudely, as did the art of other classes"—and of other faiths, he might have added. Let it be crude then; crudeness was a virtue to be cultivated, so long as it was combined with the savage vigor that had enabled the church fathers to over-

whelm the pagan rhetoricians. There would come a day when Communism was like the church triumphant. Then proletarian art would give way—as it already promised to do in Russia—to a universally human art endowed with the harmony and complexity of later Christian works like the *Divine Comedy* and the Cathedral of Chartres. Such was the dream that, in those innocent days, sustained not a few of the embattled theorists.

In practice the proletarian or revolutionary literature of the early 1930s was broad in its geographical range, which was roughly from Penobscot Bay to Puget Sound and from New Orleans to Minneapolis, with forays into Germany and China. It was excessively narrow, however, in its range of emotions.

The principal emotion would seem to be anger, whether it was felt by workers in a story or was meant to be evoked in the reader by the misdeeds of the exploiting classes. Often it took the form of revulsion and was expressed by the incantatory use of such terms as "bloated," "cancerous," "chancres," "diseased," "distended belly," "fistula," "gorged with," "maggots," "naked" (almost always used in a bad sense by proletarian writers, as in the phrase "naked greed"), "nauseating," "pus," "putrefying," "retching," "rotted flesh," "spew forth," "syphilis," and "vomit." One message all the terms conveyed or chanted was that a young writer, or anyone else who turned against the bourgeoisie, was fighting his way out of a charnel house.

The other emotions that recur in proletarian writing could be expressed in more appealing images. Second to anger (or standing before it, in many cases) was the yearning for comradeship, for a sense of communion to be attained by merging the lonely and helpless "I" in a great fellowship of the dispossessed. Third was the burning faith that this "we" must rise by hundreds and thousands, then by millions against the exploiters: "Strike!" was always the message here. Fourth and last was the hope that "we" could march arm in arm across the battlefield and into the golden mountains of the future. Meanwhile there was not much place for gentler feelings like sorrow and romantic love. These could either be mentioned in passing as additional reasons why the workers must UNITE and FIGHT for every RIGHT, including that of loving and grieving at leisure, as rich people did, or else they could be deferred from consideration till the last battle was won.

The result of ruling out so many emotions was a monotony of tone that becomes even more evident in proletarian fiction than in poems and plays of the same school. Most of the proletarian novels were cast in one mold, and the fact is that many of them deal with the same events, usually a Communist-led strike like the one in the cotton mills of Gastonia, North Carolina. Within three years after the strike was fought and lost in the summer of 1929, it had become the subject of four published novels—*Strike!,* by Mary Heaton Vorse; *To Make My Bread,* by Grace Lumpkin; *Gathering Storm,* by Myra Page; and *Call Home the Heart,* by Fielding Burke—besides contributing to the background of Sherwood Anderson's *Beyond Desire.*

Strikes in lumber mills near Aberdeen, Washington,

would be the subject of three novels: *Lumber,* by Louis Colman (1931); *The Land of Plenty,* by Robert Cantwell (1934), which can still be admired; and *Marching! Marching!,* by Clara Weatherwax (1935), which reads like a parody. Nevertheless it won a prize offered by the *New Masses* and a publishing house, the John Day Company, for the best proletarian novel submitted in manuscript. There were ninety other novels in the contest, all of which remained unpublished and unregretted, except by their authors.

As for the published novels, most of them have essentially the same plot. A young man comes down from the hills to work in a cotton mill (or a veneer factory or a Harlan County mine). Like all his fellow workers except one, he is innocent of ideas about labor unionism or the class struggle. The exception is always an older man, tough but humorous, who keeps quoting passages from *The Communist Manifesto.* Always the workers are heartlessly oppressed, always they go out on strike, always they form a union with the older man as leader, and always the strike is broken by force of arms. The older man dies for the cause, like John the Baptist, but the young hero takes over his faith and mission. Escaping from Herod's soldiery—usually with a sturdy young woman who has also been converted—the hero swears that his life will be devoted to organizing the workers for greater battles to come.

Proletarian poetry was more diversified in manners and messages than proletarian fiction, but most of it has become almost as hard to read. I do not think that its failure in this country was due to lack of talent among the poets. Some of them had, or seemed to have, more than enough to carry them through; as take for example Sol Funaroff, who edited a little magazine called *Dynamo* and often signed himself Charles Henry Newman. He was a sallow, gangling, shy, but fervent young man with a gift for bold musical constructions and another gift for interrupting them with terse imperatives. Thus, he addressed the landlords of the world as a single watchdog with a hundred heads:

> Howl, Cerberus,
> hell-hound of war
> defend your hell,
> howl and hiss your hate.
>
> Of those who have power
> I have hatred.
>
> You, thieves of today,
> what can you steal
> from those whose possessions
> are in the future?

There was Edwin Rolfe, who preferred the older iambic measures. Often he celebrated the daily lives and festivals of Communist party members in blank verse that read smoothly and effectively, until the reader stumbled over a party slogan left standing like a baby carriage in his path. ("But why not put the slogans into your own words?" I asked him when he submitted a poem to the *New Republic.* "You don't understand," he said. "Slogans are the poetry of the new age.") There was Kenneth Fearing, who invented a style of his own that was halfway between Whitman and Damon Runyon. Often he wrote with a sardonic

chuckle, as when he recounted the death of a white-collar man:

> Denouement to denouement, he took a
>   personal pride in the certain, cer-
>   tain way he lived his own, private
>   life,
>   but nevertheless, they shut off his
>   gas; nevertheless, the bank fore-
>   closed; nevertheless, the landlord
>   called; nevertheless, the radio
>   broke;
> And twelve o'clock arrived just once
>   too often,
>   just the same he wore one grey
>   tweed suit, bought one straw hat,
>   drank one straight Scotch, walked
>   one short step, took one long look,
>   drew one deep breath,
>   just one too many,
> And wow he died as wow he lived,
>   going whop to the office, and blooie
>   home to sleep, and biff got mar-
>   ried, and bam had children, and
>   oof got fired,
>   zowie did he live and zowie did
>   he die. . . .

Fearing resigned from poetry toward the end of the decade and began writing detective stories. He died in middle age, as did Edwin Rolfe, and Funaroff died young, all three without giving more than a foretaste of what one had hoped they would do. Among the poets who once belonged to the proletarian school, Muriel Rukeyser—more of a student than the others and with more music in her language—was the only one whose work developed over the years, though not in its early direction. Revolutionary verse belonged to a period of revolutionary enthusiasm and would have declined in any case as the period drew closer to its end, but we are left to wonder why it wasn't better while it flourished—in this country, I mean; some of it was very good in England and France.

One reason may have been that although there were several talented poets in the proletarian school, there was no outstanding talent like that of Aragon and Eluard in France or Auden in England. The presence there of such leaders, too self-assured to be jealous of rivals, helped to form something more than a group of poets; one might call it a poets' community. Auden in particular—"Uncle Wiz," as he was called by the younger men—attracted others into the revolutionary school by his faults as well as his virtues, but chiefly by his power of invention, which inspired others to make inventions of their own: to emulate rather than imitate. We had no poet in the United States like the Auden of the early 1930s—not even Auden himself, when he finally came to New York.

But we did have a playwright who was admired and emulated, for a time, in almost the same fashion. I am thinking of Clifford Odets in 1935, the year of *Waiting for Lefty.*

He was then a young man of twenty-eight, the son of a Jewish immigrant, a Litvak, who had gone into the printing business and had mildly prospered over the years. Odets himself was born in Philadelphia and was reared mostly in the Bronx. After leaving high school at the age of fifteen, he had quarreled with his parents, who wanted him to be a businessman, and had lived on the edge of hunger while trying to become an actor. Twice he had speaking parts in Theatre Guild shows; then he became a member of the Group Theatre, a talented company that had been assembled by Harold Clurman and others without much thought of how it could survive. Somehow it struggled on from season to season, paying its actors when a show was running and at other times providing them with food and a place to sleep.

The Group was devoted solely to art, but many of its younger members had begun to dream of being political revolutionists. Odets, a lonely man, was one of these. In Boston during the lean theatrical season of 1934, he confided his dreams to Clurman, who had become his only close friend in the company. "He wanted comradeship," Clurman says. "He wanted to belong to the largest possible group of humble, struggling men prepared to make a great common effort to build a better world. . . . None of my homilies could have the slightest effect on him. He was driven by a powerful emotional impetus, like a lover on the threshold of an elopement."

The New Theatre League had announced a prize to be given for a one-act play without scenery, designed for workers to produce at their ordinary meeting places. Odets, as he explained to Clurman, had a plan for meeting these conditions. A few days later he locked himself in a hotel room and set to work on his play, which he finished in three nights. *Waiting for Lefty* could be performed in an hour and was afterward printed in less than thirty pages, but it gives the effect of having more than its actual length—and this for a simple reason, because it presents not only the emotions but the typical characters and most of the messages that were scattered through fifty longer works of the proletarian school.

> (As the curtain goes up we see a bare stage. On it are sitting six or seven men in a semi-circle. Lolling against the proscenium arch down left is a young man chewing a toothpick: a gunman. A fat man is talking directly to the audience. In other words he is the head of a union and the men ranged behind him are a committee of workers. . . .)

That first stage direction shows how Odets has solved the problem of writing a play that requires no scenery and almost no stage properties except six or seven folding chairs. He has simply borrowed the technique of the blackface minstrel show. His interlocutor is the union president, Harry Fatt, who also doubles as a villain, and the gunman is Mr. Bones. The committeemen "seated in interesting different attitudes" are the company of minstrels, each of whom will rise in turn to do his act. But Odets has introduced a brilliant variation into his minstrel show by preparing to draw the spectators into the action and by giving them parts to play. They must imagine themselves to be taxi drivers assembled in their union hall to hear arguments from both sides and finally vote on the question "Shall we strike?"

Fatt has been speaking against a strike. He tells the hackmen that they should trust their friend in the White House, who has been working day and night. "For who?" says a voice from the audience. Other voices cry, "We want Lefty! Where's Lefty?" Fatt pounds with his gavel and says, "That's what I wanna know. . . . You elected him chairman—where the hell did he disappear?" One of the committeemen, Joe Mitchell, rises and steps forward to defend the absent leader, who "didn't take no run-out powder," he says. "That Wop's got more guts than a slaughter house." Then the lights go out, except for a white spotlight that plays on Mitchell and his wife, Edna, as they act out their story.

Mitchell has been unable to support his family on what he earns by driving a cab. He comes home to find that most of his furniture, bought on the instalment plan, has been taken away and that his two children have gone to bed hungry. Edna tells him that she will sleep with another man, for money, unless the union goes on strike. "We gotta go out," Mitchell calls to the audience as the lights come on again. Next a very young committeeman, Sid Stein, tells his story in the same fashion. He and Florrie are desperately in love, but they can't get married on the money a hackman takes home. He talks about his brother, a college graduate who has enlisted in the Navy. "They'll teach him to point the guns the wrong way," he shouts—that is, point them at other workers instead of shooting the capitalists at home. A moment later Sid kneels in despair and sobs with his head in Florrie's lap. Blackout.

A third episode is played with the house fully lighted. Tom Clayton, an older man from Philadelphia, tells how a taxicab strike was broken there and the strikers put on a blacklist. "The time ain't ripe," he says. A voice from the audience—that of his own brother—exposes Clayton as a labor spy, and he escapes down the center aisle. Two more episodes follow, both preaching the message of anger and revolt. Then, as the lights come on after a last blackout, we hear the end of a speech by another committeeman, Agate Keller, who is proud of being a Red. Fatt and the gunman try to throw him out of the hall, but he breaks away, and his fellow workers protect him. With his shirt torn to rags, Agate faces the audience again and cries, giving the clenched-fist salute, "Don't wait for Lefty! He might never come. Every minute—"

A man runs down the center aisle and jumps on the stage. "Boys," he says, "they just found Lefty."

A confusion of voices from the audience: "What? What? Shhh. . . ."

> MAN. They found Lefty. . . .
>
> AGATE. Where?
>
> MAN. Behind the car barns with a bullet in his head!
>
> AGATE (*crying*). Hear it, boys, hear it? Hell, listen to me! Coast to coast! HELLO AMERICA! HELLO. WE'RE STORMBIRDS OF THE WORKING-CLASS. WORKERS OF THE WORLD. . . . OUR BONES AND BLOOD! And when we die they'll know what we did to make a new world! Christ, cut us up to little pieces. We'll die for what is right, put fruit trees

where our ashes are! *(To audience.)* Well, what's the answer?

ALL. STRIKE!

AGATE. LOUDER!

ALL. STRIKE!

AGATE and OTHERS on Stage. AGAIN!

ALL. STRIKE, STRIKE, STRIKE!!!

Waiting for Lefty won the prize for which it competed, and it was produced on January 5, 1935, at a Sunday benefit performance for the *New Theatre Magazine.* Harold Clurman, who was there, reports in his memoirs, *The Fervent Years,* that "a kind of joyous fervor seemed to sweep the audience toward the stage. The actors no longer performed; they were being carried along as if by an exultancy of communication such as I had never witnessed in the theatre before. . . . When the audience at the end of the play responded to the militant question from the stage: 'Well, what's the answer?' with a spontaneous roar of 'Strike! Strike!' it was something more than a tribute to the play's effectiveness, more even than a testimony of the audience's hunger for constructive social action. It was the birth cry of the thirties."

The cry, whatever its nature, resounded in all parts of the country. Very soon *Lefty* was being produced on other stages, and in union halls, and even on Broadway, where it ran for months. To make a full evening it had to be combined with another play by Odets, *Till the Day I Die,* which he wrote in one night after reading a news report from Germany in the *New Masses,* and which he should have had the good sense not to print in his collected works. But it was fairly effective on the stage, and at one time the combined bill was being played simultaneously in thirty-two American cities. Then *Lefty* went to England, where it roused the same mixture of anger and boundless hope. At one performance even H. G. Wells was heard to cry in a squeaky voice, "Strike! Strike!"

But I cannot agree with Clurman's notion that *Lefty* was the birth cry of a new era. Notwithstanding its immense popularity, it was not followed by many other effective plays for the workers' theater, and there would be none that united actors and audience in that same exultancy of communication. The mood of the left-wing writers had begun to change. Already their dream of uniting with the workers to fight for a new society on American soil was giving way to fears of a new world war that Hitler might win. The Russians, who had the same fears, were trying to win allies in the West. They let it be understood that their American followers should become more respectable and should direct more of their propaganda toward the middle classes. After 1935 one heard less and less about proletarian literature, a term that embodied the notion of class warfare. The new slogan for left-wing writers was the broader and less pugnacious one of socialist realism.

Looking back after thirty years, one suspects that *Lefty* for all its faults comes as close to being a classic as anything that emerged from the proletarian school. It is still easy to read and even to admire in a dispassionate way, but not

with enthusiasm. Like the proletarian novels and poems, it belongs to what one feels was a more innocent time. To recapture the effect of its first performance, either one would have to rewrite *Lefty* in terms of a new age or else one would have to reconstitute the audience that remembered five years of depression, the banks closing, the landlord at the door, and that shouted "Strike!" with a sense of release—then again, louder, "Strike! Strike!"—as it raised a thousand clenched fists.

> *Malcolm Cowley, "While They Waited for Lefty," in* The Saturday Review, *New York, Vol. XLVIII, No. 23, June 6, 1964, pp. 16-19, 61.*

Walter B. Rideout

[*In the following excerpt from his book* The Radical Novel in the United States, *Rideout discusses ideological and aesthetic differences among the leading proletarian literary critics, and examines the role played by literary magazines the* New Masses *and* Partisan Review *in the development of American proletarian literature.*]

One of the bits of news made in the thirties by *The New Masses,* never a magazine to avoid publicity, was the opportunity that it gave—once—for a group of writers to bite their critics. In the issue of July 3, 1934, appeared "Authors' Field Day: A Symposium on Marxist Criticism," containing replies from fourteen of the more than thirty authors who had been asked by the editors "*whether the criticism of their work in THE NEW MASSES had helped them and also what they expected from Marxist criticism.*" The replies showed that almost all of these writers, who were predominantly proletarian novelists, had been annoyed by the treatment accorded their own books, and that they found *New Masses* criticism in general to be seriously defective—vague, dogmatic, or "niggardly and patronizing." In an appended reply the editors admitted some faults, denied others in an aggrieved tone, and concluded that: "After all, revolutionary criticism, quite as much as revolutionary fiction, is a weapon in the class struggle." Granville Hicks, however, felt it necessary to append a supplementary rebuttal to Robert Cantwell and Josephine Herbst, his chief detractors. There were no more authors' field days, but the one of July, 1934, threw sudden light on a whole tangle of personal and ideological tensions which, pulling and hauling within the literary Left, soon was to reinforce the different and much more compelling cause for the swift decline of the proletarian novel.

What Eastman and Dell had been to the literary rebels of the middle 1910's, Granville Hicks was now trying to be to the revolutionary writers of the middle 1930's, and he did achieve wide reputation as an interpreter of the relation of literature to society by virtue of his enormous industry and fixed convictions, his authorship of the Marxist study *The Great Tradition,* and his strategic post of literary editor on *The New Masses* from its first appearance as a weekly at the opening of 1934 to the middle of the following year, when he began to give most of his time to writing a life of John Reed. Prior to 1934, the critical policy of *The New Masses* had continued to be characterized, though decreasingly so, by the impassioned but unsystematic revolutionism represented by the emotional Michael Gold. Hicks, who had been born in Exeter, New Hampshire, had studied at Harvard, and had been a divinity student and college English teacher, was of more disciplined, perhaps overdisciplined, intellect. Although he had contributed to the 1932 symposium on "How I Came to Communism" and had written briefly on John Reed, his first considerable piece of work for *The New Masses* was an article in the issue for February, 1933, entitled "The Crisis in American Criticism," which illustrates the then rather dogmatic cast of his mind. Objecting to the "oversimplification" of Calverton's approach in *The Liberation of American Literature* because it "reduces aesthetic categories . . . to economic categories," he proposes in this article that the Marxist critics "refine" their procedure by requiring three qualities of any writer: (1) that he be concerned with the effects of the class struggle; (2) that he present experience with "intensity"; (3) that his viewpoint be "that of the vanguard of the proletariat." Evidently believing that insistence on these three essentials would represent an advance over Calverton's critical system, he concludes that this approach would give "not only a standard by which to recognize the perfect Marxian novel, but also a method for the evaluation of all literature." Obviously, however, Hicks had not progressed beyond Calverton's position, which is indeed oversimplified; for the latter critic also demanded from the writer a Marxist viewpoint and likewise paid at least lip service to the requirement of technical excellence.

It is therefore not surprising to find that Hicks's Marxist history of post-Civil War American literature, *The Great Tradition,* which is still a pioneering book of some value, should be marred by almost as much oversimplification as was Calverton's volume. One of the more peculiar aspects of the book is that, although Hicks speaks of the tradition of social criticism as "the great tradition" of American literature, both the first and, to a somewhat less extent, the second editions describe it as primarily a record of failure, compromise, or half-success; yet the chief defect in the analysis and evaluation made of these writers is the "mechanical" manner with which Hicks applies his Marxism. He apparently assumes—incorrectly, from the standpoint of actual Marxist theory—that there is a direct and immediate connection between economics and literature, and proceeds to discuss each literary figure in terms of that writer's comprehension of the contemporary socioeconomic situation, the extent to which he understood the nature of the class struggle, and the amount of devotion he displayed toward the "common man." Almost completely on the basis of this discussion, Hicks then evaluates the artistic achievement of the individual writer. For example, among current writers he dismisses William Faulkner as standing in "danger of becoming a Sax Rohmer for the sophisticated"; while he argues that Farrell's *Judgment Day* "is vibrant with a kind of awareness that Farrell had not shown before," not because he had increased his creative skill or was completing his grand design, but simply because "he moved to the left at the time he was completing the Studs Lonigan trilogy." In the face of such consistent question-begging, it is interesting to reflect that the origi-

nal edition of *The Great Tradition* received more favorable notice among the academic reviewers than among the critics on the Left. E. A. Schachner in his long article for *The Windsor Quarterly,* "Revolutionary Literature in the United States Today," blasted Hicks as being a moralist rather than a Marxist; and the visiting Englishman John Strachey tempered praise with censure when, though describing the book as distinguished and its author as "the foremost Marxist literary critic of America," he remarked that Hicks "hardly seems to pay enough attention to the merits of writers as writers . . . "

Starting from unlike beginnings, the revolutionary emotionalism of Gold and the almost puritanical dogmatism of Hicks reached, in effect, the same conclusion: that literature can almost automatically be evaluated according to the degree to which it consciously illuminates the class struggle and explicitly affirms allegiance to the proletariat. As a result, although many other Marxist critics and reviewers were by no means in complete agreement with them, the pressure of two leading shapers of *New Masses* literary policy was generally toward persuading the proletarian novelists, the less self-confident of whom would listen, that they should . . . deal with the more obvious aspects of the class struggle, melodramatize their characters into good workers versus evil *bourgeoisie,* and end on a carefully affirmative note whether the internal logic of the novel demanded such a conclusion or its opposite. Were it not for "Authors' Field Day," one might be tempted to assign both Gold and Hicks a larger share of the blame for the deficiencies of the proletarian novel.

The New Masses, however, could hardly be considered an

Granville Hicks.

organ for the literary theories of one man, and Hicks, perhaps because of his exposed position, found himself under sharp fire in his own magazine and other left-wing periodicals, particularly in *Partisan Review,* where Philip Rahv, William Phillips, and others sniped scornfully at the Hicksian line. Plans for *Partisan Review* as the voice of the John Reed Club of New York had been begun in the fall of 1933, and the first issue of this "Bi-Monthly of Revolutionary Literature," financed by John Strachey's public lecture on Literature and Dialectical Materialism, was published in February, 1934. Like most little magazines, it opened with a manifesto, this one affirming loyalty to the current revolutionary line of the Party, but insisting that the main concern of the editors would be with literature. The magazine would attack the literature of the political Right, of course; at the same time—and here was the significant point—it would "resist every attempt to cripple our literature by narrow-minded, sectarian theories and practices." That the manifesto was to be carried seriously into action was demonstrated in the same first issue by Rahv's review of Hemingway's *Winner Take Nothing,* when Rahv, while dismissing the author's subject matter as useless to the proletarian novelist, declared that the "cluster of formal creative means" which Hemingway, a "bourgeois" artist, had evolved might very well be used as a corrective to the sentimentality of much proletarian fiction.

From its first issue *Partisan Review* had become the base of operations for one side in a literary civil war which, now hidden, even sometimes from the contestants themselves, now open and violent, had been going on among left-wing writers since the very beginning of the thirties. Put simply, the cause of the war was a basic division of attitude toward the creative process, a division made public as early as 1930 by the announcement in the July number of *The New Masses* of a debate to be held between Joshua Kunitz and Michael Gold under the auspices of the (New York) John Reed Club on the subject, "Can We Learn Anything from the Bourgeois Writers?" The position each debater would take was conveniently summarized in advance. Kunitz would assert: "Are we forever doomed to relish the flat, grey stuff dished out to us by so many of our writers? We must learn from the bourgeoisie just as the bourgeoisie had once learned from the aristocracy." To this Gold would reply: "Nothing but academic banalism. There is no 'style'—there is only clarity, force, truth in writing. If a man has something new to say, as all proletarian writers have, he will learn to say it clearly in time: if he writes long enough." Neatly objectified as debate, the split, then, was between those who with Gold considered content more important than form and those who with Kunitz considered form to be quite as important as content. . . . Gold and Hicks clearly favored content; those in control of *Partisan Review*—the John Reed Club itself was deeply divided—quite as clearly did not.

By the time its third issue had appeared (June-July, 1934), *Partisan Review* had further complicated the situation by conceiving of itself as speaking for what it called the "Centrist" element among left-wing writers. In an article, "Problems and Perspectives in Revolutionary Literature," Wallace Phelps and Philip Rahv first mounted a major attack on the sectarian theories and practices of the proletarian writers themselves, practices which they now dubbed "Leftism" by literary analogy with Lenin's political polemic against extremists within his own party, *"Left-Wing" Communism, an Infantile Disorder.* "Leftism," they argued, consisted in arbitrarily imposing radical doctrine on awkward literary forms and stemmed "from the understanding of Marxism as mechanical materialism." Since literature properly makes its appeal to the sensibility, "political content should not be isolated from the rest of experience but must be merged into the creation of complete personalities and the perception of human relations in their physical and sensual immediacy. The class struggle must serve as a premise, not as a discovery." Then, shifting from primarily literary to primarily political categories, Phelps and Rahv concentrated a secondary attack on a new, opposing right-wing tendency within the Left itself, a tendency represented by writers who accepted the revolutionary philosophy only halfheartedly. So *Partisan Review* believed itself to hold a middle way which combined devotion to revolution and devotion to literature.

That such a "Centrist" group did exist, and powerfully, was in effect admitted by Joseph Freeman in *The New Masses* for September 11, 1934, though, like the public relations man he has become since leaving the Party, he asserted that unity, not difference, characterized the Left. Noting with relief that fellow travelers were being accepted far more readily into the Communist movement than they had been even as recently as the previous year, he warned against the danger that, not yet sufficiently educated in Marxism, they might actually swing the movement too far to the Right. Then he proceeded optimistically to pronounce nonexistent the conflict between what *Partisan Review* now called "Leftist" and "Centrist."

> The writers and critics who today are in or near the revolutionary movement may be divided roughly into two groups: those who have spent the last ten years primarily in the movement, and those who, during the same period have been engaged primarily in perfecting their craft. The economic crisis has united these two groups politically; on all burning questions of the day they fight side by side. It is no longer necessary to convince able craftsmen like Isidor Schneider or John Howard Lawson that it is not only permissible but obligatory for poets and playwrights to raise their voices on behalf of the struggling working-class . . . On the other hand, it is no longer necessary to convince writers who developed in the movement in isolation, during years when loyalty was the primary test, that the revolutionary writer must perfect his craft, that he must be not only revolutionary but a writer.

> The merging of these two forces promises much for the development of a revolutionary literature in the United States.

As Freeman must privately have been aware, however, the two forces had merged only in the area of politics, not in that of craft. Writer after writer appearing in *Partisan Review* attacked the "placard" or "slogan" method in fiction, insisted that a revolutionary viewpoint must grow out of rather than be imposed on a literary work, and demanded that the technical advances developed by bourgeois artists be adapted to the needs of proletarian writers. Despite Freeman's attempt at reconciliation, the struggle went on through 1934, "Centrist" arrayed against "Leftist"; and gradually the former began to gather strength throughout all the John Reed Clubs. By the end of the year *Partisan Review* could publish a triumphant communiqué on the results of the Second John Reed Club Conference, announcing that the writers' commission had unanimously denounced "Leftism": "Together they showed that a living revolutionary literature could grow only out of genuine aesthetic recreation of the class struggle." Discussion at the meetings, the communiqué went on rather smugly, indicated that "*Partisan Review* was exerting a wide influence among the young writers."

During the early months of 1935, in preparation for an event shortly to be described, the "Centrists" carried the fight into the strongest enemy position when a whole series of protests against "Leftism" began appearing in *The New Masses* itself. One of the first was Edwin Seaver's " 'Caesar or Nothing,' " which argued that: "Some of our middle-class critics have gone proletarian with such headlong momentum that today they are already several miles to the left of themselves."

> From this infantile disorder of "Leftism," this romantic demand for Caesar or nothing, derives that schematicism whose alternate names are dogmatism and sterility and which would seek to eliminate objective realities by denying them. In the field of creative work—let us say, the novel—such schematicism takes the form of offering ideas or slogans without benefit of the creative act; without, that is, clothing such ideas and slogans in flesh and blood and giving them an emotional and human propulsion so that they come to life by their own right, and not by fiat of the author's. In the field of criticism, this schematicism takes the alternate form of wish-fulfillment or denial, the attempt to deduce certain political "truths" from the novel, which are not supported by the facts or, on the other hand, the tendency to kill a book because it does not bring out certain desired "truths" which fall outside the scope of the particular work.

And Horace Gregory, although insisting that he looked for guidance to the Communist Party, went so far as to object that any revolutionary work of art was now expected to conform to the Party line of the moment.

> I believe that all important works of art *do* change in meaning, but within Left cultural groups, aesthetic standards undergo daily revision . . . Here I would say that the instrument of dialectical materialism is being made to function as a political tool, not as a standard by which we measure works of art.

The outstanding exploit of the whole campaign against the "Leftism" of Gold, Hicks, and their followers came, however, a whole year later when James Farrell published *A Note on Literary Criticism* (1936), the only extended discussion of Marxist aesthetics written from a Marxist standpoint in the United States during the thirties. Partly,

perhaps, because several extremist reviewers had called for the display of more "class-consciousness" in the un-class-conscious characters of whom he wrote, Farrell had concluded that the critics of the Hicks school were perpetuating error and should be exposed before they could do further damage. Yet much more than personal pique and a taste for disputation went into *A Note on Literary Criticism;* for, although the author rejects any claim to being professional either as critic or Marxist, his book proves him to be honestly concerned with his subject and eager for truth. Considering the eminent position held by the object of his special displeasure, it also shows him to be a man of considerable intellectual courage.

The book constitutes a simultaneous attack and defense. The attack is directed against both "revolutionary sentimentalism," as represented by Gold, and "mechanical Marxism," as represented by Hicks. Since each of these two "Leftist" tendencies in literary criticism has, in its extreme emphasis on the functional ("use-value") aspect of literature, ignored the aesthetic aspect, they have together, Farrell argues, kept Marxist criticism weak, because they substitute measurement for judgment. Hence the critic's task, which is ultimately one of judgment, of evaluation, has been avoided. Nowhere is this more obvious than in the treatment accorded "bourgeois" literature. Farrell cites chapter and verse in order to demonstrate that Marx himself would accept an important primary conclusion: "Certain works of literature possess a human worth and a carry-over power which endow them with a relatively inherent persistence-value after they have been divorced from the material conditions and the society out of which they have been created." In literature, unlike politics or economics, the categories of "bourgeois" and "proletarian" must be considered descriptive, rather than normative; for if all true works of art produced by any society have "persistence-value," the categories "are not the basis of value judgment *per se.*" One cannot, in other words, condemn a novel, as the "Leftists" do, merely on the ground that it is written from a non-Marxist point of view.

If the extremist critics have been obtuse about non-Marxist literature, the effect of their "mechanistic methods" on Marxist writing calls for even greater indictment.

> First, writers have been led to create characters out of concepts—"the general"—instead of from life with the clarifying assistance that concepts provide. The result of this has been obviousness. The characters often illustrate concepts that have not been soundly applied. Second, such work has been unduly encouraged and praised, so that it has been tacitly set up as a literary model to be followed. In order to establish such unrewarding writing as a model, critics and reviewers have gone a step farther. They have utilized such models and the concepts they present, in order to diminish the reputation and the understanding of novels that do not conform to the standards governing this type. The novels thus regarded as models have generally restated ideas that have been repeatedly developed in books, articles, pamphlets, and editorials. In other words, they are a rehash, contributing no new understanding, giving no concrete sense of

life and no help in the application of the concepts. Abstractions have merely been allowed to walk in at the wrong place.

Nor have the extremists assisted their case by arguing that all literature is propaganda. Although any literary work must ultimately spring from an ideological point of view and can certainly influence a reader, nevertheless a novel, for example, is created by a far different process than is a strike bulletin, it must be worked out by its own inner logic, and it affects the reader, not in a simple, but in a very complex way. By, in effect, lumping the novel and the strike bulletin together as "weapons in the class struggle," the mechanistic critics have failed to distinguish properly among categories and among functions. It is this failure to distinguish and then to judge which is leading revolutionary literature into confusion and sterility rather than into clarity and new life.

If Farrell's own statement of the critic's function is not strikingly original, if his dissection of the deficiencies of proletarian literature and criticism is, stylistically speaking, performed as much with a meat ax as with a scalpel, still the dissection itself was a thorough one. The extent to which he drew critical blood may, in fact, be gauged by the harshness of Isidor Schneider's review of the book in *The New Masses* and Hicks's "reply" to that review in an article entitled, with something less than accuracy, "In Defense of James Farrell." But Farrell had his supporters as well as opponents, and one of those intramural battles typical of the literary Left burned for weeks in the columns of *The New Masses,* reaching a climax, but not an end, in the issue for August 15, which contained, under the heading "The Farrell Controversy"; (1) a reply by Farrell to Schneider's review; (2) Schneider's rejoinder to Farrell's reply; (3) a letter from a subscriber defending Farrell; and (4) a communication from Morris U. Schappes attacking Farrell's "Mr. Hicks: Critical Vulgarian" in the April number of *The American Spectator.* The most important point which the controversy emphasized was that a sizable number of radical novelists and younger left-wing critics approved Farrell's attitude toward the creative process. . . .

> Walter B. Rideout, "Literature and Politics,"
> in his The Radical Novel in the United States,
> 1900-1954: Some Interrelations of Literature
> and Society, *Cambridge, Mass.: Harvard University Press, 1956, pp. 225-54.*

AMERICAN PROLETARIAN LITERATURE AND THE AMERICAN COMMUNIST PARTY

Philip Rahv

[*A Russian-born American critic, Rahv was a prominent and influential member of the Marxist movement in American literary criticism. For thirty-five years he served as co-editor of the prestigious literary journal Par-*tisan Review. *In the following essay, Rahv analyzes the relationship between American Communism and American proletarian literature.*]

There is hardly a literary critic in America who has not at one time or another taken a hand in the controversy concerning proletarian literature. Few of the contributors to this historic controversy, however, were aware of its concrete political background and perspectives. What was new about the proletarian literary movement was its emphasis on political and social relations; and in approaching this movement the critics, it is true, discussed the connection between art and politics and between art and society. But they failed to notice that it is not these general and abstract connections but primarily its specific political history which explained proletarian literature.

Like other types of literary creation, this literature undoubtedly reflected class interests, needs, and attitudes; yet unlike other types, it reflected such interests, needs, and attitudes through the coördinated medium of a political party. That party is the Communist Party, which alone of all parties in the labor movement displayed any solicitude for proletarian literature—a solicitude, needless to say, in full measure returned by its recipient.

It is impossible, in my opinion, to understand the development of this literature, its rise and fall, without understanding its relation to the Communist Party. There are other factors, of course, but all of them have been modified by this one fundamental relation. Thus the Marxist doctrine, for example, whose existence antedates that of the Communist International but in whose name the Communist literary critics habitually speak, has been generally taken as the theoretical basis of proletarian literature and its source of values. In identifying their own views—that is, the views of their party—with those of Marxism, these critics constructed a strategic mystification which had important consequences. One can place most of the books and essays dealing with Marxism and literature under the heading of this mystification, for what they actually deal with is literature and the particular interpretation of Marxism held by the official party. As such it is a perfectly legitimate subject, but the writers who use it should be aware of its real nature and hence of its limitations. Another result has been that it is the Marxist philosophy and not specifically the Communist Party which has been held responsible for the excesses and crudities of proletarian literature and which has drawn the fire of its opponents; and yet there are Marxist thinkers of reputation who believe that the theory behind this literature has nothing in common with revolutionary thought. Manifestly, a subject as intricate and contradictory as proletarian literature needs more than a purely theoretical analysis. Let us look first to its political history.

To revolutionary optimists the triumph of the left-wing in American literature seemed inevitable in the early nineteen-thirties. And, on the whole, in looking back at those years, the expectation of this triumph appears to have been based on plausible enough grounds. At face value most of the factors entering into the situation were indeed favorable to a realignment of letters along radical lines.

The suffering imposed on the bulk of the population by the

economic crisis elevated the "common man" to a martyr-dom that almost overnight integrated him into the sympathies of the literary artist. Humanized by the calamities that befell him, the "common man" now began figuring in the imaginative scheme with positive force. Notwithstanding the contempt heaped upon him for many years as a mobster and a boob, he now emerged as the ideal-carrier of fictions, invocations in verse, and critical manifestoes. In the part of petty beneficiary of a prosperous and soulless materialism he had long typified the negation of values; cast in the rôle of at once a piteous victim and militant rebel he typified their revival. And his apotheosis was consummated when writers made a practice of detaching him from his ordinary human environment in order to place him within "the glorious collectivity of the embattled proletariat."

A further causative factor was provided, of course, by the exhaustion of the literary modes current in the 'twenties. Being for the most part expressions of disillusionment with society, these modes could not cope with the demands for its reconstruction. The various regional programs, designed as they were for local uses, appeared inconsequential in the face of a national crisis involving profound spiritual and material transformations. The proletarian program, on the other hand, invoking history in all its tenses to confirm its ambitions, laid claim to a universality and radicalism of outlook poles asunder from the restricted and polite values of the past.

Furthermore, a political party existed in America, the Communist Party, which made haste to identify this literary program as a part of its own larger perspective and which welcomed into its political home all writers wishing to realize in practice their conversion to the revolutionary cause. This party, at that time virtually in sole occupation of the Marxist arena, thus became the organizer of proletarian literature and its ultimate court of appeal. The left literary magazines were published under its auspices or edited by its members. It appointed political commissars to supervise the public relations of the new literary movement and to minister to its doctrinal health. It furnished it with an initial audience and with an organizational base; and, finally, it conditioned the writers that had come under its control to conceive of the Soviet Union, its own source of strength and seat of highest authority, as the living embodiment of their hopes for socialism.

Nominally, despite the elaborate and often weirdly sectarian theories proclaimed by individual members, the program of this literary movement was quite simple and so broad in its appeal as to attract hundreds of writers in all countries. It can be reduced to the following formula: *the writer should ally himself with the working class and recognize the class struggle as the central fact of modern life.* Beyond that he was promised the freedom to choose his own subjects, deal with any characters, and work in any style he pleased. The Communist Party was seldom mentioned directly in connection with this formula of conversion. Granville Hicks's book, *The Great Tradition,* was in effect nothing more than a historical argument for the realization of this formula by American literature, whose libera-

tion from "confusion, superficiality, and despair" was predicted as the reward of compliance.

This formula, however, despite its deceptive simplicity, is actually a complicated political mechanism. Its abstract political meaning conceals multiple confusions that proved to be as beneficial to the fortunes of the Communist Party as they were pernicious in their consequences for literature. In the first place, it should be noted that this formula is empty of aesthetic principle and advocates no particular aesthetic direction; second, it establishes no defensible frontiers, so to speak, between art and politics—it merges them; third, it draws no distinctions between the politics of writing in a *generic and normative sense* and the politics of an individual writer in a particular historical period; and lastly, it fails to define in what way a writer's alliance with the working class is or is not an alliance with any particular political party of that class. Through this formula the writer was actually offered a contract of an unprecedented character, but all the specific stipulations were left to be written in after he had attached his signature to it. The principal mystification involved in this transaction consisted of the fact that while the writer thought he was allying himself with the working class, in reality he was surrendering his independence to the Communist Party, which for its own convenience had fused the concepts of party and class.

The Communist critics, sometimes deliberately and sometimes through ignorance, cultivated these mystifications, for it is with their aid that they succeeded in stuffing the creativity of the left into the sack of political orthodoxy. In their criticism, opinions as to the literary merit of a work of art were by no means ruled out, but the fundamental criteria concerned themselves with the author's loyalty to the working class and his interpretation of the class struggle. And it is exactly at that point, of course, that the literary critic resigned in favor of his party. Loyalty to the working class? Interpretation of the class struggle? What are these if not political matters, and who is better versed in political matters than the party under whose patronage proletarian literature was developing? No critic, regardless how learned in Marxism, could possibly presume to pit his own judgment against the party's political sway and reputed infallibility in the reading of the law and the prophets. To impugn the party's political authority meant to court excommunication. Thus it turned out that a novel or a play was certificated "revolutionary" only when its political ideas—existing or latent—corresponded to those of the party. And since the party had long ago awarded itself a monopoly of *correct* politics, the seemingly liberal formula that had enticed so many recruits was soon filled with a content altogether at variance with its manifest meaning. If not in origin then in function it became no more than an administrative tool, a political contrivance for imposing party views on critical and creative writing. What we were witnessing was a miniature version of the process which in Russia had resulted in the replacement of the dictatorship of the proletariat by the dictatorship of the Communist Party. Within the brief space of a few years the term "proletarian literature" was transformed into a euphemism for a Communist Party literature which tenaciously upheld a fanatical faith identifying the party with the working class, Stalinism with Marxism, and the Soviet Union with socialism. The "literary movement" droned these beliefs into its members with the result that instead of revolutionary writing—which may mean a thousand and one things depending upon time, place, and individual bias—an internationally uniform literature was created whose main service was the carrying out of party assignments. For strategic purposes, of course, the official spokesmen found it advisable to conceal their essentially factional inspiration and narrow standards under a variety of pseudonyms designed to give the appearance of flexibility, objectivity, freedom from control, etc. However (and I think I can allow myself the dogmatism of saying this), unless we understand the relation of these pseudonyms to their referents we can learn very little about left writing in America, or, for that matter, in any other country.

It is essential to understand the difference between the literature of a class and the literature of a party. Whereas the literature of a class represents an enormous diversity of levels, groupings, and interests, the literature of a party is in its very nature limited by utilitarian objectives. It cannot properly be called literature, for it tends to become a vehicle for the dissemination of special policies and views; a party is too small a unit of social life to serve as the base for the formation of a spiritual and artistic superstructure. Expressing the historic being and consciousness of an entire sector of society, the literature of a class accumulates organic traditions and norms. Confident of its past and frequently of its future as well, it permits a free exchange and conflict of feelings and ideas. A true class literature constantly strives and partially succeeds in overcoming and transcending its given social limitations; its aim is the all-human pattern and image, though this aim may be frustrated by historical needs of the opposite character. A party, however, being merely the political instrument of a class and usually of only one or several groupings in that class, must necessarily reproduce itself in literature in all its narrowness and rigidity.

But there are classes and classes, as there are parties and parties. Not all classes are capable of producing an art and literature of their own. The conception of a proletarian literature relies for its defense on abstract and formal analogies between the proletariat and the bourgeoisie. Literature is the outgrowth of a whole culture, one of its inseparable parts and manifestations. A class which has no culture of its own can have no literature either. Now in all class societies it is the ruling class alone which possesses both the material means and the self-consciousness—independent, firmly rooted, and elaborated—that are the prerequisites of cultural creation. As an oppressed class, the proletariat, in so far as it is a cultural consumer, lives on the leavings of the bourgeoisie. It has neither the means nor the consciousness necessary for cultural self-differentiation. Its conditions of existence allow it to produce certain limited and minor cultural forms, such as urban folklore, language variations, etc.; but it is powerless to intervene in science, philosophy, art, and literature. Neither is it admissible, for the purpose of proving the possibility of a proletarian culture, to compare the proletariat of today to the bourgeoisie of yesterday, when the latter

was itself oppressed. While the oppression of the bourgeoisie by the feudal regime was chiefly political, the modern property relations dominate the proletariat in a *total* fashion. Because it was already an owning class, disposing of considerable wealth and leisure, the third estate could begin creating cultural values even before its political emancipation. The proletariat, on the other hand, before it can achieve the freedom that participation in culture requires, must first institute changes in society which include its own abolition. And if that historic task is ever accomplished, it will not be the proletariat—which will then no longer exist—but a classless and stateless humanity that will shape the new culture in its own image.

Virtually all the theorists of proletarian culture are fetishists of ideology, which they naïvely equate with and substitute for culture. And since they believe that in Marxism the proletariat possesses a distinct and separate ideology of its own, they conclude that all that is lacking for the creation of an art and literature of the working class is a plan and the will to carry it into effect. But the truth is that Marxism is not an ideology *of* the working class—it is an ideology *for* the working class brought to it from without. "The history of all countries," Lenin wrote in *What Is To Be Done?*, "bears witness that the working class is capable of developing only a trade-unionist consciousness. . . . that is, the conviction of the necessity of joining together in unions, of conducting a struggle against the employer, of demanding from the government this or that legislative measure in the interests of the workers, etc. The socialist doctrine (Marxism), however, has proceeded from the philosophical, historical, and economic theories which originated with educated representatives of the owning classes, the intellectuals." Now inasmuch as proletarian literature, by the innumerable definitions of it given by its own theorists, is nothing more than the socialist doctrine transferred to the creative sphere, it follows that it is a literature produced outside the proletariat and brought to it from without. But it is impossible to conceive of a literature issuing fullblown from a doctrine—it must also have some kind of concrete political basis. That political basis is none other than the Communist Party, which conceives of itself as the guardian of the socialist doctrine and its organizational embodiment.

This analysis is confirmed by an examination of the works which the official critics have accepted as proletarian. Whether we choose Soviet novels by orthodox authors like Gladkov, Fadeyev, and Sholokhov; or recent "militant" works by the Frenchmen Aragon and Malraux; or the revolutionary prose and verse of American writers like Robert Cantwell, Fielding Burke, Michael Gold, Clifford Odets, John Howard Lawson, Albert Maltz, Jack Conroy, Ben Field, Isidor Schneider, Josephine Herbst, Kenneth Fearing, Muriel Rukeyser, Edwin Rolfe, etc.—in none of them shall we find an imagination or sensibility which is not of a piece with some variety—either plebeian or aristocratic but mostly the former—of the bourgeois creative mode. It is purely in a doctrinal-political fashion that these works differ from "the literature of another class." But even the doctrine, the one distinctive element in it, is not proletarian in any real sense; into literature as into the proletariat it is imported via a political party by "educated representatives of the owning classes" (Lenin)—the Marxist intellectuals.

It is clear that proletarian literature is the literature of a party disguised as the literature of a class. This fact explains both the speed of its development and the speed of its disintegration. Its peculiar artificiality, the devious and volatile nature of its critical principles, its artistic chaos plus its political homogeneity and discipline, its uses as a cover for organizational activities—all these are explained by the periodic shifts and changes of the "party line." The growth of proletarian literature in this country between 1930 and 1935 is precisely coincident with the growth of the party during that period, when its policy was ultra-left and opposed to any united or people's fronts. At that time the party saw the revolution as an immediate possibility, and its literature was extreme in its leftism, aggressive, declamatory, prophetic. It was intolerant of all other schools of writing and proclaimed itself to be the sole heir of the literary creations of the ages. Its practitioners were persuaded by the party-critics to turn out sentimental idealizations of the worker-types they were describing in their stories and plays. These works, most of which were quite crude as literary art, presented a silly and distorted picture of America. Despite good revolutionary intentions, their political content was schematic. Instead of giving a realistic and individualized portrayal of social experience, their authors *inferred* its characteristics by speculative methods from the theses of the Comintern about the "world-situation"; and since the Comintern had declared at that time that the workers of all countries were ready to seize power and establish socialism, they endeavored to demonstrate that the Comintern was right by showing "reality" behaving according to its directives. The better writers, of course, such as Josephine Herbst, Grace Lumpkin, Robert Cantwell, and Kenneth Fearing, avoided these fantasies by sticking to what they knew. But proletarian literature as a whole, here and abroad, followed the party in predicting and celebrating the victory of the revolution in a period when it was actually losing every battle.

At present this literature is withering away because the party no longer needs it. Since 1935 the party has acquired respectability by reconstructing itself on a reformist and patriotic basis. Having abandoned its revolutionary position and allied itself with liberal capitalism, its cultural requirements are altogether different from what they were in the past. Everything within its orbit, including the proletarian literary movement, which separates it from other reformist and left-bourgeois tendencies in being done away with in order to expedite the "building of a democratic front." That the political party which fathered proletarian literature should now be devouring it is no cause for astonishment. A certain type of internal cannibalism—witness the Moscow trials—is intrinsic to its history and necessary for the fulfillment of its peculiar tasks.

The period of the proletarian mystification of American letters is now definitely over. To say this, however, is by no means equivalent to saying that in recent years the official Left has declined in size and in influence. On the contrary, there are more writers today extending active political support to the Communist Party than ever in the past.

To read the long and diversified lists of names signed to some of the appeals or petitions issued by the League of American Writers, an organization controlled by members and sympathizers of that party, is to realize that in such centers as New York, Chicago, and Hollywood a large sector of literary opinion is in substantial agreement with the policies of the American section of the Comintern. Nothing could be more naïve, however, than to equate the popularity of these policies among writers with the triumph of the proletarian literary program. The actual process is in the opposite direction.

The official left is now engaged in reëstablishing that dichotomy between the writer as citizen and the writer as artist which it once decried as a source of bourgeois infection. It has discovered how to take advantage of a dualism between art and life that in the past it pretended to find intolerable. Why examine what a writer puts into his books when the real profit is derived from regulating his political conduct as an individual to conform with that of the Communist Party. The official Left is today primarily interested not in literature but in *authors;* from them it seeks to obtain public statements approving its political program on current issues—a favor which it is only too glad to reciprocate by guaranteeing to the works of the obliging literary men immunity from its "Marxist" criticism. (In the case of the more prominent literary personalities the rate of reciprocation is, of course, much higher. Eulogies, such as have been provided for a recent novel by Ernest Hemingway, are expected and delivered.) Thus the narrow, one-sided truism of Granville Hicks and his colleagues defining *art* as a weapon becomes in practice the many-sided opportunism of converting the *artist* into one. This takes the form of extracting from him surplus publicity-value by putting his public reputation to work in political testimonials which directly or indirectly refer back to the Communist Party or any of its agencies. Such political habits are in themselves sufficient to render insincere the attempt to introduce a radical content into literature, but in the present surreptitious abandonment of this attempt these habits are only of minor importance. If at present proletarian writing in this country is in the last stages of dissolution, it is largely because it is under political orders to commit suicide.

The experienced literary politicians who once acted as the apostles of proletarian literature would doubtless vehemently deny that they are in the midst of abolishing it. But that is exactly how their party code requires them to behave. It is now no longer news, except to fanatical Stalinists and reactionaries bent on maintaining a red scare, that the Comintern has put away its revolutionary aims and embarked on national-reformist policies; and it is no friendlier to revolutionary ideas in the cultural than in the political sphere. Its literary adherents are, of course, lagging behind the "party line." A cultural lag is to be expected. All sorts of amusing inconsistencies and atavisms are to be observed in the pages of the Stalinist literary periodicals. In a purely academic way the small fry are still permitted to play with Marxist notions. The literary movement as a whole, however, is being quickly dissolved in the body of American writing. It is a long time since we have read a programmatic article on proletarian "aesthetics" in the *New Masses,* which has replaced its former standards of evaluation with the abstract categories of "progress" and "reaction." This year only one novel and two volumes of verse were published in America that follow in any appreciable degree the accepted patterns of the proletarian literary mode.

In fiction the themes of unemployment and union organization have persisted. Being objectively present in the material of the social-minded writer, they cannot be arbitrarily cast aside; and neither does the politics of reformism make such a casting aside necessary. The question relates entirely to the political treatment such themes receive. If once, in following the official perspective, the proletarian writer transformed his positive characters—who invariably were either unemployed or on strike—into revolutionaries performing some act that symbolized the overthrow of the system of private property, today he would have to resolve their problems by attaching them to some activity of the New Deal. The new Communist orthodoxy having decreed that peace, progress, and prosperity are possible under capitalism, the writer is unable to revolutionize his characters in any concrete sense without violating the precepts of the political faith of which, presumably, he is a loyal adherent. To be really logical, the unfortunate practitioner of the "party line" in fiction would have to substitute one of the President's fireside chats or a resolution for an immediate declaration of war on Japan for those visions of proletarian upheaval and the ultra-future of the classless society which nourished his inspiration in the past.

There are certain forms of demagogy, however, which a medium as palpable as fiction—unless it degenerates to the level of pulp propaganda—excludes by its very nature. Thus the media of art, if only by that fact alone, prove their superior humanity to the media of politics. The kind of casuistry which may easily pass for truth within the pseudo-context of a political speech or editorial, will be exposed in all its emptiness once it is injected into the real context of a living experience, such as the art of fiction strives to represent. The novel is the preëminent example of an experiential art; and to falsify the experiential terms in which it realizes itself is infinitely more difficult than to falsify abstract reasoning. Whereas politics summarizes social experience, the novel subjects it to an empiric analysis. Hence the test of the novel is more rigorous, less at the mercy of manipulation and rhetorical depravity. Proletarian fiction cannot *maintain its identity* while following its political leadership into an alliance with capitalist democracy. The only alternative for a school of writing that finds itself in such extraordinary straits is to abdicate. As citizens the members of that school are still moving within the orbit of their party, but what they write is increasingly becoming a matter that concerns no one but themselves—and the individual reader and critic, of course. The orientation towards capitalist democracy has deprived the proletarian writers of those political values which alone distinguished them from the nonproletarians. If historically American literature can be said to possess an ideology that generalizes it socially, it is none other than the ideology of capitalist democracy; and it is hardly necessary to develop a proletarian literature so that it may practice

ideologically what American literature has been practicing virtually since its inception.

The other wings of cultural expression dominated by the Stalinist party are in a similar state of disintegration. That the revolutionary theater is dead no one doubts. As for Marxist criticism, it finds itself with less and less work on its hands. All that the Marxist critics can do is write conventional pieces with a slight social edge or else compose political polemics against the "counter-revolutionary fascist-aiding Trotskyites." These trenchant compositions, however, have as little in common with an analysis of art or letters as Trotskyism has with fascism. It is the absence of enemies, of course, which determines this Marxist idleness. If your critical sphere is American writing—in which there are as yet very few traces of fascism—and you have accepted the notion that your only real enemies are the fascists and that with everyone else it is necessary to coöperate, then to all intents and purposes your function as a Marxist critic has been abolished. What is left, of course, is the party-task of misrepresenting and assaulting the work of those left writers who have repudiated Russian "socialism" and the Comintern. Michael Gold, for instance, has recently arraigned John Dos Passos before the bar of "progress" and convicted him of writing nothing but *merde.* But such critical activities are exercises in the art of abuse rather than in the art of criticism.

In the last chapter of *The Great Tradition,* revised in 1935, Granville Hicks wrote that "if revolutionary writers should become convinced, on adequate or inadequate grounds, that capitalism could survive, that revolution is unnecessary or impossible, they would cease to be revolutionary writers." Given the political milieu in which Mr. Hicks works, it was rash of him to commit himself to so definite a formula, which has the virtue of proving the statement that revolutionary literature, at least as Mr. Hicks conceived it in 1935, is no longer in existence. But it passed away without the benefit of any kind of convictions, either "on adequate or inadequate grounds," on the part of Mr. Hicks' "revolutionary writers." An episode in the history of totalitarian communism, it will be remembered as a comedy of mistaken identities and the tragedy of a frustrated social impulse in contemporary letters.

Philip Rahv, "Proletarian Literature: A Political Autopsy," in The Southern Review, *Louisiana State University, Vol. IV, No. 3, Winter, 1939, pp. 616-28.*

Arthur C. Ferrari

[*In the following excerpt, Ferrari discusses the relationship between politics and literature in proletarian writings of the 1930s, paying particular attention to the role of the Communist Party-sponsored John Reed Clubs in the development of proletarian authors.*]

Editor Michael Gold's "Go Left, Young Writers," in the January 1929 issue of *New Masses,* informed his readers that a new writer was appearing. The new writer, writing in an instinctual and unpolished style, was about 21 years old, of working-class origin, and himself a worker. In that same issue Martin Russak, a young author, discussed Jack

London as America's first proletarian writer and provided a partial definition of the proletarian writer: "A real proletarian writer must not only write about the working class, he must be read by the working class." Furthermore, a good proletarian writer must possess "bitter hatred, absolute class solidarity, and revolutionary passion."

In the October issue of *New Masses,* on the eve of the Great Crash, Henry George Weiss complained that much of the poetry in *New Masses* could not be understood by ordinary workers. Perhaps a solution to the problem raised by Weiss would be provided by an organization that announced its founding in the following (November 1929) issue of the magazine. About 50 people had joined together to form the John Reed Club of New York. The announcement stated: that "The purpose of the club is to bring closer all creative workers; to maintain contact with the American labor movement," much as the club's namesake had in an earlier era.

The espousal by Gold and the others of a proletarian literature in 1929 and 1930 reflected a set of ideas that were to influence American intellectuals, literature, and literary criticism throughout the tumultuous decade that followed. *New Masses* reflected the ideology and fortunes of the U.S. Communist Party, as did the John Reed Clubs, the party's affiliated literary organizations. The Communist Party's political policy in 1930 was aimed at immediate revolution; literary policy said that the writer would aid the revolution by speaking to the proletariat, for it was the proletariat who would soon inherit the remains of decaying capitalist America and replace it with a Communist society. Of course, what seemed plausible or even probable in 1930, America's collapse as a result of the (then beginning) Great Depression, failed to occur. To those entering adulthood at this time, many things were possible as solutions to what became one of the most traumatic and tortuous crises in American history.

Marxists and non-Marxists alike saw the increasing unemployment and protest, the Hoovervilles, labor union agitation, soup kitchens, bread lines, and the apple sellers. It could indeed be time for the demise of capitalism and the rise of the workers to replace the bourgeoisie, just as they understood Marx had predicted. These were heady times for members of the Communist Party; they, after all, would lead the revolution. The party's membership grew, as did its organizing efforts.

On the literary front, John Reed Clubs spread. By 1932 there were 12 clubs with a total membership of about 900 in Portland (Oregon), Detroit, Boston, Philadelphia, Newark, San Francisco, Hollywood, Seattle, Chicago, New York, Washington, D.C., and Cleveland. One purpose of the clubs was to develop new talent among the proletariat. After all, if the proletariat was to replace the bourgeoisie and its culture with proletarian culture, members of the proletariat would have to write it.

Proletarian literature was, in part, a literature to be aimed at workers. It was to be about workers and to be read by workers. The writer was to be what some would call a propagandist. Further, recognizing that few young writers were from the working class, the John Reed Club report

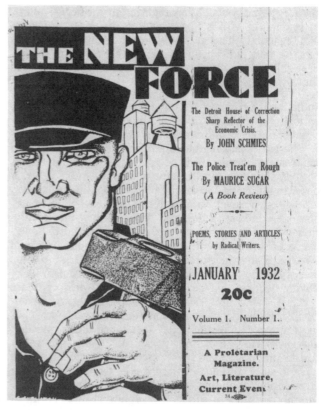

Cover for the first issue of the magazine published by the Detroit John Reed Club.

published in the January 1930 *New Masses* put forth "A New Program for Writers." Writers were to attach themselves to an industry and become thoroughly familiar with it, so that they could write "from inside."

In September 1930 editor Mike Gold spelled out in some detail the meaning of "proletarian realism," a type of literature that would reflect the life of the workers and have a clear revolutionary point. Literature would deal with real (social) conflicts, not mental anguish; it would have a social function (a point to make), not be "art for art's sake"; it would be written in as few words as possible; the action would be swift and honest; it would not be melodramatic or pessimistic; and it would reflect the courage of the proletarian experience. Here, then, were guidelines for a literature to mobilize the masses for revolution; sensitive to and reflecting their lives, it would be written so they could understand it and be moved to join the revolution against the evils of a decaying capitalism and its decadent bourgeois culture.

Proletarian literature was not the preponderant literature of the 1930s. Of about 17,000 novels published during the decade, only about 70 were proletarian. Few who wrote it are remembered today, but in its time the idea generated tremendous controversy among intellectuals. That it was taken so seriously affords the analyst an opportunity to probe the historical record for clues to the prospects and tensions of radical political and cultural convergence. Rather than asking, with Howe and Coser, "How then was it possible for writers of talent and training . . . to lend themselves to such intellectual buffoonery?" (1957), we can ask how it was that serious writers, some talented and some not so talented, attempted to unite their literary and political sensibilities—two modes of human endeavor not often united?

To begin with, we must appreciate the impact of the Great Depression. This is no place for a lengthy catalog of its effects, but coming as it did on the heels of a decade of boom and optimism, the crash and its subsequent severe depression deeply affected all levels of society. The responses of individuals and groups varied. For some, suicide or crime or mental illness; others were forced to abandon their homes and families in search of work; and others rioted. Later would come federally sponsored jobs and expansion of welfare. Labor unions increased their organizing efforts and grew, as did the Communist Party. Most people lived a life of both resignation and quiet hope.

The impact of the Great Depression on intellectuals, artists, and writers was by no means uniform, but it is fair to say that most were upset about the collapse and beset with worry about the irrationality and chaos that it implied. For some, their 1920s-based view of middle-class philistinism was vindicated. For those who had become expatriates, it signaled an opportunity to come home and help rebuild American society and culture. And for those just entering the adult world of employment (or unemployment), what were their prospects for a career as writer or poet? These were anxious, confusing days. Traditional formulas for leading one's life provided little guidance under circumstances of the Great Depression. There were decreasing outlets for young authors' publications, especially for young authors of the left, and payments for articles in magazines became smaller after 1929. To make matters worse, "The younger writers discovered that the repatriated expatriates, because they were already established in their fame, were taking up much of the available magazine space" (Rideout 1956).

Little opportunity to publish, unemployment, and disaffection from "mainstream" culture were part of the immediate context in which young would-be writers found themselves. They were troubled by problems unique to themselves as writers as well as participating in the general malaise. Writers (and intellectuals generally) searched for ideas that would solve their own and America's problems.

The solutions and the hope for a better tomorrow were provided for some by Marxism and its major vehicle in America at the time, the Communist Party U.S.A. Marxism was a coherent ideology, perhaps the only generally available coherent set of ideas in 1930, that explained the Great Depression and could provide a refuge, a sense of unity, and hope for the future. At least it seemed so at the time. Here was an intellectual home, apparently the only one for those who liked their answers whole. Marxism explained the Great Depression and provided a basis for action: join with the rising proletariat, overthrow the existing order, and help build a new, superior society. The Soviet Union provided the model of a Communist-inspired system that was enjoying considerable economic success, in contrast with the apparent failure of the American sys-

tem. And more practically, the Communist Party was seeking new members for its revolutionary movement. Intellectuals, including writers, were among the thousands who joined the party, whose membership increased steadily during the 1930s.

Interestingly, the turn to Marxism and the Communist Party by a small but noticeable percentage of intellectuals provided them with more than answers to abstract questions about the causes of the Great Depression. The party was offering them a role in building a new society and, at the same time, an audience for whom to write. The American author could solve two problems at once by "going Communist." He or she could end the traditional "outsider" status of the intellectual in America and at the same time have a ready-made audience, the proletariat. We can remember here the advice of Gold, Russak, and others that proletarian literature be written about the proletariat, for the proletariat. And we see in this convergence of political and cultural radicalism how ideas, interests, and human needs were blended and intertwined under crisis circumstances.

The meaning of proletarian literature changed subtly between 1929 and 1935, from that of a literature by the proletariat, for the proletariat, to a literature written "from a revolutionary perspective." This shift in emphasis to the writer's perspective, that it simply be sympathetic to the revolutionary destruction of capitalism, broadened the scope of what proletarian literature could be and who could write it. Under such a guideline middle-class authors could write it and the middle class might be more interested in reading it.

The importance of a middle-class readership is reflected in circulation figures for *New Masses* during the first half of the 1930s. In September 1933, when *New Masses* ceased publication as a monthly, its circulation was 6,000 copies a month. During the period 1929-33 it had stressed and contained examples of literature by and for the proletariat. When it reappeared as a weekly in January 1934, *New Masses* sold 9,500 copies; by December of that year it had increased its circulation to 25,000 copies. Not only did *New Masses* begin to publish weekly, but it reflected the changed philosophy of literature written "from a revolutionary point of view" with no restrictions on form, subject matter, or the author's or subject's class membership. This change in literary philosophy in a revolutionary journal of politics and literature appealed to a broader, more middle-class audience, and boosted circulation.

The change in literary philosophy is exemplified further by the addition of Granville Hicks as literary editor when the magazine reappeared as a weekly. Hicks's discussions of literary history and criticism followed the form (if not the content) of "bourgeois" criticism that appeared in such establishment journals as *The Nation, Saturday Review of Literature,* and *The New Republic.* His writings presented a knowledge of literature and philosophy rarely found outside the college-educated, that is, middle-class, literati.

Both of these phases of proletarian literature were not simply written about in the pages of *New Masses.* The Communist Party matched its revolutionary ideology with organization; the John Reed Clubs brought artists and writers closer to the working class and provided a training ground for new talent. The clubs accomplished this for writers with workshops, and each club had at least one "little" magazine in which authors could publish. That the John Reed Clubs had considerable impact there is no doubt. Reviewing their reports and schedules of events in *New Masses,* one finds classes and workshops in writing, graphics, photography, painting, cartooning, theater, and dance. To the young left-leaning authors or would-be authors who were up against constricted publishing opportunities for their work, the John Reed Clubs offered publishing outlets in their literary magazines.

The proletarian-literature philosophy struck a chord with relatively young, unemployed, high-school graduates of working-class background. A notable few were college-educated and wanted a career in journalism. Most were first- or second-generation Americans, a common characteristic of working-class people in the 1930s.

Other clues to the characteristics of proletarian authors (and the importance of the John Reed Clubs to their development) are provided by an analysis of authors who submitted works to a contest for the best proletarian novel published in 1934. Ninety authors, all previously unpub-

An issue of the magazine published by the Philadelphia John Reed Club.

lished, submitted works; 30 of these authors were women. The areas of the country that had the heaviest concentration of submissions were areas of active radical politics and John Reed Clubs.

The "generalizations" of the preceding two paragraphs can only summarize the scant evidence that is available. What little evidence there is, suggests that young, probably ambitious, would-be journalists, novelists, and poets from working-class backgrounds who were unemployed or unable to work in their craft were seeking whatever opportunities might appear. One admittedly self-selected sample of novelists was one-third women. It is difficult to imagine that one-third of the working novelists of the 1930s were women. Their overrepresentation among proletarian novelists indicates further the appeal of the proletarian literature philosophy to the unemployed, the young, the inexperienced, and the otherwise powerless.

Not all writers who appeared in *New Masses* or John Reed Club magazines, or who published proletarian novels, were working-class or party members. And proletarian literature was not the only manifestation of the influence of Marxism in the 1930s. Aaron cites William Phillips' characterization of the movement, in which he differentiates "older" from "younger" New Men. The older New Men consisted of such authors as Hemingway, Cowley, and Tate, and a "few confident pioneers"—Joseph Freeman, Michael Gold, and Joshua Kunitz. The younger New Men were "still in their teens or early twenties, they were idealistic and ambitious. Moreover, they considered themselves set apart by age and by cultural affiliations from the older generation of revolutionary writers" (Aaron 1961). Phillips says, further, that the older group consisted of revolutionary pioneers who did not assimilate the literary heritage of the 1920s from its literary fathers James Joyce and T. S. Eliot, as well as Cowley, Hart Crane, Kenneth Burke, and John Dos Passos.

Phillips and his friend Philip Rahv were part of a loose network (the so-called literary Trotskyists) that included James T. Farrell, Dwight Macdonald, Mary McCarthy, Diego Rivera, Edmund Wilson, Sidney Hook, and James Burnham. . . . [M]ost of these intellectuals were influenced by or sympathetic to Marxism at some time in their careers, but never joined the Communist Party or completely embraced the philosophy of proletarian literature. Their reputations (established prior to the 1930s), supported by secure literary, university, or journalistic positions, or jobs with the Federal Writer's Project, provided them with the sociological support necessary to maintain a literary-philosophical stance independent of the party's line. Aaron cites the example of Clifton Fadiman, sympathetic to the Communist Party in the early 1930s, joining the *New Yorker* as a book reviewer in 1933, which "permanently separated him from the young Marxists." It was those having lesser security, repute, training, and perhaps talent who were most involved with the John Reed Club magazines and the party's ideology of proletarian literature.

By 1934, when the philosophy of proletarian literature had been broadened to include much more than that written by the proletariat, for the proletariat, it became obvious that proletarian novels, at least, were not selling well. Moreover, there was tension over proletarian literature between the Communist Party-John Reed Clubs-*New Masses* (older New Men) camp and the *Partisan Review*-fellow travelers (young New Men) camp, as well as criticism of the proletarian literature philosophy from independent radicals, liberals, conservatives, and socialists. This tension from within and attack from without contributed to the transformation of the party's proletarian literature philosophy to one of literature written "from a revolutionary point of view."

The ideological revision was reflected in the words of poet-critic Stanley Burnshaw, who remarked that the Communist editors of *New Masses* wanted "to drive away no one who can be turned into a friend of the revolutionary movement." Referring to earlier party doctrine that "pure" art was a reflection of incipient fascism, Burnshaw defended the new policy of literature from a revolutionary perspective by suggesting that "so long as he is true to himself as a writer honestly struggling to find a way out of the crisis," his work would not amount "objectively to quiescence to the process of fascization [*sic*] now going on." Now (by 1934), good art was not necessarily incipient fascism. The "literature from a revolutionary perspective" viewpoint was reiterated by Alexander Trachtenberg, a member of the Central Committee of the Communist Party, who spoke to the New York John Reed Club in October 1934. He reminded the membership that the purpose of the clubs was to win artists and writers to the revolution, and that the party did not want to interfere with the free exercise of people's talents or absorb talented people in other kinds of work, to the neglect of their craft. This speech was a straightforward response to some of the younger New Men and fellow travelers who felt straitjacketed by the party's literary philosophy.

Both phases of the proletarian literature era were abetted by the John Reed Clubs. They brought young authors into contact with each other and with party ideology; their magazines provided training and publishing outlets; they stimulated and sustained writers' and other artists' work while providing a setting in which radical ideologues and producers of culture could commingle. But the John Reed Clubs could not overcome social and ideological differences between party and nonparty writers.

The Communist Party's change in literary policy was part of a change in broader political policy that became explicit after the Writers' Congress in April 1935. The call issued by Trachtenberg was announced in *New Masses* (Jan. 22, 1935) for the purpose of fighting the "twin menaces of war and fascism" and discussion of writers' problems. The announcement stated that "to this Congress shall be invited all writers who have achieved some standing in their respective fields. . . ." Noticeably absent from this invitation were young writers who had not achieved "some standing" in their respective fields.

The party was shifting its official political strategy from revolutionary to reformist, a move presaged by the second-phase shift in literary philosophy that attempted to broaden the appeal of proletarian literature to the middle class. The party was jumping on the Roosevelt bandwagon, supporting reformist measures, and, in general, seeking to enlarge its constituency. This was the party's Popular Front stage, dedicated to fighting fascism wherever and however necessary. One group from whom it hoped to gain adherents, and whose reputations would attract others, was writers and intellectuals. The Communist Party became interested in attracting writers, not in developing writing.

To facilitate its political goals, the party established the League of American Writers, a centralized organization run by a 17-member central committee of party members and close fellow travelers. The party was trying to attract prestigious authors such as Hemingway, Dos Passos, and Archibald MacLeish rather than to train new talent. The league's membership was open only to published professional writers, not to writers just beginning to learn their craft. In fact, the John Reed Clubs were dissolved.

The establishment of the League of American Writers ended the magazines and writing classes of the Reed Club period. Authors were asked to join hands with those whom they had previously denounced or seen denounced on the pages of *New Masses*. One case is particularly striking. In Granville Hicks's review of MacLeish's *Poems, 1924-1933* in the January 16, 1934, issue of *New Masses,* Hicks denounced MacLeish as a Nazi. In December 1935, after the policy change, MacLeish contributed to the *New Masses* antifascism issue. In March 1935, MacLeish's *Public Speech* was praised by Isidor Schneider on the pages of *New Masses* "as a 'beautiful and moving collection of poems.' " Either MacLeish changed dramatically in a short period of time, and there is no reason to believe that he did, or party political and literary policy had changed, requiring some "ideological work" on the part of true believers.

The antifascism of the Popular Front and Spanish Civil War period diverted the attention of many intellectuals from the Moscow trials and purges, and perhaps explains why there was so little controversy over the party's change in literary philosophy. It was not until the Nazi-Soviet Nonaggression Pact of 1939 that most intellectuals left the Communist Party.

This review of convergence and then divergence of Communist Party political radicalism and the radical proletarian literati has ignored until now an important strand of developments. The evolution of the *Partisan Review* from the New York John Reed Club's magazine to a more broadly based journal of politics and literature represents a schism within the proletarian literary movement that might have ended proletarian literature even if the party had not scuttled it.

I mentioned earlier the older New Men/younger New Men differences within the left. Philip Rahv and William Phillips, both younger New Men and members of the John Reed Club of New York City, founded *Partisan Review* in 1934. Ostensibly an organ of the John Reed Club, the magazine was devoted to "quality" writing, an idea that saw Marxism as a method of analysis and opposed to the party's idea of art as political propaganda. By 1936 the magazine was in the camp of the literary Trotskyites and its views were captured best by James T. Farrell's scathing attack on the party's and *New Masses'* views in his *A Note on Literary Criticism.* Farrell's book-length "note" crystallized what was soon to become both an anti-Stalinist and an anti-party aesthetic position with roots in the 1920s.

Farrell denounced Michael Gold and Granville Hicks, then accused Russian and American Marxist critics of introducing extra-literary criteria into criticism, ignoring the persistence value of art, oversimplifying art, confusing art and propaganda, stigmatizing individualism, and making foolish or irrelevant judgments because they did not take their Marxism seriously.

Granville Hicks acknowledged that Farrell had "performed some valuable services" by pointing to constricting elements in Marxist (that is, party) criticism, but argued that he should understand the sectarianism of Marxist critics as an "unfortunate but excusable reaction to the aestheticism of the bourgeois critics who had rejected 'working class experience' as 'a fit subject for literature'." . . . Farrell and the editors of *Partisan Review* come to form a "camp" when *Partisan Review* resumed publication in December 1937, after a period of cessation and a break from party influence. Their camp was anti-Stalinist politically and anti-party aesthetically, and it formally marked the end of the convergence on the left of radical political ideology and a revolutionary aesthetics.

The convergence of literary philosophy and Communist Party revolutionary politics in Depression-torn American society was facilitated by a number of factors: a major domestic economic crisis at a time when an alternative model of society was enjoying success, and a well-organized political party was providing answers to major questions (ideology) and concrete opportunities to learn the writer's craft (clubs), outlets for work (magazines and audience), and general support to young writers that eased their "blocked ascendency." The strain of blocked ascendency is often cited as a structural inducement for individuals to join a movement. This "package" of ideological, material, and sociological factors facilitated the convergence of political and literary ideas at both the cultural and the personal levels. And it was changes in these factors that led to the divergence of the political and literary movements of the 1930s.

The international situation changed with the spread of Nazism and the Moscow purge trials. Domestically, the reform programs of the Roosevelt administration tempered the worst effects of the Great Depression. The most direct impact of these reforms on the proletarian literature movement was the Federal Writers' Project, which employed writers and gave them alternatives to the John Reed Clubs, thereby providing the opportunity to write ("unblocked ascendency") in more "establishment" or "legitimate" forums. Communist Party strategy—the movement from a revolutionary to a reformist stance—in an effort to increase its constituency among the middle class and in the face of a nonrevolutionary working class, further encouraged a modification of literary ideals.

The ideological and aesthetic division among intellectuals over the propagandist nature of proletarian literature was itself an important source of divergence. Under crisis circumstances it was possible for some (especially those unemployed and unestablished) to combine literary and political ideals; the differences between literature and politics are not so "inherent" that they cannot be overcome. However, under less extreme circumstances (at least in capitalist societies and probably in Communist ones as well) the writer needs "bourgeois" freedom to seek the truth within the canons of his or her craft. Politics is about both more and less than the truth, and therefore conflicts with artistic endeavor. Perhaps politics and literature are ultimately assimilable to each other, but that awaits new developments in society and literature.

> *Arthur C. Ferrari, "Proletarian Literature: A Case of Convergence of Political and Literary Radicalism," in* Cultural Politics: Radical Movements in Modern History, *edited by Jerold M. Starr, Praeger, 1985, pp. 173-88.*

Critical attention and reader reception:

Malcolm Cowley . . . , in summing up the literary activity of the 1930's, . . . wrote: "From the very beginning, the novels of social protest received a critical attention that was out of all proportion to their popularity, considering that very few had a sale of more than 2,500 copies . . . "

Farrell, in *A Note on Literary Criticism,* was to make a neat practical point concerning the function of radical fiction: even if one accepted the premise that a proletarian novel, like all art, was merely propaganda, what was the value *as propaganda* of a piece of writing which had so slight a dissemination? This question had already been considered by Louis Adamic in an article for *The Saturday Review of Literature* entitled "What the Proletariat Reads: Conclusions Based on a Year's Study Among Hundreds of Workers Throughout the United States." Assuming the strongest justification for the proletarian novel to be that it was propaganda addressed to the working class, Adamic concluded from his conversations with workers throughout the year 1934 that 99.5 per cent of the American proletariat was not class-conscious and did not read proletarian novels at all, while a great majority of the .5 per cent of the class-conscious individuals could not afford to buy them.

> *Walter B. Rideout, in his* The Radical Novel in the United States, *1956.*

Charles I. Glicksberg

[*An American critic and educator, Glicksberg has written widely on American literature. In the following essay he asserts that on the basis of form, style, and subject matter, proletarian writings had greater merit as political propaganda than as works of literature.*]

Time lends the necessary perspective for viewing a movement objectively. Looking back upon the [1930s], we can see clearly the mistakes that were made, the excesses that were committed. The period from 1930 to 1940 was definitely Marxist in complexion. Despite strong but unorganized opposition, the left-wing movement in literature carried practically everything before it. In a time of postwar reconstruction and severe economic dislocation, the confident attack and positive views of the Marxist radicals gained many converts. Especially in the field of literary criticism was Marxism an earnest of originality, the torchbearer of truth, the inheritor of the future. Marxist writers were not slow in cashing in on their ideological opportunity. They and they alone were animated by lofty, humanistic ideals, by a comprehensive and dynamic philosophy of society which could explain every phenomenon, individual or collective, while predicting the inevitable course of history in the future. Before such powerful forces, the intellectual could put up but a scattered and ineffectual defense. Here was a great hope for mankind in the making; here was the promise of a better world. With the establishment of a collectivistic society would come not only the redemption of the proletariat but also the creation of a truly humane world culture.

"Proletarian" literature was born in the United States and in England. Learned essays were published on the dialectical qualities which distinguished, or should distinguish, proletarian drama, proletarian fiction, proletarian poetry, proletarian criticism. The emphasis, invariably, was on the militant adjective "proletarian," the symbol of salvation. Marxist critics were adept at the art of controversy; they waxed fat and strong on the incessant war of words. Authors who in their innocence strayed away from the official canons of orthodoxy, whatever these happened to be at the time, were warned about their heresies and dereliction by the watchdogs of the radical press.

In 1935, by giving its seal of approval to the policy of the United Front, the Communist International launched a movement which was bound to influence the development of culture in other countries. Liberals and workers with progressive views were now to be encouraged to join the new labor party, the object of which would be to fight the menace of fascism. That became the new battle cry, the crusading cause: Fight fascism! Even bourgeois democracy, the Comintern decided, was better than fascism, and every effort should therefore be made to preserve it. For strategic reasons, the theme of world revolution was postponed to a more expedient future.

In a mood of exaltation, liberal writers affiliated themselves with the Communist-inspired United Front. They had no conception then that they were to be used as instruments, that when the proper time came they would be unceremoniously discarded. The Communists had not abandoned and had no intention of abandoning their revolutionary program; if they spent precious time and energy honeymooning with bourgeois writers and intellectuals, it was because they needed all the support they could get at this juncture, and "culture" possessed strong propaganda value. The prestige of established writers could be utilized to support causes and advance ideas which might otherwise not receive a favorable hearing. Hence the liberal writers were valuable allies in the important task of edu-

cating and converting the masses. It was all conceived and planned as a vast propaganda campaign.

This is not to deny that many of the battles fought by left-wing critics were salutary and liberating nor to disparage the quality of some of the work they accomplished. They routed the forces of reaction. They made necessary a searching revision of aesthetics on psychological, sociological, and political grounds, and the results in criticism were highly fruitful. The myth of individualism was punctured; the social roots of the creative process were investigated and analyzed; the organic dependence of the artist on his social environment was demonstrated. Consequently many writers took courage and explored new areas of material, new depths of consciousness, new worlds of experience. They created new forms.

But the more militant among the "official" left-wing critics were far from satisfied with this consummation. They were not interested primarily in fostering a revolutionary literature but in revolutionizing society, and literature was important only in so far as it could promote that end. Culture possessed propaganda value that should be exploited to the full, but this value was ancillary to the more fundamental and difficult task of organizational work, agitation, politics, direct action, the enlightenment of the workers. Hence it was essential that literature should not only escape the blight of individualism but that it should also produce "practical" results. It should change the minds of men, it should point out the way, it should stir them to take positive action. In order to accomplish that, literature must hew to the party line.

In his brilliant polemic, *Artists in Uniform,* Max Eastman angrily and eloquently exposed the degree to which authors, native and foreign, were subservient to party dictates. At first this subservience created no untoward difficulties. In a holy war against fascism, personal sacrifices were more than justified. Besides, many of the writers were pathetically eager for political guidance and even dictation. They were too well aware of their own deficiencies: their limitations of knowledge, their confusion of purpose, their lack of clear-cut convictions. They were willing to follow wherever the embattled genius of the proletariat—which meant in practice the leaders of the party—led them. Unfortunately for their political innocence, there was no consistency in the party line, and they were hard put to it to tack and veer with the shifting winds of Comintern doctrine. What was orthodox one day turned out the next to be a vicious "bourgeois" heresy. Writers discovered that they could be banished from "proletarian" favor if they indulged in latitudinarian views. Unregenerate "individualists" at heart, a few writers would not conform, would not surrender what they were pleased to call their inalienable "right"; they refused to subordinate their art to the Spartan and expedient demands of politics. It was no easy task to keep writers within the party corral. Some of them insisted on asking too many disturbing questions. They made politically unwise or undesirable statements, and when called to account they seceded.

Then the full force of party irony and ire would be turned upon them. For the benefit of the faithful, they were portrayed as weak-kneed renegades, *bourgeoisie* who under stress reverted to type, men who were never particularly trustworthy in a political sense. Their sincerity was impugned, their character smeared, their talent held in question.

Despite this campaign of character assassination, the list of deserters continued to grow. It needed but the confirmation of Soviet Russia's trade alliance with Germany in 1939 to disillusion many others who had held on through thick and thin. They could no longer blind themselves to the truth. Many, in their desire to sacrifice themselves for something greater than the self, had ascetically obeyed all party orders. Their individual needs and aspirations were swallowed up in a higher cause. What did fame or literature matter so long as society was kept on its destined course?

But the fate of the individual does matter supremely, especially if his vocation is that of a writer. He cannot quiet his daimon or slay his talent. The task of the writer is to create; that is his mission in life. And yet writers, in spite of themselves, were led to engage in activities which bore no discernible relation to their professional role. This was justified by the rationalization that the writer can stand apart from the struggle against fascism only at the expense of sterility. By cutting himself off from the people, who are the primary source of inspiration, he commits intellectual and spiritual suicide. "It is indisputably true," declared Earl Browder, "that literature can be created today only by those who are on the side of the people against reaction, fascism and war." This is a magnificently abstract statement. Who are "the people"? What kind of "reaction" does Earl Browder have in mind? As for war, the Communists have no objection to the waging of war whenever it happens to suit their purpose. Such oratorical appeals serve to confuse the writer. How writers were affected by joining the United Front is made clear in part by Joseph Freeman who, in "Toward the Forties," declares:

> Writers have been out of work; they have been on relief and on the WPA; they have gone on strike for their own demands; they have picketed not only in sympathy with workers in other fields but for themselves; they have organized mass demonstrations, been arrested and beaten; they have sent delegations to Washington and negotiated with their employers. Their experience at work, out of work and in their trade unions has been the experience of other American workers. This direct economic experience has sharpened whatever intellectual awareness the writer may have gained about the fundamental problems of modern life. It has helped to teach him that art cannot be free while society is enslaved.

Only a few dared to ask at the time: What has all this to do with literature and the literary function?

Convinced of the truth of Marxism and the soundness of party policies, the Communist writer willingly accepts discipline. Obedience is organic because it springs from inner assent, complete faith. But the fellow traveler is in an anomalous position. How shall he choose between truth as he sees it and truth as the party critics see it? The doctrine had been drilled into him that individualism is a de-

lusion and a snare, that the cult of genius has passed. Therefore for a time the writer tended to distrust his individual impulses and values and rely increasingly on the ex-cathedra pronouncements of the Marxist pundits. But since the Marxist critics themselves followed a shifting policy in conformity with the changing demands of the political situation, their views on art were a study in contradiction.

One is justified in suspecting the value of a literary movement which flickers out at the command of political expediency. Not that the writer more than any other man is "free." But as the creative spokesman for a people, he should have some convictions of his own, a body of values that will not be dissipated by the latest wind of political doctrine.

Why, then, did "proletarian" literature suddenly fade out of the picture? Where now is the messianic fervor and fanaticism of the early '30s? As if a button had been pressed in a secret control tower, the productivity of the leading "proletarian" writers stopped. With the liquidation of the United Front, proletarian literature lost its creative vitality. The movement lost its excuse for being with the signing of the trade pact between Germany and Russia, though symptoms of decline could be detected even before that time. Silence fell upon the proletarian poets, the singing crew of the Revolution, particularly those who had embraced an ideology without previously undergoing the organic experience of conversion. In their work, wish-fulfillment and ethico-political imperatives usurped the austere labor of expression. Much of proletarian poetry in America was spoiled by sounding slogans and propagandistic clichés. Their writing was not impregnated with antecedent personal experience; their poetry sprang from a doctrine, not from a profound philosophy of life. Proletarian poetry is most convincing when it arises out of the daily struggle of living, without the infusion of cerebral complexity or doctrinaire self-consciousness.

A profound exposure of the weaknesses and contradiction inherent in the Marxist system of aesthetics is to be found in an address Waldo Frank gave on "Values of the Revolutionary Writer." It is a stirring appeal, charged with that moral passion which is characteristic of his work. It is therefore all the more significant as a document revealing with luminous clarity the dangerous fallacies involved in too orthodox and literal an application of Marxism to literature. Primarily an artist and not a politician, Waldo Frank insists that the literary work of art is not a direct incitement to action but an autonomous activity. The special function of art is to convey the true experience of the totality of life. Frank denies that direct propaganda can be effective as literature. Even revolutionary writers must not conform to the pressure of immediate ends, must not lose sight of the organic progress of mankind. They must acquire faith in the autonomy of literary art, perceive its place in the evolution of humanity and refuse to surrender their function as artists. Whatever propaganda a work of art contains is implicit in and dependent upon its effectiveness as literary art. Therefore, Waldo Frank concludes, the revolutionary writer, if he is to achieve his aim, must endeavor to see life whole.

English writers, more stable, more deeply rooted in tradition, took considerably less time to make up their minds about this problem of Marxism and its relation to art. Before the clouds of war darkened the world horizon, E. M. Forster, though he had been a valiant fighter against fascism, fulminated against the dogma that the writer must completely surrender his privacy, his periods of creative leisure and solitude. But now that a war of extermination is going on between Germany and England, he has, after examining his conscience, signified his willingness to serve his country in any useful capacity, to place his not inconsiderable talent, be it as a pamphleteer or downright propagandist, at the service of his people. The liberal ideal was brilliantly vindicated by Aldous Huxley who, in *Ends and Means,* gave a searching analysis of the Communist position; against it he upheld the thesis that the end did not justify the means.

The worm had begun to turn. Edmund Wilson, an influential American critic, returned from a visit to the Soviet Union with an unflattering account of the bureaucratic repression he found there—the oppressive atmosphere of fear, the idolatry of Stalin. His experiences there made him look once more to democratic institutions as providing hope for the future. Then, in order to sweat the Marxist influence out of his system, he set himself the ambitious task of tracing the development of Marxist thought. He dissected the vulgar interpretation of history which puts the emphasis on a monistic principle, namely, that people always act from motives of economic interest. Such a theory is based upon a mechanistic conception of consciousness. The will of individuals plays its part in the determination of the historical process. And this will is affected by passion, by deliberation. Hence Wilson concludes that the Dialectic is a religious myth which has been stripped of its divine appurtenances and applied to the evolving history of mankind. Karl Marx may admit that it is men who are responsible for the direction that history actually takes, but in practice "he keeps talking as if the proletariat were the chosen instrument of a Dialectic, as if its victory were predetermined," and thus he assumes "an extra-human power." And his followers by carrying this theory over into practice, have made fatal blunders, assuming that socialism was in any event inevitable; they have thus "acquiesced in the despotism of Stalin while he was uprooting Russian Marxism itself."

Though English writers were on the whole less severely affected by the rabies of Marxism, a number of embattled Marxist intellectuals did start a literary movement, the object of which was to create and also to lay the ideological foundation for "proletarian" writing. In fact, perhaps the most ambitious Marxist contribution in the field of literary criticism is by an Englishman, Christopher Caudwell, whose *Illusion and Reality* marks a valiant effort to judge all literature and particularly poetry in the light of historical materialism. Marxists have long maintained, though it is hard to see on what valid grounds, that dialectical materialism provides an open sesame to the understanding not only of economics and politics but also of science and literature and art. What Caudwell adds that is new is an attempt to synthesize modern scientific knowledge in the realm of physics, psychology, and anthropology and inte-grate it with the basic Marxist conceptions. It is truly an amazing book. For the intellectuals it constitutes a challenge of the first order. It provides not only a foundation for a new system of aesthetics which is a fusion of Marxism, Freudianism, modern science, anthropology, and symbolic logic; it also furnishes, or purports to furnish, a consistent and complete philosophy of the universe and of man.

The concluding chapter, "The Future of Poetry," reveals the limitations of Caudwell's extraordinary method. Bourgeois culture, he assures us, is on its last legs; it has reached its final, convulsive crisis, and the new society is emerging from the womb of the old. The proletariat, dependent and economically enslaved, can achieve freedom only by destroying the *bourgeoisie*. This class, the proletariat, is not merely the most long-suffering class of modern capitalistic society; it is the class destined to heal the wounds and cure the ills of an internally lacerated civilization. In the final struggle it will assume the leadership, play a creative role. Without understanding the deepening revolutionary crisis and taking into account the role of the proletariat in the building of society in the future, modern art, we are told, cannot be adequately comprehended. For proletarian art

> expresses the movement of the proletarian class itself, and this movement is to annihilate its existence as a class by becoming coincident with society as a whole. It was the rôle of class society to gather at one pole all consciousness and art—how then could proletarian art exist, before proletarian society has developed its own distinctive consciousness? And this could only happen in any full measure when proletarian freedom had exceeded bourgeois freedom—for consciousness is the reflection in ideology of the social product which secures its existence. Art also is a social product.

If the reader is unable to make head or tail of this farrago of Marxist abstractions, let him not be discouraged. There was a time when earnest intellectuals grappled with these dialectical formulations in the belief that they contained, even if they concealed, a profound truth, a core of precious and redemptive meaning. That belief is now badly shattered. These statements about art as a productive problem, about proletarian consciousness and bourgeois consciousness, proletarian freedom and bourgeois freedom, do not make sense. They are symbols which are arranged in the proper syntactical order, but they have no referent in reality; they are meaningless ejaculations.

The relation of literature to politics resolves itself on analysis into the relation of the writer to politics. The argument is twofold: If as a man the writer is blind to the decisive issues of his age, the fate of the social order, he falls into insincerity, he becomes a divided being, and his work is bound to be false, shallow, sterile. Second, a free, harmonious art cannot develop in a society that is based on class distinctions. Therefore the writer must lend his aid, his talent, to the revolutionary cause. There is a fallacy lurking in this argument which deceives many people. It consists in making Communism a universal philosophy valid for all types of experience, all forms of expression.

Culture as well as industry is interpreted as a function of the socio-economic order. That is, of course, simply not so. There is society and there is the universe, and man endeavors to adjust himself in his own way to each of these forces as well as to a multiplicity of interacting cultural institutions. Man creates religion, he establishes a Church, he worships the Virgin, indulges in mysticism and metaphysics, glorifies the sentiment of love, thus investing the instinct of sex with a lofty meaning and sacred dignity it does not possess in a state of nature. He feels and behaves at times in a manner highly irrational; he burns witches and makes pilgrimages; he cries out in terror at the thought of death; he acquires neuroses; he dreams heroic and absurd dreams, but he persists in dreaming; he commits suicide, sometimes for unaccountable reasons; he experiences the oppressive sense of boredom and an inexplicable nostalgia for the Absolute. To explain all this dialectically, in the mass, as the product of property relations or the level of production or the expression of "bourgeois consciousness" is a mechanical vulgarization of the complexity of human nature and the intricate pattern of history and life.

It took the intellectuals considerable time to recover from their infatuation with Marxist dogma. Some have still not recovered and are still babbling about dialectics. The greater part have regained their sanity and their creative independence. As W. H. Auden expresses it in *The Double Man:*

> We hoped; we waited for the day
> The State would wither clean away,
> Expecting the Millennium
> That theory promised us would come,
> It didn't.

In thus cutting themselves off from Communism, the writers are not acting illogically; they are not betraying "the cause"; they are not, to quote Auden once more, repenting of their last infraction by seeking "atonement in reaction." It is precisely against the absolutism of orthodoxy that their protest is directed. Expediency is not their God. Their ill-starred adventure in political engineering has taught them that there is no one road; no single political party has a monopoly of the truth. They desire as much as ever to see a rational society established, but they are no longer so certain that this can be achieved by a revolutionary seizure of power on the economic front. They perceive at long last the value of democratic institutions, they are jealously determined to retain their civil rights. If they show so much concern for the autonomy of art, it is not because they are covertly defending their "class" interests but because art is an essential expression of man and no society of the future can be complete without it.

The persistent defection of men of good will from the ranks of Communism is a portent that no dialectical rationalization can satisfactorily explain. To argue that thought is a function of the economic organization of society is to make a generalization that has little meaning or relevancy when applied concretely. It is a method of reasoning that betrays the intellectual because it denies the validity of his efforts at reaching truth. Thought does not originate and move in a vacuum but neither can it be considered a simple economic reflex. The thinker may unconsciously be conditioned by his environment and his class interests, but these influences alone will not account for the ideas he adopts.

For example, *Poetry and Anarchism,* by Herbert Read, is a declaration of independence of profound import. And the declaration gains in significance by virtue of the fact that it is primarily a confession of faith. Sincerity is hard to define and even more difficult to measure, but it is an essential quailty both in literature and politics. If political activities require a disintegration of the personality, a sacrifice of the moral principles which make up the unity that we recognize as character, then, concludes Herbert Read, the sacrifice is not worth making. The end does not justify the means. Motives are as important as results because they help to determine the results.

Herbert Read is seriously concerned about the fate of poetry. If the arts have suffered both in Russia and Germany, it is because the spirit of freedom has there been stifled. Capitalism, fascism, and Marxism have this in common: they all tend to militate against the values of poetry. The damage done by both the fascist and the Marxist rulers is that they deliberately use the poet for overt political ends. Art, however, is a fundamental need of man, particularly today when it serves to compensate for the abstractions of the intellect. The poet cannot, without renouncing his peculiar function, subscribe to an externally formulated policy or version of reality. Art as a discipline is not amenable to the control of the Dialectic.

The experiences of the past decade have been a valuable lesson for the intellectuals who hoped by violent and conspiratorial methods to hasten the inevitable birth of a collectivistic society. Their taste of official Communism, their disillusionment with party tactics and the spirit of opportunism and expediency that animated the political leaders, their recoil from the compulsive dogmas of Marxism and the doctrine of class hatred, their refusal to conform unconditionally to all bureaucratic decisions—all this made it clear that the intellectual would have to go his way alone and make his contribution to humanity on his own account and in his own way. The outbreak of the second World War, the initial success of the Nazi armies, the rapid spread of the Nazi ideology of brutal force and unconscionable hate, these opened the eyes and hastened the disenchantment of a number of fire-breathing Communists in England. For example, in his *A Faith to Fight For,* John Strachey exalts the virtues of love and faith and opposes them to the Nazi doctrine of hate and force. In short, the writer cannot place allegiance to party above allegiance to humanity. Imaginative truth supersedes political loyalty.

Charles I. Glicksberg, "The Decline of Literary Marxism," in The Antioch Review, *Vol. 1, No. 4, December, 1941, pp. 452-62.*

Joel D. Wingard

[*In the following essay, Wingard examines the 1930s polarization of the Marxist proletarian writers and critics of the political Left and the Southern Agrarians of the*

political Right. He suggests that both literary move-
ments evolved in response to the same cultural and polit-
ical stimuli, and shared thematic unity.]

In the politically charged atmosphere of American letters in the 1930s, the Rightist and Leftist poles were represented by the Southern Agrarians and the Marxist Proletarians respectively. The two groups seemed to themselves and others then, as they have seemed generally since, to be classically irreconcilable enemies: reactionaries and revolutionaries. Their differences on many counts were formidable. Two different concepts of history informed their respective visions. The Southerners looked back to an idealized past and conceived a pastoral vision of a society based upon the land, operating in a stable and traditional manner, in which class relationships were more or less fixed. The Marxists looked forward to an idealized future and conceived a democratic vision of a society based upon the machine, operating according to the "scientific laws" of dialectical materialism, in which class distinctions were eliminated. The Agrarians championed the yeoman farmer of the Jeffersonian ideal, the very man whom the Proletarians despised as a petit bourgeois individualist. The Proletarians idealized collective man as industrial worker, as a part of the machine order that the Agrarians hated. The Agrarians were staunchly anti-communist: Robert Penn Warren wanted the Agrarian manifesto *I'll Take My Stand* (1930) to be called "Tracts against Communism." The Proletarians considered the Agrarians to be incipient Fascists. The American intellectual community's perception of the Agrarian-Proletarian antipathy is evident in the pairing of John Crowe Ransom and V. F. Calverton, leading spokesmen of the respective groups, in a 1936 *Scribner's Magazine* debate over the worth of Southern culture.

The differences were real and divisive in the 1930s, but now, after nearly fifty years, the Agrarians and the Proletarians seem to have been not so much opposing as complementary groups. It is now more instructive to see them not as political enemies promoting antagonistic visions of the ideal society but as lettered allies united in the defense of a human-centered culture against the onslaught of a dehumanized modernism. Beneath the outward differences between the Agrarians and the Proletarians, we perceive certain fundamental similarities.

For one thing, the literary Right and Left in America in the 1920s and 1930s were defined by a common reaction to what each regarded as the center of modern American society and culture: a rampant and meretricious industrial capitalism and a fragmented bourgeois value system. Each group held that emphasis on the mass production and consumption of material goods for profit is inimical to the existence of a humanistic culture, particularly to the production of serious art. In his essay "A Mirror for Artists" in *I'll Take My Stand,* Donald Davidson argues that serious literature cannot survive under an economic system that views all literature as just another marketable commodity. In his well-known essay "The Profession of Letters in the South" (1935), Allen Tate complains that capitalism promotes the production of "shoddy goods" in literature because of the need for a "big, quick turnover" in the publishing business, and he decries the consequences of the

"cash nexus" between the writer and his audience. In an identical vein, the Marxist editor Henry Hart, speaking to the Communist Party-sponsored Second American Writers' Congress in 1937, pointed to "the tragedy of literary waste" that results from the evaluation of literature in terms of salability and profits.

Both the Agrarians and the Proletarians recognized that in the industrial, capitalistic age the writer no longer enjoys a happy relationship with the larger society. Isolated because money values come between him and the people, he is forced to assume the negative function of criticizing society from without rather than enjoying the positive function of affirming the ideals of the people from within a unified culture. If he does not actively criticize his society, he retreats within the world of pure art, producing the kind of literature lamented by Ransom in "Poets without Laurels" (1935)—a literature devoid of social responsibility. Indeed Davidson complains in "A Mirror for Artists" that if there were to be any art at all under industrialism, it would most probably be Romantic art, which proceeds from an "artificial or a maladjusted relation between the writer and society." Such attitudes sound like echoes of a Proletarian like Michael Gold, whom we find—in an article in the *Liberator* in 1921 entitled "Towards Proletarian Art"—regretting the "sickness" of writers under capitalism. The "art ideals" of capitalism, Gold says, have "isolated each artist in a solitary cell, there to brood and suffer silently and go mad." Or, it may be said, the Agrarian attitudes harmonize with the voice of Malcolm Cowley, supporter of the People's Front, who in the epilogue to the first edition of *Exile's Return* (1934) contends that for the last two centuries writers have suffered under capitalism from a feeling of "solitude and uniqueness, . . . [a] feeling that [has] reduced some of the best of them to silence or futility and the weaker ones to insanity and suicide."

A second similarity between the Agrarians and the Proletarians is to be discerned in their tendency to offer the same basic solutions to the cultural situation. As Marxists of one stripe or another, the Proletarian writers traced the evils of bourgeois culture to its economic base and held the economic system ultimately responsible. Thus any change for the better in American culture could come only from the bottom up, after a change in the economic system. This is the familiar Marxist argument. It agrees generally with the opening "Statement of Principles" in *I'll Take My Stand,* in which the Agrarians, objecting to industrialism's attempt to promote culture through education and philanthropy, assert that "the trouble with the life pattern is to be located at its economic base, and we cannot rebuild it by pouring in soft materials from the top." In the same statement the Agrarians reject the approach of the Harvard New Humanists on the grounds that it does not go to the economic base for a solution to the contemporary decay of culture: "We cannot recover our native humanism by adopting some standard of taste that is critical enough to question the contemporary arts but not critical enough to question the social and economic life which is their ground." Though not couched in radical jargon, this objection to the New Humanists recalls the Marxists' disdain for intellectual elitist schemes that did not penetrate to the economic base of society.

As a requirement for establishing the ideal culture, both the Agrarians and the Proletarians urged the literary artist to become actively involved in the political sphere, healing the old rift between artist-as-artist and artist-as-man. In the epilogue to the 1934 *Exile's Return,* Malcolm Cowley points out that artists must take part in the class struggle "because they are men before they are writers or painters, and because their human interests are involved, and because they can't stay out of the battle without deliberately blinding and benumbing themselves." At the 1937 American Writers' Congress, Henry Hart said that "real writers will not be content until they are at the van of life, at the head of the tide of human effort. They will write and work so that this [capitalist] society shall perish and a new and rational one succeed it." Hart added that writers must do more than just write; they must "join together"—in "a trade union in order to survive," in "a political organization in order to make their efforts to change society effective," and in "a cultural organization such as the League of American Writers, in order to learn the relationships between day to day events and the main stream of human effort." Seven years earlier Donald Davidson had made similar recommendations in *I'll Take My Stand.* Some of his phrases, like those of the Marxists, have the ring of militancy: "As in the crisis of war, when men drop their private occupations for one supreme task, the artist must step into the ranks and bear the brunt of battle against the common foe"; the writer must not forget that in the time of crisis he "is called on to play the part both of a person and of an artist," and of the two, "that of person is more immediately important"; the writer "cannot wage this fight by remaining on his perch as artist" but "must enter the common arena and become a citizen."

Although they spoke from opposing political, social, and geographical positions, the Agrarian and Proletarian voices sound nearly identical to the present-day historian. Spokesmen on either side sought to respond to the modern social disharmony by advocating a unified culture to be achieved through social cooperation and the integration of artist and society. Both the Agrarians and the Proletarians supported a humanized culture conducive to the natural expression of a literature reflecting broad social values. The Proletarians located such a culture in a post-revolutionary future, while the Agrarians found it in the southern past, which had its roots in Europe. In what distinctly resembles a Marxist statement, Donald Davidson could say in "A Mirror for Artists" that the study of the past reveals that "social conditions to a large extent direct the temper and form of art." Allen Tate could look back to the example of seventeenth-century England, when the remnants of the feudal tradition made it still possible for Milton's *Comus* to be celebrated in the "social and spiritual community" of which the poet, not necessarily famous, was an integral part. Proletarians like Mike Gold and V. F. Calverton could look back to Walt Whitman celebrating the American masses as an integrated spiritual community, seeking, no less than the Agrarians, the image of the poet as bard, symbol of cultural unity.

Unlike modern life with its endless specialization, the cultural unity of the agricultural South, the Agrarians held, extended to and was expressed in all aspects of the southern life. No craft or occupation was conducted in isolation from others. According to their "Statement of Principles" (actually composed by Ransom), southern culture embraced "the whole way in which we live, act, think, and feel." In such an atmosphere art arises naturally out of the activities of the people; it is not purchased as a commodity. Thus entertainments like the fiddling and parlor dancing celebrated by Andrew Lytle in "The Hind Tit" are honored cultural activities. Fiddling, cotton growing, home decorating, taking life easy—all are integral parts of a meaningful tradition. As Davidson puts it, the "truly artistic life is surely that in which the aesthetic experience is not curtained off but is mixed up with all sorts of instruments and occupations pertaining to the round of daily life." This was a view that the Proletarians shared. In the epilogue to the 1934 *Exile's Return,* Cowley uses language similar to Davidson's to justify "propagandistic" art: no "single type of human activity, whether it be painting pictures or smoking pipes or making money, . . . can be treated as if it existed separately from all other types." A precedent for Cowley's concept had been established by Mike Gold, who in the 1920s had repeatedly attacked the notion of cloistered art. Addressing himself to the topic of the creation of a uniquely American literature, Gold had likened such a literature to a "lusty great tree" which could never grow in the "hot-house air" of literary magazines but must have its roots "in the fields, factories and workshops of America—in the American life." The greatest American art will appear, Gold had prophesied, "when there is singing and music arising in every American street, when in every American factory there is a drama-group of the workers, when mechanics paint in their leisure, and farmers write sonnets." In a culture such as this the literary artist would not be peculiarly distinguishable from his fellow men. He would be of them, among them. As Malcolm Cowley recalls in *And I Worked at the Writer's Trade* (1978), proponents of the socialist state believed that it would abolish the oppressive feeling of "solitude and uniqueness" on the part of the artist. Cowley was in accord with the pioneer Proletarian critic V. F. Calverton, who in 1927 had said that in the Proletarian culture the artist would enjoy a "median and balanced" position: "his rank will not usurp that . . . of the discoverer of a new anesthetic, or the inventor of a new logic. He will be neither a vagrant wretch nor a deified magician."

The Agrarians and the Proletarians shared the belief that a unified cultural vision is the source and informing spirit of meaningful art. The social incidentals of their visions differed, but both groups promoted the necessity of such a vision to repair a fragmented and disintegrated modern culture. Allen Tate's argument that "a people should gather its experience round some seasoned point of view before it may boast a high culture" and that it "must be able to illuminate from a fixed position all its experience" implies that the "point of view" or "fixed position" basically consists in the relationship of people to the land. The Proletarians assumed that their unifying "point of view" found its focus in the class-consciousness of the proletariat, that the Marxist view of history brought together and explained all experience. Matthew Josephson said at the First American Writers' Congress (1935) that a "working class revolution stimulates learning, reading, and almost all cultural activities." This stimulation, he said, "indicates unmistakably the preliminary condition which in past times has always led to the flowering of a great culture." At the same Congress, Malcolm Cowley claimed that the greatest gift that revolutionary awareness could give a writer was the "unified interpretation, without which one can write neither good history nor good tragedy."

Finally, the underlying unity in the Agrarian and Proletarian movements is apparent in several modern literary and cultural figures. They are the joint heirs of the Agrarian rootedness in and love for the southern landscape and the Proletarian revolutionary fervor and desire for social change. Wendell Berry, for instance, farmer and poet, acknowledges his kinship to the Agrarian program, yet his pro-Civil Rights and anti-Vietnam War stands connect him with the Left. Berry is also an ardent environmentalist, and in his collection of essays *A Continuous Harmony* he explains his feeling that the Civil Rights movement, the anti-war movement, and the ecology movement are all part of a whole which comprehends also the vital regionalism and sense of community rooted in the land that the Agrarians promoted. (The "back-to-the-land" movement of the early 1970s grew in part out of the same rebellious consciousness which produced the New Left. More recently something of the unity of the Agrarian and Proletarian legacy may be seen in the anti-nuclear movement.) Consider another contemporary figure, one who was related to the populist movement and thus was at least indirectly an inheritor of both the Agrarians and the Proletarians: Martin Luther King, Jr. King, a deeply religious southerner of great literary power, was arguably the greatest American social revolutionary of this century. Or look at the descendants of Depression-era bard and social activist Woody Guthrie; Pete Seeger, Joan Baez, and Woody's son Arlo also demonstrate the coming together of what once seemed two separate streams, Agrarianism and Proletarianism. They have developed an art expressive of the folk yet instrumental in furthering social change. Manifesting an affinity for many of the principles of the Agrarians and the Proletarians, various latter-day figures, it would seem, demonstrate the essential similarity of two groups once seemingly so at odds with one another. From the perspective of the 1980s we may say of the Agrarians and the Proletarians what Eliot said of the Puritans and the Cavaliers in "Little Gidding": they are "folded in a single party."

Joel D. Wingard, " 'Folded in a Single Party':
Agrarians and Proletarians," in The Southern
Review, *Louisiana State University, Vol. XVI,
No. 4, Autumn, 1980, pp. 776-81.*

IDEOLOGY AND LITERARY MERIT

Granville Hicks

[*Hicks was an American writer, critic, educator, and editor. As the literary editor of* New Masses, *he was a leading cultural spokesman for the American Communist party during the mid-1930s. In the excerpt below, from a speech delivered in 1934, Hicks extols the literary merit of realism in proletarian fiction and asserts that the proletarian perspective is the most acceptable framework within which to exercise literary criticism.*]

[The] theories I shall try to expound are not isolated; they derive from and depend upon a body of thought that extends into philosophy, history, economics, and political strategy. I do not mean that the Communist party has an official position on literature; nor, if it did, could I present myself as its spokesman. I mean merely that a full statement of my views would involve an exposition and defense of historical materialism, the Marxian conception of the class struggle, Marxian economics, and the Communist program for the overthrow of capitalism and the establishment of the dictatorship of the proletariat. Of course no aesthetic theory can be properly discussed without some consideration of its philosophical foundations and its social implications, but the foundations and implications of my theory are less familiar, and perhaps, to most of you, less acceptable than those that are ordinarily taken into account in aesthetic discourse. My exposition will, therefore, seem fragmentary, and you may well be conscious of assumptions that are not shared by you and cannot, within the limits of this paper, be defended by me.

To obviate this difficulty as far as is possible, I shall approach my subject by way of a rather elementary analysis of the nature and function of literature. I should describe a work of literature as the presentation of a particular fragment of experience in the light of the author's conception of the totality of experience. The definition is neither original nor uncommon. Something of the sort is implicit in most of the definitions, from Plato's and Aristotle's to those of contemporary aestheticians. Matthew Arnold said essentially the same thing when he called literature the criticism of life; to the experience that is his immediate theme the author brings the results of a larger experience, and it is the juxtaposition of the two that gives his work its value. Indeed, the simple proposition that selection is the basis of all art implies the existence of standards, beliefs, predispositions, and prejudices according to which the selection is made; and at their highest these ideas and moods are integrated into a world-view, or, if that is too abstract and intellectual a term to describe the mental processes of an artist, into a world-attitude. . . .

It is impossible for me to state fully why I personally have chosen the side of the proletariat and why I urge other intellectuals to make the same choice. I believe that the capitalist system is inherently unstable, and that such depressions as that which has just entered its sixth year are not only unavoidable under capitalism but are certain to grow worse. Capitalism itself cannot solve the problems that, as it becomes fully developed, it creates. Only socialization of industry will eliminate these ills and permit the enjoyment of the full resources of our productive machinery. Moreover, the desperate effort of the capitalist class to maintain its privileged position results in Fascism, which sacrifices the political and cultural gains of the period of industrial expansion without achieving stability. Socialization is the only preventive of both Fascism and war, and socialization can be brought about only by the proletariat, not because of some peculiar virtue resident in factory workers, but because it is the one class that stands to gain so much by socialization and to lose so much by the perpetuation, especially in a fascist form, of capitalism that it will be willing to make the sacrifices that revolution entails.

This is, in brief, the argument that has led me to make the proletariat my point of reference. Any critic, unless he accepts the complete irresponsibility of impressionism, tries to transcend his own idiosyncrasies and speak in the name of some larger entity. To do so, he must . . . foster a kind of dual response to literature. He knows what a work of art does to and for him, but he also realizes the ways in which he deviates from what he regards as the norm, and he makes due allowance for these deviations in reaching his conclusions. So with the revolutionary critic. It has been charged that the proletariat is an abstraction, and the charge has some measure of truth, but the critic's norm is always an abstraction. Mr. Richards, for example, implies the existence of Man, with a capital letter, and the Humanists have a very precise but completely abstract conception of humanity. The revolutionary critic's idea of the normal proletarian is, in comparison, concrete and realistic, based both on an understanding of the historic rôle of the class and on first-hand experience of its spirit as displayed in crucial struggles.

I can realize how many objections might be introduced at this point, but let us see what, in practice, our conclusions involve. If we were to go to some militant leader of the working class and ask him what literature ought to do, he would probably tell us that it ought, first of all, to create a revolutionary spirit in the proletariat. Only that literature, he might well say, that prepares the class for the great task before it has any value.

This may seem a narrow and, perhaps, to some, an unworthy conception of literature. So thoroughly schooled have we been in the doctrine of the sacredness of art that we shrink from any association of literature and practical affairs. This response of ours results from the fact that any association of literature with the practical affairs of monopoly capitalism is debasing. Art under capitalism is so constantly in danger of Mammon-worship that, in order to maintain any sort of artistic integrity, we have built up these elaborate defenses. But actually in the course of human history literature has again and again been openly allied with church and state, and it may be argued that the periods of such alliance have not been unfruitful. The artists of Greece and Rome and those of the Middle Ages found no degradation in the serving of practical ends, and the rise of democracy has been aided by many of the greatest writers of modern times.

Nothing has so beclouded contemporary aesthetic dis-

course as the use of the word "propaganda." Because of its use during the war the term has come to connote chicanery and distortion. Yet it also has been employed to describe any sort of direct exhortation, and the aesthetes apply it to any work of art with a serious purpose. So often has the word been abusively hurled by aesthetes against revolutionaries that the latter have accepted the challenge and adopted the word as their own. Diego Rivera, for example, says that all art is propaganda. There is a sense of the term in which this is true, but it is not the meaning that is ordinarily understood.

Personally, I believe that the word ought to be used only in its pejorative sense, but in any case it ought to be kept out of discussions of literature. I have tried to maintain that any work of literature presents some sort of world-attitude, and that it must be judged in terms of the author's world-attitude and his success in communicating it. The most outrageous dadaist poem implies a certain attitude toward life; and the author, whether he admits it or not, wants others to adopt that attitude. If literature with a purpose is propaganda, then Rivera is right, but in that case the word is too inclusive to be useful. The conviction of most persons—that literature with a purpose one doesn't like is propaganda and literature with a purpose one does like is art—is obviously unsound. We are left, it seems to me, to hold that propaganda involves misrepresentation, and, since misrepresentation is intrinsically bad, it is unnecessary to talk about propaganda.

In serving the revolutionary cause the revolutionary writer is merely expressing his own world-attitude and fulfilling his own desires. To that extent he is like writers of all classes and all ages. And the critic, when he judges literature by its effect in preparing the proletariat for its struggle, is applying a criterion that does not differ in kind from the criteria of other critics. There is a danger, however, that he may demand immediate, concrete results. Such a demand is wrong simply because it is not in the nature of literature . . . to produce such results.

What we have to ask, it seems to me, is whether a work of literature contributes to a world-attitude that is compatible with the aims and tasks of the proletariat and whether it tends to build up a system of responses that will permit the proletarian to play his individual part in the coming struggle. We cannot approve, for example, a novel or a play that fosters an attitude of subservience. It may have incidental values, which we must point out, but fundamentally it is wrong. We cannot tolerate a defeatist literature, not merely because of the attitude it encourages, but also because, from our point of view, it distorts life by ignoring elements in human character and history that, for the proletariat, the ascendant class, make pessimism impossible. Escapism, too, must be resisted. The romantic satisfactions of the daydream are recognized as perilous by most psychologists, for they inhibit the forming of adjustments that make possible the permanent and progressive fulfilment of appetencies; but they are peculiarly menacing to the proletarian reader, both because the hardships of his present existence make them so tempting and because his future rôle is so exacting.

On the other hand, we are not to suppose that the literature of the past is to be condemned *en bloc*. Revolutionary leaders from Marx to Stalin have insisted on the preciousness of the cultural heritage with which history endows the proletariat. There is a class element in any work produced in a class society, and this bias, as found in past writers, is distressing to proletarian readers. The classic example is Shakespeare's treatment of the lower class, a treatment so derogatory that Upton Sinclair, in *Mammonart,* warns workers against reading his plays. Mr. Sinclair, I feel, underestimates the natural immunity of the modern worker to such suggestion, and he equally underestimates the valuable elements of Shakespeare's plays. The mysticism of Dostoyevsky is wholly unacceptable to the Marxist, and yet his novels are widely read in the Soviet Union. Wherever the author's class bias is negated by his insight, his work is important. In spite of both snobbishness and a quasi-mystical detachment, Marcel Proust left a richer and more detailed account of the breakdown of the leisure class than can be found elsewhere.

We recognize an element of distortion in all the literature of the past, but we see, too, much that is valid, and to that we cling. At first it seems a paradox to say that we find most enduring value in those writers who most completely responded to and represented their own times. But once you perceive that class limits cannot be transcended, you realize that human nature can best be understood in terms of the forces that at any given time condition it. The writer who sets out to rise above material circumstance and deal with the pure human spirit is occupying himself with an unreal abstraction. The great writer has always been wholly and unmistakably part of his age, and, by mastering it, has left something of value for succeeding ages.

What we demand of a writer is that he honestly confront the central issues of his own age. His world-attitude must embrace the whole of his world as his age knew it, and must organize that world in such a way as to place central issues in the center. If he does this he deserves our praise. But I hasten to repeat that literature is not primarily a matter of the intellect. It embraces the entire mind, and it must not be judged in purely intellectual terms. An author may have formulated a world-attitude that, if he were a philosopher, would be admirable, and yet his poem or story may be worthless. He may, on the other hand, have no conscious philosophy, or only a very banal one, and yet be a great writer. This is particularly necessary for me to say, for it is characteristic of revolutionary sentiment that it seems to reach the intellect first. The young revolutionary author, filled with a sense of the comprehensiveness of Marxist analysis, and unwilling to subject his imagination to the long process of quiet and largely unconscious assimilation that literature requires, is tempted to substitute dogma for experience. This explains the weaknesses of some revolutionary literature, but it is a fault that time will remedy. . . .

Certainly the vitality of contemporary revolutionary literature can scarcely be ignored. I do not hold that every novel written by a Communist is perfect and beyond criticism. I believe, on the contrary, that I am unusually sensitive to the defects of revolutionary literature because I have so vivid a conception of what it ought to be and so poignant a desire to see it realize its potentialities. But when I compare the young radical writers with the young aesthetes or the young regionalists or the young pessimists or the young romantics, I confess that the former seem to be far more alive and promising. To compare Dos Passos' career with Hemingway's, or Jack Conroy's first novel with Gladys Hasty Carroll's, or Isidor Schneider's poetry with Yvor Winters' is to see the difference between a healthy, courageous, resourceful confrontation of reality and a querulous or timid or snobbish preoccupation with petty personal problems.

But perhaps you do not agree with me; and if you do not, I suspect it is because we have different sets of values—because, indeed, our lives are organized toward different ends. I do not want to overemphasize these differences. I hope and believe that I have allies among you, and I have no desire to antagonize anyone. But I am sure that you cannot understand what I am trying to say unless you realize that I expect and desire and work for a revolution that will not only alter political and economic forms but will profoundly change the whole basis of our culture. A new class is coming into power, and the results of its emergence can only dimly be foreseen. I believe that, whatever hardships this revolution may entail, it will eventually be a powerful stimulus to cultural growth, for, by destroying exploitation and class division, it will make possible a truly human civilization. The process may be long and painful, but the goal is clear, and this is the only path by which it can be reached.

You may ask, of course, why you, who have no desire to identify yourselves with the proletariat, should be expected to show any interest in its literary achievements. I can answer on several grounds. In the first place, just as the proletariat finds in bourgeois literature, with all its class bias, a portrayal of human life that is intelligible and enriching, so the bourgeoisie can adjust itself to class differences and discover in proletarian literature a valuable extension and partial integration of experience. This adjustment is relatively easy at present because proletarian literature is still under the influence of the dominant class literature. And it is worth making the necessary effort, for, even if my theories are entirely wrong, these writers from the working class and their sympathizers are very close to movements that are affecting us all. In the second place, you ought to be willing to grant that my conception of the future may be right, and if it is right, these novels and poems, however crude, are certain to have historical importance. Finally, I must invite you to contemplate what not only Marxian theory but the practical experience of Europe has demonstrated to be the only alternative to Communism, Fascism. From my point of view, of course, it is not an alternative but merely a postponement. Nevertheless, within the span of our lives, its constitutes a kind of alternative. And if the choice does lie between Communism and Fascism, it does not seem difficult to decide which deserves the allegiance of those of us who find inspiration in the literature of the past and nourish hopes for the growth of literature in the future.

Granville Hicks, "Literature and Revolution,"
in American Literary Criticism: 1900-1950 *by*

Charles I. Glicksberg, Hendricks House, Inc., 1951, pp. 408-26.

James T. Farrell

[*Farrell was an American novelist, short story writer, and critic who is best known for his Studs Lonigan novel trilogy depicting the life of a lower middle-class Chicago man. Although he considered himself a true Marxist, he objected to the politicization of literature through the proletarian literary movement. In the excerpt below, Farrell disputes the position outlined by Granville Hicks above, asserting that literary merit cannot be determined by a work's ideological content or a critic's ideological perspective.*]

If my analysis and demonstration be acceptable, we are forced to the conclusion that some elements of the thought and the creative literature of the past survive, carrying with them some degree of æsthetic and objective validity. It is, then, safe to assume that some of the art and some of the thought of the present will retain elements of intellectual or æsthetic validity after the process of history and the passage of time have eliminated or solved the problems created by the conditions and the burning needs of our impermanent system of capitalist democracy.

Further, if this line of reasoning be correct, what becomes of the categories *bourgeois* and *proletarian* in their application to art, literature, and thought? These categories have often been applied confusingly. Thus they have been used in a descriptive sense on the one hand, and on the other they have been transferred from the status of descriptive standards to that of categories of value *per se*. . . .

Granville Hicks finds the bourgeois novel incompletely satisfying. Contrary to Isidor Schneider his adoption of a "Marxian" viewpoint has changed his literary outlook. Thus, he presents considerable detail to prove that he could not now be so impressed by Proust as he once was. He confesses: "There is no bourgeois novel that, taken as a whole, satisfies me. I am not merely conscious of omission and irrelevancies; I feel within myself a definite resistance, a counteremotion, so to speak, that makes a unified esthetic experience impossible." The present is, however, a period of transition, and we have as yet no great proletarian novels to substitute for great bourgeois novels. Thus "the reason why revolutionary writers so often seem clumsy is that they are trying to communicate the operation of what deserves to be called a new type of sensibility." In the future, they will achieve this expression in a socialist society. Until that society shall develop, "the integration toward which the revolutionary writer aims is limited by the outlook and needs of the proletariat. This means, obviously, an emphasis on class-consciousness and militancy, but the author most effectively creates such attitudes not by ignoring large sectors of life, but by integrating them with the class struggle."

Hicks spends considerable time discussing the themes about which a proletarian novelist might write; and he suggests that some themes, such as those dealing with the life of the petty bourgeoisie, will not generally satisfy the proletarian novelist. "The trouble is, of course, that such a theme does not give the author an opportunity to display the forces [the class-conscious vanguard of the proletariat and its leaders] that are working against the defeatism and incipient Fascism of the petty bourgeoisie." Withal, Mr. Hicks does not impose restrictions on the proletarian novelist in choice of themes and material. On the contrary, he is as broad as life, and even declares that the proletarian novelist may write about the past, the present, or the future. However, he thinks it most likely that the proletarian novelist, in writing about the past, will select a subject in which the feature of "relevance" is fairly obvious. He mentions probable historical subjects that clearly would be classified here—Shays's Rebellion, the Paris Commune, and the French Revolution. He predicts a future in which the proletarian novel will surpass the bourgeois novel, and he pens a prophetic picture of the future proletarian novel:

> If we can imagine an author with Michael Gold's power of evoking scenes, and William Rollins' structural skill, with Jack Conroy's wide acquaintance with the proletariat, with Louis Colman's first-hand knowledge of the labor movement, with all the passion of these and a dozen other revolutionary novelists, with something of Dreiser's massive patience, we can see what shape a proletarian masterpiece might take. It would do justice to all the many-sided richness of the characters, exploring with Proustian persistence the deepest recesses of individuality and at the same time exhibiting that individuality as essentially a social phenomenon. And it would carry its readers toward life, not, as *The Remembrance of Things Past* does, toward death.

Mr. Hicks here, as in *The Great Tradition,* reveals a strong tendency to use the categories of bourgeois and proletarian literature as standards, and within them to judge works of literature in terms of themes and of formal ideology.

Often, when they have contrasted bourgeois and proletarian literature, revolutionary critics have been pressed into a dilemma. Bourgeois literature, so-called, has developed through a long tradition, and its heritage now includes a number of great works. Proletarian literature, so-called, has not had that same historical development. Revolutionary critics, proceeding in terms of these categories, have therefore been forced to counter what has been accomplished in bourgeois literature with faith in the prospects and potentialities of proletarian literature. Through many prognostications, much theorizing, countless prophecies, we have found these critics again and again cooking up recipes for tomorrow's "great" literature. Mr. Hicks' description of a future proletarian Proust, greater than Marcel Proust himself, is one of many such prophecies. These efforts suggest a remark of Louis Grudin's. Speaking of the critic who applies standards of measurement instead of criteria of judgment, Mr. Grudin comments: "His procedure has been that of an excursion for words and notions to support his claims, wherever he could find them; and he has had to trust to the meanings he could read into already available odds and ends belonging to various fields and gathered into a makeshift critical doctrine."

We can gain a further sense of the confusion in this aspect of the critical problem by considering the views of D. S. Mirsky on James Joyce. After describing the social and ideological backgrounds and the personal history of Joyce, and proving that Joyce was introduced as a figure into the world of the international bourgeoisie by two millionaires, Mirsky asks the question whether or not Joyce offers any model for revolutionary writers:

> The answer is that his method is too inseparably connected with the specifically decadent phase of the bourgeois culture he reflects, is too narrowly confined within its limits. The use of the inner monologue (stream of consciousness method) is too closely connected with the ultra subjectivism of the parasitic, rentier bourgeoisie, and entirely unadaptable to the art of one who is building socialist society. Not less foreign to the dynamics of our [Russian] culture is the fundamentally static method in which the picture of Bloom is composed. . . . There remains still the most fundamental element of Joyce's art, his realistic grasp, his amazing exactness of expression, all that side in which he is of the school of the French naturalists, raising to its ultimate height their cult of the *mot juste*. It is this exactness which gives Joyce the wonderful realistic power in depicting the outer world for which he is famous. But this has its roots on the one hand in a morbid, defeatist delight in the ugly and repulsive and, on the other, in an aesthetico-proprietary desire for the possession of 'things'. So that even this one realistic element of Joyce's style is fundamentally foreign to the realism towards which Soviet art aims, mainly a mastery of the world by means of active, dynamic materialism—with the purpose of not merely understanding but also changing the reality of history.

These quotations reveal the widespread confusion that has accompanied the applications of such categories to literature. Mirsky assumes such a direct tie-up between economics and literature that he finds Joyce's exactitude in description to be an acquisitive and an æsthetico-proprietary desire for "things"; and that Joyce's utilization of the interior monologue is too closely connected with a parasitic element of the bourgeoisie to be usable by revolutionary writers. Such discoveries enable Mirsky to legislate for writers at wholesale on what will or will not influence them.

Michael Gold, seeking to apply these categories, extends them to the audience, applies them retroactively to dead authors, and calls upon the subconscious for abetment in his damnation of bourgeois art. And Granville Hicks, in order to establish the importance of proletarian literature, even relies on such badly subjective evidence as the flat statement that no bourgeois novel will provide him with a unified æsthetic experience. The proper duties of criticism are ignored, and the carry-over value of literature is almost completely disregarded. Functional extremism rampantly leads to one-sided formulæ, the rationalization of prejudices, and the concoction of meaningless recipes for the novelist of the classless society of the future.

Here it becomes necessary to re-emphasize a fairly apparent fact. The "bourgeois" novel has had a long history. It is possible to examine that history, to note the various types of novel that are included within the category, to arrive at some fairly accurate definitions, and even to make some fairly accurate descriptions of its growth and its methods. But with "proletarian" literature this cannot be done, because that literature is now only at the beginning of its history. It will grow and develop as part of the development of literature in general. It will not grow from the definitions of critics. In its growth it will—for some time to come—be constantly influenced by "bourgeois" literature. The assimilation will not be even and regular; it will not proceed according to the dictates of critical legislation. And since literature is a qualitative matter, and since it is æsthetic and subjective as well as functional and objective, the growth of future proletarian literature will not *per se* prove the failure of Joyce or Proust, let alone the failure of Dreiser or Melville. A proletarian classic in the future will not necessarily give rise to dispraise of *Ulysses,* any more than *Macbeth* can logically be cited in dispraise of Dante's *Divine Comedy,* or than Milton's *Paradise Lost* can be used to prove the failure of the author of *Beowulf.*

It seems to me that there are the following possible definitions of proletarian literature: it can be defined as creative literature written by a member of the industrial proletariat, regardless of the author's political orientation; as creative literature that reveals some phase of the experience of the industrial proletariat, regardless of the political orientation of the author; as creative literature written by a member of the industrial proletariat who is class-conscious in the Marxian sense, and a member of the proletarian vanguard; as creative literature written by a class-conscious member of the proletariat and treating solely (or principally) of some phase of the life of that group; as creative literature written about that group within the proletariat regardless of the author's class status or his group status within his class; as creative literature written in order to enforce, through its conclusions and implications, the views of the proletarian vanguard; as creative literature read by the proletariat; as creative literature read by the proletarian vanguard; or as creative literature combining these features in differing combinations.

Irrespective of which of these definitions or combination of definitions one applies, it remains that they do not *per se* constitute a category of value. They do not constitute an *a priori* fiat for the critical destruction of works that will not slide into such a category. Moreover, it does not follow that works of literature snugly fitting into whichever of these definitions (or combinations of definitions) one adopts will be uninfluenced by literature that is unqualifiedly non-proletarian, like Proust's works, or unqualifiedly non-revolutionary, in the political sense, like T. S. Eliot's. For there is a continuity in literature and literary influences, just as there is in thought and in science. The literary process continues whether or not we are critically conscious of it. The tightening of categories into absolutes does not destroy this continuity; it merely diverts the literary influences into a subterranean channel. In so doing, it does not subject them to the test of sensible and intelligent critical evaluation. And this is precisely the error that "leftism" has committed in its effort to harden categories and to ignore the carry-over value in literature.

Since literature is not made by definitions of categories, the definition of proletarian literature presented by our revolutionary critics is not, objectively, so important as they assume it to be. The establishment of functional categories sets up standards of measurement rather than criteria of judgment. But—as is pertinently suggested by John Dewey in *Art as Experience*—it is criteria of judgment, not standards of measurement, that are the business of criticism. And the overemphasis of definitions and categories is least relevant when it is referred to a trend in literature that is only at the beginning of its history, only now preparing to spread its wings and fly in many directions.

Any revolutionary critic who would defend himself against my analysis, and argue that the categories of bourgeois and proletarian are more than descriptive, must take one of two positions: he must admit and adopt a double standard, a dual set of criteria, or else he must favor the destruction of one at the expense of the other. If he recognizes two different sets of criteria—one for proletarian values and proletarian literature, and another for bourgeois values and bourgeois literature—he is contradicting his own position, and consistency will demand that he make adjustments of it elsewhere. He sets a wall between bourgeois values and proletarian values in literature. Not advocating the destruction of bourgeois values, he can then grant them a right to existence only as bourgeois values. For him, this position is utterly untenable; he has only one resource—and that is to recognize that these categories are descriptive.

If he adopts the other position, advocating the destruction of bourgeois values and bourgeois influences, and the creation, enlargement, and solidification of proletarian values and proletarian influences, he must answer certain questions. Where is he to find the source from which he will develop his strictly proletarian values? The answer is—in the life and the needs of the proletariat. But the proletariat does not exist in total isolation from the bourgeoisie, nor from bourgeois influences; it does not, for one thing, live free from tradition. And so, despite the critics' sternest defense, bourgeois values will be smuggled in. If barbed-wire fences are to be placed around the minds of the proletariat and its allies, what then of the stream of cultural continuity? If the critic would like to dam off this stream of cultural continuity, does he actually believe that he can? Yet it seems to me that a relentless enforcement of the view that the categories "bourgeois" and "proletarian" are disconnectably separable, that they are standards, and that the proletariat has all of its values created within the range of its own class experience, leads inevitably to that conclusion. For to say that bourgeois values are useless to the proletariat in culture, to say that proletarian values will take their place uninfluenced by bourgeois values, is to contend that the cultural values and achievements that have grown out of the past are useless to the proletariat, and must therefore be destroyed. But a relentlessly enforced leftist theory leads logically to this conclusion, and to follow it out in action and in criticism constitutes an effort toward such an achievement—if achievement it can be called. The critic who is faced with this interpretation will deny it. Yet what other conclusion can be drawn from his reasoning?

Obviously, this view was not held by the great revolutionary Marxist leaders. Further, it is a position that is today rapidly losing ground in America; though, because at one time it did exert a stronger influence on the revolutionary movement, remnants of it are still to be encountered. Such a theory is not one that preserves culture, for culture permits a more, rather than a less, conscious assimilation of the cultural heritage—which was the aim of all the great Marxist leaders.

André Gide has written:

> In every enduring work of art . . . one that is capable of appealing to the appetites of successive generations, there is to be found a good deal more than a mere response to the momentary needs of a class or a period. It goes without saying that it is a good thing to encourage the reading of such masterpieces; and the U.S.S.R., by its reprints of Pushkin and its performances of Shakespeare, better shows its real love of culture than it does by the publication of a swarm of productions which, while they may be remarkable enough in kind, and while they may exalt its triumphs, are possessed, possibly, of but a passing interest. The mistake, I feel, lies in trying to indicate too narrowly, too precisely, just what is to be looked for in the great works of the past, the lesson that is to be learned from them.

When one freezes the categories of bourgeois and proletarian and insists that they be standards of measurement in literature, one shuts out the enduring element that Gide speaks of. This is, baldly, the position of leftism when it uses its categories in such a way. And it does not sponsor a method that preserves culture. It should remain, then, that the categories bourgeois and proletarian, when applied to literary criticism, are not the basis of value judgment *per se;* rather, they are descriptive categories. Within the category bourgeois, there will be found both progressive and regressive elements. One of the fundamental duties of revolutionary criticism is, as I have already suggested in my comments on Aquinas and Spinoza, to assimilate and further the understanding of the progressive elements, and to negate the influence of the regressive ones. By performing such a task, which is his legitimate one, the critic does not dam up the stream of cultural continuity. Furthermore, his task—evaluating the literature of the present—is not simply and solely that of putting it into categories; nor that of legislating themes on the basis of such categories; nor that of grandiloquently describing future proletarian Prousts greater than Proust. It is rather the task of understanding, assimilating, evaluating, interpreting the literature of the present in a manner analogous to that in which he treats the literature of the past. And if he meets these obligations with intelligence and imagination, he is contributing toward the assimilation of cultural influences and cultural values.

James T. Farrell, "The Categories of 'Bourgeois' and 'Proletarian'," in American Literary Criticism: 1900-1950 *by Charles I. Glicksberg, Hendricks House, Inc., 1952, pp. 429-38.*

NOVELS

Madeleine B. Stern

[In the following excerpt, the critic examines several variations of the proletarian novel, tracing its development from 1929 through 1935.]

In what has been called proletarian literature, books by or about proletarians, there are several variants of a single formula, but I have preferred to group them as a single type of American propagandist literature, the picaresque novel: "picaresque", because it traces the wanderings of the hero from town to town, from one odd job to another, and "proletarian", because the peripatetic in every case belongs to the propertyless class. Within this type of writing, two variants in technique, determined by the authors' point of view, may be discerned: (1) either there is the *leit-motif* of the gradual growth of proletarian class consciousness, in which case the propagandist method would be called "delayed revealed"; or, (2) there is no development of class consciousness, in which case the propagandist technique would be designated as "concealed".

In 1929 Agnes Smedley in her autobiographical novel, *Daughter of Earth,* began the succession of picaresque proletarian works. She traced the experiences of an individual in odd jobs, fighting poverty, and gradually realizing that she belonged with her class, the proletariat, and that the only way out for that class was Socialism. This is the basic theme which became popular with American writers who believed there was a formula for propagandist alchemy.

Edward Dahlberg rehashed the formula in the following year when he sketched the odyssey of Lorry Lewis in *Bottom Dogs.* Lorry's ineffectual youth is sprinkled with diverse and short-lived positions as Western Union messenger, cattle drover, door-to-door solicitor, busboy, and sodasquirt. The Vagabondage of the twentieth-century proletarian picaro consists of "boing, sleeping in coal cars, riding . . . railroad bronchos, going to strange hotel rooms . . . walking the streets." Lorry's listlessness and ineffectuality remain, however, and unlike Agnes Smedley he is not redeemed by the salvation of union with the masses. The novel conceals the *leit-motif;* the itinerant develops no philosophy.

By a similar abstinence from articulating the necessity of revolt, the drab tale of Catherine Brody's *Nobody Starves* (1932) becomes more drab, but at the same time more disturbing. The wayfarers this time are two workers who married before the depression and were later hit by unemployment, wage cuts, and reduction of the working week in the factories of Detroit and Micmac. Throughout the period of the Wall Street crash the journalistic headlines are cheerful. "They were as heart-warming as the predictions of the fortune tellers—so encouraging to hear that there was money in your cup or in your stars though there might be none in your purse." Only once does Bill scent the basic ill: "They won't stick together, that's the trouble." On the whole, he and his companions wander about falteringly, ignorant of their status, not knowing where to go or how. Although Bill finally murders his wife in a blind attempt to annihilate the world, most of the workers in their search for a cure-all simply go to the movies.

Jack Conroy used this pattern for all it was worth in the following year when he wrote *The Disinherited.* Larry Donovan, born in the Monkey Nest miners' camp, witnesses strikes in mines and railroads, works in a steel mill in rubber and auto factories, hustles beet pulp for the Lakes Milling Company, and gradually abandons his desire to rise to a white collar job, realizing that he belongs with his class, and that their struggle is his. "I no longer felt shame at being seen at such work as I would have done once, and I knew that the only way for me to rise to something approximating the grandiose ambitions of my youth would be to rise with my class, with the disinherited: the bricksetters, the flivver tramps, boomers, and outcasts pounding their ears in flophouses." Social consciousness comes to Lorry through a German factory hand and disciple of Karl Liebknecht, as well as through his own experiences of labor and poverty, of scabs and conveyor systems.

In 1935 Conroy paralleled this work when in *A World to Win* he grooved into a similar design the career of an intellectual proletarian. Robert Hurley's youth among the clodhoppers of Green Valley is elaborated; his early and disregarded contact with Sol Abraham, the Communistic influence, is touched upon; and finally, after Hurley has undertaken various odd jobs and bucked up against unemployment, he is endowed by the author with a class-consciousness. We find the usual mid-book attitude when Robert encounters his first strike: "He did not intend to take any part in breaking up a strike, even though he did not intend to endanger his body or his comfort in helping

Jack Conroy.

to win it." It is a far cry from the expected shift when Robert attacks the policeman who pinched his brother and discovers that he too has a world to win. With his realization of the necessity of mass revolt, his thoughts become lyrical: "They sat enclosed warmly in the comradeship of sorrow and weariness and anger, fellows of the men and women—fighting, laboring, seeing—who cry out relentlessly and passionately at factory gates. . . . Their breath a whisper that will not die—the prelude to storm."

In the same year two other writers augmented the picaresque proletarian series: Edward Anderson with *Hungry Men,* and Tom Kromer with *Waiting for Nothing.* Acel Stecker, one of the *Hungry Men,* is an itinerant in flop houses, park benches, and city wharves, who spends his days grubbing tailor-made cigarettes and hitches, marrying casually, and forever hoping like his antecedent, Mr. Micawber, that something will turn up. For although he listens to the Communist disquisitions of Boots, and although he is aware that "the police work for the rich" and that "one man can pay a crooner one thousand dollars for one night and another man can't let his child give a penny to the grind organ", nevertheless Acel's ambition is to become a capitalist in a democratic society. Though he perceives that in a land of plenty there is no reason for him to live as he does, he makes no effort to band with his fellows, but simply boards another freighter for another city. Finally, Acel is acquitted from a jail sentence following a street brawl, because he refused to play "the Internationale" on the streets. At this point the reader suspects that Acel's capitalist ambitions may perhaps be realized. The concealment of propaganda in this book is unusually effective. Better than any blatant plea for Communism, this vision of a youth completely helpless in the society to which he was born, and completely unwilling to change that society, this vision propagandizes.

Kromer's *Waiting for Nothing* is another account of a man trying to get his "three hots and a flop", a man "on the fritz", running into hi-jackers, sitting around jungle fires, sleeping in missions, watching the gas hounds, living on "drags with their strings of cars", meeting prostitutes and stiffs who are trying as he is to get their "three hots and a flop". As in Anderson's book, the *leit-motif* is absent; the characters are too helpless to stick up a man even when they have a "gat", but they are not quite so Micawber-like as Anderson's *Hungry Men;* they are beginning to growl—but under their breath.

In all these novels the reader can anticipate with a fair amount of accuracy the career of the protagonist. The itinerary of the proletarian is chartered on a stereotyped pattern. The variants are few. One character works more or less frequently than another; one character develops a class-consciousness; another remains helpless, unaware, ineffectual. Of those novels which contain the *leit-motif,* Conroy's *Disinherited* is probably the best work. Of those which conceal their propaganda by sustaining their characters in the same state of economic unawareness at the end as at the beginning of their careers, Edward Anderson's *Hungry Men* would probably rank first. Of the two varieties, that which leaves the *leit-motif* unexpressed seems more effective as propaganda because it disturbs the reader more keenly, prods him more sharply with the desire to rouse these men from their chains. Possibly the strongest artistic kinship between reader and character is that felt for Conroy's Larry Donovan. But after reading a succession of novels of this type, the reader cannot but feel that the stories are twice-told tales, narrated almost as well by one writer as another. The authors themselves seem aware that they are following a formula; hence the reader senses that their rehashing of that formula is a blind alley in propagandist literature, and looks for a more valid fictional reaction to the anticipated revolution.

In all the novels we have discussed, the attempt of the authors, whether expressed or tacitly suggested, has been the burgeoning of the workers' class consciousness. In those which are now to be noticed, there is a shift in purpose toward actual labor agitation with emphasis on the basic principles of organization and sabotage. These novels are the fictional counterparts of such works as Erskine Caldwell's *Some American People,* Sherwood Anderson's *Puzzled America,* and James Rorty's *Where Life Is Better.* From the viewpoint of a worker whose class consciousness has already ripened, or is at the point of maturation, the authors investigate conditions in mills and factories before, after, or during some phase of labor agitation.

Mary Heaton Vorse, choosing a limited field of inquiry, employing the device of repetition, reports in *Strike!* (1930) the working conditions in the Basil-Schenk Manufacturing Company at Stonerton, Virginia. Recurrent scenes are given in which pickets, scabs, State Troops, and relief committees parade at cross purposes during the factory strike. We hear, in recurrent speeches, the diverse viewpoints of the Northern leader, the labor reporter, the hostile bourgeois, the mill hands. The stretch-out is followed by attempts at fraternization which in turn are succeeded by evictions, an attempted lynching, and finally a general slaughter of the laborites. Miss Vorse, without eliminating superfluities, all too adequately fulfills her promise to

> tell . . . how first they overwork them and underpay them. They underpay them so much that mothers of families have to overwork. They abuse them and mistreat them when they try to organize. Finally they evict them. It's the cycle one has to enlarge upon.

And enlarge upon it she does, leaving no element unmentioned in the rebellion against pellagra and tuberculosis, against "the stretch-out", the day of twelve hours and twenty minutes, and an average weekly wage of twelve dollars.

Despite the fact that the author limits her scope to a single factory, within that scope she makes no attempt to sift her material for large kernels of interest; in her desire to tell everything she fails because of her wealth of unselected material.

By a carefully planned delay of her introduction of a strike, Grace Lumpkin two years later not only achieved greater artistic effectiveness than Mary Heaton Vorse, but wrote a novel which marks the high water mark of the literature of labor agitation. In *To Make My Bread* (1932) the McClure family is first presented to us in their native setting in Siler's Cove. The characters are well-rounded, three-dimensional figures. We see them searching for food, smacking their lips over a confab in the general store, being born, dying. Thus, when they migrate to a factory town, we are stricken far more by their struggle against disease, poverty, and overwork than if we had never met them before. The fact that Emma, whom we knew in Siler's Cove, is mowed down by pellagra is more moving than reports of multiple pellagra cases in *Strike!* Finally, through the influence of John Stevens, the singing laborer, Bonnie awakes to the realization of the evil of the factory. She is able to calculate that the cloth she makes "for fifty cents is sold for six dollars". Ora concludes, without preliminary readings in Thoreau, that she doesn't "run the machines any more. . . . They run me". John Stevens brings them the cue to rebellion. "We must work in a strike, but there is something else. We must go beyond the strike to the message . . . that we must join with all others like us and take what is ours." And Bonnie takes up the cue, and dies proclaiming it. *Let Freedom Ring,* the play based on the novel, condenses and centralizes the action by certain modifications; the result is more compact propaganda, but less literary satisfaction. For the novel, although it eliminates non-essentials, gives us this family in full detail confronting a society against which the reader is led, in union with the McClures, to revolt.

In 1934 Robert Cantwell wrote a book which was acclaimed by some as the finest example of proletarian literature on record. Nevertheless, *The Land of Plenty* must remain a book in which Trick is the most unforgettable element. The Past Bay Manufacturing Company is placed on exhibition for the reader during the few moments in which the power behind the lights fails. During this time we witness the ineffectual circles in the air made by the sawdust taskmasters, Belcher and his overlord, Macmahon. The workers are represented by Hagen, the efficient, responsible laborer who has aged at his post. The book is a preface to strike. It compliments such studies as Albert Maltz's *Black Pit* and Mary Heaton Vorse's *Strike!,* for it is less preoccupied with the material discomforts of the workers, though these are neglected, than with the insidious influence of Carl Belcher, the "efficiency expert", who knows as little about men as about the actual working of the plant. His task he accomplishes with thoroughness: the discharging of men and the reduction of salaries.

> He was wrecking something that had been built up out of years of practice and labor, and even though they [the workers] were not conscious of it they sensed what he was doing and they were horrified and outraged as they would have been at any wanton destruction. . . .

The reader, along with the workers, is brought to the conviction that the presence of Belcher, with all of its pernicious implications, makes a strike ineluctable. Like most strike literature in America, the book is only indirectly Communistic. The strikers are accused of being Communists—which they are not. *The Land of Plenty* is a clever piece of writing; but the reader seldom finds any depths below its strategy.

In the same year, 1934, two novels appeared attacking the problems of labor agitation from different directions. In *The Foundry* Albert Halper gives a clear analysis of the conflicts between closed and open shop, and between craft and industrial unionism. The former contrast is externalized by having closed shop in the Fort Dearborn Electrotype Foundry, and open shop in Bowman House, lodged in the same building, from which the foundry receives its orders. The advantages of a Union network are evidenced on several occasions. Slavony, the tank-man, discharged ostensibly for eating a sandwich before lunch, actually for drawing a vulgar picture of boss Steuber, is returned to work through the quiet sabotage of his fellows in the Union. Again the power of closed shop is apparent when "the Big Smasher", Steuber's time-saving machine, intended to "shave three finishers off the payroll" is itself smashed. The non-union men are more easily disposed of than Slavony. Waldo, the errand boy, who liked to eat lunch during his lunchtime, and Hooper-Dooper, the janitor who felt "too young in the afternoon", are removed from the payroll without opposition. The contrast between craft and industrial unionism is clearly expounded by Karl Heitman, the "shop radical", who disparages the smug content of those entrenched in their little craft union, and bids them

> wake up to the fact that the labor movement is something bigger than our own little local; . . . it takes in everybody, yes, even the workers down in the plant below. . . . there are no scabs, only unorganised workers. . . .

The author intelligently handles the transition period between the first and second steps in organized labor, and analyses with insight the defeated, frustrated lives of the three bosses. He escapes the error of endowing every capitalist with beefy hands and trembling jowls. The book rings true. Its expositions are clear; its propaganda honest; and the canvas of life in a foundry is artistically complete.

In William Rollins's *The Shadow Before* we return to the strike proper, beginning from the inside of the Baumann-Jones Mill, and working our way out to the picket lines along the mental currents of the laborers. A ten percent wage cut precipitates a strike which the reader suspects is directed not only toward a salary raise but toward a revolution in the system which sponsored the cut. The workers who had lived their spare moments in pool rooms or movies become conscientious picketers, and find "the substitute for the old Brotherhood of Man: *class consciousness!* " The book is on the whole a mild dose of William Faulkner in Dos Passos form. Various sexual perversions are interpolated between the passages about the strike. However, the two are seldom amalgamated despite the fact that the same characters participate in both activities. Thus, though Rollins avoids the monotony of *Strike!* his episodic technique is not managed cleverly enough to attain that welding of many themes to be found, for example, in the works of Fielding Burke.

James Steele's *The Conveyor* (1935), is the fictional complement to Caldwell's *Some American People* in so far as it exposes working conditions in the Rivers auto plant. The novel is a kaleidoscope in which speed-up, accidents, labor-eliminating machinery, discarded safety devices whirl about in a bubble to be burst only by labor agitation and organization. Like his picaresque proletarian fellows, Jim is one hundred-percent American until he is forced to perceive that when the Rivers Motor Company advertises a high wage policy, it concomitantly lays off thousands of workers, and reduces the working-week of those who remain. "I guess ol' Si Rivers didn't lose no money when he put up wages. He's got ev'rybody doin' almost two men's work now. Quite a savin', ain't it?" And finally, Jim is prepared to participate in Bill's agitation for union.

Six years after Vorse's book, John Steinbeck paralleled her work with his treatment of a strike among fruit croppers in *In Dubious Battle* (1936). The point of difference is that here the perspective is candidly Communistic. Two members of the party organize a strike in Torgas Valley for higher wages, and are defeated by organized Vigilantism and strike-breaking activities which include the shooting of three strikers and the shutting off of the food supply. Leninist doctrine is applied consistently. It is stated that the mob is "stronger than all the men put together"; it is proclaimed though the strike itself ends in failure, a thousand men will have "learned how to strike", and will be ready to pool their knowledge in the days of the revolution. The compulsion which the Communists are under to employ any material that comes to hand to rouse the rebellion of the workers is reiterated in numerous episodes. Vetoed votes, burned barns, dead bodies are used as kindlewood to raise the flame. Nevertheless, the reader never actually sees a transition between Jim as an apprentice-Communist, and Jim as the competent, mature, clear-headed leader; never actually feels the mob working as a knit force. We are not sufficiently conscious of the men *en masse* to be roused to joy in their strike, to confess that though the battle is dubious, we are ready ourselves to go forth with the sword.

In the field of labor agitation certain novels rise above the recipe for strike literature, and move the reader to a disturbing sense of the necessity of revolt. This is accomplished most successfully by Grace Lumpkin in *To Make My Bread*. In the more limited realm of problems of organization Albert Halper has produced the most adequate work. The remaining novels are so caught up with tricks to amaze the reader, as *The Land of Plenty,* or so involved in the mass of detail about working conditions or the machinery of a strike, as the writings of Vorse and Steele, that they never project the reader within the rebellious consciousness of the laborer. We search then for another form of proletarian literature, not quite so limited in scope as that concerned with strikes and unionism, which may perhaps give greater opportunity to the writer to draw creative richness from the revolution.

In place of following the formula adhered to by writers of picaresque proletarian novels, or of emulating those authors who stripped the problems of American propaganda to accounts of labor agitation, some writers chose the structure of the novel inherited through bourgeois tradition in which to house their equally radical, but less limited propaganda. Such a technique began rather self-consciously when Kenneth Burke inserted in a novel sty-

listically resembling the work of Virginia Woolf, some trenchant, disillusioned remarks about the dictatorship of the proletariat. *Towards a Better Life* (1932) is a strange and beautiful piece of writing in which those emotions reserved by many writers for parenthetical statement are expanded and embroidered in verbal *petit-point*. But the novel also contains such statements as these: "The man did good for the oppressed? Then he made them oppressors", or "Oh, there is a revolutionary unction. There are the blasts of the well fed . . . comfortably summoning the people to rebel . . . They are the bankers' conscience . . . and can be kept about the house like castrated lion whelps", or "If enough men could be brought to realize their plight, then we could at their instigation have a reshuffling". No proletarian philosophy has been developed. But the author has begun to realize that the novelistic form used by Virginia Woolf to entrap the delicacies of feathers and saucepans and china, may also serve as a vehicle for conveying scattered musings on the proletariat.

In the same year Fielding Burke in *Call Home the Heart* used the novel form inherited from the nineteenth century, not merely as a dumping ground for fleeting radical cogitations, but as a broad pedestal on which to base her deeply-lodged Communistic convictions. Thus, instead of verbal insertions, we find Communism completely integrated in the life of a full-blooded character. As inevitably as her love for Britt, her bearing of children, her search for a broader life among the people of the town, does Communism enter the consciousness of Ishma. Through her contact with Derry Unthank and her experience in the mill, Ishma comes to understand the words of Dan Ogler that "no matter how glittering the front that capitalism may flaunt, at the end of its proud parade it wags the tail of a breadline". Ishma's personality is enriched by her life as a North Carolina mill worker, and she is ready to propagandize for internationalism in organized labor. "If we are pushed to the wall in spite of our union, it isn't because the union is wrong but because it isn't big enough. It's because it doesn't cover the earth. We'll do what we can to make it big enough, instead of punching holes in it." Like all of her other natural activities, Ishma's belief in the union and her devotion to Communism are not transitory interests but deeply seated forces that possess her and become more and more potent in her stride through life. Fielding Burke gives us a novel that amalgamates the emotional richness of a strong, mature woman of the hills with a profound belief in Communism. Both are inextricably welded within the frame of the traditional novel.

1932 saw the beginning of another successful effort to incorporate propaganda in the accepted novel form. James T. Farrell's Studs Lonigan, as far as his patriotism goes, is generally related to Dahlberg's Lorry Lewis, Catherine Brody's Bill, and Edward Anderson's Acel Stecker. Despite his impotence and ineffectuality, of which he is upon isolated occasions aware, Studs is congenitally blind to the social forces that inundate him. James Farrell gives his character an opportunity to speak with a radical. Let us listen to the dialogue:

STUDS: But Bolshevism means revolution.

THE RED: How else are we going to win the means of production for ourselves?

STUDS: But that's anarchy.

THE RED: What is it when guys like me all over the country carry the banner, sleep in Hoovervilles? What is it when they shoot down coal miners?

STUDS: I'm not a Bolshevik. It's against the country and the church.

Farrell throws the spotlight on Studs when he attempts a bit of thinking after witnessing the parade of workers:

> Why did these Jews and foreigners and Reds want to go on disrupting the way they did? . . . Children shouldn't be let parade with all this riff-raff, taught socialism and anarchy and atheism and ideas against God and America and the home in their tender years. . . . These youngsters should be taken away from their parents by law and placed in institutions so that they would not be contaminated with all their vile Bolshevism . . . Lonigan thought he had a bigger squawk than these people, because he was losing more. And still he wasn't a Red, was he?

Studs is the net result of his parent's advice to curse "those goddamn Jew international bankers", of his parochial school training, of the movies and can houses in which his ego can distend itself. The propagandist method is "concealed"; that is, the author never attempts to reform overtly; and the propaganda itself is subordinated to traditional devices of depicting character. Farrell details minutely, step by step, the personality of Studs, bewildered runaway, ineffectual pugilist, avid movie-goer, unquestioning Catholic, one hundred-percent American, who has nothing to lose but many corroded chains, and who will not unite with the other Lonigans of America. He is thrown living in large proportions of flesh and blood before the reader; and the reader becomes aware of the social causes of Lonigan's impotent brutality and final defeat, and of their subtly implied remedy. Although Farrell uses the modern device of the scenario script in certain episodes, in the main his technique does not depart from that of nineteenth century trilogies. His novels are constructed around a character by architectonics similar to those of *Tom Jones.* The prodigality of detail, however, includes a tacit warning of malignant social forces in America, the outcome of which are blindness, destruction, death.

In 1933 Josephine Herbst returned partially to the method of Kenneth Burke. In *Pity is Not Enough,* a novel in the formal bourgeois tradition, the author sporadically warns her protagonist that the "barbaric form of social organization with its legalized plunder and murder, is doomed to die and make room for freer society." Trexler's meditations about social idealism constitute merely an irrelevant motif in the life of this fugitive from the courts of the South after the Civil War. The fact that Miss Herbst uses a social outcast about whom to weave her novel is an important indication of the trend toward introducing revolutionary characters and concepts in the established bourgeois form. James T. Hanley in *Stoker Bush* (1936) used a similar method of telling a tale of love, desertion and

jealousy, by adopting a proletarian as his protagonist. The suggestion in the latter work is that the proletarian can stand on his own as a character in a traditional story; that he has gone beyond the need of propaganda and can take his place in literature as the prime mover of a story that might equally concern an aristocrat or a capitalist.

Waldo Frank in 1934 searched further back in the bourgeois tradition than the nineteenth century to find a form for his propagandist message. *The Death and Birth of David Markand* is actually a twentieth-century version of the medieval Quest story. In place of the Holy Grail, there is class consciousness: union with man instead of union with Christ. The devices are also medieval in their symbolism. Markand abandons his wife and children, his work in the dead body of the United Tobacco Industries, and his dead money reaped from the bondage of peons, for a strange quest. He lives in the fields and meets Deborah Gore, and the worker, Stan; like the picaresque proletarian, he alternates varied forms of labor with periodic loafing. As newspaper devil, barkeep, and politician, he comes to know workers on their own level. He fails sometimes, and spreads pain. It is through him indirectly that Stan is killed. At last David discovers John Byrne, the radical, and learns the alternatives before him:

> You've got your choice between socialist or Christian, and if you have any guts you'll *be* one or the other. If you recognize your unity with all men. . . . then you'll be a socialist. If you stand aside, denying man . . . then you'll invent God and be a Christian. . . . If you lack the guts . . . to choose, you'll shilly-shally between the two and be a bourgeois liberal.

But Byrne dies, and also David's son, both through a vague, symbolic inadequacy in David. Slowly, in and out of many blind alleys, he wanders, questing; gradually, through his work in the shambles, in barrooms, in the Batesville Steel Mill, class consciousness comes to him, and with it a new birth.

> I embrace your class. All men who want to live today must embrace it. My own life needs it to live. I have only the dead body of a class that dies: I need, that I may live, the living body of the class which is now life.

The Death and Birth has been condemned by Marxist critics for its flights into vague idealism. At the basis of such criticism there seems to lie a preconceived notion that a proletarian novel must not borrow from bourgeois tradition, and surely must not adopt medieval Christian devices. In the light of what Frank has achieved, such a condemnation appears to the present writer to be simply the "reductio ad absurdum" of pursuing Marxist criticism to its logical end. For Frank goes beneath all superficies and leaves us with the granite essentials of a man who wanders through a penumbra into light. The book is more than propaganda, for it touches the philosophy, and below the philosophy, the caverns of a human being between two worlds in travail, bringing life to the new. It couches the timely in terms of the universal. David Markand might be called an Everyman finding himself in this, our century.

It is an anticlimax to discuss after such a work, a novel

which also appeared in 1934, Arnold B. Armstrong's *Parched Earth*. By symbolistic devices, within the traditional novel form, the author flays the insidious tzar of a small town in Tontos Valley, California. Everett Caldwell has a malignant effect not only upon the workers whom he discharges by the installation of machinery, but also, symbolically, upon the town prostitute who bears him an idiot son. The character of Caldwell is condemned as much because of his baleful economic influence as because of his desire to hush up the paternity of the town idiot. He is the rugged individualist who tramples upon the fruit cutters of Slob Row, sets the price for canned fruit, and considers labor cheap, "capital god-like in its prerogatives". Hop Collins understands the evil when he declaims,

> Who in hell gives a damn about the workin'-man these days 'cept the Communists? The A. F. L. sure don't. The Wobblies is gone. The Socialists ain't been for the laborin' man since Debs' time. . . .

Feebly and hesitantly the down-trodden join with Dave Washburn, the proletarian leader, who is injured by the idiot Wally, symbol of Caldwell's deleterious power. The fact that Wally also dynamites the dam and floods the town may be interpreted as the symbolical overthrow of Caldwell and his entourage; for Hop, and Hatty who believes in him, are saved in the flood. Unless so construed, the general disaster at the end of the novel is merely a sensational collapse of all the cards in the deck, reminiscent of the close of *Tom Thumb the Great*. A symbolical interpretation indicates that Caldwell is engulfed by his own economic malice. Marxist prognostications are neatly tied up in the strings of symbolism.

Fielding Burke proved once again in 1935 that she knows better than most writers on proletarian themes how to incorporate economic issues in the normal lives of human beings. This was apparent in *Call Home the Heart* and it is equally so in the sequel, *A Stone Came Rolling*. In addition to her power of amalgamating diverse strands, the author makes those individuals who are devoted to the Communist cause so appealing, so strong and kind that the reader, though he be a dyed-in-the-wool conservative, is tricked into sympathy with their cause. Ishma has such a firm and well-controlled vision, that in caring for her, a reader must see nobility in the purpose to which she is devoted. Ishma has gone no further in her development as a Communist than in the preliminary novel. She still bewails division in labor and the struggle of workers against workers. She still upholds the belief that "all of the workers must take all of the mills at the same time". And *A Stone Came Rolling* goes no further than *Call Home the Heart*. Using the same device of incorporating radical issues in nineteenth-century fictional form, it simply repeats the message of *Call Home the Heart* in an equally forceful manner.

When Grace Lumpkin abandoned labor agitation proper and attempted to introduce Communism into a bourgeois novel form, she did not sustain her craftsmanship. *A Sign for Cain* (1935) is inferior to *To Make My Bread* mainly because the author lacks Fielding Burke's power to unite

diverse elements. Having introduced her original theme of poverty among the Southern negroes, an issue in which the building of "a new world" where "people will have plenty because there is enough for everyone" is quite congruent, the author runs off on a tangent, abandons the collective needs of whites and blacks, and pursues a problem that is purely racial. Denis, the negro, and Bill Duncan, the white editor, unite in their Communist agitations. But with the murder of Evelyn Gardner by her dissolute nephew Jim, the story is shunted off to the consideration of a strictly negro issue. The blacks, Denis and Fincents, are arrested for rape and murder, and are slain by Jim. Thus we have simply another variation on the Scottsboro case, and inter-racial Communism is relegated to mid-air. In addition to this failing, the dialogue of the Southern aristocrats is halting and melodramatic; Miss Lumpkin is more sure of herself among the workers. Hence, no doubt, her success in managing problems of labor agitation and her failure in attempting a novel in the bourgeois tradition.

In the same year Bruno Traven published *The Treasure of the Sierra Madre* (1935), a book that employs all the alluring devices of adventure stories and pulp magazines to prove that there is a curse on gold, a capitalistic curse. Only on rare occasions does Traven interrupt his exciting tale of a hunt for gold, reminiscent in its adventure of the works of London, Conrad, et al., to remind the reader that though the story is a thriller it is also an imprecation on American society. Three shiftless men band together to search for an abandoned gold mine. They work the field and hoard the nuggets.

> Those who up to this time had been considered by them as their proletarian brethren were now enemies against whom they had to protect themselves. As long as they had owned nothing of value, they had been slaves of their hungry bellies. . . . All this was changed now. . . . They had reached the first step by which man becomes the slave of his property.

After many adventures Dobbs begins to feel the curse. After slaying Curtin for his share of the gold, he, the erstwhile outcast, now "longed for civilization, for law, for justice, which would protect his property and his person with a police force. . . . " The book is the perfect "tribute" to capitalistic civilization, for in its terrifying accusation it demonstrates that even those who are in it and of it and glorify it, are tricked by it into death and failure.

Sinclair Lewis thumbed his literary nose at American society by viewing it, not as the previous writers have done, in its present form, but as it might become. Although the liberal viewpoint is sustained throughout *It Can't Happen Here* (1935) the author often accuses the Fascists from within the Fascist camp. This trick of allowing the opposition to flaunt its own iniquity instead of openly attacking it from the other side of the fence has a powerful effect, and appears in parallel works in England (*In the Second Year*) and Italy (*Fontmara*). Outside of this device, *It Can't Happen Here* differs from none of Lewis's other works which are all in the formal literary tradition. This strong polemic against American Fascism, with details borrowed from readings in Tchernavin, Billinger, Lorant, etc., loses its effectiveness because of the undecided attitude of Doremus Jessup, the raconteur. The reader, along with Jessup, hates the Corpo Fascistic state as much as Lewis, but neither Lewis nor Jessup nor the reader knows precisely what kind of state should be substituted for Capitalism, Fascism, or Communism. All three forms of government are indicted. The Russian experiment is called by Doremus, "an imagination-hating, pharisaic materialism". Capitalism and Fascism are equally antipathetic to the liberal who claims that "the worst Fascists were they who disowned the word 'Fascism' and preached enslavement to Capitalism under the style of Constitutional and Traditional Native American Liberty". Jessup is a liberal who would neither go forward to a revolutionary state, nor backward to reactionary dictatorship, nor would yet stand still. This is the type of propaganda that is unsatisfying simply because it is so very provocative. The reader's question, "What then?" must perforce remain rhetorical.

Reviewing the writings that indict American society, or analyse the class struggle, or propound revolutionary dogma within the confines of the inherited literary form, we must conclude that thus far these novels win the laurels for artistic and propagandist effectiveness. The works of Fielding Burke, Waldo Frank, James T. Farrell, and Bruno Traven bear evidence that the concept of the revolution gave a wealth of opportunity to the writer who was not completely dislodged from his literary moorings. In their own field, *To Make My Bread* and *The Foundry* are certainly as effective as many of the novels we have dis-

cussed. But one cannot help feeling that the writers who have adapted the bourgeois tradition to their immediate needs have succeeded not only in writing a convincing indictment of American society within a definite period, but also in bestowing upon their imprecations a universality and timelessness impossible within the narrower confines of the literature of labor agitation. Certainly none of the picaresque proletarian novels is comparable in artistic achievement or proselytizing power with the books we have just analyzed. Instead of following propagandist formulas, or of limiting themselves to labor agitation, Frank, Burke, Traven, and Farrell applied their literary inheritance to their observations of American society. They welded the present with the past and, finding them miscible, created novels that are now, and one feels will remain valid whenever men join against forces that oppress and annihilate.

> *Madeleine B. Stern, "America: Paradise or Paradox? Propaganda or Art? III," in* The Sewanee Review, *Vol. XLVI, No. 1, Winter, 1938, pp. 45-69.*

David D. Anderson

[*Anderson, founder of the Society for the Study of Midwestern Literature, has written critical studies of such figures as Sherwood Anderson, Louis Bromfield, William Jennings Bryan, Robert Ingersoll, and Brand Whitlock. In the following essay, Anderson traces the development of the proletarian novel, characterizing Jack Conroy's* The Disinherited *as a standard by which other works of the genre may be evaluated.*]

On October 24, 1929, the bottom fell out of a stock market already abandoned by a good many shrewd investors, but Americans not associated with Wall Street, Washington, or *Billboard* magazine hardly noticed for more than a year. Both the *Nation* and *The New Republic* denounced speculators and remained optimistic, while the *New Masses* ignored both the crash and the opportunity to point out the onset of the collapse it had predicted for so long.

But by late 1930 it was evident to most Americans that whatever was happening was more than readjustment, as politicians and pundits insisted, but a collapse of serious proportions, and decline continued; by early 1932 industrial production had fallen to half its 1929 volume, and early in 1933 the banking system collapsed, stock market prices were in single digits, and more than 12 million Americans were unemployed. For the first time in the American experience, an economic condition promised to loom as large as the Civil War in the American psyche.

But within a generation World War II had been fought and won, a new American prosperity had emerged, and the Depression, as the economic collapse of the 1930s became known, had almost disappeared from the American memory, disbelieved by those who didn't experience it and recalled with an almost nostalgic sentiment by many who did, who saw in it a somehow kinder, more virtuous America. In either case, the effects of the Depression—with a capital D—began to suffer from a problem with

---

The rise and fall of the proletarian novel:

The rise, and also the decline, of the proletarian novel in the thirties is best indicated by [the following] figures. . . . During the decade seventy examples of the form were published, fifty of them, a significantly large majority, appearing between 1930 and 1935. These fifty came chiefly in two waves, a preliminary one in 1932—eleven books—and a larger and more extended one in 1934 and 1935—thirteen and fifteen books respectively. The year 1933, with only four novels, marks a low possibly explained by the economics of Depression publishing and the draining off of the energies of writers into the 1932 Communist political campaign; while the sharp drop on the other side of 1935 to no more than six in any of the last years of the decade represents the decline. . . . A total of seventy novels over a period of ten years or even fifty over six does not represent a genuine literary *movement* even though it is greater in quantity and more concentrated in time than the prewar Socialist output; and it certainly does not lead to the conclusion that, during a time when, despite economic stagnation, an average of nearly 1900 fiction titles was published annually, Communism had "taken over" American writing. Nevertheless this body of work does represent an area of our literature worth exploring—extrinsically because it was the occasion of great furor at the time and intrinsically because it was by no means entirely given over to "desolate wastes," as it is now customarily labeled on the literary maps.

> *Walter B. Rideout, in his* The Radical Novel in the United States, *1956.*

what David G. Pugh and others have defined as "believability," a problem noted earlier by Edmund Wilson.

In his preface to *The American Earthquake,* a documentary of the twenties and thirties published in 1958, Wilson commented that it is difficult "for persons who were born too late to have memories of the depression to believe that it really occurred, that between 1929 and 1933 the whole structure of American society seemed actually to be going to pieces." It was the shock of this recognition, of this American Earthquake, as Wilson termed it, that gave rise to what appeared to be the sudden emergence of a literary movement that pridefully called itself proletarian, that flourished briefly, reaching its apex in the early 1930s, and then, confused or refuted by Stalinism, by the rise of Fascism, and the signing of a mutual non-aggression pact by Germany and Russia, faded into an oblivion that permits it to emerge only as a social, historical, or literary curiosity.

During its brief history, proletarian writing captured the leadership as well as the imagination of much of the intellectual establishment in the United States, and its effects, largely through the influence of the Federal Writers Project and the lively intellectual press of the period, were felt in every state of the forty-eight. In each, in states suffering from agricultural decline and industrial chaos, writers, young and not so young, proclaimed themselves proletarian and proceeded to write books—essays, poems, novels, plays—that they were convinced were truly proletarian.

Nevertheless, at the time and since, there has been a good deal of debate about the meaning of the term in a literary context. Although its origins are in ancient Rome and its use in English as a term for the lowest social and economic classes in the modern sense dates to the mid-nineteenth century, its literary meaning began in this century, and in use it has taken on connotations of social action and commitment rather than description. Almost invariably it has become read as Marxist, revolutionary, or communist.

What appears to have been its first literary use in America was, however, descriptive rather than ideological. For example, in *The New Republic* for September 20, 1917, in his review of *Marching Men,* Sherwood Anderson's novel of a purposeful revolutionary, Francis Hackett comments,

> The chief fact about *Marching Men* is not, however, its rhetoric, its grandiloquence. It is its apprehension of the great fictional theme of our generation, industrial America. Because the subject is barbarous, anarchic and brutal it is not easy for its story to be told. . . .
>
> . . . it seems to me, the proletarian has had small place in American fiction. Under the ban of negligible ugliness, as the eminent novelists see it, comes the majority of the people. They, the eminent ones, have principally been the children of circumspect parents. . . . Outside their view lies the life of the proletarian except as it impinges on the middle class. . . . The proletarians are in a different universe of discourse. . . .
>
> Where *Marching Men* succeeds is in thrusting the greater American realities before us, seen as by a workingman himself. It is . . . a narrative

that suggests the presence in our fiction of a man who knows our largest theme.

When Hackett's use of proletarian literature as based on subject matter is applied to other novels of essentially the same generation—Stephen Crane's *Maggie,* Brand Whitlock's *The Turn of the Balance,* Frank Norris's *The Octopus,* or Upton Sinclair's *The Jungle,* for example—it is evident that Anderson's novel was by no means the first American proletarian work of fiction, but it was apparently one of the first to be perceived as such. In *Marching Men,* Anderson's Beaut McGregor comes out of the working class to lead a mindless, non doctrinaire revolt against a dehumanized and dehumanizing system, ignoring economics in a search for the rebirth of freedom in America. However, classified in the context of a proletarian subject matter, it was to remain virtually alone until the call for a proletarian literature by Michael Gold and V. F. Calverton in the 1920s.

Four years after the publication of *Marching Men* and more than three after the October Revolution, an essay by Michael Gold appeared in the Feb. 1921 issue of *The Liberator,* the successor to the *Masses,* which had become a war casualty. In the essay, called "Toward a Proletarian Art," Gold made an emotional appeal in what he later admitted was "a rather mystic and intuitive" manner for a proletarian art and culture that would heed Walt Whitman's prophetic cry, turn to the social revolution now begun in Russia, and recognize that ". . . its secular manifestations of strike, boycott, mass-meeting, imprisonment, sacrifice, agitation, martyrdom, organization, is thereby worthy of the religious devotions of the artist." He ended by proclaiming the cultural revolution by which a proletarian culture would rise from "the deepest depths upward." No mention was made of the working class—the revolution was for artists and intellectuals—and the essay passed almost unnoticed.

By the mid-1920s, however, the concept of a proletarian literature had been taken up by leftist writers and critics, among whom the most prominent were Gold, writing in *The New Masses,* and Calverton in the *Modern Quarterly.* Both were Marxist, although both were often at war with doctrinaire Communists and both were at times called Trotskyites. Both sought to fuse in literature a new subject matter and an activist philosophy without surrendering to polemics and becoming propagandistic rather than artistic.

In 1926, in an essay in *New Masses,* Gold challenged Lenin's statement in *Literature and Revolution* that a true proletarian literature was impossible, that the proletarian dictatorship would disappear in the classless society before such a literature could evolve. He asserted that "It is not a matter of theory; it is a fact that a proletarian style is emerging in art," a style he was later to define in the term "proletarian realism." This style, he declared, "deals with the *real conflicts* of men and women . . . "; it "must have a social theme or it is mere confection . . . ": it rejects "drabness, the bourgeois notion that the Worker's life is sordid . . . ": it must reject "all lies about human nature . . . ": it must recognize that "life itself is the supreme melodrama . . . "

V. F. Calverton's concept of proletarian literature was, however, less doctrinary than evolutionary as a natural, organic development in literature and a movement toward freedom in American culture. In *The Liberation of American Literature,* published in 1932, he wrote:

> What is needed in America today is a renewed faith in the masses. American literature has to find something of that faith in the potentialities of the proletariat which Emerson and Whitman possessed in the nineteenth century. It was Emerson . . . who was so enthusiastic about the civilization which was being created in the West by men in shirt sleeves, men of unexalted station and plebeian origin, and who looked to that civilization with its democratic spirit to transform the country. It was Whitman who was ecstatic about the fact that it was democratic America which had elevated the poor man into the lord of creation, and had made the world recognize "the dignity of the common people . . . " But the faith in the common man which Emerson and Whitman entertained was faith in him as an individual and not as a mass . . . What we need today is a return to that faith in the common man, in the mass, but a faith founded upon a collective instead of an individualistic premise . . . In that belief lies the ultimate liberation of American literature—and American life.

Important to both Gold and Calverton was an insistence that the new literature be optimistic, that it celebrate the common man in the mass rather than as an individual, that it reject the prevailing naturalistic pessimism of American realism and return American literature to the note of affirmation that had characterized it in the past.

However, neither Gold's nor Calverton's pronouncements defined a clear path for proletarian literature to take, nor, significantly, did either Gold or Calverton see a place for the proletariat—the working class or its individual members—in the movement. Although both Gold and Calverton might reasonably have seen the movement as coming out of the proletariat—Gold began life as Irving Granich on Manhattan's lower East Side in 1894, an experience he described in *Jews Without Money* (1930), an autobiographical novel, and V(ictor) F(rances) Calverton began as George Goetz in 1900 in a Baltimore butcher's family—both saw the movement as intellectual and artistic, a continuation of the artistic revolution proclaimed by the Ivy League editors of the *Seven Arts* in 1916.

Nevertheless, critical and political battles over the nature and substance continued throughout the decade of the 1930s, echoes of which are with us yet. But before Gold had published his essay in *New Masses* in 1926, a proletarian literary movement had already begun, not in Greenwich Village, but among the proletariat, where it remained unnoticed by the intellectuals until after the egg laid in the New York Stock Exchange had begun to hatch. While Malcolm Cowley's young men and women were going to their exile in Montmartre and Montparnasse, or taking refuge in Greenwich Village, young writers who had come out of the proletariat or who remained in it had already begun to examine the human underside of the facade of prosperity and the human cost of the grandest spree in American history, but their work was to pass unnoticed by the *New Masses* and the *Modern Quarterly,* just as it passes unnoticed in studies of what Alfred Kazin calls "The Great Liberation" of the 1920s. Yet more than all the critical essays that call for revolution in the 1920s, they foreshadow what is to come in the 1930s.

Of the novels that anticipate Gold's and Calverton's call and that point directly to the major accomplishment of Jack Conroy, especially in *The Disinherited* in 1933, are two novels: Lawrence H. Conrad's *Temper,* published in 1924, and set in the 1920s in a Detroit heavy-industrial plant, is the flip side of the Horatio Alger myth, and G. D. Eaton's *Backfurrow,* published in 1925, is the story of a young man's failed attempt to escape the drudgery of the farm for the promised intellectual and cultural fulfillment of the city.

Temper emphasizes not the function of the factory but its drudgery and dehumanizing mindlessness and repetitiveness, much as did Sherwood Anderson in *Marching Men* and in his later industrial journalism. In the background brutality engenders mindless but covert rebellion that occasionally becomes overt violence.

In the foreground, however, the protagonist, Paul Rinelli, an Italian-American immigrant, is determined that he will rise in the system to control it, snatching power and ultimately wealth not only from the system itself but from those who would deprive him of it.

Rinelli works in various parts of the factory, each department more brutal and demanding than the others, and, rather than rising in the system, he finds the power and fury of the furnaces becoming his own, becoming part of his nature:

> . . . the furnaces and the men breathed against each other. They stood hissing all night long, and there was deadly hate in the hot breath that each one breathed out. And there was a feeling, too, that some day this would have to end, that some day one of these breaths would fail, and every man knew that it would not be the breath of the furnace. . . .

Rinelli is transferred to the blacksmith shop after a fight, but he has learned something from the furnaces:

> . . . He hated now; the fire had taught him that . . . and some day he was going to get somebody good and proper. In the meantime he took it out on the steel. What a blow he could strike!

Finally, however, Rinelli fights with a burly Scots foreman, and for the first time he is not only beaten badly but humiliated. Transferred again to a small rolling mill, in a moment's inattention he reaches out for a hot steel rod. He grasps it and faints with pain. When he awakens in the hospital his hand is a misshapen mass; a kindly company, rejecting responsibility, nevertheless lets him become a night watchman, and in the dark hours, he is free to find whatever fulfillment he can.

Here, clearly, is the underside not only of the prosperity of the twenties, but of the myths that Americans have made their own: the significance of the individual, the open society, the Gospel of Wealth. Equally denied are the later myths: the survival of the fittest, the power inherent in common causes. The reality, Conrad makes clear, is power—the power of the machine and the furnace and of whatever it is—system or group or individual—that directs it.

Conrad points out the direction that later proletarian fiction is to take: the conflict between the exploiting system and the exploited proletariat or workman. Rinelli, the individual, fights without success, but without losing, until circumstances and a human lapse determine his fate.

In the same sense *Backfurrow* depicts the underside of the American myth of escape and fulfillment that had taken Europeans across an ocean, Americans across a continent and down a river, and countless young people—epitomized by Sherwood Anderson's Sam McPherson and George Willard, Theodore Dreiser's Carrie Meeber, Floyd Dell's Felix Fay, and dozens of other fictional portrayals—to escape the fullness and drudgery of the farms and towns and to seek fulfillment not in the West of American tradition but in the city, as had their creators.

In *Backfurrow,* the protagonist is Ralph Dutton, who, at sixteen, after his grandfather's death, goes to the city, Detroit, to rise and to enjoy its books, art, and music. But he finds little work, and that low-paying, and finally no work. Broke but not discouraged, he returns to the country to work as a farmhand and save for another assault on the city. But by twenty-one he is married and at twenty-two he's a father and owner of the farm that had belonged to his father-in-law. The vagaries of weather, illness, and economics preclude prosperity or independence, and Dutton takes refuge in melancholy and finally a detachment from reality, and he sits, talking with his children, while his wife works the farm.

There is no sign of peace and pastoral plenty in the novel, but instead some of the bitterest portraits of farm life in American fiction. In fact, the publishing history of *Backfurrow* is similar to that of *Sister Carrie* a generation earlier. *Sister Carrie* had been accepted for publication by Walter Hines Page, then an editor at Doubleday. But on his return from Europe Frank Doubleday denounced it as a celebration of evil. He honored the contract, but refused to promote the novel, and it sold only a few hundred copies.

Similarly, *Backfurrow* was accepted at G. P. Putnam's while George Putnam was in Europe. On his return he was shocked by the graphic incidents in the novel. Eaton toned down some, and Putnam honored his contract but refused promotion or sale in the Putnam stores; the novel died quickly, to remain virtually unknown today.

Dutton's antagonist is neither machine nor system, as in *Temper;* it is a cosmic force determined to degrade and destroy men, a force that leads Dutton's dying grandfather to cry out, "God damn you, God," that leads Dutton to let an escaped convict go unscathed, that sees gelding as a human as well as animal condition. The novel's conclusion is, like *Temper*'s not resolution but resignation to the cycle of life and defeat that passes from generation to generation.

Neither novel is, in any doctrinaire sense, proletarian; there is no suggestion of the attempt or even the desire to revolt except on the lowest, most immediate, inevitably doomed sense. Nor is there in any way a suggestion of escape in the face of the cosmic irony that permits neither pleasure nor promise, nor, as Sherwood Anderson sought in his novels, the promise of communion with another. Instead it is clear that in spite of wives and children, each protagonist will live and die alone. The relationship of each novel to Norris and Dreiser is clear, but in subject matter, in conflict, in the suppression of dreams and hopes, in the hopelessness and helplessness, that each young man finally must accept, there is clear foreshadowing of the economic earthquake that is to come.

By the end of the decade other writers emerged who were more clearly proletarian not only in their subject matter but in a clear call for change. Among these were the Rebel Poets, originally Midwestern, in which Jack Conroy began to become prominent, the writers of Haldeman-Julius papers out of Gerard, Kansas, and eventually *The Left* of Davenport, Iowa, and *The Anvil,* edited by Jack Conroy in Moberly, Missouri. This period has been defined in detail in essays by Douglas Wixson in *MidAmerica* XI and *Midwestern Miscellany* VII, in which the prominence of authentic proletarians, particularly Midwesterners like Conroy, becomes clear.

By 1932, while some of the major writers of the twenties, particularly Sinclair Lewis and James Branch Cabell, had gone into a decline, others, such as Fitzgerald, went to Hollywood, and still others, particularly Anderson and Hemingway, attempted to man the barricades with less than successful fiction and then turned to journalism—Hemingway's exotic while Anderson tried to wrestle honestly with the Depression—major publishers began to recognize the emergence of a new critically realistic literature of the Left and a new group of writers, many from the West, the Midwest, and the South, and some were authentic American proletarians.

Significant in this recognition was the announcement that the *Scribner's Magazine* $5,000 Short Novel Contest for 1932 was won by two young writers. The first was John Herrmann, expatriate fugitive from a family tailoring business in Lansing, Michigan, former editor of *transition,* husband of Josephine Herbst, and future member of the Ware Group in Washington, to which Alger Hiss allegedly belonged. Herrmann's story, "The Big Short Trip" depicts, a generation before Arthur Miller, a salesman who loses his business to a system in decline and his son to social revolution. The salesman can only accept the inevitable, knowing that he can neither cope with nor understand the new age. The story appeared in *Scribner's* xcii (August, 1932). The co-winner was Thomas Wolfe's "A Portrait of Bascom Hawk."

While *Scribner's* was recognizing the inevitable, essays by Jack Conroy, Jim Tully, and others began to appear in *The American Mercury,* under H. L. Mencken's editorship and with his support if not sympathy. Tully had already published roadkid, hobo, underside fiction with Mencken's support; by 1933, the year in which *The Anvil* first appeared, Conroy, a refugee from the defunct Willis-Overland plant in Toledo, had returned to Moberly, where he turned the articles into a book and the book into fiction.

When Covici-Friede published *The Disinherited* in 1933, curiously it appeared between two other major but quite different works to emerge from the Depression, *Young Lonigan* (1932) and *The Young Manhood of Studs Lonigan* (1934), both by James T. Farrell and part of the great trilogy that deals with the decline and fall of a young American. It appeared, too, in close proximity to two other quite different works of the Depression, Nathanael West's *Miss Lonelyhearts* (1933) and Horace McCoy's *They Shoot Horses, Don't They?* (1935).

Farrell's novels and those by West and McCoy have much more in common philosophically with Conrad's *Temper* and Eaton's *Backfurrow* than with Conroy's *The Disinherited*. Conrad's Rinelli and Eaton's Dutton are victims not of the social system, whether in the country or the city, but of the emptiness of their own lives, the self-victimization of sex and of beliefs rooted in self-delusion, and the random violence of a universe reflected in the society around them. Neither writer sees any hope for salvation or fulfillment; the system, like the universe, simply is, and neither the individual nor a class can change it.

For West, too, reality is neither a changeable system nor a source of either belief or feeling, and to search for either will lead inevitably through suffering to the ultimate horror. Horace McCoy's novel, regarded in France as the great American Existential novel, is, like West's, neither a social protest novel nor a celebration of life or the proletariat or the revolution. Although its subject matter and characters are drawn directly out of a peculiarly American Depression phenomenon, the marathon dance, it is set in a dancehall on the Pacific south of Los Angeles, as far West as its people can go, and it lies almost within sight of the glitter of Hollywood. The people, caught up in a struggle for survival in the meaningless ritual of the dance, are hoping at once to be "noticed" and fulfill the Hollywood promise, and to survive—the hour, the day, the dance. Individual after individual collapses, and yet the dance goes on, the participants the exploited, and their survival the result of the law of the jungle in its rawest terms—cheating, fighting, holding on, knowing that there is no place to go, the dance clearly as pointless as the world, indeed the universe around them.

Jack Conroy's *The Disinherited* has much in common with the others: the failure of dreams and of myths, the stratification and exploitation of the working class, the victimization of individuals in an unfeeling system, the helplessness of the individual, the economic exile of people, the loss of faith of the sensitive protagonist Larry Donavan. The farms are as hopeless as Eaton's. The factories as brutal as Conrad's, the system as impersonal as West's and McCoy's; individuals, victims of exploitation and/or their own weaknesses, fall by the wayside. Bull Market, the prosperity of the twenties, never fulfills its promise to the workers, although many are mutely, docilely content, and little more than sustenance trickles down. But the Hard

Winter, that of the aftermath of the crash, creates what are truly the Disinherited, exiles in their own land, without either illusions or hope. Deterioration, degeneration, and death become the dreaded reality for the Disinherited.

But there is a difference. Larry Donavan, son of a miner and heir to the nineteenth century American promise loses one faith—that in the Horatio Alger myth—as he wanders picaresquely through MidAmerica, from rural Missouri to Detroit and back again, but he finds another, the cause of organization, of revolution, of the means by which a people can reclaim their inheritance. The novel, unlike the others, ends on a muted note of confidence, or romantic faith in the human ability to triumph.

The Disinherited was seen at once as the true proletarian novel, celebrating the individual, denouncing the system, pointing the way to revolution and fulfillment. It was, as Michael Gold pointed out in the *New Masses*, "a victory against capitalism . . . ", "a significant class portent, . . . " one of the "revolution-minded novels" that will make a difference.

Truly proletarian, nevertheless the novel rises above doctrine. It is at the same time a true portrayal of the underside of America that we choose too frequently to forget. It is neither a period piece nor social propaganda, but a living picture of Americans in crisis, in torment, in a set of circumstances that are unbelievable yet real, a novel that of all the genre is deserving of the literary recognition that it has finally received, just as, in the 1930s, it provided the mark by which other young writers could measure their work.

David D. Anderson, "Jack Conroy and Proletarian Fiction," in Midwestern Miscellany, *Vol. 17, 1989, pp. 33-44.*

The proletarian writer's formula:

Since many proletarian novels did have a rather formulaic inevitability in their development of plot and character, their authors were accused by hostile critics of permitting this Marxist dogma to substitute for personal insights and of writing un-American books that were more relevant to the situation in Soviet Russia. The whole canon was reduced by one cynical commentator to the following summary: "The novel began with a community of workers, on factory and farm, at first divided and unaware, then opening their eyes, hesitant and afraid, being broken and at last regrouping for final combat, having learned from defeat that there are no halfway houses, that the Party is their only ally, the owning class their only enemy, and that they have a world to win."

Sylvia Jenkins Cook, in her From Tobacco Road to Route 66, *1976.*

Claude E. Jones

[*In the following essay, the critic suggests that proletarian literature was foreshadowed in mainstream Ameri-*

can fiction that employed the same Depression-era subject matter without the Marxist political slant.]

A great deal has been written . . . concerning John Steinbeck. . . . [Since] the publication and picture production of *Grapes of Wrath*—he has been hailed as the great new prophet of proletarian literature. Critics cite the "prose epic" of the Joads as definite proof that this new light in the literary firmament is on the Labor side, that his heart bleeds for the exploited masses.

This has been said of others in the past—of Vincent Sheean and James Farrell, of Eugene O'Neill and Clifford Odets, even of Jim Tully. Some years ago it was remarked of Jack London and Stephen Crane. One would rather expect the critics, especially the socially-conscious critics, and above all the Marxists, to wait, to weigh the spirit, the ostensible purpose and the final bulk of a man's work, before they claim the new Moses. It is with this problem of the proletarian novel and its relation to some few authors, including John Steinbeck, that I am concerned here.

It would seem that whenever a creative artist concerns himself with the lower classes, with the stuff of proletarian writing, he lays himself open to criticism, usually in the form of either disgust or enthusiasm, on the score of subject matter. He is likely to be called a proletarian writer, an apostle of reform, an inciter to revolt—all because of his milieu, his setting.

There are, as a matter of fact, almost as many reasons for using such settings as the slums as there are reasons for writing at all. Further, one comes increasingly to feel that here it is not the material, but the use to which the author puts it, that really matters. Thus it is that the term "proletarian literature" is usually misleading. The critic is faced with the necessity of establishing accurate criteria for this, as for any other handy term. He must differentiate works falling within this class from those which do not quite enter it.

Proletarian literature has as theme the necessity for establishing a Marxian economy. Again, such literature almost inevitably concerns itself with what the author considers, or wants his readers to consider, the actual living and working conditions of the proletariat. Third, the theme of revolution, the overthrow of the existing economy, is usually stated, frequently by one of two characters: either (a) the protagonist himself, or (b) some other character who exercises considerable influence on the protagonist. Another feature of proletarian literature is that it has, by and large, international implications; it preaches "Workers of the World Unite", not "Workers of this Industry, in this Place, at this Time, Unite". This last, the international quality of proletarian writing, may or may not appear in the individual work; but in the whole work of any prolific proletarian writer it is extremely apt to appear.

Now, when we come to evaluate the work of any author who concerns himself exclusively, or even noticeably, with the poor, there are several points of departure. He may be a proletarian writer. On the other hand, he may be one of several other kinds of writer, or not definitely identifiable at all.

An interesting example is George Gissing. Gissing led a harsh life, a life which made him extremely bitter. Only in a few of his letters and *The Private Papers* does he get away from this bitterness. Some of his work, especially *New Grub Street* uses a failure as protagonist. This is also generally true of the tales in *House of Cobwebs.*

Further, in *Workers of the Dawn* Gissing treats a cross-section of London not far removed in type from the setting of Gorki's *Lower Depths.* Unlike the Russian, however, Gissing dwells on his wretches, savours their wretchedness, forces the reader to the conclusion that the author is personally concerned. And this is true. Gissing loathed the poor, the foul and shambling wrecks among whom he had for a while to live. They revolted him, and he dwells on their deformities, their loathsomeness, as another man would suck an aching tooth or finger a broken rib. There is in Gissing's attitude a masochism, a self-laceration, excruciatingly painful for author and reader alike. Pain affords, however, a rather popular vicarious thrill; so we read Gissing. He might, if it were not for his obvious distaste for the subject—the personal equation forced on his readers—be called a naturalist. As it is, there is no technical term for the Gissing type of thing except realism, a name lately grown flaccid with much prostitution. Certainly, Gissing is not a proletarian writer, although he frequently deals with proletarian stuff.

Another literary type frequently confounded with proletarian writing is the literature of brutality, or pain. Stephen Crane once said that pain is the proper source of all great literature, and surely much of his own writing proves that he meant it. Expiation and some self-respect come to the hero of *The Red Badge of Courage* through mental torment; the same result appears again and again in the short stories of "The Little Regiment" and "The Open Boat" and "Wounds in the Rain". But in most of these cases there is physical pain as well, usually as motivating force. Himself high-strung and easily hurt, Crane shows an almost morbid pre-occupation with such phenomena.

Crane usually deals with the lower classes—with soldiers and sailors and laborers and cowhands and poor women. In *Maggie* he traces the inevitable downfall of a slum girl; in *George's Mother,* the spiritual and moral disintegration of a poor young man. In each case, the conditioning factor is poverty. Crane's soldiers are usually nameless, are types, are unromantic. Brutality, fear, hatred, courage—these are more predominant than social grace. He handles material which another author, especially a modern, would be apt to use for preachment, to treat didactically; but he doesn't preach. Many of his characters are exploited, true, but we seldom see them, nor do they usually think of themselves, as members of a class. Frequently there is no sympathy at all. In other words, this is proletarian material without the treatment necessary for the *genre.*

Hemingway, who is preoccupied with brutality rather than with pain as such, is in some ways close kin to Crane. The brutalized frequently come from the dregs, as do many of Crane's characters; but Hemingway watches them with almost perfect detachment. In such wise do small boys hurt animals, asking themselves: "What does it feel like? What will he do now?" Only in the battered counter-espionage agent in *Fifth Column* does Hemingway learn the ultimate lesson of pain—sympathy. And *Fifth Column* is the closest the author comes to proletarian writing.

Other writers about the proletariat we have aplenty—Faulkner, Caldwell, Farrell, literally hundreds of others—but a galaxy, even a pleiade, of top-flight proletarian authors—no. A few at most; and even with some of them the classification is debatable.

Take, for example, an earlier writer interested in the masses, in labor, in revolution: Jack London. London is, as Professor Whipple points out, primarily an individualist. And a muddleheaded individualist at that—so far as his own philosophy is concerned. In him social purpose is buried under successive layers of fatty tissue: individualism, survival of the fittest, the Superman idea. London doubtless found himself occasionally sympathetic to the labor movement. He wrote essays to show the necessity of revolution, of solidarity among the workers. In the semi-autobiographical *Martin Eden* he seems to consider his protagonist a member of the proletariat, faced with their problems, forced to their conclusions. In *the Iron Heel* he shows labor prone, the iron heel of capitalism raised to stamp it out. Yet throughout all this we are unconvinced. Even in the socialistic works, the cry of the superman, the superbeast, is heard. London's humanitarianism is frequently evident, as in *In the Abyss,* but usually overshadowed by his primordialism. He is never clear-thinking enough to settle what seems to have been a nagging question for much of his adult life—the proper relationship between the Superman and the Masses. And this dichotomy forbids his inclusion among the proletarian writers.

One contemporary of London's and ours who goes the whole way is Upton Sinclair. In novel after novel he examines and vituperates the phases of Capitalist America which interest him. His panacea is Socialism, and, while it leads to industrial strife, does not with him necessarily end in world-wide revolution. The most popular, and justly so, of his novels is *The Jungle* in which, by using a protagonist who is no superman, Sinclair enlists the reader's humanitarian interest in the problem, even if he fails to satisfy the reader's intellect with the solution. The way out comes too pat, we hear the machine creak, and unless we are already indoctrinated we are not swept along.

This raises what is in some respects the most important problem faced by the proletarian writer—the necessity of selling the cure as well as establishing the diagnosis. Scenes and conditions to raise pity in the most hard-hearted reader abound almost everywhere. Given the power of description and ability to humanize characters, the writer has little difficulty in arousing the reader. This is enough for many authors, but not for the proletarian, the Marxist, creator. He must carry on, must raise the flag of revolution, must drive the reader along towards a Communist Nirvana. This is not easy, even when the reader is sympathetic, is convinced that there is a need for social therapy. Usually, he is still dubious of this cure.

Now, Communism, like any other system requiring for the most part voluntary coöperation, primarily appeals—at least in this country—to two groups.

On the one hand are those who are convinced that they are hopeless as individuals, that only by proletarian solidarity and revolution can they partake in some measure of what they feel is their just and due share of the world's goods. This group as a whole is not intellectual; it does not form a high percentage of what is referred to, somewhat loosely, as the "Reading Public". The author who would live by the proletariat must confine himself, by and large, to writing for labor papers and for the little theatre groups nourished by union and party organizations. He must, in other words, confine himself to simple media, employ simple techniques, forego the pleasure, or advantages, or inner necessity (and sometimes all three) of individualism. He must identify himself with the Cause, explain it, not criticize it, and do the work which his hand finds to do. Such a writer rarely reaches his peers—his mental peers. At least that has usually been true in this country.

The second group comprises, for the most part, intellectuals who are sympathetic, or at least familiar, with Communist doctrine. For them, the proletarian author employs techniques, utilizes material, aimed at the "Reading Public", especially at that part of it which is not yet thoroughly indoctrinated. Of course, if he is clearly enough identified with the movement, if his solutions follow the somewhat strictly drawn party line, he will be received with acclaim by those who are already convinced, whether or not he is a competent artist. This appears in the *New Masses* reviews; and the reverse, in Mr. Hicks's *The Great Tradition.* To be of much value to his party, to his movement, however, the proletarian artist must go beyond this. He must convince the wavering, the not-quite-sure, even the previously unsympathetic, reader. And herein lies the real test of his power.

Readers are easily convinced that a given situation is bad. This is done, for the most part, by appeals to emotion. And it is for emotion that most of the "Reading Public" reads. Grant that Mr. R. P. is convinced—he is even on fire to assist some particular group of the downtrodden, the "underprivileged". The author suggests that only one solution exists—a complete reversal of the social structure. These "creatures in God's image", this "Man with a Hoe", must take control of the government, must reorganize industry, farming, business. The writer appeals to the reader's "common sense".

"Look," he says, "here is a horrible situation. This cannot be permitted to go on, can it? No, of course it can't. What can we do about it, you and I? Nothing. Nothing at all. The world has always been full of humanitarians like you and me. And what good did they do? Very little. No, my friend, we can't do anything. It is up to the masses. They're the ones who have to act, to organize, to take over. Let's help them, let's make it easier for them. But, of course, probably your job, certainly your bank balance and your investments and your insurance, won't be worth a damn after we succeed."

And the reader, who is still feeling sympathetic towards the poor, miserable downtrodden victims of what the author calls Social Injustice, thinks, "Terrible. Such conditions mustn't be permitted. Time for the government to do something. Or we'll have a revolution. As this writer fellow says. But if we do what he wants, everything I've worked for will go to smash. Anyway, he's trying to convert me, so things probably aren't as bad as he paints them."

Mr. R. P. is just naturally suspicious of systems. And of the writers who propose systems.

Most authors interested in the proletariat are content to draw their picture. This may be true because of the difficulties I have mentioned. One suspects that it usually is. For the most part, one feels that the artist, like Mr. R. P., is shocked by what he sees—but more strongly because at first hand—and is driven to use the material because of its inherent power. On the other hand, he may feel that others more practical than he will find a way to effect reform.

Reform literature—lashing at an evil without suggesting the perfect antidote—is of long and distinguished heritage in English. Its practitioners have included such diverse figures as Swift and George Eliot, Johnson and him whom we call Langland, Shelley and Harriet Beecher Stowe, Whitman, and Dickens. And surely few, if any, of the great satirists and social-novelists who have written in the English language had intellectual or doctrinaire roots in the proletariat, however clearly they might see its problems and however sympathetic they might be towards its misery.

Take, for example here, Herman Melville. The author of *Billy Budd* and *White Jacket* had an axe to grind, and grind it he did with many sparks. The American Navy had, he felt, too many short-comings, and he—having served in it before the mast—was the obvious person to bring these defects to the attention of the American taxpayers who foot the Navy bill. In *White Jacket* he not only points out these injustices and warns against their perpetuation, but he suggests reforms. These are not to be brought about by overturning the social system, however, but by the intervention of a civilian legislature goaded on by indignant readers of Melville's book. Americans would never permit such conditions to prevail, Melville felt—and the sequel proved him right. The reforms he suggested were carried out—possibly because of his presentation of the case, pedestrian though that case frequently was in his hands. American literature, particularly what is becoming known as the "economic" or reform novel, abounds in such presentation of social ulcers. And, as here, the appeal is usually emotional, at least for the most part of any given work. And the work's success is frequently in inverse ratio to the amount of expository criticism to be found therein.

All of which brings us to an American who is writing now—who has made considerable din in contemporary literature, whose voice is even now heard in the land. John Steinbeck. He is not one crying in the wilderness although one fears that there are many groups who wish that he were.

Steinbeck started, innocuously enough, with two novels which did not even ripple the pond of American criticism. One, based on the life and exploits of the buccaneer Sir

Harry Morgan, reminds the reader of Defoe's *Colonel Jacques* without the oldster's sympathy with his protagonist's opportunism and bourgeois morality. Steinbeck's Morgan is unloving, unlovable and unloved—like O'Neill's Marco Polo in some ways. And this unsympathetic, in some places excoriating, treatment of middle-class morality and ideals, is the only link between proletarian writing and this early effort. *The Cup of Gold* died almost stillborn like Crane's *Maggie,* and like it was republished only after the author's success. *To a God Unknown,* the other early novel, is in some ways of foretaste of the later Steinbeck—what with its California setting, the metaphysics of its mythos, the supernatural qualities of its protagonist. It is, in part at least, allegorical; the allegory is of the land and parallels older myths personified in the Indian scenes.

All this is a far cry from proletarian literature, from propaganda writing in general and the economic novel, but the early work, especially *To a God Unknown,* is important, one feels, because it suggests an approach and foreshadows a treatment.

The success novels—*Tortilla Flat* and *Of Mice and Men* (the latter in play as well as novelette form)—deal with California also. Steinbeck was shocked at the reception accorded the former, which seems to have been gathered to the bosoms of the socially indignant (it is *not* a propaganda novel), the searchers for the picturesque, and lovers of the "off colour". Steinbeck knew his characters, the *paisanos,* and loved them; he wrote of them with understanding and affection—and was shocked by what faddists did to his work, as well as what critics said of it. *Of Mice and Men,* on the other hand, proved readily understandable to the reading and theatre publics and resulted in the author's elevation to a Writer of Importance. It, too, concerns Steinbeck's California—and if to the socially-conscious it is a study of proletarian conditions and, especially in the person of the Negro, of minority problems, to almost everyone else it is simply a swift moving tale of psychopathic phenomena (*Sanctuary* was a success, too), of horror and sudden deaths, of man's love for man.

Then came the prelude to the wide social study—in the form of a novel concerning a strike, *In Dubious Battle.* Conservatives and radicals alike called the author names, insisted that his treatment was unfair, untrue—was intended to whitewash Communism on the one hand and to paint it at its very worst on the other. The novel presents a situation only too frequent in California. Unfortunately for the enthusiasts among his readers, Steinbeck is aware of certain shortcomings—shortcomings from the humanitarian standpoint, that is—on both sides. Here Labor is as unscrupulous as Capital—the strike settles nothing and proves little. True, it teaches the workers to organize, it shows them their potential of power. Yet labor loses, one protagonist is murdered and his co-worker uses the dead body as a symbol and a slogan. The reader's delicacies, his humanitarian sympathies, are outraged; he is left with the taste of blood and gall in his mouth. But one feels that for the author this novel presents a Californian situation, handled on both sides as it is in California, and that the moral, if any, is that Californians could, and should, find a more satisfactory answer to this ever-present problem. This is, one is sure of it despite the author's objectivity, not a study of labor movements in the abstract, of proletarian universals, but of a specific sore spot in one particular place.

Two other works must be considered here. First is *Pastures of Heaven,* which is built, like William March's excellent war novel *Company K,* out of short stories. The technique is akin to that employed in *Tortilla Flat,* but the continuity is provided by geographical location—a valley in California—rather than by the reoccurrence of principles, as was true in the earlier work. The stories show considerable range of material and attitude, but the predominant feature is the life of typical California farmers in a California valley.

The other item is the pamphet republication, called *Their Blood is Strong,* of a series of newspaper articles concerning the itinerant laborers known as Okies. It is, of course, meant to arouse sympathy in California for her problem children, the harvest nomads. The results sought are two-fold—establishment of decent camps, and state restraint on what the author clearly feels to be the rapacity of certain groups who are held responsible for: first, the presence of the Okies; second, the problems which these migrants now face. The solution lies in the hands of the state; she must clean up this mess, eradicate this blot. It is a Californian problem which must be solved by Californians.

The Long Valley, a collection of short stories and sketches, is also Californian. Only one or two of the parts might be set elsewhere. What critics agree to be the best parts of the book—"The Red Pony" and "The Leader of the People"—are necessarily of the far West, and treat the growth and ideology of a boy whose family own and operate a ranch there. "The Vigilante" and "The Raid" hark back, in subject matter at least to the type of material found in *In Dubious Battle.* "Breakfast" might be taken *verbatim* from *The Grapes of Wrath,* as "The Murder" and "Johnny Bear" might well come from *Pastures of Heaven.* Others of the stories concern California people, and bring out a feature predominant in *To a God Unknown* and *Pastures of Heaven*—the author's love and sympathy for, as well as identity with, the earthy people of his own state.

In time the interest shown in *Their Blood is Strong* gave birth to Steinbeck's most ambitious novel so far, *The Grapes of Wrath.* According to the critics, this is an example of that amorphous and incongruous genre, the prose epic. It is, as a matter of fact, the chronicle of an Okie family's westing trek. How seriously the author intends it to be taken as a documentary novel, a record in fiction, appears from the fact that fifteen of the thirty chapters (only a sixth of the book by actual page count, however) are intermediary, or expository, and have no direct relationship with the plot concerning the Joads themselves.

Roughly, the novel falls into three parts: The Departure, The Trip, and The New Home. It begins with a dust storm in Oklahoma and ends with a California flood. The Joads cover a great deal of ground—geographically, emotionally, and economically. They appear early in the book as good stock for settlers—Americans of long standing; they are hardworking and frugal, tough and courageous. The

System (specifically, the Banks) combines with agricultural conditions to drive them West. These people can, we feel, make a go of it if given any opportunities whatever.

The Westward movement is drawn in all its length and breath. The reader follows these latter-day pioneers mile by weary mile, facing their social problems, evolving their emergency code of ethics, marvelling—as the author frequently does—at their stamina, their unfailing courage, their vast kindness. This is the crucible in which their qualities are fused. Good stock for California.

The third, and last, section treats the end of the road. Deluded by advertisements for workers, driven by screaming necessity, the Okies come face-to-face with the California agricultural system at last. Here, in the Promised Land, they meet hatred, scorn, and above all fear. Shunted from job to job, from county to county; kept on the move lest they organize or try to settle, they live in filth, they are shamelessly exploited. Here in the Land of Plenty they starve, are foully housed, go insufficiently clothed. Something is wrong here, radically wrong. The dazed Okies hurry from will-o'-the-wisp job to mirage job, picking up a dollar or two here and there during harvest time. Sometimes they can even eat meat, buy milk for the babies; but usually this is impossible. Once they enjoy a breathing spell in a government camp and here, says Steinbeck, is a solution, a practical solution. (He had presented it earlier, in *Their Blood is Strong.*) But they must move on.

The Joad family disintegrates—only father, mother, Rosasharn and the youngsters are left. Then comes the season of no crops, the season of rains. Washed out of their temporary quarters, they seek shelter in a barn, where Rosasharn gives of her breast milk to a dying man. This, Steinbeck seems to say, shows the indomitable courage, the unquenchable humanity of the Okies. Outside the barn, a new crop is breaking the ground. Inside, a dying man is being revitalized by the mother-spirit. Here are hope and Spring after the long winter. The grapes of wrath—sown in Oklahoma, budded on the westward journey, and ripened in California—need stamping out. This must be done with improved living conditions, with a chance to settle down.

The Grapes of Wrath crosses the State Line, it is true. Yet the crossing is westward, into the State from without. There comes a vast influx of new blood, of potentially valuable citizens. Help these new-comers to find a home, let them live as human beings, as worthy citizens of a state to which God has been good, and in time they will be a blessing where now they seem a curse. They will be our friends who are now our enemies. On these we may build solidly, they are strong oak for the building. This is the theme of the novel, not "Workers of the World, Unite"! This problem is a *State* problem, to be faced and eventually solved by the citizens of the State. The Okie is not adrift amid the rapids of a vaguely defined Capitalist system. The solution is not revolution, but love and understanding. The community mind must solve a community problem. The threat of radical organization is there—but it is a threat, not a promise. Steinbeck, here as earlier, is not a doctrinaire, but a Californian urging other Californians to solve a problem, the importance and magnitude of which has not, heretofore, been made apparent to them. This is his work, his gift—in terms of the State.

Truly, I doubt that Steinbeck is a proletarian writer, just as I doubt that London was, or the others whom I have mentioned. Further, I cannot help feeling that the proletarian novelist gives to fortune hostages which many artists are unwilling to give—and rightly so, from their standpoint. I also think that some criteria of proletarian writing are not sufficiently regarded by critics who are over-free with the term. In any treatment of such writing, or of any artist as possible professor or precursor of the type, the critic should begin with a clear statement of what he feels to be the *sine qua non* of the genre. Further, he should apply these criteria to other writers, and evaluate them according to these standards.

> Claude E. Jones, "Proletarian Writing and John Steinbeck," in The Sewanee Review, Vol. XLVIII, No. 4, Autumn, 1940, pp. 445-56.

Harold Strauss

[Strauss was an American editor associated for many years with the publishing house of Alfred A. Knopf. In the following excerpt, he offers an overview of the development of the American proletarian novel and suggests that it met with mainstream critical disfavor in part because proletarian writers relied on the stylistic traditions of the bourgeois novel instead of devising new literary methods.]

The proletarian novel is in disfavor at the moment, and I shall not revive the futile and narrow controversy that raged around it during its brief blossom-time and that degenerated into partisan bickering over the place of propaganda in art. There are other factors of far greater importance. The proletarian novel, as we knew it a few years ago, bore within itself the seeds of its own destruction because it sprang not from the vision of the proletariat, or of society in general, as a creative force but from despair and disillusionment. It invented no new methods of its own, but adopted the decadent technique of photographic realism.

Proletarian novels . . . are more than documentary; they are vivid portrayals of a time, a place, and a people in a period of crisis, torment, and self-searching. . . . They recreate a folk-drama difficult, as Edmund Wilson commented, for those who did not experience it, to believe in as human experience.

—David D. Anderson in MidAmerica, 1982.

Vernon Parrington points out that what he calls "natural-

ism" emerged in response to a darkening social outlook, and he defines it as "a pessimistic realism that sets man in a mechanical world." The photographic realism of the proletarian novelists is a specialized development of naturalism, its *reductio ad absurdum.* For it not only sets man in a mechanical world but limits his response to that world to the simple recording of sense perceptions. It allows reflexes, of course, but it rejects all generalizations of sensory experience; therefore it denies the novelist the right to interpret the experiences of his characters. It denies him the privilege of omniscience and the right to make judgments of behavior. Instead it seeks, to the ultimate capacity of language, to bring the reader directly into the mind of a central character, who acts as a reporter, or means of perception; consequently it strives also to limit the horizon of consciousness, physically and intellectually, to the sense perceptions of that character.

The mere description of this method already makes clear the extent to which writers who use it have turned their backs upon the novelist's onetime mission of clarifying and ordering human experience. For, implicit in the rejection of the right to judge behavior, one perceives the perverse notion that chaos is more profoundly meaningful than order. Those very novelists, the proletarians, who presumably wished to survey the orderly pattern of stress and strain in society, by a curious process of rationalization have pledged themselves to the disorderly technique of photographic realism.

The reasons for this literary collision between end and means lie in the origins of the proletarian novel. Although there have been many novels about factory workers ever since factory production displaced handicraft, although there have been many strike novels since Zola's *Germinal,* and although there is much speculation in the writings of Marx, Engels, and Lenin on proletarian literature, proletarian novels were not named and consciously produced in quantity in America until the onset of the great depression. Jack London preached the war of the classes in *The Iron Heel* and *The Revolution* thirty years ago, but his Spencerian optimism, his faith in man's perfectibility, and his concept of evolution made it little likely that he would be accepted as a fountainhead of tradition by the post-war pessimists. Dreiser and Anderson concerned themselves with workers enslaved to machines; but their approach was humanitarian and their solution individual rebellion rather than the organization of the proletariat as a creative force.

Dos Passos represents the transition. His *Three Soldiers* (1921) is the work of an idealist disillusioned by the war, the protest of an individual against the regimentation of the war machine. But in *The 42nd Parallel* (1930) he makes a confused and awkward beginning at a true proletarian novel. There are many conflicting elements, but it is clear, in his references to the I. W. W. and in his many biographies of young men unable to rise in life, that he is groping towards a radical world view. The first American books consciously written and consciously reviewed as proletarian novels were, in all probability, *The Disinherited* (1933), by Jack Conroy, and Robert Cantwell's *Land of Plenty,* which came out the following year and was the better of the two. They were the first to take the truly Marxist position that it does not lie within the power of capitalists to order society more benevolently, and that workers must find their own salvation.

The effect was instantaneous. The vogue flared. The magazines of the Left carefully encouraged each newly converted apprentice, whether he had any craftsmanship or not. Only a few musty reactionaries continued a discussion of artistry that seemed tenuous indeed in a world troubled by urgent material problems. The trend of fashion was revealed not so much in the lists of best-sellers, where established authors continued in their accustomed ways, but in the complete capitulation of amateurs and neophytes. Restless adolescents who could no longer afford to take their maladjustments to Paris for a year or two found their first feeble literary efforts swept into the limelight. Their books might not sell, and they might go unpaid for their short stories—but the reviews were balm for their souls. Art was declared to be a weapon, but it strangely resembled a cure for greensickness.

Not all Marxist criticism was applause for neophytes. Such serious critics as Hicks, Gold, Freeman, and Strachey tried to set up standards for a Marxist analysis of literature. They discovered that writers such as Joyce, Proust, and Lawrence were decadent bourgeois. Strachey dismissed them thus: "Contemporary writers are a part of existing civilization; existing civilization is a bourgeois civilization; and bourgeois civilization is in headlong decline. This fully accounts for the peculiar characteristics which we notice in its greatest writers." But Strachey had recognized only a part of the conclusion indicated by the logic of his own words. If existing civilization was bourgeois, the development of a proletarian literature in America would be an impossibility for many years to come. Even if, in 1932, the revolution, like a lot of other things, seemed just around the corner, common sense should have suggested that an educational time lag would have to intervene between the revolution and the beginnings of a proletarian culture.

Nevertheless, serious Left-wing critics, for political reasons, made a vigorous attempt to extend and to apply the materialistic axioms of Marxist philosophy to literary technique. The strike novel appeared theoretically to offer the best opportunities for materialism; but in practice it soon became apparent to everyone except a few dogmatists such as Granville Hicks that while the philosophical results were interesting, the literary results were almost nil. Most novels of strikes were bad novels; they were bad because their very concern with material circumstance made them superficial, melodramatic, and sensational in the same way that a similar concern with material circumstance on the part of the "pulp" magazines often makes them superficial, melodramatic, and sensational.

And the strike formula itself proved unmanageable; it invariably crucified the novelist upon its climax, of which victory for the workers was the shaft and defeat the beam. Victory always produced suggestions of Utopianism, while defeat led to the mood of pessimism that no true revolutionary can abide. That defeat was the resolution most commonly chosen tells us much about the temper of the novelists. We are now close to the nub of the matter: proletarian novelists were torn by an inner emotional disturbance which vitiated and made ineffectual most of their work. Living in a bourgeois society, they found themselves driven to expound a pessimistic tale, although as revolutionists their natural attitude should have been optimistic. They involved themselves in incredible verbal acrobatics, for they were forced to explain how the workers, while they were realistically losing strikes, were theoretically winning the revolution.

The strike novel of that type was soon abandoned. Some radical novelists in whom pessimism predominated passed on by easy stages into the recording of sense perceptions with its gloomy, more passive implications. Endlessly they photographed the sufferings of the workers, but they ceased to bring these sufferings to the point of direct social action—strike and revolution. Their work they proudly called the literature of protest. But their readers often failed to perceive the protest. A writer such as Erskine Caldwell was widely received as a humorist.

Meanwhile, certain less doctrinaire critics, among them Malcolm Cowley and Alan Calmer, began to explain, quite rightly, that American proletarian novels had been ineffectual simply because their authors were incompetent. They pointed out the power of such European radicals as André Malraux, who, in *Man's Fate* and *Days of Wrath,* developed problems of behavior in the ethical, immaterial terms that are traditional to the novel. They looked hopefully towards American work of this nature.

Thus the circle was closed. The pessimists and the optimists, the realists and the idealists, each in their own way returned to a tradition of the bourgeois novel—the pessimists to a rarefied naturalism, and the optimists to the ancient drama of the individual's pursuit of his dreams. Such was the history of American proletarian fiction that followed the depression, in practice and in theory. The forces that shaped its brief course must now be accounted for. I shall try to show that the eager young revolutionaries of this period blighted their chances at the outset by taking over, blindly and uncritically, the hand-me-down technique of disillusioned bourgeois novelists. Unless they had had genius, which always rises above its environment, they could have done little else, for they themselves were disillusioned bourgeois.

To understand their failure we must sample the temper of the times, and speculate upon the nature of the novel and its potentialities. There are as many definitions of the novel as there are approaches to it. With these we need not concern ourselves. As Bernard DeVoto is fond of saying, any literary device is acceptable if it works. But we mean something quite definite when we say that a device "works." When we say this of a novel, we mean that it is a cultural entity which performs a tangible and recognizable function in our society. Critics may balk at stating this function, for any such statement tends to suggest limitations incompatible with the myth of creative freedom. Yet it can be simply stated.

Ever since men began to live in groups and mastered words, the art of narration has had a very definite social function. The primitive hunters who gathered around the evening campfire, the epic poets who sang the glories of tribal heroes, the dramatists who put human experiences upon a stage, and finally the novelists—all these masters of words spoke or wrote with the same purpose. Narration, whether as a hunter's campfire boast, epic, play, or novel, has always been, and, I think, always will be, an examination of *human behavior in crucial circumstances.* By amassing and comparing various accounts of the fashion in which men have overcome obstacles, we have been able to develop certain principles for successful action. The examination of past behavior in crucial circumstances becomes a guide to action in the future. These circumstances, even in fantasy, must have a likelihood of occurrence sufficient to induce the reader to lend his credence. In the circumstances of the crisis is the outer, physical world: the framework of economic or social determination, if you wish. But in the modes of human behavior there are subjective, pragmatic, moral as well as sensory elements, out of a comparison of which morality emerges. Morality is forever in danger of becoming codified and dogmatic; it must be continuously refreshed and adjusted to evolving outer conditions. For the accomplishment of this high function the novel is superbly suited, for of all the forms of narration it affords most fundamentally an opportunity for comparison of the broad reaches of human experience.

There is no doubt that in the case of a strike novel the strike itself is adequate, even beguiling as a crucial circumstance, for in a strike the very existence of the worker often hangs in the balance. It is just as natural for strikers to swap yarns over a glass of beer as it was for primitive hunters to boast, over a flagon of mead, of the dragons they had conquered. Here it is not the crucial circumstances that are wrong; rather, what is wrong is the refusal of proletarian novelists to deal with variants of human behavior and to make the essential comparisons. This refusal in the cases that have been mentioned was based upon theories of the materialistic determination of human action. There can be but one flat course of action open to a worker and one to a capitalist, according to the Marxists. Therefore the proletarian novel was confined in the strait jacket of a dogmatic philosophy. Instead of finding itself free to examine behavior qualitatively in the crux of a strike, it was forced to report quantitatively upon a mass of sensory experience to which was ascribed the ultimate power of determining the action.

The great problem of determinists was one of motivation. How were the workers to be forced to strike? As yet there were none but theoretical mainsprings of proletarian action. Utopian motives were rejected. If the workers could not be pulled ahead by dreams, they might be prodded from behind by suffering. The workers were shown to be trapped by life; they were shown to suffer and suffer until they struck. A strike was presented as a natural tropism of the proletarian amoeba.

In such an approach to human motives, there can be no just weighing of experience. There can be no vision of the proletariat as a creative force, no drama of moral choice, and no pondering of the good way of life. There is only re-

porting. It would be quite impossible for a writer dominated by such concepts to probe the effect of dream and desire in the mind of a worker. He simply uses flat characters who are either all scab or all hero. He cannot deal with choice, and therefore he selects his characters among those who have the least choice in their way of life.

But there are hopeful signs. A few Left-wing novelists have learned that the dangers of such strike novels, with their fatuous endings, can be avoided only by stating the inherent social problem in terms of its action upon individuals. The concept of mass action is being abandoned as unworkable, although the alternative has not yet been fully grasped. The behavior of individuals is a complex business which is only partly describable in terms of material fact; more often a man responds far more powerfully to symbols, slogans, morals, ideals—which are abstractions of experience that the mind makes for itself by associative, educative, and conditioning processes, and which are many steps removed from the crude sensory impressions. This means simply that a novelist, if he deals with human behavior as a whole, must deal with much that is not explicit.

But the prime quest of Left-wing writers was an immediate and explicit determinism. They worked themselves into a curious position, for while their philosophers were insisting that morals and ideals, along with everything else in society, were conditioned by the methods and ownership of the means of production, some of their novelists were denying the very existence of such abstract controls over human behavior. If they had read Engels they would have learned, as Edmund Wilson points out in *The Triple Thinkers,* that there is "a superstructure of higher activities . . . which are not, as is sometimes assumed, wholly explicable in terms of economics." The body of proletarian novelists, however, were not competent Marxists, but frightened pessimists who hoped, by referring all human behavior directly to sensory experience, to banish their intuitions of chaos. Failing to discover any ready-made proletarian morality, their poor imaginations balked at the necessity of creating one. They eventually learned that the strike novel was unsatisfactory; they do not yet see that accurate reporting of the organization of the workers is no substitute for an attempt, however feeble, at forming a few concepts of the good proletarian way of life.

In short, the radicals confused philosophical materialism with the apparent materialism of photographic recording. They left out of consideration the fact that a man can react as violently to a totem as to a pinprick and that any true report of his behavior will include both types of reaction. Such an omission imperils the prime cultural function of the novel—the comparison of motives. The novel can offer no adequate account of human behavior in crucial circumstances if only a fragment of the motivation of that behavior is admitted into the account. In order to answer the eternal question, "what happens when?" a writer must know something about the things that impel human beings to action, as well as something about the physical structure of society. The orthodox Marxists have schooled themselves so rigidly in the latter that they have neglected the former, and are the merest children when they are forced to deal with it.

The error is not merely a matter of false logic. It is a basic rationalization, for the radicals had a deep-rooted inclination towards the methods of photographic realism long before they were generally adopted. The truth of the matter, the human factor behind all this theoretical confusion, is that the majority of our radical writers were not the fruit of a suddenly burgeoning proletarian culture; they were merely bourgeois in revolt against the contradictions and inhumanities of capitalism. They were the Bohemians, the Greenwich Villagers of 1910, the Left-Bankers of 1920, the maladjusted, the dissidents, the intellectuals. And as such they are to be understood in terms of literary tradition, rather than in terms of Marxism.

There is, then, no proletarian literary tradition in this country. There is only a tradition of revolt against puritanism. The idea of a proletarian literature was imposed on this tradition from the outside. The novelists themselves employed the technique of photographic realism because they were a part of the mainstream of twentieth-century literature.

The story of this literary technique starts with Hemingway, for it is the most refined expression of the mood of the "lost generation," to which he belongs. The photographic realist invariably has an emotional distrust of the common, basic symbols and generalizations of the world to which he was born. Hemingway, ridden by this distrust, pointed the way. His mind, tutored in post-war realities, rejected its heritage of American ideals. As he prodded into the complexities of human behavior, he discovered an impasse, a contradiction between belief and fact which inhibited action—and action for him was writing. He felt repression and defeat. He was no longer attuned to the moral themes of his community. He had to cast out a whole mess of stiffly codified Victorian beliefs which he thought were wrong. He had to retrace his own education and conditioning. He had to go back to basic sense perceptions; and symbolic of this process was his journey from the Parisian Left Bank to the arenas of Spain, to see pain and death in its simplest and most violent form.

In their own fashion, all our young realists have made, figuratively, a journey to Spain. Whenever a young man discovered that neither the bedroom nor the battlefield, neither the sweatshop nor the sanctuary, were what he had been taught to believe they were, he made such a journey to Spain. In the end, he came to regard direct sensory experience not as merely a corrective for outmoded or unfounded moral generalizations, but as a substitute for all morality.

Hemingway still achieved a certain breadth of vision by looking at the world through the eyes of a variety of characters. He used plural means of perception. There was still an element of comparison in the several points of view which he developed. But his successors tried to simplify experience still further. The photographic realist now employs a single means of perception, in order to obtain a perfect amoral reference to the universe. We are asked to

follow the tropisms of this creature as he responds to the casual stimuli of his environment.

It was John Dos Passos, in *The 42nd Parallel,* who first developed pure sensory impressionism in the mind of a single observer. While he appeared to be borrowing a cinematographic technique from the movies, actually he took the "stream" from the stream-of-consciousness method and applied it to the method of Hemingway. He offered a stream of sense perceptions which could be examined only through one means of perception.

What Hemingway and Dos Passos began, a number of writers influenced by them carried further. *Gas-House McGinty,* Farrell's worst book, is also the best example of the pure stream-of-sense-perception novel. It expresses nothing but the confusion of a writer in a world that is changing too fast. It simplifies life by conventions which make the broaching of complexities impossible. The author makes a case history, a chart, if you please, of simple, describable, uncontroversial impressions that the senses of an ordinary human being receive in the course of daily living. By this surrender to a deterministic philosophy, his confused spirit escapes the more exacting demands of other, less passive views of life.

The workers and the unemployed have become the favorite characters of the photographic realists, for the urgencies of the dispossessed are immediate and simple. However blameless they may be for their plight, however enslaved by the system, their minds, as described by these writers, are dulled by suffering, their sensibilities necessarily dulled, their imaginations dulled, their spirit dulled; only their sensory nerves are keenly operative, and then only to trace the horrible and unvarying record of hunger. They present a highly simplified problem in human dynamics, and therefore they appeal as characters to the timorous, doubt-haunted novelists who seek merely to record sensation.

Their distrust of all symbols and generalizations extends even to word symbols. That is why they describe over and over again the olfactory attributes of an outside toilet or the tactile and visual attributes of a syphilitic scab on the leg of a Bowery bum. But if we allow a general uniformity to primary human sensations, we can leave the checking of minor individual variations to scientists. From novelists we desperately need some ray of light on the patterns of human behavior under the proddings of more complex stimuli. We don't particularly need an analysis of bad plumbing smells. But we need very deeply to know why such smells, as a symbol of frightful slum conditions, turn one man into a revolutionary, another into a determined riser-in-life, another into a utopian dreamer, and another into a criminal. But the characters of these photographic realists are, as we have said, more acted upon than acting. Therefore their behavior can throw no light on such problems.

This is the crux of the matter. My contention is that this passivity produces an effect that is morbid and subjective in our fiction, and not the social objectivity that must be demanded of a good revolutionary novel. The photographic realists, unsettled by their own social and psychological maladjustments, have done more to distort the subject-object relationship than the hordes of moralizing bourgeois philistines whom they have attacked.

The processes of sense perception have, of course, a governing importance in literature as in life. I am criticising here only the distorted impression of experience and behavior that is given by novelists who attempt to reduce them to streams of sensations. This technique will not survive the simplest biological or psychological tests. It is merely the device of young men taught to dream of great deeds, but confounded by the confusion of a world they never made. It is just as distortionate of human experience as the strangely similar attempt of Huysmans to make a direct approach to sensory impulse.

Breadth must be sought in literature rather than narrowness. A changing society must create its own mythology as it goes along, and its own morality, of which the mythology would necessarily be a concrete expression. To whatever material elements the Marxist may be able to reduce the mythology of the bourgeoisie, he cannot afford to deny that a myth can drive a man to action. The legend of the opportunity of every man to rise in life may be economic nonsense, but it has stirred the imaginations of millions of young Americans. It has driven them to action. How the action came about and whether it was well or poorly rewarded are questions for novelists; for the critic the point is that the myth was an important and effective synthesis into a handy symbol of the historic experience of America in the days when it had an open frontier. It is by such symbols that men live.

If it is to survive, proletarian literature must recognize all forms of human motivation. It should employ any method, the best possible method, and not exclusively the hand-me-downs of the disillusioned bourgeoisie. Which is to say that the proletarian novel should not be any particular kind of novel at all in respect to technique, but simply a novel that expresses a specific world view.

Harold Strauss, "Realism in the Proletarian Novel," in The Yale Review, *Vol. XXVIII, No. 2, December, 1938, pp. 360-74.*

GASTONIA

Sylvia Jenkins Cook

[*In the following excerpt from her book* From Tobacco Road to Route 66, *Cook discusses* Strike!, *the first of the so-called Gastonia novels to be published, and explains the significance of the textile workers' strike in Gastonia, North Carolina, which became a recurring theme in American proletarian literature.*]

In both the factual and the fictional history of the poor white in the thirties, no name has acquired a richer symbolic significance than that of Gastonia. Before the events that occurred there in 1929, this North Carolina cotton-

mill town was a byword among southern manufacturers for the fruits of industrial progress—reckoned not only in numbers of looms and spindles in the mills but also in the concomitant prosperity of the area's churches. After the Communist-led strikes, mob violence, and bloodthirsty reprisals, Gastonia became a symbol to the rest of the country of the horrors of southern capitalism and a cynical comment on North Carolina justice. It also became the focus of a brief experiment in southern proletarian literature by providing the inspiration for at least six novels of political insurrection among poor white textile workers: *Strike!,* by Mary Heaton Vorse; *Call Home the Heart,* by Fielding Burke; *To Make My Bread,* by Grace Lumpkin; *Gathering Storm,* by Myra Page; *Beyond Desire,* by Sherwood Anderson; and *The Shadow Before,* by William Rollins. The attention of sympathetic writers was directed to Gastonia not merely by the *New Masses,* which was offering fulsome prescriptions for the proletarian novel, but also by the general tenor of the reporting in liberal periodicals such as the *Nation,* the *New Republic,* and the *Outlook and Independent. . . .*

As is frequently the case when one name is used to evoke all the passionate emotions and conflicting philosophies of an era, what happened at Gastonia was neither a typical example of the efforts to unionize the southern worker (a process achieved, if at all, by the AFL rather than the Communists), nor was it even the most extreme example of the violent atrocities committed in the name of the law (strikers at nearby Marion suffered a much higher death toll). What Gastonia did offer was a histrionic confrontation of communism and capitalism, a dress rehearsal for class war, with the *Daily Worker* and the mill owners performing so zealously in their antagonistic roles that they almost upstaged the confused proletarians, who were agonizing over their choice of a battle hymn between "Solidarity Forever" and "Praise God from Whom All Blessings Flow." No revolutionary could have hoped for an enemy so blatantly prepared to pervert law and justice, so openly a friend to tactics of blackmail and terror as the officials and lawyers of the Loray mill and *Gastonia Gazette* were. No jealously paternalistic owner could have advised the Communists to more condemnatory courtroom behavior in the eyes of the South than the propaganda speeches, advocating atheism and the violent overthrow of the government, that one of their Party-instructed witnesses chose to make. Indeed, both sides seemed to cooperate in presenting to the world verification of all the suspicions it had about the mill owners' use of racial, sexual, and religious prejudices to buttress a corrupt economic system and in furthering the public's considerable misgivings about the integrity of the Communists' compassion for these workers, whom they so easily involved in strikes and so readily abandoned afterwards.

The ramifications of the Loray mill strike upon all the habits and beliefs of the tightly knit community made it a favorite research project for journalists and sociologists; there was even more tempting material for fiction writers in the romantic background of the mill workers, their close folk ties with their former mountain life, the flamboyant rhetoric of the public life of the South, the macabre courtroom incidents of the trial, the pervasive violence of the town, and the vicious assassination of the strikers' ballad maker. This was the essence of stirring left-wing journalism—or of dramatically updated local color fiction. . . .

The first of the Gastonia novels to be published, Mary Heaton Vorse's *Strike!*, is a transitional work between the journalism and the fiction of Gastonia. Like several of the other novelists, the author was a reporter with a background of radical activism, fiction writing, and journalism. Her literary career had begun in 1908 with the publication of *The Breaking In of a Yachtsman's Wife,* which was followed by a regular stream of light fiction and anecdotes, notable mainly for their humor and charming characterizations. Then in 1920 came *Men and Steel,* a harrowing description of the tyranny of coal, iron, and steel over the lives of people who worked the machinery of production. The uniformly favorable reception of her work up until this time changed abruptly to the accusation of propagandizing, but Vorse's sympathy for the labor movement was unweakened by this transparent shift. She covered the Gastonia events for *Harper's* and must obviously have been working simultaneously on the novel and the reports. In fact, *Strike!* appeared so precipitately in 1930 that it outran the actual Gastonia incidents on which it was based. Thus while periodicals reviewed the noble martyrdom to which the novel brought Fred Beal and his companions, they were simultaneously reporting on their news pages the less heroic bail-jumping that concluded the factual organizer's southern career. The fictional massacre was based on events at Marion, North Carolina, rather than Gastonia, but apart from this final extra indulgence in emotional catharsis, the novel adheres closely to the events of the Loray strike and points its own honesty with rather naive naming devices. Fred Beal becomes Fer Deane; the Manville-Jenckes company, which owned the mill, becomes the Basil-Schenk company; and Violet Jones, the union traitor, becomes Violet Black. The novel's reportorial accuracy and its exclusive concentration on the strike itself as the touchstone of all activity is achieved by presenting the events through the responses of Roger Hewlett, a northern journalist on his first southern labor assignment. His business is to record and synthesize the seemingly random and capricious moods and movements of the strikers, but he is also the *bildungsroman* hero who slowly emerges from his bourgeois intellectual cocoon to find at the end his true allegiance, declassed and denationalized, with the workers of the world.

As one of the earliest proletarian novels in America, *Strike!* holds little promise of radical innovations in technique to match the ideology; the novel is heroless, or rather it has as multiple hero the entire body of strikers, but otherwise it is quite conventional in form and style. Its dramatic content derives not only from the violent historical episodes but from a fascination with mass psychology in a city divided into two hostile armed camps. The emotions of the strikers fluctuate with remarkable cohesiveness between extremes of confidence and despair; the passions of the mob ("Everyone was mob who hated the Union") are more adulterated: "They were at once menacing and ridiculous. . . . They wasted their fury in futilities." Both groups are shown to be extremely unstable and

susceptible to the rumor and rhetoric of the moment, which the strikers hear at their frequent union "speakings" and the mob obtains from the local newspapers and Chamber of Commerce. Vorse naturally makes every effort to differentiate the quality of persuasion offered by these hostile sources—the repeated calls for nonviolence by the union leaders, the gushing benevolence and sentimentality from the bosses that thinly disguises greed and fury. The moral is that "Collectively human beings are at their best or their worst. They climb perilous heights of beauty and sacrifice together. And together they revert to the hunting pack, creatures aslaver for blood."

Union versus mob represents the central struggle in *Strike!*, but the simple proletarian allegory that should emerge from the confrontation does not materialize. The amorphous mob is an effective villain, spreading violence and terror throughout the community, but the multiple hero is a curiously modern image of irony, confusion, and inner contradictions. It is first of all a union that does not know how to strike. The startling ignorance among southern workers about this means of industrial protest causes both sides to view the action as one of much greater significance than a mere method of bargaining; it is for them apocalyptic—each side believes it to be the final struggle against anti-Christ. The problems of organizing the South are suggested in the miserable comment of Fer Deane, " 'I wisht I was North. I wisht I was leading a strike of fellers I was ust to.' " This remark is symptomatic of an aspect of *Strike!* that made it less than satisfactory to the *New Masses*. This was a considerable skepticism about the appropriateness of traditional Communist strike methods both for the poor whites and other classes in the South and a sharp eye for the shortcomings, rivalries, and animosities of the Party members who carried out the plans. Thus, though her emotional sympathies are correct, the *New Masses* noted the absence in Vorse's book of the "dynamic logic that made the Carolina textile worker stand up in his proletarian dignity with a copy of the *Daily Worker* in his hand." Her workers cower in confusion behind their leader. "The long years in the mill village, the paternalism under which they had lived, had taken initiative from many"; they put themselves in the hands of organizers and relief workers with the same childlike confidence that they had abandoned themselves to the mills. Those who understand that it is their fight can scarcely be restrained from using guns. The leaders, trapped between apathy and violence, between adoration and vilification, are "burdened with the hatred of the comfortable people and equally burdened with the devotion of the mill workers, a load of love and hate too heavy for their shoulders." The strikers see the union not as a rational means of organizing but as something mystical, more akin to religion, a power that exists independently of them: " 'It's kinda like salvation. You belong to the Union, and somehow or other, you're saved.' " Indeed, they hold meetings patterned on the revivalist practice of testimonials, where mass enthusiasm is whipped up by personal accounts of dramatic conversions: " 'I heard a voice asayin' to me, "jine the Union! jine the Union!" . . . an' one day it come to me, I just couldn't beah to yere that voice acroakin' to me no longer, an' I started in an' with my lame leg, I run for two miles an' I nevah stopped runnin' til' I got to Union headquarters an' jined up.' " But it is not merely such mental attitudes that portend trouble from the beginning for the northerners—the southern poor whites are virtually unable physically to sustain a strike. They have no savings to rely on, no homes of their own if the mill evicts them from its housing, and since whole families must work in the mill in order to live, there are no alternative sources of income. The union becomes instantly a charitable organization, and as the more able-bodied workers slip embarrassedly back to the hills and mills—" 'they ain't scabbin' in their hearts' "—it is left with the care of cripples and babies, the old and the weak, an ironic solidarity of nonworkers.

However, when the strike finally collapses, Vorse suggests that in addition to southern obstacles, the defeat is aided by that heresy for which the Communists themselves had coined the term "male chauvinism." All the way down the chain of command from organizers to picketers, there is keen evidence of sexual jealousy and resentment. The clash is symbolized mainly in the altercations between Fer Deane, the good-humored and rather lazy union leader idolized by the workers yet dreaming of escape from the strain, and his assistant, Irma Rankin, superior perhaps in energy and orthodoxy and arrogant in anticipation of martyrdom. Irma constantly criticizes Fer's weaknesses as a leader—" 'he hasn't the caliber to organize the *South!* . . . He has no *drive!*' "—but her hostility is clearly an affair beyond union tactics. "There was a continuous pull and strain between them of a man and woman fighting for supremacy over each other." Irma and the relief worker Doris defend the militancy of southern women to a point where it begins to hurt the strike, since the southern men have a quite contrary notion of their women and will not be led by them in the picket line. When Fer orders the young mill girls to fraternize with the soldiers, Irma contends he is confusing these workers about their "natural enemies"; bitterness between them rises to a climax when Fer gains credit for the famous tent colony over which the women had labored so hard. In controversial matters of race and religion, the Communist organizers endorsed a policy that split them from the southern workers and could only be reconciled with a few; but in their theory of sexual equality, they split among themselves as well and were unable to effect their own policy without a distrust so profound that it almost ruined the strike. There is a final irony too in this struggle, for it is Fer who becomes the reluctant martyr of the whole affair, while Irma and Doris live on to organize again.

Perhaps to try to counteract the negative effect of this male-female rivalry, Vorse introduces two love stories which in their excruciating sentimentality destroy some of the journalistic integrity of *Strike!* without adding any compensatory fictional quality. One affair, between a local girl Lissa and Fer Deane, is largely a reward for Lissa for finding a field for the tents. The other is between a local organizer and the ballad singer Ella May Wiggins, here known as Mamie Lewes. These two lovers are brought together by their passion for the union and held apart by their dedication to it: " 'We got too much to do to get mixed up this away.' " One lover from each couple is sacrificed to the guns of the mob, but the romances gain melodrama rather than dignity from their historic setting, and

the composite hero of the novel becomes fragmented by this sudden emphasis on the private lives of characters we knew only in public.

The trial incidents are used effectively to add to the sense of southern grotesquerie of the whole affair by depicting it as a parody of courtliness, "a stately ritual, an eighteenth century affair. . . . A bloodless duel with feints and parries. An elaborate structure built of courtesy and culture, something between a duel and a minuet." The result of this elegant game is the bloody effigy of the murdered man wobbling slowly in on wheels. It is like the mob singing hymns as they destroy food and supplies for the children—horrifying but also incongruously ridiculous. In her anatomy of the strike, this ironic sense of the contradictory emotions it encompasses is the most successful aspect of the novel. The whole movement of the strike, as well as the mob action, seems to be pervaded by chaos, hesitation, and whim, and there is little effort to idealize the general progress of union principles or distort the attitudes of opponents. However, this is scarcely a vindication of the *New Masses*'s judgment that the book lacks dynamic logic: the objective ideology of the strikers does advance, albeit unevenly, against the subjective limitations of the individuals involved. The author is clearly partisan, but in dissecting the strike she manages to give both external journalistic accuracy and a sympathetic portrayal of the inner tensions without resorting to propagandizing and deception. If the purely aesthetic successes of *Strike!* are very limited indeed, it nevertheless achieves through the form of the novel a sense of the local, irrational, very human aspects of Gastonia that the fine journalism could not so effectively explore.

> *Sylvia Jenkins Cook, "The Gastonia Strike and Proletarian Possibilities," in her* From Tobacco Road to Route 66: The Southern Poor White in Fiction, *The University of North Carolina Press, 1976, pp. 85-97.*

Joseph R. Urgo

[*In the following essay, Urgo examines the Gastonia novels from a feminist perspective.*]

In 1934 Granville Hicks, literary editor of the *New Masses,* wrote a seven-part series for that journal entitled "Revolution and the Novel" in which he outlined, often pedagogically, how a writer with proletarian sympathies might go about writing a revolutionary novel. In his opening article, Hicks assured young novelists that their art form "is to have a prominent part in the literature of the transition period" between capitalism and the classless society. Subsequent articles concerned individualism and collectivism in the novel, the dramatic and biographical formula, characterization possibilities, selection of plots and settings, the issue of documentation and authenticity, and, finally, an optimistic concluding article urging novelists to keep at it. "All I want to do," Hicks claimed, "is to indicate the variety of methods" open to young writers. Hicks affirmed the place of proletarian literature as "an indispensable instrument for intensifying and organizing the vague impulses toward rebellion that are the foundation of the revolutionary state of mind."

The early 1930's was characterized by a confidence among Leftist writers that the revolution would not be long in coming. All intellectual activity, then, had to be turned toward preparing for and maintaining the inspiration necessary to carry out the final conflict. All other concerns, for instance, the "woman question," were either consciously or unconsciously made subordinate to the seemingly greater and more imminent struggle between American economic classes. Characteristically, then, Hicks' seven-part series does not address the possibilities of redefining or even criticizing sex-role stereotyping in fiction, or the potentiality of revolutionary literature to contribute to women's liberation.

The low priority given women's issues among American Leftists in the 1930's is the subject of a recent article about the Communist Party. Robert Shaffer cites the "lack of an independent mass woman's movement, and the seemingly overriding nature of the economic crisis and the fight against fascism" as contributing factors to the low degree of women's activism in the thirties. "The Party's major goal," Shaffer writes, "was always to have women fighting 'side by side' or 'shoulder to shoulder' with men against capitalism."

Despite the subordination of feminism to other issues in the Communist Party, however, women did find in the Party structures that encouraged their activism in the class struggle and which more than occasionally allowed feminist concerns to be articulated. Allowing for "its important weaknesses," Shaffer concludes, "the CP's work among women in the 1930's was sufficiently extensive, consistent, and theoretically valuable to be considered an important part of the struggle for women's liberation in the United States." Feminist issues were not among the Communist Party's primary concerns in the 1930's, but they were nevertheless on the agenda. Given the absence of an autonomous women's organization in that period, moreover, the presence of an identifiable women's faction within the CP's structure becomes historically significant.

Shaffer's article suggests that in order to understand women's history in the Left in the 1930's, historians must look for evidence of feminist activism within structures which admittedly gave women's issues low priority. Although the Communist Party "did not adequately recognize the importance or difficulty of achieving women's liberation," it did address women's concerns when women raised them. Of course, some of the ways in which feminist concerns were addressed in the Communist Party in the 1930's may, in 1984, seem regressive. However, as Shaffer further concludes, this is more a function of the lack of organization among feminists:

> a consciousness of liberation does not arise fully coherent and in a neat package, but in partial and even contradictory ways. An analysis of the CP's policies on women must always be grounded in the perception of those policies by the women involved. We cannot ignore as duped, or misled, those many women who have written that they gained increased awareness of their po-

tentialities as women through participation in the CP. Neither can we forget those who complained of the CP's apparent unconcern for their particular problems of housework and child care.

Feminist issues were articulated in the 1930's, according to Shaffer, through such Leftist periodicals as *Women Today, Working Woman,* and in the *Daily Worker,* which carried a regular column on women. In addition, women were writing scholarly books about women in the thirties, including Grace Hutchins' *Women Who Work* and Mary Inman's *In Woman's Defense.* In this paper a third area in which feminist concerns were articulated in the 1930's is suggested, proletarian literature of female authorship. In the thirties women contributed significantly to the new literary genre and, I would contend, often included within their revolutionary plots the special concerns of their sex.

This essay examines a small body of proletarian fiction by women—four novels about the same contemporary event—for evidence of special women's concerns existing beneath the surface of the novels' thematic and plot objectives. In the absence of a women's movement in the 1930's, female writers did not have the structures toward which their characters could lean to express their feminism any more than did the women in the Communist Party of that decade. Proletarian literature, as revolutionary literature concerned with reshaping and redefining society, no doubt provided one literary framework in which female writers could legitimately express feminist protest.

Granville Hicks' series on proletarian fiction did not address the "woman question" as an issue appropriate to the new genre. Nor were Leftist or other reviewers of the novels discussed here sensitive to their feminist elements. This is not surprising, of course, given the low currency of women's issues in the press and among Leftist organizations in the thirties. However, it is this absence of feminist structures in the 1930's which makes the feminist elements in radical novels so interesting today. Although women's issues in the novels studied here do not, to borrow Shaffer's phrase, "arise fully coherent and in a neat package," they are easily identified when the novels are read with them in mind. Once articulated, these elements may provide important ideological links between the more salient periods in women's political and intellectual history occurring before and after the proletarian decade.

In the late 1920's, the Trade Union League developed a three-part strategy for organizing American textile workers. In 1926-1927, factories were struck in Passaic, New Jersey, followed in 1928 by strikes in New Bedford, Massachusetts, and culminating in statewide strikes in North Carolina in 1929. The strikes in North Carolina were particularly violent, especially those taking place in Gastonia County in the spring and summer of 1929, and received national media attention. "After the Communist-led strikes, mob violence, and bloodthirsty reprisals, Gastonia became a symbol to the rest of the country of the horrors of southern capitalism and a cynical comment on North Carolina justice." To many Leftists, Gastonia became a symbol of imminent class warfare in America.

After World War I, textile companies in the Northeast

moved into the South, attracted by the prospects of cheap labor, tax incentives, and proximity to raw materials. Workers were drawn from among mountain people "who came down to the factories because of the promise of, to them, higher wages and the glamour of town life after their isolation." Once moving into the mill towns, however, the economic dreams of these workers were shattered by high rents and high prices, the necessity that the entire family work, and the extremely dangerous and physically exhausting nature of textile labor. The American Federation of Labor was present in North Carolina in 1929; however, that organization had been either unable or unwilling to effect any real progress in worker conditions. Into this scenario entered organizers from the National Textile Workers in the spring of 1929.

The violence with which North Carolina authorities met the strike and the intransigence and courage displayed by the workers in the face of superior state forces resulted in Gastonia's becoming "a cynosure for radical sentiment" in the 1930's. "Not since the battle in Homestead have workers replied with greater determination and courage to the attacks of the armed forces of the capitalist class," wrote the *New Masses* of Gastonia. The guns in Gastonia were "shots heard round the world." The events in North Carolina were given extensive treatment in the *New Masses,* including political analyses, eyewitness accounts, poetic interpretations, and excerpts from Gastonia novels. "The attention of sympathetic writers was directed to Gastonia not merely by the *New Masses,*" however, "but also by the general tenor of reporting in liberal periodicals such as the *Nation,* the *New Republic,* and the *Outlook and Independent.*" The liberal press, although hardly supportive of revolution, did not like to see the capitalist state supported by such blatant uses of its power.

Gastonia provided literary inspiration for six novelists as well: *Strike!,* by Mary Heaton Vorse; *Call Home the Heart,* by Fielding Burke; *To Make My Bread,* by Grace Lumpkin; *Gathering Storm,* by Myra Page; *Beyond Desire,* by Sherwood Anderson; and *The Shadow Before,* by William Rollins. All six novelists saw in Gastonia a structure through which a larger purpose could be served. In each of the novels, Gastonia is given as the focus of the universal class struggle, as a set of real events operating within the context of Marxist ideology. In this way, the novels take a singular, actual event and offer literary and ideological interpretations which can, in turn, be applied to the reader's own experiences and beliefs. Gastonia was already a symbol of class struggle in America before these novels were written; what the novels do is articulate reasons why Gastonia had universal significance, and demonstrate ways in which that significance could be understood and applied to the lives of readers.

In his discussion of ideology and literature, John M. Reilly observes the special relationship between the Gastonia novels and the development of political, especially Leftist, fiction in America. "Novelists almost invariably describe their mode of writing as a way of telling the truth," Reilly states. "Thus, while the authors of the novels about the Gastonia strike worked to reveal what they thought of as the genuine truth about Gastonia, it was a truth perceived

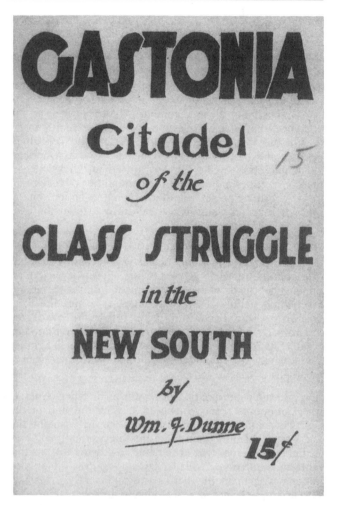

Pamphlet about the Gastonia, North Carolina, textile workers' strike of 1929, written by the editor of the Daily Worker - *the official newspaper of the Workers Party of America.*

by means of an imaginative pattern—their ideology." Hence, the novels are attempts, in varying degrees, to fit Gastonia into the theoretical pattern of Communist ideology, and "were intended as anticipations of political action throughout the country." Differences in emphases and selectivity of events in the six novels reflect a variety of ideological sympathies among the novelists drawn to the Gastonia symbol.

Four of the six Gastonia novels were of female authorship, and these extract from the North Carolina events issues of particular relevance to women. The condition of women in the Gastonia story—farm women forced by economic necessity into factories, the high rate of infant mortality, violence directed toward female strikers—stands out today as an important part of the Gastonia symbol as perceived by the four women novelists. The "woman's side" of the story was not commented upon by the *New Masses,* however, except as further proof of the evils of capitalism, just as rape would be considered another instance of the enemy's barbarity in warfare. During the Gastonia riots the state police and militia were particularly cruel toward the women on the picket lines, a phenomenon included in all four novels examined here.

The analysis which follows reads the novels specifically for their treatment of women in an effort to synthesize the feminist elements within them. Brief summaries of each author's career and the critical reception of each novel precede analysis to provide historical and literary context. I am not as concerned with the surface events of the novels, the presentation of the Gastonia strike, class issues, and Communist ideology, as I am with the more implicit themes of feminism, raising the woman question, in these four proletarian novels. A brief discussion of the two Gastonia novels by men is included in the conclusion in order to amplify my claim that the novels of female authorship contain a wholly distinct set of concerns, reflecting an autonomous view of the events at Gastonia.

Strike! (1930)

Mary Heaton Vorse's *Strike!* was published in 1930, one of the earliest examples of the "instant book" which paperback book publishers would perfect thirty years later. In fact, Vorse finished writing *Strike!* before the events in Gastonia had ended; thus, while her strike organizer was martyred the real-life organizer fled to Russia while out on bail. Vorse, who covered the strike as a reporter, probably wrote the novel in between filing press releases. She was forty-four when the book was published.

From 1912 through 1950, Vorse was a major figure in the labor movement. Although she was among the more energetic and versatile Leftist activists of her time, she never joined a radical political party and shied away from confining her labor allegiance to any specific ideology. Late in her life she would attribute what she perceived as her failings to the dependency of her children and grandchildren who, Vorse claimed, kept her from fulfilling her activist calling. In order to support these dependents she was compelled to write what she called "lollipops," or romantic, light fiction. Her disdain for such fancy is evident in *Strike!,* which is practically devoid of lollipops.

Whatever her personal misgivings, by 1929 Vorse was an important interpreter of labor issues in America. By the time she arrived in Gastonia she had almost twenty years of labor journalism experience behind her, beginning in 1912 when she covered strikes in Lawrence, Massachusetts. Vorse was drawn to Lawrence out of sympathy for the condition of workers' children there; she would continue to center her strike reports around the effects of labor on the quality of workers' lives in America. At Gastonia, Vorse found what were probably the worst labor conditions in the country in 1929.

The *New Masses* published an excerpt from *Strike!* the month before it was released. In November 1930, reviewer Walt Carmen gave the book an enthusiastic reception, stating that "people will argue whether this is literature, propaganda, or art, or proletarian art." Carmen does conclude that the story was worth telling, however. Sinclair Lewis, writing in the *Nation,* agreed that the book was "more a statement of facts than a novel," but pointed out that "she tells the truth—and dramatically." Although finding "not much to be said for its merits" as a novel, the

Saturday Review of Literature saw a "moral purpose" in keeping the events of Gastonia in the public eye. The *New York Times* had virtually the same response, criticizing the novel's "lack of direction and unity" while praising its journalistic function. Appearing so soon after the events it described, *Strike!* could be accepted by the liberal press as a topical, secondrate piece of fiction. The confusion of the *New Masses'* reviewer reflects that journal's lack of articulation of a theory of "proletarian literature" at the time of *Strike!* publication. *Strike!* may have been among the novels which led the *New Masses* to formulate such a theory four years later.

Strike! is by no means a good novel. It reads tediously and is repetitive, and it includes entirely too many events to allow it a necessary coherence. However, there is one thread which runs through the novel, even if not always in view, and that is the relationship between the strike organizer, Fer Deane, and "his girl," Irma Rankin.

Through the characters Irma and Fer, Vorse presents a specific comment on sexism within the Communist Party, and a more general comment on individualism and collectivism. The critique of the Communist Party emerges from the two characters' own interaction. Irma is presented as being "tougher" than Fer, a "potential" leader who is not a leader, because she is female. Relations between Irma and Fer are characterized by "a continuous pull and strain between them of a man and woman fighting for supremacy over each other." Roger Hewlitt, the reporter in the novel, observes the intense "role-bound" fight for dominance between the two Communists. Irma is not in equal competition due to the "role-bound" nature of the contest. The uneven competition drives Irma to complain about Fer behind his back (to Roger, usually). Vorse says Irma's strategy was designed to "dominate Fer, to put something over on him. In a way, to diminish him."

By casting Irma as something of a spoiler, Vorse may be commenting on the wasted talent in labor organizations (Irma's last name, Rankin, is a play on "rank and file"), and in the Communist Party, by virtue of the sexual exclusiveness of their leadership. Vorse intimates that it is dangerous for the movement to prohibit significant female participation. According to Robert Shaffer's study of women in the Communist Party, females complained that male organizers often "discouraged women from joining the CP" and "intimidated or ignored the few women members." As Shaffer states, "sexism within the CP was a problem for many woman members—and would be members." Through her characterization of Irma and Fer, then, Vorse illuminates a very real problem within the Communist Party in the 1930's.

In her one direct confrontation with Fer, Irma backs down from him, but not without first calling into question the Party's exploitation of women. Irma sees the young mill girls flirting "arm-in-arm" with the state militia and complains to Fer about such fraternization, arguing that it "confuses their minds." Fer snaps at her: "You read that in a book. . . . You better go and read another book, Irma, that will tell you about winning over the military." Irma, objecting to the use of the young girls' bodies in the class struggle, is rebuffed by Fer, who accuses her of being naive. By "confuses their minds" Irma refers to compromising Communist ideology with sexist tactics. Fer, the strike organizer, is unreceptive to such concerns. Interestingly, the historical strike organizer at Gastonia quarreled with Party officials over strategy, and was criticized for not maintaining a purist position on tactical matters.

In the scene which immediately follows the Irma-Fer confrontation, Vorse uses Fer's character to offer a general criticism of individualism. It is individualism which allows Fer to abuse Irma, according to Vorse, and only collectivism will end such sexism. Fer is about to address a crowd of strikers when, faced with their collective strength, he feels "his own smallness and inadequacy." Here the man who could dominate Irma in an individualistic, "role-bound" struggle is revealed before the collective in all his insignificance. Fer, despite his averred Communist beliefs, never emerges as a true collectivist in *Strike!*. An individualist to the finish, Fer is given a true hero's death by martyrdom at the end of the book. His death is not without irony, however, as the "hero" Fer is soon forgotten by the people and replaced by a myth, "a composite of all virtues which he had not possessed." Heroes, individual achievers, and even individualism in general, in Vorse's view, are myths. Men become leaders by tactical successes (as Fer's over Irma), but in fact are no more than personifications of collective beliefs.

The traditional American conception of manhood, the individualist, is held up by Vorse in contrast to the joining, cooperating spirit among the proletariat. A general disappointment with men runs throughout *Strike!* Irma observes that "the women are pluckier than the men," that they have "fighting stuff in them, these women." It is women like Ma Gilfin who are behind the strike, after all. She tells her reluctant sons to "jine or git," and they join. Even the bourgeois woman, Mrs. Parker, tells Roger that "men have no courage anymore," although she is referring to their softness toward the strikers. "If the police and the law act too slowly," she says, "I believe in men showing their manhood." This is the bourgeois myth of masculinity: lawless, violent, independent. It is directly contrasted by Vorse to the more productive and humanistic spirit shared by the collectivity of workers.

Vorse ties sexism within the Communist Party to latent individualism among its male leadership through the characterization of Fer Deane. The women in *Strike!* are more inclined to collectivist politics and true Communism, and the men are in need of their guidance. However, the position men enjoy as leaders in the Party results in the stifling of the participation of women, and the loss of important female contributions to Party efforts. By prohibiting women from reaching positions of leadership within its structures, the Communist Party handicaps itself and actually works against its own goals. As Sylvia Cook has pointed out, the final irony in the Irma-Fer relationship is that Fer is martyred while Irma is left to continue the struggle. The individualist receives his hero's death, while the collectivist lives on to fight again.

To Make My Bread (1932)

Heterosocial relations in Grace Lumpkin's Gastonia novel are less explicit than in Mary Heaton Vorse's, but they are at the same time more important to the book's theme. *To Make My Bread* is chiefly concerned with the effects on women of the transition from mountain to mill life. Lumpkin is as blatant in her politics as Vorse (it is the mill owner who grinds the bones of the workers "to make my bread"), but it is not Communist ideology which informs the drama of the novel.

Grace Lumpkin grew up in the South. As a government home demonstrator, she worked among the types of people described in her novel and grew sympathetic to their plight as mill workers. She became a Communist fellow-traveler in the 1930's, writing for the *New Masses* and developing her own fiction. In 1953, however, she adjured her radicalism before a Senate subcommittee, testifying that Communist critics pressured her into infusing her work with Leftist propaganda.

To Make My Bread, published when Lumpkin was thirty, was well-received by contemporary critics. The *New Masses* gave it an extended review in which it was judged as "definitely in the line of the literature of the revolutionary proletariat." Lumpkin was faulted, however, for writing the book from the perspective "of the backward workers" instead of from the point of view of a true "revolutionist," and thus getting some of her ideology backward. Robert Cantwell welcomed *To Make My Bread* as proof that there is such a thing as proletarian literature, even though he found the book "propagandistic." He considered it, however, "very good, very effective propaganda; I cannot understand how anyone could read it and not be moved by it." Mary Heaton Vorse, writing in the *New Republic,* called it the best book written on Gastonia yet, praising its "almost epic scope." The *New York Times* declared that *To Make My Bread* was "one more milestone on the road to the return of 'social consciousness' in American fiction." The *Times* liked the subject matter, style, and technique of the novel, calling it "not in any way propagandistic."

The range and types of reviews received by Lumpkin are testimony to her ability to provide multiple themes in her work. The enthusiasm of the *Times,* for example, may be due to the classic American "fall from grace" the mountain people experience in moving to an industrial setting. The qualified praise from Leftist critics is equally attributable to Lumpkin's refusal to commit herself, until the end of the book, to proletarian rebellion. In any case, none of the contemporary reviews picked up on what Sylvia Cook points out as the book's main emphasis, the "dialectical debate" among feminists "between the adherents of solidarity with other movements . . . and those who believe that no economic or social equality can ever exist without a prior radical revision" of heterosocial relations.

The weakness and vulnerability of women due to the physiological burden of childbearing forms the tragic theme of *To Make My Bread.* The novel opens as Emma McClure is about to give birth. Unable to get help due to a "wailing snowstorm" outside, Emma must enlist the aid of her own father, Grandpap, for the delivery. Her husband is dead. The birth is presented in violent imagery, compared to the slitting of a pig's throat, and strongly affects the entire family. It marks the first time that Grandpap has "known fear"; it reveals to Kirk, Emma's son, that his mother is a "beast"; it reminds Emma that she has no close woman friend to help her at this most basic female function. Having her father delivery her dead husband's son underscores the complete domination of her body by males; Kirk's judgment only adds humiliation to her subservient position.

The parcelling of the female body and functions among dominating males is repeated symbolically later in the book. While Minnie, a local mountain girl of dubious morality, is giving birth to a boy baby of dubious paternity, the men outside the house are cutting up and dividing the body of a "she-bear." Echoing the birth scene in Chapter One, one possible father of Minnie's child has deserted her. The burdens of childbearing and child-raising are women's alone. Even Emma's daughter, Bonnie, must raise her children alone while her husband deteriorates. Men receive the spoils of this particular women's burden—just as they divide up the carcass of the she-bear—and assume none of the responsibilities. Only male babies are born in *To Make My Bread;* the women characters simply exist.

There are three types of male characters in Lumpkin's book. There are weak men, like Basil who deserts his family for selfish personal gain, and Robert who is physically injured in the mill. There are defeated men, like Grandpap, the mountain man whose "rugged individualism" is anachronistic in an industrial society. And there are sensitive men, such as Emma's son John, who gradually grows to socialist awareness. Three types of women inhabit Lumpkin's world as well. Emma and Bonnie are strong women: they do what they have to do, and make gradual progress toward social activism. There is the evil woman, college-educated, who uses her sexuality to tempt good John away from unionism. And there is the whore, Minnie, who is driven to prostitution by social forces beyond her control, and by making the mistake of loving too many men.

John's altruism is a result of his ability to learn from the right people—both men and women—and of his willingness to treat all people as human beings and not according to the societal roles they play. John successfully fuses the ideals and example of his rugged Grandpap with the strength and sensitivity of his sister Bonnie. When he meets Ruth, he is not taken in by her beauty and education and quickly realizes that she is attempting to seduce him away from unionism. He also visits Minnie as a human being, not as a whore, and remains friends with her despite her pathetic condition. John treats both of these women not in accordance to their status—Ruth's intelligence and beauty, Minnie's degradation—but in accordance to his judgment of them as people. He stands in direct contrast to his brother, Basil, for example, who treats women as objects existing for his own personal gain and satisfaction. Basil marries an "ugly" woman for her money and slips out of his wife's bed at night to stay at Minnie's house as a paying customer.

Although *To Make My Bread* centers on women and the woman's burden, its political heroes are exclusively male

and it expounds no feminist ideology. Women are presented as stronger and more durable than men, but politically less important. The book is tragic in the sense that it depicts women as potential reformers who are handicapped by their fecundity. By demonstration rather than exposition, *To Make My Bread* presents this female contradiction as inhibiting social progress. In *Strike!,* Mary Heaton Vorse attributed women's subjugation to Communist Party chauvinism and regressive individualism on the part of male members; Grace Lumpkin's emphasis is not on male chauvinism but on women themselves and the female childbearing function. In her novel, Lumpkin sees the progress of the world in the hands of women who can inspire men to greatness, even if they must suffer and die while doing it. Bonnie emerges as the striker's songwriter, whose songs keep the men and women on the picket lines strong. She is killed at the end of the book, as the historical Gastonia's Ella May Wiggins was actually martyred, and her brother John pledges to continue the struggle with her martyrdom as inspiration. Bonnie will be the source of John's strength in his future labor activism.

Gathering Storm (1932)

Sylvia Cook states that *Gathering Storm* was "so ideologically 'correct' that it was almost wholly ignored by reviewers to the right of the *New Masses.*" The book is a virtual showcase of Party doctrine with almost no literary merit. A recent critic calls it a "zealous work in which ideology is preferred without any check by the author's knowledge of the way human beings think and perceive." *Gathering Storm* is particularly disappointing because Myra Page later wrote fairly good Leftist fiction. *Moscow Yankee,* for example, tells the story of an American worker's "coming into consciousness" in the Soviet Union through his work in a Soviet factory and his love affair with a Russian woman.

Myra Page is the most educated of the four novelists studied here, receiving her Ph.D in sociology at Minnesota University in 1928. Her dissertation concerned Southern textile mills. Her Master's Degree was in political science at Columbia, where she studied yellow journalism. Between her M.A. and Ph.D., Page returned to her home state of Virginia and worked as a union organizer in department stores and silk mills. Finding the YWCA-sponsored organizing program too conservative, Page resigned after a short stay in Virginia and moved to Philadelphia to work with the Amalgamated Clothing Workers Union. After completing her dissertation, Page traveled to Europe and the Soviet Union, working as a journalist.

Given her education and work experience, Page is open to the charge that her Gastonia novel is a self-conscious amalgam of what she read and what she hoped to do. *Gathering Storm* was published when she was thirty-two. Twenty years later, Page was blacklisted and unable to find an American publisher to print her fiction. She kept working, however, taking her husband's name and publishing four biographies between 1956 and 1964.

According to *Book Review Digest, Gathering Storm* was reviewed by only two major publications, the *New Republic* and the *London Times.* The *New Masses* found the book burdensome for its preponderance of detail, but exemplary of the "understanding of one who has studied Marxism and Leninism." The reviewer, however, mentions neither Gastonia nor the book's literary merit. "*Gathering Storm* is one of our first novels of and for the workers," she claims. "It is essentially regional in background, which is good." This is odd praise, since the novel jumps from Gastonia to New York, Chicago, and Russia in an effort to suggest the international significance of the story. In a brief note in the *New Republic, Gathering Storm* is dismissed as "a political and agitational novel" which covers too much ground and too many tangential issues. It should have centered on "the particularly brutal and open exploitation of the textile workers," which it does well, but incompletely. The *Times Literary Service* had a similar judgment of *Gathering Storm,* finding it on the whole painfully propagandistic.

The Crenshaw family is the center of *Gathering Storm.* In an almost misogynist opening tale, the heroine's grandmother tells her how the Crenshaws came to the mills from the mountains. Marge's grandfather did not want to go, so the grandmother "sabotaged" the potato patch. Having spoiled the year's crop, the family was forced to leave the mountains. This variation on the Garden of Eden story (although this Paradise was not so Edenic) points to the female side of the family as somehow responsible for the family's suffering under industrialization. "From the beginnin' thar was trouble," Granma says, " 'n it's been nothin' but trouble and worriment ever since."

Marge and her brother, Tom, form points of sex-role comparison in the novel. Tom, disillusioned with mill life, goes North to find success. Marge cannot do this because she is female. Instead, Marge gets Bob, a persistent suitor who wants Marge and a family. Marge refuses and vows never to have children ("weighing you down, sucking your spirit"). But Marge's resolution cannot survive the pressure Bob puts on her at the outset of the World War, and she marries him before he joins the army. One woman can hold her own against one man, Page suggests, but not against the overwhelming force of the masculine military institution which lends legitimacy to otherwise unfair and uncivil male demands on women. Bob leaves Marge pregnant before he leaves for war. While Bob is away, Marge tries to abort the pregnancy using a primitive method. Again, war destroys civil relations between men and women, and male demands upset the natural relation between a woman and her body. The baby, a girl, is born sickly, and Marge, "of little milk," is unable to prevent its dying in infancy. Meanwhile, Tom's career as a Communist is well underway in New York City. Significant to Marge's story, Tom is jailed for his opposition to the war. He is also overcoming his racist indoctrination and rising within Party ranks. Page's view of sex-role stereotyping in capitalist America is displayed by her juxtaposition of the stories of the Crenshaw siblings: Marge's subordination to masculine institutions and her struggle with her body, and Tom's active opposition to those institutions and his role in the larger class struggle. Tom has chosen his cause; Marge's destiny is determined by her physiology.

When men and women interact in *Gathering Storm,*

women invariably become pregnant as men move from abusive sex mania to depleted obsolescence. Page suggests that the labor movement and Communism may save everyone from these traps. Bob returns from the war a candidate for the lost generation (he "wandered about the house as though looking for something he couldn't find") and totally useless to Marge. He does manage to get Marge pregnant again before dying. The child is, as was the widow McClure's and the unwed Minnie's in *To Make My Bread,* a healthy boy. Marge moves in with her sister, who has a drunken, shiftless husband who "won't let her be." She has entirely too many children already, so Marge tells her to put salt and pepper in her husband's food to "quiet him." Now that Marge, as a widow, is free of her husband, she gradually becomes involved in the labor movement and identifies it with her own untapped potential. However, Page does not follow this through except for an isolated instance of Marge "saying a word" to a rally, or getting arrested in a mass arrest on a picket line. What Page found significant was the wasted potential of women like Marge. In this sense Marge resembles Vorse's Irma Rankin: potential leaders stifled by sex-role typification.

Marge's brother Tom falls in love with Bessie, a Russian immigrant of considerable labor experience in America (sweatshops, garment strikes, Chicago shirtwaist strike). Similar to Irma in *Strike!,* Bessie fell out with her male union leaders over policy and tactics. As if to show there is a "radical mystique" in women, Page describes in detail Tom's impression of Bessie as "a picture of glowing brown eyes in a rounded face, topped with black curly hair and a small sturdy figure with quiet moving gestures." Sounding a bit like the description of an ice cream sundae, this description of Bessie stands out as the only detailed statement of the physical attributes of a female character in the four novels. Bessie had something Tom had "never seen in a woman." Presumably, she differs from the American women in the novel not only in appearance but in the control she exerts over her body. She does not suffer the stifling ailments of women such as Marge, she does not get pregnant, nor is she sexually tormented by her man, Tom Crenshaw. She certainly does not suffer any of the societal limitations which plague the other female characters in *Gathering Storm.* During the War, the United States government deports her as "dangerous" because she is a radical. The reader should understand her threat to American society both on political as well as heterosocial grounds.

Gathering Storm raises feminist issues but is ultimately disappointing in its handling of them. The childbearing trap, treated thoroughly by Lumpkin, is thrown away by Page in a series of trite circumstances and cliches. But the novel is more important for what it attempts than for what it achieves. It is significant that Marge's sickly, unwanted child is a girl and the healthy, fatherless child is a boy. In *Call Home the Heart,* considered next, this phenomenon becomes almost emblematic. The societal limitations suffered by Marge in *Gathering Storm* are made to appear pathetic by the introduction of Bessie, who suffers no such limitations. But the differences between the two women cease to be pathetic and emerge as political when we remember that Bessie was raised in Russia. In Russian society, Page suggests, the Communist way of life produces a new kind of woman with none of the fragility and social importance of American women. Just as Page juxtaposes sex-role destinies through her creation of the Crenshaw siblings, Marge and Tom, she contrasts the destinies of two women from opposing economic systems. Considered as personified symbols in an ideological dialectic, Page's characters emerge as significant statements in proletarian fiction. While they may be disappointing literary creations, they do indicate a strong authorial sense of the connection between economic revolution and heterosocial redefinition.

Call Home the Heart (1932)

Tilford Dargan grew up in Kentucky and Missouri and attended a teacher's college in Nashville and Radcliffe College in Boston. She lived ninety-nine years and was sixty-three when *Call Home the Heart* was published. All of her social fiction was published under the pseudonym "Fielding Burke"; she used her own name for her poetry and short stories. She received a literary prize for her fiction in 1916 and an honorary doctorate from the University of North Carolina in 1924. Antecedents of Dargan's political writing have been traced to her earliest efforts. In the first years of the twentieth century, she wrote about industrial oppression and the conflict of emotional commitments among working people in dramatic form.

Call Home the Heart was Dargan's first novel. In the *New Masses,* it was given extensive treatment and judged among "the pioneer novels in the literature of the American working class." Robert Cantwell found Dargan "breaking new ground" in fiction but faulted the novel for poorly presenting the strike as a "dramatic conflict in itself." Cantwell attributed the shortcomings of *Call Home the Heart* to the lack of an articulated theory of proletarian fiction. *The New Republic* found the novel guilty of a "distinctively American romanticism" even though it was too cumbersome to qualify as a work of art. Only the *New York Times* addresses the heroine herself, pointing out the struggle between her longings to "see more of the world" and the inescapable realities of her social and economic condition.

The *Saturday Review of Literature* praised *Call Home the Heart* for finally dealing with Gastonia "not in the form of drab economic propaganda . . . but in a powerful story of men and women." Sylvia Cook identifies a typical Dargan theme in the novel—the undermining of societal causes by the love between a man and a woman "which constantly threatens their loyalty and concentration." There is a "whole pattern of feminist discontent" in *Call Home the Heart,* moreover, which eluded contemporary critics and which is the unifying theme in the novel.

Call Home the Heart stands apart from the novels previously discussed here as a work of considerable artistic merit. Ishma Waycaster emerges as the only "whole" character in the novels. Her naming, for Ishmael the outcast, also brings to mind Melville's Ishmael. For Ishma, however, the Leviathan lurks in the mill town, calling her away from her mountain home and toward something she cannot identify:

> Ishma: Why does every body think a girl's got to marry? I'm going to have something else.
>
> Britt: Have what?
>
> Ishma: I don't know.

Circumstances—commitments to family, poverty, a tireless suitor—force Ishma, as Marge in *Gathering Storm,* to compromise, and marry Britt. Throughout the novel, in fact, Ishma's plans are foiled by uncontrollable external events. She has a child every year for the first years of her marriage, which increases her discontent as much as it enhances the happiness of Britt. Finally, faced with her brother's decision to leave the mountain (again, recall Marge's brother Tom), Ishma decides to leave. Prodded on by an old boyfriend who still loves her, Ishma fulfills her girlhood dream to see the life of a city. Ishma uses Red, the old suitor, to get to the mill town. Here Dargan cynically ties the fate of her heroine to yet another male figure, and makes possible the charge that Ishma prostitutes herself off the mountain. The exchange of services is made explicit by Ishma, who repeatedly refers to fulfilling her side of the "bargain" with Red by living with him.

Dargan views Ishma's brush with Communism and Communist ideology in general with a critical eye, unlike the treatment of Communism in the other novels. What Ishma wanted most of all in life was "to count, to be a part of something real," namely, the emergence of Communism as a force among workers. Communism, a rally speaker proclaims, "is a great mother, calling us to peace and plenty." Ishma pursues the "great mother" by studying world history and Marxist ideology and going to work for a union organizer, Amos Freer. Ultimately, however, Ishma cannot become a Communist due to her latent American racism. When her activities force her into close proximity with Negroes (she is hugged by a black woman after saving the woman's son), a revulsion sweeps over her, and she flees back to the mountain. Dargan was not about to accept the pretensions of contemporary Leftists who claimed to have the answer to the American race problem.

Sylvia Cook claims that Ishma's venture presents the feminist point that there will never be a Communist state without a prior change in the relations between men and women. While this is certainly a valid inference, it is not Dargan's strongest statement. There is a point in the novel at which Ishma gains the knowledge for which she has been searching. She visits a wealthy farmer, Abraham Beasley, "a self-made man" who followed the paradigmatic path from rags to riches. He tells his story to Ishma, but adds to it his consciousness of how lucky he was, and of what an exception his story is to the actual farmers' plight. He is, therefore, a Communist now, who advocates cooperative farms. When Ishma leaves Beasley she is an enlightened woman:

> Gradually she became possessed of a secret. Every sordid and ugly life had its hidden war in the service of a dream; its struggle behind drab, matter-of-fact; its timidity and pride, fearing to be found out. That was the mystery she had so often seen in chilled, coffined faces.

Ishma's main struggle is not with Britt (he actually defends her right to leave him and pursue her dream when he pummels the preacher who speaks out against her), but with herself. After Vennie, her child, is dead, and after Red falls in love with another woman, Ishma is completely free. With her new freedom she pursues an active life in the Communist movement, but ultimately fails due to her revulsion toward Negroes. Finally getting herself to a point at which she believes she is emancipated, Ishma discovers yet another obstacle, racism. In this sense, then, the novel is intensely individualistic, suggesting that progress lies in personal catharsis rather than political panacea, and denying there is any such thing as freedom. In other words, before assuming that simple "independence" will free her to effect social change or participate in radical politics, the individual woman must reach an understanding of herself which is conscious of all the oppressive distinctions handed down to her by the patriarchal social order. Dargan's feminist emphasis is not upon heterosocial relations so much as upon the self-knowledge and self-understanding of individual women.

The burden of childbearing faced by women is given particularly effective attention in *Call Home the Heart*. Ishma is alienated from her children in the mountains, considering them as one shackle after another, preventing her escape from the mountain. When she arrives in the mill town with Red, she is pregnant. This unwanted child is a girl. Despite Ishma's firm decision to have no children in the city, Vennie, Britt's legacy to her, continues to be a burden, a quiet vengeance. The child is born sickly and weak, and incapable of existing without Ishma's presence. Therefore, even after birth, Ishma must continue to literally "carry" the child with her constantly. The burden of childbearing, from Lumpkin's *To Make My Bread,* and the symbol of the girl-child as the result of a particularly unwanted pregnancy (*Gathering Storm*) begin to emerge as identifiable symbols triggering ideological significance in these four women's novels. Childbearing occurs neither as symbol nor as event in the Gastonia novels by men, discussed in the conclusion below. In *Call Home the Heart,* it is only after Vennie's death and Red's diversion to another woman that Ishma is free to discover her "secret." But Dargan's novel is ultimately tragic, not polemical: in order to find "truth," woman must be free of the burden of childbearing and search it out alone. The "truth," however, is that everyone has his or her burden to bear.

In the two Gastonia novels written by men, sexuality and sexual adventurism play central roles in the action of the novels' various side plots. Sherwood Anderson's *Beyond Desire* makes an explicit call for some sort of new understanding between the sexes and has what might be considered a vaguely feminist undertone. But Anderson is not about to assign clearly recognizable roles of aggressor and victim to males and females in his novel. *Beyond Desire* leaves one feeling that there is something dreadfully wrong with the way the sexes interact and that the problem is much more fundamental to human existence than are the artificial institutions of the economy. In William Rollins' *The Shadow Before* things are much simpler. Ramon Viera, the Portuguese upwardly-mobile section-hand in the mill, has sex with nearly all the central female

characters, and emerges from the novel as an industrial Don Juan of sorts. The marriage between Mr. and Mrs. (mill foreman) Thayer is formal at best, with Mr. Thayer's real spouse being the mill, and Mrs. Thayer's real lover being Ramon. The Thayer's daughter, Marjorie, loses her virginity (and she does consider it a loss) to the mill owner's son, Harry Baumann, who considers her just another sexual score. In scenes bordering on the pornographic, Rollins presents male violence and female submission as natural aspects of relations between the sexes. Women in the strike do little more than cook and worry, as does Micky, over which man made them pregnant. Micky is torn between her love/hate relationship with Ramon (he used to be her lover, but now he's on the side of management and has eyes for Marjorie Thayer—Micky will still have sex with him on demand, of course), and her love/hate relationship with Harry (she loves him but he is, after all, the mill owner's son). In the end Micky gets neither boy. She is left with a pregnancy, however, which she suspects must be Ramon's doing since Harry, the good bourgeois boy, used "precautions."

If sexual relations in Rollins' novel sound like a side show, then I have related my sense of the book effectively. There is no indication that the maker of *The Shadow Before* finds anything wrong with heterosocial relations, or that the way in which the sexes interact in any standard "tough guy" novel is of questionable mimetic value. There is certainly no sense that Rollins considers a redefinition of society's economic base to be connected in any way to a redefinition of sexual alignments. Rollins' admiration of the working class leads him to portray it as more sexually vigorous—the bourgeois characters are as bored with sex as they are with life in general—but the world reflected in his novel offers a clear acceptance of the kind of human sexuality one finds in Mickey Spillane.

Relations between the sexes in Anderson's *Beyond Desire* are of such central importance to the novel that the strike seems almost like a side show. The book even makes the explicit claim that the first step in any social or economic revolution must be to end "the queer old enmity between men and women." The quest for personal sexual fulfillment is shared by all of Anderson's major characters, and the search for a mate motivates male and female radicals alike. Women, however, are presented as the more radical sex because their traditional, subordinate position in patriarchal society allows them to see social inequities more readily. Having no power to lose, women easily accept the connections among economic, social, and sexual redefinitions. But feminist issues are kept at the level of private frustration and not articulated as ideology in the novel. Anderson thus avoids the issues of power and patriarchy which are so obviously crucial to the Gastonia novels written by women. Anderson's Ethel, for instance, who is "in revolt against men," is *really* angry and frustrated that the right man has not yet come along. Moving from sadomasochistic fantasies to a lesbian encounter with her age-equal stepmother, Ethel finally opts for a quiet companionate marriage to the cynical Tom Riddle. As with Tilford Dargan, Anderson's primary interest lies with the individual, not the class. His twin themes of sexual redefinition and industrial oppression merge in the character of

Molly, the young mill worker from the mountains. In the mill, Molly exchanges sex for a chance to rest during the work day, giving herself to a mill foreman for short naps in the stockroom. This experience radicalizes Molly and she later joins the strikers wholeheartedly. When Molly meets Red, the one character in the novel who moves from ambivalence to fatalistic extremism, the reader expects a climatic relationship which will demonstrate what Anderson has been leading up to throughout the novel.

Anderson allows the physical consummation but not the ideological union. With intentions perhaps more artistic than polemic, Anderson's novel resists simple reduction; like Dargan's novel, it moves away from any radical self-satisfaction. Red refuses to stay with Molly after they have sex together ("It was time now for men to prove themselves in a new way") and associates his feelings for Molly with weakness, not strength. Hence, Red really learns nothing in the novel: he leaves Molly to pursue a lone hero's death, sacrificing himself in a selfish attempt at martyrdom. But his devotion to the cause is dubious at best as he acts primarily to assuage his own self-anger and sense of cowardice. Molly is left clutching the Communist Party activist; in preventing him from the same masculine folly which Red commits, she stands for the collective power of men and women over the illusory strength of the individual man.

Sexuality in Anderson's novel is presented as life's primary force. Lesbian overtones dominate female friendships, male homosexuality is hinted at between Red and his economics professor, and sexual adventurism characterizes all of life's stages after adolescence. Marriage is presented as a kind of refuge from the horrors of sexual experimentation common to the experiences of the unattached. *Beyond Desire* reflects an inhumane and chaotic state of sexual affairs in the world common to all social and economic classes. If there is a thematic or ideological plea in Anderson's novel, it is articulated in the following meditation of Ethel's:

> Sometime there might be a good life on earth but the time was a long, long way off. It implied some new kind of understanding between men and women, an understanding grown more general among all men and all women, a sense of the oneness of human beings not realized yet.

Finding peace with one's sexual desires and impulses is the single most compelling force in the lives of Anderson's characters, male and female alike. The force manifests itself in countless ways—from masculine brute sexuality to feminine alienation and hostility, from adventurism to prudery, from obsession to resignation. Anderson does not, however, see the issue of sexual redefinition as a fundamentally feminist one. Dargan's point is potentially radical in implication: she sees personal catharsis as a necessary precept to social change. Anderson remains a romantic: if enough people fall in love, men and women might work this thing out.

Where Rollins is oblivious to the place of heterosocial redefinition in a radical world view, Anderson is nearly consumed by it. Rollins seems to have missed what every other Gastonia novelist saw, in varying degrees, as one of the historical event's more crucial aspects: sexual radicalization. Anderson presents human sexuality in all its complexity and is sympathetic to a feminist perspective. But neither author succeeds in presenting the issue—obviously or obsessively—from the perspective of a woman. For example, the issue of childbearing, the obvious result of chaotic sexual relations and adventurism, barely appears in either male author's novel despite the relatively high degree of sexual interaction. In the novels by women, one brief relation with a man often leaves the female character pregnant. In reading the Gastonia novels as a group, then, the reader gets a clear sense of contrasting, often opposing perspectives. Aside from their importance to the proletarian fiction genre, the Gastonia novels provide a neat case study for what Lesley Dretar Urgo has called a distinctive and autonomous woman's voice in literature.

The four novels by women examined here demand critical attention as distinctly female perspectives on an historical event of importance to labor history. The perspective which emerges from the four novels is at odds with Walter Rideout's general conclusion about proletarian novels and human relations:

> The number of successful marriages is extremely large in this fiction, and the workers' sexuality is almost always considered in a matter-of-fact way as evidence of healthy vigor.

Rideout's rule, no doubt statistically true for proletarian novels as a whole, is not true of the four novels analyzed in this essay. Even in the two novels by men discussed above marriages are not common experiences among workers—although sexuality, as pointed out, figures highly. In the women's novels, however, there are no "successful marriages," if success is understood as something which contributes to human happiness. Marriage is better understood as a compromise of aspirations. The "sexuality" of the characters is almost nonexistent, unless men who "won't let her be" and women who cannot stop having babies are sexy. Marriage is a compromise, childbearing is the price paid for that compromise, and fecundity symbolizes the futility of female ambition.

The four novels by women as a whole demonstrate an insistence upon more consideration from the Left of women's needs than the Left was giving. Women are consistently portrayed as frustrated activists battling the same sexism and sex-role traps in the labor struggle as they do under capitalist patriarchy. Even within the Communist Party, as Mary Heaton Vorse shows in *Strike!*, women were excluded from positions of leadership despite their qualifications, and in some cases, superior understanding of Party doctrine. In particular, the individuality denied women under patriarchal capitalism makes women prime candidates to lead in the conversion to a collectivist society. Generations of submission have made women reactionary collectivists.

Implicit in the plots of all four novels is an identifiable feminist protest. Vorse's Irma should have been a leader in the strike instead of just plain "Fer's girl"; Page's Marge, who promises her grandmother she will never quit, is not even the master of her own body; Lumpkin's women are "vessels of life," forever serving men; and Dargan's Ishma, back on the mountain, feels she has "betrayed humanity" by her racism and her love for Britt. Identifying childbearing as the chief threat to personal freedom, furthermore, is a direct challenge to mainstream ideology which idolizes that female function. In Emma that function is as endless and violent as the "wailing snowstorm" outside; to Ishma it is the symbol of Britt's continuing hold on her.

The treatment of motherhood in the novels is more complex, however, than the simple burden of it. The mothers of the heroines, for instance, do not fare well at all. Ishma's mother is condemnatory, Marge's mother is no more than a shadow, and Emma has little to do with her daughter, Bonnie. (In *Strike!*, there are no mothers among the main figures.) Perhaps the uniform protest against motherhood expressed by the heroines is rooted in their personal conception of the failures of their own mothers. Grandmothers, however, are idolized (Marge's gives her a lifetime of inspiration) when they are present. The complexity of the female novelists' portrayal of motherhood might indicate the contradictory emotions that function produces in women. Seeing motherhood as a threat to her own freedom, yet recognizing its fundamental purpose in getting herself born, the female novelist finds herself confronting what is often considered by men an obvious positive force with a stinging ambiguity and conflicting motivation.

The feminist elements which are present in the four novels studied here appear in a much more subtle fashion—the image of Ishma running about town carrying the fragile Vennie—than do the proletarian themes. This may indicate a willingness to sublimate feminist protest in the name of Leftist solidarity, it may have been a problem of articulation, or it may have been so apparent to the writers as a fact of life that bluntness was inappropriate. On the other hand, a polarized image emerges from the perspectives of the two male authors. Rollins sees nothing at all feminist in Gastonia; Anderson sees sexual relations as the historical event's main legacy. But what might have been an artistic revelation of sorts for Sherwood Anderson was nothing quite so visionary to the four women novelists. In their novels, female subjugation through the realities of childbearing, sexism, dominating males, and a societal structure which assumes male primacy, is a basic function of existence without which the novel's mimetic function would fail. Whereas the speeches, slogans, and proclamations of the Communists were foreign to the given world order and therefore demanded various propagandistic and polemical devices, female subordination to patriarchy was better expressed thematically. Collectivity and massive strikes were new forces in society calling for new language and new literary forms; female subordination and patriarchal power structures are older than capitalism itself. It is their feminist content which makes the Gastonia novels by women truly a form of subversive fiction.

Rollins' novel ignores completely those issues which can easily be ignored by a male. The man's novel, like a man's life, can exist oblivious to or ignorant of any feminist content. Anderson's novel raises feminist issues, but its perspective on chaotic and often horrifying sexual interaction

in America borders on the visionary. Vision, however, is not called for in the women's Gastonia novels; there sexual oppression is understood as being among life's fundamental truths. In creating the mimetic world of their novels, the novelists demonstrate that sexism and female subjugation are normative parts of their universe, in tune with the unnatural order of things in a patriarchal world. If we are to recover the thoughts of intellectual and activist women in the 1930's in order to more fully understand the history of feminist ideology, one place to begin is with their fiction. We may find there, as I have attempted here to demonstrate, that a woman's perspective and life experience produces artistic creations quite distinct from a man's.

Joseph R. Urgo, "Proletarian Literature and Feminism: The Gastonia Novels and Feminist Protest," in The Minnesota Review, *Vol. 24, Spring, 1985, pp. 64-84.*

DRAMA

Richard J. Altenbaugh

[Altenbaugh is an American educator and critic. In the following essay, he traces the evolution of proletarian drama and American labor college theater troupes during the 1920s and 1930s.]

The stock market crash of 1929 and the subsequent Great Depression generated many radical efforts to dramatize the struggles of the working class. Plays began to assume themes of social reform, liberty, rebellion, social injustice, anti-fascism, and anti-war. Radical plays were produced in New York City by Artef (1927–37, 1939, 1941), the Theatre Collective (1933–36), the Theatre Union (1933–37), the Actors Repertory Theatre (1934–37), and, on a national basis, the Federal Theatre (1935–39), a WPA backed experiment. The New Theatre League, formed in 1935, previously known as the League of Workers' Theatres, represented the culmination of this theatrical activity. Across the country, some 300-400 theatres became affiliated with the New Theatre League, a United Front organization consisting of liberals, socialists, and communists.

Several theatre companies, such as the Workers' Laboratory Theatre, Artef, and, to a certain extent, the Theatre Union, relied upon the "agitprop" mode of drama: " . . . portable productions whose actors brought their settings and costumes to union meetings, strike headquarters, street corners, parks, or workers' social affairs. Their repertory, one-act pieces for the most part, consisted almost entirely of political satires in which the capitalist in a silk hat was the invariable villain and the worker in overalls the shining hero." Although somewhat elementary in its approach, agitprop served a didactic purpose by emphasizing a social class theme and appealing to social activism among its proletarian audiences. Malcolm Goldstein explains that "Some of the earliest agitprop skits were realistic but crude, but more were a blend of chanted dialogue and mass-movement in which the actors, performing in unison, symbolized the working-class solidarity necessary for the overthrow of the bosses." Agitprop dispensed with the complexities of human character and, instead, concentrated on easily recognizable symbols in a fashion not unlike the expressionistic theatre out of which it had grown.

The theatre of agitation and propaganda originated in the Soviet Union about 1920 and was later used by workers' movements in Germany. In the United States, this and other forms of proletarian drama stemmed from workers' organizations and the workers themselves: "The cultural leadership of the working class has definitely passed out of the hands of sympathetic intellectuals into those of the revolutionary workers themselves to whom it is a truism that the class war exists in the cultural field as in any other." Drama, an art form, became a means of organizing workers and generating social change.

Among the various workers' organizations, several American labor colleges utilized a dramatic format that appeared to embody distinct agitprop characteristics. During the 1920s and 1930s, radical workers who were dissatisfied with the existing social order and the social institutions that supported it, particularly the public school system and the American Federation of Labor, fashioned the labor college movement. These schools functioned to train labor leaders and activists to organize and to lead workers and their unions in working toward a new social order. The labor colleges offered a full-time, co-educational, residential, and structured education program for worker-students. More importantly, the labor drama, among the many educational activities of the labor colleges, resembled agitprop and served as a vital pedagogical tool.

Brookwood Labor College opened for classes in September of 1921 in Katonah, New York. Work Peoples' College preceded Brookwood by some fourteen years and evolved from a Finnish folk high school in Duluth, Minnesota, to a workers' school that primarily served the Finnish immigrant, working-class community. Commonwealth College, founded in 1923 in Louisiana and moved to Arkansas in 1925, became known as the "Brookwood of the Southwest." When Lucien Koch, a Director at Commonwealth, cogently summarized the school's purposes as "educating leaders for a new society," he also delineated the generally radical aspirations of the labor college movement. Most labor college students came from working-class backgrounds and, although in their twenties, lacked extensive formal schooling. The teachers reflected a broad background and included professors, workers, and poets. With support from socialists, industrial unionists, and liberals, the labor colleges maintained an education program that emphasized conflict and solidarity through a variety of social issues and pedagogical techniques combining classroom interaction with off-campus, militant activities such as participating in strikes and staging labor dramas.

Proletarian drama functioned as an integral part of the educational process at the labor colleges. Brookwood first employed labor drama in an experiment during the fall of

1925 as part of the "increasing interest of the trade union movement in popularizing and dramatizing labor's problems and achievements through such agencies as motion pictures, pageantry, and dramas." Brookwood, at first, lacked the facilities to rehearse and stage plays; students and teachers soon remedied the situation by converting an old barn into a theatre. At Commonwealth, drama began as an informal endeavor which grew from Sunday evening programs devoted to singing, dancing, and plays. Early dramatic efforts did not appear to emphasize "social" themes, but were performed solely for entertainment purposes. According to the *Commonwealth College Fortnightly*, the school's newspaper, "Modern Drama" became a formal part of the curriculum during the 1927-28 school year. The course description noted its purposes and content: " . . . a study of drama from the standpoint of its psychological and social import. The plays used will be selected from Strindberg, Ibsen, Shaw, O'Neill, and other contemporary playwrights." Commonwealth staged its first social drama during the Christmas celebration of 1927 at the school for farm neighbors and their children. The holiday pageantry included a "tableau" that portrayed the trials and tribulations of the masses: "The shifting scenes of the tableau depict modern working class problems in a Biblical setting. A cotton farmer is dispossessed because he cannot pay his taxes; a negro is lynched because of an alleged assault upon a white woman; strikers are starved into submission; workers become machines. As Capital lashes Labor behold! a new star appears in the sky. The Glad Evangel is born to make men free." Commonwealth's plays were often produced "with its stage at one end of the dining space with a few simple flats, a cyclorama and two baby spots." Labor drama at Work Peoples' College, unlike that at Brookwood and Commonwealth, never became a part of the curriculum, but operated as an extracurricular activity for students and teachers.

The labor drama served several purposes. A. J. Muste, Brookwood's first Director, described it as "a means of self expression, making the Labor Movement more vital to the workers themselves; it may interpret the Labor Movement for the public in more sympathetic and appealing terms than abstract reasoning can do; it may be a means of entertainment, particularly in isolated regions where the pool room and blind tiger are the only means of diversion." Commonwealth likewise saw a similar role for drama and by 1932 labor drama, labor art, and labor literature became a major emphasis in the school's curriculum: "The basic idea behind these courses was to get across to potential organizers how they could use drama, art, and literature as an appeal to exploited laborers, to convince them of the hopelessness of their current situation and of the necessity of forming militant labor unions if they hoped to better their lot." In addition to social class consciousness raising, propaganda, and recreation, the workers' play gave worker-students some practical background in play production and selection, acting, coaching, interpretation, lighting, staging, set construction, costume design, and play composition. Writing in 1927, Jesse Slaughter, a Brookwood student argued " . . . that labor drama created by workers and expressing the true working-class spirit, is of tremendous significance and value to Labor, and that it can be easily, effectively, and successfully done by students who have had practical experience in all the various phases of labor dramatics." Therefore, labor drama within the labor college setting functioned as a multi-faceted "educational tool."

Why did the students and teachers at the labor colleges adopt the labor drama? That is, why did they purposefully avoid studying and staging standard drama? Rosa Knutti, an instructor at Work Peoples' College, praised playwrights such as Shaw, Ibsen, Gorky, and O'Neill, but insisted: "The theatre . . . is a means to an end. Classified as art, it concerns itself in providing entertainment; as propaganda, it provides something to think about." For Knutti, most plays utilized what she termed the "bourgeois formula" which tended to romanticize working-class life by portraying a harmonious, albeit at times strained, relationship between labor and capital. This bourgeois drama stressed the view ". . . that if the poor are poor it is the fault of their stubbornness or laziness, or etc., and the rich, though they be rich and masters of workers' destinations, are still good-hearted and are well supplied with the milk of human kindness." In this manner, entertainment acted as "subtle propaganda in the name of art." Knutti, however, saw the need for workers' drama which exposed the drab existence and the harsh realities of working-class life. Proletarian drama at the labor colleges consciously avoided the "bourgeois formula" and, instead, endeavored to supply thought-provoking entertainment framed in class-conflict assumptions: "There is material for drama in the experiences and thoughts and emotions of workingmen and women that other people do not know and that the workers themselves do not really appreciate because they are too close to it." As a result, labor college students and teachers wrote and staged labor dramas that reflected working-class culture.

The themes of labor drama encompassed working-class struggle, unionization, sexism, social class solidarity, racism, and work conditions, among others. The Brookwood Players produced their first plays at the school on December 12-13, 1925. Among the three one-act dramas, David Pinsky's *A Dollar* satirized money and status by depicting a wandering and indigent acting company that finds a dollar bill lying in the middle of a country road. The players worship the dollar: "We must contemplate the dollar with religious reverence . . . A dollar is spread out before us—a real dollar in the midst of our circle, and everything within us draws irresistibly . . . Remember you are before the Ruler, before the Almighty. On your knees before Him and pray. On your knees . . ." Eventually, one of the actors, the "Villain," grabs the dollar and declares himself the ruler. A scuffle (revolution) over possession of the dollar ensues, and they ultimately agree to equally divide the dollar among them. The theme of social class conflict as a means of attaining an equal distribution of wealth is made clear in the following—although somewhat anticlimatic—passage: ". . . let there be blood . . . You are to give the dollar up to all of us. At the first opportunity we'll get change and divide it into equal parts." The other plays included *Peggy*, by Harold Williamson, which portrayed the tragic lives and struggles of poor white southern farmers, and *The People*, by Susan Glaspell, which illustrated the trials and tribulations of an impoverished radical mag-

azine. The magazine, not surprisingly, attempted to raise the social awareness of workers and ultimately to generate the "social revolution." The twelve member cast of *The People* reflected the diverse student body at Brookwood. It consisted of seven nationalities and numerous trades, including needle and textile workers, plumbers, miners, and teachers. The Brookwood Players later performed these dramas at the Labor Temple in New York City.

Labor college students and teachers found that a dearth of suitable plays and prohibitive royalty fees inhibited their dramatic efforts. Accordingly, they began to compose many of their own one-act "social dramas." A Brookwood student, Bonchi Friedman, a Russian immigrant and a member of New York Local 248 of the Amalgamated Clothing Workers, wrote a play entitled *Miners*. Twenty-five Brookwood students presented the play in February of 1926 before the national workers' education conference held annually at Brookwood. This performance was reported in *Labor Age*, the unofficial organ of Brookwood: "There was the real stuff of life in that play— the loyalty of workers to their union; the sacrifice not only of self but what is infinitely harder, of one's family; resentfulness of workers who have no alternative but violence against the schemes of the capitalist boss; mob action that is well intentioned but dangerous unless held steady by clear-sighted leaders—these things were as the author of the play had seen them." Meanwhile, Commonwealth College, too, discovered that it could not afford to pay royalties for published dramas and decided to write and to stage its own plays. For example, *Risen from the Ranks, Or from Office Boy to President*, written by Harold Coy, a Commonwealth teacher, attacked the "Horatio Alger myth" and the "Hoover Depression." At Work Peoples' College, students wrote dramas in the playwriting class and created "labor skits that the school and other labor groups can use. It will not aim at anything more pretentious than the one-act play."

Because of the geographical proximity of Brookwood to New York City, Brookwood's labor dramas tended to treat themes most relevant to urban, industrial workers. *The Tailor Shop*, a one-act musical written, arranged, and choreographed by Brookwood students, clearly illustrates the power and the benefits gained by garment workers through unionization. The play opens in a garment shop with "The Song of the Workers":

> In the sweat shop days, we'd not dare to play
> But we'd slave from dawn to dark
> For the eight-hour day which our union gained
> Makes us ready for a lark,
> Still we get too tired if we work eight hours
> Without pause for rest and play
> But if you watch us here and now
> To join work and play we will show you how.

Individual workers, such as the Cutter, the Needle-Hand, and the Button-Sewer, follow and sing various songs that relate to their work. The Machine-Operator sings the following lyrics praising the union:

> What a trade, what a movement,
> Now I can see how they built it
> And planned all for me.

I never knew what a worker goes through,
There's nothing the union can't do.

Union I swear by you.
You've made my dreams come true.
Since I began first to sew,
You made things better I know.
I didn't join right away,
I waited till I was swayed.
I don't know any way I can ever repay—
Union I swear by you!

The entrance song of the Boss is, not surprisingly, "Get Back To Work." This is followed by his singing of "The Owner of A Union Shop" to music from "My Gallant Crew," from Gilbert and Sullivan's *H. M. S. Pinafore*. In the song, the Boss laments his loss of control over the workers because of the union: "I used to work my girls twelve hours [a day], Till the union made you [them] stop." The play ends with the workers ridiculing their Boss and his "aping" of the bourgeoisie. While unorganized workers in the garment industry who saw this play easily recognized the strength and self-assurance derived from a union, an implicit theme existed as well. Female workers represented a significant portion of the workforce in the garment industry. Similarly, the cast of *The Tailor Shop* consisted of female garment workers who were organized and were consequently treated better. The message for female industrial workers was evident.

While the themes of Brookwood's plays appealed to urban industrial workers, Commonwealth College productions focused on the plight of rural, agricultural workers, particularly in Arkansas. They presented *Can You Hear Their Voices?* in February of 1932 to some 300 local farmers. Written in 1931 by Hallie Flanagan, a Vassar College instructor, and Margaret Ellen Clifford, a teaching assistant, the play consciously followed the agitprop genre. The Experimental Theatre at Vassar College first produced the drama and it was subsequently adopted by Artef and numerous other worker and college groups. A representative from the New Theatre League introduced the play to the Commonwealth group. The drama, based on factual material, unfolds with a group of apolitical, southern tenant farmers facing a drought and imminent starvation. They become politicized after they are refused bank credit and government relief. The farmers finally turn to the Red Cross for help—the farmers refer to it as "charity"—but are refused because of bureaucratic red tape. The play culminates when the angry farmers and their families storm the Red Cross station, attack its local chairman, and take the food. This agitprop drama clearly illustrates the process of revolutionary politicization and the results of farmer solidarity. As Raymond and Charlotte Koch, former students, teachers, and administrators at Commonwealth, recall, the play was a decided hit among the school's "farmer neighbors, who had no difficulty understanding what it said about drought, hunger, and lack of credit."

The solution of farmers' problems through collective action, as expected, delineated an important theme. *Get Goin' George*, written and produced in 1938 by the students and staff at Commonwealth for the Arkansas Farmers' Union, depicted the dilemma of an apolitical farmer, George Thompson. In the play, George faces foreclosure, but because of the efforts of the Farmers' Union George retains his farm by refinancing the mortgage, and at a lower interest rate. The key phrase of the play appears in Scene Three when Mr. Gray, the Farmers' Union organizer, states: "When the farmers learn to organize, their problems will be a lot easier for them." In this case, the farmers are organized and it is this solidarity which saves George's farm. Like *The Tailor Shop*, the benefits of collective action were clear to the farmers who viewed the play.

Commonwealth also used drama to attack racism, a major impediment to unionization in that region. *We Are Not Alone*, a one-act "Commonwealth Labor Play," written by students of the Labor Drama class in 1938, dramatized the case of "Bubbles" Clayton and Jim Caruthers, known as the "Blytheville Boys," who had been sentenced to death. The play takes place in the death cell of Tucker Farm, Arkansas, where Clayton and Caruthers, both black men, await their executions. The theme of racism, and the concomitant racist judicial system, is evident throughout the play. The drama ends with an appeal to unions, churches, and "every mass organization" to send protests to the Governor and the Attorney General of Arkansas, and to send donations to the President of the local office of the Little Rock National Association for the Advancement of Colored People.

In July of 1932, Commonwealth College presented *What Price Coal?* on campus and later staged it for groups of miners. Some four years earlier, Brookwooders had performed the same play to raise donations for striking miners. Written in 1926 by miners from Sub-District No. 5 in Illinois, the play was "dedicated to the twenty-five hundred coal miners . . . needlessly killed in the coal mines of America every year" and illustrated the work hazards faced by coal miners. The plot unfolds in the kitchen of a miner's home in the Illinois coal fields. It is morning and Jack, a coal miner, prepares to leave for the mine. Before he departs he asks Mary, a housekeeper and companion for his mother, for an answer to the previous evening's marriage proposal. The affection between Jack and Mary is apparent and she teasingly makes him wait until he returns from the mine that evening. Job conditions in the mine are revealed through their discussion about his lunch pail:

> JACK. Have you put the lid on tight?
>
> MARY. Sure I put the lid on tight. Why?
>
> JACK. The rats ate most of my dinner yesterday. They got the lid off some way. But rats in a mine have to have food too. I guess they were as hungry as I was.

After Jack leaves, his mother, Ellen, tells Mary about the tragic death of her husband in a mine explosion, and she senses danger for her son. According to Ellen, miners and their families grew hardened to death and injury because it represented an almost daily experience: "We're used to it here. Men are always being killed in coal mines. And there is hardly a day goes by that some of them don't get hurt. And some of the ones that are only hurt would be better off dead. They go about the rest of their lives crippled or blind . . . just a burden to themselves and everybody else." To make matters worse, miners could not escape by abandoning the mining town to find another job because of their indebtedness to the company store. The foreshadowing reaches fruition when the alarm bell sounds at the mine signaling a mine explosion. Jack's dead body is carried in and the final line of the play is: "What a price to pay for coal!"

Work Peoples' College maintained scripts for some 200 plays in Finnish and English and furnished a play rental service. Plays with such titles as *Shades of Passaic* and *Food* are representative of their proletarian themes. Rents and royalties ranged from a few cents to ten dollars and a variety of individuals and workers' clubs rented the plays. Students also staged dramas in nearby towns in order to raise money for the school. By 1935, the school's play inventory was valued at $635.40. Unlike Work Peoples' College, Commonwealth supplied its "labor skits" free of charge.

The Brookwood Players not only performed dramas for other Brookwood students, workers' education teachers, and many New York City workers, but travelled thousands of miles in performing their plays. The Brookwood Players presented a play written by a second-year student, Edith Kowski, entitled *An Open-Shop Summer* at Columbia University for the League for Industrial Democracy on December 28-29, 1927. In 1932, Brookwood students embarked on a nine-day, 800-mile tour with *Mill Shadows*, written by Brookwood instructor Tom Tippett and based on the violent 1929 Marion, North Carolina, textile workers' strike. Some 2,800 people "enthusiastically received" the play in Connecticut, Pennsylvania, Maryland, New Jersey, and Washington, D.C.

The labor drama at Brookwood eventually became incorporated as part of the chautauqua program sponsored by the school. The chautauquas consisted of plays, songs, skits, and other educational entertainment:

> With complete unanimity our worker audiences agreed that a labor movement which moves must have its drama and its marching songs. It must appeal to the heart as well as the head; to the emotions as well as the intellect. All of the sugar-coated movies have not permanently hypnotized the workers so that they cannot recognize and welcome real labor culture. Economics with tears and history with footlights in place of footnotes can be successfully taught by this new method of MASS EDUCATION, and the thousands that would never think of enrolling in formal classes. Our plays hold the mirror of social struggle in the United States . . . up to the workers; they recognized themselves and took new heart for the struggle.

In 1934, twenty-three members of the Brookwood student body formed three different companies and toured fifty-three cities, covered some 4,300 miles, and performed before as many as 14,500 workers. During April and May of 1935, Brookwooders appeared ninety times to a total audience of over 20,000 people. The sponsors included locals of nineteen international unions, thirteen central labor unions, six unemployed organizations, six workers' education groups, seventeen locals of the Socialist Party,

and twelve miscellaneous labor or liberal associations. Yet, Brookwooders sometimes found themselves not always welcome. In a few towns, "local vigilantes" closed the hall just hours before the show was scheduled to begin.

In 1936, Brookwood also assisted the New Theatre League in presenting *Let Freedom Ring,* by Albert Bein, by supplying a bus for transportation. This actually represented a joint effort by the New Theatre League, Brookwood, and the Executive Council of the United Textile Workers of America. The six-week tour presented Bein's play of Carolina hillfolk-turned-mill workers throughout industrial New England. The play was staged thirty-three times before approximately 22,000 workers, many of whom were on strike. As the *New Theatre* reported it in 1936:

> If an awareness of the mutual aid which theatre and labor can give each other is growing among the unions, the same may be said of the theatre. Much good work has already been done by the New Theatre League, the Theatre Union, and the touring companies sent out by Brookwood Labor College, towards building a theatre based on trade union support. The *Let Freedom Ring* tour proved that the possibility of enlisting this support is available wherever labor is organized. When touring companies go out with the endorsement of an International, the various locals cooperate by rallying not only their membership, but the rest of the community as well, to its support.
>
> A strong social theatre can only become a reality when the theatre recognizes the need of cooperation with organized labor and achieves that cooperation, and when labor realizes the powerful ally it has in the theatre and utilizes it effectively.

In contrast to Brookwood, audiences for Commonwealth's plays primarily consisted of farmers. Rural audiences in Arkansas and Oklahoma applauded *Until the Mortgage Is Due* by William Cunningham, a Commonwealth teacher, that satirized the agricultural crisis during the Great Depression. However, because many members of Commonwealth's audiences adhered to Christian fundamentalism, some of the school's theatrical efforts flopped. The successful Broadway play *1931* by Claire and Paul Sifton was one such instance. Commoners first learned of the play from a New Theatre League representative. First produced by the Group Theatre at the Mansfield Theatre in New York City, the play illustrated the experiences of Adam, a proud urban warehouse worker. The drama opens as Adam is fired from his job because of a fight with the foreman. Adam appears confident at first, but encounters numerous problems finding another job. Adam obviously symbolizes the millions of unemployed workers during the depression. As the play progresses, he is forced to postpone his marriage, fruitlessly searches for work, falls victim to corrupt labor agents, loses his apartment, panhandles on the streets, and finally, in desperation, attempts to mug an "elegantly dressed" gentleman. Adam's ebullience at the beginning of the play is gradually eroded until he is reduced to begging for food at a soup kitchen and is faced with the realization that his fianceé has become a prostitute because she lost her job. The play

Brookwood Labor College production of Sitdown, *a play about auto workers by William Titus (on platform).*

ends when Adam regains his pride by becoming the vanguard for a workers' revolution. Yet, as the Kochs remember it, the drama's message was lost on the religiously conservative rural audience when it satirized the subjection of hungry people to the soul saving ritual of a Salvation Army-like minister. To the dismay of the Commonwealth players, this scene did not generate hisses from the audience. Instead, the audience responded with "Amens." Commoners quickly discovered that it became counterproductive to mock any kind of religious expression with Christian fundamentalist audiences.

In conclusion, the historical example of proletarian drama at the labor colleges clearly illustrates how workers used the theatre to aid their struggles. The plays fit the agitprop mode by attempting to arouse the social consciousness of the audience as well as the participants. Agitprop, of course, was made popular at the time by a number of radical theatre groups, and historical evidence points to some contact between the labor colleges and these theatre groups. A representative from the New Theatre League, it may be recalled, introduced *Can You Hear Their Voices?* and *1931* to the Commonwealth Players. At Brookwood, Tom Tippett participated on the executive board of the

Theatre Union and Brookwooders assisted the New Theatre League in its production of *Let Freedom Ring*.

The labor drama represented an important part of the social and educational purposes and programs of the labor colleges. Labor college students were expected to take their theatrical skills back to their unions and communities in order to share their talents with working people. Helen G. Norton of Brookwood, perhaps, best summarized this point:

> [the students] are keeping in mind at Brookwood that labor plays will be most popular and effective not where there are fine theatres and professional actors and expensive scenery, but among local unions and groups of workers where the Woodman's hall or a church will be used; where red calico curtains will be pushed back and forth on baling wire; where coal oil lamps; or at best, acetylene, will light the stage, where costumes will come, not from a theatrical house, but out of old trunks; and where tired workers and sleepy children will have to rehearse at night—which means they must have plays easy to memorize and give. The workers' story thus can be made attractive . . .

In 1932, the *Commonwealth College Fortnightly* recorded that former students were organizing workers' theatres in Chicago and in the East. Harry Lessin had gone from Commonwealth to acting with the Blue Blouses, a workers' theatre in Chicago, and eventually joined the Workers Laboratory Theatre in New York. Proletarian drama also functioned to remind workers of "their relationship to the world of work as a whole." In this sense, labor plays provided entertainment as well as agitation and propaganda instruments. That is, the power of collective action, as evinced in the labor drama, ameliorated the social and economic problems of workers and farmers. The lessons to be learned by industrial and agricultural workers from this educational experience were quite clear.

> Richard J. Altenbaugh, "Proletarian Drama: An Educational Tool of the American Labor College Movement," *in* Theatre Journal, *Vol. 34, No. 2, May, 1982, pp. 197-210.*

JOURNALISM

David Peck

[*In the following essay, the critic examines proletarian journalism, or reportage, of the 1930s.*]

In his talk on "Reportage" at the first American Writers' Congress, in April of 1935, Joseph North defined this "new" journalistic form as "three-dimensional reporting. The writer . . . helps the reader feel the fact", and cited as examples Agnes Smedley's reports on revolutionary China, John Spivak's series of articles on 1934 America, Meridel Le Sueur's "I Was Marching", and other work by John Dos Passos and Albert Halper. When *Proletarian Literature in the United States: An Anthology* appeared six months later, North repeated his definition in the "Preface" to the 50-page "Reportage" section (this kind of journalism, he wrote, "helps the reader *experience* the event recorded") and included pieces by Smedley, Spivak, Le Sueur, and Dos Passos, as well as his own "Taxi Strike", to prove his point. A third of a century later, when North came to edit "an anthology of the rebel thirties" from the *New Masses,* his "Reportage" section included articles by Erskine Caldwell, Jack Conroy, Dorothy Parker, Richard Wright ("Joe Louis Uncovers Dynamite"), and Ernest Hemingway ("Who Murdered the Vets?"), as well as pieces by Spivak ("A Letter to President Roosevelt"), Dos Passos ("The Unemployed Report"), and "Taxi Strike" again. In his "Introduction" to the anthology, Maxwell Geismar wrote that "perhaps no decade since the Thirties has given rise to so much good writing in that genre—and raised the genre itself, at its best, to an art form". As for the examples of reportage in this *New Masses* collection, Geismar argued that

> documentaries are at the core of the volume and are equally of historical importance and permanent literary value. They bring the period back

directly and immediately: the poverty, the suffering, the pain, the social misery of, then as now, the richest and most powerful nation in the world . . .

Possibly the most neglected literary genre of the otherwise overmined 1930s may be its proletarian journalism. We have uncovered other literary movements from the period, including the two forms closest to this reportage (the proletarian novel of the first half of the decade and the documentary journalism of the second), but we still have not talked very much about their precursors: the articles and exposés in the late 20s and early 30s that revealed conditions for the poor and unemployed in early Depression America and that led to the proletarian novels and documentary journalism we remember today. There were, particularly in the first years of the Depression, a great number of these factual reports of socioeconomic conditions in America, by writers who got inside them (and, in some cases, actually emerged from them): articles and books on the jobless, the homeless, and the hungry by those who had, at least in part, experienced those conditions.

There existed of course a tradition for this kind of social journalism, from the 1920s and even earlier. In his American Writers' Congress paper, North cited John Reed and the Muckrakers as direct influences, but he could as easily have noted the 20s labor journalism of Mary Heaton Vorse, John Spivak, and others who wrote from the perspective of the disenfranchised or the voiceless. What is distinctive about the proletarian reportage of the early 1930s is that it is a recognizable form—or at least part of one.

When Mike Gold took over as sole editor of the *New Masses* in June of 1928 (the radical magazine had been edited collectively for its first two years), he began a campaign to get workers to write of their lives:

> Write. Your life in mine, mill, and farm is of deathless significance in the history of the world. Tell us about it in the same language you use in writing a letter. It may be literature—it often is. Write. Persist. Struggle.

What Gold was looking for, of course, was proletarian literature, but what he got, and what the *New Masses* started printing, were confessional pieces like "Inside the Reformatory" and "A 5 and 10 Cent Store Girl" as well as proletarian short stories. At the same time, as economic conditions worsened in the late 1920s for those at the bottom, more and more professional writers like North, Vorse, Dorothy Day, and others began writing articles on strikes, prisons, and unemployment for the *New Masses*. By the early 1930s, there were regular examinations of socioeconomic conditions in America in the magazine, written from the point of view of the classes suffering under those conditions: articles by Gold, Josephine Herbst (on Scottsboro), Ben Field ("The Black Belt"), Meridel Le Sueur ("Women on the Breadlines"), and other writers, professional and not.

But this kind of social reportage was not confined to radical journals like the *New Masses:* more liberal journals like *The Nation* and *The New Republic* also published examples of this form in the early 30s. Sometimes the articles were actual experiences of poverty conditions; at other times they were accounts by writers who had dressed "down" to get the story (Garland O Ethel's "Soup Line in Seattle", for example, in the February 25, 1931, *Nation*). *The Nation* regularly carried reports on Depression America in the early 30s by associate editor Mauritz A. Hallgren, as well as occasional pieces like "I'm Tired of Beans" (by "Workless") or "Hunger—1931", "A Dirt Farmer Wonders", and "One of the 6 Million" (all from 1931). *The New Republic,* similarly, carried articles with titles like "No Help Wanted", "An Arkansas Farmer Speaks", and "I Want a Job" (all from 1931), as well as regular examination of conditions in rural and urban America by editors and contributors like Bruce Bliven ("On the Bowery"), Sherwood Anderson ("Factory Town", also from March 1930), Edmund Wilson, Malcolm Cowley, Dos Passos, and others. Many of these occasional articles on Depression America would be collected into the books we know today as *the* social journalism of the 1930s: Wilson's *The American Jitters* (1932), for example, or Sherwood Anderson's *Puzzled America* (1935). But there were other volumes of proletarian reportage in the 1930s, less well-known today, perhaps, but equally useful in uncovering 30s America: *Harlan Miners Speak* (1932), a "Report on Terrorism in the Kentucky Coal Fields Prepared by Members of the National Committee for the Defense of Political Prisoners", a Committee that included Anderson, Dos Passos, and Theodore Dreiser; Lauren Gilfallen's *I Went to Pit College* (1934), another report on mining conditions in the South, this one by a young college graduate; Mary Heaton Vorse's *Labor's New Millions* (1938); *These Are Our Lives* (1939), "As Told by the People and Written by Members of the Federal Writers' Project of the Works Progress Administration in North Carolina, Tennessee, and Georgia"; and Ruth McKenney's *Industrial Valley* (1939), "a true story of Akron, Ohio" between 1932 and 1936.

We can actually define two levels or stages of this proletarian reportage of the 1930s. First, there were accounts of working-class experiences by those who were there: reports from the Bonus Army or Gastonia printed in the *New Masses,* for example, and written by participants. John Mullen's "Mushrooms in the Foundry" (reprinted in *Proletarian Literature in the United States*) is a brief account of a closed factory by "a steel organizer" and one of the pickets. Robert Carter's "Boys Going Nowhere", in the March 8, 1933, *New Republic,* is a vivid account of young hobos, written by one of them; Victor Castle's "Well, I Quit the Job at the Dam", printed in the August 26, 1931, *Nation,* is written by "a worker at Boulder Dam". Most of these accounts by workers were written in the late 20s and early 30s; by the mid-30s, "worker-correspondents" had mostly given way to professional writers covering the same subjects, even in the *New Masses.*

On the second level are those accounts of proletarian experiences by professional writers, both those with working-class backgrounds and middle-class writers who were inspired by the plight of the poor (or by the nagging of militant editors like Mike Gold) to get closer to actual Depression conditions. Gold himself falls into the first category:

his *Daily Worker* columns like "Night in a Hooverville" and "In a Home Relief Station" have a certain authenticity because they have been written by someone familiar with poverty and hunger himself. But most of the professional proletarian reportage of the 1930s was produced by writers with middle-class backgrounds; the articles of Wilson, Dos Passos, Anderson, Cowley, and others, in *The Nation* or *The New Republic,* certainly fall into this category. Frank G. Moorhead's "Broke at Fifty-Five", in the May 13, 1933, *Nation,* is another example, an account of unemployment by a formerly successful farm journal editor.

The difference between the two levels of proletarian reportage—between actual accounts of Depression conditions or pieces by professional writers—is that the middle-class writer may have to come *down* to the experience to describe it. James Agee's *Let Us Now Praise Famous Men* (1941) is certainly the best-known example of the documentary journalism of the 1930s, and it is a good example of the second level of proletarian reportage as defined here. But, as Tom Wolfe has complained about the book, "It uses no point of view other than his own." Agee gives us the tenant-farmer experience, but it is from his point of view *among* them.

Regardless of level, the definition for proletarian reportage is the same: journalism that attempts to give Depression conditions *from the perspective of those who are suffering them.* Proletarian reportage is 30s social journalism that tries to get inside working-class experience: the conditions of the poor, the unemployed, and the hungry from their point of view. North would undoubtedly broaden that definition (as his selections and discussions of proletarian reportage cited earlier show) to include those writers who are looking at Depression situations, and revolution, internationally: Smedley on China, for instance, or Josephine Herbst on Cuba. But it is easier to limit proletarian reportage to this country. It is less easy to define that national journalistic movement. Certainly not every writer who contributed to proletarian reportage did it consistently: some of Wilson's pieces in *The American Jitters,* for example, are on other subjects, and even some of those on socio-economic subjects are not from the point of view of people suffering them. Hemingway did not write many other pieces like "Who Murdered the Vets? (A First-Hand Report on the Florida Hurricane)". Proletarian reportage is slippery and constantly threatens to slide off into labor or social journalism without a working-class perspective. Finally, it is easiest to say that proletarian reportage is social journalism written, at least in part, from the point of view of the victims of the Depression.

But what is most important here is that this journalism helped to open up the literature of the 1930s. By exposing the underside of American capitalism, and giving voice to its victims, the proletarian reportage of the early 1930s provided subjects and materials for the novelists and journalists who followed. A book like *The Grapes of Wrath* is only possible after the ground has been prepared by journalists (Steinbeck among them) who described the Joads and the other disenfranchised of the Depression for middle-class readers.

What is most interesting about proletarian reportage, from a scholarly point of view, is how literary historians writing today about the 1930s ignore it. In his chapter on "Documentaries, Fiction, and the Depression", in *Radical Visions and American Dreams* (certainly one of the more important recent studies of the radical culture of the 1930s), Richard Pells does not acknowledge any precursors when he starts to talk about the "extraordinary number of artists and critics"—including Wilson, Anderson, Dos Passos, James Rorty, and Theodore Dreiser—who "interrupted their other work to travel around America in search of the thoughts and aspirations of ordinary people . . . " Their aesthetic, Pells tells us, was "rigorous objectivity". Nowhere here is there anything on North, Vorse, Gold, Spivak, Le Sueur, or the dozens of other proletarian journalists who preceded these more famous writers in their travels through the "union halls and assembly lines" of America. Pells concludes this long chapter with a 5-page analysis of *Let Us Now Praise Famous Men*. Only Agee, Pells concludes, "was ever able to fuse the demands of radicalism with the concerns of art into a unified statement of the decade's social, cultural, and moral ideals".

William Stott's *Documentary Expression and Thirties America* is a much more complete and thorough analysis of all documentary forms in the Depression (including film, which Pells ignores). Stott discusses Gold's early proletarian campaign in the *New Masses,* and North's address to the first American Writers' Congress, and he has a whole chapter on "Documentary Reportage: Radical", in which he mentions Wilson, Le Sueur, Vorse, Spivak, Tillie Lerner's "The Strike", and several of the other writers and pieces considered here. The problem is that Stott does not recognize a distinctive proletarian reportage. (For one thing, his numerous journalistic categories—"informant narrative", "participant observer", "worker narrative"— tend to complicate the genre unnecessarily and dispel any sense of radical purpose or unity in the 1930s.) And that problem goes back to Stott's definition of documentary:

> . . . documentary treats the actual unimagined experience of individuals belonging to a group generally of low economic and social standing in the society (lower than the audience for whom the report is made) and treats this experience in such a way as to try to render it vivid, 'human', and—most often—poignant to the audience.

What is missing from Stott's otherwise useful definition is perspective: trying to render this "experience" from the point of view of those who are suffering it.

Stott's limitation—and this is true of a great number of the commentators on the radical 30s—is that he is not terribly sympathetic with this part of the subject of his inquiry. "What is remarkable in the radical reportage of the thirties", Stott concludes this chapter, speaking of Edmund Wilson, "is the *size* of the distortion, the discrepancy between the facts and the lessons that purport to be implicit in them."

> The radical reportage of the thirties was characteristically 'primitive' in its emotionalism, and distorting and reductive in its vision of the world. That it was bespeaks the fanaticism of the

time and, even more, its reckless despair: in making a new order, *nothing* of the old order was worth saving.

Stott closes his study of Depression documentary with a long analysis of "a classic of the 1930s", and the one work that was, in Stott's and others' opinions, successful: Agee's *Let Us Now Praise Famous Men*.

It is interesting to note that a contemporary journalist can be more sympathetic to the proletarian reportage of the 1930s than a literary historian. In casting about for the forerunners of the New Journalism of the 1960s, Tom Wolfe came up with a number of "Not Half-Bad Candidates", including early 30s social journalism:

> The 'reportage' school of the 1930's, which was centered about the magazine *New Masses;* theoreticians such as Joseph North had in mind a new journalism as fullbodied as anything I've been talking about, but most of the work degenerated into propaganda of a not very complex sort; it amuses me that North complained that literary people were calling his boys' new journalism 'a bastard form'.

—which is of course a complaint that Wolfe and his New Journalistic contemporaries repeated in their time. It is also noteworthy that Wolfe, unlike Pells and Stott and other academic critics, finds *Let Us Now Praise Famous Men* "a great disappointment" that suffers from Agee's "extreme personal diffidence".

The only way to combat the ignorance of a Pells or the criticism of a Stott is to look at the proletarian reportage itself. But before examining a few pieces of the genre, it may be beneficial to return to North's two definitions, in his American Writers' Congress address and in his short preface to the "Reportage" section of *Proletarian Literature in the United States: An Anthology.*

Taken together, North's two definitions of "reportage" give us analyses of the genre that are still useful. Like the writers of the New Journalism, North's writer of reportage "not only condenses reality; he must get his reader to see and feel the facts". Such a goal demands "artistry", North argues, for reportage

> requires many of the same characteristics as the novel, the short story. It requires delineation of character, of locale, of atmosphere . . . In brief, reportage is the presentation of a particular fact, a specific event, in a setting that aids the reader to experience the fact, the event.

The contrast North establishes is between the writer of reportage and the "bourgeois" journalist, who sees "the fact, the event" as a "corpse". Writers of reportage give the historical context for every story; they "know there is a past, a present and a future, and they estimate the relation of the event to the factors surrounding it". The best examples of 30s reportage thus contain "both an analysis and an experience, culminating in an implicit course of action".

North sees a double heritage for this form: "The term reportage has come to us from Europe, particularly from the Soviet Union; yet it is a peculiarly American form." When we limit North's discussion to journalists in this country (i.e., eliminate writers like Agnes Smedley on China), his definitions are still valuable. Specifically, the writers of proletarian reportage fuse Marxist analyses with what we would today call a New Journalistic style: they generally describe their subjects from a 30s Marxist point of view (what North called "an analysis and an experience, culminating in an implicit course of action") and they write in an experimental style (North's "artistry"). In short, the writers of proletarian reportage were the radical New Journalists of the 1930s (which is why Wolfe deigns to label them "Not Half-Bad Candidates").

The four pieces of proletarian reportage we will consider here are all from 1934, they are all about strikes and labor conditions, and they all fulfill the definitions given above: they deal with working-class experiences from a working-class perspective, they make a radical analysis, and they experiment with style and structure. They show, finally, that the proletarian reportage of the 1930s, despite what the critics say, constitutes a distinctive and influential literary genre of the 1930s.

John L. Spivak's "A Letter to President Roosevelt" is a very emotional and effective piece of reportage. Spivak is writing the letter for an illiterate 15-year-old girl who works in the cotton fields of California's Imperial Valley. Her family lives in what looks like an outhouse in "a typical migratory workers' camp", where the girl's baby sister, sick with scarlet fever, sleeps on the only bed and the other four members of her family sleep on the floor. The only water is four miles away.

> She doesn't mind picking cotton bolls for thirty-five cents a day and she doesn't mind the filth and dirt and starvation but she is worried about that electric light in the shack.

It costs 25c a week to use the electric light, Spivak writes, and the girl and her family can't afford it.

> She is going to have a baby and suppose it comes at night and there is no light? She is going to have a baby in this little outhouse where her mother and father and brothers live, this little outhouse with the sign SCARLET FEVER over its door. What she wanted to ask you is if you could possibly get in touch with somebody and have them not charge them twenty-five cents for the use of the electric light—especially when somebody's sick or expecting a baby.

But Spivak also manages to tell us, in the midst of all the details of suffering, about conditions in the Imperial Valley for other workers, about the Cannery and Agricultural Workers Union ("the Communist union"), and about how

> the strikes were almost always won. That's because the workers felt a lot like this little girl: no matter what happened it couldn't be worse than it was. If the Communists help them then they would be Communists.

Spivak asks the girl whether she thinks President Roosevelt is helping poor people like herself.

> 'No sir, not yet. Things very bad for us. But he got lots to do and he never hear about cotton pickers. I wanted to write and tell him hurry up

because I going to have a baby and things very bad for us. He do something for poor people if he know how things very bad, eh?'

Spivak assures her that the President "will be glad to hear from you". But the girl cannot write; she dropped out of school at 8 or 9 to begin working in the fields. Spivak answers that he will write the letter for her, and, in a technique common to the reportage of the 30s, goes back over many of the details of her poverty. He concludes:

> That is all, Mr. President. I don't know whether you will ever see this but I just wanted to keep my promise; and if you do see it you'll know why 'red agitators' are making more headway here than anywhere I've been so far in this country.

"A Letter to President Roosevelt" demonstrates dramatically the strengths and limitations of proletarian reportage. There is little between us and the poverty and suffering here. While the events are narrated by Spivak, his naive, ironic tone does not shield us, and we experience painfully the feelings of these victims of American capitalism's failure to care for its own workers. Spivak's account includes both a radical *analysis* of labor conditions in the Imperial Valley and an innovative *style* (a letter detailing the writer's encounter with the Mexican girl, her own language, etc.). Like so much of Spivak's journalism in the 1930s (and, as Stott tells us, Spivak was considered "America's greatest reporter" in the 30s), "A Letter to President Roosevelt" is an effective and poignant confrontation with conditions in Depression America from the point of view of its victims.

Joseph North's "Taxi Strike" is prefaced by a "Hackie's Fable", in which a cab driver has to pay the company for the ghost who has ridden his cab around Central Park. " 'Who's it you gonna keep?' " the cabbie's wife demands at the end of this fable, " 'Me or the company?' "

The piece itself describes the largest strike in industry history: "Forty thousand cabmen abandoned their wheels for the sake of an independent union, and against the strait-jacket of a company union." North captures the "juicy lingo" of New York cabbies: " 'The beauty part of it is, kid, we're making history for the whole woild. The eyes of the woild is on us—the New York hackies.' " North describes the strike and details the confrontations between strikers and police from inside the action, but also manages to give the complex causes for the cabmen's strike action. The piece closes with an analysis of how "race hatred melts in the crucible of class struggle" (as white and Negro hackies vow to work together) and with a young cabbie describing the district Communist convention of an earlier evening.

> The lad with a palm cross on his lapel raises his eyebrows. 'Three hundred bucks!' He shoots a few left hooks in the air. 'If the Communists are wit' us, I'm wit' them. Left hook!' he shouts. The others chorus, 'Left hook . . . left hook . . . '

In *No Men Are Strangers*, North's 1958 autobiography, he retells many of the incidents from "Taxi Strike", and how he wrote them, but he also tells us—what is not in the essay—that "the strike was lost". "Several days after my story appeared", North continues, "a solid, handsome young man with an aureole of blondish hair above a high forehead called on me at the office."

> The name, he said, is Clifford Odets, and with a boyish grin, described himself as 'an indigent actor and an aspiring playwright.' My taxi piece had inspired him, he said, to try to do a play about the strike. Would I tell him more about the hackies?

North spends an evening telling Odets his strike stories and "Some months later in January 1935 I sat enchanted watching Odets' play *Waiting for Lefty* . . . " For North, "Odets had caught a moment of history, their history." But it was also a moment inspired by North's piece of proletarian reportage. Several of the elements in North's article—from the "Hackie's Fable" at the beginning to the "left hook" ("uppercut" in Odets) at the close—find echoes in the more famous proletarian play. Here is a clear example of where the proletarian reportage of the early 1930s led directly to other, more widely viewed literature in the Depression.

Tillie Lerner's "The Strike" describes the days leading up to the 1934 San Francisco general strike. It opens:

> Do not ask me to write of the strike and the terror. I am on a battlefield, and the increasing stench and smoke sting the eyes so it is impossible to turn them back into the past.

Through her militant (and teary) eyes we watch the sequence of events: the strike of longshoremen, which closes the port of San Francisco; a rally of 20000 in solidarity with the strike; and "the massacre" (as Harry Bridges calls it here) of "Bloody Thursday", when police killed two strikers and dozens were injured on both sides. Like North, Lerner identifies with the strikers, but she gets even closer to them:

> I saw the people, I saw the look on their faces. And it is the look that will be there the days of the revolution. I saw the fists clenched till knuckles were white . . .

At times the narration actually slips into the voices of the strikers themselves:

> . . . it's all right Nick, clutching your leg and seeing through the fog of pain it is a police car has picked you up, snarling, let me out, I don't want any bastard bulls around, and flinging yourself into the street, still lying there in the hospital today—

Of all the writers of reportage here, Lerner is the most experimental in style and language, mixing points of view, as she does in the passage above, or fusing headlines (like Dos Passos) into her own narration, as she does here:

> LAW—you hear, Howard Sperry, exserviceman, striking stevedore, shot in the back and abdomen, said to be in dying condition, DEAD, LAW AND ORDER— . . .

In part because of this style, no doubt, "The Strike" has real energy and power. Lerner has captured much of the frantic, bloody sense of what this strike must have been

like. There is not as much analysis of causes here (except for a few complaints by workers about bad conditions), but there is a great deal more description of what it *feels* like to be in a strike. Like Meridel Le Sueur below, Lerner takes us *inside* this experience. She closes the piece:

> The rest, the General Strike, the terror, arrests and jail, the songs in the night, must be written some other time, must be written later . . . But there is much happening now . . .

"I Was Marching" is Meridel Le Sueur's story of her initiation into the militant working class. In her introduction to a recent collection of Le Sueur's writing from five decades, Elaine Hedges places the essay into a 30s context:

> 'I Was Marching' is an example of reportage, that special kind of journalism developed by the Left in the thirties. Described as 'journalism with a perspective', and as 'three-dimensional reporting' intended to make the reader see and feel the event, it eschews the presumed objectivity of traditional journalism. Often it adopts elements of the short story, emphasizing character, carefully selected detail and image, and narrative line.

"I Was Marching" opens with the statement, "I have never been in a strike before", and carries the narrator through the process of joining the strike until, in the last line, "I was marching". The struggle throughout the piece is between the individualistic, middle-class narrator and the mass of anonymous, charged strikers. Slowly, as the narrator gives up her individuality to the larger group, she gains a new vitality and purpose.

At the beginning of the story the narrator stands outside the factory looking into "the huge black interior and live coals of living men . . . "

> The truth is I was afraid. Not of the physical danger at all, but an awful fright of mixing, of losing myself, of being unknown and lost.

Inside the plant, she realizes, "they were acting in a strange, powerful trance of movement *together*". She witnesses something of the violence of the strike and recognizes "In these terrible happenings you cannot be neutral now." She enters "the dark building", but still doesn't identify herself: "I wanted to be anonymous." She holds onto this identity, but also senses the energy, the "current", and slowly the "I" of the narrator becomes the "we" of the strikers. She is given a job in the strikers' kitchen and swings "into the most intense and natural organization I have ever felt". Caught up in the tension of the scene, "I seemed to have no body at all except the body of this excitement."

Another bloody confrontation occurs, two strikers are killed, and the narrator is swept up with the rest into action.

> I have the brightest, most physical feeling with every sense sharpened peculiarly . . . I feel most alive and yet for the first time in my life I do not feel myself as separate.

She joins with thousands of other strikers and sympathizers in a memorial march for the slain.

> I felt my legs straighten. I felt my feet join in that strange shuffle of thousands of bodies moving with direction, of thousands of feet, and my own breath with the gigantic breath. As if an electric charge had passed through me, my hair stood on end. I was marching.

Le Sueur has described the strike and strikers from the inside and, at the same time, she has described her own initiation into the revolutionary working class. The individual has become part of the group, and Le Sueur's language and imagery carry this transformation poetically. (The metaphors of heat and electricity here remind us of Henry Roth's *Call It Sleep* and other proletarian works of the 30s which use similar imagery to portray the *charged* quality of the radical Depression experience.) We know, after reading "I Was Marching", what it would be like to observe a bloody strike; but we also know—what is even more important for middle-class readers—what it would be like to *join* in that strike. "I am putting down exactly how I felt", Le Sueur writes toward the beginning of this article, "because I believe others of my class feel the same as I did." Readers of "I Was Marching" witness the events of the strike at the same time as they experience, with her, the narrator's "conversion" from middle-class to working-class identity.

If there was an immediate value to the proletarian reportage of the 1930s, it was probably this: that middle-class readers could experience working-class life and gain sympathy for those suffering most in the Depression. Proletarian reportage helped Americans learn early what the Depression was like for that "one-third of a nation" hit hardest by all the socioeconomic collapses of the 1930s. It was not only proletarian reportage that provided this function, of course. Proletarian fiction (Roth, Gold's *Jews Without Money*) and proletarian drama (Odets' *Waiting for Lefty*) also helped to alert middle-class America to the hopeless condition of the poor, the hungry, the homeless. But this distinction is finally unimportant for, as Peter Lisca has argued, "The line between social documentation and fiction has never been so hazy . . . " as it was in the 1930s.

> Often what was intended as social documentation and reportage had a literary value achieved only rarely in proletarian fiction—Ruth McKenney's *Industrial Valley* being an example.

It was in fact proletarian reportage that helped to pave the way for the proletarian and social fiction that followed in the 1930s.

The four selections above demonstrate what Joseph North—the first and probably the last theoretican of proletarian reportage in America—has called "the almost infinite flexibility of this form". In a variety of styles, proletarian reportage carried readers into the new and growing world of the working, often non-working, class. It moved between our mostly middle-class lives and the increasingly revolutionary conditions in Depression America. It helped us to discover ourselves. For this if nothing else, we should recognize the work of Joseph North and the other journalists who helped to develop the proletarian reportage of the 1930s.

Postscript: In 1983 *The Nation* instituted "While Someone Else Is Eating", a series of articles "about the human costs of President Reagan's policies", and "about how some people are being made to live in America today. The writers featured are all novelists or poets." But the series has its roots in a journalism about poverty and hunger written in this country 50 years ago.

> *David Peck, "Joseph North and the Proletarian Reportage of the 1930s," in* Zeit schrift F [. . u]r Anglistik und Amerikanistik, *Vol. 33, No. 3, January, 1985, pp. 210-20.*

PROLETARIAN LITERATURE IN THE UNITED STATES

Joseph Freeman

[*Freeman was a Russian-born journalist, editor, poet, author, and critic well known for his support of American proletarian writers in the 1920s and 1930s. A Socialist from the age of seventeen, Freeman was the co-founder of* New Masses *and the* Partisan Review, *and was active in forming American anti-Nazi organizations. In the following excerpt from his introduction to* Proletarian Literature in the United States, *he recounts the development of proletarian literature and offers a defense of proletarian literature as art.*]

Whatever rôle art may have played in epochs preceding ours, whatever may be its function in the classless society of the future, social war today has made it the subject of partisan polemic. The form of polemic varies with the social class for which the critic speaks, as well as with his personal intelligence, integrity, and courage. The Communist says frankly: art, an instrument in the class struggle, must be developed by the proletariat as one of its weapons. The fascist, with equal frankness, says: art must serve the aims of the capitalist state. The liberal, speaking for the middle class which vacillates between monopoly capital and the proletariat, between fascism and communism, poses as the "impartial" arbiter in this, as in all other social disputes. He alone presumes to speak from above the battle, in the "scientific" spirit.

Wrapping himself in linen, donning rubber gloves, and lifting his surgical instruments—all stage props—the Man in White, the "impartial" liberal critic, proceeds to lecture the assembled boys and girls on the anatomy of art in the quiet, disinterested voice of the old trouper playing the rôle of "science." He has barely finished his first sentence, when it becomes clear that his lofty "scientific" spirit drips with the bitter gall of partisan hatred. Long before he approaches the vaguest semblance of an idea, the Man in White assaults personalities and parties. We are reading, it turns out, not a scientific treatise on art but a political pamphlet. To characterize an essay or a book as a political pamphlet is neither to praise nor to condemn it. Such pamphlets have their place in the world. In the case of the liberal critic, however, we have a political pamphlet which pretends to be something else. We have an attack on the theory of art as a political weapon which turns out to be itself a political weapon.

The liberal's quarrel with the Marxists does not spring from the desire to defend a new and original theory. After the ideas are sifted from the abuse, the theories from the polemics, we find nothing more than a series of commonplaces, unhappily wedded to a series of negations. The basic commonplace is that art is something different from action and something different from science. It is hard to understand why anyone should pour out bottles of ink to labor so obvious and elementary a point. No one has ever denied it, least of all the Marxists. We have always recognized that there is a difference between poetry and science, between poetry and action; that life extends beyond statistics, indices, resolutions. To labor that idea with showers of abuse on the heads of the "Marxists-Leninists" is not dispassionate science but polemics, and very dishonest polemics at that.

The problem is: what, in the class society of today, is the relation between art and society, art and science, art and action. It is true that the specific province of art, as distinguished from action or science, is the grasp and transmission of human experience. But is any human experience changeless and universal? Are the humans of the twelfth century the same in their specific experience as the humans of the twentieth? Is life, experience, thought, emotion, the same for the knight of 1300, the young merchant of 1400, the discoverer of 1500, the adventurer of 1600, the scientist of 1700, the factory owner of 1800, the banker of 1900, the worker of 1935? Is there no difference in the "experience" grasped and transmitted by Catholic and Protestant poets, by feudal and bourgeois playwrights, by Broadway and the Theatre Union? Is Heine's social experience the same as Archibald MacLeish's? Is the love experience of Pietro Aretino the same as T. S. Eliot's?

We may say that these are all personal differences: experience is an individual affair and individuals differ from age to age. Yet nothing is more obvious than the social, the *class* basis of fundamental differences. Greeks of the slave-owning class, for all their individual differences, had more in common with each other than any of them has with the bourgeois poets of the Romantic school; the Romantics, for all their individual differences and conflicts, had more in common with each other than with individuals of similar temperament in Soviet letters or American fiction.

Art, then, is not the same as action; it is not identical with science; it is distinct from party program. It has its own special function, the grasp and transmission of experience. The catch lies in the word "experience." The liberal critic, the Man in White, wants us to believe that when you write about the autumn wind blowing a girl's hair or about "thirsting breasts," you are writing about "experience"; but when you write about the October Revolution, or the Five Year Plan, or the lynching of Negroes in the South,

> **A party card does not automatically endow a Communist with artistic genius. But once there is the man with the specific sensibility, the mind, the emotions, the images, the gift for language which make the creative writer, he is not a creature in a vacuum.**
>
> —*Joseph Freeman*

or the San Francisco strike you are not writing about "experience." Hence to say: "bed your desire among the pressing grasses" is *art;* while *Roar China,* Mayakovsky's poems, or the novels of Josephine Herbst and Robert Cantwell are *propaganda.*

No party resolution, no government decree can produce art, or transform an agitator into a poet. A party card does not automatically endow a Communist with artistic genius. Whatever it is that makes an artist, as distinguished from a scientist or a man of action, it is something beyond the power of anyone to produce deliberately. But once the artist is here, once there is the man with the specific sensibility, the mind, the emotions, the images, the gift for language which make the creative writer, he is not a creature in a vacuum.

The poet describes a flower differently from a botanist, a war differently from a general. Ernest Hemingway's description of the retreat at Carporetto is different from the Italian general staff's; Tretiakov's stories of China are not the same as the resolution on that country by a Comintern plenum. The poet deals with experience rather than theory or action. But the social class to which the poet is attached conditions the nature and flavor of his experience. A Chinese poet of the proletariat of necessity conveys to us experiences different from those of a poet attached to Chiang Kai Shek or a bourgeois poet who thinks he is above the battle. Moreover, in an era of bitter class war such as ours, party programs, collective actions, class purposes, when they are enacted in life, themselves become experiences— experiences so great, so far-reaching, so all-inclusive that, *as experiences,* they transcend flirtations and autumn winds and stars and nightingales and getting drunk in Paris cafés. It is a petty mind indeed which cannot conceive how men in the Soviet Union, even poets, may be moved more by the vast transformation of an entire people from darkness to light, from poverty to security, from weakness to strength, from bondage to freedom, than by their own personal sensations as loafers or lovers. He is indeed lost in the morass of philistinism who is blind to the *experience,* the *emotion* aroused by the struggle of the workers in all capitalist countries to emancipate themselves and to create a new world.

Here lies the key to the dispute current in American literary circles. No one says the artist should cease being an artist; no one urges him to ignore experience. The question is: what constitutes experience? Only he who is remote from the revolution, if not directly hostile to it, can look upon the poet whose experiences are those of the proletariat as being nothing more than "an adjunct, a servitor, a pedagogue, and faithful illustrator," while the poet who lives the life of the bourgeois, whose experiences are the self-indulgences of the philistine, "asserts with self-dependent force" the sovereignty of art. Art, however it may differ in its specific nature from science and action, is never wholly divorced from them. It is no more self-dependent and sovereign than science and action are self-dependent and sovereign. To speak of art in those terms is to follow the priests who talk of the church, and the politicians who talk of the state, as being self-dependent and sovereign. In all these cases the illusion of self-dependence and sovereignty are propagated in order to conceal the class-nature of society, to cover the propagandist of the ruling class with the mantle of impartiality.

In the name of art and by the vague term experience, accompanied by pages of abuse against the Communists, the ideologues of the ruling class have added another intellectual sanction for the *status quo.* What they are really saying is that only *their* experience is experience. They are ignorant of or hate proletarian experience; hence for them it is not experience at all and not a fit subject for art. But if art is to be divorced from the "development of knowledge" and the "technique of scientific action," if it is to ignore politics and the class struggle—matters of the utmost importance in the life of the workers—what sort of experience is left to art? Only the experience of personal sensation, emotion, and conduct, the experience of the parasitic classes. Such art is produced today by bourgeois writers. Their experience is class-conditioned, but, as has always been the case with the bourgeoisie, they pretend that their values are the values of humanity.

If you were to take a worker gifted with a creative imagination and ask him to set down his experience honestly, it would be an experience so remote from that of the bourgeois that the Man in White would, as usual, raise the cry of "propaganda." Yet the worker's life revolves precisely around those experiences which are alien to the bourgeois aesthete, who loathes them, who cannot believe they are experiences at all. To the Man in White it seems that only a decree from Moscow could force people to write about factories, strikes, political discussions. He knows that only force would compel *him* to write about such things; he would never do it of his own free will, since the themes of proletarian literature are outside his own life. But the worker writes about the very experiences which the bourgeois labels "propaganda," those experiences which reveal the exploitation upon which the prevailing society is based.

Often the writer who describes the contemporary world from the viewpoint of the proletariat is not himself a worker. War, unemployment, a widespread social-economic crisis drive middle-class writers into the ranks of the proletariat. Their experience becomes contiguous to or identical with that of the working class; they see their former life, and the life of everyone around them with new eyes; their grasp of experience is conditioned by the class to which they have now attached themselves; they write from the viewpoint of the revolutionary proletariat; they create what is called proletarian literature.

The class basis of art is most obvious when a poem, play, or novel deals with a political theme. Readers and critics then react to literature, as they do to life, in an unequivocal manner. There is a general assumption, however, that certain "biologic" experiences transcend class factors. Love, anger, hatred, fear, the desire to please, to pose, to mystify, even vanity and self-love, may be universal motives; but the form they take, and above all the factors which arouse them, are conditioned, even determined, by class culture. Consider Proust's superb study of a dying aristocracy and a bourgeoisie in full bloom; note the things which rouse pride, envy, shame in a Charlus or a Madame Verdurin. Can anyone in his senses say that these things— an invitation to a party at a duke's home, a long historical family tree—would stir a worker to the boastful eloquence of a Guermantes or a Verdurin? Charlus might be angry at Charlie Morel for deceiving him with a midinette; could the Baron conceive what it is to be angry with a foreman for being fired?

Art at its best does not deal with abstract anger. When it does it becomes abstract and didactic. The best art deals with specific experience which arouses specific emotion in specific people at a specific moment in a specific locale, in such a way that other people who have had similar experiences in other places and times recognize it as their own. Jack Conroy, to whom a Proustian salon with its snobbish pride, envy, and shame is a closed world, can describe the pride, envy, and shame of a factory. We may recognize analogies between the *feelings* of the salon and those of the factory, but the objects and events which arouse them are different. And since no feeling can exist without an object or event, art must of necessity deal with specific experience, even if only obliquely, by evasion and flight. The liberal critic who concludes that all literature *except proletarian literature* is equally sincere and artistic, that every poet *except the proletarian poet* is animated by "experience," "life," "human values," has abandoned the search before it has really begun. The creative writer's motives, however "human" they may be, however analogous to the motives of the savage, are modified by his social status, his class, or the class to which he is emotionally and intellectually attached, from whose viewpoint he sees the world around him.

Is there any writer, however remote his theme or language may seem at first glance from contemporary reality, however "sincere" and "artistic" his creations may be, whose work is not in some way conditioned by the political state in which he lives, by the knowledge of his time, by the attitudes of his class, by the revolution which he loves, hates, or seeks to ignore? What is the *real* antagonism involved in the fake and academic antagonism between "experience" on the one hand and the state, education, science, revolution on the other? This question is all the more significant since the best literary minds of all times have agreed on some kind of social sanction for art, from Plato and Aristotle to Wordsworth and Shelley, to Voronsky and I. A. Richards. Recent attempts to destroy the "Marxo-Leninist aesthetics" fall into a morass of idealistic gibberish. The term "experience" becomes an abstract, metaphysical concept, like "life" or the "Idea" or the "Absolute." But even the most abstract metaphysical concept, like the most fantastic dream, conceals a reality. . . .

Art varies with experience; its so-called sanctions vary with experience. The experience of the mass of humanity today is such that social and political themes are more interesting, more significant, more "normal" than the personal themes of other eras. Social themes today correspond to the general experience of men, acutely conscious of the violent and basic transformations through which they are living, which they are helping to bring about. It does not require much imagination to see why workers and intellectuals sympathetic to the working class—and themselves victims of the general social-economic crisis—should be more interested in unemployment, strikes, the fight against war and fascism, revolution and counter-revolution than in nightingales, the stream of the middle-class unconscious, or love in Greenwich Village.

At the moment when the creative writer sits at his desk and composes his verses or his novel or his play, he may have the illusion that he is writing his work for its own sake. But without his past life, without his class education, prejudices, and experiences, that particular book would be impossible. Memory, the Greeks said, is the mother of the muses; and memory feeds not on the general, abstract idea of absolute disembodied experience, but on our action, education, and knowledge in our specific social milieu. As the poet's experience changes, his poetry changes. The revolutionary Wordsworth, Coleridge, and Southey become reactionary with age and advancement by the ruling powers; the Goethe of *Goetz* becomes the Goethe of Weimar; the T. S. Eliot of *The Hippopotamus* becomes the T. S. Eliot of *Ash Wednesday;* the Lewis of *Babbitt* becomes the Lewis of *Work of Art;* the O'Neill of *The Hairy Ape* becomes the O'Neill of *Days Without End.*

The free exercise of the personality in human relations and in art is not in itself a bad thing. The social revolution aims to make these goods, like the more material goods upon which they are dependent, accessible to all rather than to a few. But as long as the mass of mankind consists of exploited workers, peasants, and "whitecollar slaves," the art that springs from "love and pride" is bound to be a limited art and in times like ours a false art. Such an art can have little real meaning for those who fight for bread. It is not from the Kremlin that the worker learns to be more interested in strikes than in "love and pride," but from life itself.

When socially-owned machines will be the slaves of men instead of men being the slaves of privately-owned machines, we may begin to think seriously about a "pure" art. Until that time, art cannot help being, consciously or unconsciously, class art. The cloak of self-dependence and sovereignty no more deprives art of its class character than the cloak of self-dependence and sovereignty deprives the state of its class character, or the image of the all-knowing omni-present god deprives the church of its class character. . . .

Like all new art, revolutionary art is bound to start crudely, as did the art of other classes when they were new. To begin with there are bound to be revolutionary novels as sentimental as the *New Heloise;* the artist's energies are too absorbed in the search for intellectual and emotional clarity for him to achieve immediate perfection of form. As the proletariat grows stronger, as it is educated by its struggle for power, its art and literature will grow stronger and better. In Russia we have in seventeen brief years seen the development of proletarian literature from the early agitational verses to *And Quiet Flows the Don;* in America from the sentimental socialist novels of Upton Sinclair to the mature works of the novelists represented in this volume. The vast, creative experiences of the revolutionary workers and their intellectual allies must of necessity produce a new art, an art that will take over the best in the old culture and add to it new insights, new methods, new forms appropriate for the experience of our epoch.

Every writer creates not only out of his feelings, but out of his knowledge and his concepts and his will. However crude or unformulated or prejudiced his philosophy may be, it *is* a philosophy and it colors his works. The revolutionary movement in America—as in other countries—is developing a generation which sees the world through the illuminating concepts of revolutionary science. The feelings of the proletarian writer are molded by his experience and by the science which explains that experience, just as the bourgeois writer's feelings are molded by his experiences and the class theories which rationalize them. Out of the experiences and the science of the proletariat the revolutionary poets, playwrights, and novelists are developing an art which reveals more forces in the world than the love of the lecher and the pride of the Narcissist. For the first time in centuries we shall get an art that is truly epic, for it will deal with the tremendous experiences of a class whose world-wide struggle transforms the whole of human society.

American writers of the present generation have passed through three general stages in their attempts to relate art to the contemporary environment. Employing the term *poetry* in the German sense of *Dichtung,* creative writing in any form, we may roughly designate the three stages as follows: Poetry and Time, Poetry and Class, Poetry and Party.

From the poetic renaissance of 1912 until the economic crisis of 1929, literary discussions outside of revolutionary circles centered on the problem of Time and Eternity. The movement associated with Harriet Monroe, Carl Sandburg, Ezra Pound, Sinclair Lewis, Sherwood Anderson, Gertrude Stein, Ernest Hemingway was one which repudiated the "eternal values" of traditional poetry and emphasized immediate American experience. The movement had its prophet in Walt Whitman, who broke with the "eternal values" of feudal literature and proclaimed the here and now. Poetry abandoned the pose of moving freely in space and time; it focused its attention on New York, Chicago, San Francisco, Iowa, Alabama in the twentieth century.

The economic crisis shattered the common illusion that American society was classless. Literary frustration, unemployment, poverty, hunger threw many writers into the camp of the proletariat. Once they were compelled to face the basic facts of class society, such writers of necessity faced the problem of poetry and class. It was impossible to share the experiences of the unemployed worker and continue to create the poetry of the secure bourgeois. Poetry, however, tends to lag behind reality. Suffering opens the poet's eyes but tradition ties his tongue. As a member of society he was forced to face the meaning of the class struggle; as a member of the ancient and honorable caste of scribes, he continued to be burdened with antiquated shibboleths about art and society, art and propaganda, art and class.

In the past five years many writers have fought their way to a clearer conception of their rôle in the contemporary world. At first they split themselves into apparently irreconcilable halves. As *men,* they supported the working class in its struggle for a classless society; as *poets,* they retained the umbilical cord which bound them to bourgeois culture. The deepening of the economic crisis compelled many writers to abandon this dichotomy. The dualism paralyzed them both as men and as poets. Either the man had to follow the poet back to the camp of the bourgeoisie, or the poet had to follow the man forward into the camp of the proletariat. Those who chose the latter course accepted the fact that art has a class basis; they realized that in a revolutionary period like ours poetry is inseparable from politics. The choice was influenced chiefly by the violence of the class struggle in America today; it was also influenced by echoes of that struggle in the realm of letters. On the one hand, there were writers trained in the revolutionary movement with definite ideas on the question of poetry and class, who reasoned with the hesitant and the confused; on the other, it became more and more evident that the writers who proclaimed the "independence" of poetry from all social factors were themselves passionate and sometimes unscrupulous political partisans. The poet poised uncertainly between the two great political camps of our epoch now saw that it was no longer an abstract question of art and class, but the specific challenge: which class?

The solution of this problem raised new ones. The working class is itself divided, and the poet feels the cleavage acutely. He now faces the question of poetry and party. There are those who say: I am, both as man and poet, on the side of the proletariat, but I cannot get mixed up with the party of the proletariat, the Communist Party. The poet cannot be above class, but he must be above party. There are others who say with Edwin Seaver: "The literary honeymoon is over, and I believe the time is fast approaching when we will no longer classify authors as proletarian writers and fellow-travellers, but as Party writers and non-Party writers." . . .

In the past five years [1930-1935] American proletarian literature has made striking progress. The arguments against it are dying down in the face of actual creative achievement. Life itself has settled the dispute for the most progressive minds of America. The collapse of the prevailing culture, the pressure of the economic crisis, the ruthless oppression of monopoly capital, the heroic struggle of the workers everywhere for the abolition of man's exploitation of man—this whole vast transformation of the world through the inexorable conflict of social classes has produced a new art in this country which has won the respect even of its enemies. Abstract debates as to whether or not the revolutionary movement of the proletariat could inspire a genuine art have given way to applause for the type of drama, fiction, poetry, and reportage included in [*Proletarian Literature in the United States*].

Literature inspired by the revolutionary working class is, broadly speaking, no new thing in America. It would be possible to issue an anthology taking us back to the early works of Jack London and Upton Sinclair, to John Reed, Arturo Giovannitti, and Floyd Dell. The present generation of revolutionary writers is, however, by force of circumstances, even more acutely aware of the class struggle. It is the offspring of the World War, the October Revolution, the Five Year Plan, the social-economic crisis of capitalism everywhere, the growing world-wide movement of the workers for a classless communist society. These factors have given our generation its own specific features; it is a generation sobered and strengthened by the intense conflict between two civilizations, a conflict in which all are compelled to take sides.

Moreover, the literary movement represented by the writers in this volume has already had a profound influence on American letters. The theatre, the novel, poetry, and criticism, have felt the impact of these invigorating ideas; even those writers who do not agree with us have abandoned the ivory tower and begun to grapple with basic American reality, with the social scene.

Revolutionary literature is no longer a sect but a leaven in American literature as a whole, as was evidenced by the American Writers' Congress last spring. There, for the first time in the history of our country, leading writers met to discuss specific craft problems, general literary questions, and means of safeguarding culture from the menace of fascism and war. A literary congress was possible in this country only when in the writer's mind the dichotomy between poetry and politics had vanished, and art and life were fused. Similarly, the publishing houses, theatres, and magazines, themselves not interested in revolutionary ideas, are turning more and more to the left-wing where writers find the basic ideas which give solidity and direction to their work.

This is a recent phenomenon in American culture, arising out of the historic conditions under which we live.

> *Joseph Freeman, in an introduction to* Proletarian Literature in the United States: An Anthology, *edited by Granville Hicks and others, International Publishers, 1935, pp. 9-28.*

James Thurber

[Thurber was a celebrated American critic and humorist best known for his essays, stories, and cartoons published in the New Yorker *magazine during the 1930s and 1940s. In the following review of* Proletarian Literature in the United States, *he focuses his comments on the an-*

thology's fiction selections, suggesting that most are generally unconvincing and without humor, depth, or authenticity.]

The old bitter challenges to the bourgeois as critic, writer and human being (in answer to the old bitter challenges of the bourgeois to the proletarian as critic, writer and human being) ring out right at the start in Joseph Freeman's introduction to *Proletarian Literature in the United States.* Nothing, I am afraid, will ever change this. We shall all meet at the barricades shouting, or writing, invective at the top of our voices. Interspersed, of course, with sound arguments (to which the other side will not listen). The bourgeois writer and critic and the proletarian writer and critic do not seem to be able to meet, sanely, on a forum. Their meeting place is the battlefield. They are cat and dog, Smith and Roosevelt. This cannot, I suppose, be changed and it is a rather melancholy reflection. Out of it are bound to come distortion, exaggeration and, what is probably worse, triviality. But it presents a colorful, if meaningless, free-for-all, which members of both armies, being human beings born of war, are bound to find rather more pleasurable than deplorable.

Mr. Freeman sets himself a large and important task in his introduction and, in great part, he discharges it well, the great part being an explanation of, and argument for, the values of revolutionary art. But here and there the old urge springs up, the old bitter desire to take irrelevant cracks at bourgeois literature (without specific instances) and at the more intimate emotions of the bourgeoisie, all the more intimate emotions of all the bourgeoisie. He hates to use the word "love" in relation to them. Thus he speaks of "lechery" and of "flirtations"; when he does use the word "lovers" he joins it up with "loafers." This petty bitterness—it seems almost a neurosis—disfigures his arguments. He writes:

> Every writer creates not only out of his feelings, but out of his knowledge and his concepts and his will . . . . The feelings of the proletarian writer are molded by his experience and by the science which explains that experience, just as the bourgeois writer's feelings are molded by his experiences and the class theories which rationalize them. Out of the experiences and the science of the proletariat the revolutionary poets, playwrights and novelists are developing an art which reveals more forces in the world than the love of the lecher and the pride of the Narcissist.

Well, there you are: the old slipping out of a sonorous and imposing argument into what is nothing more than a hot-tempered jibe, a silly sweeping insinuation. It is odd how that kind of thing has somehow or other become one of the major points in the literary battle. Studies of the effects of class backgrounds and social concepts upon the emotions belong in such works as *Middletown,* or in articles by themselves, but they should scarcely be flung helter-skelter into an analysis of the kind Mr. Freeman sets out to write, particularly if they degenerate into what has the thin ring of an absurd personal insult. So much of the critical writing of both proletarians and bourgeoisie sounds as if the writer were striking back at some individual who has been striking at him. I am afraid that is too often the case.

Schoolgirls; boys behind the barn. And literature can go die, on the barricades, or behind the barn.

But this is not getting into the book, which is divided into Fiction, Poetry, Reportage (that's what they call it, don't look at me), Drama and Literary Criticism. It contains selections from the work of proletarian writers in the past five or six years. I have read it with great interest and I believe anybody with any sense of what is going on, would also. I was mainly interested in the fiction; first, because it takes up more than a third of the volume; second, because, of the five divisions, I care most for fiction.

The fiction here I found uneven: sincere generally, sometimes groping, often hysterical or overwrought, now and then distinctly moving. The only thing in this section that I think can last is John Dos Passos' "The Body of an American" from *1919.* Many of the other authors have the fault of whipping themselves up to a lather, or whipping their characters up to a lather, whereas Dos Passos whips his reader up to a lather. Somewhere in this book there should be a critical piece on his method. It might well have been put in, under Literary Criticism, in place of Mr. Gold's famous attack on Thornton Wilder, which seems as dated as the Dempsey-Carpenter fight, or in place of Phillips' and Rahv's "Recent Problems of Revolutionary Literature," which loses its points in a mass of heavy, difficult and pedantic writing. For what some of these proletarian writers need to learn is simply how to write, not only with intensity, but with conviction, not only with a feeling for the worker but a feeling for literary effects. Even the Erskine Caldwell of "Daughter" (by which flabby story he is unfortunately represented here) might learn from Dos Passos. Compare (and you'll have to read both pieces to see the really important difference) Caldwell's refrain: "Daughter woke up hungry again . . . I just couldn't stand it" with Dos Passos': "Say buddy can't you tell me how I can get back to my outfit?" The first flops, the second gets you.

Many of the stories are simply not convincing. I have read several two or three times to see if I could discover why. I think I found a few reasons. You don't always believe that these authors *were there,* ever had been there; that they ever saw and heard these people they write about. They give you the feeling that they are writing what they want these people to have said. This seems to me an important point. It is not the subject matter, but the method of presentation, I believe, which has raised the bourgeois cry of "propaganda." Proletarian literature must be written by men and women with a keen ear and eye for gestures and for words, for mannerisms and for idioms, or it fails. Jack Conroy catches perfectly the words of the Negro in his "A Coal Miner's Widow" (particularly in the fine paragraph beginning " 'Scuse me!"); but I don't feel reality—I vaguely feel some literary influence—in most of Ben Field's "Cow." And he should be forever ashamed of having written this sentence: "He said something about her being without either and without clothes, but for the sake of somebody who liked him, as he had been unable to get her off, he had had all added." But then read his "The Cock's Funeral" in the first issue of *Partisan Review* and *Anvil;* it is fine, and it has what nothing in this anthology has: humor. Some of the richest humor in the world is the humor of the American proletariat.

I think Albert Halper fails to make his scab taxi-driver come to life. I did not believe the driver and I did not believe his fares; I believed Mr. Halper's sincerity; and that is not enough. More care and hard work, in watching and listening and writing, is what was needed here. The driver is not nearly so good as Joseph North's driver in his reporter piece called "Taxi Strike," and Mr. North's study is far from excellent. I believe both Halper and North might profit by an examination into the way Robert Coates or St. Clair McKelway handles such pieces. I can tell you that their observation and their writing is hard, painstaking, and long. Nobody, however greatly aroused, can successfully bat off anything.

Now I *did* believe Albert Maltz's "Man on a Road" (minor note: I am told that no user of "you-all" ever addresses a solitary person as "you-all"). This story is written with sympathy and understanding but also with detachment (and oh, my friends, and oh, my foes, in detachment there is strength, not weakness). Mr. Maltz leaves the clear plight of his victim undefiled by exaggeration, anger and what I can only call the "editorial comment" which seeps into some of the other pieces. You remember the man on the road after you have forgotten most of the figures in the book. Mr. Maltz knows how to make his reader angry without demanding that he be angry. And if this is not the procedure of class, it will forever remain the dictate of art.

I thought that the dialogue in Grace Lumpkin's "John Stevens" had an artificial sound—one gets to thinking more about the writer than about her people, more about her faults than about what is troubling her characters. I can understand why the Communist literati bewail the loss to the cause of Ring Lardner—as they should also bewail the straying of John O'Hara. In this kind of story an ear like theirs is worth more than rubies. To go on: there is too obvious strain and effort in Tillie Lerner; she grabs tremendously at the reader and at life and fails to fetch the reader and fails to capture life. William Rollins Jr. has a deplorable affection for typographical pyrotechnics: caps, italics, dashes. It makes his story almost impossible to read. I was reminded, in trying to read it, of what an old English professor of mine, the late Joseph Russell Taylor, used to say: you can't get passion into a story with exclamation points. But Mr. Rollins deserves credit for one thing, at least: he is the only writer in this book who uses "God damn" in place of "goddam." Josephine Herbst, so often authentic, writes: "A newsboy sang out, 'Big Strike at Cumley's, night crew walk out, big strike threatened, mayor urges arbitration.'" That is what she wanted to hear a newsboy sing out but it is not what any newsboy in this country ever sang out. I grant the importance of the scenes on which all these stories are based, but they cannot have reality, they cannot be literature, if they are slovenly done—merely because there is a rush for the barricades and proletarian writers are in a hurry. Art does not rush to the barricades. Nobody wants to believe that these authors sat in warm surroundings hurriedly writing of things

they had never seen, or had merely glimpsed, yet that is often the impression they give.

At the end of the fiction section is the worst example of failure in method and effect, Philip Stevenson's "Death of a Century." What might have been sharp satire is a badly done, overwrought and merely gross burlesque. Even burlesque must keep one foot on verisimilitude. It grows better out of healthy ridicule than wild-eyed hate. In the poetry and drama departments there are fine things (*Waiting for Lefty* among them). The reportage section is, in some instances, excellent and it should have been widely expanded, preferably at the expense of the literary criticism, almost all of which could have been left out. There is, as I have said, not a note of humor in the anthology, not even in Robert Forsythe's piece on the Yale Bowl.

> *James Thurber, "Voices of Revolution," in* The Critic as Artist: Essays on Books 1920-1970, *edited by Gilbert A. Harrison, Liveright, 1972, pp. 305-10.*

Bernard De Voto

[*De Voto, a literary critic and historian, was editor of the* Saturday Review of Literature *and a longtime contributor to* Harper's Magazine. *In the following review of* Proletarian Literature in the United States, *he defines the functions of proletarian literature and offers an overview of* Proletarian Literature in the United States.]

Some of the inclusions in [*Proletarian Literature in the United States*], the first offering of the Book Union, are surprising to a middle-class reader: if they are proletarian literature then a good many American writers have been speaking prose without knowing it, and an excellent proletarian anthology could be assembled from people who would be alarmed if they found themselves classified as anything but boorjoy. Some of the omissions are even more surprising and make one suspect that some of Mr. Freeman's six editors have applied the principle he quotes from Edwin Seaver—have divided authors into Party writers and non-Party writers and let it go at that. If you are a Trotskyite, it appears, you may write about the exploited as much as you please but you will not produce proletarian literature. Which may be sound dogma but is confusing.

Some confusion is implicit in any attempt to make an anthology of class literature, but it is increased here by unsatisfactory definition. Mr. Freeman's otherwise excellent introduction fumbles pretty badly when he undertakes to tell us just what proletarian literature is. Messrs. Phillips and Rahv are more illuminating—their "Recent Problems of Revolutionary Literature" is one of the best things in the book—but they too ignore a fundamental principle.

Class literature, the literature of any class whatever, quite apart from its esthetic function which may in part at least affect all classes, must serve at least one of two functions. First and most important, there is the function of heightening and unifying the sentiments of the class which it represents. It may confirm or increase their group-consciousness, step up their solidarity, make stronger their sense of power and injury and communion, and create, propagate and enliven those vital myths, beliefs, ideals, aims, dogmas, slogans, personifications, purposes and sanctions which are at once the bonds that hold the class together and the energy that makes action possible. Second, there is the interclass function. Literature may be an agency of attack on other classes or of conversion among them. It may assist disintegration, weakening the other classes by making them pity or fear the class it represents, giving them a sense of shame or guilt or futility, hammering at their doubts with ridicule or horror or terror. Or it may proselytize among them, converting the essentially religious symbols of its own myths into symbols acceptable among the religions it invades, and carrying the position by outflanking it with visions of the greater glory to come—or the equivalent in the eschatology of the period.

These functions are usually quite distinct. Only rarely and only in great literature will they coalesce. A work of genius may well fuse them, achieving symbols that are both incandescent for its own class and immediately authoritative for other classes. But the usual disparity between them is especially marked in proletarian literature. For the proletariat is composed of the least educated, least sophisticated, least intellectually complex elements of society. The fact may be distasteful to champions of the proletariat, but it must be taken into account by writers and critics, whatever their class. Literature, to be "live" for most of the proletariat, must employ simple, crude, naïve symbols, must work primarily with caricature or sentimentality or invective or the pink spot or the offstage violin, must use the simplified technique of the pulp story and the sex movie and the cheap melodrama if it is to be understood and effective in its most important function. No sophisticated art of the proletariat is possible till the proletariat becomes sophisticated, yet the more faithfully and effectively literature serves this function, the less effective it must be in the other one. That is why literature that can really inspire the proletariat will, except by accident, continue to be written by actual proletarians for a long while yet. That is why intellectuals who join the movement from outside will continue to be effective writers principally as they are evangelists or propagandists among the heretics.

Such considerations must be kept in mind while reading the present collection. It contains, for instance, a number of exhibits which demonstrate that some proletarian authors can write as badly as any on earth—that they can be clumsy, derivative, imitative, sprawling, uncorseted, priggish and damned dull. But, considering the purposes of the anthology, that judgment is in part irrelevant, since the esthetic shortcomings of such writing may facilitate its class function. Thus Tillie Lerner's "The Iron Throat," which is crude and awkward, and Grace Lumpkin's "John Stevens," which is as mawkish as any temperance apologue in a Methodist weekly, may conceivably serve the primary purpose of class literature far better than, say, the subtleties of John Dos Passos which only sophisticates can appreciate.

By the more usual criteria, the fiction selections are the worst in the volume, drama esthetically the best, and literary criticism the most interesting. The fiction is badly chosen. Any bourgeois critic could have made a better showing for proletarian literature from novels of the last five years, frequently from the same writers represented here. Much of it is either plain bad or pretentiously bad. A good deal of it vindicates bourgeois Hollywood by painting up its goblins of the exploiting class in shapes and colors accommodated to the mental age of eight. On top of this, a surprising amount of it is tricked out with the arty spellings and punctuation that Dos Passos took over from Joyce, and one wonders why such an accessory of decadent capitalist art is essential to the literature of the workers. Ben Field's "Cow" would be first-rate stuff if the author were a Trotskyite or a millionaire, and no pitch of Party orthodoxy could make Philip Stevenson's "Death of a Century" anything but lousy.

Poetry goes better but is uneven. Eliot—who is probably to be classified as Fascist—is imitated in it almost as often as Dos Passos is in the fiction; and, whatever their ardor, such people as H. H. Lewis, Norman MacLeod and Charles Henry Newman are bad poets. Kenneth Fearing and Horace Gregory, on the other hand, are very good ones. They are too mannered and elliptical to be much read by the proletariat and will be acclaimed chiefly in infidel parts. Isidor Schneider and James Neugass work far more directly with the emotions and symbols of the class for which they speak: they are within the myth-making function of proletarian literature. But probably the truest class poetry of all is that which, rather ambiguously, is called Folksongs. More of it might well have been included, and surely there should have been selections from the Little Red Songbook.

Proletarian literature in America has so far had its finest artistic achievement in the drama. *Black Pit, Waiting for Lefty, Stevedore,* and *They Shall Not Die,* are represented here. They are accompanied by Alfred Kreymborg's *America, America,* which does not live up to them. The section called "Reportage" (Mr. Freeman assures his audience that the term has Moscow's *nihil obstat*) contains some excellent writing but one wonders why it was included. It must be intended solely as an exhibit, for reportage fully as sympathetic to the workers appears regularly in the capitalist press. Meridel LeSueur's "I Was Marching" is easily the best of it.

The essays grouped under "Literary Criticism" can mean nothing to the general proletariat, but they are more interesting to an inquiring infidel than anything else in the book. Here is where the theology of proletarian literature is formulated, its canon determined and the tests to be applied to it for orthodoxy set forth—with holy water and exorcisms to reveal the presence of Fascism. It varies, of course, in intelligence and maturity, and includes one bit of collegiate smarty-pants that tends to discredit the serious work it appears with. But the sum is valuable and arresting: here, so far as literature is an offensive weapon, is the actual front of class aggression. Here is where the myths, dogmas and philosophies of history are being selected, validated and implemented. This dialectical department is, and is likely to remain for a long time, the most active field of proletarian literature and, in its secondary function at least, the most important.

The collection has the defects of a first attempt, and the solid virtue of putting into one book a number of representative selections. It has one serious blemish: the biographical identification of authors is much too brief. If, as we are told, writing is to be classified as Party and non-Party literature—Christian and pagan, Mormon and Gentile, Eddyite and M.A.M.—then we boorjoys want to know whether a writer presented to us as proletarian has taken out his papers. Does he or doesn't he belong to the Party? So far as we are concerned the question of whole-hog honesty is a typical middle-class sentimentality. But conceivably the proletariat might feel the same curiosity in a more realistic frame of mind.

> *Bernard DeVoto, "Proletarian Literature in the United States, by Joseph Freeman," in his* Forays and Rebuttals, *Little, Brown, and Company, 1936, pp. 334-39.*

Kenneth Burke

[*Burke is an American educator and critic known for his unorthodox approach to literary criticism in which he blends perspectives from anthropology, psychology, and Marxist ideology. In the following excerpt, he offers an in-depth examination of* Proletarian Literature in the United States, *characterizing it as reflective of proletarian life in America and a significant contribution to American culture.*]

Were every material want to be satisfied, people could live as moral beings (without pride) only by developing *subtler* concepts of necessity. In a civilization of mechanical slaves, for instance, they might revert to Grecian concepts of effort. They might focus their attention upon the ultimate task, the development of the "perfect citizen" (shaped for the playing of his rôle as member of a collectivity). But that too would be toil—and if the toil were avoided, the God of wrath, speaking through history, would once more pronounce his curse, and the proud architecture of the State would crumble.

It is for such good reasons, I think, that this new literary movement devotes particular attention to the poignancy of unemployment, and of employment under conditions of intolerable conflict. Turning to the works [in *Proletarian Literature in the United States, An Anthology*], you will unquestionably find such subjects painfully overstressed. The strike, the lock-out, bad working conditions, the witting or unwitting agents of "exploitation," the physical and mental rigors of joblessness, the *organizing* of protest (whereby the forces of anger and anguish may not be allowed to follow their natural chaotic bent, but may be directed into rational, socially useful channels of expression)—a continual harping upon such grim themes is bothersome to us, in so far as we have been taught that we have a *right* to anesthesia. And this reviewer admits that, but for the nature of his task, he would not have read the book continuously, but would have turned to it now and then, wisely interspersing it with material more in the "glorification of the American girl" tradition. I know of

one critic who, though avowedly "proletarian" in his sympathies, read the anthology while convalescing in a hospital, and developed such a "blockage" that he has not been able to review it at all. Lamentations may be more gratifying to write than to read.

Our resistance, particularly to the work of the less imaginative contributors, is justified for another reason. They are not able to "transcend" the partisan "leads" supplied by their philosophy. Their philosophy makes them quick to recognize a *propaganda situation,* and they proceed with great efficiency to build a work that emphasizes it. In fact, they become so intent upon the emphasizing of the *situation,* that they overlook the *humane* development of character. Their characters are formed in haphazard fashion, for the specific partisan purpose at hand, like the distortions of a political cartoonist. Hence, if the situation itself is burdensome to the reader, there may be nothing else in the work by which the writer can cajole him. One may hypothetically picture the two opposite procedures: that of the "partisan" writer, who begins by discovering a "propaganda situation," and proceeds to exploit it by inventing characters to fit; and in contrast, there is the "imaginative" writer, who might begin with an attachment to some very appealing character, and in the course of depicting him, might show him at work in some propaganda situation, such as the harboring of a labor leader hunted by vigilantes. Ultimately, there need be nothing at odds between the two approaches: an expression that is not truncated will encompass both. But if the partisan factor is emphasized with too much greed, it may lead to schematization of character, with nothing of appeal in so far as the situation itself lacks appeal.

An extreme instance of this is Philip Stevenson's story, "Death of a Century." Some of Stevenson's stories in the old *American Caravan,* prior to his "efficient" development of the partisan approach, were very appealing in the subtlety of their humaneness. But here he attempts to project, through an entire piece, a feeling people sometimes experience when seeing pictures and hearing stories of Rockefeller in extreme old age. He imagines a fabulously wealthy capitalist, now in his dotage, a living mummy surviving for a time after a successful revolution in the United States. Venomously, literal in his settling of scores, the author attempts to wreak symbolic vengeance upon his villain by picturing him as a victim of both revolution and old age. Not only is the result childishly repellent in the simplicity of its wish-fulfillments. It is so naïvely partisan that it defeats its purpose as partisanship. One grows indignant at the author's treatment of senility. In trying to discredit capitalism by identifying it with a decrepit old man, he quite unintentionally reminds us that no social change can remove the pathetic feebleness of age—and the more vengeful he becomes, the sorrier we feel for the scapegoat of his vengeance. Thus, the character is thin at best, and in so far as it takes on fullness, it does so at the expense of the propagandistic purpose.

There is a compensatory feature of the "propaganda situation" that should be noted, however. Whereas, in its overemphasis, it can serve as imaginative restriction, it does contribute one virtue to even the least pretentious contributions in the book. For I think that the strong sense of the propaganda situation is linked with the strong sense of an *audience* one gets when reading this anthology. This literature is written *to* people, or *for* people. It is *addressed*.

So much by way of introduction. The volume is compendious, and uneven. Yet perhaps we should single out for comment some of the more representative texts.

Robert Cantwell's story, "Hills Around Centralia," is a good example of a crucial propaganda situation embodied imaginatively. It is based upon the poignancy of the Crucifixion theme (the "benefactor" persecuted as "malefactor"). Irony of clashing moralities. The author "weights" his material propagandistically by showing us, first, the morality of the vigilantes in action, and then slowly widening our conception of the total scene by a sympathetic portrait of the strikers. Tactfully, he permits us to see how the interests of the vigilantes have led them to misinterpret the nature of a riot, while their grip upon the channels of education and publicity serves to shape "neutral" opinion in their favor. The two opposing worlds (of vigilantes and strikers) are eventually "synthesized" by a bridge device, being brought together when some impressionable boys, who had been bewilderedly subjected to the vigilante views, come upon two strikers hiding in the woods (overtones of the "little child shall lead them" theme). The author's choice of sides is made atop the ironic, the relativistic—hence, "propaganda" in the fullest sense, because profoundly humane. Strict "proletarian" morality could not be so "shifty." It would be pitted squarely against the enemy. But the farthest-reaching *propaganda* (as a device for appealing to the enemy, and not merely organizing his opposition by the goads of absolute antithesis) requires the more ambiguous talents of the diplomat (who talks to an alien camp in behalf of his own camp).

The excerpt from Jack Conroy's novel, *The Disinherited*, reveals upon analysis that the author, for all his superficial roughness, can be very sensitive in the delicacy of his formal progressions. For his tendentious situation, he draws upon our sympathies for a courageous, hard-working, but victimized mother. The "argument" falls into three parts: (1) we see the mother rejecting the thin-lipped charity that would separate her from her children; (2) we get an effectively ironic association when the son, resolving to be a "man," hears the other children playing "hide and seek," and yearns to join them; (3) the mother rigorously at toil. The chapter is rhetorically rounded off with something that might be called a coda. Apparently at a tangent, Conroy falls to telling of an incident unrelated to the matters at hand—and when he has finished, he suddenly reveals its application to his theme. It becomes a bitter device for rejecting "those canned Western Union greetings" for Mother's Day. If the reader is not moved by this turn, at once surprising and prepared, he is blessed with a tougher skin than is your present correspondent. Conroy evidently likes to think of himself as a "diamond in the rough" sort of writer; but the correctness of his form reveals a sense of propriety in the best sense of the word.

Ben Field's "Cow" is interesting as a problem in propaganda because of its vigorous attempt to combat anti-Semitism by destroying the stereotype image of the Jew and assembling a different cluster of traits in its stead. Perhaps he approaches his task a little too head on. Hence, those who respond strongly to the stereotype will tend to feel his portrait as "false," since his zeal for reconstruction gets him into the "statuesque" rather than the "humane." But its attainments may be felt despite its defects—and one must recognize the justice of its inclusion in a book of this kind, representing the attitudes of a group which, like the many religious bodies of the Hellenistic period, recruits its members by cutting on the bias across traditional distinctions of nationality and race.

Albert Halper's "Scab!" suffers from an O. Henry patness in the "well-made" conversion of the last two lines. But it makes one notable contribution in the search for propaganda situations. Halper adds this particular twist: he establishes his own point of view by showing a man who sins against it in spite of himself. He "weights" his material by giving a sympathetic plea for the strikebreaker while at the same time causing the strikebreaker to revolt against his own rôle. Obviously, such internal conflicts, that match external conflicts, provide a good opportunity for the dramatic—and Halper develops the possibilities with complexity, complexity enough in fact to have spared us the bluntness of the ending.

Albert Maltz's "Man on the Road" is a remarkable mixture of dream-magic and realistic shrewdness. The man with the glazed eyes, standing at the approach to the tunnel, conveys to us the overtones of the "pit," and of "living death." Yet the fact that the author built his ominous dreaming about a worker dying of silicosis (his politics prompting him to see the "news" in the West Virginia disaster without waiting for the story to "break" in our headlines) indicates how deep an author's enlistment in a practical cause may go. We observe how a writer may on occasion tie even his dreams to a party line.

I might close my reference to the story section by a mention of an excerpt, complete in itself, from Edwin Seaver's novel of white-collar workers, "The Company." Seaver has evidently learned much from Sherwood Anderson, whose lyric mode of story-telling he applies to his idylls and laments of metropolitan life. He is particularly good at finding simple themes that suggest complex connotations. In some ways, the tendentious situation embodied in his portrait of Aarons places us strategically at the very "narrows" of the propaganda issue. Aarons works for a public relations counsel—and the public relations counsel is the proletarian propagandist in reverse. He is purely and simply the historic devil. For whereas (the proletarian propagandist would enter the region of overlap between) his group and the people for the purpose of enlisting the people *in behalf of* social change, the public relations counsel would work in this same marginal territory *to obstruct* social change. Hence the subtlety of the situation which Seaver economically depicts for us, as we see Aarons, with a revolutionary interest in this region of overlap, employed by a man whose business it is to manipulate this same region for reactionary purposes. We watch Aarons making himself at home in this schizoid state. We see him undermining the simple loyalty of the others in the office, until their self-cynicism impairs the convincingness of their copy, while Aarons has learned to harness his detestation. From the very violation of his own beliefs, he derives a perverse strength, and is finally commended by his boss in the presence of those whose confidence in themselves he has destroyed. The bowing of the head, the theme on which this brief story ends, is mutely eloquent.

I have considered the stories at some length, since they lend themselves particularly well to an analysis of the tactics underlying propagandist art. Turning to the poetry section, we note that the lyrics necessarily possess, in their *epistolary, polemic* ingredient, a level of relevance beneath which they cannot sink. There are such incidents as May Day, the burning of the books, the execution of Sacco and Vanzetti to be commemorated; there is a definite need of encouragement to equip one for the intricacies of "class struggle"—hence the strongly recitative, oratorical note that pervades this form, a form rapidly becoming almost bereft of gravitational pull. To borrow a word from capitalism, we may note that there is a "market" for occasional verse, devotional verse, and the ritualization of dogma. These poets are at the stage where Commodianus was in the upbuilding of Catholic poetry. One feels behind them the pressure and sincerity of hunger (sometimes hunger literally, more often hunger in its wider, metaphorical aspects). Much of this verse is not written merely for the eye, or even for the ear, but for the mouth. Thus, though most of these atheistic poets would be scandalized at the thought, I should say that their verse is primarily concerned, in secular guise, with the mimetics of prayer. For prayer, we are told by the shrewdest of our naturalistic explainers-away, derives the force of its appeal from the first experiences of childhood when the child learns "word magic," the influencing of reality by speech (as when it summons its nurse by calling for her). Its obverse is the anathema. So we get here the building of character by the "magical" devices of petition, plaint, and curse.

Let me mention, "among those present," such pieces as: Kenneth Fearing's three declamatory poems, an amalgam of politics and sentiment. Robert Gessner's "Cross of Flame," vigorously realizing for us the incidents before the Reichstag fire. Michael Gold's "A Strange Funeral in Braddock" ("listen to the story of a strange American funeral"); and his "Examples of Worker Correspondence" suggest good possibilities, if the poet can resist the temptation to convert his wise lameness into a mannerism. Horace Gregory's "Dempsey, Dempsey," employing for polemic purposes the psychoanalytic account of the "identification" process. Alfred Hayes' "In a Coffee Pot," interesting for its transformation from the theme of *one man's unemployment* to the theme of *organized group resistance,* an "extension device" also well utilized in Langston Hughes' "Ballad of Lenin." James Neugass' "Thalassa, Thalassa" (a serviceable "idea," as he incongruously draws upon our connotations of ancient Greece when celebrating a strike of Greek freighters at Buenos Aires, though it is far better as an invention than in its working out). Kenneth Patchen's "Joe Hill Listens to the Praying," a work conducted on three levels: the sermon, Joe Hill, the poet's comments. Edwin Rolfe's "Unit Assignment," a homely but accurate account of an incident in the spreading of the doctrine. Muriel Rukeyser's "City of Monu-

ments," the imaginative opposing of tomb and sprout. Isidor Schneider's "Portrait of a False Revolutionist" ("He'll chant red song / like a cricket all day long")—also one should note his use of the Brecht-Eisler "you must be ready to take over" theme in "To the Museums." The middle class writer's concern with scruples, in Genevieve Taggard's "Life of the Mind, 1933" and "Interior." Don West's "Southern Lullaby" (which Mr. Brooks had condemned for its sentimentality, an unfavorable diagnosis one could rephrase favorably, or part-favorably, by saying that the author undertakes the strategic feat of incongruously introducing politics into the least political of themes). And two anonymous Negro pieces, which well illustrate how the moods of the spiritual can be drawn upon for "modern" purposes.

The "reportage" section is excellent. Perhaps it maintains the highest average of quality in the whole anthology. Nor is this an accident. I sometimes wonder whether, when Communists speak of "reality," they mean purely and simply "news." And there is a notable accuracy here. The early bards were hardly more than news peddlers. Later, when the bourgeois order became established, the resistance to the democratization of news was stubborn and powerful (since private access to news gave one a distinct commercial advantage). And Communists feel, of course, that "the news" is still being tampered with, to an extent that prevents people from seeing, in the proper proportions, the "realities" of the historic process now under way. Each of these eight items has much to recommend it. I should mention in particular the strange circumstantiality of Meridel Le Sueur's "I Was Marching." It has an almost mystical cast, that may result from the hysterical suppression of terror. Nor can one read Agnes Smedley's "The Fall of Shangpo" without being fascinated. She carefully depicts the dreadful upheavals of the human mind as archaic ways of thought are jammed brutally into new situations. John Mullen's "Mushrooms in the Factory" is brief, with a surprising touch of fancy in its ingenious way of revealing the workers' attachment to their place of work despite the many good reasons for alienation. Perhaps John L. Spivak's "A Letter to the President" is the most vulnerable article in this section. Spivak learned his trade doing "sob sister" work for MacFadden. He has brilliance, and the events he is describing make an authentic claim upon our sympathies—but it would take no princess to be disturbed by the pea of his early training beneath the twenty mattresses of his politics.

The inclusion of Clifford Odets' *Waiting for Lefty* among the plays would be enough to make the drama section valuable. I spoke earlier of the tendency to *begin* with propaganda situations and work towards character. This method of construction is more natural to the dramatist— and in *Waiting for Lefty* it flowers. Odets builds characters with strict reference to their functional necessity; his efficiency is sometimes astounding. This functional or formal emphasis prompts him to make unexpected discoveries. When the crooked labor leader says, for instance, that it is "only an hour's ride on the train" to Philadelphia, a voice pipes up: "Two hours!"—and these simple words carry an enormous load. They are *eloquent* in their place, because they are rich with promise. In their trivial stubbornness, they show you which way the arrows are pointing. You are amused—and there is a strong promise that your attitude of vengefulness towards the crooks will subsequently be permitted fuller expression.

Marxism is above all an inducement to drama. It is a dramatic theory of history, for it clearly and unmistakably names the vessels of good and evil (you can't make good drama without the assistance of a villain in goading forward the plot). It is loquacious, litigious, rhetorical. In our theatres at least, the revolution has already taken place, as the old hack producers of the "give the public what it wants" school had already brought on the fatal crisis in culture, darkening one house after another by their inability to have the least notion as to what the public wants. In addition to full-sized plays, requiring considerable commercial organization, there are many short skits being produced without scenery, in political gatherings of one sort or another. At their poorest, they merely confirm the audience's prejudices, as a war play in war times. But often they "transcend" these simpler requirements, attaining a wider comic or tragic scope—and there is no reason why, as audiences develop, the talent they enlist should not develop also.

As for the specific works in this collection: Odets's *Waiting for Lefty* and Alfred Kreymborg's *America, America!* (somewhat in the manner of a morality play) will probably appeal best when read, though all the pieces can disclose virtues to those who also watch for *theatric* possibilities.

I agree with Newton Arvin that the section on criticism seems least developed. The dramatic invitation to "make a choice" may lead the critic to make his choice too soon. Here enters the problem of "suspended judgment," as against the invitation to the dramatics of invective. In fact, if one reads Michael Gold's "Wilder: Prophet of the Genteel Christ" purely as a fiction, he is likely to enjoy it much better. I could even imagine Wilder enjoying it, if he were able to think of it as a Cicero thundering against a Catiline. And in "Eagle Orator," Malcolm Cowley administers very deft punishment to Paul Engle's earlier work, "American Song." For criticism of a non-pyrotechnic nature, we should signalize Edwin Berry Burgum's appreciation of Spender, Auden, and Lewis, written from the standpoint of their serviceability in shaping revolutionary attitudes. And the essay by the younger critics, William Phillips and Philip Rahv, bears testimony that they understand the complexity and indirectness involved in the "imaginative assimilation of political content." Indeed, I believe that their reservations would require them, editors of the Communist *Partisan Review,* to be less friendly towards some of the political matter in this anthology than I have been. We should also include here a reference to Joseph Freeman's introduction which, though prolix and unnecessarily defensive, contains many acute formulations.

In conclusion: As one particularly interested in the *processes* of literary appeal, I have generally tended to consider the volume from this standpoint. I have been vague about "absolute" tests of excellence, for I frankly do not know what such tests might be. Particularly in works of a controversial nature, the imponderabilia of emotional

bias strongly influence our aesthetic judgments. Hence, in dealing with a book of this sort, I thought it better to place the emphasis upon the matter of functions, which are neutral, available to anyone, like a theory of ballistics. But in the course of discussing processes, I have also found it necessary to touch somewhat upon the "way of life" that gives them meaning.

For the anthology does represent a way of life—and in this congregational feature lies the power and the promise of the "proletarian" movement as a contribution to our culture. In this movement, there is the customary high percentage of unexalted moments, as regards the field of literary representation, and even more so as regards the field of practical relationships. But taking what we have, I think we may see how the "proletarian" sort of emphases and admonitions can provide a lasting and essential stimulus to the formation of the national "consciousness."

> *Kenneth Burke, "Symbolic War," in* The Southern Review, *Louisiana State University, Vol. II, No. 1, Summer, 1936, pp. 134-47.*

Allen Tate

[*Tate was an American critic closely associated with the Agrarians, who were concerned with literary, political, and social issues, and were dedicated to preserving the Southern way of life and traditional Southern values. In particular, they attacked Northern industrialism and its attendant proletarian labor movement as they sought to preserve the Southern farming economy. The following is Tate's response to Marxist critic Kenneth Burke's review and assessment of* Proletarian Literature in the United States.]

In this brief essay I shall try to raise a few questions suggested by Mr. Kenneth Burke's able paper, "Symbolic War," published in the Summer, 1936, issue of *The Southern Review.* Mr. Burke alone of the extreme left-wing critics seems to me to possess the historical and philosophical learning necessary to the serious treatment of the literary problems of Marxism: before his "conversion" to Communism he had subjected himself to a rigorous critical discipline. Although Mr. Burke is a political partisan, he approaches the new radical literature in the spirit of inquiry, and for that reason, I suppose, he was subjected to some bitter obloquy by his colleagues at the American Writers' Congress held in New York in April, 1935. At this congress Mr. Burke was attacked for describing the class-struggle as a myth competing with other myths for supremacy in the modern world: at that stage of the discussion Mr. Burke was compelled to say, "I was speaking technically before a group of literary experts, hence I felt justified in using the word in a special sense. A poet's myths, I tried to make clear, are *real*"—an effort that won only moderate success before an audience of which Mr. Granville Hicks, as a literary expert, was a member.

In "Symbolic War" Mr. Burke begins: "Poetry, I take it, is a matter of welfare—as religion and politics are matters of welfare. And welfare, in this imperfect world, is grounded in material necessities." It is true enough to be a truism, and for that reason the statement is very likely, if it mean anything, to turn out to be as false as it is true. The chief trouble is in the term "matter." The phrase "is a matter of" may mean "depends upon," "is a reflection of," or "is a way of achieving"; but these phrases all mean something different. I am not chopping Mr. Burke's logic. I am pointing out that the ablest logician in the Communist camp, when confronted with the question of the economic base of literature, is driven to subsume so much under so vague a general term that he ends up with the assumption of a "truth" that it is his business to prove. The burden placed upon "welfare" is more than it can be made to bear.

Mr. Burke goes on to say: "The dispossessed man is in a different 'environment' from the man who enjoys the fruits of the society's wealth. He has a different 'relation to the productive forces.' And in so far as this situation sharpens his fears, hopes, and conflicts, it helps to condition his 'morality.'" That is to say, under finance-capitalism we do not have a community of culture because we do not have an ordered society in which every member has an economic stake. Within the general "culture" we get the beginnings of a new "culture" that may or may not replace the old. There is thus the rise of "class-consciousness." But Mr. Burke is aware there is no one-to-one relation, in the individual person, between his economic class and his morality. "We can belong," he says, "in as many classifications as scientists or philosophers care to invent." And this fact is largely due to another fact—that our "economic environment," our specific relation to the "forces of production," is not our total environment. For Mr. Burke insists upon a distinction between the merely historical environment—an abstraction resulting from the simplification of our personal situation into a historical pattern, Marxism, agrarianism, etc.—and the "human environment"; this latter, Mr. Burke calls the "resources of the body itself" from which rise certain "superstructural counterparts," love, hate, desire for mobility, intelligence. (I cannot see mobility as coördinate with love, hate, and intelligence, but it is worth recording that Mr. Burke is the first Communist critic to come to my notice who seems to allow any autonomy to intelligence apart from the allengrossing economic environment of the orthodox Marxist.) In some sense the relation of the superstructure of love, hate, intelligence, to the "resources of the body" corresponds to the superstructure of culture that a class erects upon its economic environment. I wish Mr. Burke had pursued this correspondence further and had isolated the dynamic factor at work in each relationship. I think we shall see in a moment that Mr. Burke is here almost a pure determinist, that the economic environment of the class and the human environment, the "resources of the body," respectively condition or perhaps actually effect the rise of their superstructures of general culture and personal experience. And it is this determinism, it seems to me, which cripples Mr. Burke's theory of literature, making it possible for him to take seriously certain modern works that merely illustrate new combinations of economic forces; I refer to such examples of "proletarian" writing as are contained in *Proletarian Literature in the United States*. Apart from the contributions by Edwin Seaver and Robert Cantwell, that volume seems to me to be almost worthless; and so it seems to Mr. Burke, but his own political bias commits him to the respectful consideration of unfavorable analysis which is too often mollified by *but* and *perhaps*. Of a very bad story he writes: "Ben Field's 'Cow' is interesting as a problem in propaganda because of its vigorous attempt to combat anti-Semitism by destroying the stereotype image of the Jew and assembling a different cluster of traits in its stead. Perhaps he approaches his task a little too head on."

Of the conflict between the economic environment and the human environment Mr. Burke says: "Many of the recent literary battles hinge about this issue." Let us see in just what terms Mr. Burke understands the issue as it affects literature.

> The presence of this "human" environment, the "natural" frame of reference that is wider than the "historical," may be discussed as the tendency of the poet to "transcend" the peculiar economic necessities of his times. Not even a fish could be said to live in a totally different environment from man. The "moralities" of man and fish must tend to overlap, destroying the symmetry of complete differentiation, in so far as both "classes" live by respiration and locomotion. A happy translator might do a fairly reputable job at turning a fish's delight in gills and fins into a glorification of lungs and legs.

I very much fear that in this passage Mr. Burke has committed himself to the metaphorical logic of popular journalese. (His partial awareness of this is in the quotes around "transcend.") If the historical environment is the product of historical and scientific method, it is, on its necessarily quantitative basis, infinitely wider than the human environment; so the poet in achieving the human point of view probably engages in a procedure that can in no wise be conveyed by the verb *to transcend*. He is more likely proceeding to his objective with an entirely different quality of intelligence from that employed in isolating the economic or historical environment, a kind of cognition which differs from the historical not merely in being wider or narrower but in being, apart from physical range, intensive. Mr. Burke is, of course, in the passage about the fish, adumbrating a theory of the universal in art: it is preëminently an eighteenth-century theory couched in a biological analogy dear to the nineteenth. The universal is the general average of observation drawn from the *widest* possible field. It is not a universal of implicit intensiveness, but a universal of scientific formulation. Instead of a proposition like "Man is vile," we get "Man is a vertebrate."

But Mr. Burke is aware that this kind of formula in literature has its dangers, not because it is an inadequate formula but because its adherents may push it too far.

> The oversimplifying advocate of "proletarian" art would stress the historic environment to the exclusion of all else (and would then invent all sorts of subterfuges and epicycles to explain a liking he might have for Dante or Aeschylus, perhaps finally deciding that they were "workers" in their field). And the oversimplifying advocate of the universally human would lay all emphasis upon the continuity of "man's burden" throughout the ages, as he incessantly confronts the critical events of birth, growth, love,

union, separation, initiation, sorrow, fear, death, and the like.

I do not know if Mr. Burke is driven into the subterfuges that he seems a little jibingly to attribute to his colleagues; I gather that he is not. Nor is he committed to the catalogue of spurious universals that he finds in the repertoire of the nonproletarian writer. I cannot imagine why Mr. Burke ridicules his own theory, but I should like to guess why: he does not believe in it, but he cannot allow himself to think up any other because he has previously subscribed to a theory of the relation of the human and the economic environments, a theory that misleads him into the belief that the human is wide and abstract, the historical narrow and concrete, and that the latter may be transcended by the former, and indeed must be transcended at least, one supposes, to a certain degree, if the artist is to escape the stigma of mere contemporaneity, a stigma earned by an excessive zeal for propaganda.

The question that arises here, and it is a question that I should like to see Mr. Burke undertake to answer, is the extent to which the artist, *qua* artist, must transcend the mere historical environment. That is to say, in what proportion shall the two environments be mixed? In Mr. Burke's analysis of the artist's situation into these two environments, the question that I have just posed must, I think, be necessarily asked in those terms—the terms, not of fusion, but of mixture. Mr. Burke asks: "Might we not suspect that, unless men were brutes or gods (and Aristotle reminds us that they are not either) they must inevitably exemplify imagination and propaganda both?" That sounds reasonable. But what does "exemplify" mean; and are imagination and propaganda coördinate terms? Upon close examination most of Mr. Burke's propositions about this problem of propaganda turn out to be merely rhetorical logic—when he is not actually ridiculing his own terms. The distinction between imagination and propaganda is rhetorical. When a critic as astute as Burke falls afoul of terms we are entitled to look for a very dark nigger hiding in the rhetorical woodpile.

That nigger, as I dimly see him, looks like this: he is the effort of a profound critic to conceal from himself the true nature of his problem in order to justify the literary practice of his political allies. One more quotation and my exhibit of this tendency in Mr. Burke's essay—a tendency that does not appear in *Permanence and Change*—will be complete:

> One may hypothetically picture the two opposite procedures: that of the "partisan" writer, who begins by discovering a "propaganda situation," and proceeds to exploit it by inventing characters to fit; and in contrast, there is the "imaginative" writer, who might begin with an attachment to some very appealing character, and in the course of depicting him, might show him at work in some propaganda situation, such as the harboring of a labor leader hunted by vigilantes. Ultimately, there need be nothing at odds between the two approaches: an expression that is not truncated will encompass both. But if the partisan factor is emphasized with too much greed, it may lead to schematization of charac-

ter, with nothing of appeal in so far as the situation itself lacks appeal.

That too looks sensible—but to me the whole passage is meaningless. Is the artist rendering his subject, or is he merely mixing ingredients—is he at liberty to *emphasize* this and to pass over that? (Mr. Burke's verbs will bear watching.) And what is Mr. Burke going to do about the writer who begins "with an attachment to some very appealing character" whose life is so lived that he has never seen a labor leader and never even heard of vigilantes? I personally know dozens of people, of fathomless interest as characters, who are like that. Will Mr. Burke reply with the orthodox Communist reply, that such a writer, dealing with such characters, is outside the Great Tradition, that he is frivolous, irrelevant, and a disguised apologist of capitalism—simply because implicit in this writer's characters there is no "propaganda situation," because the writer ignores the "economic environment" as it is defined by the Marxists? I do not think that Mr. Burke will say this; but I am not sure.

Mr. Burke's aesthetic standards are offended by the propagandist excesses of his colleagues; but the only warning that he issues to them in "Symbolic War" is an appeal for moderation; he asks them *not to go too far.* He asks them not to mix too much of the ingredient of propaganda into the gruel of art. He does not ask them to do some fundamental aesthetic thinking that might eliminate altogether the need for compromise between the different pairs of antinomies that he describes: propaganda and imagination, historical and human environments, etc.

How far is too far? Mr. Burke must obviously be an opportunist in this, since on principle he cannot establish a point at which the poet must eschew propaganda; Mr. Burke will have to decide each case as it appears. And it seems to me that this is due to the underlying significance of his dichotomy between propaganda and imagination, between the historical and the human environments. For, in the long run, from whichever end of the dilemma the artist may begin, he is cut off, under Mr. Burke's theory, from the exercise of the critical intellect.

It is astonishing to observe that political revolutionists evince such timidity in aesthetic theory. Mr. Burke's theory of literature is the standard eighteenth-century belief in the inherent dignity of the subject: some subjects are good, some bad. It is too large a field of discussion to describe here, yet the equivalent for literature of Mr. Burke's "historical environment" is the decorous subject that from the time of Addison dominated criticism until the time of Matthew Arnold. The very use of the term "sincerity" by many Communist critics today is closely related to Arnold's notion that it is the same as high seriousness. On this point Mr. Cleanth Brooks is instructive:

> If Arnold states that high seriousness "comes from absolute sincerity," one remembers Coleridge's objection to the play of wit because it implied "a leisure and self-possession incompatible with the steady fervor of a mind possessed and filled with the grandeur of its subject." Indeed, Arnold's high seriousness amounts to little more than this *steady fervor.*

The steady fervor about the Cause—Victorian morality or Marxian doctrine—cannot admit of critical examination; and, under Mr. Burke's theory, least of all can it admit of the exercise of the critical wit which tends to place all "causes" in the whole context of experience. The steady fervor cannot be fused into an integral expression of sincerity and intelligence; they come together in a mixture.

I have indicated that Mr. Burke sees in his "historical environment" the concrete reality, and in the "human environment" the wider abstract medium through which artists transcend the merely local view. Yet it is apparent that the act of transcending carries the artist over into a very thin realm of miscellaneous emotions in which Mr. Burke obviously feels very little conviction; he is aware of a vague duty to do justice to the eternal verities—love, union, hate, and the rest. They are all, of course, only a miscellany of Platonic abstractions, and although Mr. Burke calls them the "human environment" they actually have no environment at all: they were once the decorous subjects of eighteenth-century poetry and criticism. They were susceptible to the application of Coleridge's steady fervor. I need not quote exhibits of the poetic language appropriate to that zeal: criticism in the last twenty years has sufficiently described the state of the poetic vocabulary at the end of the nineteenth century. From the neo-classical belief in decorum there is a direct development of theory and practice through the Romantics and Victorians into a belief in the higher decorum, which makes the poet the "unacknowledged legislator" and, for Arnold, the Teacher.

And that is all that Mr. Burke's theory, it seems to me, allows him to be. The poet may be a purveyor of the eternal verities, and thus I suppose a capitalist poet in the "traditional" culture; or he may be concerned with the historical environment of Marxism—in which case he is still a teacher.

Mr. Burke's scheme of the two general procedures possible to the poet seems to me vulnerable at two points. First, the distinction between the human environment and the historical environment is a distinction without a difference. They are both realms of practical abstractions for the service of the will—the will of the individual prophet-teacher and the will of the radical reformer. And secondly Mr. Burke's scheme offers only a mechanical explanation of the relation of the poet to his material: in making the poet's apprehension of "ideas" explicit and self-conscious he commits himself to a theory closely resembling that of Mr. Paul Elmer More. The anomaly of this association of names disappears when one remembers that there has been no general revolution in criticism since Dryden. For, after the rise of materialism under Hobbes and Locke, the poet lost confidence in his own special function—the whole and inutile creation of the human experience—and began to compete with the scientist, until at last the poet has begun *to be* a social scientist. The practical abstraction has usurped the whole realm of the poet. Criticism for two hundred years has been based, not upon Shakespeare, for whom the "idea" has no meaning apart from the concrete experience, but upon the weaker side of Milton, upon his professed mission as Teacher and not upon his performance as a poet.

The mechanism of the abstract idea underlying Mr. Burke's theory has dominated our criticism for two centuries. Its dominion over Mr. Burke's intelligence witnesses the absence of revolutionary critical thought in a political movement whose avowed aim is revolution. If among the American Communists there were any radical thinking in literary criticism I think Mr. Burke would be aware of it, or we might expect him to supply it. Mr. Burke's case for the "proletarian" writers is persuasive, but it is not convincing on the special ground of their originality. Some of these writers are interesting, but they are interesting, from the strict critical point of view, not for their zeal in reform, but rather for whatever merit they have achieved as writers. They have most of the merits and most of the defects of other writers living within the mentality of the present age.

The test of the economics of literature is in the long run the test of time. And time here signifies not merely the stability of an economic system but the continuity of a certain way of life. Whether a Communist economic order in America—whatever it may do in Europe—can achieve a continuous pattern of life is debatable; it is debatable equally for and against. Finance-capitalism has developed on the economic side in well-defined and predictable directions; on the social, moral, and religious side there has been steady deterioration. A system of production may be made to work a high efficiency without in the least effecting for society a moral pattern durable enough for men to depend upon; without, moreover, making any sort of pattern necessary or desirable. This is indeed inevitable when men have no moral control over the method of production. And here it is difficult to see any fundamental moral difference between the giant corporation of the present and the giant supercorporation, which is the state, of tomorrow.

Communist literature gives us no clue to such a difference. In Mr. Burke's own analysis of the situation of the American Communist writer, the novelist and the poet must be preoccupied, directly or indirectly, with the "historical environment," a picture of men abstracted into two warring classes, capitalist and worker. That is the subject of greatest "reality" to the Communist writer. Yet so far as successful works of literature are concerned the test of their reality is not the historical and political conviction of the authors, but the works themselves. It is probable that political conviction transformed into the reality of experience based upon a definite, and not merely a hoped for, order of life is the matrix of literature. There is no evidence that Shakespeare was aware, in terms of modern historical thinking, of the conflict of dying feudalism and rising capitalism. For him it was an inexhaustible subject—but not in those terms.

Allen Tate, "Mr. Burke and the Historical Environment," in The Southern Review, *Louisiana State University, Vol. II, No. 2, Autumn, 1936, pp. 363-72.*

FURTHER READING

Anthologies

Hicks, Granville; Gold, Michael; Schneider, Isidor; North, Joseph; Peters, Paul; and Calmer, Alan, eds. *Proletarian Literature in the United States: An Anthology.* New York: International Publishers, 1935, 384 p.

> Compilation of representative works of American proletarian fiction, poetry, reportage, drama, and literary criticism.

Swados, Harvey, ed. *The American Writer and the Great Depression.* Indianapolis: The Bobbs-Merrill Company, 1966, 521 p.

> Collection of works and excerpts widely representative of Depression-era American writers, and includes samples of proletarian writing of the 1930s.

Secondary Sources

Aaron, Daniel. *Writers on the Left: Episodes in American Literary Communism.* New York: Harcourt, Brace and World, 1961, 460 p.

> Consideration of the left-wing American writer from 1912 through 1940 explores the roots of proletarian literature, the appeal of Communism to American intellectuals during the 1920s and 1930s, and the ultimate dissolution of the literary movement based in Marxism.

Anderson, David G. "Michigan Proletarian Writers and the Great Depression." *MidAmerica* 9 (1982): 76-97.

> Overview of four novels published between 1924 and 1938 and a discussion of their importance in documenting midwestern American experience during the 1920s and 1930s.

Angoff, Charles. "The Proletarian Bohemia." In his *The Tone of the Twenties and Other Essays,* pp. 228-47. South Brunswick, N. J.: A. S. Barnes and Co., 1966.

> Anecdotal recollections of the 1930s American subculture of proletarian writers, editors, and political activists from a right-wing perspective.

Barnes, L. "The Proletarian Novel." *Mainstream* 16, No. 7 (July 1963): 51-7.

> Discussion of the 1963 reprint of Jack Conroy's *The Disinherited* (1933) and its relationship to renewed academic interest in the proletarian novel during the 1950s and 1960s.

Canby, Henry Seidel. "The March of the Ideologies." In his *American Memoir,* pp. 315-19. Boston: Houghton Mifflin Company, 1947.

> Recalls the proletarian movement in American literature, asserting that "labor leaders and spokesmen for the underprivileged" did not read proletarian novels and, generally speaking, "had never heard of them."

Guttmann, Allen. "The Brief Embattled Course of Proletarian Poetry." In *Proletarian Writers of the Thirties,* edited by David Madden, pp. 252-69. Carbondale: Southern Illinois University Press, 1968.

> Traces the development of proletarian poetry from 1929 to 1939.

Hicks, Granville. "The Failure of Left Criticism." *The New Republic* 103, No. 11 (9 September 1940): 345-47.

> Retrospective consideration of the aesthetic and political limitations of Marxist literary criticism of the 1930s. Hicks concludes: "There was nothing wrong in our belief that the world had to be changed and that we could help to change it. There was something naive in our faith that literary criticism would be a major weapon in the struggle."

Hoffman, Frederick J. "Aesthetics of the Proletarian Novel." In *Proletarian Writers of the Thirties,* edited by David Madden, pp. 184-93. Carbondale: Southern Illinois University Press, 1968.

> Considers the aesthetic value of proletarian novels.

Klein, Marcus. "The Roots of Radicals: Experience in the Thirties." In *Proletarian Writers of the Thirties,* edited by David Madden, pp. 134-57. Carbondale: Southern Illinois University Press, 1968.

> Presents a brief overview of *Proletarian Literature in the United States,* the 1935 anthology considered to be the most representative collection of works characteristic of the proletarian movement in American literature.

Ledbetter, Kenneth. "Henry Roth's *Call It Sleep:* The Revival of a Proletarian Novel." *Twentieth Century Literature* 12, No. 3 (October 1966): 123-30.

> Critical reassessment of Henry Roth's 1934 novel *Call It Sleep.* The critic asserts that the work is "perhaps the most authentic and compelling expression the American proletariat has received."

Madden, David. *Proletarian Writers of the Thirties.* Carbondale: Southern Illinois University Press, 1968, 278 p.

> Collection of essays focusing on individual authors and general characteristics of the proletarian movement in American literature.

Pearce, Sharyn. "The Proletarianization of the Novel: The Cult of the Worker in Australian and American Fiction of the Depression." *Southerly* 48, No. 2 (June 1988): 187-200.

> Analyzes the influence of American proletarian literature on Australian proletarian literature, which reached its peak in the 1950s.

Pugh, David G. "Reading the Proletarians—Thirty Years Later." In *The Thirties: Fiction, Poetry, Drama,* edited by Warren French, pp. 89-95. Deland, Fla.: Everett Edwards, Inc., 1967.

> An examination of proletarian literature and its role as interpreter of Depression-era political and economic reality to 1960s readers who found proletarian writings hard to believe.

Rideout, Walter B. "Class War" and "Art is a Class Weapon." In his *The Radical Novel in the United States: 1900-1954,* pp. 132-224. Cambridge: Harvard University Press, 1956.

> Extensive consideration of the role of proletarian fiction during the social and economic upheaval of the 1920s and 1930s in the United States. Rideout focuses on writers' use of style, symbolism, and subject matter, and on the social context in which proletarian novels were written and received.

Widmer, Kingsley. "The Way Out: Some Life-Style Sources of the Literary Tough Guy and the Proletarian Hero." In *Tough Guy Writers of the Thirties,* edited by David Madden, pp. 3-12. Carbondale: Southern Illinois University Press, 1968.

  Discusses the archetype of the hobo in American culture and its influence on the development of both "tough guy" and "proletarian hero" figures in 1930s American literature.

Wilson, Edmund. "The Literary Class War: I." *The New Republic* 70, No. 909 (4 May 1932): 319-23.

  Early analysis of the controversy within the proletarian movement about how to evaluate proletarian art and literature. Wilson argues for judging works on the basis of artistic merit and achievement rather than lauding or dismissing them primarily on political and philosophical grounds.

Additional coverage of American proletarian literature is contained in the following source published by Gale Research: *Dictionary of Literary Biography Documentary Series,* Vol. XI.

Art and Literature

INTRODUCTION

Since classical times commentators have maintained that there are significant parallels between literature and the visual arts. The mutual influence between writers and other artists has resulted in paintings based on works of fiction, drama, and poetry, as well as literary works inspired by or emulative of pictorial styles. Much critical discussion has focused on defining essential similarities and differences between literature and the arts. Early commentators tended to espouse the view, *"Ut pictura poesis"* (Poetry is like painting), expressed by the Roman poet Horace in his treatise *Ars Poetica*. Gotthold Lessing's 1766 treatise *Laokoön, oder uber die Grenzen der Maleri und Poesie* (*Laocoön: An Essay on the Limits of Painting and Poetry*) is one of the first modern attempts to challenge this idea and to define the basic differences in representation imposed by the differing natures of literature and the visual arts. Comparing the account of the death of the priest Laocoön that appears in the second book of Virgil's *Aeneid* to a Greek sculpture treating the same theme, Lessing argued that the depiction of a succession of events in time is the concern of poetry, while the portrayal of objects in space is the realm of the visual arts. In the early twentieth century, with the advent of Cubism and other non-objective or non-naturalistic artistic styles and the attempts of such writers as Gertrude Stein and James Joyce to transcend the concept of linear narrative structure, the question of the interrelation between literature and the visual arts has assumed growing importance for critics. Such commentators as Joseph Frank suggest that literary works which juxtapose differing images of a character or situation and depend on the reader to draw connections or infer a succession of events in time exhibit "spatial form." According to Frank, such texts demand that readers suspend judgment or interpretation until the moment they have apprehended an entire work and are thus able to "see" its meaning in much the same way a viewer sees the meaning of a painting in a single moment. Proponents of this theory maintain that the limits traditionally believed to distinguish the expressive capabilities of literature and the visual arts have begun to erode. Other commentators assert that the idea of spatial form is merely an analogy for the processes by which readers understand any text. The concept of spatial form in literature and the idea of a relationship between literature and the visual arts continue to inspire discussion between the art world and the literary world. As Stanley Kunitz writes, "In his panegyric of Delacroix, Baudelaire noted that it is 'one of the characteristic symptoms of the spiritual condition of our age that the arts aspire, if not to take one another's place, at least reciprocally to lend one another new powers.' A century later the observation seems much more pertinent than at the time it was made."

OVERVIEWS

Edward Allen McCormick

[*McCormick is an American educator, translator, and critic. In the following excerpt from the introduction to his 1962 translation of Gotthold Lessing's* Laocoön *(1766), McCormick traces the history of the art-literature comparison from classical times to the present.*]

The origins of the problem [of defining the relationship between visual art and literature] which Lessing attempts to solve in his *Laocoön* reach back to the very beginnings of art criticism. Among the ancients, it was Aristotle with his doctrine that all arts are arts of imitation who first attempted a separation and classification of the arts. In his *Poetics* he distinguishes between the rhythmical arts (dancing, poetry, and music) and the arts of rest (painting and sculpture). Unfortunately, however, he says nothing further about the basic differences between poetry and painting.

The first direct reference to the problem of the relation of the arts to one another is the often quoted and more often misunderstood saying of Simonides that poetry is a speaking picture and painting a mute poem. This "witty antithesis," as one critic [W. G. Howard in his *Laokoon*] has called it, attained such popularity that its validity was for many centuries hardly ever seriously questioned. Needless to say, its effect was a virtual obliteration of the demarcation line between the two arts.

Another attempt to formulate the relationship between painting and poetry is to be found in the *Ars Poetica* of the Apuleian poet Horace. This work, which was quite obviously not intended to present a complete theory of poetry, made the seemingly harmless statement that both poet and painter have equal freedom to attempt whatever they deem worthy of portraying in their works. His actual words, however,

> pictoribus atque poetis
> quidlibet audendi semper fuit aequa potestas,
> ["Poets and painters have always had an equal
> license to venture anything at all"]

were taken to mean that both arts were basically alike, and hence their aims and achievements likewise. To make matters worse, his *ut pictura poesis* was snatched out of context and made into the argument par excellence for the homogeneous nature of painting and poetry:

> Ut pictura poesis; erit, quae, si propius stes,
> Te capiat magis, et quaedam, si longius abstes.

["Poetry is like painting: one work seizes your fancy if you stand close to it, another if you stand at a distance."]

This, later aestheticians maintained, implies only that Horace extends the similarity between visual art and poetry to include everything except the obvious fact that the one employs color and lines and the other words and rhythm.

There are a few additional writers of antiquity who might be mentioned in connection with Lessing's essay, but none of them goes beyond a few general remarks on the distinctions between the arts, nor do they ever develop a reasonably clear system of aesthetics. Plutarch, it is true, devotes considerable space to the differences between poetry and the visual arts, [in his *On the Glory of Athens*], but he comes to the conclusion that such differences lie principally in the material with which the two arts work rather than in their nature and aims. Another Greek author, Philostratus the Elder, remains for the most part in the narrow tradition of avoiding any excursion into the field of aesthetic philosophy, with one exception. In his *Life of Apollonius* he suggests that the visual arts owe their origin not only to the imagination, but also to imitation. This latter, we are told, can work only with that which it sees, while the imagination can go further and express the unseen also.

The list of classical authors who broached the problem . . . might be enlarged—Longinus, Pliny the Elder, Quintilian, and Lucian, for example, all made various remarks of a very general nature which touched on some aspect of the theory of arts—but their contribution to the development of a critical art theory was extremely limited. Indeed, it can be said that of all the writers of antiquity only one made a serious attempt to get at the real nature of and inherent differences between the arts. In his twelfth *Olympian Oration,* Dio Chrysostomus (born *c.* A.D. 40) compared Homer with the sculptor Phidias in their treatment of the god Zeus. Some of the conclusions reached by the Greek rhetor anticipate Lessing's *Laocoön* to such a degree that, despite Lessing's failure to mention this writer in his essay, we may safely assume that he was acquainted with the *Orations* at the time the *Laocoön* was written. A comparison of the two works, which would not be to our purpose here, shows quite clearly that a number of Dio Chrysostomus' propositions, although generally not pursued very far, contain the essence of what Lessing later says in his *Laocoön*.

As has been pointed out, however, Dio represents a singular exception among the ancients in his attempt to confront the problem of the relationship of the arts to one another in a critical manner. The bulk of the evidence is unfortunately on the other side: *Ut pictura poesis* and Simonides' "witty antithesis" held the field for many hundreds of years, and the confusion that reigned in the arts, especially with respect to poetry and its dependence on painting, tended rather to increase until the time of Winckelmann and Lessing.

From the end of the first century until the close of the Middle Ages there was scarcely any attempt to develop a critical theory of the arts or to continue what the ancients had begun. Architecture, painting, and sculpture, which had long held supremacy in the arts under the ever growing influence of Christianity, were obliged to overstep their natural limitations time and time again in order to express ideas not aesthetically compatible with their inherent nature. Christian concepts of virtue, constancy, etc., had to be personified and thus made accessible to the Christian flock. Medieval literature, too, as soon as it shed its Latin garb and became "popular," joined the other arts, especially painting, in admitting allegory and symbolism on a grand scale. Painting was still considered the nobler art, however, and so poets borrowed freely from it and attempted to "paint" in their works.

This was the state of affairs at the close of the Middle Ages. Painting, or more precisely the visual arts in general, had succumbed to what Lessing terms the mania for allegory, and poetry to the mania for painting or description, as well as for allegory. During the Renaissance we again encounter attempts to cope with aesthetic problems in a critical way but, as was to be expected, the writers of the sixteenth century and later those of the seventeenth sanctioned the practice of ignoring the limits of poetry as opposed to painting. The Italian Luigi Dolce, for example, examines in his *Dialogo della Pittura* the works of Titian, Michelangelo, and Raphael with respect to invention, design, and use of color. A number of his conclusions do not differ sharply from the views held by the ancients. According to Dolce, a poet is at the same time a painter, and hence a good poet will necessarily be a good painter. Common to both is the element of imitation; the painter imitates by means of lines and colors, the poet by means of words. The former is limited to what his eyes can see, while the latter is able to represent not only what he sees, but also what is revealed to his spirit. Despite the fact that Dolce calls good poets good painters and asserts that Virgil based his account of Laocoön's death on the statue, which he had before him, he is prepared to accept a mutual dependency of one art on the other to a considerable degree. Painters, he stresses, get their subject matter ("invention") from the poets and vice versa. He does not, however, inquire into the basic dissimilarity of the two arts, and in this important respect at least he fails to modify the common doctrine of the Renaissance as it had been inherited from antiquity.

Medieval allegory and the mania for description, meanwhile, continued to hold sway in poetry and, to a lesser degree, in painting. Some thirty years after Dolce's *Dialogo* appeared, Edmund Spenser published the first three books of his *Faerie Queene* (1590), in which both tendencies, or manias, as Lessing calls them, are everywhere evident. To a greater or lesser degree Drayton, Dryden, Milton, and Pope all followed this tradition, which reached its high point in the eighteenth century with the publication of Thomson's *Seasons*. In the field of criticism the dictum *ut pictura poesis* was closely adhered to in eighteenth-century England, notably by Addison, Hurd, and Joseph Spence. The last-named, a good friend of Alexander Pope, attempted to explain the Greek and Roman poets through an examination of the relics of ancient art [in his *Polymetis*]. While Lessing's attack on Spence is not always fully justified (for example, Spence actually anticipated Lessing in his dictum that the poet was superior to the artist in his power to imitate the transitoriness of motion; and he is generally not quite so willing to identify poetry with painting as Lessing claims), the English critic does seem to go rather far in his attempt to prove that every poetic description was based on some ancient statue or picture.

Another Englishman of considerable importance to the development of aesthetic theory was James Harris (1709-80), whose *Three Treatises, the first concerning Art, the second concerning Music, Painting, and Poetry, the third concerning Happiness,* was published in 1744. In the second treatise he attempts to show the similarities and dissimilarities of music, painting, and poetry, and to determine which is to be considered superior to the other two.

The Laokoon Group, *marble. This Hellenistic sculpture, discovered on the Esqualine Hill in Rome in 1506, depicts Laokoon, a priest of Apollo, and his two sons struggling against attacking serpents. Gotthold Lessing, in his* Laokoon *(1766), cited the group, which was known for its dynamic facial expressions and compositional tension, as an example of the limitations of the plastic arts in favor of poetry because the sculpture was meant to be viewed only from the front.*

Proceeding from Aristotle's statement that all arts are arts of imitation, he shows how the media of each limit its powers to imitate fully. Painting, says Harris, can imitate only by means of color and figure. It can represent only one moment in time. Although it is motionless it can indicate motions and sounds as well as actions which are known (i.e., history). Poetry imitates by means of sound and motion, but since sounds stand for ideas, poetry is able to imitate to the extent that language can express things. Consequently, poetic imitation includes everything. Its materials are words, and words are "symbols by compact of all ideas." Harris concludes that poetry is superior to painting because it is not restricted to the depiction of short, momentary events but may imitate subjects of any duration. In sentiments, too, it is the only medium. From the summary just given it is obvious that Harris follows tradition in most respects and has little to say that is strikingly original. His claim of the greater power of poetry to represent actions and express feelings is, however, new and was no doubt of some influence on the *Laocoön*.

In France, too, we find a continuing belief in the dependence of poetry on art, although there was no lack of attempts to develop a critical theory of the arts. One of the earliest such attempts in modern times was the Latin poem, *De arte graphica,* by Charles du Fresnoy, which appeared in 1668. Its opening words, *ut pictura poesis,* betray its message. Fresnoy accepts both this saying of Horace and the antithesis of Simonides and goes on to show how the arts of painting and poetry are similar in their essential features. Other early critics, e.g., de Piles, Watelet, and Coypel fail to break with the doctrinal tradition taken over from Dolce and his contemporaries. There is, however, a shift of emphasis (such as we have already seen in Harris' *Treatises*) which becomes evident from the eighteenth century on. In the work of Abbé Jean Baptiste du Bos, *Réflexions critiques sur la poésie et la peinture* (1719), we encounter the usual belief in the equality and homogeneous nature of poetry and painting as well as the Horatian *ut pictura poesis,* which he uses as the motto of his work. Despite this apparently slavish acceptance of the traditional theory of aesthetics, however, du Bos attaches special significance to the ability of the two arts to arouse emotion. Both poetry and painting, du Bos claims, seek to arouse passions, or rather are copies of real passions, and these copies or imitations should affect us in the same way as would the objects imitated. But there are differences between the two arts in the means through which they arouse our emotions. Painting represents only a single moment, and its signs are coexistent; poetry, on the other hand, produces its effect in a series of instants. Accordingly, the poet may depict a more complex passion than may the painter, who can treat only subjects in which effects are due to relatively simple causes and are revealed in some visible aspect of the body. Du Bos thus shows the superiority of poetry over painting in the representation of the sublime, and it is in this most important point that we can see how deeply indebted Lessing was to this French critic's work.

Another Frenchman to whom Lessing owes a considerable debt is Philippe de Tubières, Count Caylus, whose *Tableaux tirés de l'Iliade, de l'Odyssée d'Homère et de l'Énéide de Virgile, avec des observations générales sur le costume* is severely criticized in the *Laocoön*. It is unnecessary to comment here on the contents of this important work since Lessing himself discusses it at considerable length. It should be pointed out, however, that his aim of opening up new sources of inspiration for contemporary artists—the real purpose of Caylus' book—and the tendency on the part of many critics to see in the *Tableaux* a striking anticipation of Lessing's own conclusions tend to offset what is undoubtedly too harsh a judgment in the *Laocoön*.

In eighteenth-century Germany, where most writers followed the models of contemporary English poets and turned with passion to painting in poetry, two Swiss-German critics raised descriptive writing to the dignity of a theory. In their struggle to uphold the ideals of English poetry, Johann Jakob Bodmer and Johann Jakob Breitinger, in their *Discourses of the Painters* (1771-72), turned against a French-inspired pseudoclassicism in German literature, represented by Johann Christian Gottsched. Rejecting Gottsched's doctrine (which owed a great deal to Boileau) that poetry must be restricted to the realm of the natural and ruled by the intellect, they argued for the admission of the supernatural and the acceptance of emotions as vital forces in poetry. Valuable as were the critical works of these two men to the progress of German literature, and despite the fact that they occasionally made some clear distinctions between painting and poetry, *ut pictura poesis* still lay at the base of their program. According to them, poetry is a kind of painting, and the poet is simply a painter who appeals to the imagination and has a greater range of subjects than the painter or sculptor.

Two other Germans, Mendelssohn and Winckelmann, must be added to this list of critics who dealt with the problem [of defining the relationship between art and literature]. The first of these, Moses Mendelssohn, was a contemporary and friend of Lessing. His essay, *On the main principles of fine arts and belles-lettres* (first version in 1757), produced a deep impression on Lessing. In the second part of this work, which deals with the kinds of art which produce aesthetic pleasure, we encounter ideas and definitions which were to pass directly into the *Laocoön*. Mendelssohn classifies the arts according to their media of expression:

> Symbols, by means of which an object may be expressed, may be either natural or arbitrary. They are natural if the association of the symbol with the object designated is derived from the nature of the object itself. Conversely, those symbols which we call arbitrary have in their very nature nothing in common with the object designated. . . . The fine arts, under which we generally understand poetry and rhetoric, express objects by means of arbitrary symbols, through audible tones and words.

The subject matter of the fine arts is, according to Mendelssohn, more limited than that of belles-lettres (*schöne Wissenschaften*). Its symbols affect either the sense of hearing or that of sight. Natural symbols, which appeal to the sense of sight, are either consecutive or simultaneous (coexistent) and express beauty either through motion or through form. The former is the case in the art of dancing, the latter in those arts which employ lines and figures. Painting employs surfaces; sculpture and architecture employ bodies. Since the painter and the sculptor express beauties as they exist motionless side by side, they must choose that moment which serves their aims to best advantage.

It is perhaps significant that little of Mendelssohn's theory and classification of the arts is actually new or original. Du Bos, as we have seen, also defines aesthetic symbols as natural and arbitrary, or artificial, and a number of other critics not touched on in this brief survey, e.g., Diderot, Shaftesbury, or de Piles, were at least as advanced in their approach to the *Laocoön* problem as was Mendelssohn. Despite these shortcomings, if they can be termed that, Mendelssohn represents the "supreme moment in a stage of transition," as one critic aptly says:

> He came nearer than his predecessors—even Diderot—to a systematic separation of the arts on the basis of their symbols of expression. . . . moreover, he suggested the very example with which Lessing begins his discussion, and at the same time first called Lessing's attention to the epoch-making work in which these examples were used in support of an opinion with which Lessing could take issue. [Howard, *Laokoon*]

The work with which Lessing takes issue in his *Laocoön* is the *Thoughts on the Imitation of Greek Works in Painting and Sculpture* (1755) by Joachim Winckelmann. This disciple of Greek beauty and simplicity in art was instrumental in leading the arts out of the artificialities of baroque and rococo into which they had fallen in the seventeenth and eighteenth centuries. However, he was at the same time as one-sided in his doctrine as any of his predecessors had been. Most of his observations on art were based on Greek statuary that he had seen himself. Logically they should have been applied to the other arts with extreme caution, but this was unfortunately not the case. Winckelmann tended to ignore the differences between painting and sculpture. Beauty was beauty of form, especially of human form, and of contour; the all-important aspects of pictorial art, color and light, were neglected in his eagerness to apply the laws of sculpture to painting and poetry as well. For these arts, he says, are merely different ways of expressing the same thing. And as to their limits, he explains, "It does not seem contradictory that painting should have as wide boundaries as poetry, and that consequently it ought to be possible for the painter to follow the poet, just as music is able to do this."

It is against this claim of inherent similarity among the arts as well as against the now deeply rooted tradition of granting painting the first place among them that Lessing speaks out in his *Laocoön*. Each of the arts is subject to its own laws, and if one art is actually superior to the others, then it is not painting, but poetry with its infinitely wider domain.

> *Edward Allen McCormick, in an introduction to* Laocoön: An Essay on the Limits of Painting and Poetry *by Gotthold Ephraim Lessing, translated by Edward Allen McCormick,*

1962. Reprint by The Johns Hopkins University Press, 1984, pp. ix-xxviii.

G. Giovannini

[*In the following essay, which was first presented as a lecture at a meeting of the Modern Language Association of America in 1948, Giovannini surveys critical studies that measure the parallelism between the plastic arts and literature.*]

Determining a fruitful method for the study of literature in its relation to the other fine arts depends on the affinities general theory has discovered among the arts, and on how readily the affinities can be concretely illustrated. From ancient times there has been much speculation about the harmony of the arts, an urgency to reduce them to a simple system of common qualities, ends, or principles governing the making of art objects, which in turn will differentiate the fine arts from nature and from the practical arts. But much of the speculation has not been utilized for the concrete and analytical comparison of art objects different in kind. The failure may in part be ascribed to the slow development, especially in literary study, of a method for the concrete and close analysis of an art object in terms of its own specific context. Literary study has strongly tended to detail the historical context, probably more so than studies in the other arts where concrete analysis, like Wölfflin's in his *Principles of Art History*, of structural features of the art object as such is not exceptional. The failure, however, may also be due to the highly abstract nature of the speculation on the harmony of the arts, to the kind of vagueness found, for instance, in a passage in Cicero's *Pro Archia* (I.2) which became a commonplace in discussions of harmony: "Indeed, the subtle bond of a mutual relationship links together all arts which have any bearing upon the common life of mankind." By Cicero's generalization presumably only some arts are bound by a relationship to life; but when one considers what human activities are not so bound, the generalization becomes so sweeping as to be meaningless.

Similar vagueness is found in comparisons drawn among some of the arts. Simonides' popular saying that painting is silent poetry and poetry a speaking picture is a typical statement of affinity which cloaks the abstract with metaphor and often minimizes the large question of differences and their relevance to the differences in the effects produced by like elements in two arts. In his commentary on Simonides' epitome ["On the Fame of the Athenians," *Moralia*], Plutarch, for example, while recognizing the differences in material (words and colors) and in the manner of imitation (painting by means of design depicting an action as if now happening and poetry narrating it as having happened), minimizes the differences and suggests a vague identity of purpose in the two arts, namely, vividness in the imitation—an affective quality which, if at all analyzable, refers more to the descriptive parts of poetic and historical narrative than to narrative as such. The quality does not account for the putative affinity between painting and poetry in its generic sense, and the analysis of color words in poems and coloring in painting would very likely establish only an incidental relationship between particular poems and paintings. Moreover, vividness in painting is limited to the quality of the colors and the light and shadows, and of their disposition—matters which can be perceived and measured with a degree of exactness. But in literary art the term tends to imply an aggregate of elements and becomes, with reference to the affinity between the two arts, a confusing metaphor. The confusion can be illustrated from Dryden's *A Parallel of Poetry and Painting,* which in one place details the affinity mentioned by Plutarch and concludes by equating "strong and glowing colours" with "bold metaphors." But Dryden equates much more: the outline of the fable in epic and dramatic poems is, like the naked lines in paintings, dressed up by colors, which are "The words, the expressions, the tropes and figures, the versification, and all the other elegancies of sound, as cadences, turns of words upon the thought, and many other things," among them special tropes and figures functioning like lights and shadows in painting "to lessen or greaten anything." In this theory coloring is everything but the outline of the fable, and for the practical purpose of comparing objects from the two arts the generalization is sterile. The "secret friendship," as it was sometimes called, between the two arts is lost in a complex of elements, some of them referring to the relationship between poetry and music and the rest to purely literary phenomena.

The theory of harmony grounded in the classical doctrine of the arts as modes of representation—the most enduring of the theories, often banished from modern speculation only to creep back into discussions of the arts as modes of expression or of imagination—has not been fully exploited theoretically, nor implemented for the practical end of the analysis of art objects different in kind. The development in Aristotelian terms of a methodology for the synoptic analysis of the arts has been embarrassed by controversies over the meaning of imitation in the *Poetics,* and by the difficulty of fitting architecture, modern music, and abstract painting and sculpture into the basic meaning of imitation as some kind of likeness, or of a reordering of elements of reality into a structure immediately perceptible as ontologically different from the reality itself. The development since the Renaissance has largely been un-Aristotelian; for while in Aristotle the emphasis falls heavily on the reordering itself as the formal cause of the imitative arts—Aristotle in some places saying that the order of art need not be, and in other places, must not be the order of reality—in modern theory emphasis has fallen on the reality imitated and the values, primarily ethical or social, deriving from the reality, informing all the arts, and reducing them to modes of experiencing broadly social phenomena. It may very well be that the communal material of the arts, as Cicero implies and John Dewey thinks [in *Art as Experience*], is human and social; that all the arts, as the neoclassicists and romantics maintained, are the image of man and nature; or that they are ways of knowing reality—in the words of Taine "une sorte de philosophie devenue sensible" [*Histoire de la littérature anglaise*]. But such large generalizations yield little that can be concretely used for a close comparative analysis of the fine arts, especially of their formal elements. They raise the problem of the socio-ideological origins of art, and without solving it they tempt the speculator to assume

there are general laws governing the production of the arts as organisms of a culture. But conditions of time and milieu are so complex in a given period as to make generic laws of origin and function of dubious value. Baroque art, for example, has been analyzed as the spirit and the instrument of the Counter-Reformation, but the term has been also applied to a great deal of Protestant art.

In a survey of the problem of the interrelations of the arts, Paul Maury [in his *Arts et littérature comparés*], while warning against the danger of vague and facile analogizing which ignores the vast differences in the formal aspects of the several arts, overlooks the differences and seeks for a harmony in the social and ideological, and suggests the need for an encyclopedic parallel history of a common and socio-ideological origin of the arts. But such a parallel history, besides duplicating the work of social history and the history of ideas, would be premature; for though a milieu is the inescapable condition in which the artist works, there is no established principle universally applicable in determining the coextension and intimate connection of the fine arts with social phenomena. Maury voices the popular view that to ignore their social aspects is to falsify the arts. This may be true of some arts, architecture, for example; or of some types of literary art like the realistic novel. But there are worse falsifications, and the familiar one of ignoring the formal aspects and their relation to meaning within the context of the art object is suggested in the comparative method Maury proposes, which would very likely utilize the arts merely as documents illustrative of social phenomena, or crudely lump them together as symbols of a time-spirit.

Reducing the arts to a sign of some kind of reality external or internal to the artist is a simplification subjecting the arts to a confusion with reality itself, making them the vehicles of life-experiences different only in degree of refinement and intensity from actual experiences. The concept of harmony based on the rapport of the arts with reality is a philosophical concept which raises the question of the truth-value of art objects and glosses over the more important matter clearly seen by Aristotle that all sorts of distortions and errors are allowable to satisfy the demands of artistic design. To Aristotle there is no absolute necessity that a painted stag have horns; a stag without horns can be justified by the artistic design. The fine arts, as distinguished from truth-finding activities, are one in their freedom from the obligation to reality which governs science, history, and philosophy. From the history of the fine arts it appears that reality is often merely a suggestion for design. "The ballet-girl," says Degas, "is merely a pretext for the design," and Marc Chagall explains the headless milkmaid in one of his paintings by a reference to the demands of design: " . . . it occurred to me to separate her head from her body because I found that I needed an empty space in that particular place."

To say that the arts have design which may have only a tenuous relation to reality is rather obvious, but the statement bears repetition to suggest the possibility that just as design determines the kind of shape which reality takes in art, so also design may determine meaning within the context (interrelational meaning), which is not necessarily the meaning we normally attach to a reality (extrarelational). When, for example, the Inquisition censured Veronese's painting "The Feast in the House of Simon" for the inclusion of a dwarf, parrot, dog, and "similar buffoonery," it did not see that these figures, as Veronese tried to explain during the cross-examination, have an ornamental signification appropriate to the design of a magnificent feast in a magnificent household. The accommodation of meaning to the design, and the possible distortion of meaning by the design, are seen in Wordsworth, who in his early poetry makes contradictory or apparently contradictory statements about the child's responses to nature. In *Tintern Abbey* the child is described as enjoying nature in a purely sensuous, thoughtless way, with "no need of a remoter charm, By thought supplied, nor any interest Unborrowed from the eye." In *The Prelude,* however, the child experiences a sensuous pleasure qualified by thought emerging from the "giddy bliss" before nature: there are "Gleams like the flashing of a shield." The discrepancy can be explained by the character of the design in each poem. In the first three paragraphs of *Tintern Abbey* the design centers the attention so exclusively on the distinctive features of maturity that when the child appears in paragraph four a sharp contrast is artistically necessary. In *The Prelude* the design is a shifting back and forth among the various levels of experience, causing meanings to overlap; and accordingly, the child's experience is not wholly thoughtless, but foreshadows maturity. It may of course be said that meaning also determines the design; but the design once adopted, it imposes the obligation to carry it through, so that there is always the possibility of a modification of the meaning originally intended (whatever that was) to the demands of structural consistency.

The rapport of the arts with reality is delicate and complex; and it is doubtful that the problem of the harmony of the arts can be solved by considering them signs of reality. Reality varies so much from art to art and from art object to art object that a classification according to subject matter appears impractical, and the reduction of subject matter to a common feature—social, ideological, etc.—appears vague and unconvincing, as, for example, in the work of Spengler. A theory of harmony which moves in the direction of abstracting the extrarelational, i.e., of considering reality and its meaning as part of a structure outside the art object, seems to be dealing with the irrelevant. This is not to say that the extrarelational is unimportant, or that, as Clive Bell contends [in his *Since Cézanne*], the arts are one in that they are singularly and absolutely detached from life, but to suggest that the extrarelational becomes relevant when the direction is reversed and reality and its meaning are seen as interrelational, i.e., as elements informing the total structure of the art object itself.

Provision for both the interrelational and extrarelational is made in some modern speculations on harmony, like those of [Charles Morris, "Aesthetics and the Theory of Signs (*Journal of Unified Science,* 1939) and Etienne Souriau, *La correspondance des arts*], and it is suggested by Aristotle. The *Poetics* does not make imitation, in its basic sense of a rapport with reality, coextensive with all the fine arts; only some kinds of music, for example, are imitative. In Aristotle the emphasis falls so heavily on the

art object as ontologically distinct from the reality imitated that the implication is twofold: (1) that though in the imitative arts the design has a dual aspect—it is a sign of itself and a sign of a reality outside itself—it is the design as such which distinguishes them, for in one place the *Poetics* alludes to a common experience: when the object painted is unknown to the beholder, the painting still pleases for its workmanship, color, technique; and (2) that the non-imitative arts, some kinds of music and presumably architecture, have design in common with the imitative arts. This theory provides for a harmony of all the arts from the highly abstract to the highly imitative. In this theory, as in Morris's theory of aesthetic signs, art objects are things-in-themselves with a value immanent in the formal organization. Souriau, who develops this theory and cogently reasons that even in the imitative arts the pleasure derives from the design and not from the representational element, suggests that what is called content and its meaning be studied contextually as elements affecting the design, the study of harmony then becoming the study of formal elements in themselves and as expressive of interrelational meaning.

. . . . .

While the theory of harmony based on design is generally adequate and has the virtue of keeping the attention on the structure of the art objects compared, it has not detailed the comparable elements of design in the various arts, nor clarified how, for example, the principle of unity and diversity operates in the various arts with varying degrees of complexity. The need for clarification and detail on a theoretical level is apparent from comparative studies of literature and the other arts. What is described as a common element in two art objects is likely to be an element actually given (i.e., perceptible to sense) in one object and objectively analyzable in it, and not given in the other but merely suggested in the affective response and applicable to the object only by way of metaphor. As will be clear from the examples which now follow, even though comparative analysis of art objects different in kind lacks a detailed theory of comparable elements to guide it, the method can be very much improved by more awareness of what is relevant and analyzable and by a recognition of the limitations to which comparative analysis is subject.

The element of time is not only common to literature and music; in recent speculation—that of Souriau, F. E. Halliday, John Peale Bishop—it is claimed as common to the spatial arts as well and advanced as a valid basis for a parallelism between the verbal and visual arts. Architecture and a free-standing statue cannot be grasped as a whole in one glance: we must move around a statue and in and around a building before the whole is apprehended. Moreover, three dimensional art changes with changes in light and seasonal changes. In painting, so Bishop contends, perspective or distance is the equivalent of time. But this is the vaguest sort of parallelism. For a literary object unfolds in time in a precise manner by a sequence of beginning, middle, and end; it is apprehended in terms of this sequence, which governs the structure of the part as well as the whole and permits verification of change and progression of meaning and rhythmical structure as data of a temporal form. The fact that we move around a statue or follow the line of perspective in painting may induce a sense of change and progression, but only as a by-product of the act of perception. In literary art the sense of time is controlled by elements analyzable as temporal within the object.

Lessing's careful distinction between temporal and spatial forms, and the corresponding difference in the effect produced by different internal structural relations, have been ignored in some recent scholarship on comparable elements—scholarship apparently influenced by the concept and the metaphorical language of Spengler's time-space logic. Bishop claims that since space (as well as time) is a deeply rooted concept of the mind, it inevitably informs poetic structure, and cites *Anthony and Cleopatra* and the poetry of T. S. Eliot in illustration, forgetting that the spatial verbally pictured informs some poetic structures and not others, and that the spatial is not (excepting in figure-poems) a thing given as in painting, but suggested by symbols ordered temporally. The method Bishop suggests, a method based on the notion of time and space as comparable or quasi-identical, has been applied to the poetry of Keats by Robert Stallman [in his "Keats the Apollinian," *University of Toronto Quarterly,* (1947)] and to modernistic verse and prose fiction by Joseph Frank [in his "Spatial Forms in Modern Literature," *Sewanee Review,* (1945)]. In Stallman's analysis, the *Ode on a Grecian Urn* is plastic art and the Chapman sonnet pictorial art spatially conceived. What is analyzed, however, in these and other poems of Keats, is not the technique of the visual arts verbally imitated, but a concept of timelessness (pure-present time, it is called) which is supposed to be a denial of time and a predication of space. Aside from the question whether this concept is actually a part of the meaning structure of Keats' poetry, the method seems to encourage vagary and confusion. The metaphorical is rendered metaphorically; for example, the metaphors of darkness in Keats are predications of space and denials of time. While the method does successfully uncover in Keats' poetry a strong visual sense and a static quality as of objects resting in space, it confuses abstracted content with technique, so that it seems logical to assert that, since we do visualize the Grecian Urn, the art of the poem is plastic. But of course spatial visualization may be effected by a conventional descriptive technique which bears no resemblance to the technique of plastic art.

A similar confusion in method appears in Joseph Frank's analysis of the work of Joyce, Pound, Eliot and other writers as spatial form, so called because the literary object, *The Waste Land,* for example, frees itself from the limitations of the temporal sequence governing conventional literary art by in one place juxtaposing fragments temporally or logically belonging in another place. Though the fragments follow one another in time, their meaning does not depend on their temporal relation in the sequence, but on the "simultaneous perception in space of word-groups which, when read consecutively in time, have no comprehensible relation to one another." The discontinuous sequences are supposed to effect the apprehension of the whole in a moment of time, of "pure time," which is not time at all and therefore must be space. The logic is ques-

tionable. But what is more important, the method confuses the final operation of perception fusing disparate fragments into a whole with a technique which is spatial only in the sense that the fragments are found in different places. The method does not take into account the fact that the whole finally visualized is of a certain kind and has a certain kind of meaning because it has been built up and controlled by a temporal sequence, however much broken. Moreover, it is not an imitation of spatial art which explains the apparently instantaneous fusing of fragments in *The Waste Land,* but a technique of concentration and rapid shift without transitions, a technique which is probably a development of elements within a literary tradition.

The attempt in these studies to discover comparable elements is unconvincing because the method is insufficiently grounded in what is relevant and analyzable. Irrelevancies have plagued comparative studies of the arts: verse-dialogue is orchestration in poetry; eye rhyme is evidence of plastic art in poetry; the blue in Keats' poetry is a Reynolds blue, etc. This kind of vagary is a possible indication that comparative analysis has not advanced much since Spence's *Polymetis* and the arbitrary analogizing like that of Haydon, who described the Elgin marbles as "essentially Shakesperian" [*Lectures on Painting and Design*]. In the studies of Manwaring, Hussey, Binyon, Tinker, and Larrabee, terms like chiaroscuro, Claudian, sculpturesque, high coloring, when applied to literary art are largely emptied of their technical significance in the visual arts and are often confined to description of general similarity in content [E. W. Manwaring, *Italian Landscape in Eighteenth Century England,* Christopher Hussey, *The Picturesque;* Laurence Binyon, *Landscape in English Art and Poetry;* C. B. Tinker, *Painter and Poet;* S. A. Larrabee, *English Bards and Grecian Marbles*]. While the assimilation of the terminology of the visual arts is theoretically justified, in practice the terminology, which has a precise sense in the visual arts, has paradoxically resulted in impressionism and inconsistency. A passage in *Windsor Forest,* for example, is classified by Manwaring as close to the Claudian and therefore the picturesque; the same passage is classified by Hussey as generalized description, having "no visualization," "no trees worthy the name, but saplings of Raphaelite origin," though it is not clear why the Raphaelite is non-visual, for the Claudian in landscape poetry is elsewhere so loosely applied as to make any passage with a few details visual and picturesque.

These studies are admirable for their wealth of historical information on the confusion of the literary and visual arts, and for their illustration of the parallel development of a relish for detail in poetry, the novel, and painting. But the parallel amounts to little more than the fact that some painting and poetry relished details of nature ignored by neo-classic art, or that novelists copied the scenery of Claude's paintings. In these and other studies, like those of Chew, Fairchild, and Praz, when there is a venturing beyond the fact of a communal subject matter into comparable elements of design, the problem of how verbal imagery and rhythmical patterns can overcome the limitations of a temporal form to suggest pictorial or sculptural effects is ignored [Samuel C. Chew, *The Virtues Reconciled: An*

Iconographic Study; A. H. R. Fairchild, *Shakespeare and the Arts of Design;* Mario Praz, *Studies in Seventeenth-Century Imagery*]. It is probably the neglect of this problem which is the cause of the confusion of a similar effect produced by similar subject matter in art objects different in kind with some assumed similarity in the design. Larrabee, for example, attributes to poems in some way involving sculpture in content a sculptural quality which upon analysis appears to be a generic and literary quality of clarity of expression. Without a detailed analysis of compositional patterns, terms like sculptural, statuesque, linear, will not explain how the clarity of "sculpture-poems" is distinctive, but merely symbolize an affective response which, if left unchecked, will entangle itself in irrelevancies.

One of the important tasks of the analyst of comparable elements in literature and the other arts is to distinguish between what is actually given and is an affinity, and what is not given but suggested; and further, to distinguish between what is suggested by way of analogy and is analyzable, and what is the by-product of perception, or of a mood, and is irrelevant. Rhythm, for example, is given in both literary and musical art as movement and ordered sound; as movement simply it is also given in the dance, but only suggested in the other arts. The problem of distinguishing may seem complicated; for at times what is suggested is so strongly suggested as to appear given. Melody, with which the verbal arts have been associated from antiquity, is, for example, strongly suggested in poetry. But though verse may be so read as to describe a melodic line, the "melody" is indefinite; and the task of the analyst remains the same—in this instance to distinguish between the sound structure given in the words and what in the structure suggests a melodic patterning comparable to musical tune.

What is needed is not a new method for the study of comparable elements, but a recognition and development of distinctions such as these, which will keep comparative study from deteriorating into a description of unanalyzed or unanalyzable affective states. There are already a variety of methods, especially in the German scholarship described by Wais and examined critically by Wellek [Kurt Wais, *Symbiose der Künste;* René Wellek, "The Parallelism between Literature and the Arts," *The English Institute Annual 1941*]. A new method is possible only after theory has clarified and particularized generalizations about a community of the arts, and this it has not done. When theory has attempted particularization of the components of design (harmony, proportion, contrast, balance, rhythm, complexity, integration), they are discovered to be synonyms of the generic principle of similarity in dissimilarity. What is needed is more detailed comparative analysis grounded on the fact that the extensive differences in the materials used (words, stone, pigments, etc.) impose on each art a complexity peculiar to it and outside the area of affinity. It is interesting to note that very detailed analyses, like Webster's parallel of Greek art and literature [*Greek Art and Literature, 530-400 B.C.*] and Neider's of Keats' *Ode to A Nightingale* and the andante movement of Brahms' First Symphony [*Brahms and Keats: a Parallel*] indicate that the area of analyzable affin-

ity is relatively small. Webster shows that Greek literature, plastic art, and vase-painting have in common a few simple devices effecting a transition among parts; his study suggests that the complexity of the whole is beyond the scope of comparative analysis and analyzable only in terms of its own art. Similarly, the embryonic Pindaric form Neider by comparative analysis uncovers in Keats' ode and Brahms' andante is abstracted form which contextually loses its homologous character and falls outside the area of affinity.

Leland Schubert, in his extensive study of fine-art devices in Hawthorne's fiction [*Hawthorne the Artist*], tries to enlarge the area on the psychological theory that, however dissimilar the arts are objectively considered, they are one in the similar or identical impact they produce on the imagination; and so it is possible to speak, he argues, of sculptural plasticity, architectural mass, etc., in Hawthorne's prose. But aside from the question of the soundness of his theory and the fanciful comparisons which the method encourages (for example, the comparison of *Dr. Heidegger's Experiment* with Ravel's *Bolero*), it is again interesting to note that the more his analysis enters into the structure of the literary object, the more the area of affinity becomes restricted and the terms of comparison metaphorical. Plasticity, for example, becomes descriptive, not of a quality of the prose structure as such, but of the contents of the image.

It appears from these studies that comparative analysis is limited: the object in its complexity escapes from exact parallelism into the heritage of its own art with its own conventions and techniques. Since the literary object has a structure in part determined by literary conventions, a distinction should be made between what is part of a literary heritage and what is not and may be accounted for by reference to the heritage of another art. Henry James' *The Ambassadors* probably owes much to impressionistic painting, and a parallel is appropriate. But the wonderfully rich description of surfaces in the novel is obviously more than a picture; unlike a painting it is not self-contained. It develops the hero's intelligence and is part of a complexity which, in its successful coordination of the physical and psychological, escapes parallelism and uses a technique developed within the traditions of the novel.

The failure to make this distinction leads to the kind of unconvincing comparison in which what has an adequate explanation from a literary point of view is subjected to elaborate analysis in terms of another art. For instance, Bernard Fehr in his studies of neo-classic and baroque art ["The Antagonism of Forms in the Eighteenth Century," *English Studies,* 1936] tries to account for the structural features of a set of couplets from Pope in terms of Palladian architecture and describes one line which reads, "Paints, as you plant, and as you work, designs," as "a symmetrical one-line arrangement of Euclidean gracefulness: two outposts in the same garb (*paints* and *designs*) at either end, supported each towards the middle by two links of equal length and of the same kind (*as you plant,* and *as you work*) knocking from opposite sides against a peg (*and*) which seems to have been fixed there to mark the exact middle." Since the line from Pope has a simple and adequate explanation in literary terms as an arrangement of elements into a chiasmus, the elaborate architectural analogy seems superfluous.

The distinction between what is explainable in literary terms and what is better explained in terms of another art suggests a systematic and close analysis by which elements verifiable as affinities can be isolated, and then examined within the organization of the total structure of the literary object. The isolation of affinities may furnish material making more precise the nature of the relationships between literature and the other fine arts; and by the integration of affinities the literary object will not be lost sight of. The effort at close analysis in the scholarship summarily discussed in this paper is not always discriminating, but the examples cited in illustration of its limitations are not intended to discredit this scholarship; for only by such effort can general theory be furnished with empirical data for the formulation of workable definitions of the relations of literature to the other fine arts. A more soundly grounded theory of what is relevant is needed to answer the objection [registered by Jean-Paul Sartre in his "What is Writing?" *Partisan Review,* XV, 10 (Jan. 1948)] that parallelisms among the arts are a fiction and "to 'talk literature' in the argot of the painter" a current fashion.

> *G. Giovannini, "Method in the Study of Literature in Its Relation to the Other Fine Arts,"* in The Journal of Aesthetics and Art Criticism, *Vol. VIII, No. 3, March, 1950, pp. 185-95.*

René Wellek

[*Wellek is an Austrian-born American critic and essayist who is best known for his important critical works,* Theory of Literature *(with Austin Warren, 1949) and* A History of Modern Criticism *(1955, 1966). Wellek's critical theory differentiates between an "intrinsic" and "extrinsic" approach to critical analysis and emphasizes the necessity of viewing a work of art as an entity in and of itself rather than as the result of properties exterior to the work, such as the social or cultural environment in which it is created. In the following essay, which was presented as a lecture at the English Institute's annual meeting at Columbia University in 1941, Wellek offers an overview of comparisons between literature and the plastic arts and argues that such comparisons must be based on analyses of the structures of artifacts rather than such subjective criteria as the emotional impact of the works on their audiences.*]

The title of my address, "the parallelism between literature and the arts," may sound, I fear, somewhat cryptic and vague. I chose it because I could not think of a simple title which would clearly indicate my problem: what use is there, for the study of literature, in the comparisons and parallels drawn between literature and the arts? Which of these methods are legitimate and have led to illuminating results? Are we justified in assuming a unitary time-spirit which pervades all the arts of a given period and makes parallels between the arts not only possible but also necessary? These are large questions, and I should like to define my problem even more narrowly, as I . . . don't want to indulge in too general aesthetic speculations or theories belonging properly to a philosophy of history.

I am thus not concerned with the question of the manifold relationships between the arts. There is no particular theoretical problem in the fact that the arts are in constant interrelationship, as are all human activities. Literature has sometimes drawn inspiration from paintings or pieces of sculpture or music. Other works of art have become the theme of poetry just as any other piece or section of reality. In surveying the history of English poetry alone we need only to think of the tapestries and pageants which seem to have inspired Spenser, the paintings of Claude Lorrain and Salvatore Rosa which influenced eighteenth-century landscape poetry, or recall Keats's "Ode on a Grecian Urn". . . . I need not stress the fact that literature can become the theme of painting or that music, especially vocal and program music, has drawn on literary inspiration, just as literature, especially the lyric, has coöperated closely with music. There is an increasing number of studies of medieval carols or Elizabethan lyrics which stress the close association with the musical setting, and in art history a whole group of scholars (Erwin Panofsky, Fritz Saxl, and others) has grown up who study the conceptual and symbolic meanings of works of art and thus frequently also their literary relations and inspirations. . . .

I can only touch briefly on one problem: the question of the confusion of the arts. This is the topic of Lessing's *Laokoön and Irving Babbitt's New Laokoön:* whether one art should or should not try to achieve the effects of another art—whether poetry, for example, can make visual descriptions or achieve musical sound effects. As a matter of history the arts have tried to borrow effects from each other, and the critical question whether they are always successful or whether that success is desirable may be left unanswered today.

What I want to discuss is not a new and esoteric question. It dates back to antiquity. Simonides, as reported by Plutarch [in his *On the Fame of the Athenians*], was the originator of the phrase "painting is mute poetry and poetry speaking painting." In the eighteenth century innumerable comparisons were made between the composition of Spenser's *Faerie Queene* and the glorious disorder of a Gothic cathedral. Then August Wilhelm Schlegel stressed the sculpturesque qualities of classical literature and the pictorial qualities of modern romantic poetry [in his "Vorlesungen über schöne Litteratur und Kunst, Erster Teil (1801-2), Die Kunstlehre," in *Deutsche Literaturdenkmale des 18. und 19. Jahrhunderts,* ed. by B. Seuffert]. To Schelling is usually ascribed the saying that "architecture is frozen music" [*Vorlesungen über Philosophie der Kunst,* published in *Sämtliche Werke*]. These parallels became more and more concrete and widespread in the nineteenth century; for instance, the German dramatist Otto Ludwig [in his "Über Shakespeares Komposition," in his *Werke,* ed. by A. Stern] drew an elaborate comparison between a sonata and a Shakespearean drama. These analogies have found more and more favor also with academic and analytical scholars. Early in this century the well-known German art historian August Schmarsow did much to introduce the term "rhythm" into architecture, and he even drew up an amusing scheme of an alcaic verse pattern for which he claimed decorative value [in his *Kompositionsgesetze in der Kunst des Mittelalters*].

In 1915 the famous Swiss art historian, Heinrich Wölfflin, published his *Principles of Art History,* a book which was destined to influence literary history profoundly. Wölfflin tries to distinguish between Renaissance and baroque art on purely structural grounds. He constructed a scheme of contraries which are applicable to any kind of picture or piece of sculpture or architecture in the period. Renaissance art, he showed, is "linear," while baroque art is "pictorial." "Linear" suggests that the outlines of figures or objects are drawn clearly, while "pictorial" means that light and color blur the outlines of objects and are the principles of composition. Renaissance painting uses a "closed" form, a symmetrical, balanced grouping of figures or surfaces while baroque prefers an "open" form: an unsymmetrical composition which puts emphasis on a corner of a picture rather than on its center or points beyond the frame of the picture. Renaissance pictures are "flat" or, at least, composed on different recessive planes, while baroque pictures are "deep" or seem to lead the eye into a distant and indistinct background. Two further such contraries are developed in detail and it is argued that these principles of composition can be found in all art and must be found always in this combination and this temporal sequence. Wölfflin's brilliant formal analyses of pictures soon excited the envy and competition of literary historians. In 1916 Professor Oskar Walzel, fresh from the reading of Wölfflin's *Principles of Art History,* attempted to transfer to literature the categories established by Wölfflin's contrast between Renaissance and baroque art. Walzel took one of these pairs of contraries, the "closed" and "open" form, and applied it to Shakespeare [in his "Shakespeares dramatische Baukunst," in *Jahrbuch der Shakespearegesellschaft,* LII (1916)]. Studying the composition of Shakespeare's plays he came to the conclusion that Shakespeare belongs to the baroque, as his plays are not built in the symmetrical manner found by Wölfflin in Renaissance pictures. The number of minor characters, their unsymmetrical grouping, the varying emphasis on different acts of the play—all these characteristics are supposed to show that Shakespeare's technique is the same as that of baroque art, while Corneille or Racine who composed their tragedies around one central figure and distributed the emphasis among the acts according to an Aristotelian pattern, belong to the Renaissance type. Thus, on the basis of a single criterion, transferred from painting to drama, Shakespeare and Racine exchanged places. Actually we have learned only what we knew long before, that is, that Shakespeare violated the unities. But it would be unjust to criticize Oskar Walzel too severely; he himself realized the limitations of the method and in his little book on *Wechselseitige Erhellung der Künste* (1917) puts its claims very cautiously and modestly.

But these restraints were thrown to the winds by Oswald Spengler, who was then writing his amazing work of analogizing ingenuity, *The Decline of the West* (1918). Most scholars today profess to ignore Spengler, and there is no necessity to warn against his extravagances. But one should not underrate his enormous direct and especially indirect influence on the effort to set up analogies among the arts. He revived and deeply impressed on recent scholars the concept of organic, necessary evolution from flowering to decay and erected into a dogma the idea that a period is a closed organic whole. He claims [in *Der Untergang des Abendlandes,* 1923] I, 151. that it is possible from the scattered details of ornaments, architecture, writing, or from scattered data of a political, economic, and religious nature to reconstruct the history of whole centuries or to divine from details of the artistic forms the contemporary constitution of a state and from the mathematics of a time to draw conclusions as to economic conditions. Everything in Spengler thus parallels everything. Where there is a discrepancy, Spengler knows how to resolve it into some higher whole. The analogizing between the arts breaks out into a veritable riot of metaphors. Spengler speaks, for example, of the "visible chamber music of the bent furniture, the mirror rooms, pastorals and porcelain groups of the eighteenth century," he mentions the "Titian style of the madrigal," and refers to the "*allegro feroce* of Franz Hals and the *andante con moto* of Van Dyck," and he elaborately compares Rembrandt to the music of his times. In Rembrandt he finds a "*basso continuo* of the costume, above which play the *motifs* of the head." All this may be very ingenious and amusing, but at closer inspection it amounts to little more than assertions that certain moods induced by a picture suggest the mood of some musical composition, which, to support the theory, must be contemporary. In isolation this is a harmless game, but Spengler's method, prepared as it was by suggestions in Schlegel and others, soon found its scholarly glorification in "Geistesgeschichte," a large-scale movement in German scholarship of the last twenty years. The term is sometimes used as referring to any type of "intellectual history," and thus in its broader sense it remains outside our discussion. But usually, to quote one of its exponents, "Geistesgeschichte" aims to "reconstruct the spirit of a time from the different objectivations of an age—from its religion down to its costumes. We look for the totality behind the objects and explain all facts by this spirit of the time" [M. W. Eppelsheimer, "Das Renaissance-Problem," in *Deutsche Vierteljahrschrift für Literaturwissenschaft und Geistesgeschichte*], Thus a universal analogizing between the arts is at the very center of the method which has stimulated a veritable flood of writings on the "Gothic" man, the spirit of the baroque, and so forth. Most relevant to our purpose are the attempts to transfer terms originally defined in art history to the history of literature. Today periods in the history of literature, instead of being, as they used to be, either political concepts transferred to literature or literary terms and slogans, have come more and more under the spell of the divisions in art history.

The term "baroque" is the most obvious case in point. Fritz Strich, Arthur Hübscher, and Herbert Cysarz have interpreted German seventeenth-century literature in terms of the baroque in the fine arts, and the method has been applied also to the English seventeenth century. There is a whole book by Paul Meissner called *Die geisteswissenschaftlichen Grundlagen des englischen Literaturbarocks* (1934), which seems to me, in spite of its

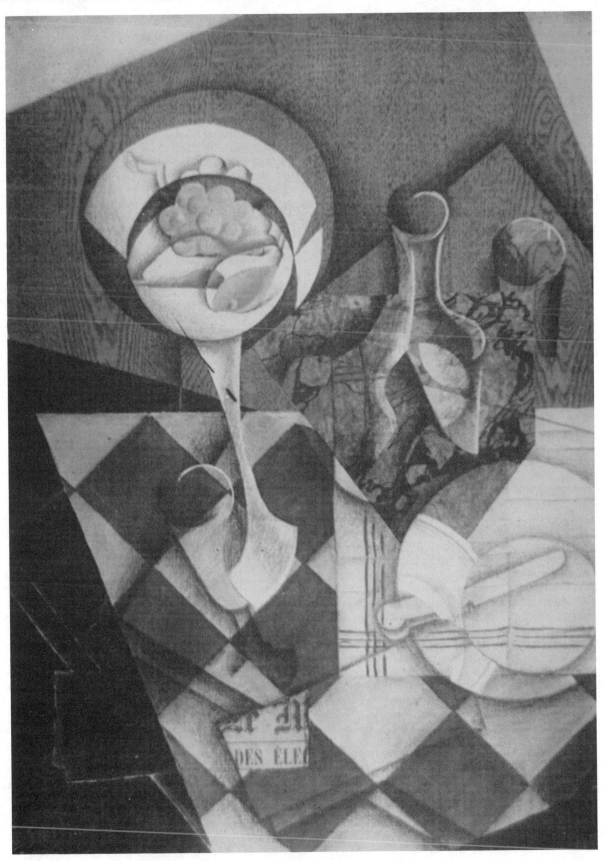

Juan Gris, Still Life with Fruit Dish, *oil and* papier collé *on canvas, 1914.*

learning, the *reductio ad absurdum* of the method. Meissner defines the baroque as a conflict of antithetic tendencies and pursues this formula for the "time-spirit" relentlessly through all human activities from technology to exploration, from traveling to religion. All the wealth of materials is nicely ordered into categories such as expansion and concentration, macrocosmos and microcosmos, sin and salvation, faith and reason, absolutism and democracy, "atectonics" and "tectonics." A method of universal analogizing arrives at the triumphant conclusion that the baroque age showed conflict, contradiction, and tension throughout its manifestations. There were active men interested in conquering nature and praising war, there were passionate collectors, travelers, adventurers; but there were also contemplative men who sought out solitude or founded secret societies. Some people were fascinated by the new astronomy, while others analyzed personal states of mind like the diarists or drew the individual features of men like the painters of portraits. There were those believing in the divine right of kings and others believing in an equalitarian democracy. Everything exemplifies, thus, the principle either of concentration or of expansion. If you want concentration in literature, you are presented with the plain style of prose stimulated by the Royal Society after the Restoration. If you want expansion, you are shown the long sentences of Milton or Sir Thomas Browne. Mr. Meissner never stops to ask whether the very same scheme of contraries could not be extracted from any other age. Nor does he, of course, raise the question whether we could not impose a completely different scheme of contraries on the seventeenth century and even on exactly the same quotations culled from his wide reading.

Similarly Ludwig Pfandl, in his very learned and informative *Geschichte der spanischen Nationalliteratur in ihrer Blütezeit* (1929), which is also available in a Spanish translation, gave us a slightly varied formula for the baroque in Spain. It is supposed to show how the innate Spanish dualism of realism and idealism was during the baroque age "expanded and exaggerated" in an antithesis of naturalism and illusionism. Under these categories a varied scheme of subdivisions of symbolism, the cult of genius, the humanization of the supernatural, and so forth, marshals a wealth of information which, however, frequently amounts to no more than telling us that there were nuns and prostitutes, beggars and rich men, in seventeenth-century Spain; that some people danced the indecent *zarabanda*, while others (or the same) went to masses, that some professed the creed of Epicurus, while others were pessimistic and melancholy, had headaches (*jaqueca*), and thought of death.

The phrase "the baroque Shakespeare," tentatively proposed by Walzel, has caught on amazingly. In a book by Helene Richter, *Shakespeare der Mensch* (1923), Shakespeare is made out to be a typical baroque man. Even his career described a curve or zigzag line: he reached his aims always by devious ways, and this is, of course, an "unmistakable analogy to the baroque." Miss Richter also applies one of Wölfflin's principles to the *Merchant of Venice.* The composition of baroque pictures in diagonals leading the eye toward a distant prospect in the rear is there paral-

leled. "The diagonal of ideas connects the foreground of concrete vital truth with backgrounds of world-wide distance and extension." But even this verbiage was easily surpassed by later German scholars. In *Shakespeares Macbeth als Drama des Barock* (1936) Max Deutschbein presents us with several graphic pictures of the composition of *Macbeth.* A very nice ellipse is drawn with the words "Grace" and "Realm of Darkness" written around it, and "Lady Macbeth" and "Weird Sisters" placed at the focal points. We are then told that this represents the "inner form" of Macbeth which determines the baroque character of the drama, because the baroque style "has a pronounced predilection for the oval groundplan, as shown frequently in the groundplans of baroque churches and castles." Here, then, a completely arbitrary geometrical pattern is drawn up by the ingenious professor, and then this drawing is used as a proof for the baroque character of *Macbeth,* as the ellipse is supposed to be a specific form of baroque architecture. To dismiss this whole undertaking, it is not even necessary to doubt whether the ellipse is so frequent in baroque churches as Deutschbein seems to imply.

Bernard Fehr, in a series of articles in English on the "Antagonism of Forms in the Eighteenth Century made a similar attempt to interpret poetry in terms of architecture. He takes eight lines from Pope's *Moral Essays* and then draws parallel lines for each verse which he interrupts wherever there is a caesura. The result is that these lines, in his own words, "make up a body of equidistant parallels like the string courses and cornices of a Palladian building." Moreover, "the rhyme scheme *aa, bb, cc* . . . breaks up the parallel into a flight of couples to be compared to the colonnades of the pavilions so fashionable in Pope's day." Mr. Fehr never asks the question whether any set of end-stopped lines, rhymed or unrhymed, with any place for the caesura would not lend themselves to exactly the same depiction in parallel lines and thus invite the same comparison with Palladian architecture or whether any couplets should not be, on the same principle, compared to colonnades of pavilions. Mr. Fehr, however, is not content with having demonstrated the parallel between Pope's verse and a Palladian building. He picks a passage from a poem by David Mallet, which happens to be a long pseudo-Miltonic period in blank verse, and represents it, by the same method, as a serpentine line. Thus Mallet and Thomson and many others who wrote blank verse with long sentences overflowing the limits of a single line are shown to be baroque, for convolutions and cork-screw pillars are baroque and look exactly like the picture of the verse drawn by Mr. Fehr. But Mallet's lines lend themselves to a further analogizing with architecture. The sentence quoted has clauses and even subclauses, and these suggest to Fehr "in opposition to Pope's double rows of columns, the broken frontage of a baroque building and the recesses and advances of its groundplan, such as may be noted in Blenheim Castle." "This presupposes," he continues ingenuously, "that we look upon a principal sentence as a movement on the front vertical plane, and that anything interrupting an initial or later stage of this movement— from the slightest appositional adjunct or adverbial phrase to the longest subordinate clause—is to be taken as a recess." With the same method any writer who uses subordinate clauses, from Demosthenes and Cicero down to Mr. Fehr himself, could be proved to be baroque. The whole amazing jugglery is only possible because he takes seriously the purely graphic arrangement of a line on a page in print and devises a completely arbitrary translation into architectural terms, which has not even the merit of being specific. No wonder that he comes to such conclusions that all run-on-line blank verse is baroque, that therefore Wordsworth is baroque, while Keats mysteriously "adapted his eyes to a pre-baroque mode of seeing." Thus the baroque has finally stretched to include both Shakespeare and Wordsworth, and almost everybody, with the exception of the strictest classicists, between them.

This foray of art history or rather pseudo-art history into the study of literature is not, of course, confined to the baroque. There is, for example, a book by Friedrich Schürr, *Das altfranzösische Epos* (1926), which in its subtitle tells us that it is a contribution to the history of the style and inner form of Gothic. In the text the parallelism between a Gothic cathedral and a French epic poem is pursued with relentless vigor. For example, the widespread use of parallels and repetitions in action, themes, and motifs in the epic is quoted as argument for an architectonic composition of these epics which can be easily enough demonstrated to agree with the "principle" of all Gothic art: "repetition with variation," which we find in the flying buttresses, pillars, and pointed arches of the Gothic cathedrals. That pattern and variation are devices of practically all art of all times is an objection which is not even considered by Mr. Schürr. There are other books of this type, one by Friedrich Brie [entitled *Englische Rokokoepik*] on the rococo epic in English literature which centers in the *Rape of the Lock* and many studies trying to transfer the term "Empire," "Biedermeier" or "impressionism" from painting and decorative arts to literature.

Most widely known is possibly Fritz Strich's attempt in his *Deutsche Klassik und Romantik* (1922) to describe the opposition between German classicism and romanticism by an application of Wölfflin's categories evolved for the Renaissance and the baroque. The baroque characteristics hold good for romanticism, the Renaissance for classicism. Strich's special contribution is the interpretation he gives to Wölfflin's contraries of closed and open forms. "Closed" form means to him complete, perfect classical form, which expresses a longing for timeless values; while the "open," unfinished, fragmentary or blurred form of romantic poetry expresses man's longing for the infinite, for eternity. Thus, by a simple equivocation between finished and finite, unfinished and infinite, an elaborate structure of metaphysical implications is erected and much opportunity for clever juxtapositions is gained.

It would not have been worth while to discuss these books if they were merely isolated perversions on the fringes of scholarship. Actually all the books mentioned are thoroughly representative of a much larger literature written by the most prominent scholars of Germany, many in high academic positions, and,—it would be unjust not to recognize it,—by scholars of real learning and comprehension. "Geistesgeschichte" is, besides, not a local phenomenon any more, but is spreading to publications in English,

though, on the whole, the greater common sense and ingrained empiricism of most non-German scholars have saved them from some of the worst quibbling, extended metaphors, and easy formulas of the Germans. The few writers who have used the term "baroque" in English literature have been extraordinarily cautious. In his studies of the *Baroque Style in Prose* Morris William Croll has proceeded by strictly empirical methods: he has analyzed and observed with great sensitivity the types of prose rhythm and sentence structure current in the seventeenth century. The term "baroque" is used to label the ornate style of the age. Parallels to painting occur only as illustrations, for example, in analyzing a loose sentence by Sir Thomas Browne, Mr. Croll suggests [in "The Baroque Style in Prose," in *Studies in English Philology; a Miscellany in Honor of Frederick Klaeber*] that it "closely parallels the technique of an El Greco composition, where broken and tortuous lines in the body of the design prepare the eye for curves that leap upward beyond the limits of the canvas." Wölfflin's "open" form is obviously in the mind of the author, but no far-reaching conclusions or speculations are tied to these remarks. Austin Warren, also, in his book on *Richard Crashaw: a Study in Baroque Sensibility* (1939), though he describes Bernini's St. Theresa and uses the term "baroque," carefully keeps to an analysis of the actual poems in terms of their verse, imagery, and symbolism. There is no particular objection to the use of this term as an alternative to metaphysical, concettist, and so forth, as long as we give it a strictly literary meaning.

Somewhat earlier Mr. F. W. Bateson, to whom we are all indebted for the *Cambridge Bibliography of English Literature,* took up the term "baroque" but applied it to eighteenth-century Miltonic poetry, in his stimulating book on *English Poetry and the English Language* (1934). Thomson, Young, Gray, and Collins make on him the same impression as baroque architecture by their orderly disorder and artificial excitement. He characterizes them in terms quoted from Geoffrey Scott's *Architecture of Humanism* (1914), a book which, partly under the influence of the early studies of Wölfflin, described baroque architecture along the lines of distinctions between picturesque versus linear, and unclear versus clear forms. Mr. Bateson also argues that the eighteenth-century term "sublime," as expounded by Burke, in its love of the obscure and confused is a description of the baroque and that the function of the invocations, personifications, and stock phrases in Thomson, Young and the others is "identical with that of baroque ornament." One might ask whether all poetic diction, including that of the Scottish Chaucerians and the Italian sonneteers and even the Silver Latin poets would not, according to the same criteria, have to be considered "baroque ornament." Baroque thus loses any useful connotation and becomes a term for anything decorative, tawdry, and conventionalized.

[Beverly] Sprague Allen's two-volume study of *Tides in English Taste* (1937) examines the relationships between the arts in concrete terms, only rarely attempting speculations about far-reaching parallelisms. Mr. Allen suggests such similarities as those between the still fundamentally Gothic architecture of the Tudor period with the early Tudor drama, full of medieval remnants, overlaid by imitations of Seneca. He sees also a parallel between the Palladian adaptations of Tudor houses and the "improving" of Shakespeare during the Restoration. More doubtful seems a parallel he draws between the rococo in the arts and the eighteenth-century attack on the unities in the drama. The similarity is merely in the dissatisfaction with rigid symmetrical form. Even more fanciful is the parallel recently drawn by the eminent Italian scholar, Mario Praz, between Milton and Poussin [in *Seventeenth Century Studies Presented to Sir Herbert Grierson*]. He tries to show that Milton preferred design to color and tells us that Poussin modeled his figures first in wax in order to study their attitudes before he painted his pictures. But then Signor Praz goes on to say that

> Milton also modelled his verse in wax before working it in English. The wax pattern of Milton was the Latin construction; he handles so to say the classical flesh of the words before dressing it in English attire . . . his sentences marched at the pace of Roman legions; there was an enchanted air about it all, as in Poussin's pictures.

As a matter of fact, Milton did not write first in Latin and then in English; and the similarity between Poussin's wax figures and Milton's search for Latinized constructions seems very remote. Nor is there much light in the comparison of Milton's sentences with the pace of Roman legions or in a purely emotive statement that "there is an enchanted air about it all" in Milton as in Poussin. Mr. Laurence Binyon, in a chatty lecture on *English Poetry in Its Relation to Painting and the Other Arts* (1918), spoke of the "organ-music" of Milton's rhythm, which seems hardly compatible with the pace of Roman legions, and had paralleled Milton with both Michelangelo and Veronese rather than with Poussin. A German scholar [Gustav Hübener, in his *Die stilistische Spannung in Miltons Paradise Lost*] compared the tension and bold arch of Milton's sentences with the cupola of St. Paul's Cathedral, while Mr. Herbert Read is reminded of Dryden by the buildings of Sir Christopher Wren.

Mr. Read, in his express discussion of "Parallels in English Painting and Poetry," published in his volume of essays *In Defence of Shelley* (1936), compares Turner with Keats, while Mr. Binyon thought rather of Shelley. But these are all only vague impressions, and there is also little more than a comparison of landscape types and moods in Mr. Read's statement that "an early landscape of Gainsborough's matches the unrhymed rhythms of Collins' 'Ode to Evening,' whilst the still freer and more naturalistic treatment of Gainsborough's later landscapes approaches to the poetic objectivity of Wordsworth." Only once, in his survey of the whole history, does Mr. Read attempt a structural parallel between painting and poetry. He compares Anglo-Saxon ornament with Anglo-Saxon meter.

> I wish to suggest that the same spirit which expressed itself in linear emphasis in the case of drawing, when it came to verse expressed itself in alliteration. Alliteration is a horizontal movement across the structure of verse; it is linear abstraction within verbal expression. In a corresponding way, the play of lines in a drawing will show a continual repetition of the same motive, a kind of linear alliteration.

Mr. Read does not see that the term "horizontal" applied to alliteration refers purely to the graphic picture on a page and might be applied to any repetition within a verse, for instance, the repeated accents of normal blank verse which would be even more regularly placed than the alliterations. The view that repetitive ornament is a kind of alliteration could be equally upheld as to classical columns, Gothic arches, meanders and arabesques, in short to any repetitive device, and thus the whole parallel falls to the ground. I don't want, however, to press these statements, but merely to take them as examples. They show how parallelisms between poetry and painting are spreading and that most of them point only to the slightest and most tenuous thematic or emotional similarities.

I should have created a wrong impression, if this little survey of books and examples were understood to imply a wholesale dismissal of the problem. I am rather pleading for clear distinctions between the different methods in use and a scheme of relationships and emphases. A clarification of the place and function of each special method and a realization of their difficulties and limitations may help us in formulating a new approach. Let me attempt such a sketch.

Most of our criticism in literature and the arts is still purely emotive: it judges works of art in terms of their emotional effect on the reader or spectator and describes this effect by exclamations, suggested moods or scenes, and so forth. However disguised, much criticism amounts to the labeling of works of art by emotional terms like "joyful," "gay," "melancholy," and so forth, or, in modern psychological terms, as inducing a balance of impulses—a "patterning" and "ordering" of our mind, to use the terms introduced by Mr. I. A. Richards. Many parallels between the fine arts and literature amount to an assertion that this picture and that poem induce the same mood in me: for example, that I feel light-hearted and gay in hearing a minuet of Mozart, seeing a landscape by Watteau, and reading an Anacreontic poem. But this is the kind of parallelism which is of little worth for purposes of scholarly analysis: joy induced by a piece of music is, not joy in general or even joy of a particular shade, but is an emotion closely following and thus tied to the pattern of the music. We experience emotions which have only a general tone in common with those of real life, and even if we define these emotions as closely as we can, we are still quite removed from the specific object which induced them. I cannot see any light in Mr. Richards's main theory, that poetry and art put into order the chaos of our impulses. He is driven to admit [in his *Principles of Literary Criticism*] that a balanced poise might be achieved by a bad as well as a good poem, by a carpet as well as a sonata, and thus has nothing to do with the actual object of our study: the work of art. Parallels between the arts which remain inside the individual reactions of a reader or spectator and are content with describing some emotional similarity of our reactions to two arts will, therefore, never lend themselves to verification and thus to a coöperative advance in our knowledge.

Another common approach is the intentions and theories of the artists. No doubt, we can show that there are some similarities in the theories and formulas behind the different arts, in the neoclassical or the romantic movements, and we can find also professions of intentions of the individual artists in the different arts which sound identical or similar. But these intentions may not have any definite relation to the finished work of art; they may go far beyond it, they may contradict its results, or they may fall short of the accomplished object. They can at the most serve as a useful commentary or as signposts pointing to problems, but they require much analysis and interpretation to be of any use in the comparison of the arts. A good example is the professed classicism of most baroque artists. Bernini, for example, gave a lecture to the Paris Academy, asserting that he followed the Greek sculptors, and the architect of a most rococo building, the Zwinger in Dresden, Daniel Adam Pöppelmann, wrote a whole little book demonstrating the agreement of his building with the chastest principles of Vitruvius. Similarly, the metaphysical poets in England never thought of their own work as deviating from classical standards, nor did they ever invent a distinct aesthetic for their extremely different practice except that they spoke about "strong lines" and praised wit and obscurity. "Classicism" in music must mean something very different from its use in literature for the simple reason that no real classical music (with the exception of a few fragments) was known and could thus shape the evolution of music as literature was actually shaped by the precepts and practice of antiquity. Likewise painting, before the excavation of the frescoes in Pompeii and Herculaneum, can scarcely be described as influenced by classical painting in spite of the frequent reference to classical theories and Greek painters like Apelles and possibly some remote pictorial traditions which must have descended from antiquity through the Middle Ages. Sculpture and architecture, however, were to an extent far exceeding the other arts, including literature, determined by classical models and their derivatives. Thus theories and conscious intentions mean something very different in the various arts and say little or nothing about the concrete results of an artist's activity: his work and its specific content and form.

How little decisive for an understanding of a concrete work of art may be the approach through the personality of the author can best be seen in the rare cases when artist and poet are identical. For example, a comparison of the poetry and the paintings of Blake or Rossetti will show that the character, not merely the technical quality of their painting and poetry, is very different and even divergent. I think of the grotesque little animal which is supposed to illustrate "Tiger! Tiger! Burning bright." Without daring to dogmatize about Michelangelo, I would venture the opinion that in structure and quality there is little comparison between his *Sonnets* and his sculpture and paintings, though we can find the same Neoplatonic ideas in all and may discover some psychological similarities. This shows that the "medium" of a work of art (an unfortunate question-begging term) is not merely a technical obstacle to be overcome by the artist in order to express his personality, but a factor pre-formed by tradition and thus has a powerful determining character which shapes and modifies the approach and expression of the individual artist. The artist does not conceive in general mental terms, but in terms of concrete material; and the concrete medium has its own history, frequently very different from that of any other medium.

More valuable than the approach through the artist's intentions and theories is a comparison of the arts on the basis of their common social and cultural background. Certainly it is possible to describe the common temporal, local, or social nourishing soil of the arts and literature and thus to point to common influences working on them. But many parallels between the arts are possible only because they ignore the utterly different social background to which the individual work of art appealed or from which it seems to be derived. The social classes either creating or demanding a certain type of art may be quite different at any one time or place. Certainly the Gothic cathedrals have a different social background from the French epic; and sculpture frequently appeals to and is paid for by a very different audience from the novel. Just as fallacious as the assumption of a common social background of the arts at a given time and place is the usual assumption that the intellectual background is necessarily identical and effective in all the arts. Literature, because it shades off almost imperceptibly into the vehicle of science and philosophy, is in closest touch with the technical philosophy of a time. But even there the assumption that poetry mirrors the thought of an age is not always true, as witness the gulf between the poetic thought of the romantic age in England and the prevalent common-sense and utilitarian philosophy of the time. It is even more hazardous to interpret painting in the light of contemporary philosophy: to mention only one example, Károly Tolnai has attempted to interpret the pictures of the elder Brueghel in evidence of a pantheistic monism paralleling Cusanus or Paracelsus and anticipating Spinoza and Goethe [Charles de Tolnay, *Pierre Bruegel l'Ancien*]. Even more dangerous is an "explanation" of the arts in terms of a "time-spirit," a sort of mystical integral which is positively vicious when hypostatized and made absolute and is useful only as a pointer toward a problem. But the German "Geistesgeschichte" has usually merely succeeded in transferring criteria from one series to the whole and has then characterized the times and in them every individual work of art in terms of such vague contraries as "rationalism" and "irrationalism." The genuine parallelisms which follow from the identical or similar social or intellectual background scarcely ever have been analyzed in concrete terms. I want only to suggest that we have rarely had studies which would concretely show how, for example, all the arts in a given time or setting expand or narrow their field over the objects of "nature" or how the norms of art are tied to specific social classes and thus subject to uniform changes or how aesthetic values change with social revolutions. Here is a wide field for investigation which has been scarcely touched and promises concrete results for the comparison of the arts. Of course, only similar influences on the evolution of the different arts can be proved by this method, *not* any necessary parallelism.

Obviously, the most central approach to a comparison of the arts is based on an analysis of the actual objects of art, and thus of their structural relationships. There will never be a proper history of an art, not to speak of a comparative history of the arts, unless we concentrate on an analysis of the works themselves and relegate to the background studies in the psychology of the reader and the spectator or the author and the artist as well as studies in the cultural and social background, however illuminating they may be from their own point of view. Unfortunately it seems to me that hitherto we have had scarcely any tools for such a comparison between the arts. Here a very difficult question arises: what are the common and the comparable elements of the arts? I hardly need to say that I see no light in a theory like [Benedetto] Croce's, which concentrates all aesthetic problems on the act of intuition, mysteriously identified with expression. [In his *Aesthetic*] Croce asserts the nonexistence of modes of expression and condemns "any attempt at an aesthetic classification of the arts as absurd" and thus *a fortiori* rejects all distinction between genres or types. Nor is much gained for our problem by John Dewey's insistence in his *Art as Experience* (1934) that there is a common substance among the arts because there are "general conditions without which an experience is not possible." I am not prepared to deny that there is a common denominator in the act of all artistic creation or, for that matter, in all human creation, activity, and experience. But these are solutions which do not help us in comparing the arts. More concretely, Theodore Meyer Greene, in his *Arts and the Art of Criticism* (1940), defines the comparable elements of the arts as complexity, integration, and rhythm, and he argues eloquently, as John Dewey had done before him, for the applicability of the term "rhythm" to the plastic arts. I have no time to enter into this controversy, but it seems to me that it is impossible to overcome the profound distinction between the rhythm of a piece of music and the rhythm of a colonnade, where neither the order nor the tempo is imposed by the structure of the work itself. Complexity and integration are merely other terms for "variety" and "unity" and thus of only very limited use. Few concrete attempts to arrive at such common denominators among the arts on a structural basis have gone any further. Mr. Birckhoff, a Harvard mathematician, in a book on *Aesthetic Measure* (1933), has with apparent success tried to find a common mathematical basis for simple art forms and music and he has included a study of the "musicality" of verse which is also defined in mathematical equations and coefficients. I have my doubts whether the problem of euphony in verse can be solved in isolation from meaning, and Mr. Birckhoff's high grades for poems by Edgar Allan Poe seem to confirm such an assumption, but his ingenious attempt, if accepted, would tend rather to widen the gulf between the essentially "literary" qualities of poetry and the other arts which share much more fully in "aesthetic measure" than literature.

Thus, the application of Wölfflin's *Principles of Art History* to literature is the one concrete attempt to find a common ground among the arts based on an analysis of structure. Wölfflin's analysis is frequently admirably concrete and sensitive. Used with caution, his terms "open" and "closed" form, "linear" and "pictorial," "flat" and "deep," and so forth seem to point to real distinctions in the history of art, illuminating for the contrast between the High Renaissance and the baroque. The art historians will have to decide whether the terms are particularly useful in analyzing the arts of other times and places, but one cannot suppress the obvious criticism that Wölfflin provides us with only one set of contraries which applied to the whole history of the arts seems a clumsy instrument of distinction. But transferred to literature and thus deprived of the concrete meaning attached to them by Wölfflin, these concepts seem to lose almost all meaning. They help us merely to arrange works of art into two categories which, when examined in detail, amount only to the old distinction between classic and romantic, severe and loose structure, plastic and picturesque art: a dualism which was known to the Schlegels and to Schiller and Coleridge and was arrived at by them through ideological and literary arguments. Wölfflin's one set of contraries manages to group all classical and pseudoclassical art together, on the one hand, and on the other to combine very divergent movements such as the Gothic, the baroque, and romanticism. This theory seems to me to obscure the undoubted and extremely important continuity between the Renaissance and baroque, just as its application to German literature by Strich makes an artificial contrast between the pseudoclassical stage in the development of Schiller and Goethe and the romantic movement of the early nineteenth century, while it must leave the "Storm and Stress" unexplained and incomprehensible. Actually, the German literature at the turn of the eighteenth and nineteenth centuries forms a comparative unity which it seems absurd to break up into an irreconcilable antithesis. Thus, Wölfflin's theory may help us in classifying works of art and establishing or rather confirming the old action-reaction, convention-revolt, or see-saw type of dualistic evolutionary scheme, which, however, confronted with the reality of the complex process of literature, falls far short of coping with the complex pattern of the actual development.

The transfer of Wölfflin's pairs of concepts also leaves one important problem completely unsolved. We cannot explain in any way the undoubted fact that the arts did not evolve with the same speed at the same time. Literature seems sometimes to linger behind the arts: for instance, we can scarcely speak of an English literature when the great English cathedrals were being built. At other times music lags behind literature and the other arts; for instance, we cannot speak of "romantic" music before 1800, while much romantic poetry preceded that date. We have difficulty in accounting for the fact that there was "picturesque" poetry at least sixty years before the picturesque invaded architecture or for the fact, mentioned by [Jakob Burckhardt, in his *Die Kultur der Renaissance in Italien*], that *Nencia,* the description of peasant life by Lorenzo Magnifico, preceded by some eighty years the first genre pictures of Jacopo Bassano and his school. Even if these few examples were wrongly chosen and could be refuted, they raise a question which, I think, cannot be answered by an over-simple theory according to which, let us say, music is always lagging by a generation after poetry. Obviously a correlation with social factors should be attempted, and these factors will vary in every single instance.

We are finally confronted with the problem that certain times or nations were extremely productive only in one or two arts, while either completely barren or merely imitative and derivative in others. The flowering of Elizabethan literature, which was not accompanied by any comparable flowering of the fine arts, is a case in point, and little, it seems to me, is gained by speculations to the effect that the national soul, in some way, concentrated on one art or that, as M. Legouis phrases it in his *History of English Literature,* "Spenser would have become a Titian or Veronese had he been born in Italy or a Rubens or Rembrandt in the Netherlands" [E. Legouis and L. Cazamian, *Histoire de la littérature anglaise*]. In the case of English literature it is easy to suggest that Puritanism was responsible for the neglect of the fine arts, but that is scarcely enough to account for the differences between the productivity in very secular literature and the comparative barrenness in painting. But all this leads us far afield into concrete historical questions which I have not time to argue in full.

I merely wanted to suggest further problems in order to support my conclusions. The various arts—the plastic arts, literature, and music—have each their individual evolution, with a different tempo and a different internal structure of elements. No doubt they are in constant relationship with each other, but these relationships are not influences which start from one point and determine the evolution of the other arts; they have to be conceived rather as a complex scheme of dialectical relationships which work both ways, from one art to another and *vice versa,* and may be completely transformed within the art which they have entered. It is not a simple affair of a "time-spirit" determining and permeating each and every art. We must conceive of the sum-total of man's cultural activities as of a whole system of self-evolving series, each having its own set of norms which is not necessarily identical with those of the neighboring series. The task of art historians in the widest sense, including historians of literature and of music, is to evolve a descriptive set of terms in each art, based on the specific characteristics of each art. Thus poetry today needs a new poetics, a technique of analysis which cannot be arrived at by a simple transfer or adaptation of terms from the fine arts. Only when we have evolved a successful system of terms for the analysis of literary works of art can we delimit literary periods, which, as I showed in my lecture ["Periods and Movements in Literary History," in *English Institute Annual, 1940*], can be best conceived in terms of dominant systems of norms, and not as metaphysical entities dominated by a "time-spirit." Having established such outlines of strictly literary evolution, we then can ask the question whether this evolution is, in some way, similar to the similarly established evolution of the other arts. The answer will be, as we can see, not a flat "yes" or "no." It will take the form of an intricate pattern of coincidences and divergences rather than parallel lines.

Thus, to summarize briefly, I should like to argue that the current methods for the comparison of the arts are of little value. They are based either on vague similarities of emotional effects or on a community of intentions, theories, and slogans which may not be very concretely related to the actual works of arts. Or, more usefully, they are based on a community of antecedents in the social or general cultural background, but even here the community is frequently merely presupposed, and the mysterious unifying

"time-spirit" is usually little more than a vague abstraction or empty formula. Finally, most usefully, this community among the arts has been and should be studied in the structural relationships between the arts, but, in practice, the one widely used scheme for the approximation of the arts, Wölfflin's series of contrary concepts, leads only to the establishment of a very general community between the arts and literature by the distinction of two stylistic types and their supposed alteration in the course of history. The vaguely emotive, the fancifully metaphorical, and the drearily speculative analogizing between the arts should be recognized as blind alleys, and the problem should be approached anew.

It might sound distressingly vague and abstract, if I should suggest that the approximation among the arts which would lead to concrete possibilities of comparison might be sought in an attempt to reduce all the arts to branches of semiology, or to so many systems of signs. These systems of signs might be conceived as enforcing certain systems of norms which imply groups of values. In such terms as signs, norms, and values I would look for a description of the common basis of the arts. But I propose such a distant solution only hesitatingly, knowing very well that this would involve the presentation of a system of aesthetics which I am not prepared to develop today.

> *René Wellek, "The Parallelism between Literature and the Arts," in* English Institute Annual, *1941, AMS Press, 1965, pp. 29-63.*

DEFINITIONS

Howard Nemerov

[Nemerov was an acclaimed American poet, fiction writer, critic, and educator known for the broad range of subjects treated in his poetry, especially his concern with ideas and thought processes. In the following essay, Nemerov maintains that poet and painter share mutual aims: "Both . . . want to reach the silence behind the language, the silence within the language."]

There are affinities between poetry and painting, and perhaps the words 'image' and 'language' will help focus these as well as the differences. Painters make images, poets make images; the painter too has language, though not perhaps in so explicit a sense as the poet does; the palette for a given landscape, say, acts as a negative kind of syntax, excluding certain colors from the range of possibility; and as a positive kind as well, indicating the possibilities of gradation in getting from earth through river through forest to sky.

Both poet and painter want to reach the silence behind the language, the silence within the language. Both painter and poet want their work to shine not only in daylight but (by whatever illusionist magic) from within; maybe even more from within than by daylight, for many of their works in times now past had not the object of being viewed in daylight but went to do their magic in caves, in tombs, among the dead, and maybe as a substitute for daylight.

The poet walks through the museum and among so many and so diverse conceptions and manners of treatment he sees, he hears, especially two things: silence and light. Viewing the picture frames as windows, he looks into rooms, out of rooms into landscapes—what the Chinese call 'mountain-water pictures'—and knows from the silence that he is seeing the past, the dead, the irrevocable; and he knows something else, that what he sees is not only the past, the dead, the irrevocable, but something that had the intention of being these things from the moment of its conception: something that is, so to say, past from the beginning. Hence the great silence common among so many differences of subject and execution; hence, too, the solemnity of the museum, crowded with solitudes; the dignity of painting, that stands in a sort of enchanted space between life and death.

He sees also that the light in these rectangles appears to come from within. In the work of an unknown master he sees the thin veil of a small waterfall in sunlight—amazing! He leans in to look closer, the threads of water become white paint mixed with a little gray on a gray ground—amazing again, not quite in the same way, that crossing-point, that exact distance, within which illusion becomes paint, beyond which paint becomes illusion again. Whereas in the painting of a river by Vlaminck, the thin, pale surface of the water, bearing the thinnest and most shivering of pale reflections, is made by means of the heaviest, thickest, grossest applications of paint, made with a virtuosity that is able to make colored dirt produce effects of light. Amazing again.

His own art, in the comparison, begins to seem the merest pitifullest chatter, compounded of impatience and opinion. On thoughts like this, the poet finds it best to hasten from the museum, that marvelous tomb-temple wherein the living are privileged to look so deeply into what is no more, experiencing their own mortality as a dignified silence not without its effects of grandeur and austerity; though all this *looking deeply,* that so magicks the beholder, is done on a plane surface.

Out in the day again, he thinks about the matter some more. First about some poems of his own time, especially some he cares for, that have a relation with painting or drawing. There is Auden's 'Musée des Beaux Arts,' with its reflections that rely on Brueghel, on *The Fall of Icarus* and on the *Massacre of the Innocents.* There is John Berryman's 'Hunters Returning at Evening,' also referring to Brueghel; there is Randall Jarrell's emblem drawn from Dürer's *Knight, Death, and Devil* ; there is even one of his own, composed and called after René Magritte's *The Human Condition (I).* These things have a relation to painting, and they are not painting. It would be interesting to speculate what that relation might be.

It is not, certainly, that the poems speak about the paintings they refer to; no, for the poems offer relatively bare and selective descriptions; no art student sent to the muse-

um would dare come back with such descriptions, which sometimes hardly serve to identify the paintings. No, the poems speak about the silence of the paintings; and where the poet was lucky his poem will speak the silence of the painting; it too will say nothing more than: It is so, it is as it is. The poem, too, when it works, is a concentrated shape illuminated by an energy from within; its opinions do not matter, but it matters. Here, too, he observes, all that happens happens while the poem, like the painting, lies flat on a plane surface, the surface of the page.

From the other side, he is reassured to think, ever so much of painting comes from poetry, refers to poetry, and is poetical in its own nature as well as in its subject matter. Not only the biblical subjects, for example, but the various conceptions and styles that transfigure the subjects, that poetize upon the Crucifixion, say, with respect to an eternal glory in so many medieval masters, a superhuman grandeur in Michelangelo, a bitter suffering in Grünewald, the light of an ordinary day in Brueghel.

So both painter and poet are makers of images, and traditionally there is a connection between the images they make. And when we say they *make* images, we do not seek to distinguish, for the present, the component of invention from that of discovery.

And both painter and poet write in languages. This seems at first to mark a decisive and unbridgeable difference, the difference in their languages. But it invites a little further thought.

Surely the painter's language has the dignity of being the oldest ever written down. Minerals, plants, the liquids of the body even to blood, all gave up their substance many thousand years ago to the representation by signs of perceptions based upon fear, desire, hunger, dreams, and a certain decorative and geometrizing distance from all these, a certain coldness. Whereas writing came much later. Writing in an alphabet wholly independent of pictorial elements is usually dated not much earlier than the middle of the second millennium B.C.

Perhaps nothing in the alphabet cannot also be seen in nature: O in a hole, W or M in a distant flying bird, Y in the branching of a tree, and so on. But that's not pertinent. What really matters is that no alphabet could exist as long as these signs were seen exclusively as belonging to nature; they had to be got out of nature, so that you could write C without any thought of the curve of the shoreline, S without thinking about snakes, any letter without thinking of it except as a letter—something that had never before been, something in effect literally 'nonsensical' that yet could 'make sense' of the realms to which its immense range of combinations was applied. If the conservative element in society got as mithered as it did at the advent of 'abstract art' at the Armory Show of 1913, imagine its probable resentment at so great an innovation as the alphabet: 'It don't look like anything I ever seen,' 'A child could do stuff like that if he thought it worth the bother,' and so on.

With respect to painting, E. H. Gombrich, who has written so beautifully against the grain of an abstract age about the miraculous thing that is representation, suggests that perhaps painting too arose out of coincidences in nature— as the alphabet did, but in the opposite direction. The earliest cave drawings might have been, he speculates, those in which a peculiar form of the rock itself was first *recognized* as resembling an animal, and then modified by artistic means with a view to increasing the degree of this resemblance; rather as the earliest portrait statuary, too, employed the human skull itself as armature—a thought that even yet retains a depth of sinister magical intent.

And the development of painting might be conceived of as having three main branches. The first would be in the direction of greater fidelity to appearances, ending in the peculiar magic of the waxworks, which so clearly and instantly distinguishes itself from the magic of art. The second would be in the direction of ornament, rhythm, pattern, figuration, of an abstract character. And the third would be in the direction of language, of alphabet and the codifying of signs, ending in the magic of writing; the process is indeed perceptible in the history of Chinese writing; while in Egypt, though writing and painting were clearly distinguishable, yet writing remained a species of representational drawing, though abstract and conditioned by the introduction of specifically linguistic and nonrepresentational signs.

It will be worthwhile to remember here Coomaraswamy's (Ananda Kentish Coomaraswamy, *Christian and Oriental Philosophy of Art*) demonstration that in traditions of sacred art, the medieval Christian as much as the Hindu, painting was treated as linguistic; the characters of iconography were dictated at least as much by the codified formulas of priesthoods as by any free observation of the visible world; which offers an answer, and a good one, to the question of how, in a world without photography, the features of gods and saviors become so quickly fixed and invariant.

In both languages, then, of writing and of painting, the shapes and substances of the earth rose up and assumed a mental and a spiritual quality, conferring upon the mind that brought them forth a thrilling if somewhat frightening power of detachment from the world as viewed by the prehuman mind, or at least the mind that was before these things were.

Maybe the comparison has to end there. For push and pull as we may, writing and painting *did* separate off from one another. Might they ever come back together? Ought they ever to come back together? If their very different but immense powers were to fuse into something not really much like either—what then?

We do already have an instance in which this happens: the making of maps, charts, diagrams, blueprints . . . where the representing of the visible, at which painting is supremely capable, is accomplished in parallel with the strict and abstract syntax of writing able without modification of its own nature to transmit an indefinite variety of messages, which is the supreme contribution of written language. Might this somewhat elementary compound of writing and painting have still some way to go in the world?

I should like to make a rather wild leap at such a question, and hope to be going in a forward direction. Writing and painting could come together, though I don't know in the least what their offspring would look like. (Possibly it would not *look* at all.) It is here that I get the vaguest glimmer of a hint from music, or from some thoughts about music. Proust touches the thought [in *The Remembrance of Things Past*], but almost at once lets it go:

> And just as certain creatures are the last surviving testimony to a form of life which nature has discarded, I asked myself if music were not the unique example of what might have been—if there had not come the invention of language, the formation of words, the analysis of ideas— the means of communication between one spirit and another. It is like a possibility which has ended in nothing.

Another writer, François le Lionnais (*The Orion Book of Time*) also encourages this sort of speculation, also without demonstration, when he says that certain music—his examples are the Elizabethan virginalists, J. S. Bach, Schumann, Anton von Webern—'consists not only of fluctuating sound patterns capable of delighting the ear but also of psychological hieroglyphics not yet decoded.'

The vaguest glimmer of a hint, and one which I am, at least at present, unable to take any further, though perhaps some of my readers may. For this of 'hieroglyphics' and 'decoding' has its charms, because the arts have always had, in addition to their popular side, their deep affinity for mystery and the esoteric, for the secret which is also the sacred.

Howard Nemerov, "On Poetry and Painting, with a Thought of Music," in his Figures of Thought: Speculations on the Meaning of Poetry & Other Essays, *Godine, 1978, pp. 95-9.*

Stanley Kunitz

[*Kunitz is an American poet, critic, and translator. In the following essay, Kunitz discusses the affinities between poetry and painting, maintaining that "Painting and sculpture, drama and dance, prose and poetry, in their overlapping and combining, continue to press towards a dissolution of boundaries."*]

One reason why I stay in New York, though I suspect that it impairs my prospects for longevity, is that so many of my artist friends live here. By and large I prefer the company of painters and sculptors to that of poets, who tend to be rather surly and withdrawn. The romantic impressions that I had of studio life as a boy were, of course, naïve and highly colored, but still they had an element of truth in them. Artists flock to the metropolis mainly because the museums and the galleries and the money are there, but also, I propose, because they are temperamentally gregarious. Every art movement is a testimonial, at bottom, to the vitality of a complex of friendships.

If I should say to a painter that I envy his art because the poet at his desk is never free from mental struggle, whereas the artist finds a measure of satisfaction and release in the sheer physical activity required of him, the rhythm of his body, I know from experience that this compliment will be taken amiss, so that I try, not always successfully, to suppress it. Painters, especially in their youth, have such a good time together that I sometimes wonder why they want poets around at all, but the history of these associations is so redundant in modern times—witness Keats-Haydon, Baudelaire-Delacroix, Rilke-Rodin, Apollinaire-Picasso, Eluard-Picasso, Breton-Aragon, Lorca-Dali, etc.—that it would be difficult to believe that the gratifications are not mutual.

The great lesson that Rilke, with his fragility and neurasthenia, learned from contact with the abounding energy of Rodin was the importance of hard work: *"Il faut toujours travailler."* What artists discover in poets is more tenuous; perhaps it is largely a state of nervosity and awareness, a capacity for being nothing and experiencing everything. The most extraordinary evidence of the natural affinity between poet and painter is the number of creative spirits who have combined in themselves both talents. In the heyday of Surrealism and Dadaism, movements that belonged as much to literature as to art, poet-painters and painter-poets sprang up in Paris by the dozen. Here, where the arts have been more compartmentalized, we can nevertheless identify the painter Marsden Hartley as one who wrote poems, and the poet E. E. Cummings as one who painted pictures. Michelangelo and Blake are the most notable examples of the type, but if we reach back to the eighth century in China we can locate their progenitor in the person of Wang Wei, preeminent among the T'ang poets and father of the southern school of Sung landscape painting, of whom it was said that "his pictures were poems and his poems pictures." The same could apply to Buson who, ten centuries later, flourished in Japan as a master in the *haiku* style.

To Japanese readers the effectiveness of the seventeen-syllabled *haiku* is largely dependent on the silences that surround the images, which are presented sparely, without subjective coloration. Here is my version of a famous one by Buson:

> On the great bronze bell
> At noon a white butterfly
> Motionlessly sleeps.

Stillness on stillness, as the most ephemeral of creatures folds its wings on the temple-bell that waits in readiness to announce the Eternal. In the highly formalized tradition of Japan the painting, or sketch (*haiga*), that serves as a companion piece, is executed in a quick breath, just as the *haiku* was written, and with a minimum of brushwork, allowing for the eloquence of white space in the same way that the poem uses what is left unsaid. A single poetic experience is rendered simultaneously in two media; the same rhythmic life courses through picture and script.

But the Japanese artist is working within the limits of a visual convention, so codified that each line he draws, each area he washes belongs recognizably to pictorial vocabulary. The contemporary western artist, who lacks a comparable convention, is presented with a poem that does not seem to require his services, since it is a self-sufficient form, much more fully articulated than its oriental counterpart. He must not only define the nature of his relationship to the poem and his understanding of it—not always a simple matter, given the complications and contradictions of the poetic voice—but he must also justify his tinkering with it. And—what is most formidable among these challenges—he must invent a style of graphic translation that enables him to register his variable sense of the poem. If he does less than this, he has not done much.

The easiest way out for the artist is to make a literal illustration of the poem. Let the poet speak of a monkey in a banana-tree and, sure enough, there it is drawn by hand for you—whee! that monkey in that banana-tree—on the same or on a facing page, just as in a first-grade primer. What could be more boring?

A more interesting strategy is that of interpretation of the text, the offering of a visual commentary, which in itself constitutes an act of criticism and may even go so far as to supply a counter-statement to the poem. I can conceive, for example, of a drawing or painting derived from the previously quoted *haiku* of Buson that would not even faintly suggest a temple-bell or a butterfly, but that might be born of the mood occasioned by the contemplation of these images. The artist might enjoy the poem and yet not yearn for Nirvana, in which case he might be impelled to break the spell of inaction that gives the lines their enchantment and to set the whole page whirling with his greed for life. Such a response is by no means restricted to the figurative artist. As for those artists who appear, on the surface, to be working abstractly but whose forms somehow manage to suggest landscape or figures descriptive of the poem's content, I am inclined to categorize them as illustrators without conviction. The bolder effect would be to pass beyond illustration and, even, interpretation in order to attempt something more: namely, the re-embodiment of the poem in terms of the graphic imagination. To achieve this end the materials supplied by the poetic imagination, predominantly images and words, must first of all be destroyed or fragmented in the process of experiencing them. Only then, I venture, when images break into line and color and words into calligraphy, can the poem begin to be reconstituted in a different medium.

In his panegyric of Delacroix, Baudelaire noted that it is "one of the characteristic symptoms of the spiritual condition of our age that the arts aspire, if not to take one another's place, at least reciprocally to lend one another new powers." A century later the observation seems much more pertinent than at the time it was made. Painting and sculpture, drama and dance, prose and poetry, in their overlapping and combining, continue to press towards a dissolution of boundaries. And all the arts grow increasingly restless, not only in their impatience with traditional categories, but even more radically in their rejection of a concept of aesthetic limits. At this moment of transit, while the style of an age, or at least of a generation, is evolving, it seems to me imperative that poets and painters should continue their civilized discourse. When the poetic imagination is confined to poetry alone, it runs the risk of withering. Given that circumstance, no art—least of all, painting—could hope to flourish. In Leonardo's words, which need to be restudied, "Painting is a form of poetry made to be seen."

Stanley Kunitz, "The Sister Arts," in his A
Kind of Order, A Kind of Folly, *Atlantic-
Little Brown, 1975, pp. 131-34.*

Northrop Frye

[*A Canadian critic and editor, Frye was the author of
the highly influential and controversial* Anatomy of
Criticism *(1957), in which he argued that literary criticism can be scientific in its method and results and that
judgments are not inherent in the critical process. Believing that literature is wholly structured by myth and symbol, Frye viewed the critic's task as the explication of a
work's archetypal characteristics. In the following essay,
which was originally presented in Italian as a paper at
the Conference of the Associazione Internazionale per gli
Studi di Lingua e Letteratura Italiana in Toronto, Canada, in 1985, Frye argues against the existence of an art-
literature parallel on the basis that "one art cannot
really do what another art is especially equipped to do."*]

I should like to approach the relation of literature to the
visual arts through some of the general principles involved, and hence I am not confining myself to Italian examples. Also, if I am to keep the discussion contained
within the limits of a short introductory paper, I shall be
able to discuss only one of the visual arts: the one I choose
is painting.

The verbal and musical arts that address the ear are presented as temporal experiences, where we move along with
the presentation from beginning to end. Those that address the eye, including painting, sculpture, and architecture, are presented spatially. But before long we realize
that there is something accidental about the presentation,
that every art has both a temporal and a spatial aspect. We
may, by studying the score, perceive a musical composition as simultaneous, spread out all at once in front of us,
as it were. We may also see a painting or other spatial
work of art as an instant of arrested movement.
T. S. Eliot speaks of how "a Chinese jar / Moves perpetually in its stillness." Literature seems to be closer to the
visual arts than music, as it depends on imagery as well
as rhythm. We may think of it as midway between the musical and the visual. We experience this double context
most obviously in drama, where we not only hear a narrative but often a background of music as well, along with
seeing a spectacle on the stage. But even if we are silently
reading a work of literature, there is still a metaphorical
hearing and seeing that is never wholly out of our consciousness.

The metaphorical "hearing" of literature, more particularly poetry, is often expressed in metaphors of music.
Thus Milton's *Lycidas* has in its invocation the line
"Begin, and somewhat loudly sweep the string," implying
that the poem has a *mezzoforte* musical accompaniment
on a lute or lyre. At the end we read

> Thus sang the uncouth swain to th' oaks and rills
> While the still morn went out with sandals gray:
> He touch'd the tender stops of various quills
> With eager thought warbling his Doric lay.

The word *quills* implies the use of a reed or a kind of rustic

oboe, called an "oat" earlier in the poem. Milton had a
good deal of musical taste and knowledge, but the impossibility of singing and playing a wind instrument at the same
time does not seem to bother him. *Paradise Lost,* again,
invariably uses the metaphor of singing whenever the poet
appears in his own person.

But when the process of reading or listening to a body of
words in time is ended, we make an effort to understand
what the body of words conveys, in a simultaneous or
comprehensive act that we metaphorically call "seeing."
Someone about to tell a joke may begin with some such
formula as "Have you heard this?" Once we hear it, we
"see" the joke; we "grasp" (turning to another group of
tactile metaphors) the essential point or meaning of the
joke, or what Aristotle would call its *dianoia.* But once we
"see" the joke we do not want to hear it again. Similarly,
we may read a detective story in order to identify the murderer at the end, but once we "see" who the murderer is,
we normally do not want to read the book again until we
have forgotten his identity.

If, on the other hand, we are presented with something as
complex as *King Lear,* we hear or read the play, and make
a tentative effort to understand what it all means. This effort soon falls to pieces; its inadequacy becomes oppressive; we read or listen to the play again, and attempt a
more satisfactory understanding. Such a process, if one is
professionally concerned with studying literature or
drama, may go on for the whole of one's life. Any feeling
that we have "seen" the meaning of a work of literature
in a final and completely adequate way implies a rather
low estimate of it. This conception of "seeing" a body of
words is so deeply involved in our response to literature
that the metaphor of "structure," literature studied as a
simultaneous pattern, has become a central critical term.

The metaphor of "seeing," however, has two frames of reference. It may refer us to a conceptual meaning, an understanding which is a gestalt of apprehension, but in itself,
when expressed, is primarily another kind of verbal structure. Thus the fable is a story we listen to like other stories,
but understanding it is a matter of understanding a
"moral," the reconstruction of the story in conceptual or
didactic verbal terms. Most allegories call for a response
of this kind also. Here the seeing is a response of simultaneity that appears to take place in some kind of conceptual
space. Sometimes a poet will indicate what kind of response he expects by providing a suggested moral of his
own to his fable, as with Gray's "On a Distant Prospect
of Eton College": "No more: where Ignorance is Bliss, /
'Tis Folly to be wise." Another example would be the
"truth is beauty" proposition at the end of Keats's "Ode
on a Grecian Urn," where the urn itself suddenly comes
to life and speaks, in the figure of speech technically
known as prosopopoeia. This is the same figure of speech
that is employed in Anglo-Saxon riddles, where a visual
object describes itself verbally and challenges the reader
to guess its identity. The Grecian urn in itself, apart from
the poem, belongs to the visual arts, and suggests that a
verbal moral can be attached to a pictorial image as well
as to a story. This is what is done in the emblem, where

an allegorical picture is the occasion for verbal commentary.

Poetry depends heavily on concrete sense experience, and has a limited tolerance for the language of argument, thesis, or proposition. Within the last century we have had a series of manifestos directed against the moral and didactic type of writing where the act of understanding, being itself verbal, keeps the literary work "logocentric," in the current phraseology. Thus Valéry adjures the poet to "wring the neck" of rhetoric, meaning by "rhetoric" the alliance of poetry and oratory that seems to evoke only a verbal response. In English literature the early years of this century produced the movement known as Imagism, which demanded that the response to the total meaning, or what we may call the theme, of a poem should be at least metaphorically pictorial. Imagism was a minor movement in itself, but similar tendencies led Eliot, for example, to praise the "clear visual images" of Dante, contrasting him in this respect with the blind Milton to the latter's disadvantage. William Carlos Williams, though working in a very different idiom from Imagism, formulated the principle that forms the title of the last poem in Wallace Stevens's *Collected Poems:* "Not Ideas about the Thing but the Thing Itself." In prose fiction it is a very common device to have some visual emblem represent the simultaneous meaning or theme of the novel. Examples include Henry James's *The Golden Bowl,* D. H. Lawrence's *The White Peacock,* and Virginia Woolf's *To the Lighthouse.*

The geometrical shapes of the letters of Western alphabets make it difficult to assimilate the literary and pictorial arts as completely as can be done in the Orient, where calligraphy often seems to bridge the gap between writing and drawing. However, there are enough experiments with shape poems and concrete poetry to indicate a considerable interest in this area. There is much less to note on the musical side: poets are no longer as liberal with metaphors of harps or lyres or lutes, or even singing, as they used to be. We occasionally run across the term *voice* as a metaphor for hearing, as in Herbert Read's *The True Voice of Feeling* or Malraux's *Les Voix du silence,* but these are critical works.

But the combination of verbal and visual appeal, with each art functioning by itself, has had a long history in our tradition. Its more modern forms begin with Hogarth's sequential pictures on a verbal program, such as *Marriage à la Mode* and *The Rake's Progress,* and reach their highest development in the illuminated books of William Blake, where we have again a sequence of plates that may show any proportion of verbal and visual material, from a plate that is all text to one that is all design, and anything in between. These are not illustrated poems, for illustration punctuates a verbal text and brings it to periodic halts: in Blake there is a continuous counterpoint of the two arts from beginning to end. On a popular level an easy-going intermixture of drawing and text forms the staple of young readers today, the comic book, where one art continually feeds on the other, so that the deficiencies in each art by itself are less noticeable.

We next notice that in our cultural traditions the specifi-

cally biblical and Hebrew influence, the one that underlies the religions of Judaism, Christianity, and Islam, has in common a reverence for the spoken word of God and a corresponding distrust in any association of deity with the eyesight. Moses turns aside to see why the burning bush does not burn up: the visual stimulus is merely to awaken his curiosity, and it is the voice that speaks from the bush that is important. God constantly speaks in the Bible, and there seems to be no theological difficulty about hearing his voice. But the editorial and redacting processes in the Old Testament seem to get very agitated where any suggestion of a vision of God is concerned. We are solemnly adjured to make no image either of the true God or any of the gods concocted from nature, and this commandment has led to the practical extinction of representational painting in all three religions at various times, more particularly in Islam. In Christianity, any swing back to the primitive revolutionary fervor of the first Christian age has been normally accompanied by iconoclasm, in both Western and Eastern churches. In the *Clementine Recognitions* St. Peter enters a building decorated with frescoes, and it is noted with emphatic approval that he is totally indifferent to the impressions of pictorial art. Of course the Bible is full of imagery, as full as any work of literature would be. But apparently this imagery is intended to be internalized, and assimilated to the silent hearing which is the approved response to the Word of God.

The attitude of Plato toward the arts of *techne,* painting and sculpture particularly, was not greatly different: he began the critical tendency to regard the painter as simply a master of representational illusion that lasted until after the Renaissance. But in a polytheistic religion we must have statues or pictures to distinguish one god from another, and in Greek culture we see two powerful emphases on the visual: the nude in sculpture and the theater in literature. For, whatever the importance of the music and poetry heard in a theater, the theater remains primarily a visual presentation of literature, as its derivation from the Greek word for seeing (*theaomat*) shows. In contrast, the iconoclastic tendencies in Christianity are often accompanied by a strong dislike of the theater, and complaints about the moral indecency of portraying naked bodies need no elaboration of reference. Again, in Homer a god or goddess will appear to a hero in the guise of someone he knows well: the Christian notion of a uniquely portentous incarnation of a deity in a human form is very remote from the Homeric world.

At the same time the transition from hearing to seeing metaphors that we noted in the encounter with literature also seems to operate in religious texts and rituals. In the Christian mass the Collect or scripture readings are followed by the elevation of the Host; the Eleusinian mysteries culminated, we are told, in exhibiting a reaped ear of corn to the initiates; Zen Buddhism has a legend that the Buddha, after ending a sermon, held up a golden flower, the only member of his audience who got the point being, naturally, the founder of Zen. The Christian Bible ends with the Book of Revelation, a tremendous vision of the whole order of nature being destroyed and succeeded by a new heaven and earth. Though a very imperfectly visualized book, it is said to be a "vision," and clearly follows the religious tradition in which the crucial transition from physical to spiritual life is described in the visual metaphor or "enlightenment." Similarly Job remarks, at the end of his long ordeal, "I have heard of thee by the hearing of the ear: but now mine eye seeth thee."

When the relation of the art of words and the art of drawing and coloring becomes less metaphorical and more concrete, the tension between them greatly increases. The elaborate descriptions of paintings that are occasionally found in literary works belong to a specific rhetorical device, usually called ecphrasis, which is often considered a sign of "decadence," or whatever term we use to indicate that the writer has embarked on what we consider a misleading path. Many such descriptions belong to late classical fiction: the romance of Leucippe and Clitophon, by Achilles Tatius, is triggered by a picture, elaborately described, of the rape of Europa, which leads a bystander to tell his story to another bystander. However, when he ends the story eight books later, the author has forgotten his opening and does not return to it. It is usually a woman's nudity that a writer counts on to hold his reader's attention in such a device, but even so his resources are limited. Two heroines are exposed naked to a sea monster in *Orlando Furioso,* but despite the fullness of Ariosto's description, the reader is apt to conclude that, in a verbal setting at any rate, one luscious nude is very like another. In still more elaborate examples, such as the shield of Achilles in Homer, we quickly forget about the connection with the visual arts—that is, we stop asking ourselves if it is really possible to get all that on a painted or carved surface, and simply accept the shield for what it is: a description of a calm world at peace that forms a beautiful contrast to the weary hacking of bodies that is the foreground action. It has been a generally accepted principle, since Lessing's *Laokoon* at least, that one art cannot really do what another art is especially equipped to do. The principle involved here is quite distinct from the one implicit in Blake's illuminated poems: there we have two arts running side by side, each doing its own work, and not one art attempting to reproduce the effect of another in its own medium.

The same principle would apply to the attempt in painting to imitate verbal effects, but there the issue is more complex. In the Middle Ages, when the church was the chief patron of the visual arts, an elaborate code of iconography prescribed at least the content of the picture. There were verbal reasons for presenting one saint as bald and another with hair, and for supplying martyred saints with the instruments of their martyrdom—Catherine's wheel, Laurence's gridiron, and the like. When in the Renaissance the market for secular painting began to expand, the situation was not very different: painting the birth of Venus or the apotheosis of Louis XIV is equally a commitment to a verbal program. Still later come the anecdotal pictures of the eighteenth and nineteenth centuries, which are part of the development of the visual arts known as illustration.

We have said that verbal media internalize the imagery they use, so that the reader is compelled to build up his own structure of civilization. The illustration relieves the strain of this by supplying a readymade equivalent for the reader's mental picture: hence its proverbial vividness, as

expressed in the journalistic cliché that "one picture is worth a thousand words." In the nineteenth century books were illustrated to an extent hardly conceivable today, when the development of film and television has obviated the need for most of it. What's the good of a book, inquires Lewis Carroll's Alice, without pictures or conversations? The same close association with words is present in paintings themselves: the Pre-Raphaelite movement in Britain, for example, was primarily a development of painting as illustration—to medieval romance, to Shakespeare, to contemporary life, to the Bible.

A contradiction seems implied in what we have said thus far. We have spoken of the iconic art of the Middle Ages, and also of the prejudice against representational art of any kind that pervades the biblical religions, and accounts for the recurring movements of iconoclasm. The explanation is that the Word of God, or doctrine of the church, being verbal, is, we said, supposed to be internalized, and the status of the painting or sculpture related to it depends on the previous existence of that internalization. If there is none, the picture or whatever could be an idol, something that brings us to a reverent full stop in front of something presented as both objective and numinous. But in the biblical tradition nothing objective can be numinous: art is a creation of man and nature a creation of God, and no deities lurk in either. If the internalized verbal structure is already there, however, the picture becomes an icon, intended to elicit meditation instead of closing it off. The same principle, working inside the Christian tradition, makes for a progressive domestication of the major religious figures. We go from the great Torcello Madonna, who seems a million years old with no sign of aging, through the highly stylized Byzantine figures like the Rucellai Madonna of Duccio to the comparatively humanized Madonna of Giotto, and from there to the still more familiar quattrocento Madonnas, who look so much more like simply attractive young women with their babies.

In later periods of painting we become increasingly aware of the principle stated by William Carlos Williams in relation to literature: "The classic is the local fully realized, words marked by a place." Substituting "pictures" for "words," we see the principle operating in Dutch realism, including the realism of landscape in Hobbema and Ruisdael, in the first generation of French impressionism, in the earlier Barbizon school, in the southern English landscape tradition headed by Constable. Such movements in painting are opposite in tendency to what is called the "picturesque," the search for a particular spot (often called "unspoiled") that lends itself to certain pictorial conventions, again usually verbal in origin. In our day the picturesque has been mainly taken over by photography, but a contrast remains between two approaches to visual art: that of the tourist looking in from the outside and that of the native looking out from the inside. Such contrasts are more familiar in culturally new countries, including Canada, but picturesque bandits and gypsies have been celebrated by European painters too. The picturesque is typically a conservative idealized vision, and hence rather distanced: if it comes much closer it turns into the genuinely realistic. John Ruskin, who in this respect was more of a lay preacher using pictures as moral documents than

Piero di Cosimo, Simonetta Vespucci, *wood, ca. 1480.*

a critic making objective analyses of works of art, is full of denunciations of the picturesque that gets too close to its subject. Thus in *Stones of Venice* he contrasts Holman Hunt, who "loves peasant boys, because he finds them more roughly and picturesquely dressed, and more healthily coloured, than others," with Murillo's drawing of a beggar's dirty foot, which "is mere delight in foulness."

The issue involved here takes us a long way. Traditionally, the painter has been judged by his representational skill: there are Greek legends about painters painting grapes that birds would peck at, and the Elizabethan critic Puttenham says that the artist of painting or carving is "only a bare imitator of nature . . . as the marmoset doth many countenances and gestures of a man." It is somewhat chastening to realize how triumphant the tradition of painting has been, in the face of such infantile critical theories. The justification for the theories was that, as Sir Thomas Browne said in the seventeenth century, "Nature is the art of God"; hence in theory all the original part of the painter's work had already been done. And yet the painter often agrees with such critics, maintaining that he paints only what he sees, and just as he sees, without realizing how impossible this is. What he sees he sees from within the conventions of painting in his day, which in turn are determined by a cultural and social framework. Any frequenter of art galleries can determine, with a little practice, what century any picture he is looking at was painted in, and this clearly could not be done if it were true that any painter in any age could simply reproduce nature at second hand. The development of photography has complicated this situation, but has not essentially changed it: photography has its conventions and fashions also.

In any case the assumption that painting is essentially representation has persisted up to a century or so ago, and it is part of the assumption that the painter is permitted only selection, not recreation. The selective process is supposed to operate on a quasi-moral principle: what the painter selects to record should, traditionally, be the "beautiful." The trouble is not only that beauty, at least the beauty that is connected with erotic feeling, is proverbially fleeting, but that conventions of beauty are fleeting also. Whatever is considered beautiful in any given period of culture tends to imprison itself within an increasingly narrowing convention. A beautiful body should be only a body in good physical condition between the ages of eighteen and thirty, and in a white society it must be obviously white. Even in the nineteenth century it was widely assumed that the Greeks had invented beauty, and that Asian and African artists had deliberately made a cult of the grotesque and hideous out of sheer perversity.

This constant closing off of the beautiful in academic dead ends and blind alleys is accompanied by a corresponding exhaustion of resources in the techniques of producing it. We recall Browning's melancholy monologue of "the faultless painter" Andrea del Sarto, obsessed with a sense of futility and disillusionment not merely in his personal life but in his painting as well. It has been remarked that probably nobody in Andrea's own time would have understood that faultlessness could itself be a fault: the point is, however, that technical perfection implies a convention

narrowing so rapidly that there is soon nothing left to explore within it. When such perfection is reached it becomes mechanical, and there is nothing to do but abandon the convention and try something else. Nobody would call Magnasco, or for that matter even Caravaggio, a faultless painter, but they were exploring pictorial conventions that Andrea del Sarto could not have dreamed of.

We should not be surprised to find a fairly consistent tradition of revolt in the painting of the last two centuries or so, first against the tyranny of verbal conventions, then against the assumption that the painter's primary function is to represent nature, which makes the content of the picture and the "accuracy" of its representation functional elements in criticism. The landscape painters in England, Turner, Constable, Bonington, and their impressionist successors in France, were in the forefront of the struggle against too exclusive a demand for emblems, illustrations, and other forms of subservience to the verbal. By the end of the nineteenth century this resistance had spread to the dominance of representation itself. One of the commonest stories about twentieth-century painters, ascribed to both Picasso and Matisse and doubtless many others, is the response to the complaint that a picture, let us say of a fish, was not a fish: "Quite right: it is not a fish, it is a picture." The issue at stake here is, of course, the autonomy of painting, the right of the painter to deal only with the pictorial shapes and colors that belong to his art.

The development of the verbal arts has followed parallel directions, though the sequence is harder to trace because as long as literature uses ordinary words, it can never be as abstract or autonomous as painting or music can be. Some representational aura will still cling to the words, however strong the embrace of their metaphorical context in poem or story. Also, the external forces trying to dominate literature mostly take the form of other verbal structures. But the same resistance to conventionalizing standards of beauty, to an idealizing representationalism that stays well away from its subject (unfortunately there is no exact literary equivalent of "picturesque"), to the tyranny of religious or political anxieties, has operated in literature as well as in the visual arts.

One result of this is that instead of making a sterile and canonized ideal beauty the model for the artist, the entire spectrum of cultural traditions, from the most primitive to the most sophisticated, from the most immediate to the most exotic, is spread before him as a source of possible influences. A contemporary artist without a strong sense of inner direction would be more likely to suffer from agoraphobia than claustrophobia. A by-product of the same expansion has been the breaking down of the barrier between the work of art and the ordinary visual object. The *objet trouvé* may be not only the subject for a picture but the art object itself; in collage the picture is not painted but assembled from pictorial data; pop art and similar developments are based on the principle that anything may become a work of art when a consciousness is focused on it. In the Renaissance it was assumed, not only that nature was the art of God, but that the order of nature was a metaphorical book, a secondary Word of God, and that the properly instructed man could read its riddles for almost any purpose, magical, medical, scientific, or religious. A rather similar assumption, that nothing exists merely as itself, seems to inform the visual arts today, however different the context. A well-known picture by Boccioni, *The Street Enters the House,* may serve as an allegory for an age in which the separation of works of art inside buildings from miscellaneous objects outside on the street is breaking down.

The oldest paintings we possess, and the oldest works of any art by many thousands of years still extant, are the Paleolithic paintings and drawings in the caves of southern France and northern Spain. The firmness and assurance of the drawing would be impressive anywhere, but in such surroundings, with such formidable difficulties of positioning and lighting, they are little short of miraculous. There were doubtless representational motives for drawing the animals of the hunt on which the food supply depended, but this can hardly have been the entire motivation, as some of the figures are human beings, probably sorcerers, clothed in animal skins. Wherever we turn in studying this art, we are constantly brought up against the cave itself, as a shrouding maternal womb containing the embryos both of human society and of the beings of the natural environment to which that society was most closely related. The persistence of the cave setting for fresco painting in Anatolia, India, Etruscan Italy, and many other places makes us wonder whether painting may not have a special relationship to the sense of something embryonic, present within the human imagination but suggesting the outlines of a human civilization not yet born.

Whatever may be thought of this, the sense of something unborn and embryonic turns up recurrently in the history of painting. We see it in the grotesque fantasies of Hieronymus Bosch and Brueghel, in the naive staring faces of primitive painters, in the melting or deliberately incongruous shapes of the surrealists, in the spidery childlike scrawls of Miró and Klee. It is as though, in Klee's words, the painter "places more value on the powers which do the forming than on the final forms themselves." We are very far away here from the notion of the painter as a supermonkey reproducing the art of God in nature. In the cultural history of Canada painting was the first of the arts to come to maturity, and it formed a very important aspect of the exploring and settling of the country. Perhaps a worldwide metamorphosis of the visual arts indicates the coming of a new age in man's attitude to the globe he inhabits.

A corresponding metamorphosis of the verbal arts would probably come later, though some elements of it can already be glimpsed. In the Western tradition literature seems to have run through a cycle beginning with myth and romance and ending with an ironic realism which disintegrates into various forms of paradox, such as the theater of the absurd. In our day we see many signs of the cycle being repeated: the retelling of the great myths, the reshaping of romance formulas in a science fiction setting, the revival of a primitive relation to a listening audience in rock and ballad singing. But nothing repeats exactly in history, and in any case the end of a cycle does not compel us to repeat the same cycle, but gives us a chance to transfer to another level.

It is obvious that most of the movements in the arts mentioned above are political statements. Many of them are regarded as bourgeois erosions of socialist values in Marxist societies, even though they often assert those very values in a democratic setting. It seems to me that behind the political statement lies a fundamentally antipolitical attitude, an anarchism tending to break down all social mythologies devoted to promoting special social interests. Such an attitude may be unrecognized by the individual artist himself, or may even be the exact opposite of what he thinks he is trying to do. The movement known as dada, which arose after the First World War, was explicitly anarchist in this sense as a total movement, whatever the variety of social opinion within it. At present we are confronted by a movement in all the arts which, for all its tremendous creative variety, has incorporated the spirit of dada within it. Such a movement is to be welcomed, as long as we see it not as a kind of extreme unction for the bourgeois soul or as a morbid preoccupation with chaos for its own sake, but as the opportunity for renewed imaginative energy and a new freedom in seeing the world.

> *Northrop Frye, "Literature and the Visual Arts," in his* Myth and Metaphor: Selected Essays, 1974-1988, *edited by Robert D. Denham, University Press of Virginia, 1990, pp. 183-95.*

Jan Mukařovský

[*Mukařovský was a leading Czechoslovakian linguist and semiotician who gained international renown for a theory of aesthetics based on semiology, in which he relates the meaning of artworks to the social and historical context in which they were created. In the following essay, which was first published in Czech in 1941, Mukařovský addresses some aspects of the interconnection between literature and the plastic arts.*]

Comparative literature owes its origins to the Romantic interest in the historical and geographical heterogeneity of cultural activities. In the course of its development it has created a number of methods, each of which has entailed not only a different modus operandi but also a different approach to material, a different conception of it. Sometimes the path of a certain theme or thematic element (motif) is traced through different literatures; sometimes the literary activity in a broad cultural sphere differentiated into a number of national literatures is examined with a unifying vision. The questions arise as to what is the center of this activity, what the impulses originating from it, and how do literatures bound into a unity of a higher order influence each other. Furthermore, the question of the general regularity of literary activity and its historical variations arises. In the last few decades the foundations for a comparative study of literary forms have been laid. In connection with the comparative study of the literary form we should mention Jakobson's fruitful idea of investigating those literary forms which are closely tied to language, for example, meters in literatures related by language (such as Slavic). The influence of language for the differentiation of literary development is thus revealed. It appears that even slight differences between kindred languages determine the completely different natures and developments of the same meter in two linguistically related literatures. Even in more complicated literary phenomena, for example, in international literary movements (such as Symbolism), we can often deduce to a considerable degree the heteromorphism of such a movement in different nations from differences in their linguistic systems.

The above methods of study are not, of course, the ultimate ones which comparative literature is capable of deriving from its basic orientation. Neither has structuralism, penetrating the methodology of literary theory, threatened comparativism with its presupposition of the immanent development of every individual literature; rather it has enriched its possibilities. Structuralism proceeds from the presupposition that every compared literature comprises an individual structure. The contribution of structuralism is that it does not compare individual facts as independent values but as representatives of the literary structures into which these facts are incorporated. Comparison thus eliminates the risk of fortuity and the arbitrary interpretation of the compared facts. In each case, even the most detailed ones, its object is, in fact, entire developmental series and their polarity. The concern for polarity, for the tension between comparative series (literatures), however, causes structuralism, unlike older comparative scholarship, to take into account not only similarities between the matters compared but also, and above all, their differences (an example of this being the comparative studies of metrical schemes that we mentioned above).

Polarity manifests itself not only among different literatures but primarily within each literature itself. The essence of literary structure lies in the polar tension among individual components, the tension that maintains the structure in constant developmental movement. From the standpoint of structuralism, therefore, there is not a substantial difference between the comparative study of several literatures and the study of a single literature; even within a single literature the scholar is always compelled to make comparisons. It is impossible, for example, to understand the developmental dynamics of a given literature without taking into account the influence that the tension between verse and prose exerts upon this development. Prose continuously adopts its artistic devices from verse, altering their function and appearance in terms of its intrinsic preconditions (the difference between rhythmic and nonrhythmic speech) and its current developmental situation, and poetry borrows from prose in the same way.

If, however, the scholar decides to take into account this and similar tensions, he will approach his material in exactly the same way that a comparativist deals with the literatures compared. In the case mentioned, prose and verse appear as two independent developmental series interpenetrating and repelling one another. The assignment of individual poets within the development of a given literature also requires the comparative method: the poet in question appears to be determined by his polar relation to predecessors, contemporaries, and younger poets (consider Šalda's famous scheme: Vrchlický-Neruda, Vrchlický-Zeyer, Vrchlický-Březina). If comparative study thus penetrates

more deeply the very kernel of literature than seems to be its primary design, we may obviously presuppose that it can expand in the opposite direction as well, namely, into the sphere where artistic literature touches upon other arts.

Neither do the relations among individual arts, including literature, differ from those among individual national literatures. Similarly, as individual literatures usually differ from one another most conspicuously through language, the individual arts differ from one another according to material. Czech literature, for example, differs from German, French, and Russian literature primarily (if we disregard, of course, other differences) in the fact that its material is the Czech linguistic system with such and such individual features that both make possible and limit artistic creation in this language. Likewise, literature as one of the arts differs from painting and music in its material, the boundaries of which it cannot overstep and from which it draws its typical developmental possibilities. As early as 1766 Lessing discovered (in his *Laocoön*) the delimitation of the arts according to the nature of their material. In the spirit of his time he interpreted this limitation as a directive for artists, whereas the real development of art shows that every art sometimes strives to overstep its boundaries by assimilating itself to another art. Boundaries are, however, uncrossable, not *de iure* but *de facto,* for material can never give up its nature. Other questions of contact among the arts also find their analogues within literature. For example, the transposition of a theme from one art to another (painting, drama, film with a theme adopted from literature or vice versa) has some aspects in common with the transfer of a theme from one literary structure into another or even from one literary genre into another. Thus the transition from the comparative study of literature to the comparative theory of the arts is likewise continuous with the connection between the comparative study of literature and the study of a single literature. There is an uninterrupted scale of correlations and tensions from the polarity among individual components of a literary work to the polarity between literature and the other arts, and only a total survey of this multiply stratified scheme of forces would yield a complete picture of the "internal" development of literature as an art. In the following section we shall attempt a more detailed characterization of the relations which link the individual arts to one another as well as a closer examination of the situation of literature within this interplay of forces.

. . . . .

What links the individual arts to one another is the community of their goal. In general the arts are activities with a prevailing aesthetic consideration; what separates them from one another is the difference in material. Both these circumstances manifest themselves simultaneously and, of course, dialectically, creating a basic antinomy in the relation among the arts. Community of goal leads to the fact that every art—as we have already said—sometimes strives to attain through its own means the same effect that another art attains. Sometimes literature seeks to portray like painting, sometimes it strives to achieve the semantic polyvalence of music (to which the perceiver can attribute

Georges Braque, Face et profil, *canvas, 1942.*

a large number of meanings and can at the same time oscillate among manifold meanings). At such a moment, however, the character of the material intervenes. A word remains a word, and by copying painting, literature attains only the discovery of a new possibility (in some cases, a

new configuration of possibilities) of the artistic exploitation of the word. For example, if the verbal imitation of painting emphasizes shades of color and light, this tendency necessarily manifests itself in linguistic material as an excessive need for terms (most often adjectives and substantives derived from them) expressing colors and lights. To achieve necessary variety foreign words can be adopted, and the exploitation of foreign borrowings as a literary device can thus be increased. The differentiation of expressions signifying colors and lights can also be achieved through unusual derivations, and derivation is therefore elevated to a means of poetic effect.

Let us cite another example. One of the important factors in the "imitation" of music by poetry can be the euphonic organization of speech sound elements in combinations which repeat; the phonological composition of a text which, of course, does not resemble a series of tones except for its temporal succession is thus deautomatized. Of course, it also happens that an art striving to achieve an effect characteristic of another art has at its disposal an element common to this art and utilizes it for "imitation." If Hlaváček entitled one of the poems in the collection *Pozdě k ránu* with the line "Svou violu jsem naladil co možná nejhlouběji" ("I tuned my viola as low as possible"), he expressed not only the figuratively musical orientation of the collection but also (perhaps involuntarily) the real tonal level of the voice that his poems compel during an oral reading. Here the tonal level of the voice has been exploited (by means of the syntactic, phonological, and semantic composition of the text), or, more precisely, the differences among the three tonal levels which every individual has at his disposal. Hlaváček's poems force the reader to remain on the lowest of these levels. Despite the fact that tone is a factor common to the human voice and to music, it is exploited in a poem in a completely different way than in music. Musical melody is based on variations in tone; the "musicality" of the poem, however, has made it necessary to remain as much as possible on the same tonal level, has required vocal monotony.

An art inclining toward another art can never, therefore, transcend its own essence. There are even cases in which this impossibility itself becomes an object of poetic effect. Thus Nezval has created the impression of the fantastic in a poem of his *Absolutní hrobař* (the cycle "Bizarní městečko" No. 6) by transposing the perspective of a picture into the poem.

The imitation of one art by another is not unambiguous. If, after a certain time in the course of development, the same two arts encounter each other several times, the imitating art can focus attention each time on a different aspect of the other art. For example, during the period of descriptive poetry, poetry sought, in its contact with painting, support for the predominance of static (descriptive) over dynamic (plot) motifs. On the other hand, in the period of Parnassianism and especially in the period of literary Impressionism immediately following it, it was a matter of the imitation of color which, as we have already suggested, especially influenced the selection of words. There is neither a totally passive nor totally active party in the contact of the arts with one another. The same art which inclined toward another in one period itself becomes an object of imitation in another period. For example, theater and film have alternated between activity and passivity in very rapid succession several times during the last few decades. In its beginnings film sought support in theater (the

photographed theatrical scene, theatrical acting in film), it then influenced theater itself (lighting, the dynamicity of scenic space), but finally, in the period of the soundtrack, film has again attempted to become, in part, theater (theatrical dialogue). As for literature, sometimes it has been the object of imitation in relation to music (program music), sometimes it has sought support in music itself (Symbolism). Neither is painting always simply a model with respect to literature, for in certain periods it itself seeks a poetic effect, sometimes by attempting narrative, sometimes by pursuing lyrical emotiveness, and sometimes by striving for the painterly equivalent of poetic metaphor, metonymy, and synecdoche.

There are not only temporary encounters but also permanent contacts among the arts. It is precisely here that the tension among the arts is most conspicuous. For literature, illustration and vocal music, in particular, constitute such an area of interconnection. In both these cases, the problem of the transposition of literary devices into music and painting is raised again and again with the same urgency. Frequently, however, the opposite problem also occurs: the transposition of musical and painterly devices into literature. A picture is not always an illustration of a literary work, for sometimes a literary work is an illustration of a painting; the poetic word is not always the foundation of music, for sometimes music is the basis of the poetic word. The materials of the participating arts and their expressive possibilities collide with one another in illustration and vocal music especially. The histories of these two fields show how differently their materials can be interrelated and how diversely they can project themselves into one another.

Quite often arts meet in the person of the artist himself. Thus a literary talent is often combined with a talent for the visual arts, especially painting (Wyśpiański, Josef Čapek), or for music (Nezval). Even more frequent are cases in which the second art remains a dilettantish activity (Mácha, Pushkin). These cases are not less interesting than the former for the study of the interrelations between literary structure and the structures of other arts. There are also cases in which the poet is the illustrator of his own writings (Karel Čapek in his travel books); here the question of the interpenetration of word and picture is of the utmost urgency.

Finally, we should mention that the encounters of the arts need not always have the character of an influence of one upon the other, for they can appear as a quite extraneous competition and struggle for popularity. For example, during the last few decades we have witnessed a competition between film and theater in which film had the upper hand for a while, whereas theater now enjoys this advantage. Painting and sculpture have frequently been in a similar competitive tension. Sometimes competition has to do with different branches of a single art; in literature, for example, a predilection for poetry alternates with a predilection for prose. If we continued this consideration of competition among the arts, it would of course lead us into the sociology of art. Nevertheless, some of the factors which are decisive in this competition can have their source in the development and state of artistic structure (for example, verse will probably be more popular when it stresses the emotiveness of poetic expression than when it renounces emotive effectiveness); others can have their source in the epistemological range of the artistic work which is closely connected with its structure (the art that at a given moment is based upon an epistemological stance accessible to the broadest strata will be more popular than the others).

Meeting and struggling in the course of their development, the arts enter into very complex relations which influence the character of the entire set. Thus during the period when Symbolism began to incline toward music, painting (or at least some of its movements) also sought support for its tendency toward the harmonization of colors in music. Consider, for example, one of Karel Hlaváček's reviews ["Výstava českých akvarelistů roku 1896" (The 1896 exhibit of Czech watercolorists), *Dílo Karla Hlaváčka* 3 (1930)]:

> "Thinking and feeling artists are returning to the reduction of natural color tones, to the basic unshaded levels of pure, rich, singing colors. They are returning to where Japanese art is clearly preeminent. Depth, airy perspective, motion, and rest—all these can be expressed by simple, pure and broad primary and secondary tones resolved by the crystal corundumlike prism of the artist's soul. From the entire symphony of colors, viewed and heard, the modern watercolorist chooses only broad, harmonious tones in a minor key in order to express the present state of his soul. And if you give the same color symphony to several modern watercolorists, each of them will sing a different aria from it. . . . "

At the turn of the century, however, architecture also approximated literature and music. As late as 1929 Ozenfant treats the last relics of this aesthetic trend ironically [in *Foundations of Modern Art*]:

> "The architect's client, when he dreams of his future house, has a whole poem in his bosom. He rocks himself with dreams of the perfect symphony he will dwell in. He unburdens himself with some architect. And the ordinary architect is all fire to be a second Michael Angelo. Under pressure, he puts up an ode in concrete and plaster that generally turns out very different from what the client brooded over: whence arise conflicts: for poems, particularly those engendered by others, are uninhabitable."

After all, all the arts are always interrelated in particular ways so that they are bound into a structure of a higher order. Even if two arts do not confront one another head on at a given moment, they feel their common existence and react to one another. For instance, it is quite possible that when poetry "imitates" music, it simultaneously exhibits detectable traces of a kinship with the visual arts. We have in mind the state of poetry in the Symbolist period when poetry demonstrated a certain affinity to the movement in the visual arts called Art Nouveau at the same time as it was approximating music (we shall deal with Art Nouveau in poetry in more detail in the following section). The structural makeup of all the arts is thus as complex and dynamic as that of any individual art. It is

also hierarchically organized and even has its dominant component if one of the arts in a certain period is felt to be the art κατ' εξοχην, the most essential one, the representative of artistic creation in general. During the Renaissance, for example, the visual arts held such a position; during Romanticism, literature enjoyed this status. If the entire structure of the arts undergoes a change, the relations among its individual components, indeed the components themselves, also undergo a change. Thus the interrelation of literature and theater changed when film became a member of the set of the arts (I gather that the influence of film can be seen, for example, in the fact that the relation of theater to narrative literature has become more intense: the frequent staging of novels); indeed, even the intrinsic structure of these arts has changed as a result of the influence of film. Despite this perpetual changeability in the hierarchy of the arts, certain constants underlie the relations of individual arts. For instance, under any developmental situation literature is closer to music (with which it is connected through the sound aspect) and painting (with which it has in common the capacity of expressing the phenomena of external reality through signs connected in a continuous contexture) than to sculpture and architecture.

The concept of the interrelation of the arts as we have depicted it in the previous paragraphs is based upon the contradiction between the commonality of aim and the difference in material of the individual arts. In this it differs from the former concept, the typical expression of which, at least as far as literature is concerned, may be found in the appropriate chapters of Oskar Walzel's *Gehalt und Gestalt im Kunstwerk des Dichters* (1923) and in his earlier study *Wechselseitige Erhellung der Künste* (1917). Walzel's concept reduces the unity of the arts to the undynamic parallelism of artistic configurations, in the given case, of the literary configuration with the painted and musical ones. Its difference from the contemporary concept lies in the fact that Walzel tries his utmost to remove from sight the specific distinctiveness of the individual arts. He thus devotes much space to the weakening of the division between the temporal arts (literature, music) and the spatial arts (visual arts). He does this in such a way that, with a polemical thrust against Lessing, he discovers the element of successiveness in the perception of the visual arts as well.

There is no doubt that Walzel's achievement was developmentally necessary and progressive in its time. In Walzel the dogma of the nontransgressiveness of the boundaries between the arts yields to the unprejudiced study of the correlation between individual arts. From the modern standpoint, however, it is equally clear that Walzel's method goes too far in its direction away from Lessing. In rejecting the *dogmatic* separation of the arts, Walzel loses sight of their *factual* delimitation by the nature of their material. He applies to literature the principles created by Wölfflin for the analysis of works of visual art, finding it quite possible to seek the differences between linearity and the "picturesque" in the verbal aspect of literature. Such an application of terms adopted from the theory of the visual arts to literary devices can be, of course, only figurative and therefore ambiguous. Proof of this is the fact that

Walzel himself admits a dual possibility in applying the aforementioned opposition. The difference between linearity and the picturesque can, according to him, correspond either to the difference between a literary technique emphasizing the contours, in some cases the plasticity, of objects and one emphasizing colors, or to the difference between a literary style which articulates distinctly and one which weakens the articulation by obliterating the transitions between syntactic units, sentences, and so on. It is obvious that it is a matter of a mere analogy, in the discovery of which quite a lot of leeway is left to the scholar's fantasy. Walzel himself, of course, frequently arrives at very valuable results, but this is often for reasons of clairvoyant perception rather than methodological precision.

The adoption of the periodization of the visual arts, especially architecture, by other arts stems from an attitude similar to Walzel's, though not completely identical with it. This method is based upon the presupposition of a common epistemological and psychic tendency from which all the arts of a certain period arise. In all of the artistic creation of a given period there is the same will toward form (*Formwille*—Worringer's term) which renders its works similar to one another. Periodization following that of the visual arts has enjoyed considerable success in the history of literature (and elsewhere): such terms as Gothic literature or Baroque literature have the value of technical terms today. The advantage is obviously that the styles of the visual arts in their rather distinct periodization lend support to the division of the much more continuous development of the other arts. In recent years, however, attempts have been made to work out this method in detail. Not only the great epochs but also the secondary temporal segments of literary development are designated by terms adopted from the history of the visual arts: the literature of the Empire, the Biedermeier, and so forth. Nor is this detailed confrontation of literature with the visual arts without value. It is like projecting a sharp light from the side so that the aspects of literature which have previously escaped our attention are now revealed.

There are, however, certain dangers, among which the principal one is that regard for the specificity of literary material and for the autonomous development of literature will be neglected in this confrontation. The developmental boundaries need not be the same in every detail in all the arts, and the character of individual periods is also usually different in different arts. Let us take as an example Impressionism in painting. In its beginning Impressionism was parallel to Naturalism in verbal art (an effort to grasp reality without the veil of conventions); however, in its later phases it is related to further stages of literary development. Its effort at suggestiveness (the landscape as "the state of the soul") brings it closer to poetic Symbolism; the laying bare of devices (for example, individual styles of painters, color-patches) renders it similar even to more recent literary movements. Nevertheless, Impressionism does not give up the basic unity of its approach throughout the entire period of its development. The consistent application of the developmental divisions of the visual arts to literature would necessarily lead to the separation of phenomena related from the standpoint of literature, the application of phenomena alien to one another, and so forth.

Must we therefore abandon the confrontation of literary development with the development of the visual arts? We think not (and it would also be wrong to give up the advantages which result from this confrontation). It is only necessary that the scholar look for dissimilarities as well as similarities between these two developments. Only if he takes into account these similarities and dissimilarities at the same time, will he avoid the danger of deforming the material under study. In the following section we shall attempt to present an example of a developmental study oriented in this way.

. . . . .

The subject of the comparison that we are attempting here is the way in which the movement in the visual arts called "Secession" [in Czechoslovakia; the English and French equivalent is Art Nouveau; the German, *Jugendstil*] projected itself into the development of literature at the turn of the century. First we must make a few brief remarks about the nature of this movement.

Art Nouveau is rooted in the craft industry, and its origin derives from the revolt against the imitation of historical styles. Tendencies of this kind first appeared in France and especially in England where the revival of the artistic craft was proclaimed by Ruskin and put into practice by Morris. For central Europe this movement is usually marked by the years 1895-1905. From the craft industry Art Nouveau penetrated the visual arts, and we may thus speak about Art Nouveau painting, sculpture, and architecture. Here, however, the boundaries are not definite. Recently there has been an effort to broaden the notion of Art Nouveau; for example, van Gogh, Gauguin, Munch, and the Czech artist Preisler are included among Art Nouveau painters today.

We could enumerate many of the features of Art Nouveau, especially if we took into account heterogeneous peripheries of this vaguely defined movement, but we shall limit ourselves to the most essential of them. Above all, Art Nouveau is characterized by a tendency toward ornamentation. For the Art Nouveau artist the ornament is not something additional and optional but the very essence. We can already find emphasis on the importance of the ornament in Morris's theoretical discussions. He supports his thesis with interesting arguments. Figure painting is without any doubt the highest form of the art of painting, but pictures representing man and his activities frequently arouse human passions and instincts; indeed, sometimes they even cause suffering and dread. This tires the body and the soul, and like an animal man longs for rest, while at the same time he resists fatigue. He is therefore reluctant to experience tragic feelings day after day and hour after hour. On ordinary days he must accordingly surround himself with an art which, though perhaps not worse than high art, is less exciting. This is why he covers the walls of his home with ornaments reminding him of the face of the earth and the innocent love of animals and people who spend their days between work and repose. This is how Morris expresses himself about ornamentation in a lecture on decorative painting, and his essay reveals the very foundation of the Art Nouveau attitude. Though we do not claim that every Art Nouveau artist would agree with this opinion word for word, we can, nevertheless, deduce from it that the dislike for strong emotional fluctuations and for the strong force of will which such fluctuations necessarily cause is inherent in the very essence of Art Nouveau. For Art Nouveau, emotion seems to be a monotonous mood, sometimes a bit asthenic, qualitatively characterized as dreaming, weariness, resignation. The supple ornamentation of Art Nouveau is the expression of this mood and the means of its evocation. A predilection for line and plane is closely associated with the ornamentality of Art Nouveau.

The *line* of Art Nouveau is a continuous curve without sharp breaks and without geometrical regularity, a curve that evokes in the viewer an impression of undulatory, pacific movement through a sympathetic motor reaction. This curve is found not only in ornaments and paintings but also in the construction of furniture, and even in architecture (the contours of walls, gables, etc.). Some favorite motifs of Art Nouveau painting—hair, streams of smoke, hands outstretched sideways and upwards, dangling twigs—are linked to its linearity. A predilection for the *plane* finds its application especially in Art Nouveau painting but elsewhere as well, for example in architecture (the flat facades of Art Nouveau buildings). Color compensates for the monotony of the plane. The color-patch gains coherence after the trembling quiver of Impressionism: firm contour is furnished by the line. Art Nouveau color is a value in itself rather than a mere characteristic of an object. Even the craft industry of this period frequently chooses colors that conflict with the usual coloration (indeed, sometimes the designation) of an object (for example, pink or blue furniture in Art Nouveau kitchens). The essential requirement of Art Nouveau color is the interrelation of the colors of a painting, of an ornament, or even of an entire interior. The harmonization of colors or their contrast is the means of achieving this interrelation;

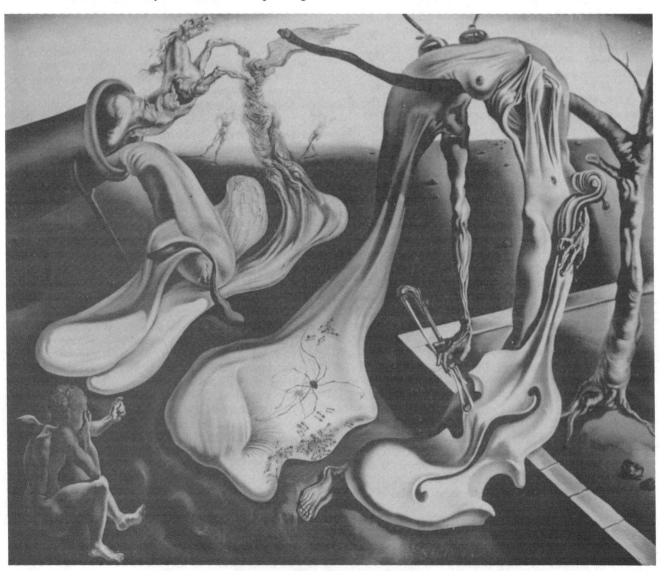

Salvador Dali, Cauchemar de violoncelles mous, *canvas 1940.*

harmonization is sometimes produced by the decomposition of light. Decomposition and harmonization lead to the selection of unusual, even previously non-existent, shades of color. The emphasis on the shading of color is one of the most characteristic features of Art Nouveau.

A predilection for a combination of heterogeneous materials is connected with this passion for color—for example, colored tiles, colored glass, colorful mosaics, polished stones, and metals combined in surprising compositions on the facades and in the interiors of Art Nouveau buildings. A predilection for materials themselves thus arises. Unlike the later conception, however, this predilection concerns primarily the optic impression that a material creates.

Finally, we must mention the Art Nouveau concept of stylization. Seeking to detach itself from historical ornamental formulae, Art Nouveau favors natural shapes (leaves, flowers, the human or animal body) which, however, it arranges according to the principles of proportionality, symmetry, and eurhythmy. Thus arise shapes subtly oscillating between the imitation of reality and ornamentation. The contradiction between reality and artifact is therefore felt more sharply in Art Nouveau than in other periods. There are even theoretical writings about this phenomenon. Stylization becomes the central feature of Art Nouveau perception, and not only in the visual arts; gestures, forms of social contact, and clothing are stylized. Through stylization Art Nouveau penetrated the whole of life, all of its expressions and activities, and it is thus not surprising that we can find its reflection in artistic activity other than the visual arts.

Having briefly characterized Art Nouveau, let us now turn our attention to the Czech literature contemporary with it, the literature of the years 1895-1905. What was happening in Czech poetry at this moment? It was about 1895 that the generation of the Symbolists and Decadents gained ascendancy. Sova's collection *Soucit i vzdor,* with which "the anteroom of his poetry ends" (Šalda), was published in 1894. The year 1895 brings Březina's *Tajemné dálky.* In 1896 Hlaváček publishes the book *Pozdě k ránu,* and Karásek ze Lvovic publishes *Zazděná okna.* The situation is not, of course, so simple. Besides the generation of the Lumírians, whose profile was already unalterably complete (but whose younger members—the trio O. Auředníček, J. Borecký, and J. Kvapil—had prepared the way for Symbolism), we find the unique figure of Machar here. The contradiction between Machar and Symbolism provides the basic scheme of the developmental plan for a long period: poets such as Neumann, Dyk, and Bezruč are, each in his own way, syntheses of this antinomy.

From this point up to the [First] World War, the development of Czech literature continues without any further distinct generational division, but it is richly differentiated by strong personalities. Previously accustomed to the system of leading individuals (Hálek and Neruda in the Máj school, Vrchlický and Čech in the generation of Ruchovians and Lumírians), Czech poetry at this time acquires a new, unusual organization. There are a number of equally important poets interconnected and separated by complex relations. This individualizing differentiation of poets as a whole was accompanied by a strong upsurge in criticism. Šalda's *Boje o zítřek* [Battles for tomorrow] (1905) shows graphically that the purpose of this critical effort was not only the struggle for a new conception of poetry and its task but also the need to impose some order upon the individualizing process of literature. Šalda never stops repeating that individuality and the individual cannot do without internal regularity, that they are not natural phenomena but values which must be created by a great ethical and artistic effort. This volcanically restless activity and its mediation gave birth to the particularity of the Czech cultural awareness, basing it for the moment on the personal responsibility of individuals to themselves.

At first glance nothing is more alien to this maximally active contemporary attitude than the playful and relatively passive nature of Art Nouveau. We would be unjust to every one of the poets of this period (at least every outstanding one) if we declared Art Nouveau as the basic feature of his profile. As long as the historian does not distort actual conditions, there is no chance for a section called "The Literature of Art Nouveau" to appear in the history of Czech literature. And yet . . . In 1896 *Almanach secese* [Almanac of Art Nouveau] appears under the editorship of Stanislav K. Neumann. In his introduction the editor declares: "I invited all of the modern camp [to contribute], independently of any faction, whether they stood in either of its wings or alongside of it, as long as they did not stand against it." Thus we find the names of Březina, Hlaváček, Karásek, the pseudonym of Dyk, and even the name of Zeyer among the contributors. It would therefore appear that Art Nouveau made the claim of being synonymous with modernism. Even more conclusive for the influence of Art Nouveau on poetry is the way in which Šalda formulates his ideal of the self-determining poetic figure [in "Osobnost a dílo" [Personality and the work], *Boje o zítřek*]: "But the kingly artist and the chaste donor of a blossom and a second, who gave only overflowing froth, gave infinitely more: he gave his *height,* the highest height which he ever reached and thereby his entire *depth,* for froth is the blossom of the depth and its measure. . . . There are no greater artists than the artists of the froth of life." The inner order of artistic individuality required by Šalda takes on the form of contemporary stylization, a purely Art Nouveau stylization, as the motifs of the *blossom* and the *froth,* both borrowed from the typical stock of ornaments of Art Nouveau painting, indicate. . . .

Let us now consider literature itself. Here we cannot present a detailed comparison of literature with Art Nouveau in the visual arts, and this is certainly not the aim of this essentially theoretical essay. We shall therefore attempt to illustrate our assertion by means of only a few characteristic passages selected at random from the poems of the period around 1895-1905. The reader who wishes to get a more complete picture should consult the anthology *Modern Czech Poetry,* in which the material is lucidly arranged. From today's standpoint this anthology could quite easily bear the subtitle "Art Nouveau in Czech Poetry."

We have spoken about the linearity of Art Nouveau. In

looking for a reflection of this visual artistic feature in literature, we do not wish to interpret it figuratively as Walzel did. In Czech poets of the turn of the century there are plentiful examples of landscapes *actually* perceived linearly, hence examples of the verbal transposition of painted works:

> Klid bílých linií se tiše krajem snoval
> v šat slabě vzdmutých ploch a lesů mrtvých
>   ladem;
> let ptáků v azuru čar sítě nerýsoval.

> The calm of white lines was moving quietly
>   through
> the landscape
> into the garment of the slightly raised planes and
> the forests dead in fallow;
> the flight of birds was not sketching nets of lines
> in the azure.
>
> (Březina, "Siesty," *Tajemné dálky*)

> Kraj vymřel dokola. Je mrtvo. Nikde ruchu.
> Vše tichu podléhá. V snů jemně modrý klam
> Klid spících linií se kreslí v měkkém vzduchu.

> The countryside has died out all around. It is
> deathlike. Not a sound anywhere.
> Everything is subject to silence. Into the fine
> blue mirage of dreams
> The calm of slumbering lines is sketched in
> the soft air.
>
> (Karásek ze Lvovic, "Hudba siesty," *Zazděná
>   okna*)

> Je večer sladký, lípy dech
> petřísnkých voní na valech,
> a polo bdí a na půl dříma
> v oparu světel obrys čar
> barvami do mlh vhozenýma,
> pohádka, smutek, polotvar.

> The evening is sweet, the linden's breath
> wafts sweetly on the Petřín ramparts,
> and half-awake and half-asleep is
> the contour of lines in the midst of lights
> like colors thrown into fog,
> a fairy tale, sadness, a half-form.
>
> (Sova, "Praha, věčná stráž," *Zápasy a osudy*)

We could not explain the similarities among these three landscape depictions if we did not take into account a common source, the linear perspective of the Art Nouveau visual arts. Moreover, there is the fact that Sova evidently conceives the landscape as a plane ("a contour of lines"); thus even in this respect he follows the model of Art Nouveau painting.

In the enumeration of Art Nouveau features in the visual arts we have also spoken about the passion of Art Nouveau for color and coloration. The verbal transposition of natural colors and colors found in painting is not a rare phenomenon in literature; nevertheless, if we find a predilection for grasping individual shades of color among the poets of the turn of the century, we can safely assume the kinship of poetry with Art Nouveau color technique:

> Sen modří šedivých ve stínech sněhu ožil,
> však záře usnula ve zrůžovělých žlutích.

> A dream of gray blues has revived in the
> shades of snow,
> but the glare has fallen asleep in pinkened
> yellows.
>
> (Březina, "Siesty," *Tajemné dálky*)

Březina's lines apostrophizing autumnal days demonstrate the tendency toward the shading of color even more distinctly:

> Svůj rozestřete lesk a plajte v chladný říjen
> svou září karmínův a minií a sien.

> Spread your luster and blaze into cold October
> with your glare of carmines and miniums and si-
> ennas.
>
> ("Říjen," *Tajemné dálky*)

The designations "carmine" and "minium" refer to two shades of the same color, red. This fact as well as the explicit naming of color shades (not just the colors: red, brown) attests to the Art Nouveau conception of coloration. And if we read (at a distance of thirteen years from *Tajemné dálky*) in Růžena Svobodová's *Černí myslivci* the sentence "It was after the great rains, the warm earth breathed white vapors, the vapors created blue mists, lightly ultramarine, which cajoled amorously about the crowns of trees, filled up the valley, shaded the bluish forests, piled up unevenly, cloudlike in the foreground of the picture, and created a subtle harmony of bluish-green"—if we read this sentence which varies the same color (blue) four times, we feel that we are still within the range of Art Nouveau.

The internal cumulation of colors into colored chords which we frequently encounter among poets of the turn of the century reminds us of the harmonizing effort of the color technique of Art Nouveau painting and ornamentation:

> A v jeden akvarel skvrn rozteklých teď splývá
> Krev s černí spálenou a karmín s línou šedí
> A slunce vyrudlé jak plátek staré mědi
> se kalné, znavené v kraj jednotvárný dívá.

> And into a single watercolor of run-together
>   patches
> Blood now merges with burnt black and carmine
>   with lazy gray
> And the sun faded like a piece of old copper,
> dull, tired, looks into the monotonous land-
>   scape.
>
> (Karásek ze Lvovic, "Kalný západ," *Zazděná
>   okna*)

In this stanza no fewer than five colors (blood, black, carmine, gray, copper) mingle in the depiction of a sunset. At the same time three of them (blood, carmine, copper) are shades of the same basic color. And we should not forget the attendant circumstance that watercolor painting (about which these lines speak) is one of the techniques favored by Art Nouveau painters.

Another example reads:

> Za horkých červnových dnů, kdy všechno
>   plápolá zlatem,
> a bílí holubi s radostným chvatem
> třesavě nad strání krouží,

tu mladé dívky se šťastným smíchem do trávy se
  hrouží
a shora dolů se to kotálí,
jak plamínky v trávě když zapálí
červené, žluté a bílé.

During the hot July days, when everything flares
  up in gold,
and white doves with a joyful haste
shakily circle above the hillside,
then young girls immerse themselves in the grass
  with happy laughter
and roll down the hill,
as if little flames were lit in the grass
red, yellow and white.
             (Neumann, "Stráň chudých lásek," *Kniha
                          mládí a vzdoru*)

In the overall coloration of the picture, the triad of red, yellow, and white creates an intentional color chord. We find an analogous color harmony, bordering, however, almost on contrast, in the following poem by Machar:

Na hoře město. Zdí tré pásů chrání
bezpečnost jeho. Prvá natřena jest
svítivou barvou, jak ji má krev lidská,
ta druhá mrtvou černí tmavé noci
a třetí modrá, jako bývá nebe,
když slunce slábnouc mdle jen usmívá se.

On the hill a town. Three belts of walls protect
its safety. The first is painted
a shiny color, like that of human blood,
the second the dead black of dark night
and the third is blue, as the sky usually is,
when the sun growing weak only weakly smiles.
            ("Krajina asijská," *V záři hellenského
                          slunce*) . . .

We thus conclude our brief comparison of Art Nouveau in the visual arts with Czech literature of the years 1895-1905. If we have not quoted all of the outstanding poets of this period, this does not mean that we could not find traces of Art Nouveau in their works as well. There is abundant material, but the purpose of our study has not been the investigation of concrete artistic phenomena; rather we have been concerned simply with illustrating the theoretical assertions developed in the first two sections A more consistent study would prove without a doubt the thesis that although Art Nouveau in the visual arts projected itself into literature very effectively, it neither created a special movement nor limited its influence to only one of the purely literary movements but scattered its colorful light over the entire range of the literature of its time. Art Nouveau intervened at the moment when the development of literature, if it tended at all toward a different art, had music, not the visual arts, as its goal. Moreover, the aggressive vividness of Czech poetry and cultural life of this period did not coincide with the languor of Art Nouveau. Despite all of this, or rather in conjunction with it, Art Nouveau intervened effectively in the fate of literature, complicating an already complex development. At a moment of extreme individualization its leveling influence affected almost all poets without exception. For the theoretician of literature the moral of the story is the following: If we study the relation between literature and another art, the influence of this other art must not be evaluated as a mechanical transposition of an alien periodization into literature but as a complex transference of an external impulse into the immanent development of literature, as a reflection which can strike literature at the most varied angles of incidence and with the most diverse results.

> *Jan Mukařovský, "Between Literature and Visual Arts," in his* The Word and Verbal Art, *edited and translated by John Burbank and Peter Steiner, Yale University Press, 1977, pp. 205-34.*

W. J. T. Mitchell

[*Mitchell is an American critic and educator. In the following excerpt, which was originally presented as a lecture at a conference on literature and the visual arts at Dartmouth College in 1984, he examines the generic differences between texts and visual artworks.*]

Emerson once noted that the most fruitful conversations are always between two persons, not three. This principle may help explain why the dialogue between poetry and painting has tended to dominate general discussions of the arts, and why music has seemed something of an outsider to the conversation. All the arts may aspire to the condition of music, but when they set out to argue, poetry and painting hold the stage. One reason for this is that they both lay claim to the same territory (reference, representation, denotation, meaning), a territory that music has tended to renounce. Another reason is that the differences between words and images seem so fundamental. They are not merely *different* kinds of creatures, but *antithetical* kinds. They attract to their contest all the dualisms and binary oppositions that riddle the discourse of criticism, the very discourse that takes as one of its projects a unified theory of the arts, an "aesthetics" which aspires to a synoptic view of artistic signs, a "semiotics" which hopes to comprehend all signs whatsoever.

Despite these ambitions for theoretical unity, then, the relation between verbal and pictorial signs seems to resist stubbornly the attempt to make it a matter of neutral classification, a mere problem in taxonomy. Words and images seem inevitably to become implicated in a "war of signs" (what Leonardo called a *paragone*) in which the stakes are things like nature, truth, reality, or the human spirit. Each art, each type of sign or medium, lays claim to certain things that it is best equipped to mediate, and each grounds these claims in a certain characterization of its "self," its own proper essence. Equally important, each art characterizes itself in opposition to its "significant other." Thus, poetry, or verbal expression in general, sees its signs as arbitrary and conventional—that is, "unnatural"—in contrast to the natural signs of imagery. Painting sees itself as uniquely fitted for the representation of the visible world, whereas poetry is primarily concerned with the invisible realm of ideas and feelings. Poetry is an art of time, motion, and actions; painting an art of space, stasis, and arrested action. The comparison of poetry and painting dominates aesthetics, then, precisely because there is so much resistance to the comparison, such a large gap to be overcome.

This gap has two important functions in discussions of the arts and their symbol systems: it lends an air of tough-minded common sense to assertions of difference between the arts, and it gives an air of paradoxical daring and ingenuity to assertions of sameness or transference. The topic of the text-image difference provides an occasion for the exercise of the two great rhetorical skills, wit and judgment, "wit," as Edmund Burke noted, being "chiefly conversant in tracing resemblances," and judgment concerned mainly with "finding differences." Since aesthetics and semiotics dream of a theory that will satisfy both the need to discriminate artistic signs and to identify the principles that unite them, both these approaches to the topic have established themselves as traditional alternatives within the discourse of criticism.

The mode of wit, the "tracing of resemblances," is the foundation of the *ut pictura poesis* and "sister arts" tradition in criticism, the construction of analogies or critical conceits that identity points of transference and resemblance between texts and images. Although these conceits are almost always accompanied by acknowledgments of differences between the arts, they are generally perceived as violations of good judgment that criticism ought to correct. . . .

In my view, the problem is that we have not gone nearly far enough in our exploration of text-image relations. William Blake, whose testimony on the Sister Arts question deserves to be taken seriously, said that "you never know what is enough until you know what is too much." I'd like to pursue this road of excess by urging that we abandon our cautious reverence toward the generic laws that divide image from text and inquire into the foundations of those laws: How were they instituted? What values and interests do they serve? And what power gives them authority over artistic and critical practice?

The first step in the examination of these laws is the realization that they are metaphors, figures of speech, and not (as we sometimes suppose) straightforward, literal propositions about the arts or the media. We tend to think that to compare painting and poetry is to make a metaphor, while to differentiate poetry from painting is to state a literal truth. But the differentiation of the arts follows the classic pattern of figurative discourse: it tries to explain something we think we don't understand (in this case, the difference between text and image) by comparing it to something we think we *do* understand (the difference, say, between the natural and the conventional, or the temporal and the spatial). Actually, a moment's reflection should suggest that we sister arts scholars know a great deal more about images and texts than we do about these profound abstractions. The figures we employ in our theoretical discriminations between text and image serve more to mystify than to clarify the difference.

In suggesting that these judicious discriminations are figurative, however, I do not mean to assert that they are simply false, illusory, or without efficacy. On the contrary, I want to suggest that they are powerful distinctions that affect the way the arts are practiced and understood. I do mean to imply, however, that they are literally false, or (more generally) figuratively true. My argument here will be two-fold: (1) there is no *essential* difference between poetry and painting, no difference, that is, given for all time by the inherent natures of the media, the objects they represent, or the laws of the human mind; (2) there are always a number of differences *in place* in a culture which allow it to sort out the distinctive qualities of its ensemble of signs and symbols. The difference between texts and images is not a matter about which we are likely to be mistaken in a practical way; the most rabid "sister arts" scholar is perfectly capable of telling the sisters apart. The problem arises when we try to give a theoretical account of these differences, an account that will regulate our critical practice and stand free of the polemical debates that have so often accompanied this subject.

There seem to be four basic ways in which we theoretically differentiate texts from images: by perceptual mode (eye versus ear); by conceptual mode (space versus time); by semiotic medium (natural versus conventional signs); and by function or "grammatical" mode (the distinctions of modern symbol theory, reflected in such antitheses as replete versus differentiated, autographic versus allographic, analogical versus digital). We have, in short, an embarrassment of riches when it comes to theories about the differences between texts and images. And each of these models of difference has a long tradition. The most ancient is probably the semiotic, with its classic articulation in Plato's *Cratylus* and its modern redactions in writers like E. H. Gombrich and the followers of C. S. Peirce. The perceptual distinction between the visual and the aural is hardly less influential, however, and has its classic statement in Leonardo's *Paragone,* where the sovereignty of the eye redounds to the everlasting advantage of images over texts; the very same perceptual figures are mobilized to make the opposite argument later in Edmund Burke's aesthetics of the sublime. The model of conceptual mode has, as we might expect, the greatest aura of rationality and modernity about it. Time and space resound with the authority of Newton and Kant; when combined with Lessing's notion of temporal and spatial "signs," they offer a homology between the physical, the subjective, and the aesthetic.

Then, finally, there is the functionalist approach, the one which says that the difference between images and texts is nothing essential, not grounded in the nature of things, the mind, or the senses. It's just a matter of different ways of using significant marks. This, I suppose, would have to be called the "post-modern" or "anti-foundationalist" approach, and its most systematic theorist is Nelson Goodman, although some would argue that the pragmatic lineage of Peirce's semiotics places it with the "functional" or "grammatical" approach to symbol classification. The fortunes of this mode of analysis are difficult to predict. While it is capable of great subtlety and has the revolutionary effect of "de-centering" the text-image debate by surveying all sorts of media and information systems, it has the disadvantage of being formidably technical and thus is hard to mobilize in the service of public discussions of value in the arts. Semiotics, one suspects, may go the way of Renaissance rhetoric with its passion for names and distinctions, while the ancient categories of nature and convention, time and space, eye and ear will persist.

They cannot persist in quite the same way, however, once we have bitten the functionalist apple, for it is precisely this turn to the grammar of the text-image difference that reveals the figurativeness of the traditional distinctions, reveals them as functional categories that serve our values and interests. Functionalism clears the ground for a fifth way of studying the difference between texts and images, the mode of historical criticism that I offer in this essay. This approach to the text-image difference is less concerned with establishing a true theoretical account to regulate the comparative study of texts and images than it is with asking what gives rise to the resistance to this study. What is it that makes the relation of texts and images a matter for polemical dispute rather than neutral, technical description? What is it that makes the "confusion of the arts" and the media seem such a threatening prospect? Why is the notion of "spatial form" in literature regularly associated with fascism by critics like Frank Kermode and Robert Weimann? Why does the "sisterhood" of the arts seem more aptly described as a struggle between contending sexes, classes, or nations?

There are two ways the historical critic can answer these sorts of questions. The first is simply to study very closely the historical context of the various engagements in the long war between texts and images. One can read Leonardo's *Paragone* as a document of this war at the level of professional prestige. Leonardo was attempting to raise painting to the level of a liberal art along with literature, and he found the logic of his argument leading toward a claim for the infinite superiority of the visual arts, a claim grounded in the rational, scientific sovereignty of the eye over the ear. Or one can read Lessing's attempt to regulate textual and pictorial boundaries as a nationalistic argument that invokes the superiority of temporal values (which all happen to be associated with the culture of Northern Protestant countries like Germany and England) and the inferiority of spatial, pictorial values (associated with Southern Catholic countries, and particularly with the "false delicacy" of France). In modern polemics, one finds the national associations of time and space replaced by ideological terms: "space" becomes a code-word for Modernism, which is linked in turn with the destruction of narrative, syntactic, and logical continuity, the irrational reverence for formal patterns and mythic images and the loss of a sense of history, all linked in turn with fascism.

All these particular examples, however, only leave us bewildered and in need of a more general explanation. We may have a sense that the difference between texts and images has a strong tendency to get involved in professional, national, or ideological conflicts, but we still don't quite understand why this should be so. What is it about *this* seemingly innocent difference that makes it the focus of so much energy? The answer, I think, lies in the peculiar status of imagery in Western culture, its role as an object of peculiar reverence and fear. We live in a culture that has a deeply entrenched tradition of iconoclasm and iconophobia. Prohibitions against graven images, against "idols" of the tribe, the market place, and the mind are a consistent theme in Western critical discourse, and they generate an iconoclastic rhetoric that comes into play every time the power of images is challenged, whether it is the image-making power of advertising and political propaganda, the power of image-dominated media like television and the movies, or the temptations of metaphor and analogy in critical discourse.

Not that it's hard to find reasons for being an iconoclast: in the presidential election of 1980, all the polls told us that the electorate preferred the policies of one candidate, but it nevertheless voted for the other because (as a professional movie actor) he had a "better image." If we want to understand the difference between texts and images, however, we have to do more than simply exercise the rhetoric of iconoclasm; we have to examine the way it exercises us, shaping our criticism with tropes and intentions we may not want to acknowledge. These tropes form a kind of secondary system of figurative associations that cluster around the figures of difference between texts and images and give them their ideological, polemical charge. These figures, I want to suggest, are variations on differences in class, race, and gender.

The link between semiotic and class difference is as easy to grasp as the difference between literacy and illiteracy. Images are the code of the illiterate. They served as a *biblia pauperum* in the middle ages, providing the vulgar laity with an outward, sensory expression of history and doctrine, while the inward, spiritual sense was preserved in the texts of the clergy. Arguments for the "naturalness" of imagery regularly invoke their efficacy with pre-literate subjects: the fact that children can recognize pictures before they can read words, or that travellers who can't speak native languages can read pictographic road signs seem to suggest that images provide a universal, lowest common denominator in the semiotic universe. Images are the medium of "the masses" and are thus filled with a revolutionary potential that must be suppressed or exploited.

A similar appeal to "natural" coding is frequently made to associate images with non-Western or "primitive" cultures and racial "others." Histories of human knowledge since the Enlightenment have regularly described the history of writing as an evolutionary progress from pictographic to hieroglyphic to alphabetic notation. Picture-writing, along with physical gesture, is seen as the most primitive form of expression and is frequently linked with idolatry and fetishism. The "nature" that underwrites this version of the natural sign is, of course, irrational and superstitious. But the racial "other" is frequently brought in to testify on behalf of the *rational* naturalness of another kind of sign—the photograph. I like to call this testimony the "what do the natives say?" strategy. It shows up with ritual regularity whenever Ernst Gombrich wants to demonstrate that photographs, and Western illusionistic pictures in general, are truly natural signs.

But most subtle of all is the connection between the text-image difference and the categories of gender. I do not know of any place where this association is made directly, but the pattern is unmistakable in the aesthetics of Burke and Lessing, where the text-image difference is linked to gender by way of the categories of sublimity and beauty. The sublime, needless to say, is the masculine mode, based in sensations of obscurity, fear, and overwhelming power, while the beautiful is the feminine mode, based in pleasure, love, and a sense of weakness, even contemptibility. Not surprisingly, images turn out to be the appropriate medium for the beautiful, and words for the sublime. For Lessing, the French attachment to pictorial values is a sign of effeminacy and "false refinement." The spatial character of the visual arts is a way of legislating their confinement to the "narrow realm" of bodily display and preventing them from invading the "wider sphere" of literature, the spiritual realm of time, action, and history. Blake, with his keen eye for the human images embodied in the most refined abstractions, saw clearly what lay behind the reification of space and time in eighteenth-century criticism: "Time & Space are Real Beings a Male & a Female Time is a Man Space is a Woman" [from his poem "A Vision of the Last Judgment"].

The sexual basis of the text-image difference is simultaneously disguised and revealed by the traditional trope of "sisterhood." This figure suggests equality, but actually enforces a discrimination between the superior literary sister, who, as a "speaking picture," combines the positive virtues of the arts, and the inferior pictorial sister, who is "mute poesy," defined principally by what she lacks. Painting did not even achieve the status of step-sisterhood, much less personhood, until the sixteenth century, and then only on terms which kept it inscribed within invidious distinctions between the intellectual and the sensual, the spiritual and the bodily, the pure and the impure. The association of painting with cosmetics and the lure of the "painted woman" was never far from the surface of Sister Arts rhetoric. Like the two women who personify Pleasure and Duty in emblematic renderings of "The Choice of Hercules," Painting and Poetry present the artist with a choice between the vanity of outward appearance (often signified by a mask or mirror) and the purity of inner truth (generally signified by nakedness or a text).

How then was it possible for painting to achieve sisterhood on anything like equal terms with poetry? In order to make this step, the "naturalness" of the image had to be conceived in a duplicitous fashion, linked simultaneously with irrational sensuality and with the rational representation of the senses; the mirror in the hands of the sinister sister had to be read, not as an emblem of vanity and illusory appearance, but of rational representation. The mask had to be replaced with the compass, the emblem of *geometria* and *perspectiva*. Leonardo's *Paragone* brings this duplicity out in the open: painting is to be preferred to poetry because it is the medium of rationality and science. The technique of linear perspective guarantees that painting will provide true representations of the visible world, in contrast to language, which relays nothing but rumor, tradition, and opinion through the unreliable sense of hearing. For Leonardo, image is to text as substance is to shadow or as "facts" are to "words." But Leonardo's argument [in *Treatise on Painting*] for the epistemological superiority of painting leads him to the inevitable paradox: painting is not only better at telling the truth than poetry; it is also better at telling lies. In its mastery of illusion "painting even deceives animals, for I have seen a picture that deceived a dog because of the likeness to its master . . . likewise I have seen a monkey that did an infi

nite number of foolish things with another painted monkey". Even more sinister is the ability of these scientific, rational images to make monkeys out of men: "men . . . fall in love with a painting that does not represent any living woman," and they may be "excited to lust and sensuality" by the vivid illusion of lewd scenes. But the most dangerous effect of the image is its ability to lure men into the sin of idolatry:

> If you, poet, describe the figure of some deities, the writing will not be held in the same veneration as the painted deity, because bows and various prayers will continually be made to the painting. To it will throng many generations from many provinces and from over the eastern seas, and they will demand help from the painting and not from what is written.

Leonardo cannot acknowledge that his argument for the rational truth of painting entails an argument for its deceptiveness and that its status as a "natural science" has its obverse in a nature of animal lust and primitive fetishism. His strategy for keeping these two aspects of painting separate is clear: "we" will not be fooled by these images; only those from the "provinces" and "from over the eastern seas" will be taken in.

What are we to make of all these figures of the image as the medium of the cultural, racial, and sexual other? What effect do they have on the practice of the arts, and on practical criticism of the arts? Should we try to eliminate this rhetoric and replace it with neutral, technical terminology free of ideological associations? This seems to be one of the goals of modern symbol theory: semiotics aspires to be a "science of signs" that will regulate the comparative study of things like texts and images and keep us from going "too far" with our critical and artistic mixing of media. While I admire the almost scholastic rigor of semiotics, I must express some reservations, both about its claims to be a "science" and its efficacy as a guide to practice. Semiotics, at least in its recent versions, has never abandoned the mystique of the image or icon as "natural sign." Thomas Sebeok's essay, "Iconicity," is perhaps the clearest expression of this mystique, grounding the character of imagery firmly in the realm of animal behavior. This strategy revives the ancient fable that measured the merit of painting by its ability to get birds to mistake painted grapes for real ones. The problem with this fable and its modern redactions in zoosemiotics is twofold: first, it confuses the perception of a sign as such with being taken in by an illusion, two things that strike me as logically incompatible. To see an image as such requires seeing it as a representation or sign; to be taken in by an image is to stop seeing it as an image. The birds of Apelles and Xeuxis were not seeing images; they were seeing grapes. The notion of a "natural sign" in this sense is a contradiction in terms, albeit a powerfully persuasive one. As such, it is better understood as a symptom of repressed desire, not as a critical concept on which to base a theory of imagery.

The second problem with the animal behavior approach is more on the order of a misgiving than a logical objection. In a system of differences that is continually regulated by ideological appeals to class, race, and gender difference, the difference between man and animal ought to come as no surprise: it is the "bottom line" of the text-image difference as a boundary between the human and the non-human. In Enlightenment anthropology, the imputation of idolatry and fetishism to "primitives" regularly proceeded by a denial of their humanity (idolatry is a "brutish" worship), accompanied by a denial of manhood (the idolater's "impotence" in relation to the Western observer seen as a consequence of his phallic power being consigned to a fetish object).

If we cannot purge these ideological categories from critical discourse, and especially that criticism concerned with the relations of texts and images, what then should we do? My suggestion is that we study their movements, expose them to the light of critical and historical analysis, and try to clarify their effect on the criticism and practice of the arts. I do not think we will ever find a method that protects us against going "too far" in mixing the media that our categories insist on keeping separate. But we may be able to see more concretely what is at stake in violating or observing these distinctions. My own work on image-text relations in the eighteenth and nineteenth centuries has convinced me that these categories provide a basic link between the great social upheavals surrounding the French Revolution and the transformation in artistic and critical practice that accompanied them. English Romanticism, I believe, constructs its poetics around an iconoclastic, antipictorialist rhetoric that privileges invisibility and voice and associates imagery and visibility with inferior, threatening "others"—most notably the French and their culture of painting and rational speculation. Indeed, the iconophobia of English Romanticism goes so deep that even the text is not enough of an antidote to the idolatrous temptations of the image. Insofar as texts are printed, making language visible, they *are* images. Insofar as the printed word was (in Hazlitt's phrase) a "remote but direct" cause of the French Revolution, it had to be countered with a poetics of voice, a literature of "man speaking" (not writing) "to men."

We need not go back to the French Revolution, however, to see the difference between voice and visibility presented as a political struggle; the war between vision and voice is a central feature of a definitively "modern" medium, the movies. It is a commonplace in film criticism that the movies have overturned all the traditional categories of image-text division. Erwin Panofsky, as a good Kantian, saw the "unique and specific possibilities" of the film medium as "dynamization of space and spatialization of time." But Panofsky also makes it clear that this hybridization of aesthetic categories is not to be understood as a compromise between the values of text and image, but a clear victory for the power of imagery. The ur-fact about the movies for Panofsky is not narrative or dramatic representation, but simply the "moving picture": "in the beginning . . . there were the straight recordings of movement. . . . The imitation of stage performances was a comparatively late and thoroughly frustrated development". Walter Benjamin would make this sort of observation part of his argument for the revolutionary character of film. But Panofsky's sense of the "original" character of film is threatened continually by the incursion of textual elements, the most significant, of course, being the human

voice. Panofsky's account [in his 1947 essay "Style and Medium in the Motion Pictures"] of his strategy for containing this threat to the dominance of the image is worth quoting in full:

> In a film, that which we hear remains, for good or worse, inextricably fused with that which we see; the sound, articulate or not, cannot express any more than is expressed, at the same time, by visible movement; and in a good film it does not even attempt to do so. To put it briefly, the play—or, as it is very properly called, the 'script'—of a moving picture is subject to what might be called the *principle of coexpressibility*.

Panofsky neutralizes the threat of word to image by pretending that the word adds nothing, makes no real difference. The "principle of co-expressibility" might as well be called the "principle of redundancy," for the word "cannot" express more than the image. Even more significant, it will "not even attempt to do so" in a "good film." The law of the genre implies and enforces a law of taste.

But consider a film that violates Panofsky's law throughout, and then has been criticized for precisely this reason. The film is *Sunset Boulevard,* the story of an aging silent-film queen, Norma Desmond (played by Gloria Swanson), who hires a young writer, Joe Gillis (William Holden), to help her "polish up" her enormous, illiterate script of *Salome.* Norma hopes that she will make her "return" in this costume epic under the direction of Cecil B. DeMille; Joe Gillis hopes that he will make enough money to save his car from the finance company and maintain the mobility he needs to peddle his own scripts to the movie industry ("losing your car in Los Angeles is like having your legs cut off," he says at one point). The basic conflict of this story clearly allegorizes the very issues that Panofsky is concerned with: the struggle between the pure, expressive, moving image (Norma Desmond, the screen "idol") and the verbal invader who must be subjected to the "principle of coexpressibility." When the writer tells Norma that her script "needs dialogue," she scoffs, reminding him that she has always been capable of saying everything with her face and gestures. She rapidly takes over the young writer's life, using him to fill the void left by the death of her pet monkey. (In Joe's first encounter with Norma, she mistakes him for the man from the pet cemetery who has come to dispose of her dead pet. The link between the ape and the speechless mimicry of Norma's image-dominated world should be clear.)

Joe is not completely alone in this film in his disgust with the image-dominated world of Hollywood. He has a girlfriend who works as a reader for Paramount. She tries to get him out from under Norma Desmond's spell by offering, not just herself, but her help as editor, muse, and co-author. She believes in Joe's writing so much that she is willing to work for nothing and asks for none of the credit of authorship. She will remain invisible in Joe's unwritten script. Joe is too weak to break away from his Circe-Medusa-Salome; he is paralyzed with self-pity and disgust with himself for becoming a male whore to this fading screen idol, selling both his pen and his penis. Meanwhile, "Max" (Eric von Stroheim) looms in the background, the ex-husband, ex-great film director, who gave up his career to become her butler-chauffeur. And over it all looms the invisible presence of Joe's voice, telling his story of castration, paralysis, and death, relieved only by the cold comfort of the ending, where his body is gently pulled from the pool ("they're always gentle with you after you're dead in Hollywood"), its image now safely photographed for the scandal sheets.

The interesting thing about *Sunset Boulevard,* then, is the way it formally enacts the conflict that it dramatizes. Joe may have been transformed into what Benjamin would call an "effigy" of himself—literally as corpse, figuratively as photographic image—but his voice lives on to speak with the authority of the dead. The film opens at its chronological ending, Joe's disembodied voice-over telling us his story from his vantage point face down in Norma Desmond's swimming pool. This voice plays a sardonic counterpoint to the film images throughout, warning us against being taken in by false versions of the story peddled by Hollywood image-makers. Where are we, as audience, placed in relation to all this? In an impossible position, at the bottom of Norma Desmond's swimming pool, looking up at the floating body of our narrator, intermittently dazzled by the flashbulbs of the photographers above.

What are we to make of all this? *Sunset Boulevard* is a film against the movies, an expression of hatred and fear of the primal origins, the natural, generic necessities of the medium, especially as understood by Panofsky. It is the film of an *auteur,* a film story-teller, writer, and director who wants to keep the film image under control. It is pure film iconoclasm, anti-Panofsky, and yet confirming Panofsky. Joe's voice is completely absorbed in the lurid images he narrates; his literate comparison of Norma to another famous deadly aged virgin (Dickens' Miss Havisham) only confirms the triumph of the female image. Just when we think that he will have the last word, his narrating voice falls silent, and Norma Desmond descends her staircase, euphorically posturing for the reporters and police photographers. As the spotlights pick her up, she imagines that her "return" as a potent film idol is at hand, and she has the last words of the film: "I'm ready for my close-up, Mr. DeMille."

Consider, then, the questions *Sunset Boulevard* raises about the relationship between texts and images. Does the film confirm Panofsky's "principle of coexpressibility," making words redundant and impotent in the face of the eloquent image? Or does its dramatic and formal representation of this principle as an atavistic feminine monstrosity and its counter-image in the "good sister," the complaint muse of literature, suggest that all these formal choices are really ideological impasses? If Joe Gillis is a Hercules at the crossroads, choosing between Pleasure and Duty, Image and Text, the femme fatale and the benevolent muse of literary virtue, what choices does the film leave its audience and its *auteur?* Can or should we make images into texts and texts into images, as the eighteenth-century aestheticians dreamed? Or have we already gone too far?

W. J. T. Mitchell, *"Going too Far with the Sister Arts,"* in Space, Time, Image, Sign: Essays on Literature and the Visual Arts, *edited by*

James A. W. Heffernan, Peter Lang, 1987, pp. 1-10.

Modern literary criticism and formal discussion of the visual arts have proceeded along separate paths and there often appears little scope for a *rapprochement.* They can join forces most easily in the study of the history of ideas, but such inquiries do not readily insist upon the crucial differences that exist between figurative and verbal expression, with the consequence that the individual work of art is neglected, its special and unique properties lost amid the ideal entities.

—*John Dixon Hunt in the preface to his* Encounters: Essays on Literature and the Visual Arts, *1971.*

Louis A. Renza

[*In the following excerpt, which was originally presented as a lecture at a conference on literature and the visual arts at Dartmouth College in 1984, Renza replies to the essay by W. J. T. Mitchell excerpted above, asserting that Mitchell's arguments fall prey to the same political problems that they criticize.*]

Professor Mitchell's paper focuses on the politically unconscious binary oppositions that mark all critical discussions, past and present, which attempt to compare painting and literature or, in the language of [his essay], images and texts. Even egalitarian semioticians, we are told, unwittingly commit elitist crimes in the dark of their analyses. If such critics would treat the two arts as coequal examples of different systems of signs, they nevertheless tend to regard pictorial images as "natural" signs. This apparently neutral division of semiotic labor between natural and conventional signs, that is, in fact situates "images" in the politicized context of a Western iconoclastic tradition that leads one to fear and thus denigrate being "taken in by an image."

Like the other politically motivated views of the arts he cites, this one demonstrates how assiduously Mitchell's own criticism would guard the artistic border from theoretical extremes. If his criticism works to expose the manifest and latent puritanism behind certain theoretical postulations of the difference between the arts, it does not inversely espouse the critical libertinism implicit in poststructuralist efforts to unify the arts under the banner of "textuality." In short, he would not *in theory* mix these media. Thus, his discussion of the movie *Sunset Boulevard* adopts Panofsky's idealized plea for the "coexpressibility" of the arts to stage what Mitchell maintains throughout his paper is the "antithetical" relation between the verbal and pictorial arts. Ostensibly marrying both media, film ironically reinscribes the war between these arts or, considered as a chain of political signifiers, also the war between the sexes and classes. For example (although Mitchell does not use this example), wouldn't the masses seeing *Sunset Boulevard* at the time define or at least refer to it as a (pictorial) "movie" rather than as a (literary) "film"? Mitchell's allegorical analysis of *Sunset Boulevard* ends in an ideological stand-off between Panofsky's anxiety about the word's iconoclastic reduction of the image (traditionally and here particularly represented by the woman) and Mitchell's observation, in effect, that this *film* does not allow the male word (represented by Joe's voice) to have the last word, but rather subsumes the word "in the lurid images" of the *movie* itself. One could argue, in other words, that insofar as this movie "confirms the triumph of the female image," it smuggles into its audience's perception a revisionist sexual politics along with an ideologically coded meta-artistic message.

Still, Mitchell's "reading" of this movie expresses a recognition that, if only by the example of *his own* critical discussion, images cannot stand alone but, in the end, need protection *from* language *by* language. Such protection, I would suggest, also belies the apparent neutrality of his own critical stance or border-patrolling of both the warring arts and their warring critical exponents. His discussion entails the same kind of political or culturally self-interested maneuvering as those critical theories he proposes we "study" and "expose . . . to the light of critical and historical analysis," at least to compensate for our inability "ever [to] find a method that protects us against going 'too far' in mixing the media that our categories insist on keeping separate." Here "study" seems to function as a kind of trope in Mitchell's criticism that would neutralize the *anxiety* over "going 'too far' in mixing the media." Mixing media clearly threatens the traditional separation of the arts which, as we can see from his discussion of *Sunset Boulevard,* his criticism tends to maintain. Indeed, despite his explicit argument that "there is no *essential* difference between poetry and painting" (2), since this distinction is a matter of variable ideological figuration, Mitchell sometimes tends to regard this difference as inescapable, pre-ideological, or infrastructural—perhaps as "essential" after all. Words and images, he tells us at the beginning of his paper, not only "seem" fundamentally different but "are" antithetically so.

Wishing to protect this difference even as he would consign it to the domain of figuration and/or ideologically polemical causes, Mitchell's discussion supports the generally conservative premise (if not the particular political implications) of the various theoretical distinctions previously drawn between the arts that he reviews and exposes to historical analysis in his paper. His criticism perforce preserves even as it politically deconstructs these theories, and it does so precisely in the face of that most egregious critical exponent of mixing the two arts, semiotic criticism. On the one hand, Mitchell discusses such criticism as if it were primarily defined by a "technical" methodology "almost" possessing "scholastic rigor," although he also claims to admire this criticism "as a complex and venerable discipline." On the other hand, he virtually reduces

semiotic criticism to a soon-to-be-defunct fad—that is, in comparison with the more enduring (hence truer?) critical "categories" that seem better able to discuss both arts in the same theoretical context: "Semiotics, one suspects, may go the way of Renaissance rhetoric with its passion for names and distinctions, while the ancient categories of nature and convention, time and space, eye and ear will persist."

But Mitchell surely knows that despite his wish to deny the privilege accorded to text-oriented theories of the two arts, his own perspective partakes of that heretical brand of semiotic criticism loosely termed "poststructuralist." And as his very thesis reminds us, his own critical act no less than his hypostasis of a "venerable" if restricted mode of semiotic criticism must have ideological repercussions of a kind similar to those he discerns in past and present comparative discussions of these arts. I would cite one such repercussion here: in its poststructuralist guises, semiotic criticism happens to define the dominant mode of present *literary* criticism which, one can relevantly speculate, threatens to subsume any discussion purporting to address the pictorial arts. In this context, Mitchell's paper itself seems less neutral than "motivated"—to use an aggressive semiotic term—in a figurative war fought not so much between the arts as between the kinds and subject matter of his and other critical discourses.

Thus, we can at least wonder whether his proposed "historical criticism" does not itself pivotally take place within a synchronically construable political-academic scene of critical writing. And we can also wonder whether Mitchell's deconstructions of privileged binary terms like literary, temporal, modern, and/or male images are not themselves "motivated" performative tropes in his particular narrative. His paper purports to recover the equal value of critically underprivileged terms like pictorial, spatial, primitive, and female images. Yet, like Leonardo's *Paragone,* which he cites as arguing for the superiority of painting over literature, Mitchell's final analysis of *Sunset Boulevard* suggests, as we have seen, the superiority or "the triumph" of—along with their respective artistic analogues—the "female image" over the male image. Indeed, we could take his analysis one step further and argue that this movie (any voiced-over movie, for that matter) represents the "narrating voice" as an *acoustic* rather than strictly *verbal* image—that is, as an image whose apparent presence or immediacy makes it more akin to the medium of visual images than even the "visual" medium of written discourse. "Space filled with sound," Erwin Straus has noted, "is enough to establish a connection between viewer and picture."

In any case, Mitchell's cinematic example in effect makes the case for *literature's* anxiety before pictorial art rather than the reverse situation, which in his paper constitutes the pretext for his deconstructions. And one can easily cite similar examples of an inscribed, perhaps unconsciously self-promoting artistic civil warfare in movies. The sheer visual display and details of Stanley Kubrick's *2001* exist at both the thematic and performative expense of a debased discourse represented, say, in the monotones of an eventually castrated Hal as well as in the stereotyped language of the movie script's characters. Indeed, Kubrick's movie *Barry Lyndon* not only effects this same visual reduction of language but does so explicitly in relation to the *literary* text by Thackeray.

Virtual assaults on literature and words, such examples clearly resist demonstrating how "texts" are always egregiously privileged figures—the "bad guy" representing an ideologically revered, authoritarian, or patriarchal "Western culture" with "a deeply entrenched tradition of iconoclasm and iconophobia"—in the political drama staged by Mitchell's critical narrative. English Romantics, as Mitchell claims, may have raised their privileged poetic "voices" against the pictorialist-political threat posed by the French Revolution. But then certain male American Romantic writers seem inclined to privilege the rhetoric of image over text, even if to do so ironically points to the inadequacies of their own texts. Poe, for example, argues [in his essay, "Nathaniel Hawthorne"] for the semiotic potency of the short tale on the basis of pictorial criteria: ideally, it results from a "design" that itself results in a (virtual) "picture . . . at length painted which leaves in the mind of him who contemplates it . . . a kindred art". Or Hawthorne frames *in writing* the image of a woman embroidering a scarlet letter—i.e., an image qua image—as taking precedence over the poetic (and largely unrepresented) vocalisms of her guilty, patriarchal, and would-be iconoclastic Christian lover.

Moreover, one could also argue that the pictorialist rhetoric of such writers functions as a kind of ideological trope. That is, like "nature" for Emerson, their notion of pictorial immediacy in writing effectively counters the perceived dominance of a text-oriented *English* Romantic culture vis-a-vis the desire for American artistic independence. Mitchell's thesis, in other words, here needs to go at least far enough into areas of investigation where the picture or image possesses, despite evidence to the contrary and our own political temptations to think otherwise, a certain recuperable authority within specific historical contexts of aesthetic theory. The oppressed status of the visual image is by no means as certain as Mitchell seems to suggest. Do Jackson Pollock's a-pictorial paintings or "motion" pictures derive their visual energy paradoxically from destroying visual images—by "doing" painting as if it were a kind of writing, a kinetic scripting with brush instead of pen? Or do they preempt the material base of writing or textuality in the sense of aggressively reasserting writing's inescapable origins in as well as influence by the visual-perceptual medium? Iconoclasm or Iconophilia?

Surely an interartistic *critical* writing such as exemplified in this volume can leave us with the same kind of question. Itself condemned to writing, such criticism inevitably tends to fantasize dramas in which it overcomes or at least insists on its equality with what it imagines as *its* more imaginative double in writing: "literature." In disarming this antagonist and recovering its power by allying itself with minority or underprivileged "images," this *criticism* would become *ut pictura*. But in the process of using this strategy inscribed within the civil war of the *literary* arts, such criticism also effectively tends, albeit heroically like the Chartrean text of Henry Adams, to reinstate a hierar-

chical difference, this time with the pictorial arts as the protagonist heroine.

Mitchell's critical approach, then, truly provocative in its citation of interartistic warfare and the often subtle, ideologically biased critical theories that fuel it, can only prolong such warfare, not explain or lead to a negotiated settlement of it. But if his paper fails to resolve the politicized difference between the arts, it succeeds in sketching out fertile zones of critical inquiry: questions about whether this very war does not constitute a pretext for taking self-interested political stances; or about how, analogous to ekphrastic literature like Keats's "Grecian Urn," painting paradoxically can itself inscribe language or verbal image; and not least, questions that wrestle with the fact that the terms we use to discuss the pictorial arts, literary terms like "analogy," "inscription," and even "reading," necessarily but also accurately mix these media.

Literature, after all, as Professor Mitchell has argued elsewhere, strives to become spatial, and not just in the modernist era. According to Edward Casey, literature depends on various kinds of verbal repetition—for example, "repetitive patterns [that] delimit and guide the movements of the reader's imagination. Without the shaping force of repetition, this imagination is tempted to wander aimlessly beyond the bounds of the work and its world." And if literature is always already spatial, painting is no less temporal, though perhaps not in the usual way critics argue for this temporality. Unlike literature, a painting *presupposes* such repetition, the optical as well as aesthetic-perceptual repetition entailed in simply looking at it. But what happens, as *must* happen, when one leaves a particular painting behind? The necessary afterimage of a painting, of course, exists in time—in a medium of memory akin to the comparatively insubstantial medium of literary or textual imagery. Painting here willy-nilly *becomes* a kind of literature, just as literature, at least in its less iconoclastic moments, would become a kind of painting.

The difference between these arts, then, might better be considered not as a civil war but rather as each art's inevitable doubling of the other through a disjunction of time: as the contingent difference accruing between two modes of imagery in the process of becoming each other. In other words, here the arts themselves would seem to go too far in making images into texts and texts into images. Or is such a proposal already too "literary"—that is, already charged with the assumptions of narrativity and the (political) privilege accorded to time Mitchell uncovers in Lessing's classical mode of differentiating the two arts?

Mitchell's thesis thus has the value of continually reminding us that discussions of the difference between "the sister arts"—epistemological, phenomenological, or whatever—cannot escape the political ideology such criticism unwittingly serves behind the mask of a desire for "neutral classification". But for this very reason, the difference between painting and literature must remain stubbornly elusive even to a politically self-conscious criticism such as Mitchell espouses. Or is this elusive difference itself the "blind" agenda of his paper—namely, to occupy the space of this difference and thus prevent critical theory, which he historically associates with patriarchal activity, from having its way or "going too far" with his after all genderized topos—the *sister* arts? In that case, "Going Too Far With the Sister Arts" attempts not only to make one of the sisters equal to the other, but also to protect this *pair* of arts from the serpent that would enlist them in the politics of critical knowledge and its repeated wars against the pleasure of creation.

> *Louis A. Renza, "Response to W. J. T. Mitchell," in* Space, Time, Image, Sign: Essays on Literature and the Visual Arts, *edited by James A. W. Heffernan, Peter Lang, 1987, pp. 11-15.*

INFLUENCE OF VISUAL ARTS ON LITERATURE

Jeffrey Meyers

[*Meyers is an American educator, critic, and biographer. In the following excerpt, he discusses the process by which the novelist creates written images using painting as a source of inspiration.*]

'A characteristic symptom of the spiritual condition of our century', writes Baudelaire [in his *The Life and Work of Eugene Delacroix*], 'is that all the arts tend, if not to act as a substitute for each other, at least to supplement each other, by lending each other new strength and new resources.' Aesthetic analogies express this inherent relationship of the arts, and add a new dimension of richness and complexity to the novel by extending the potentialities of fiction to include the representational characteristics of the visual arts. The novel is essentially a linear art which presents a temporal sequence of events, while painting fixes reality and produces a simultaneity of experience. Evocative comparisons with works of art attempt to transcend the limitations of fiction and to transform successive moments into immediate images.

Comparisons with works of art in the modern novel are similar to the literary use of metaphor, symbol, archetype or myth, for they evoke a new depth of meaning through suggestive allusion. Aesthetic analogies can intensify ordinary life and elevate the significance of commonplace reality. Art throws life into relief, as it were, focusing the familiar and clarifying the vague, for as Proust writes [in his essay "John Ruskin"], 'Painting can pierce to the unchanging reality of things, and so establish itself as a rival of literature.'

Through numerous specific allusions we know what visual images the novelists had in mind when making their analogies. Their visualisation was based on paintings they knew well, and determined by their memories and impressions. Yet the novelists demand a knowledge more specialised and a memory more precise than even the most cultured and careful reader can command. By reproducing the paintings visually, by describing them verbally, by interpreting them inconographically, by looking at them

with the same attention and intensity as the novelists, we can attempt to see what they saw and make that ideal correspondence between their visual images while writing and those in our minds while reading.

This correspondence concerns the widest implications of perspective—the way an author shapes his vision of the world and enforces his way of seeing on the reader. Virginia Woolf observes [in her *Walter Sickert: A Conversation*] that 'painting and writing have much to tell each other; they have much in common. The novelist after all wants to make us see.' And in a letter to a painter [Jacques Raverat, 3 October, 1924] she says, 'I rather think you've broached some of the problems of the writers too, who are trying to catch and consolidate and consummate (whatever the word is for making literature) those splashes of yours.' Through a careful examination of the paintings the novelists used as sources of inspiration we can see how the paintings are transformed by their imagination and can understand how their creative process works.

Stendhal employed Guercino's *St William of Aquitaine* in *Le rouge et le noir* (1830) and George Sand used Holbein's *Dance of Death* in *La mare au diable* (1846) to portray character and emphasise themes, but modern novelists are pre-eminent in the use of this technique. . . . Hawthorne is the first English-language novelist to use aesthetic analogies, but his approach to art is rather naive. He seeks imaginative inspiration in Guido Reni's sentimental idealisation of Beatrice Cenci, but remains completely uncritical about the blatant faults of the painting and exhibits the same defects as Reni. *The Marble Faun,* an obviously weak novel, . . . [provides] a contrast to the more sophisticated techniques developed by later writers like Henry James. For James studies and learns from Hawthorne, and adopts the 'international theme' of Americans alienated in Europe that becomes dominant in his own work. James finds in Bronzino's morbid Mannerism and Veronese's splendid materialism an accurate reflection of the ambiguous value of wealth in *fin-de-siècle* London and Venice.

When Forster writes his Italian novels at the turn of the century the example of James, whom he later discusses in *Aspects of the Novel,* is paramount. Forster expresses the spirit of San Gimignano and Florence through Ghirlandaio and Giotto, and he exploits the satiric and ironic aspects of their religious subjects. He defines his characters through their responses to the paintings and reveals their approach to life through their approach to art. Though Lawrence writes extensively about Italy and could say [in his *Sea and Sardinia*], with James and Forster, 'Italy has given me back I know not what of myself, but a very, very great deal', his greatest books are rooted in England; in his first novel and then in his best one, he uses English paintings as the thematic centre of his work. In *The White Peacock* the obscure work of Greiffenhagen portrays a Pre-Raphaelite and Theocritan lyricism that represents an unobtainable kind of love. In *The Rainbow* Fra Angelico's paradisal angels, which link the generations of Brangwens, symbolise a quest for the connection between the material and spiritual worlds and helps the characters develop a 'visionary awareness'. And Lawrence sees in Mark Gertler's

Merry-Go-Round an expression of the decadence of modern society, dominated by the chaos and violence of war, that he describes in *Women in Love.*

French writers have studied the relation between painting and literature since the eighteenth century, and the important tradition of Diderot, Stendhal, Fromentin, the Goncourts, Baudelaire and Zola culminates in the aesthetic novels of Huysmans, Proust and Lampedusa. Count Robert de Montesquieu is the model for both Huysmans' Des Esseintes and Proust's Charlus; and Huysmans' sensibility and luxury, his refined taste and lapidary prose, his decadence and neurasthenia are all reflected in Proust's novel. [In Joris-Karl Huysmans' *A Rebours*] Des Esseintes' box of purple bonbons also seems to foreshadow Marcel's *madeleine:* 'he would place one of these bonbons on his tongue and let it melt; then, all of a sudden, and with infinite tenderness, he would be visited by dim, faded recollections'. Huysmans uses Gustave Moreau's *Salome* to symbolise a perverse fantasy that allows an escape from the hideous vulgarity of the contemporary world. In Proust, Mantegna and Botticelli transform aesthetic perceptions into moral truths; and Vermeer embodies the perfections of an Impressionist painting, and provides a moral touchstone that helps to evaluate the characters. The influence of Proust is present in Lampedusa's use of symbolic *objets d'art* to illustrate and prophesy the love of Tancredi and Angelica. Like Guido Reni, Greuze exhibits a rather banal hypocrisy, but Lampedusa significantly places Greuze in the context of a decadent cultural tradition that is analogous to feudal Sicily; and *Le fils puni,* which mirrors the death of Prince Fabrizio, reveals the ironic triumph of *bourgeois* over aristocratic values.

Dostoyevsky has a profound ideological effect on both Mann and Camus. Adrian's dialogue with the devil in *Doctor Faustus* is modelled directly on Ivan's discussion with Satan in *The Brothers Karamazov.* And Prince Myshkin's humane ideas about executions influence Camus' attack on capital punishment in 'Réflexions sur la guillotine' (1957) and *Resistance, Rebellion and Death* (1961), as well as the theme of guilt and redemption in *The Fall.*

The paintings in Dostoyevsky, Camus and Mann express the traditional values of a period of high culture and religious faith that contrast with modern nihilism. Dostoyevsky was deeply moved by the ghastly Holbein which reinforces the analogy between Christ and Myshkin and dramatises a crisis of faith by casting doubt on the divinity of Christ. Camus replaces the drama we normally find in fiction with the tension of a moral and philosophical argument; and the Van Eyck portrays the salvation of mankind that is, ironically, denied in the guilt-ridden world of *The Fall.* In Mann, Dürer relates Nazism to the era of Faust and Luther by expressing an archetypal Germanic demonology, and visualises the themes of artistic sterility and apocalyptic destruction.

Though an awareness of the paintings that form the symbolic core of the work contributes to an understanding of all the novels, the function of the pictures in Hawthorne, Forster, the early Lawrence, Huysmans and Lampedusa is *relatively* less important than in James, the later Lawrence, Proust, Dostoyevsky, Camus and Mann, where a thorough knowledge of their aesthetic models is essential for a full comprehension of their works. . . . [A] thorough knowledge of the visual qualities of the paintings as well as the artist, his time and the whole cultural tradition in which they were created—the biblical sources and saints' legends; the biographies of the secular subjects (Beatrice Cenci and Mohammed II); the history (the restoration of Giotto and Nazi theft of Van Eyck); the critical reputation (Ruskin's ideas on art influenced Hawthorne, James, Forster, Lawrence and Proust); and especially the reasons why the authors were attracted to the paintings, their response to them in their journals, letters and essays, and even their personal feelings about the artist (Lawrence's attitude toward Gertler)—all these elucidate the themes, characters, structure and imagery of some of the most famous and difficult novels in modern European literature.

> *Jeffery Meyers, in an introduction to his* Painting and the Novel, *Manchester University Press, 1975, pp. 1-4.*

Adelia V. Williams

[*In the following excerpt, Williams discusses the role of poesie critique ("critical poetry"), a poetic genre established by Charles Baudelaire with his writings concerning the Salons in nineteenth-century France, in the reciprocal inspiration between painters and poets.*]

The inaugural issue of the Surrealist magazine *Minotaure* appeared in 1933. Conceived by Swiss art publisher Albert Skira, the revue provided a forum for the avant-garde artistic movements of the day. Its contributors encompass a complete array of the foremost artists and writers of the era. A kind of manifesto that figures in the first three issues reveals the journal's interdisciplinary mission:

> It is impossible today to isolate the plastic arts from poetry. The most characteristic modern movements have closely linked these two domains.
>
> (Il est impossible d'isoler aujourd'hui les arts plastiques de la poésie. Les mouvements modernes les plus caractéristiques ont étroitement associé ces deux domaines.)
> [Albert Skira, *Minotaure* I, No. 1 (1933)]

Prevalent also is an interest in ethnography, archaeology, and non-Western cultures which aims beyond description toward serious investigation outside the traditional artistic and literary canon.

Some thirty years after co-editing *Minotaure,* Skira initiated the *Sentiers de la création* series, for which he asked a wide variety of authors, artists, and composers to explore their personal creative itinerary and sensibility toward other art forms. These volumes attest to the importance of the visual arts for such diverse writers as Roland Barthes, Philippe Sollers, Michel Butor, Louis Aragon, Jean Starobinski, Eugène Ionesco, Claude Simon, René Char, Jacques Prévert, Francis Ponge, and Roman Jakobson. Yves Bonnefoy, Jean Tardieu, and Henri Michaux also contributed essays to the collection; their texts are indicative of three strikingly divergent stances.

Bonnefoy's *L'arrière-pays* (1972) is a poetic and personal meditation on the history of art, which the poet views metaphorically as a search for a "true place," a transcendent site. Illustrated primarily with reproductions of sixteenth and seventeenth century Italian and French paintings, especially landscapes, the volume evokes the Florentine Renaissance and Roman baroque. Tardieu's *Obscurité du jour* (1974) is a multifaceted effort to translate the pictorial into literary terms, and is principally illustrated with reproductions of twentieth century drawings and paintings. Like Tardieu, Michaux experiments with the common ground of words and images. *Emergences-résurgences* (1972), illustrated almost entirely by the author, is an exploration of both literary and plastic creation, a voyage within interior space in search of new, and hitherto unexplored territories.

Writings such as those found in the *Sentiers de la création* series have often been referred to as *poésie critique,* a general term for the art writings of literary figures. Said to begin with Charles Baudelaire's *Salon* of 1845, the genre continues with increasing dynamism into our own century, from Apollinaire's *Calligrammes* (1918) and his critical writings on modern art, through the works of the Surrealists, to the efforts of poets of the post-war generation. However, even the most cursory of reviews of the *poète critique* tradition reveals a wide variety of disparate endeavors, demonstrating both the richness and the vagueness of the appellation.

Although nineteenth century writers of all the genres investigated the plastic arts (including Gautier, Stendhal, Balzac, Zola, the Goncourt brothers, Huysmans, and Jarry), it was Baudelaire who enlarged the scope of the poetic medium through examination of the plastic arts. He inaugurated the modern poet's preoccupation with the arts by documenting the *Salons* (1845, 1846, 1859) and finally composed his paean to Constantin Guys, *Le peintre de la vie moderne* (1859), a celebration of the transitory heroism and eternal beauty of the modern age. In the first *Salon,* Baudelaire outlines a theory of modernity. The essay calls for, while exemplifying, a critique of traditional art criticism as subversive as Manet's break with prescribed pictorial conventions in *Olympia* nearly two decades later. Baudelaire's most compelling contribution to the *poésie critique* genre is the notion advanced in the *Salon* of 1846 that the ideal form for extolling pictorial language and an artist's virtuosity is a poem or an elegy. This view was realized in the 1859 poem *Les phares* where the poet evinces, rather than describes, the style and features of eight European masters: Rubens, Leonardo, Rembrandt, Michelangelo, Watteau, Goya, and Delacroix. This last Romantic genius ultimately became Baudelaire's painter of predilection. In *Exposition universelle de 1855* Baudelaire writes:

> Another very great and vast quality of M. Delacroix's talent, and which makes him the preferred painter of poets, is that he is essentially literary.
>
> (Une autre qualité, très grande, très vaste, du tal-

ent de M. Delacroix, et qui fait de lui le peintre aimé des poètes, c'est qu'il est essentiellement littéraire.)

Then, in *L'oeuvre et la vie d'Eugène Delacroix* of 1863, the poet affirms:

> One of the gauges of the spiritual state of our century is that the arts aspire to replace one another, or at least to reciprocally lend new force to one another.
>
> (C'est . . . un des diagnostics de l'état spirituel de notre siècle que les arts aspirent à se suppléer l'un à l'autre, du moins à se prêter réciproquement des forces nouvelles.)

Indeed, as the post-Romantic sensibility moved away from lyricism and self-consciousness, it began to encompass a global view of nature and esthetics. Curiosity in the correspondences among cosmic matters, as evidenced, for instance, in the synesthesia of Baudelaire's sonnet "Correspondances," seems to have lead to an interest in interartistic phenomena as well.

This interest is apparent in the works of Arthur Rimbaud, Jules Laforgue, and Stephane Mallarmé. While Rimbaud neither wrote on art nor frequented the *milieux* of contemporary artists, visual elements clearly influence his poetry. This is most apparent in the sonnet "Voyelles" in which the spectrum joins with the five vowels in a vocalic color theory. Markedly influenced by medieval iconography, the images of *Une saison en enfer* (1873) and *Illuminations* (1874) are intensely visual *tableaux* of fantastic scenes.

Rimbaud's eventual importance for the Dadaist and Surrealist painters and poets is paramount. In the 1931 *History of Dada* Georges Ribemont-Dessaignes describes the pre-eminent poisition of Rimbaud within the Dada framework:

> The case of Rimbaud was on the order of the day . . . to the point where each of the group struggled to find a means of adapting Rimbaud's experiments to his own needs.

Max Ernst, the inventor of *frottage,* the pictorial equivalent of automatic writing, comments in *Au-delà de la peinture:*

> Just as the role of the poet, since the celebrated "letter of the seer," consists in writing under the influence of that which is thought (is articulated) in him, the role of the painter is to capture and to project that which is seen in him.
>
> (De même que le rôle du poète, depuis la célèbre "lettre du voyant," consiste à écrire sous la dictée de ce qui se pense (s'articule) en lui, le rôle du peintre est de cerner et de projeter ce qui se voit en lui.)

During roughly the same period as Rimbaud's poetic career, Jules Laforgue and Stéphane Mallarmé wrote on behalf of the Impressionists' cause. Mallarmé also collaborated with Edouard Manet in 1875 on his own translation of Poe's *The Raven.* However, Mallarmé's most significant and influential contribution to interdisciplinary explorations is his breaking with traditional verse and experimentation with the typographical arrangement, and ultimate derangement, of a text. He first expressed a three-dimensional image of the page in the vision from the sonnet "Le vierge, le vivace et le bel aujourd'hui" of shattering a sheet of paper. His last poem, the pivotal and labored *Un coup de dés jamais n'abolira le hasard* (1897), is the prototype of this treatment of the blank page. In his essay on *Un coup de dés,* Paul Valéry stresses Mallarmé's attention to the page as a literary unit:

> All of his inventiveness, deducted from years of analyzing language, the book, and music, is founded on the consideration of the "page" as a visual unity.
>
> (Toute son invention, déduite d'analyses du langage, du livre, de la musique, poursuivies pendant des années, se fonde sur la considération de la "page," unité visuelle.)

Mallarmé had spoken of the double nature of the word as both essential and immediate in *Crise de vers* of 1895. For the poet, the suggestive, physical and rhythmic properties of words override their literal meaning. Exemplifying this view, *Un coup de dés* betrays the intermediary nature of poetry situated between visual and musical composition. The poem aspires to the non-representational quality of music, in much the same way as the earliest non-figurative paintings will do two decades later.

In a deliberate confusion of the spatial, textual and diagrammatic dimensions within the physical bounds of the printed page (what Mallarmé refers to in the preface as the "Simultaneous vision of the Page" ["Vision simultanée de la Page"]), the poem emphasizes its own materiality, construction and creation, a notion aptly expressed by the poet in the famous rejoinder to Degas, "One does not make verse with ideas. . . . *but with words.*" (Ce n'est point avec des idées que l'on fait des vers. . . . *C'est avec des mots*") [cited in Valéry's essay on *Un coup de dés*]. For the first time in poetry, the reader/viewer experience is a participatory one, inexorably intertwined with the facture of the work of art, as well as with the actual time required to complete it. Here, poem, page, line of verse, word, even letter, become material objects.

This perception of literature as matter had been illustrated by Mallarmé in his unfinished *Le livre,* where he advances the concept of the book as a "total expansion of the letter" ("expansion totale de la lettre"). *Le livre,* and by extension *Un coup de dés,* also exemplifies the Mallarméan cosmology in which the entire world is ultimately reduced to a book.

The impact of Mallarmé's last poem reverberates throughout our own century in both literary and plastic works. In his essay on Marcel Duchamp's *The Bride Stripped Bare By Her Bachelors, Even* (1915-1923), arguably the most influential post-modern work of art, Mexican poet Octavio Paz concludes, "The direct antecedent of Duchamp is not to be found in painting but in poetry: Mallarmé. The work that most closely resembles the *Large Glass* is *Un coup de dés.*" In poetry, Guillaume Apollinaire most completely pursued Mallarmé's experimentations with the text's multidimensional possibilities in *Calligrammes* (1918), the

first of which, *Lettre-Océan,* was published in June 1914. Apollinaire's typographical derangement of a text bears witness to the aspiration of evincing the voluminous intensity of spatial dynamics, especially empty space, and to tread a realm inherently forbidden and unattainable to any writer.

Apollinaire's calligrammatic poems are matched in importance by his critical writings on art. As a champion of twentieth century esthetics and plastic ideas, Apollinaire is often viewed as the quintessential *poète critique.* For [L. C. Breunig and J.-Cl. Chevalier in an introduction to their 1965 edition of Apollinaire's *Méditations esthétiques: Les pointres cubistes*]:

> . . . Apollinaire's originality was to have extended the domain of modern poetry to art criticism . . . Apollinaire thus inaugurated for the twentieth century the *poésie critique* genre.
>
> (. . . l'originalité d'Apollinaire est d'avoir étendu le domaine de la poésie moderne à la prose de la critique d'art . . . Apollinaire a inauguré ainsi pour le XXe siècle le genre de la *poésie critique.*)

Like his predecessors Baudelaire and Mallarmé, Apollinaire's oeuvre includes a substantial corpus of essays and articles dedicated to contemporary art and artists, as well as poetry which seeks to appropriate pictorial techniques. As Baudelaire had continued the tradition among men of letters since Diderot of chronicling the *Salons,* Apollinaire, in a modern variation, documented the *Salon des Indépendants* and the *Salon d'Automne.* More than a critic, however, Apollinaire was a keen and astute witness to one of the most vibrant periods of art production this century has known. What marks his art writings is the fact that he recognized the import of both the revolutions occurring in the art world, such as the distinction between nonrepresentational and representational art, and the specific personalities responsible for the modern temper. These are the most influential artists of the first half of the century: Henri Rousseau, Pablo Picasso, Henri Matisse, Fernand Léger, Wassily Kandinsky, Piet Mondrian, Georges Braque, Alexandre Archipenko, Francis Picabia, Pierre Bonnard, André Derain, Raoul Dufy, Robert Delaunay, Giorgio de Chirico, and Marcel Duchamp. His copious and perspicacious writings on art ushered in nearly all of the monumental *avant-garde* movements: Simultaneism (what Apollinaire called *Orphisme*), Cubism, Fauvism, Futurism, the taste for primitivism, London's Imagism, and the earliest years of Dada and Surrealism. It was, in fact, Apollinaire who coined the term *Surréalisme* in 1917 when writing about Cocteau's "poéme scénique," *Parade.*

Apollinaire's modern and innovative sensibility toward the arts greatly influenced many of his contemporaries. Blaise Cendrars, well acquainted with Delaunay's theory of simultaneous color contrasts, Duchamp's conceptual experiments, and the Cubists and Futurists, also experimented with simultaneist poetry. His *La prose du Transsibérien et de la petite Jehanne de France* (1913), dubbed the first simultaneous book, combines poetry with Sonia Terk Delaunay's abstract painted images in a scroll-like work

The "debut" cubist painting: Pablo Picasso, Les demoiselles d'Avignon, *canvas, spring, 1907.*

sharing the dimensions of the Eiffel Tower. Max Jacob, himself an accomplished artist, collaborated with Picasso on an illustrated volume of *Saint Matorel* (1910) and with Derain on *Les oeuvres burlesques et mystiques de Frère Matorel, mort au couvent* (1912). He and Pierre Reverdy adapted Cubist principles to poetry. In addition, Reverdy wrote on the art of Braque, Gargallo, Gris, Laurens, Léger, Matisse, and Picasso beginning in 1923.
Tristan Tzara first chronicled these early achievements of

poésie critique in the seminal essay of 1953, *Picasso et la poésie.* Here, Tzara systematically traces the evolution of the genre from the late nineteenth century, showing it to be at the vanguard of the monumental breakthroughs in the plastic arts. Tzara astutely points out that, though Baudelaire often missed the mark in his estimations of contemporary artists, he engendered the definitive break with academism. Zola, continuing along these iconoclastic lines, eloquently defended his much-derided friend Edouard Manet. Following this practice, Apollinaire published a laudatory article for Picasso in *La plume* in 1905. Moving from Mallarmé's typographical derangement to that of Apollinaire, and from Cézanne's study of form to Picasso's *Les demoiselles d'Avignon* (1907), Tzara binds the nineteenth century creators to the modern movement. Their discoveries lead to the Cubist poetry of Jacob and Reverdy. Tzara posits the Dada movement as a direct successor to these efforts, especially in their shared interest in so-called "primitive" art.

Apollinaire's exemplary writings paved the way to an unprecedented sensitivity among poets toward interrelations among the arts. Though a large number of modern French writers, including Proust, Paulhan, Sartre, Bataille, Malraux, Genet, Ionesco, Simon, Robbe-Grillet, and Butor, have been studied within the *poésie critique* genre, the interest in the plastic arts of these novelists, thinkers, and playwrights is eclipsed by the engrossing predilection for the arts evidenced by modern poets. Among the most notable examples are Valéry, Cocteau, Claudel, Artaud, Jouve, Perse, Queneau, Char, Ponge, Frénaud, Du Bouchet, Dupin, Pleynet, and the Surrealists: Breton, Eluard, Aragon, and Desnos. Far from remaining a uniform presence in literary expression, the genre appears in a multitude of manifestations which include such diverse productions as book collaborations between poets and artists, known as artists' books or *livres de peintres,* critical and esthetic prose writings, museum and gallery exhibition catalogue prefaces, poetry inspired by painting or which otherwise seeks to emulate plastic works and techniques, and visual works by painter-poets.

Clearly, the questions raised by *poésie critique* are not merely relegated to problems in representation or ekphrasis. As the visual arts have moved further away from narrative toward a more suggestive, non-representative, hence poetic, quality, poetic discourse too has aligned itself more closely to this non-anecdotal, metapoetic impulse. While historically the distinction between the visual and discursive realms from Aristotle to Lessing corresponds to a philosophy of mimetic art, conversely, the fusion of semantic and visual fields correlates to non-literary strategies in both arts. In addition, visual artists have increasingly investigated and ultimately exploited the temporal domain traditionally denied them while, significantly, abandoning discursive strategies. Concurrently poets have continued to explore the spatial potential of the word. These dual processes take root in Mallarmé's poetry which aspires to the non-representative ambitions of music, thus resembling abstract painting. The modern temper in poetry and painting has progressed from an emphasis on the work of art as a complete self-referential entity to the work as a self-conscious ongoing process. In art, this phenomenon has resulted in a profusion of heterogeneous art forms: collage, the Readymade, assemblage, the mobile, kinetic sculpture, sound sculpture, performance art, book art, and video art. In poetry, it has resulted in the multiform *poésie critique* genre.

The Dadaists and Surrealists, with whom the interplay of the plastic and the poetic culminated, most clearly and fully continued Apollinaire's example. Both groups sought to divest themselves of distinctions among media, genres, and modes of expression, and so led the way for the artistic developments of the years between the two world wars. The salient works of the period attest to the perpetual interaction between poetry and art, showing once more the diversity and innovative nature of *poésie critique.*

Among the first examples of the Surrealist contribution to the genre are the 1922 Paul Eluard—Max Ernst collage collaborations, *Répétitions* and *Les malheurs des immortels,* the veritable prototypes of the *livre de peintre.* These are textual and pictorial *découpages* whose effect of unfamiliarity and disorientation is indeed a literal/literary/figural illustration of Lautréamont's celebrated image of the fortuitous encounter of a sewing machine and an umbrella on a dissecting table. This collage technique was most eloquently and accurately articulated by Louis Aragon, the first to recognize the difference between the Cubist collages of Picasso, Braque, and Gris, and Ernst's Surrealist collage. Aragon observes that while in the former the artist attempts to graft reality onto the picture, a practice especially evident in the insertion of words onto the pictorial space, in the latter, visual elements behave like words in poetry in an atmosphere of ambiguous meaning.

Aragon's *poésie critique* writings were collected in the posthumous volume *Ecrits sur l'art moderne* of 1981. The art writings of Robert Desnos from 1922 to 1944, poems, aphorisms, and essays collected in *Ecrits sur les peintres,* also treat Ernst, as well as Picasso, Picabia, de Chirico, Duchamp, Man Ray, and Masson. *Donner à voir* of 1939, a collection of thoughts and poems on numerous artists, including Ernst, Picasso, and Miró, best exemplifies the more experimental critical writings of Eluard. A capital text for *poésie critique, Donner à voir* aims at liberating both reading and vision by inserting the visible into the legible. On the *poéte critique,* Eluard later wrote, "It would be prodigious for a critic to become a poet, and it is impossible for a poet not to be, in part, a critic. . . . I consider the poet to be the best of all critics." ("Il serait prodigieux qu'un critique devînt poète, et il est impossible qu'un poète ne contienne pas un critique. . . . je considère le poète comme le meilleur de tous les critiques.")

In 1928 Breton published *Le surréalisme et la peinture,* a treatise on the failure of art criticism throughout history, and on the innovations of contemporary artists who direct their subject matter toward an inner vision. Its opening line, the cogent dictum, "The eye exists in the savage state," ["l'oeil existe à l'état sauvage,"] encapsulates the group's aspiration toward the privileging of the visual image. Breton's preferred artist is Pablo Picasso whom he appropriates for the Surrealists, as Apollinaire had done to illustrate his own esthetic preoccupations with modernism. Breton credits Picasso with having introduced poetic principles to painting by veering away from the traditional referential nature of painting. In its playfulness, Picasso's painting embodies the creative freedom toward which the Surrealists aspired. The Spanish artist figures prominently for all of the poets of the group. Eluard considers him at length in *Donner à voir.* Aragon's 1924 *Hommage à Pablo*

Picasso praises the artist for embodying the modern spirit. For Desnos too, Picasso represents the new vitality of modern art and the exaltation of the imagination. And yet, it must be said that in more technical terms, Picasso's overwhelmingly intellectual, conceptual approach to art seems antipodal to, for example, the automatism of the Surrealist esthetic. His is, indeed, a painting of ideas, as Tzara describes in *Picasso et la poésie,* and appears, therefore, more closely allied with the tenets of Dada.

Nonetheless, the Surrealist poets, by choosing to align themselves with Picasso, who with Duchamp symbolizes the century's most influential artistic impulse, clearly established themselves at the fore of the modern movement. The intense activity among the Surrealist poets, painters, and sculptors played the central role for the convergence of the verbal and visual idioms in twentieth-century French letters. All subsequent attempts at blending plastic and literary creation can be said to find their source, if only indirectly, in the Surrealist ideology. In many ways the review *Minotaure* represents the culmination of the Surrealist agenda toward fusing poetic and plastic elements.

Yves Bonnefoy, Jean Tardieu, and Henri Michaux, although marginally linked to Surrealism, are all indebted to the Surrealist poets for their pioneering efforts toward fusion of the arts. Both Michaux and Tardieu allude to Eluard's idea of "donner à voir" when writing about art, while Bonnefoy considers Surrealism to be the most important contemporary contribution to European art. In their discussions of Surrealist artists, the poets express the central problematics of their own concerns with pictorial and linguistic representation. Bonnefoy's "poetics of presence" and his discussion of mimesis hinges on Giacometti's last Surrealist piece, *The Invisible Object.* Tardieu's attempt to write painterly poems are linked to the images of letters of Max Ernst who created the frontispiece for *Obscurité du jour,* Tardieu's theoretical writings. The disconcerting oxymorons of Ernst intrigued Michaux as well, when he discovered them at an exhibit of Surrealist art in 1925 at about the time he himself began to paint. Additionally, Michaux's essay on René Magritte is fundamental to the understanding of Michaux's own pictograms. Though Magritte, unlike Michaux, is a representative painter, both create an ambiguous representation which challenges the very principles of mimesis by revealing its simulacrum.

Michel Foucault, in his book *Ceci n'est pas une pipe* on Magritte and the evolution in the West from mimetic art to calligrammatic art, and the ultimate dissolution of painting, treats these very questions. Foucault traces the development from the classical hierarchy in which verbal and visual elements exist in and as two distinct spaces, to their intersection in the twentieth century in the works of Klee, Kandinsky, and Magritte. In the works of these three artists, gesture, the seminal element in writing, obliterates the fenestral and Albertian functions of painting. The canvas becomes an appropriate space for words.

Concomitant with this pictorial revolution is a progression toward a critique of the conventions of language and adoption of Oriental matrices. Though the East is especially ev-

ident in Michaux's outlook, the questions raised by Asian esthetics are equally important to Bonnefoy and Tardieu. Bonnefoy, who has written on the non-mimetic quality of Zen art in an essay on photographer Cartier-Bresson, as well as on Japanese poet Basho and on haiku, has provocatively confronted the questions of perspective and representation. Tardieu, who cites Japanese and Chinese calligraphy in *Obscurité du jour,* and whose first attempt at painterly poetry was inspired by the Chinese painter-poet Wang Wei, treats the questions of gesture in calligrammatic expression.

For Foucault, the calligram is a double cipher, in that it combines letter and figure while simultaneously, and this is the essential paradox, "unraveling" or annulling the separate functions of each mode of expression which had been for centuries the bedrock of representation in art and literature. Though only Jean Tardieu specifically mentions the calligram, both he and Michaux explore the convergence of word and image by turning to Asian models: particularly Chinese calligraphy, and in the case of Michaux, the chanted syllables of the Hindu yantra. The calligram exists in an ambiguous space as is true also in Chinese painting, poetry and calligraphy, an aspect of particular salience to the work of Henri Michaux. . . . With all three poets, we discern a "double cipher" through which visual and verbal elements are funnelled and combined. The calligram's double function, by which it exceeds pure language or pure image alone, is analogous to the efforts of these poets who seek, in disparate ways, to explore the many approaches to the problematics of representation.

> *Adelia V. Williams, in an introduction to her* The Double Cipher: Encounter Between Word and Image in Bonnefoy, Tardieu and Michaux, *Peter Lang, 1990, pp. 1-21.*

Wylie Sypher

[*Sypher is an American educator and critic. In the following excerpt, he discusses the influence of techniques employed by Cubist painters on literature of the early twentieth century, maintaining that both painters and writers sought in their works to redefine the relationship between art and life.*]

Pirandello's "desperate theatricality" was not a laboratory fully equipped for research into the new perspectives in reality; and his plays seem to be artful rather than art, perhaps resembling some of the experiments Picasso should have performed in his studio, not in public. Yet Pirandello, like Picasso, was seeking a "way beyond art" and, like the scientists, accepted reality as a continual transformation where fiction impinges on fact, where art intersects life. In writing of Picasso, Gertrude Stein explains that "because the way of living had changed the composition of living had extended and each thing was as important as any other thing . . . the framing of life, the need that a picture exist in its frame, remain in its frame was over. A picture remaining in its frame was a thing that had existed always and now pictures commenced to want to leave their frames and this also created the necessity for cubism." The cubists changed the status of the easel picture and deliberately, as modern artists, broke open the boundaries between their composition and the process going on outside the frame; the easel painting was no longer a work of art isolated from the world about it. To emphasize the relevance of their interlocking planes to the situation outside, they "bled" their composition, or sometimes arbitrarily cut off their constructions without completing the motif or extending it to the edge of the canvas. Thus they affirmed Whitehead's principle that there is no isolated or independent existence, that the whole is constitutive of each part and each part constitutive of the whole. Art is no longer a window into another world but an aspect of reality, a mode of transformation, another angle on process. The obliteration of punctuation in Apollinaire's "calligrams" is the same sort of elision between images that occur simultaneously, like the montage of rhythms in Delaunay's whirling colored disks.

Cubist paintings had the enormous advantage, which nineteenth-century illustrative or symbolist painting did not have, of *approaching* reality without attempting either to identify art with things or to alienate art from things. This is the difference between the cubist *découpage* and *découpage* in Degas, who relied on the camera-shot, the excerpt from life, for unexpected quotation. The cubist quoted otherwise, by collage or the inserted clichés of the studio. Thus the cubist separation of painting from actuality, when it occurs, is shown to be arbitrary, not deceptive; the limits of cubist representation are not set by the limits of the canvas, for by implication cubist painting belongs to the world outside. The canvas is no longer "other." Neither the romantics nor the realists were able to make this adjustment of art to life. Apollinaire was exact in saying that cubist structures are endowed with the fulness of reality; they gave up the nineteenth-century "game of art" to pass "beyond painting." The cubists were able to *situate* the art-object more satisfactorily, more intelligently, more provocatively than at any time since the renaissance—when painters also tried to bring the art-object into adjustment with real space by means of deep perspective.

Many novelists like Aldous Huxley and Philip Toynbee have used the cubist simultaneous perspective, but no modern writer has been more concerned with situating his narrative than André Gide, who has been called cubist, but only in the trivial sense that he liberated the novel from conventionalities. This is the Gide who surprises us as Picasso has often sought to surprise; but, as Ozenfant remarked, surprise works only once. There is more in Gide than surprise, for his novels are not mere revolt but experiments with new means of representing reality. Gide constantly examined the transformations of fact to fiction and the effects of the Discontinuity or Uncertainty Principle: there he followed current scientific theory even more successfully than Valéry, who doubtless knew science far better.

Much of Gide's "fiction" is a factual record seen from a certain angle and thus transformed. As he suggested in *Les Caves du Vatican* (1914) "fiction is history that *might* have taken place, and history is fiction that *has* taken place." *Les Cahiers d' André Walter* (1891) was his early attempt to give a fictional dimension to autobiography, and four

years later in *Paludes* he explained, "I arrange facts in such a way as to make them conform to truth more closely than they do in real life." The ground of Gide's fiction was usually his *Journals,* equivocal testaments produced somewhere between Gide's life and Gide's art in a domain where cubist sculptors created what has been called "The Object Purified" or "The Object Dissected." Are we, for example, to think that the episode in *La Porte Étroite* (1909) when Jérome finds Alissa weeping because of her mother's adultery is fact or fiction? We know that here, as in *L'Immoraliste* (1902), Gide was consciously treating in some duplex way the events he mentions not only in his *Journals* but also in that more tantalizing "record" *Et Nunc Manet In Te.* Gide's ingenious transformations of actuality to fiction culminated in *Les Faux-Monnayeurs* (1919-1926); and at once he complicated these transformations by printing *Le Journal des Faux-Monnayeurs,* which is for the most part Gide's own journal documenting the writing of the novel. Deliberately Gide turned his back on the modern quest for myth in literature and devoted himself, instead, to the cubist problem of the distance of art from actuality. "What will attract me to a new book," he says in the *Journal des Faux-Monnayeurs,* "is not so much new characters as a new way of presenting them. This novel must end sharply, not through exhaustion of the subject, but on the contrary through its expansion and by a sort of blurring of its outline." The blurring occurs precisely along the margin between art and life. As he said in his tenth Imaginary Interview, the novelist can dispose of his materials as he sees fit, but his materials are actualities—"You cannot do without them."

Beginning, like a cubist painter, with actualities, Gide then affirmed the difference between actuality and the representation of actuality. When Gide was very young, another writer asked him, "If you had to sum up your future work in a sentence, in a word—what would that word be?" Gide replied, "We must all represent." From the first he saw that representation is a challenge to actuality. Any representation is a counterfeit that daringly invites us to detect what is fraudulent in resemblance. It is an act of defiance in which the artist stakes his skill in rendering a notion of reality. The counterfeiting becomes a creative act. Gide based *Les Faux-Monnayeurs* on Oscar Wilde's paradox that nature imitates art: "The artist's rule should be never to restrict himself to what nature proposes, but to propose nothing to nature but what nature can and should shortly imitate." So Gide accepts the significant motif from the decadents and symbolists and yet amends art-for-art into the more penetrating inquiry of the relation between art and life.

What Gide finds is that life is not art, that art is not life, that art cannot occur without life, but that life may be less significant than art: life and art are two aspects of consciousness, perhaps. The cubists were working in the same direction, for as Juan Gris told Kahnweiler: "My aim is to create new objects which cannot be compared with any object in actuality. . . . My *Violin,* being a creation, need fear no competition." Here was the trouble with the novel, Gide thought—it had always been clinched to actualities (*cramponné à la réalité*). Defoe and Stendhal had written "pure" novels by a kind of counterfeiting that interested

Gide, who says in *Journal des Faux-Monnayeurs:* "On the one hand, the event, the fact, what is given from without; on the other hand, the special effort of the novelist to write his book with these. And *there* is the real subject, the new axis that unbalances the narrative and projects it toward the imaginative. In brief, I see this notebook where I record the composing of the novel, turned entire into the novel itself, forming the main interest, for the greater irritation of the reader." This is a novel centering in a novelist (in some respects Gide himself?) who is writing a fiction about the very events in which he himself, as novelist, is involved. All relations in Edouard's novel are reflexive and at the same time open to actuality, uncertain, shifting.

It has been said that the great cubist achievement was *camouflage*. In cubist painting and Gide's stories the relations between the painted object and the object, between plot and autobiography, are unresolved and reciprocating. Similarly in the film which "broke with the theatre," Eisenstein presented a "graphic conflict" by montage: "Headlights on speeding cars, highlights on receding rails, shimmering reflections on the wet pavements—all mirrored in puddles that destroy our sense of direction (which is top? which is bottom?)."

Edouard says he sets himself before reality like a painter. Later Strouvilhou asks why modern painting has gone so far ahead of literature by daring to discard the fine subject. Curiously, Strouvilhou is wrong. Painting did not outdistance *Les Faux-Monnayeurs,* which, like Pirandello's comedy-in-the-making, surrenders the fine subject and dismantles plot with its cause-and-effect certainties while the cubists were setting about their diffractions of reality. *Les Faux-Monnayeurs* is an inquiry, like Picasso's *Arlésienne,* into the innumerable transitions between the object and the conception of the object. Gide personally seems not to have seen the resemblance, being insensitive to contemporary painting. One of his friends was surprised that he admired Chardin. "It was natural," Gide remarks, "that but little gifted to like painting instinctively, I should attach myself particularly to a painter whom I could like only quite specifically for the qualities of which I had been most particularly deprived. . . . There are few painters who more authentically taught me to enjoy painting." Evidently Gide liked Chardin for the same reason he liked Defoe: they both confidently offer the actualities Gide did not permit himself. In *Les Faux-Monnayeurs* Edouard does not set himself in front of actuality like Chardin and Defoe but, instead, like Braque, La Fresnaye, and early cubists who destroyed things, then formally rebuilt them to compete with the actuality they had demolished. Gide notes that his novel "must not be neatly rounded off, but rather disperse, disintegrate."

In 1937 Gide wrote "Some Reflections on the Relinquishing of Subject in Plastic Arts," in which he says he was never tempted to take still lifes by Chardin or Cézanne for "actual objects." Gide knew that the cubists were eager to explore the contradiction between the object and their representation of the object. Cézanne wanted his paintings to be solid *and* artificial "like paintings in museums." Braque used to take his paintings out into the fields "to have them meet things," to see whether his representation could hold

Pablo Picasso, Man with a Violin, *1911.*

its own against the natural world from which he had excluded it. Picasso also exchanged actuality for representation, stating in his painting what the world is *not*. At the outer margin of cubist purity Mondrian protests that "art has been liberated from everything that prevents it from being truly plastic"—a last corollary to the significant motifs of Art Nouveau. For all these painters art is an equivalent. More consciously than any other novelist Gide practiced an art of counterfeit, which is a camouflage of the "document" (the journal) and a representation of the document at some uncertain level of fiction. As Edouard explains about the false ten-franc piece, "It will be worth ten francs so long as no one recognizes it to be false." Gide asks whether we recognize it. First Edouard writes in his journal that he has never been able to invent anything; then he corrects himself: "Only this remains—that reality interests me inasmuch as it is plastic, and that I care more—infinitely more—for what may be than for what has been." The textures of actuality over against the textures of fiction—that is the problem in Gide's research, which repeats in the novel the cubist analysis in the *tableau-tableau,* the art-form in the making.

Picasso has asked whether anybody ever saw a "natural" work of art. His own paintings, he claims, are a course of destructions: "I do a picture—then I destroy it. . . . In each destroying of a beautiful discovery, the artist does not really suppress it, but rather transforms it . . . makes it more substantial." The novel Edouard intends to write will be a sum of destructions, or a "rivalry between the real world and the representation of it which we make to ourselves. The manner in which the world of appearances imposes itself upon us, and the manner in which we try to impose on the outside world our own interpretation—this is the drama of our lives." It is a drama nineteenth-century art, with its anxiety about nature, never wrote; the nineteenth century either tried to find the drama in nature or else, with the symbolists, refused nature, but did not welcome the rivalry of the mind with what nature offers. This rivalry produces a style—which is more than a technique: it is an assertion that man takes a *view* of nature. Trying to justify his method, Edouard says he would like his book to be as close to *and as far from* actuality—as human and fictitious—as Racine's *Athalie*. Edouard allows himself no finer subject than Strouvilhou's painter; everything will go into his novel, yet the result will not be reportage. There will be no suppressions, but only a translation of events into fiction: "What I want is to represent reality on the one hand, and on the other that effort to stylize it into art." The artist's struggle, which causes style, is "between what actuality offers him and what he himself desires to make of it." During his cubist phase Picasso studies how the features of *Man with Violin* transform themselves into his conception. [According to Max Ernst in his *Beyond Painting*] The painter or novelist becomes "a spectator at the birth of his work." Here is another facet of the double-consciousness of modern man, the *dédoublement* of existential experience.

Bernard objects about Edouard's novel: "A good novel gets itself written more naïvely than that." Bernard misses the point—this is not the nineteenth-century "good novel," for the modern artist is aware of actuality in a new way. In fact Edouard says actuality "puts him out." He must, like Braque, compete with it. Edouard is trying to liberate his narrative from easy identifications. His journal (which is, in part, Gide's novel) uses a tactic of collage by imposing excerpts from life (documents!) upon a fictional texture for the sake of affirming the competition between fiction and history. Apollinaire calls this tactic the cubist "enumeration of elements," of which actuality is merely one. Edouard says his novel will be a "formidable erosion of contours." The erosion had begun in the cubist destruction of objects; for, as Picasso said, if they are damaged by representation, "so much the worse for objects." Edouard transvalues the document as the cubists transvalued ordinary things like bottles, tables, newspapers. For the cubist, objects are residual; they are borrowed into another order of reality.

The cubists gave counterfeit a prestige, recovering the formalities of artistic vision by passing objects through a repertory of planes, not by reportage. The skill of the counterfeiter exerts itself against great pressures from the world outside. His resistance to this world is the warrant of his art, since actuality must be used only as collage—a fragment that guards the integrity of representation. Cubist painting is an impartial examination of textures, a résumé of the various levels of identity at which things appear. Apollinaire said that the great revolution in art Picasso achieved almost unaided "was to make the world his rep-

resentation of it." Cézanne's proto-cubism was solid geometry, entirely untheoretical, a realization of the strength of the world, the thick contours of houses and dovecotes and hills, the mass of trees, roads, sea, rocks, and headlands. Of its own weight, almost, this world fell open into shifting planes that dazzle in Braque, Gris, and Picasso, who make many hypothetical adjustments by a cinematic vision through which things flicker, come and go, recede and approach, yet are held in formal composition. As the artist penetrated nature by his thought, cubism turned conceptual in its approaches and structures. Cézanne's volumes were leveled to planes until the object, at first dismantled, was reconstructed on the surface of the canvas within two dimensions, an entirely pictorial displacement with *ruptures subites des plans géométrisés*. The erosion of contours was complete, and cubism, disciplined by the mind, went from its massive to its transparent, synthetic, cinematic phase.

This is how Gide erodes his events and characters. Edouard complains that the novel, too long hindered by fidelity to facts, must be stripped of its encumbrances—its "literature." Now that photography, he argues, has "freed painting from its concern for a certain sort of accuracy," the phonograph should rid the novel of nineteenth-century dialog. He does not describe his characters; he is concerned only with the "formal adjustments" in his fiction. The cubist world and the world of *Les Faux-Monnayeurs* are not the world we ordinarily know. Just when we are about to feel Braque's things, reassuringly, "there," they disappear in a complex of planes, lines, colors, with interpolations of wood, paper, cloth, which are—and are not—within the composition, and are only one more insolent value in reality. Gide's fiction uses all the simulated and literal textures of cubism. Is Edouard's notebook a fiction? If so, then what is the status of Gide's own journal, transcribed into the formalities of Edouard's novel-in-the-making? More annoying, what is the status of Alfred Jarry, that legendary *fauve* let loose in person, pistol and all? This *trompe l'oeil* is a sardonic version of the outworn actualities of the novel. What of the coiners themselves, whom Gide "borrowed" from stories in the daily press? And what of Edouard's scandalous closing remarks about Boris: Edouard will not use Boris' suicide in *his* novel—"I have too much difficulty in understanding it. And then I dislike police court items. There is something peremptory, irrefutable, brutal, outrageously real about them." Wherever these facts are most obviously used as facts they appear fictional. In contrast to the collage-figure of Jarry, the figure of Lady Griffith is deliberately set "outside the action," like the Son in Pirandello's play [*Six Characters in Search of an Author*]. What are the relations between Gide's journals, the intermediate *Journal des Faux-Monnayeurs*, the journals displaced into Edouard's notebooks, and Gide's encompassing fiction—if it be fiction? In his notes Gide said he wanted this book to be "a crossroad—a meeting of problems."

Apollinaire said that the cubist analysis of the object is "so complete and so decisive of the various elements which make up the object that these do not take the shape of the object." Gide disliked the naïve logic of the older novel and admired Defoe's ability to gain a fictional perspective on literal facts. However useful, Defoe's experiment with actuality was limited. Gide experiments with other dimensions, from the internal dimension of Edouard's journal to the wholly unexpected Thackeray-like intrusion when he remarks to us by shocking direct address, "I am afraid that Edouard, in confiding little Boris to Azais' care, is committing an imprudence." To vex us again Gide opens another fictional dimension when Edouard records in his notes for his novel-in-the-making (which is, reflexively, these notes themselves) how he submitted these notes to Georges for scrutiny ("I wanted to know what Georges' reaction might be; . . . it might instruct me"). These mirror-inversions are so complicated that reality becomes only a theoretical perspective upon reality.

Gide treats the events in *Les Faux-Monnayeurs* at a distance that gives him *access* to actuality without any naturalistic false resemblances and encumbrances. Edouard complains that previous novels have been like pools in public gardens: "their contours are defined—perfect, perhaps, but the water they contain is captive and lifeless. I wish it now to run freely. . . . I choose not to foresee its windings. . . . I consider that life never presents us with anything which may not be looked upon as a fresh starting point, no less than as a termination." He wants his novel to end with the phrase "might be continued." Comparably, Gertrude Stein left unfinished her *Making of Americans* when she was convinced that her cinematic fragments had caught the rhythms of reality. *Les Faux-Monnayeurs* closes with Edouard's wish to know Caloub, the boy who was only casually mentioned at the start of the book. Caloub's unfinished profile carries the fiction "outside."

Edouard says that for him "Everything hangs together and I always feel such a subtle interdependence between all the facts life offers me, that it seems to me impossible to change a single one without modifying the whole." This means there can be no isolated stress on "big" events, no major crisis, no emotive fragments, no melodramatic passages; the perspectives are too complex to allow this heavily personal accent. Neither Gide nor the cubist painter needs the climax. That would be romantic. The cubist view of the world is an unexcited sense of possible meanings and contours. This undisturbed perception is the privilege of classic art, which makes its formal arrangements without being victimized by its emotional momentum. The cubist novel, the cubist painting displace and adjust their figures arbitrarily with, perhaps, the control of Racine's drama, or with any of the classic disciplines that destroy, then reconstruct, the world.

The cubist imagination, or Racine's, brings the world clearly and firmly into focus between our sensations and our ideas. Gide's experiment was to find out precisely where he must set the plane of his fiction, which must purify facts by ideas of these facts. This is what the nineteenth-century realists never determined, for they accepted Courbet's belief that "the art of painting should consist solely of the representation of objects visible and tangible to the artist." Gide began by distancing autobiography, like Picasso insisting there are no concrete or abstract forms in art but only more or less successful lies which

occur when actualities are transposed to representation. Picasso's art, or Gide's, is a counterfeit erected arbitrarily between the physical world and the formations of thought. This it shares with "pure" science. For the modern painter, novelist, and scientist the world exists to be violated by the mind, which excerpts from it what it needs. The cubist counterfeit does not refuse the splendor of things and events. But it can also approach the condition of music. Edouard says, "I can't see why what was possible in music should be impossible in literature." It is possible, as Gide must have known when he hoped his novel would be like a fugue. The cubist, subduing the world by the activity of his mind, achieves fugue-like variations upon the themes reality affords.

To have art approach music was the aim of the symbolists. But the symbolist distance from actuality is not the cubist distance. The symbolist imagination—a belated romanticism—demolished the world by feeling, emotively possessing objects as hieroglyphs for a state of soul. The symbolist imagination suffers among its own ruined images of things. The cubists revered the world as the symbolists and fauves did not—for the fauves were often inheritors of the symbolist emotional distortion. The violence of the cubist imagination is intellectual; objects are destroyed at an impersonal distance, as if by theorem. Cubist refractions of objects are "disinterested." The cubist painting or novel is not the art of fugue in the nineteenth-century sense that art is music; for then music meant emotional suggestion. Poe and Baudelaire wrote musical compositions, but did not purify their music of their emotional involvements. It was left for the cubists to detach themselves from their moods, to speculate dispassionately about objects, to gain nuances by thought and vision rather than by feeling. Braque said, "I love the rule that controls emotion." Cubist color, like cubist line, has architectural, not emotive, value. Some have complained that cubism dehumanizes art; Ortega y Gasset feared it did.

The cubists were not really *fauves* in spite of their close kinship; for the fauvists were descendants of the first romantics, and fauvism approached a style only when it was decorative, or when it used rhythm and color architecturally and mastered its urgent vision as Van Gogh did under the still glare of a southern sun. Then the ornamental motifs of the Nabis and Art Nouveau were endowed with monumental presence. Matisse, the greatest fauve, inscribed romantic feeling in joyous liberated flat patterns; composition, he said, is reducing violent movement to decoration. The cubists passed from plane to plane without romantic impetus. Their fugal compositions are neutral in tone—intelligent variations upon a few themes worked out in series: figures with guitar, harlequins, tables, carafes, fruits, and the furnishings of urban life. The cubist investigated the uses of actuality by diffractions and discontinuities, a structure of contrasting textures adjusted within monochromatic transparencies and reflections as if within receding mirrors. With cubist asceticism Gide reduced mannerisms of style until his surface is "pure," for, as he decided, in this novel "everything must be said in the most neutral way" (*la manière la plus plate*). His statement is as disinterested as a Braque *nature morte*. His narrative refuses sensuous color, purple passages, romantic inflections. It has the lucid quality of Braque's manipulation, the facile touch of a gallic hand.

He will improvise, improvise upon an ordinary motif until he has examined its possibilities. Like the cubist, Gide is impartial. What he called his irresolution, an incapacity or unwillingness to endorse any one perspective, was typical of the cubist temperament, the indecision of the early twentieth-century intellectual who, having accepted the notion of relativism, was aware of all the attitudes that could be held, but perhaps not acted upon: neutrality in art and life, and a clever investigation of alternative angles on every problem. In 1932 Gide wrote, "Each of my books up to now has been the exploitation of an uncertainty." Gide discovered, along with the cubists, the artistic value of impromptu. He notes again: "Everything in me calls out to be revised, amended, re-educated." Picasso has a cubist temperament—mercurial in his experiments, his diversities, his departures, and his returns. Another cubist, André Lhote, once said, "Each aspect of an object demands a new perspective, a new space to create."

Under such scrutiny the cubist object gradually tended to disappear. Once the figure broke up into planes, these planes broke up, and there was no way to halt the destruction short of reabsorbing these smaller and smaller facets into the neutral continuum of process, which is featureless. We see the fragmentation beginning rather savagely in Picasso's *Demoiselles d'Avignon* (1907) and ending in the depersonalized, minutely fractured passages of *Man with Violin* (1911). After the first bold—nearly fauvist—regard of the object, cubism diffused its momentums, accepting what Whitehead calls the "startling discontinuity of spatial existence," which also appeared in the quantum theory and cinematic *découpage*, syncopation, and the "collision of independent shots." Gide intended the action in *Les Faux-Monnayeurs* to be a continual discontinuity: "every new chapter should pose new problems, serve as a new beginning, a new impulse, a plunge ahead." His law of composition was, "Never keep on—Ne jamais profiter de l'élan acquis." Begin again. Check the velocity. Break the rhythm. Try another profile. His novel is a form of "creative incoherence." From *André Walter* on Gide gave himself and his characters to the ethical impromptu, *la vie spontanée.* "Inconsistency. Characters in a novel or play who act all the way through exactly as one expects them to . . . This consistency of theirs, which is held up to our admiration, is on the contrary the very thing which makes us recognize that they are artificially composed." Thus Edouard explains his psychology. Or again, Protos in *Caves du Vatican:* "Do you know what is needful to turn an honest man into a rogue? A change of scene—a moment's forgetfulness suffice . . . a cessation of continuity—a simple interruption of the current." The *acte gratuit* is a psychological mechanism congenial to the cubist artist, who in his readiness to shift perspectives takes the impromptu approach. At the close of the nineteenth century Pater had urged the artist to be inquisitive: "What we have to do is to be forever curiously testing new opinions and courting new impressions." The cubist turned this *fin de siècle* aesthetic receptivity into a principle of style.

Gide's art has the excitement of interruption, of fracture.

His fiction is a daring intellectualism that constantly reorganizes appearances into adjustments that look very strange, if not inexplicable, to the older logic of continuity. As Gris said, "Cubism is a state of mind." As Braque said, "Art is made to disturb." Gide repeats: "My role is to disconcert."

Gide's detachment is not hostile or in any way emotional, but cubist. His distance from the events he presents is not determined by intensity of feeling; he does not betray disillusion; he is not surprised; he does not exclaim. Instead, his tone is exploratory, uncommitted. The very question of "sincerity" vexes him: "I am never anything but what I think myself—and this varies so incessantly that often, if I were not there to make them acquainted, my morning's self would not recognize my evening's. Nothing could be more different from me than myself." So remarks Edouard, underscoring what Gide says in his journals. This "dissociation of sensibility" in Gide is not tormented (that would be romantic) because he recruits, indifferently, from all ranges of possible experience without predisposition. His protestant scepticism and scruple are a disguise for a discontinuity of temperament and inconsistent motives—his outlook is a "flat" perspective that is not cynical but open to alternative angles. Gide is capable of sympathy, of crime, of faith, of blasphemy, but never of unintelligence. The cubist invents with disconcerting curiosity, by severe and ingenious experiment.

Before the cubists investigated the world we did not know what an object is *capable of.* Chardin must have surmised; but he was not venturous enough. Defoe must have guessed; but his research was local. Gide systematically investigates his moralists and immoralists, subjecting them to irresistible strains suddenly and cleverly applied. Man in the cubist novel, like the object in cubist painting, is capable of all features, and at the same instant. Yet Gide's curiosity is not the bohemian curiosity of Baudelaire and Rimbaud, which was essentially a means of escaping from the world, or rejecting it. Gide says, instead, "I love life, but I have lost confidence in it."

Cubism was a sign of destruction as well as creation. Both cubist and fauvist destructions of the world suggest possibilities of splendor and disaster the nineteenth century could hardly have imagined—even after the flaming devastations of Turner's painting. When Gertrude Stein first flew over the American landscape in 1934-35 she understood what art means for our century, for the air-vision gave her a new and terrifying perspective:

> . . . when I looked at the earth I saw all the lines of cubism made at a time when not any painter had ever gone up in an airplane. I saw there on the earth the mingling lines of Picasso, coming and going, developing and destroying themselves, I saw the simple solutions of Braque, I saw the wandering lines of Masson, yes I saw and once more I knew that a creator is contemporary, he understands what is contemporary when the contemporaries do not yet know it, but he is contemporary and as the twentieth century is a century which sees the earth as no one has ever seen it, the earth has a splendor that it never has had, and as everything destroys itself in the

twentieth century and nothing continues, so then the twentieth century has a splendor which is its own and Picasso is of this century, he has that strange quality of an earth that one has never seen and of things destroyed as they have never been destroyed.

(Picasso)

First the artist's destruction of the world, the painted object, the prose fiction. Then the larger and more public destructions, Guernica and Hiroshima. Cubism was an art of frightening conceptions.

Wylie Sypher, "The Cubist Novel," in his Rococo to Cubism in Art and Literature, *Random House, 1960, pp. 295-311.*

SPATIAL FORM IN LITERATURE

John Peale Bishop

[*Bishop was an American poet and critic who is sometimes associated with such Southern Renaissance authors as Allen Tate and Robert Penn Warren. The emphasis on color in Bishop's poetry and his criticism concerning the arts evidences his life-long interest in painting. In the following essay, which was originally delivered as a lecture at Princeton University in 1940, Bishop upholds Lessing's ideas concerning the limits of poetry and painting, stating: "succession in time is the sphere of the poet, as space is that of the painter."*]

I shall begin this essay by quoting a passage from one of the *Reactionary Essays on Poetry and Ideas* by Allen Tate. He is speaking of the confusion which results when the common center of experience, out of which the separate arts achieve their special formal solutions, disappears. Then the arts, deprived of their proper sustenance, begin to live one on another. "Painting," he says, "tries to be music; poetry leans upon painting; all the arts 'strive toward the condition of music'; till at last seeing the mathematical structure of music, the arts become geometrical and abstract, and destroy themselves."

The passage occurs in an essay on my own poetry. And it is because Mr. Tate feels, quite rightly, that in some of my poems I lean very far toward the painters, finding in an art not theirs solutions which are possibly proper only to them, that he has asked me here this evening. There may have been malice in his invitation. He may have asked me here only to witness my confusion. But the confusion is not mine alone. It has perhaps always existed. It was present, we know, in the mid-eighteenth century, when Gotthold Lessing wrote his famous essay on the limits of painting and poetry, which he called the *Laokoon*. The distinction that Lessing made still seems to hold good. It would still seem to be sound to say that succession in time is the sphere of the poet, as space is that of the painter. And yet, paradoxically enough, it is with that movement in the arts which Lessing did something to initiate that the

confusion becomes serious. I do not want to make too much of Lessing. There is a tendency among critics to play up their predecessors; in order to increase the prestige of criticism; they ascribe to the critics of the past a power for creation which in all probability they never had. However, Lessing was in at the beginning of a movement of which we have not yet seen the end. And it is worth considering his position for a moment, if we are to understand why the clarity of his distinction between poetry and painting should have been followed by a century in which these arts are confused as they had not been before in the history of the West.

Now one of the reasons why Lessing, whose distinctions are so clear, gave rise through his influence to such confusion is that he was, as any of his contemporaries would have been, interested in the means which each art employed in what he called its imitations, only in so far as they limited the artist in his choice of subjects. It was possible for him, in the eighteenth century, consumed as he was by admiration for the Greeks and Romans, to take the means for granted. We cannot. And more, we know that for the artist the assumption of limitations is the beginning of liberation and that, in the complete work of art, while we always know what the means are, we never know what the end is. I can say how Shakespeare wrote *Full Fathom Five*. I cannot possibly tell you what he wrote. All I can say is that it is poetry. I can make out from the canvas, stroke by stroke, how Cézanne painted, but if I were to tell you that what he had painted was some apples and a tablecloth, you would know that I had said nothing.

The art of poetry is, like that of music, made manifest in a control of time. The poet has words to work with, and words are his only sounds; it is by controlling their sequence in time that he seems to control time; it is upon their sensuous disposition that he must depend to convey a sense of duration. A painter is known by his spatial power. What he does when he applies paint to canvas is to create, from what was without depth, an illusion of enduring space. Only a moment in any action can be shown within that space. What goes before and after that moment in time, which must be seen in space, can at most be imagined.

Let us go back before the great modern confusion to see what happens in that space. I am going to take the painting of a battle, which is all action, one of the several paintings which Paolo Uccello made of the Rout of San Romano, that one which is now in the National Gallery in London—or was before it was buried against air raids—and which is reproduced in Thomas Craven's *Treasury of Art Masterpieces*. The horsemen press in from the left with their lances lifted, under white banners tormented by the wind. The white charger of the turbaned swordsman in the foreground rears, snorting in the delight of battle. The lance of the fantastically helmeted Florentine is already lowered to meet the oncoming Siennese. At the right, the fighters on each side are hacking at one another, with swords, across their horses' heads. On a far hillside can be seen, beyond the fray, foot soldiers, and above them on the hill, made small by distance, two more horsemen. The moment the painter has chosen to depict is that of first contact between the Florentines and the Siennese, a moment all action, a moment composed in space of many actions, and yet, in point of time, but a moment. The motion of the warriors is motionless, the plunging of the horses arrested. What has been is, and, in what is actually seen, what is about to be is foreseen. The spatial imitation of a moment (and that is all the Rout of San Romano is) is still an imagination of time.

We cannot ignore time in a painting, and particularly we cannot ignore it in Paolo Uccello. For Uccello it was who introduced perspective into European painting, and perspective is the means which allows the painter to include in his composition the consciousness of time; for it is by means of perspective that we see the distance one from another of objects in space; and all distance, like astronomical distance, may be expressed as time. But, however great the temporal element, it has been converted in Uccello's composition into terms of space. That is why the Rout of San Romano is one of the truly great paintings of the European tradition. The opposing bodies of men and horses are not pitted against each other merely in battle; they are here opponents in space. The lifting and lowering of lances, the raising and breaking of swords, all those movements which in life could not have achieved their meaning unless in time, are here brought into spatial relations, and create their meaning by simply being. And all are under complete control. Since their aim is to kill, all these movements, were they living, would be violent. The impression they convey is one of absolute calm. Man has been added to nature. The order of art has been imposed on human disorder.

In Paolo Uccello's battle we have the actions of time set before us as a complex of space. The poet who wishes to present a battle should have no trouble in rendering the succession of actions. But a battle must take place somewhere.

And one might suppose that Shakespeare could show us how it is done. The difficulty is really to find a battle in Shakespeare's plays. It would seem that nothing would be easier, for we carry away from his plays the impression that they resound from beginning to end with the conflict of arms, so long a reverberation do words like Philippi, Agincourt and Bosworth leave in our ears. But when you go through the plays, looking for the poet's equivalent to the painter's Rout of San Romano, you discover that the poet was almost as wary of fighting as his Falstaff. He is at times forced on the very field, but when he gets there, he, as likely as not, pretends like Falstaff that he has slaughtered his bravest enemy, while actually he has merely gone through the motions of fighting. His failure is not one of valor; for he does not fall. He is simply discreet enough to know that real battles are always fought in real space and that an imaginary battle must take place in imaginary space. He can imagine space, but his danger, since he was a dramatic poet, was that the space he had imagined could be confounded, at what ridiculous risk he knew, with the real stage on which his actors stood, hacking at one another with the theatre's harmless swords.

> O! for a Muse of fire, that would ascend
> The brightest heaven of invention;

> A kingdom for a stage, princes to act
> And monarchs to behold the swelling scene.
> Then should the warlike Harry, like himself,
> Assume the port of Mars; and at his heels,
> Leash'd in like hounds, should famine, sword,
>   and fire
> Crouch for employment. But pardon, gentles all,
> The flat unraised spirits that have dar'd
> On this unworthy scaffold to bring forth
> So great an object: can this cockpit hold
> The vasty fields of France? Or may we cram
> Within this wooden O the very casques
> That did affright the air at Agincourt?

Obviously not. All that the cockpit ever held was a company of actors and all that ever did affright the air in that wooden O were the words of the poet. What then does Shakespeare do? Since he can't put the battle of Agincourt on the stage, he diverts the interest to something he can show. Agincourt was one of the most interesting battles ever fought. But while it is being prepared for, while it is being forced into conclusion, the attention is centered on the relation between the sovereign and subject. Not only was this profoundly interesting to Shakespeare—and presumably to his audience—but it was a relation which could perfectly be shown in a succession of scenes, which present now one aspect, now another, but which never, even in the sum, exceed the possibilities of the stage.

The poet, though his art is one of time, cannot get away from space. For our minds are so made that space is a necessary concept. The greatest expanse of space which Shakespeare ever attempted to put on the stage is in *Antony and Cleopatra,* where, if we but listen to the words, we shall hear the tramplings of armies over three continents. But it is a space that we hear; it comes to us in names, and if we see a plain before Actium, it is only in the mind's eye. Of the battle itself we have only the noise of a sea-fight and then a short report in which we are told how Cleopatra fled:

> She once being loof'd,
> The noble ruin of her magic, Antony,
> Claps on his sea-wing, and like a doting mallard,
> Leaving the fight in height, flies after her.
> I never saw an action of such shame;
> Experience, manhood, honour, ne'er before
> Did violate so itself.

The action at Actium becomes the act of Antony; the issue of the battle has already been decided where for the poet decision is possible: in Antony's violation of his own manhood. And that being the work of time, it is perfectly possible for the poet to handle it, his medium being words and his art being so to control them that they create by their sensuous succession an illusion of time.

What conclusions are we to draw from this? The poet of *Antony and Cleopatra* has not been limited, in staging that ancient tragedy, to a sequence of actions in time. Shakespeare's subject demanded that his actions range over the whole of the known and subjugated world, and we may suspect that what attracted Shakespeare to that particular tragedy at a time when, as a poet, he must have been conscious as never before of his powers, was its spaciousness. Certainly beyond any other of his plays *Antony and Cleo-*

patra is conceived in space and charged with the emotions which arise from its contemplation. He is limited by his means, for verses are only articulate sounds, which must so follow one another that they create time in a sensuous flow, which, unlike time itself, is under the control of the poet. He is not limited in his subject. The battle, which we should expect, had Lessing been as sound as he seemed on the limits of poetry and painting (since a battle is composed of nothing but actions successive in time), to have been a most appropriate subject for the poet, has actually been presented much more successfully by the painter as a conflict of bodies immobilized in space. What we are concerned with in Shakespeare's play is what is happening to Antony, and Actium is only a point in the long process, whose significance, since Antony is a living man, only time can let out. And Shakespeare was not at a loss when it came to making the life of Antony, which, in so far as it is history, belongs to the past, into the continuous present which is poetry. His means is verse. Shakespeare, I think it is safe to say, was not much interested in action for its own sake, but no poetry was ever written in which more happens, for in no other does so much more happen within the words in a given moment of time. A great deal also happens in the Rout of San Romano, but what counts is not the conflict or armies which prompted the painter, but the use of their lineaments and colors to control space. The exhilaration and the calm which is produced by art is due to the sense it gives of release from the conditions of living, not by its denying those concepts without which life is to us inconceivable, but by controlling them. Only through the means of art can the conviction be created that man controls time and space. It is in the means of art, then, that we must look for its end.

Lessing's contention that each art is at its best where its power is least to be disputed is doubtless still sound. Each artist is limited by his means, but in those limitations is the source of his power. Why not then, asked Picasso, make the means the end? The power of the painter is shown only in his ordering of space. Why should he not then limit himself to paintings in which the spatial relations should be apparent, in which indeed nothing else should appear? When all is said and done, the subject signifies nothing, the subject is merely a pretext; why not then discard the subject, or if the subject refuses to disappear, let its own life dissolve so that nothing is left but living form?

An Impressionist like Monet had devoted his long life to preserving in pigment the changing appearance of an hour. And Impressionism, conscious of the moment of mutability, had at last, as Lhote said, committed plastic suicide and been drowned like Ophelia among the water-lilies which are the last great work of Monet's age. Picasso for a time at least sought nothing else but form, for nothing in art is permanent but form.

If we look at such a painting of Picasso's as *The Three Musicians* we cannot but be aware that in this canvas space has been superbly created. The whole composition seems to have been made up of surfaces which, like those of plane geometry, are without a third dimension, and yet the illusion of depth is there. If we look closely we can see how

it has been produced, by color and by lines, though no one line leads us more than a little way. There is in the painting nothing that we should ordinarily call perspective; there is at most only a primitive approach to it. To find anything that is so nearly a pure creation of space, we should have to go back to Paolo Uccello. In the *Rout of San Romano* the perspective is still primitive, though for not the same reason as in the work of Picasso. Picasso greatly admires Uccello and would probably admit that his art has been influenced by the Italian. And it is almost certain that we would not now find so much satisfaction in the *Rout of San Romano,* if we had never seen a Picasso. For the art of the present can contribute to the art of the past. History is not a one-way road. But it will not do to allow this contrary traffic to confuse us. The artist of one century can never repeat the art of another.

Paolo Uccello replaced a visible world, where all was disorder, with a world of sensuous form and color, where all is disposed according to some invisible source of order. Pablo Picasso projects an invisible world, in which all is disorder, with a world of abstract form and color, where all is arranged according to some purely material order. Man is so made that he cannot conceive the world except as time and space. But there is a great difference in the world of Italy in the fifteenth century, when time seemed to have been conquered by a dream of eternity, and our own world, in which we suppose a conquest of space through material, not to say mechanical means.

That abstract painting was incomplete was soon clear, but what it lacked, what Picasso had so lately and with absolute logic eliminated, was not clear. At least it was not clear to anybody that counted, until Chirico brought back perspective. But he did not bring back the elaborate perspective that had been lost. The aim was no longer *trompe d'oeil,* but in Cocteau's perfect phrase, *trompe d'espirit.* And it was to be tricked in exactly the way we are tricked in dreams into believing that what is past is present. Picasso had also painted much from memory: his harlequins, his guitars, his three musicians all are memories of Spain when he was a young man. But Chirico's recollections have something of the quality of hallucination; his paintings are excursions into a childhood spent, for all his Italian parentage, in Greece. There is, of course, a difference between painting an object or a person remembered and attempting to paint memory itself. Picasso is sound and sane; Chirico is a man under compulsion and perhaps a little mad; Salvador Dali simulates paranoia. But the point is not there; the point is that the contemporary mind cannot pretend that it is without the consciousness of time. But when time reappeared in the early paintings of Dali it was most self-conscious. It came back marked on those marvellous limp watches in a painting called *The Persistence of Memory.* And not only has Dali restored perspective. He uses it with a skill that is nothing short of ostentation.

The presumption is that perspective was brought back into painting to satisfy an emotional need. Certainly those empty squares with their arcades in shadow, those streets deserted of all but statues of Chirico, or the immense plains of Dali, where small muscled shapes of men cast disproportionate shadows, are sources of disquietude. I cannot altogether say why they trouble us. But it is not at all necessary for the purpose that I should. I merely want to suggest that the moment a painter insists upon his third dimension of perspective, he has already introduced a fourth, which is time. And when time appears in a painting, it comes somewhat as the messenger in a Greek play comes, not by chance, but as an instrument of necessity.

I have stayed long over the painters, because it is more difficult to discern the temporal element in painting than it is to discover why the poets have never been able to get along without the concept of space.

> Here is no water but only rock
> Rock and no water and the sandy road
> The road winding above among the mountains
> Which are mountains of rock without water
> If there were water we should stop and drink
> Amongst the rock one cannot stop or
>   think. . . .

This is the Dali desert before Dali. In this passage from [T. S. Eliot's] *The Waste Land,* images of space do occur, but successively and not as they would in one of Dali's paintings: simultaneously. And the dry rocks and the sandy road winding toward the mountains where there is still no water are but symbols of a spiritual drought, due to the disappearance of faith in the truth of Christianity, which is itself a disaster of time. The early poems of Eliot are often situated with great care in space. In *Sweeney Among the Nightingales* Apeneck Sweeney, that extraordinary sensual man, is found in a Parisian dive; but for a moment we are also allowed to see him standing on the great earth itself:

> The circles of the stormy moon
> Slide westward toward the River Plate. . . .

It is an earth still dark with the tragic blood of Agamemnon:

> The nightingales are singing near
> The Convent of the Sacred Heart,
> And sang within the bloody wood
> When Agamemnon cried aloud,
> And let their liquid siftings fall
> To stain the stiff dishonoured shroud.

On Sweeney's sordid surroundings the poet suddenly intrudes with the terror of time.

The pure poet is one for whom a poetic solution is possible for any problem which his life imposes upon him. A pure painter is likewise one for whom the solution of any problem is in painting. Shakespeare is such a poet; Uccello, such a painter. Once the problem is solved, it no longer exists as a problem; it is present in the solution, but solely as a force, as a tension. The public is interested in problems; it is seldom interested in the solution; it is seldom interested in art.

The ultimate question concerning any work of art is out of how deep a life does it come. But the question that must first be asked is whether it has a life of its own. And the life of art is in its form. There have been poets among the painters. Chirico is one. There have been poets who not only leaned on the painters, but picked their pockets and stole their palettes as well. Baudelaire was one. But Chirico does not write verse, while in Baudelaire all his colors have their correspondences in sound.

When all the arts strive toward the condition of music, painting becomes abstract and poetry attempts to live on its own technical resources. This is behaving like the child who copies the answers from the back pages of his arithmetic book without having consulted the problem. But that behavior is at the moment unlikely. Today the artist is more like the child who from his schoolroom desk looks first at the window beyond which lies life with all its turmoil and play, and then at the enclosing walls and the door that is slow in opening. In the meanwhile the problem waits, unsolved, but not insoluble. But the problem is one which demands to be solved on its own terms, not those of the playground or the street.

It is the mind that imposes these conceptions of time and space. It is his art that confines the poets to the conventions of time, as it is the art of the painter that holds him to a conventional space. The mind is free; but it is the mind of a condemned man.

John Peale Bishop, "Poetry and Painting," in The Collected Essays of John Peale Bishop, *edited by Edmund Wilson, Charles Scribner's Sons, 1948, pp. 175-83.*

Joseph Frank

[*Frank is an American educator and critic. In the following excerpt, he examines evidence of spatial form in modern literature.*]

Lessing's *Laokoon,* André Gide once remarked, is one of those books it is good to reiterate or contradict every thirty years. Despite this excellent advice, neither of these attitudes toward *Laokoon* has been adopted by modern writers. Lessing's attempt to define the limits of literature and the plastic arts has become a dead issue—one to which respectful reference is occasionally made, but which no longer has any fecundating influence on esthetic thinking. One can understand how this came about in the nineteenth century, with its passion for historicism, but it is not so easy to understand at present, when so many writers on esthetic problems are occupied with questions of form. To a historian of literature or the plastic arts, Lessing's effort to define the unalterable laws of these mediums may well have seemed quixotic; but modern critics, no longer overawed by the bugbear of historical method, have begun to take up again the problems he tried to solve.

Lessing's own solution to these problems seems, at first glance, to have little relation to modern esthetic thinking. The literary school against which the arguments of *Laokoon* were directed, the school of pictorial poetry, has long since ceased to interest the modern sensibility; and many of its conclusions, particularly when based on the plastic arts, grew out of a now-antiquated archeology whose discoveries, to make matters worse, Lessing knew mainly at second-hand. But it was precisely his quixotic attempt to rise above history, to define the unalterable laws of esthetic perception rather than to attack or defend any particular school, which gives his work the perennial freshness to which André Gide alluded. Since the validity of his theories does not depend on their relationship to the literary movements of his time, or on the extent of his first-hand acquaintanceship with the artworks of antiquity, it is always possible to consider them apart from these circumstances and use them in the analysis of later developments.

In *Laokoon,* Lessing fuses two distinct currents of thought, both of great importance in the cultural history of his time. The archeological researches of Winckelmann, his contemporary, had stimulated a passionate interest in Greek culture among the Germans. Lessing went back to Homer, Aristotle and the Greek tragedians, using his first-hand knowledge to attack the distorted critical theories, supposedly based on classical authority, which had filtered into France through Italian commentators and then taken hold in Germany. At the same time, as Wilhelm Dilthey emphasizes in his famous essay on Lessing [*Das Erlebnis und Die Dichtung*], Locke and the empirical school of English philosophy had given a new impulse to esthetic speculation. Locke tried to solve the problem of knowledge by breaking down complex ideas into simple elements of sensation, and then examining the operations of the mind to see how these sensations were combined to form ideas. This method was soon taken over by estheticians: the focus of interest shifted from external prescriptions for beauty to an analysis of esthetic perception. Writers like Shaftesbury, Hogarth, Hutcheson and Burke, to mention only a few, concerned themselves with the precise character and combination of impressions that gave esthetic pleasure to the sensibility. Lessing's friend and critical ally, Mendelssohn, popularized this method of dealing with esthetic problems in Germany, and Lessing himself was a close student of these works and many others in the same general spirit. *Laokoon,* as a result, stands at the confluence of these intellectual currents: Lessing analyzes the laws of esthetic perception, shows how they prescribe necessary limitations to literature and the plastic arts, and then demonstrates how Greek writers and painters, especially Homer, created masterpieces by obeying these laws.

His argument starts from the simple observation that literature and the plastic arts, working through different sensuous mediums, must therefore differ in the fundamental laws governing their creation. "If it is true," Lessing wrote, "that painting and poetry in their imitations make use of entirely different means or symbols—the first, namely, of form and color in space, the second of articulated sounds in time—if these symbols indisputably require a suitable relation to the thing symbolized, then it is clear that symbols arranged in juxtaposition can only express subjects of which the wholes or parts exist in juxtaposition; while consecutive symbols can only express subjects of which the wholes or parts are themselves consecutive." Lessing did not originate this formulation, which has a long and complicated history; but he is the first to use it systematically, as an instrument of critical analysis. Form in the plastic arts, according to Lessing, is necessarily spatial, because the visible aspect of objects can best be presented juxtaposed in an instant of time. Literature, on the

other hand, makes use of language, composed of a succession of words proceeding through time; and it follows that literary form, to harmonize with the essential quality of its medium, must be based primarily on some form of narrative sequence. Lessing used this argument to attack two artistic genres highly popular in his day: pictorial poetry and allegorical painting. The pictorial poet tried to paint with words, the allegorical painter to tell a story in visible images: both were doomed to fail because their aims were in contradiction with the fundamental properties of their mediums. No matter how accurate and vivid a verbal description might be, Lessing argued, it could not give the unified impression of a visible object; no matter how skillfully figures might be chosen and arranged, a painting or piece of sculpture could not successfully set forth the various stages of an action.

As Lessing develops his argument, he attempts to prove that the Greeks, with an unfailing sense of esthetic propriety, respected the limits imposed on different art mediums by the conditions of human perception. But to understand the importance of Lessing's distinction it is not necessary to follow the ramifications of his argument, nor even to agree with his specific judgments on individual writers. Various critics have quarreled with one or another of these judgments, thinking that, in doing so, they were in some way undermining Lessing's position; but such a belief was based on a misunderstanding of *Laokoon*'s importance in the history of esthetic theory. It is quite possible to use Lessing's insights solely as instruments of analysis, without proceeding to judge the value of individual works by how closely they adhered to the norms he laid down. And unless this is done, as a matter of fact, the real meaning of *Laokoon* cannot be understood. For what Lessing offered was not a new set of opinions, but a new conception of esthetic form.

The conception of esthetic form inherited by the eighteenth century from the Renaissance was a purely external one. Classical literature—or what was known of it—was presumed to have reached perfection, and later writers could do little better than imitate its example. A horde of commentators and critics had deduced certain rules from the classical masterpieces—rules like the Aristotelian unities, of which Aristotle had never heard—and modern writers were warned to obey these rules if they wished to appeal to a cultivated public. Gradually, these rules came to form an external mold into which the material of a literary work had to be poured: the form of a work was nothing but the technical arrangement dictated by the rules. Such a superficial and mechanical notion of esthetic form, however, led to serious perversions of taste—Shakespeare was considered a barbarian even by so sophisticated a writer as Voltaire, and Pope found it necessary in translating Homer to do a good deal of editing. Lessing's point of view, breaking sharply with this external conception of form, marks out the road for esthetic speculation to follow in the future.

For Lessing, as we have seen, esthetic form is not an external arrangement provided by a set of traditional rules: it is the relation between the sensuous nature of the art medium and the conditions of human perception. Just as the natural man of the eighteenth century was not to be bound by traditional political forms, but was to create them in accordance with his own nature, so art was to create its own forms out of itself, rather than accepting them ready-made from the practice of the past. Criticism was not to prescribe rules for art, but was to explore the necessary laws by which art governs itself. No longer was esthetic form confused with mere externals of technique—it was not a straitjacket into which the artist, willy-nilly, had to force his creative ideas, but issued spontaneously from the organization of the art work as it presented itself to perception. Time and space were the two extremes defining the limits of literature and the plastic arts in their relation to sensuous perception; and it is possible, following Lessing's example, to trace the evolution of art forms by their oscillations between these two poles.

The purpose of the present essay is to apply Lessing's method to modern literature—to trace the evolution of form in modern poetry and, more particularly, in the novel. The two sections will try to show that modern literature, exemplified by such writers as T. S. Eliot, Ezra Pound, Marcel Proust and James Joyce, is moving in the direction of spatial form. This means that the reader is intended to apprehend their work spatially, in a moment of time, rather than as a sequence. . . .

. . . . .

Modern Anglo-American poetry received its initial impetus from the Imagist movement of the years directly preceding and following the first World War. Imagism was important not for any actual poetry written by Imagist poets—no one knew quite what an Imagist poet was—but rather because it opened the way for later developments by its clean break with sentimental Victorian verbiage. The critical writings of Ezra Pound, the leading theoretician of Imagism, are an astonishing farrago of keen esthetic perceptions thrown in among a series of boyishly naughty remarks, whose chief purpose, it would seem, is to *é pater le bourgeois*—to startle the stuffed shirts. But Pound's definition of the image, perhaps the keenest of his perceptions, is of fundamental importance for any discussion of modern literary form. "An image" Pound wrote, "is that which presents an intellectual and emotional complex in an instant of time." The implications of his definition should be noted—an image is defined not as a pictorial reproduction, but as unification of disparate ideas and emotions into a complex presented spatially in an instant of time. Such a complex is not to proceed discursively, according to the laws of language, but is rather to strike the reader's sensibility with an instantaneous impact. Pound stresses this aspect by adding, in a later passage, that only the instantaneous presentation of such complexes gives "that sense of sudden liberation; that sense of freedom from time limits and space limits; that sense of sudden growth, which we experience in the presence of the greatest works of art."

At the very outset, therefore, modern poetry championed a poetic method in direct contradiction to the way in which Lessing had said language must be perceived. By comparing Pound's definition of the image with Eliot's well-known description of the psychology of the poetic process, we can see clearly how profoundly this conception has influenced our modern idea of the nature of poetry. For Eliot, the distinctive quality of a poetic sensibility is its capacity to form new wholes, to fuse seemingly disparate experiences into an organic unity. The ordinary man, Eliot writes, "falls in love, or reads Spinoza, and these two experiences have nothing to do with each other, or with the noise of the typewriter or the smell of cooking; in the mind of the poet these experiences are always forming new wholes." While Pound had attempted to define the image in terms of its esthetic attributes, Eliot, in this passage, is describing its psychological origin; but the result in a poem was likely to be the same.

Such a view of the nature of poetry immediately gave rise to numerous problems. How was more than one image to be included in a poem? If the chief value of an image was its capacity to present an intellectual and emotional complex simultaneously, linking up images in a sequence would clearly destroy most of their efficacy. Or was the poem itself one vast image, whose individual components were to be apprehended as a unity? But then it would be necessary to undermine the inherent consecutiveness of language, frustrating the reader's normal expectation of a sequence and forcing him to perceive the elements of the poem juxtaposed in space rather than unrolling in time.

This is precisely what Eliot and Pound attempted in their major works. Both poets, in their earlier work, still retained some elements of conventional structure. Their poems were looked upon as daring and revolutionary chiefly because of technical matters, like the loosening of metrical pattern and the handling of subjects ordinarily considered non-poetic. Perhaps this is less true of Eliot than of Pound, especially the Eliot of the more complex early works like "Prufrock," "Gerontion" and "Portrait of a Lady"; but even here, although the sections of the poem are not governed by syntactical logic, the skeleton of an implied narrative structure is always present. The reader of "Prufrock" is swept up in a narrative movement from the very first lines:

> Let us go then, you and I,
> When the evening . . .

And the reader, accompanying Prufrock, finally arrives at their mutual destination:

> In the room the women come and go
> Talking of Michelangelo.

At this point the poem becomes a series of more or less isolated fragments, each stating some aspect of Prufrock's emotional dilemma; but the fragments are now localized and focused on a specific set of circumstances: the reader can organize them by referring to the implied situation. The same method is employed in "Portrait of a Lady," while in "Gerontion" the reader is specifically told that he has been reading the "thoughts of a dry brain in a dry season"—the stream-of-consciousness of "an old man in a dry month, being read to by a boy, waiting for the rain." In both cases there is a perceptible framework, around which the seemingly disconnected passages of the poem can be organized. This was one reason why Pound's "Mauberly" and Eliot's early work were first regarded, not as forerunners of a new poetic form, but as latter-day *vers de société*—witty, disillusioned, with a somewhat brittle charm, but lacking that quality of "high seriousness" which Matthew Arnold had chosen as the touchstone of poetic excellence. These poems were considered unusual mainly because *vers de société* had long fallen out of fashion: there was little difficulty in accepting them as an entertaining departure from the grand style of the nineteenth century. In the "Cantos" and "The Waste Land," however, it should have been clear that a radical transformation was taking place in esthetic structure; but this transformation has been touched on only peripherally by modern critics. R. P. Blackmur comes closest to the central problem while analyzing what he calls Pound's "anecdotal" method. The special form of the "Cantos," Blackmur explains, "is that of the anecdote begun in one place, taken up in one or more other places, and finished, if at all, in still another. This deliberate disconnectedness, this art of a thing continually alluding to itself, continually breaking off short, is the method by which the "Cantos" tie themselves together. So soon as the reader's mind is concerted with the material of the poem, Mr. Pound deliberately disconcerts it, either by introducing fresh and disjunct material or by reverting to old and, apparently, equally disjunct material." Blackmur's remarks apply equally well to "The Waste Land," where syntactical sequence is given up for a structure depending on the perception of relationships between disconnected word-groups. To be properly understood, these word-groups must be juxtaposed with one another and perceived simultaneously; only when this is done can they be adequately understood; for while they follow one another in time, their meaning does not depend on this temporal relationship. The one difficulty of these poems, which no amount of textual exegesis can wholly overcome, is the internal conflict between the time-logic of language and the space-logic implicit in the modern conception of the nature of poetry.

Esthetic form in modern poetry, then, is based on a space-logic that demands a complete re-orientation in the reader's attitude towards language. Since the primary reference of any word-group is to something inside the poem itself, language in modern poetry is really reflexive: the meaning-relationship is completed only by the simultaneous perception in space of word-groups which, when read consecutively in time, have no comprehensible relation to each other. Instead of the instinctive and immediate reference of words and word-groups to the objects or events they symbolize, and the construction of meaning from the sequence of these references, modern poetry asks its readers to suspend the process of individual reference temporarily until the entire pattern of internal references can be apprehended as a unity. This explanation is, of course, the extreme statement of an ideal condition, rather than an actually existing state of affairs; but the conception of poetic form that runs through Mallarmé to Pound and Eliot, and which has left its traces on a whole generation of modern poets, can be formulated only in terms of the principle of reflexive reference. And this principle is the link connecting the esthetic development of modern poetry with similar experiments in the modern novel.

For a study of esthetic form in the modern novel, Flau-

bert's famous county fair scene in *Madame Bovary* is a convenient point of departure. This scene has been justly praised for its mordant caricature of bourgeois pomposity, its portrayal—unusually sympathetic for Flaubert—of the bewildered old servant, and its burlesque of the pseudo-romantic rhetoric by which Rodolphe woos the sentimental Emma. At present, it is enough to notice the method by which Flaubert handles the scene—a method we might as well call cinematographic, since this analogy comes immediately to mind. As Flaubert sets the scene, there is action going on simultaneously at three levels, and the physical position of each level is a fair index to its spiritual significance. On the lowest plane, there is the surging, jostling mob in the street, mingling with the livestock brought to the exhibition; raised slightly above the street by a platform are the speech-making officials, bombastically reeling off platitudes to the attentive multitudes; and on the highest level of all, from a window overlooking the spectacle, Rodolphe and Emma are watching the proceedings and carrying on their amorous conversation, in phrases as stilted as those regaling the crowds. Albert Thibaudet has compared this scene to the medieval mystery play, in which various related actions occur simultaneously on different stage levels; but this acute comparison refers to Flaubert's intention rather than to his method. "Everything should sound simultaneously," Flaubert later wrote, in commenting on this scene; "one should hear the bellowing of the cattle, the whisperings of the lovers and the rhetoric of the officials all at the same time."

But since language proceeds in time, it is impossible to approach this simultaneity of perception except by breaking up temporal sequence. And this is exactly what Flaubert does: he dissolves sequence by cutting back and forth between the various levels of action in a slowly-rising crescendo until—at the climax of the scene—Rodolphe's Chateaubriandesque phrases are read at almost the same moment as the names of prize winners for raising the best pigs. Flaubert takes care to underline this satiric similarity by description, as well as by juxtaposition, as if he were afraid the reflexive relations of the two actions would not be grasped: "From magnetism, by slow degrees, Rodolphe had arrived at affinities, and while M. le Président was citing Cincinnatus at his plow, Diocletian planting his cabbages and the emperors of China ushering in the new year with sowing-festivals, the young man was explaining to the young woman that these irresistible attractions sprang from some anterior existence."

This scene illustrates, on a small scale, what we mean by the spatialization of form in a novel. For the duration of the scene, at least, the time-flow of the narrative is halted: attention is fixed on the interplay of relationships within the limited time-area. These relationships are juxtaposed independently of the progress of the narrative; and the full significance of the scene is given only by the reflexive relations among the units of meaning. In Flaubert's scene, however, the unit of meaning is not, as in modern poetry, a word-group or a fragment of an anecdote, but the totality of each level of action taken as an integer: the unit is so large that the scene can be read with an illusion of complete understanding, yet with a total unawareness of the "dialectic of platitude" (Thibaudet) interweaving all levels, and finally linking them together with devastating irony. In other words, the struggle towards spatial form in Pound and Eliot resulted in the disappearance of coherent sequence after a few lines; but the novel, with its larger unit of meaning, can preserve coherent sequence within the unit of meaning and break up only the time-flow of narrative. (Because of this difference, readers of modern poetry are practically forced to read reflexively to get any literal sense, while readers of a novel like [Djuna Bournes's] *Nightwood,* for example, are led to expect narrative sequence by the deceptive normality of language sequence within the unit of meaning). But this does not affect the parallel between esthetic form in modern poetry and the form of Flaubert's scene: both can be properly understood only when their units of meaning are apprehended reflexively, in an instant of time.

Flaubert's scene, although interesting in itself, is of minor importance to his novel as a whole, and is skillfully blended back into the main narrative structure after fulfilling its satiric function. But Flaubert's method was taken over by James Joyce, and applied on a gigantic scale in the composition of *Ulysses.* Joyce composed his novel of an infinite number of references and cross-references which relate to one another independently of the time-sequence of the narrative; and, before the book fits together into any meaningful pattern, these references must be connected by the reader and viewed as a whole. Ultimately, if we are to believe Stuart Gilbert, these systems of reference form a complete picture of practically everything under the sun, from the stages of man's life and the organs of the human body to the colors of the spectrum; but these structures are far more important for Joyce, as Harry Levin has remarked, than they could ever possibly be for the reader. Students of Joyce, fascinated by his erudition, have usually applied themselves to exegesis. Unfortunately, such considerations have little to do with the perceptual form of Joyce's novel.

Joyce's most obvious intention in *Ulysses* is to give the reader a picture of Dublin seen as a whole—to re-create the sights and sounds, the people and places, of a typical Dublin day, much as Flaubert had re-created his provincial county fair. And, like Flaubert, Joyce wanted his depiction to have the same unified impact, the same sense of simultaneous activity occurring in different places. Joyce, as a matter of fact, frequently makes use of the same method as Flaubert—cutting back and forth between different actions occurring at the same time—and usually does so to obtain the same ironic effect. But Joyce had the problem of creating this impression of simultaneity for the life of a whole teeming city, and of maintaining it—or rather of strengthening it—through hundreds of pages that must be read as a sequence. To meet this problem, Joyce was forced to go far beyond what Flaubert had done; while Flaubert had maintained a clear-cut narrative line, except in the county-fair scene, Joyce breaks up his narrative and transforms the very structure of his novel into an instrument of his esthetic intention.

Joyce conceived *Ulysses* as a modern epic; and in the epic, as Stephen Dedalus tells us in *The Portrait of the Artist as a Young Man,* "the personality of the artist, at first sight a cry or a cadence and then a fluid and lambent narrative, finally refines itself out of existence, impersonalizes itself, so to speak . . . the artist, like the God of creation, remains within or beyond or above his handiwork, invisible, refined out of existence, indifferent, paring his fingernails." The epic is thus synonymous for Joyce with the complete self-effacement of the author; and, with his usual uncompromising rigor, Joyce carries this implication further than anyone had dared before. He assumes—what is obviously not true—that his readers are Dubliners, intimately acquainted with Dublin life and the personal history of his characters. This allows him to refrain from giving any direct information about his characters: such information would immediately have betrayed the presence of an omniscient author. What Joyce does, instead, is to present the elements of his narrative—the relations between Stephen and his family, between Bloom and his wife, between Stephen and Bloom and the Dedalus family—in fragments, as they are thrown out unexplained in the course of casual conversation, or as they lie embedded in the various strata of symbolic reference; and the same is true of all the allusions to Dublin life, history, and the external events of the twenty-four hours during which the novel takes place. In other words, all the factual background—so conveniently summarized for the reader in an ordinary novel—must be reconstructed from fragments, sometimes hundreds of pages apart, scattered through the book. As a result, the reader is forced to read *Ulysses* in exactly the same manner as he reads modern poetry—continually fitting fragments together and keeping allusions in mind until, by reflexive reference, he can link them to their complements.

Joyce intended, in this way, to build up in the reader's mind a sense of Dublin as a totality, including all the relations of the characters to one another and all the events which enter their consciousness. As the reader progresses through the novel, connecting allusions and references spatially, gradually becoming aware of the pattern of relationships, this sense was to be imperceptibly acquired; and, at the conclusion of the novel, it might almost be said that Joyce literally wanted the reader to become a Dubliner. For this is what Joyce demands: that the reader have at hand the same instinctive knowledge of Dublin life, the same sense of Dublin as a huge, surrounding organism, which the Dubliner possesses as a birthright. It is such knowledge which, at any one moment of time, gives him a knowledge of Dublin's past and present as a whole; and it is only such knowledge which might enable the reader, like the characters, to place all the references in their proper context. This, it should be realized, is practically the equivalent of saying that Joyce cannot be read—he can only be re-read. A knowledge of the whole is essential to an understanding of any part; but, unless one is a Dubliner, such knowledge can be obtained only after the book has been read, when all the references are fitted into their proper place and grasped as a unity. Although the burdens placed on the reader by this method of composition may seem insuperable, the fact remains that Joyce, in his unbelievably laborious fragmentation of narrative structure, proceeded on the assumption that a unified spatial apprehension of his work would ultimately be possible.

In a far more subtle manner than with Joyce and Flaubert, the same principle of composition is at work in Marcel Proust. Since Proust himself tells us that, before all else, his novel will have imprinted on it "a form which usually remains invisible, the form of Time," it may seem strange to speak of Proust in connection with spatial form. He has, almost invariably, been considered the novelist of time *par excellence*: the literary interpreter of that Bergsonian "real time" intuited by the sensibility, as distinguished from the abstract, chronological time of the conceptual intelligence. To stop at this point, however, is to miss what Proust himself considered the deepest significance of his work. Obsessed with the ineluctability of time, Proust was suddenly visited by certain quasi-mystical experiences—described in detail in the last volume of his work, "Le temps retrouvé"—which, by providing him with a spiritual technique for transcending time, enabled him to escape what he considered to be time's domination. By writing a novel, by translating the transcendent, extra-temporal quality of these experiences to the level of esthetic form, Proust hoped to reveal their nature to the world—for they seemed to him a clue to the ultimate secrets of reality. And not only should the world learn about these experiences indirectly, by reading a descriptive account of them, but, through his novel, it would feel their impact on the sensibility as Proust himself had felt it.

To define the method by which this is accomplished, one must first understand clearly the precise nature of the Proustian revelation. Each such experience, Proust tells us, is marked by a feeling that "the permanent essence of things, usually concealed, is set free and our true self, which had long seemed dead but was not dead in other ways, awakes, takes on fresh life as it receives the celestial nourishment brought to it." This celestial nourishment consists of some sound, or odor, or other sensory stimulus, "sensed anew, simultaneously in the present and the past." But why should these moments seem so overwhelmingly valuable that Proust calls them celestial? Because, Proust observes, his imagination could only operate on the past; and the material presented to his imagination, therefore, lacked any sensuous immediacy. But, at certain moments, the physical sensations of the past came flooding back to fuse with the present; and, in these moments, Proust believed that he grasped a reality "real without being of the present moment, ideal but not abstract." Only in these moments did he attain his most cherished ambition—"to seize, isolate, immobilize for the duration of a lightning flash" what otherwise he could not apprehend, "namely: a fragment of time in its pure state." For a person experiencing this moment, Proust adds, the word "death" no longer has meaning. "Situated outside the scope of time, what could he fear from the future?"

The significance of this experience, though obscurely hinted at throughout the book, is made explicit only in the concluding pages which describe the final appearance of the narrator at the reception of the Princesse de Guermantes. The narrator decides to dedicate the remainder of his life to re-creating these experiences in a work of art; and this work will differ essentially from all others because, at its foundation, will be a vision of reality that has been refracted through an extra-temporal perspective.

Viewing Proust as the last and most debilitated of a long line of neurasthenic esthetes, many critics have found in this decision to create a work of art merely the final step in his flight from the burdens of reality. Edmund Wilson, ordinarily so discerning, links up this view with Proust's ambition to conquer time, assuming that Proust hoped to oppose time by establishing something—a work of art—impervious to its flux; but this somewhat ingenuous interpretation scarcely does justice to Proust's own conviction, expressed with special intensity in the last volume of his work, that he was fulfilling a prophetic mission. It was not the work of art *qua* work of art that Proust cared about—his contempt for the horde of faddish scribblers was unbounded—but a work of art which should stand as a monument to his personal conquest of time. This his own work could do not simply because it was a work of art, but because it was at once the vehicle through which he conveyed his vision and the concrete substance of that vision shaped by a method which compels the reader to re-experience its exact effect.

The prototype of this method, like the analysis of the revelatory moment, occurs during the reception at the Princesse de Guermantes. After spending years in a sanatorium, losing touch almost completely with the fashionable world of the earlier volumes, the narrator comes out of seclusion to attend the reception. He finds himself bewildered by the changes in social position, and the even more striking changes in character and personality among his former friends. According to some socially-minded critics, Proust intended to paint here the invasion of French aristocratic society by the upper bourgeoisie, and the gradual breakdown of all social and moral standards caused by the first World War. No doubt this process is incidentally described at some length; but, as the narrator takes great pains to tell us, it is far from being the most important meaning of the scene. What strikes the narrator, almost with the force of a blow, is this: in trying to recognize old friends under the masks which, as he feels, the years have welded to them, he is jolted for the first time into a consciousness of the passage of time. When a young man addresses the narrator respectfully, instead of familiarly as if he were an elderly gentleman, the narrator realizes suddenly that he has become an elderly gentleman; but for him the passage of time had gone unperceived up until that moment. To become conscious of time, the narrator begins to understand, it had first been necessary to remove himself from his accustomed environment—or, what amounts to the same thing, from the stream of time acting on that environment—and then to plunge back into the stream after a lapse of years. In so doing, the narrator found himself presented with two images—the world as he had formerly known it, and the world, transformed by time, that he now saw before him; and when these two images are juxtaposed, the narrator discovers, the passage of time is suddenly experienced through its visible effects. Habit, that universal soporific, ordinarily conceals the passage of time from those who have gone their accustomed ways: at any one moment of time the changes are so minute as to be imperceptible. "Other people," Proust writes, "never cease to change places in relation to ourselves. In the imperceptible, but eternal march of the world, we regard them as motionless in a moment of vision, too short for us to perceive the motion that is sweeping them on. But we have only to select in our memory two pictures taken of them at different moments, close enough together however for them not to have altered in themselves—perceptibly, that is to say—and the difference between the two pictures is a measure of the displacement that they have undergone in relation to us." By comparing these two images in a moment of time, the passage of time can be experienced concretely, in the impact of its visible effects on the sensibility, rather than as a mere gap counted off in numbers. And this discovery provides the narrator with a method which, in T. S. Eliot's phrase, is an "objective correlative" to the visionary apprehension of the fragment of "pure time" intuited in the revelatory moment.

When the narrator discovers this method of communicating his experience of the revelatory moment, he decides, as we have already said, to incorporate it in a novel. But the novel the narrator decides to write has just been finished by the reader; and its form is controlled by the method that the narrator has outlined in its concluding pages. The reader, in other words, is substituted for the narrator, and is placed by the author throughout the book in the same position as the narrator occupies before his own experience at the reception of the Princesse de Guermantes. This is done by the discontinuous presentation of character—a simple device which, nevertheless, is the clue to the form of Proust's vast structure. Every reader soon notices that Proust does not follow any of his characters through the whole course of his novel: they appear and re-appear, in various stages of their lives, but hundreds of pages sometimes go by between the time they are last seen and the time they re-appear; and when they do turn up again, the passage of time has invariably changed them in some decisive way. Instead of being submerged in the stream of time—which, for Proust, would be the equivalent of presenting a character progressively, in a continuous line of development—the reader is confronted with various snapshots of the characters "motionless in a moment of vision," taken at different stages in their lives; and the reader, in juxtaposing these images, experiences the effects of the passage of time exactly as the narrator had done. As he had promised, therefore, Proust does stamp his novel indelibly with the form of time; but we are now in a position to understand exactly what he meant by the promise.

To experience the passage of time, Proust learned, it was necessary to rise above it, and to grasp both past and present simultaneously in a moment of what he called "pure time." But "pure time," obviously, is not time at all—it is perception in a moment of time, that is to say, space. And, by the discontinuous presentation of character, Proust forces the reader to juxtapose disparate images of his characters spatially, in a moment of time, so that the experience of time's passage will be fully communicated to their sensibility. There is a striking analogy here between Proust's method and that of his beloved Impressionist painters; but this analogy goes far deeper than the usual comments about the "impressionism" of Proust's style. The Impressionist painters juxtaposed pure tones on the canvas, instead of mixing them on the palette, in order to leave the blending of colors to the eye of the spectator.

Similarly, Proust gives us what might be called pure views of his characters—views of them "motionless in a moment of vision" in various phases of their lives—and allows the sensibility of the reader to fuse these views into a unity. Each view must be aprehended by the reader as a unit; and Proust's purpose is only achieved when these units of meaning are referred to each other reflexively in a moment of time. As with Joyce and the modern poets, we see that spatial form is also the structural scaffolding of Proust's labyrinthine masterpiece.

Joseph Frank, "Spatial Form in Modern Literature," in The Sewanee Review, *Vol. LIII, No. 2, April-June, 1945, pp. 221-40.*

Mario Praz

[*An Italian educator, critic, and translator, Praz is best known for his writings on the Baroque and Romantic periods, and for his pioneering study* The Romantic Agony, *which explores the tradition of sadism in literature, art, and music. In the following essay, Praz analyzes spatial relationships between modern art and literature.*]

The general panorama offered by the first half of our century is one of such a variety of experiments that it would be easy to lose oneself among them. However, parallel lines of development can be observed in the various arts. There has been an anti-art with the Dada movement, an anti-architecture with Le Corbusier, an anti-novel in France with Robbe-Grillet and the *nouvelle vague*. The same problems face writers, sculptors, and architects. To give expression to the sense of nothingness, of the void, has been attempted—to quote only a few names—by Rothko in painting, Antonioni in the film, Kafka in the novel, Beckett on the stage. Cézanne told Emile Bernard to "see in nature the cylinder, the sphere, the cone." Picasso has represented a figure both *en face* and *en profil* in the same view; architects have spoken of a fourth dimension. Giedion (on whom Picasso's paintings doubtless had an influence) sees the history of architecture as a progression from the bidimensional to the three-dimensional and so on, without knowing, of course, that a parody of pluridimensionality had already been written in the Victorian era by Edwin A. Abbott, in *Flatland*.

Interpenetration of planes in painting, sculpture, and architecture; interpenetration of words and meanings in the language of Joyce; an attempt, in Lawrence Durrell's *The Alexandria Quartet*, at a "stereoscopic narrative" obtained by means of "passing a common axis through four stories" [*Clea*] ("to intercalate realities . . . is the only way to be faithful to Time, for at every moment in Time the possibilities are endless in their multiplicity" [*Balthasar*]). In the films of Alain Robbe-Grillet (*Last Year at Marienbad* and *L'Immortelle*), as Bruce Morrissette has remarked [in "The Evolution of Narrative Viewpoint in Robbe-Grillet," in *Novel: A Forum in Fiction* I, 1 (Fall 1967)], "two or more characters appear twice in different parts of a panoramic camera movement, creating a strange effect of continuity between two moments of time and two spatial locations which on a realistic level could not be proximate . . . a willingness to accept, in fiction, some of the same formal liberties and absence of conventional justifications that prevail in modern pictorial style (from abstract to op) and musical compositional methods (from serial to chance)." Quotations which seem to float like alien bodies in the sentences of Ezra Pound's *Cantos* and Eliot's *The Waste Land;* collage in the paintings of Braque, Max Ernst, and others. "The noises of waves, revolvers, typewriters, sirens, or airplanes," explained Erik Satie, the musician contemporary with the Cubists, in commenting on his ballet *Parade,* subtitled *Ballet Réaliste,* "are in music of the same character as the bits of newspapers, painted wood grain, and other everyday objects that the Cubists frequently employ to localize objects and masses in Nature" [quoted by Harold Rosenberg in *The Ancient Object; Art Today and Its Audience*]. Picasso's career could be put side by side with Joyce's, in the manner of Plutarch's *Parallel Lives of Greeks and Romans.* The painter also started with spirited imitations of traditional styles: he could be as civilized as Ingres, as primitive as an African sculptor, as solemn as an archaic Greek, as subtle in color effects as Goya. In both painter and writer we find the general contraction of the historical sense and that intoxication with the contemporaneity of all historical styles which can be compared to the experience of drowning, a giddy simultaneous rehearsal of one's whole life. Picasso's *Les Demoiselles d'Avignon* attempted, long before Joyce, the elaboration of a new language through the fusion of unreconcilable manners. The left-hand figure in that picture speaks the language of Gauguin, the central section is conceived according to the flattened planes of Iberian sculpture, the right-hand portion betrays the influence of African masks with their saw teeth and sharp spines; whereas Cézanne is responsible for the hatching filling the space between the figures. But this contamination of styles is by no means confined to Joyce and Picasso; Picasso is not alone among modern painters in his ability to be at the same time Raphael and Cimabue. Incidentally, a trait common to Joyce, Picasso, and another representative genius of our time, Stravinsky, is that while they have derived from many sources, nearly everybody since has derived from them. Ezra Pound could be both Chinese and Provençal, and T. S. Eliot could write sententious Elizabethan English as well as musical comedy songs, as he demonstrated in "Sweeney Agonistes." *The Waste Land* is an even more composite product than *Les Demoiselles d'Avignon.* Viewed as pastiches, all these works of art take us back to the atmosphere of the circus and to the performances of the tightrope walker: there is a deliberate masquerading and prancing, with the constant danger of losing one's balance and falling from the flying trapeze into the void, or merely into the sawdust of the arena. There lurks behind all these experiments the suspicion that the artist is just "shoring fragments against his ruins." There is no proper succession governing the episodes of *Ulysses* but rather simultaneity and juxtaposition, just as in cubist paintings the same form reappears, mixing with others, the same letter of the alphabet or the same profile popping up here and there in a perpetual rotation whose final result is immobility. All this helps to give the structure of the book the appearance of the spatial and temporal interpenetration aimed at by futurists and cubists.

However, the juxtaposition of different languages was for Joyce only a first step toward the creation of an ultrasonic language, a language that falls on deaf ears as far as common mortals are concerned. In *Finnegans Wake* Joyce, having completely freed himself from the tyranny of mimesis, has made a Dublin publican, Earwicker, the recipient of the whole past history of mankind, and a universal linguist in his dream language as well, which on an incomparably larger scale repeats the experiment of Lewis Carroll's "Jabberwocky" "C'est"—remarks J.-J. Mayoux in "L'hérésie de James Joyce" [in *English Miscellany* (1951)]—"une langue de *lapsus,* très exactement, c'est à dire de *glissements.*" The demon of association, conjured up by Lewis Carroll for fun, has received from Joyce the chrism of psychoanalytical science; the artist has dived into the night of dream psychology, revealing a phantasmal world that might have been one of the discarded alternatives at the beginning of things. But this is exactly what Picasso has done with forms in his escape from the accepted patterns of beauty. Behind the world of forms as it exists, just as behind the world of words with which we are familiar, there is an infinity of unrealized possibilities that God or nature, or whatever you like to call the supreme vital principle, has rejected. By a perversion of the process described by Michelangelo in his famous sonnet "Non ha l'ottimo artista alcun concetto," Joyce and Picasso have searched in the marble block for all the unlikely and illegitimate forms hidden within its entrails; theirs has been an anti-creation in the same sense that the gospel preached by the Antichrist was an inverted gospel. No wonder Mayoux says of Joyce's work: "Le néant, l'esprit du néant pénètre tout," and calls him "fils spirituel du Mallarmé du *Coup des dés;* chercheur d'absolu, enchanteur maléfique, puissant et stérile, engendreur de fantômes et d'incubes."

To take the relatively simple instance from *Finnegans Wake* that Edmund Wilson examines first: "Amengst menlike trees walking or trees like angels weeping nobirdy aviar soar anywing to eagle it!"; the last seven words represent the sentence "Nobody ever saw anything to equal it" telescoped into an ornithological simile. Picasso, repeating a process which can be traced to Giuseppe Arcimboldi, represents a lady's hat like a fish, giving an ichthyological turn to the hat, just as Joyce reads an ornithological content into a plain sentence. Salvador Dali sees a lady's hat like a shoe, and imagines Mae West's face utilized as a room, with her lips as a sofa and nose as a fireplace; he telescopes Velázquez' infanta into the summit of a Hindu temple, whose shape the infanta's farthingale has recalled. Picasso sees a stork with forks for legs, a shovel for wings, a nail for beak, and the blade-shaped head of a screw for a comb; out of an old weathered bicycle seat and a rusty handle bar he makes an impressive bull's head; a toy motor car becomes the muzzle of a monkey. No doubt Freud's influence has to be taken into account in these developments of suggestions which we find first in Rimbaud and Lautréamont and later in Raymond Roussel, the author of *Impressions d'Afrique* and *Locus Solus.*

In spite of its shortcomings, the chief of which is its monotony, *Finnegans Wake,* according to Wilson, has succeeded in one respect: "Joyce has caught the psychology of sleep as no one else has ever caught it, laying hold on states of mind which it is difficult for the waking intellect to re-create, and distinguishing with marvelous delicacy between the different levels of dormant consciousness."

No such delicacy can be found in the fashionable offshoots of Dali's surrealism, which also purports to be based on dream psychology. In *The Secret Life of Salvador Dali* we read of a masquerade at the Coq Rouge which had as its theme "A surrealist dream": at a certain moment a huge slaughtered ox was brought into the ballroom, its belly kept open with crutches and stuffed with a dozen gramophones, and Gala, Dali's wife, appeared in the role of *cadavre exquis,* carrying on her head a doll representing a real baby with its entrails eaten by ants and its brain clawed by a phosphorescent lobster. Most of Dali's compositions are actually such *cadavres exquis,* and what else but a *cadavre exquis* is Joyce's ornithological sentence we read a moment ago, and a thousand others? And Gertrude Stein's famous sentence "Toasted susie is my icecream" is similarly a *cadavre exquis* of the first magnitude.

In his *The Dehumanization of Art* Ortega y Gasset observes a change of perspective in most modern artists:

> From the standpoint of ordinary human life things appear in a natural order, a definite hierarchy. Some seem very important, some less so, and some altogether negligible. To satisfy the desire for dehumanization one need not alter the inherent nature of things. It is enough to upset the value pattern and to produce an art in which the small events of life appear in the foreground with monumental dimensions. Here we have the connecting link between two seemingly very different manners of modern art, the surrealism of metaphors and what may be called infrarealism. Both satisfy the urge to escape and elude reality. Instead of soaring to poetical heights, art may dive beneath the level marked by the natural perspective. How it is possible to overcome realism by merely putting too fine a point on it and discovering, lens in hand, the micro-structure of life can be observed in Proust, Ramón Gómez de la Serna, Joyce. . . . The procedure simply consists in letting the outskirts of attention, that which ordinarily escapes notice, perform the main part in life's drama.

The same mesmerized attention to magnified minutiae that we find in Salvador Dali we come across in many a modern writer as well. William Empson's critical method as expounded in *Seven Types of Ambiguity* (1930), by exploring all possible meanings of the words and thus opening strange vistas through the pages of a classic, has imparted to these words a tension, a dramatic irony, not unlike a surrealist effect (as when, for instance, Dali combines two figures of women in seventeenth-century Dutch costumes in such a way that they form together the head of Voltaire: a well-known optical trick of the end of the nineteenth century, frequently combined with erotic and macabre details, e.g., bodies of naked women forming a skull). Empson's love of misprints, which he finds illuminating because they suggest buried meanings, can also be paralleled with the deliberate surrealist cult for solecism in the forms of things (wet watches, limp cellos, telephone receivers used as grills, etc.). When Empson remarks that

"the practice of looking for ambiguity rapidly leads to hallucinations," he seems to be formulating the very process of surrealist inspiration, as illustrated, for instance, in Raymond Roussel's *Comment j'ai écrit certains de mes livres.* Another aspect of this mesmerized attention to minutiae is offered by the hairsplitting analyses of structural criticism, an extreme and indeed preposterous instance of which is Roland Barthes' *Système de la Mode,* where the analysis of clothes takes the form of a minute survey of the tailoring language. It is in fiction, however, that we are likely to find obvious parallels with surrealist technique. William Sansom's *The Body* offers a number of illustrations of experiments which are verbal counterparts of the techniques of Dali, Max Ernst, and Eugène Berman. Take, for instance, this scene, which is uncannily like a hallucination in the manner of Max Ernst:

> But in that house there was a third figure—and this I saw suddenly through the French windows. I stopped, stooped rigid—searched for this figure which suddenly I knew was there, but could not exactly see. A second before I seemed to have seen it. Then again I caught it—in the detached glass windscreen of a car propped against the sundial there stood reflected, motionless, the figure of a man. Dark and glassy in the windscreen lay reflected blue of the sky and a picture of the façade of the house above—though mostly of the verandah rail just above that garden room itself. The figure was standing with its hands on its sides, right against the white curled iron and creepered rail; it wore a dressing gown; its face seemed to stare directly down into mine; it was Bradford.

This second passage illustrates Sansom's attention to magnified minutiae:

> In the fresh morning air, in the still room without fire or light, in that motionless new grey daylight I sat and stared at the blacklead. After a few minutes, long minutes, I remember my eyes moving nearer to my boots. Nothing stirred—but in the stoneset solitude I suddenly grew conscious of my living body. Inside those black boots there were feet and toes and on the toes greyish-yellow hairs. There was a corn on one toe, a patch of hard skin along the side of the other foot. Inside the boot, inside the sock, there was life. And in this knowledge I understood clearly how all the time, motionless in a motionless room, my body was slowly, slowly falling to pieces. A gradual, infinitesimal disintegration was taking place. Nothing could stop it. Pores that once had been young were now drying up, hairs were loosening in their follicles, there was an acid crusting the backs of my teeth and my stomach. And what horrors persisted in the unseen entrails, among all those unbelievable inner organs? My fingernails were growing, phlegm accumulated itself on the membranes of my throat and nose—all the time steadily, relentlessly, a quiet change was taking place, the accelerating decadence of forty-five years.

From Henry Green [in his *Concluding*] (though, generally speaking, the counterpart of Green's writing is to be found rather in abstract art), we take this vision reminiscent of

Dali; while the last portion seems to be in the manner of Meredith:

> He looked down on a girl stretched out, whom he did not know to be Merode, whose red hair was streaked across a white face and matted by salt tears, who was in pyjamas and had one leg torn to the knee. A knee which, brilliantly polished over bone beneath, shone in this sort of pool she had made for herself in the fallen world of birds, burned there like a piece of tusk burnished by shifting sands, or else a wheel revolving at such speed that it had no edges and was white, thus communicating life to ivory, a heart to the still, and the sensation of a crash to this girl who lay quiet, reposed.

Desolate landscapes of a kind which surrealist paintings have vulgarized are a salient feature of Eliot's *The Waste Land:*

> A rat crept softly through the vegetation
> Dragging its slimy belly on the bank
> While I was fishing in the dull canal
> On a winter evening round behind the gashouse
> Musing upon the king my brother's wreck
> And on the king my father's death before him.
> White bodies naked on the low damp ground
> And bones cast in a little low dry garret,
> Rattled by the rat's foot only, year to year.

Another trait Eliot has in common with the surrealists, particularly Max Ernst with his fondness for collage, is the practice of quoting a classic in an apparently unrelated context; in the passage we have just read, we find a quotation from *The Tempest* and, in the lines that follow, a conglomeration of quotations from Marvell's "To his Coy Mistress," Day's *The Parliament of Bees,* a modern Australian ballad, and Verlaine. Picasso's quotations are more cryptic. In his *Girls by the Seine* the pattern of Courbet's famous painting of the same title can be dimly descried, like a wire contrivance supporting a firework. Georges Braque's quotation of the portrait of Simonetta Vespucci by Piero di Cosimo has partly reversed the color pattern, making the profile of the girl black against a white, moonlike face, whereas in the earlier painting the white profile is outlined against a black cloud. In Max Ernst's *Une Semaine de bonté* the sphinx appears at the window of a nineteenth-century train compartment, within which a lion-faced gentleman wearing a bowler is seated, and one sees the naked legs of a corpse. In one of Hans Erni's photomontages one of the Magi as painted by a fifteenth-century Swiss artist, Konrad Witz, appears against the background of a sanatorium, a modern corridor with a view on Swiss mountains.

In the fifth section of *The Waste Land* we come across another surrealist landscape:

> Who are those hooded hordes swarming
> Over endless plains, stumbling in cracked earth
> Ringed by the flat horizon only
> What is the city over the mountains
> Cracks and reforms and bursts in the violet air
> Falling towers
> Jerusalem Athens Alexandria
> Vienna London
> Unreal

Then there comes to the foreground a figure which reminds us of Dali's *Cauchemar de violoncelles mous:*

> A woman drew her long black hair out tight
> And fiddled whisper music on those strings.

The chaotic landscape described in the next passage bears the mark of sterility and is peopled with nightmares, again a typical surrealist treatment:

> And bats with baby faces in the violet light
> Whistled, and beat their wings
> And crawled head downward down a blackened wall
> And upside down in air were towers
> Tolling reminiscent bells, that kept the hours
> And voices singing out of empty cisterns and exhausted wells.

The revolt against the traditional perspective that had prevailed in European painting since the Renaissance produced the well-known intersections of time and space in cubism: Picasso's simultaneous presentation of the side and front view of a face. A parallel to this revolutionary change is to be found in the dislocation of the time sequence in fiction, the most conspicuous example of which is William Faulkner's *The Sound and the Fury.* In 1939 Sartre hailed in Faulkner's novel the introduction of the fourth dimension into literature, and then himself produced, in *Le Sursis* (1945), a narrative based on the technique of the Americans Dos Passos and Faulkner. This technique has since been popularized, for instance by Anouilh in *L'Alouette.*

In few modern writers can the parallel with painting be followed so closely as in Gertrude Stein. Her tricks of repetition and childlike sentences belong to the same current of innovation which made Matisse discard the traditional syntax of painting in favor of a return to infantile vision, an extreme sequel to Wordsworth's address to the "best Philosopher . . . Eye among the blind." The close contact of Gertrude Stein with avant-garde painters, particularly Matisse and Picasso, is well known, as is Picasso's contact with Apollinaire and Max Jacob; at the time of *The Making of Americans* Gertrude Stein stated that she was doing in writing what Picasso was doing in painting. On the other hand, one of Matisse's nudes might easily be a fit illustration for these lines from a poem by Gertrude Stein:

> If you hear her snore
> It is not before you love her
> You love her so that to be her beau is very lovely
> She is sweetly there and her curly hair is very lovely
> She is sweetly here and I am very near and that is very lovely
> She is my tender sweet and her little feet are stretched out well which is a treat and very lovely.

Matisse's synthetic childlike simplicity is also present in this passage from [Stein's] *Ida:*

> Ida returned more and more to be Ida. She even said she was Ida.

> What, they said. Yes, she said. And they said

why do you say yes. Well she said I say yes because I am Ida.

It got quite exciting.

And just as the man in the street wonders whether Matisse can draw, so the press where Gertrude Stein had *Three Lives* printed sent to inquire whether she really knew English.

For Donald Sutherland, "it can be said that the difference between Gertrude Stein and Proust is the difference between Cézanne and the impressionists. The complexities of accident, light, and circumstance are reduced to a simple geometrical structure, a final existence addressed to the mind" [Sutherland, *Gertrude Stein*].

He continues:

> Allowing certainly for his analytical gift and his splendors of construction, the presented continuity in Proust is a continuity of perception, of registration, like the surface of an impressionist painting; while in *The Making of Americans* the continuity is one of conception, of constant activity in terms of the mind and not the senses and emotions, like the surface of a cubist painting. . . .

> As the three-dimensional abstractions of Cézanne were flattened into the two dimensions of cubism, so the biographical dimension of *Madame Bovary* was flattened into the continuous present of *The Making of Americans*. As in straight narrative art the story functions as a plane, the continuous present of interior time was for Gertrude Stein a flat plane of reference, without concern for depth. Solids and depth concerned both Flaubert and Cézanne, but not at this time Gertrude Stein or Picasso. The change to plane geometry was an advance in simplicity and finality, to absolute elementalism. It contains some interesting motifs for future writing and painting, as for example the use of the letters of the alphabet, the simple juxtaposition of heterogeneous objects, the use of a concrete recognizable object in the midst of abstractions. But the main similarity between cubism and this period of Gertrude Stein's writing is the reduction of outward reality to the last and simplest abstractions of the human mind. . . .

> 'A Curtain Raiser' happens to correspond to the extremely simple and dry and tense cubist drawings done by Picasso at the same time (1913). . . . Gertrude Stein said much later that her middle writing was painting, and this is true even when no objects are mentioned [*Everybody's Autobiography*].

> She seriously created, in the midst of our world, which was falling away under habits and memories and mechanisms of words and ideas, a new reality. The elements of that reality were implicit in the life of the 20th century—the intense isolation of anyone and anything, the simple gratuity of existence, the fantastic inventiveness, and the all but total lack of memory—but it was Gertrude Stein who made that implicit reality most distinct and positive and completely real to the

reading mind, as Picasso made it clear to the eye . . . Gertrude Stein and Picasso have isolated quality and movement, and made them articulate, she in words, and he in line and color. . . . They are . . . classical in their insistence on an absolute present free of progress and suggestion, and their use of the flat plane.

Gertrude Stein herself, in *The Autobiography of Alice B. Toklas,* has moreover acknowledged a similarity of aim with Juan Gris:

> Gertrude Stein, in her work, has always been possessed by the intellectual passion for exactitude in the description of inner and outer reality. She has produced a simplification by this concentration, and as a result the destruction of associational emotion in poetry and prose. . . . Nor should emotion itself be the cause of poetry or prose. They should consist of an exact reproduction of either an outer or an inner reality.

> It was this conception of exactitude that made the close understanding between Gertrude Stein and Juan Gris.

> Juan Gris also conceived exactitude but in him exactitude had a mystical basis. As a mystic it was necessary for him to be exact. In Gertrude Stein the necessity was intellectual, a pure passion for exactitude. It is because of this that her work has often been compared to that of mathematicians and by a certain French critic to the work of Bach.

Next to the mannerism of repetition, which finds illustration in Gertrude Stein, comes the mannerism of telegraphic language, with suppression of parts of speech, elliptical constructions, and so on. Before Pound advocated economy of speech by the suppression of articles and pruning of adjectives, the Italian futurists had given abundant instances of this, and Marinetti in the 1912 *Technical Manifesto of Futurist Literature* declared:

> Syntax was a kind of monotonous cicerone. We must suppress this intermediary, so that literature may directly become one thing with the universe. After free verse, here we have at last loose words. . . .

> Get yourself ready to hate the intellect, by reawakening in yourselves divine intuition, through which we shall overcome the apparently irreducible hostility which separates our human flesh from the metal of engines.

Another Italian who belonged for a time to the futurist movement, Ardengo Soffici, assuming in his *First Principles of Futurist Aesthetics* (1920) that the function of art consists in refining and sharpening the sensibility, concluded that the artistic language was tending to become a slang which needed only the slightest hints to be understood; therefore the modes of expression could grow more and more concise and synthetic, taking on a more intimate and abstract character to the point of becoming a conventional script or cipher. The artist and the public would find satisfaction no longer in working out a detailed representation of lyrical reality, but in the sign itself that stands for it. Therefore a few colors and lines in painting, a few forms and volumes in sculpture, a few words in poetry would be able to set in motion wide repercussions, infinite echoes. A meeting of two colors on a surface, a single word on a page would give an ineffable joy. He foresaw the ultimate destiny of art in the abolition of art itself through a supreme refinement of sensibility such as would render its manifestations useless. One need only look at Piet Mondrian's compositions or listen to Webern's music to see how well the Italian futurist movement coincided with the trend of abstract art. Apollinaire's *Calligrammes* (1918) and Soffici's *Chimismi lirici* (1915, second edition 1920) were already a form of abstract art, violent dissociations of the sentence from any subject matter, its reduction to a mere pattern for the eye and patter for the ear. Similar devices were used by Gertrude Stein: mysterious initials, mistakes and corrections in the midst of sentences, "cryptograms." E. E. Cummings' poems (in which Ezra Pound's ideas about the appearance of the words on the printed page and William Carlos Williams' theory that "the poem, like every other form of art, is an object" reach their extreme development) put one in mind of the achievements of Mondrian, Kandinsky, and Klee in painting: they elaborate a free technique in which the very signs take the place of imagery. Cummings' *technopaignia* are indeed poetry and painting at the same time, a new application of the Alexandrian principle *ut pictura poesis,* as can be seen in the following instance [from *Poems 1923-54*], which I choose not because of its particular merits but for its brevity:

```
the
   sky
         was
can dy lu
minous
            edible

spry
    pinks shy
lemons
greens     coo l choc
olate
s.

     un der,
     a lo
co
mo
      tive     s pout
                            ing
                              vi
                               o
                            lets
```

But the closest approach to Mondrian is represented by Gertrude Stein's set of statements abstracted from reality, by her celebrated poem "A rose is a rose is a rose is a rose," and by "Are there Six or Another Question": she "developed a sense—past rhythm, past movement, past vibration—of sheer happening as an absolute" [Sutherland, *Gertrude Stein*].

The nearest the art of fiction comes to abstract art is in the novels of Henry Green. He applies to prose an essentially poetic technique which has derived many hints from Hopkins and Auden: for instance, the concentration on a few

An example of a pictorial poem by futurist poet Filippo Marinetti, who authored the first manifesto of Futurism in 1909. Marinetti sought a liberation of the word, as well as the image, from the constraints of the Italian artistic and literary tradition.

significant features, the abolition of the article, the telegraphic language. The very titles of his novels are models of concision: *Living, Party Going, Nothing, Concluding*—single words in the middle of a page, almost taking on the function of a dot of color in an abstract painting. A passage from *Living* may remind one, on the other hand, of Chagall: "Here pigeon quickly turned rising in spirals, grey, when clock in the church tower struck the quarter and away, away the pigeon fell from this noise in a diagonal from where church was built and that man who leant on his spade. The very atmosphere of Green's novels, the substitution of a much subtler arabesque of conversations and inconclusive episodes (not without a certain resemblance to Ronald Firbank's elegant distortions) for a plot in the current sense of the word, the flattening of personal traits in the characters, so that they may be molded upon the arabesque and become almost indistinguishable from the pattern itself, the placing of the story almost outside a definite time and space (as in *Concluding*), and in some cases (in *Nothing,* for instance) the nearly total absence of descriptive passages—all these features contribute to the impression of abstract art. Occasionally, as in the following passage from *Back,* a faint echo of Gertrude Stein mingles with a surrealist sense of the macabre:

> But as it was he went in the gate, had his cheek brushed by a rose and began awkwardly to search for Rose, through roses, in what seemed to him should be the sunniest places on a fine day, the warmest when the sun came out at twelve o'clock for she had been so warm, and amongst the newest memorials in local stone because she had died in time of war, when, or so he imagined, James could never have found marble for her, of whom, at no time before this moment, had he ever thought as cold beneath a slab, food for worms, her great red hair, still growing, a sort of moist bower for worms.

Henry Green's novels seem to belong to the kind of *divertissements* "translating everything into subtlety and elegance" [Hauser, *Social History of Art*] which are typical of every mannerist phase in the history of literature and art.

On a lower artistic level, the same characteristic is to be found in Christopher Fry's plays. The artist seems to give himself up to private juggling in a world whose sole significance is as a storehouse of possible patterns. As an Italian follower of Laforgue, Aldo Palazzeschi, had put it as early as 1910 in the conclusion of a poem, "Lasciatemi Divertire (Canzonetta)," in which he indulged in verbal clowning:

> i tempi sono cambiati,
> gli uomini non dimandano più nulla
> dai poeti:
> e lasciatemi divertire!

The purpose of art as stated by Green in *Pack My Bag,* quoted below, is very near that outlined by Soffici in his *First Principles of Futurist Aesthetics:*

> Prose is not to be read aloud but to oneself alone at night, and it is not quick as poetry but rather a gathering web of insinuations which go further than names however shared can ever go. Prose should be a long intimacy between strangers with no direct appeal to what both may have known. It should slowly appeal to feelings unexpressed, it should in the end draw tears out of the stone.

It is not difficult to see how closely this aiming at the greatest possible rarefaction of style coincides with the aim of abstract art. "A gathering web of insinuations," an intimacy able to "draw tears out of the stone": there are people who can be intensely moved by a geometric pattern of Malevich or Mondrian; Plato himself had acknowledged the spell of pure geometric figures. Schoenberg worked in the same direction in the musical field, and a parallel can be drawn, as Melchiori draws it, between Green's later novels (*Nothing* and *Doting*) and Schoenberg's final stage in the atonal method, the affirmation of an abstract classicism based on pure form, the perfect and perfectly empty musical construction of the hero of Thomas Mann's *Doctor Faustus.* But such abstract reflections of the modern world—the remark is again Melchiori's—have a peculiar poignancy, due perhaps to despair: for these artists are tightrope walkers, and the surrounding void endows their juggling with an aura of tragedy.

Klee's abstract art indicated to Rainer Maria Rilke the solution of a problem with which he was absorbed: the relation between the senses and the spirit, the external and the internal. [In "Die Verwardlung des Sichtbaren, Die Bedeutung der modernen Bildenden Kunst für Rilkes späte Dichtung," in his *Zarte Empirie*] Herman Meyer, who has studied Rilke's affinity to Klee, both in attitude and in the means of expressing it in art, has drawn a parallel between Klee's abstract art and Rilke's symbolic language in the *Duino Elegies.* The symbol does not develop out of elements derived from reality, but is a message in cipher. Such are, for instance, in the tenth elegy, the figures of stars used as signs; here there is a close analogy with Klee's enigmatic language in cipher. Rilke has described this process of abstraction in a letter to the painter Sophy Giauque, in speaking of Japanese poetry: "Le visible est pris d'une main sûre, il est cueilli comme un fruit mûr, mais il ne pèse point, car à peine posé, il se voit forcé de signifier l'invisible."

I have refrained, except for a few hints, from drawing parallels between modern music and the other arts, partly because, as I have already had occasion to say, similarities between music and literature are often deceptive. As Edmund Wilson aptly remarked apropos of the supposed musical character of *Finnegans Wake:*

> Nor do I think it possible to defend the procedure of Joyce on the basis of an analogy with music. It is true that there is a good deal of the musician in Joyce: his phonograph record of *Anna Livia* is as beautiful as a fine tenor solo. But nobody would listen for half an hour to a composer of operas or symphonic poems who went on and on in one mood as monotonously as Joyce has done in parts of *Finnegans Wake,* who scrambled so many motifs in one passage, or who returned to pick up a theme a couple of hours after it had first been stated, when the listeners would inevitably have forgotten it. [Wilson, *The Wound and the Bow*]

Parallels between the visual arts and literature, on the contrary, seem to me very appropriate: here the fields are closer, and this can be argued—as we have seen—from cases of painters who are also good writers and writers who can draw. But whereas, as I said at the beginning, parallels of this sort seem to be almost obvious in past ages, they are not so obvious in modern art, because the "énormité devenant norme" and the "sauts d'harmonie inouïs" are violently striking when expressed on a canvas or in metal and stone; on the printed page they are not so staggering. Even a page of *Finnegans Wake* is more accessible than most abstract painting; one can guess why that page was written, but the first reaction to most modern painting is precisely to wonder why it has been done at all. The Victorians, as we know, could enjoy "Jabberwocky" but they would have packed Mondrian, Malevich, and Kandinsky off to the lunatic asylum, and would have seen no difference between Klee's pictures and those made by mad criminals. I feel, however, that there is a close relationship between the development of art and literature also in the modern period, one may even say, chiefly in the modern period, when creation goes hand in hand with an overdeveloped critical activity debating problems which are common to all the arts.

> *Mario Praz, "Spatial and Temporal Interpenetration," in his* Mnemosyne: The Parallel Between Literature and the Visual Arts. *Bollingen Series XXXV, Princeton University Press, 1970, pp. 191-216.*

FURTHER READING

Secondary Sources

Babbitt, Irving. *The New Laokoon: An Essay on the Confusion of the Arts.* New York: Houghton Mifflin, 1910, 259 p.

Studies Gotthold Lessing's 1766 essay on literature and the plastic arts, *Laocoön,* as a problem in comparative literature whose roots lie in the classical theories of art developed during the Renaissance. Babbitt extends his study to examine literature and the arts since Lessing's time, and asserts that Romanticism gave rise to a "confusion" of the proper boundaries between literature and the visual arts.

Cutler, Anthony. "Acrobats and Angels: Art and Poetry in the Cubist Period." *The Emory University Quarterly* XX, No. 1 (Spring 1964): 52-56.

Discusses the impact of Cubism on painting and poetry in the 1920s. Cutler states: "Traveling beyond the descriptive, the analytical, the decorative, and the sentimental mode, [painters and poets of the 1920s] determined the truth of what is now a truism: That an object can be beautiful without reference to anything extrinsic."

Czerniawski, Adam. "Poets and Painters." In *The Mature Laurel: Essays on Modern Polish Poetry,* edited by Adam Czerniawski, pp. 225-39. Bridgend, Wales: Poetry Wales Press, Seren Books, 1991.

Studies the effect of painting on three Polish poets' imagery.

Frank, Joseph. "Spatial Form in Modern Literature," Parts II and III. *The Sewanee Review* LIII, Nos. 3, 4 (July-September 1945; October-December 1945): 433-56, 643-53.

Second and third parts of an essay by Frank excerpted above. Frank analyzes the structure and technique of Djuna Barnes's novel *Nightwood* (1937) as an example of spatial form in literature and proposes that in modern literature "Just as the dimension of depth has vanished from the plastic arts, so the dimension of depth has vanished from history as it forms the content of these works: past and present are . . . locked in a timeless unity which . . . eliminates any feeling of historical sequence by the very act of juxtaposition."

———. "Spatial Form: An Answer to Critics," *Critical Inquiry* 4 (Winter 1977): 231-52.

Addresses various criticisms of Frank's 1945 essay on spatial form in literature.

Hatzfeld, Helmut A. "Literary Criticism through Art and Art Criticism through Literature." *The Journal of Aesthetics and Art Criticism* VI, No. 1 (September 1947): 1-21.

Hatzfeld defines current methods of analyzing parallels between the arts, demonstrates the inadequacies of these methods, and argues for the development of a new critical-theoretical approach.

Kermode, Frank. "A Reply to Joseph Frank." *Critical Inquiry* 4, No. 3 (Spring 1978): 579-88.

Response to Joseph Frank's 1977 defense of his theory of spatial form in literature. Kermode disputes Frank's theory, arguing that " 'spatial form' seems to be only a weak figure for the process, compounded of memory and prediction, by which we understand utterances of whatever length."

Laude, Jean. "On the Analysis of Poems and Paintings." *New Literary History* III, No. 3 (Spring 1972): 471-86.

Examination of the relationship between poetry and painting that asserts, "poetry and painting constitute series which, each one taken separately, are linked not to each other but to an identical sequence of a common cultural area."

Lessing, Gotthold Ephraim. *Laocoön: An Essay on the Limits of Painting and Poetry.* 1766. Translated by Edward Allen McCormick. Baltimore, Maryland: Johns Hopkins University Press, 1962, 259 p.

Classic essay on the relationship between literature and the visual arts.

Mitchell, W. J. T. "The Politics of Genre: Space and Time in Lessing's Laocoon." *Representations* 6, No. 6 (Spring 1984): 98-115.

Discusses strengths and faults of prominent critical theories about the art/literature relationship and "[proposes] a new way of conceiving of the space-time problem in the arts, as a dialectical struggle in which the opposed terms take on different ideological roles and relationships at different moments in history."

———. *Iconology: Image, Text, Ideology.* Chicago: The University of Chicago Press, 1986, 226 p.

Series of essays that consider various historical definitions of "image" and the difference between images and texts.

Mukařovský, Jan. "Art as Semiological Fact." In *Calligram: Essays in New Art History from France,* edited by Norman Bryson, pp. 1-7. Cambridge: Cambridge University Press, 1988.

Semiological analysis comparing and contrasting the ways art and literature function as communicative signs.

Neumann, Alfred R., compiler, and Erdman, David V., editor. *A Bibliography on the Relations of Literature and the Other Arts, 1952-1967.* 1959. Reprint. Rev. ed. New York: AMS Press, 1968.

Selected bibliography of works regarding the relationship between literature and the arts.

Smitten, Jeffrey R. and Daghistany, Ann, eds. *Spatial Form in Narrative.* Ithaca, N. Y.: Cornell University Press, 1981, 271 p.

Collection of essays discussing spatial form in narrative fiction.

Steiner, Wendy. *The Colors of Rhetoric: Problems in the Rela-*

tion between Modern Literature and Painting. Chicago: The University of Chicago Press, 1982, 263 p.

Considers reasons for the art-literature comparison and endeavors to "show the crucial position played by the painting-literature comparison in our attempt at understanding aesthetic—and even critical—meaning."

Yau, John. "Poets and Art." *Artforum* XXIII, No. 3 (November 1984): 85-88.

Interviews four contemporary poets, who discuss their relationship with the artistic community and their thoughts about writing art criticism.

Crime in Twentieth-Century Literature

INTRODUCTION

Crime and criminality have figured prominently in literature since ancient times. In Greek and Shakespearean drama, the image of the criminal was that of an individual trapped by destiny and character flaws in a web of crimes against man and nature. By the mid-nineteenth century literary depictions of crime were influenced by rapidly changing social conditions in Europe and the United States, particularly the rise of real-life crime among the burgeoning underclasses of urban areas, and the criminal was often portrayed as a member of the poverty-stricken masses fighting for survival. Inspired in part by Feodor Dostoevski's characterization of Raskolnikov in *Crime and Punishment* and Friedrich Nietzsche's theory of the superman—a superior human being not held to conventional morality due to his or her "will to power"—twentieth-century writers such as Albert Camus and Jean Genêt raised questions in their works about the nature of crime and guilt. Summarizing the enduring appeal of the criminal figure, Robert Langbaum has written: "Not only in literature but also in the sensational stories on the front pages of newspapers, the criminal becomes a mythological figure who, like the tragic hero of old, acts out for us the unrealized potentialities of our own nature and raises, in the punishment he takes upon himself, the questions about guilt and innocence which in our own lives most of us contrive never to face."

REPRESENTATIVE WORKS

Broch, Hermann
  Die Schlafwandler (novel trilogy) 1931-32
    [*The Sleepwalkers*, 1932]
Brown, Charles Brockden
  Wieland (novel) 1798
  Arthur Mervyn (novel) 1799
Camus, Albert
  L'étranger (novel) 1942
    [*The Stranger*, 1946; also published as *The Outsider*]
  La chute (novel) 1956
    [*The Fall*, 1956]
  "Reflections on the Guillotine" (essay) 1959
Capote, Truman
  In Cold Blood (novel) 1965
Conrad, Joseph
  Lord Jim (novel) 1900
Crane, Stephen

"The Blue Hotel" (short story) 1898
Defoe, Daniel
  Moll Flanders (novel) 1721
Döblin, Alfred
  Berlin Alexanderplatz (novel) 1929
    [*Alexanderplatz, Berlin: The Story of Franz Biberkopf*, 1931; also published as *Berlin Alexanderplatz*, 1978]
Dostoevski, Feodor
  Zapiski iz myortvogo doma (memoirs) 1862
    [*Buried Alive; or, Two Years' Life of Penal Servitude in Siberia*, 1881; also translated as *The House of the Dead; or, Prison Life in Siberia*, 1911]
  Prestuplenye i nakazanye (novel) 1866
    [*Crime and Punishment*, 1886]
Doyle, Arthur Conan
  A Study in Scarlet (novel) 1888
  The Adventures of Sherlock Holmes (short stories) 1892
Dreiser, Theodore
  An American Tragedy (novel) 1925
Fitzgerald, F. Scott
  The Great Gatsby (novel) 1925

Genêt, Jean
  Journal du voleur   (memoirs)   1949
    [*The Thief's Journal,* 1954]
Gide, André
  L'immoraliste   (novel)   1902
    [*The Immoralist,* 1930]
  Les caves du Vatican   (novel)   1914
    [*Lafcadio's Adventures,* 1928]
Hemingway, Ernest
  "The Killers"   (short story)   1927
Hesse, Hermann
  Demian   (novel)   1919
    [*Demian,* 1923]
Howells, William Dean
  A Modern Instance   (novel)   1882
  The Rise of Silas Lapham   (novel)   1885
Kafka, Franz
  In der Strafkolonie   (novella)   1919
    [*In the Penal Colony,* 1941]
  Der Prozess   (novel)   1925
    [*The Trial,* 1936]
Mann, Thomas
  "Tonio Kröger"   (short story)   1903
  Bekenntnisse des Hochstaplers Felix Krull   (novel) 1954
    [*Confessions of Felix Krull, Confidence Man,* 1955]
Melville, Herman
  The Confidence Man   (novel)   1857
Musil, Robert
  Der Mann ohne Eigenschaften. 3 vols.   (unfinished novel)   1930-43
    [*The Man without Qualities,* 1952]
Nabokov, Vladimir
  Lolita   (novel)   1955
O'Connor, Flannery
  "A Good Man Is Hard to Find"   (short story) 1953
Orwell, George
  "Decline of the English Murder"   (essay)   1946
Poe, Edgar Allan
  "Murders in the Rue Morgue"   (short story)   1841
  "The Mystery of Marie Rogêt"   (short story)   1842
  "The Gold Bug"   (short story)   1843
  "The Purloined Letter"   (short story)   1845
Puzo, Mario
  The Godfather   (novel)   1969
Sartre, Jean-Paul
  Saint Genêt, comédien et martyr   (nonfiction)   1952
    [*Saint Genêt, Actor and Martyr,* 1963]
Wright, Richard
  Native Son   (novel)   1940

EVOLUTION OF THE CRIMINAL FIGURE IN LITERATURE

Theodore Ziolkowski

[*An American educator and critic, Ziolkowski is best known as the author of* The Novels of Hermann Hesse

(1965) and as the editor of numerous English translations of Hesse's works. In the essay below, excerpted from his book Dimensions of the Modern Novel *(1969), Ziolkowski examines the figure of the criminal in twentieth-century literature.*]

[In Alfred Döblin's *Berlin Alexanderplatz,*] Franz Biberkopf is an ex-convict who has spent four years in prison for manslaughter. [In Hermann Broch's *The Sleepwalkers,*] Wilhelm Huguenau is a deserter who gets by, unpunished, with six months of swindling, rape, and murder. [In Franz Kafka's *The Trial,*] Josef K. is arrested and executed for his "guilt" a year later. [In Thomas Mann's *The Magic Mountain,*] Hans Castorp regards his experiences on the Magic Mountain as an "adventure dans le mal." [In Andre Gide's *Lafcadio's Adventures,*] Lafcadio pushes a man out of a speeding train as an "acte gratuit." Jean Genêt has become the darling of the intellectuals, thanks in part to the efforts of his staunchest admirer, Sartre. And surely more than one reader felt a tickle of irony at the recent report (in *Die Zeit,* October 10, 1967) that Döblin's most conspicuous literary heir, Günter Grass, had visited Tegel Prison in Berlin in order to read selections from *The Tin Drum* to the inmates. This obsession with criminality (both in literature and in life) will undoubtedly give pause to future cultural historians, yet it is by no means exclusively a modern phenomenon.

A morbid fascination with crime seems to number among the basic human traits, and writers through the centuries have never been slow to gratify this taste in appropriate literary forms. Enterprising reporters of the fifteenth and sixteenth centuries traveled around Germany singing their *Zeitungslieder* ("newspaper songs"), which recounted the gory details of the latest crimes in seven-line strophes. As soon as they had captured the attention of an avid audience, they sold their songs in the form of broadsheets or *fliegende Blätter.* Debased versions of these ballads survived into the seventeenth and eighteenth centuries; they were known as *Bänkelsang,* because the balladmongers stood on benches at local fairs to sing their *Moritaten* (a corruption of *Mordtat* or "act of murder"). In England, meanwhile, prison chaplains did a flourishing business in the sale of firsthand accounts of the confessions of notorious criminals. These chronicles, known loosely under the collective designation of "Newgate Calendars," provided in turn the inspiration for many of the Newgate novels of the nineteenth century, which traditionally incorporated a daring prison escape into their reports of criminal adventures.

By the middle of the eighteenth century this pastime had advanced from the marketplace to the salon. In 1734 Gayot de Pitaval began publishing the twenty volumes of his *Causes célèbres* from the tribunals of Paris, a work that was to exert its attraction for over two centuries and on such connoisseurs of crime as Schiller, E.T.A. Hoffmann, and Ernst Jünger. Thirty-five years later, Pitzval's successor introduced a new edition with a rationalizing appeal to the favorite catchwords of the Enlightenment: "In general, I shall endeavor to unite, in my selection of *Causes célèbres,* the clear, the precise, the curious, the instructive, the reliable, the useful and, finally, the pleasant" [M.J.C. de la Ville, *Continuation des Causes Célèbres et Intéres-*

santes; avec les jugements qui les ont décidées, 1769]. But the rationalistic vocabulary scarcely conceals the underlying fascination with crime that made this collection one of the most popular works of the century. By 1782 it had been translated into German, and in 1792 Schiller prefaced a four-volume selection (Jena, 1792-1795) with praise for "the important gains for the study and treatment of humankind" that could be obtained from the perusal of criminal cases. In 1842 the lawyer-turned-writer Willibald Alexis published the first volume of his *Neuer Pitaval,* with cases gleaned from the law courts of the entire continent. Before his retirement in 1860 Alexis edited twenty-eight volumes of the series, which by 1890 had grown to sixty volumes, providing an inexhaustible source of material for Hebbel, Fontane, and other contemporary writers.

The *Causes célèbres,* that Enlightenment police gazette, was merely one of the new forms devised for indulging a more refined public taste for crime. (On another literary level altogether, Rousseau's *Confessions* accustomed the public to the most shocking disclosures of the intimate details of guilt.) By the end of the eighteenth century the literary market in Germany was choked with a miasma of *Ritter- und Räuberromane* (novels of knights and robbers) boasting such titles as *Thaten und Feinheiten renomirter Kraft- und Kniff-genies (Deeds and Ruses of Famous Geniuses of Strength and Roguery;* published in two volumes, Berlin, 1790–1791). An entire generation of hack writers, capitalizing on the revolutionary fervor of the times and portraying their heroes as titanic figures, made a living by describing in these works the more colorful or terrible deeds of the notorious "Sonnenwirt," Schinderhannes, and other criminals of the century. All of these works, and the Newgate novels as well, had at least two things in common. They focused on the criminal and his deeds; and they viewed the criminal with sympathy, as a kind of people's hero who dared to defy an unpopular authority. The criminal in these works is often related by descent to the picaresque rogue of the sixteenth and seventeenth centuries as well as to the titanic hero of the German *Sturm und Drang:* Goethe's *Götz von Berlichingen,* Schiller's *Räuber,* and the like. The hero of Heinrich Zschokke's *Aballino, der grosse Bandit (Aballino, the Great Bandit,* 1794), which in translation helped to popularize the figure of the "noble brigand" in France, is a lineal ancestor of the "good" outlaws who gallop across our television screens every night.

The year 1828 saw the appearance of the work that was to change these concepts radically: the four-volume *Mémoires* conventionally (though wrongly) attributed to François Eugène Vidocq (1775-1857). Vidocq was a onetime crook who had shrewdly calculated that it would be more to his advantage to work for the law than against it. In 1806 he offered his services to the Paris police and rapidly rose from the status of stool pigeon to the rank of chief of the Sûreté. He and the associates he recruited among other ex-convicts astounded Paris both by the number of criminals they apprehended in the lawless days of the Restoration (over eight hundred in one year) and by the daredevil methods they employed. Suddenly the "deeds and ruses" of the pursuer began to match and surpass those of the pursued. Whether or not Vidocq wrote the *Mémoires,* his

exploits inspired Eugène Sue, Dumas, Hugo, Dickens, Poe, and Gaboriau, and marked a turning point in popular crime literature. For with Vidocq, interest began to shift from the criminal to the "detective"—a designation that did not gain currency in English until Dickens' *Bleak House* (1852).

It is unnecessary, for our purposes, to make subtle distinctions between the *roman policier* and the detective story, between *Kriminalroman* and *Detektivroman.* It does not matter whether the detective works by ratiocination, brute strength, or animal cunning. The important point is simply that popular sympathy was displaced, generally speaking, from the criminal and was now firmly on the side of his pursuer, whose methods in themselves were often scarcely preferable to those of the men they hunted. (In this respect, Mickey Spillane's Mike Hammer and Ian Fleming's James Bond are direct descendants of Vidocq and his gang of "police.") For without this shift of emphasis, without the transformation of the criminal from a titanic hero into a guilty man, the criminal would be useless as a metaphor and symbol in much modern literature.

By the time Poe's "Murders in the Rue Morgue" appeared in 1841, the romance of crime, which had flourished for centuries, had been in effect relegated to the cheap counters. In the detective story, the crime and the criminal have been reduced to a constant, not to say irrelevant, factor. Here, virtually all interest is focused on the analytical powers or physical prowess of the detective; the crime is either merely a *fait accompli* that precipitates the narrative or the threat that the hero seeks to avert. The author's originality exhausts itself in the creation of ever new heroes: from Poe's Dupin through Sherlock Holmes, Hercule Poirot, and Father Brown, down to the latest Negro and rabbi sleuths of John Ball and Harry Kemelman. No one can forget Inspector Maigret, but who remembers the criminals he pursues? The titanism that characterized the criminals of old has been drained off into the detectives, and with a few notorious exceptions, crime, like the rest of society, has become institutionalized and faceless. We remember famous crimes—the Great Train Robbery, or the Valentine's Day Massacre—but the individual criminals have faded into anonymity, like Jack the Ripper, who is known only through his deeds. The criminal, in other words, has become the gangster, with all the collectivity implied in the term. It is perhaps not going too far to suggest that the titanism of evil, continued in the *Volksbücher,* the shilling pamphlets, and the penny dreadfuls of the nineteenth century, was deflected into the genre of horror fiction, which manifested itself on a literary level in *Frankenstein, Dracula,* or *Dr. Jekyll and Mr. Hyde.* But the criminal of modern popular literature is almost invariably condemned to a pallid existence.

Truman Capote's *In Cold Blood* (1965) is symptomatic of the fate of the criminal. In this "true account of a multiple murder and its consequences," it is the monstrosity of the crime, its absurdity, and the details of the investigation that fascinate the reader. In comparison with Dick Turpin, Jonathan Wild, and other criminals of the past, the two slack-jawed perpetrators of the Kansas murders are anything but titanic figures. To be sure, Truman Capote was dealing with reality; he did not invent a fictional situation. But the very fact that he chose to record this particular crime is characteristic of the turn that the literature of crime has taken. We no longer expect criminals to be titanic; they are merely sordid.

The entire development just outlined here is based, of course, on popular literature of crime—on folk ballads, chronicles, trivial romances, detective stories, works written for the gratification of public taste. Yet its history, which has often been recorded, is linked in a very direct way to literature of another order altogether. And a grasp of this history is essential, I believe, to certain distinctions that must be made if one is to understand properly the role of the criminal in modern literature. Before the shift in public sympathy around 1830, a clearly defined genre featuring the criminal as a titanic man had emerged. This genre, with its distinct characteristics, has survived on a literary level right down to the twentieth century, even though popular crime works underwent the transformation we have noted. Around 1900, before the criminal had become the wretched creature of the present but after he had become an outlaw and an outsider who no longer engaged public sympathy, he emerged in a different literary role: as a metaphor for the artist himself. During the last forty years, finally, he has made his appearance in a third guise, stripped of all titanism and grandeur, but representative by his very sordidness of elements that many writers sense in our society. These three types exist side by side in the novel of the twentieth century: the criminal as Titan, as Narcissus, as Everyman. We can understand this phenomenon if we begin by considering a constellation of writers that may at first glance seem incongruous: Diderot, Schiller, Hoffmann, Dostoevsky, Nietzsche, and Genêt.

. . . . .

Diderot's *Neveu de Rameau* seems to be one of the earliest examples of a literary preoccupation with the criminal. "If I knew history, I would show you that evil has always come into the world through some man of genius." This fashionably titanic association of genius and evil, which anticipates a favorite theme among the romantics of succeeding generations, is gradually refined into a more specific definition of the sublimity of the criminal. "If it is important to be sublime in any aspect of life, then especially so in the case of evil. People spit on a little scoundrel, but it is impossible to deny a kind of respect to a great criminal: his courage astonishes you, his atrocity makes you shudder. We esteem above all his unity of character." In reading Diderot, one must not fail to take into account the rhetoric of the situation; Rameau's nephew is purposely trying to shock his interlocutor. At the same time, we note a certain tone that is scarcely present in the popular literature of the times. For here it is not merely the criminal act that fascinates, but the phenomenon of criminality as such. Moreover, the criminal is regarded with aesthetic detachment as a worthwhile object of contemplation—so much so that the narrator is distinctly perturbed by the unusual attitude of Rameau's nephew and soon concludes his story: "I began to have great difficulty in tolerating the presence of a man who discussed a horrible action, an exe-

crable crime, in the same manner as a connoisseur of painting or of poetry examines the beauties of a work of taste, or as a moralist or a historian extols and demonstrates the circumstances of a heroic action."

Titanism, objective detachment, and focus on the criminal mind rather than the criminal act—these are precisely the characteristics that show up in ["Der Verbrecher aus verlorner Ehre; Eine wahre Geschichte"] Schiller's fictionalized case study (an eighteenth-century "non-fiction novel," if you like) of Johann Friedrich Schwan, the notorious outlaw known to his time as "der Sonnenwirt." "In the entire history of man," Schiller says in introducing his tale, "no chapter is more instructive for heart and mind than the annals of his errors. In every great crime a relatively great force was in motion." Men with a more sensitive understanding of human nature, he continues, will value the experience that can be obtained by contemplating this realm of criminals; they will fit it into their theory of psychology and evaluate its significance for the study of ethics. The attitudes of titanism and objective contemplation are developed consistently throughout the story. But Schiller is even more explicit than Diderot regarding the shift of emphasis from the criminal act to the criminal mind. "His thoughts are far more meaningful to us than his deeds, and the sources of these thoughts even more than the consequences of those deeds." For "that which is merely horrible is in no way instructive for the reader." Schiller is not merely commenting in passing on the phenomenon of criminality, like Rameau's nephew; he is writing a story—indeed, a "true story" that had been recounted in numerous other versions by contemporary writers who were not so contemptuous of horrible deeds. Schiller's tendency to linger on motivation and meaning rather than on the deeds themselves distinguishes his story from such sensational and popularizing treatments as J. F. Abel's *Tale of a Robber* (*Geschichte eines Räubers,* 1787) or G. I. Wenzel's drama *Crime from Infamy* (*Verbrechen aus Infamie,* 1788).

But in Schiller we find a new motif, one that was absent from Diderot's reflections: the thought, derived from Rousseau and the *Sturm und Drang,* that man is basically good and has been corrupted only by the forces of society. Thus, in his *Avertissement* for the first performance of his drama *Die Räuber,* Schiller outlined Karl Moor's fate as follows: "Unrestrained ardor and bad company ruined his heart—they dragged him from vice to vice. . . . " This notion, dear to the trivialized rationalism of the later eighteenth century, made its way even into the popular literature of the times. It provided the theme for Restif de la Bretonne's *Le paysan perverti* (1775) as well as for Ludwig Tieck's *William Lovell* (1793-1796). In the potboiler about "der Bayrische Hiesel" that Tieck and his preceptor Rambach wrote for the *Thaten und Feinheiten renomirter Kraft- und Kniffgenies,* we read: "through circumstances, situation, and convention a misshapen monster was formed out of such a lovely material." But here it is merely a sentiment tacked onto the blood-curdling adventures of the criminal-hero.

In Schiller this rationalistic theme is announced in the title: his hero is a criminal, after all, because he has been bereft of his honor ("Der Verbrecher aus verlorner Ehre," 1786). But Schiller's version would not be of such interest to us if it restricted itself to the shallow behaviorism that underlies most other works of the day. To be sure, it is the story of a good man corrupted by circumstances. But Schiller does not stop with external motivation. Like dozens of other heroes of rationalistic crime literature, Christian Wolf is caught poaching and sent to prison. But he is not merely damned by circumstances; he reflects on his position and consciously chooses a life of crime. "I wanted to do evil; that much I can vaguely recollect. I wanted to deserve my fate." It is this decision, this shift from the act to the essence, that distinguishes Schiller's tale. "So he has chosen the worst. He had no other choice. His life is all laid out: it will be a journey to the end of misfortune. He will later write: 'I decided to be what crime made of me.' Since he cannot escape fatality, he will be his own fatality; since they have made life unlivable for him, he will live this impossibility of living as if he had created it expressly for himself, a particular ordeal reserved for him alone. He wills his destiny; he will try to love it." This quotation comes not from Schiller's story, but from Sartre's study of Jean Genêt [*Saint Genêt; Actor and Martyr*]. Yet it could have been written for Schiller's "Sonnenwirt."

Christian Wolf, to be sure, is not Genêt; he repents at the end. But this striking parallel of initial motivation exhibits another characteristic that gradually emerges in the literary treatment of crime. The criminal is born uncorrupted; but once his development has been deflected from the normal path, he begins to *will* his criminality. The act of crime becomes secondary; it is merely a manifestation of a titanic impulse consecrated to evil. This is precisely the phenomenon that Ernst Jünger noted in his *Paris Journal* after reading the first volume of the *Causes célèbres:* "The greatest crimes are based on combinations that, logically considered, are superior to the law. Moreover, the crime shifts more and more from the deed into the essence in order to attain levels at which it exists as the abstract spirit of evil in pure cognition. Finally even interest vanishes—evil is done for the sake of evil. Evil is celebrated."

This set of characteristics—titanism, the good man corrupted, the will to crime, the criminal mind rather than the criminal act as a worthy object of aesthetic contemplation—is carried over into the works of romanticism whenever they are concerned with crime. Kleist's tale of "Michael Kohlhaas" and his terrible vengeance repeats the formula of Schiller's story almost exactly. But romantic *Naturphilosophie* soon imprinted its stamp on these works, distinguishing them unmistakably from the products of rationalism. For if the theories of rationalism seem to anticipate modern sociology and criminology, the attitude of Brentano's "Tale of Good Kasperl and Pretty Annerl" (1816) or of E. T. A. Hoffmann's "Fraülein von Scuderi" (1819) anticipates psychoanalysis.

Hoffmann's story, based in part on the *Causes célèbres,* is a forerunner of the detective story inasmuch as it proceeds analytically from a mysterious series of crimes, through the drama of an innocent man wrongly accused, to the solution of the mystery. But Madame de Scudéry is not so much a sleuth as a mother-confessor: she does not deduce;

she is informed. The titanism of the tale is still invested wholly in the goldsmith Cardillac, a demonic figure doomed to murder and theft by powers of nature over which he has no control. It is here that the narrator's interest lies, with the innocent man whose "evil star" (a symbolic leitmotif repeated often throughout the work) drives him to crime. Hoffmann's theory of criminality is based on the belief that a child's character is affected by the experiences of the mother during pregnancy. Cardillac's mother, during her first month, succumbs at a court ball to the blandishments of a cavalier wearing a magnificent diamond necklace. Just as she is about to embrace him, her eyes riveted greedily on the flashing jewels, her lover collapses and falls dead on top of her. After months in bed at the point of death, she eventually recovers and gives birth to a seemingly healthy and normal son. "But the horrors of that terrible moment had affected *me*. My evil star had risen and shot off the spark that ignited within me one of the strangest and most destructive passions"—an unconquerable lust for gold and jewels. This fateful proclivity leads Cardillac into the profession of goldsmith, and he becomes the most accomplished master in all France. But the criminal impulse shows up whenever he is forced to part with one of his creations: he has no rest until he is able to recover it, by theft or even by murder if necessary. In the figure of Cardillac, Hoffmann has concentrated all the characteristics of the criminal-hero that we noted in Diderot and Schiller; but by shifting responsibility for Cardillac's criminality from society to nature itself, he has given his work the characteristic twist that marks it as the product of a romantic writer.

Schiller and Hoffmann—these are the two names in German literature that meant most to Dostoevsky, who was himself inordinately fascinated with crime and criminality. This obsession, discernible even in his earliest works, was catalyzed by his experiences in the Siberian prison of Omsk, where the author gained the materials and insights that were to inform all his major works. His account of those years, *The House of the Dead* (1862), is a document virtually unmatched in literature until the revelations of Jean Genêt. Yet though Dostoevsky's first hand knowledge of criminals vastly exceeded that of his predecessors, it is easy to recognize traditional patterns beneath the variety of types that he records. It is symptomatic, first of all, that Dostoevsky chose to cast his memoirs in a fictional form. This device permitted him to exploit the immediacy of first-person narrative and at the same time assured him the detachment necessary for the objective contemplation of the criminal mind. As Ernest J. Simmons has pointed out [in *Dostoevsky: The Making of a Novelist,* 1962], artistic selection is apparent throughout the work. The effect of aesthetic unity is further enhanced by the theme stated explicitly on the last page: "After all, one must tell the whole truth; those men were exceptional men. Perhaps they were the most gifted, the strongest of our people. But their mighty energies were vainly wasted, wasted abnormally, unjustly, hopelessly."

The titanic quality of the criminal, proclaimed here as a general principle worthy of Diderot or Schiller, is documented again and again by such specific cases as those of Petrov and Orlov. "I can confidently say that I have never in my life met a man of such strength, of so iron a will as he," Dostoevsky writes of the latter. "We saw in him nothing but unbounded energy, a thirst for action, a thirst for vengeance, an eagerness to attain the object he had set before him." *The House of the Dead* in itself would be sufficient evidence of the romantic conception of the criminal, that of a titanic man corrupted by external forces and now willing his evil, which places Dostoevsky in the tradition of Schiller and Hoffmann. But the real confirmation comes later, in the five great novels. The clearest example is *Crime and Punishment,* for in that work, as Gide noted in his lectures on Dostoevsky, the division between the thinker and the doer has not yet been established. This distinction, which produced those later heroes who regard action as a compromise of their thought, appealed greatly to Gide, Hesse, and others. Raskolnikov, however, is still a hero after the pattern of the criminals in *The House of the Dead,* a man who translates his thought into the act of murder.

Crime and Punishment represents both a critique and an ultimate deepening of the pattern established in earlier works. It is a critique to the extent that it unmasks Raskolnikov's titanic dream of Napoleonic glory, his theory of "ordinary" and "extraordinary" people, as fallacious. And Dostoevsky's belief that the criminal generates spontaneously within himself the moral demand for his own punishment amounts to a mystical intensification of the more trivial rationalistic belief in the criminal's simple repentance. To a certain extent Raskolnikov anticipates the later heroes who disdain action, for he lives to realize how miserably his own act has failed. The act itself, though rendered in meticulous detail, is reduced in importance. Dostoevsky shows us, as R. P. Blackmur has persuasively demonstrated [in "*Crime and Punishment:* Murder in Your Own Room," in *Eleven Essays in the European Novel,* 1964], how Raskolnikov becomes the product of his own crime. Unlike the Napoleon of his imagination, who creates his own world by his bold deeds, Raskolnikov is himself transformed by the miserable murders he commits. This is certainly what Garine, the hero of André Malraux's *The Conquerors* (1928), has in mind when he disparages the feeling of remorse so common in Russian novels. "These writers all have the failing of not having killed anyone. If their characters suffer after having killed, it is because the world has scarcely changed in their eyes." For a true assassin, Garine reasons, there are no crimes—only separate murders. The assassin's world has changed, and he sees reality from a different perspective, where the concept of crime no longer has any meaning.

In Raskolnikov's case, however, the opposite occurs. Instead of changing from a man with a moral conception of crime to an assassin who refuses to acknowledge the existence of crime, he is forced to recognize the hollowness of his titanic dream and accedes to a feeling of remorse for his act. It is his act that transforms Raskolnikov, in this sense, into a criminal in his own mind. Before the murders he refused to contemplate the possibility of crime for an extraordinary man. The story of his punishment, however, is the story of the gradual growth within him of the awareness of his own guilt and his need for expiation. It is this feeling that prompts him to badger Porfiry, leading him

ever closer to the fact that he is the murderer, and that finally produces his confession. In this novel, then, the romantic pattern has been preserved in its essential structure, but it has undergone a remarkable transformation in depth and meaning. The criminal-hero is suddenly charged with so much meaning, his motivation becomes so complex, that the old pattern can scarcely accommodate him. Because of Dostoevsky's dualistic vision of the world, the criminal can no longer be viewed with total objectivity; he belongs, at least in part, to the character of the author himself. And for this reason Raskolnikov awakens a different response in the reader, who views him objectively and at the same time tends to become involved in his crime. As a result of this important shift, certain writers of the next generation were able to see the criminal in a new light, as a metaphor for the artist himself. But the original romantic tradition continued beyond Dostoevsky into the present.

Nietzsche's wholly titanic view of the criminal was conditioned almost entirely by his reading of Dostoevsky. In his letters and works of 1887 and 1888, just after he first discovered the Russian writer, he returns again and again to *The House of the Dead.* In the notes subsequently published as *The Will to Power* he asserted that "Dostoevsky was not unjustified when he said of the inmates of those Siberian prisons that they constituted the strongest and most valuable segment of the Russian people." Then, with a characteristically Nietzschean twist, he goes on to blame contemporary civilization for its lack of titanic criminals. "If in our own times the criminal is a badly nourished and withered plant, that fact merely discredits our own social circumstances; in the days of the Renaissance the criminal thrived and won for himself his own brand of virtue— virtue *à la Renaissance, virtù,* a moral-free virtue."

Toward the end of *Twilight of the Idols* (1888), again with reference to Dostoevsky, whom he calls "the only psychologist from whom I had something to learn," Nietzsche devotes a section to an analysis of the criminal. "The criminal type is the type of the strong man under unfavorable circumstances, a strong man who has been made sick." In a passage reminiscent of Schiller and the Enlightenment he maintains that "it is our tame, mediocre, castrated society in which a natural man, coming from the mountains or the adventures of the sea, necessarily degenerates into a criminal." The criminal shares with all great men the feeling of alienation from society; but unlike Napoleon, for instance, he has been unable to prove that he is stronger than society and hence becomes a criminal. In a letter of December 7, 1888 to Strindberg, Nietzsche remarked that the history of criminal families "inevitably can be traced back to a man who was too strong for a certain social niveau," and he went on to cite a contemporary example. "The most recent big criminal case in Paris provided a classic type: Prado exceeded his judges and even his lawyers in self-control, *esprit,* and boldness." In these passages and many others Nietzsche clearly regards the criminal as a titanic figure corrupted by society. There is a tentative identification with the genius and the artist, but since the criminal is a strong man who has failed in his aspirations, Nietzsche tends to regard him with objective detachment and sympathy rather than to identify with him.

Jean Genêt's novels and plays, and especially his autobiographical *Journal du Voleur* (1949), constitute the most powerful documents of the titanic image of the criminal in the twentieth century. "Though they may not always be handsome," Genêt announces in his opening paragraph, "men doomed to evil possess the manly virtues." One could almost speak of life imitating art, for it is Genêt's aesthetic consciousness that endows his sordid world with its heroic dimensions. This becomes particularly conspicuous when Genêt is talking about such great criminals as Stilitano, who (his homosexuality aside) bears a striking resemblance to Dostoevsky's Orlov: "Perhaps his power alone was enough for Stilitano to inspire respect without having to perform a bold deed." "Stilitano was handsome and strong, and welcome at a gathering of similar males whose authority likewise lay in their muscles and their awareness of their revolvers." The phallic imagery with which Genêt embellishes these figures—indeed, with which he endows the whole world of the criminal, including the prison buildings themselves—merely emphasizes their titanism. (Phallic imagery has been an aspect of titanism at least since Schiller.) But in Genêt the romantic titanism is carried one step further: he creates a veritable myth of criminals and criminality. Thus his book begins with a lament over the abolishment of the penal colonies in Guiana. "The end of the penal colony prevents us from attaining with our living minds the mythical underground regions." On the last page Genêt denies that he has attempted to make of his book "a work of art, an object detached from an author and the world." Yet, like *The House of the Dead*, these memoirs are vouchsafed a high degree of artistic unity by the theme that pervades them: the war between the criminal and society intensified to the level of myth. As a result, the work is in no sense a simple confession, an outpouring of feeling. By mythicization and aesthetic shaping, Genêt manages to treat his own life and those of his fellow criminals with a high degree of objectivity.

In Genêt's case the initial impulse to crime came from the outside world, from society, which cast him in his role by calling him a thief. Until that point the little boy who stole had regarded his thefts as isolated acts; but society, by giving it a name, forced upon him a role which became his *raison d'être*. "If he has courage," Genêt reasons, "the guilty man decides to be what crime has made him. Finding a justification is easy; otherwise, how would he live?" Hence society is necessary to the criminal; he can assert himself only by breaking its laws. "No doubt, the culprit who is proud of what he is owes his singularity to society but he must already have had it for society to recognize it and make him guilty of it. I wanted to oppose society, but it had already condemned me, punishing not so much the actual thief as the indomitable enemy whose lonely spirit it feared." For this reason Genêt the thief felt frustrated in Nazi Germany. " 'It's a race of thieves,' I thought to myself. 'If I steal here, I perform no singular deed that might fulfill me. I obey the customary order; I do not destroy it. I am not committing evil.' "

Again and again the criminal act is transmuted into a mythic deed, a gesture of evil against the morality of society. Hence the act itself is reduced in significance. The

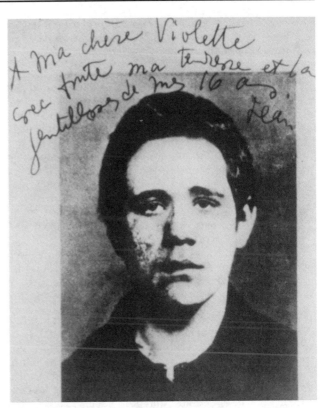

Photograph inscribed by Jean Genet to Violette Leduc soon after his incarceration for theft at Mettray reformatory.

pursuit of evil becomes a goal in itself. "Toward what is known as evil, I lovingly pursued an adventure which led me to prison." In Genêt we find assembled once again all the characteristics of the genre: the titanism of the man corrupted by society, the resulting will to crime, and an interest in criminality replacing that in the criminal act. The fact that he chose to translate this entire autobiography into a myth assures Genêt the final characteristic necessary for the work: a point of view which regards the criminal as an object worthy of contemplation for its own sake. He does not simply record his life. He reflects upon its deeper significance within the framework of the morality that gives it its meaning. There is a pronounced continuity of tradition in evidence here, arising with eighteenth-century rationalism and culminating in the autobiography of this twentieth-century criminal. Genêt would surely not have objected to having Schiller's words printed at the head of his works: "In the entire history of mankind no chapter is more instructive for heart and mind than the annals of his errors." And Schiller, I believe, would not have turned away from Genêt.

Theodore Ziolkowski, "A Portrait of the Artist as a Criminal," in his Dimensions of the Modern Novel: German Texts and European Contexts, *Princeton University Press, 1969, pp. 289-331.*

Eric Hobsbawm

[An English critic and educator, Hobsbawm is the au-

thor of numerous books about the history of the working classes. In the essay below, he discusses the criminal as a heroic and mythic figure in literature and popular culture.]

In any society in which men are exploited, oppressed and alienated, the free man is necessarily a hero and an ideal; and the free man most familiar to most people is the criminal. This is not merely because official society will classify any rebel against it as a criminal if he is sufficiently serious in his rebellion (so that "bandit" has become the most familiar modern euphemism for a guerrillero who has not yet won) nor because in many societies those who live outside the iron compound of the social order are thrown into the same social milieu as the criminals, notably artists and dissident intellectuals. The medieval poor student and wandering scholar-poet belonged among the rogues and vagabonds like the actor and the entertainer, and may well have occupied the same position of neutrality and immunity as does the recognized musician among the *tsotsis* of the Johannesburg African quarters.

It is also because the idealization of the outlaw transforms even the non-rebellious, non-ideological criminal himself—robber, gangster or thief—into a sort of hero. He is free from Adam's curse, work. He resists the strength of the oppressor. Isaac Babel's Benia Krik is all that the traditional ghetto Jew is not: strong, brave, flaunting his defiance in the face of Cossacks and policemen. He takes from the rich, which obscures the fact that he also takes from the poor; he scatters his booty freely, which leads to the illusion that he gives to the poor among whom he lives and from whom he is sprung. Above all, he breaks the commandments by which men are as enslaved as by the laws. That is why the murderer has always attracted the shy awe of the non-criminals, whose persistent fascination by him has long made the fortunes of the publishers of broadsheet ballads and popular newspapers.

On the other hand any genuine human community abominated the breaker of the communal bond. Where community and society coincide, as in certain primitive tribes, the criminal can be no more idealized than the parricide or matricide in the unbroken family or the strike-breaker in the trade union. Cain became a hero only among the Romantics. In so far as modern societies have bonds as well as internal strains and divisions, the same is true: the traitor may be a figure of awe, but he is not a hero except to those who deliberately put themselves outside the bounds of their community. His name is famous but abhorred, like Guy Fawkes. A large cycle of books and films has been created about Al Capone, but not about Benedict Arnold.

This double attitude towards the criminal has determined his place in popular and literary mythology. In the simplest cases he is either totally rejected as a Judas or simply not considered to be a criminal at all (except by some irrelevant outside criteria), like the traffic offender among the motorized classes. He may be both at the same time like the grain-speculator in peasant society, who is a smart businessman among his peers but personified evil to the labouring poor. At a slightly more complex level his criminality is accepted, because the law punishes him, but he is not a "real" criminal, because he does not break the commandments of his own people or class. On the contrary, because he breaks the oppressors' law and the bounds of poor men's lives, he is a rebel and hero.

This is the social zone in which the the great ballads and epics of the bandit-hero and "bad man" flourish: Robin Hood, Janošik, Rosza Sandor, or at a lower and more hopeless level, the Negro Samson Stagolee, who "caused" the San Francisco earthquake by pulling down the city when refused a drink because of his colour. (For among the most oppressed of all, as Brecht's Pirate Jerry shows, the fantasy of rebellion easily turns into the fantasy of universal destruction.) Among the non-political, unskilled or peasant poor, especially those cut off by colour, religion or social isolation, the criminal hero is a permanent and accepted part of myth and life. Like the Carpathian Jewish bandit Josif Polyansky he is aware of his role, singing as the police take him to jail:

> Look at me girls
> Here comes a man
> If you want sons
> Look at me girls.

The image of the great criminal among the poor and the socially disoriented of the modern big city slum is fundamentally not very different from this.

At the other extreme, that is to say among the classes for whom the criminal has no attraction and the policeman is the guarantor of law, order and civilization, the situation is not quite so simple. For one thing, as the immense vogue of the British detective novel—a purely middle-class creation—shows, the forces of established order are haunted by its instability. This is perhaps why they have to exorcise the threat over and over again by the imagined apprehension and punishment of relays of incredibly subtle and dangerous malefactors. And perhaps also why it must be shown that the breakdown of the official machinery of order—the ever-baffled police—is not such a terrible disaster. For the private detective, the clubman hero or bourgeois terrorist (Hannay, James Bond or Bulldog Drummond) is in the last analysis powerful enough to redress the balance between order and anarchy.

But how terrible and ubiquitous that threat is! Characteristically it is, in Britain, not primarily a threat to property, which is adequately safeguarded by insurance companies. The main subject of the detective novel is not robbery or fraud, but the breakdown of the moral order in its most flagrant form, murder. It does not come from outside but from within the circle of order. It may at first sight seem comprehensible and even to engage our sympathy. But it must not: anybody who substitutes his own judgment and action for the law breaks down its fragile structure. The murderer, however ostensibly sympathetic, becomes a monster who murders time and again, as he does in every detective novel, for purposes not entirely explicable by the technicalities of maintaining suspense. The British detective novel, in fact, is not only reassurance but a call to conformity and solidarity to those who personify the social order in times when all conspires to undermine it.

This is one of the many complexities of the criminal image which are the product of modern middle class society, though the most characteristic product of liberal criminology, the thesis that the criminal is mentally disturbed or an object of pity, has made no impact on either the upper or the lower class criminal myth. For this reason the student of the criminal's social image will find the period from the eighteenth century to the present vastly more interesting than all previous ages put together. Two fundamental facts determine its complexity and ambiguity, both reflecting an unprecedented difficulty in actually defining what is criminal: the nature of private enterprise and the nature of modern urban civilization.

The first discovery of the unbiased observer of a rising business society was that it turned accepted morality upside down. By all traditional European standards the businessman was immoral and criminal, turning what had hitherto been vices (selfishness, shamelessness, greed, avarice, hypocrisy) into virtues. Yet he was "respectable" and claimed, perhaps correctly, to build a richer and fuller society on this basis of vice, while repressing the old-fashioned criminal who seemed to be doing much the same thing. The paradox—that of Mandeville's *Fable of the Bees*—dominated eighteenth-century England, the golden age of the criminal in literature. Moll Flanders, Roxana, Jonathan Wild, *The Beggars Opera* and the myth-figure of Dick Turpin all date back to it.

What *was* the difference between Macheath and Walpole, between Peachum and the respectable merchant? Critics can strip layer upon layer of ambiguity off a masterpiece like Gay's and still leave the answer in suspense, because life left it so. At the same time in the decaying aristocratic society of France a corresponding paradox emerged. The underworld of rogues, entrepreneurs and cheating servants, among whom the nobleman moved freely, secure in his status, emerged into the open, for birth no longer immunized the social order against brains and beauty. The age of John Law was the age of Gil Blas. Manon Lescaut was the contemporary of the actress Adrienne Lecouvreur, whose burial as a vagabond caused Voltaire to protest. Cagliostro might have met Figaro, and presumably did meet his ambiguous creator.

The French and Industrial Revolutions introduced yet another complexity into the literary myth, which Professor Louis Chevalier has recently studied in his *Classes Laborieuses et Classes Dangereuses:* the fusion between crime and social revolt. The labouring poor and the criminal outcasts were no longer separable. Beneath and around the upper and middle world there now swirled the menacing dark flood of growing urban proletariat in growing uncontrolled cities, part of whose reaction to and rebellion against its fate took the form of a crime-wave. This fusion of the poor with the underworld appears in French literature from the late 1820s. Eugène Sue's *Mystères de Paris,* the bestseller of 1842-43, was to have been a sentimental progressive's novel about the labouring poor, and turned insensibly into one about the criminal poor, an evolution also observable in Dickens (e.g., *Oliver Twist*). This increasing attention to the squalor and gangsterism of the new slums fostered the concept of the populace as a mob, ready to break out, burn and ravish; a theme also found in Dickens. At the same time those who lived in the slums

were now seen, for good or evil, not as an excrescence on the social body but as its main substance. They were "the people". The two shadows of crime and revolution merged into one among the romantic writers.

But the romantics' crime was more than Engels's "earliest, crudest and least fruitful form of [the working man's] rebellion". It was also the ubiquitous symbol of all individualism, at once the logical expression of a society based on self-interest and a rebellion against it. Napoleon and the numerous Napoleons of business and crime belonged to the same species. Once the hood of bourgeois hypocrisy was stripped off, this was evident, at least to Stendhal and Balzac. But crime was not merely a mode of bourgeois accumulation. It was an equivalent expression of individualism. It was a form of power, as in the murderer Lacenaire, who haunted the French romantic imagination, and also a form of aesthetic creation: murder as a fine art. The master-criminal, the secret plotter against civilization, the ostensibly meek secret superman, acting out his or her fantasies in crime, have descended to modern crime fiction from the Paris of 1815-48. And so has the modern detective (Vidocq's *Memoirs* came out in 1828), for he is in turn the criminal creator and power-exerciser, only with reversed signs.

By 1848 all but one of the main ingredients of the modern literary myth of the criminal were ready, though they had not yet been combined in the British middle-class detective novel or the American crime-story, which has since become the definitive expression of this myth for western city society. (For reasons which are still obscure none of the other major western cultures developed an equivalent myth. Why, for instance, did the same ingredients in their Russian form develop so very different a combination of criminality and literature in Dostoevsky and in Gorki?) The missing ingredient was the formal fusion of crime and respectable society, which is the chief American contribution to the genre.

For the most powerful of the modern criminal concepts, and the one which dominates the public and library myth of the criminal today, is not that businessmen are as bad as criminals, but that criminals are as good as businessmen; that in fact they *are* businessmen. The policeman paid off by the gangster, the gangster as the formal boss of city or state; in extreme cases (as in many films) the illegal operator—notably the gambler—as the very type of the successful and admirable man; or even (as in Raymond Chandler) as the real force of social order in a corrupt society: these have turned crime from a Beggars' into a Millionaires' Opera.

There is no longer any virtue or any vice. There are no longer any formal slaves or serfs. The pursuit of happiness has reached its end, but for the pursuers it is not a happy end. For they are less happy than the illiterate peasant-rebels for whom the brigand was the hero and champion of the just and not of the affluent society.

Eric Hobsbawm, "The Criminal as Hero and Myth," in The Times Literary Supplement, *No. 3095, June 23, 1961, p. vi.*

On the relationship between real and fictional crime:

There was, and is, a feeling in some quarters that writers who use real crime may be unthinking accessories before the fact of subsequent crimes. . . .

The imitative syndrome is one of the few, the precious few, psychological notions concerning errant behaviour that deserve to be taken seriously. But, looking specifically at murder, what does one do about it? Ian Brady and Myra Hindley, the "Moors murderers", may have been excited towards evil by books, records, and relics relating to the Nazis. So should we ban commerce in anything to do with Germany in the 1930s and early '40s? . . .

I know of no factual books on crime, nor any crime novels based on fact, that have caused gentle readers to try their hand at murder. And I can think of none that, for sure, has put ideas into unimaginative, already-criminal heads. Graham Young, a fully-fledged murderer (and an inmate of Broadmoor) when Agatha Christie's novel *The Pale Horse* was published in 1961, may have been struck by the fact that the original means of poisoning outlined in that tale was available to him on his release; but *The Pale Horse* was pure fiction. (As far as I am aware, Mrs Christie resorted to reality in only one of her novels, *By the Pricking of My Thumbs.*)

I would argue that books that reconstruct or filch from real cases are more likely to be cathartic than incendiary. Generally, the message that comes across is either that "crime does not pay" or that the rewards are small compared with the risks.

Jonathan Goodman, in his "Fictions of Murderous Fact,"
Encounter, *January 1984.*

Robert Langbaum

[*Langbaum is an American critic and educator. In the essay below, he examines criminal psychology as reflected in Albert Camus's* The Fall *and Meyer Levin's* Compulsion.]

In the history of literature, as in history generally, the revolution of one generation becomes the orthodoxy of succeeding generations; and the truths which men of genius painfully draw from experience become easy platitudes for their second- and third-rate followers. I say this in answer to Edmund Fuller's telling attack in the last issue of *The American Scholar* on what he calls "The New Compassion in the American Novel"—the "new compassion," that is, for criminal and antisocial as against respectable, law-abiding characters. Although compassion for wrongdoers is at least as old as Christianity, the "new compassion"—the compassion involving judgment not only of the criminal but also of the law he is breaking—goes back to the beginnings of romanticism. It goes back to Goethe's Faust who, with the approval of God, makes a pact with the Devil in order to taste all experience. It goes back to Dostoevsky, whom Mr. Fuller uses as a stick with which to beat such contemporary American novelists as James Jones, Paul Bowles and Charles Jackson. Mr. Fuller is

right in attacking the merely mechanical exploitation of an inherited literary theme. He is wrong, however, in seeing in what are simply inferior novels "the absolute end product of ethical relativism"—for this seems to imply an attack on the theme itself.

Unlike our contemporary novelists, Dostoevsky "was not," says Mr. Fuller, "neutral in the conflict between good and evil." True. But Dostoevsky does not speak with Mr. Fuller's certainty about the distinction between good and evil. His novels show the saint and sinner bound together by a moral intensity which distinguishes them from other people. Mr. Fuller understands that "all of us are involved in the guilt of mankind. . . . But you have to have a standard of values," he says, "in order to see how corrupt, warped, misdirected values destroy themselves and others." True again. But where do you find the standard of values on which we can all agree? That is the central and distinguishing question of the modern literary movement from the eighteenth century to our own day. The question is how to find values in a world where tradition has been rejected, where we cannot accept values on faith. In other words, how far can we carry the freedom to which modern man is committed? At what point must the free man place limits on his own freedom?

The question opens the way to a kind of moral experimentalism. And this is where the criminal, the satanic hero, "The Outsider"—to borrow the title of Colin Wilson's relevant but careless study of the criminal among other Outsiders in literature—plays his part. Whatever the truth about actual criminals, the criminal as a literary figure is significant because he seems to carry to the extreme at least one side of human nature, and in so doing he carries his own moral freedom to that verge where individual self-realization comes into conflict with society. The criminal is on one side, therefore, a good test case as respectable people are not. The artist and the saint are also test cases on the other side, and modern literature is always trying to show that the two sides have more in common with each other than either has with respectable people. That is because respectable people, it is implied or stated in much of this literature, have not carried any human potentiality to an extreme and have therefore not taken advantage of their moral freedom. *Respectability*—in the sense at least in which the word figures in modern literature—is not a state you choose. It is the state you find yourself in when you have stopped short of moral choice.

Not only in literature but also in the sensational stories on the front pages of newspapers, the criminal becomes a mythological figure who, like the tragic hero of old, acts out for us the unrealized potentialities of our own nature and raises, in the punishment he takes upon himself, the questions about guilt and innocence which in our own lives most of us contrive never to face. The mythology of crime may as a matter of fact be the only really compelling mythology left us. Although a comparable mythology has in modern times evolved around the artist, the mythology of the artist has not a comparable appeal to all classes of men. Readers and writers of all classes, high-brow, low-brow and middle-brow, are attracted to crime stories. The difference in the quality of the stories depends on how far the writer can go in connecting the criminal with the rest of us and even—if the writer has intellect and imagination enough—with a whole world-view: a world-view which, whether it be original or orthodox, must be discovered or rediscovered through the facts of the case. Thus crime stories range from novels of automatic violence which excite without illuminating—novels Mr. Fuller quite rightly deplores—to a novel like Dostoevsky's *Crime and Punishment* which shows the vilest crime as a transaction of love in which victim, aggressor, policeman and society all need each other to fulfill the Christian ritual of sin and redemption.

The case for the modern interest in crime is beautifully made in Albert Camus' latest novel, *The Fall,* which in itself offers a wry comment on that interest. Camus' hero is a highly successful Parisian lawyer who makes a specialty of defending, often without a fee, criminals who are fundamentally justified, "noble murderers" as he calls them. He is, in other words, the very model of enlightened respectability, of the kind of reader who finds edification in reading crime stories and understanding the criminal's side of the case. But then this hero comes to realize that he is himself a criminal whose aggressive weapon is his morality. He has used the guilt of others to establish, without any risk to himself, his own innocence, his own Eden, as he puts it. He has arranged for himself a moral invulnerability that protects him from involvement with the rest of humanity and enables him to experience the highest pleasure of all, the enjoyment of one's own nature.

The man's doubts begin one night when, full of self-satisfaction, he hears laughter floating down the Seine, laughter he feels to be directed against himself. From that time on he hears laughter everywhere, always, he feels, directed against himself. Finally, again at night, he sees a woman drown herself in the Seine, and he is ambiguously unable or unwilling to rescue her. The incident or lack of incident dramatizes for him the crimes of omission he has been committing all his life. His awareness of guilt constitutes his Fall which, like Adam's, is paradoxically fortunate in that it initiates him into the moral life, the knowledge of good and evil. Crime has for Camus' hero the same significance that it has for those of us who—lacking, as Camus says, "the energy of evil as well as the energy of good"—read crime stories to learn something about our own untested nature.

Camus' hero gives up his practice in Paris and goes to Amsterdam, where we find him as the novel opens in a tough waterfront bar, the hangout for scum from all over the world. He is telling his story to a Frenchman, a Parisian, of his class and education, also involved in the law; in short, the counterpart of himself and like himself distinctly out of place in that bar. Now our hero has taken to defending the downright criminals who hang out in the bar, criminals whose motives are as bad as their deeds. He does this to make sure justice does not work perfectly. "If pimps and thieves were invariably sentenced, all decent people would get to thinking they themselves were constantly innocent, *cher monsieur.*"

Why Amsterdam? Because Amsterdam, partly reclaimed from the sea itself, is the edge of Europe, the place where civilization meets primeval chaos, where Europe reaches out in romantic longing for the East, a longing which fulfills itself as imperialistic domination. Amsterdam is the city of waters; and water is the original reality, not only biologically but morally—there are the waters of baptism and of hell. "Have you noticed that Amsterdam's concentric canals resemble the circles of hell? The middle-class hell"—the ante-hell, we realize by later references, of those souls in Dante who were neither for God nor against Him and were therefore not worthy to get into hell itself. Clearly the author has done everything he could to universalize his crime story. Yet it cannot be said that the symbolism, nor for that matter the novel itself, quite comes alive dramatically. We hardly notice this, however, for the book has plenty of life—the life of a first-rate mind engaged in passionate thought.

The book is a dramatic monologue and therefore reminiscent of Browning, who likewise used the form to investigate morality's many cunning passages. Taking Browning as model, we find in Camus' book all the elements of a great dramatic monologue. Characteristic, for example, is the speaker's repudiation of his own utterance. He reveals in the end that he hasn't after all changed, that his latest moral posture, the confession of common guilt, gives him an even more devastating advantage over others. "We are in the soup together. However, I have a superiority in that I know it." Also characteristic is the moral autonomy whereby the speaker judges and punishes himself. He reveals in the end that he has consented to harbor a stolen Van Eyck, *The Just Judges,* in the hope that one of the people to whom he tells his story will turn out to be a policeman who, by arresting him for the theft he did not commit, will enable him to expiate the crimes he has committed, crimes which do not fall within the provisions of the law. His present auditor, then, is:

> Not a policeman; that would be too easy. What? Ah, I suspected as much, you see. That strange affection I felt for you had sense to it then. In Paris you practice the noble profession of lawyer! I sensed that we were of the same species. Are we not all alike, constantly talking and to no one, forever up against the same questions although we know the answers in advance? Then please tell me what happened to you one night on the quays of the Seine and how you managed never to risk your life.

The utterance accomplishes nothing. The speaker is brought face to face in the end with that counterpart of himself which he must find in every auditor, that counterpart to whom he speaks in order to learn something about himself, to hear again his own story and self-judgment. As in all dramatic monologues, there is no reversal, no way out through external events or judgment, and therefore no answer, no meaning in the logical sense. There is only the logic of character carried to its ultimate conclusion. "Logic is easy," M. Camus says elsewhere, "almost impossible is logic to the bitter end." Logic to the bitter end leads to that dead end where all dramatic monologues arrive. But beyond logic is art. And Browning, in his best dramatic monologues, breaks through the impasse by offering us life itself, the reality and vitality of the speaker.

Camus, too, wants us to admire in the end the speaker's bitter bravery. He offers us, however, an undelineated consciousness from which there emerges no character to believe in. This makes Browning an Existentialist in effect and Camus, at least in this book, an Existentialist in theory only. But then Camus goes to a farther verge than Browning; he looks into nothingness as Browning does only once (in *Childe Roland*)—and from that bourn few authors manage to bring their heroes back alive.

. . . . .

"The French," says Lytton Strachey in the brilliant *Virginia Woolf & Lytton Strachey Letters,* "the French seem to me a melancholy race—is it because they have no imagination, so that they have no outlets when they find themselves (as all intelligent people must) vis-à-vis with the horrors of the world? There's a sort of dry desperation about some of them which I don't believe exists with the English—even with Swift." The remark—significant coming from Strachey who was enamored of the French mind and did everything he could to import its qualities into English literature—applies beautifully to Camus and the French Existentialists with their "logic to the bitter end."

In spite of Strachey's remark, however, it is the clear, dry vision he and Virginia Woolf have in mind when they reject over and over in these letters a hypocrisy and sentimentality which they identify as Victorian—"the Victorian horror" they call it. Envisioning the literature of the future, *"At last,"* says Strachey, "it'll tell the truth, and be indecent, and amusing, and romantic"; and Virginia Woolf says, "The danger lies in becoming too kind." We see what she means when, after a cruel account of the literary pretensions of a self-educated clerk and the peculiarities of a theosophist couple (types that sentimentalists, whether Victorian or contemporary, would treat as lovable eccentrics), she cries out in pain:

> Why is it that human beings are so terribly pathetic? . . . But can you explain the human race at all—I mean those queer fragments of it which are so terribly like ourselves, and so like Chimpanzees at the same time, and so lofty and high minded, with their little shelves of classics and clean china and nice check curtains and purity that I can't see why it's all wrong.

The cry of pain shows that genuine reverence for the mystery of human existence which can emerge only after the very worst has been taken into account.

Was it in pursuit of such knowledge that James Yaffe and Meyer Levin made novels this year out of one of the most gruesome crimes on record, the Leopold-Loeb murder case of 1924—the case of two brilliant and wealthy University of Chicago students who kidnapped and murdered a little boy, and then tried to collect ransom, for no apparent motive except to get a thrill and to apply a pseudo-Nietzschean theory about the rights of "supermen"? It would be difficult to ascribe the pursuit of knowledge or any other intent to Mr. Yaffe who, in *Nothing but the Night,* renders his story less significant and even less sensational than the case itself—he changes the murderers from university to prep school students, omitting their philosophical rationalizations and turning their overt into la-

tent homosexuality. Mr. Levin, on the other hand, in *Compulsion,* does everything he can to give his story the widest possible significance. A fellow student of the murderers, and the reporter who wrote the story largely responsible for their apprehension, Levin has, we are told, been pondering the meaning of the case for the last thirty years. By introducing himself into the novel as Sid Silver, the reporter, who is in many ways a counterpart of the murderers (Sid is also a prodigy who graduates from the University at eighteen, also Jewish and a member of their circle, sharing many of their ideas; one of the murderers, Judd Steiner, falls in love with Sid's girl)—Levin introduces the point of view by which to show the connection between the criminals and the rest of us.

"Judd Steiner, someone like myself," Sid thinks. "If we were in so many ways alike, surely I would come to understand him. And yet he had done that most incomprehensible, that most horrible murder." In the world of this novel where no one is religious, where everyone with brains is a scientific materialist and determinist and the fashionable chatter is about free love and free experience, Judd sees in the murder an opportunity "to test the farthest human experience, dispassionately, as in a laboratory," and says, as he pours hydrochloric acid over the dead boy's body, "I hereby baptize and consecrate nothing to nothing." Are the two murderers, Judd and Artie, carrying the ideas of the age to a bitterly logical conclusion? We soon see that their ideas are attempts to explain to themselves psychological motives they themselves do not understand. We learn that the boys suffered traumas in childhood, that they are emotionally arrested, and that the crime is for both a compulsive ritual and hence apparently motiveless.

The motiveless crime is the kind that interests modern writers because it suggests, first of all, that man has a soul, that he does not merely respond automatically to material needs; and then it forces us to look so deeply into human motivation as to uncover compulsions which seem to be of the soul itself—compulsions which raise again the question that goes back to Greek tragedy, the question about the mysteriously inextricable connection between fate and free will. Levin manages to maintain the general significance of the crime by suggesting that the ideas of the age are, like the ideas of the murderers, symptoms of a psychological deficiency, that the age itself suffered a trauma in the war, that "we are," as Artie's girl says, "the generation that refused to grow up." Sid, in trying to understand why this crime "seized the public imagination as a crime beyond other crimes," suggests that "this crime had meanings that would project far into our time." The author even connects the crime with the start of Capone's rule in Chicago and the abortive Hitler putsch in Munich; but here, it must be admitted, his intention outstrips the success of his execution.

He does very well, however, in portraying the frenzied inquisitiveness, part sexual, part moral, which attends the case and gives it the religious significance—the significance of a ritual sacrifice—which crime really has when it is treated seriously in modern literature. In the passionate mob that swarms around the courthouse the morning the sentence is to be delivered, every person carries "the hidden sense that the disposition would symbolically apply to his own darkest impulse. *If I let myself do something even as awful as this, how much would I be punished? Would I die for it?"*

In a foreword Mr. Levin tells us that in using for his story an actual crime which seems to epitomize the thinking of an era, he is following in the great tradition of Stendhal's *The Red and the Black,* Dostoevsky's *Crime and Punishment* and Dreiser's *An American Tragedy.* The comparison with Dreiser is the most appropriate because Levin does not, like Stendhal and Dostoevsky, see further than his age; like Dreiser, he uses the ideas of his age to explain an apparently inexplicable crime. I should say that Levin's ideas are almost up-to-date, for the reader who knows his Freud is likely to be several jumps ahead of the novel and to find certain of the stunning psychological revelations anticlimatic.

Compulsion is, as it were, the *American Tragedy* of the 1950's in that it adds to Dreiser's physical and sociological determinism a psychological determinism which plumbs such mysterious depths in human nature as to raise doubts about determinism itself. The change of intellectual climate is dramatized in the figure of the defense attorney, the famous old determinist, Jonathan Wilk (Clarence Darrow in the actual case). Wilk tries to save the boys from hanging by pleading that, though they are legally *sane,* their psychological abnormality is a mitigating condition. But Wilk does not dare go so far as to say what he really means, that "no one was responsible for any crime." Wilk's philosophy is not, as the prosecuting attorney points out, distinguishable from Judd's. Yet Wilk does not like Judd and Artie; for he has spent his life defending victims of economic and social conditions, and these two rich boys are victims in a new sense. Wilk pleads that if Judd and Artie had been from impoverished homes, the court would agree that there were mitigating conditions and act accordingly. That is the particular refinement of the law which Wilk (and Dreiser) had fought for. Now Wilk (and Levin) is fighting for a refinement of the crude legal line between *sanity* and *insanity,* for a recognition by the law that so-called sane people do not always know what they are doing or why. The final enigma is posed when the judge, an intelligent man, decides that since the plea of psychological abnormality applies to all criminals and raises the whole question of human responsibility and legal punishment, the reason he will save the boys from hanging is their youth.

The enigma raises all the ultimate questions about the commensurability of free will and fate, guilt and retribution—questions which used to be raised in tragedy where the committer of violence is a god or king, a maker of the law, and which in modern times have been raised in plays and novels where the committer of violence is a criminal, a breaker of the law. The fall of a god or king reinforces the moral order by showing that even the greatest must succumb to it. But the fall of the criminal is not remarkable; what is remarkable is our sympathy for him—a sympathy which causes us to question the moral order itself. Tragedy—which belongs to a world where the moral order is regarded as fixed—shows how the greatest individual becomes even greater at the point where he succumbs to the moral order. At its best, the crime story—which belongs to a world where the moral order is regarded as evolving—shows how the most lawless individual breaks through the order of his society only to discover a new morality or rediscover an old one.

> Robert Langbaum, *"Crime in Modern Literature,"* in The American Scholar, *Vol. 26, No. 3, Summer, 1957, pp. 360-70.*

CRIME AND SOCIETY

M. E. Grenander

[Grenander is an American critic and educator. In the essay below, she examines how the depiction of crime in American fiction relates to social and political realities in American society.]

Crime, a recurrent literary theme in many countries since the fraternal murder in Genesis, has been a pervasive constant in American fiction from the early days of the Republic. To deal with it in an article, I have slighted popular literature, which reflects the prevailing ethos, in order to concentrate on enduring works, which subject their culture to searching criticism. I shall, however, briefly indicate the norms promulgated in three genres of popular fiction which lean heavily on crime before turning to more fundamental critiques.

WESTERNS, SPY THRILLERS, AND DETECTIVE STORIES

The western story reflects a frontier society's desire for an uncomplicated system of law and order, easily understood and administered, coupled with distrust of nuances of right and wrong which are difficult to decipher and interpret. The common man of the western plains always wins. The spy story also operates in a matrix of accepted values. The spy in popular thrillers is always either good or bad, depending on whether he is "ours" or "theirs." The sympathetic portrayal of a foreign agent working to subvert American values would be unconscionable to readers of mass fiction. The detective story has a more complicated history. Edgar Allan Poe invented it in his "tales of ratiocination": "The Murders in the Rue Morgue" (1841), "The Mystery of Marie Rogêt" (1842-43), "The Gold-Bug" (1843), and "The Purloined Letter" (1845). Their appeal lay in working out answers to a puzzle which was only incidentally a crime. However, since the person who solved it was usually a detective, tales and novels in this form came to be called "detective stories," a term Poe himself did not use.

Since Poe's time, the detective story has split into two categories, the classic and the hard-boiled, each with distinguishing characteristics. The classic detective story's appeal is almost totally intellectual. But the tough-guy detective novels of Dashiell Hammett, Raymond Chandler, and their followers elicit, like the western, a gut reaction favoring macho simplicities. The plot of both species proceeds along a clearly marked path, with the actual crime committed in the early pages and the detective methodically reasoning from effect to cause, in order to discover who committed the crime and why—revelations that are not conveyed to the reader, except through clues on which he can exercise his own wits, until the end of the story. The criminal then meets justice, which may be highly idiosyncratic rather than conventional. Its manner is immaterial; the reader wants the puzzle solved, and when his suspense is ended, he is satisfied.

The classic detective solves a puzzling crime set in the framework of a society's fundamental values. The tough-guy detective plays his role against a corrupt backdrop, but he, too, corrects a perceived injustice. Like the western hero, he triumphs single-handedly, often using extralegal methods to satisfy the average man's yearning for a justice he can comprehend, and reflecting an urbanized version of the frontier code. Neither species of detective story leaves the moral loose ends lying about with which high art teases our minds; and, almost by definition, neither can probe society's values for us. The detective story must share, not challenge, its readers' assumptions; otherwise they will not care about the solution of its puzzle. Although Nero Wolfe, in Rex Stout's *The Doorbell Rang* (1965), does take on the FBI as his adversary, such a confrontation could occur in popular fiction only when doubt about the FBI was already widespread in society.

WHAT IS A CRIME?

In serious fiction, defining crime is crucial. In the real world, whatever the state calls a crime *is* a crime, and popular fiction tends to agree. "Right feeling," however, may not agree; and serious fiction is on the side of right feeling. The legality of chattel slavery is a cautionary example of the bad guidance our laws have sometimes offered. Hence, literature can be of tremendous importance in challenging current definitions of criminality. The victimless crimes frequently taken for granted in popular fiction are almost never examined from a legal point of view in high art: adultery, drug addiction, prostitution, gambling, and drunkenness. On the other hand, certain actions seem always to have been regarded as criminal in the fiction of American literary masters. These actions have involved threats to life, to the person, to liberty, to property, and to the society itself. The consensus on these as "crimes," whatever their legal status may be, accords with the view that, fundamentally, all "customs and institutions" are built on a bedrock of "universal, deep mental structures" [Gunther S. Stent, "Limits to the Scientific Understanding of Man," *Science,* 21 March 1975].

Victimless crimes

Nicholas Meyer's recent best seller about Sigmund Freud and Sherlock Holmes, *The Seven-Per-Cent Solution* (1974), reflects contemporary mental health ideology in its attitude to Holmes's drug addiction. But even though drug addiction, prostitution, gambling, drunkenness, and adultery are sometimes crimes in popular literature, they have not been in serious American fiction. Indeed, victim-

less crimes are often not reprehensible even in pop literature.

Although the high-minded hero of Charles Brockden Brown's early *Arthur Mervyn* (1799) is zealously bent on reforming prostitutes, Stephen Crane analyzed their plight more searchingly in *Maggie: A Girl of the Streets* (1893), relating it to harsh family treatment, poverty, and male chauvinism. However, a sentimental stereotype of the prostitute with a heart of gold, along with the gentlemanly gambler and the amusing drunkard, had already begun to emerge in semi-popular fiction. Bret Harte made a career of presenting these stereotypes, which turned conventional cultural values upside down, in such local color short stories as "The Luck of Roaring Camp" (1868), "The Idyl of Red Gulch" (1869), "The Outcasts of Poker Flat" (1869), and "Tennessee's Partner" (1869). In "The Blue Hotel" (1898) Crane portrays a professional gambler as mannerly, just, and moral; and Margaret Mitchell continued the tradition of the wise and kindly prostitute in *Gone with the Wind* (1936).

Drunkenness and adultery are special cases. Although the former is not a crime per se in fiction, actions harming others which are exacerbated by drunkenness are. Adultery has seldom been represented as criminal, even though statutes against it are still on the books in many states (including New York). But since it may have very serious consequences, popular sentimental literature of the nineteenth century imbued it with pathos and melodrama; and three great American novels subjected it to searching analyses: Nathaniel Hawthorne's *The Scarlet Letter* (1850), Henry James's *The Golden Bowl* (1904), and Robert Penn Warren's *All the King's Men* (1946). By and large, however, since World War I, adultery has seldom been taken seriously in popular literature, where it tends to be treated as a lighthearted jest. It is not portrayed as criminal even in the fiction of John O'Hara, John Cheever, and John Updike, where it is a staple element.

Threats to life, to the person, and to liberty

Although American fiction writers have always taken murder seriously, they may explore refinements in its definition. Thus, James Gould Cozzens's *The Just and the Unjust* (1942) deals with the trial of defendants who are legally guilty of first-degree murder, although they did not actually kill their victim. Harper Lee's *To Kill a Mockingbird* (1960) treats rape conventionally from the orthodox male point of view, but it is examined much more searchingly in Richard Wright's *Native Son* (1940) and Robert Traver's *Anatomy of a Murder* (1958). The psychological destruction of the victim as an aftermath of her experience is underlined in William Faulkner's *Sanctuary* (1931) and its sequel, *Requiem for a Nun* (1951), and is given a particularly poignant twist in Vladimir Nabokov's *Lolita* (1955), where the victim is a child.

Kidnapping is important in *The Just and the Unjust,* but it is slavery as a crime against humanity that has fired American writers—in Mark Twain's *Adventures of Huckleberry Finn* (1884), Herman Melville's *Benito Cereno* (1855), and Warren's *All the King's Men.* Much of the pathos of *Huckleberry Finn* lies in Huck's unquestioning belief that he is committing a crime by not surrendering Jim to the authorities. He does not doubt the morality of the law; he simply decides to break it. But the very conventional Tom Sawyer goes along only because he knows that Jim is free, manumitted in his dead mistress' will. Both Tom and his creator were playing it safe. Mark Twain wrote his novel about an antebellum society years after the abolition of slavery. Moreover, helping the kindly and paternalistic Jim flee to freedom is hardly an offense to right feeling.

Melville, however, said "NO! in thunder" to slavery while it was still legal by showing its victims reacting with murderous violence in *Benito Cereno,* which turns the institution upside down. A band of African Negroes who are cargo on a South American slaver have mutinied, killing the whites or holding them hostage. The experience of the Castilian Chilean captain, Don Benito Cereno, as a helpless slave forces him to recognize the horror of human bondage. Although he is rescued from the insurrectionists, he cannot cope with the ethical inferno he has glimpsed and succumbs to his monstrous vision.

This novella, written while slavery was under statutory protection in the United States, was created with great subtlety so that the horror of what the blacks do is fully apparent. Nevertheless, Melville was mounting an extraordinarily effective attack against the perverted laws which allowed so intelligent and resourceful a person as Babo, leader of the mutineers, no role except that of a slave. *Benito Cereno* poses mutiny and murder against the evils of a legalized crime against humanity. Something similar is done in our time by Ken Kesey, whose *One Flew Over the Cuckoo's Nest* (1962) uses murder to criticize the psychiatric torture and enslavement institutionalized in contemporary society.

Threats to property

Theft in American fiction sometimes finances flight from intolerable circumstances, as in Theodore Dreiser's *Sister Carrie* (1900), Willa Cather's "Paul's Case" (1905), and Faulkner's *The Sound and the Fury* (1925). More sophisticated thefts occur as early as *Arthur Mervyn,* where Thomas Welbeck's forgery and fraud are portrayed as outright villainy. In some cases, however, "white-collar" crimes have been left shadowy—as in F. Scott Fitzgerald's *The Great Gatsby* (1925)—or they raise refined ethical questions, underlining the gray area they occupy. Melville's novella *The Confidence-Man: His Masquerade* (1857) was based on the activities of an actual New York criminal, who prefaced his touch by asking his intended victim, "Are you really disposed to put any confidence in me?" His query created the generic name for the class of criminal he typified. At the time, some observers pointed out that his crimes were made possible not by stupidity but by generosity, a moral dilemma Melville's fable explores.

William Dean Howells's interest in the relationship of social problems to economic questions underlies his exploration of white-collar crimes in *A Modern Instance* (1882) and *The Rise of Silas Lapham* (1885). The corporate bribery of Judge Montague Irwin when he was the state's attorney general plays a key role in *All the King's Men.*

Threats to society

Fiction may present the betrayal of a subculture which threatens the parent society. Long before Mario Puzo's popular *The Godfather* (1969), Ernest Hemingway's classic "The Killers" (1927) presented this inversion of values. But crimes threatening the social order itself (riots, mutiny, treason, and revolution) are the most fundamental a society can face, since they deal with its very existence. The resourcefulness and courage of one man or a small handful of men control incipient riots in *Huckleberry Finn, To Kill a Mockingbird,* and *Native Son.* Walter Van Tilburg Clark's *The Ox-Bow Incident* (1940) portrays a mob lynching, and Ralph Ellison's *Invisible Man* (1952) an explosive riot. In all these novels, a mob forms when it perceives that justice has not been, and is not going to be, done. Its perception may or may not be accurate; however, if its complaints are handled with dispatch and firmness, the danger of its eruption into violence is greatly lessened.

Analyses of both treason and revolution require such an epic approach that most fiction has not attempted them. Exceptions are Edward Everett Hale's harrowing short story, "The Man without a Country" (1865), and James's *The Princess Casamassima* (1885-86), which includes magnificent portrayals of the cold-hearted dedicated revolutionary, the inept bumblers who tend to surround such a figure, and the women of high rank drawn into the revolutionary cause through boredom. More fundamentally, James's novel presents the revolutionary's classic dilemma: a given society's values and graces are inextricably intertwined with its misery and injustice.

Mutiny, a microcosmic threat to the social order, has been more manageable. Melville's *Benito Cereno* and *Billy Budd* (ca. 1890) examine it with extraordinary penetration and subtlety. World War I was the background for Hemingway's *A Farewell to Arms* (1929) and Faulkner's *A Fable* (1954); World War II, for Herman Wouk's *The Caine Mutiny* (1951). *Billy Budd* and *The Caine Mutiny* are of special interest in portraying mutineers sympathetically, but nevertheless unequivocally holding them accountable for their crime.

THE CRIMINAL

Habitual, occasional, manipulated, and inadvertent

American fiction has dealt with both the habitual criminal, whose offenses are a way of life with him, and the individual who, for whatever reason, commits an isolated crime. Examples of the former are found in Mark Twain's *Pudd'nhead Wilson* (1894), Willard Motley's *Knock on Any Door* (1947), *Anatomy of a Murder,* "The Killers," and, of course, the rash of current popular fiction dealing with Mafia figures. There is a depressing sameness about all these petty criminals, described in *The Just and the Unjust:* their principal problem was "how to make a living; and criminals who made good ones were as rare as millionaires. The rank and file could count on little but drudgery and economic insecurity." Nerve-racked and in perpetual danger, they would "kill a man in a paroxysm of malignity and terror as soon as look at him."

Fiction also portrays characters who commit an occasional isolated crime, exemplified by Lieutenant Frederic Manion, in *Anatomy of a Murder,* who kills his wife's rapist; Hurstwood in *Sister Carrie,* a responsible businessman who commits an atypical theft; Clyde in Dreiser's *An American Tragedy* (1925), who drowns his pregnant lower-class girl friend in order to free himself for a socially advantageous marriage; and the badly trained dentist in Frank Norris's *McTeague* (1899), who murders his wife. The aristocratic Judge Irwin in *All the King's Men* once accepted a lucrative bribe; self-righteous Adam Stanton in the same novel murders the unscrupulous governor he discovers is his sister's lover. The adolescent in "Paul's Case" commits a single embezzlement in order to have one gaudy fling before he commits suicide. The protagonist in Faulkner's "A Rose for Emily" (1930) murders her lover, but continues to hold her head high. All these are characters who are not professional criminals, but are impelled to their isolated crimes in order to safeguard what they perceive as respectability in a law-abiding society whose code they subscribe to.

A third type of criminal may become the cat's-paw for a more intelligent one who escapes the consequences of action he has initiated. The fanatic's killings in Charles Brockden Brown's *Wieland* (1798) were triggered by a ventriloquist, and Steven Maryk is maneuvered by Tom Keefer in *The Caine Mutiny* into a breach of discipline leading to his court-martial. Mr. Wilson was told by Tom Buchanan that Jay Gatsby owned the hit-and-run car that had killed Mrs. Wilson. The murders of Willie Stark and Adam Stanton in *All the King's Men* are also committed through manipulation.

Finally, there is the inadvertent misdeed which is a criminal accident, like Billy Budd's blow at Claggart and automobile manslaughters such as those in *The Great Gatsby* and *The Just and the Unjust.*

Criminal psychology

Miriam and Donatello in Hawthorne's *The Marble Faun* (1860) offer an example of the "deepening tangle of dark impulses and mixed motives" described by the narrator in *Anatomy of a Murder.* The relation between the criminal's ethical principles and his passions gives us three different kinds of motivation. If both impel him, he will be completely stable; he *wants* to commit a crime, and he has embraced principles which justify it. Although the later may deviate from the principles of his society, giving rise to the legalistic concept of "insanity" discussed later in this article, the criminal holding them will suffer no pangs of conscience; he can act with cold efficiency and complete ruthlessness.

Criminals whose passions and principles coalesce are Tom in *Pudd'nhead Wilson;* Hemingway's gangsters in "The Killers"; and Nick Romano, the young Chicago hoodlum in *Knock on Any Door.* Paul Muniment, the revolutionary chemist in *The Princess Casamassima,* is quite prepared for murder to further his goals. *McTeague* presents two paired psychopathologies in the Zerkows and the McTeagues, both of which result in the wives' brutal murder by their husbands. The adolescent in "Paul's Case" feels

no remorse after embezzling his employer's funds, nor does the necrophiliac Emily Grierson after poisoning her faithless lover in "A Rose for Emily." The murderous Misfit in Flannery O'Connor's "A Good Man Is Hard to Find" (1953) says, "I ain't the worst [man] in the world. . . . I never was a bad boy that I remember of." In *Billy Budd,* a tantalizing attempt is made to present the evil Claggart's "natural depravity" as a phenomenon that has puzzled the courts, giving rise to "the prolonged contentions of lawyers with their fees" and the "yet more perplexing strife of the medical experts with theirs." The passions and principles of Bigger Thomas powerfully coincide in *Native Son.* He smothers the drunkenly comatose Mary Dalton in terror at being discovered in her bedroom, then stuffs both her hacked-off head and decapitated corpse into the roaring furnace. Although her murder was accidental, he draws psychic strength from it, justifying his crime as an existential choice affirming his personality. He also rationalizes it as an expression of race hatred, but shortly rapes and then murders his Negro mistress, Bessie, battering her head in with a brick and throwing her body down an air shaft. In the concluding pages of the novel, faced with impending death, he says, "What I killed for I *am!*"

Two types of more ambivalent motivation are found in criminals whose principles war with their passions. Such characters are in conflict and extremely unstable. Hyacinth Robinson, the young bookbinder in *The Princess Casamassima* who becomes embroiled in a revolutionary cadre, exemplifies those who justify their crime intellectually but recoil from it. Hyacinth's revolutionary ethics support the duke's assassination; when the crunch comes, however, his humane instincts prevent him from killing his intended victim. The obverse character has right principles, but overwhelming passion drives him to an act he knows is evil. Great artists have been fascinated by the psychological complexities of such a character, who will inevitably be gnawed by conscience. Shakespeare and Moussorgsky have given us the archetypes in Macbeth and Boris Godunov, but American fiction offers less grand examples: the murderer swayed by religious mania in *Wieland* and *The Scarlet Letter*'s Arthur Dimmesdale, consumed by remorse.

Criminal responsibility

Few writers have presented criminals not responsible for their own destinies, since the term *character,* as literary critics use it, derives from the moral choices an individual makes throughout his life. Depriving him of responsibility, for good or ill, dehumanizes him into a driven puppet to whom the reader can have only a vaguely humanitarian response. The rare instances of such a fictional agent seem to be embodiments of contemporary intellectual movements. A possible reason for Wieland's manipulation by ventriloquism into killing his family may be that Brown wrote the novel during the heyday of the great Austrian hypnotist, Franz Anton Mesmer (1734-1815). In the late nineteenth century, writers following Zola were fascinated by the doctrines of naturalism, whose tenets of determinism and overpowering instincts were used by Stephen

Crane and Frank Norris to account for the murders in "The Blue Hotel" and *McTeague.*

Although current biomedical research demonstrates that neural circuits are "anything but diffuse and non-selective," scientists in the 1930s believed that the nervous system was functionally almost infinitely malleable. Their views supported an organismic psychology which put almost total stress on family and social factors as conditioning determinants for behavior, theories with important consequences for sociology and penology. If delinquency were directly attributable to adverse cultural influences, then crime would simply be the result of the criminal's upbringing. This reductionist doctrine, beguiling in its simplicity, found its way into fiction. Two novels, in particular, dramatized it explicitly: *Native Son* and *Knock on Any Door.* A more sophisticated exploration of blame-shifting occurs in *The Caine Mutiny,* which makes the point that no matter how good a seaman an officer is, he must also understand and deal effectively with his fellows. Thus, although it was "really" Keefer who was responsible for the *Caine* mutiny, Maryk nevertheless pays an appropriate penalty by having his dreams of a naval career dissipated because he had unwisely trusted a shallow coward.

Indeed, Maryk's fate underlines a paradox about nearly all the protagonists discussed in this section whose creators have attempted to divert criminal responsibility from their shoulders. With the single exception of Crane's gambler in "The Blue Hotel," all the murderers meet death as the appropriate punishment for their brutal crimes: Wieland commits suicide, McTeague dies horribly under the desert sun, Romano and Thomas are both electrocuted. In every case, despite the authors' lip service to doctrines which attempt to absolve criminals from the consequences of their actions, the reader feels that justice has been done.

THE VICTIM

Fiction rarely portrays crime as the victim sees it. One reason, since the crime is frequently murder, is that he simply disappears from the scene, although he may not disappear from the plot: Barney Quill, dead before *Anatomy of a Murder* begins, permeates the novel. The victim may be someone who deserved to die, like the macho rapist Quill, or over whose loss the reader can feel few pangs, such as the brutal policeman in *Knock on Any Door* or Bob Ewell in *To Kill a Mockingbird,* stabbed barely in time to prevent his killing the Finch children. On the other hand, fictional portrayals of murder victims, when they do occur, seize the imagination powerfully. Trina McTeague's grisly death is painted with harrowing intensity, as is the family murder in "A Good Man Is Hard to Find."

Such examples offer clues for a relatively arcane area of investigation: to what extent do the victim's own attitudes and behavior contribute to his demise? After the witnesses in "The Blue Hotel" tumble into the street, "the corpse of the Swede, alone in the saloon, had its eyes fixed upon a dreadful legend that dwelt atop of the cash-machine: 'This registers the amount of your purchase.' " The white Mary Dalton in *Native Son,* whose condescending pseudo-doliberalism toward her father's new black chauffeur takes the form of getting drunk with him so that he has to carry

her to her bedroom and put her to bed, invites her death. Claggart in *Billy Budd* solicits his own destruction by falsely accusing the Handsome Sailor of fomenting mutiny. Barney Quill courts murder by raping the wife of the man who subsequently killed him.

More subtly, fiction suggests that the victim may fail to exercise ordinary prudence in an intimate situation, treating someone dangerous with unwary compassion. A pathetic example of this tendency is revealed by the horrified Bessie Mears in *Native Son,* whose premeditated murder by Bigger Thomas occurs after he has coerced her into joining him in an extortion scheme based on Mary Dalton's death. She agrees to go off with him to a deserted building, where he rapes and beats her, throwing her body down an air shaft. The point is made explicit by his own lawyer, Boris Max. He consistently describes Bigger not as a responsible individual, but as the symbol for a collective entity so bestialized that "at the sight of a kind face it does not lie down upon its back and kick up its heels playfully to be tickled and stroked. No; it leaps to kill."

THE WITNESS

Graphic examples of human slaughter in fiction, as witnesses actually perceive it, emphasize the concrete incident or dramatize specific clues. In "A Rose for Emily," the "witnesses" are the Jefferson townspeople; what they see is not the crime itself, but signs from which a particularly bizarre necrophilic murder is inferred. It is never made explicit, however; the reader himself is forced to be a witness, drawing his own conclusions. Other crimes or their immediate aftermath are vividly described. Thus Trina McTeague discovers Maria Zerkow's body with the throat cut; her coming upon Maria's corpse ominously foreshadows the discovery that someone will later make of her own. In "The Blue Hotel," a small group in a western saloon witness the braggart Swede's murder. When the gambler's knife shot forward, "a human body, this citadel of virtue, wisdom, power, was pierced as easily as if it had been a melon. . . . The bartender found himself hanging limply to the arm of a chair and gazing into the eyes of a murderer." Another direct account is presented in *All the King's Men.* Dr. Adam Stanton, discovering that his sister is the governor's mistress, shoots Willie Stark and is immediately gunned down by his bodyguard. The description by Jack Burden, the narrator, is peculiarly poignant because he is inextricably tangled with all these characters.

APPREHENDING THE CRIMINAL

The detective

Poe's "The Murders in the Rue Morgue" and "The Purloined Letter" created the detective's special attributes, emphasizing his analytical or deductive powers. Sometimes he is a member of the official force; sometimes a professional private detective, like Nero Wolfe; sometimes merely a dilettante with a loose, informal police connection who dabbles in crime for the sheer joy of solving its puzzles, like Poe's C. Auguste Dupin himself. His idiosyncrasies set him apart from the ruck of mortals. Dupin is a bookworm, fond of nocturnal rambles through the Paris streets, who shutters his house during the day and lives by candlelight. Nero Wolfe, so immensely obese that he rarely stirs from his New York City brownstone, is an orchid fancier and a dedicated gourmand. David Wilson is an educated eastern lawyer, whose whimsical deadpan humor alienates him from the literal-minded yokels of Dawson's Landing. Ostracized and lonely, he takes up fingerprinting as a hobby and, through this means and his native wit, solves the murder in *Pudd'nhead Wilson*. Although the classical detective is, above all, an intellect, like Dupin or Nero Wolfe, the hard-boiled detective employs violence as his primary weapon. He is a very tough guy, cynical in his attitude toward his fellow mortals, and often displaying superhuman prowess at the bottle and in bed. Although he tends to be an expert marksman and a good fighter, he has no Marquis of Queensberry scruples. His physical skills are brutal and ruthless, more those of the barroom brawler than the adroit boxer.

The police

Fictional police, whether city, county, or state, are usually remarkably efficient. Their procedures frequently involve large numbers of professional personnel, sophisticated and expensive technology, and even effective extra-legal measures. However, unless one of their number is himself the detective, they lack imagination and tend to be intellectually pedestrian. The relationship between key officials in a police force and the analytical detective or lawyer (such as Perry Mason in the Erle Stanley Gardner series) is, therefore, apt to be one of grudging mutual respect. Again, Poe's tales furnish an outline, with Dupin describing the Parisian police and their prefect as attaining their surprising results with an ordinary criminal through "simple diligence and activity." But a felon whose cunning is "diverse in character from their own" foils them.

Dupin's condescending attitude appears also in *Anatomy of a Murder*, which describes "alert good-looking young state police troopers" with their accurate charts and measurements as being like eager math professors. The Chicago police in *Native Son,* however, are impassive functionaries. They methodically protect Bigger Thomas, who has murdered two women in particularly brutal fashion, from an angry mob. In both *Native Son* and *Knock on Any Door,* the Chicago police are white. By the time of Saul Bellow's *Herzog* (1964), however, they are blacks, still functioning with the stolid efficiency described in Wright's novel.

Although ruthless police brutality is seldom emphasized in the classic detective story, it is apt to be shared with the hero himself in the hard-boiled species. In serious fiction, procedures outside the law may achieve a rough justice. The Chicago force in *Knock on Any Door* use violent methods to identify and apprehend the murderer, clearly guilty but against whom only circumstantial evidence exists. In *To Kill a Mockingbird,* the county sheriff exculpates the reclusive Arthur Radley by making up a complicated accidental-death story to account for the stabbing of Bob Ewell.

The FBI

Although city police, county sheriffs, and—especially—state troopers are often treated with respect and some admiration, the Federal Bureau of Investigation has come in

for a severe drubbing. *The Doorbell Rang* pits Nero Wolfe against J. Edgar Hoover and his minions. With its widespread cadre of highly trained agents, costly electronic surveillance gadgetry, and nationwide tentacles, the FBI is one of the most formidable adversaries the portly detective has ever come up against. His abhorrence of and contempt for the powerful agency and its unscrupulous tactics are given extensive coverage in this popular novel, which concludes with an unnamed figure (clearly Hoover) ringing Wolfe's doorbell to admit defeat.

The FBI also appears in an unfavorable light in a serious novel, *The Just and the Unjust.* Its agents, with extensive legal education and experience, know just how much they can get away with in torturing a suspected criminal, Stanley Howell, into admitting his guilt. Hard-faced and efficient, they are careful to leave no marks on his body as a record of what they have done, but reduce him to such a physical wreck that his attorney has to ask for repeated recesses. Judges, attorneys, and local police all suspect what has happened and regard the FBI agents with distaste.

THE TRIAL

Although detective stories conclude with the apprehension of the culprit, on the assumption that due punishment will be meted out once he is caught, serious fiction often examines the trial, a "fascinating pageant" where his legal guilt or innocence is established. Both *The Just and the Unjust* and *Anatomy of a Murder* center on trials; and trials are significant in *Billy Budd,* "The Blue Hotel," *Knock on Any Door, To Kill a Mockingbird,* and *The Caine Mutiny. Anatomy of a Murder, Knock on Any Door,* and *The Just and the Unjust* describe the trial as an intensely partisan contest in which lawyers seek not truth but victory. In revealing imagery, it is a "snarling jungle"; a savage, "primitive, knock-down, every-man-for-himself" combat; a "damned hard battle" for "survival itself." Other metaphors are of a show, play, or "raw drama" whose "main actors lose all if they fail." In the trial as duel, the opposing lawyers, whose weapons are their "wits and brains," are "masters of overstatement, flamboyantly fighting for victory, for reputation, for more clients, for political advancement, for God knows what."

The reader of American fiction can pick up a certain expertise about courtroom tactics and strategy. Both *To Kill a Mockingbird* and *The Just and the Unjust* emphasize that aimless fishing on cross-examination is usually foolish and dangerous. Although the jury is an incalculable element, another bit of lore is that it telegraphs its findings as soon as it comes into the courtroom, never looking at a defendant it has convicted. Its verdict is supposed to be based on factual evidence brought out by the opposing lawyers combined with law relayed by the judge. However, following this procedure does not always give the result readers feel is just. Hence, the jury (to the exasperation of lawyers, judges, and reviewing bodies) may render a verdict which, although not in accord with the evidence and the law, nevertheless satisfies the reader's gut desire for equity.

The prosecuting attorney

According to Paul Biegler, the narrator of *Anatomy of a Murder*, "being a public prosecutor was perhaps the best trial training a young lawer could get . . . , but as a career it was strictly for the birds." Mitchell Lodwick, prosecuting attorney in this novel, is a clean-cut but inexperienced young man elected for his glamor as a football star and war veteran. Abner Coates of *The Just and the Unjust* and his superior, Martin Bunting, the district attorney, are honest, logical, and straightforward, doing a workmanlike and completely persuasive job. Kerman and Buckley, the prosecutors in *Knock on Any Door* and *Native Son*, are very different types—unsympathetic, driving careerists bent on swelling their records with convictions. Both see their duty as one of protecting society by upholding its laws. When necessary, Kerman clothes his disreputable witnesses in presentable clothes; and he coaches them with cajolery and threats, acquiescing in their being beaten up by the police to get their testimony. Nick Romano's counsel describes prosecutors as not caring "if a man is innocent or guilty. They're out to make a record for themselves." However, *The Just and the Unjust* gives a different slant: "A miscarriage of justice, with some good, brave man in the interesting and dramatic plight of standing trial for what he never did" is an implausible thousand-to-one chance, given the detailed process by which a prisoner is indicted and brought to trial.

The defense attorney

Defense lawyers, whatever their ethics or abilities, are portrayed as infatuated with the law. Although money is their primary professional motivation, they all want desperately to win their cases. Biegler says that "a lawyer caught in the toils of a murder case is like a man newly fallen in love: his involvement is total." Boris Max, Bigger Thomas' Communist lawyer in *Native Son*, is more the personification of a dialectical thesis than a fully characterized individual, but in his single-minded adherence to collectivist ideology he is sincere. In this respect he resembles the wise, scholarly Atticus Finch, in the sentimental and rather dated *To Kill a Mockingbird*, who is otherwise unique. Max and Finch, however, are unlike most criminal defense lawyers in American fiction, who tend to be at best indifferently honest. More typical than either is the defense attorney in *Anatomy of a Murder*, who considers truth only as a last resort. According to *The Just and the Unjust*, which presents lawyers more favorably than most American fiction, an attorney is a "professional liar."

Defense lawyers, if successful, are incomparably better paid than prosecutors. Good examples are Servadei and his partners, prominent shysters in *The Just and the Unjust;* and the amusing old windbag in *Anatomy of a Murder*, Amos Crocker, who weeps and roars his way through filibusters instead of making jury arguments. However, the fullest characterization of the type is Andrew Morton, who takes up Nick Romano's case in *Knock on Any Door*. A skillful mouthpiece for organized crime, he has luxurious, well-staffed offices and a magnificent home on Chicago's Gold Coast. Although he knows quite well that Nick murdered the policeman Dennis Riley in a particularly brutal fashion, he does not hesitate to spin an elaborate web of false testimony in an effort to secure an acquittal, going even farther than Kerman in suborning perjury. His tactics are so shrewd that the reader expects their success until Nick breaks down on the witness stand and confesses.

The defense attorneys in *Anatomy of a Murder* and *The Caine Mutiny*, Paul Biegler and Barney Greenwald, are somewhat more ethical, being careful to stay within the letter of the law. However, they do not hesitate to violate its spirit. Biegler artfully coaches his client, Frederic Manion; and Greenwald, Steve Maryk's lawyer in *The Caine Mutiny*, establishes that Lieutenant Commander Philip Queeg, against whom Steve had mutinied, was a "neurotic" and "paranoid." Greenwald's ploy gets Maryk acquitted at the general court-martial, but he is deeply ashamed of what he has done. At the subsequent victory dinner, he shows up drunk and says that if he were writing a novel its hero would be Captain Queeg. "You're guilty," he announces to Maryk. "I got you off by phony legal tricks."

The most admirable defense lawyers in the fiction I have studied are Parnell McCarthy in *Anatomy of a Murder* and Harry Wurts in *The Just and the Unjust*. McCarthy, most of whose own clients have fallen away because of his drinking, is Biegler's learned and industrious assistant. Wurts is a buffoon in his personal life, and his sterling qualities as a trial lawyer tend to be further obscured because the novel is told from the prosecution's point of view. But he is resourceful, bold, and acute. He has a real feel for the law, a passionate faith in the adversary process through which legal justice operates, and an acute insight

Dust jacket for Richard Wright's Native Son.

into the psychology and foibles of the ordinary men and women who become jurors.

The judge

Judges come off far better in American fiction than do lawyers, being wise and humane scholars who attempt to administer even-handed justice. Since our legal system charges them with instructing the jury in matters of law, they are often impartial founts of legal knowledge and may state the thesis in didactic novels and stories. Even Montague Irwin in *All the King's Men* had been, except for his single lapse, a "just judge" who had "done good." Others, like Judge Weaver in *Anatomy of a Murder* and the homespun Judge Taylor in *To Kill a Mockingbird,* are able, learned, and seldom reversed. *The Just and the Unjust,* with its three judges, gives us the fullest description of judicial attitudes and proprieties. The curt, severe Judge Vredenburgh is irascible, but he is also astute, competent, and fair. Judge Irwin, the "reserved and aloof" president judge, is strict, but has an air of "austere sweetness." Hating facts as symptoms of the "folly and unreason pandemic in the world," he balances them precisely against the statutes; but opposes any legislation which would enhance "the principle, false among free men, of preventing a choice instead of punishing an abuse." His rambling charge to the jury impresses on them what they need to know, his circumlocutions giving them time to mull over each point. It is, however, Abner's invalid father, Judge Coates, who presents the novel's thesis, pointing out the importance of the jury in granting an equity that impersonal law may not provide.

Probably the most famous judge in American literary history is Captain the Honorable Edward Farfax Vere, commanding officer of H.M.S. *Indomitable* in 1797, when mutiny was a constant threat. A handsome young impressed seaman, Billy Budd, was falsely accused of mutiny in front of Vere by the mysteriously depraved master-at-arms, Claggart. Unable to speak because of a stammer which afflicts him during moments of great stress, Billy knocks Claggart down, inadvertently killing him. "Fated boy!" breathes the appalled Captain Vere. Although he feels an almost paternal fondness for the luckless sailor, he appoints a drum-head summary court-martial to try him for murder during an act of mutiny. After the trial—whose facts are not in doubt—he reminds the members of the court what naval law prescribes, and they bring in the inevitable verdict. Starry Vere then reports it to the prisoner in a long and presumably emotional last interview. That his course was the right one is borne out by subsequent events. Billy Budd dies blessing Captain Vere, mutiny is averted, and an authorized naval publication approves the salutary promptness of the punishment. The point of Melville's story is that in the affairs of men time, place, and circumstance render necessary a judgment which may run contrary to the scruples of that higher justice only the absolute rectitude of eternity can afford.

The jury

American fiction makes its most telling point about our legal system in defense of the jury's key role in the vast, lumbering machinery of the law. Even *To Kill a Mocking-bird,* which presents the jury in a negative light, concedes its educational value. Although juries preserve a rough equity, they are neither particularly wise nor able. The unpredictability of their verdicts is stressed repeatedly, but is paradoxically the very quality that makes a jury trial democratic, since its weathervane results are never preordained. Yet, as Biegler tells Manion,

> "Even jurors have to save face. . . . If the judge—who's got a nice big legal face to save, too—must under the law virtually tell the jurors to convict you, . . . then the only way they can possibly let you go is by flying in the face of the judge's instructions—that is, by losing, not saving, face."

This is precisely what happens in *The Just and the Unjust,* where these theories are given their fullest expression. Two issues confront the jury: (1) Was Frederick Zollicoffer murdered? (2) Was he murdered in the course of a kidnapping? As Judge Vredenburgh carefully instructs the jurors, if they believe the evidence points to a "yes" vote on both these questions (and it clearly does), they are legally bound to bring in a verdict of first degree murder against Zollicoffer's kidnappers. Such a verdict, at the time and place in which the novel occurs, would have resulted in the execution of the two defendants. However, they did not actually fire the shots that killed the victim. That action was performed by their leader, subsequently captured and shot in an attempted escape. The dry, matter-of-fact district attorney, Marty Bunting, methodically explains the obvious to the bored jury. If they believe what the evidence establishes, they should bring a verdict of first-degree murder against Howell and Basso and assign the death penalty. But to the judge's exasperation and the dismay of the district attorney and his assistant, they bring in a verdict of second-degree murder, whose maximum sentence is twenty years' imprisonment. Even the defendants' city shyster, Servadei, recognizes their decision as "the caprice of a lot of stubborn yokels who could not be counted on to play the game according to the rules."

The scholarly President Judge Irwin then delivers a long, stern lecture to the confused and sulky jurors, stating that it would be inappropriate to thank them, since they had failed to understand their position and their responsibilities and had not discharged their duty properly. He then makes a nod in an outrageously implausible direction: "You had a right to find, if that was what the evidence meant to you, that neither of these men took part in any kidnapping." Since the evidence could not possibly support this conclusion, he ends by giving them a wintry smile and an indication of what their consciences must support: "You were sworn to give a true verdict according to the evidence."

The Just and the Unjust traces the way in which the jury arrives at its preposterous decision, what the immediate consequences of such a verdict are, and how its larger implications support our system of criminal justice and our society as a whole. Why did this willful jury astoundingly find against reason, law, and fact for second-degree murder, when its verdict obviously should have been first-degree murder? The novel suggests a number of answers.

To begin with, though killing Zollicoffer, a drug peddler and low criminal, was,

> of course, a crime, his death was no loss—even a gain—to society at large. Thinking along this line, a jury might do something silly, like deciding the defendants were not so bad after all. . . . To counter with law or logic was hard, for in adopting such a line of thought, a jury already had declared the intention to abandon both. Collective entities—a jury, a team, an army, a mob—often showed a collective apprehension and a collective way of reasoning that transcended the individual's reasoning and disregarded the individual's logic. The jury, not embarrassed by that need of one person arguing alone to explain and justify what he thought, could override any irrelevancy with its intuitive conviction that, irrelevant or not, the point was cogent.

Another reason is advanced by an FBI witness, "a liar but . . . certainly no fool," who "thought the jury was jibbing at executing two men for something they argued a third man had really done." Harry Wurts, the dedicated and skillful defense attorney, had underlined this point in addressing the jurors. He described as barbarous, futile, and disgraceful eighteenth-century laws making scores of crimes punishable by death. They were eventually abolished, he says, because juries refused to "bring in verdicts of guilty. Jurors might not be able to make the law; but they had something to say about justice."

Wise Judge Coates, however, puts the jury's decision in its broadest context. "A jury has its uses. . . . There isn't any known way to legislate with an allowance for right feeling. . . . Justice is an inexact science" mediating the ancient conflict between liberty and authority. Although the Finch family in *To Kill a Mockingbird,* bitterly disappointed at the jury's verdict, discuss the possibility of changing the law so that "only judges have the power of fixing the penalty in capital cases" or even of doing away with juries entirely, Judge Coates undermines these naïve notions.

> "The jury protects the Court. It's a question how long any system of courts could last in a free country if judges found the verdicts. It doesn't matter how wise and experienced the judges may be. Resentment would build up every time the findings didn't go with current notions or prejudices. . . . A jury can say when a judge couldn't, 'I don't care what the law is, that isn't right and I won't do it.' It's the greatest prerogative of free men. . . . They may be wrong, they may refuse to do the things they ought to do; but freedom just to be wise and good isn't any freedom. We pay a price for lay participation in the law; but it's a necessary expense."

These theories are implemented in "The Blue Hotel." In that story, the gambler who killed the Swede got a light sentence because "there was a good deal of sympathy for him in Romper." However, the negative side of the equation hinted at by Judge Coates is provided by the rather peculiar jury in *To Kill a Mockingbird,* which includes no townspeople, only farmers, no blacks, and no women. Perhaps in part because of its unrepresentative composition,

its verdict is only too predictable, but nevertheless flouts both evidence and law. Still Atticus Finch regards it as the "shadow of a beginning. That jury took a few hours. An inevitable verdict, maybe, but usually it takes 'em just a few minutes."

INSANITY AND CRIME

Ambiguity vexes the whole question of insanity and crime. On the one hand, fiction probes rather deeply into the aberrations I have described under "Criminal Psychology" without suggesting that they excuse their possessors from responsibility for their actions. On the other hand, insanity as a legal concept nearly always results in a perversion of justice for two quite contradictory reasons. Although an insanity defense may allow the perpetrator of a crime to be freed (as in *Anatomy of a Murder*), it may also, quite to the contrary, result in abrogation of his constitutional rights and a far more severe punishment than he would have received had he been declared sane and guilty. This is what happens in *One Flew Over the Cuckoo's Nest.*

Insanity and *sanity* as legal ploys in fictional works are terms with so little relevance to questions of criminal responsibility that shrewd lawyers can manipulate them in almost any direction they choose, capitalizing on the absence of consensus among psychiatrists. Thus, although Barney Greenwald believes that Steve Maryk has foolishly allowed himself to be misled by the venal Tom Keefer, he nevertheless agrees to defend him and cynically maneuvers "expert" witnesses into indicating that Captain Queeg, who had been pronounced medically sane by three navy psychiatrists, was a paranoid neurotic. The labels Greenwald pins on Queeg can then be distorted to justify Maryk's actions.

"Insanity" can also be applied to the defendant. Paul Biegler in *Anatomy of a Murder* constructs the entire case for Frederic Manion, being tried for killing his wife's rapist, on a plea of temporary insanity, a "decently plausible legal peg" for the jurors to hang an acquittal on. Manion learns his lesson so fast and so thoroughly that he successfully cons not only the judge and jury but even his own attorney, and the gambit works. The jurors find Manion "not guilty by reason of insanity"; he is released from custody on a writ of habeas corpus and, in a matter of minutes, walks out of the courtroom a free man.

Nevertheless, the comments on this book by the psychiatric scholar, Professor Thomas S. Szasz, are instructive. Dr. Szasz writes that although the jury's refusal to convict Manion "makes sense," his crime had "nothing to do with insanity." Szasz goes on to point out that "if the defense of insanity is sustained, . . . there are two basic possibilities" for the defendant, with an outcome like Manion's rare and becoming rarer. Much more likely is the alternative that acquitting him by reason of insanity will warrant his transport to an insane asylum after his trial, to be confined there until " 'cured' or until 'no longer dangerous to himself and others.' " Accordingly, Szasz recommends abolition of the insanity plea on two grounds: (1) it should not be used to excuse crime; (2) its consequences for the defendant are customarily dire [Thomas S. Szasz, *Law,*

Liberty, and Psychiatry, 1963; *Ideology and Insanity,* 1970].

American fiction supports his reasoning. Pretty Boy Romano, the murderer in *Knock on Any Door,* is adamant against being pronounced insane. His celebrated lawyer, Andrew Morton, announces: "We can build a case on insanity or temporary insanity." Romano, however, refuses: "No. I ain't going to cop no plea on insanity! Leave that angle out, see!" Bigger Thomas reacts the same way when the state's attorney tries to elicit his cooperation by suggesting a hospital examination to determine that he's "not responsible." Bigger's angry reaction is immediate: "He was not crazy and he did not want to be called crazy. 'I don't want to go to no hospital.' " Although both Romano and Thomas are electrocuted for their murders, *One Flew Over the Cuckoo's Nest* suggests that acquittal by reason of insanity would have been more horrible. McMurphy, who has naïvely chosen a mental hospital in preference to the prison farm after committing a minor offense, gradually realizes the unlikelihood that he will ever be released. Subjected to a series of technologically refined tortures, he is finally murdered by a fellow-inmate to rescue him from the empty existence awaiting him after part of his brain has been surgically destroyed.

PUNISHMENT

Punishment in American fiction covers a wide spectrum. It may not be assigned at all, as in the case of a shy recluse in *To Kill a Mockingbird* who stabbed the murderous drunk assaulting his neighbor's children. It may take the form of blocking the defendant's career plans after his acquittal (Steve Maryk in *The Caine Mutiny*). It may entail imprisonment, either short-term (as in Manion's case) or long-term (Tom Robinson in *To Kill a Mockingbird* or Yakov Bok in Bernard Malamud's *The Fixer* [1966]). It may involve indefinite incarceration in a mental hospital, with such ancillary tortures as electroshock and lobotomy (*One Flew Over the Cuckoo's Nest*). Or it may involve execution: hanging in *Billy Budd* and Ambrose Bierce's "An Occurrence at Owl Creek Bridge" (1890); electrocution in *Knock on Any Door* and *Native Son.*

Death is by no means the worst of these punishments. After the protagonist of *Knock on Any Door* began his relentless criminal descent, he was neither attractive nor sympathetic; yet, once sentenced, he achieved a brief integrity, recognizing what he had become and what he had done to his family. He is brave and composed at his actual electrocution. In death Nick Romano becomes, if not a hero, at least someone whose stoicism compels a measure of admiration. Peyton Farquhar, the captured Confederate spy, faces hanging with manly resolution. As his neck breaks, he has a vivid fantasy of escaping to be reunited with his wife and family. Consequently, his last moments are happy ones. Billy Budd goes even beyond Farquhar's experience, achieving a brief glory when he hangs. Just before he dies, he says clearly, "God bless Captain Vere!"— words enhanced by his spiritualized appearance as his body swings in the mystically rosy dawn.

Extended imprisonment is a much worse prospect for the condemned criminal than death. Manion tells Biegler that he'd "sooner die" than spend his days in prison. Tom Robinson, falsely accused of rape and convicted, cannot stand confinement. He makes a futile, desperate dash for freedom from the prison farm, where he is being held pending his appeal, and is promptly gunned down by the guards. A wrenching account of a long, tortured imprisonment makes up the bulk of *The Fixer.* Since the novel's setting is anti-Semitic Czarist Russia, this punishment has no direct relevance to American society, but it does reveal a distinguished modern American writer's attitude toward the crippling psychological effect of prolonged detention and the extraordinary resources a prisoner must call upon to withstand it.

Probably the worst punishment a criminal can undergo, as portrayed in American fiction, is incarceration in a hospital for the insane. Even mass fiction is beginning to hint at this. Richard Condon's mystery thriller, *Winter Kills* (1974), for example, portrays a ruthless industrial magnate delivering the ultimate threat: being "locked away for a long time" in a mental institution, "and I'm going to . . . see that you get a prefrontal lobotomy to help you wait for the years to go past." A gruesome account of the harrowing effects such a commitment can have is presented in *One Flew Over the Cuckoo's Nest.* The protagonist in this novel, who has unwittingly exchanged the limited hardships of a prison farm for the Kafkaesque horrors of a mental hospital, gradually comes to understand the capricious and arbitrary nature of the length of his confinement and the punishments that can be visited upon him. After being subjected to repeated electric shock convulsions which impair his memory, he undergoes a lobotomy which destroys his personality. Rather than allow this hollow shell to endure as an object lesson to those who confront the institution's staff, his best friend, another patient, murders him and escapes.

CONCLUSIONS

Certain tentative generalizations emerge from this rapid survey. Literature for a mass audience tends to confirm accepted values. Critical examination of these values in such fiction serves as a warning signal that sizable numbers of people are already beginning to doubt them. The negative treatment of the FBI in a popular detective novel is a cautionary example to the literary historian who remembers how widely read Harriet Beecher Stowe's *Uncle Tom's Cabin* (1852) was before the Civil War.

At a more fundamental level, high art diagnoses cancers in the body politic still unnoticed by most people. The horrors brought on by slavery in *Benito Cereno* are analogous to the institutionalized repression of *One Flew Over the Cuckoo's Nest.* If we follow this line of thinking, serious fiction suggests questions to which social scientists, including criminologists and penologists, should direct special attention. The dubieties that trouble the mind after one reads widely in the American fiction portraying crime indicate issues of basic importance to society. The exploration of values our literary masters have undertaken forces us to reexamine cultural assumptions that, in our everyday lives, we often take for granted.

M. E. Grenander, "The Heritage of Cain:

Crime in American Fiction," in The Annals of the American Academy of Political and Social Science, *Vol. 423, January, 1976, pp. 47-66.*

On the attitudes toward crime reflected in the detective story:

As the detective story shows, aesthetic and scientific attitudes toward crime are by no means irreconcilable, since both depend on a certain detachment from intense moral feeling. On the popular level, the figure of Sherlock Holmes with his combination of artistic and scientific skills and interests constitutes an imaginative synthesis of aesthetic intuition and empirical rationalism. The romantic image of the outlaw as rebel is, in one sense, an extension of the aesthetic approach, for it differentiates the bandit's admirable nobility of character and intention from the dark reality of his deeds. The romantic image also shares with the scientific approach to crime a concern with criminality as a social phenomenon. For the melodramatist, the brigand symbolized a state of social evil, just as for the scientific criminologist the criminal was evidence of a poor environment or a defective heredity. Though there are perhaps more points of similarity between the various nineteenth-century views of crime than appear on the surface, it is nonetheless quite apparent that, by the beginning of the twentieth century, a number of basic ambiguities had developed in the understanding and representation of crime. Though the concept of crime as a function of social context rather than individual morality was becoming ever more widely accepted, a residual moralism continued to dominate public attitudes. This was especially strong in America where one could find a traditionally religious and moralistic movement like Prohibition existing cheek by jowl with a romanticizing of the bootleggers who evaded that same law.

John G. Cawelti, in his Adventure, Mystery, and Romance; Formula Stories as Art and Popular Culture, *University of Chicago Press, 1976.*

Beth Kalikoff

[*In the following essay excerpted from her book* Murder and Moral Decay in Victorian Popular Literature, *Kalikoff examines popular crime fiction written between 1870 and 1900.*]

"There is nothing in this world that has not happened," detective Martin Hewitt remarks, "or is not happening in London." A world-weary Sherlock Holmes echoes Hewitt's observation: "There is nothing new under the sun. It has all been done before." [Late nineteenth-century] crime fiction reflects this grim perception of crime as unchanging, ever-present, relentlessly repetitive. In many novels and stories that feature murder, crime is highly organized and implacable. The calculating, cold-blooded murders of mid-Victorian popular genres are replaced by a larger, more completely amoral threat to decent society. . . . Late-century murderers in popular fiction kill for more removed and distressing reasons. Individuals or gangs murder for religious or intellectual—

occasionally even aesthetic—motives. The accounts of conspiracies, gangs, and cults in popular writing stress the stark proficiency, inhumanity, and moral depravity of late-century murder.

Detectives and their criminal counterparts show strong and ominous resemblances to each other; virtuous and murderous impulses are often lodged within one person. In order to combat highly organized professional criminals, police and detectives adopt criminal methods. But sometimes the crime solvers become criminals themselves for other reasons than the desire to see rough justice done. For revenge, for love, or for sport, detectives discard their professional responsibilities with alacrity, occasionally even using their special knowledge to escape punishment. Their liability to moral failings and human passions eliminates the final protection against thieves and murderers. Their deductive powers and their attention to the minutiae of crime only further undermine any hope for safety and justice. Holmes's special knowledge—of exotic cigarette ash, for example—might have helped him to become a master criminal, as he sometimes muses; the more adeptly police and detectives solve crimes, the better equipped they are to commit them.

Like police and detectives in late-century popular fiction, ordinary characters are also capable of extraordinary criminality. No one is incorruptible and no trusted member of the community or family is above the most hateful deeds or motives. In earlier fiction, sly murderers like Hortense, the maidservant in *Bleak House*, or Madeline Smith, who killed her former lover to protect her future marriage, shock because they are unexpected and incongruous; their crimes erupt from within protected middle- or upper-class settings. By the end of the century, friends, lovers, servants, and relatives are exactly those who commit murders: it is no longer incongruous for anyone to kill. Late Victorian popular fiction reflects a disintegration of faith in human nature and despair at the prospect of curbing crime. "There's the scarlet thread of murder running through the colorless skein of life," Holmes intones, and the very blandness of the "skein" becomes a constant threat of violent crime.

A Study in Scarlet, "The Sign of Four," "The Five Orange Pips," and "The Final Problem" are Sir Arthur Conan Doyle's most significant contributions to the late-century literature of conspiracy. In *A Study in Scarlet,* a man is killed violently, the word "RACHE" painted in blood on the wall above his body. "There was something so methodical and so incomprehensible about the deeds of this unknown assassin," Watson shudders, "that it imparted a fresh ghastliness to his crimes." Holmes discovers that RACHE refers to a secret criminal society that is not involved in this murder, a blind to conceal the identity of the murdered man and the motive for the crime. Later, the man is identified as Drebber, and his secretary, Joseph Strangerson, is also killed. After the surprise arrest of Jefferson Hope, the American who committed the crimes, the story unfolds in flashback: Hope killed both men because they caused the death of his fiancée, Lucy Ferrier, years ago in Utah. Drebber and Strangerson were Mormons, and Lucy's father had been murdered by them because he refused to permit his daughter to marry into the Mormon faith and become one of a group of wives.

Doyle depicts the Mormons as cold, frightening, and all-powerful religious fanatics. They kill those who believe differently or who present obstacles. The Ferriers come to live among them after being saved by Mormons in the desert. Converting to Mormonism is a condition of their rescue: "Better far that your bones should bleach in this wilderness than that you should prove to be that little speck of decay which in time corrupts the whole fruit," the spokesman for the Mormons says ominously. Ferrier becomes a useful and respected member of the Mormon community, although he would not "set up a female establishment after the manner of his companions." Lucy falls in love with Jefferson Hope after he saves her when a bull gores her horse. But John Ferrier is told that Lucy has interested the sons of two important Mormons, Drebber and Strangerson, and that she must choose between them in thirty days or else: "It were better for you . . . that you and she were now lying blanched skeletons upon the Sierra Blanco, than that you should put your weak wills against the orders of the Holy Four."

Unfortunately for the Ferriers, this warning is not hollow. The devotion to the Mormon creed is obsessive and inhumane; individual preferences must be erased for the common "good," lack of conformity punishable by death. A retributive force within the Mormon camp, called the "Danite Band," polices the behavior and speech of the faithful: "Even the most saintly dared only to whisper their religious opinions with bated breath, lest something which fell from their lips might be misconstrued, and bring down a swift retribution upon them." No one knew the members of this avenging group: "The very friend to whom you communicated your misgivings . . . might be one of those who would come forth at night with fire and sword to exact a terrible reparation." The band was conceived as a way to punish recalcitrants who wanted to leave or distort the Mormon faith; yet soon "it took a wider range" and a shortage of women was followed by "fresh women" who "bore upon their faces the traces of an unextinguishable horror."

Horribly efficient, the "Danite Band" strikes mysteriously. After insulting the two young Mormon suitors who come to wrangle over marrying Lucy, John Ferrier starts receiving bizarre warnings. The first is a note pinned to his bed covers while he sleeps: "Twenty-nine days are given you for amendment, and then—." Every day a new warning appears in a different place, counting down the days, and Ferrier can not stop them or find out how they are posted: "Sometimes the fatal numbers appeared on the walls, sometimes upon the floors, occasionally they were on small placards stuck upon the garden gate or the railings. . . . A horror which was almost superstitious came upon him at the sight of them." Ferrier sends a desperate message to Hope, who arrives two days before the month is out. Although Hope sneaks the Ferriers out of Mormon territory, he returns from fetching food to discover Ferrier dead and buried beneath a newly dug grave identified by a handmade sign. Lucy has been kidnapped. Hope's pioneering ingenuity is no match for the Mormons' relentless

organization. He cannot prevent Ferrier's murder or Lucy's marriage to Drebber; by the time he locates her, she has "pined away and died," and he spends the next twenty years pursuing Drebber and Stangerson to revenge the deaths of the Ferriers. Finally, nearly dead himself from an aortic aneurism, Hope achieves his life's aim.

"The Sign of Four," "The Five Orange Pips," and "The Final Problem" also focus on organized gangs and criminal alliances. In "The Sign of Four," Major Sholto dies of shock when seeing a threatening face in the window, and his son is killed later; the murderer leaves a note reading "The sign of the four" by Bartholomew Sholto's body. Greed and revenge animate these fatal events. Four men sign a treasure map indicating vast riches that are inaccessible because Jonathan Small, their leader, was in prison; two officers who learn of the treasure rob the men, and Bartholomew Sholto, one conspirator's son, is killed by Small's savage associate. As in *A Study in Scarlet,* alliances quickly become criminal with fatal consequences for innocent people. "The Five Orange Pips" presents the fatal "outrages" of the Ku Klux Klan, who murder opponents after sending them a warning "in some fantastic but generally recognized shape—a sprig of oak-leaves in some parts, melon seeds or orange pips in others." Like the "Danite Band," the KKK is omnipotent and fearfully effective: "So perfect was the organization of the society, and so systematic its methods, that there is hardly a case upon record where any man succeeded in braving it with impunity, or in which any of its outrages were traced home to the perpetrators." Although Holmes discovers the identities of two KKK murderers, he does not uncover the entire group to which they belong.

In "The Final Problem," organized crime is given a face: that of "the Napoleon of crime," Professor Moriarty. Brilliant, evil Moriarty invents the most various and sophisticated crimes in London; as with the "Danite Band" or the KKK, criminals under his direction may be captured without impeding the murderous activities of the whole organization. Holmes is frustrated by Moriarty's invisibility, which seems to accentuate his triumph over the great detective: "The man pervades London, and no one has heard of him. That's what puts him on a pinnacle in the records of crime," Holmes explains to Watson. His evil intellect directs a vast criminal network: "He is the organizer of half that is evil and of nearly all that is undetected in this great city. . . . He sits motionless, like a spider in the centre of its web, but that web has a thousand radiations, and he knows well every quiver of each of them." His anonymity is a taunting reminder of his brilliance, and only Holmes, a genius of the same order, even knows Moriarty exists.

The Valley of Fear (1915), written near the end of Doyle's career as a crime writer, returns to the theme of conspiracy with chilling energy. Dangerous, impulsive McMurdo joins Lodge 341 in Vermissa (a "most desolate corner of the United States of America") by undergoing a savage ceremony. McGinty, the "Bodymaster" of the Lodge, "sat at the head with a flat black velvet cap upon his shock of tangled black hair, and a coloured purple stole round his neck; so that he seemed to be a priest presiding over some diabolical ritual." It was "difficult to believe" that the ordinary members of the Lodge "were in very truth a dangerous gang of murderers, whose minds had suffered such complete moral perversion that they took a horrible pride in their proficiency at the business." Whatever ideological, political motives inspired their early crimes have degenerated into a few desultory remarks about differences among the classes. The Lodge members have sunk into the most ruthless, inhumane crimes, and their murders develop their own aesthetic:

> To their contorted natures it had become a spirited and chivalrous thing to volunteer for service against some man who had never injured them, and whom in many cases they had never seen in their lives. The crime committed, they quarreled as to who had actually struck the fatal blow, and amused one another and the company by describing the cries and contortions of the murdered man.

After being branded, McMurdo becomes a full-fledged member of the Lodge. Dissension in the ranks is quelled before it begins; one brother whose conscience has not atrophied frets: "Whatever we say, even what we think, seems to go back to that man McGinty." After reducing Vermissa's population further, the Lodge is finally halted by McMurdo, a wily detective in disguise. But years later, he is murdered, and Holmes recognizes the hand of Moriarty, whom the American gang consulted and to whom it contracted the murder of McMurdo. Even Holmes can not save this courageous, virtuous man. The story ends on a dark note as Holmes broods about Moriarty's success: " 'I don't say that he can't be beat. But you must give me time—you must give me time!' We all sat in silence for some minutes while those fateful eyes strained to pierce the veil." It is no wonder Holmes needs time; he is called upon, as Christopher Clausen observes, to defend "an entire social order . . . deeply threatened by forces that only he is capable of overcoming" ["Sherlock Holmes, Order, and The Late-Victorian Mind," *Georgia Review* 38, No. 1 (Spring 1984). Secret societies mean more than the sum of their individual victims. Crime is relentless and hydra-headed, as in earlier Doyle stories.

In order to combat crime that is so organized and ruthless, police and detectives adopt criminal methods. At times they circumvent, bend, or merely avoid the law when traditional systems of justice can not reach the criminals. "I shall be my own police," Holmes announces in "The Five Orange Pips," and with biblical appropriateness, he sends the killers their own warning; although the pips never reach the murderers, they go down on a ship in mysteriously severe gales. Holmes shares many qualities with Raffles, the debonair creation of Doyle's brother-in-law, E. W. Hornung. Although both are outsiders who are smarter than the rest of society, Raffles is a criminal, Holmes a detective. "Between them the two brothers-in-law evolved a conception of crime as a perfectly planned military operation," one critic notes [Anthony Curtis, preface to E. W. Hornung's *Raffles: The Amateur Cracksman*, 1899]. After seeing Holmes force open the catch of a locked window, Inspector Gregson remarks: "It is a

mercy that you are on the side of the force, and not against it, Mr. Holmes!"

The worry about inept police that characterizes late-century nonfiction becomes, in popular fiction, the uneasy suspicion that police detectives are corrupted by desires for publicity and bureaucratic advantage rather than for justice. In the Holmes stories and Israel Zangwill's *The Big Bow Mystery* (1892), the authors depict police as competitive thieves of credit. Capturing dangerous criminals and understanding what causes their behavior is secondary to receiving public acclaim for brilliant detective work, work that is often done by others. Not only are Inspectors Gregson and Lestrade less than smart, they also are distressingly plagued with petty rivalries; as Holmes observes: "They have their knives into one another. . . . They are as jealous as a pair of professional beauties." The police constantly steal credit from Holmes, and the sycophantic tone of the newspaper articles that often conclude one of Sherlock Holmes's brilliant demonstrations of deductive reasoning act as ironic epilogues:

> It is an open secret that the credit of this smart capture belongs entirely to the well-known Scotland Yard officials, Messrs. Lestrade and Gregson. The man was apprehended, it appears, in the rooms of a certain Mr. Sherlock Holmes, who has himself, as an amateur, shown some talent in the detective line and who, with such instructors, may hope in time to attain to some degree of their skill. It is expected that a testimonial of some sort will be presented to the two officers as a fitting recognition of their services.

Officers receive applause even for the wrong guess; after Inspector Athelney Jones arrests innocent Thaddeus Sholto, a newspaper article sings his praises: "The prompt and energetic action of the officers of the law shows the great advantages of the presence on such occasions of a single vigorous and masterful mind." The inspectors' dishonesty is minor and amusing; the implication that their top priority is rising in the ranks of Scotland Yard rather than helping to halt criminal activities is not.

The vanity and bureaucratic ambition that cause Scotland Yard inspectors to steal credit from Holmes and from each other seems to infect every character in *Michael Dred, Detective: The Unravelling of a Mystery of Twenty Years* (1899). Using a now well-worn convention, authors Marie and Robert Leighton present a victim whom every character in the novel has good reason to kill. Choleric and mean-spirited Lord Luxmore is murdered, and police arrest his daughter Lena's suitor, the virtuous but poor Paul Wingrove, for the crime. Wingrove had argued openly with Luxmore about his refusal to permit Lena to marry him. However, a duplicitous butler, a vengeful housekeeper who is jealous over Lord Luxmore's upcoming marriage, an erratic and secretive daughter, Beatrix (Lena's younger sister), and a ne'er-do-well aristocratic cousin, Reginald, all have sturdy reasons for wanting Luxmore dead. The possibilities for criminal alliances among them are almost infinite. Dred, the mysterious and moody detective Wingrove consults, uncovers evidence that points in turn to each member of the household and every character. The coroner, in his investigative capacity, addresses

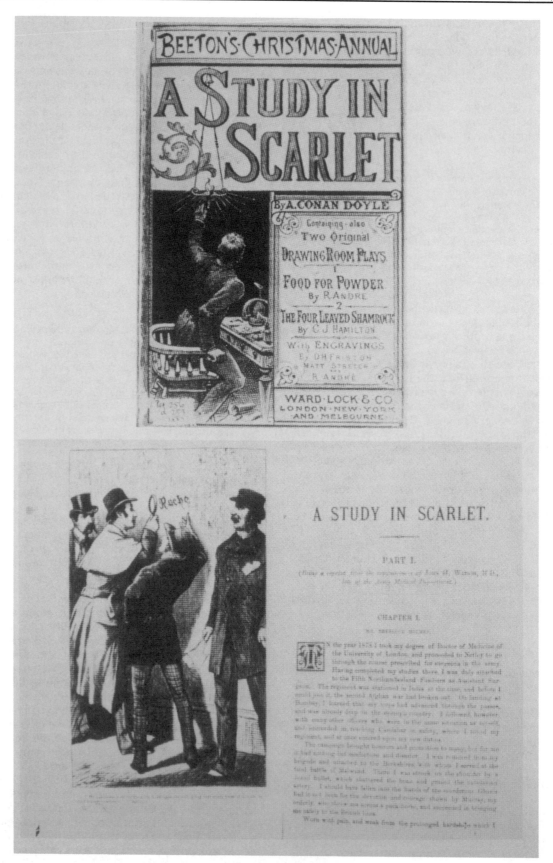

Cover and opening pages of the first publication of the first Sherlock Holmes novel, 1887.

the possibility of conspiracy, although he is not aware of the multiplicity of motives that would inspire such plots:

> There appears to have been a remarkable unanimity among the various members of the household in desiring that on this particular evening the rooms should be left in darkness—a unanimity which would suggest, were such a thing not practically impossible, that every member of the family was accessory to the crime, either before or after the fact.

As it turns out, Luxmore has been killed twice, and each of his murderers had no knowledge of the other. Mrs. Vayne, the malicious housekeeper, gave him arsenic to prevent his marriage. When Dred, in love with Luxmore's fiancée, entered the room shortly after, he found the victim in what seemed to be a fit and poisoned him on the spot using a syringe. Although no conspiracies actually existed, the Luxmore residence was alive with motives to murder Lord Luxmore, and only Lena, a stock melodramatic heroine who is less convincing a character than her selfish family and associates, grieves at his death. The grotesque "double" murder might well have been a quadruple crime, and the seething atmosphere of hatred, fear, and greed nurtured a kind of contagious criminality.

In *Michael Dred,* both hero and detective share the criminality of the other characters. Charming, self-sacrificing Paul Wingrove eagerly eavesdrops on Dred's courtship of Luxmore's former fiancée without shame: "I desired to gain information, and I had—and have still—too much at stake to care how I gained it. There is no way of meeting cunning except with equal cunning." Dred's courtship is desperate, sickly: "If you were the worst and cruellest woman living—if you were guilty of the blackest of crimes—I should not love you less." Later, Dred sends Paul a confession, explaining how he killed Luxmore—he removed the dying man's shirt and injected poison into his body—while pretending to help him. With ruthless efficiency, Dred spends the next weeks trying to endanger everyone who might be suspected of the murder he committed: "I occupied myself in accumulating evidence indiscriminately against any and every other person who could possibly be implicated in the affair. I felt no malice against any one of those whom I endeavoured to convict." Because it is not vengeful, Dred's pursuit of the other characters is perhaps even more distressing.

The most successful detectives in late-century crime fiction are those who recognize the inexorable way in which evil runs through "the colourless skein of life." "There is a strong family resemblance about misdeeds, and if you have all the details of a thousand at your finger ends," Holmes tells Watson, "it is odd if you can't unravel the thousand and first." Holmes's observation and his general ennui imply that a boring brutality infests Victorian London. Crime and criminals are the norm, not the deviation. Mrs. G., the dogged detective in Andrew Forrester's *The Unknown Weapon,* shares Holmes's suspicion of human nature: "We have to believe every man a rogue till, after turning all sorts of evidence inside out, we can only discover that he is an honest man. And even then I am much afraid we are not quite sure of him—." Grodman, the wry investigator of *The Big Bow Mystery,* concurs: "All men—

and women—have something to conceal, and you have only to pretend to know what it is."

Detectives could not possess too cynical a vision of human nature. Readers of late Victorian fiction repeatedly witness the homicidal natures of "decent" as well as underworld characters. In "The Poisoner," investigator Paul Beck is saddened but unsurprised to learn that Susan, "a quiet, shy little body" beloved for her placidity and good nature, is a two-time murderer. After she and her accomplice, Dr. Coleman, are discovered, she commits suicide, and her romantic death jars with what the reader now knows to be her terrible ruthlessness:

> Behind the bright chintz curtains, on the white counterpane, Susan Coolin lay dead—soft, pure, and beautiful as a white lily. The wealth of light golden hair lay scattered loose on her pillow like a saint's halo—a tender smile was on her dead lips. She seemed a statue of sleeping innocence, carved by a master-hand.

"It's wonderful," observes Beck, "that a fiend should look so like an angel." Especially grotesque is her lack of viciousness; we never really see what lies beneath her gentle exterior except when she flees, terrified, as Beck invites her to eat a piece of poisoned cake she intended for someone else. Unlike Lady Audley's sotto voce triumph, or the energetic lust of Edith Archbold, we have no way to understand Susan's evil; one character concludes that Dr. Coleman "tempted her to this," and her devotion to him may be one explanation, but it is insufficient. Similarly, in "Murder by Proxy," jovial, affectionate Eric commits a murder and does his best to indict his cousin for the crime, while pretending to save him. Only under Beck's canny questioning does Eric break down, changing to a nearly bestial killer in a matter of moments; a voice escaped him, "a voice unlike his own—loud, harsh, hardly articulate; such a voice might have been heard in the torture chamber in the old days when the strain on the rack grew unbearable." Like Sweeney Todd, Eric falls in a timely fit after confessing. But where even his less-than-bright apprentice suspects Todd of crime, Eric remains untarnished by his beleaguered cousin's accusations. Only Beck figures out the truth, and his complete lack of faith in human nature makes him an acute detective.

Israel Zangwill's *The Big Bow Mystery,* a distinctive story that was greatly popular in its time, illustrates many late-century themes in popular crime fiction, especially the corruption of the police by desires for publicity, the criminality of the detective, and the murderer's impersonal motive. In this novel, suspicion of and contempt for the police are palpable. When observing that there were no suspects in the shocking murder of middle-class philanthropist Arthur Constant, the narrator dryly remarks: "The police could not even manufacture a clue." George Grodman, a famous former inspector of Scotland Yard, is summoned to Constant's room by his neighbor Mrs. Drabdump when Constant, her tenant, does not awaken. Grodman lives to humiliate his successor, posh and progressive Edward Wimp. Unconcerned with Wimp's effectiveness as a detective, although Wimp indeed is notorious for "putting two and two together to make five," Grodman fears that his own accomplishments will fade because of his successor's good fortune or deceit: "He [Wimp] almost threatened to eclipse the radiant tradition of Grodman by some wonderfully ingenious bits of workmanship." Grodman writes a letter to the *Pell Mell Press,* taunting Wimp for his inability to quickly solve the case: "The Department has had several notorious failures of late. It is not what it used to be. Crime is becoming impertinent." A letter signed "Scotland Yard" retorts that Grodman's "judgment is failing him in his old age," and the rivalry continues even at Christmas dinner; Wimp has invited Grodman so that he might pump him for information. Grodman attends for the same reason.

The drama of agitator Tom Mortlake's arrest by Wimp at a working-class gathering, where Gladstone is to dedicate a portrait of Constant, is followed by the excitement of Mortlake's conviction, over working-class and liberal protests. But to Grodman, it is all merely background to his professional duel with Wimp. At the moment Mortlake is convicted, Grodman feels no pity or outrage, although he knows Mortlake is innocent: "Wimp had won; Grodman felt like a whipped cur." Grodman is ready to have Denzil Cantercot, the ghostwriter of Grodman's best-selling memoirs, arrested to punish him for bringing information about the murder to Wimp. (Even Grodman's book, *Criminals I Have Caught,* is false, written entirely by Cantercot, who receives no credit for it.) Although their competitiveness and dishonesty is humorous, Wimp is morally corrupt—he will arrest anyone to get credit for solving the crime—and Grodman turns out to be corrupt *and* criminal.

Like other detectives in late Victorian fiction, Grodman breaks the law. The night before Mortlake's execution, after Grodman had organized several unsuccessful actions for his release, the former detective visits the Home Secretary. During a lengthy, abstract lecture on the vagaries of evidence and human psychology, he informs the Home Secretary that since Mrs. Drabdump *expected* to see Constant dead when she and Grodman burst into his room, that is what she saw, although Constant was really only "sleeping the sleep of the just" under the influence of a sleeping powder Grodman had given him the night before for his toothache. When Grodman cries out as if he saw something horrible, "a mist as of blood swam before Mrs. Drabdump's eyes. She cowered back . . . she shut off the dreaded sight with her hands. In that instant I made my cut." Thus, Grodman commits murder in front of a witness and confesses only to thwart Wimp's victory. Saving the innocent Mortlake is secondary:

> That Wimp should achieve a reputation he did not deserve, and overshadow all his predecessors by dint of a colossal mistake, this seemed to be intolerable. . . . As the overweening Wimp could not be allowed to go down to posterity as the solver of this terrible mystery, I decided that the condemned man might just as well profit by his exposure.

Grodman kills Constant for the pleasure of devising a crime that can not be solved. Where Lord Luxmore deserves his death, Constant is preternaturally good, and Grodman's decision to kill him is simply perverse: "I do not know when I have ever taken to a man more. . . . It

is a pity humanity should have been robbed of so valuable a life. But it had to be." He shares with Cantercot an appreciation of the aesthetic: "And yet criminals would go on sinning, and giving themselves away, in the same old grooves—no originality, no dash, no individual insight, no fresh conception!" He longed to show criminals "their lack of artistic feeling and restraint." Grodman is eventually robbed even of his confession when the Home Secretary reveals that last-minute evidence clearing Mortlake had arrived just before Grodman did, and the former detective shoots himself. Yet Grodman comes dangerously close to achieving his goal, and only an ironic twist of plot prevents him from getting away untouched.

Robert Louis Stevenson's *Dr. Jekyll and Mr. Hyde* (1886) may be the most vivid late-century work exposing the criminality of human nature. Although Nabokov warns the reader against interpreting Stevenson's work as an allegory about warring decency and wickedness in ordinary people ["Dr. Jekyll and Mr. Hyde," in *Lectures on Literature,* 1980], Stevenson himself invited such an interpretation. "The gnome is interesting, I think," he wrote to his American friend, W. H. Low, "and he came out of a deep mine, where he guards the fountain of tears. . . . The gnome's name is JEKYLL AND HYDE: I believe you will find he is likewise quite willing to answer to the name of Low or Stevenson." The novel abounds with monstrous imagery—Jekyll's "other" is variously described as "some damned Juggernaut" and "something troglodytic"—but Jekyll's similarity to ordinary people, not his freakishness as Hyde, emerges as more deeply distressing. Hyde, the murderer and brutal half-man, exists within Jekyll embryonically before the good doctor ever conceives of the experiment that helps to conjure him up in fact. Reserved, rational Utterson, Dr. Jekyll's lawyer, suspects an evil he cannot name, and goes to Dr. Lanyon to inquire about their philanthropic, strangely preoccupied, mutual friend. Lanyon has had a falling-out with his fellow medical man because of Jekyll's theories: "It is more than ten years since Henry Jekyll became too fanciful for me. He began to go wrong, wrong in mind." We learn, when reading Jekyll's confession, that his dangerous proclivities existed even before Lanyon's disapproval of his impractical experiments.

The doubleness of his nature was an accomplished fact by the time Jekyll reached "years of reflection":

> And indeed the worst of my faults was a certain impatient gaiety of disposition such as has made the happiness of many, but such as I found it hard to reconcile with my imperious desire to carry my head high, and wear a more than commonly grave countenance before the public. . . . I concealed my pleasures. . . . I stood already committed to a profound duplicity of life.

As he begins to consider his own duality, Jekyll comes to believe that "man is not truly one, but truly two." He is, he realizes, "radically both" sides of the duality, and Hyde springs directly from the evil side of the doctor's nature. Hyde does not victimize the doctor because of his respectability, but because of his amoral desires. Stevenson's reference to Jekyll's secret pleasures "hints at the stereotype of the 'respectable' gentleman's . . . peccadilloes in the upper regions of the Victorian underworld" [Michael Wheeler, *English Fiction of the Victorian Period 1830–1890*, 1985]. Jekyll's experiments release "the beast within."

Jekyll is not morally different from other citizens, but his medical knowledge enables him to become entirely his bestial self. He knows he must choose between his two natures:

> Strange as my circumstances were, the terms of this debate are as old and commonplace as man; and it fell out with me, as it falls with so vast a majority of my fellows, that I chose the better part, and was wanting in the strength to keep to it.

Tellingly, it is as Jekyll, not as Hyde, that he eventually "was once more tempted to trifle with my conscience; and it was as an ordinary secret sinner that I at last fell before the assaults of temptation." After Hyde has brutally murdered Sir Danvers Carew and Jekyll resolves never to indulge his other self again, he reflects one day: "I was like my neighbours; and then I smiled, comparing myself with other men, comparing my active goodwill with the lazy cruelty of their neglect." At that "vainglorious" thought, he turns into Hyde. His unconscious is his murderer, and he is afraid to sleep: "If I sleep, or even dozed for a moment in my chair, it is always as Hyde that I awakened." By ordinary standards, Jekyll is, as a philanthropist and friend, a good person; his eruption into Hyde is caused by his slyness and his humanity. Moreover, Hyde's wickedness is stronger than Jekyll's virtue. This essential possibility for evil we keep repressed, but sooner or later it will burst out.

Detectives and philanthropists are as dangerous as those they seek to capture or reform. Behind this late-century belief in the essential criminality of human nature is a loss of faith in divine justice. As Hyde, Jekyll scrawls terrible blasphemies in a pious work, and Utterson is partly right when he concludes at first that his friend is driven by some past sins: "In the law of God there is no statute of limitations." But if characters in late-century fiction believe in God, they only believe in a punishing deity; events are generally considered to be ruled by an amoral, careless fate. "Chance!" observes Mrs. G. "In the history of crime and its detection chance plays the chief character." Tormented Jefferson Hope tries to discover whether human events are determined randomly or purposefully when he confronts Drebber. Instead of shooting or strangling him, he gives him the choice of two pills, one poisoned: "Choose and eat. There is death in one and life in the other. I shall take what you leave. Let us see if there is justice upon the earth, or if we are ruled by chance." Drebber's death suggests that justice exists, but, as Umberto Eco notes, "in fictional possible worlds things go better" ["Horns, Hooves, Insteps: Some Hypotheses on Three Types of Abduction," in *The Sign of Three: Dupin, Holmes, Peirce,* ed. Umberto Eco and Thomas A. Sebeok, 1983]. And even in the possible world of Jefferson Hope, belief in a beneficent, guiding presence is compromised by the shadow of the "Danite Band," Lucy's awful marriage and death, and

Hope's blighted life. Justice is not divine; instead, it is a lucky toss of the dice.

> *Beth Kalikoff, "Fiction, 1870-1900," in her* Murder and Moral Decay in Victorian Popular Literature, *UMI Research Press, 1986, pp. 157-68.*

LITERARY PERSPECTIVES ON CRIME AND PUNISHMENT

Edward Sagarin

[*Sagarin is an American educator and critic. In the following excerpt from his* Raskolnikov and Others: Literary Images of Crime, Punishment, Redemption and Atonement *he argues that literary depictions of crime and criminals can offer valuable insights into the study of criminology.*]

Among the most significant sources to which one goes for answers to age-old questions about the human condition, about the meaning of being a human being, about the nature of humanity and of the societies and cultures in which we live, is the legacy of literature, in the form of drama, poetry, and novels. Poverty and wealth, bereavement following death, forces that bring people together and drive them apart in a family, the nature of love and of war—all are depicted in the two millennia of literary work that is our heritage. Where are fatalism, incest, remorse, and self-punishment more forcefully portrayed than in Sophocles? Who can enlighten us more on the meaning of love than a long list of writers from Ovid to Lawrence? Where is the social evil arising from feuds between families and clans, and even by extension between nations, portrayed in all its tragic implications with greater understanding than by Shakespeare in *Romeo and Juliet*?

In this body of literature crime, redemption, and themes closely related hold a central position. For literally thousands of years, at least back to the era when the Old Testament was probably evolving as an oral literature, sin and the reaction against it—the reactions of both God and society—have been described, analyzed, and studied. In the earliest scenes of the Bible there is transgression and banishment, followed soon thereafter by fratricide, committed by the son of Adam and Eve. Thus humanity was only in its second generation—at least in this symbolic rendering of the origin of our species—when the first recorded murder occurred, and to this day the stigma borne by the transgressor is referred to as the mark of Cain.

Sexual violations were abundant in the Old Testament: seduction, incest, homosexuality. Problems of crime held the attention of Greek dramatists, Roman poets, and the writers of the Renaissance. Shakespeare delineated conspirators plotting murder, their suspicions, their consciences, entering into the minds and thoughts of Hamlet and his mother and uncle, of Lucrece and her attacker, and others. It was not only crime that dramatists and storytellers were depicting here, it was often suffering and atonement, expiation and redemption.

These are some of the major literary images, and side by side with them there grew up a body of thought, philosophic and later social scientific, concerned with the same themes. It was a dramatist but it might well have been a philosopher who wrote, *Homo sum; humani nil a me alienum puto* (Publius Terentius Afer, generally known as Terence: *I am a man; I count nothing human as alien to me*). But just what could be called human—was it anything that a human being had ever done or had the capacity to do?—remained unanswered by Terence, although it was a problem pursued by both philosophers and the builders of literature. There were in fact two bodies of literature growing, each looking at the same phenomena but in different ways, and they were not as entirely separate as at one time they might have appeared to be. After all, Rousseau was a novelist, as was Voltaire, and philosophic works, even scientific ones, were often written in the form of poetry.

There was a bifurcation, however, and literature in the artistic sense separated from social philosophy and social and behavioral science. If at times the former appears to be the more insightful, it is not to say that the latter is unproductive or that its contribution to this body of thought is unneeded, but that there was a parallel or complementary rather than a redundant development.

Criminology as a separate field of study flowered in the eighteenth and nineteenth centuries. It had been preceded by philosophic and theological inquiries into the nature of sin and transgression, and by the growth of criminal law and the rich and informed studies of the philosophy of law and of punishment. The interest in social science as science, given its great impetus in France and England during the first half of the nineteenth century, spurred the development of criminology. Then Darwin published *The Origin of Species,* and the era of evolution, anthropology, and biology was reflected in the growth and refinement of criminological thought, particularly in Italy.

In its parallel development with poetry, novels, and dramas dealing with the same basic issues that held the attention of criminologists—the motivations of people who transgress the laws, the nature of the reactions against them, and the struggle of such people to redeem themselves—criminology appears to have learned less from the literary masters than they had to teach, and the reverse is also true. Two groups of thinkers, both looking at the same object, were going their separate ways. Here and there one finds an exception, a major figure who bridges the gap, not by being both novelist and scientist or philosopher but by interweaving the knowledge of the two fields in a manner beyond what had previously been accomplished. Perhaps no one comes to mind in this regard more quickly than Freud, who drew upon Sophocles, Shakespeare, Dostoevsky, and Goethe and who in turn so strongly influenced Lawrence, Kafka, Joyce, and perhaps one might say all of twentieth-century literature.

Despite the rich influence that literature had on psycho-

analysis and that the latter had in turn on the former (as witness the road from Sophocles and Dostoevsky to Freud and then from Freud to Joyce and Lawrence), it can nonetheless be stated that the two roads toward an understanding of humanity were parallel but hardly visible to each other. Only indirectly and unsystematically, on rare occasions, did the rich treasures of one group illuminate and fertilize the work of the other.

In 1959, C. P. Snow noted that in Western societies there were two cultures, one consisting of scientists (he was referring to physicists and chemists and not social scientists) and the other of writers, and that the two were totally ignorant of each other's work:

> I felt I was moving among two groups—comparable in intelligence, identical in race, not grossly different in social origin, earning about the same incomes, who had almost ceased to communicate at all, who in intellectual, moral and psychological climate had so little in common that instead of going from Burlington House or South Kensington to Chelsea, one might have crossed an ocean [*The Two Cultures and The Scientific Revolution,* 1959].

It was not merely that they were not communicating with one another; it was, Snow contended, that "the intellectual life of the whole of Western society is increasingly being split into two polar groups." There were literary intellectuals at one pole, and at the other the physical scientists.

It is perhaps less true of social scientists, in that they stand as a bridge or an island between the two poles, deeply interested in and involved in the work of physicists and chemists and certainly not unaware of what writers, the literary intellectuals, are saying about the social world. But it is also true that the relevance of literary output for social science and of social science for literature is more immediate, more complex, more demanding than Snow's two poles allow. So that if we now begin to think of three cultures and not two, with social scientists occupying a midway position between the other two, we find that to the extent that these groups represent what Snow called different cultures, the consequences can be even more disastrous than he had thought.

Criminology is a part of this midway culture, and at this point it is probably true that criminologists have more to learn from the literary world than the reverse. To say that criminologists have largely ignored the body of belles lettres, with the psychoanalysts as significant exceptions, is not to deny that some attention has been given to the problems posed and the answers proposed in works of fiction. The distinguished criminologist Gilbert Geis, in an essay on Jeremy Bentham [in Hermann Mannheim, ed., *Pioneers in Criminology,* 1972], writes that Bentham presumably "does not consider the possibility that an outlawed act might actually serve to increase human happiness, . . . [that] the dilemma so brilliantly portrayed by Dostoevsky in *Crime and Punishment* in which a murder is defined, with considerable justification, as a social good by its perpetrator [is] thus morally justifiable." Geis draws attention here to an important issue, and he goes to a novelist, not a criminologist, for an elaboration and a portrayal of it. That the study of Dostoevsky is exceptionally fruitful for the criminologist can be seen from the manner in which Geis, or another reader, could take the statement on the definition of the crime by its perpetrator as morally justifiable, and carry it further, noting that it was only when Raskolnikov abandoned this vision of his own act that he was able to move toward rebirth.

Dostoevsky is mentioned almost in passing by America's renowned criminologist Marvin E. Wolfgang, in an essay on Cesare Lombroso, often considered the founder of scientific criminology: "By his supporters Lombroso has been referred to as a scientific Columbus who opened up a new field for exploration, and his insight into human nature has been compared to that of Shakespeare and Dostoevsky. Perhaps these encomia are exaggerations" ["Cesare Lombroso," in Mannheim, ed., *Pioneers in Criminology,* 1972]. What Wolfgang is here suggesting is that Lombroso's disciples had such a high opinion of him that they compared his insights into human nature with those of Dostoevsky (let us leave Shakespeare aside), and since such eulogistic remarks are thought of as possible exaggerations, the logic of the statement is that Dostoevsky's insights at least equalled if they did not surpass those of our greatest criminologists.

But was Dostoevsky himself a criminologist? Or Conrad or Faulkner . . . ? Or Kafka, Camus, Sartre, Tolstoi, each for one work or many, or Proust for his colossal study of sex deviance, a field so closely related, at least at the time he wrote, to the concept of crime? Without conceding that there is any justification for the two cultures, or the three, to fail to communicate with one another and to draw from others and hence enrich themselves, it is still worthwhile to note the distinction between the literary intellectuals and the social scientists, even when they examine the same phenomenon. If, as Wolfgang contends, . . . Dostoevsky had insights into human nature surpassed by few, and specifically into the mind of the criminal in committing the act, in punishing himself, and in searching for redemption, what distinguishes him from the social scientist?

The distinction between novelist and social scientist is a difference of métier and method. What is involved here may well be two entirely different ways of portraying the same human behavior, and with it, entirely different ways of looking at, understanding, and explaining it. Sociology is itself an art form, writes Robert Nisbet, in an essay in which he contends that sociologists have been portraitists very much like those who use canvas or put words on paper [*Sociology as an Art Form,* 1976]. Both look at social types, and both at social milieux. At the same time that sociologists were examining urbanization and its concomitant poverty and slums, cities and their squalor were the subject of the novels of Balzac, Gissing, Dickens, Zola, and many others. Novelists were describing workers' lives in factories and at home, and what better portrait of workers can one find than in the writings of Marx and Engels? The two groups, the literary artists (and others traditionally termed artists) and the social artists were using different techniques in looking at the same objects, in conveying the same messages, and in reaching similar conclusions.

In the eighteenth and nineteenth centuries the lines of similarity were even greater, for many novelists were not yet dependent upon metaphor, which is probably the hallmark distinguishing art from exposition, explication, and science.

Perhaps Nisbet is here a bit sanguine, his examples all too nicely chosen to fit into his theme. If one arbitrarily demands that a work of art must be contemplated as a thing of beauty, that it must, to qualify as art, be not only metaphor but also inspire a sense of esthetic appreciation, then only a few social scientists would qualify as artists (Nisbet would, it might be added, more than an overwhelming number of his colleagues). He even stops to take to task one eminent sociologist for his failure not as an artist but as a scientist—for the failure to have empirical evidence of a scientific nature from which he can draw the intuitive conclusion that he does. That is precisely the license permitted to the artist, never to the scientist; the novelist does not need proof, he can convince us by intuiting the truth. In that sense, sociology is not an art form and should not aspire to be one; what is needed is the communication that Snow found lacking, so that sociology and art can draw inspiration from each other.

Criminologists have indeed given the world portraits of criminals and, in addition, of the detectives and police, of families of prisoners, and of victims. While many of these are in the form of endless tables and statistical correlations, sometimes important even when boring but seldom punctuated by anything deserving to be called insightful, this has not always been the case. Some criminologists and other social scientists have made portraits that differ only slightly from what Daniel Defoe had sought to accomplish with *Moll Flanders.* That book, in fact, is not only in the criminological tradition, it may well be a forerunner of such later works as descriptions of criminals by Hutchins Hapgood, of a professional thief by Edwin Sutherland, of a safe-breaker by Bill Chambliss, or of a professional fence by Carl Klockars. There is something of a straight line, a common intellectual core and alliance, that goes from Defoe to Oscar Lewis, from *Moll Flanders* to *The Families of Sanchez.*

With the exception of Lewis, the writers wrote what came to be known as "own story" criminology, a technique developed by the prominent sociology department at the University of Chicago earlier in this century. Researchers ventured forth into the real world of hoboes and denizens of the slums and described what they found, sometimes in their own words and on occasion in the words of the subjects living there (itself a small difference, as an examination of a third-person narrative like Dostoevsky's and a first-person tale, as told by Defoe in *Moll Flanders,* will illustrate). Yet there are several differences that separate Defoe's *Moll Flanders* from Sutherland's *Professional Thief,* and although at this point the techniques of criminologist and novelist almost converge, they do not quite become identical. Three distinctions seem apparent.

First, Defoe's work is offered as fiction, Sutherland's as edited autobiography (with some slight changes to protect informers and preserve anonymity). That Sutherland may have more fiction in the work than he allowed or believed would not negate a basic difference.

Second, Defoe presents the story with a minimum of commentary, while Sutherland makes a running commentary as a sociologist-criminologist throughout the work. In fact, Sutherland's notes and analytic remarks are at least as important (if not more so) as the autobiographical confession of the thief, Chic Conwell. . . . It is true, also, that Defoe departs from storytelling in its pure form more than a modern novelist would do, because the art of refraining from explication was not yet fully developed when he wrote.

Third, Moll Flanders is offered to the reader as one person, with one set of experiences. Whereas Chic Conwell is *explicitly* presented not as one particular professional thief but as one who represents many, an entire genre, Moll is *implicitly* portrayed in a similar manner. This is so in the sense that all art is universalistic in its implications: it never says something about just one character, one situation, or one setting; it talks about the human and social condition.

What, then, distinguishes the criminologists, or all social scientists, from novelists and other artists? Above all, it is method. The criminologist has come to a conclusion about crime and related subjects through studies based on selected (preferably carefully and scientifically selected) samples rather than on one or several individuals (Freud and theories drawn from a single case notwithstanding). The samples are or aspire to be representative; just of what and whom is not always clear, but the idea of being representative is a *sine qua non* for the social scientist. The work of the scientist must be reproducible, not an easy task in the nature of social science, but the claim that the work is science implies that it could be replicated, giving the same results if all conditions were the same.

The criminologist takes several people, or large numbers, teases out the similarity of conditions, isolates the patterns of repeated factors, and makes a presentation from which conclusions are drawn. The writer, or for that matter the painter, has studied humanity in a unique but unsystematic manner. He has learned about the world by living in it, absorbing and illuminating its appearances and realities, a technique not foreign to the social scientists, particularly those influenced by the work in Chicago when that university's ascendancy was undisputed and those who have adopted the less empirical, more qualitative approach of participant-observation. But the social scientist, even when venturing forth to learn about the world by living in it rather than by merely asking questions about it, so often naively believing in the truth of the respondents, does so with training for this task, with previous systematic study of the people whom he is researching, with knowledge of former studies and how they were conducted, and with an obligation to test what he finds by comparison of his results with related and competitive theory and research.

It might appear, at first glance, that the scientist has the superior method, and if he has not revealed truths as penetrating as those limned by the artist, perhaps science has not attracted thinkers as great as those who have utilized literature as a method for dissemination of their thought. Such an answer is doubtful. Yet if the minds have been as great, and the method superior, why is it difficult to find criminologists with insights into human nature comparable to those of Shakespeare and Dostoevsky? Actually, the superiority of one method of perceiving or presenting information should not concern us, for both methods, in the hands of profound thinkers, are necessary, each for different reasons, to yield complementary portraits and the understandings that can be derived therefrom.

Artists and novelists on the one hand, criminologists and related behavioral scientists on the other, use different means to arrive at their results, different methods to explain them. The method of presentation favored by the artist is metaphor. The meanings are implicit, and they became more so with the development of literary style and the evolution of the novel as an art form. The method favored by the behavioral scientist is that of explication, and if this is the abandonment of metaphor, then it is difficult to sustain the concept of social science, whether sociology or any other, as an art form.

Dostoevsky, Faulkner, Conrad, and such other writers . . . as Kafka, Camus, and Genet portray for us people, social worlds, events, and circumstances from which we readers can deduce significant social meanings. The criminologist locates a representative sample, the novelist creates a representative character.

"In Dostoevsky's *Crime and Punishment,* based upon his own experiences with police and prison," writes Nisbet, "Raskolnikov is not only a highly memorable individual but also the image of a class or type Dostoevsky was fascinated by." Then Nisbet proceeds to contend that with Raskolnikov and numerous other characters from Balzac, Tolstoi, Dickens, and others, "we are dealing with a distinct, unforgettable *individual.*" But they are individuals who are also social types. To emerge as an individual is a necessity for the success of the novel as an art form, but were the individual not a social type, he would represent only himself and fail to give the reader a vision of humanity, as conceived by the author. Dostoevsky, like Conrad, Defoe, and others, chooses these individuals to be representative. The criminologist would not be permitted such liberties. He would have to establish their representativeness.

In the instance of interpretation, both novelists and criminologists have to be speculative. The portraits, characters, events, and settings of the novelist are like the data that the criminologist uses, but while the novelist offers only intuition to justify his choice, the sociologist cites statistical formulations and a body of material that has been culled from what has come to be called methodology. The criminologist brings forth the data from which he draws conclusions, but there is nothing in the data that demands those specific conclusions. Other conclusions might be equally justified, and sometimes are, with canons of scientific method, rules of induction and deduction, concepts of parsimony and falsifiability that the social scientist must fall back on to justify his interpretations. The novelist draws no conclusions, in the sense in which the scientist deliberately organizes his data into logical structures that invite succinct summary statements. The literary artist presents us with no statistics on per capita income and crime rates to ponder, but may describe the staggering difficulties the poor and the guilt-ridden must face in coping with mere survival.

The writer of fiction embodies his ideas with characters whose life rhythms punctuate the social reality of statistics with an immediacy and a poignancy unsuited to a scientific monograph. To depict reality solely in terms of equations and documents—and *solely* is not what the responsible social scientist does, whatever stereotypical images the public may hold of him—represents an insolence and a futility if the point of research is, after all, to communicate ideas. The insights the artist may bring to his project do not merely dramatize reality but inform us as well and deepen our knowledge of the world and of humanity. For example, Raskolnikov is not a cipher of a political creed, the creature of a polemicist. He does not transform his outrage at social injustice into terrorism but instead he crushes the skull of a helpless old woman. Even here, the deed, for all its abjectness, comes through as understandable. Dostoevsky shows Raskolnikov as a victim of a callous and insensitive social system, but he is in no way exculpated because he was victim before he became victimizer.

Though the modes of work of the literary artist and scientist are distinctive, these blur before the deepest and most fundamental goals of each: to make the world meaningful and comprehensible. The artist, whatever his medium, and the scientist, whatever his discipline, provide order to the world in such ways as to attribute logic and meaning to it. Both set in motion new kinds of associations between ideas and emotions and in so doing not only enhance our grasp of the world of men and women but add to it new dimensions in the experience of living.

In both art and science, the interpretations are inherent in the work, but the artist stops to allow readers and critics to continue without his aid. Both artist and sociologist can be said to be offering data; and while they differ in whether they will make explicit their interpretations, in neither instance should the interpretations be confused with the data.

Lord Jim, abandoning a ship and several hundred people to their fate, is an individual, and if he were not, readers would never be caught up in his sorrows or concerned about his destiny. He is only one person, but the fact that Conrad has chosen this person to portray, and not another, is itself a statement about that writer's involvement with human issues. The moment that readers visualize Jim as a sailor who deserted his ship, they have ceased to confine him to the status of the individual and have begun to ponder human frailty, indecision, and the meaning of lost honor. How representative Jim is of humanity, or even of a part of it, only the reader can decide: it is fundamentally a question of whether Conrad's vision of the world is a profoundly convincing one. But when criminologists describe a group of prisoners, convicted burglars, or victims of violent crime, the readers know, or are at least supposed to know, how many such people have been seen, how they

have been studied, what questions were asked, what observations made, what information elicited. The representativeness of the sample can be challenged, in a manner somewhat similar to the challenge that some would make as to whether Jim, Meursault, and Temple Drake represent more than themselves.

Thus the same problems are raised in the two cultures, but not by the same people and not in the same way. What seems to be occurring here is that two groups of thinkers are each bringing their own methods and techniques to focus on the same phenomenon. In different historical periods when great philosophical conceptions of humanity and the world became popular, science and literature reflected these trends in their approaches and productions. In writing about the Romantic movement, Edmund Wilson in *Axel's Castle* observed that in the seventeenth and eighteenth centuries artists and scientists "examined human nature dispassionately, in the same lucid and reasonable spirit, to find the principles on which it worked. Thus, the theories of the physicists were matched by the geometrical plays of Racine and the balanced couplets of Pope."

But Racine was not a Newton, nor was Newton a poet. In the problems to which these essays are addressed, we would not say that Dostoevsky was a great criminologist, or a criminologist at all, or that his contemporaries who were studying crime were artists, but only that some novelists and criminologists had profound insights into the nature of crime and the criminal, attained through dissimilar methods, usually without each other's aid, and often arriving at mutually consistent conclusions.

There are, then, two portraits, or types of portraits, as Nisbet would contend. But unlike Nisbet, I prefer not to see sociology as an art form (ironically, this statement is itself a metaphor) or the novelist as a social scientist, but to regard the two as complementary observers and thinkers, elaborating on the same aspects of the human condition but utilizing different techniques to attain the same goals: to make the human experience more comprehensible and meaningful.

The alienation of these two cultures from each other is certainly not complete and total, and one need not resort to the example of Freud to be convinced of that. The works of sociology not infrequently quote, as examples and illustrations, from novels, the better to elaborate on abstract themes: from Sinclair Lewis, for one, to depict the nature of smalltown American life in the 1920s, and especially its enforced and devitalizing conformity; from Kafka, to demonstrate the meaning and nature of bureaucracy; from Dickens, on social class and poverty in nineteenth-century England; from Dostoevsky's *Brothers Karamazov,* on power. And others. The American muckrakers included journalists and novelists—Lincoln Steffens, Ida Tarbell, Stephen Crane, Theodore Dreiser, Upton Sinclair—who portrayed a sector of society and various types of social problems, and sociologists have learned from them. Without the body of their works, who knows where sociology would be today. But let us not exaggerate: the impact has not been overwhelming.

Nor are novelists immune from the influence of the social scientist. A few have gone to the sociologists for their source material. For the most part, these have been among the minor writers, Marquands and not Joyces. That the great writers have drawn from psychology and psychoanalysis while contributing to the development of those fields only highlights the potential in a similarly symbiotic relationship with criminology.

The world has not been entirely impoverished by the gap between the two cultures, for in a more general sense, and in a variety of direct and indirect ways, knowledge accumulated by social scientists and expressed in their visions of the world has strong influence on literature. Over the past hundred years, Freud and Marx may have been the two prime examples of social thinkers who deeply affected the world of letters, but many others can be named: Charles Darwin, the Webbs, Lenin, and probably even more Trotsky, Gunnar Myrdal, György Lukács, David Riesman, Frantz Fanon, and perhaps the name of a criminologist might be found were the list lengthened sufficiently.

The bridges between the two cultures may be tenuous, constituting a fragile and inadequate connection, and it would seem to me that it is the world of criminology, not the world of letters, that has suffered. For Dostoevsky, who cannot properly be described as a criminologist, was nonetheless one of the most profound thinkers on crime and punishment, on suffering and redemption, whose creative work could enrich all of criminology, as it did the thinking of Freud, if criminologists would study it.

[The] issues of crime, sin, redemption, and atonement need not necessarily be conceived in terms of either literary metaphors or scientific idioms. Rather, the expression and elucidation of these themes is greatly enhanced in terms of a network of concepts borrowing freely from both literary and scientific genres. Following the work of some twentieth-century philosophers, such as Wittgenstein, Russell, and, later, the other "ordinary language" analysts, it is possible to speak of varieties of human action without reducing them to the language of behaviorism or the sometimes impenetrable discourses of other scientific disciplines.

The method of analysis developed by the linguistic school tends to show that human action, including criminal actions and events, depends on more than one "language-game." The behavioral and social scientific discourses constitute only one of these games, guided by specific rules which define "behavior" as something observable and logically connected with other empirical parameters. Yet, despite the power and prestige of these idioms, the word *behavior* and the concepts it represents and symbolizes do not exhaust the meaning of the word *action*. Within the scientific paradigms, the term *behavior* commits its users to speak of "contingencies," "control," "deterrence," "incapacitation," and who knows what other terms, still undreamed of at this time. Eliminated from the scientific discourse are perfectly intelligible ideas and concepts concerning beliefs, desires, hopes, and ambitions that belong to another "language-game."

Undoubtedly some ideas from one language-game can be translated into another. Nevertheless, each mode of analysis with its special ontological base and assumptions has its own coherence and structure which is not always congenial and receptive to ideas and information emanating from other systems of thought. Such ideas as conditioning, aversion, reinforcement, deterrence, and rehabilitation, making up the vocabulary of contemporary criminological research, must remain "translations" in ordinary language systems and thereby suffer a loss of meaning. But what about fear, guilt, violence, remorse, hatred, and self-hatred? These notions reside in another idiom having more kinship with ethical and political questions than with the behavioristic languages of the sciences. Science and technology may lead to a set of policies, but not to moral perspectives. Scientific "grammars" of action do not have a monopoly on meaningfulness and coherence, and a retreat into them as the sole means of understanding, discussing, and coping with crime would be disastrous because, among other things, the scientific enterprise would lose its breadth should it deprive itself of opportunities to cross-fertilize with art and humanism.

The word *literature* has a double meaning. In one sense it refers to belles lettres and in another to the accumulated scientific writings on any subject. The former is literary, the latter almost never so, and on the subjects of crime and punishment, both literatures are vast. As prose, literature in the literary sense, developed in forms of tale, story, or novel, showed an early interest in crime but went off in at least three different directions. One of these was the novel of the rogue, an often delightful creature whose peregrinations we follow, whose capers amuse us, even when the acts themselves are violations of the law. The rogues were central characters in many of the picaresque novels, and Tom Jones represents, as much as does any single character, this type of fictional person. In more recent times, André Gide delighted readers with Lafcadio (in *Lafcadio's Adventures,* also translated as *The Caves of the Vatican*), and Thomas Mann with Felix Krull.

If the rogue is a transgressor, his sins are small. Raskolnikov is no Tom Jones, and Conrad was dealing with problems far different from those that engaged Fielding. We can only laugh at Felix Krull, or laugh with him, thief though he is, especially when the woman who seduces him, begging in vain for masochistic treatment at his hands, finds that she can receive this only by his stealing more from her. In the picaresque novel the protagonist was more hero than antihero; although he was a scoundrel, he was more a rascal or a wastrel than a criminal. His actions amuse and titillate the reader, they do not appall and outrage. If they are transgressions, they are minor ones in a world of abundant enormities.

In another direction entirely, often traced to Edgar Allan Poe, criminality in literature became a source of novels of suspense. These were mystery stories, sometimes macabre, and in Europe this literary strand went off in the direction of the Gothic novel, more somber than suspense-laden and designed to fill the reader with an eerie chill of terror. In France the mystery was called *le roman policier,* and some have classified *Crime and Punishment* in such a category.

However, the difference is too great to permit the mystery novel and the fiction that delves into the mind of the criminal to be categorized as one. In the former, the reader is not left in suspense with regard to the meanings of human action as an abstraction; the wonderment, so often contrived, is over what those actions were and who committed them. It is a genre which, on some rare occasions, overlaps great literary treatments of crime, particularly when there is uncertainty as to whether or not the protagonist will be apprehended. For example, the "whodunit" element is not entirely absent from Faulkner; it is simply unimportant to an appreciation of his work. In a powerful novel like Richard Wright's *Native Son,* the reader is never left in doubt as to whether Bigger is the murderer. There is an entirely different kind of suspense involving how the memory of the event will weigh upon him, how it will motivate him in his actions during the hours and days that follow the murder, and whether he will justify the act and find inner peace.

Aside from the picaresque novel and the mystery, then, one is left with a huge legacy of works that illuminate, certainly as profoundly as the criminological literature, the propensity and capacity of humans to sin and to err, and their search for redemption and expiation.

> Edward Sagarin, "In Search of Criminology Through Fiction," in his Raskolnikov and Others: Literary Images of Crime, Punishment, Redemption, and Atonement, *St. Martin's Press, 1981, pp. 1-17.*

On the relationship between the publication of crime stories and the process of criminal execution:

The ritual of execution provided the criminal with a platform, metaphorical and literal, from which to make his words public; the gibbet authorized this amplification and publication of the criminal's tale. While the execution of a criminal is quite different from the publication of a fictionalized criminal tale, I would like to suggest that the reading public for the book and the crowd at the execution had much in common, as did these two diverse forms of publication. The ritual of execution was in fact linked to print, since the dying speeches of criminals were recorded and published as a matter of course following or even preceding executions. Likewise, accounts of executions were transformed into ballads, flying sheets, and pamphlets to be read by those who were not present. These printed works "were the sequel to the trial; or rather they pursued that mechanism by which the public execution transferred the secret, written truth of the procedure to the body, gesture and speech of the criminal," as Foucault writes. Both the execution and the criminal novel require, indeed presuppose, the observing presence of the crowd—who Foucault maintains was actually the protagonist of the execution—or the reader. The centrality of crowd and readership emphasizes the notion of publication inherent in the rituals of punition and publishing.

> Lennard J. Davis, in his *"Wicked Actions and Feigned Words: Criminals, Criminality, and the Early English Novel,"* Yale French Studies, *1979.*

Albert Borowitz

[*Borowitz is an American attorney and literary critic whose works include* Fiction in Communist China *(1955),* Innocence and Arsenic: Studies in Crime and Literature *(1977), and* A Gallery of Sinister Perspectives: Ten Crimes and a Scandal, *from which the essay below is excerpted. Here, Borowitz examines literary treatments of capital punishment from the eighteenth to the twentieth centuries.*]

One of the most fiercely contested fronts of the continuing conflict over capital punishment in the United States is statistical. In the case of *Gregg v. Georgia,* the Supreme Court of the United States was asked to decide issues of life and death on the basis of econometric studies of Prof. Isaac Ehrlich that concluded, contrary to earlier findings, that capital punishment has a deterrent effect on murder and that "an additional execution per year over the period in question [1933–1969] may have resulted, on average, in 7 or 8 fewer murders." In the winter of 1975–76 the *Yale Law Journal* published critiques of Ehrlich's work, together with his rejoinders, and strong words were exchanged about the appropriateness of statistical "regression" analysis to criminal conduct, the accuracy of Professor Ehrlich's theories as to the variables influencing the murder rate, the quality of his data, and the validity of his statistical technique.

The decision of the Supreme Court in *Gregg,* 428 U.S. 153 (1976), did not resolve the controversy. While holding that capital punishment was not under all circumstances "cruel and unusual," the Court rejected the statistical studies on deterrence as "inconclusive." However, the majority opinion stated that for some murderers "the death penalty undoubtedly is a deterrent"; and that "retribution," the second principal "social purpose" of the death penalty, is neither "a forbidden objective nor one inconsistent with our respect for the dignity of man."

There is a distinctly American flavor to the econometric debate over deterrence. As Dwight MacDonald pointed out many years ago in his essay "The Triumph of the Fact," Americans are enamored of statistics whether they relate to batting averages or to major political or social issues. Ironically, it does not appear likely that Professor Ehrlich's conclusions, even if confirmed by further research, will be a decisive influence on the judgments the courts and the state legislatures must make on the retention or abolition of capital punishment. Prof. Jon K. Peck, in trying to moderate the opposed views of Ehrlich and his critics, has pointed out the relative insignificance of capital punishment as a deterrent even under Ehrlich's own equations: a one percent change in per capita income produces a greater effect on the homicide rate than a one percent increase in the number of executions. Professor Ehrlich has himself emphasized that he has not advocated the use of capital punishment and that "the issue of deterrence is but one of a myriad of issues relating to the efficiency and desirability of capital punishment as a social instrument for combating crime."

Therefore, as we await further reports from the statisticians, we will continue, as our ancestors have done, to listen to other voices on the issues of capital punishment.

Those who take some guidance from the minds and hearts of our great writers will find that the literature of capital punishment is a primary source to be consulted.

The eighteenth century was for the English a heyday of crime and the Golden Age of Deterrence. England's so-called "Bloody Code" (which was not adopted in the American Colonies) imposed the death penalty for hundreds of crimes from murder to trivial shopliftings. The frequent public hangings which were carried out in London in the name of deterrence did nothing to stem an enormous tide of violent crimes and thefts, and appeared to serve the principal function of public amusement, not only for the working classes (who were generally given a holiday on "hanging day") but for the educated as well. The same age that produced this savagery also gave us Henry Fielding and Samuel Johnson.

Henry Fielding, who is known to us all as the author of *Tom Jones,* is remembered in the history of criminal law as a tough-minded and compassionate justice of the peace of Middlesex County and the City of Westminster (Greater London). Regarded as a founder, with his blind brother John, of London's police force, Fielding was faced with a terrible conflict between his recognition of the inhumanity of the frequent executions under the "Bloody Code," and his abiding faith that capital punishment, properly applied, could have a deterrent effect on the rising crime rate.

Fielding set down his thoughts on criminal punishment in his treatise *An Enquiry Into the Causes of the Late Increase of Robbers* (1751). Quoting Lord Hale, he postulated that the principal end of all punishment was less to punish for past offenses than to "deter men from the breach of laws, so that they may not offend and so not suffer at all." The humane goal of punishment then was to make punishment unnecessary at some point in the utopian future. Only with that hope in his heart could Fielding be reconciled to the infliction of capital punishment for petty thefts, for "no man indeed of common humanity or common sense can think the life of a man and a few shillings to be of an equal consideration, or that the law in punishing theft with death proceeds (as perhaps a private person sometimes may) with any view to vengeance. The terror of the example is the only thing proposed, and one man is sacrificed to the preservation of thousands."

And so the kindly Fielding set about the task of proposing how the terror of punishment could be maximized. First, the sovereign must renounce his prerogative of mercy and decline to pardon criminals under death sentence, for "pardons have brought many more men to the gallows than they have saved." Second, reforms must be introduced into the manner of execution, since a convicted thief, far from fearing death, often viewed his execution as a source of glory rather than shame, and the procession to the gallows at Tyburn (the site of the modern Marble Arch) as a triumph.

The greatest cause of the convict's bravado Fielding found in the very frequency of executions in the city—"the thief who is hanged to-day hath learned his intrepidity from the example of his hanged predecessors." The design of those who made executions public had been to add the punishment of shame to that of death, but experience had been contrary: the mob found diversion and the convict an easy heroism. One way of preventing frequency of executions was to attack the roots of crime, and Fielding in his treatise suggested a broad store of remedies—restraint of the passion for luxury, drunkenness and gambling; improvement of provision for the poor; stricter punishment of receivers of stolen goods; and improved administration of criminal justice.

While these goals were being pursued, the performance of executions should be modified. Executions should not be delayed so long that public resentment of the crime cooled and that the punishment itself became the sole subject of contemplation. "No good mind," Fielding wrote, "can avoid compassionating a set of wretches who are put to death we know not why, unless, as it almost appears, to make a holiday for, and to entertain, the mob." He also proposed that executions be to "some degree private" so that, taking added intensity from the imaginations of the excluded public, they could assume the terror of the off-stage murders of classical drama. Terror should also be heightened, Fielding wrote, by giving execution the highest degree of solemnity. He suggested that at the end of the trials the Court of Old Bailey be adjourned for four days; that a gallows be erected in the area before the court; and that all the convicted criminals be brought down together to receive sentence and be executed forthwith in the presence of their judges. Fielding had little room for appellate courts in his scheme of things.

Samuel Johnson, unlike Fielding, announced himself an enemy of those who tinkered with the time-honored festival of public hanging. In 1783, he lamented to Sir William Scott the abolition of the procession to the hanging site at Tyburn:

> The age is running mad after innovation; and all the business of the world is to be done in a new way; men are to be hanged in a new way; Tyburn itself is not safe from the fury of innovation. . . . it is *not* an improvement; they object, that the old method drew together a number of spectators. Sir, executions are intended to draw spectators. If they do not draw spectators, they don't answer their purpose. The old method was most satisfactory to all parties; the publick was gratified by a procession; the criminal was supported by it. Why is all this to be swept away?

Perhaps Dr. Johnson was speaking in jest, but he appeared to be saying that the public found Tyburn more entertaining than terrifying. Abolitionists often quote his comment that he had seen pickpockets working the crowd around the gallows though their trade was punished by hanging. In any event, Johnson's mind was so palatial that it echoed with inconsistencies. He displayed his delightful ability to take every side of an issue in his comments on the effect of a prospective execution on the mind of condemned criminals. In 1769 Boswell mentioned to him that he had seen the execution of several convicts at Tyburn and that none of them seemed to be under any concern. "Most of them, Sir," Johnson explained, "have never thought at all." This observation hardly provides a psychological basis for the eighteenth-century belief that prospective criminals may be deterred by the risk of execution. However, in speaking of the forthcoming execution of the clergyman Rev. Dodd for forgery, Johnson took an opposite position in his famous quip: "Depend upon it, Sir, when a man knows that he is to be hanged in a fortnight, it concentrates his mind wonderfully."

The efforts Johnson made in the unsuccessful campaign to save Dodd from the gallows may show more clearly where his heart lay on the use of capital punishment—at least in cases of nonviolent crime—than do his casual comments to his friends. He drafted Dodd's speech before sentencing at the Old Bailey, petitions of Dodd and his wife to the king and queen, and even a farewell address to Dodd's fellow convicts.

In the appeal to the king that Johnson wrote for Dr. Dodd, he begged that the sentence be commuted to exile and referred to the "horrour and ignominy of a publick execution" and to "the spectacle of a clergyman dragged through the streets, to a death of infamy, amidst the derision of the profligate and the profane." Johnson sought no credit for his humane intervention but on the contrary enjoined Dodd to keep secret his authorship of the numerous petitions and letters he had written for the prisoner.

Literary history also tells us that Gary Gilmore was far from the first condemned man to announce a preference for execution over imprisonment. A melodramatic precedent was recorded by Frances Trollope in her comments on an execution in Cincinnati in *Domestic Manners of the Americans* (1832). A great throng assembled for the hanging, not for traditional merrymaking as in eighteenth- or nineteenth-century London but to witness a novelty, for Mrs. Trollope notes that her informants told her no white man had ever been executed at Cincinnati. The convict, who had been condemned on the testimony of his own son, turned down an offer of reprieve from the governor of Ohio, saying to the sheriff, "If any thing could make me agree to it, it would be the hope of living long enough to kill you and my dog of a son: however, I won't agree; you shall have the hanging of me." The sheriff on the day of execution assumed his alternate office of hangman, but with his watch in one hand and in his other the knife for cutting the rope, made one last effort to obtain the criminal's acceptance of the offered commutation. Unlike Gilmore, the Ohio convict had a last minute change of heart, and when "the hand was lifted to strike, . . . the criminal stoutly exclaimed, 'I sign'; and he was conveyed back to prison, amidst the shouts, laughter, and ribaldry of the mob." Mrs. Trollope concluded: "I am not fond of hanging, but there was something in all this that did not look like the decent dignity of wholesome justice."

In the early nineteenth century a group of law reformers led by Sir Samuel Romilly mounted an attack on England's Bloody Code that finally succeeded in reducing the number of capital provisions from over 200 to 15. The battle for the absolute abolition of capital punishment was to be waged for the next century and a half. Among the outstanding voices raised in the cause of abolition during the Victorian period were those of Dickens and Thackeray.

Thackeray anticipated Dickens's more famous abolitionist writings by several years. Thackeray's essays on the death penalty, which I discuss in a chapter of *Innocence and Arsenic: Studies in Crime and Literature,* were the product of a highly personal blend of morbid fascination with public hanging and an intense, almost hypochondriacal empathy with the hanged man. His 1839 article on the execution of Sebastian Peytel, which he had unsuccessfully sought to attend, presents many of his principal arguments against the death penalty. First of all, Thackeray, like Balzac who had also interested himself in the case, was not sure that Peytel was guilty of the murder with which he was charged. He urged that we should "at least, be sure of a man's guilt before we murder him." In his peroration against the execution of Peytel, Thackeray forcibly put other arguments: that the execution does not deter others from crimes and is a source of entertainment rather than moral profit; and that imprisonment is an adequate alternative means of protection of society.

The scope of Thackeray's opposition to capital punishment widened in his "On Going to See a Man Hanged" (1840) written after he finally attended a hanging (of the murderer Courvoisier) and found he could not bring himself to look. The question of doubtful guilt did not now condition his views since the hanged man's guilt was conceded. But Thackeray's strong personal identification with Courvoisier was now supported by the insight that hanging was pornographic: that it brutalized the public by appealing to its sensual instincts. He was left with "an extraordinary feeling of terror and shame," springing from his partaking with 40,000 others in "this hideous debauchery, which is more exciting than sleep, or than wine, or the last new ballet."

Thackeray and Dickens saw each other in the crowd at Courvoisier's hanging but neither could catch the other's eye. Dickens did not react to the sight with the emotional immediacy of Thackeray. Indeed, public executions continued to exert on him what he called the "attraction of repulsion." Philip Collins in his admirable work *Dickens and Crime* has defended Dickens against the charge of being a "masculine Madame Defarge," but the fact is that he attended three or possibly four executions. Thackeray, so far as we know, gave up death as a spectator sport after the Courvoisier execution, and once turned down an invitation to a foreign beheading, commenting, "*j'y ai été* [I've been there already], as the Frenchman said of hunting."

Despite the ambivalence of the emotions that were stirred by Dickens's observation of executions, the Courvoisier hanging undoubtedly had a great impact on his conscience. He recalled the scene vividly six years later in the first of a series of four long articles to the *Daily News* in which he advocated the total abolition of capital punishment. He wrote of the effect of the execution on the crowd in attendance: "No sorrow, no salutary terror, no abhorrence, no seriousness; nothing but ribaldry, debauchery, levity, drunkenness, and flaunting vice in fifty other shapes. I should have deemed it impossible that I could have ever felt any large assemblage of my fellow-creatures to be so odious." In his arguments against capital punishment, Dickens emphasized as had Thackeray its tendency to barbarize and desensitize the community. He also quoted several examples of hangings of the innocent, including a report of a New York Select Committee. (Six years later in *Bleak House* Dickens satirized the desire of the public to see murder avenged by the execution of *somebody* regardless of guilt or innocence: the "debilitated cousin" opines to Inspector Bucket in his slurring style that he "hasn't a doubt—zample—far better hang wrong fler [fellow] than no fler.") Dickens also cited statistics that abolition of the death penalty in certain foreign countries had not led to increases in their murder rates. As an additional blow to the deterrence theory, he cited a favorite statistic of abolitionists: that according to a prison chaplain in Bristol, only 3 of the 167 prisoners he had attended under sentence of death had not been spectators at public executions.

The uniqueness of Dickens's articles, however, lies not in the assembling of these arguments but in the application of his fictive imagination to the potentially harmful role of the gallows in shaping the evil resolves of the would-be murderer. He noted that for the murderer with exhibitionistic instincts the death penalty and its attendant notoriety, far from acting as a deterrent, in fact provided an incentive. The "ill-regulated mind" of the murderer actuated by revenge, Dickens argued further, might impel him to kill on the basis of the mechanistic calculation that capital punishment, by demanding life as the price of a life, had removed the "base and cowardly character of murder" and that society by hanging him would receive its just bargain. Pursuing this line of thought, Dickens feared that the prospect of hanging might also incite the wife-murderer who could feel that his crime was not the cowardly slaughter of a woman but a heroic challenge to the shadow of the gallows and a response to its dark fascination: "Present this black idea of violence to a bad mind contemplating violence; hold up before a man remotely compassing the death of another person, the spectacle of his own ghastly and untimely death by man's hands; and out of the depths of his own nature you shall assuredly raise up that which lures and tempts him on." Later in the forties Dickens abandoned his advocacy of total abolition of capital punishment, but passionately urged an end to public hanging in his famous letters to *The Times* which were inspired by the obscene behavior of the crowd at the hangings of Frederick and Maria Manning.

Dickens emphasized that his writings against capital punishment and public hanging were not inspired by sympathy for the criminal, whom he claimed (in an article against flogging) to hold "in far lower estimation than a mad wolf." It was as a novelist rather than as a wavering abolitionist that Dickens taught most persuasively that the passion to save and conserve life is a communal force that binds and enhances society however worthless may be the individual whose life is saved. In *Our Mutual Friend,* a doctor, with the help of four tough habitués of a riverside tavern, does his human best to revive the villainous Rogue Riderhood, who has fallen into the Thames. The onlookers are rewarded by a sign of returning life in a man they despised before and would despise again: "See! A token of life! An indubitable token of life! The spark may smoulder and go out or it may glow and expand, but see! The four rough fellows seeing, shed tears. Neither Riderhood in this

world, nor Riderhood in the other could drag tears from them; but a striving human soul between the two can do it easily." This passage can do much to explain how many people can favor capital punishment in principle but hope it will never be applied, or struggle to save a Gary Gilmore from an overdose, though knowing that in another room a firing squad will claim him.

Prior to World War II George Orwell made a poignant contribution to the literature of capital punishment with "A Hanging" (1931), his eyewitness description of an execution in a Burmese prison yard. Recreating the horror of the scene with a novelist's eye for cumulative physical detail—the last-minute incursion of a prancing half Airedale, the "bobbing gait" of the slight Indian prisoner on his way to the gallows, his reiterated prayer cry of "Ram! Ram! Ram!" answered by the howls of the dog—Orwell recalled a minute action of the convict that brought home to him the meaning of what was being done. During the procession to the place of execution, in spite of the tight grasp of two warders, the condemned man "stepped slightly aside to avoid a puddle on the path." Orwell, who "had never realized what it means to destroy a healthy, conscious man," now saw "the mystery, the unspeakable wrongness, of cutting a life short, when it is in full tide." He wrote of the prisoner during that last walk: "His eyes saw the yellow gravel and the grey walls, and his brain still remembered, foresaw, reasoned—even about puddles. He and we were a party of men walking together, seeing, hearing, feeling, understanding the same world; and in two minutes, with a sudden snap, one of us would be gone—one mind less, one world less."

After the war two works urging abolition of the death penalty were published in this country by influential European writers, Arthur Koestler's "Reflections on Hanging" and Albert Camus' "Reflections on the Guillotine." Both writers were inspired by traumatic personal experience. "In 1937, during the Civil War in Spain," Koestler wrote in his preface, "I spent three months under sentence of death as a suspected spy, witnessing the executions of my fellow prisoners and awaiting my own." Camus recalled that when he was a child his father arose in the dark to attend the execution of a brutal murderer who had slaughtered an entire family of farmers. One of the few things Camus knew about his father was that this was the first time he had wanted to witness a guillotining. He never forgot his mother's account of his father's return:

> He never told what he saw that morning. My mother could only report that he rushed wildly into the house, refused to speak, threw himself on the bed, and suddenly began to vomit. He had just discovered the reality concealed beneath the great formulas that ordinarily serve to mask it. Instead of thinking of the murdered children, he could recall only the trembling body he had seen thrown on a board to have its head chopped off.

Koestler's book (unlike Camus' shorter essay which relied on Koestler for much of its factual foundation) is in large part a history of the development and function of capital punishment. As Dickens and other nineteenth-century predecessors had done, Koestler devotes many pages to showing that the deterrent effect of the death penalty has

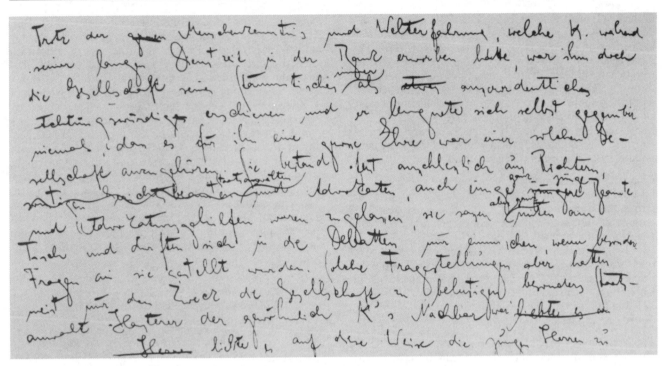

Part of a page from Franz Kafka's manuscript of The Trial.

not been established and that there has been a discouraging number of judicial errors in capital cases. Koestler's sketch of the growth of the Bloody Code in eighteenth-century England is illuminating. He points out the paradox (which he regards as relevant to the dialogue on punishments which continues in our time) that the English opted for more and more severe penalties because they feared that the alternative of a stronger and more efficient police system posed a greater threat to their freedoms.

The heart of Koestler's argument for abolition is philosophic. Rejecting the validity of the deterrence theory, he concludes that the force behind retention of the death penalty is a desire for vengeance: "Deep inside every civilized being there lurks a tiny Stone Age man, dangling a club to rob and rape, and screaming an eye for an eye. But we would rather not have that little fur-clad figure dictate the law of the land." Koestler rejected retribution not only emotionally but also on the basis of principles of moral philosophy. He observed that neither religion nor philosophy had ever resolved the question whether man is moved to act by free will or predetermination. If murder was blindly predetermined by heredity, environment or other factors, Koestler argued, "vengeance against a human being is as absurd as punishing a machine." On the other hand, even the acceptance of freedom of the will left unanswered "the problem of evil: the fact that evil has been included in the [higher] design." In sentencing for all offenses other than murder, the administrators of the law could compromise with the determinist view by finding gradations of culpability and letting the punishment fit the crime. But Koestler pointed out that the death penalty left no room for compromise. Its "rigidity and finality" presupposed an absolute criminal responsibility which philosophical concepts did not support.

Camus' arguments are less abstract and to me much more moving. He begins, perhaps with a degree of irony, by parting company with the reformers since Fielding: if we really mean business about deterrence, we should guillotine in public so that we will all be confronted with the horrible actuality of execution rather than reading the euphemistic death reports in the morning papers while downing our coffee. Public execution was necessary if the guillotine was to make an example, Camus argued, but he doubted that it deterred either the crime of passion or those who lived by crime. In that crowd in which Camus' father stood "there must have been a considerable number of future criminals who did not run home and vomit." It could not be denied that men fear death, but Camus believed such fear could be overmastered by human passion or neutralized by the criminal's instinctual optimism—that he will not be caught, will not be found guilty, will not be sentenced to death, or will not be executed.

Rejecting the deterrent function of the guillotine, Camus brands it a form of revenge that is "as old as man himself, and usually goes by the name of *retaliation*." But capital punishment more than matches murder, he adds. Rarely does murder have the degree of cold premeditation or impose such agonized waiting in which "torture by hope alternates only with the pangs of animal despair." If there were to be a real equivalence, "the death penalty would have to be pronounced upon a criminal who had forewarned his victim of the very moment he would put him to a horrible death, and who, from that time on, had kept him confined at his own discretion for a period of months. It is not in private life that one meets such monsters."

Camus tests the strength of his own belief in abolition by raising the question whether he would forbid application of the death penalty to "irrecoverables" such as mass murderers. Even in this case he decides against capital punishment, fearing judicial error (as in the case of Marie Besnard) or the pressures of public opinion (as in case of terrorist acts judged in the light of "accidents of the times . . . and of geography"). But even "monsters" he would not subject to the "absolute" punishment of death since there is no absolute innocence. As a matter of logic he would deny to no man the right of reparation by his later life in a secularized world which has lost faith in the possibility of redemption beyond the grave.

Camus' ultimate arguments are social and political. Capital punishment is wrong in Camus' view because it "destroys the human community united against death" (a community Dickens had sketched in small as the four men cheered by the revival of Rogue Riderhood). Moreover, our civilization defines itself, Camus concludes, by the fact that "for thirty years crimes of State have vastly exceeded crimes of individuals" not only through war but also political killings. He urges that the abolition of the death penalty is the first step in the denial of the right of the State to destroy its citizens.

The literature of capital punishment often dwells on the clumsiness of the tools of death. We read of the headsmen who missed; of the (almost literally) immortal Half Hanged Smith; of the ingeniously contrived "new drop" which was new but did not drop; of the electric chairs with defective circuiting. Doubts continue, we are told, that even the guillotine brings instant oblivion, and at least a qualm of credulity is aroused by the tale that the cheek of the severed head of Charlotte Corday, when slapped by the assistant executioner, flared with indignation. If one's mind is in close balance on the death penalty, it is tempting to divert the issue of "cruel and unusual punishment" from the fact of death to the means of killing. One might even become nostalgic over the days when a cup of hemlock was passed to troublesome philosophers. But death, however painless, remains the issue. John Webster's *Duchess of Malfi* reminded her executioner of this when he attempted to terrify her with the sight of her own coffin and the cord with which she was to be strangled:

> What would it pleasure me to have my throat
> cut
> With diamonds? or to be smothered
> With cassia? or to be shot to death with pearls?

> *Albert Borowitz, " 'Under Sentence of Death':*
> *Some Literary Views on Capital Punishment,"*
> *in his* A Gallery of Sinister Perspectives: Ten
> Crimes and a Scandal, *The Kent State University Press, 1982, pp. 144-54.*

On the difference between the portrayal of crime in popular and serious literature:

If one thinks of a work of art which deals with murder, *Crime and Punishment* for example, its effect on the reader is to compel an identification with the murderer which he would prefer not to recognize. The identification of fantasy is always an attempt to avoid one's own suffering: the identification of art is a sharing in the suffering of another. Kafka's *The Trial* is another instructive example of the difference between a work of art and the detective story. In the latter it is certain that a crime has been committed and, temporarily, uncertain to whom the guilt should be attached; as soon as this is known, the innocence of everyone else is certain. (Should it turn out that after all no crime has been committed, then all would be innocent.) In *The Trial,* on the other hand, it is the guilt that is certain and the crime that is uncertain; the aim of the hero's investigation is not to prove his innocence (which would be impossible for he knows he is guilty), but to discover what, if anything, he has done to make himself guilty. K, the hero, is, in fact, a portrait of the kind of person who reads detective stories for escape.

The fantasy, then, which the detective story addict indulges is the fantasy of being restored to the Garden of Eden, to a state of innocence, where he may know love as love and not as the law. The driving force behind this daydream is the feeling of guilt, the cause of which is unknown to the dreamer. The fantasy of escape is the same, whether one explains the guilt in Christian, Freudian, or any other terms. One's way of trying to face the reality, on the other hand, will, of course, depend very much on one's creed.

> *W. H. Auden, in his "The Guilty Vicarage," in* The
> Dyer's Hand and Other Essays, *Random House, 1962.*

WRITINGS BY CRIMINALS

H. Bruce Franklin

[*Franklin is an American critic and educator. In the following excerpt from his* Prison Literature in America: The Victim as Criminal and Artist *he surveys fiction and nonfiction writings by American convicts.*]

Personal narratives of the lives of criminals—both fictional and actual—made their appearance along with colonialism and large-scale mercantile capitalism in the sixteenth century. Ever since, they have been developing as an integral part of the culture of capitalist society. In fact, the principal literary form of the capitalist epoch, the novel, originated as extended prose narratives of the lives of criminals.

The modern novel first appeared in the form of picaresque fiction, in sixteenth-century Spain. Whereas *Don Quixote* (1605-15) was to mark the transition from feudalism to capitalism by parodying the aristocratic hero of feudal romance, the picaresque novel was already embodying this same transition by presenting the life story of what was to become the bourgeois hero, the self-made man who begins as an outlaw and, living by his own wits and energy, tries to make it for himself on a grand scale. At the very pinnacle of Spanish imperial power came *Lazarillo de Tormes* (1554), which broke away entirely from the maidens fair and knights errant of medieval romance; it is the tale of the archetypal Lázaro, who, cast out as a boy, lives among beggars, thieves, and swindlers, becoming cynical, self-seeking, and independent. In the next half-century, some of the outlaws and bandits, usurers and confidence men springing up amidst the collapse of feudalism were beginning to transform themselves into powerful and respectable merchants. The first full-length realistic novel in European literature, Mateo Alemán's *Guzmán de Alfarache,* presents this rise of the bourgeoisie in microcosm. In Part 1 (1599), the picaresque hero Guzmán details his adventures as a street urchin, a beggar, a gambler, a thief. In Part 2 (1604), he steals his way to a fortune and becomes a wealthy merchant. He is then found out, loses his fortune, and is imprisoned. Then he repents, gets a new wife, and starts on the way up again, this time by being her pimp. Down he falls again, now becoming a galley slave. Tortured by the captain of the ship, he is approached by his fellow galley slaves, including Moors, to be part of a planned rebellion. He manages to get a private word with the captain, betrays the would-be rebels, and is rewarded with his freedom. *Guzmán de Alfarache* thus epitomizes the underlying quest of the bourgeois epoch—to escape from rags to riches. And its archetypal man who makes himself by living by his wits is the living embodiment of the underlying epistemological, and even ontological, vision of bourgeois culture—"*I* think, therefore *I* am." Descartes was just eight years old when this criminal hero has the wit to achieve his own freedom by betraying his fellow slaves.

From that moment until the present, real criminals and imagined criminals have been narrating their lives at length in European literature and in the literature of the European colonies, including such places of exile for transported convicts as America and Australia. Throughout this literature, certain features have been consistently present and for a long time were predominant. One is a special relationship between the narrator, whether fictional or actual, and the presumed audience. The criminal narrator characteristically is confessing his or her crimes, and this confession, especially its moral lesson, is ostensibly the purpose of the whole narrative. In Daniel Defoe's *The Fortunes and Misfortunes of the Famous Moll Flanders,&c. Who was Born in Newgate, and during a Life of continu'd Variety for Threescore Years, besides her Childhood, was Twelve Year a Whore, five times a Wife (whereof once to her own Brother) Twelve Year a Thief, Eight Year a Transported Felon in Virginia, at last grew Rich, liv'd Honest, and died a Penitent* (1722), Moll Flanders tells us in all earnestness that her "publishing this Account of my Life, is for the sake of the just Moral of every part of it, and for Instruction, Caution, Warning and Improvement to every Reader." Obviously, however, most readers are not perusing the intimate details of Moll's criminal life, or those of any of the countless other rogues, for the purpose of moral betterment. Whatever "Instruction, Caution, Warning and Improvement" the readers may hope to find is largely about the details of how professional criminals operate, the better to avoid their wiles (or, perhaps, to learn their craft). The main interest lies in vicarious participation in their thrilling, sordid adventures.

The criminal narrator is sharply marked off from the readers. He or she speaks as a lone "I"—an outlaw, a desperado, a deviant, or a member of an alien underworld—to society in general, or, more usually, a respectable reading public, incarnate in the reader. This relationship has much in common with that between the authors of the slave narratives and their audience, or between Melville and his audience, as he explicitly defines it in the first paragraph of *Typee.* The most extreme alternative to such a relationship lies in the songs of Black slaves and convicts, because there the audience is none other than the artists themselves.

America in its very origin was a society abounding in criminals and ex-prisoners, including those Puritans who came from the prisons of old England to New England. Throughout the eighteenth century, the shortage of labor in America and the heavy crime rate in England combined to make the transportation of felons to the American colonies a major component of British penology. All the colonies, especially Virginia and Maryland, received continual mass shipments of convicts to serve as cheap labor, usually for a seven-year indenture. The conditions and the death rate on these sea passages approached those for African slaves. This practice ended only with the American Revolution, after which Australia became Britain's main convict colony. And lawlessness was the essence of colonial life, for the colonies prospered through the mass murder of the native peoples and the theft of their lands. Whatever domestic tranquility reigned on the farms and in the villages that sprang up on the conquered land, there was always the frontier to provide more bloody conquest, an area beyond all laws except those which grew directly out of the barrel of a gun. So it is no surprise that by the early nineteenth century the lives of criminals were becoming an especially popular American literary form. In eighteenth-century England, novels about criminals flourished among their more-or-less authentic biographies and autobiographies. In America there was very little picaresque fiction, but there were many narratives about actual criminals. Perhaps people felt little need to create fictional criminals to supplement the ones all around them.

The earliest literature by convicted American criminals of which I am aware is purely confessional. The author offers himself as an example for all other members of society to shun, and he seeks forgiveness not in this world but the next. An example is a broadside by Philip Kennison, published in Boston in 1738, "The Dying Lamentation and Advice of Philip Kennison, Who Was Executed at *Cambridge* in *New-England* (for burglary) on Friday the 15th day of *September,* 1738. . . . All written with his own hand, a few days before his death." For forty stanzas, Kennison elaborates on his exemplary predicament:

> Good People all both great & small,
>   to whom these Lines shall come,
> A warning take by my sad Fall,
>   and unto God return.
> You see me here in Iron Chains,
>   in Prison now confin'd,
> Within twelve Days my Life must end,
>   My Breath I must resign.

This purely confessional mode continued throughout the nineteenth century and on into the twentieth. For instance, James A. Clay's *A Voice from the Prison; Or,*

Truths for the Multitude and Pearls for the Truthful (1856), written during his incarceration in Augusta, Maine, consists of 362 pages of moralizing based on his reformation; and *Echoes from the Living Grave. By a Convict in Sing-Sing Prison* (1869) is merely a conversion tract dedicated "to all prisoners" as "a beacon to guide them out of the midnight darkness of Sin and Unbelief into The Glorious Light of the Gospel." Toward the end of the nineteenth century, Hiram Peck McKnight, a prisoner in the Ohio Penitentiary, compiled an anthology of pious poems by himself and other inmates, *Prison Poetry* (1896). We even have an occasional throwback to this archaic tradition today, such as convicted Watergate conspirator Charles Colson's book about his religious conversion, *Born Again* (1976). But whatever wider significance this confessional mode may once have had, it had become of little consequence even by the middle of the nineteenth century.

By then the dominant mode of autobiographical convict narrative was confessional only in the conventional manner of the picaresque novel. In fact, the earliest known extended narrative by a convicted American criminal reads just like a tale told by a fictional picaro. This book, which compares favorably in quality with all but a very few picaresque novels, is *A Narrative of the Life, Adventures, Travels and Sufferings of Henry Tufts* (1807). It is yet one more discovery by Thomas Wentworth Higginson, who described it in a penetrating essay, "A New England Vagabond," in *Harper's Monthly Magazine,* March 1888 (later included in his *Travellers and Outlaws,* 1880). Tufts sprinkles occasional pious sentiments of confession throughout the narrative, and concludes by offering himself as a "negative example" to steer his readers from "the monster sin" to a life of "virtue": "Should any of the rising generation, by a perusal of my story, learn to avoid those quicksands of vice, on which I have been so often wrecked, I shall feel myself amply compensated for the trouble I have taken in its compilation." But the real purpose of his long tale is obviously not to reform but to entertain his readers. As Tufts narrates his roguish escapades in crime and love, he also gives a vivid, priceless picture of life in the American colonies of the northeast in the latter half of the eighteenth century. After some minor thievery in his native New Hampshire, making love "with ardor" to a "damsel" who unfortunately becomes pregnant, marriage to another of his lovers, more thievery, and his first of many stays in jail, Tufts runs off in 1772 to live among the Indians in Sudbury, Canada, where "I successfully prosecuted my amour" with a "beautiful savage." Later he enlists as a private in the revolutionary army, passes counterfeit money, practices Indian medicine as a herb doctor, commits countless burglaries, makes love with many women while keeping several as wives, passes himself off in a church as a "saint" although publicly denounced by a young female parishioner who declares that Tufts had "first surveyed my face, then my feet, then my whole person, in such a carnal way and manner, that I perceived he had the devil in his heart." Tufts then discovers his true calling, that of a horse thief, which he describes in such meticulous detail that his narrative sometimes sounds like an instruction manual, and pursues his criminal and amatory adventures until he barely escapes hanging and achieves reformation.

In the next few decades personal narratives by American criminals were to become commonplace. Just as Tufts gives us an irreplaceable view of late eighteenth-century American life from its seamy side, these narratives do the same for early nineteenth-century American life. Most of them are also told in the picaresque mode. They are often far more realistic than most early American fiction, and the wide-ranging activities of their rascally heroes give authentic scenes of early American experience filled with frankness, vitality, and intimate detail. A good example is *Sketches of the Life of William Stuart, The First and Most Celebrated Counterfeiter of Connecticut, Comprising Startling Details of Daring Feats Performed by Himself—Perils by Sea and Land—Frequent Arrests and Imprisonments. . . . As Given by Himself,* "Printed and Published by the Author" in Bridgeport, Connecticut, 1854. Though he acknowledges "I am the hero of my own story," Stuart professes that "my heroism was displayed in direct opposition to the laws of the land," and he then mouths the conventional confession expected of all rogues who narrate the thrilling stories of their lives: ". . . if I stand now as a beacon to warn the young and ambitious against vice and crime, my history will be a gain to the world." After some more pious professions, Stuart launches his fine narrative of counterfeiting and other wild adventures covering even more territory than Tufts. Around 1807 he works a con game in the South as partner with a free Negro who runs away to rejoin Stuart each time Stuart sells him, until one day when he fails to reappear. Later our hero ships out on a privateer aiding South American states in revolt against Spanish rule. Stuart, as expected, tacks on the usual self-condemning moral at the very end.

By the time Melville published *The Confidence-Man* in 1857, the lives of famous "bad men" were a staple in the literary diet of America. As the passengers board his Mississippi River steamboat, they are given a wide choice of narratives about bloodthirsty outlaws and bandits. But Melville, who sets this scene in a book displaying all the tricks of riverboat confidence men and counterfeiters as a synecdoche for the criminality of capitalism itself, suggests that these passengers are being warned about the wrong kind of criminal:

> . . . still another versatile chevalier, hawked, in the thick of the throng, the lives of Measan, the bandit of Ohio, Murrel, the pirate of the Mississippi, and the brothers Harpe, the Thugs of the Green River country, in Kentucky—creatures, with others of the sort, one and all exterminated at the time, and for the most part, like the hunted generations of wolves in the same regions, leaving comparatively few successors; which would seem cause for unalloyed gratulation, and is such to all except those who think that in new countries, where the wolves are killed off, the foxes increase.

The adventures of horse thieves, highwaymen, rustlers, bank robbers, counterfeiters, riverboat gamblers, and assorted confidence men were narrated both as sensationalist tales by professional writers and as picaresque confessions by themselves. Meanwhile, another kind of "criminal" was also publishing autobiographical narratives, often involving revelations of life in prison. These were what we would now call political prisoners.

Some of the earliest political prisoners were rebels who had risen up in open class warfare against semifeudal land tenure in the New York State Anti-Rent Wars of 1839-46. One of the imprisoned leaders of the Anti-Renters, Mortimer Belden ("Little Thunder"), improvised songs, accompanied by his fiddle, for his fellow inmates. His "The Prisoners in Jail (Lines Composed in the Columbia County Jail, July 9, 1845)," reprinted in the Anti-Renters' journal, *The Albany Freeholder,* protested against both prison and the oppression that led to their incarceration. Among the fourteen stanzas are these:

> The sheriffs will out with their array of men,
> The County will find them what money they
>   spend;
> They will seize upon prisoners, and into the
>   cell—
> If there's anything worse, it must be in Hell,
>   In these hard times.
>
> And there they will keep them confined in the
>   jail,
> Without any liberty for to get bail;
> They will do as they please in spite of your
>   friends,
> And God only knows where this matter will end,
>   In these hard times.
>
> The judges and jurors are a very fine crew,
> They take the poor prisoners and drive them
>   right thru;
> The sheriffs will falter, all hell they don't fear,
> They will bring them in guilty if they prove
>   themselves clear,
>   In these hard times.

Most political prisoners prior to the Civil War were jailed for antislavery acts. Some of these people were conscious abolitionists, such as George Thompson, who was incarcerated for over four years, during which he wrote *Prison Life and Reflections* (1847) and *The Prison Bard; Or, Poems on Various Subjects. Written in Prison* (1848). Others were just individuals like Lewis W. Paine, a white machinist from the North working in Georgia, who decided to help a slave escape; Paine describes his decision and resulting imprisonment in *Six Years in a Georgia Prison* (1851).

These autobiographies by antislavery political prisoners have much the same intention as the narratives by escaped slaves: both attempt to use the authors' personal experience as a means of awakening the audience to the real nature of slavery and activating them to join the struggle against it. They attack the existing legal structure of society, which defines the slaveowners as respectable citizens and those who subvert slavery as "criminals." Thus both these autobiographical forms are diametrically opposed to the narratives of the lives of professional criminals, which are presented ostensibly as warnings about outlaws and confirmations of the conventional definition of crime.

Viewed in the light of these contrasting forms, *The Confessions of Nat Turner* appears fundamentally different from the kind of document it is usually taken to be. Here a slave who has led a major revolt against slavery does not manage to escape and to write or tell his own narrative. Instead he falls into the clutches of the slaveowners, who not only try him, convict him, and execute him as a criminal, but actually force him to present the story of his life in the form of a conventional criminal confession. Rather than the voice of a rebel against slavery, *The Confessions of Nat Turner* is a narrative constructed by Thomas R. Gray, its white recorder and publisher, to fit into a widely read popular genre, the lives of bloodthirsty outlaws and bandits. A political prisoner is thus transmuted into a conventional criminal.

Gray's introduction sarcastically introduces "this 'great Bandit,' " and claims that the purpose of publishing this narrative is "the gratification of public curiosity." Gray describes "Nat Turner, and his band of ferocious miscreants" as "remorseless murderers." This was a "fiendish band," Gray tells us, and "no cry for mercy penetrated their flinty bosoms." As usual in this confessional mode, this criminal now "frankly acknowledges his full participation in all the guilt." Nat Turner's "own account" is offered as "an awful, and it is hoped, a useful lesson." The underlying moral purpose of publishing this document is explicitly the preservation of slavery and the social status quo, exactly opposite from the narratives of imprisoned abolitionists and escaped slaves:

> It is calculated also to demonstrate the policy of
> our laws in restraint of this class of our popula-
> tion, and to induce all those entrusted with their
> execution, as well as our citizens generally, to see
> that they are strictly and rigidly enforced. Each
> particular community should look to its own
> safety, whilst the general guardians of the laws,
> keep a watchful eye over all.

Prior to the Civil War, two types of narratives by criminals were well established: one by the amateur or professional criminal writing in a confessional, often picaresque, mode, the other by the political reformer imprisoned as a criminal for an act many readers would commend. *The Confessions of Nat Turner* represents perhaps the earliest example of one form of overlap between these two types. Since Nat Turner was not a reformer but a revolutionary, his captors define him as just another criminal, an especially vicious and dangerous criminal. Until the rise of anarchism in the early twentieth century, autobiographical narratives by convicted revolutionaries were rare. But by the early 1860s another kind of overlap between the two forms was beginning to emerge, as some common criminals began to write the narratives of their lives, particularly their lives in prison, with a political perspective. Rather than wallowing in guilt, or professing to wallow in guilt, about their own crimes, these convict authors began to turn a critical gaze upon society. In these early works by prisoners the key question of much later prison literature was already beginning to emerge: Who is the real criminal, the prisoner or the society that imprisons people?

The modern prison system, based on the religious concept of the "penitentiary," developed first in the United States, in the late eighteenth and early nineteenth centuries, and then rapidly spread to Europe. Its first implementation, under the leadership of Pennsylvania Quakers, was in the solitary cells established in 1790 in the Walnut Street jail in Philadelphia for the purpose of meditation and reformation; this is often referred to as the birthplace of the modern prison system. The first prison physically designed to achieve total isolation of each inmate was the Eastern State Penitentiary, better known as Cherry Hill, in Philadelphia, constructed in 1829 with cells laid out so that no prisoner ever saw another person but his guards.

Initially, this system was administered by idealists who encouraged what they believed to be moral growth among their captives. There were even a few successful examples of reformation, such as George Reno, who in 1844 published in Philadelphia, under a literary pseudonym, *Buds and Flowers of Leisure Hours, by Harry Hawser, Sailor, &c.,* a collection of rather well-executed poems, including a very moving antislavery piece entitled "On the Dying Slave." In his preface, Reno asserts that the author "regards his confinement at Cherry Hill the happiest event of his life."

The "separate system" represented by Cherry Hill was being rivaled by an alternative, designed specifically for exploiting mass convict labor, the "silent system," under which prisoners were housed in solitary cells but worked together all day as an ideal source of cheap reliable labor, under rigorous enforcement of the rule that all convicts must maintain total silence. The model for this system was set up at Auburn, New York, in 1825, where they initiated the "lockstep" so that guards could maintain strict control as the prisoners marched back and forth between their cells and their industrial workshops.

Neither of these two competing systems apparently produced many successors to George Reno; extremely few subsequent prisoners have much good to say about any of the variants of modern prisons. (The last published work I have been able to find by someone confined under the "solitary system" is *Selections from the Writings of Jesse Harding Pomeroy, Life Prisoner Since 1874,* published in Boston in 1920; Pomeroy began his forty-three years of solitary confinement at the age of fourteen and was not released into the general prison population until 1917; his pathetic writings include a Rip Van Winkle experience, "My First Movie Show.") In fact, as industrial capitalism rapidly developed in the middle of the nineteenth century, the prisons rapidly shed much of their early pretense of being places of reformation and became frankly acknowledged as places of cheap mass production. With this shift, literature by convicts became increasingly a form of protest literature against the brutality of prisons and sometimes against the prison system itself.

A remarkable early work in this genre appeared in the first years of the Civil War, shortly before the mass use of convict labor to replace slavery. This book, *An Autobiography of Gerald Toole, the State's Prison Convict, who murdered Daniel Webster, Warden of the Connecticut State Prison, on the 27th of March, 1862 (Written by Himself) Being a Full Confession of Crimes for which he was sent to the State Prison . . . ,* was published in 1862 in Hartford, Connecticut. The title would seem to indicate that this is a confession in the same vein as *The Confessions of Nat Turner,* and, as in that earlier work, the criminal's "confession" is framed by the legal documents which preceded his execution. The main difference between the two works comes from the fact that Toole is actually speaking for himself, not having someone else narrate his alleged "confession." Hence Gerald Toole, unlike Nat Turner, has the opportunity to articulate a political defense of the "murder" he committed. His position is precisely the same as the one Frederick Douglass presents in describing his physical attack on the "nigger-breaker" Edward Covey and the one that Melville presents in White Jacket's preparations to murder his captain; it is the uprising, as a basic act of self-defense, of the slave against his oppressor. In fact Toole was defending himself against exactly the same punishment as the one that menaced Douglass and Melville—a flogging.

Despite the misleading title, Toole confesses nothing, including the "Crimes for which he was sent to the State Prison," an alleged arson of part of the building which housed his small shop. In the main body of his story, he tells not of his own guilt but of the viciousness of the guards and prison officials, and of their slave-driving management of the convict labor. Along with Melville's "The Tartarus of Maids" (1855) and Rebecca Harding Davis's *Life in the Iron Mills* (1861), this stands as one of the first American literary narratives set inside an industrial workshop. And Toole describes the actual scene of production in words that recall Melville's picture of the life-robbing paper factory in "The Tartarus of Maids":

> In the shop were about thirty men whose pale, emaciated looks showed that the very life blood was being worked out of them. They were all working at boot making. The coffers of unblushing contractors are filled from the labors of these poor convicts who work from dawn to dark.

Toole is set to work and then severely flogged for failing to produce twelve pairs of boots in a day. The next day, his back and shoulders still oozing blood, he is again being driven off to the flogging dungeon for punishment. As Captain Webster starts pushing him with a heavy mounted stick to the place of his torture, Toole stabs him with a shoe knife. "At that time had Webster twenty lives, I should have taken them," Toole tells us with defiance and dignity. Toole is stomped, beaten, and whipped "until my whole body became one mass of torn flesh," then tortured for a week, convicted of murder, and executed at the age of twenty-four. Toole's autobiography is not a confession at all, but a justification of his act of rebellion against what he perceived as a criminal system.

Just as the flogging of slaves is often central to personal narratives and fiction about slave life, and the flogging of seamen is often central to nineteenth-century literature about sailor life, the flogging of prisoners is a common theme in many works of convict literature for the next hundred years. Many readers of this book may not comprehend the severity of this punishment; a flogging is not what is usually thought of as a spanking or a paddling or a switching. It is administered with a long, heavy strap often weighted at the tip with metal; many prisoners describe guards and "captains" practicing by breaking bricks with a single blow of this whip. Prison literature contains innumerable scenes of convicts being flogged to death. I do not wish to inflict on the readers many of the detailed descriptions of floggings found in prison literature from the 1860s through the 1970s. These descriptions become increasingly appalling, and increasingly excellent as narrative prose, as our literary standards move toward approval of concrete, realistic detail and away from emotional adjectives. Whenever flogging is mentioned, the reader might envision the experience as described, with the purity and precision of a simple modern style, by Dale Woodcock in *Ruled by the Whip; Hell behind Bars in America's Devil's Island—the Arkansas State Penitentiary* (1958):

> I was given twenty-seven lashes as I lay on the concrete floor. The warden threw his weight behind each lash and pulled on the whip as it struck my buttocks, thus twisting and tearing the skin. Soon blood and skin together were flipped away at every blow. . . . Blood was pouring from my rectum.

In the period immediately following Toole's autobiography, prison literature began to present prisoners as a definite category of being in society, rather than merely individual criminals being punished. Less than a decade after Emancipation, there appeared a personal narrative by an anonymous convict who saw prisoners as the most oppressed people in society, *An Illustrated History and Description of State Prison Life,* published in Toledo, Ohio, in 1871. The author describes himself as writing in a cell in Southern Indiana State Prison "not for compensation or fame, but in defense of the most unfortunate being on earth, the convict." He tells a grisly tale of torture, convict labor, and the routine rape of female inmates by prison officials, concluding with an ardent plea to the reader to do something about reforming or abolishing prisons.

Up through the first half of the nineteenth century, literature by convicts, except those convicted of political crimes, had appeared as the words of *criminals,* whether they were sincerely confessing to help their readers avoid their life of sin or merely conventionally confessing to entertain their readers with their life of rascality. But with the development of prison as a systematic means to achieve its professed goals of punishment and reformation, and its practical purpose of cheap convict labor, literature by convicts more and more appeared as the words of a new subclass in society, *prisoners.* By the turn of the century, this shift is quite striking.

Even in works primarily intended to use an individual convict's own life as a means of exploring the sociology and psychology of the *criminal,* the main interest often shifts to the sociology and psychology of the *prisoner.* For example, *The Autobiography of a Thief,* recorded by Hutchins Hapgood (1903), starts off as a narrative of criminal life but soon becomes an investigation into prison life. The anonymous author tells us that he was born of "poor but honest parents" in 1868, but "I have been a professional thief for more than twenty years. Half of that time I have spent in state's prison. . . ." He tells of his crimes and his various imprisonments, including stretches in Sing Sing and the Dannemora asylum for the criminal insane. He documents the viciousness of the prison system and describes the new class of being it is creating. For example,

here he shows the responses of prisoners to an environment designed to deprive them of love and human affection:

> Convicts, particularly if they are broken in health, often become like little children. It is not unusual for them to grow dependent on dumb pets, which they smuggle into prison. . . . The man in stir who has a white mouse or robin is envied by other convicts, for he has something to love.

The very same year these words were being published, 1903, another ex-convict writer was explaining that his own personal descent, at the age of eighteen, into this subclass below the industrial proletariat had been the turning point in his life. Rather than making him a crippled and pathetic victim, this experience had converted him from "rampant individualism" to revolutionary socialism. Jack London describes this change in his life in "How I Became a Socialist," first published in *The Comrade* (March 1903). According to London, "no economic argument, no lucid demonstration of the logic and inevitableness of Socialism affects me as profoundly and convincingly as I was affected on the day when I first saw the walls of the Social Pit rise around me and felt myself slipping down, down, into the shambles at the bottom." The decisive event had come in 1894, when, as a tramp "I strayed into Niagara Falls, was nabbed by a fee-hunting constable, denied the right to plead guilty or not guilty, sentenced out of hand to thirty days' imprisonment for having no fixed abode and no visible means of support, handcuffed and chained to a bunch of men similarly circumstanced, carted down country to Buffalo, registered at the Erie County Penitentiary, had my head clipped and by budding mustache shaved, was dressed in convict stripes, compulsorily vaccinated by a medical student who practised on such as we, made to march the lock-step, and put to work under the eyes of guards armed with Winchester rifles."

London's crime was the same as that of Melville's Bartleby. But by this point, forty years later, imprisonment for vagrancy was not intended merely to get nuisances out of sight; prisoners were now used as part of a slave labor force, even if they preferred not to work. London's experiences as a tramp and as a prisoner led him to his understanding of how both groups form a critical part of the surplus army of labor essential to the survival and growth of capitalism, as he explains at length in "The Class Struggle" (*The Independent,* November 5, 1903) and "The Tramp" (*Wilshire's Magazine,* February 1904). In the latter article he shows how thin a line separates the employed worker from either the tramp or the criminal:

> The tramp is one of two kinds of men: he is either a discouraged worker or a discouraged criminal. Now a discouraged criminal, on investigation, proves to be a discouraged worker, or the descendant of discouraged workers; so that, in the last analysis, the tramp is a discouraged worker. Since there is not work for all, discouragement for some is unavoidable.

In 1907-08, London published *My Life in the Underworld* as a series of articles in *Cosmopolitan Magazine,* narrating his life as a tramp and his month as a convict in the Erie

County Penitentiary. In "Pinched: A Prison Experience" (July 1907) and "The 'Pen': Long Days in a County Penitentiary" (August 1907), he explains in vivid detail how his arrest, his so-called trial, and what he lived through in prison shattered all his earlier concepts of the police, the laws, the criminal justice system, and his own relation to them all. He shows how this experience led directly to his political and social analysis. But here he is less concerned with his analytical procedure than his emotional response, for his adolescent, naïve, heroic, superman view of himself had collapsed beneath the iron heel of the American state, and he had come to *feel* what it is like to be part of the class routinely crushed at the bottom of this society:

> I saw with my own eyes, there in that prison, things unbelievable and monstrous. And the more convinced I became, the profounder grew the respect in me for the sleuth-hounds of the law and for the whole institution of criminal justice. My indignation ebbed away, and into my being rushed the tides of fear. I saw at last, clear-eyed, what I was up against.

The same year as this autobiographical narrative, London put all these ideas and feelings into the novel I regard as his masterpiece, *The Iron Heel,* perhaps the first vision of the fascist nightmare which was to haunt the rest of the twentieth century, at least through the present. Jack London imagined capitalism, faced with socialist revolution, turning its whole society into one gigantic penitentiary.

As long-term prisoners began to write of themselves as a subclass, as that category of slave laborers provided for in 1865 by Article 13 of the Constitution, they began to express a sense of being branded as outcasts, of being treated as less than human, caged up and walled off in the midst of society. This dehumanization is summed up for them in the practice of assigning numbers to convicts to substitute for their names. Thus American convicts become the first people actually to experience the exact form of what was to become that recurrent nightmare of the twentieth century—living as a nameless number in a society of numbers.

Their situation, however, was even worse than this nightmare, for their numbers also separated and distinguished them from a surrounding society, stigmatizing both them and their families. "Mourn Not for Me (To His Wife)," a poem published by two prisoners, James Stell and John Null, in *Convict Verse* (1908), expresses this double branding and alienation:

> Mourn not for me because my shame
> Is hedged by towered walls,
> And black across my humbled name
> A hated number falls.
>
> Weep for yourself, and not for me;
> Dear, all your flood of tears
> Can never set the captive free
> Nor cleanse his sullied years.
>
> . . . . .
>
> Weep not for me; for always, wife,
> The angry coals of shame
> Burn deepest in the guileless life
> That bears the branded name.

In the same year, a novel entitled *9009* (1908), written as an indictment of the prison system by James Hopper and Fred R. Bechdolt (neither of them convicts as far as I know), achieves a bone-chilling effect by consistently using "9009" as the name of the protagonist. (Eugene Zamiatin's enormously influential Soviet antiutopian novel *We,* with its city-state in which all citizens have numbers for names, was not to appear until 1924.) This was rapidly becoming a convention used, and somewhat overused, by prison writers in books with purposes as varied as these: *Life in Sing-Sing* (1904) by "Number 1500," who still resents being incarcerated with "cheap criminals"; *Thru the Mill, by "4342"; A Prison Story That's Different* (1915), a rather dry but quite informative circumstantial account of Minnesota State Prison at Stillwater; *A Tale of a Walled Town, and Other Verses by B. 8266, ——Penitentiary* (1921), a collection of the author's archaic religious poetry.

The significance of having a number for a name, and the estranged relationship between the prisoner-author and his audience, form part of the design in *An Open Letter to Society from Convict 1776* (1911). This thoughtful, well-constructed disquisition on the prison system by a seven-time loser carries the form of the prison narrative to a logical, if rather bizarre, extreme: a 160-page letter addressed from this author with a patriotic, revolutionary pseudonym to "My Dear Madam Society." Convict 1776 asserts that he does "not in the least justify crime, whether it is committed by us against you, or by you against us." His analysis, however, proceeds from the fact that "the greater part of our offences is against your accepted suitor, Mr. Dollar."

In order to understand what all this is, it may be helpful here to see, through contrast, what it is *not.* Except for London, these white prisoners see themselves first as isolated individuals, then as members of some social subclass defined by their alienation from the rest of their society. As I discussed at length in the preceding chapter, this is not at all the situation of Black prisoners, whose situation is qualitatively little different from the rest of their people. A personal narrative published during this same period, the opening years of the twentieth century, displays how this Black situation contrasts starkly with the white.

This remarkable document, "The New Slavery in the South—An Autobiography, By a Georgia Negro Peon" (1904), transcribed by a reporter "who took the liberty to correct the narrator's errors of grammar and put it in form suitable for publication," chronicles the development of a plantation from chattel slavery to convict slavery. The twentieth-century illiterate Black narrator opens his story just like the narrative of a nineteenth-century fugitive slave: he confesses that he knows neither the date of his birth nor the identity of his father. He figures he must have been born during the Civil War: "I reckon by this time I must be a little over forty years old"; "I never knew who my father was or anything about him." When he is about ten years old, he is "bound out" to a plantation owner. Around the age of seventeen or eighteen, he goes to a neighboring plantation and hires himself out. His former contractor immediately reclaims him, and gives him "thirty lashes with a buggy whip across my bare back" for running off. At the age of twenty-one, he is allowed to contract himself for annual terms. When the owner dies, his son takes over:

> . . . this son had been serving at Atlanta in some big office to which he had been elected. I think it was in the Legislature or something of that sort—anyhow, all the people called him Senator. At the end of the fifth year the Senator suggested that I sign up a contract for ten years; then, he said, we wouldn't have to fix up papers every year. I asked my wife about it; she consented; and so I made a ten-year contract.

Shortly thereafter, the Senator has constructed a "long, low shanty" with "a double row of stalls or pens" which "looked for all the world like stalls for horses":

> Nobody seemed to know what the Senator was fixing for. All doubts were put aside one bright day in April when about forty ablebodied negroes bound in iron chains, and some of them handcuffed, were brought out to the Senator's farm in three big wagons. They were quartered in the long, low shanty, and it was afterward called the stockade. This was the beginning of the Senator's convict camp.

The narrator tells us that "when I saw these men in shackles, and the guards with their guns, I was scared nearly to death. I felt like running away, but I didn't know where to go." He and the other peons under contract had considered themselves "free laborers"; they meet, and send a representative with a threat to quit. Then they learn just how much difference there is between Black convicts and free Black people:

> Word came back that we were all under contract for ten years and that the Senator would hold us to the letter of the contract, or put us in chains and lock us up—the same as the other prisoners. It was made plain to us by some white people we talked to that in the contracts we had signed we had all agreed to be locked up in a stockade at night or at any other time that our employer saw fit; further, we learned that we could not lawfully break our contract for any reason and go and hire ourselves to somebody else without the consent of our employer, and, more than that, if we got mad and ran away, we could be run down by bloodhounds, arrested without process of law, and be returned to our employer, who, according to the contract, might beat us brutally or administer any other kind of punishment that he thought proper. In other words, we had sold ourselves into slavery—and what could we do about it? The white folks had all the courts, all the guns, all the hounds, all the railroads, all the telegraph wires, all the newspapers, all the money, and nearly all the land—and we had only our ignorance, our poverty and our empty hands.

The Senator begins to add additional stockades, bring in more convicts, and buy more land:

> Within two years the Senator had in all nearly 200 negroes working on his plantation—about half of them free laborers, so-called, and about half of them convicts. The only difference between the free laborers and the others was that the free laborers could come and go as they pleased, at night—that is, they were not locked up at night, and were not, as a general thing, whipped for slight offenses.

But all this is in the relatively happy days of "contract" labor, when there was still some faint distinction between the "free laborers" and "the other prisoners." The real "troubles of the free laborers began at the close of the ten-year period." Then they discover that, since they all had been compelled to buy all their food, clothing, and other supplies on credit from the Senator's commissary, they were now debt peons. Henceforward, "we were treated just like convicts." He is locked up in one of the filthy stockades, which "were but little more than cow lots, horse stables or hog pens." When he is put in the stockade, his nine-year-old son is given away to someone in South Carolina and his wife is taken into the "Big House" to serve as one of the white men's mistresses. The antebellum split between house slaves and field slaves is reproduced:

> . . . the poor negro women who were not in the class with my wife fared about as bad as the helpless negro men. Most of the time the women who were peons or convicts were compelled to wear men's clothes. Sometimes, when I have seen them dressed like men, and plowing or hoeing or hauling logs or working at the blacksmith's trade, just the same as men, my heart would bleed and my blood would boil, but I was powerless to raise a hand. It would have meant death on the spot to have said a word.

What kind of crime had these convicts committed? The narrator learns that the great majority were convicted of the usual minor offenses established to provide a constant flow of cheap convict labor. The most common crime of convicts on the Senator's farm, and several other convict farms in the area, was adultery, committed in a certain county in south Georgia "way down in the turpentine district":

> . . . I learned that down in that county a number of negro lewd women were employed by certain white men to entice negro men into their houses; and then, on certain nights, at a given signal, when all was in readiness, raids would be made by the officers upon these houses, and the men would be arrested and charged with living in adultery.

To the Black convict or peon, imprisonment did not mean becoming an alien being isolated from the rest of his people but rather becoming the typical representative of his people. Even during the early years of the twentieth century, some white prisoner-authors began to perceive their own situation as not entirely different. *Convict 1776* shows a class perception of social reality when he argues to Madam Society that "the vagrancy laws should be strictly enforced against the tramp and the millionaire alike." John Carter, whose poems were published in *Century Magazine, Harper's Weekly, The Bellman, The Smart Set, Cosmopolitan,* and *Lippincotts' Magazine,* divided his collection of prison poems, *Hard Labor, and Other Poems of Prison Life* (1911), into two sections indicating a perception of society to be expressed by the Black Panther Party half a century later. The poems about life in prison he places in the section entitled "Under the Lash"; the poems about "free" life he places in the section entitled "In the Greater Prison." Then in 1912 appeared a very influential work by a convict who claims that he is not a criminal, though he is a burglar, because he belongs to an entire social class driven to "crime" in order to survive—Donald Lowrie's first book, *My Life in Prison.*

Lowrie writes as a poor person to "the taxpayers and the conscientious citizens of the community," hoping to move them toward the reformation of prison and society. His first words establish the relationship between himself and his reader, and between the two social classes embodied by them:

> I was broke. I had not eaten for three days.
>
> I had walked the streets for three nights. Every fibre of my being, every precept of my home training protested against and would not permit my begging.
>
> I saw persons all about me spending money for trifles, or luxuries. I envied the ragged street urchin as he took a nickel in exchange for a newspaper and ran expectantly to the next pedestrian. But I was broke and utterly miserable.
>
> Have you ever been broke?
>
> Have you ever been hungry and miserable, not knowing when or where you were going to get your next meal, nor where you were going to spend your next night? . . .
>
> If you have not felt each and all of these things, it will, perhaps, be futile for you to read what they brought to one who has felt them. . . .

Lowrie's books did have some effect on the movement toward prison reform and were also studied by later prison authors, as attested to in the confessional, picaresque autobiography of the professional thief Jack Black, *You Can't Win* (1926), when he praises "Donald Lowrie, whose writings did for American prisons what John Howard's did for those of England."

And already another kind of convict was writing not from a reformist but a revolutionary perspective. These were prisoners serving time for revolutionary political crimes, and they brought into the prisons a theoretical class perspective, even though some of them lacked the proletarian class experience of most "common" criminals.

An important early book by a committed revolutionary was Alexander Berkman's *Prison Memoirs of an Anarchist* (1912). In 1892 the Carnegie Steel Corporation locked out the Iron and Steel Workers union from its Homestead, Pennsylvania, plant. Henry Frick, the company's superintendent, brought in a boatload of three hundred Pinkerton gunmen to put down the protesting strikers. A pitched battle was fought, in which ten men were killed, and the three hundred Pinkertons surrendered as "prisoners of war" to the armed workers. The workers, however, were then crushed by thousands of Pennsylvania state militiamen. Berkman, hearing of the outrages committed against the defeated workers, went to Homestead, where he shot and stabbed Frick in an unsuccessful assassination attempt. Imprisoned, Berkman narrates the story of his own actions in the Homestead strike, then carefully interrelates the class oppression of the workers and his fellow prisoners. He dedicates his book "To all those who in and out of prison fight against their bondage."

My main concern throughout this chapter is with people who became creators of literature because of their incarceration as victims of American society. Although there are many twentieth-century prisoner-authors convicted for outright political crimes whose perception of society has been deeply intensified, if not fundamentally altered, by their prison experience, I am essentially limiting my analysis to "common criminals" whose understanding of their own situation developed directly as a consequence of their crime and punishment. The reader should, however, be aware of the rich and ever-increasing body of twentieth-century writing by political prisoners, dating at least from Berkman. These include such notable early works as Carlo de Fornaro's *A Modern Purgatory* (1917) a narrative of life in the New York City Tombs by "an artist, writer, editor, revolutionary"; *A Fragment of the Prison Experiences of Emma Goldman and Alexander Berkman in the State Prison at Jefferson City, Missouri, and the U.S. Penitentiary at Atlanta, Georgia* (1919); *Bars and Shadows: The Prison Poems of Ralph Chaplin* (1922), including some fine sonnets by this leading I.W.W. organizer; *In Prison* (1923) by Kate Richards O'Hare, who spent fourteen months in the Missouri State Penitentiary and became committed to prison reform; *Wall Shadows: A Study in American Prisons* (1927) by Frank Tannenbaum, whose many years of work on prison reformation began while he was serving a year for unlawful assembly in 1913-14; and Eugene Debs's *Walls and Bars* (1927). (Debs's cellmate in the Atlanta Penitentiary, the forger Roger Benton, devoted a chapter of his own book, *Where Do I Go From Here?* [1936] to "A Man Named Gene Debs," "the most Christ-like man I have ever met in my life.")

Another group of convict writers beyond the main scope of this chapter are those who were professional writers before they became convicts. One of the most popular and prolific American authors, Julian Hawthorne, who published close to forty books of fiction, essays, and biography, far more than his father Nathaniel, was sent to the Atlanta Federal Penitentiary (for mail fraud) at the age of sixty-seven and the height of his career. He served almost a year. When he got out, he immediately began work on *The Subterranean Brotherhood* (1914) a narrative of prison life, written with more passion and commitment than any of his other works I have read. In his preface, Hawthorne declares that "these chapters were begun the day after I got back to New York from the Atlanta Penitentiary" and that he worked on the book without interruption until it was complete. "Though I had read as much in 'prison literature' as most people," he discovered that he had very little conception of what life in prison really meant. His experience leads him to the "radical and astounding" conclusion that there is only one solution:

"nothing less than that *Penal Imprisonment for Crime be Abolished.*" Julian Hawthorne penetrates, through his experience, to part of the historical significance of the prison system:

> Before the Civil War there were some millions of negro slaves in the South, whom to set free we spent some billions of dollars and several hundred thousand lives. It was held that the result was worth the cost. But to-day we are creating some five hundred thousand slaves, white and black, each year. . . .

Hawthorne repeats the deeply held belief of "every convict and ex-convict": "Let every judge, attorney general, district attorney, and juryman at a trial spend a bona fide term in jail, and there would be no more convictions—prisons would end."

This last statement is borne out by still another group of prisoner-authors I pass over without much attention, the prominent and respectable citizens who suddenly awake to find themselves convicts. For example, Charles Stuart Wharton, former Illinois congressman, for many years an assistant district attorney in Cook County, and then a prominent businessman, was convicted of being an accomplice in a spectacular armed mail robbery in 1928. After serving his two-year sentence at Leavenworth, he describes that institution and prison in general, to which he had sent many a criminal, in *The House of Whispering Hate* (1932):

> Leavenworth is a great mill through which men pass in an endless chain to be turned out as ex-convicts. It is as useful as a sausage machine which grinds up meat with poison. Most of the men it sends forth will be a burden on their communities, and the few who can ever benefit themselves or the world at large after their release are made fearful by the brand upon them.

The literature about prison experience written by highly educated, formerly respectable convicts, even that by a leading professional author such as Julian Hawthorne, rarely matches the quality of writing, at least by late twentieth-century standards, of much proletarian and lumpenproletarian prison literature (just as the slave songs of the nineteenth century now seem to us finer literary creations than most of the elegant poetry of the literary periodicals). These respectable citizens tended to follow the archaic literary models then in fashion, and their prose is therefore generally lifeless, vague, effusive, humorless, verbose, and now rather difficult to read. Many of the "common" criminals, however, wrote with direct, economical, colloquial, often raw prose, filled with frank realism and spiced with humor; their books still bubble with life.

There was, however, one formerly respectable citizen who, by learning the lingo of his fellow criminals and convicts, was to achieve a wide popularity and deep, though perhaps transitory, influence on the writing of fiction. This was William Porter, whose strange career was to anticipate much literature by twentieth-century criminals just as the equally strange career of his sidekick Al Jennings, also once a respectable citizen, was to echo much literature by nineteenth-century criminals.

Al Jennings was one of the last of the famous outlaws of the Wild West, leader of the daring Jennings Gang of train robbers. Fleeing to Honduras with $30,000, he there met Bill Porter, on the lam from a bank embezzlement charge. The two traveled around Mexico and Central America together, Porter living off the loot of Jennings, who at one point shot a man about to stab Porter. Both eventually ended up in the State Penitentiary at Columbus, Ohio, where each began serious writing. Jennings's life story, *Beating Back* (1914), was one of the final tales of the nineteenth-century picaros, with its thrilling adventures and detailed how-to-do-it accounts of robbing trains. Much earlier, while still in prison, Porter was smuggling out his characteristic short stories to be published under the name O. Henry. Some of his best-known stories were published in this manner, including "A Blackjack Bargainer," "A Fog in Santone," "An Afternoon Miracle," "Money Maze," "No Story," "The Enchanted Kiss," "Hygeia at the Solito," "Rouge et Noir," "The Marionettes," and "The Duplicity of Hargraves."

O. Henry did not publish as an acknowledged prison author. In fact, it was not until after his death in 1910 that it became widely known that he had been a convict who had served almost four years in the state penitentiary. Then, however, he did influence the direction of prison writing, more by personal example than through his already somewhat outdated trick-story technique. From this point on, prison writers began to see possibilities in fiction as well as autobiographical narrative, essays about crime and prison, and lyric poetry; they began to think of themselves as potential professional authors rather than just criminals with their own tale to tell. Of course, this process would no doubt have taken place anyhow, but for aspiring convict authors O. Henry was a supportive patron saint.

In the 1920s, novels and short stories by prisoners started to develop, especially after H. L. Mencken actively began to encourage convicts to submit their material to the *American Mercury*. This fiction of course varied widely in both quality and intention.

Some of it was romantic and escapist, like Howard D. Bolling's novel *The Mystery of the Cumberlands* (192?). Bolling was born and reared in the foothills of the Cumberland Mountains in Virginia. While traveling through Winona, Missouri, he was accosted without cause by the town marshal, who, pistol in hand and not identifying himself, demanded Bolling's surrender. Bolling pulled his own gun, killed the marshal, and was sentenced to thirty-five years in a Missouri prison. He wrote *The Mystery of the Cumberlands* in prison, partly to raise money to reopen his case. The novel is a strange and rather fascinating tale of a wild, mysterious boy named "D," born to a strong, heroic mountain woman. "D" grows up to become a kind of savior-adventurer not only in his native Cumberlands but in Africa as well.

More typical fantasy was churned out by Jack Callahan, who describes the facts of his own life as a gangster, a prisoner, and an author in *Man's Grim Justice: My Life Outside the Law* (1928). Callahan makes little pretense to moral reformation as he narrates his own lurid adven-

The stockade around Omsk Prison Camp, where Feodor Dostoevski was incarcerated.

tures. He seems especially to enjoy telling of a shootout in a boxcar where he and his pals kill three "bad niggers," the "notorious nigger, 'Brooklyn Shine,' " and "two other coons, 'The Riverside Shine' and 'Boston Yellow.' " Callahan writes hard-boiled prose with great skill, and he is not totally devoid of moral sensibilities, as shown in his concluding sketch, a brilliant and shocking description of the hideous execution of a Black prisoner in the electric chair, which comes out as a far more criminal act than Callahan's own killings. Because of Callahan's extraordinary frankness, the description of his own career as a writer of fiction is exceptionally revealing.

His first venture as an author was an autobiographical article "on how a bank burglar attained success in the automobile business." He "pounded out" this article, giving it a suitable "inspirational twist," and then went wild with joy when it was published. He decides to become a "great writer" by creating stories about criminals. With straight-faced ironical humor about both himself and his editors, he tells of his early success:

> . . . I began my crook serial. I wrote myself into the story. I called it "The Philanthropic Bank Burglar." I was robbing banks and building hospitals with the money I got. I was a burglar with an ideal. Prisons were all wrong. Criminals should be treated in hospitals by psychiatrists and pathologists. I was sending all the money that I got out of the banks to a well-known pathologist. I was sending it anonymously and he was building a hospital with it. I had celebrated detectives on my trail all through the story and just about the time that they were going to capture me, the reader read "continued in the next

installment." I had learned how to leave readers "hanging in the air" gasping for breath, and I was sure that I was a great novelist when the readers began writing me letters complimenting me on the "marvelous Philanthropic Bank Burglar."

> But I was not so good on endings. I killed the detective at the end of the story. One of the Editors said that wouldn't do, that I would have to change the ending.

> "We must have a moral in the story," he said, "and the moral of this story should be defeat. A burglar should never succeed."

> So I switched the ending. I had myself killed by the detective! Needless to say I didn't like that ending. I preferred killing the dick to being killed.

This kind of fantasy fiction by convicts, in which a loser can imagine himself a winner, reached its full development almost half a century later, when it was no longer necessary to point toward the moral that crime doesn't pay. E. Richard Johnson, serving forty years in Stillwater Prison, Minnesota, for a hold-up killing, churns out hard-boiled crime novels at a rapid rate: *Silver Street* (1968), *Mongo's Back in Town* (1969), *The God Keepers* (1970), *Case Load-Maximum* (1971), *The Judas* (1971). In some the criminal-protagonist ends up like Callahan's philanthropic bank burglar. But in *The Judas,* the hero—and first-person narrator—is a professional killer who single-handedly wipes out the really mean criminals in Kansas City and lives to enjoy his trade. (Johnson writes a more honest kind of fiction in *Cage Five Is Going To Break*

[1970], a novel of brutality and betrayal set on a prison farm.) The highest artistic achievement in this genre is almost certainly Edward Bunker's *No Beast So Fierce* (1973), which carries the fantasy of the world-defying criminal explicitly to a Nietzschean level; I shall discuss this novel and its significance in the final chapter.

Quite a different kind of fiction develops from the reformist tendency still dominant in prison autobiographical narratives of this period. For example, the bank robber Ernest Booth, who published his autobiography, *Stealing through Life,* in 1929, went on much later to write a protest novel against prison and the legal machinery of which it is a part, entitled *With Sirens Screaming* (1945).

Booth, along with Robert Joyce Tasker, author of *Grimhaven* (1928), Victor Folke Nelson, who wrote *Prison Days and Nights* (1933), and the prolific Jim Tully, were all encouraged by H. L. Mencken; their sketches and tales appeared frequently in the *American Mercury* between 1925 and 1933. Five sections of *Stealing through Life* appeared first in the *Mercury,* including the lead piece for September 1927, "We Rob a Bank," a marvelous description of his own feelings during a bank stick-up and getaway. Then a couple of years after the publication of his autobiographical narrative in book form, Booth made one final appearance in the *Mercury,* "Ladies in Durance Vile" (April 1931), fine sketches of life in the women's section of Folsom Prison. The last sketch points forward to his novel. It tells of an eighteen-year-old woman unwittingly trapped as the "accomplice" of her youthful husband, whom she had known only three days, because "under California law *all* accomplices, regardless of how far they were removed from the crime, are equally guilty with the principals." Mary is serving life for a murder her husband committed during a bank robbery she knew nothing about; he is due to be hanged in the same prison. Booth describes the final day, with the prison awash in a "ghostly grey fog" that "drifted off the bay and shrouded the tops of the walls":

> From my hunched-up position on the railing I glanced up at the lighted window with the vent. The leaf was out. The window showed two figures pressed against it. Mary, also, had seen the warden pass. . . . I visualized that girl up there in a room filled with silent women. She, too, was waiting.
>
> The huge weight of the trap dropped with ponderous decisiveness. Through the salt-bitter air that thud came with a sickening hard finality. More minutes dragged through my benumbed mind.
>
> Again the warden appeared, now walking rapidly through the fog, as though he would lose in it a pursuing ghastliness. . . . A gentle murmur rose in the cells. The prison stirred. Life moved again in the women's department. I heard the whirring of sewing-machines. At the window there was no shadow. The leaf had been replaced in the vent.
>
> Down through the awakening life there came the brown autumnal voice of Grace: "Get to work girls! Get at your tasks!"

> Suddenly her voice rose in harshness: "Mary, go on in and get to work! Go on! Go on! There's nothing more to wait for. It's all over!"
>
> Then through that thin pane of glass and out into the heavy fog, there came Mary's cry: "All over?" And all the bleakness of the endless years before her was in her final anguished scream: "Over? God no! It's just *starting!*"

Booth transmutes this material, but still uses it for reformist purposes, in *With Sirens Screaming.* In this earnest and somewhat dated novel, a young World War II veteran and his seventeen-year-old sweetheart unwittingly commit a crime just by traveling together. She is held as a juvenile delinquent. He is imprisoned on a morals charge, escapes, commits a crime, becomes involved in a prison riot, is convicted for another crime that he did not commit, and is sentenced to capital punishment, as Ann, his lover, here tells in protest against his fate and the system which determined it:

> "Mark is unjustly condemned to die. Actually, he has not committed a crime. Trying to get married, we were treated like children. Mark escaped, so he could see my mother and get her to withdraw the charge against him. During a rainstorm he took an overcoat. For that he was given a life sentence. In Folsom Prison he was near by when a guard was cut with a knife. For that he has been tried and now the State will kill him. . . . All he wanted to do was marry me, live honorably, work hard, and be a credit to his parents and the country he has served."

This protest in some ways is actually a retreat from the consciousness of much previous writing from prison, because it is directed primarily against the inflexibility of a legal system which victimizes an innocent individual, not a people or a social class. On the other hand, the novel can also be read as a forerunner of the protest movement against the oppression of youth, with even that movement's individualist anarchism and escape to a fantasy of life outside society. Faced with an implacably unreasonable society, Ann, unlike Mary, her model in real life, turns into a heroic figure of action. She pulls a gun in prison, and forces the warden to come with them to cover Mark's escape. She leads Mark to a well-stocked mountain cabin in an idyllic wilderness setting. At the end, the two lovers are preparing to live in this wilderness while the machinery of state, "with sirens screaming," is trying to apprehend them and all other youthful threats to the well-being of society.

The main ex-convict contributor to the *American Mercury* was Jim Tully, who published no fewer than thirteen stories and sketches in its pages between 1925 and 1933. Tully, born of a poverty-stricken Irish immigrant family in 1888, had become a "road-kid" at the age of eleven, and his adventures in the ensuing twelve years as a hobo, circus roustabout, prisoner, and professional prizefighter provided the materials for all his early books, which ranged from novels to autobiographical narratives, mostly falling someplace in between. *Emmett Lawler,* an autobiographical novel, appeared in 1922, but his real reputation began in 1924 with the publication of *Beggars of Life,* which described his initiation into the life of a hobo, his first arrests, and the lives and deaths of people on the fringes of society—tramps, jailbirds, and prostitutes.

Beggars of Life displayed all the main characteristics of the style and method Tully was to use in his subsequent twenty-four books: fast-paced, episodic, alternating between cynicism and sentimentality, tough and ostensibly detached on the outside but obviously filled with compassion, always aligned with the victims and misfits against organized society. Here, for example, is his description of a lynching in a western town:

> I left the good woman's home and walked toward the centre of the town, carrying a "handout" which solved my eating problem for the day. As I reached the court-house square, a crowd yelled madly. They stood in front of the court-house jail yelling loudly at someone inside. Some broken iron bars hung from a third story window. Soon the end of a rope was thrown from the window to the waiting crowd below. Many men grabbed it. Framed in the window, with a rope around his neck, and men screaming behind him, was a negro, with eyes as big as eggs.
>
> "Kill the nigger! Kill the nigger!" yelled many voices. "Pop his neck. Make it crack."
>
> The negro's face writhed in fear, as women, men and children hurried from all directions into the square.
>
> A terrific shout went up, and the rope was jerked by many men. The black body shot into space, whirled, and fell crashing into a tree. "Don't shoot," screamed a voice.
>
> A man untangled the wriggling body, and, shaking and horror-stricken, it fell to the ground. They dragged the half-conscious negro to the business square, where a fire burned slowly.
>
> He was placed upright above it, his armpits in heavy post-like crutches.
>
> As the shoes were ripped off, the blaze burned his feet. He wriggled his body frantically as more fuel was placed on the fire and the flame shot upward. "Not too fast," yelled a voice. "Let him burn slow." The doomed Ethiopian's eyes rolled swiftly as the poles were knocked from under him and his body fell into the fire. A blood-curdling "Ouch, ouch, O God! Oh, ouch, O God, O God hab mercy."
>
> "We'll mercy you—you black bastard," yelled a man.
>
> The poles were made upright, and the negro's armpits were fitted into the crutch-like end of them. Wriggling loose, the black mortal tried to eat fire to end his agony. That boon was denied him. A club crashed his wrist. His head went on his breast. His eyes closed a moment, and as the blaze shot higher, they opened in awful pain.
>
> The clothes burned first, and then the flame ate the hair from his skull. The ears charred and

> melted on his head. He moaned in prolonged and dying pain, "ooooo-ooch, oo-oh-oh-oh."
>
> The burnt body fell from its moorings, and the poles dropped over it. Kerosene was thrown on the hissing fire.
>
> Sick at heart, I turned away. Some children skipped the death-rope gracefully.

At the end of the book, Tully assures us that "I am no reformer, but a weary writer who has been living in the memory of adventure." In 1928, *Beggars of Life* was dramatized by Maxwell Anderson with the appropriate title *Outside Looking In.*

Tully's *Jarnegan* (1925) was a fast-moving novel about a supermasculine figure, something of a self-fantasy, who kills a man in a fist fight, is imprisoned, but eventually becomes a successful Hollywood director. *Circus Parade* (1927), consisting of fictionalized sketches of Tully's life as a roustabout in a traveling circus, was another sensation, chosen by the Literary Guild and banned in Boston. One of the tendencies in Tully's fiction is brought out in an extreme form in this book. Tully's sense of all his fellow outcasts as misfits and oddities leads to an art which always threatens to convert even the most sympathetic characters into caricatures. In *Circus Parade,* his misfits are actually turned into freaks, like "the female Hercules," the love-starved giantess who kills herself over unrequited love, or the "repressed but deeply emotional" beautiful young woman who converts herself into "the Moss-Haired Girl."

Shanty Irish (1928), a book dominated by the fine portrait of his Irish grandfather, describes Tully's impoverished childhood. *Shadows of Men* (1930) is, in Tully's own words, about "the tribulations, vagaries, and hallucinations of men in jail." *Blood on the Moon* (1931) brings the story of his life up through his career as a prizefighter and his decision to become a writer; it ends with the words, "In ten years my first book was published." *Laughter in Hell* (1932) is a novel about an Irishman who kills his wife and her lover. *The Bruiser* (1936) returns to Tully's days as a pugilist, and *A Hollywood Decameron* (1937) describes his life in the movie capital, where he went in the early 1930s, soon to become a publicist for Charlie Chaplin and ultimately to get rich doing articles for screen magazines. His final works included the novel *Biddy Brogan's Boy* (1942) and a series of short biographies of famous contemporaries, *Dozen and One* (1943), introduced by Damon Runyon, who describes Tully as at least "among the first five" of living writers.

During his days on the road, Tully spent a total of about five years in jail, almost all on vagrancy and similar charges. In other words, his "crime" was much like that of Bartleby, a refusal to fit into the workaday world of his society. This was not merely his crime but also the center of vision in his literary art. The category of literature I have established as a touchstone in this chapter about literature by criminals, the picaresque, is precisely the one in which Tully places his own literary achievement. Tully does not, however, see himself as a conventional picaresque novelist imagining the life of an outlaw and outsider, but as one of these beings actually opening up communication with polite society. As he puts it in the introduction to *Blood on the Moon* (1931):

> To those critics, however kind, who contend that I am a novelist trying to find myself, I will here answer for the first and only time. If I have not been able to invent a new medium in my picaresque books, I have at least been strong enough not to conform to one that is outworn.
>
> I did not study the people in these books as an entomologist does a bug on a pin. I was of them. I am still of them. I can taste the bitterness of their lives in the bread I eat today.

Tully's literary vision of the victim as the criminal is developed most fully in *Shadows of Men,* his book about life in jail. *Shadows of Men* opens with the chapter "Sapping Day" (which had appeared in the *American Mercury* in 1929), presenting in microcosm Tully's sense of a world divided between good citizens who are really vicious monsters, and their no-good victims, who are really good-hearted misfits. It takes place in Kansas, and Sapping Day is a ritualized mass brutalization of the tramps and vagrants:

> Lined up on each side of the lane, hundreds of men awaited us. They were well supplied with clubs, stones, and long rattan whips.
>
> At a signal we started to run.
>
> On both sides of us were the leering and tobacco-stained faces of rustics, old, middle aged, and young. The lashing of long whips could be heard on naked skin. The hoboes grunted and staggered on. We, the despised and rejected, ran as if it were part of the day's work.
>
> We had not gone far when two old vagabonds fell exhausted to the ground.
>
> A group of rustics gathered about them.
>
> Mud was thrown in their aged faces. They tried to ward off the brutality by holding their arms over their eyes. They were kicked in the sides. Hard hands slapped viciously against their hollow cheeks.
>
> "We'll teach you, damn you, to stay away from honest men," a rustic in a rubber collar shouted. As if to better shield themselves from the fury, the two old codgers turned on their stomachs and buried their faces in the mud.
>
> A farmer spat tobacco juice in their ears.
>
> They took it in silence.

At the end of the chapter "Sapping Day," Tully and the other vagrants are arrested on the charge of "having no visible means of support" and booked into jail, the scene of the main narrative. *Shadows of Men* concludes with a sketch restating the theme of the opening festivities in Kansas, "A California Holiday" (originally written in 1928 on assignment for the *American Mercury*), the hanging of an innocent convict in San Quentin, accompanied by all the solemn rituals of officialdom. From first to last,

the book displays the victimization of the "criminal" by law-abiding society.

The vision of the loner, the outsider, the outlaw, the scapegoat persecuted and tormented by society is carried to its logical extreme in *Philosophy of the Dusk* (1929), an autobiographical and speculative narrative by Kain O'Dare, a professional criminal who had become a short-story writer. O'Dare, hanging from his thumbs in a midwestern penitentiary, being tortured to make him betray a fellow prisoner, perceives himself as reliving the experience of Christ:

> My thumbs were being torn out of their sockets. I was dripping wet with sweat. Every bone in my body was aching. I was gradually slipping away into some vague world. Little flashes were appearing in the darkness. My mother was speaking to me. My sister was speaking to me. I was a child again. And I remembered a story that I had heard when I was a child.
>
> It was the story of Christ nailed to the cross. Bleeding. Taking a repentant thief into paradise. I knew much how Christ must have felt, with his hands nailed high and his feet nailed low. And I knew in the bottom of my heart that Christ had never been a squealer, and that he would have helped John Gaber to escape so he could have reached the bedside of his dying wife.

Not all prison writers saw themselves as loners or as part of an outcast class. In one of the most famous prison narratives of the 1920s, *The Twenty-Fifth Man. The Strange Story of Ed Morrell, the Hero of Jack London's "Star Rover"* (1924), Ed Morrell does describe his own experience of unspeakable torture in San Quentin and Folsom in terms very much like those used by Kain O'Dare, and he does dedicate much of his subsequent life to aiding prisoners. But Morrell's original crimes came from an identification with the very people Tully perceived as part of the hostile organized society, the working class and small property owners. Morrell had been involved with people who had been dispossessed by Leland Stanford's railroad and who were fighting back with night robberies of railroad funds. When his lover's father was jailed in this war, Morrell organized a successful jail-break, during which a sheriff was wounded, leading eventually to Morrell's imprisonment as a lifer, first in Folsom and later in San Quentin. There he helped, as the "twenty-fifth man," to organize a prison mutiny, which was betrayed. During weeks of unimaginable torture, he experienced an almost mystical vision of his future mission in life, prison reform. Eventually pardoned, Morrell became an indefatigable worker for his "New Era Penology" and a writer of short stories on the side. *The Twenty-Fifth Man,* his major work, is introduced by George Hunt, the first governor of Arizona, who praises the courage of Morrell and the many others who had unsuccessfully fought back against the plundering of California by the railroad magnates.

The autobiographical narratives by prisoners in the 1920s were gradually leading toward a more radical social analysis. Toward the end of the decade, Charles Patrick Murphy, a lifer in the Idaho State Penitentiary who had previously published three books of autobiographical and other writing, brought out *Shadows of the Gallows* (1928), a lengthy and cogent analysis of crime, its causes, and the history of its punishment. Murphy perceived the so-called criminals as the people on the bottom, the victims of the real criminals, those at the top:

> For thousands of years the whip, the chain, the rack, the gibbet, and the sword, have been used to uphold the laws made by robbers, idlers, and by ambitious lunatics, to punish the "crimes" of the ignorant and the weak.

The prison system rested solidly on the belief that convicts were not human beings, and this assumption permeated all aspects of the institutions, with only rare exceptions. So the spectacle of prisoners actually publishing books which were being received as literary achievements or intelligent social analysis or both was fundamentally threatening. These books posed the same kind of subversive threat that narratives by fugitive slaves had presented in the years between 1830 and 1860; for the practices of the modern prison system, and perhaps that system itself, like slavery, could not last if society recognized its victims as intelligent human beings.

In the economic boom times of the 1920s, however, there was not much opportunity for prisoners to link up with radical social forces in the society as a whole. Then came the Crash of 1929, and immediately a wave of suppression swept over the convicts trying to write from inside the prison to the people outside. This sudden shift of policy was described in 1945 by Herman K. Spector as merely a reaction to the success of prison writing in the 1920s: "Ironically enough, their flurry of success set off a counterflow of reaction and prohibition, during which California adopted the policy that convicts were in prison 'to be punished, not to make money' " ["What Men Write in Prison," *Tomorrow,* December 1945]. Certainly the prison authorities did not want to see their inmates making money during the Depression. Did they also fear the lines of communication being opened between prisoners inside the walls and the millions of angry people on the other side? Whatever their motives, their new policy of suppression for a while had devastating results, as Miriam Allen De Ford describes in "Shall Convicts Write Books?," an article published by the *Nation* in late 1930: " . . . cells were searched all through *San Quentin*—not for narcotics or knives, but for manuscripts," and all those found were removed and presumably destroyed.

The suppression was by no means entirely successful. A large breakthrough was made when Robert E. Burns's *I Am a Fugitive from a Georgia Chain Gang!* suddenly became a national sensation in 1932, the same year that scores of coal miners striking in Harlan County, Kentucky, were imprisoned for "criminal syndicalism," a year in which over a quarter-million acres of land in the United States were under cultivation by convicts.

Burns had been launched into national prominence before he wrote his best-selling book; what made it so popular and influential was not only its horrifying revelations about convict labor but also the extraordinary circumstances of Burns's life. Before World War I, Burns had been a successful young accountant. He enlisted, served in a medical detachment at the front, and returned a fairly

typical case of what was then called "shell-shock." Drifting into penniless desperation, he was more or less forced by another man to participate in a grocery store holdup which yielded $5.80. He was sentenced to six to ten years on a Georgia chain gang. A Black convict, who "had been in the gang so long and had used a sledge so much that he had become an expert," deformed Burns's ankle shackles for him; Burns slipped them off his emaciated legs and made a hair-raising escape, eventually ending up in Chicago. It was then 1922. By 1929, Burns was a prominent editor and businessman in Chicago. Then he was betrayed as a fugitive, and Georgia's successful request for extradition aroused a national storm of protest. He was sent to La Grange, the toughest stockade among the 140 chain-gang camps of the state, "a place shunned by everyone of Georgia's 5,000-odd felons." There this well-educated, now widely respected white businessman and journalist comes to share the fate of the most brutally oppressed men in Georgia. He becomes part of a minority in what he calls "hell":

> As I was locked in the bull pen, a guard changed the figures on a small blackboard to read:
>
> | White prisoners | 33 |
> | Black prisoners | 69 |
> | Total | 102 |
>
> I made the thirty-third white convict in the worst chain-gang camp of them all.

Burns escapes once again. And like the fugitive slaves of the nineteenth century, he once again heads north. When *I Am a Fugitive from a Georgia Chain Gang!* was published in 1932, Burns was living a furtive existence under false names in New Jersey.

Burns precisely details the various forms of torture on the chain gang: the "jack," "a relic of the ancient Spanish Inquisition"; the sweat box, in which the prisoner can neither lie nor stand nor sit; the "pickshack," a ten-pound hinged steel bar locked on and around the calf of the leg in addition to shackles and chains; the "necklace," a massive iron collar with five feet of heavy chain; and of course the routine sadistic floggings. He describes the daily horrors of prison life: the crushing labor, the absence of any nourishing food, sleeping in chains, having to get permission to wipe the sweat off your face, rarely being allowed to wash, and so on. And just as foreign to Burns's accustomed life is the intimate contact with Black people, to whom this life is not at all uncommon. So Burns's narrative serves as a kind of surrogate, bringing many readers from his own social class and millions of other white Americans into touch with convict labor and, to some extent, with the Black culture developing within it.

Other prison narratives by white men had reported to their basically white audiences about Black songs. In *You Can't Win,* Jack Black on the night of his first arrest hears "a colored woman" prisoner "singing a mournful dirge about 'That Bad Stackalee' "; he tells us that he later learned "that this song is a favorite among negroes when in great trouble, such as being locked in jail, being double-crossed by a friend, or parting with their money in a dice game. At such times thirty or forty verses of 'Stackalee' invariably restores the laughing good humor and child-like confidence of the wronged one." In *Shadows of Men*, Jim Tully describes a condemned Black convict singing a modern version of a song that we saw as a slave song recorded by William Wells Brown in *Clotel*, but Tully takes this singing merely as evidence that "the Negro" was facing "the meaningless futility of his chaotic life with the laughter of a fool":

> "Hang up de fiddle an' de bow,
> Lay down de shobel an' de hoe,
> Dey's no moah stealin' fo' pooh ol' Ned,
> He's goin' wheah de bad niggahs go."

Burns, however, reporting from inside convict slave labor, the matrix of many Black songs, understands their true significance:

> Just as day was breaking in the east we commenced our endless heart-breaking toil. We began in mechanical unison and kept at it in rhythmical cadence until sundown—fifteen and a half hours of steady toil—as regular as the ticking of a clock.

> In the chain gangs, human labor has been synchronized as the goose step was in the German Army. When using pickaxes, all picks hit the ground at the same time, all are raised and steadied for the next blow with uncanny mechanical precision. So it is with all work, shoveling, hammering, drilling. The convict bodies and muscle move in time and in unison as one man. The tempo and speed is regulated by the chanting of Negro bondage songs, led by a toil-hardened Negro of years of servitude as follows:

> "A long steel rail," croons the leader.

> "Ump!" grunt all the rest in chorus as pickaxes came down.

> "An' a short cross tie," croons the leader.

> "Ump!" grunt all the rest in chorus as pickaxes come up.

> "It rings lik' sil-vah," croons the leader.

> "Ump!" goes the chorus as the picks come down.

> "It shin's lik' go-old," croons the leader.

> "Ump!" and all the picks come up.

> And so it goes all day long, with the torrid rays of the blazing monarch of the skies adding their touch of additional misery.

> This working in unison is called "Keeping the lick."

Later Burns tells us that the usual "lick" was sixteen per minute, a very precise measure of a certain kind of musical time.

Burns by no means feels at one with his Black fellow prisoners. He not only habitually refers to them as "niggers," but when he protests against Georgia's violations of its own penal regulations, one of his complaints is that con-

trary to the law "whites and Negroes worked side by side." Nevertheless, he has many passages of deep sympathy for the special oppression of the Black prisoners, and he understands that their servitude, unlike his own, is part of the history of a people. When two Black convicts flee in desperation, he perceives their predicament historically, even echoing Frederick Douglass's definition of their white pursuers as "beasts of prey":

> Two illiterate Negroes, battling for freedom in the wilds of Georgia's swamps, hunted by white men like beasts of prey. For more than two hundred years the woods and swamps of Georgia have witnessed similar exciting scenes.

> And even before that in the wilds of Africa the tragedy was enacted, the purpose the same, the result foretold.

And he does not see the hell of convict labor as something unique to the South but as part of "Twentieth Century America, the land of ideals, human justice, liberty and progress."

During this period, relatively little literature was published by women prisoners, partly because far fewer women than men were in prison and partly because their typical crimes—prostitution, shoplifting, drug addiction, begging, check passing—were merely part of the humdrum daily activity of poverty rather than the thrilling adventures of train robbery, bank stick-ups, professional forgery, and burglary. The real-life counterparts of Stephen Crane's "Maggie: Girl of the Streets" were not publishing their stories. If there were any happy hookers like Xaviera Hollander, they were certainly not convicts. And after all, even Moll Flanders had told her tale from the vantage of a now reformed—and wealthy—character.

One notable woman criminal who was something of an author was Bonnie Parker, but she wrote as a defiant fugitive, not a convict. Her famous doggerel ballad "Bonnie and Clyde," published by the Dallas *Morning News* on May 23, 1934, shortly after she and Clyde Barrow were shot to death in a police ambush, does illustrate one tendency in early twentieth-century prison literature, a mixture of rebellion against the state machinery with a sense of guilt and doom. As she puts it in some of the key stanzas:

> Now Bonnie and Clyde are the Barrow gang,
> I'm sure you all have read
> How they rob and steal and how those who
>   squeal
> Are usually found dying or dead.

> There are lots of untruths to their write-ups,
> They are not so merciless as that;
> And they fight because they hate all the laws,
> The stool pigeons, spotters and rats.

> They class them as cold-blooded killers,
> They say they are heartless and mean;
> But I saw this with pride that I once knew Clyde
> When he was honest and upright and clean.

> But the law pestered them, fooled around
> And kept locking him up in a cell;
> Till he said to me, "I will never be free,

So I'll meet a few of them in hell."

They don't think they are too tough and desper-
    ate.
They know that the law always wins;
They've been shot at before, but they do not ig-
    nore
That death is the wages of sin.

Quite different from Bonnie Parker, both as a criminal and as an author, was Agnes Smedley. Her crime was aiding friends from India in their struggle for independence from British colonialism. In 1918 she was arrested, charged with violating the Neutrality Law, and placed in solitary confinement in the Tombs for about nine months. There she wrote her first published narratives, *Cell Mates*, sketches of fellow women prisoners. This experience as a prisoner helped shape her future as one of America's most internationally respected writers of the 1930s and 1940s. Smedley's books about the Chinese revolution—*Chinese Destinies* (1933), *China's Red Army Marches* (1934), *China Fights Back; An American Woman with the Eighth Route Army* (1938), *Battle Hymn of China* (1943)—are just beginning to come back into acclaim in America after their suppression in the 1950s, but their international reputation has never waned. Her autobiographical novel *Daughter of Earth,* originally published in 1929, reappeared in 1935 with a long new section describing her imprisonment and its effects on her consciousness. Since the reissue of *Daughter of Earth* in 1973, many teachers of literature have come to regard it as the finest proletarian novel of the 1920s and 1930s, and a few make even larger claims for it.

The imprisonment of women convicts is the main subject of two autobiographical narratives published in the mid-1930s: the anonymous *Female Convict* (1934) and Edna O'Brien's *So I Went to Prison* (1938). These two books offer a startling, and most revealing, comparison.

Edna O'Brien is another one of those examples proving Julian Hawthorne's contention that prisons would not survive if enough respected citizens ever experienced them from inside. What makes O'Brien's narrative extraordinary is her sex. She had been vice-president and treasurer of a small manufacturing company. Then in the heady days of the late 1920s she began to branch out as a professional speculator on the stock market. Her first "radical" act was having a stock ticker installed in her office; in this man's world of business, "a ticker in a woman's private office was radical." When the Crash came, she found herself unable to deliver some stock due to a friend, a wealthy woman doctor. She thought little of this until early 1933, when she was arrested for grand larceny, in a case making the front pages of the New York newspapers. Convicted in 1935, she served a year in the State Prison for Women at Bedford Hills, New York. For her, the main torments of prison are merely the routine physical discomforts, the personal indignities, and the deprivation of her normal luxury and freedom. Nevertheless, she becomes a passionate opponent of penal imprisonment, wondering "Why do we keep deluding ourselves that herding people behind bars prevents crime?"

Female Convict is a far more powerful book. One of seven children, the anonymous narrator tells how she grew up in her family of ten "in two rooms on the top floor of a tenement," with "two grimy windows" through which seeped "the foul odors of the stockyards." The physical prison conditions described by Edna O'Brien would have been a welcome relief from the childhood experienced by this woman. Her family "had but three beds for ten people," and "there was absolutely no privacy"; " . . . in order that my father or brother might sleep for their work the next morning, my little sister and I played on the roof or on the street until two or three in the morning." They had "no electric lights, no bathroom, no heat":

> In the hall-way was a dirty sink with the only running water in the house. The only toilet facilities were in the back yard. The place was used by twelve families, some of them as large as our own. The yard was a rubbish pile, consisting of the garbage thrown from the windows of the tenements which looked out upon it. An ugly heap of refuse, sardine and tomato cans, beer bottles, whiskey flasks, old shoes and rags. A stable, a junk-yard and a box factory flanked our row of tenements. And across the street stood a kosher slaughter-house.
>
> A row of saloons and booze joints down the street kept the neighborhood in a constant uproar with rum-hound rows and drunken brawls. On Saturday nights the sidewalks were lined with drunks and tipsters. . . . Early every morning, at five o'clock, we were awakened by the bleating of sheep, and the cries of the cattle, as they were driven down the street to the slaughter-house.

This is the norm of her prose: terse, precise, straightforward, unsentimental, clear, drawing its enormous strength from the reality of its remembered physical and psychological detail. It is a prose that flows naturally from her class experience, a prose that makes many of the would-be proletarian novels and plays of the 1930s seem hollow imitations. When she does generalize on the basis of her experience, it has the ring of truth, even when she uses language that has been purposely discredited, such as "the unabating exploitation of the masses." For in her next sentence she reminds us, "When I speak of the exploited class I speak from experience."

There is nothing roundabout or abstract in her own understanding of both the causes of crime and the various schemes for punishing or eliminating it. She cuts directly through to the heart of the matter:

> Gangsters? They were grown as naturally in the alleys and gutters of our slum neighborhood as mosquitoes grow in a swamp. Now when I pick up a paper and read of one more noble crusade against gangsters, I smile—and understand. To whip up a crusade against gangsters is as ludicrous as to organize an army of mosquito-swatters while the swamplands where they multiply are left untouched.
>
> Society makes gunmen and then gets excited when their guns go off.

"I understand," she adds, because "I saw how my own brother became a gangster."

Her father drank "to defend himself . . . against the hopeless cage of poverty which permanently imprisoned him. When drunk he was vicious." When Jack, her oldest brother, was nineteen, he returned home with the news that he had been laid off from the automobile parts factory because they had just installed new automated equipment. The result was the experience that makes her perceive the "criminal" as the desperate victim:

> That night my father happened to be drunk. When he learned of Jack's discharge he was enraged. He threw Jack out of the house and told him not to come back until he had another job. Jack was on the street without a nickel. He did the only thing he could think of—went to a poolroom dive and slept that night on a pool-table. There he met a gang of unfortunate slum lads like himself—most of them farther down the road of ruin than he. Two months later Jack was caught in a hold-up and sent to Joliet for ten years.

> Jack's story is the story of thousands of unlucky lads whom our social order labels criminals.

Soon after, her father, who worked in the Gary steel mills, is "burned alive by a wave of fiery iron." She is forced to leave high school. Before long, she is writing bad checks to survive. She is arrested, put in jail for six months awaiting trial, and is then sent to prison on a sentence of seven years maximum.

What oppresses her about jail is not, as it would be later for Edna O'Brien, primarily the physical conditions, though these are bad enough. What makes jail and prison qualitatively more hellish than the cage of her childhood poverty is the relationships among the human beings. This comes out initially as she sits on a bench at her first dinner, where she witnesses a racist incident that fills her with a profound "loathing for the place":

> I squeezed in between a burly negress and a thin-faced, tired little woman. The latter gave a snarl of protest and poked me with her elbows.

> The former was very friendly. "What's yo' name, honey?"

> "Call me Eleanor," I replied.

> "Mah name's Mary, dey call's me Black Mary. Whatta yo' all up for, Eleanor?" she queried.

> "I guess you'd call it forgery," I replied. We became quite chummy. I rather liked Black Mary. Hers was a frank, friendly face. . . .

> The coffee-pourer for some reason had overlooked my companion, Black Mary. She held up her tin cup. "Give me some of dat dere chicory-soup, Mamie," said Black Mary, with a friendly grin.

> "You dirty nigger, you got your coffee," said the woman with the pot in her hand, and as she passed behind Black Mary she gave her a vicious

kick to emphasize it. Black Mary sat up straight with a cry of pain.

> "Please, mam, don't do dat to me. . . . Ah ain't had a bit a coffee . . . ah swear ah ain't. . . .

> She didn't finish the sentence. The prison flunky came back and gave Black Mary a resounding smack alongside the jaw with a dirty towel she was carrying. With an oath, Black Mary leaped to her feet. They closed in a furious, rough-and-tumble fight. The rest of the prisoners began to cheer and yell, stamping their feet and pounding the table with their tin cups.

> "Bite her ear off, Black Mary," some of them cried.

> Others yelled, "Kill that nigger, kill that nigger." . . .

> The whole thing sickened me. I got up and left the table, my meal practically untouched. I went back to my cell, with a loathing for the place that burned in my heart like fire.

When she arrives in prison, she is marched in company with the other new "fish" to visit the warden's office. Her description of this "sorry-looking crew," in "our gray prison dresses" without "a scrap of underwear or a stocking in the gang," gives a brilliantly vivid picture of the kinds of women confined as criminals in the cages of the "penitentiary":

> Directly behind Red-frotz [the matron] walked Laura, the Candy Kid, seventeen year old shoplifter, prostitute and drug-addict, an inveterate thief, pretty as a picture.

> Then Rebecca, thirty year old Jewess, diseased, heavily sentenced after a fourth offence at shoplifting.

> Next Old Lady Cuno, eighty-seven, arrested for begging, always swearing in German and smelling like a fish factory.

> Following her, Stephanie, the Czechoslovakian girl, with swarthy complexion and large black eyes, with her deep guttural voice, an all-around crook and shoplifter.

> Then back of her, Dora Coningsby, drug-addict and prostitute, with the needle-pocked body.

> Next "Bugs," an old Irish woman who smoked a pipe and swore like a trooper, and had a habit of spitting in your face if she was angry.

> Following "Bugs," Big Bertha, a burly dark-complexioned drug-addict, with her mottled hair in curlers and skirts above her bare knees.

> Then Pauline, the most beautiful girl in the prison, kleptomaniac, graduate of Vassar, with the background of a fine family, up the second time for cashing bad checks.

> Behind her, Lillian Johnson, six feet tall, pretty but a badly diseased prostitute.

> Then the Kid from Georgia, a nineteen year old

girl taken from a sailor's dive, very badly diseased with red spots all over her body.

After her Rachel Endres, whose husband had framed her, then myself, followed by Ethel Kingsley, morose murderess, who had killed her husband in a row about another woman, and at the end of the rogue's gallery line Joan Barnum, bootleg queen, up for ten years for shooting a policeman.

Thus we lock-stepped down the iron stairs to the warden's office.

Once in the office of the warden, she discovers one practical reason why the women were allowed to wear only their prison dresses:

"The first law of this prison," he continued, putting his hand on my shoulder, and gradually running it down my side, a smirk of sensual pleasure playing upon his leather-like countenance, " . . . is to obey at all times . . . to obey your superiors . . . to fit in to your surroundings without fault-finding or complaint. . . ." His hand had now progressed below my skirt, and he was pressing and patting my naked thigh . . . "because unruly prisoners are not wanted here and they are apt to get into trouble. . . ."

The main human relationship she has to cling to during her prison life is the love of the man who awaits her outside. At one point even this literally turns into a nightmare. One night she is pleasantly dreaming of her lover, when, as she describes in a splendid piece of narrative art, the dream becomes increasingly hideous until she awakes to find her body almost completely covered with cockroaches. Eventually she manages to escape from prison and rejoin her lover, who flees with her out west. *Female Convict*, like most of the nineteenth-century slave narratives, and like *I Am a Fugitive from a Georgia Chain Gang!*, thus comes to the reader from the mouth of a fugitive being hunted by the law.

> H. Bruce Franklin, "A History of Literature by Convicts in America," in his Prison Literature in America: The Victim as Criminal and Artist, revised edition, Oxford University Press, Inc., 1989, pp. 124-78.

FURTHER READING

Anthologies

Haworth, Peter, ed. *Classic Crimes in History and Fiction.* New York: D. Appleton, 1927, 286 p.
Collects fictitious and historical stories and vignettes about crime.

Secondary Sources

Bernheimer, Charles. *Figures of Ill Repute: Representing Prostitution in Nineteenth-Century France.* Cambridge, Mass.: Harvard University Press, 1989, 329 p.
Contains discussion of the criminal aspects of prostitution represented in the art and literature of nineteenth-century France.

Borowitz, Albert. *Innocence and Arsenic: Studies in Crime and Literature.* New York: Harper and Row, 1977, 170 p.
Collection of essays on crime in literature.

Boyle, Thomas. *Black Swine in the Sewers of Hampstead: Beneath the Surface of Victorian Sensationalism.* New York: Viking, 1989, 273 p.
Examines various nineteenth-century sensationalist publications, some centering on crime.

Davis, Lennard J. "Wicked Actions and Feigned Words: Criminals, Criminality, and the Early English Novel." *Yale French Studies* 59 (1979): 106-18.
Asserts that the early English novel was considered dangerous not only because of the tendency of writers to feature criminal activity in their plots, but also because the novel form "was specifically associated with the fear of threatened violence and social unrest from the lower classes."

Frohock, W. M. *The Novel of Violence in America.* Boston: Beacon Press, 1964, 238 p.
Examines the depiction of violence in the novels of several twentieth-century American writers.

Goodman, Jonathan. "The Fictions of Murderous Fact." *Encounter* LXII, No. 1 (January 1984): 21-6.
Provides a brief history of English true-crime fiction.

Gossett, Louise Y. *Violence in Recent Southern Fiction.* Durham: Duke University Press, 1965, 207 p.
Argues that the violence and grotesqueness portrayed in contemporary Southern writing are manifestations of fears of social disorder.

Hall, Roger Allan. "Frontier Dramatizations: The James Gang." *Theatre Survey* XXI, No. 2 (November 1980): 117-28.
Analyzes popular late nineteenth- and early twentieth-century dramatic recreations of the story of Jesse James and his gang.

Logan, Malcolm. "Glorifying the Criminal." *Scribner's Magazine* XC (July-December 1931): 43-6.
Argues that twentieth-century criminals and gangsters used popular literature, newspapers, and film to create myths out of their otherwise unromantic activities.

Newton, H. Chance. *Crime and the Drama, or Dark Deeds Dramatized.* New York: Kennikat Press, 1927, 284 p.
Discusses theatrical renderings of real-life crimes in early twentieth-century popular drama.

Papke, David Ray. *Framing the Criminal: Crime, Cultural Work and the Loss of Critical Perspective, 1830-1900.* Hamden, Conn.: Archon Books, 1987, 255 p.
Contains discussion of nineteenth-century American criminal memoirs in a work that examines the "crime-related products [that] traveled every avenue into the cultural marketplace" of that period.

Thompson, Jon. *Fiction, Crime, and Empire: Clues to Modernity and Postmodernism.* Chicago: University of Illinois Press, 1993, 200 p.

Addresses how late nineteenth- and twentieth-century crime fiction affirms the values of imperialistic cultures and provides "myths of the experience of modernity."

Watson, Colin. *Snobbery with Violence: Crime Stories and Their Audience.* London: Eyre and Spottiswoode, 1971, 256 p.

Examines early twentieth-century popular crime fiction.

Williams, Daniel E. "Rogues, Rascals and Scoundrels: The Underworld Literature of Early America." *American Studies* XXIV, No. 2 (Fall 1983): 5-19.

Traces changes in the portrayal of criminals in early American crime literature from the pre- to post-Revolutionary War eras, concluding that early Puritan efforts to warn society of the wrath of divine punishment gave way to a celebratory image of the criminal after Americans had become rebels and criminals during the war.

Wilson, A. D. "Crime and the Stage." *The Spectator* 156, No. 5624 (10 April 1936): 659-60.

Contrasts representations of crime in Greek tragedy with those in modern drama.

Wood, Grace A. "Crime and Contrition in Literature." *Contemporary Review* 198 (July 1960): 391-97.

Analyzes sin and repentance in modern dramatic interpretations of the ancient Greek story of Orestes.

Indian Literature in English

INTRODUCTION

"Indo-English" and "Indo-Anglian" are terms used by critics to denote literature written in English by natives of the Indian subcontinent. Both terms distinguish literature composed by native Indians from literature written about India by British authors, which is usually referred to as "Anglo-Indian" literature. British contact with the Indian culture dates back to 1600 with the charter of the British East India Company. Gradually, the English language was introduced to India's native population by merchants and Christian missionaries. Throughout the 1790s and 1800s, most of the Indian subcontinent came under the control of the British Empire. During that time, generations of Indians, especially from the wealthy upper classes, began receiving formal English education, often as preparation for careers in the administration of the British government. Many native Indians attended universities in England. The first works of Indo-English literature were largely attempts to emulate the works of English Romantic and Victorian writers. In the 1930s and 1940s, social realism and nationalist concerns began to dominate much Indian literature in English. Writers such as Mulk Raj Anand, R. K. Narayan, and Raja Rao created fiction set in contemporary India that addressed the various concerns of India's large, poverty-stricken underclass, including the inequities of the Hindu caste system and the desire for an independent, self-governing India. These three, regarded as the "founding fathers" of the Indian novel in English, continue to write today, and two generations of Indian novelists working in English have followed them, including important women writers such as Kamala Markandaya and Anita Desai. Since India won independence from British rule in 1947, the novel in English has continued to be an important vehicle for artistic expression among Indian writers. Poetry, another important form of Indian writing in English, has also continued to flourish in the hands of poets such as Nissim Ezekiel and Kamala Das.

Although generally accepted now, Indian writing in English has in the past been a subject of controversy. India has over a hundred regional, indigenous languages, including Assamese, Bengali, Hindi, Gujarati, Kannada, Malayalam, and Tamil, and some consider English an inappropriate vehicle for communicating the concerns and the flavor of Indian life, especially since it is not usually the first language of those who choose to write in it. The charge that Indo-English authors write for a Western audience rather than an Indian one is still heard, although it is less common than it was only two decades ago. Those who defend Indo-English literature claim that the use of English gives Indian writers a broader audience and greater recognition, as well as helping writers to avoid the divisive issues of regionalism which might accompany poetry and fiction in one of the indigenous tongues.

REPRESENTATIVE WORKS

Abbas, Khwaja Ahmad
  Inquilab; A Novel of Indian Revolution   (novel) 1977
Anand, Mulk Raj
  The Untouchable   (novel) 1935
  Coolie   (novel) 1936
  The Big Heart   (novel) 1945
  Two Leaves and a Bud   (novel) 1946
  The Private Life of an Indian Prince   (novel) 1953
  Morning Face   (novel) 1968
Bhattacharya, Bhabani
  So Many Hungers   (novel) 1947
  A Goddess Named Gold   (novel) 1960
Chatterjee, Bankim Chandra
  Rajmohan's Wife   (novel) 1935
Chattopadhyaya, Harindranath
  Blood of Stones   (poetry) 1944
  Siddhartha: The Man of Peace   (drama)   1956
  Masks and Farewells   (poetry) 1961
Currimbhoy, Asif Ebrahim
  Darjeeling Tea?   (drama) 1971
  The Hungry Ones   (drama) 1977
Daruwalla, Keki N.
  Crossing of Rivers   (poetry) 1976
Das, Kamala
  Summer in Calcutta   (poetry) 1965
  The Old Playhouse, and Other Poems   (poetry) 1973
Derozio, Henry Louis Vivian
  Poems   (poetry) 1827
  The Fakeer of Jungheera: A Metrical Tale and Other Poems   (poetry) 1828
Desai, Anita
  Cry, the Peacock   (novel) 1963
  Voices in the City   (novel) 1965
Desani, G. V.
  All About Mr. Hatterr   (novel) 1948; also published as *All About H. Hatterr,* 1951
Dutt, Romesh Chunder
  Lays of Ancient India   (verse translations) 1895
  The Slave Girl of Agra: An Indian Historical Romance   (novel) 1922
Dutt, Toru
  Bianca; or, The Young Spanish Maiden   (unfinished novel) 1879

A Sheaf Gleaned in French Fields (poetry and verse translations) 1882

Ezekiel, Nissim
  The Unfinished Man: Poems Written in 1959 (poetry) 1960
  Hymns in Darkness (poetry) 1976

Gandhi, Mohandas K.
  An Autobiography; or, The Story of My Experiments with Truth (memoir) 1929

Ghose, Aurobindo
  Songs to Myrtilla, and Other Poems (poetry) 1923
  Savitri (poem) 1950
  Savitri: Two Scenes (drama) 1951

Ghose, Kashiprosad
  The Shair, and Other Poems (poetry) 1830

Ghose, Manmohan
  Love Songs and Elegies (poetry) 1898

Ghose, Sudhindra Nath
  And Gazelles Leaping (novel) 1949
  Cradle of the Couds (novel) 1951
  The Vermillion Boat (novel) 1953
  The Flame of the Forest (novel) 1955

Gokak, V. K.
  In Life's Temple (poetry) 1965

Jhabvala, Ruth Prawer
  Esmond in India (novel) 1958
  Heat and Dust (novel) 1975

Joshi, Arun
  The Strange Case of Billy Biswas (novel) 1971
  The Apprentice (novel) 1974

Kailasam, Tyagaraja Paramasiva
  Karna: The Brahmin's Curse (drama) 1946

Kiran, Amal [pseudonym of Kaikhushru Dhunjibhoy Sethna]
  The Adventure of the Apocalypse (poetry) 1949

Krishnamurti, M.
  The Offering (poetry) 1926

Lal, P.
  Sun: Poems (poetry) 1975

Malgonkar, Manohar
  Distant Drums (novel) 1960
  A Bend in the Ganges (novel) 1965

Malik, Keshav
  The Rippled Shadow (poetry) 1959
  Poems (poetry) 1971

Markandaya, Kamala
  Nectar in a Sieve (novel) 1954
  Some Inner Fury (novel) 1955
  A Handful of Rice (novel) 1966

Moraes, Dom F.
  Poems: 1955–1965 (poetry) 1965

Mukherji, Dhan Gopal
  My Brother's Face (novel) 1925

Nagarajan, Krishnaswamy
  The Chronicles of Kedaram (novel) 1961

Naidu, Sarojini Chattopadhyay
  The Bird of Time: Songs of Life, Death, and the Spring (poetry) 1912
  The Broken Wing: Songs of Love, Death, and the Spring, 1915–1916 (poetry) 1917
  The Feather of Dawn (poetry) 1961

Nandy, Pritish

In Secret Anarchy (poetry) 1976
  Anywhere in Another Place (poetry) 1979

Narayan, R. K.
  The Dark Room (novel) 1938
  Swami and Friends (novel) 1942
  Waiting for the Mahatma (novel) 1955
  The Man-Eater of Malgudi (novel) 1962
  The English Teacher (novel) 1971
  The Painter of Signs (novel) 1976

Nehru, Jawaharlal
  Jawaharlal Nehru, an Autobiography: With Musing on Recent Events in India (memoir) 1936

Parthasarathy, R.
  Rough Passage (poetry) 1976

Rajan, Balachandra
  The Dark Dancer (novel) 1958
  Too Long in the West (novel) 1961

Rao, Raja
  Kanthapura (novel) 1938
  The Serpent and the Rope (novel) 1960
  The Cat and Shakespeare (novel) 1965

Rau, Santha Rama
  Remember the House (novel) 1956

Rushdie, Salman
  Midnight's Children (novel) 1982

Sahgal, Nayantara Pandit
  Prison and Chocolate Cake (memoir) 1954
  A Time to Be Happy (novel) 1958
  From Fear Set Free (memoir) 1963

Singh, Gopal
  The Man Who Never Died (poem) 1969

Singh, Khushwant
  Mano Majra (novel) 1956; also published as *Train to Pakistan*

Singh, Puran
  The Bride of the Sky: A Poetic Play, and Other Poems (poetry) 1976

Srinivas, Krishna
  The Bud and the Blossoms (poetry) 1954
  He Walks the Earth (poetry) 1972

Tagore, Rabindranath
  Gitanjali: Song-Offerings (poetry) 1912

Varma, Monika
  Green Leaves and Gold (poetry) 1970

Venkataramani, K. S.
  Murugan the Tiller (novel) 1927
  Kandan the Patriot (novel) 1934

OVERVIEW

Uma Parameswaran

[*In the following excerpt, Parameswaran provides a historical overview of Indian literature in English.*]

The story of Indo-English literature is similar to that of many other literatures that were born in the wake of the colonial and missionary expansions of the 18th and 19th centuries. It is a bastard child of Britain and a British colony, having, characteristically enough, Christian missionaries as foster-parents. What makes Indo-English culture different from many other offshoots of the colonial and missionary empires is that it is only a minor facet of the complex, crystalline structure that characterizes Indian civilization. Similarly, Indo-English literature is only a minor chapter in the history of the country's literatures. Sanskrit and Tamil had a written literature long before the beginning of the Christian era and an oral tradition predating the written by a thousand years. Indo-English writing seems immature and insignificant when placed alongside India's classical literatures. Even compared to the modern vernacular literatures which have made rapid and remarkable strides in the last hundred years, Indian writing in English is only a minor unit. And compared to the promise of its beginnings and the fine achievement of contemporary writers, the future appears bleak, offering little but the prospect of extinction. Even so, Indo-English literature is worth critical study because it is a distinct entity and has produced writers of great calibre, such as Rabindranath Tagore and Raja Rao.

Like other Anglo-colonial literatures, Indo-English literature was until recently ignored by Britain except for occasional patronizing criticism, and disclaimed if not ostracized by the native people. But within the last decade the tide has turned in favour of Commonwealth literatures. They have become the focus of interest among critics and casual readers. More significant contributions have been made in the creative and critical fields of almost every Commonwealth literature in the last decade than in the hundred years preceding it.

However, unlike other Anglo-colonial literatures, Indo-English literature seems destined to die young. This Cassandrian prognostication about its imminent extinction is based on a realistic appraisal of current political trends and educational statistics, not on baseless pessimism. Indo-English literature has owed its existence to a peculiar concatenation of political circumstances, and the political scene today precludes any optimism regarding the continuance of English.

The early missionaries had introduced English education to bring more converts quickly into the Christian fold; the British had subsidized English education in order to consolidate their power through native loyalists. Both had claimed altruistic rationales. Similarly, Indian politicians of today have banished English, ostensibly on such high-sounding principles as strengthening of national identity and perpetuation of regional sub-cultures. But their policy is rooted in practical selfishness that seeks to consolidate their own power. That they have erected a Babel and set in motion a process of divisiveness seems to be of minor importance.

A brief survey of certain landmarks in Indian history will throw light on the origins and future of Indo-English literature.

The two most significant dates in this context are 7 March 1835, and 14 September 1949. On 7 March 1835, the council under Governor-General William Bentinck passed a Minute on education making English the medium of instruction in government-subsidized schools; in effect the Minute made English the official language of British India. This administrative move was the culmination of a social movement which in turn had been set in motion by the political fact of British paramountcy in the subcontinent. At the head of the social movement stood Raja Rammohun Roy (1774-1833). A titan among men, Rammohun Roy ushered India into a new age. He regenerated Hinduism by breaking down outdated traditions, revolutionized social values by condemning polygamy and widow-immolation, advocated far-reaching fiscal reforms, championed the freedom of the press, and, what is most relevant here, urged the introduction of English education. His energetic canvassing for the cause of English education drew the support of Thomas Babington Macaulay. As president of the Committee of Inquiry into Public Instruction, Macaulay's voice carried the issue, and the Orientalists who had been advocating Arabic and Sanskrit education were defeated. Macaulay's speeches on the subject exhibit the idealism and rhetoric for which early Indo-English writers admired him; they also show the qualities of self-interest, political foresight, altruism, and arrogance which characterized the British attitude towards their colonies. All of these traits, except self-interest, are present in the concluding lines of Macaulay's speech to the British House of Commons in 1833:

> It may be that the public mind of India may expand under our system till it has outgrown that system; that by good government we may educate our subjects into a capacity for better government; that, having become instructed in European knowledge, they may, in some future age, demand European institutions. Whether such a day will ever come, I know not. But never will I attempt to retard it. Whenever it comes, it will be the proudest day in English history. To have found a great people sunk in the lowest depths of slavery and superstition, to have so ruled them as to have made them desirous and capable of all the privileges of citizens, would indeed be a title to glory all our own. The sceptre may pass away from us. . . . But there are triumphs which are followed by no reverse. There is an empire exempt from all natural causes of decay. Those triumphs are the pacific triumphs of reason over barbarism; that empire is the imperishable empire of our arts and our morals, our literature and our laws.

Indian writing in English had started a generation earlier but now, after the country-wide introduction of English education under Governor-General Bentinck, it gathered considerable momentum. Bengal led the way. Today its star is set, but let it not be forgotten that between 1800 and 1940 this eastern province produced more numerous and greater writers, leaders, reformers, artists, saints and thinkers than the rest of the country put together. Among those who wrote in English are Henry Derozio (1809-31), Romesh Chunder Dutt (1848-1909), Aru Dutt (1854-74), Toru Dutt (1856-77), Rabindranath Tagore (1861-1941), Manmohan Ghose (1867-1924), Aurobindo Ghose (1872-1950) and Sarojini Naidu (1879-1949). The writing of these earlier figures is characterized by Victorian ideals and Romantic diction even though several of them lived well into the 20th century.

Partly owing to certain educational policies and partly because of innate Indian reverence for tradition, Victorians held the field in India long after they had been eclipsed in their native England. As late as the 1930s Indian orators continued to speak in the vein and vocabulary of the old masters—Macaulay, Carlyle, Burke; Indian writers continued to model themselves on Scott and Dickens. It was only after the 1920s that such writers as Mulk Raj Anand and Raja Rao discarded the highflown diction of the earlier generation and started developing an Indo-English language that transmitted the flavour of the vernacular. But these writers could also command the King's English if they so wished. Some other good writers, such as Balachandra Rajan and Kamala Markandaya, adhered for the most part to correct English usage. Still others, like R. K. Narayan and K. Nagarajan, did not consciously cultivate either of these styles but rather wrote in the language naturally spoken by the average educated Indian. The language used by their characters, and occasionally by themselves, has cliches, officialese, Babuisms and picturesque translations of vernacular phrases and idioms. However, these writers differed from Anand and Raja Rao in that theirs was not conscious experimentation but spontaneous naturalness.

While the major writers of the entire 200-year span have had a knowledge of the language and of their art, the minor writers have fallen short of one or the other. The minor writers till the 1930s wrote pleasing, correct English even though their art was imitative and mediocre. After the 1930s there was rapid deterioration in the standard of English, and we have a plethora of fiction that falls outside the pale of literature even though it is classified in libraries as literature. This deterioration was due to the growing antagonism for the language of the rulers; the national movement was gathering impetus during the thirties, and the boycott of the language was in line with the boycott of everything British. When India gained independence in 1947, this antagonism culminated in the abolition of English in schools, and the imposition of Hindi. On 14 September 1949, the constituent assembly, after several days of acrimonious debate, passed Clause 343 of the Constitution which made Hindi the official language of the Union. English was to be concurrently used till 1965.

During the 15-year period granted for the transition from English to Hindi, there were periodic debates and demonstrations by pro-English, non-Hindi-speaking groups. Today there is silence on this front because the fervour for English has been replaced by frenzied fervour for the regional language and fanatical antagonism towards Hindi. Tamilians, who were the staunchest supporters of English, are now busy throwing out all languages other than Tamil from Tamil Nadu (Madras state). It is difficult to decide which is the more absurd and impractical step—the current trend in Tamil Nadu to substitute unknown but pure Tamil words for long-accepted, simple English words ("perundu" for "bus"), or lexicographer Raghuvira's Hindi in which long-accepted English words are given their exact meaning in simple Hindi by means of long compound words (for example, "electric bulb" being translated as "light-throwing round egg" and "necktie" being rendered as "loincloth for the neck").

English, then, has been discarded by the government and the masses. Though it continues to survive, the end obviously is near unless some radical political upheaval changes the trend. It is periodically pointed out that some of the best works in Indo-English literature have been written after independence. David McCutchion, for example, begins his volume of critical essays [*Indian Writing in English,* 1964] with: "By a strange irony, Indian literature in English has been flourishing since Independence more successfully than it ever flourished before." It is not at all strange; on the contrary, it is most natural and could not have been otherwise. In the earlier decades there were weighty issues to be taken up—a nation to be aroused, freedom to be won—and all talent went into the more urgent cause of nationalism. Another factor is that higher education spread to smaller towns and villages only in the 1920s and 1930s, and this was the period in which some of the best writers of today had their education. Let us remember that *all* the successful writers of today were born in the days of the British Raj, and even the younger writers have had English as the medium of instruction at school and university. Once the pre-independence generation dies we might still have a few Indians writing in English, but they are likely to be even more alien to the heartbeat of Indian life than today's expatriate writers. Once English is ousted from schools, and it has been ousted from numberless areas already, the shade of Joseph Conrad (frequently conjured up by McCutchion and others) notwithstanding, the chances of a thriving Indo-English literature are slim indeed. That is why I set A.D. 2000 as the dirge date for Indo-English literature. I hope time proves this prediction wrong.

Whatever the future may hold for Indo-English literature, enough works of merit have been published in the last hundred years to warrant study. This study is an attempt to evaluate and document certain representative south Indian writers of Indo-English fiction.

By "south Indians" are meant writers in English whose linguistic origin lies within the geographical bounds of the present states of Tamil Nadu, Kerala and Karnataka (Mysore), the regional languages of which are Tamil, Malayalam and Kannada respectively. Since most of the writers studied are Tamilians, occasional references to vernacular works are drawn from Tamil literature.

By "Indo-English" fiction is meant fiction written by Indians in English: this term is not the same as "Anglo-Indian" fiction, which denotes fiction written by Englishmen who spent a fair part of their lives in India and set a fair number of their works in India. John Masters, for example, is an Anglo-Indian novelist. [In a footnote the critic states: "K. R. Srinivasa Iyengar popularized the term 'Indo-Anglian' because it can be used both as adjective and as substantive. Contemporary Indo-English critics use both terms, 'Indo-English' and 'Indo-Anglian'; however, all seem to agree that a distinction should be drawn between 'Anglo-Indian' and these terms."]

Indo-English writers may be said to fall into one of four categories: early writers, native-talents, native-aliens, and a fourth group which consists of writers whose work transcends chronological or nationalistic categorization. The early south Indians, born before 1880, were of the first generation in the south to take up English education. Genuinely grateful to the British for having introduced them to the literature and philosophy of the West, they felt impelled to justify the ways of men to the new gods; to build the bridge of which E. M. Forster speaks in *A Passage to India,* the bridge that has never been built between the British and Indians. The early novelists give us conducted tours of India, past and present, in a language copied from the works of the English Romantics and Victorians.

The second group of writers, most of whom happened to be born between 1895 and 1910, had their early education before the struggle for independence had initiated any antagonism for the English language. When they started their literary careers, circumstances encouraged them to speak in their natural voice; they were not overly anxious to write for the British reader because the growth of English education assured them an audience from among their compatriots. They did not feel compelled to build bridges because the increasing momentum of the national movement precluded the necessity, and even the possibility; they were not inclined to imitate English writers or to use King's English because they realized that Indian literary traditions could be adopted and adapted to let them express themselves in a language that was now one of the many Indian languages. In short, native-talents, as I call these writers, are unanglicized Indians who write best about unanglicized Indians.

The third group of writers is somewhat younger than those in the preceding set. These too had their education during the British Raj, but, unlike native-talents they went abroad early in life. Partly owing to their foreign education, to their own inclination, and to the fact that their families had already been anglicized to a greater extent, these writers became alien to the heartbeat of Indian life and, at best, have only a cerebral awareness of it. They may be called native-aliens. Most of them—Kamala Markandaya, Santha Rama Rau and Balachandra Rajan—to name only south Indians, are expatriates. Raja Rao is the only expatriate who cannot be called a native-alien. Though he left India at the age of 19 and has spent much of his life since then outside India, he remains essentially Indian. Among south Indians he stands alone, the only writer who has transcended categories—chronological, generic, and national.

Till 1940 there were only sporadic reviews in newspapers and lectures. The pioneer in the cause of systematic criticism is K. R. Srinivasa Iyengar. A leading reviewer through the thirties, Srinivasa Iyengar published two volumes in the forties that formally turned the sod for Indo-English criticism. These two volumes—*Indo-Anglian Literature* (1943) and *The Indian Contribution to English Literature* (1945)—are priceless bibliographical sources for the study of lesser writers. His *Indian Writing in English* (1962) is a basic and indispensable reference book. One must keep in mind, however, that Srinivasa Iyengar is a generous critic; he has a word of praise for everyone. Any unfavourable comment he has is tempered with a favourable one. More serious is his questionable choice of quotations because of which some writers (Manjeri Isvaran, for example) suffer. Another shortcoming in this indisputably useful volume is that his critical lens not only sees some good even in the most mediocre of writers but is coloured by his admiration for the poetry and philosophy of Aurobindo, the composer of the modern epic *Savitri.* This last quality has been lambasted out of all proportion by certain Indian critics such as P. Lal, Nissim Ezekiel and Jyotirmoy Datta in their reviews and references to Srinivasa Iyengar's books.

Between 1945 and 1965 there was a sharp division of opinion among both critics and writers about the worth of Indo-English literature. Several writers turned to the vernacular, repeating the sentiments of Michael Madhusudhan Dutt (1827-73) who said: "Let those who feel that they have springs of fresh thought in them fly to their mother-tongue."

Interestingly enough, a comparison of the English and Tamil works of such novelists as Shankar Ram and K. S. Venkataramani shows that they were more successful in Tamil though they started their literary careers with English writing. One of these bilingual writers, Masti Venkatesa Iyengar, is now a strong activist in the anti-English lobby and advocates that English be rooted out altogether because it has stifled regional languages.

Generally, those who maintained that there is no worth in Indo-English literature were more voluble than those who attempted to justify it. Indo-English literature was suspect for several reasons. There was the charge of anti-nationalism as already mentioned. There was the charge that these writers were profiting from the prestige gained by India after independence in the comity of nations and on the eagerness of Americans to pay handsomely for anything Indian, the more legendarily Indian (that is, the more full of nautchgirl-maharaja or poverty-sacred bull motifs) the higher the price. There was also the charge that the style and vocabulary of Indian writing in English was borrowed or colourless. Chalapathi Rau's caustic comment [in "The Indo-Anglians," *The Illustrated Weekly of India* (26 May 1963)] is representative of this group:

> Writing is close to life, but the Indo-Anglians have little to do with life, its lustiness . . . its gorgon splendours. The Indo-Anglians crawl about like the crabs and jellyfish and earthworms of our intellectualism; they are singers of self-praise. . . . Indian writing in English is at its best, composition, and the best of it is translation. . . . We have no prose; we have strings of words, gawkishly arranged like beads. There is no rhythm; there is at best a street-walker's gait.

On the other side we have supporters of Indo-English literature who through articles and university courses promote the cause. One such group consciously coming together under a banner is Writers' Workshop. Founded in 1958, it consists of "a group of writers who agree in principle that English has proved its ability, as a language, to play a creative role in All-India literature."

On yet another side we have those who, either through ignorance of vernacular literatures or through error of judgment, feel that English writing is and will be superior to other Indian literatures. M. E. Derrett, author of one of the very few full-length thematic studies on any aspect of Indo-English literature, exemplifies this view [in "Why Write in English?" *Times Literary Supplement* (10 August 1962)]:

> Expression in English can bring a sense of release to the Indian intellectual as he endeavours to express the deepest turns and twists of his own mind. . . . Whatever its future form, it seems certain that the Indian novel in English will surpass its counterpart in the regional languages.

By 1962, when the above was written, it was evident that English, and consequently the Indo-English novel, was to be ousted from India, and also that the major vernacular literatures were drawing abreast of or had already outstripped Indo-English literature. The modern novel which had been launched by vernacular writers in mid-19th century had attained a superior degree of achievement as early as the 1930s. To name just a few of the well-known writers, we have Bankim Chandra Chatterjee (1838-94) and Saratchandra Chatterji (1876-1938) in Bengali; Prem Chand (1880-1936) and Mahavir Prasad Dvivedi (1868-1938) in Hindi; and R. Krishnamurthi (1899-1954) and R. Mahadevan (1913-57) in Tamil. It is true that all these novelists were in varying degrees indebted to English literary traditions but their work shows that the vernacular novel had come into its own earlier than the Indo-English novel. A study of these and more recent novels shows that because of the rapid adaptation of literary experiments conducted in Western literatures and because of their contact with the essential Indian life, the contemporary and future vernacular novel is likely to be more prolific and popular than the Indo-English novel and at least as good.

> *Uma Parameswaran, in an introduction to his* A Study of Representative Indo-English Novelists, *Vikas Publishing House Pvt Ltd., 1976, pp. 1-14.*

ORIGINS AND MAJOR FIGURES

C. Paul Verghese

[*In the following excerpt, Verghese examines the influence of English education on the origins of English writing in India.*]

A study of the problems of the Indian writer in English is intimately bound up with the historicity of the development of English as the official language during British rule, and as an important common medium of expression among the cultured Indians of the time, and occasionally also as the vehicle of creative expression for a few Indian writers. It is, therefore, relevant here to trace the history of English education in India, though briefly, and to examine how far the acceptance of English by the educated and cultured Indians during the early days of British rule in India was spontaneous and natural.

Though the early British Government in India encouraged Indian learning in their own interest, they had no scheme or even a remote suggestion of introducing any system of Western education under Government supervision or control. This is evident from the controversy that arose between the Anglicists and the Orientalists, both of whom were enthusiastic about the promotion of education in India. The Anglicists pleaded for the introduction of Western education in India, which according to the 'Filtration Theory' then popular, would gradually percolate down to the rest of the community. The Orientalists, on the other hand, wanted the Government to build upon the existing foundations of Indian language, philosophy and science. Indian opinion was divided, a considerable section actively supporting the Anglicists. Men like Ram Mohan Roy found no use for the traditional system which had, as a result of centuries of neglect, sunk into stagnation.

In 1823 a Committee of Public Instruction was appointed by the Government to go into the question of disbursing educational funds and to concert measures for imparting better instruction to the people. Steps were taken to establish a Sanskrit College in Calcutta. Against this, Ram Mohan Roy, who at his own expense had established several schools to teach the young men of Bengal through the medium of English, protested in a petition to the Governor-General, Lord Amherst. In his appeal he pleaded for the imparting of the best and the most modern European education through English.

A significant landmark in the history of English education in India was Macaulay's Minute on Education. In this Macaulay after giving his interpretation of the Act of Parliament providing for 'the revival and promotion of literature and the encouragement of the learned natives of India and for the introduction and promotion of a knowledge of the sciences among the inhabitants of the British territories', expressed a low opinion of Classical Sanskrit and Arabic literature. One need not attach any great importance to the supercilious strictures which Macaulay passed on India's ancient learning; for he was completely ignorant of Oriental literature. But his eloquent advocacy of English education is quite pertinent. He said:

> We have to educate a people who cannot at present be educated by means of their mother-tongue. We must teach them some foreign language. The claims of our own language it is hardly necessary to recapitulate. It stands pre-eminent even among the languages of the West. . . . In India English is the language spoken by the ruling class. It is spoken by the higher class of natives at the seats of Government. It is likely to become the language of commerce throughout the seas of the East. . . .

The main objective of Macaulay was indeed the creation of a separate class of scholars. He hoped that the new class of English-educated men would 'refine the vernacular dialects' and 'make them fit vehicles for conveying knowledge'. This, however, did not come true. Perhaps it was because all available funds for purposes of education were utilized for instruction through the medium of English and no encouragement was given to instruction through the regional languages, and consequently, no suitable textbooks came to be written in these languages.

In his Minute Macaulay showed that the demand for English education was far greater than that for Sanskrit and Arabic. Then he proceeded to answer the claims of the Orientalists. While doing so, he asserted that no public encouragement should be given to the Christian missionaries. But in his heart of hearts Macaulay too wanted Hindus to imbibe Christian teaching. However, he was against the sort of proselytizing tactics resorted to by the missionaries.

Complete anglicization of India was Macaulay's ultimate aim, and he had absolute faith in this. He equated the process of anglicization with civilization, and Christianity was an integral part of that civilization he believed in. In this task of 'civilizing' India, it was easy for Macaulay to get the support not only of the Christian missionaries but also of the great bulk of the English mercantile community in Calcutta. The latter believed that English education would pave the way for permanent commercial bonds between India and England.

In his Minute, Macaulay also answered the argument of the advocates of Oriental learning that Indians could not 'attain more than a mere smattering of English'. He observed:

> This is not merely an assumption, but an assumption contrary to all reason and experience. . . . There are in this very town natives who are quite competent to discuss political or scientific questions with fluency and precision in the English language. I have heard the very question on which I am now writing discussed by the native gentlemen with a liberality and an intelligence which would do credit to any member of the Committee of Public Instruction.

Macaulay's recommendations for English education were fully approved by Bentinck. And on 7th March 1835 it was decided that 'the great object of the British Government ought to be the promotion of European literature and science among the natives of India; and that all the funds appropriated to education would best be employed on English education alone'. Till 1838 Macaulay remained President of the Public Instruction Committee and did everything in his power to implement his scheme. He believed that European knowledge would soon be reflected in the Indian languages and hoped that some at least of those persons enlightened by English education would have 'the inclination and the ability to exhibit European knowledge in the vernacular dialects'. This hope was fulfilled only in part. There is no doubt that the contact with the English language and literature was fruitful to the regional languages in so far as it led to the growth and development of creative literature in these languages. But these languages even today are deficient in the literature of modern subjects like medicine, engineering, economics, law and politics. At the time of the introduction of English ed-

ucation in India, these languages did not have the necessary vocabulary and flexibility to serve as vehicles of useful knowledge. Macaulay then hoped that the Indian languages would develop in course of time to become suitable media for the dissemination of European knowledge. But the English-educated elite who he expected would use these languages for the communication of Western sciences and thought to the others, did not show any inclination to undertake the task. This was because there was no demand for scientific books in the Indian languages. And this in turn was due to the fact that higher learning was imparted through the medium of English and that the system of education had been for a very long time excessively literary and insufficiently vocational.

Macaulay's Minute on education may imply an effort at imposition of English on Indians. But Indians were not unwilling to receive English education. Basing his views on what is recorded in Srijut Brijendranath Banerjee's *Sambadpatre Sekaler Katha*, K. K. Datta asserts that enlightened Indians in the early nineteenth century had come 'to realize the need of linking their countrymen with the progressive cultural forces of the outside world'. Extracts from contemporary Bengali papers like *Samachar Darpan, Samachar Chandrika, Bangaduta* etc. published in *Sampadpatre Sekaler Katha* are quoted extensively by Datta in support of his view [as expressed in his *Dawn of Renascent India*].

There is thus enough evidence to show that many years before Macaulay's Minute, there was an enthusiasm among the people for the study of the English language. It is true that English education was desired by the people as it was an essential qualification for employment in the public services and that it was this incentive that brought about the great enthusiasm for the study of English language and literature. Nevertheless, the fact remains that their enthusiasm was quite natural inasmuch as the desire for learning came from the people themselves and they were not compelled to acquire a mastery of the English language.

This interest in Western learning, however, was by and large confined to the sphere of knowledge and did not extend to the realm of religion. And Macaulay's prediction that the young men educated under the new system would be 'Indians in blood and colour, but English in taste, in opinions, in morals, and in intellect' never came true in any significant measure, though the introduction of education on Western lines in this country made its powerful impact on the minds of educated Indians and sowed the seeds of rational and scientific approach to life.

Besides the enthusiasm shown in general by the people for English education in the first three decades of the nineteenth century, there was a keenness among the gifted men to try their hand at literary composition in English. In this connection may be mentioned the names of Ram Mohan Roy, Henry Louis Vivian Derozio, Kashiprosad Ghose and K. M. Banerji.

Ram Mohan Roy was the first Indian of any importance to write in English. He was well versed in several languages; besides Sanskrit, Persian, Bengali and English, he had some Arabic also. He had a remarkable fluency in the English language and wrote very effective prose. His polyglottic attainment did not act as a drag on his power of expression in English; he wrote and spoke forceful English. Besides starting secondary schools and leading a successful campaign against *sati,* he edited newspapers in English, Bengali and Persian. His theological writings and *The Precepts of Jesus, the Guide to Peace and Happiness* are proof enough of his mastery of English.

Ram Mohan Roy addressed himself in English chiefly to the English people, the British Government and Parliament on various matters of political and social reform such as the abolition of *sati* and the introduction of English education in India. Some of his writings were intended for the small English-educated intelligentsia in India who looked up to him for guidance. There were also the tracts setting forth his views on religion, which he wrote in his theological controversies with missionaries and orthodox Brahmins. The bulk of his writings is, therefore, polemical. But it is evident that he wrote with conviction and taste. Whether he was defending the precepts of Jesus or the teachings of the *Vedas,* his reasoning was always convincing and clear. In his English writings he used a vocabulary that was at once intelligible and finely discriminated. He carefully avoided monotony by varying his constructions, and adapted his style to meet the demands of the occasion. The style that he used in his memorials and petitions to the Government was different from the one he employed in his replies to those with whom he engaged in religious controversies. If his petitions are noted for their forceful presentation of views in well-balanced, sinuous sentences, his rejoinders to theological adversaries are full of cut and thrust, and characterized by a certain appropriate rhetorical vehemence. Ram Mohan Roy wrote what we may today call a utilitarian prose. His style was the standard prose of a cultivated late eighteenth century gentleman. Clarity and exactness were his aims. He used prose purely as a medium for the effective communication of ideas. It compares favourably with prose of similar purpose written by his English contemporaries.

Henry Derozio who came to be associated with the Hindu College of Calcutta in May 1826 was a poet who though of mixed Portuguese and Indian descent loved India ardently and gave expression to this sentiment in no uncertain words in his sonnets, "The Harp of India" and "To India—My Native Land". Derozio may be said to represent the first echo in India of Western ideas that had begun to take root in Indian soil. His poems have the flavour of English romantic poetry, but they constitute the first expression of Indian nationalist thought besides revealing his high sense of patriotism.

A wistful melancholy pervades most of his poems. Their themes are either death, freedom, patriotism, love or the transitoriness of life. Sometimes the poet is even caught in a mood of escapism as in "Evening in August". Of his narrative poems, "The Fakir of Jhungheera" is the best. Derozio's ardour for social reform shows itself in this poem which tells the story of a Brahmin widow who escapes *sati* by being carried away by a robber-chief, only to become a widow again. The poem is full of Byronic echoes, but is yet competent narrative verse. "The Maniac Widow" and "The Bridal" are noted for their pathos.

Derozio's personality as revealed in his aspirations, in his sorrows and in his style is that of a pale, derivative romantic poet. We find in him only the trappings of romantic tradition without the imagination and insight to create a world-view of his own. The genuine romantic outlook [according to C. M. Bowra in *The Romantic Imagination,* 1957] 'insists that a man must exploit to the utmost what is characteristically his own, and especially his individual vision and special inspiration. It places little trust in the forms and techniques which other poets have fashioned for common use . . . ' We cannot say that Derozio submitted himself to these exacting demands. Even in the expression of high ideals of liberty, freedom and patriotism, let alone his wistfulness, obsession with death and mood of escapism, he was content to be the echo of his romantic masters. Perhaps this was inevitable in the inherent dilemma that he faced as an Anglo-Indian who declared himself to be an Indian with cultural moorings neither in India nor in England. His fumbling with the Indian myth was also perhaps due to this dilemma. However, it should be said to his credit that he was the first Indian to attempt to write romantic poetry in English and that he made a small start in the right direction to give expression to an Indian personality through the medium of English, though his achievement was not much and seems negligible today.

Kashiprosad Ghose published a regular volume of verse entitled *The Shair and Other Poems* in 1830. Though the work has little intrinsic poetic quality, yet it made a very favourable impression on several Englishmen of the time. For example, in *The Literary Gazette* of November 1, 1834, D. L. Richardson, then a prominent member of the staff of Hindu College, quoting one of Kashiprosad's poems wrote: 'Let some of those narrow-minded persons who are in the habit of looking down on the natives of India with arrogant and vulgar contempt read this little poem and ask themselves—could they write better verses not in a foreign tongue but their own?' The praise is perhaps more valuable as a graceful gesture on the part of a generous Englishman than as any true indication of Ghose's literary merit. However, the point we should remember is that Indians had begun to use English as a medium of creative expression even before the days of Macaulay.

K. M. Banerji who came under the spell of Christianity and took holy orders also belonged to the small group that wrote in English before the system of English education was introduced in India. He wrote a play called *The Persecuted* in 1832. It deals with the conflict of the English-educated Indian with the conservatism of the orthodox society. Banerji also rendered great service to the Bengali language and literature by publishing *Vidyakalpadarum or Encyclopaedia Bengalensis* in thirteen volumes.

The question may now be asked whether the decision of 1835 in favour of English education in India was well taken. The choice before the British Government in 1835 was to use English or Sanskrit or Arabic as the medium of instruction; it was at any rate not a choice between English and one of the regional languages; for these languages, it had been admitted on all hands, were grossly inadequate to serve as a medium of European learning. Sanskrit was the medium of all Hindu religious and higher knowledge, and this education in pre-British India was restricted to Brahmins who enjoyed the monopoly of all higher learning. Among the Muslims higher education was not the monopoly of a section, but it was imparted in Arabic, an alien language, and Persian taught in the Madrasah was only the language of Islamic culture and administration. Both Arabic and Persian were foreign to the people at large. And the schools that existed were just centres where the three R's were taught to the common people. So, the most suitable medium of instruction in European learning which became the concern of not only the Anglicists and British Orientalists but also the enlightened Indians, in the circumstances, was English. Once the decision to use English as the language of administration and to prepare India to accept Western institutions was taken, there was no alternative but to impart learning in English. And as English was the passkey to Government service, there was the enthusiasm of the people to impel the Government to ensure the progress of English education. Commenting on the enthusiastic response to English education, C. E. Trevelyan [in his *On the Education of the People of India,* 1838] observed: 'The curiosity of the people is thoroughly roused and the passion for English knowledge has penetrated to the most obscure, and extended to the most remote parts of India'.

It is true that Macaulay's 'Filtration Theory' did not, however, succeed except in so far as it created an elite class of English-educated Indians—a loyal English-admiring community—some of whom had a vested interest in the British rule in India. It is also true that in spite of the later educational reforms such as those contained in the Wood Despatch and the declared intention of the British administration in India to educate the masses through the Indian languages, no great progress in that direction could be achieved. Perhaps this was because the introduction of Western education in India was primarily motivated by the political, administrative and economic needs of Britain in India. There were other motives too, and it was these that gained the support of British statesmen and leaders of English thought for English education in India; they were convinced that British culture was the best and that India, therefore, should be anglicized culturally. Both the English Anglicists and the English Orientalists believed in this civilizing mission of England. They believed that European learning would make the Indian people gladly accept British rule. Albeit these motives dictated by self-interest, English education in India was a progressive act of British rule; for it was secular in character and liberal in essence. We may, therefore, ask the question: how did it justify itself in ways other than supplying to the Government English-knowing clerks and competent civil servants and how did it benefit India as a whole?

The spread of English education enabled India to have a common language in which her educated classes could freely exchange their views and ideas, and which in subsequent years proved very valuable as a medium of expression at various national congresses and conferences, and

helped to bring about a socio-religious revolution leading to the modernization of life in India and a certain measure of unity among the different linguistic regions of modern India. As K. M. Panikkar points out [in *The Foundations of New India,* 1963] if the new education had been through Indian languages, India instead of being unified 'would have split into as many different units as there were languages in India, and would have repeated the pattern of Europe with its conglomeration of mutually hostile units within the same Christian community'.

Knowledge of English helped the educated Indian to imbibe the strong currents of world culture and reinforce his knowledge so as to develop a world outlook and perspective. He was able to overcome the isolationist conception of Indian culture and view Indian national development as a part of world development. In other words, the educated Indian's knowledge of English gave him access to modern European literature, thought and science. He became familiar with a galaxy of profound thinkers and great scientists of the West—Locke, Adam Smith, Godwin, John Stuart Mill, Carlyle, Ruskin, Spencer, Darwin and a host of other giants of science and philosophy. Through English translations he could study the philosophical systems of the world and assimilate the social theories of thinkers like Plato and Diderot. Not only did he gain access to the immense wealth of English literature but his knowledge of English also led him through the corridors of other European literatures and helped him to study the works of literary artists of the first rank such as Chekhov, Dostoyevsky, Turgenev, Emile Zola, Balzac and Flaubert.

The impact of the West inevitably brought about changes in the cultural and social life in India. There were a good number of Indians who had acquired Western knowledge and had developed an enthusiasm for it. The scientific truths which they had learnt impelled some of the more enlightened among them to strive hard to modify the structure of traditional knowledge, beliefs and social customs; for the cultural and social life in India at the time of the Western impact on her was at a very low ebb and was fast deteriorating. Hinduism, which was generally speaking the religion of India, had been a bundle of contradictory faiths and beliefs, and had permitted a number of socially harmful customs. Cut off from the whole development of learning and science which took place in Europe from the seventeenth century onwards, Indian learning had lost its vitality. A great awakening now came over India. English education was not merely a catalyst but was mainly instrumental in bringing about this renaissance. That is why Sir Jadunath Sarkar [in his *India Through the Ages,* 1962] describes the Indian renaissance as 'the greatest gift of the English'.

Western scholarship thus helped India in the nineteenth century in her momentous task of self-discovery and self-understanding and brought about an awakening in the spiritual, religious, social and literary spheres of Indian life. Treating Indian renaissance as a part of the general renaissance of Asia, K. M. Panikkar [in *Asia and Western Dominance,* 1953] distinguishes four broad characteristics of the movement. According to him the Indian awakening was the work of thinking men at the top who had received Western education, rather than 'a movement starting from the bottom'. In the second place, the efforts at social reform always involved religious reform. Also, the transformation was the result of an attempt to assimilate the learning and thought of the West. A fourth characteristic was that there was an emphasis on the growth of nationalism.

The religio-social awakening developed an All-India nationalism and the consequent creation of an Indian image, which prevented the dismemberment of India into tiny linguistic units. Before the advent of the British, India had none of the conditions regarded as essential for the development of a political-national consciousness. [According to the 1939 *Report of a Study Group of the Royal Institute of International Affairs on Nationalism*] these conditions are:

> (*a*) the idea of a common government whether as a reality in the present or past, or as an aspiration of the future;

> (*b*) a certain size and closeness of contact between all its individual members;

> (*c*) a more or less defined territory;

> (*d*) certain characteristics clearly distinguishing the nation from other nations and non-national groups;

> (*e*) a certain degree of common feeling or will associated with a picture of the nation in the minds of the individual members.

The nineteenth-century English historians thought of India as a complex of many nations which became a unified political entity only under British rule. The fact has been acknowledged as recently as 1955 in the *Report of the States Reorganization Commission.* It is, however, true that India as a whole had an ancient civilization, but that was almost similar to the European civilization with different well-knit linguistic groups forming themselves into nations.

If the prerequisites for a natural development of national consciousness are absent, the alternative is propaganda. In India the task of stimulating an all-India consciousness was performed by a group of Western-educated Indian social and religious reformers who had imbibed modern ideas and ideals through English and believed that they ought to work for conditions conducive to the development of a national consciousness, either through social reforms or religious revival. Foremost among them were Vivekananda and Tilak. An important feature of their effort was that they tended to lay great emphasis on the identification of nationalism with Hinduism.

Contact with the West, the desire of enlightened Indians to revive the culture of the past and the growing demand for social reform had their influence on the creative minds of the time. Writers in the Indian languages who were mainly bilingual began to introduce characteristics of English prose while writing in these languages. The evolution of a prose style and its development encouraged these writers to adopt modern forms of literature such as the novel, the short story and the drama. These forms were practically non-existent in the Indian literature before the

nineteenth century; there were only the fable and the romance. Barring the classical Sanskrit drama and the semi-dramatic forms in the regional languages, there was no flourishing Indian drama or theatre. In almost every Indian language, the first novel was written after the middle of the last century. The first novel in Bengali, *Alaler Gharer Dhulal* (The Spoilt Child) by Pyaricharan Mitra, modelled on Fielding's *Tom Jones* was published in 1858. But the credit for creating a popular taste for the novel in Bengali must go to Bankim Chandra Chattopadhyay whose first novel *Durgeshnandini* (The Chieftain's Daughter) came out in 1865. Bankim's first novel was, however, *Rajmohan's Wife,* a romantic tale of domestic life in an East Bengal village of the nineteenth century, written in English; this was published in 1864. It is not known for certain why he chose to write all his subsequent novels in Bengali. Perhaps it was because in Bengali he could be the pioneer of a new form of art by creating his own standards or importing them from the English novels he had read, especially the novels of Scott whose influence is evident in his historical novels.

The first Malayalam novel *Kundalata* by T. M. Appu Nedungadi was published in 1887. The novel shows unmistakable influence of well known English works. For its story and characterization it is indebted to certain portions of Shakespeare's *Cymbeline* and Scott's *Ivanhoe.* Though *Kundalata* is the earliest novel in Malayalam, yet it is O. Chandu Menon's *Indulekha* published in 1889 that is claimed to be first one having all the requisites of an excellent novel. It is even today given the pride of place as the best social novel in Malayalam. Equally outstanding is the work of C. V. Raman Pillai whose *Marthanda Varma* is the first Malayalam historical novel. He too like the author of *Kundalata* not only drew his inspiration from Scott's *Ivanhoe* but took characters as models for his novel. This tendency to model their novels on some of the outstanding English works was generally displayed by almost every early writer of novels in the regional languages, and is proof enough to show that the novel as a literary form in India is a product of the British impact.

That the modern Indian drama is heavily indebted to English literature and other European literatures through translations is a fact acknowledged by the literary critics in the regional languages. In Malayalam, for example, the impact of Western plays was felt towards the turn of the century. At first it expressed itself through translations of *The Taming of the Shrew* and *King Lear.* Translations of *Othello, The Merchant of Venice, The Rivals, Oedipus* and *Ghosts* soon followed. Ibsen's influence became quite pronounced in subsequent years, and original plays came to be written following the technique of Western plays.

The short story, biography and autobiography too, like the novel, came into being in Indian literatures as a result of Western contact. Poetry, however, did not have to make a new beginning; there was substantial output of poetry in every Indian literature. But there was no variety in it and poets had followed the tradition of writing religious epics. The British impact widened the horizon of poets in every Indian language. They began to break with tradition, writing lyrics and short narrative poems. For example, the Malayalam poets, V. C. Balakrishna Panikkar, Kumaran Asan and Vallathol Narayana Menon, discarding the practice of writing *Maha Kavyas,* began to write *Khanda Kavyas* and *Laghu Kavyas* in the manner of English lyrics. Before the influence of English literature was felt, Malayalam poetry could boast of only a few *Sandesha Kavyas* like Kerala Varma's *Mayura Sandesham,* a few *Maha Kavyas* like K. C. Kesava Pillai's *Kesaviyam* and a few *Attakathas* and *Thullals,* apart from some religious and devotional poetry.

English education thus affected the Indian cultural, religious and literary traditions in such a way that there was a great awakening transforming Indian ways and traditions. This awakening yielded beneficial results in the realm of literature; for there was a rejuvenation of Indian literatures through the adoption of new literary forms and genres from the West. Apart from this rejuvenation, there was also the beginning of Indian creative effort in English. The credit for this should certainly go to Derozio though his achievement as well as that of others in this early period of Indian writing in English cannot be regarded as praiseworthy.

C. Paul Verghese, "The Beginnings," in his Problems of the Indian Creative Writer in English, *Somaiya Publications Pvt Ltd, 1971, pp. 1-17.*

English viewed as a "de-Indianizing" influence:

Those interested in English have become a body of people with certain interests, with certain dispositions and with corresponding arguments for defending its continuance and the writing in English produced by us. Our writing in English is intimately connected with the habits of the educated, and it is from this class our reading public for it is formed, which knows English without knowing its literature. We must not forget that our point of view must be a point of view in the interests of our life. Not that English must not be used but that, I hold, it must not be used in accordance with the interests its long use by us has created. We have now a prejudice in favour of English and its advantages, which is so deep-rooted that the indispensability of English for us is an article of faith for the educated. It may be suggested summarily that the mind of the educated, in the wake of the dominant trends of our recent history, is formed on the basis of a liking for English, of ideals to reform our life, of determination to change it, though we evade its true claims because we are more keen on personal success. In this disposition of our mind are inherent the ideals of European Liberalism and the Enlightenment. Such a mind stands opposed to the value of our languages, of our religion, our metaphysics, our great rituals, our music, and our folk-spirit, in short, our life.

T. V. Subba Rao, in his Indian Writing in English: Is There Any Worth in It? *Koodal Publishers, 1976.*

K. R. Srinivasa Iyengar

[*Iyengar is an Indian educator, critic, editor, and trans-* *lator who founded the School of English Studies at Andhra University, as well as the University's Post Graduate Center in Guntar, which later became Nagarjuna University. A prolific writer, his works include a study of the Indian poet Rabindranath Tagore and English translations of Tamil and Sanskrit works. In the following excerpt, he places Indian literature in English into the context of Indian literature as a whole, and briefly discusses some of the major figures in the development of Indo-English poetry and prose.*]

A first look at the Indian literary scene is likely to prove most bewildering. It is said that there are nearly two hundred languages and thrice as many dialects in the Indian subcontinent. Many of these have their own literatures, either oral or written. And all are implicated, to a greater or lesser extent, in the abiding life currents of the people. Some of the languages are kept alive mainly on account of their religious associations, while others are no more than a means of intercourse at particular social levels. There is, first of all, Sanskrit, which is both a sacred and a classical language to the Hindus; it is not a "dead" language by any means, for scholars still write in Sanskrit, and in the symposium entitled *Contemporary Indian Literature* (1955), sponsored by the National Academy of Letters, Sanskrit literature occupies more space than any other of the fifteen literatures represented in it. Pali is held in veneration by the Buddhists, and Ardhamagadhi by the Jains; Arabic is the holy language of the Muslims; as the dogmas of the Christian Church are preserved in Latin, it is of especial significance to the Indian Catholics; and the Parsis, too, have their own sacred language. There is, finally, English, which is now both a spoken and a written Indian language with a considerable vogue in the whole country. We have thus, on the one hand, a group of "classical" literatures—Sanskrit, Pali, Ardhamagadhi, Arabic, Persian, Latin—which are cultivated by certain sections, large or small, of the people of India; and, on the other hand, a number of living languages and literatures—Assamese, Bengali, English, Gujarati, Hindi, Kannada, Kashmiri, Maithili, Malayalam, Marathi, Oriya, Punjabi, Sindhi, Tamil, Telugu, Urdu—that play an active part in the life and thought of the seething population of India. Bengali, Urdu, Punjabi and Sindhi are also the "living" languages of Pakistan, besides, of course, the "classical" languages.

These are the many literatures in India: these are all Indian literatures; but is there such a thing as "Indian literature"? Is "Indian literature" no more than the artificial sum of a miscellany of literatures, or is it verily a living, recognizable entity, endowed with life in every limb and with a heart and soul as well? Indian literature is somewhat akin to a garden. Nature, man, the march of history, the play of chance, all have taken a hand in making this garden. One marks the individual trees, one is attracted by the flower here, the fruit there; but one takes in no less the garden, admiring its relations and proportions and inferring its unifying and harmonizing soul. However dazzling in its richness or baffling in its complexity, modern Indian literature is but the outcome of a long, long process of evolution and growth. Again and again, behind the seeming complexity, the forces of unity and harmony are seen to prevail. Various are the scripts in India, but most of them are said to derive from a single parent, Brahmi. Most of the languages are themselves descended from either primitive Aryan or primitive Dravidian speech. By a slow process of evolution—variation, assimilation and evolution—the ancient Sanskritic dialects have become modern Assamese, Bengali, Gujarati, Hindi and so on, not to mention, perhaps, Burmese and Sinhalese. Similarly the language of the ancient South Indians split up in the fullness of time into modern Tamil, Kannada, Telugu and Malayalam. Sanskrit has influenced all along these two groups of languages, and at this distance of time it is impossible for the modern Indian languages or literatures to divorce completely this vital Sanskrit element in them. In more recent times other influences, too, have helped to enrich the Indian languages and literatures. In medieval India, Muslim influence was widespread and fruitful. The Muslims brought with them Arabic and Persian, and many words from these languages gained general currency throughout India, so that Hindus and Muslims together built a new, cosmopolitan culture, a notable product of which was Urdu literature. From Amir Khusraw in the thirteenth century to Muhammad Iqbal in the twentieth, Urdu literature has had a continuous and meritorious history. Likewise, the Western impact has also markedly influenced India's literary history. The Christian missionaries brought with them the Bible, set up printing presses and issued the Bible in the various languages of India. Nay, more: the Elizabethan Jesuit, Thomas Stephens, wrote in Marathi-Konkani an epic of the life of Christ; another Jesuit, the Italian Beschi, achieved the tour de force, *Tembavani,* in Tamil. There was a cross-fertilization of ideas and cultures and there was a spurt of intellectual activity and new writing in the languages of India, including Indian writing in English. The modern Indian literary renaissance had begun and was presently in full swing.

Indo-English literature is a significant part of this renaissance and an interesting by-product of the Western impact on Indian culture. It is really a Janus-faced phenomenon. There is, in the first place, the literature created by the Englishmen who have responded to the call of the East and have made India the theme of their writings. This literature may be called Anglo-Indian literature, and men of letters like Sir William Jones, H. H. Wilson, John Leyden, Sir Edwin Arnold, F. W. Bain, Meadows Taylor, Rudyard Kipling, E. M. Forster, Edward Thompson, L. H. Myers, J. R. Ackerley and Rumer Godden have made their varied contributions to this interesting and still-growing literature. Then there is, in the second place, the literature created by Indians in English, and this unique Indian contribution to English literature is nowadays referred to as Indo-Anglian literature.

A century and a quarter ago, having wavered long between a purely Oriental and a purely Western system of education, India took the plunge at last on March 7, 1835. On the advice of Thomas Babington Macaulay, Lord William Bentinck's Government decided to employ all funds available for cultural purposes on "English education alone," and so English became in due course the official language of India, and schools and colleges sent forth, year after year, increasing numbers of young men and women who could speak and write in English. Indian lawyers and judges and administrators, journalists, professors and publicists soon found themselves reasonably at home with English and thereby created conditions favorable to the birth and growth of Indo-Anglian literature.

Indo-Anglian literature is thus a matter of recent history. But so is Australian, Canadian or even American literature. Besides, Indo-Anglian literature is also strictly contemporaneous with the modern phase of the various regional literatures of India, several of our writers of today and yesterday being equally proficient in two or three languages and wielding with mastery both English and a regional language. The British impact, while it no doubt brought about, for a time, national discomfiture, also created certain conditions favorable to the renaissance in life and literature. Novel conditions and ideals, strange forms of life and letters, both attracted and repelled, and the tensions proved conducive to the birth of a new literature in Bengal, in Maharashtra and in the other linguistic regions in both North and South India. Drinking deep in the springs of English literature, Bengali youths wished to lisp in English and also to give Bengali a new vigor and versatility. The same thing happened in other parts of the country. Indian writing in English was still Indian writing and had close affiliations with Indian writing in Bengali or Tamil or Hindi. Like any modern regional literature, Indo-Anglian literature is thus unquestionably Indian literature, with a manifoldness of achievement almost as striking as that of any of the other Commonwealth literatures. The late C. R. Reddy declared [In K. R. Srinivasa Iyengar's *Indo-Anglian Literature,* 1943]:

> Indo-Anglian literature is not essentially different in kind from Indian literature. It is a part of it, a modern facet of that glory which, commencing from the Vedas, has continued to spread its mellow light, now with greater and now with lesser brilliance, under the inexorable vicissitudes of time and history, ever increasingly upward to the present time of Tagore, Iqbal and Aurobindo Ghose, and bids fair to expand with our and our humanity's expanding future.

The very divisions of this literature would broadly correspond to the divisions into which the other Indian literatures, in their modern phase, conveniently fall:

> 1820–1870: *The Beginnings*—the age of the great pioneers.
>
> 1870–1900: *The Renaissance in the Spirit*—the age of the religious and literary awakening.
>
> 1900–1920: *The Era of Political Awakening*—the age of "Home Rule" and "Bande Mataram."
>
> 1920–1947: *The Era of the Gandhian Revolution*—the modern "Heroic Age."
>
> 1947-: *The Era of Independence*—the age of recovery and reconstruction.

This is by no means an absolute scheme of division, but rather a convenient way of studying the period of a century and a half of writing.

Raja Rammohun Roy (1774–1833) was not only the father of Indo-Anglian literature; he was also, and in very truth, the "Father of Modern India." Rammohun was a self-made man with a purpose in his life and an unfaltering sense of direction. While still a young man he left the East India Company's service and became a servant of the nation. Then he carried his mission to England, made the necessary contacts and moved the powers that be to do the right thing by India. Whether in England or in India, he was restlessly active, and there was not a department of life—religion, social reform, education, journalism, public administration—which did not receive the beneficial impact of his personality. He was no unbeliever, but a devout Hindu, and his Hinduism went back to the pristine purity of the Vedas, leaping over the unhealthy encrustations of the intervening centuries. He was a sturdy nationalist, and he wisely saw that it was not in obscurantism, but in the assimilation of Western knowledge and techniques that India's progress lay. The plight of Indian widows, the darkness of superstition, the miasma of ignorance, the general backwardness of the country, all stirred him to action; and writing—whether in Bengali or in English—was for him a form of action. By 1823 he had fully matured, sharpened his dialectical instruments, tested his friends and rethought his ends and means. Some disillusion he had no doubt experienced, but it had also given a new dimension to his experience and a mellowness to his intelligence. A staunch advocate of English education, he was also a master of lucid English prose. His determined and forceful personality revealed itself in books like *Precepts of Jesus* (1820) and numerous prose tracts and pamphlets. While in England he contributed on request a brief autobiographical sketch to the *Athenaeum and Literary Gazette.* He died at Bristol in 1833.

If Rammohun was the first Indian to write English prose with self-confidence and an easy mastery, Henry Derozio (1809–1831) was the first of the Indo-Anglian poets. Half-Indian, half-Portuguese, Derozio had a chequered career; but as a teacher of English literature and as an iconoclast he exerted a powerful influence on his wards. He has left behind him a creditable body of verse in English, including the narrative poem "The Fakir of Jungheera." His sonnets and lyrics are competent, being compounded of genuine feeling and careful craftsmanship. However, creditable as are his achievements in poetry, his work is to be cherished even more for the great promise underlying his actual output, and E. F. Oaten aptly compares him with Keats, for "in both men there was a passionate temperament combined with unbounded sympathy with nature. Both died when their powers were not fully developed."

Another pioneering Indo-Anglian poet was Kashiprosad Ghose (1809–1873), whose *Shair and Other Poems* (1830), however, reveals little intrinsic poetic quality. A far more talented poet, Michael Madhusudan Dutt (1827-1873), came to be acclaimed as the Bengali Milton in recognition of his epic *Meghanad Badha* (1845); he wrote in English also, and his *Captive Ladie* (1849) is a brisk narrative poem, with Byronic echoes, on Prithvi Raj and Samyukta, the hero and heroine who symbolize the deathless chivalry and romance of the Rajput race. An English rendering of *Meghanad Badha* appeared in 1879.

During the last three decades of the nineteenth century India underwent a splendorous awakening of the spirit. The importation of Christianity had led to considerable rethinking and heart-searching, and movements like the Brahma Samaj, Arya Samaj and Prarthana Samaj gained numerous adherents. The Theosophical Movement established its headquarters at Adyar, near Madras, in South India. And there arose the new star at Dakshineshwar, near Calcutta—the power and personality of Ramakrishna Paramahamsa who shone as the exemplum of the quintessential best in Hinduism. Ramakrishna's disciple, Swami Vivekananda, carried the message of the Vedanta even beyond the shores of India, and his luminous discourses in English have been translated into almost every modern Indian language. It was during these stirring times that the precocious Aru and Toru, the brothers Manmohan and Aurobindo and the "civilian" Romesh Chunder contributed the first inspiring chapter to the history of Indo-Anglian poetry. It was during this period, too, that Bankim Chandra Chatterjee, a Bengali civil servant, published a series of quite remarkable novels in Bengali, not a little inspired by Sir Walter Scott. Bankim's novels have been translated into English as well as the various regional languages, and he has been a focal point in India's literary renaissance. His novel *Anand Math,* and especially the song "Bande Mataram" included in it, have played a truly notable part in the political and cultural awakening of the country.

After a brief but intense period of education in France and England, Toru Dutt (1856–1877) and her elder sister, Aru, plunged (in Edmund Gosse's words) into "a feverish dream of intellectual effort and imaginative production." Inevitably they broke under the strain, dying before their prime at the ages of twenty-one and twenty-two respectively. But already they had left for posterity a body of verse astonishing in promise and striking in achievement. Their English renderings of French lyrics of the Romantic school, *A Sheaf Gleaned in French Fields* (1876), are both felicitous and moving, and Gosse felt that "if modern French literature were entirely lost, it might not be found impossible to reconstruct a great number of poems from this Indian version." Aru Dutt's rendering of Victor Hugo's "Morning Serenade" has been justly and universally praised:

> Still barred thy doors! the far east glows,
> The morning wind blows fresh and free.
> Should not the hour that wakes the rose
> Awaken also thee?

Toru Dutt's *Ancient Ballads and Legends of Hindustan* (1882) appeared posthumously and more than ever ensured her place in "the great fellowship of English poets." She left, besides, a complete romance in French and an incomplete one in English, besides numerous letters to an English friend. Of Toru's occasional sonnets and poems, "Our Casuarina Tree" is perhaps the most popular—and deservedly so. Its eleven-line stanza is worthy of Keats himself, while its organization as a whole and its music of sound and ideas make it a noble piece of writing, giving us a taste of what she might have done had not the race of her life been so quickly run.

Romesh Chunder Dutt (1848–1909) was a capable administrator and a voluminous writer. Two of his Bengali novels appeared in English with the titles *The Lake of Palms* (1902) and *The Slave Girl of Agra* (1909). His treatises on the economic and cultural history of India, valuable as they are, are of less abiding interest to us than his English verse renderings of India's national epics, the *Mahabharata* (1898) and the *Ramayana* (1899), which are still among the best efforts of their kind. Romesh Chunder adopted the *Locksley Hall* meter, and in his hands it rings and chimes to admirable effect. In *Lays of Ancient India* (1894), likewise, Romesh Chunder included English verse translations of selections from India's ancient sacred and secular poetry. Certainly he was an adroit versifier, and his condensed versions, especially of the *Mahabharata* and the *Ramayana,* notwithstanding their limitations, remain commendable performances. In portraiture or dialogue, in description or in exhortation, in depicting the horrors of war or in delineating the primary human emotions, always—or almost always—Romesh Chunder proves that he is not unworthy of his great originals, and we need not doubt that he will have a secure place in Indo-Anglian literature.

The brothers Manmohan and Aurobindo Ghose both started writing poetry while studying in England. Manmohan Ghose (1867–1924) published, along with Laurence Binyon, Arthur Cripps and Stephen Phillips, a volume of poems entitled *Primavera* (1890), which received high praise at the time. Oscar Wilde knew Manmohan and described him as "a young Indian panther in evening brown." After his return to India, he became a Professor of English in the University of Calcutta and published *Love Songs and Elegies* (1898), containing some of his best work. His posthumous *Songs of Life and Death* (1926) included the two remarkable sequences "Immortal Love" and "Orphic Mysteries," and it is said that he left much more behind him, though it is to be feared that most of it is now irretrievably lost. In Manmohan the culture of Europe—and not alone the culture of modern England—and the serenity and spiritual awareness of India met and fused to splendid effect. He was as much at home with Theocritus, Meleager or Simonides as with Milton, Landor or Keats. He was, in a manner of speaking, the complete poet—almost nothing else than a poet. An enigma still, he is unquestionably (in Laurence Binyon's words), "a voice among the great company of English singers; somewhat apart and solitary, with a difference in his note, but not an echo."

Manmohan's younger brother, Sri Aurobindo Ghose (1872–1950), had a career unthinkable in any country except India where (in the words of a reviewer in the *Times Literary Supplement*) "the tradition of retirement from the world, for study and meditation, was already ancient in the times of Gautama Buddha." Having taught for a time at Baroda and subsequently played a prominent part in politics, he lived for over forty years a life of retirement at Pondicherry, founded the now-famous Ashram and passed away in his seventy-ninth year. Aurobindo is without question the greatest figure in Indo-Anglian literature and one of the literary giants of all time. The two sumptuous volumes of *Collected Poems and Plays* (1942) do not adequately represent his many-sided poetic genius, but they include a blank-verse play, *Perseus the Deliverer,* the narrative poems "Urvasie" and "Love and Death" and a number of lyrical poems that effectively draw upon his own spiritual experiences. Poems like "Thought the Paraclete" and "The Rose of God" are in a class apart, being *mantric* in utterance, prayerful in their intensity and exaltation. Posthumously an unfinished epic in hexameters, *Ilion,* and three full-length blank-verse plays—*Vasavadutta, Rodogune* and *Vaziers of Bassora*—have appeared, rather in the class of *Perseus* and distinctly and reminiscently Elizabethan in cast and even in language. However, Sri Aurobindo's poetic magnum opus is the epic, *Savitri* (1950), described by the poet himself as "a legend and a symbol." Although the "legend" of Savitri and Satyavan is taken from the *Mahabharata,* Aurobindo has grafted on it a symbolism derived from his own metaphysics of the Life Divine and the purposes and processes of his own integral Yoga. Savitri starts, no doubt, as an apparently limited human being, subject to the defeats, dichotomies and half-knowledges of our terrestrial world—brave, beautiful, yet obviously human too—but on the eve of her great ordeal she looks inward, tears veil after veil of blinding appearance, rejects the pale or colored reflections that claim to be the Self, passes by the Mother of Sorrows, the Madonna of Might and the Mother of Light, turns away from both the emphatic Denials and the arrogant Affirmation, till at last her purposive divinity achieves full expression and she sees in a flash the whole arc of her earthly mission. It is an extraordinary story of spiritual action—namely, the defeat of Death, the expulsion of Darkness, the liquidation of Ignorance. Written in blank verse of a singular purity and strength, *Savitri* rhythmically swings from the first line to the last with the puissance and deliberation of a *mantric* chant. One small extract alone can be given here to indicate the quality of the verse. As Savitri, having met Satyavan in the woods and fallen in love with him, returns to her father's place, Rishi Narad finds her transfigured by love and breaks out ecstatically:

> Who is this that comes, the bride,
> The flame-born, and round her illumined head
> Pouring their lights her hymeneal pomps
> Move flashing about her? From what green
>   glimmer of glades
> Retreating into dewy silences
> Or half-seen verge of waters moon-betrayed
> Bringst thou this glory of enchanted eyes?

It is too early, perhaps, to make a definitive assessment of this spiritual epic of nearly 24,000 lines. But Professor Raymond Frank Piper is surely right when he describes *Savitri* as "the most comprehensive, integrated, beautiful, and perfect cosmic poem ever composed . . . the most powerful artistic work in the world for expanding man's mind towards the Absolute."

Sri Aurobindo is, besides, a master of prose, and his style is often reminiscent—but not imitative—of the lords of language like Sir Thomas Browne, Edmund Burke and Cardinal Newman. His most famous work, *The Life Divine* (1941), has been described by Sir Francis Younghusband as indisputably the greatest work produced in his time, while the editor of the *Times Literary Supplement* has remarked that the book generates "vast circles of peace."

Aurobindo's other prose works include *Essays on the Gita, The Synthesis of Yoga, The Human Cycle, The Future Poetry, The Foundations of Indian Culture, The Secret of the Veda* and *The Ideal of Human Unity;* massive sequences of these appeared originally in *Arya,* the Indian monthly philosophical journal (1914–1921), and have since appeared, revised, in book form. The Aurobindonian touch is ever unmistakable, and there is a "global" quality in his prose style that comprehends, caresses and convinces at once. The Aurobindo canon is already of Himalayan proportions and acclaims him a veritable Titan in letters. His influence on Indian writers is not easily commensurable. Not only is there an Aurobindonian school of Indian writers of English verse, but many poets of yesterday and today in the various regional languages have also been profoundly influenced by him. Subramania Bharati in Tamil, Sumitranand Pant in Hindi, Puttappa, Gokak and Bendre in Kannada, Sundaram in Gujarati, Nishikanto and Dilip Kumar Roy in Bengali, are among the many poets who have sought inspiration at the Aurobindonian fount. As for the Aurobindonians who cultivate English verse, K. D. Sethna (*Artist Love,* 1925; *The Secret Splendour,* 1941; *The Adventure of the Apocalypse,* 1949), Dilip Kumar Roy (*Eyes of Light,* 1948), Nirodbaran (*Sun Blossoms,* 1947), Nishikanto, Romen and Nolini Kanta Gupta (*To the Heights,* 1944) stand in the vanguard.

Rabindranath Tagore (1861–1941), another Titan, belongs primarily to Bengali literature, but he has a place—and a prominent place at that—in Indo-Anglian literature as well. The award of the Nobel Prize for Literature to him in 1913 was but the beginning of a drama of recognition on a world scale to which there cannot be many parallels in literary history. He was a poet, dramatist, actor, producer; he was a musician and a painter; he was an educationist, a practical idealist who turned his dreams into reality at the Visvabharati University at Shantiniketan; he was a reformer, a philosopher, a prophet; he was a novelist and short-story teller and a critic of life and literature; he even made occasional incursions into nationalistic politics, although he was essentially an internationalist. He was a darling of versatility, and his fecundity and vitality were amazing. His active literary career extended over a period of sixty-five years, and he probably wrote the largest number of lyrics ever attempted by any poet. Next only, perhaps, to Mahatma Gandhi, Tagore has been the supreme inspiration to millions in modern India. It was when he was past fifty that he published *Gitanjali* (1912), a collection of prose lyrics based on his own Bengali originals. In his memorable Introduction to the book, W. B. Yeats wrote:

> These lyrics . . . display in their thought a world I have dreamt of all my life long. . . . As the generations pass, travellers will hum them on the highway and men rowing upon rivers. Lovers, while they await one another, shall find, in murmuring them, this love of God a magic gulf wherein their own bitter passion may bathe and renew its youth.

Other collections followed, and there appeared, in due course, *Collected Poems and Plays* (1937). Mahatma Gandhi's celebrated "march to Dandi" to defy the salt laws inspired Tagore's poem "The Child" in 1931. This was a prophetic piece of writing. Tagore wrote many plays too: *Chitra, The Post Office, Sacrifice, Mukta-Dhara* and several others—yet it is not the logic of careful plotting, but the music of ideas and symbols that is the soul of these dramas. His novels and short stories, too, have been translated into English, notable among these being *Hungry Stones* (1916), *The Home and The World* (1919), *Broken Ties* (1925) and *Binodini* (1959). Some of his philosophical discourses, however—*Sadhana* (1913) and *The Religion of Man* (1930)—were originally delivered in English, the latter as the Hibbert Lectures. The distinctive quality of Tagore's writing, the religious slant, may be summed up and defended in his own words:

> In India the greater part of our literature is religious, because God with us is not a distant God; he belongs to our homes as well as to our temples. . . . He is the chief guest whom we honor. In seasons of flowers and fruits, in the coming of the rain, in the fulness of the autumn, we see the hem of His mantle and hear His footsteps. We worship Him in all the true objects of our worship and love Him where-ever our love is due. In the woman who is good we feel Him; in the man who is true we know Him; in our children He is born again and again, the Eternal Child. Therefore, religious songs are our love songs, and our domestic occurrences . . . are woven in our literature as a drama whose counterpart is the divine.

Like Tagore, Sarojini Naidu (1879–1949) too has inspired a whole generation of Indian writers of English verse, and her three collections, *The Golden Threshold* (1905), *The Bird of Time* (1912) and *The Broken Wing* (1917), form an impressive trilogy of poetic promise and poetic achievement. Although it was as an English poet that she first caught the attention of the public, in course of time the patriot in her exceeded the poet, and she played a notable part in the struggle for independence, coming to occupy some of the highest positions, official and unofficial, in the public life of India. As a poet Sarojini Naidu particularly excels in describing with a coloring of the imagination familiar things like a June sunset, the full moon, nightfall in the city, temple bells, the palanquin bearers, the Coromandel fishers. The light touch, the easy lilt, the delicate phrasing never fail her. She can also scent the immensities and imponderables in the spiritual world, and her best poems—"To a Buddha Seated on a Lotus" and "The Flute-Player of Brindavan," for example—achieve the fusion of the real and the ideal and bring together both earth and heaven. Her most ambitious work is *The Temple,* a trilogy of lyric sequences, each of eight poems, and subtitled "A Pilgrimage of Love." The vicissitudes of this "pilgrimage" petrify us into awed attention. The glow, the surrender, the ecstasy; the recoil, the resentment, the despair; the reaction, the abasement, the acceptance—all are here. She lived for another thirty years, but as a poet she ceased to be.

Harindranath Chattopadhyaya was her brother, and his

first book of poems, *The Feast of Youth* (1918), received great praise at the time; he has not been idle since then, for poems and plays have appeared at regular intervals. His work, however, is unequal; while the facility is unfailing, the inspiration is fitful. But in the 209 lyrics of *Spring in Winter* (1956) the poet has recorded the transforming experience of a renewal of youth and love, and the lover's varied moods and fancies give this sequence an orchestrated unity. It is nearest in quality and urgency of utterance to his first volume, for it commemorates the birth of a second spring and tries to capture the splendor of the setting sun.

Of other Indo-Anglian poets of yesterday and today we can here make only a passing mention. Behramji Malabari (1853–1912), Nagesh Vishwanath Pai (*The Angel of Misfortune,* 1904), Ram Sharma (1837–1918), Brajendranath Seal (*The Quest Eternal,* 1936), P. Seshadri (1887–1942), Uma Maheswer (1902–1942), G. K. Chettur (1898–1936), V. N. Bhushan (1909–1951), B. N. Saletore (1897–1923), not to mention Swami Vivekananda (1862–1902), were all distinctive poets for one or another reason. The poets of today come under various groups: there are the lyricists of the Spirit, the Aurobindonians, already referred to; there are the traditionalists, Fredoon Kabraji, Armando Menezes, Adi K. Sett; there are the experimenters and rebels, Manjeri Isvaran, P. R. Kaikini, Cyril Modak; there are the new poets, Nissim Ezekiel, Dom Moraes (whose first book, *A Beginning,* 1957, won for him the Hawthornden Prize), P. Lal, K. Raghavendra Rao, R. L. Bartholomew, Mary Erulkar, A. K. Ramanujam, B. Rajan and Nilima Devi. Of particular interest are recent attempts to project through the English medium the multiverses of modern Indian poetry. Prema Nandakumar's *Bharati in English Verse* (1958) contains free renderings of forty-one of the Tamil poems of Subramania Bharati. *Modern Indian Poetry* (1958) and *Modern Telugu Poetry* (1956), edited by Rajeswara Rao and Chaya Devi, are co-operative undertakings, even like the special Indian issue of *Poetry* (January, 1959). *Modern Indian Poetry* includes seventy-five poems from seventy poets representing contemporary India's fourteen languages; and it is commendable as a blow struck for India's cultural unity and self-awareness. One interesting feature of all these anthologies is worth stressing: in a majority of instances the English renderings are done by the poets themselves, thus testifying to the fact that most of our writers are purposively bilingual.

Although fiction by Indians in English—either in the original or as translation from the original Bengali or some other Indian language—had been appearing since the last quarter of the nineteenth century, it was only during the 1920's and 1930's that Indo-Anglian fiction definitely came to its own. K. S. Venkataramani, Mulk Raj Anand, R. K. Narayan, Raja Rao, S. Nagarajan, Shanker Ram, Jogendra Singh, Dhan Gopal Mukherji, A. S. P. Ayyar, Ahmad Ali, D. F. Karaka—these, among others, showed that it was possible to essay English fiction on Indian themes. By the beginning of the Second World War, Narayan and Anand at least had each a body of writing to his credit that was of high quality and hinted at even better things to come.

With the war coincided India's own final struggle for independence, and presently freedom came, and the "partition of India" and its terrible consequences. A new age began with its excitements, ardors and achievements—also its setbacks, frustrations and humiliations. It was an invitation to the creative writer, and especially the novelist. Who would catch, like the drizzle in the sunshine, the multi-colored view of the nation awakening from its long nightmarish past? Who would record our epics of achievement, who would indite the lyrics of high endeavor, the satires of self-deception or the grim elegies of failure?

While some of the writers who won recognition in the thirties and the early forties (Anand, Narayan, Bhabani Bhattacharya, Manjeri Isvaran) have retained their fecundity and popularity, the new arrivals (Kamala Markhandaya, Sudhin Ghose, Santha Rama Rau, Khushwant Singh, B. Rajan) have given the contemporary literary scene both the stir of variegated excitement and the promise of future achievement. No doubt the valiant struggle for independence highlights many of our fictional experiments from Vankataramani's *Kandan the Patriot* (1932) to Markhandaya's *Some Inner Fury* (1956). Ahmad Abbas' *Inqilab* (1955), Venu Chitale's *In Transit* (1950), Narayan's *Waiting for the Mahatma* (1955) and Lambert Mascarenhas' *Sorrowing Lies My Land* (1955) also draw upon India's (the last, Goa's) struggle for freedom. The social context and the perennial human situation, of course, provide matter for many more novels, while there are not wanting novelists who exploit the bizarre, the mystical and the fantastical.

Sudhin Ghose's *The Vermilion Boat* (1953) is a fantasy with an undercurrent of serious intention. The narrator is evidently a student, a Bengali variation of James Joyce's Stephen Dedalus, and he "covers" Calcutta (as Stephen covers Dublin) and enacts a voyage through Hell and Purgatory, in the end finding his Heaven in the arms of the long-desired and strangely attractive Anglo-Indian girl, Roma. There is a vivid description of two menacing masses of men, Hindus and Muslims, about to start a bloody struggle:

> Wolves, when hunting in packs, I have been told, know no fear. . . . The men on both my flanks looked like such wolf packs. . . . They appeared to me more frenzied than fierce wolves; they had the ferocity of the beasts that hunt and the cunning of the creatures that crawl.

When one remembers what happened during the terrible months of 1946–1947, the prepartition and postpartition horrors that swept the country, Sudhin Ghose's description may pass for no more than understatement. Elsewhere, however, the writing borders on the eerie and the wholly unpredictable. In this and in his other novels (*And Gazelles Leaping, The Flame of the Forest* and *Cradle of the Clouds*), Ghose has contributed something really new to Indo-Anglian fiction.

Of the veterans, Anand has given us *The Big Heart* (1945) and *The Private Life of an Indian Prince* (1953). The former describes (like the earlier *Untouchable,* 1935) a single day in the life of a community of hereditary coppersmiths, while the latter explores the private life of Victor the "prince" who runs against all sorts of difficulties in trying to reach adjustments with the national government at New Delhi after the British withdrawal from India. Narayan's *The Financial Expert* (1952) is in a light vein, and the principal characters, Margayya and Dr. Pal, are hardly more than caricatures. His more recent novel, *The Guide* (1958), tells the story of Raju, a man with a past who is trapped into playing the saint in spite of himself. Bhabani Bhattacharya's *So Many Hungers* (1948) and *He Who Rides a Tiger* (1954) are both located in the famine-ridden Bengal of the later years of the recent war. The former is a forceful exposure of the man-made famine in Bengal, a famine that took a toll of two million innocent men, women and children. The latter novel is lighter in tone, and Kalo's practical joke on society is pure entertainment. His *Music for Mohini* (1957), however, is a sensitive study of domestic life.

Of the new arrivals, Kamala Markhandaya is the author of three novels, one of which, *Some Inner Fury,* has been mentioned earlier. Her first novel, *Nectar in a Sieve* (1955), recalls K. S. Venkataramani's *Murugan the Tiller* (1927). It is a story of village folk—the apparently hopeless story of helpless people—but the narrator-heroine, Rukmini, is drawn firmly, and she is revealed (or, rather, she reveals herself) as the veritable Mother of Sorrows. Two other Indian novels have a similar theme, Shivarama Karanth's *The Return to the Soil* (1955), translated from the original Kannada by A. N. Murthy Rao, and Vyankatesh Madgulkar's *The Village Has No Walls* (1959), translated from the original Marathi by Ram Deshmukh. The Indian peasant has his roots in his village, and when he is forced to leave it, he is like a man who has lost his soul. The tenacity of his attachment to the soil is the theme of many an Indian novel, and characters like Murugan in Venkataramani's novel or Vencatachalam in Shanker Ram's *Love of Dust* (1938) are prototypical of Indian peasantry. In her second novel, *Some Inner Fury,* Kamala Markhandaya delineates the love of an Indian girl for an Englishman, and woven into this central theme are other strands—the conflict between the old and the new and the "Quit India" movement launched by Mahatma Gandhi in 1942. Not the least of Kamala Markhandaya's claims to recognition are the purity and suggestiveness of her English style. These are clearly exhibited in *A Silence of Desire* (1960), the story of a Hindu couple's near-destruction as a result of their general despair and their inability to help one another.

Among other recent novels of note are Santha Rama Rau's *Remember the House* and Anand Lall's *The House at Adampur* (both 1956), Nayantara Sahgal's *A Time to Be Happy* (1958) and B. Rajan's *The Dark Dancer* (1959). A novel that stands rather apart is Khushwant Singh's *Train to Pakistan* (1956), which is a pointed reminder of the hells let loose in the Punjab at the time of the fateful partition of India. The arbitrary cutting of a country into two (or three) was an act of evil, and evil could only engender more and still more evil. Once the wind of communal differences had been sown, how was one to escape the whirlwind that uprooted masses of humanity, mangled them and threw them aside in a heap? Crime—reprisal—more crime. Was the chain reaction to go on indefinitely?

But men's normal nature is love, not hate; and after the violence of the storm is spent, calm must descend at last. The ruffian, Juggat Singh, loves the Muslim girl, Nooran, and at the cost of his own life he, a Sikh, saves a train carrying her and other Muslim refugees from India to Pakistan.

In other forms of literature, too, notable work is being done, not least by Indian writers in English. Although the scope for Indo-Anglian drama is limited, good plays have been written by V. V. Srinivasa Iyengar, T. P. Kailasam, Bharati Sarabhai, Fyzee-Rahamin, J. M. Lobo-Prabhu, Purushottam Tricamdas and Harindranath Chattopadhyaya. *Nala and Damayanti* (1928) by Vasudeva Rao is a tour de force, being a verse drama in five acts and twenty-seven scenes. Another unusual play is P. A. Krishnaswamy's *The Flute of Krishna* (1950). Bharati Sarabhai's *The Well of the People* (1943) and the more recent play in prose, *Two Women,* are obviously inspired by Mahatma Gandhi's life and the waves of thought generated by his ministry amongst us.

Literary criticism has not been much in evidence, although N. K. Sidhanta's *The Heroic Age in India* (1929), Humayun Kabir's *Poetry, Monads and Society* (1941), V. K. Gokak's *The Poetic Approach to Language* (1953), K. D. Sethna's *The Poetic Genius of Sri Aurobindo* (1947) and S. C. Sen Gupta's *Towards a Theory of the Imagination* (1959) are excellent in their kind. Notable autobiographies have been published by Mahatma Gandhi, Jawaharlal Nehru and Nirad C. Chaudhuri (*The Autobiography of an Unknown Indian,* 1951). Nagesh Pai, S. V. V., R. Bangaruswami, Iswara Dutt, Narayan and Shanta Rungachary have written "light" essays touched with humor or satire, while Pothan Joseph, Khasa Subba Rau and "Vighneshwara" (N. Raghunathan) have won a national renown as columnists with a striking individuality of their own. Finally writers on philosophy like Vivekananda and Radhakrishnan, historians like Jadunath Sircar, polished speakers like Nehru and V. S. Srinivasa Sastri, journalists like M. Chalapati Rau and Frank Moraes, one and all of them have enriched this unique literature and given it both width and depth, variety and vitality.

Of the prose writers listed above (and the list is by no means exhaustive), several stand out as masters by reason of their thought and the uncanny sufficiency of their style for the many demands made upon it. Mahatma Gandhi (1869–1948) wielded a prose style that has been rightly praised for its effortless ease and its utter simplicity. A serenity, a beautiful tranquillity marks almost everything that he wrote. It is the model of the clear and simple style, as clear and pure and healthy as fresh water. Jawaharlal Nehru's writing (*An Autobiography,* 1936; *Glimpses of World History,* 1939; *The Discovery of India,* 1946) is like the man himself, and all his culture, all his humanity, all his integrity, are mirrored in it. Professor Radhakrishnan (*An Idealist View of Life,* 1932; *Eastern Religions and Western Thought,* 1939) commands a rich and colorful style, and this man of "words and wisdom" can always find the right words to convey the ranges of his experience and the movements of his thought. Torrential in speech as he is facile in writing, Professor Radhakrishnan is the Platonic dream of the philosopher as man of affairs come true in present-day India. Srinivasa Sastri (1869–1946) was the liberal statesman and enlightened humanist par excellence, and his spoken as well as written prose was invariably warmed by his humanity and touched by the light of his mind, as may be seen, for example, in his *Lectures on the Ramayana* (1949). Another master, too, must be mentioned here—Rajaji (C. Rajagopalachari). He is a great dialectician, with a marvelous austerity in expression; and he is also a *bhakta,* with an emotional and spiritual side to his personality. His recent English adaptations of the *Mahabharata* (1951) and the *Ramayana* (1957) give us the essence of these ancient Indian epics, flavored with the spices of the current intellectual idiom. He is an equally accomplished writer in Tamil, and his popular expositions, short stories and fables have given him an abiding place in the hearts of his people.

Indo-Anglian literature began as a hothouse plant. It has not, even now, shed its strangeness. Yet it would be wrong to describe it as an "alien" literature. It is fallacious to argue that, because English is the mother tongue of Englishmen, Indians must not use it in the medium of their creative efforts or that such efforts must necessarily fail or result in only very inferior work. As Sri Aurobindo once pointed out, "as time goes on, people will become more and more polyglot and these mental barriers will begin to disappear." England *is* abroad, and English literature is being created, not in England alone, but also in Nashville, in Johannesburg, in Melbourne, in Toronto, in Pondicherry, in New Delhi. Indo-Anglian literature has now taken firm and deep roots in the Indian soil, and it is branching out in many directions. At its best, Indian writing in English compares not unfavorably with the best writing in Australia, Canada or even in the United States and England. It may, therefore, be confidently hoped that, as in the past, in the future also, the Indo-Anglian writer will primarily aim at projecting a total view of India— interpreting her aspirations and hopes and recording her ardors and achievements—not only before the outside world, but also before the diverse linguistic groups within the country. There is no reason why Indo-Anglian literature should not, in the fullness of time, grow with the growth of the various regional literatures, giving and taking freely, and so achieve a position comparable to the distinctive national literatures like modern American literature and become an individual expression of the Indian genius and a means to national unity and international understanding.

K. R. Srinivasa Iyengar, "India," in The Commonwealth Pen: An Introduction to the Literature of the British Commonwealth, *edited by A. L. McLeod, Cornell, 1961, pp. 115-41.*

THE INDO-ENGLISH NOVEL

A. V. Krishna Rao

[*In the following excerpt, Rao provides an overview of the history, themes, and major authors of the Indo-English novel.*]

Although the Indo-Anglian novel has been a relatively delayed manifestation of the modern Indian imagination, it has always been instrumental both in an artistic rendering of the contemporary social reality and also in reflecting the changing national tradition as a complex of inherited values and acquired habits of attitude, taste and temperament. The Indo-Anglian novel, properly speaking, made its first uncertain, but significant start in the Thirties, when most of the vernacular literatures in India had already achieved a full expressive power in the medium of fiction reflecting the universal consciousness of change as well as the constantly expanding horizons of national aspiration. Stalwarts such as Bankim, Premachand, Sarat, Phadke and Veeresalingam had already achieved a synthesis of the Western novel form and the indigenous narrative prototypes, besides also, in the process, transforming fiction into a faithful vehicle of individual and national sensibility. The factors behind the maturation of the vernacular Indian novel were many; but most important of all was the quickening of the national consciousness into new areas of tension, thereby pressed to express its own released energies as political independence in the life of action, and as creative autonomy in the life of the imagination. The two impulses, more often than not, combined themselves into a single force for a comprehensive change. In the result, the transition from the utilitarian to the aesthetic use of the English language, especially in the field of fiction, has been natural and smooth. Sensitive without being self-conscious, audacious without being coy, the Indian writer could transport the assurances of an achieved national identity in fiction to a new dimension of the creative effort, which at one time might have caused dismay in the native writer, and suspicion in the alien reader. The assurance of a fully developed indigenous, or vernacular tradition in fiction has reduced the area of self-conscious ambivalence in the writing of Indo-Anglian fiction, conferring on its remainder the necessary symbolic strength of cultural paradox.

Since the Thirties, the Indian novel written in English has not only established itself on the native soil but has also been the spearhead of progressive ideas and experiments in the novel. Moreover, it has also acquired a status of meaningful independent existence in the complex body of Indian Literature, providing, as it were, a direct access to the Indian mind and heart, which is denied to outside readers by the language barrier, inherent in the vernacular literatures. Thus, it is by no means an irrelevant undertaking for a serious student of literature to venture an exploratory analysis of the Indo-Anglian novel, in terms of the cultural values and the patterns of change that have affected them. The Indo-Anglian novel has been a product of change; it has also become the major vehicle of the consciousness of that change.

The mood of the Thirties in India was a complex of traditional certitudes and transitional uncertainties, at once nostalgic and rebellious, contemplative and impulsive. India was moving into a new dimension in her cultural life, and the First World War imprinted the seal of history on the factors of a whole culture's modern transformation. Describing the national ferment that was the aftermath of the First World War, Jawaharlal Nehru observes [in his *Discovery of India*]:

> The peasantry were servile and fear-ridden; the industrial workers were no better. The middle classes, the intelligentsia, who might have been beacon-lights in the enveloping darkness, were themselves submerged in this all-pervading gloom . . . There was no adjustment to social purpose, no satisfaction of doing something worthwhile, even though suffering came in its train . . .

Earlier still, the British impact on the national life during the nineteenth century was almost traumatic. The political subjugation of India in the nineteenth century cannot be conceived, however, as her cultural capitulation. That the senescent and the tottering civilisation of Victorian India should prove its vitality and resilience so strongly that the rejuvenated nation could immediately strike a perfect stride in almost every department of human culture is perhaps one of the happily rewarding ironies of recent world history; and, understandably enough, the cultural collision between India and England had resulted in the emergence of a new India with a larger vision of the world. The political paramountcy of Britain in India had yielded the rich fruit of an Indian Reformation and Renaissance. This cultural movement was not a purblind craze for the perpetuation of obsolescent and obscurantist social values. It was essentially nonpolitical in origin, and was a radical revaluation of the traditional ideas. Over and above everything else, it meant a cultural reorientation and a literary stimulation, the English language offering a passage to the West no less than a passage to India. Thus in the words of the French historian, Amaury De Riencourt [in his *Soul of India*]:

> India's century-old cultural stagnation came to an end in the nineteenth century. What took place was a cultural awakening. . . . India experienced a cultural Indian Summer. . . . It laid the foundation of modern India and indirectly shaped India's latter-day political awakening. All through the nineteenth and early twentieth centuries, this cultural development was almost exclusively literary and non-scientific.

The creative stimulus and potency of the English cultural contact cannot be overemphasised, although, sometimes, the intellectual mood among the Indians in the early stages was one of the abject adulation for the West, and needless denigration of whatever was Indian. The manifest product of this exaggerated adoration of the West was an Indian version of the European Reformation. Raja Ramamohan Roy and Keshubchandra Sen, Veeresalingam Pantulu and Venkataratnam Naidu, among a host of other social reformers, were basically oriented towards the reformist urge. Gandhi came at the end of this line, although

by the time he came to it a new content far more diverse, varied and demanding in its elements had entered into the emerging ethos of the Reformation. India's age-old quest for truth was no longer merely metaphysical and spiritual; it became radically reoriented to the awareness of the more concrete, if tragic world of man's earthly destiny.

The impulse arose subsequently to look, with fresh vision and insight, at India's historical heritage, and to retrieve out of the historical chaos, a pattern of order inclusive of the permanent elements of Indian thought and culture not subject to the denuding forces of Time, or the corrosive influences of Western civilisation. The primary product of this impulse was the Indian Renaissance, pioneered by Ramakrishna Paramahamsa and Dayanand Saraswati, Swami Vivekananda and Swami Rama Tirtha. Sri Aurobindo's concept of a new evolutionary spiritual revolution was the natural culmination of the Indian Renaissance. A corollary development of the Indian Reformation and Renaissance was the active re-emergence of the native genius for synthesis underlying the permanent character and structure of Indian civilisation.

The assimilative and inclusive temper of Indian culture and civilisation has been reflected in a blend of ideas and attitudes in such modern personalities as those of Tagore and Nehru. Universal unity is the Tagorean conception of Harmony and Beauty. The idea of universality, which in Tagore becomes embodied in his artistic sensibility, acquires in Nehru's doctrine of *Panch-shil* its natural Indian historical extension. Thus, as the historical perspective unfolds itself, the dialogue of ideas in Indian thought reveals the prevalence of the basic dynamic essences of Indian culture.

The situation of the writer in the Thirties was conducive to imaginative work only in so far as the latter was inseparable from the national situation in general. In the Indian tradition, in contrast to the Western, the writer, although universally respected, has never sought to build for himself a separate identity. The Indian artist, by and large, has preferred anonymity to individual recognition, because for him Art is more a spiritual discipline than the egocentric expression of a mere individual. In Indo-Anglian art pressures of individual sensibility have always been effectively transformed into the flowing pulses of the collective cultural life. This tendency has persisted in the modern imagination too, but under the impact of the new climate of ideas and forces for change, it has taken on a new orientation. The Indo-Anglian novel thus made its debut in the Thirties.

The growth of the Indian sensibility in modern times traces a broad arc of development, and is marked out by three distinguishable phases. First, the writer articulates the general experience, and his own subjective compulsions are artistically identified with the general drama of life. Next, having absorbed the general weight of life into his own consciousness, he seeks to utter his private truth of the felt life. Lastly comes a stage of synthesis in which the public and private components of life become integrated and raised to the level of the universals—myth, vision and prophecy.

Tagore's development as an artist is a case in point. His poetry reflects the adventures of the individual consciousness in communion with the universe. In his plays he experiments with the higher symbolism of the finite individuality of Man in the process of extending itself into the infinite, ineffable and immortal Truth of the Cosmic Purpose. Tagore's novels offer an intellectual and aesthetic middle-ground, as it were, holding in exquisite balance the sensitive truths of the private vision and the solid verities of the public experience. As in the matter of modern intellectual history, so in his artistic output, Tagore always stands for synthesis and for the power of a mediating vision, anchored in Beauty and hence inevitably rooted in Truth and Goodness as well. Thus, where Gandhi stands for the empirical vitality of Truth and for Non-violence as Goodness in action, both individual and collective, and where Sri Aurobindo denominates Truth as productive of the Good in terms of its own evolutionary supra-mental dynamic, Tagore takes his stance at a point of intellectual mediation which reflects itself as aesthetic Beauty. Thus the achievement of Tagore, whether his work is considered Indian or Indo-Anglian, comes to assume a central significance in the historical development of all modern Indian literature, particularly fiction. Whatever be the contribution of the contemporary Indo-Anglian novelists to the establishment of Indo-Anglian fiction, historically speaking, Tagore was the father of the Indian novel in the best sense.

In his article in 'The Aryan Path' (April, May, June 1961) on Tagore, D. V. K. Raghavacharyulu has made one of the most significant critical pronouncements in his appraisal of Tagore's achievements as a dramatist when he says,

> Tagore effected a fruitful synthesis in his career and achievement between our Renaissance and Reformation. As a child of the Indian Renaissance, he emphasised the values of intellectual and imaginative creation. As a product of the Indian Reformation, he stressed the need of relating the enlightenment of outward nature with the illumination of the inner spirit . . . All the artistic output of his long life was a projection of this quick pulse of national consciousness into the enduring moulds of vital imagination.

This is indeed no less true about Tagore, the novelist. Being in the midst of the turbulent times of the late nineteenth century and the early twentieth century, Tagore naturally reflects the contemporary ideas and counter-ideas in all his works—more particularly in his novels. His are novels of ideas without the taint of propaganda; despite the particular thesis in most of his novels, the characters are free in their action and organic in their development.

A careful scrutiny of his novels reveals two concurrent ideas of special significance to his countrymen; one is the Upanishadic ideal of the Universal Man, the Enlightened soul but not the materialistic robot of a mechanical civilisation; the other is the image of woman, symbolising the sensitivity and energy of Prakriti, the Universal Mother, but certainly not the sensual nymph of a hedonistic society. These are the two basic ideas of the Indian national

consciousness that Tagore presents in his novels against the contemporary background of hatred and violence, vice and superstition.

It was the Age of Renaissance and Reformation. The reactionary forces of conventional society were up against the social reformers and liberal philosophers. On the other hand, the few educated Indians were but the brown version of the white snobbery and the complex of superiority. It was, in the words of Krishna Kripalani, 'an age of toadies and of reactionaries, those who aped the Western ways and those who sought consolation in the bondage of immemorial tradition and dogma'. Thus we see that the novels of Tagore inevitably constitute the imaginative rendering of the contemporary social history. And Tagore's greatness as a novelist lies in his artistic detachment while painting the canvas in diverse hues.

If Tagore's fiction moves in a universe of discourse that comprehensively sums up the various evolutionary cycles of the modern Indian sensibility, he has achieved a creative maturity that could contemplate the battles of the outside world by persistently remaining above the battle. Other writers began their careers while the battle for reality was demanding clear-cut loyalties, unambiguous fervours and active impulses. The post-Independence novel clearly marks out a new phase of emotional and intellectual growth in Indian literature; and the dislocations, the distempers and disenchantments of the post-war and post-Independence India have gone into the making of an Indian 'Lost Generation' which has had its impress on the Indo-Anglian novel, too.

Some Indo-Anglian novelists such as Balachandra Rajan present in their novels the predicament of the present day young men and women who feel uprooted, suffering a continued crisis in culture, and some of them actually living in a cultural vacuum. Rajan's *Too Long In The West* (1961) dramatises the dichotomous personality of the modern, Western-educated young woman, Nalini, who is looked upon by her countrymen as a sophisticated, unconventional and rebellious cultural expatriate; Nalini who has stayed so long in the West that her confined consciousness in a traditional society becomes suddenly liberated and expanded. But her return to the 'old world' in India from the Columbia University in the New World uncovers the hiatus between tradition and modernity. Nalini is the representative of the 'lost generation' in modern India, although it is significant that in India there was, strictly speaking, no lost generation as a direct consequence of the First World War. There was only intellectual agitation as Nehru has observed in *The Discovery of India*. Hence, it is a curious irony that the younger generation in India after the advent of Independence should feel 'lost' to the traditional culture. Their flippant purposelessness is phenomenal as reflected, for example, in the novels of R. P. Jhabvala, herself a 'naturalised' citizen of India. The incomplete personalities—the result of, perhaps, a lamentable lacuna in their general education—of these modern young men and women are reflected in the novels of R. P. Jhabvala and other contemporary novelists. This desideratum, this lack of fiery idealism, has even corrupted the once venerable Congressmen despite the inspiring leadership of Gandhiji.

One finds this post-Independence disease of spiritual torpor and loss of moral moorings to be quite deep-rooted if one glances at the Chairman of the District Congress Committee who appears in Manohar Malgoankar's *Distant Drum* (1960). The army officer Kiran is confronted with a piquant situation when Lalaji, the District Congress Chairman, requests him to give the *shamiana,* the big tent meant for the use of the army only; Kiran, a conscientious officer refuses to oblige as the army *shamianas* cannot be used for political shows. Says Lalaji:

> Coynelsaab . . . the paalitical party aaf which you taak so lightly is ruling thish country today. The days aaf treating us as a sheditious aarganization are gone. Now the party and gournment are the shame.

Another aspect of the Indo-Anglian novel is the credo of Nationalism, appearing in different phases. Much of the 'Anglo-Indian' fiction has frequent references to the Great Revolt of 1857 which, incidentally, marks the end of an age, but heralds the beginning of a new era—an era of National Struggle, fought by millions of politically-conscious intellectuals as well as the simple-minded peasants.

Most of the Indo-Anglian novelists have dealt with one aspect or the other of the historic non-violent battle for India's Freedom, fought under the banner of the Indian National Congress. The militant spirit of the Great Revolt of 1857 seems to have dissolved into the potentially peaceful force of the Congress. It is true that the Movement had occasionally taken violent turns as for instance, in August, 1942, and also in 1947, when the Hindu-Muslim communal riots caused untold misery and unhappiness to millions of Hindus, Muslims and Sikhs. The *Satyagraha* Movement, or the passive resistance in the Thirties—the Dandi Salt *Satyagraha* especially—by and large, forms the theme of many a novel.

Almost all the Indo-Anglian novels have one or more of the following nuclear ideas, predominant in them: the Evil of Partition; the Cult of 'Quit India'; and the Gandhian Myth.

It is a significant fact that the Image of Gandhi is present in all the three types of novels, though the details and emphasis may vary. As Dorothy M. Spencer says in her book, *Indian Fiction in English,* 'Political events and issues of over a hundred year period are reflected in various ways, both direct and indirect in the literature'.

Kushwant Singh's *Train to Pakistan* (1956) describes with biting economy of phrase, mathematical precision and graphic detail, the horrors of Partition. It is a vivid and exciting novel that tells us of the 'rioting, bloodshed and murder on the Indo-Pakistan border'. Mano Majra is a small Punjabi village with a mixed population of Muslims and Sikhs. They live peacefully together without any religious rancour until, one day, a train comes there, loaded with hundreds of Muslim corpses; Muslims naturally look askance at their own honest and friendly neighbours. Shortly afterwards, another train reaches Mano Majra— this time filled with dead bodies of Sikhs. The baneful result of the two-nation theory and the consequent Partition is unmistakably clear. The communal Frankenstein gulps down hundreds of thousands of people in the Punjab. Finally, it is decided that all the Muslims of Mano Majra should evacuate and migrate to Pakistan. Some of the Sikhs thirsting for revenge hatch a deadly conspiracy with a view to butchering all the migrating Muslims who occupy practically every inch of the running train. Juggut Singh, the hero of the novel, foils the plot by sacrificing himself, for the sake of Nooru—his Muslim love—who happens to be on the train. And, 'the train went over him, and went on to Pakistan'. A keener study of the novel reveals two central motifs: first, the train, a modern contrivance to convey and communicate, symbolises the most disturbing element of modern civilisation when it comes loaded with the dead bodies of the rival communities to the obscure traditional and quiet village in the Punjab— the village of Mano Majra. Secondly, however indirectly, the derogatory image of Gandhi in the new India is strikingly present, as illustrated by the reverie of Hukum Chand, the Magistrate:

> He is a great man, this Mr Nehru of yours. I do think he is the greatest man in world today. And how handsome: Wasn't that a wonderful thing to say? 'Long ago we made a tryst with destiny and now the time comes when we shall redeem our pledge, not wholly or in full measure but very substantially'. Yes, Mr Prime Minister, you made your tryst. So did many others—on the 15th August, Independence Day.

Bonophul's *Betwixt Dream And Reality* (1961) takes us from the Punjab to Bengal to witness the ghastly deeds, perpetrated by both the communities. Jotin, the young and dreamy idealist is the hero who, 'being stunned, agitated, incredulous', recalls to his mind the entire historical record, showing the Hindu-Muslim unity and amity for the past so many centuries. There is not much of a story as the hero nervously indulges in mere imaginative invocation of the past, and semi-conscious conversation with other shadowy characters. He visualises that Pakistan is a sheer political absurdity, if not impossibility. And 'his mind is giving shape to India that is yet to be, the India of his dreams, freed from foreign domination and from the coils of damned unrighteousness', while in the streets below, people fanatically revel in mutual murders and massacres. Jotin wakes up to see a truncated India, drenched in blood, somehow surviving the vivisection.

Yet another novel which refers to the communal frenzy of the Partition Riots is Padmini Sengupta's *Red Hibiscus* (1962). But mainly it is a social novel with the national Movement in the background.

The second type of novels deals with the cult of violence, symbolised in the August Revolution following the passing of the Quit India Resolution by the Congress. Gandhi's message, 'Do or Die' was much misunderstood by the ardent and impetuous youths of the country; the movement gradually took a violent turn, after the arrest of Gandhi and other leaders. In fact, there is in our literature a full and faithful documentary representation of this last violent and revolutionary attempt to attain independence. For example, Phadke's *The Whirlwind* (1956) is not only 'a story of men and women, of villages and cities, it is a story of a nation' as well, and it describes the heroic struggle that rocked the foundations of a mighty empire. The hero of the novel is the youthful, dynamic and resourceful college student, Syam who gives a new, but simple interpretation to Gandhi's call—'Do or Die'. He, however recognises his mistake later, for, he says to his friends, 'that Gandhi disapproves of violence of any kind and in any shape', and that it must stop forthwith. Their revolutionary activities are halted; the Whirlwind of Revolution and the terrorist orgy is blown away. Syam finally resolves to retire to his village and serve the people without longing for any lucre. This is, perhaps, the most sympathetic account of the August Revolution, generally condemned by Gandhi and other Congress leaders.

Kamala Markandaya's *Some Inner Fury* (1957) is a tragic political novel, in spite of the hero and heroine who try their best to rise above the tide of popular unrest and uprising. It is, in a sense, as Iyengar observes in his *Indian Writing in English,* 'a tragedy of politics'. The tender romantic mosaic of Mira and Richard is violently pulled to pieces by the terrific typhoon of the 'Quit India' campaign. With all her love for Richard, Mira finds it impossible to sever her relations with the rather impulsive people of her own race and so resolves her own tragic problem of life. She is convinced that the forces that have pulled them apart have been too strong. Throughout the novel the revolutionary spirit of the movement is in evidence. Much as she loathes violence, she helplessly finds herself defending her adopted brother, Govind, a terrorist desperado who is accused of murdering her brother, Kitsamy. Markandaya efficiently exploits the violent situations of the national struggle for the artistic purposes of her novel. The tragedy is all the more poignant because of Mira's other personal misfortunes. She finds happiness in her idyllic love for Richard, however short-lived it may be. She looks on, and later silently and forlornly follows the mob which breaks into the court and carries away the prisoner, Govind.

Another novel which is not political, in the sense that it deals with the decadent and degenerate feudal society, is Anand Lall's *The House At Adampur* (1958); yet it is not completely divorced from politics as the hero of the novel, Jai Singh, is a serious and sincere Congress Worker. Besides, the reactions of the wealthy lotus-eaters of Delhi to the National Movement in its various stages are graphically represented. Chapter Six in Part I of the novel brings out the most significant and the prominent event of the Movement under the leadership of Gandhi—The Salt Satyagraha. And Chapter Twenty-Eight in Part II deals with the Quit India Movement. The attitude of the loyalist upper classes of Delhi is represented by Dewan Ramnath who wonders whether the 'villagers and scavengers' that are taking part in the Gandhian politics are going to work for 'us' in the old way. Despite the lack of conviction in the novel, *The House At Adampur* brings out an important aspect of recent history to the fore. Thus, the National Movement has definitely influenced and fostered the growth of an Indo-Anglian novel that is thematically national. To call it merely a political novel is perhaps to minimise its significance in the Indian context. Strictly speaking, the Freedom Struggle simply provided for a spontaneous and artistic ventilation of what Middleton Murry might call 'the originating impulses' of the Indo-Anglian novelists. These are seminal; after all, the writer cannot, and should not write sitting in an ivory tower. John McCormick observes [in *Catastrophe and Imagination,* 1957]:

> To the genuine novelist, war and politics are facts of the real world to be faced, interpreted, and imaginatively projected in his work.

Although it is sometimes argued that India through the ages has shown little historical consciousness, Modern India has found herself in a complex situation in which the notions of Time and the concepts of historicity have been forced on a culture wedded to eternity and spirituality. The result has been on the one hand a sense of continuous crisis, and on the other a continuous assurance of the possibility of the way-out of the crisis. The Western Tragedy elaborates the idea of a consciousness in tension, but represents the human fulfilment as something always short of final consummation. The quest for consummation rather than the subtle drama of consummated Being is the essential feature of Western literature. The Indo-Anglian novel is unmistakably Indian in the sense that like all other forms of Indian literature, it commits to imaginative expression the actuality of a life continued beyond the contingencies of conflict as well as the substances of plot. For instance, R. K. Narayan, above all other Indian writers, illustrates this point of individual existence in a continuum of Time. Superficially, the structure of his novels appears to be a medley of comedy and tragedy, violence and nonviolence; melodrama and sentimentality. But when seen in the light of what is native to the genius of Indian Literature, there is an Indian wholesomeness, because the constant pattern underlying the structure of his novels is the mode in which crisis and consummation intermingle and yield up contingent and artistically envisioned realities to the permanent structures of Life. This peculiar attitude to Life and Reality specifies and defines the characteristic universe of discourse and the corresponding fictional idiom in the Indo-Anglian novel, particularly in its treatment of historical and cultural change.

It is agreed that in Modern India, especially after the First World War, there has been a great ferment of change in our intellectual attitudes. The old attitudes to tradition have been either radically altered, or arbitrarily rejected, or fondly resuscitated according to the nature and disposition of individuals and groups. But, the consciousness of change has been universal; and, it is on this basis that an authentic Indo-Anglian Literature, particularly novel, has been developed. Change, the nature of Change, the drama of Change and the significance of Change—these are the issues that have been singly or collectively raised in our literature. The final emergent attitudes and responses are, however, neither uniform nor ultimate. But they are worthy of careful study not only as the indexes of modern India's complex fate, but also as illustrations of the paradoxical quality of all experience that gets rendered as Vision in Art. Some Indo-Anglian novelists have protested against the evil uses of the past in the hope of a comfortable present on which a meaningful future may be based.

They have been chroniclers of social change and their art has consequently been representational and realistic, sometimes extending itself into an unflattering naturalistic art of exposure, exposition and didacticism. Mulkraj Anand has brought this tendency to almost cruel perfection in his novels which are essentially novels of Experience.

Other writers such as Kamala Markandaya have attempted to get beneath the social surfaces in contemporary welter, and discover a pattern of ordered experience in terms of the hidden, but living springs of human sensibility. Their works at a first glance appear to be comedies of manners, or social or domestic chronicles; but, more closely approached, a subtler mechanism of analysis and exploration may be discovered to be at work. In the novels of Kamala Markandaya, it is not the whole body of experience that is offered, but its essences as they are strained through precisely defined and sharply focused individual sensibilities caught in the process of external change and inner response. While Mulkraj Anand offers even adventure as experience, especially social experience, Kamala Markandaya offers every experience as an adventure of the individual sensibility.

A third group of writers stabilize their vision of experience in terms of fixed symbols or constant patterns of abstraction in a changing world of concrete appearances. Starting from this limited, controlled world, their art presses forward towards new horizons and in the final analysis makes the whole life fully available to Art which extends and fulfils itself as vision. Apparently tenuous and deceptively unambitious, R. K. Narayan as the central writer of this group, has risen to great heights of achievement because of the very intensity of his art—an art whose self-effacing quality liberates itself into the realms of dignified splendour free from the tyranny and triviality of mere facts.

Finally, if R. K. Narayan applies the controls and disciplines of Art to the run-away vitalities of life so as to forge order out of chaos, and meaning out of *maya,* Raja Rao has taken a broader cosmopolitan canvas, arresting life neither in time, nor in space, but letting them confer upon themselves an epic movement of their own magnificence and majesty in eternity. Even as the American pair of Hawthorne and Melville, although moving in opposite directions, had arrived at a similar goal, and in the process brought the American novel to maturity, so, too, the Indian pair, R. K. Narayan and Raja Rao have continued in their new-found medium of the Indo-Anglian novel the 'Great Tradition' of the Indian literature. Raja Rao's uses of the past are both complex, composite and significant, and his achievement is to be found mainly in establishing a cultural and aesthetic symbolism in the Indo-Anglian novel.

The emergence of the Indo-Anglian novel has thus significantly coincided with the coming into focus of the Indian consciousness those seed-ideas and germinal intellectual patterns which had previously remained on the nebulous plane of mere intellectual history. The mental absorption and imaginative proliferation of modern India's cultural synthesis form the natural substructure of the novels of the four representative Indo-Anglian novelists—Mulkraj

Anand, Kamala Markandaya, R. K. Narayan and Raja Rao. The *Triveni* or the triple streams of Indian thought as symbolised by Sri Aurobindo with his philosophy of the spiritual evolution of Man, Mahatma Gandhi with his faith in the marriage of ethics and politics in the sanctum of Truth and Non-violence, and Tagore with his sage outlook for a Universal Man, is the *summum bonum* of the Indo-Anglian fictional philosophy. The four novelists not only sum up the major achievements of the Indo-Anglian novel, but also represent the changing patterns of national tradition as they have come to be projected as the archetypes of modern India's new awareness of herself and of the world.

> *A. V. Krishna Rao, in an introduction to his* The Indo-Anglian Novel and the Changing Tradition: A Study of the Novels of Mulk Raj Anand, Kamala Markandaya, R. K. Narayan and Raja Rao, 1930-64, *Rao and Raghavan, 1972, pp. 9-26.*

On the documentary function of Indian literature in English:

It seems to me indisputable that set against the achievement of world literature in all ages—which is the field open, after all, to those who read for purely literary reasons—the contribution of Indian literature in English is as yet insignificant. It is not scornful to face this fact, but it naturally follows that most of those who interest themselves in this literature read it *because* it is Indian. This has curious consequences, not yet I think sufficiently taken into account. Among the main tasks of those who criticize or comment on this literature, therefore, must be to examine the circumstances which produced it, establish the limits of its authenticty, and assess the extent to which it is derivative from non-Indian sources. Some take offense at this 'documentary' approach, which appears patronizing and unsympathetic, but in fact we read all literature not only for aesthetic or vicarious emotions, but to learn about our fellow men, and to the extent that nations are idiosyncratic we learn about national behaviour this way too. Even that most original creation of Indian literature in English, G. V. Desani's *All About H. Hatterr,* is as fascinating a document as it is a literary experience, and indeed can hardly be appreciated without a knowledge of the background of the way English is used in India. But the fascination of Indian writing in English lies more in the phenomenon itself (of literary creativity in a language other than the surrounding mother tongue), than in its documentation of Indian life, which may be hopelessly misleading.

> *David McCutchion, in his* Indian Writing in English, *Writers Workshop, 1969.*

William Walsh

[Walsh is an English educator, critic, and editor. His works include R. K. Narayan: A Critical Appreciation *and book-length studies of Commonwealth literature and Indian literature in English. In the following excerpt, Walsh examines the work of the three "Founding*

Fathers" of the Indian novel written in English: Mulk
Raj Anand, Raja Rao, and R. K. Narayan.]

In the nineteen-thirties a number of Indian novelists began
to write in English—genuine novelists, that is, for whom
the art of fiction was an end in itself and not just a means
for communicating other kinds of truth. Fifty years later
it is clear that this was a form peculiarly suited to the Indian sensibility and one to which Indian writers have made
a distinct and significant contribution. I shall deal with
three writers who are distinguished not only for their own
work but as the inaugurators of the form itself since it was
they who defined the area in which the Indian novel in English was to operate, drew the first models of its characters
and themes and elaborated its particular logic. Each used
his own version of an English freed from the foggy taste
of Britain and transferred to a wholly new setting of brilliant light and brutal heat.

The three are Mulk Raj Anand (b. 1905), Raja Rao (b.
1909) and R. K. Narayan (b. 1907). Mulk Raj Anand's
first novels, containing some of his best work, appeared between 1935 and 1940: *Untouchable* (1935), *Coolie* (1936),
Two Leaves and a Bud (1937), *The Village* (1939) and
Across the Black Waters (1941); he had, in fact, written a
considerable amount before this; for example, a study of
Persian painting and a book about curries! Rao has written
only three novels—*Kanthapura* (1938), *The Serpent and
the Rope* (1960) and *The Cat and Shakespeare* (1963)—
as well as a volume of short stories (1947);
R. K. Narayan's first novel *Swami and Friends* came out
in 1935 and he has published steadily ever since.

Mulk Raj Anand was born in Peshawar in 1905. He was
educated at Punjoot University and University College
London, with a final year at Trinity College, Cambridge.
In her essay 'Mulk Raj Anand and the Thirties Movement
in England' [in *Perspectives on Mulk Raj Anand,* 1978]
Gillian Packham writes: 'Mulk Raj Anand was not the
typically well-heeled young Indian sent to complete his
education in London. His love of study and his poor relationship with his father had led him to escape his father's
petit bourgeois conditions. With the encouragement and
the material support of the poet Iqbal, his college principal
and his mother, he arrived in London in 1924, a poor student forced to earn his living by working in Indian
restaurants. . . . ' He completed a doctoral thesis on
'Bertrand Russell and the English Empiricists' in 1928
and he lived in England for twenty-one years. As Gillian
Packham's perceptive essay demonstrates, Mulk Raj
Anand became an essentially thirties man in thought and
sensibility, politically committed to Marxism if not to Soviet Communism, involved with the Unity Theatre and
the left-wing literary movement of the period. He even
wrote plays in which, says Gillian Packham, 'two characters would talk out an issue for five hours, regardless of
time or act divisions'. Mulk Raj Anand regarded himself
as a rational humanist rather than a Marxist but his ideas
on art—he is clearly not a thinker, let alone an original
one—are almost comically reminiscent of the Left Book
Club at its most ingenuously youthful. 'All art is propaganda. The art of Ajanta is propaganda for Buddhism.
The art of Ellora is propaganda for Hinduism. The art of
the Western novel is propaganda for humanity against the

bourgeoisie. Gorky as a humanist dared to speak of man,
man's condition, not to say how awful it is, but he also suggested what man could be. And thus he did propaganda
for man.'

But however derivative Anand's thought may have been
his feeling was genuine and his own and his experience of
the poor in India and in Britain gave him every warrant
for it. His fiction is, of course, exclusively concerned with
India. He is passionately involved with the villages, the ferocious poverty, the cruelties of caste, the wrongs of
women, and with orphans, the untouchables and urban
labourers. He writes in an angry reformist way, like a less
humorous Dickens and a more emotional Wells of the personal sufferings induced by economic injustices. It is really
economics he is writing about, even when the subject is
caste. His sharp well-organized early novel *Untouchable*
was very highly thought of by E. M. Forster. It is a fascinating combination of hard material, intense, specific
theme and throbbing Shelleyan manner. The action, occupying a single day, is precipitated by a great 'catastrophe',
an accidental touching in the morning. Everything that
follows is affected by it, even the innocent and vividly realized hockey match. Of the three solutions hinted at to the
problem of the untouchable—Christ, Gandhi and main
drainage—it is the last which is most favoured by Anand.
He is a committed artist, and what he is committed to is
indicated by Bashu's mockery in *Untouchable:* 'greater efficiency, better salesmanship, more mass-production,
standardization, dictatorship of the sweepers, marxian
materialism and all that.' 'Yes, yes,' is the reply, 'all that,
but no catch-words and cheap phrases, the change will be
organic and not mechanical'.

Organic standardization, unmechanical mass-production,
advertisement without catch-words—how clearly this
kind of thing confirms Mulk Raj Anand's deficiencies as
a thinker and the capacity of his Marxist enthusiasms to
glide gaily across the most deeply entrenched differences.
This, together with his furious indignation, unself-critical
ideology and habit of undue explicitness, make him a writer whose work has to be severely sieved. Like other writers
impelled by social motives, however worthy, whose attitude to life is all too patently dominated by theory, he has
the habit of preaching at the reader and trapping him into
sharing his unexamined motives. But when his imagination burns, and the dross of propaganda is consumed, as
in *Untouchable, Coolie* and *The Big Heart* (1945), there is
no doubt that he is a novelist of considerable power.

Even politics—that is, even politics as abstract, rigid and
doctrinal as this—can be humanized by the ingathering
and melting capacity of the Indian mind. It is something
working right through *Coolie* where Anand shows himself
to be one of the first of Indian writers to look on the savagely neglected, despised and maltreated Indian labourer
with an angry lack of resignation. The novel combines an
acid indignation at the condition of the poor with a Dickensian vivacity in physical registration and a delicate sense
of the psychology of Munoo, the waif-hero, in particular
of the rhythms of his growth from child to adolescent.
Munoo's victim role brings home to one the passive quality of the Indian poor in what Anand shows to be a mark-

edly static and hierarchical society, just as the immense distances from Simla to Bombay, covered in the boy's enforced journeys, convey in a way quite new in Indian fiction the continental vastness and variety of India.

In a perceptive note on Anand's fiction [in *Commonwealth Literature,* 1979], Anna Rutherford writes: 'Anand's characters invariably fall into three classes: the victims who are usually the protagonists; the oppressors, those who oppose change and progress; and the good men. Under the last category fall the social workers, the labour leaders, all those who believe in progress and can see how modern science can improve the lot of the sufferers and help bring about the equality of all men.' While this shrewd observation is an accurate account of some of the more Marxist protest fiction, it is hardly adequate for the novels, like *Across the Black Waters* or *The Private Life of an Indian Prince* (1953), in which there is a subtler distribution of forces and a more complicated division of sympathies. *Across the Black Waters* is the middle part of a trilogy published between 1940 and 1942, the other volumes being *The Village* and *The Gourd and the Sickle,* in which the peasant boy Lal Singh is taken from his North Indian village and a life stifled by suffocating layers of custom and religion into the ferocity of the Great War in Europe and then back to India and a new political stance. Anand, whose father was a soldier, shows himself to have a fine apolitical understanding of the soldier's life, and its instantaneous transitions from excessive boredom to extreme danger. He conveys, too, without any sense of superiority the soldiers' muzzy bafflement and anger at the politics and honours of war. *The Big Heart,* on the other hand, answers more closely in structure to Anna Rutherford's analysis. The theme of this distinctly Dickensian novel is stated in the first sentence.

> In the centre of Amritsar is Kucha Billimaran, a colony of traditional coppersmiths called Ihuthiars, now uprooted and on the brink of starvation due to the advent of the factory and the consequent loss of their traditional occupation.

The contrast of the two worlds, vividly delineated, is a splendid vehicle for Anand's largeness and generosity, qualities which soften the rigidity of the formal structure pointed to by Anna Rutherford and certainly prevent any sense of imposition or distortion. The ideological and organizational friction between money and craft is the more intense because it is ultimately located in one individual, Ananta. He feels the attractions of both kinds of life. On the one hand, he has an artist's fulfilment in the craft of working the intractable metal with a skill honed over generations. On the other, he appreciates what industrialization could do for the half-starved coppersmiths. Moreover, Ananta suffers not only the oppression of the capitalists but also the moral prejudice of the poor because of the window he lives with. The inward friction which frays Ananta is related to that which Anand himself suffers as an artist, the tension between art and ideology, which he has managed to assuage in only a handful of his novels.

One of this group is certainly *The Private Life of an Indian Prince* published in 1953 and revised in 1970. At first glance the material of this novel would make it a ripe subject for the Marxist side of Mulk Raj Anand: a depraved and neurotic monarch, a corrupt court, an impoverished and mutinous people, and a tense and critical period of Indian history. In fact, in spite of the very occasional radical *longeur,* the novel is refreshingly free from politics of the oppressive, ideological kind. Anand shows a powerful empathy for the morbid and suffering character of the maharajah. Indeed there is evidence that traumatic events in Anand's own life, the break-up of a marriage, the loss to another of the woman for whom his marriage had ended, informed his sense of Victor's personality and his feelings for his predicament to such a degree indeed that the author seems both possessed by and possessed of the prince's character. Such self-projection makes all the more necessary the device of the candid confidant, the Maharajah's personal London-trained physician, Dr Shankar, which Anand uses, deftly and economically, to ensure balance, distance and control. In most of his fiction Anand shows very much a nineteenth-century conception of the novel, seeing it as an organization based on a double foundation of character and circumstance: a character which has to be clearly defined and then developed, largely through the causality of other forces, social circumstances and influences, usually of a harshly oppressive sort. This is a pattern which is present in *The Private Life of an Indian Prince* but less insistently so than usual. The Rajput tradition of autocracy, the family tradition of self-indulgence, his profligate education and his promiscuous upbringing, the servility of advisers, the overwhelming influence of the Prince's prostitute mistress—much of the vicious disorder of the character of Vicky is attributed to these and other external influences. But the relationship between the Prince and Dr Shankar makes it possible to concentrate on the self-created chaos of the Prince's personality, so that he is seen to be much more than the echo of his past and the mere effect of the influence of others. It is the autotelic quality of the Prince's mental and moral ruin which finally stamps itself on the reader's mind in spite of the elaborate delineation of external influences, conditions and causes which form the substance of the many conversations between him and Dr Shankar. It is this which pulls him towards the status of tragic hero and away from that of pathetic victim. In the end he finishes, I suppose, somewhere between the two, but closer to hero than victim. The rhythm of his progress towards utter mental collapse is defined with precision and informed conviction, as indeed is the whole personality of the dissolute, stricken protagonist.

Anand also has his share of the Victorian gift for creating a gallery of minor figures, each of which has its particular flicker of life. The women, for example, are remarkably well done: the illiterate prostitute mistress, Ganga Dasi, with whom the Prince is hopelessly infatuated, who exists solely on the plane of instinct and animal cunning and whose musky presence can almost be smelt; the virtuous and neglected Maharani, the wife who has given Victor a son and who travels from Sham Pur to Poona to care for her husband in the insane asylum; the young shop assistant June whom Victor seduces in London: each of these has an individual life of her own, plays a significant part in Victor's downfall and in the design of the novel. The same is true of the men, particularly of the political figures whether of the lightweight provincial kind or the more powerful national sort of politician. There is an especially strong, even menacing portrait of Jardar Patel.

The most interesting and the most complex character in the novel is Dr Shankar. The Prince for all his neuroses, extravagance and moral insensibility is after all a straight-forward, uncomplicated figure. Dr Shankar is the narrator, the focuser of the reader's attention, the surrogate conscience of the Prince, and his interpreter and analyst. Above all he is the moral man whose every act or judgement is made against the presence, or at least the possibility of a moral standard. The novel is not, in consequence, simply the documented case-history of a collapsing mind, but the dramatized conflict of a human and tragic kind, conducted implicitly through Dr Shankar's scrupulous effort to refine his own moral sense and explicitly in his relationship with the Prince, where he struggles continually to nourish a moral sense in one who proves finally incapable of supporting it. Dr Shankar's moral sense may be derived from limited sources, from progress, science, humanism of a commonsensical kind, but it is a worthy one and fitted for its purpose in the novel, which is to provide another, moral dimension in an aimless world of privilege and cruelty.

I have referred more than once to Victorian characteristics in Anand's work. The reader should imagine an Indian writer of Anand's type and period as stepping instantaneously from a Victorian ethos, from Victorian style, prose and feeling into the leftish, progressive world of the thirties. But Anand did not thereby shed all his Victorian habits and manners. One which persists is his extraordinary Victorian fluency of communication, which has in it something both Victorian and Russian (Anand was influenced by Russian novelists). E. M. Forster was a critic of the purest taste and the most candid expression, and in arguing in the Preface to the novel, not altogether convincingly, that the conclusion of *Coolie* was really integral with the story in spite of 'being too voluble and sophisticated in comparison with the clear observation which has preceded it', made this essential point in the one word 'voluble'. Creation appears to be no agonizing struggle for Anand and communication is something he engages in with an unstrained and vivid enthusiasm and much of the facility of a nineteenth-century Russian novelist.

Mulk Raj Anand does not have the profound commonsense of Narayan which enhances both actuality and myth, the fact and the poetry of life. He does not have that sense of the metaphysical nature of man we find in Raja Rao. But he has a deep feeling for the deprived, a grasp of the social structure of his society and the clearest vision of its injustices and malformations. When his imagination burns and the propagandist is forgotten, he is a novelist of considerable power.

Raja Rao is an Indian and a novelist; but these generalities apart, he is as a novelist as different from Mulk Raj Anand as it is possible to be.

It would be hard to conceive of two writers more different from one another than Mulk Raj Anand and Raja Rao:

the former a man of the future committed to science and Marxist humanism who sees the past as a brutal drag on progress and enlightenment; the latter with a profound sense of the richness and creativity of the past, metaphysical, poetic, traditional. And yet there is more than one significant similarity. In his first novel *Kanthapura* (1938) Raja Rao remarks in the introduction—which was written, he tells us, at the instance of his publishers—on those very qualities of volubility and pace I referred to as characterizing Anand's manner. 'The tempo of Indian life must be infused into one English expression. . . . We, in India, think quickly, we talk quickly, and when we move we move quickly. There must be something in the sun of India that makes us rush and tumble and run on.' Anand met this requirement, as M. K. Naik shows in his acute and patient study of the short stories [*Perspectives on Mulk Raj Anand*], with a whole battery of devices. Indian locutions, idioms and images are rendered directly into English. Even the Indian vernacular is translated immediately into English. Anand's English, says Naik, shows its Indian origin in its 'oriental opulence, its passion for adjectives, its tendency to use more words than are absolutely necessary and its fast, galloping tempo'. As one would expect of a temperament like Raja Rao's, his method of realizing an Indian sensibility in the English language is subtler than Mulk Raj Anand's. His technique is much less extractable from the text, and is more incorporated into the body of the fable. His writing is closer to speech, and he is able to use the rhythms of speech—and particularly the intimate, sharing rhythm of folk speech—to indicate character, feeling and a vast tissue of assumptions and beliefs. It is a method which works beautifully in a story like *Kanthapura* concerned with the intensity of village life, with its physical immediacy, its traditional swaddling, and its religious murmurations.

E. M. Forster thought *Kanthapura* the best Indian novel written in English, and this is one of his many judgements for which a case could still be argued. Later critics have assigned this equivocal laurel to Raja Rao's second novel, *The Serpent and the Rope,* published in 1960. Although Raja Rao is by no means a prolific writer this elaborate work gives no impression at all of any constricted or meagre talent. On the contrary it strikes the reader with its flowing abundance and endless intricacy. The action or, perhaps, since external events do not have a high status in the novel, I should say the scene swerves from India to France to Britain and takes in a large number of authentic, sharply realized characters, French, Indian and Russian. In essence the novel is a philosophical meditation on the nature of existence in which the drama lies in the activity of meditation and not in the action, plot or progression we are used to in a European novel. For Raja Rao, experience naturally falls into a series of antinomies—life and death, being and becoming, knowing and unknowing—and the inner debate about the nature of existence is seen as the tension between appearance and reality, figured as the serpent and the rope. The examination of this central question of human life is done through the intense diagnosis of its hero Rama, Southern Indian, Brahmin, intellectually brilliant, spiritually sensitive and tubercular. His relationship with his French wife Madeleine, their disintegrating marriage and the subtle nexus with his mother-in-law

(Little Mother) are beautifully realized but the novel's primary concern is with laying bare Rama's individuality and his predicament. 'His choice is between the serpent—unreality masquerading as reality, seductive because it is apparently verifiable—and the rope—reality hidden because man sees through the serpent's eyes.'

The defect of this remarkable novel, which at the very least extends our concept of what the novel can be, is that Coleridgean fault of unstoppable fluency. Raja Rao does go on and on, and being intellectually lively and curious he thrusts upon us scholarly information and innumerable reflections on masses of subjects; Asian, European, religious, historical and mystical. Presumably the point is to show both the range of Rama's consciousness and the absolute relevance of the appearance—reality distinction, but even the most attentive and appreciative reader can find his concentration drooping.

The Serpent and the Rope is a rich and complex creation. Its defects are a tendency to slip too easily into formlessness or into the ineffable. There are also attempts, which fail, to employ Sanskrit rhythms in English. And if there is sometimes too tenuous a connection between the novel's highest flights and the humble details of ordinary existence, it is still clearly the work of a writer of exemplary integrity and of an artist with a pure and impressive talent. A fine and delicate vehicle for that talent is *The Cat and Shakespeare* (1965) which is much freer from the somewhat inhuman unattachment of *The Serpent and the Rope*. It is a *novella* of 117 pages marked by a patterned complexity and a subdued sardonic poetry.

The basic concern animating the fable is not much different from that in *The Serpent and the Rope*. It shows itself here as a scrutiny of being and individuality and, in particular, as the active contemplation of the ways in which appearance and reality approach one another, jostle, mimic and supplant one another, as they do in the narrator's relationships with his wife-like mistress and his money-driven business-woman wife. The reader is invited 'to weep on every page, not for what he sees but for what he sees he sees'. But not simply to weep because the questioning tone—which is mild on the part of the story-teller Ramakrishna Pai, and is caustically comic on that of his neighbour and fellow Ration Office clerk, Govindar Nan—opens the door to both simple gaiety and philosophical, or more precisely epistemological wit. And one notes also that while the questioning note in the narrator's tale is puzzled and plaintive, the interrogation of existence and its enigmas by Govindar Nan implies more positively that there may well be answers to these problems hidden in the traditional wisdom of the Hindus, and even that he quite possibly possesses the key to it.

In this story Raja Rao shows a gift for design less evident in the more diffuse and sometimes theoretical *The Serpent and the Rope,* and conspicuously absent in one of his final works, *Comrade Kirilov* (1976), which presents in rather essay-type form the opposing attractions of cerebral Soviet Marxism and historical Brahminical wisdom in the mind of a South Indian Brahmin, though without ever making a living union out of the two elements. But in *The Cat and Shakespeare* both the major themes and the smallest details fit vitally together. There is no separate conceptual cloud hovering over the story; no vague disconnected wash of feeling around its edges. The racial and poetic wisdom which is everywhere implicit, the evidence of Brahminical thought, the profoundly philosophical vision are all absorbed in, and sustained by, the particulars of the fable. The characters, Ramakrishna Pai, Govindar Nan, Horaham, John, Saroja and Shantha are both psychologically convincing and lucid and effective symbols; each is in Henry James's terms, 'a strikingly figured symbol' because each is also 'a thoroughly pictured creature'. And this is also true in its degree of the other details of the story, the Ration Office, the Ration Books, the cat, the rats, the work. They are also symbols which work, symbols with bite. Moreover the innumerable literary and philosophical hints and suggestions, the analogies, the muted quotations, the remote, insinuated connections which echo and re-echo throughout are used with that musical propriety, wholly different from merely explicit or pedagogic pointing, which is the infallible evidence of an authentic art.

It seems fitting to end these remarks on a genuinely 'difficult' writer with his own modest and concise account of his work.

> Starting from the humanitarian and romantic aspect of man in *Kanthapura* and *The Cow and the Barricades* [his early volume of short stories]—both deeply influenced by Mahatma Gandhi's philosophy of non-violence—I soon came to the metaphysical novel, *The Serpent and the Rope* and *The Cat and Shakespeare,* based on the Vedantic conceptions of illusion and reality. My main interest increasingly is in showing the complexity of the human condition (that is, the reality of man is beyond his person), and in showing the symbolic construct of one human expression. All words are hierarchic symbols, almost mathematical in precision, on and of the unknown. [*Contemporary Novelists,* ed. James Vinson, 1972].

R. K. Narayan is the author of a substantial body of fiction, some dozen or more novels, all of them remarkably even in the quality of their achievement. The world established in these novels (although 'established' is too harsh a term for the delicate skill in implication everywhere evident) impresses the reader with its coherence, its personal stamp and idiom. The action is centred in the small town of Malgudi in Mysore—small by Indian standards, that is—and although the physical geography is never dealt with as a set piece but allowed to reveal itself beneath and between the events, one comes to have a strong feeling for the place's identity. The detail suggests, surely and economically, the special flavour of Malgudi, a blend of oriental and pre-1914 British, like an Edwardian mixture of sweet mangoes and malt vinegar: a wedding with its horoscopes and gold-edged, elegantly printed invitation cards; tiny shops with the shopkeeper hunched on the counter selling plantains, betel leaves, snuff and English biscuits; the casuarina and the Post Office Savings Bank; the brass pots and the volumes of Milton and Carlyle; the shaved head and ochre robes of the *sanyasi* and Messrs Binns' catalogue of cricket bats. Especially is this true of the details of public life, of the shabby swarming streets and the stifling by-lanes, the cobbles of Market Road and the sands on Sarayu bank, the banyan tree outside the central Cooperative Land Mortgage Bank (built in 1914), the glare of Kitson lamps and the open drain down Vinayah Mudali Street. Even the names strengthen this double quality: Nallappa's Grove and Albert College, Mill Street and the Bombay Ananda Bhavan (a restaurant), Kabir Street and Lawley Extension, the Mempi Hills and the Board School; while Malgudi Station is both Euston and the East and the Krishna Medical Hall both ancient and modern medicine.

But although these novels convey so full and intimate a sense of place, they are not in any limiting way regional. They send out long, sensitive feelers to the villages where the inhabitants are 'innocent and unsophisticated in most matters excepting their factions and fights', and to the cities where they are 'so mechanical and impersonal'. They concern themselves too with such varied spheres of interest as business, education, journalism, film-making, money-lending. One must not, of course, exaggerate this matter of the scope of reference. Narayan does work by focusing his attention sharply. Part of his strength is never to ignore his instinct for limitation. But he has the serious artist's gift for achieving representativeness by concentration. His preoccupation is with the middle class, a relatively small part of an agricultural civilization and the most conscious and anxious part of the population. Its members are neither too well off not to know the rub of financial worry nor too indigent to be brutalized by want and hunger. They may take their religion more easily than the passionately credulous poor, but even in those with a tendency towards modernity one is always aware under the educated speech of the profound murmur of older voices, of 'Lakshmi, the Goddess of Wealth, the spouse of God Vishnu, who was the Protector of Creatures'.

Narayan chooses for his heroes—modest, un-selfconfident heroes, it is true—members of the middle class who are psychologically more active, and in whom consciousness is more vivid and harrowing. They have some room for independent, critical existence; but there is always a tension between this and that deep source of power, the family where the women rather than the old represent 'Custom and Reason' and know 'what is and what is not proper'. The family, indeed, is the immediate context in which the novelist's sensibility operates, and his novels are remarkable for the subtlety and conviction with which family relationships are treated—those of son and parents, and brother and brother in *The Bachelor of Arts* (1937); of husband and wife, and father and daughter in *The English Teacher* (1945); of father and son in *The Financial Expert* (1952), of grandmother and grandson in *Waiting for the Mahatma* (1955).

It is against the presence of the town, finely and freshly evoked, and amid a net of family relationships, each thread of which is finely and clearly elaborated, that Narayan's heroes engage in their characteristic struggles. The conditions of the struggle vary from novel to novel, the stress is highly particularized, the protagonist may be a student, a teacher, a financial expert, a fighter for emancipation. One still discerns beneath the diversity a common pattern, or predicament. What is so attractive about it is the charm and authenticity of its Indian colouring; what makes it immediately recognizable is that it seems to belong to a substantial human nature. The primary aim of all these characters is to achieve, in the words of Chandran in *The Bachelor of Arts*, 'a life freed from distracting illusions and hysterics'. (The 'distracting illusions' are in the Indian tradition; the freedom from 'hysterics' is the cool qualification introduced by Narayan. The complete phrase suggests the subdued association of seriousness and comedy which distinguishes the tone of these novels.) At first the intention is obscure, buried under the habits of ordinary life, personal responsibilities and—since this is India—a heavy, inherited burden. The novels plot the rise of this intention into awareness, its recognition in a crisis of consciousness, and then its resolution, or resolutions, since there are more often than not several mistaken or frustrated efforts at a resolution.

This theme—it does not seem extravagant to call it the aspiration towards spiritual maturity—is sustained throughout Narayan's work. Clearly it is one with its own special dangers. How easily it could slide into formlessness or puff itself into grandiosity. It is a remarkable achievement—given such a theme and an Indian setting—that Narayan's work is singularly free of pretentiousness. A cool sympathy, a highly developed sense of human discrepancy, a rare feeling for the importance and the density of *objects*—these check any straining after undue significance or any tendency to lapse into a search for large truths about life. In particular each stage of the impulse towards maturity is defined with meticulous accuracy in minutely specified circumstances, so that the reader is left not with a vague scheme of some dialectical progress but the conviction of an individual living his chequered, stumbling life. Let me give an illustration of this. Here is an example of one of these young men—it is Krishna and it occurs on the first page of *The English Teacher*—at the beginning of his development when what I have called the impulse or aspiration is still too dim to be recognized and when it simply produces vague feelings of dissatisfaction and irritable moods of brooding and analysis. 'The urge had been upon me for some days past to take myself in hand. What was wrong with me? I couldn't say, some sort of vague disaffection, a self-rebellion I might call it. The feeling again and again came upon me that as I was nearing thirty I should cease to live like a cow (perhaps, a cow, with justice, might feel hurt at the comparison), eating, working in a manner of speaking, walking, talking, etc.—all done to perfection, I was sure, but always leaving behind a sense of something missing.'

The same mild hopelessness, the same domestic accidie, is to be seen in Srinivas in *Mr. Sampath* (1949), a man so bogged down in indecision that 'the question of a career seemed to him as embarrassing as a physiological detail'. 'Agriculture, apprenticeship in a bank, teaching, law—he gave everything a trial once, but with every passing month he felt the excruciating pain of losing time. The passage of time depressed him. The ruthlessness with which it flowed on—a swift and continuous movement; his own feeling of letting it go helplessly, of engaging all his hours in a trivial round of actions, at home and outside.' It is present in the lighter, less formed character of Chandran in *The Bachelor of Arts:* 'Chandran emerged from the Professor's room with his head bowed in thought. He felt a slight distaste for himself as a secretary. He felt that he was on the verge of losing his personality'. Even in *The Guide* (1958), Narayan's most complex novel, where the lines of development and of narrative are folded in subtler convolutions, one comes across this feeling of being lost in a pointless, endless routine, although here it is expressed in the nervier, more sophisticated manner proper to this 'advanced' character. 'But I was becoming nervous and sensitive and full of anxieties in various ways. Suppose, suppose—suppose? What? I myself could not specify. I was becoming fear-ridden. I couldn't even sort out my worries properly. I was in a jumble'.

The issue from this malaise comes about through some critical event which precipitates a crisis of consciousness and a new effort of will. In *The English Teacher* the event is the illness and death of Krishna's wife, but more often it is a meeting or series of meetings. The meetings may be disconcerting or terrifying, bewildering or exalting. In *The Financial Expert,* Margayya, perhaps Narayan's most brilliant single comic creation, gradually realizes his desire for a life 'freed from illusions' (but for him this means ironically a life dedicated to the cult of money—not money which with gross simplicity is spent across the counter of a shop but money as a beautiful living force) in a series of encounters: first with Arul Doss, the dignified peon of the Cooperative Bank who shows up Margayya's utter insignificance, then with the strangely impressive priest in the seedy temple who rehearses him in rituals for propitiating the Goddess of Wealth, then with Dr Pal, 'journalist, correspondent and author', whose 'sociological' work, *Bed Life* (later changed to *Domestic Harmony*), combining the Kama Sutra with Havelock Ellis, eventually makes Margayya's fortune, and finally Mr Lal, the large, astute, but fundamentally uncomprehending businessman. The effect of these meetings, the effect of Sriram's exalting meeting with Gandhi in *Waiting for the Mahatma* or Chandran's baffling meeting with the middle-aged rake in Madras in *The Bachelor of Arts,* is to wake the character from 'an age-old somnolence', from what he now sees to have been his illusory and hysterical past and to determine him wholly in favour of a completely new life.

If the analysis of the subject's struggle to extricate himself from the habitual, dreamy automatism of his past—and in a country like India where the influence of the given is so powerful, the severity of the effort required must be arduous and intense—if this shows Narayan's gift for serious moral analysis, then the various solutions adopted by his *personae* in the search for another, more conscious life, exhibit his remarkable comic talent. (Not of course that the fiction offers a neatly logical division just like this. The serious and the comic flow in and out of one another throughout in an intricate, inseparable alliance.) Tracts of human experience are looked at with an affectionately ridiculing eye, and with that kind of humour in which the jokes are also a species of moral insight. Such treatment brings out the note of the bizarre, of human queerness, in the activities of many sorts of people: businessmen, print-ers, teachers, holy men, press agents, money-lenders. At our most commonplace we are all exotic if scrutinized by a fresh eye. The range is impressive but it has to be said that it follows naturally on Narayan's reading of the key experience at the heart of his novels. Since it was a meeting, the intervention of human difference, human otherness, into the hero's narcissistic world which first shattered it for him, he feels in response that he has to break out of his solipsistic circle into a novel, even a deliberately alien, field of action. To evoke so much variety with such casual, convincing authority and to make it also organic and functional testify to a notable and original talent.

Sometimes these solutions end in a moment of illumination like Krishna's vision of his dead wife in *The English Teacher*—'a moment for which one feels grateful to Life and Death'—or in a total reversal like Margayya's bankruptcy, or even for Raju in *The Guide* in death. Often they show a character now more solid yet also more conscious, more finished, yet more sensitive, accepting, though with misgivings and backslidings, the responsibilities of ordinary life. Always they conclude on a note of acceptance. The following lines towards the end of *Waiting for the Mahatma* convey the feeling, although it is usually quieter and more implicit than this. 'For the first time these many months and years he had a free and happy mind, a mind without friction and sorrow of any kind. No hankering for a future or regret for a past. This was the first time in his life that he was completely at peace with himself, satisfied profoundly with existence itself. The very fact that one was breathing, feeling and seeing seemed sufficient matter for satisfaction now'. 'Accepting' indeed, is the word which best defines the attitude, not just here but Narayan's attitude generally in the face of his experience. 'Welcome' would be too shrill and hearty, 'resignation' too passive and submissive. In any case his attitude is too nimble with irony for one or the other. And that irony, it should be noted, is an irony of recognition, not an irony of correction.

Perhaps irony is too sharp a word for the calm scrutiny turned on these ardent young men and earnest old ones. Irony has a social reference and the characters in these novels seem to be tested against something deeper than conscious, formulated standards. And irony is in place in the presence of corruption; but all these people, even the seedy, the stupid and the vain, retain a core of essential innocence. The naïveté of being human: that is the daring subject of this decidedly self-effacing writer.

For Narayan is not a pushing or intrusive novelist. He has no anxiety to be tugging at our sleeve or to be giving us a knowing look. He has no message, no doctrine. The half-baked is not an item in his diet. The acceptance of life, which his art expresses, has no doubt a root in the national condition. One feels that a more than individual sensibility—more than simply personal categories and feelings—is operating under the surface. But his acceptance, a kind of piety towards existence, is not simply an inherited temperament with its corresponding technique of passive reflection. It is something that has to be worked towards, grown up to, gradually matured. Nor is it—as I mean to imply by calling it 'piety'—in any way rapt or mystical but altogether homely and human. It includes delight in the expressive variety of life, cognisance of its absurdities, mockery at its pretensions and acknowledgement of its difficulties. And like other kinds of piety and other sorts of tradition, it tends to focus itself in objects. Objects become hallowed with more than their own nature and invested with singular and lasting importance. This appreciation of the weight, the form, the value of *things* is both a feature of the temperament sustained throughout these novels and a device of the art employed in their construction. It pins down and solidifies the lightness and fluency of a manner that might otherwise be too evasive, too 'spiritual'. The effect of Krishna's clock, of his father's 'steel pen with a fat green wooden handle' and his ink made up by hand in a careful, yearly ceremony, or of Sriram's teak and canvas chair, is to help to enclose the souls of these people in flesh, pitted, worn and ordinary flesh. Here is an example of this particularizing power of objects at work, a passage from *Mr. Sampath* which gives a new meaning to the words 'an object of sentimental value'.

> He prayed for a moment before a small image of Nataraja which his grandmother had given him when he was a boy. This was one of the possessions he had valued most for years. It seemed to be a refuge from the oppression of time. It was of sandal wood, which had deepened to a darker shade with years, just four inches high. The carving represented Nataraja with one foot raised and one foot pressing down a demon, his four arms outstretched, with his hair flying, the eyes rapt in contemplation, an exquisitely poised figure. His grandmother had given it to him on his eighth birthday. She had got it from her father, who discovered it in a packet of saffron they had bought from the shop on a certain day. It had never left Srinivas since that birthday. It was on his own table at home, or in the hostel, wherever he might be. It had become part of him, the little image. He often sat before it, contemplated its proportions and addressed it thus: 'Oh, God, you are trampling a demon under your foot, and you show us a rhythm, though you appear to be still. May a ray of that light illuminate my mind.' He silently addressed it thus. He never started his day without spending a few minutes before this image.

The permanence of objects makes them a protection against the oppression of time. Clearly the direct reference here is to the Indian scene, to the hard agricultural tradition, the vast distances, the ruthless climate, the terrible poverty. But it seems to me to have as well, like so much in Narayan's writing, a measure of the wider validity that belongs to genuine works of art—the universal imprisoned but visible in the particular. In utterly different conditions, where nobody's grandmother could have handed down an image of Nataraja discovered by her father in a packet of saffron, we are probably like Srinivas and 'grasp the symbol but vaguely'. And yet as we contemplate its proportions we are not, I think, deceived in detecting through the appearances of stillness and strangeness a rhythm, the common and extraordinary rhythm of life.

Narayan's novels belong to a difficult *genre,* the serious comedy. Success in it calls for a sensibility preserved from

ambivalence or fracture, an unusual unity in the point of view as well as a social tradition in which the comic and the sad are not sharply marked off one from the other. It requires too a certain equanimity, an evenness of temperament and manner, to hold back both the exaggeration of farce and the one-sidedness of sentimentality.

I feel it would be wrong to end my consideration of the senior Indian novelists in English, the founding fathers of the *genre,* without a note on G. V. Desani, a writer of the same generation as Mulk Raj Anand, Raja Rao and R. K. Narayan and the author of one extraordinary book. He has an unusual background. He was born in Nairobi in 1909. He was a Reuters correspondent, a lecturer for the British Ministry of Information during the Second World War, a BBC broadcaster and then for some twenty years the inmate of monasteries in India, Burma and Japan. From 1960 to 1968 he was a newspaper columnist in India and since 1969 he has been a Professor of Philosophy in the University of Texas. The extraordinary book is *All About H. Hatterr* published in 1948 and revised in 1970. (Desani's other writings consist of a few short stories and a prose poem in dramatic form, *Hali* (1950), which most modern readers would find vague, idealistic in a gaseous way and intolerably rhetorical.) *All About H. Hatterr* is a turbulent, deflationary, bawling, magnificently irregular account of the weird self-education of the fantastic H. Hatterr. It is written 'in what may be termed', says Anthony Burgess in his enthusiastic and cogent introduction, 'whole language, in which philosophical terms, the colloquialisms of Calcutta and London, Shakespearian archaisms, whinings, quack spiels, references to the Hindu pantheon, the jargon of Indian litigation, and irritability seethe together.' To this catalogue we should also add as influences Rabelais, Chaucer, Kipling, Wilde, Joyce, *The Magnet,* and P. G. Wodehouse. This tumult of sound and semi-sense—in which an organizing principle is associated, frank, oblique or hidden—is subject, as Anthony Burgess also makes clear, to the control of an intricate pattern: seven meetings with seven sages in seven cities; seven lengthy lessons and seven energetic bouts of learning; seven superbly comic discussions of seven aspects of living with his friend Benneroji; seven efforts to teach the lesson to others—it is worthy of a wild-eyed Indian Joyce but one whose humorous sanity, however disillusioned, is never cynical.

There would seem to be very little in common between G. V. Desani, the master of the absurd, and Mulk Raj Anand, the novelist as social reformer, Raja Rao the novelist as metaphysical poet and R. K. Narayan, the novelist as moral analyst. They would certainly find his whole manner and approach relentlessly bantering and self-mocking, and his choice of narrator, an enlightened clown and auto-didact, the son of a European seaman and an Indian woman from Malaysia, utterly alien. And yet threading their way through the comic rhetoric and the welter of quips and literary allusions are themes all these novelists are concerned with: the nature of individuality, the development of the person in a society weighed down by inherited assumptions, the relationship of appearance and reality, the cogency of the ancient Indian myths, the cyclical swirl of existence. But most pointedly they all share a debt to the English language and to English literature and to its power to serve and to express distinguished talent of such various kinds. Each has his own way of acknowledging this debt. G. V. Desani's is shown in his delicious account of his arrival in England.

> All my life I wanted to come: to the Poet-Bard's adored Eldorado, to England, the God's own country, the seat of Mars, that demi-paradise . . . And now I have arrived.
>
> The realization made me feel humble, and O. H. M. S. post-haste, thank Almighty for same.
>
> Forgetting all reserve, forsaking all Do-as-Romans-do etiquette, and in full view of Liverpool's sardonically inclined docker population and the vastly jocose ship's sailor-company, I greeted the soil, both in the true English and the Eastern fashion.
>
> I took off my tropical-lid, the sola-topi, in sincere salutation, and next, without a waterproof, in my white drill shorts, I knelt on the mud-beds of the old country the soft depths of its textilopolis County Palatine, aye, keeper, luv, the blessed wet earth of Liverpool, Lancs., in a thousand salaams.

> *William Walsh, "Fiction: The Founding Fathers—Mulk Raj Anand, Raja Rao and R. K. Narayan," in his* Indian Literature in English, *Longman, 1990, pp. 62-97.*

Janet P. Gemmill

[*In the following essay, Gemmill explores the theme of "the city as jungle" in several representative Indo-English novels.*]

The temptation is strong to approach Indo-English novels set in Indian cities as case studies in urbanization. For instance, in *Coolie* by Mulk Raj Anand, the student of urban problems finds all he has been taught to look for. Anand's novel vividly describes the confused plight of the typical urban migrant in Bombay: a single young man who suffers from "too little sleep under too poor conditions after too much work at too low pay." Although written in the thirties, *Coolie* offers a still accurate description of the highly mixed character of land use in the typical Indian city. The malodorous pickle factory in Cat Killers Lane epitomizes the tendency for industrial areas to appear almost anywhere in an urban area, with small operations carried on in unsuitable structures objectionable to those in nearby residences. In addition, Anand presents a highly realistic picture of the various forms of low-income housing available to the urban migrant: the three-storied *chawl* with whole families crammed into single rooms, and *bustees* or collections of huts which spring up like mushrooms on any vacant piece of land.

Yet, as A. K. Ramanujan has warned [in "Toward an Anthology of City Images," in *Urban India: Society, Space and Image,* 1970], to use literary examples to illustrate such urban manifestations as overcrowding, slums and modernization is to misuse literature, for in doing so "we bring our categories to it and take them out again, with no new insight gained from the give and take." Rather, suggests Ramanujan, with literature we must enter the realm of symbolic values expressed through facts functioning as "objective correlatives." [In a footnote, the author states that the term was coined by T. S. Eliot to indicate an "object or image which represents a particular feeling or sensory experience."] In a novel, every action, every description functions as an aspect of the writer's vision, having passed through the filter of his imagination and been found to be accurate in a symbolic sense. Indeed, the symbolic truth of a particular city as represented by a novelist may supercede in importance the literal representation of that city.

The literary image of a city is the product of an individual sensibility reacting to a place and attempting to recreate the sense of what it means to be there. The literal representation of that place is significant only insofar as it corresponds to or gives rise to the symbolic representation. Yet the writer has certain mimetic demands to be met. First, his readers will not suspend their disbelief long enough to accept false images of a familiar city. Second, the writer's own commitment is to represent, as clearly and truthfully as possible, his own awareness of what it might be like for a particular character to interact with the place itself and with others in that place. The image of a city offered by a novelist coalesces as a demand for truth met on many levels: physical description that approximates what is actually to be found there; awareness of a city's "soul" which expresses itself in the relationship of activities, buildings, and space to each other; the sense of what it is like to live in that environment if one is a young urban migrant, a middle-class writer, or a struggling tailor, among others; the ultimate significance of choosing or having to live one of those lives in that environment; and the value judgments, transformed by metaphor, which a particular writer forms in his attempt to make sense of the phenomenon that is the city.

How are we to distinguish these various demands for literal and symbolic truth in our discussion of the city in the Indo-English novel? Some of these levels are subjective, arising out of the vision of a particular writer; others are more objective, representing the shared elements of a culture in which the writer is one participant among many. The first two levels have to do with the literal representation of a city, presumably shared by all who come in contact with that place. Physical description that approximates what is actually to be found there is an objective element, verifiable by anyone who makes an empirical observation. The sense of a city's soul seems to verge on the subjective, yet we observe a certain universal relationship between the spatial patterns of a city and its observer. The third level, however, the sense of what it is actually like to live in a particular environment for a particular person, has a double expression. The experience of those who live in a city is at least partially verifiable in an objective sense through sociological measurement or analysis of political and economic patterns. Yet the artificial world of place and character created by the novelist is clearly the product of individual perception and imaginative interpretation. Here, the writer's "negative capability" to project himself into another's way of thinking and being is crucial.

The fourth level, the significance of having or choosing to live a particular lifestyle is certainly a matter of subjective evaluation. The writer pronounces judgments upon the characters he has created and attempts to consider the worth of their interaction with each other and with the environment in which they find themselves. Finally, the fifth level, that of symbolic thought, is also entirely the subjective creation of the writer. His value judgments are converted into metaphors which may occur as static images or as objective correlatives in the actions of particular characters.

In this chapter these five levels of meaning are employed to study four Indo-English novels set in Bombay, Madras, and Calcutta, cities built by the British, and functioning originally as Presidency towns. What vestiges of their colonial origin affect contemporary symbolic representation of these cities? What is the ethos that springs from their common origin? We are less concerned about physical description, as it approximates what exists in the real world, than with awareness of a city's soul and the value judgments, however transformed by symbol and metaphor, which a particular writer makes in his attempt to understand a particular city.

Bombay, Madras, and Calcutta share a common history as major urban centers which evolved during the period of British rule. Begun respectively in 1667, 1639, and 1696, they were not indigenous Indian cities, but were built by the British for the express purpose of maintaining trading connections with India. Thus, the three cities have a common reference system. Neither sacred nor ceremonial cities, they are not oriented toward a sacred place, or the cardinal points of the compass, as an indigenous Indian city might be. Their orientation, rather, is toward the ocean; their earliest function was that of port. Until the early nineteenth century, the factories of the East India Company were the nuclei of military, commercial, and governmental activities in these cities. From their beginnings, the form of the three cities was designed to meet the Company's principal pursuit of trade and commerce.

An old Indian proverb notes three things that make a city, "*darya* (river), *badal* (cloud, meaning adequate rainfall), and *badshah* (the king)." Of the Presidency towns, Calcutta was built alongside a river. Madras was located at the mouth of a river, and Bombay, although not intimately associated with a river, occupied a water surrounded site. Each city contained a fort built for the protection of the traders and their defending armies against the encroachment of competitors and the native population. In both Calcutta and Madras, a large open space surrounds the fort, symbolizing physical separation between the native population and the colonial power. Historically, the ethos of these cities was one alien to the Indian. It had no link with sacred values, but was essentially commercial in tone.

The British evolved a new urban form in India after 1750. Writing of Madras, Susan Lewandowski describes the new form as "intrinsically Western, characterized by the separation of work and residence—related in part to the growth of an industrial mentality, and an ideology of individualism becoming prevalent in the European world" [in "Changing Form and Function in the Ceremonial and Co-

lonial Port City in India: An Historical Analysis of Madurai and Madras," *Modern Asian Studies* II, No. 2 (1977)]. Each of the three cities developed an area recognizable as a central business district with concentration of banks, insurance offices and other commercial facilities, with law courts and public offices located nearby. Little residential land occurred in the central area, in contrast with the traditional Indian city, where both commercial and residential land uses reach maximum intensity in a central bazaar. Residential areas, moreover, were sharply demarcated as European or indigenous. European-planned residential sectors include large bungalows with garden compounds on wide streets, a pattern reflecting concerns for space and the isolation of the nuclear family. Native residential areas, on the other hand, continued to be densely populated with narrow streets and closely built houses clustered about temples and other small ceremonial foci.

The new urban form in India had its genesis partly in the baroque city of Europe with its strong bias toward law, order and precision. Law, backed up by administrative and military power, confirmed the status of colonial rulers and secured their privileges. Order was based not on blood ties or neighborhood affiliations, but on subjection to the ruling power. New additions to the city were laid out on mathematical lines often with straight avenues, uniform block units, and radiating streets. The broad avenues designed for wheeled vehicles stretched the market out along traffic lines instead of providing local points of neighborhood concentration.

In the seventeenth and eighteenth centuries, when Calcutta, Madras and Bombay were expanding rapidly, the city was regarded as representative of social order. Its very form a declaration of a society organized by rational contract. The cities which the British built in India contrasted strongly with indigenous cities marked by narrow crooked streets, overcrowded lanes, and buildings set on top of one another to accommodate more people wherever space was needed. The wide boulevards and grid streets of the British were declarations of the rational mind at work. European man had ceased to believe that anything irrational might intentionally interfere to disturb his own systematic designs, and he set out to prove it by organizing the political and economic framework of his colonies accordingly.

Today, the early aim of the British—to bring light and order to a seemingly chaotic civilization—seems heavy-handed and absurd, though we know that many Indians welcomed British educational and legal systems. What is more, the admirable vestiges of that rational spirit have given way to new kinds of chaos inevitably linked with certain changes brought about by the British, including industrialization, the introduction of a monetary system of exchange, and social egalitarianism, to name only three.

Twentieth-century Indo-English novelists perceive clearly that the early changes wrought by the British were alien to the Indian psyche. But through symbolic thought, they also point out that in more recent stages British-built cities and institutions have become as alien and ironically more chaotic than those they were originally intended to replace. The urban cycle has come full circle, from jungle to "jungle." Perhaps these ideas can best be understood by examining four novels in order to determine how the historical evolution of the British-planned city surfaces in the symbolic thinking of the contemporary Indo-English novelist.

The first novel is *Coolie,* written by Mulk Raj Anand in 1935 (Hind Pocket Books, Delhi), prior to the departure of the British and the granting of independence. Anand's treatment of colonial elements tends to reflect the strong demands for independence being made at that time. We perceive a sense of alienation as Munoo, a hill boy who has previously worked in Daulatpur, comes to Bombay:

> Munoo emerged from the Central Station. Before him was Bombay; strange, complex, Bombay, in whose streets purple-faced Europeans in immaculate suits, boots and basket hats rubbed shoulders with long-nosed Parsis dressed in frock-coats, white trousers, dome-like mitres; in which eagle-eyed Muhammadans with baggy trousers, long tunics and boat caps mingled with sleek Hindus clothed in muslin shirts, dhotis and white caps; in which the saris of Parsi women vied with the colourful loads of garments on rich Hindu women and put to shame the plain white veils of purdah women and the flimsy frocks of masculine European women; in which electric motor-horns phut-phutted, victoria and tram bells tinkled tinga-linga-ling; in which was the press of many races, and the babble of many tongues which he did not know at all.

The essential quality is that of strangeness. Never having been in a large city before, much that Munoo encounters is new, but the cosmopolitan presence of Europeans and Parsis, both of whom are dressed peculiarly and speak unfamiliar languages, contributes to Munoo's sense of being a stranger in a strange land.

He is struck by the hugeness of the architecture, particularly in the central part of the city where institutional structures reflecting the values of the colonial power impose themselves upon the landscape.

> He looked around to measure the strength of his frame against the world. The huge domes and minarets of the General Post Office on his right, the vast domes and minarets of the railway station on his left, the great domes and minarets of the University and the Law Courts beyond, all vying with each other to proclaim the self-conscious heights attained by their architecture, challenged him to decide which of them was the most splendid, not knowing in their vanity that he was only a modest hill-boy impetuously impelled by every big building to believe it to be great, and easily daunted by such grandeur into believing himself completely insignificant and small.

Here, we observe the writer simultaneously offering physical description in approximation of what is actually there, and also making value judgments by insisting on a symbolic relationship between the huge buildings and the smallness of the young urban migrant. Thus, the ethos of Bombay is further transformed by the imagination of the writer attempting to convey a sense of how the city diminishes the individual.

In another passage, Munoo sits at the foot of a marble statue of Queen Victoria. This time the writer goes further, ridiculing the colonial power which foolishly thought to win the hearts and minds of the Indian people by proclaiming the Queen as Empress of India, yet not saying that in so many words. What he presents instead is the objective correlative of a crow cawing defiance to the world from Queen Victoria's crown, where it hops and flutters after relieving itself. A further use of an objective correlative follows to symbolize the rapaciousness of those who flock to Bombay in quest of jobs and wealth. In an unguarded moment, the boy allows the crow to steal a bag of sweets from his hand. And then a swarm of crows came:

> . . . soaring over his head, and cawing brazenly, fell on the sweets which had dropped out of the bag onto the pavement, and fluttered back to their eminent perch on Queen Victoria's head, in her arms, and around her large proportions.

Anand uses the phenomenon of insolent hordes of birds which cluster in cities hoping for a handout from the wastefulness of urban living, as a symbolic statement about the urban dweller and his city, including the role of the British in creating Bombay and patterning it according to Western values.

Munoo's first job is at the Sir George White Cotton Mills in Bombay, and his foreman is an Englishman with a scarlet bulldog face and a small waxed mustache. Jimmie Thomas, the virtual master of the factory, functions as the employer's agent to engage workmen, the chief mechanic, moneylender, and landlord for the workers. By satirizing Thomas, Anand makes a value judgment concerning the essential worth of Munoo's British employers. "Why did you not bring the whole of your village, ooloo, rogue!" said Jimmie Thomas, who had acquired the Indian accent, manner, and swear words. His sarcasm is immediately contrasted with the naivete of an innocent job applicant who says, "I will write a letter to some more people, Huzoor, if you need more workers." Jimmie Thomas is thus presented as the foreign victimizer of the innocent Indian peasant, and thus the objective correlative of the British presence in India.

In his first encounter with the machines in the spinning mill, Munoo experiences at first their poetry and then their oppressiveness.

> He lifted his eyes to the horizontal, circular, cylindrical, octagonal, diagonal shapes of the different parts of the machine. The first impact was fascinating. Then the bold gesticulation of a hundred knobs and shafts of the engine deafened him with its uproar.

In the end the machine devours his tunic as he struggles to take it off. With a traditional Indian metaphor, Anand describes the machine as "a many-headed, many-armed god" that chuckles with laughter at the joke it has played on him. The factory, under the management of the British, is seen ultimately as a source of destruction for the naive indigenous worker who does not understand its workings.

In Bombay, Munoo also experiences an initiation into the low life along Grant Road:

> Munoo followed Ratan enthusiastically into the quaint, narrow, old street whose dirt was hidden by the dark, whose unsavoury smells mixed with the perfume of the flower-stalls, and whose squalor was camouflaged by the forms of the thickly painted, profusely bejewelled, gorgeously attired women who sat on low stools, padded with cushions, in the windows and balconies, over curious little shops, smiling strange smiles and winking at the swarms of men who walked along, leisurely, gaily dressed and chewing the betel leaf or betel nut, while they looked out for a whore.

Even in the house of the prostitute, Piari Jan, the British are not absent, for on the walls hang "large oleographs of His Majesty King Edward VII and his eldest son, the King-Emperor George," along with lithographs of Hanuman and photographs of Piari Jan in her prime. The selection of pictures on the wall of the whorehouse is an ironic juxtaposition providing a value judgment of the city and its British rulers.

Munoo's experiences in Bombay terminate with a strike which his friend Ratan helps to foment. Sponsored by the All India Trade Union Conference, the strike is superseded by a Hindu-Muslim riot. A crowd gathers in Bhendi Bazaar, where a speaker exhorts Hindus to "show our Maratha courage to these circumcised Muhammedans." Munoo, still the innocent Punjabi hill boy, is bandied about by forces which he can neither understand nor control, forces generated by the urban environment. Attempting to maintain order is a young English officer in khaki, followed by ten Indian policemen leading a baton charge. Yet communalism is beyond the control of the British, as Munoo himself succumbs to the blows of a towering Pathan and wakens to find himself rescued by the Social Service League, a kind of Salvation Army operation that "rescues" beggars, paupers, and coolies from the streets where they sleep. Here again, we taste the flavor of satire aimed at a well-meaning British institution that misconstrues its humanitarian effort.

There is no end to Mulk Raj Anand's caricaturing of the British. Though his story is essentially that of the urban migrant, the writer constantly links the destructive power of the city with its British creators and administrators. It is somehow their fault for having unleashed the forces of urbanization which draw Munoo to the city and finally destroy him. He dies symbolically in Simla, the British hill station where he has pulled rickshaws for British memsahibs and thus contracted tuberculosis. In Anand's novel, the city and the British are one. Bombay is a British creation, and it is they who are responsible for its death-dealing atmosphere.

So Many Hungers, by Bhabani Bhattacharya (Jaico Books, Bombay, 1947), contrasts the city of Calcutta with the surrounding villages of Bengal. Set during World War II, the novel examines the economic relationship between an urban society and its rural hinterlands, as complicated by the war induced famine. The British are responsible for the government's scorched earth policy as well as for the buying up of rice from village stores, which in turn leaves the peasants hungry and destitute. In huge numbers they flock to Calcutta, only to join the thousands of hungry and homeless already sleeping on the city streets. We trace the rural-urban relationship through the figures of a Westernized Calcutta family and their poorer village relatives, linked by the figure of a Gandhian leader whose ideals are nearly forgotten in the struggle for mere existence.

The village is idealized in Bhattacharya's novel. City-dwellers, by comparison, are affluent consumers of luxury goods. Thus, the mother of the Westernized city family says of her sons' needs:

> Sugar, too. Clothing. I must get white English drill for the father and you two boys. And tinned butter, tinned fish. Strange tongues you children have. The river of Bengal choked with fish—every kind, large and small—still you fancy the year-old shapes packed in tins, both you and Kunal. The strong smell!

In contrast, Devata the Gandhian says of the villagers:

> On his petty income the landed peasant can have just enough of his own rice to eat, no reserve for lean days. And the *kisans*—they must always be hungry save for a spell of two or three months in the year, when they earn meals and a wage for field work. The hundred million *kisans* of India must always be hungry. It is a rare gracious day to have the stomach full.

Indeed, it is the peasants who receive our sympathy as we watch them abandoning homes and land to make their way to the city in search of non-existent food. Meanwhile the wealthy of that city speculate in foodgrains and make a financial killing from the starving peasants of Bengal.

The manners of the villagers are also idealized. The young urban scientist comes to visit relatives in the village and is embarrassed when Kajoli insists on removing his leather shoes and washing the dust off his feet. Devata reminds him that "she is a well-bred peasant girl. She has a legacy of manners as old as India. How could she give up her manners and proprieties to suit your new-fangled city ideas? You are a respected visitor in the house." By contrast, the urban dweller is devoid of compassion as well as manners. Bhattacharya describes an artist in a railway station sketching a dead mother with her young baby still suckling at her breast. When the ticket collector says to the artist, "She is dead," the artist replies, "Hoon," and goes on sketching. When the railway man reprimands the artist for his lack of pity and human feeling, the artist merely begs to be left in peace. The crowd at the station is unwilling to do that, however, and rush upon the artist beating him with their fists.

To the villagers, Calcutta is a miraculous place where food and jobs abound. The peasants, as they begin to migrate there in quest of elusive necessities, never lose their faith in the city.

> Then the men trekked the meadows and roads, ten thousand village streams flowing citywards. Ahead was the city, shining bright as a lighthouse. The city had never grown a blade of corn. The city had eaten out of the green bowl of the peasant's fields. The city, having taken the harvests, would spare a little for the peasant folk who had ever filled the bowls? The city would

not let the food-growers famish? Move on to the city. Move on. Drag your sore feet and move on.

When a young mother tries to bury her baby alive in order to spare him the pain of starvation, she is comforted by a vision of the city as a place of giving and healing:

> Why, girl, you can go to Calcutta city . . . You will get milk aplenty in the wonder city, and rice, and a new sari to put on. Calcutta city has money to spare. The people have kindness in their hearts to spare for poor folk. You will be looked after. You will find work, big wages! Nothing to worry about—nothing. One day when your child has grown and he is employed in a jute mill—think of that proud day!

The act of comforting is a human act which belies the irony of the comforter's vision. The naivete of the villagers is compounded by their need to believe in miracles.

Calcutta holds the promise of miracles precisely because of the mystifying technological innovations of the British. Telegraph lines, railroads, and motorized vehicles all went their way to rural areas from the city. Moreover, the city possesses the magical presence of lights that come on at the flick of a switch. Kishore, Kajoli's young husband, fantasizes a visit to the city:

> Why, one day, when he had money, they would go to the city of cities a-visiting, he and the girl, his wife. What streets! What crowds! Like people in a fair. And the illumination! So many lights on each street. No lamps of oil, mind: lights of great power, lightning-white; so many lights that night was no darker than daytime. And the cinema plays! How he would love to take the girl, his wife, to a cinema play!

Calcutta is endowed with the metaphor of light, not only because of the presence of electric lights, but because the city represents the apex of civilization. Such thinking echoes the Enlightenment view of the European city, and having been propounded by the British city-builders, persisted among rural people long after disillusionment had set in among the city-dwellers themselves. So the weary peasants, moving on foot toward Calcutta, see fireflies in the dark as "a sign, a message from the Image of Light. On to the city of a million lights! The city of humanity. The city of civilized living." Thus Bhattacharya deepens the irony, for even the City of Light cannot handle a crisis of such immensity as this famine.

The image of the city as an enlightened place persists even after the village relatives arrive in Calcutta in an army ambulance. Ironically, Kajoli's miscarriage saves the family from immediate collapse and transports them to a situation of greater misery. Yet in the mother's mind,

> the hospital to which Kajoli had been taken had the grand look of a king's mansion. Yet, the poor and needy were cared for in the wonder city. And why not? The city had money to spare and jingle. The people had great kindness in their hearts, like that young khaki-clad military doctor. There would be food. Onu would go to school—city folks were all set on book learning.

Such an idealized vision of the city, however, persists only momentarily once the peasants join the army of hungry pavement dwellers in Calcutta.

Their first impression of the city is one of enormous buildings rising steeply everywhere, "each one big enough to swallow all the men and women of Baruni village." Traffic seems overwhelming and assaults their rural sensibilities with its noise and startling variety of vehicles: "Motor-wagons of five hundred shapes and sizes. Tram-cars. A short, stout motorcycle darting off like an arrow with a fierce roar loud enough to burst one's eardrums." The ceaseless rumble of traffic oppressed their nerves.

Life in the city meant searching for food in new places. The famine migrants picked through rubbish cans for fruit skins and vegetable peels. Stalks, peels, and rotten vegetables were steamed together over a fire. Still others caught and ate rats. Thus advice is given to the newly-arrived village mother: "Those garbage cans—they are our food-bowls, mother. We pick out of them before the city's scavenger folk come with their vans. Sometimes we pick at night—less competition. I saw two women fighting like animals over a dust-bin—it happened yesterday." Bhattacharya notes the changes such competition evokes in the ordinarily generous peasant. He offers a vignette of two boys fighting a dog for an empty jam tin with sweet syrup clinging to its inside. Onu defeats the dog, then shares unwillingly, one side of the tin with his former opponent, a smaller child. Bhattacharya comments,

> It was truly an act of self-sacrifice. And it was, truly, a second victory . . . Destitutes and dogs in those days often fought for possession of the rich city's ten thousand rubbish heaps, in which scraps of rotting food lay buried. It was not every time that the destitutes won, routing the dogs on the streets and the dog within themselves.

Acts of the human spirit are rare when survival is at stake, and this, suggests the author, constitutes the metamorphosis of the peasant to the city-dweller.

The Bengal famine of 1943 was man-made, a scarcity intensified by lack of rationing, the destruction of forty thousand country boats, and inflated currency. The British, ironically the champions of freedom abroad, were seen in India as "eaters of freedom." Yet the situation in the early forties was but a temporary one, intensified by fear of Japanese invasion. Many people died unnecessarily, but villages which had been torn apart were put back together again and the rural areas restored, until the next outbreak of violence which came with Partition in 1947. Bhattacharya's picture of Calcutta and its hungry peasant refugees now seems like a premonition of what was to come in the sixties and seventies as new waves of refugees flocked to the city from East Pakistan, as well as from villages that held no occupational promise for their young men. Yet as Bhattacharya presents Bengal in 1943, it was very much the province of the British.

British mismanagement of the famine is treated as consistent with their inhumanity as colonial rulers, a view which intensifies the nationalist sentiments at work in both *Coolie* and *So Many Hungers*. Rahoul speaks sarcastically to a group of students in the Quit India Movement: "Imagine two million Englishmen dying of hunger that was preventable, and the Government unaffected, uncensored, unrepentant, smug as ever! In the village, an uneducated fisherman wonders who might be the "Japanese folk" threatening to invade and is told, "Aliens . . . aliens all—Engraze and German and Chinee and Japanee." The fisherman replies, "Aliens all. Why don't they keep to their own hearth? What madness calls them across the seven blackwaters to the homes of harmless folk whose door-sills they darken?"

Calcutta, the City of Light built by the British, is in Bhattacharya's novel, in the process of becoming a city of darkness. The city of civilized living is in metamorphosis to the jungle, habitat of beast, an image which it assumes in Anita Desai's novel of twenty years later. Yet the transformation in 1947 was seen as momentary, a creation of the British. With a new dawn of independence on the horizon, there was hope for the restoration of light. Bhattacharya, however, merely hints at the promise of freedom. Rahoul, imprisoned by the British for his speechmaking, envisions Calcutta as a "vast swamp of suffering and struggle" where "the four-petaled lotus of the people" would break into bloom. The swamp of Calcutta's past is evoked and joined with a sacred image—the lotus—and subtle Marxist terminology—"of the people." Symbolically, Bhattacharya points out as the novel ends that the British still hold the key to Rahoul's chains and those of his people, but their spirit remains free.

Kamala Markandaya, in *A Handful of Rice,* written in 1966 (Hind Pocket Books, Delhi), shows us a Madras no longer inhabited by the British. Their vestiges are there in George Town, the area adjacent to the Fort, which skirts the docks. Yet George Town is now an outlet for the black marketeer and an unproclaimed clearing house for wine, hashish, and exotic fabrics. Ravi, the young urban migrant, moreover, sleeps at first in the railway station, in the waiting room, for lack of other lodging. The writer thus reminds us of the great railway system constructed by the British for their own convenience in getting goods out of the country and themselves to various hill stations.

A memory of the British haunts the women of Madras. Though convenient to their house, Ravi's young wife Nalini refuses to go to a stretch of beach with fine white sand because there the British Tommies came, "storming down from St. Thomas' Mount to maraud and rape . . . and once they had attacked a high-born Brahmin lady . . . stripped her and tied her to a stake in the sand; and when she was rescued she had killed herself for the shame of it." When Ravi objects that there are no Tommies left, so why not go there now, Nalini replies, "Because of the terrible aura of things left behind." Thus, suggests Markandaya, the ghosts of the British stalk the city of Madras, creating a kind of urban folklore that affects the behavioral patterns of superstitious young women.

There is also the section of the city known as Nungabakkam, where Apu's most important customers live:

> It was quiet here, with large cool detached houses, and dancing patches of shade from spreading tamarind trees and gulmohur such as never lined the streets where they lived, and in the shade an

occasional slab of stone or a concrete bench where people could sit.

One knows who has built these houses and laid out the garden suburbs and why, yet there is here no attempt to satirize the British, as in the value judgments made by Anand. In Markandaya's novel, the emphasis is on the contrasts between the struggling lower class and the affluent families, both European and Indian, who live in these spacious colonial bungalows with wide verandahs. Their original function as "oases of cultural space" is perpetuated in modern Madras through the economic class structure of the city.

The picture of Madras in Kamala Markandaya's novel is that of a smaller, less terrifying city than Bombay or Calcutta. The parts of the city are referred to in terms of quarters or districts that allow one to proceed to one's final destination by personal inquiry. Yet like the larger cities, Madras is the seat of a money economy, and man in that environment "is reckoned with like a number, like an element which is in itself indifferent." Ravi, the hungry young man who has given up ties to his ancestral village, becomes almost by necessity a city-dweller, confronting the problem of eking out an honest existence through the unfamiliar profession of tailoring, and taking upon his shoulders the burden of a growing family overcrowded in its living space. The problems of hunger and poverty are similar to those he has left behind in the village, yet in an urban setting they are intensified and worse, unrelieved by kinship ties or agricultural exchange. As a city dweller, Ravi balances on the precarious edge of respectability, threatening to crash through momentarily into violence and crime as existential responses to an impossible situation. Although *A Handful of Rice* is set in Madras, it is first a novel about the lower-class city dweller. His environment is important only insofar as it is the cause of his problem and the stage upon which his life is played.

The dream of leaving the village and emigrating to the city was one that had obsessed Ravi as it had his brothers and all the young men he knew, "joining the exodus to the cities because their villages had nothing to offer them." But there is an irony in urban migration in South India: "The cities had nothing either, although they did not discover this until they had arrived; but it held out before them like an incandescent carrot the hope that one day, some day, there would be something." Even Ravi's father, a poor tenant farmer, had held that hope as had the father of Apu, Ravi's father-in-law, "who had joined an earlier Exodus from his village following the recurrent famines at the turn of the century." The city is represented as a vast magnet with unlimited drawing power to which there was no counterweight that the village way of life or its people could apply. The passing of the train through the village once each day was an ever-present reminder of the way to the city.

Simultaneously, the urban place is viewed as a stronghold of evil, a place of temptation in the eyes of the villagers. When Ravi's father comes to Madras to negotiate his son's marriage with Nalini, he comments, "In a big town like this there are so many temptations . . . which fortunately do not come one's way in a village." The jutka driver agrees, saying there were "indeed many pitfalls in a town, traps specially set to seduce your men away from right into wrong." Ravi, in return, is repulsed by the way the older generation "gathered every evil they could think of and laid it at the feet of a town, as if they were making an offering to some black god."

During the birth of his son, as Ravi paces the streets, he is acutely aware of how unconsoling the urban landscape is. In the village, "there was something about the land, mortgaged though it was to the last inch, that gave one peace, a kind of inner calm, that he was acutely conscious of lacking as he gazed at the narrow, hard bustling and indifferent street." Kamala Markandaya here consciously evaluates the effect of the city on the psyche of the urban migrant. The city is presented as the negative antithesis of the village with its open fields, soft earth, leisurely pace, and intricate kinship ties.

The problem of housing in Madras is vividly depicted by Markandaya through Ravi's various living arrangements. Ravi becomes a pavement dweller like millions of other urban migrants. He worked all day and "it was a matter of chance where he slept. A bench in the park, an empty six-by-two space in a doorway, the veranda of an empty house, the pavement, all in turn had served to bed down on." It is not merely the lack of money which prevents Ravi from renting a room: "The city was so crowded, rents so high, that even men with decent incomes searched for years, squashing themselves and their families on to whichever relative had managed to secure some foothold in some house."

Even after he becomes part of Apu's family with Nalini as his wife, they cannot talk to each other at night or indulge in love-making without evoking a pounding on the door. Their room, through which everyone must pass to reach the kitchen, is not theirs even in the night, for the needs of others intervene—milk for a fretful baby or a poultice for an old man's ills. Even when Ravi constructs a straw hideaway on the roof for himself and his wife, it is invaded by other members of the extended family.

The writer thus illustrates the stress undergone by traditional values in an urban setting. First Apu expels his non-productive son-in-law, who by stealing the old man's savings, gives him reason to abbreviate his hospitality. Later, it is Ravi who, as head of the family, is oppressed by inflated rice prices in the face of additional children and declining income. He expels the parasite Varma and the cripple Kumaran, and we are made to realize that the traditional values of extending one's home to kin have completely collapsed under the conditions of urban life.

Other values collapse also as Ravi becomes part of a brick-throwing mob on Nabob's Row at the end of the story. The mob stands before an elegant women's shop with floor-to-ceiling show windows, the name EVE written in large gold letters above. The shop is full of luxury goods for women: beaded bags, brocade sandals, and the quilted coats, with an enormous price mark-up, made by Ravi and Apu. The shop, frequented by European women for the most part, is a symbol of the affluent and their oppression of the poor. Ravi does not participate in the shattering of

the great glass window, yet its shards symbolize the shattering of his own willingness to work quiescently for too little pay.

Ravi lacks the energy to throw a brick at the mannekins in the window, and we see that in the end the city has robbed him of his ability to assert his rights. Ravi's reluctance to hurl a brick accompanied by his final words, "I don't feel in the mood today . . . but tomorrow, yet tomorrow," suggest a mood of hope deferred. The lot of the urban poor, implies Markandaya, is to be tantalized by extremes of wealth which are always beyond their reach. The city juxtaposes extremes of wealth and poverty in a more abrupt way than does the village, and that juxtaposition is a source of perpetual agony.

Markandaya's most frequently used metaphor for the city is that of the jungle, "a man-made jungle, full of snares and traps and unkept promises." The city is a place which turns mild, well-bred but jobless students into screaming agitators, and respectable tradesmen into brick-throwing bandits. The jungle metaphor is associated particularly with Damodar, the small-scale black marketeer, who through cunning and persistence finally attains great wealth and power. At the end, he is contemptuous of the changes wrought in Ravi by poverty, worries, respectability, and hard work. "You're empty. No heart, no spleen, no lights, no guts. Something's been at them . . . What was it, termites?" Ravi is no longer fit for competition in the jungle. In the struggle for survival of the fittest, he is the weakling, unable to cope with the urban environment which is slowly but surely devouring his hopes, his family, and his very being. *A Handful of Rice* makes of the British-influenced commercial ethos of Madras a metaphor, insisting upon the city as jungle, a wild chaotic world in which civilized values have ceased to matter and the unwary are destroyed. The Enlightenment vision of the city as a symbol of social order is thus replaced by the nineteenth-century European view of the city as the epitome of vice, a place of poverty, squalor and upper-class hardheartedness. In a curious inversion of images, the city returns to jungle: that which it was before the British came.

Anita Desai, in *Voices of the City,* written in 1965 (Hind Pocket Books, Delhi), offers us a somewhat different angle on Calcutta. Here we are dealing with a different kind of urban migrant, who comes from an aristocratic background in the northern reaches of India, close to the Himalayas. A brother and two sisters encounter Calcutta as a destructive force, a personification of the goddess Kali, who both gives life and takes it away. The city is presented as a force acting upon the minds of those who come to her, a metaphoric representation of the intense nervous stimulation experienced by the city dweller. It could be any city, but it happens to be Calcutta, where the "rapid crowding of changing images" and "the sharp discontinuities in the grasp of a single glance" are more extreme than in any other city in the world.

Desai reinforces this sense of discontinuity through frequent vignettes of Calcutta as seen from a moving train or through the eyes of a person walking rapidly down a city street. Always, one is struck by the sharp contrasts in onrushing impressions as scene after scene flashes before the reader's eye:

> The streets where slaughtered sheep hung beside bright tinsel tassels to adorn oiled black braids, and a syphilitic beggar and his entire syphilitic family came rolling down on barrows, like the survivors of an atomic blast, then paused to let a procession of beautifully laundered Bengalis in white carry their marigold-decked Durga—or Lakshmi, or Saraswati, or Kali—on their shoulders down to the Ganges, amidst drums and fevered chanting. In one shadowy doorway an old crone lit a fire, mumbling. Beneath a brief canvas roof a skeletal old gnome with electric white hair served *kebabs*, still sizzling on their red-hot spikes, first to an urchin who had his day's earnings knotted at his crotch, and next to a party that waited in a long American car drawn up to the pavement.

The very juxtaposition of opposing images and sounds, briefly experienced, conveys perfectly the psychological assault that occurs from constant exposure to an overcrowded city.

A persistent impression in Calcutta is the sense of overpopulation. Desai comments that the crowd is everywhere—passive, but distressed, till there is reason for anger, and then "a sullen yellow flame of bitterness and sarcasm starts up." Even then it is anger that "broods and festers like a pus-filled boil," occasionally erupting into student strikes and burned trams. Monisha, condemned to life behind the confining walls of a conservative extended family, is oppressed by the crowds in the streets: "From all sides their moist palms press down on me, their putrid breaths and harsh voices. There is no diving underground in so overpopulated a burrow, even the sewers and gutters are choked, they are so full." The imagery here is that of animals living in holes in the ground, not unlike the jungle metaphor in *A Handful of Rice*. Thus, Desai presents Calcutta symbolically as an overwhelming experience of superstimulating images.

This particular city, built by the British in a most unlikely location, carries with it a memory of its birth out of the swamp along the Hooghly River. From its earliest days, Calcutta bore the reputation for being "an indistinguished mass of filth and corruption equally offensive to human sense and health." Building upon this historical memory, Desai personifies Calcutta as a monster born in the marsh and having, as a result, certain inhuman qualities that prey upon the people who live there. "On all sides the city pressed down, alight, aglow and stirring with its own marsh-bred, monster life that, like an ogre, kept one eye open through sleep and waking." Dharma, an artist who loses his child to cholera and becomes profoundly depressed, refuses to repudiate the city. He still needs "the Calcutta earth, the Calcutta air" though "these are the very things that poisoned him. . . ." The unhealthy swamps which first gave rise to the city are linked with the current unsanitary water supply to create an everpresent aura of disease.

Amla, the young woman artist, comes to Calcutta to work and is immediately struck by the transformation which the city has wrought upon her brother Nirode and her sister Monisha. In the garden of her aunt's home, she senses the corrupt spirit of Calcutta:

> It was a dampness and a darkness that swarmed with uneasy, dissatisfied spirits, all sighing, complaining and warning, warning the young and living of the city's gory history, of slow mortality, of the swamps that flank it, the corruption that rose from it in historic odours and seeped first into the business houses, then into the rich houses that were founded upon these businesses, and the rag-and-thatch huts that huddled beneath the high walls, finally invading the tired and listless mind, then laying waste all that was fine and moral.

Calcutta is repeatedly referred to as a monster that "lived no normal, healthy, red-blooded life but one that was subterranean, underlit, stealthy and odorous of mortality." The city as monster, believes Amla, has captured and enchanted, or perhaps disenchanted, both her brother and sister.

Monisha, the married sister, has opted for the orthodox Hindu role of wife in the household of a wealthy old Calcutta family. Deprived of the intellectual stimulation of the city by her traditional lifestyle, she looks out on Calcutta from her balcony and feels herself a prisoner shrinking away to nothing. "I grow smaller every day, shrink and lose more and more of my weight, my appurtenances, the symbols of my existence that used to establish me in the eyes of this world. I am already too small to be regarded much by anyone. I will be invisible yet." It is Monisha who realizes that Calcutta is the city of Kali, goddess of death. By committing suicide, Monisha allows herself to be a sacrificial victim, that her brother and sister might survive and make of tormented consciousness something with which to resist the city.

Desai relies less on objective correlative, and perhaps too heavily on metaphor, to convey her awareness of the city's soul and its effect upon those who dwell there. The city is described as a toothless hag that "holds its head between its knees and grins toothlessly up at me from beneath a bottom black with the dirt it sits on." Thus, the mad, toothless hags seen along the pavements of Calcutta are converted into a personification of the city. Another face of Calcutta, suggests Desai, is the dull, vacant, hopeless face of the rickshaw coolie, the street sweeper, and the beggar child with his limbs cut off at the joints. Through the sensitive mind of the brother, Nirode, the writer presents Calcutta as a creature with two faces—one rapacious, one weary. How is he to respond, he wonders, with loathing or compassion? The ambivalence is paralyzing. Dharma tells Nirode, "There can be no phoenix in the heart of such destruction. The anarchistic genius of Calcutta is intrinsically negative." Calcutta emits a unique sense of her own terribleness.

Literal description of a physical place is of little consequence in Desai's novel. Nor is there much action in *Voices in the City*. The symbolic truth of Calcutta as a disease-ridden enchantress dominates instead. The writer employs sensitive, educated characters who reflect upon their urban experience and indulge in constant interpretative value judgments and metaphoric images of Calcutta. Thus the writer projects into the minds of her characters an almost frantic attempt to make sense of the overstimulation, the overcrowding, and the filth that is Calcutta. Their perceptions suffice for an instant, then fail in the face of new experience. They barely succeed in surviving and do so only by understanding that their mother's failure to care for them, and their failure to care for each other, are somehow linked to the inability of Calcutta's inhabitants to care for anything save their own survival.

The outcome of the novel suggests that if one is to live meaningfully in such an environment, he must will himself into human involvement and creative triumph such as Amla's illustrations or Dharma's portraits. What is possible but difficult is retaining one's individuality, summoning the utmost in uniqueness to preserve a personal core. To outwit the destroying goddess, one has to exaggerate the personal "in order to remain audible even to himself.

If Clifford Geertz [in *The Interpretation of Cultures,* 1970] is right in suggesting that symbolic activities represent attempts to provide orientation for an organism which cannot live in a world it is unable to understand, then the constant symbolizing in these four novels is the result of writers trying to make sense of their own experience. The city, in particular, is a traumatic, exciting, destructive element in the experience of modern man. Life in the city is characterized by intensified sensory stimulation, depersonalized relationships, brutal competition for economic gain, and the atrophy of individual culture. At the same time, life is easy in the sense that stimulations, interests, uses of time and consciousness carry the person in a stream where he has no need to swim for himself. The contrast with the slow, habitual rhythms of village life is enormous and ultimately disturbing. In more recent novels, these concerns take precedence over symbols that are rooted in experience with the British, even in novels dealing with the Presidency towns.

The contemporary Indo-English writer, in his attempt to make sense of these disturbing contrasts, creates an image of the city that will somehow enable him to dwell there. He seeks to overcome the sense of chaos which the city evokes in him by creating a symbolic world in which characters interact with each other and with the place in which they live. If the creation is successful, he has succeeded in establishing meaningful literary order out of chaotic literal experience. In the process, he brings something new into existence—a way of understanding the city—that ultimately contributes to the collective treasure chest of culture. His vision thus becomes available to others as they, in turn, attempt to make sense of their lives. And so we rummage in the treasure chest trying on and casting off symbols. We are casual, even playful in our reading, yet the quest is one of desperation: somewhere is the symbol that will ease the chaos. Then we will know how to respond.

> *Janet P. Gemmill, "The City as Jungle in the Indo-English Novel," in* India: Cultural Patterns and Processes, *edited by Allen G. Noble*

and Ashok K. Dutt, Westview Press, 1982, pp. 45-68.

Meenakshi Mukherjee

[Mukherjee is an Indian educator, novelist, and critic. In the following excerpt, she examines the theme of the encounter between East and West as it is portrayed in several Indian English novels.]

In the complex fabric of contemporary Indian civilization, the two most easily discerned strands are the indigenous Indian traditions and the imported European conceptions. Almost every educated Indian today is the product of the conflicts and reconciliations of two cultures, although the consciousness of this tension varies from individual to individual. What is generally true of the educated Indian is especially true of the Indian writer, because a writer is concerned with the springs of human action and with the motivation behind human behaviour. Thus he is more aware than others of the elements that make up his personality. At the present point of Indian history, a writer's analysis of his self necessarily involves the evaluation of his own attitude towards these two aspects of his being— one inherited from birth, the other imbibed through education.

This cultural conflict—or synthesis, as the case may be— has for some reason always assumed a vital significance for the Indian novelist who writes in English. As early as 1909, Sarath Kumar Ghose wrote a novel called *The Prince of Destiny* dealing with this inter-cultural theme where the hero, the prince of a native Indian state, has to choose between the love of an English girl and marriage with an Indian princess. And as late as 1960, J. M. Ganguly's *When East and West Meet* shows that the East-West motif has not yet exhausted itself. In the intervening half-century a number of novelists have attempted to study this encounter at various depths of meaning. In some novels the West appears as a character, in some others as an attitude or a set of values. In the novels written during the Gandhian era, we find the East-West theme operating as the conflict between pre-industrial modes of life and mechanisation, as in K. S. Venkatramani's *Murugan the Tiller* (1927) and in V. V. Chintamani's *Vedantam, the Clash of Traditions* (1928). In the years following Independence, however, a number of novels have appeared where the conflict between the two cultures is not on the social but on the personal level, whose theme in broad terms may be called an individual's search for identity in a changing India. The definition of 'East' as well as of 'West' varies from novel to novel, but each tries in its own way to grapple with the problem that has continued to concern the Indo-Anglian novelist for more than fifty years. One is struck by the unabating interest shown by these novelists in the inter-action of the two sets of values that exist side by side, and often coalesce, in twentieth century India.

To a certain extent, this interest is noticeable also in novels of the period written in the Indian languages. S. H. Vatsayan has noted in a survey of modern Hindi literature that "the search for a satisfactory attitude towards the west and of an emotionally and spiritually significant image of the east" marks the Hindi novels after the Second World War. But the Indian novelist in English is more seriously and consistently involved with the East-West theme than his counterparts in the Indian languages, if only because his very choice of language indicates an awareness of and exposure to a culture other than the traditional Indian. We assume that an Indian, when he writes in English, does so only because it comes most naturally to him. As Balachandra Rajan has argued, the real necessity of a writer is the necessity to render his individual vision without compromise into a public language—"If that language happens to be English the creative choice must be respected and one should judge by results rather than by dismal prophesies of what the result must fail to be." The need to realize oneself creatively in English, however, presupposes a familiarity with the language which goes along with a greater degree of exposure to western culture than what the average educated Indian undergoes. The latter, in spite of all his English education, is usually more at home in his regional language. The majority of Indo-Anglian writers today (with one or two notable exceptions), it will be observed, have had at least part of their education abroad. Because of their intimate experience of a culture other than their own, they are made aware of their Indianness as well as of the difference in the two systems of values: one rather acquired, the other inherited and often taken for granted. Not all Indians educated abroad develop this awareness, but a writer certainly is likely to be more sensitive in his responses than other men. The intercultural nature of his own being becomes for such a writer a theme of profound interest. Therefore, the search for one's identity is found to be a common and recurrent theme in Indo-Anglian fiction.

There may be other reasons for the Indo-Anglian writer's concern with the East-West theme. One could argue, that this theme is no more than a manifestation of the Indo-Anglian writer's constant awareness of a western audience. The East has to be deliberately interpreted and defined for this supposed audience, hence the need for this dialectical and contrastive theme. This is a nebulous charge, which has to be examined in specific novels before it can either be accepted or rejected as a worthwhile generalization. The fact that the Indo-Anglian novelists are generally more closely acquainted with western culture seems to be a more valid reason of this concern. The Indians who have learned the English language merely as part of the educational curriculum, as something not really connected with their daily life, need not be seriously affected by the western values to which this language introduces them. It is as easy for them to discard the acquired values as it is for them to take off their western clothes at the end of a working-day. But for those who have had a more intensive exposure, the confrontation of these two kinds of values becomes a major concern.

There are a few examples among Indo-Anglian writers of those for whom the confrontation has not resulted in any tension, creative or otherwise, who have been able to write as if the acquired values alone can sustain their view of life. D. F. Karaka is an example of this kind of Indo-Anglian writer. He must be the only Indian novelist to write a novel set in England using only British characters. Karaka's *Just Flesh* (1941) undoubtedly displays the author's intimate knowledge of English life and culture, but it makes no contribution either to English or to Indian literature because it nowhere comes to grips with reality. His second novel, *There Lay the City* (1942), is set in Bombay, but its narrator admits he "touched the great city only on the fringe, mentally, spiritually and physically," while he dreamt of London streets, the *bois* of Paris, or of "the cobbled streets of a little Spanish town." The bullet lodged between his heart and lung as the result of an accident in Europe remained there both literally and metaphorically. In his last novel, *We Never Die* (1943), Karaka makes a belated attempt at writing about an Indian village. But it remains a purely theoretical exercise, far removed from the real predicaments of rural India, and the solution that is suggested at the end is too facile to be taken seriously.

Another group comprises novelists for whom the intercultural tension exists, but does not seriously affect the course of events in their fictional world. R. K. Narayan and K. Nagarajan are two examples of writers who have been able to write about life as it is known to them, in their particular areas of the earth—Malgudi and Kedaram—without the need to indulge in any generalizations about what is Indian and what is western. Their characters are that curious blend of the east and the west which all Indians are, but they refuse to sift the elements. Their refusal to take sides, to justify, to explain or to condemn, is responsible for a good deal of their success as novelists.

Then there is the curious case of Manohar Malgonkar, for whom the conflict is not between East and West, but between the sense of justice, fair play and integrity (exemplified by the British in India) on the one hand, and on the other, inefficiency and servility, dishonesty and a sense of inferiority, which by Malgonkar's definition are typically Indian. It is true that none of his novels hinges entirely on this conflict, but even a casual reading of his four novels will make the basic pattern of contrasts clear. British public school code of conduct constitutes the norm in Malgonkar's novels and, let it be said to his credit, the norm is maintained consistently.

His choice of theme in the first novel, *Distant Drum* (1960), was lucky, because the Indian Army is a direct inheritance from the British and still adheres fairly closely to the British system of values. In *Combat of Shadows,* his second novel, Malgonkar bypasses the problem of reconciling British values with Indian characters by making his central figure an Englishman. Henry Winton, the tea-planter is a healthy young man of the hunting and shooting type, and in spite of the difference in race and nationality, he is essentially of the same species as Kiran Garud, the squash-playing, upright military officer of *Distant Drum.* Abhay Raj, the hero of the third novel, *The Princes* (1963), is again another version of Kiran Garud, though a much weaker one. Having been born in a princely family, Abhay Raj is subject to a special princely code of conduct. But this conduct is not very different from Kiran Garud's code of honour or Henry Winton's ideals of masculine life. And the more enduring ideals of Abhay Raj's life, by his own admission, are derived from two Englishmen: his private tutor, Mr. Lawrence, and the principal of his college.

As a contrast to these decent, clean and honourable young men, there is the other type of character, who appears in every Malgonkar novel in various guises. Servile before superiors, arrogant before subordinates, thoroughly untrustworthy and corrupt, these characters all correspond to Gyan Talwar's analytical description of himself in *A Bend in the Ganges:* "Was it part of the Indian character itself? Did he in some way represent the average Indian, mixed up, shallow and weak?" The I.N.A. brigadier in the same novel represents the type physically: "He was soft and fat and dripping with perspiration . . . He was the embodiment of all that was servile in India . . . How many such creatures did India possess? Thousands upon thousands." This contrast between the fairness of the British and the pettiness of Indian officials forms a running theme in *A Bend in the Ganges.* If Gyan Talwar was the only person to observe this contrast, it could have been attributed to his personal inferiority complex. But all the characters repeat the observation, until it begins to look like a statement of the author's own point of view. Almost everyone in the novel shudders, like Debi Dayal's father, "to think what the nationalists would make this country." Not surprisingly, the nationalists in all the novels are invariably like Lala Vishnu Ram of *Distant Drum* who is constantly boasting, "I yam the Chairman aaf the Dishtrict Caangress Committee"—and just because Malgonkar completely withholds his sympathy from all the characters who are not "rich and wellborn" or do not share the British public school virtues, these characters remain either entirely comic or merely unreal. As characters they never become as fully realized as those the author favours. In this sense there is no real conflict in the novels of Malgonkar.

But apart from these three kinds of exceptions (represented by Karaka, Narayan and Malgonkar), the majority of Indo-Anglian writers have found a creative challenge in this tension between two civilizations. A few have confronted it with some measure of success, while some have reduced the intercultural dialectic into a narrow national commitment. The duality of culture as it exists in India today can either be a source of a strength to the writer, providing him with a double-bladed instrument with which to conquer India's hydra-headed reality; or it may be a serious handicap, because writing about a society in which different sets of values are flowing into each other, each at a different level of internal change, cannot be an easy task. To make out of this flux, where no single standard exists for all, a coherent social context for a novel, calls for exceptional qualities of organization and selection.

Confrontation with the West for the discovery of one's own country, and of one's own self: this is not an infrequent motif of contemporary Indo-Anglian novels. Homecoming after a sojourn abroad and consequent readjustment and revaluation of the terms in which to face life constitute the major issue in a number of these novels. Although the level on which this revaluation takes place varies considerably, the recurrence of the theme itself is sig-

nificant. In both the novels of B. Rajan, the protagonist's return home after a period spent abroad forms an important incident. Raja Rao's *The Serpent and the Rope* begins with Ramaswamy's coming back to India after spending some years in France, and his metaphysical definition of the re-discovered country. Santha Rama Rao's young heroine Baba Goray has just returned from school in England as *Remember the House* opens. In most of these cases there is an autobiographical element in the apprehension of the predicament of the person who has returned, though in the case of the more successful novels the autobiography does not interfere with the integral design of the work. In each case the protagonist's awareness of two civilizations intensifies his concern with his own identity. They are all in search of their true image, torn between the traditional values they have absorbed from childhood and the new values of their education has bestowed upon them. In each case, the novel ends with the resolution of their dilemma through a definite act of will.

Then there is the homecoming in novels where it is not the central incident, nor does it affect the protagonist personally, but incidentally it illustrates the interaction between two cultures. The return of Kitsamy in *Some Inner Fury* and the homecoming of Laila's cousins in *Sunlight on a Broken Column* are examples of this interaction at a rather superficial level, because the impact of the West upon these characters is presented very incidentally. Kitsamy, we are told, submits to the family priest's benediction on his return with ill-concealed annoyance—"his face took on a faint insolent impatience as if he was above all this sort of thing and amazed that we were not"—while for Laila's cousins, Kemal and Saleem, "the ten years of estrangement had no significance. Centuries of kinship swallowed them up in a moment." These two examples indicate the different levels on which the intercultural theme can be treated in a novel, ranging from the attitudes of a novelist of manners who is concerned with the shallow stereotypes to those of a more serious analyst; for some, the encounter of two civilizations results in a dilemma that must be solved in order to define the self.

In this distinction between eastern and western values, we tread dangerous grounds. Apart from the fact that after two centuries of proximity it has become increasingly difficult to demarcate precisely between the two traditions as available in India, such patent oppositions tend to prove disastrous in fiction insofar as they oversimplify action and conflict. Nevertheless, in spite of the constant overlapping and interchangeability of values, some kind of basic difference does exist between the two civilizations. Granting that in literature each writer has to make his own definition of what is for him the West and what is East, it would probably not be out of place here if we try to make, as a starting point, a tentative definition of the two value systems.

The American sociologist Clyde Kluckohn has indicated one way of defining this vague term 'values' when he says, "It should be possible to construct in general terms the views of a given group regarding the structure of the universe, the relation of man to the universe . . . and the relations of man to man. These views will represent the group's own definition of the ultimate meaning of human life." Sociologists, anthropologists and philosophers have tried many times to define the precise nature of Oriental and Occidental value systems. Among these definitions, the most comprehensive and least controversial seems to be the one suggested by Cora Du Bois. She sums up the entire issue in three questions, the answers to which—in her opinion—will indicate the value system of a particular culture. These questions are:

(1) What is man's relation to nature?

(2) What is man's conception of time?

(3) What is man's relation to man?

In posing these essentially metaphysical questions, she is raising universal queries for which men in all cultures have sought explicit answers. The answers they have selected from the total range of possibilities, and the consistency among the answers, constitute the basic premises of their varying value systems, their 'way of life'.

With regard to the first question, namely, man and nature, we find man can either accept the forces of nature as invincible or he can strive to master nature through the application of science in the form of technology. As for a concept of time—the second question—man can either look backward to a lost golden age or forward to an even more perfectible world; that is, have belief in progress. As for the third question, society can either be envisaged as a strict hierarchical order where each man performs duties allotted to him, or man can look upon himself primarily as an isolated individual, charged with cherishing and developing his unique potentialities.

It must be remembered, of course, that each of the questions asked above has more than two alternative answers. In reducing the complex issues involved in these answers to two opposed viewpoints we certainly over-simplify the cultural diversity of the human race. But we may at least tentatively accept these opposed alternatives—as philosophers such as Charles Morris and Ethel Albert, and a cultural anthropologists like Cora Du Bois have done—as representative of the mutual opposition of eastern and western values. These alternatives may therefore be treated as a working hypothesis for the examination of a particular aspect of the Indo-Anglian novel, though ultimately, East and West are subjective terms interpreted differently by different writers.

The heroes of Mulk Raj Anand are rugged individualists who suffer because they refuse to conform. Munoo the coolie, Bakha the untouchable, Bikhu the chamar, Lal Singh of the trilogy—all are persecuted by society for their non-conformity, but all of them are indomitable in spirit. Anand wrote in *Apology for Heroism:* "I am conscious that much of my insistence on the role of man in the universe derives from European Hellenism. For the traditional attitude of India in this regard is essentially non-human, super-human: 'This atman . . . is the same in the ant, the same in the gnat, the same in the elephant, the same in the whole universe' so says the Brhadaranyak Upanished". But for Anand the novelist, the atman in each man is

something rare and precious. It is clear on which side of the East-West dialect Anand takes his stand.

If we take Cora Du Bois' first question in relation to Anand's work, what is man's relation to nature—it is easily answered. Belief in man's power to master nature through a rational technology is evident in every novel of Anand. While others in the village take the filth and drought and misery as inevitable, Anand's nonconformist heroes rebel against the existing conditions because they have faith in the possibility of controlling nature for man's benefit. "The seasons will be changed by man. There will be water from the wells, with electric pumps . . . and medicines will renew the earth," proclaims Gauri towards the end of *The Old Woman and the Cow.* If the majority of the villagers in Anand's world share the traditional fatalism about nature's cruelty to man, his protagonists stand out as rebels and visionaries who believe in the prospect of improvement. They suffer because they cannot accept and be resigned, yet often find themselves unable to act. Added to the suffering imposed upon them by society is their own helplessness. Lal Singh is from his boyhood fired with a vague idealism and desire to change his village; these ideals find concrete objectives when he sees a French farm for the first time, observes the advanced methods of cultivation, notices the resulting prosperity. Like Bakha, Lalu admires the white man with a naive adulation. Even amid the stress of actual battle in the trenches, he "felt curiously thrilled to be among them, for in spite of their haggard faces the tommies had not lost that look of exalted sahibhood." This sahibhood consists in the efficiency of the white man, his ability to act, to use science to change existing conditions to suit his own convenience. For this reason, the machine is such a dynamic symbol in Anand's work.

The answer to the second question formulated by Cora Du Bois (namely, what is man's concept of time?) is found in equally unambiguous terms in Anand's work. While the older people sit mourning their fate, speaking nostalgically of the good old days and the debased state of affairs at present, Anand's young people—village adolescents (Bakha, Munoo, Lalu, Bikhu) as well as city labour leaders (Anant in *The Big Heart,* Ratan in *The Coolie*) and patriotic poets, doctors or wise men (Iqbal Nath Sharshar in *Untouchable,* Puran Singh Bhagat in *The Big Heart,* Dr. Mahindra in *The Old Woman and the Cow*)—all look towards the future to a more perfectible world. On the second page of *The Village* Lalu is found arguing with his father about the advantages of the goods train over the bullock cart which his father still prefers. From this point onwards Lalu becomes a representative of the forces of modernity or progress. Lalu, along with the other protagonists of Anand, shares the values of his creator, and these values are in sharp opposition to the traditional values of an Indian village.

But the issues raised by the third question—'What is man's relation to man'—are the most important in a discussion of Anand's work, because a crusade against caste with its faith in a hierarchical society has always been the motivating force of Anand's writing. Though he writes mostly of villages where life is strictly compartmental, where a man is labelled from birth, his victim-heroes invariably rebel against the social mechanism. Lalu as a gesture of defiance eats in a Muslim cookshop—which is almost the replica of an incident in *Coolie* where Munoo does the same thing for the same reason. Anand believes in the intrinsic merit of each individual quite apart from his caste and profession, and he has never tired of propagating universal brotherhood through his novels.

Thus Anand leaves us in no doubt of his position regarding man's relation to nature, time, and fellow human beings. He is a rational humanist, in the western tradition, believing in the power of science to improve material conditins, in progress and in the equality of all men, and his manifest intention is to propagate his beliefs through his novels. Judging how far he succeeds in the artistic realization of his intentions is for the literary critic a far more important task than the evaluation of the intentions themselves.

First of all Anand seems to simplify the conflict between tradition and modernity by creating clearly distinguishable sets of characters, withholding his sympathy from some, while deluging others with compassion. His characters fall neatly into three types: the sufferers, the oppressors and the good men. Usually the protagonist is the sufferer-in-chief. All money-lenders, priests, and landlords, i.e., people with a vested interest in resisting change or progress, come under the second category. The Sahukar, Mohant Nandgir and Hardit Singh in the trilogy are examples of this triple figure of evil which appears in every Anand novel under different names. The good men, an assortment of labour leaders, social workers, poets and idealistic doctors, are all advocates of the benefits of the machine and the need for progress and equality. Dr. Mahindra (*The Old Woman and the Cow*) emphasises the use of medicine and soap and the need for cleaning up the village; Iqbal Nath Sharshar (*Untouchable*) speaks of mechanizing the mode of the disposal of garbage which will ultimately eradicate caste; and Puran Singh Bhagat (*The Big Heart*) voices Anand's opinion when he says, "But don't let us forget that for all their sins the English at least had the Bible and Browning in their background . . . Our merchants are descended—let us be honest—from a caste-ridden society with an utter contempt for the lower orders ingrained in them as part of their dharma."

Anand's dice, therefore, are heavily loaded; there is a too obvious taking of sides, and the patent opposition between two neatly divided groups does not express truth which is often complicated and elusive.

Anand is free from what the Bengali critic and wrier Annanda Sankar Roy has called the East-Past complex and there is no nostalgia or sentimentality in his attitude towards Indian traditions. If the rejection of the superstitions and narrowness of traditional life involves the loss of the strength that a continuity of culture provides, it is for Anand a deliberate choice. He substitutes the international doctrine of socialism for the myth of the race, but this is preceded by an exposure to a number of viewpoints, great deal of soul-searching and a certain intellectual process, the record of which can be found in his *Apology for Heroism*. However, when he imposes his convictions directly upon his heroes, who are usually country-bred or unsophisticated people without the advantage of his wide background, the characterization fails because instead of becoming fully rounded individuals they become mouthpieces of the author's ideas. Anand's characters are lonely misfits—not lonely in the tradition of the modern European protagonist of fiction, whose loneliness is a form of intellectual alienation, but lonely because they do not arise out of the soil they inhabit, because Anand has stuffed them with his own beliefs. They lack the necessary background, are thereby rootless, and appear somewhat unreal.

Anand was at the height of his power in the 'thirties and early 'forties, when a sociological approach to literature was very much in vogue both in India as well as outside. [These] two decades were predominantly the period of public concern in literature. The Independence movement, the uplift of the downtrodden, the reform of social evils: these public preoccupations were followed, in the next decade, by a concern with one's own self that was basically a private search. Trends in literature do not confine themselves to specific dates and years, but the shift of interest from the public to the private sphere may be regarded as a characteristic of the 'fifties and the 'sixties. This private search often constituted a quest for a satisfactory attitude towards the West, and for a realistic image of the East that would at the same time be emotionally valid. This search has taken varied and complex forms. At its lowest, it has often descended into sentimental chauvinism and neurotic rejection, at its highest it has attempted a re-integration of personality, a revaluation of all values.

We shall now examine five examples of novels which basically deal with the same theme—a quest for the self—and in doing so necessarily touch upon the east-west conflict at different levels of meaning. The novels are *Remember the House* (1956), *A Time to be Happy* (1957), *Some Inner Fury* (1957), *The Dark Dancer* (1959), and *Sunlight on a Broken Column* (1961). This chronological sequence may be accidental, but one notices that these novels were published in close succession, all towards the end of the 'fifties. It is significant that another major novel to deal with the same theme, Raja Rao's *The Serpent and the Rope*, also appeared during this period.

[Santha Rama Rau's] *Remember the House* is a first novel and, like many Indo-Anglian first novels, is autobiographical in technique, if not in substance. The central conflict of the adolescent heroine is between two ideals of life. As in B. Rajan's *The Dark Dancer* the west here appears in person, and Alix Nicoll, the narrator's American friend who makes happiness her goal in life, represents one side of the conflict. The other side does not have a similar concrete personification but the heroine's mother is the closest to an embodiment of the truly Indian values. The narrator, Baba Goray, briefly infatuated with the American way of life, finds the ideals of 'enjoyment', 'success' and 'happiness' supremely desirable. But all the time she is aware of the basic incompatibility of these ideals with what she has always been taught. The difference between the two modes of life is rather obviously pointed out in an explanatory passage:—

She (Alix) held up the glass. "To happiness," She said laughing. I sipped my lemonade and laughed with her. In Jalnabad, I thought, no one made a point about happiness. We were given, and we accepted almost without thinking, certain precepts. The importance of the family, the one we were born to or the one we are married into. Our place in a certain structure, a pattern of life, or birth, of marriage, children, peace and death . . . Within our frame-work we would make our happiness . . . It was never suggested that we pursue happiness. We were not encouraged to waste our time.

Reiterating the same difference between two ideals of life there is this brief conversation between mother and daughter much later in the novel:—

"Now are you happy?" Baba asks.

"Is happiness what you want?" She asked me with infinite compassion. . . . "Oh my poor child".

It can be observed in passing that other Indo-Anglian novelists also have insisted that happiness is not an Indian goal. One remembers Nalini in Rajan's *Too Long in the West* who, when asked by Ernest, her American admirer, "Don't tell me you are happy in this mud-bath" answered, "It isn't a question of happiness."

In *Remember the House,* contrasted with the serenity of the heroine's mother, Alix has an effervescent vitality that is intoxicating. Baba's friendship with her however does not last long—but even after their parting Alix's effect does not wear off easily. Baba stumbles through another infatuation, before she reaches the bed-rock of sensible values. Santha Rama Rau intends to convey that Baba's sudden interest in the south Indian school teacher was merely a fancy based on the western conception of love, and did not have any basis in reality. At the end Baba's marriage with Hari, the steadfast, undemonstrative old friend, approved of by the family, is in fact the triumph of traditional values over a temporary infatuation.

A variation on the same theme, personal fulfilment as opposed to loyalty to the family, is found in Attia Hosain's *Sunlight on a Broken Column,* another first novel by a woman novelist. The conflict here does not resolve neatly along East-West lines, though the heroine's quest for her personal destiny itself is a result of the impact of the west on her. The west, if it appears explicitly at all does so in terms of ideas rather than of persons. The theme of the novel, until the last part where it badly disintegrates—is Laila's journey from the acceptance of traditional family values to questioning and rebellion. Her search for her own personal fulfilment, goes against the expectation of her family. When Laila takes the decision of marrying Ammer against the will of her family she has this unpleasant encounter with a favourite aunt:—

I wept the last time I was with her.

"Phuphi Jan, I have done nothing wrong."

She was cold and unyielding and drew away from me.

"You have been defiant and disobedient, You have put yourself above your duty to the family."

. . . . I know that understanding was impossible between us. She was part of a way of thinking that I had rejected.

Unlike the heroine of Santha Rama Rau, Laila chooses to defy tradition. In the conflict between society and the individual, the latter wins. But even in this novel the triumph is temporary. From the disintegrated reminiscence of the last part one gathers that Laila's marriage with Ameer was cut short by Ameer's death, and even during its brief duration the marriage was made uneasy by the disparity in their social and economic situations. At the end Laila comes back to the deserted family house, and in an orgy of sentimentalism, rediscovers her cousin Asad, who, apparently, has been waiting for her all his life. One can see that Attia Hosain's heroine also finally follows the same pattern as the heroine of Santha Rama Rau: rebellion, romantic quest, final submission to traditional values.

There is a very large streak of nostalgia in both these novels as well as in Kamala Markandaya's *Some Inner Fury.* Mira in Markandaya's novel recalls wistfully the laughter and the happiness of her father's home, the gulmohurs and the peace which later she chose to renounce in order to move in a circle she would create for herself. In *Remember the House,* as the very title indicates, the memory of a particular house in distant Jalnabad becomes a sentimental motif in the structure of the novel. The expansive inclusiveness and tolerant co-existence in her grandmother's large household where the narrator had spent her childhood remains a fixed focal point to which her thoughts return again and again as if to the roots of her being during the confusing search for identity. As in the case of Jalnabad in Santha Rama Rau, Hasanpur in Attia Hosain's *Sunlight* stands for a deep sense of belonging.

Jalnabad or Hasanpur thus give a local habitation and name to a vague feeling of nostalgia about a way of life that seems to be passing away. This feeling is compulsive and can be seen even when this way of life is deliberately rejected. For example, in *Sunlight on a Broken Column* as well as in *Some Inner Fury* the protagonists themselves consciously break away from the kind of life they are nostalgic for. They struggle against this way of life to seek their personal fulfilment in another sphere created by themselves. And in both cases, love for a man is the incentive for rebellion. R. K. Narayan has pointed out the absence of the eternal triangle in the Indian social context. But it seems to me that in the Indian context the triangle is very much present in another sense; only the third side of the triangle is provided not by a human being, but by a more powerful and less defined force—the joint family, tradition, orthodoxy. The joint family is a formidable force even when the love interest is absent and in Indo-Anglian fiction it has served a number of functions at the same time. It represents the voice of authority and tradition and serves as a microcosm of the hierarchical society which the individual has to rebel against in order to attain his personal identity. Just as society has various levels based on caste, the joint family has various levels of authority, different roles being allotted to individuals. The hero of B. Rajan's *The Dark Dancer,* speculates on the correctness of his self assertion: "It was blackmail to say . . . he should not protest simply because his protesting might hurt others. Iron out the man for the convenience of the Machine." Krishnan rebels for the time being, as do Laila in *Sunlight on a Broken Column* and Mira in *Some Inner Fury.* The joint family may be a static force to rebel against but at the same time the joint-family also stands for security, relaxed comfort and a kind of sharing of joys and sorrows, qualities which Hasanpur and Jalnabad embody. Finally at times it acts as a chorus—commenting on the actions of the individual, e.g., in the remarks of uncle Kruger in *The Dark Dancer* or of Aunt Abida in *Sunlight on a Broken Column.* Thus the institution of the joint family is very conveniently used by the Indo-Anglian writer, in order to get a close view of the struggle between self and society. Society which is vague and amorphous becomes a concrete experience in the joint family.

The conflict between the two cultures of East and West is nowhere so obviously spelled out as in Nayantara Sahgal's first novel *A Time to be Happy* and nowhere is the resolution so unambiguous and simple. Here the protagonist is Sanad Shivpal. He is the son of a rich man, a product of a public school, an executive in a mercantile firm, a good tennis player: in short, the stereotype of a particular social class. His problem is that of regaining his roots, of belonging: "it occurred to him that his parents had gone to a great deal of trouble and expense moulding him to be a figure that would never have any reality" and the dilemma is restated for further emphasis when Sanad mourns his fate: "I don't belong entirely to India. I can't. My education, my upbringing, and my sense of values have all combined to make me un-Indian. What do I have in common with most of my country-men?" His self-pity arising out of a sense of alienation and rootlessness is a very common theme in Indo-Anglian literature, even though it is not always so explicitly stated. We remember Laila in *Sunlight on a Broken Column* breaking out into a burst of self-pity at the sight of an ugly shape in *burqua* heaving into a curtained car: "She is closer to the people than us, sitting, standing, eating, thinking and speaking like them, while we with our Bach and Beethoven, our Shakespears and Eliot, put 'people' into inverted commas"; and Krishnan in *The Dark Dancer* trying to unite himself to things "that are real and rooted, that belong to India," even if he does not.

Alienation in all these cases necessitates sentimentalization of the objects one has been alienated from. In the case of Sanad Shivpal in *A Time to be Happy* it becomes an obsession to know the 'people' and the way he does it is the most unconvincing element in this novel of naive conflicts. In each of the three novels (*Remember the House, Sunlight on a Broken Column* and *A Time to be Happy*) the resolution comes through marriage. In *Remember the House* after some blundering misadventues Baba marries the right person and settles down to a life that adheres to the traditional code. In *Sunlight on a Broken Column* Laila achieves selfhood by marrying the man of her own choice even if it means defying convention and loyalty to

family, though the resolution is later weakened by the fact that after Ameer's death Laila rediscovers a cousin of hers, and probably marries him. This in effect means a return to the family she had forsaken. In *A Time to be Happy* Sanad attains his goal of coming close to the "people" by marrying the unsophisticated, non-westernized daughter of a college lecturer and by (incredible as it might seem) learning Hindi and spinning.

Kusum, Sanad's wife, conforms to that type of idealised Indian womanhood to which Premala of *Some Inner Fury* and Kamala of *The Dark Dancer* also belong. All of them derive their strength from service and sacrifice and they believe in non-violence as a creed and in right action rather than happiness. In *Some Inner Fury* although the central figures are an Indian girl and a young Englishman, they are merely themselves, and not intended to be representatives of two cultures. If any one is representative of Indian culture it is not the heroine, but Premala with her Eastern calm and acceptance. The impact of the West is also seen more clearly on the minor characters than on the protagonist herself, in Kit, for example, Mira's westernized brother in the civil service whose "feeling for the West was no cheap flirtation . . . it was understanding and love," or at the other extreme, Govind, to whom the Western way of life "was the product of a culture which was not his own—the culture of an aloof and alien race, twisted in the process of transplantation from its homeland and so divorced from the people of the country as to be no longer real". Between the two extremes of love and hatred for the West stands Roshan who, the author tells us, understands the West "but she belonged to the East also." This to the author seems to be the golden mean. Roshan's case is offered as the solution of a dilemma that is essentially complex.

To talk of West and East with capital W and E, as Kamala Markandaya does, is always a dangerous abstraction, especially in fictions where abstract notions must never obscure the particular and concrete realization of individual human experience. Kit, because he is entirely a product of the west becomes more of a stereotyped *burra sahib* than a living character, and his actions and responses are predictable. Premala, Kit's wife, who feels ill at ease in westernized environments is idealized to the extent of being unreal. West, here as in Nayantara Sahgel's novel has a very limited connotation. In each case it means the external forms and empty rituals of westernized living in India—a variation of Forster's Chandrapore Club—more trivial, because it is an ineffectual imitation. This, of course, is the most superficial definition of West possible, and if nothing else, this limited definition seriously hampers the quality of these novels.

Some Inner Fury also attempts to work out another familiar dilemma, familiar at least in fiction, thanks to E. M. Forster, between personal relationship and racial prejudice. In the other three novels discussed above, the resolution came through marriage and there was an element of choice for each protagonist. But in this novel the climax is brought about by riot and violence in which Mira is separated from Richard. Because Mira is not a free agent, and has no power of self-determination, this novel cannot be regarded as the quest for self-discovery as the other three can. Mira is merely the victim of forces beyond her control, the forces of history as it were. As she leaves Richard in the midst of the angry mob, she thinks:

> Go: leave the man I loved, to go with these people. What did they mean to me, what could they mean, more than the man I loved? They were my people those others were his. Did it mean something then—all this 'your people' and 'my people'? . . . I know I would go, even as I know Richard might stay. For us there was no other way, the forces that pulled us apart were too strong.

Though rather melodramatic, these lines carry a faint echo of the famous last line of a *A Passage to India*: "The earth did not want it . . . the temples, the tank, the jail, the palace . . . they didn't want it, they said in their hundred voices, 'no, not yet', and the sky said, 'no, not there' ",—reminding us that *Some Inner Fury* also ends on the note that the East and the West cannot meet because the forces that pull them apart are too strong.

The name of Forster tends to stray into any discussion of East-West relationship in fiction, but comparison or contrast with him is not very relevant in the present context because what he attempted in his masterpiece was something very different from what most Indo-Anglian writers are trying to do. Personal relationship—communication between, and understanding of, men who happen to belong to two races—is part of Forster's theme in *A Passage to India* while the Indo-Anglian novelist more often than not is trying to reconcile within himself two conflicting systems of value. In this tension between two views of life any easy solution is bound to be an inadequate one as the four novels discussed above demonstrate.

B. Rajan's *The Dark Dancer* comes closer to the crux of the problem than any of the novels analysed so far. But even here one feels dissatisfied with the treatment of the theme and the denouement. Krishnan's alienation is apparent from the very beginning. After two years in Cambridge "he was coming back to an indifferent sky, an anonymous teeming of houses". His indifferent attitude towards his family which was ready to arrange his life for him, his cynical view of the society around him, and his lack of involvement in his surroundings, all these mark him as an outsider right away. The outsider as protagonist is a recurrent figure in much of twentieth century fiction in Europe and in America. We have celebrated examples of the artist as an alien (*Portrait of the Artist as a Young Man*), the Negro or the Jew as an outsider (as in Ralph Ellison's *Invisible Man* or Saul Bellow's *Herzog*), or the sensitive adolescent as an outsider (as in J. D. Salinger's *Catcher in the Rye*). In a similar way, the Indian who has spent a considerable time abroad may become an alien in Indian society. One advantage of this device is that if the protagonist does not belong to the society he writes about, he can be more objective in his evaluation of it. But Krishnan is not an outsider in this sense, because his nonconformity does not influence his actions. In spite of his constant hair-splitting and analysis of the unreasonable demands of society, he submits to every family decision. Secondly, he wants very much to belong, which is indicat-

ed by at least two deliberate actions: his taking part in the non-violent demonstration by the seaside and his agreeing to an arranged marriage. His failure in both merely shows that estrangement cannot be overcome merely by accepting the symbols of belonging. The civil disobedience march is ruined by Krishnan's active show of violence, and his marriage by his wavering of will between Cynthia, on the one hand, who for him represented individuality, selfhood, who urged him to 'be and not belong', and his wife on the other, who represents the strength of acceptance and belonging. About his wife Krishnan thinks: "Kamala's Indian, intensely so, not simply in what she knows and does but deep down, in ways that I can only sense, and don't even want to understand." Krishnan is temporarily attracted towards Cynthia because her insistence on the importance of the self counterbalanced Krishnan's own streak of resignation. Like Baba's infatuation with the Nicolls in Santh Rama Rau's novel, Krishnan's infatuation with Cynthia is based on the fact that she has qualities that are lacking in Krishnan's own personality. Krishnan himself analyses the differences between them thus: "She [Cynthia] came from a tradition which included non-conformity and dissent among its attributes . . . His on the contrary was a back ground completely conformist, where the map of one's life was drawn even before one's first cry." From accepting the family's decisions he passes on to accepting Cynthia's decisions, which is easy, because she has a stronger will, until Krishnan suddenly realises the mistake of his choice. The reason they finally break their relationship is trivial and unconvincing. During his visit to a temple Krishnan suddenly discovers that while the priest would bless him, he would not bless Cynthia. This leads to a sudden realization of the basic difference between him and Cynthia. Cynthia fails in the tug-of-war between loyalties and Krishnan goes back to his wife, who to drown her own unhappiness is serving the people of the riot-ravaged area of Shantipur. He thus finds the right path, learns abandonment of the self from Kamala, and even when she dies trying to save a Muslim woman Krishnan finds serenity and meaning in life.

The resolution of Krishnan's East-West dilemma ultimately hinges on his choice between Cynthia and Kamala, and the two women are more representatives than convincing individuals. Cynthia with her stubborn individualism, her sense of fairness, her nonconformity, is an embodiment of British liberal humanism while Kamala, like the earth, with her source of mysterious strength, her belief in non-violence and right action rather than happiness, her patience and self-sacrifice is an idealised portrait of Indian womanhood. But even more than the static nature of the characters, the real weakness of the novel lies in the fact that Krishnan's final resolution does not arise out of the conflicts and tensions that he goes through. Rather it comes as a preconceived solution, that has nothing to do with the series of crises described in the book. One knows from the way Kamala is presented that she is India, and she is bound to win ultimately and she does, even though she has to die for it.

In Raja Rao's *The Serpent and The Rope* (1960), the East-West theme assumes a depth and validity not achieved before in Indo-Anglian fiction. Here East, however, is no general term: it is India, Brahminical India, which represents the quintessence of of advaita philosophy. India at all other levels is excluded. The moral puritanism of India is rejected as something essentially weak:

> I hated this moral India . . . Lakshmi was not India. Lakshmi was the India that accepted invaders, come Muslim, come British, with sighs and salutations. Lakshmi would not read the Mahabharata the whole night, cut her finger, and annointing her Lord with her young blood burn herself alive.

Industrial, metropolitan India is equally rejected as irrelevant: "Bombay . . . simply had no meaning to a Brahmin like me . . . Bombay had no right to exist." The modern, cosmopolitan India of the northern cities is rejected as alien to the traditional pattern of Indian life:

> I could not understand the northerners going from strict purdah to this extreme modernism with unholy haste. We in the south were more sober, and very distant. We lived by tradition . . .

But the West is considered in more general terms. The Provençal taxi-driver, the Parisian notary, the Russian scholar, the Spanish refugee, the British students, Ramaswamy's French wife, however different from each other as characters, all partake of a single value system which may be regarded as "western" in its insistence on the particular and the concrete, on the personal and the immediate—in other words, in its recognition of the object as something outside oneself.

The complex and amorphous theme of the novel has been summed up in one concise sentence by a reviewer: "In the marriage of Rama and Madeleine, two contrary worldviews, two contrary epistemologies, come together, and the novel is a study of that encounter." In spite of their sharply differentiated attitude towards life, Ramaswamy and Madeleine have one striking similarity as characters: they are both intensely self-conscious about the epistemologies they represent. Hardly ever do they regard themselves or each other simply as individual human beings. Instead, they are constantly interpreting their own and each other's actions in terms of their national and cultural differences, invariably ending up with generalizations about "Indian" and "Western" traits of character. Thus when Madeleine is indignant about some social or political injustice and Ramaswamy fails to be aroused, he attributes it not to their differences in temperament, but to his "thin Brahmin blood" and her "warm southern blood". When Ramaswamy feels an affection for Catherine and talks to her like an elder brother, he hastens to explain, "I acted no doubt from my Indian instinct . . . Left to himself the Indian would go on tying *rakhi* to every woman he met, feel her elder brother, protect her love . . . " Even minor events and small actions like buying a pepper-grinder or carrying a suitcase are invested with Madeleine's "Frenchness" ("I must use it some day—you know, I am French and nothing should be useless") or Ramaswamy's Indianness ("How incompetent we two Indians felt before things") Ramaswamy's inability to deal with the practical side of life, his haphazardness ("like the towels in the bathroom that lay everywhere"), is attributed not to any personal shortcoming but to his Indianness. This representative burden falls most heavily upon their personal relationship. When Madeleine is impatient with Ramaswamy's heavy seriousness and his refusal to grapple with tangible reality, she does not regard these as characteristics of an individual human being; these are related immediately to the larger cultural, philosophic and religious background of the country of his origin. Madeleine writes to him "I wondered whether I could really love you—whether anyone could love a thing so abstract as you . . . I wonder if Indians can love." And when Madeleine feels no warmth for Ramaswamy's family in Hyderabad, a group of people whom she has never met, she thinks it is because of her reading of Gide and Sartre that she cannot conceive of a large and loose unit as a family.

But in spite of their representative function, both Ramaswamy and Madeleine are completely convincing and recognisable as individuals. Their self-consciousness about culture and history and heritage is the way they have been conceived of as characters and it sets them apart from other characters in the novel. Whether Ramaswamy represents India or he symbolises decadence may lead us to fruitless discussion. Those who share Ramaswamy's Brahmanical background, his traditional childhood of hymns and rituals, and his advaitic grounding, will easily identify him with India. Those who do not have this background will inevitably feel uncomfortable at his excessive emotionalism with regard to certain objects and gestures (for example: the cows of Benares, the touching of the feet with kumkum). This diametric opposition in reactions has been present in all evaluations of *The Serpent and the Rope*.

But if Ramaswamy is regarded as a fictional character and not the embodiment of Raja Rao's philosophy of life, then in his predicament we see just another variation of the familiar east-west motif—only, this variation touches many depths and spreads out to cover many aspects. As the title suggests, the novel involves two ways of apprehending reality: the recognition of the object as object, and the recognition that the object exists because the perceiver perceives it. The novel merely presents the confrontation of these two modes, but does not come to a definite preference of one over the other. Madeleine slowly excludes Ramaswamy from her life, and Ramaswamy brings his burden of infinite pathos back to India. And there is just a hint towards the end that in Travancore he might find a new mode of apprehending reality and a new meaning in life. With admirable restraint, Raja Rao has steered clear of the facile solution of concocting an easy assimilation of the two cultures. If there is an enduring solution, it is a private solution, and may not yield its secret to any public discussion.

Meenakshi Mukherjee, "East-West Encounter," in her The Twice Born Fiction: Themes and Techniques of the Indian Novel in English, *second edition, Heinemann Educational Books, New Delhi, 1971, pp. 65-98.*

INDO-ENGLISH POETRY

John B. Alphonso-Karkala

[*Alphonso-Karkala is an Indian-born Canadian educator, novelist, and critic. In the following excerpt, he provides an overview of nineteenth-century Indian poets writing in English and discusses their major works.*]

In the nineteenth century there appeared no significant Indo-English poet, though a number of Indian writers published their exercises in English verse. The reason is not difficult to find. The Indians were, no doubt, dazzled by the works of such British poets as Shakespeare, Milton, Dryden, Pope, Wordsworth, Byron, Scott, and Tennyson, whom they eagerly read, studied, and admired; but they were unable to express their own innermost thoughts and feelings freely in a foreign language. Thwarted in their ambition, these English-educated young men remained outsiders, at home neither with the vernacular Indian poets nor with their foreign masters. Yet the desire to express possessed them. Hero-worshipping the British poets, and piously imitating their form and meter, even at times their themes and moods, the Indo-English poets of the nineteenth century recollected their emotions almost in futility. Nevertheless their verses, however, lacking in originality, are indicative of the sincerity of their attempt. An examination of these early compositions, therefore, is helpful not so much in discovering any great literary merit in them, but in appreciating the magnitude of the difficulties which the Indians faced in writing English verse.

During the [English East India] Company's administration in the first half of the century, some writers attempted English verse, moved by the literary renaissance that occurred in Bengal with the introduction of English education. The boyish enthusiasm of Henry Derozio, the much-laboured homework in prosody of Kashi Prosad Ghose, and the ardent search for originality of Michael Madhusudan Dutt, in the absence of creative boldness, resulted only in volumes of imitative verse. Yet, after the administrative change-over from the Company to the British government, and in spite of the extension of English education throughout India in the second half of the century, there appeared no literary movements in the rest of India similar to the one that took place in Bengal. Besides, in the absence of the revolutionary temper of Bengali reformers and the dedication to art and letters of such families as the tradition-bound Tagore family or the newly converted Dutt family, the 'educated' Indians outside Bengal did not involve themselves seriously in the reform movement, nor did they use English verse to express their attitudes, thoughts, and feelings. Even the Christian influence, filtering through missionary schools and conversion to Christianity, while moving many Bengalis and the whole of the Dutt family to imitate the English poets, did not very much disturb the Gujaratis, the Maharastrians, or the Dravidians. On the whole, therefore, outside of the Dutt family, Indo-English poetry did not flourish in the second half of the century, or what little was published was of no significance.

Foremost among Indian writers of English verse is Henry Derozio, poet, patriot, and educator, who started his career with an exuberant faith in man and nature but was pursued by tragedy from the very beginning. However, before his death at the age of twenty-three [From cholera], he wrote poems, taught in a college, edited journals, and shook the intellectual world of Calcutta.

Henry's fame as a poet rests upon his two volumes of verse, which were published before he joined the Hindu College. Thereafter, although he wrote a critique of Kant, translated some of the works of de Maupertuis, and edited four journals, he did not write verse. He is not a great poet, nor even a good one; but one may ask how many of the works of the great poets were published before they were nineteen. If Henry's verses are examined here, it is only to see out of what imitative origins Indo-English poetry emerged and developed during the nineteenth century.

Henry attempted to write English verse in school. In his 'prologue' to the play which his school was producing, he imitated the rhymed couplet of the late eighteenth-century English poets. Presenting the members of the dramatic company, he compares the inexperienced actors to 'new fledged birds . . . unus'd to soar.' Being familiar with Shakespearean theatrical tradition, he is conscious that their 'schoolboy effort' will not stand comparison with 'mighty Kemble' and 'Siddons.' What one sees in these verses is not so much the poetry but the earnest attempt of a schoolboy of fourteen to be poetically articulate:

> As new fledged birds, while yet unus'd to soar,
> Tremble the airy regions to explore,
> Mistrust their power, yet doubting dare to fly
> And brave the dazzling brilliance of the sky—
> So, the poor train who now are to appear,
> Shrink ere they try—perplex'd 'tween hope and
>   fear—
> And th' your smiles bespeak indulgence certain
> Still, still they dread the raising of the curtain.
> No mighty Kemble here stalks o'er the stage,
> No Siddons all your feelings to engage,
> But a small band of young, aspiring boys
> In faintest miniature the hour employs.
> Shall then, as first we spread our ardent sails,
> Like the thin Nautilus to catch the gales!
> By stormy frowns our feeble bark be toss'd
> And having fondly dared be poorly lost?
> No—we will trust, tho' rude be our display,
> You will remember it is the first essay
> Of schoolboy effort in the rolls of time,
> Yet ever witnessed in this orient clime—
> We ask but this—and surely 'twill be granted—
> Praise, if 'tis due—indulgence when 'tis wanted.

It is clear from the prologue that though his verses are weak imitations, his images are brilliant and his own. Perhaps, in his last line Henry instinctively wrote a prologue to the whole of Indo-English poetry of the nineteenth century, for most of the authors who wrote verse were echoing either consciously or unconsciously, the same sentiment, seeking recognition for their 'first essay of schoolboy effort' or indulgence, when they failed.

In his *Poems* (1827), published in spite of John Grant's advice to the contrary, Henry progressed from his amateur exercises to better verse with control over meter, imagery, and stanza form, though essentially remaining an imitator. More than all of his poetic embellishments, what is striking in his verse is his passionate nationalism. With a profound and reverent admiration for the ancient, rich lore of India, and in spite of his Eurasian origin, Henry remained 'wholly Indian in spirit and aspired to be India's national bard.' His deep and sincere desire to belong to India's great poetic tradition becomes evident when he humbly invokes: 'Harp of my country, let me strike again!'

The Harp of India

Why hang'st thou lonely on yon withered
   bough?
Unstrung forever, must thou there remain?
Thy music once was sweet—who hears it now?
Why doth the breeze sigh over thee in vain?
Silence hath bound thee with her fatal chain:
Neglected, mute, and desolate art thou,
Like ruined monument on desert plain:
O! many a hand more worthy far than mine
Once thy harmonious chords to sweetness gave,
And many a wreath for them did Fame entwine
Of flowers still blooming on the minstrel's grave;
Those hands are cold—but if thy notes divine
May be by mortal wakened once again,
Harp of my country, let me strike again!

The imagery of an unstrung harp hanging from a withered tree in a deserted place and a young wayfarer stretching out his hand towards it, vividly portrays the Indian decadence at the beginning of the century. Unlike his Eurasian community, which clung more to Europe and the ruling class than to India and her masses, Henry boldly asserts his Indianness in his last dramatic line.

In another poem, lamenting the fate of the 'fallen country,' the young poet asks, 'Where is that glory?' Feeling the need of cultural roots for a renaissance in India, he proposed to 'dive into the depths of time' in order to bring forth some 'small fragments of those wrecks sublime.' His sonnet apostrophising India, clearly brings out his deep and genuine concern for the future of his Native Land:

To India—My Native Land

My country! in thy days of glory past
A Beauteous halo circled round thy brow,
And worshipped as a deity thou wast.
Where is that glory, where that reverence now?
The eagle pinion is chained down at last,
And grovelling in the lowly dust art thou:
Thy minstrel hath no wreath to weave for thee
Save the sad story of thy misery!
Well—let me dive into the depths of time
And bring from out the ages that have rolled
A few small fragments of those wrecks sublime,
Which human eye may never more behold;
And let the guerdon of my labour be,
My fallen country, one kind word for thee!

It is not only his country that he loved with a romantic passion, but also his profession of teaching and his young pupils. He taught his students as no ordinary teacher would. He seems to have watched closely the miracle of blossoming minds, 'expanding like the petals of young flowers.' For in another eloquent sonnet he gave poetic expression to his vision of the new generation that was growing out of the Hindu College:

Sonnet to the pupils of the Hindu College

Expanding like the petals of young flowers
I watch the gentle opening of your minds,
And the sweet loosening of the spell that binds
Your intellectual energies and powers,
That stretch (like young birds in soft summer
   hours)
Their wings to try their strength. O! how the
   winds
Of circumstance, and freshening April showers
Of early knowledge, and unnumbered kinds
Of new perceptions, shed their influence,
And how you worship Truth's omnipotence!
What joyance rains upon me, when I see
Fame in the mirror of futurity,
Weaving the chaplets you are yet to gain—
And then I feel I have not lived in vain.

His imagery of blooming flowers or of young birds attempting to soar, fuses with the young minds of his pupils. Unloosening themselves from superstition and ignorance, they were attempting to see a new India in the broad light of learning. Perhaps, in the 'mirror of futurity' Henry saw a vision of India yet to come that made him feel he had not lived in vain. By his enlightened reformative zeal, by his exalted patriotism, by his abundant sense of humility (the true index of a mind potentially great), Henry implanted European ideas and questioning attitudes among India's youth to help them to recover their cultural glory. He himself led the way in giving in his poems the first articulate expression to the nationalist sentiment of renascent India.

In his longer work, *The Fakir of Jungheera, a Metrical Tale* (1828), Henry attempts to tell a long tale, combining adventure and romance and exposing the social evil of sati. The theme and setting of this long poem render him worthy of regard 'as a minor but genuine member of the Romantic Movement.'

The Fakir of Jungheera is the story of Nuleeni, a young Brahmin widow. Nuleeni is about to be burned on the funeral pyre of her husband; but within her is a fierce conflict between her misplaced sense of religious 'duty' and her own desire to live. Suddenly she is carried away by a robber-chief (a kind of Robin Hood) to be his bride. In the mountain retreat,

Her robber-lover and young Nuleeni share
Each bliss as perfect as the heart may bear.

Though Nuleeni and her lover 'quite forget mortality,' their happiness does not last long. With a band of men, Nuleeni's father and her relatives attempt to rescue her. In the battle Nuleeni's second husband, who had snatched her from death, himself dies, thus leaving her widowed a second time. Unable to bear the sorrow or to face her relatives, Nuleeni finally finds peace in death, as she breathes her last on the battle field, lamenting over her husband's body.

In this poem Henry experiments with a variety of metrical forms in his effort to present the various incidents of the story in their appropriate moods. After opening the first canto in iambic four-foot simple narrative, he switches to brisk dactylic lines to present a chorus of women who are coaxing Nuleeni to ascend joyfully her husband's funeral pyre:

> Happy! thrice happy! thus early to leave
> Earth and its sorrows, for heaven and its bliss!
> Who that hath known it at parting would grieve
> Quitting a world so disastrous as this!

When the ceremony of sati is about to begin, Henry uses trochees to present the chanting priests and the chorus of Brahmins, whose singing would effectively drown a cry or even a sigh from Nuleeni's soul in agony:

> Scatter, scatter, flowrets round,
> Let the tinkling cymbal sound,
> Strew the scented orient spice
> Prelude to the sacrifice.

Thereafter he takes up again the slow moving narrative verse for describing the scene or to add his own comments on the scene until he comes to the battle scene in the second canto, when he uses the galloping anapestic measure to keep up with the quick moving action:

> Each robber has taken his sabre and shield,
> And bounds like a blood-hound new-slipt to the
>   field.
> Heard ye the horrible roar of the gun?
> Destruction is raging, the battle's begun.
>
> . . . . .
>
> The youthful, the gallant are falling around
> Like corn just reaped on the damp, cold ground,
> And the blood flows fast of the fallen and falling,
> As if it came forth at the spear-point calling.

In the first quarter of the nineteenth century when Britain was taken up by the romantic vogue, it was, perhaps, inevitable that the Indo-English poets would be caught by that contagious enthusiasm. Though Henry uses all the essential ingredients of a romantic tale in the manner of Byron or Moore, at times even accepting pre-Wordsworthian poetic diction, what is more important in his poem is his theme—his attempt to expose the social evils of a decadent society with greater subtlety than Raja Rammohun Roy's outright denunciation. The inhumanity of sati, the false morality of the women, and the hypocritical chanting of the Brahmins he depicts with such an understanding, 'real yet manly pathos, imaginative thought and musical and appropriate diction', that one wonders whether a Hindu would have written in the way he did. At a time when Eurasians were not accepted either by the Europeans or by the Indians, Henry, a child of two cultures, identified himself with his native land and wrote purely on Indian themes with a reformer's zeal. A century later, however, Edward Oaten thought kindly of him as the 'most famous of those of our Indian fellowmen who are neither exclusively European nor Indian,' but, sharing the blood of both, 'put all the pathos and passions of his sensitive nature into his metrical tale, *The Fakir of Jungheera*.' Henry has to be admired for what he might have been had he lived longer, for the promise of his greatness is much greater than the quality of his actual output.

The first Indian to write English verse was Kashi Prosad Ghose (1809-1873). Born in rural Bengal, Kashi Prosad first went to school at the age of fourteen, but he studied the English language so diligently that he mastered it in a few years. While at the Hindu College, he surprised his teachers by writing a lengthy review in English of the first four chapters of Mill's *History of British India*. After leaving college in 1829, Kashi Prosad wrote poems in English, some of which were published in local periodicals like the *Literary Review* and the *Calcutta Monthly Magazine*. Besides writing prose and poetry both in English and Bengali, he also edited an English weekly, *The Hindu Intelligence*, from 1845 to 1857.

Kashi Prosad's collected poems were published under the title *The Shair, or Minstrel and Other Poems* (1830) in Calcutta. These immature verses, lacking originality and sincerity, only indicate to what extent he was influenced by the minor love poets of the late Elizabethan age:

> I would I were the zephyr sweet,
> To kiss thy face and round it play;
> And when thou sigh'st for love, to greet
> Those sighs, and steal their sweetness away.
>
> I would I were the whiteness pure,
> That clings unto thy bosom's swell;
> That others I'd to madness lure,
> While I myself there safely dwell.

Another young enthusiastic imitator of English verse was Richardson's pupil, Rajanarian Dutt (1824-1889), who dedicated his work *Osmyn: An Arabian Tale* (1841) to his teacher. Rajanarian was faced with double difficulties: he was attempting to tell an Arabian tale in English verse by diligently imitating English heroic couplets, a form which had been exhausted in England by that time.

After the early experiments in Indo-English poetry by Henry Derozio, Kashi Prosad Ghose, and Rajanarian Dutt, the imitative tradition was carried a step further by Madhusudan Dutt, whose fame primarily rests on his Bengali epic poem, *Meghanad Badha*. Though Madhusudan is considered the first great figure in the Bengali renaissance, he holds but a secondary rank among Indo-English poets. His English verses seem the accidental expressions of a genius driven to exile by his conversion to Christianity. When he started to write in his native Bengali, the English Muse went out the window.

Michael Madhusudan Dutt (1824-1873), son of a lawyer, Raj Narayan Dutt, was born in Jessore district of Bengal. After his early education in his home town, he entered the Hindu College in Calcutta at the age of thirteen, where he distinguished himself by his command of English and by winning several scholarships, prizes, and medals. Being more gifted than Kashi Prosad or Rajanarian, Madhusudan did not struggle through books of prosody, but playfully wrote satires on his companions and epistles to his friends. Some of his poems he sent to the *Blackwood's Magazine*, dedicating them to the prophet of the English romantic movement, William Wordsworth. However, his greatest admiration was for Byron.

Madhusudan's English verses include two long poems, *The Captive Ladie* and *Visions of the Past*, some sonnets and a few lyrics, all of which he wrote before he left for England. *The Captive Ladie*, Madhusudan's best known English poem, was written while he was working as a journalist and was first published in the columns of the *Madras Circulator and General Chronicle.* When it was later issued as a book, it was accompanied by the *Visions of the Past* (1849).

The Captive Ladie deals with one of the most popular legends of Indian history, that of Prithviraj, the king of Delhi, who ruled in the eleventh century, just before the beginning of a series of Afghan raids into India. The subject of the poem is the jealousy and rivalry for supremacy in northern India between Prithviraj and the king of Kanouj. When the latter celebrated the time-honored 'feast of victory', almost all the contemporary princes, with the exception of Prithviraj, accepting Kanouj's overlordship, attended the feast. Highly incensed at the refusal of Prithviraj, the king of Kanouj ordered an image to be made to represent the absent chief. On the last day of the feast, Prithviraj and his followers, entering the palace in disguise, carried away not only the image but also the Princess Royal, whose hand he had solicited in vain. The fair princess was, however, retaken and confined in a solitary castle from which her lover effected her escape and married her. The King of Kanouj never forgave this insult. When Mohammed of Ghizni from Afghanistan invaded Prithviraj's kingdom of Delhi, Kanouj sternly refused to aid his son-in-law in expelling the foe. Unsupported, Prithviraj could not stop the Afghan invader; his kingdom was sacked. But before the Moslems could enter the city next morning, Prithviraj and his captive princess killed themselves by mounting a funeral pyre.

Madhusudan narrated the medieval legend in octosyllabic meter, a form which Walter Scott and Lord Byron had made popular in England. He followed his English masters closely in style and mood:

> There's light upon the heaving stream,
> And music sweet as heard in dream,
> And many a star upon its breast
> Is calmly pillo'd unto rest,
> While there, as on a silver throne,
> All melancholy, veil'd, alone,
> Beneath the pale moon's colder ray,
> The Bride of him—the Lord of Day
> In silence droops, as in lone bower
> The love-lorn maid at twilight hour!

Abandoning Kashi Prosad's models, Madhusudan wrote verses free from moralizing or conventional description of nature. At times he even tried to be dramatic in his descriptions. For instance, in the second canto, opening with the Moslem siege of Delhi, Madhusudan describes the marauding hosts led by Mohammed of Ghizni seeking 'dark vengeance.'

> A thousand lamps all gaily shine
> Along the wild extended line;
> And loud the laugh and proud the boast
> Swells from that fierce, un-number'd host;
> And wild the prayer ascends on high,
> Dark Vengeance! thine impatient cry—
> 'Oh! for a glimpse of Day's fair brow.
> To crush yon city tow'ring now,
> To make each *cafir*-bosom feel,
> Th' unerring blade of Moslem steel!
> By Allah! how I long to be,

> Where myriads wreaths in agony,
> And make each wretch with rolling eyes
> Call on false gods,—then curse and die.
> Meet pilgrim for the dire domain,
> Where *Eblis* holds his sunless reign!'

Against the Muslim savagery and wanton destruction, Madhusudan depicts a touching domestic scene. Prithviraj knows that his besieged city is doomed to fall, but he refuses to sue for peace or survive the disgrace. When he implores his royal bride, the Captive Ladie, to fly away, she makes a spirited reply in which the ancient 'spirit of Hinduism flames up and illumines' even in non-Indian metrical form:

> Oh! never,—never will this heart
> Be sever'd, Love! to beat apart!
> I fear not Death, tho' fierce he be,
> When thus I cling, mine-own to thee!
> For in the forest's green retreat,
> Where leafy branches twine and meet,
> Tho' wildly round dread *Agni* roars,
> Like angry surge by rock-girt shores,
> The soft gazelle of liquid eye
> Leave not her mate alone to die!

Madhusudan showed considerable freedom in using English meter. He was able to describe a scene vividly, or express a deeply felt emotion in tense diction. He embellished his English verse, at times by literally translating Sanskrit descriptive phrases, such as 'the bride of him—the lord of Day [sun]' to suggest a water lily; at other times, by making allusions to persons, or places, or incidents in the *Ramayana,* or the *Mahabharata,* or the *Puranas*—'young Krishna with his maidens fair,' referring to gopis, the milk-maids; or 'Jamuna, the holy stream.' What is significant in Madhusudan's work, therefore, is his bold attempt to use Indian material and to synthesise Sanskrit diction and English language, a promising development for Indo-English poetry. This process was further intensified in the second half of the nineteenth century by the illustrious Dutt family.

Madhusudan's second composition, *Visions of the Past* (1849), is a fragment containing thirteen pieces in blank verse. They were published in book form along with *The Captive Ladie.* These 'visions' deal with Christian themes: primeval innocence, the temptation of man, his fall, and his redemption. Madhusudan, considerably influenced by Milton's epic grandeur, attempted to capture his poetic method and mood. Though his English verse did not rise above mediocrity, he succeeded in writing his well known epic when he turned to his mother tongue, Bengali. Nevertheless, traces of Milton's influence can be seen in his *Visions.* For example, in portraying the 'gloomy majesty' of Satan, Madhusudan depicts 'a form of awe' in half a dozen broken lines, supported by Miltonic similies:

> But there was one amidst that sunny throng—
> And there he came as some dark visag'd cloud
> Careering on in gloomy majesty—
> Which dims the tranquil smile of every star
> And wings its lightless path along the sky;
> A form of awe he was—and yet he seem'd
> A sepulchre of beauty—faded—gone—

Mould'ring—where memory, fond mourner,
    keeps
Her lonesome vigils sad—to chronicle
The past—and tells its tale to coming years!
Or—like a giant tree in mighty war
With storm, on whirl-wind car and fierce array,
Blasted—and crush'd—of all its pride bereft—
Or like a barque which oft had walk'd the deep,
In queen-like Majesty—had proudly brave,
But by the fiery hand of some dread fiend,
Nurs'd in the starless caves of Ocean, shorn
Of all its beauty on the boundless surge—
A phantom of departed splendour—alone!

Although Henry Derozio and Kashi Prosad Ghose were the pioneers in writing English verse, it was Michael Madhusudan Dutt whom the succeeding generations of Indo-English poets in Bengal followed and admired. Outside Bengal, there appeared no Indo-English poet until the last quarter of the nineteenth century, when some promising verse were published but the promise was never fulfilled. Behramji Malabari's *The Indian Muse in English Garb* was published in Bombay in 1876; but thereafter he deserted his muse in favour of journalism. Vesuval Nowrosji, after publishing in Bombay his *Courting the Muse* (1879), ceased to write English verse. Nothing more was heard of Indo-English poetry in west and south India until the last decade, when two more minor volumes were published: A. M. Kunte's *Rishi* (1890) and T. Ramakrishna Pillai's *Tales of Ind* (1895). With the exception of Behramji Malabari, Indians outside of Bengal did not write Indo-English poetry of any significance. On the other hand, in Bengal, even though the majority of the poets were within the Dutt Family, there were a few others who published verse: P. C. Mitra, *The Spiritual Stray Leaves* (1879); Jotindra Mohan Tagore, *Flight of Fancy* (1881); Nabokissen Ghose (Pseudonym: Rama Sharma), *The Last Day* (1886); Manmohan Ghose, Poems in *Primavera* (1890), and *Love Songs and Elegies* (1898). Among these, only Manmohan Ghose achieved recognition as a poet.

Behramji [Merwanji Malabari (1853-1912)] wrote prose and verse in both Gujarati and English, but his only contribution to Indo-English poetry is *The Indian Muse in English Garb,* containing thirty-two short poems, published when he was only twenty-two years old. His verse differs from that of other Indo-English poets in his choice of themes. While other Indo-English poets were generally writing English verse on legendary, historical, or national themes, Behramji wrote verses welcoming or addressing the British royalty, or expressing his concern for social reform, or recalling his own early childhood days. In a number of occasional poems, dedicated to the members of the British royal family, Behramji seems more British than the British themselves in exalting royalty. Perhaps, he wrote them with an eye on securing royal patronage or impressing local Englishmen. For example, in 'An Humble Request', he asked Queen Victoria, 'Heaven directed Sovereign', accustomed to a 'graceful Tennysonian muse,' whether she would care to peruse his verses; when the Prince of Wales visited India, Behramji wrote a poem glorifying 'the lord elect, found fit in Heaven's sight'; when the Prince Consort died, Behramji assured 'the bleeding heart' of the Queen of 'her nations' proud esteem!' Young

Behramji was, perhaps, aspiring to become a national poet of British India!

Nevertheless, Behramji wrote a number of other poems concerning social problems, especially the misery of young women suffering under the unjust customs and practices against which he was to carry on an unceasing campaign later on in his life. In all these poems, his main theme remained the child-widow, 'made orphan by a husband's hand, and widow by a sire's!' As verse they are but poetical exercises, though the novelty of a Parsi youth writing English verse surprised the Bombay public.

However, in spite of imperfections due to the immaturity of the author, the poem 'A Sketch', recalling Behramji's early life, is, perhaps, the best in the whole collection. In this poem, closely imitating the eighteenth-century satirists in style, Behramji gives an autobiographical account of himself up to his twenty-first year. His early education in Surat was a kind of apprenticeship to a bohemian way of life from which he learnt one thing: to observe human nature. Out of this experience he drew vivid pictures of his school days and striking portraits of his eccentric teachers, making generous allowances for their weaknesses and shortcomings. His first encounter with a teacher was when he was six years old. It was the common practice among the Parsis of that time to entrust their children to Mobeds, who, while working at their looms, gave children oral lessons in the sacred writings of Zoroaster. Accordingly, Behramji was sent to a venerable centenarian, Minochehru Daru, a Parsi 'priest, patriarch and a man of skill,' from whom Behramji learned to pray and to weave:

> High time 'twas thought, now in my heart to
>   breed
> Some pious notions of Zoroaster's creed,
> A likely man they found, a weaver wise,
> Advanc'd in years, and moral exercise.
> White, white his all, but red his blinking eyes!
> A man mysterious of the Magus tribe—
> A close astrologer, and a splendid scribe—
> A faithful oracle of dread Hormazd's will—
> A priest, a patriarch, and a man of skill.
> A master weaver, and—to close details—
> He weav'd long webs, and Lord! he weav'd long
>   tales!
> Hard murd'rous words, that wisdom's lips defied,
> Would thick portentous from his nozzle glide!
> And here we struck, tho' long and hard we tried;
> He cursed and caned by turns, we humm'd and
>   cried!
> This could not last; our mutual failings seen,
> He left his preachings and we left our dean.

Behramji's admiration for Alexander Pope becomes evident in his use of antithesis, wit, and satiric humour; but his subject matter, nevertheless, remains essentially very much close to his own Parsi community. In his brilliant word pictures, though he depicts a priest and a patriarch rather irreverently, a reader could not fail to see an imaginative grasp and genuine appreciation of character by a poet who was only twenty-one years old. In the same vein, he continues to describe his second teacher, Narbheram Mehtaji, 'fearless and fear-inspiring,' who was no better than the first, but a different sort, with whom Behramji could not stay for more than three months. Thereafter, he was sent to the Parsi Panchayat School in Surat for religious and secular instruction, where he remained for a year. In this school Behramji found a third teacher strikingly different—another Daru by name, a man of about forty-five years, a 'very ungodly man of god,' and 'the terror of city imps and street arabs.' Behramji describes him with lively humour:

> A zealous man he was, a man of parts,
> With scanty science, but a host of arts.
> With pointed paws his fierce mustache he'd twirl,
> And at the culprits the direst vengeance hurl.
> His jaws he'd rub, his grizzl'ed beard he'd peck,
> Till rubb'd and peck'd, the whole appear'd a wreck,
> Which in a polish'd glass, he then would quiz,
> And look complacent at his mottl'd phiz!

>   . . . . .

> But woe betide the hour, if e'er his meal
> Was late; that would his hidden traits reveal.
> His zeal rose higher, as his stomach fell;
> And hard his fervour on our skins would tell!
> Sharp went the whizzing whip, fast flew the cane;
> And he fairly caper'd in his wrath insane!
> He chanted pray'rs, oh Lord, in such gruff tones,
> 'Twould set on rack the hoar Zoroaster's bones!
> Then came his comments, cook'd with such abuse,
> As would a Rabelais' gross sense confuse!
> He shrick'd and stagger'd in his zealous rage,
> Till he look'd an actor on a tragic stage!
> And when our whines, the neighb'ring women drew,
> The man of zeal, at once persuasive grew!
> Expounded doctrines, in a fervid breath,
> Preach'd patience, virtue, truth and tacit faith!
> Thank God, I'd then too small religious wit,
> To understand that canting hypocrite.

After studying carpentry for a year, because 'his mother belonged to a Bhansali or house-building family.' Behramji returned to more schooling at the hands of another teacher. But things changed with the death of his mother, who exercised a great influence upon the young poet. He recollected his mother as 'a picture of self-sacrifice,' whose memory he enshrined in a poetic tribute.

During her life-time Bhikhibai had done everything in her power to mould the character of her wayward son, often pleading in vain for his reform. It was only on her deathbed she triumphed; for there, suddenly, Behramji realized that she had passed away, leaving him friendless and alone to face the world at the age of twelve. 'I became an old, old man,' he wrote afterwards. 'All my past associations were discarded.' With poignant feelings he recollects his mother's death in his autobiographical 'Sketch':

> One day the sun as his decline began,
> Declin'd the sun of this my earthly span!
> Her latest breath below my safety sought—
> To bless her orphan was her dying thought!
> No tear I shed, when first my loss I view'd
> My sense was smother'd and my soul subdu'd.

> She had clasp'd a child, with sad emotions wan;
> But when the clasp relax'd, there was left a man.

In spite of this change, young Behramji never completely outgrew his youthful idealism. In almost prophetic couplets, he outlined the goal of his future life in his poem 'Manhood's Dream':

> There's pleasure luring me to ruin; I'll never the siren heed;
> If once my soul is wrecked, she's naught but shame to wed indeed;
> But no, I'd honest death prefer to being Pleasure's knave;
> So up and on to glory, soul,—glory or the grave.

Unlike other Indo-English poets, Behramji was initiated into poetic art not by any school teacher but by the Khialis (street singers) of Surat. Khial (literally means 'thought' or 'fancy'), considered one of the varieties of desi (local) romantic music as opposed to the margi (classical), was developed by Buddhist musicians and was later taken up by the Muslims; but in Gujarat it acquired a particular kind of meter. A Khiali, that is, one who signs a khial, is a kind of a poet-philosopher who could sing religious legends, devotional songs, historical ballads, love tales, or sometimes even satirical verses on contemporary persons and events. They were folk-poets who had the genius to compose verses on the spot in community singing or a singing contest with their equals.

Among the Khialis there were two sects: one held that female energy was superior to the male, while the other held a contrary view. Accordingly, the former worshipped Kali and the latter, Siva. When the Khialis belonging to the two opposing sects got involved in a singing contest in a bazaar, they usually challenged each other in impromptu verses to answer knotty questions in history, science, or metaphysics; rejoinders and counter-attacks followed freely, all in good humour, in extempore verse. When the controversy became heated, there was a tendency to descend from high and lofty philosophy to vulgar satire and abuse. They often indulged in ribald and obscene songs unworthy of the founders of their respective schools. At such points, even the uninitiated youngsters joined the contest till it ended in a street fight.

Behramji was drawn to the contests by the music and the poetry. Joining one of the sides in the contest, he often indulged in extempore verse-attacks on the opponents. Though he did not understand or care for their philosophy, he, no doubt, appreciated the poetry of the Khialis, enjoyed participating in their contests, and was thrilled by composing his own verses. Some of Behramji's khials were included in his collection of Gujarati poems, *Niti Vinod*. On the other hand, Behramji's interest in English verse was not roused by the Khialis but by the Rev. (Mr.) Dixon of the Irish Presbyterian Mission School in Surat. Under Dixon's guidance he read widely in English literature, specially the poets. Being imbued with the satiric humour of the Khialis, he found the eighteenth-century English satirists to his liking and imitated them rather faithfully. Though he modelled his rimed couplets on Dryden and Pope, he nevertheless shows his fondness for occasional Miltonic inversions, like 'wrath insane,' or 'man mysterious,' or for the dancing rhythm of lines with medial caesura:

> Sharp went the whizzing whip
> fast flew the cane.

Behramji attempted to write English verse with the enthusiasm of a high school youth, drawing mainly from his personal experience.

Several of the poems in *The Indian Muse in English Garb* were composed in Surat. His keen mind and minute observation helped him to portray with bold, broad outlines characters with whom he had come directly in contact. The vividness of detail, the satiric description, and his impish delight are some of the characteristics that distinguish his riming couplets. He alone, among Indo-English poets, ventured to write satiric verse, perhaps, because, being a Parsi, he had the natural advantage over his Hindu or Moslem compatriots; for the Parsis are generally more given to satiric humour and are more caustic even in their conversations than any other community.

Behramji was conscious that he was writing in a foreign language, yet instead of making a meek apology, he boldly asserts that he was only taking advantage of the 'world language':

> To an observant mind it cannot be a secret, that English which bids fair, at no distant date, to become a world language, has so far identified herself with our best interests, that, what with speaking and writing, we have almost grown to thinking in English.

He further argued that English, having become the current language in India, and having opened doors to European civilization, had replaced Sanskrit and Persian as the language of culture. It was no fault of Indians, therefore, that they essayed to turn the blessings of the foreign language to some account. 'It is in this spirit', he wrote, 'that the writer would have his verses viewed by the Englishmen and the natives; everything else he would leave to their candour. The merit of his work is as modest as its scope is limited.'

A more disciplined Indo-English poet of the nineteenth century, outside of Dutt family, was Manmohan Ghose (1867-1924), who because of his education in England was able to write verse with ease and skill.

[Manmohan's] verses were praised by English poets and critics. It was no small achievement for an Indian to be so recognized. By living in England in his early youth, and cultivating the language of the natives from his childhood, Manmohan had grown up with English as his mother-tongue. His interest in poetry was aroused early in school. The companionship of young English poets kindled his poetic flame. But it was Greek poetry that moulded his taste. He had sought out on his own, outside of books prescribed in the school, Greek poets like Theocritus, Meleager, and above all Simonides. His early poems, an echo from the Greek, reflect Manmohan's attempt to fuse expressive imagery with music and serene movement. He could see free birds flying 'with music in their wings'; or watch the colourful sunset hour when 'heavens grow hea-

venlier'; or recalling the steadfast stars that 'remember to appear,' he could underline the sadness in his heart at the disappearance of his lover:

A Lament

> Over thy head, in joyful wanderings
> Through heaven's wide spaces, free
> Birds fly with music in their wings;
> And from the blue, rough sea
> The fishes flash and leap;
> There is a life of loveliest things
> O'er thee, so fast asleep.
> In the deep West the heavens grow heavenlier,
> Eve after eve; and still
> The glorious stars remember to appear;
> The roses on the hill
> Are fragrant as before:
> Only thy face, of all that is dear,
> I shall see no more!

The note of sadness (specially at the passing away of youth and summer), pervades all of Manmohan's poems. In 'Raymond and Ida' two lovers, kept warm by a 'cheerful flame' in a dark room, whisper their dread at the approaching winter:

> My dreaming heart is stirr'd
> Sadly the winter comes!
> The wind is loud: how weird,
> Heard in these darken'd rooms!
> Speak to me, Raymond; ease this dread
> I am afraid, afraid.

However, it is in his longer poem in the anthology that Manmohan transcends earthly sadness to reach the understanding of the Upanishadic sages when he tries to see in the cycles of Nature greater cycles of life and death. Whether it is the 'vernal visitation of the rose,' or the falling of a thousand-year-old oak, whether it is the ebb and flow of life in plant, bird, fly, or man, Manmohan sees Nature manifesting its purpose, irrespective of whether or not man understands or appreciates it. Despite man's attempt to comprehend manifested Nature in terms of nama-rupa (name and form), Manmohan comes to the realization in typical Indian fashion when he concludes that Nature carries on its unceasing work 'unfathom'd and unknown':

Mentem Mortalia Tangunt

> Now lonely is the wood:
> No flower now lingers, none!
> The virgin sisterhood
> Of roses, all are gone;
> Now Autumn sheds her last leaf:
> And in my heart is grief.
> Ah me, for all earth rears
> The appointed bound is placed!
> After a thousand years
> The great oak falls at last:
> And thou, more lovely, canst not stay,
> Sweet rose, beyond thy day.
>
> Our life is not the life
> Of roses and of leaves;
> Else wherefore this deep strife,
> This pain, our soul conceives?
> The fall of ev'n such short-lived things
> To us some sorrow brings.

And yet, plant, bird, and fly
Feel no such hidden fire.
Happy they live; and die
Happy, with no desire.
They in their brief life have fulfill'd
All Nature in them will'd.

. . . . .

Why thirst the spirit so
For life? What moves it thus?
'Tis *her* voice; yes, I know,
'Tis Nature cries in us:
'Tis no unholy strife of ours
Against forbidding powers.

. . . . .

So in the chrysalis
Slumber those lovely wings;
So from the shell it is
The dazzling pearl she brings:
Her glorious works she works alone,
Unfathom'd, and unknown!

This high seriousness of Manmohan to express oriental metaphysics in chiselled English verse led Oscar Wilde to speak of him as 'the young Indian of brilliant scholarship and high literary attainment who gives some culture to Christ Church. Wilde went on further to suggest that Indo-English literature, perhaps, would establish, in due course of time, a closer and more just and lasting bond of union between England and India:

> His [Manmohan's] verses show how quick and subtle are the intellectual sympathies of the oriental mind, and suggest how close is the bond of union that may some day bind India to us by other methods than those of commerce and military strength.

Manmohan seems to have felt a sense of living in exile both in England and in India though the feeling became more acute during his last few years in India. In his impressionable days, in spite of his feeling at home in the literary world of England, he seems to have experienced, during cold and dark winter seasons, some moments of home-sickness and romantic yearning for his own country. In his poem 'Myvanwy' he gives expression to his longing for the tropical land of 'meridian suns and ardent summers' which he hardly knew:

> Lost is that country, and all but forgotten
> Mid these chill breezes, yet still, oh believe me,
> All her meridian suns and ardent summers
> Burn in my bosom.

On his return to India Manmohan found himself in a completely different world—a world in which he became more and more isolated socially and culturally. The Indian men of letters, agitated by the nationalist movement, were seeking inspiration from Sanskrit literature. The Indo-English writers were attempting to re-express ancient Indian culture or interpret contemporary Indian life. Though Manmohan continued to write English verses, they were composed in surroundings from which they drew no natural nourishment. For him England remained 'the nursing-mother of imagination and the dear home of the muses.'

In that island set in silver sea, he saw his 'gardens of bliss,' to which he longed to return:

> In the gardens of bliss
> The nightingale did moan,
> And it seemed his throat
> Throbbed for me alone.

There is no doubt that Manmohan loved the countryside and regarded Nature as the loveliest of all muses. But the countryside for him was always the English countryside of elm, oak, and beach; the seasons were the English seasons when spring wafted 'reprive of death.' In a poem addressed to the month of April with its flowering flag, haunting water falls, and cuckoo-calls, Manmohan, singing in bubbling rhythm, attempts to find joy through 'windowed paradise':

April

Oh to be flowery,
   Dripping and balmy,
Call up the showery
White clouds, an army!
Shallow and freshet flush
Green as the grasses lush;
By shady soft degrees
Thicken the leafy trees
   To reach out dreamily
Wall and lane over,
   Till in fresh groves are heard,
In the green clover,
   Warbling their lays each bird
Over and over.
   Curd wild brooks creamily;
Let not the bulrush lag,
Quicken the flowering flag,
   Till in reeds stilly
Soon the wild swan shall nest
Preening his dazzling breast
   By the oped lily.
Make listening echo sweet
   By the full waterfall,
Dimly and oft repeat
   The haunting cuckoo-call.
With all that shady is
   Hasten to bower the land!
Elm, oak, and tall beach grand
Of dim isles that lady is
   Where greenness shall hover,
And where a tall thin mist
Rises, the green wheat whist,
Chatters the crake; make tryst
   Fond lass and lover!
Haste, April, upon city streets to blow
   Thy purest, warmest breezes; fly beneath
With flower-girl's rags, poor beggary's basket stow
with lordliest gold of daffodils aglow.
I will not love thee, save with sighing breath
On pale, worn cheeks thou waft reprive of death.
   Come in a wash of fragrance, let sick eyes
   See leaves bud, bird-song hear through windowed paradise.

When his isolation was intensified by suffering, Manmohan sought to identify himself with nature's 'steadfast sorrower', the willow. With restrained rapture he seeks communion with the willow tree in order to learn from it the artless art of transmuting still sadness into expressions of beauty:

> Willow sweet, willow sad, willow by the river,
>   Taught by pensive love to droop, where cease-
>   less waters shiver,
> Teach me, steadfast sorrower, your mournful
>   grace of graces,
> Weeping to make beautiful the silent water-
>   places.

Manmohan wrote poems on various themes, such as nature, seasons, love, death, and the home-sickness of the soul. Whatever his theme may be, his poetry has two distinctive characteristics: an undeniable technical perfection in writing verse and a note of sadness. His short, clear cut lines, his happy phrases, and finely set images appear effortless. His stanzas glide smoothly, conveying their melancholy directly to the reader's heart. George Sampson felt that Manmohan was 'the most remarkable of Indian poets who wrote in English.' Being educated in England, he absorbed the subtleties of the language so completely that 'a reader of his poems would readily take them as the work of an English poet trained in the classical tradition.' To the end of his life, remaining a lover of European literature and art, self-exiled Manmohan dreamed of returning to England and appropriately died on the day he was scheduled to sail.

Manmohan Ghose completes a curious cycle in the tradition of Indo-English poetry in the nineteenth century. It was started in 1820's by Eurasian Henry Derozio out of the fusion of two cultures. Though Henry was brought up in an English household, he attempted to identify himself in his writings with the traditions of India. Subsequent writers like Kashi Prosad Ghose, Rajanarian Dutt, and Behramji Malabari absorbed more and more of English culture and tradition. They were educated under English teachers. In the mid-century the Indo-English poets, after their education in India, visited England and came in direct contact with English life and letters, but wrote their verses mainly in India. In the last quarter, however, a reversal occurred. Young Indians went to England for their education till one of them (Manmohan Ghose) grew up in England, picking up the language of the natives as his own mother-tongue and writing verse in the company of English poets. Though Manmohan's verses were published in England, they may, in fact, be considered as properly belonging to the category of Indo-English poetry.

> *John B. Alphonso-Karkala, "Indo-English Poetry," in his* Indo-English Literature in the Nineteenth Century, *University of Mysore, 1970, pp. 34-66.*

R. Parthasarathy

[*Parthasarathy is an Indian poet and critic. In the following essay, he discusses the tradition of Indo-English poetry that is emerging from what began as merely "the borrowed voice of the English poets."*]

Quite often I find myself in the situation, at least hypothetically, when I am asked: 'How representative is Indian English verse of the literatures of India?' Not being an apologist by disposition, I shall try here not to appear defensive in offering to formulate some responses.

It is true that Indian English verse has a past that is best forgotten. There are far too many skeletons in the cupboard for the poet to feel comfortable or secure today. By persisting to speak in the borrowed voice of the English poets, the Indian poets lost, over the years, the use of their own voice. Here is a sample from ['Perseus, the Gorgon Slayer,' by] Manmohan Ghose (1869-1924):

> Whither fled Sleep, whither fled that soft Power
> World-stilling, when from Iris' side he rose
> From sentinelling the hush'd awful head
> Of brooding and thought-task'd Omnipotence.
> Where went he spreading his wide dewy wings
> To deepen slumber o'er the world's unrest.
> Far as to Oxus river, and where rolls,
> Where mighty Indus rushes. He had left
> To fade with ebbing light each noble stream
> And from Night's gloaming step, the dusk ad-
>   vance
> Of silence, to drink first of silver rest
> In glassing the bright peace of Hesperus!

The allusions Ghose uses are not taken from the deposits of a common Indian tradition. And, therefore, for the reader, the validity of what is said is immeasurably lost, since it is outside his comprehension. We can only throw up our hands in despair, and exclaim: 'Milton! should'st *thou* be living at this hour?' It isn't the use of English that is appalling; it is the erosion of sensibility. Ghose was, of course, an extreme case of 'colonialitis'. In 1916, eight years before his death, he wrote to Laurence Binyon:

> For years not a friendly step has crossed my threshold . . . and with Indians my purely English upbringing and breeding puts me out of harmony; denationalised, that is then the word for me.

On the criticism of Indo-English poetry:

Contemporary Indo-English poetry has little precedent in the past, except obvious, though tenuous, points of contact in regard to certain thematic motifs. The temptation, therefore, is to place the twentieth-century poet alongside his nineteenth-century counterpart and in smaller waters make him appear a leviathan. Moreover, since this poetry emerged as a distinct entity only in the sixties, critics who look for streamlined historical evolution in this poetry—of its emergence, the progressive growth and the eventual efflorescence—are applying inapplicable criteria. Therefore, any approach to this poetry must make judicious use of traditional frames applicable to literary genres and infer the paradoxes inherent in its rather abrupt maturity perceptible during the last decade.

> *M. Sivaramkrishna in "The 'Tongue in English Chains': Indo-English Poetry Today."* Indian Poetry in English: A Critical Assessment, *edited by Vasant A. Shahane and M. Sivaramkrishna, Macmillan, 1980.*

Instead of being told to stop composing pastiches of the English poets, he was in fact commended by Binyon:

> No Indian had ever before used our tongue with so poetic a touch, and he would coin a phrase, turn a noun into a verb with the freedom, often the felicity, of our own poets. But he remains Indian.

More than one Indian English poet has been ruined by such adulation. Ghose's *Selected Poems,* with an introduction by A. Norman Jeffares, was published in 1974 by the Sahitya Akademi, and in the following year he was honoured with a monograph in the 'makers of Indian Literature' series.

It is an unfortunate truism of the Indian English literary scene that responsible criticism is the exception rather than the rule. What exists, such as the few studies of individual poets, is invariably laudatory in tone and makes embarrassing reading. There is no evidence in them of either scholarship or the critical faculty at work. Those who write are familiar with *only* English (or American) literature; their terms of reference are borrowed from that literature. The exercise becomes, as a result, inappropriate and futile. Familiarity with at least one of the Indian literatures would have offered a perspective in which to evaluate the work.

In spite of there being a *history* of Indians writing verse in English for over a hundred and fifty years, Indian English verse has no *tradition* to speak of. And during that long period, none of the poets helped to establish an indigenous tradition, involving the whole history of verse in one or more of the Indian languages. In fact, the history of Indian English verse is the history of lost opportunities. None of the poets seriously took up its challenge, and attempted to write verse that was authentically Indian in inspiration and was also, at the same time, artistically viable.

The Indian renaissance, of which Rammohun Roy (1772-1833) was the representative spokesman, touched only a handful of educated Indians. There is no evidence to show that it represented a general awakening of the Indian people. The poets failed to question, examine or reflect on the upheaval that was taking place as a result of the British conquest of India. The verse is, therefore, feeble and emasculated. It has the vitality, or what was left of it, of an enslaved nation:

> My country! in thy day of glory past
> A beauteous halo circled round thy brow,
> And worshipped as a deity thou wast.
> Where is that glory, where that reverence now?
> Thy eagle pinion is chained down at last,
> And grovelling in the lowly dust art thou:
> Thy minstrel hath no wreath to weave for thee
> Save the sad story of thy misery!

However, ever since the withdrawal of the British from India, Indian English verse has become increasingly separated from English literature to become a part of the mainstream of the literatures of India. It has, in effect, today acquired an obstinately national or regional bias. Such a bias is imposed on the poet by the culture and society of which he is an integral part. What the Kannada writer, U. R. Anantha Murthy, says is relevant in this context:

> We all write in the Indian languages, and this fact has a profound consequence on what we actually do in our languages, however much we expose ourselves to the West in search of ideas and forms. . . . If the ideas that are still not of my language are embodied in my language creatively, then they become a part of the living tradition of my language. [From his "Search For an Identity: A Viewpoint of a Kannada Writer," in *Identity and Adulthood,* edited by Sudhir Kakar, pp. 107-09, 1979]

This is the special concern of the ecology of language, that is, the 'study of interactions between any given language and its environment' In Indian English literature, the interactions have been in the reverse direction: English has interacted with Indian languages in the minds of bilingual speakers and with Indian society in which it continues to be used. It has, as a result, undergone the inevitable process of acculturation, and the outcome of this long process of indianization of English is Indian English. The Indian context has nativized the company that English words traditionally keep in their non-Indian settings, thus helping to form new, typically Indian, collocations. These collocations mark Indian English as distinct from other varieties of English. Further, in the Indian context, as in the West African context, there developed a form of pidgin English. The pidginization of English was initiated with the first contact of Indians and Englishmen during the earliest phase of the East India Co. I think it would be useful to keep in mind here J. R. Firth's comment on Indian English:

> Most Indian English is badly overdrawn. But it is kept going by the Government, and though it has therefore a certain local currency, it has no gold backing. English literature up to and including Addison is not a suitable security on which to issue current tokens of speech in the twentieth century. Babuism is not by any means confined to India. It is the common danger lurking in all purely literary education, and especially perilous if the languages are alien to the social life of the learners. [from *Speech,* 1930, 1964]

The Indian context of situation provides the parameters of appropriateness for Indian English, and these parameters indicate the extent of deviation. In the linguistic history of India, this phenomenon is consistent with the past linguistic assimilations of this country, for example, the indianization of Persian, the dravidianization of Sanskrit and the sanskritization of the Dravidian languages.

Successive conquests for about eight hundred years, beginning with the rise of Muslim power in 1175 to the close of the raj in 1947, disrupted the continuity of the Hindu tradition. Our literatures have not been immune to the onslaught. The last great works in Sanskrit and Tamil, for instance—Jayadeva's *Gitagovinda* and Kamban's *Iramavataram*—appeared in the twelfth century. The raj especially struck at the roots of the Indian psyche, and it hasn't been fully assimilated by us. Our languages did not have the resources to come to grips with the modernization initiated by the raj.

The work of A. K. Ramanujan (*b.* 1929) offers the first indisputable evidence of the validity of Indian English verse. Both *The Striders* (1966) and *Relations* (1971) are the heir of an anterior tradition, a tradition very much of this subcontinent, the deposits of which are in Kannada and Tamil and which have been *assimilated* into English. Ramanujan's deepest roots are in the Kannada and Tamil past, and he has repossessed that past, in fact made it available, in the English language. I consider this a significant achievement, one almost without a parallel in the history of Indian English verse. Ramanujan has, it seems to me, successfully conveyed in English what, at its subtlest and most incantational, is locked up in another linguistic tradition. He has, as a result, indicated the directions Indian English verse is likely to take in the future.

'Prayers to Lord Murugan' is an 'imitation' of the *Tirumurukarrupatai* in which the Tamil poet, Nakkirar (fl. 7th cent.) sings the praises of Murugan, the Dravidian god of youth, beauty, love and war. Also known as Skanda and Karttikeya, Murugan is represented as a six-faced god with twelve hands, riding on a peacock, holding a bow in one hand and an arrow in another. With the rise of bhakti literature by about A.D. 600 in the Tamil country, he is displaced by Siva and Vishnu. There was, however, a revival of the cult of Murugan towards the beginning of the sixteenth century. In Ramanujan's poem, Murugan is vividly invoked in the tradition of Tamil heroic verse. The *arrupatai* is a kind of poetical composition in which bards, having received favours from Kings, *direct* others to seek their patronage. But in the *Tirumurukarrupatai* the bhakta who has received the grace of Murugan shows others the way to salvation. Even the *arrupatai* form of Nakkirar's hymn is preserved, albeit ironically:

> Lord of new arrivals
> lovers and rivals
> arrive
> at once with cockfight and banner-
> dance till on this and the next three
> hills
> women's hands and the garlands
> on the chests of men will turn like
> chariotwheels
> O where are the cockscombs and where
> the beaks glinting with new knives
> at crossroads
> when will orange banners burn
> among blue trumpet flowers and the shade
> of trees
> waiting for lightnings?

'Prayers to Lord Murugan' can be seen as being embedded in, and arising from, a specific tradition. It is the first step towards establishing an indigenous tradition of Indian English verse. And it can be established and kept alive only if Indian English verse increasingly aligns itself with the literatures of India.

Arun Kolatkar's (*b.* 1932) deepest roots are again in the Marathi past. He has made a considerable dent in the tradition of the bhakti poets, notably Tukaram (1598-1649) and Namdeo (1270-1350), in his appropriation of that tra-

dition in *Jejuri* (1976). Apparently, the poem is about the poet's irreverent visit to the temple of Khandoba at Jejuri, a town 50 km. southeast of Pune in Maharashtra. In reality, however, the poem oscillates between faith and scepticism in a tradition that has run its course. Khandoba is, in fact, Mailar in Karnataka and Murugan in Tamil Nadu. It is a fortuitous coincidence that both Ramanujan and Kolatkar should have chosen to resuscitate Indian English verse by invoking the same popular folk deity. Lord of the hills and of shepherds, Khandoba is represented wrapped in a blanket and riding on a horse, with a sword in one hand. He has two wives, Mhalasa and Banai. A dog usually accompanies him. To this day, people from all over Maharashtra flock to his shrine. 'A Song for a Vaghya' (worshippers traditionally dedicated to Khandoba) has its roots in the *abhang* (short devotional poem):

> Khandoba's temple
> rises with the day.
> But it must not fall
> with the night.
> I'll hold it up
> with a flame for a prop.
> Don't turn me away.
> I must have my oil, ma'am
> Give me a drop
> if you can't spare a gram.
> This instrument
> has one string.
> And one godawful itch.
> As I scratch it,
> it gives me just one pitch.
> But if it plays
> just the one note,
> who am I to complain
> when all I've got
> is just a one-word song
> inside my throat?
> God is the word
> and I know it backwards:

Jejuri points the way to the future precisely because it has a firm hold on a specific tradition. Kolatkar has, like Ramanujan before him, contributed significantly to the making of an indigenous tradition for Indian English verse.

In 1972 I spoke of my resolve to write in Tamil in a poem ['Homecoming 1'] which is now regarded as 'paradigmatic of the entire Indian English poetic milieu' [according to M. Sivaramkrishna in 'The "Tongue in English Chains": Indo-English Poetry Today,' in *Osmania Journal of English Studies* 13, No. 1 (1977)]

> My tongue in English chains,
> I return, after a generation, to you.
> I am at the end
> of my dravidic tether,
> hunger for your unassuaged.
> I falter, stumble.
> Speak a tired language
> wrenched from its sleep in the *Kural,*
> teeth, palate, lips still new
> to its agglutinative touch.
> Now, hooked on celluloid, you reel
> down plush corridors.

Sivaramkrishna commented, 'if the Indian English poet of the nineteenth century had his tongue firmly entrenched in English chains, it is the unchaining of this that is suggested here'. In attempting to formulate my own situation, perhaps, I stumbled upon the horns of dilemma. From the beginning, I saw my task as one of acclimatizing the English language to an indigenous tradition. In fact, the tenor of *Rough Passage* is explicit: to initiate a dialogue between myself and my Tamil past. 'Homecoming', in particular, tries to derive its sustenance from grafting itself on to whatever I find usable in the Tamil tradition—from the *Kural* (3rd or 4th cent.) to the *Nalayiradivyaprapantam* (5th-9th cent.). Something that had eluded me over the years, I was eventually able to nativize it in English—the flavour, the essence of Tamil mores. The result is 'a Tamil poem written in English' ['Homecoming 3']:

> And so it eventually happened—
> a family reunion not heard of
> since grandfather died in, 59—in March
> this year. Cousins arrived in Tiruchchanur
> in overcrowded private buses,
> the dust of unlettered years
> clouding instant recognition.
> Later, each one pulled,
> sitting cross-legged on the steps
> of the choultry, familiar coconuts
> out of the fire
> of rice-and-pickle afternoons.
> Sundari, who had squirrelled up and down
> forbidden tamarind trees in her long skirt
> every morning with me,
> stood there, that day forty years taller,
> her three daughters floating
> like safe planets near her.

I am aware of the hiatus between the soil of the language I use and my own roots. Even though I am Tamil-speaking and yet write in English, there is the overwhelming difficulty of using images in a linguistic tradition that is quite other than that of my own. If the images used are drawn from the deposits of a common tradition, the validity of the work is at once recognized by the reader. I believe that if a writer thought long and hard enough on his own use of language, even if it is English, sooner or later, I think, through the English language, he will try to come to terms with himself as an Indian, with his Indian past, with his environment, and the language will become acclimatized to the Indian environment.

I'd like to think that every time a poem is written it appropriates, in a sense, all the poems that have ever been written in that particular language. This cannot be said of an Indian English poem, because there is no tradition to relate it with. If, however, the poet has access to an Indian language, though he may not find himself writing in it, he can gradually try to appropriate that tradition though he writes in English. This would, of course, mean reconciling ourselves to having Kannada English verse, Tamil English verse and so on—all inalienable segments of a pan-Indian mosaic that we know as the literatures of India. When that happens, the severed head, Indian English verse, will no longer 'choke to speak another tongue'.

Orissa is the hub of Jayanta Mahapatra's (*b.* 1928) icono-clastic perambulations. Through his translations of Oriya verse, he has successfully assimilated in his own work its literary tradition. He produces strange, evocative poems

when he trains his poetic eye on the improverished landscape of Orissa, overburdened with an intolerable past, such as the unorthodox rites centred around the temple of Jagannath at Puri, the celebrated seat of Krishna bhakti in eastern India. To its festival of *ratha-yatra* flock thousands of pilgrims when the idol of Jagannath is brought out in the car for his 'symbolic tour of the world to study the state of mankind'. The emptiness of traditional rituals is obliquely exposed in 'The Faith':

> In these indistinguishable mornings
> like pale-yellow hospital linen,
> a legless cripple
> clutters up the wide temple street,
> the quiet early light crouched in his palms.
> What sentence of old
> moves him toward the furious wrinkled walls?
> The Puri priest standing in indulgent sunshine
> plays a small ridicule across the melting festival
> safe in place above a pile of hard-eyed ancestors.

Another bilingual poet, Kamala Das (*b.* 1934) works out her emotional and sexual traumas in poems of unexceptionable frankness reminiscent of the medieval *Sahaja* (Skt. 'spontaneous') poets who espoused free love as a means of realizing oneself. The classic expression is found in Chandidas (fl. 15th cent.) [from *Love Songs of Chandidas: Rebel Poet-Priest of Bengal,* translated by Deben Bhattacharya, 1967]:

> What god is that
> Who moulded me a woman?
> I am always alone
> Being married and watched.
> Since falling in love
> Is a disgrace for me,
> I must then kill
> My meaningless life.
> I am not free
> To open my mouth
> But I am in rapture
> With another man.

Traditionally, Nayar women were sexually uninhibited because of the practice of *marumakkathayam* ('matrilineal system of inheritance and succession'). And Katnala Das' forthright treatment of sexual relations [in 'The Old Playhouse'] is an offshoot of her Nayar background.

> It was not to gather knowledge
> Of yet another man that I came to you but to
>   learn
> What I was, and by learning, to learn to grow,
>   but every
> Lesson you gave was about yourself. You were
>   pleased
> With my body's response, its weather, its usual
>   shallow
> Convulsions. You dribbled spittle into my
>   mouth, you poured
> Yourself into every nook and cranny, you em-
>   balmed
> My poor lust with your bitter-sweet juices

If the recent work of Nissim Ezekiel (*b.* 1924), Keki N. Daruwalla (*b.* 1937) and Gieve Patel (*b.* 1940) is any indication, its thrust is not towards shaping an indigenous tradition but in its relevance to the contemporary Indian situaation. Ezekiel's statement about himself [in 'Naipaul's India and Mine,' in *New Writing in India,* 1974] could be extended to include Daruwalla and Patel:

> I am not a Hindu and my background makes me a natural outsider: circumstances and decisions relate me to India. . . . I cannot identify myself with India's past as a comprehensive heritage or reject it as if it were mine to reject. I can identify myself only with modern India.

> They write with irony and humour about the experience of living in India today. Their stance is critical as they explore and celebrate, after the tortuous labyrinths of solitude and disillusion, the sense of finally coming home, of coming to terms with India.

It is a measure of Ezekiel's integrity as a man and poet that he recognizes and accepts his unenviable situation. *Hymns in Darkness* (1976) reveals his increasing concern with the nature of religious experience, even though he is 'not a religious person in any conventional sense'. Unlike Ramanujan, he is not questioning the validity or otherwise of a traditional faith. He is simply content to evoke luminously but ironically the configurations of his experience [in 'Hymns in the Darkness 3']:

> He has seen the signs
> but not been faithful to them.
> Where is the fixed star of his seeking?
> It multiplies like a candle
> in the eyes of a drunkard.
> He looks at the nakedness of truth
> in the spirit of a Peeping Tom.
> Changing his name would be no help.
> He is the man
> full of his name.

The landscape of northern India sometimes erupts with unexpected violence in Daruwalla's poems; at other times, it broods over them like an ominous Himalaya [as here in 'Death of Bird']:

> I broke my gun in two across the back
> of an ash-grey dawn. A brown bird left the crags
> flying strongly, and as its shadow crossed us
> it shrieked with fear and turned to stone
> dropping at our feet.

He is one of the few poets to have successfully rehabilitated the topography of the land in his work.

Unable to accept present-day India as it is, and unable to relate themselves comprehensively to traditional India, these poets fall back on irony to disclose the contradictions inherent in the Indian situation.

The literatures of India are increasingly conditioning Indian English literature and, therefore, familiarity with even one of them would appreciably enhance our understanding of the latter. The history of Indian English verse is therefore the history, on the one hand, of a growing relationship between two traditions and two languages and, on the other, of the reshaping of English to express the Indian experience. The tension of this dialogue has produced and is still producing significant and often excellent writing. To understand Indian English verse is to understand the traditions involved and how they interact. The individ-

ual work is for us the only focus of value. If, however, it is valid, its value will be outside the personal and traditional, and reach out to the universal. For the present, it appears to me, every poet has to make the imaginative grasp at identity for himself; and if he can find no means in his tradition to sustain him, he will have to start from scratch.

> *R. Parthasarathy, "Indian English Verse: The Making of a Tradition," in* Alien Voice: Perspectives on Commonwealth Literature, *edited by Avadhesh K. Srivastava, 1981. Reprint by Humanities Press, 1982, pp. 40-52.*

INDO-ENGLISH DRAMA

M. K. Naik

[*Naik is an Indian educator, critic, and editor who specializes in the study of Indian literature in English. He has edited several anthologies of critical commentary on the subject, including* Perspectives on Indian Drama in English, Critical Essays on Indian Writing in English, *and* Indian Response to Poetry in English. *He has also written book-length studies of T.S. Eliot, Raja Rao, and Mulk Raj Anand, as well as a history of Indo-English literature. In the following essay, Naik examines the reasons for the shortage of Indian drama written in English.*]

The story is told of a London bookseller who, upon being asked to supply a copy of F. O. Matthiessen's *The Achievement of T. S. Eliot*, is reported to have asked, 'What achievement?' A similar question has often been asked in respect of Indian drama in English—though in a different spirit altogether—and the answer, though likely to be far different in this case, is equally obvious: If Indian writing in English is the Cinderella of literature in English, Indian drama in English has always been, along with criticism, one of the twin Cinderellas of Indian writing in English. A [1972] bibliography of Indian writing in English lists as many as 777 separate titles under poetry, 664 under fiction and a paltry 173 under drama. The bibliography of Indian drama in English appended to the present volume brings the story up to date, but it advances the score only to about 400. Actually, of these three forms, only poetry had a clear start of about half a century, for its career began with Kashiprasad Ghose's *The Shair and Other Poems* (1830); while the first novel and play in English appeared in the same century, more than forty years later: Toru Dutt's novel, *Bianca or the Young Spanish Maiden* in 1878, and Michael Madhusudan Dutt's play, *Is This Civilization?* in 1871. But since then, the 'pocket theatre' has clearly left the theatre far behind in the development of Indian writing in English. Fiction has already produced masterpieces like *Untouchable, The Serpent and the Rope* and *The Guide.* Why has Indian drama in English been unable to grow similarly and bear rich fruit?

Several factors are responsible for the arrested growth of

drama. At the outset, there is the fundamental problem of the indissoluble relationship between drama and the theatre—a relationship which constitutes at once a signal advantage and a limitation for drama vis-a-vis other literary forms. Drama is a composite art in which the written word of the playwright attains complete artistic realization only when it becomes the spoken word of the actor on the stage, and through that medium reacts on the mind of the audience. A play, in order to communicate fully and become a living dramatic experience, thus needs a real theatre and a live audience. Of all writers, it is truest to say of the dramatist: 'He must communicate or he will die.' It is precisely the lack of these essentials that has hamstrung Indian drama in English all along.

A glance at the development of drama in India during and after the raj is instructive. The first theatre in Bombay, the Bombay Amateur Theatre, was built in 1776 on a spot 'where a tank of impure water existed before' (and the curse of that 'impure water' has perhaps plagued the English theatre in India ever since). The plays presented here were 'in the main the comedies of the later Georgian playwrights'. This theatre, soon crippled by financial difficulties was finally sold by public auction in 1835. *The Bombay Gazette* (12 September 1835) protesting against the sale considered the 'day not distant when Bombay itself would become the theatre of British enterprise . . . and when the genius of Hindoostan would again raise its head in renovated youth invigorated by the mighty auxiliaries of European literature and science'. 'If then', the editor asked, 'an Indian Shakespeare should arise, shall there be no stage to call forth the creations of his fancy? Shall his genius sleep and its first fruits be lost to his country?' (A hundred and forty years later this complaint is still valid today, as far as drama in English is concerned.) When the Grant Road Theatre opened a decade later, in 1846, Mrs Deacle, in her inaugural address, indicated the kind of entertainment she proposed to offer: 'Old wines made mellow and improved by age/New fruits but late from the London stage.'

These early theatres had naturally no room for plays originally written in English by Indians, though *The Bombay Telegraph and Courier* (10 January 1852) hoped that amateur writers would try their hand at new dramatic compositions and that scenes from Indian history would 'become as familiar to the playgoing Englishman as those derived from the histories of Greece and Rome'. *The Oriental News* (16 October 1853) even 'announced confidently that life in the (Bombay) Presidency provided ample material for farce writers. It also quoted a whole incident from Satara's history which, it asserted, contained within it all the elements of tragedy'. We soon find a young Indian following this advice. In 1866, C. S. Nazir wrote what is perhaps the earliest Indian verse play in English, *The First Parsi Baronet,* but it was an isolated effort, and Nazir soon became actively associated with the Victoria Natak Mandali, which specialized in Gujarati and Hindustani plays.

Several European touring companies visited and performed in Bombay during the latter half of the nineteenth century. These included the Fairclough Company, the Lewis Dramatic Company, Norville's Our Boys Company, the Loftus Troupe, the Willard Opera Company and the Dave Carson Troupe. The plays staged were mostly comedies, farces and operas (very rarely tragedies)—all imported from Britain. Of these, only Dave Carson, the self-styled 'only Anglo-Indian comedian in the world' (*The Bombay Gazette,* 25 April 1877) made any attempt to use Indian material for his farcial comedies. Among the popular items in his repertoire were a 'burlesque of the eccentricities sometimes witnessed in a mofussil magistrate's court', 'scenes in the Bombay Police Court', and 'The Bombay Palkheewala', his biggest song-list being the 'Bengalee Baboo'—a tune which bands continued to play till the end of the century at Hindu weddings and on Parsi New Year's Day.

Many amateur dramatic groups and clubs also flourished, especially during the 1860s and 1870s, notably the Parsi Elphinstone Dramatic Society, the Kalidas Elphinstone Society, the Shakespeare Society of Elphinstone College, the Bombay Amateur Dramatic Club, the Thespian Club, the Orphean Dramatic Club, etc. A pointer to the great interest created by this dramatic activity among the students of the time is provided by a letter published in *The Times of India* on 7 May 1864. Signed 'J.D.S.', it complained that young Parsis spent a 'major portion of their time in attending the club and preparing their parts of the performance instead of allotting their time towards the preparation of their school lessons'.

The upshot of this many-sided dramatic activity in Bombay was not, however, the growth of drama in English, but the rise of modern drama in Marathi and Gujarati. Annasaheb Kirloskar's epoch-making production of *Sakuntala* in 1880 successfully launched modern Marathi drama, and English drama on the Bombay stage slowly declined in the face of the challenge from vernacular dramatic activity. The story of the growth of modern drama in the two other important centres of early British influence, namely, Calcutta and Madras, runs along similar lines. The first play was staged in Calcutta in 1795

> through the enterprise of a Russian music director, Lebedoff . . . assisted by one Goleknath Das. . . . The first Bengali drama performed, *Chhadma-besh* (was) adapted from an English drama called *Disguise.* . . . It was not until 1832 that Prosonna Kumar Tagore . . . began to stage Bengali dramas adapted from some of the best Sanskrit plays. This continued . . . until 1851, to which can be traced one of the earliest original Bengali dramas, *Kirtibilas,* a social play by Pandit Jogendra Nath Gupta. [Narendra Dev in 'Drama in Modern Bengal' in *Drama in Modern India and the Writer's Responsibility in a Rapidly Changing World,* 1961]

By the end of the nineteenth century, the Bengali theatre was already well-established, whereas drama in English in Bengal had to remain content with a solitary play, Madhusudan Dutt's *Is This Civilization?* (1871). (Some of Sri Aurobindo's plays were written by the turn of the century, but they were published much later.) The career of modern drama in Madras is much briefer. In 1875, the Madras Dramatic Society was established, enabling amateur Europeans to give performances in English. The Oriental

Drama Club followed in 1882, and the first Indian amateur dramatic society in southern India, The Sarasa Vinodini Sabha, was founded by Krishnammachary of Bellary in 1890.

By the early twentieth century, the theatre movement in the Indian languages had already gathered momentum under the influence mainly of British drama, whereas the theatre in English received no chance to develop at all. From 1940 onwards, one finds several dramatic organizations launched, but none devoted exclusively to drama in English. Among these were the Indian People's Theatre; the Indian National Theatre established under the leadership of Kamaladevi Chattopadhyaya during World War II (its first production was a ballet based on Nehru's *The Discovery of India*—but that is the only service done by it to Indian writing in English); Ebrahim Alkazi's Theatre Unit; and the Bharatiya Natya Sangha affiliated to the World Theatre Centre of UNESCO.

Several regional amateur theatres have also flourished from time to time. These include Sombhu Mitra's Bohuroopi Group in Bengal; the Hindi Natya Parishad, the Kalakendra, Rangabhoomi and Nat Mandal in Gujarat; the Prithvi Theatres and the Mumbai Marathi Sahitya Sangha in Bombay; the Telugu Little Theatre and the Andhra Theatre Foundation; the Seva Sangha in Madras; Dishantar in Delhi, etc. It is highly significant that the Little Theatre Group was established in 1947 as an English theatre, but changed over to Bengali, in 1953.

After the attainment of Independence, the first Five-Year Plan encouraged the performing arts as an effective means of public enlightenment, and the National School of Drama was established under the directorship of Alkazi. Institutions for training in dramatics were founded in big cities: Rukminidevi Arundale's Kalakhestra at Adyar, Madras and Mrinalini Sarabhai's Darpana in Ahmedabad being notable examples. Drama departments started functioning in several universities including Baroda, Calcutta, Punjab, Annamalai, Mysore, etc. The annual National Drama Festival was started in New Delhi hy the Sangit Natak Akademi in 1954. Visits of foreign troupes are arranged from time to time by the British Council and the U.S. Information Service. With so much encouragement coming from so many quarters, drama in the Indian languages has 'fared sumptuously' and put on flesh; but drama in English has had to remain content only with the crumbs fallen from its rich cousin's table. With the exception of Gopal Sharman's Akshara Little Theatre in New Delhi, an occasional performance or two is what Indian plays in English usually have, even in big cities like Bombay. Paradoxically enough, some of these plays like Gurcharan Das' *Mira*, Partap Sharma's *A Touch of Brightness* and Asif Currimbhoy's *The Dumb Dancer* have successfully been staged in the West—a fact which has provoked the jealous ire of some of the supporters of Indian-language playwrights who have been complaining of the unfair advantage the medium of expression confers on the Indian playwright in English, conveniently forgetting the latter's plight in his own country.

This lack of opportunities to subject his plays to the acid test of a living theatre in his own country (an Indian play in English staged abroad may succeed simply as an exotic *tour de force*) has done incalculable harm to the art of the Indian dramatist in English. All too conscious as he is of the fact that his play is not going to be staged after all, he perhaps allows his dramatic vision to be insidiously warped in the embryo itself. The primrose path to artistic miscegenation is always inviting. This process is clearly seen at work in most of our verse plays. Denied the discipline of the theatre, the playwright in English is easily led to forget the vital distinction pointed out by T. S. Eliot [in his *The Three Voices of Poetry,* 1953] between the 'voice of the poet addressing an audience' which makes for dramatic poetry and the 'voice of the poet when he attempts to create a dramatic character speaking in verse', which constitutes genuine poetic drama. It is precisely the blurring of this essential difference that has made most of Harindranath Chattopadhyaya's verse plays like *Eknath* and *Tukaram* dramatic poetry and not authentic verse drama. T. P. Kailasam is similarly carried away by the temptation to poetize, though he had actually a far better command of the dramatic medium.

It is also significant that Kailasam and Sri Aurobindo invariably cast their full-length plays in the age-old Shakespearian mould, without at all pondering whether the form was still artistically viable in the modern context. A parallel that comes immediately to mind is that of the Romantic and Victorian poets who copied the Shakespearian verse play with similar results. It was only by discarding the Shakespearian framework that Eliot and Fry were able to give a new lease of life to stageworthy verse drama. It is arguable that an original mind like Sri Aurobindo and an inventive one like Kailasam would perhaps have consciously tried to evolve a new dramatic form in keeping with the Indian ethos, instead of borrowing the ready-made Shakespearian one, if only they could have written English plays for being actually staged and not for being simply read.

As for prose drama, the case of Currimbhoy shows how the continued lack of the discipline of the living theatre corrupts even genuine dramatic talent and corrupts it absolutely. His recent play, *Om Mane Padme Hum* (1972) should be a veritable nightmare to any producer, howsoever resourceful; it might well defeat even a combined team of Stanislavsky, Gordon Craig and Jean-Louis Barrault. Within its limited range of two Acts, the play involves innumerable changes of scene within single scenes (there are as many as eighteen in Act I, scene i); there are a number of flash-backs and dream-sequences; and some scenes, as the playwright himself points out, 'need screen shots', for example, 'scenes of the torrid rivers being crossed' 'a few thousand Chinese troops entering', etc. Finally, there are two scenes which will create dramatic history if the play is ever staged; the first actually shows the copulation between a 'beautiful aristocratic lady' and a 'huge hairy monkey' and the second, the dismembering of a dead body 'completely, limb by limb, into small pieces'. In his introduction to the play, Faubion Bowers remarks, 'Currimbhoy has let his mind run riot over the stage.' One wishes the playwright had been more concerned with making it possible for his characters to present a viable dramatic experience through the spoken word. Currimbhoy has certainly done this in his earlier plays, which show commendable respect for the actual requirements of the theatre. In his *Doldrummers* (1960) and *Goa* (1964), the setting remains the same throughout; and in *The Dumb Dancer* (1961) the flashback is used sparingly and theatrical experimentation is well within the bounds of possibility. These plays have been successfully staged both here and abroad. It is in his recent plays like *Darjeeling Tea* (1971), *Sonar Bangla* (1972), etc., that Currimbhoy has recklessly been subjecting the dramatic art to a strain it cannot bear. It is possible to suggest that this playwright's development would perhaps have been in the direction of more viable drama, had his plays been staged regularly.

The *cri de coeur* of the playwright in English could thus be: 'A theatre! A theatre! My life for a theatre!' As K. R. Srinivasa Iyengar points out [in his 'Drama in Modern English,' in *Drama in Modern Indian and the Writer's Responsibility in a Rapidly Changing World,* 1961], 'There must be numberless . . . plays and playlets written with a view to being only read, and hence either unpublished or buried in second-hand book-stalls or in old or defunct magazines and newspapers.' R. K. Narayan's play, *The Watchman of the Lake,* first published in 1940, is a glaring example. And if this is the case with a reputed author, one can imagine the plight of playwrights in English who are still-born for want of a theatre.

But the playwright in English cannot conveniently escape censure by laying all the blame for his lack of solid achievement upon the theatre that could not be. He himself is equally to blame in his own artistic practice. It is a shocking fact that he has mostly written as if he belonged to a race which has never had any dramatic traditions worth the name, and must therefore solely ape the West. Actually what a rich and varied dramatic tradition he can draw upon! Drama was the 'fifth *Veda*' for the ancient Hindus, and Indian classical drama which flourished for ten centuries and more can safely challenge comparison with its counterparts anywhere in the world. And even when this tradition was broken after the Muslim invasion, it did not die but was absorbed into folk forms in several Indian languages actually gaining fresh vitality in the process, by drawing closer to the common man. Thus arose folk forms like *Fatra* and *Navtanki* in Bengal; *Bhand Fashn* in Kashmir; *Rasadhari* plays in Mathura; *Ramalila* in northern India; *Bhavai* in Gujarat; *Lalita, Khele, Dashavtar* and *Tamasha* in Maharashtra; *Yakshagana, Bayalata, Attadata, Doddata* and *Sannata* in Karnataka; *Veedhi-natakam* in Andhra Pradesh; and the *Kutiyattam, Mohiniattam* and *Kathakali* dance dramas in Kerala. It is, of course, true that these popular forms remained mostly in an oral tradition and that when drama began to be written in the modern Indian languages after the establishment of British rule, the model was not this folk tradition but first Shakespeare and then Ibsen and Shaw, just as it is now Brecht and the Absurd drama. But during recent years vernacular Indian drama has been increasingly turning to folk forms and tapping their springs of vitality with splendid results. Girish Karnad's use of the *Yakshagana* in the Kannada play, *Hayavadana* and Vijay Tendulkar's of *Dashavatar* and *Khele* techniques in the Marathi play, *Ghashiram Kotwal;* the adaptation of *Bhavai* in two Gujarati plays—Dina Gandhi's *Mena Gurjari* and Bakul Tripathi's *Leela;* the employment of the *Fatra* motif in Utpal Dutt's *Fokumareswara* and Badal Sarcar's *Evam Indrajit;* and Habib Tanvir's presentation of *The Little Clay Cart* in a neo-*Navtanki* style, etc., are prominent recent examples. An American dramatic critic who recently visited India has said that 'At the moment, the vitality and independence of India's folk theatre exceeds that of any other in Asia.'

Unfortunately, the dramatist in English has seldom thought of experimenting in this direction, and when he has occasionally tried to do so, he has only been guilty of using these traditional elements as little more than clever and exotic gimmicks which can be depended upon to impress a gullible foreign audience which has no familiarity with the genuine article. The *Kathakali* Dancer and 'The Self-Whipper and his Drummer' in Partap Sharma's *The Professor Has a War Cry* (1970), for instance, add nothing substantial to the content of the play, except providing some rather confused symbolism. The *Kathakali* dance is far more central to Currimbhoy's *The Dumb Dancer* (1961) where the dancer protagonist has played Bhima's role so conscientiously that he has come to identify himself with the Pandava prince, thus becoming a split personality. But here again, the playwright's passion for sheer technical virtuosity has led him to neglect the basic dramatic values to the detriment of a potentially rich artistic conception. The playwright in English has thus failed to enter into the spirit of these folk forms, while his counterpart in the Indian languages has succeeded and secured vital artistic leverage. This failure is all the more galling, since modern African playwrights writing in English have already shown the way to success. As Efna Sutherland, the Ghanaian playwright who has successfully used traditional African forms like the *Anansi* folk tale in writing plays in English, observes, 'In order for African drama to be valid, it has to derive lots of its impetus, its strength from traditional African forms . . . because they exist. What we must do is to find out what they are, and how we can use them.' [quoted by Ama Ata Aidoo in *African Writers Talking,* 1972.]

It is, however, hardly fair to blame the playwrights alone for this failure. Earlier playwrights are tarred with the same brush. Surprisingly enough, though firmly grounded in the Indian tradition, Sri Aurobindo and Kailasam never seem to have attempted drawing upon either the Sanskrit or the folk modes, even in plays in which the setting and the characters were drawn from classical times. Their model, as noted earlier, was Shakespeare and not Kalidasa; and the history of English verse drama has always shown that no post-Shakespearian playwright who has modelled himself on Shakespeare can escape the transformation of his still small artistic voice into an echo. Most Indian verse drama in English is a vast whispering gallery of Shakespearian echoes. For instance when Polydaon in Sri Aurobindo's *Perseus the Deliverer* goes mad after his downfall and starts raving, Shakespeare seems to take over, for Polydaon's ravings clearly recall those of Lear. When, in the same play, Smerdas the merchant cries, 'I have eaten/An drunk of terror', one immediately recognizes Macbeth's voice here (cf. 'I've supped full with horrors'). Similarly, when Kailasam's Karna, in the play *The Curse,* lies dying, the spirit of the typical Shakespearian tragic hero hovers unmistakably over him. In the context of these examples, the confession (accompanied by a warning to younger playwrights) recently made by Adya Rangacharya [in 'Classical Indian Drama and Modern Indian Theatre,' in *Indian Drama,* 1974] one of the pioneers of the modern drama in Kannada, makes very significant reading:

> I was one of those who first opened the doors of the Indian theatre closed for centuries. In my enjoyment of the fresh breeze that suddenly started blowing in from the West, I forgot that the breeze could give me only fresh energy. Unthinkingly, we opened our theatre and bewitched by the breeze we forgot it and just walked over to the Western theatre. It would make me happy if youngsters learn from our mistakes. . . . My plea to lovers of modern Indian drama is first, to study classical Indian drama and make a reassessment of it.

This advice is even more relevant to the situation of the playwright in English than it is to that of his counterpart in the Indian languages.

In addition to the failure to exploit the potentialities of traditional Indian dramatic modes, there is also the equally disastrous failure to make creative use of the rich fund of myth which our tradition readily affords to any modern Indian writer. T. S. Eliot breathed new life into the moribund verse play by going back to ancient Greek myths and boldly transporting the Eumenides to a country-house in North England, inviting Hercules to a cocktail party in London, and transforming Ion into an English confidential clerk, and Oedipus into a British elder statesman. The artistic advantage of running 'a continuous parallel between antiquity and contemporaneity' and thus administering a shock of recognition which reveals the modern human condition is abundantly available to the Indian playwright in English; but he does not seem to have made full use of this potent artistic strategy. Kailasam no doubt chose his subjects from *The Ramayana* and *The Mahabharata,* and was even daringly iconoclastic in his treatment of traditional figures like Arjuna and Keechaka. Thus, in *The Purpose,* he boldly presents Arjuna not as the perfect archer of legend, but as an indifferent one, and extremely selfish as a man. Similarly, his Keechaka in the play by the same name is not the villain of tradition but a brave hero genuinely in love with Draupadi. But in spite of this, Kailasam remained content with only limited innovation and never progressed further in the much more challenging direction of harnessing ancient myth and legend to a revelation of contemporary life. A comparison between his *Keechaka* and K. P. Khadilkar's Marathi play, *Keechaka-vadha* (1907) is highly revealing. Khadilkar successfully makes the Keechaka story a political allegory of the days of the partition of Bengal during the British regime, and his Keechaka stands for Lord Curzon, then Viceroy of India. This adds a new dimension to the old legend. No playwright in English appears to have used this technique on an extensive scale. (Gopal Sharman, who in his *Ramayana* makes some attempt to do so, is a possible exception.)

If the playwright in English has neglected myth, he has likewise failed to make full creative use of his extremely complex historical heritage. In spite of his penchant to ape his Western masters, he has conveniently forgotten how effectively Anouilh, Fry, Robert Bolt and others have used historical material for modern drama. There are of course isolated exceptions like Gurcharan Das' *Larins Sahib,* Lakhan Deb's *Tiger Claws* and Dilip Hiro's *To Anchor a Cloud;* but there has been no regular school of plays of this type. Our most prolific playwright, Asif Currimbhoy, is seen to be more busy with current politics in plays like *Inquilab, Sonar Bangla* and *Om Mane Padme Hum* than with ancient history, except in that ambitious but rather amorphous experiment, *Om.*

One major hurdle which the playwright in English is supposed to encounter is that of language. It is often said that we have so few actable English plays because a dialogue in English between Indians will not sound convincing except when the characters are drawn from an urban, sophisticated milieu, or are actually Anglo-Indians, whose mother tongue is (supposed to be) English. Some playwrights have thus scrupulously confined themselves to the urban milieu, and have also taken an extremely limited view of the use of English by employing 'babu English' exclusively as a source of some rather cheap comedy. Dnyaneshwar Nadkarni is right when he complains [in his 'Butcher the Ando-Inglians' (*sic*) in *Enact,* 85-86 (January-February 1974)] that 'English as the non-Convent-trained people speak it in this non-English country has been made a thing to laugh at on the Indo-Anglian stage. . . . This is a shared snobbery between the playwright, the producer, and the audience.'

It will indeed be suicidal, if the playwright takes so narrow and short-sighted a view of the problem of a viable dialogue for his plays. Actually, the much-dreaded difficulty is more apparent than real. If Raja Rao can make a rustic Indian grandmother (in *Kanthapura*) talk in a kind of Indian English which recaptures the very feel of the soil—and that too not merely for superficially comic purposes—why should his counterpart in the theatre feel shy to emulate his example? When Shakespeare makes his Romans speak in Elizabethan English, we do not bat an eyelid; when Shaw's St Joan speaks in English, no one asks whether the French girl held a certificate of proficiency in that language; and when Brecht makes the good Woman of Setzuan express herself in German, we are not horrified. Nearer home, when a play about Krishna was written in any of the Indian languages (and there is hardly any Indian language without one) did either the playwright or the audience raise the question, whether the author of the *Gita* could possibly have used any of these Indian vernaculars? It would indeed be patently absurd to demand that all characters in Indian drama in English must, in order to qualify, produce a certificate that (a) English is their mother tongue or (b) they normally use it in their everyday social intercourse. As Dr Johnson has pointed out [in his 'Preface to Shakespeare,' in *Johnson on Shakespeare,*] 'The truth is that the spectators are always in their senses, and know from the first Act to the last, that the stage is only a stage and that the players are only players.' In making his Indian characters speak in English the playwright need therefore have no qualms at all. Let him first create living characters in live situations, and the language will take care of itself. Gurcharan Das has said [in an interview with R. Parthasarathy in *The Indian Express* (7 July 1973)] that 'The English theatre in India will have to project the kind of hybrid English we speak interspersed with Indian expressions. My approach is that the characters should speak the English that is spoken in India, using expressions like *'Kya yar'*, *'Chalo'*, *'Bhai'*. And actors can bring about a revolution in spoken English.' That is one way, and there may be other and more subtle ways also like that of Narayan's fiction to impart an Indian flavour to a dialogue in English.

The actual achievement of Indian drama in English has thus remained poor so far owing to numerous reasons. But this does not mean that this kind of drama has no future at all, though many in India seem to be convinced that it is a hot-house plant which cannot survive long. In a recently held National Seminar on Drama, several participants were of the view that the 'Indo-Anglian theatre had absolutely no relevance for India, and if not dead, should be so,' Dnyaneshwar Nadkarni, in a fit of righteous indignation, has even gone to the length of declaring: 'Butcher them (the Indo-Anglian playwrights), castrate them, and force them to write in their native Hindi or Urdu or whatever Indian languages their fathers and mothers used to speak.' Apart from the futility of performing the second and the impossibility of carrying out the third operation, after the playwrights writing in English have duly been butchered at the behest of this critic, surely the one thing Indian literature can certainly do without today is provincial little Herods. Actually, the playwright in English need not be a rival or an enemy of the playwrights in the Indian languages. He can learn much from them and can also contribute something distinctly his own. He can, however, do so only if he succeeds in overcoming the temptation to play to a foreign gallery by concocting fake orientalism; the greater temptation to bedeck himself with sundry plumes stolen from Brecht and Beckett; and the greatest temptation of all—which is 'the greatest treason'—to turn into a literary snob whose spiritual home is the modern wasteland of Europe and who, therefore can have no roots in his own culture. Given these conditions and given a theatre, there is no reason why we should not have a school of genuine and worthwhile Indian drama in English.

Fanciful as it may superficially sound, the playwright in English is, in many ways, virtually in the same position as the Sanskrit playwright of classical times. Ancient Sanskrit drama had a limited appeal to a circle of the cultivated. [A. B. Keith in his *Sanskrit Drama* (1924) maintains that] 'Such an audience, however, acted as a stimulus to refinement and elaboration.' Again, it used a language which was not a 'normal living language', thus providing unlimited scope for experimentation with words. The audience of the playwright in English is also restricted, and English is not a 'normal living language' in India. It is for the playwright in English to make fruitful use of these conditions in the manner of his ancient forbears, turning his professional limitations into artistic assets. When he does so, the jesting critical Pilates who now ask 'What achievement?' will have to stay for an answer.

M. K. Naik, "The Achievement of Indian Drama in English," in Perspectives on Indian Drama in English, *edited by M. K. Naik and S. Mokashi-Punekar, Oxford University Press, 1977, pp. 180-94.*

CRITICAL PERSPECTIVES ON INDO-ENGLISH LITERATURE

Feroza F. Jussawalla

[*In the following excerpt, Jussawalla surveys the criticism generated by Indian writing in English.*]

In 1833, two years before T. B. Macaulay introduced his famous minute on English education in India (1835), Raja Rammohun Roy, the first of Indian writers in English, died in Bristol. Amongst all the other historical implications of Macaulay's minute lies the fact that it gave birth to a plethora of literary activity in English as also the critical activity about the use of English by Indians. It was Macaulay who recognized that English could be learned quickly and learned well in India:

> We have to educate a people who cannot at present be educated by means of their mother-tongue. We must teach them some foreign language. The claims of our own language it is hardly necessary to recapitulate. It stands pre-eminent even among the languages of the west. . . . In India English is the language spoken by the ruling class. It is spoken by the higher class of natives at the seat of government. It is likely to become the language of commerce throughout the seas of the East. . . .

He praised the English competence of the people he knew:

> There are in this very town [London] natives who are quite competent to discuss political or scientific questions with fluency and precision in the English language. I have heard the very question on which I am now writing discussed by the native gentlemen with a liberality and an intelligence which would do credit to any member of the Committee of Public Instruction.

However this opinion is taken, whether as the patronizing amazement of the British at the Indians' English language ability or as genuine admiration and encouragement, Macaulay's statement can be considered the first critical opinion on the use of English by Indians.

Before Macaulay, Christian missionaries had been teaching English in schools and colleges around the country. Indians on their part were eager to obtain a Western education and to link their countrymen with the changing world. This Westernization led to two ironies. In Bengal, the English learned led to a flurry of literary activity that developed into the Bengal Renaissance. Christian missionaries' efforts at translation and the codification of the Indian languages led to the vernacularization of English, as it began to absorb vocabulary and rhythms from the vernaculars. This fact of the natural Indianization of English was soon to become an important part of the criticism of Indian Writing in English. The biggest irony, however, was the impetus to creativity in English. By the early part of the nineteenth century, Indian literary activity in English had already begun. Henry Derozio (1809-1831), Kashiprosad Ghose (1809-1873), Michael Madhusudan Dutt (1827-1873) and Bankim Chandra Chatterjee (1838-1894) were some of the early Indians to use English for their creative and social purposes. By the latter half of the nineteenth century educated Indians were using English for all purposes from mundane government work to poetry.

Yet, just as the government work was modeled on the British patterns, Indians modeled their poetry on that of the British. The poetry that flourished closely imitated Victorian poetry in form, and Indian subject matter was often tortured into fitting this form. Romesh Chunder Dutt (1848-1909), for instance, took to translating the *Ramayana* convinced that the meter of "Locksley Hall" was particularly well suited to this purpose. The moulds for future Indian-English literature were beginning to set—imitation was soon to become an important method for Indian writers in English. Cousins of Romesh Chunder Dutt, Aru and Toru Dutt were educated in European girls' schools. The sisters started with writing English sonnets and translating French lyrics into English. After Aru's death, Toru collected their poems in a volume entitled *A Sheaf Gleaned in French Fields.* In 1875, in an attempt to turn back to her native traditions, Toru Dutt began to learn Sanskrit. By 1882 she published a translation of tales from the *Ramayana* and *Mahabharata* entitled *Ancient Ballads and Legends of Hindustan.*

Aru and Toru Dutt are also considered the first of expatriate Indian writers who expressed some alienation from India. After all, they had started with the typically Indian disdain of things Indian and began their literary efforts in a European mode. On their return to India after their schooling they yearned for "the free air of Europe, and the free life there." Their poetry, whose audience at this time was certainly Western or the small handful of English-speaking Indians, was very well received by the British critics. According to H.A.L. Fisher, it was by force of "native genius" that Toru Dutt was to be "enrolled in the great fellowship of English poets." Yet from the tone of the criticism, it seems that the British critic was responding to the curious fact of a native Indian writing poetry in English more than to the quality of the poetry.

Professor C. D. Narasimhaiah, one of the critics of Indian Writing in English who has written about the Dutts, documents Edmund Gosse's reaction to the Dutts' *Sheaf Gleaned in French Fields.* Gosse records that one day in 1876 while he was in the office of Professor Minto, editor of *The Examiner,* a book arrived for review with a "wonderful little postmark on it."

> This shabby little book of some two hundred pages, without preface or introduction, seemed especially destined by its particular providence to find its way hastily into the waste-paper basket. . . . A hopeless volume it seemed, with its queer type, published at Bhowanipore, printed at the Sapthikasambad press! But when at last, I took it out of my pocket, what was my surprise and almost rapture to open such verse as this. . . . When poetry is as good as this it does not matter whether Rouveyre prints it upon Whatman paper, or whether it steals to light in blurred type from some press in Bhowanipore. [Quoted by C. D. Narasimhaiah in *Awakened Conscience: Studies in Commonwealth Literature,* 1968.]

Gosse was praising verse which imitated Cowper, who himself would not be ranked among the best English poets. Behind the acceptance seemed to be a desire to support even the manifestation of an ability on the part of an Indian to compose poetry in English.

The mere acceptance of poetry by Indians simply because it was written in English existed even before Gosse's review of Toru Dutt's book. D. L. Richardson wrote about Kashiprasad Ghose's collection of verse in *The Literary Gazette* of November 1, 1834, "Let some of those narrow-minded persons who are in the habit of looking down on the natives of India with arrogant and vulgar contempt read this little poem and ask themselves—could they write better verses not in a foreign tongue but their own?" This early criticism of Indian literature in English marks some of the trends that have persisted in the literature and its criticism.

Two major habits that were pressed upon the Indian authors were the forcing of Indian subject matter into European forms and the imitation of the trendiest of these European forms. The literature was already responding to the criticism. In addition, the audience was seen as an European audience hungry for an oriental element in their lives. The exoticism of Indian myth and culture was soon to be exploited even further. As they met with critical acclaim abroad, Indian writers seemed to be writing for the Western critics who were amazed and patronizing of their achievements. Much of that amazement resulted from what seemed to be wonder at the ability of these writers to write in English, a second language, and at their ability to use the European forms of poetry and later, the novel. At the same time, Indian writers themselves manifested an ambiguity towards their Indian roots. Aru and Toru Dutt had seen themselves as fortunate to know and use European languages. The questions of nationalism versus alienation became inextricably linked both with the development of the literature and its criticism.

In the twentieth century as British and Indian critics began to evaluate the literature written in English, a major critical question was forced to the forefront. Should, and indeed *could,* Indians use the English language for creative purposes?

In his introduction to Rabindranath Tagore's *Gitanjali* (1913), translated from the Bengali by the author himself, Yeats wrote:

> I have carried the manuscript of these translations with me for days, reading it in railway trains, or on top of omnibuses and in restaurants

and I have often had to close it lest some stranger should see how much it moved me.

But when Tagore started writing poetry in English, Yeats reacted to the sentimentality in his style. In 1935, he lamented in a letter to William Rothenstein:

> Damn Tagore, we got three good books and because he thought it more important to see and know English than to be a great poet he brought off sentimental rubbish. No Indian knows English. Nobody can write music and style in a language which is not their own . . . [reproduced in *The Letters of W. B. Yeats,* 1955].

This dictum, coming from Yeats, the Irish poet writing in English, became a significant issue both in the formulation of Indian writing in English and in its criticism.

The theme of whether Indians can use English and whether their style should be shaped by the usage they admired—that of the British and at that time, of "Burke, Sheridan, Disraeli, Gladstone and Macaulay"—is a question that has continually occupied critics of Indian Literature in English. This question pervades Professor Narasimhaiah's criticisms of the individual writers he brings together in *The Swan and the Eagle* (1969) which together with Professor K. R. Srinivasa Iyengar's *Indian Writing in English* (1962; revised 1973) was one of the major and influential critical works on Indian Writing in English:

> Now what holds writers so divergent as those whose work is examined here, together? First and foremost, their writing is the expression of a distinct, identifiable sensibility *which is Indian, and the language, foreign in the sense that it is not picked up on the mother's lap but learnt assiduously by a most sensitive exposure to its practitioners* in a wide-ranging variety of speech and writing in India and abroad. (italics mine)

But then, Professor Narasimhaiah states that he does not have time for "such futile and fatuous questions as: Can Indians write in English? Or what future has English as a medium for creative activity in India?" Yet, he spends the entire introductory chapter defending Indian writing in English against these very same questions. His treatment of the early Indian writers—Sarojini Naidu, Toru Dutt, Aurobindo, among others—is concerned with keeping them from being "dubbed exiles in their own country" and with showing their greatness, in spite of their "Georgian effusions."

Additionally, in *The Swan and the Eagle,* Professor Narasimhaiah is also preoccupied with establishing Indian writing in English as an "Indian" endeavor, and an endeavor of quality. Before him, Professor K. R. Srinivasa Iyengar in his monumental history, *Indian Writing in English,* had also pleaded for the literature to be given "a dog's chance at least!"

> The Indian critic should make allowances, be satisfied with what appears rather less than the whole arc of the Indian way of artistic expression; and the English critic too should make allowances and be prepared for surprises, elaborations, and seemingly strange similitudes.

Professor Iyengar has been condemned by a new generation of critics and writers for his inability to establish critical standards for Indian writing in English. And, for the early Indian writing in English there was indeed a lack of critical discrimination. For instance, R. K. Narayan (1907—) received a generally subjective and impressionistic criticism which emerged from the assumptions that had already been developed. Critics thought that Indian literature in English would be best if it could be cultivated within British patterns by those educated abroad so that their English language-use conformed with British /American norms.

Some of the above-mentioned attitudes of the Indian critic can be seen in Professor Narasimhaiah's record of his own early response to Narayan. This record is interesting in showing the prejudices implied in the Indian critical response to literature written by Indians in English:

> I was surprised, because of their otherwise inclusiveness, to find myself endorsing fully the reviewers' first flush of enthusiasm for *a novel by an entirely unknown quantity from colonial India. All the more surprising when one realized that R. K. Narayan has not been educated in any of the older or the more modern redbrick universities of England or America,* no, not so much as visited them until 1951, and, I believe, had scarcely left South India; *had learnt English mostly from Indian teachers, themselves ill-equipped for their calling; spoke Tamil at home, a sort of Kannada in the streets* and English with a South-Indian accent in educated circles; did not pass examinations at school or college with any credit to himself or the institutions which are now seen contending to own him as their product. (italics mine)

Some of the critical prejudices revealed in Professor Narasimhaiah's evaluation of Narayan are: 1) the literature could not be any good if it did not imitate what was produced abroad; 2) it could not be any good if it was written in English by someone who had not been abroad—implicit in this is the judgment that Indians could not use English effectively by themselves; 3) the writer could not produce great literature if he was not concerned with "the profounder" issues which could range anywhere from Indianizing English, to expressing Indian philosophical problems, to dealing with the current nationalistic issues. The denigration of Narayan on this score comes through again as Professor Narasimhaiah describes Narayan's simple style:

> It suited Narayan's shy temperament to withdraw from these serious questions and concern himself with mediocrity—like the sun it shines everywhere and [is] easy to exploit by one whose gifts for it were unquestionable.

This assessment of Narayan by Professor Narasimhaiah reveals the criticism of Indian literature in English taking two rather complicated forms. Indian critics, though willing to accept encouraging Western opinion, felt that Indian literature should be patterned after British literature. At the same time, Indians should attempt to make the English language their own. For, nationalist criticism indicated that the Indians should shake off this yoke of imperialism, but if it could not be thrown off, it should be incorporated into Indian nationalism. Those who persisted in writing literature in English, particularly in what seemed to be an unvaried English, were seen as alienated, and their perspective on India was considered suspect.

Another twist to this already complicated situation developed when critics attempted to show the Indianness of those writers who were considered alienated. For example, the generation of critics after Narasimhaiah immediately began an attempt to show that writers writing in English, albeit not a "redbrick English," were indeed Indian and nationalist.

Mrs. Mukherjee, for instance, attempted in her *The Twice Born Fiction* (1971) to describe the *Indianness* of Narayan's fiction. The form and technique of Narayan's novels she felt was much more closely rooted in Indian myths—a pattern of order-disorder-order, "the familiar pattern of the tale from the *Puranas* where a demon gets too powerful, threatens the heavens with his elemental forces of disorder, but finally goes up in the air like a bubble in the sea, leaving the universe as calm as before." She illustrated this Indianness particularly with *The Man-eater of Malgudi* where the character of the taxidermist Vasu is that archtypical rakshasa bringing disorder, and the theme plays on the alternating dance of order and disorder.

Having established the Indianness of theme in Narayan, Mrs. Mukherjee shows that Narayan's simple, unobtrusive style is part of his vision which encompasses the common Indian man in the street and in this she establishes the Indianness of his style. His style creates the character and the environment of the particular locale it describes. In this it is integral to that Indian locale. By contrast she shows that most other efforts to convey Indianness through stylistic experimentation remain "icing on a cake or embroidery on a sari."

Mrs. Mukherjee sees that the paradox which characterizes Indo-Anglian fiction is that, with perhaps the single exception of Narayan, most Indian novelists are "constantly aiming at an Indianness bereft of temporal and spatial values." This is perhaps the direct result of a criticism that calls for writers to be preoccupied not just with the "large" issues of life, but with "Indian" issues, particularly those of language. Mrs. Mukherjee does not equate the creation of an "Indian English" with Indianness. She concludes as follows:

> The future of Indo-Anglian fiction seems to lie in the direction of further authenticity through exploiting the particular, local and regional reality—without, of course, the calculated 'documentation' or 'explanation'—rather than through that straining to find another of the very few available 'all-India' themes.

She urges the Indian writer in English "to grapple with the particular, the concrete and the immediate."

Contrarily, another type of critical opinion, also exemplified by the treatment of Narayan, is embodied in Uma Parameswaran's *A Study of Representative Indo-English Novelists* (1976). Uma Parameswaran focuses on South In-

dian writers, whose representativeness remains obscure. Through an introductory, expository approach, she intends to show that Raja Rao is the "excelsior" of Indian fiction in English and that Narayan has been awarded indiscriminate admiration. This indiscriminate admiration she feels is one of the faults of Indian criticism in English that arises from an inability to be critical because of an effort to establish a national identity. At the same time that she rejects Narayan's focus on the ordinary Indian man, she praises him for creating Malgudi in concrete particulars, ignoring that what makes Malgudi real is the "national identity" of the characters who people it. She faults Narayan's treatment of Gandhi in *Waiting for the Mahatma* for not being nationalistic enough and favors Raja Rao's *Kanthapura*.

The varying attitudes expressed in the criticism of R. K. Narayan exemplify in small part the failure of the criticism of Indian Writing in English to look at a writer and his art in the context of his milieu. Various labels had been used to describe Narayan—the Indian Jane Austen or the Indian Chekhov—but Narayan is in a class all his own, combining the skills of those two literary giants and at the same time creating his own fictional world. Through his career of over fifty years Malgudi town has grown as familiar to Narayan's readers as Yoknapatawpha county is to Faulkner's. From *Swami and Friends* (1935) to *The Painter of Signs* (1976) and *A Tiger for Malgudi* (1983), readers around the world have lived with the characters from Malgudi, felt with them, and seen the history of India evolve from the coming of Gandhism (*Waiting for the Mahatma,* 1950) to the coming of "American ways" (*The Vendor of Sweets,* 1967). His best-known work *The Guide* (1958) was made into both a movie and an unsuccessful Broadway production—both versions disliked by Narayan himself.

Narayan's choice of language is straightforward, traditional English. English for him is a tool for the man who can use it. Contrary to other Indian writers, Narayan has always felt that English was a very adaptable language—"it is so transparent it can take on the tint of any country" [quoted in *R. K. Narayan,* 1973]. Narayan's descriptions of South Indian life come through with an effectiveness that would make any effort to convey such an essence through language variations superfluous, for they are just descriptions of universal moments that occur in a specific context.

Narayan is probably the only Indian writer writing in English who has successfully avoided the self-consciousness implicit in the situation of being an Indian writer writing in English. He successfully resisted the attempt to shape his writing according to the criticism as it was developing later or according to current literary fashions and fortunately did not let criticism affect its course. The example of his critical treatment shows that the criticism of Indian Writing in English was not concerned with the artistic quality, the permanence or the "morality" (as John Gardner would call it), of the work in question.

What Uma Parameswaran praises in Raja Rao as truly nationalistic was Raja Rao's early response to the call to make the English language one's own—the effort to Indianize English. Mindful of the nationalism at home and of the general call to ban English from their daily lives, most Indian writers, whose only medium of expression in some cases may have been English, responded with efforts to Indianize the English language. Raja Rao was one of these.

In 1938, Raja Rao (1909—) wrote his now familiar foreword to his novel *Kanthapura* expressing precisely the problem of writing in English:

> The telling has not been easy. One has to convey in a language that is not one's own the spirit that is one's own. One has to convey the various shades and omissions of certain thought-movement that looks maltreated in an alien language. I use the word "alien," yet English is not really an alien language to us. It is the language of our intellectual make-up—like Sanskrit or Persian was before—but not of our emotional make up. We are all instinctively bilingual, many of us writing in our own language and in English. We cannot write like the English. We should not. We cannot write only as Indians. We have grown to look at the large world as part of us. Our method of expression therefore has to be a dialect which will someday prove to be as distinctive or as colorful as the Irish or the American. Time alone will justify it.

In *Kanthapura,* an oral tale told by an old crone of the coming of Gandhism to her village, Rao attempted to capture the rhythms of Indian speech in English. Told in the lyrical, lilting voice of the village crone, *Kanthapura* gave the English language a new rhythm, so skillfully developed that it seems to have been a unique achievement in Indian literature in English. Raja Rao's two other novels, *The Serpent and the Rope* (1960) and *The Cat and Shakespeare* (1965), both resort to conventional English, varied only for dialogue. But *Kanthapura* set the tone for several attempts to Indianize English and seemed to become for the critics a touchstone by which to judge the use of the English language.

G. V. Desani's (1909—) *All About H. Hatterr* (1948) manifests a deliberate attempt to capture Indian English and follows as perhaps the next most important work in the trend towards Indianizing English. It is much less successful than *Kanthapura* and comes off as "mumbo-jumbo" almost impossible for most readers to read. In part the language is meant to fit the character of H. Hatterr, who is of mixed blood and mixed cultural backgrounds. As Anthony Burgess wrote in the introduction to the 1970 Bodley Head re-issue, "it is the language that makes the book, a sort of creative chaos that grumbles at the restraining banks." Burgess makes a comparison with the language of Joyce. In fact, both in the language and in the rambling "stream of consciousness" technique of the novel, the influence of Joyce is evident. However, Desani does not transcend stylistic imitation. It is no puzzle that, as Burgess observed, the book went underground and became a "coterie pleasure." The language itself becomes an obstacle for readers both in India and abroad. But in the very fact that it was a Joycean imitation and a variation of the Indian language, the book was considered a 'tour-de-force' by Indian critics. Indian subject matter was being

forced into the trendiest European forms in this imitation of European models.

Mulk Raj Anand's (1905–) friends among the Bloomsbury intellectuals saw in him quite early the effort at language variation. Anand began his career by attempting a Joycean stream-of-consciousness "tract" written in a Tagorean manner! In "Why I Write?" [from *Indo-English Literature,* 1977] he describes his first attempt:

> I wrote the story ["The Lost Child"] in the early hours of the morning, in my room in Trinity College, Cambridge, facing the Backs. I read it to a friend next morning, with native Punjabi enthusiasm, but "Mr. Shivaramakrishna" was a South Indian cynic and condemned it out of hand as "Tagorian sing-song rubbish".
>
> As I had used many onomatopoetic words in this prose narrative, I felt that his verdict may be correct.

Anand got the same reaction from his Bloomsbury friends when he read them his confessional narrative turned into a novel about Bakha, the untouchable:

> they felt that I had borrowed the technique of word-coinage from James Joyce's *Ulysses* and made the narrative rather literary, and that the novel was a prose form, not an epic poem like Milton's *Paradise Lost.* Only one thing they liked about my fictional narrative: that it faced the poverty, the dirt and squalor of the "lower depths" even more than Gorky had done. And I was confirmed in my hunch that, unlike Virginia Woolf, the novelist must confront the total reality, including its sordidness, if one was to survive in the world of tragic contrasts between the "exalted and noble" vision of the blind bard Milton and the eyes dimmed with tears of the many mute Miltons.

The Untouchable (1935) became the first of a trilogy which included *Coolie* (1936) and *Two Leaves and a Bud* (1937) and moved away from Joycean word-coinage in an attempt to realistically portray the milieu of the untouchable and consequently, Indian-English speech. Anand's answer to critics who sought to nationalize English seemed to be realism: capturing the "higgledy-piggledy" English mixed with Indian languages as spoken in the Indian streets. This style has often been misinterpreted as relying not on the realistic portrayal of the language as Anand heard it but on stylized transliteration and coinages. Anand himself has refuted this charge in his essay "Pigeon-Indian: Some Notes on Indian-English Writing" [in *Aspects of Indian Writing in English,* 1979]. Realism had become Anand's hallmark and he espoused it steadfastly. In a succession of works, he remained consistent in his portrayal of the wronged poor: *The Village* (1939), *Across the Black Waters* (1940), *The Barber's Trade Union and Other Stories* (1944), *The Big Heart* (1948), *Seven Summers* (1951), *The Old Woman and the Cow* (1960), *The Road* (1961), *Morning Face* (1968). Eventually his realism aided the development of a style suitable to portray his characters. Anand had begun to use an English generously sprinkled with Indian words.

Yet Anand's efforts to make English his own did not meet with the critical approval that Rao's efforts did. Mrs. Mukherjee dismisses his style in *The Twice Born Fiction* as does C. Paul Verghese in his *Problems of the Indian Creative Writer in English* (1970). Professor Verghese labels Mulk Raj Anand's adapting of English to portray the vernacular as a "drawback." He sees Anand's attempt to evolve an Indian English as a "vulgarisation" (Verghese's word) of English words into words like "vagabondizing" (Anand's word) or into coinages like "gooder"! He concludes then:

> Anand's practice of indiscriminate use of Hindi words and of the vulgarisation of English words does not create the illusion of reality he aims at for the simple reason that the dialogue itself is in English and that it is known that the villagers and coolies cannot speak English. This device will be successful and have a humorous effect in a regional language novel in which all the characters speak their own mother-tongue. An Indian novelist in English should employ his skill in *contriving* a dialogue that is at once natural and lively, supple and functional. He may even catch the speech rhythms and the turns of phrases used by all kinds of people in the village and translate some of the abuse, curses, imprecations and proverbs to advantage. (italics mine)

What we see here is not a description of the problems of the Indian creative writer in English, but an enactment of the prejudices of the Indian critic of creative writing in English by Indians. While they wish the Indian writer to nationalize English, they wish him to create a *new* vernacular rather than portray the existing one which would only reinforce the Western prejudice that Indians in general do not use English well. Again, the last sentence quoted wants the writer to follow the Raja Rao mode. This is another vivid example of the family quarrel between the critics and the writers.

Much of the dichotomy of the critical response to Indian literature in English is intensified in the quarrel over the more recent and new writers, both poets and novelists. Critics seem not to have known what to do with Kamala Markandaya, (1924—) for example, who wrote with solid command of the English language. And this is what on the one hand critics had wanted, someone who could use the English language as the British would. But then, could this be a sign of alienation? After all, should she not then follow the current mode in modernist British fiction or in nationalist Indian fiction to be experimental stylistically? Her situation is particularly disconcerting. Married to an Englishman, she wrote about India from abroad and with a perspective identified as Western. The themes in her fiction often depict the difference between the Eastern and Western views of life, as in *The Coffer Dams* (1969), and *Two Virgins* (1973). Even her earlier works, *Nectar in a Sieve* (1954), *Some Inner Fury* (1955), and *A Handful of Rice* (1966) describe India through Western eyes, while they remain essentially accurate portrayals of urban and rural poverty. Juxtaposed with the critical perspective of her as an alienated writer, as the Commonwealth writer overseas, Kamala Markandaya sees herself as having "the blessing and the bane of duality."

Markandaya's work, though, is seen by the critic C. Paul Verghese as the embodiment of another problem faced by the Indian creative writer: "The creation of an Indian Consciousness." For Verghese the problems of the Indian creative writer are the effort to portray a vision of India without seeming like a salesman of exotica, an effort to convey an Indian consciousness through English and an effort to portray a vision of life that expresses Indianness. The "Indian consciousness" is loosely defined:

> If by the term 'Indian consciousness' we mean the awareness that India historically has her own cultural identity, then to project the image of India not only means to transmit her own cultural identity, but also create an awareness of this identity in the minds of her own people and the rest of the world.

Through a study of the treatment of hunger and poverty, of village life and Indian society in the works of novelists such as Kamala Markandaya and Khushwant Singh, Verghese finds the Indian novelist lacking in the portrayal of the "Indian consciousness."

Such a criticism overlooks the fact that the social background of contemporary India emerges from two contrasting traditions—the Indian and the British. The contrast manifests itself also as the pull between tradition and modernity and often as the difference in perspective of expatriate writers and local writers. Kamala Markandaya, Balachandra Rajan, and Santha Rama Rao are some of the authors Mrs. Mukherjee discusses within this context of a dual tradition. The problem of alienation, expatriation, and Indianness is a major critical criterion that seems to have developed apropos the work of the writers just mentioned.

A writer who uses her double perspective on this mixed society deriving from two parent cultures as an arch perspective is Ruth Jhabvala (1927—), winner of both the Booker Prize and the MacArthur fellowship. Mrs. Jhabvala, in a career of about twenty years, developed while living in India, has continuously explored and described upper middle-class Indian life—particularly as she saw it in New Delhi. Her *Esmond in India* (1958) is almost an allegory for contemporary Indian civilization. Gulab, the Indian girl married to the Englishman Esmond, is an embodiment of India. Shakuntala, the young college girl with whom Esmond later develops a relationship, is the personification of the new India—modernized, sprightly and yearning for achievement—embarrassed by the slower and more traditional counterpart. Esmond, despite his knowledge of Indian culture, civilization and languages, remains the foreigner unable to understand the simultaneous existence of the modern and the traditional, attracted only to exoticism and unable to fit in. Mrs. Jhabvala seems to concede that such is the position of the foreigner in the levels of Indian society she explores. This experience is the exclusive metier of her ironic art, an achievement by a foreigner. Nationalistic critics and writers in India have rejected her because of her perspective on India. Nissim Ezekiel describes the reception of *Heat and Dust* (1976):

> Indian reviewers dwelt on the India of *Heat and Dust*, on the character of the Indian Nawab or

Prince who has an affair with the wife of a British Civil Servant stationed in his town, and on the explicit and implicit commentary on Indian mores as well as the Indian setting, things Indian generally. For them, there could be no separation between these and the quality of the novel, its authenticity, its literary authenticity. English reviewers seemed to ask only how such matters were used within the novel's pattern of events, what light they threw on the writer's perceptions of character and conduct. The intercultural encounter was secondary, minor and interesting but not in any way disturbing. *Heat and Dust* did not generate any heat or raise any dust in England. It did both in India, partly because of the Booker Prize which put on the novel the stamp of English approval, naturally without any concern for Indian sensibilities. The gulf between the two viewpoints seems unbridgeable. [From "Two Readers and Their Texts," in *Asian and Western Writers in Dialogue: New Cultural Identities,* 1982.]

The Indian critical response described here can perhaps be considered typical of the nationalist Indian critics who search for any indication to perpetuate a family quarrel.

Because of a newer critical emphasis on theme and subject matter, among the new generation of novelists the question is not "Should we use English?" or "How can we Indianize English?" but rather "How best can we use the English language to reflect our society and culture?" With the newer novelists, Manohar Malgonkar, Nayantara Sahgal and Anita Desai, experimentation focuses on form and structure but only if there can be an effective interweaving of subject matter. Manohar Malgonkar's novels include *Distant Drum* (1960), *Combat of Shadows* (1962), *The Princes* (1963), and *A Bend in the Ganges* (1964). Nayantara Sahgal's novels from *A Time to be Happy* (1957) to *Situation in New Delhi* (1977) reflect the changing political history of India from the independence movement to the present. Modernity versus tradition, an important theme in Sahgal's novels, permeates Anita Desai's fiction too. The novels of both take a metaphoric look at westernization, particularly its effects on traditional Indian women.

A recent, prominent Indian novel in English, Salman Rushdie's *Midnight's Children* (1981) expresses an alienation from contemporary, political India and concentrates heavily on stylistic innovation. *Midnight's Children* more than any other recent novel seems to respond too readily to criticism that calls continuously for stylistic imitation and innovation. Nayantara Sahgal, writing out of the 1975 period of "Emergency," adequately summed up the state of the Indian novel:

> There has been both experiment and achievement in Indian writing, and as far as English is concerned, some experimentation with the use of the language itself and the emergence of a "distinct Indian English." But the novelist has far to go in evoking and arousing feeling. Perhaps this is because the Indian has far to go in experience . . . the major part of the creative battle may yet be ahead. For the Indian writer must now come to grips with problems he has avoided. The present stifling situation may com-

pel him to define his values, desert the simple solution and the luxury of detachment, and bring Indian fiction into its maturity. [In "New Chapter for Indian Writers," *Far Eastern Economic Review* (August 20, 1976).]

To attain such a maturity a new criticism may very well have to emerge. It is not sufficient to develop a style that reflects the chaos of the political situation as Rushdie's work does. The message is lost in the stylistic mire. It is important for the criticism to shape a literature that both expresses its context and develops a viable language for the expression of this context.

Indian poetry in English contends with the same critical prejudices and subsequently the same problems of imitation and nationalism as does the fiction just described. There has been a resurgence of interest in writing poetry since the 1950s. P. Lal in 1951 published in the *The Sunday Standard* his credo for new poetry. This later reappeared as the introduction to *Modern Indo-Anglian Poetry* (1959) edited by himself and K. R. Rao. Lal wanted to move away from the vague, mystical, Tagorean poetry of spirituality. According to him poets ought to come to terms with "concrete images" and concrete experience and so he urged the development of the "private voice" and "realistic poetry." Even as late as 1968, Lal was re-echoing his attempt to get Indian writers to reject the examples of the past:

> By the "past's inadequacy and undependability", we meant largely the stilted Victorian poetic style of Sri Aurobindo, and the Romantic fireflies dancing through the *Neem* of Sarojini Naidu. . . . Tagore himself was not unguilty of allowing the soft-scented, Pre-Raphelite lilies of the English *Gitanjali* to circulate among Georgian and Edwardian readers as samples of the East's mystic incense. *No wonder, then, that we thought style to be all important. The old style was deficient in sensibility, and, for our purposes, clumsy and intractable. The style had to be changed, scrapped if necessary, and a new one fashioned to meet the change in sensibility. This was the only way any important break-through could be effected in getting English to play a meaningful role in Indian literature.* (italics mine)

Ironically, however, the only writers P. Lal gave any credence to were Sri Aurobindo—whom he had previously condemned—and G. V. Desani, Raja Rao, and Bharati Sarabai, an Indian playwright writing in English. Desani was praised because Eliot praised him and because he attempted the Joycean task. This in itself was indicative of a new imitative tendency manifest in Indian writing. Though Lal saw himself as the perpetrator of a new tradition, one that would effectively blend style and content in Indian poetry, he was simply following, as H. M. Williams points out [in *Indo-Anglian Literature: 1800-1970, A Survey,* 1976] in the footsteps of the modernist tradition—some several years too late:

> In place of the English and Indian romantic poets came the dominating figures of T. S. Eliot, Ezra Pound, the later Yeats, W. H. Auden, Wallace Stevens and Dylan Thomas, of all of whom

much of the new poetry was plainly derivative if not slavishly imitative. It became common to come across the Eliot poem, the Dylan Thomas poem, etc. in Indian journals and in the slim volumes that issued from Indian publishers of English poetry. In the nineteen-fifties 'classicism' replaced Aurobindian and Tagorean romanticism; and symbolism and the surrealism of Dylan Thomas quickly occupied the place vacated by the fairly simple, uncomplicated muses of the previous decades.

In an attempt to establish the poetry he wanted to develop, P. Lal founded the Writers Workshop in Calcutta, a circle of poets drawn from all over India. The Writers Workshop both published their works and put out *Miscellany,* the Workshop's magazine which provided a forum for the exchange of ideas. Both through *Miscellany* and his anthology, *Modern Indian Poetry in English* (1969), Lal established a credo aimed at explaining why Indian poets wrote in English. The questionnaire and the anthology seemed to be developed primarily to refute the Bengali poet Buddhadeva Bose, who claimed in his entry in *The Concise Encyclopaedia of English and American Poets and Poetry* that Indian poets could not use the English language effectively, and secondarily, to refute the Whorfian critics' claim that Indian writing in English is a contradiction since one could not write poetry in a language in which one did not experience reality. Lal attempted to communicate to the critics who championed the vernaculars that there was no alienation from Indian culture or anglomania in the poets' choice of English. Rather it was a practical choice resultant from the accidents of history.

Subsequently, the critical treatment of the poets has focused on whether they continue in an imitative strain and on whether they can write poetry effectively in English. Despite their attempts to break from the past and to "affirm their faith in a vital language," C. Paul Verghese, for instance [in *Problems of the Creative Writer in English,* 1971], judges that modern Indian poets in English continue to imitate. According to Verghese, experimentation is "the vogue and tradition a taboo" among the new poets, yet Verghese makes no effort to place these writers in the *tradition* of the modernism they are imitating. At this point he misses an opportunity to point the direction towards a genuinely new and Indian creative writing in English. In discussing P. Lal, Professor Verghese points out that "Eliot of course is Lal's master." Here he means to criticize Lal for being imitative but does not show by concrete example of image or line Eliot's influence or that of other modernists on Lal or other Indian poets. The critic seems caught between pointing out the imitative tendencies and offering a 'pat on the back' for a good imitation as he does with Moraes' symbolist poems. It is easy to see how a criticism of this nature affects the direction of subsequent literature. Conversely, Kamala Das is considered "full of metrical, syntactical and linguistic defects, but there is no doubt that a genuine poetic talent is at work in much of what she has written." Her strength lies in her freedom from literary influences and in simply expressing her "self." Her genuine Indian voice emerging through language variation receives lesser praise even from Verghese, since it does not fit effectively in the contemporary

"vogue." Thus, the pundits seem to stand opposed to the poets in every way, yet by rewarding imitative tendencies even though they are labelled as such, Indian criticism can be seen as adversely shaping the future of this fledgling literature.

The poets who emerged from the charmed circle of the Writers Workshop were all academics—Nissim Ezekiel, Shiv Kumar, Pritish Nandy, among others. Well-schooled in modernist traditions, they soon produced modernist-influenced works and they have been criticized [by H. M. Williams in *Indo-Anglian Literature: 1800-1970, A Survey,* 1976] for an "irritating propensity for erudite reference." Among the poets of this generation two stand apart—Kamala Das, who has published with the Writers Workshop but is not from the academy, and Dom Moraes. Fiercely independent, their poetry does embody the freshness of their individual voices and concerns. Kamala Das claims no influences—only the struggle to create her own voice. Though Moraes' poetry does show his roots in the "Waste Land" tradition, he has helped articulate the critics' concern for the effective use of English by Indian poets.

David McCutchion, one of the Western critics writing about Indian poetry in English during the 1960s, had raised the issue [in *Indian Writing in English: Critical Essays,* 1969] of whether a differing concept of the rhythm of the English language affects the poetry written by Indians in English. Moraes extended this critical concept to the currency of the English language usage by Indians. McCutchion had also studied the "Indianness" of both the criticism and the literature, and in a controversial essay/talk, Moraes attributed to the failure of the criticism, the declining standards in the literature. In "The Future of Indian Literature in English is Pretty Dim," *Onlooker* (July 15/31, 1976) Moraes argues that "a really dramatic fall in standards in Indian Writing in English" could be attributed to the lack of a "proper critic" to provide the poets and novelists with a genuine criticism. In answering Moraes, though, Professor Narasimhaiah [in "Literary Criticism: European and Indian Traditions," *Literary Criterion* 7, No. 1 (Winter 1965)] is extremely defensive, though he, too, had previously admitted the important role of criticism:

> I would like to think that responsible criticism might have made a tremendous difference to our literatures, and if it has not done so it may be that we have merely degenerated into cataloguing and classifying and wrangling over grammatical subtleties, allowing the song to slip through our fingers.

The failure of critical standards becomes even more obvious in the later criticism. Just as the Indian writers seemed compelled to imitate the British writers of the previous generation, younger Indian critics continue to imitate the older generation of Indian and sometimes Western critics of Indian writing in English. An interesting example of the tendency to follow current fashions even in criticism is Nissim Ezekiel's retitling of his previously mentioned article on Jhabvala's *Heat and Dust.* "Two Readers and Their Texts" is much more fashionably au courant than "Cross Cultural Encounters in Literature."

While they criticize the older generation of critics for dropping too many British names and of writing in circumlocutions, these younger pundits do not essentially break these habits themselves. Kamta C. Srivastava's blanket criticism of Indian patriarchs is delivered in their style and the circumlocutions do not seem to be satirical in intent:

> A weakness for precision, so it seems to say, comes from a poor appetite for gush and effusion, which according to its better known practitioners, judging from their unstated but demonstrated tenets, is all that Indian criticism ought to strive for. What is needed, in their terms, is a telling criticism which should be capable of shocking its readers into submission by the din and colour of its words, the garish novelty of concept and lexis, not to speak of the innocent, by-the-way distortions of sense and meaning of its subject of study [in "English Literature and Indian Criticism" in *Meru* (no date) Quarterly Review of Literature and Culture].

While criticizing Dr. Mokashi Punekar, an Indian poet and critic, for obfuscating critical tenets, Srivasta proceeds to do exactly the same thing:

> Obscurity that is meaningfully accessible to sensitive exploration is legitimate and poetically desirable. Obscurity that resists comprehension comes from conceptual or notional opacity, or from a collocation of words that does not show words to advantage, and prevents interflow and interanimation of meanings.

This critical passage is similar to the "linguistic sculptures" of the imitative creative writers.

The imitative tendency is not surprising. The younger pundits are trained in the traditions of the patriarchs who were themselves concerned with following Western trends. Yet, at the same time, these younger pundits do constitute a revolt in criticism—a recognition that Indian critics' name dropping and a tendency to do *'puja'* and *'darshan'* among themselves was dangerous [in a footnote, the critic explains that "*puja* and *darshan* refer to religious activities that require making offerings and benefitting by visual interaction respectively"]. While seemingly oblivious to the larger developments in criticism, they do ask for closer readings of texts and for interpretations to be based on a word-by-word analysis of the text, rather than interpretations based on large general issues such as race, moment, and milieu, the Taine-ian aesthetic which Professor Iyengar had espoused. Such a criticism, however, also constitutes an imitation of the West which does not consider whether close reading is a critical method suited to Indian literature written in English, which is so much a product of its race, moment, and milieu. It shows again "a too-ready acceptance of the Western ethnocentric assumptions" of criticism whereas "a good close reading ought to take social and linguistic context into account." Even a word-by-word reading must see each word in the context of Indian English and the context of the Indian environment. In the Indian situation, close reading can lead to parochial wranglings over the localized meanings of words, far from what was originally meant by close reading.

For example, Ujjal Dutta attempts a "close reading" in an effort to disparage Professor Narasimhaiah's critical style [in "Amiable Expertise: Trends in Indo-English Criticism," in *Meru*]. He criticizes Narasimhaiah's claims that Sarojini Naidu was genuinely Indian based on her use of the phrase "the wing of halcyon wild," which he feels belies any Indianness. Placing the poem within its moment and milieu and not just in its race would have helped Ujjal Dutta recognize the implicit Indianness in the Victorian imitation of the vocabulary. Instead of demonstrating Professor Narasimhaiah's "parochialism," this critical essay simply demonstrates the parochialism of blind imitation—the need to jump on the most fashionable critical bandwagon in the West. Instead of asking "Must Indian poetry in English always follow England?", as David McCutchion did, we should ask, "Must Indian criticism of Indian writing in English always follow the West?" In following critical and literary fashions set in the West, the criticism has forced the literature into forms molded in the West by virtue of applauding those works that best approximated Western literary fashions. . . .

In developing a critical voice and method of their own, the Americans managed to achieve literary independence. Like the Americans in Hamlin Garland's *Crumbling Idols,* the Indians must also strain for a literary freedom: "It has taken the United States longer to achieve independence of English critics than it took to free itself from old-world political and economic rule. Its political freedom was won, not by its gentlemen and scholars, but by its yeomanry; and in the same way our national literature will come in its fullness when the common American rises spontaneously to the expression of his concept of life." Indian critics are hampered by a preconceived conception of literature and thus are unable to bring a fresh perspective to their own unique literature. They prevent the common Indian from rising to a spontaneous expression of his socio-cultural linguistic contexts by emphasizing the more elitist stylistic and intellectual traditions. Indo-English criticism needs to develop a terminology of its own and to aid in the free development of its literature.

> *Feroza F. Jussawalla, "Family Quarrels," in his* Family Quarrels: Towards a Criticism of Indian Writing in English, *Peter Lang, 1985, pp. 1-40.*

MODERN INDO-ENGLISH LITERATURE

Prema Nandakumar

[*Nandakumar is an Indian writer, critic, and translator. In the following excerpt, she provides an overview of Indo-English fiction and poetry written after India won its independence from Britain in 1947.*]

Kashiprosad Ghose published in 1830 a volume of English verse, *The Shair and Other Poems*. This first book of Indian verse in English displayed conventional metres controlling conventional imagery:

> Region of bliss! Irradiate gem of night!
> Soother of sorrows! Orb of gentle light!
> For still, resplendent Moon! whene'er we see
> Thy placid face, and fondly gaze on thee,
> Its gentleness upon the wounded soul
> Exerts a healing power and calm control.

It was a long while ago. Even the 'Sepoy Mutiny' was yet to be. But a beginning had been made. Nearly a century and a half after, faced with a growing voluminous mass of Indian writing in English, we are now able to discuss periods and trends, theory and aesthesis, individual styles and group significances. Already many reputations have been made, and many have fallen. A good deal of writing considered significant and effective by contemporary standards now appears powerless and inane. Some writers lost in obscurity have ridden to the forefront in the estimation of succeeding generations. And some titans have continued to stay on their pedestals. Meanwhile, India has become a free nation, for the British left our land twenty-five years ago. But English has continued in India, and the quarter-century of independent India has further enriched Indo-Anglian literature. It is with this 'modern period' that this essay is concerned.

Though a critical approach is unavoidable when dealing with literature written in the immediacy of our experience, no doctrinaire distinctions can be made yet. We can but map out certain major achievements, refer to a few significant publications, and limn a few distinctive trends. This survey is no inclusive history. Post-Independence Indo-Anglian literature is certainly vaster than what a brief survey can hope to indicate.

The authentic voice of a people is heard in their poetry. Indo-Anglian writers of verse have been many ever since a beginning was made by Derozio and Michael Madhusudhan. Indo-Anglian poetry reflected shaded brilliance in the poets now famous—Manmohan Ghose and Sarojini Naidu—and reached its apotheosis in Sri Aurobindo who was still an active poet when India became independent. His poetry is full of spiritual symbolism. A keen lyricist who limned the contours of the spirit, his poetic career spanned half a century. A good deal of what he wrote in his yogic retreat at Pondicherry was published only posthumously. However, his monumental epic *Savitri* in English blank verse appeared in a complete edition in 1950. Based on the familiar Savitri Upakhyana in the *Mahabharata,* the epic is a detailed exposition of Sri Aurobindo's world-vision, and the original legend and the spiritual symbolism are forged together throughout the twelve Books that make the epic. In the words of Dr. K. R. Srinivasa Iyengar:

> The story, derived from the familiar *Mahabharata* episode, is simplicity itself but simplicity doubled with sublimity. A young man, Satyavan by name, dies a year after his marriage, and his wife, Savitri, armed by the power of her love, struggles with Death, and secures her husband's release from mortality and returns to the earth. The death of Satyavan also means the defeat of Truth, the eclipse of light through the invasion of darkness; and Savitri's is the light of love that defeats the darkness and achieves the recovery of Truth. Nay more: Savitri not only accomplishes the recovery of Satyavan from "death", she also compasses the recovery of the soul and Nature from the partial and temporary darkness that have overtaken them.

Significantly enough, the first canto of the epic was published on 15 August 1946, one year ahead of India becoming an independent nation. Titled 'The Symbol Dawn', this canto describes a physical dawn as well as a symbolic one. Night gives place to Day, ushering in the light of life for mankind. Man too, in his evolutionary ascent, leaves behind him the corridors of inconscience and reaches a higher consciousness poised for greater achievement. And likewise the nation too, after centuries of bleak incertitude, might hope, perhaps, for a new life of energy and creative endeavour in the wake of political independence.

Sri Aurobindo was truly a Lord of the English language whether he wrote prose or verse. The blank verse of *Savitri* has a steely definiteness about it with each line almost achieving metrical and semantic self-sufficiency. The spiritual action of *Savitri* sweeps on the wings of the mystic muse, and this is most significant in the first canto which Sri Aurobindo himself characterised as 'a key beginning and an announcement'. The central idea about the movement from night to day is brought out by a series of brilliant images.

> The persistent thrill of a transfiguring touch
> Persuaded the inert black quietude
> And beauty and wonder disturbed the fields of
>   God.
> A wandering hand of pale enchanted light
> That glowed along a fading moment's brink,
> Fixed with gold panel and opalescent hinge
> A gate of dreams ajar on mystery's verge.
> One lucent corner windowing hidden things
> Forced the world's blind immensity to sight.
> The darkness failed and slipped like a falling
>   cloak
> From the reclining body of a god.

Sri Aurobindo's was a powerful poetic personality that drew within its orbit countless practitioners of verse in the Indian languages, thus giving rise to a distinctive Aurobindonian school in Indo-Anglian literature. K. D. Sethna, Dilip Kumar Roy, Nirodbaran and V. K. Gokak are among the more important poets who reflect the influence of Sri Aurobindo. They are all competent poetic craftsman and have also a spiritual bent of mind. K. D. Sethna's imagery is purely Aurobindonian in *The Adventure of the Apocalypse* (1949):

> But when the Great Self glows
> Like a golden cosmic rose,
> The petals fanning out
>   from one sweet core,
> No strangeness anywhere
> Remains for stare and stare
> Seeking to itself a door.
> The central Eye of eyes

Can shut in all-repose
For the Great Flower knows
Its perfume of paradise.

In Life's Temple contains V. K. Gokak's poems written after 1947. Many of the deeper currents in Gokak's poetry are inspired by Sri Aurobindo's philosophy, as for example 'Recognising an Avatar':

His words are runes
That unfold their meanings slowly
To the rapt ear of Time.
But they are charactered on Time's forehead
And the whole universe may read them.
His deeds are seeds sown by the wayside.
They spring into a colonnade
And fructify after a thousand years.
You recognise the Divine
In your own heart's lotus-flame
For there he abides for ever.
As you ascend into the higher realms of being,
You see the Divine as Infinity.
More vast, more ample, more manifold,
The higher you climb.

There is the desire to know the Self even in younger poets like Romen, Themis and Prithwindra belonging to this group, and they all record their visions and experiences with a sense of ecstasy and fulfilment. Thus Chitra in a short lyric:

The strident blows and terrors
Of your unannounced coming,
The mortal rigours and fatigues
Of your unexplained going—
These, when I understand—
Thanks to a thoughtful friend—
I mind no more.
My psyche is ashore.

The Aurobindonian tradition is a widening stream of poetry with its perennial source in the Himalayas of Spirituality. These poets believe in no rash experiments merely for the sake of novelty, and are usually content to use traditional patterns to convey spiritual truths. There are, however, others who have tried to make a break with the kind of clarity and finish achieved by Manmohan Ghose, Sarojini Naidu and Sri Aurobindo. This 'movement' was spearheaded by P. Lal, a Calcutta Professor of English, himself an accomplished lyricist who also organised the Writers' Workship. In an eight-point credo, P. Lal and his Workshop group decried the poetry of their Indo-Anglian predecessors and proclaimed the emergence of a 'stripped, non-slush poetry' that would aim at 'precision of expression'. Some good poetry has been written by these Workshop poets, but their credo has largely been mere bravado. Apart from a dozen or so of the more successful among them, the rest have fallen an easy prey to misplaced 'modernism'. Commenting upon the much-publicised rebellion of these poets, M. K. Naik observes:

> . . . . the fact remains that the strain of imitation is equally strong in many of them, who seem to have merely exchanged the King Log of Milton-Shelley-Tennyson for the King Stork of Pound-Eliot-Yeats. It is especially Eliot who is 'too much with' these poets, for poetry for them seems to be almost synonymous with 'Eliotry.'

Their 'dutiful genuflection to the post-war European gods' notwithstanding, bright patches of originality often catch the eye in the poems of P. Lal, Nissim Ezekiel, R. Parthasarathy, Keki Daruwalla, A. K. Ramanujan and Kamala Das. Dom Moraes, who won the coveted Hawthorndon Prize in 1958 is outside this group, and has continued to keep up his youthful zest and invoke brilliantly clear images:

In my lady's chamber
Once I found a skull.
It helped her to remember
That she was beautiful.
If I find the moral
That is all my wish.
Men have fetched up coral
When they have trawled for fish.

A. K. Ramanujan has achieved wide recognition as an original lyricist and sensitive translator. His first collection of poems, *The Striders* (1966), won a Poetry Book Society recommendation. Things happen to him that provoke his anger or frustration, and so his recordings radiate a grim humour:

I have known
That measly-looking man,
not very likeable. . . . .
Sitting at the window of the local bus,
Suddenly make. . . . .
A poem.

Nissim Ezekiel is a dedicated practitioner of poetry. *A Time to Change* (1951), *Sixty Poems, The Unfinished Man* and *The Exact Name* (1965) contain his best work. His sensitivity has a bitter edge, as is revealed even in a recent poem, 'He Contemplates His Self-doubt and the Scepticism of His Readers':

Sell what you have if you must
but do not buy it; customers
are shrewd, even when they don't complain
they doubt, and sense their discontent.
Who says he is a poet? How much
does he really know, or is he
one of those who cheat with words
and sometimes money, counterfeiter
caught by critic-cops at dead of night?

There are scores of young lyricists who have turned out fine lines of poetry like Pradip Sen, Deb Kumar Das, Suresh Kohli, Jayanta Mahapatra, S. Mokashi-Punekar and Pritish Nandy. But women writers from the Workshop have been rather a disappointment. There are a few exceptions, however. Monika Varma's poems in *Green Leaves and Gold* (1970) are vibrant with something deeply felt, iridescent with the Indian scene and moving in their turns of phrase. 'Rain Days' indicates 'the time to read poetry':

This is the time of bittern and egrets:
notches against leaden skies.
This is the time lightning whips,
and thunder cries, rolls, screams,
cracks roads of iron
and rumbles anger against hill and plains.

Her nature poetry is rich in associations. She can also

touch our hearts with pity and the suggestion of deeply-felt tragedy. 'An old house once lived' is now in shambles:

> One should not return to old haunts:
> no Manderley of fiction
> is as true as life's truth.
> Only a chimney stack remains
> reminding of cold nights, roasted chestnuts,
> potatoes roasted by small hands;
> and violated, the piano lies spreadeagled,
> the keyboard on the floor.
> I shall not return. . . .
> no, not again.

And there is Kamala Das, author of *Summer in Calcutta* (1965), who burst upon the Indo-Anglian scene like a daring fascinating spectre of unconventionality blowing to smithereens the traditional reticences of Indian womanhood. Her weird wordiness has not lost its capacity to send shock-waves in her more recent *The Descendants* (1968). The title poem draws into its vortex the countless victims who have voicelessly yielded to the commitment of youth:

> We have lain in every weather, nailed, no, not
> To crosses, but to soft beds and against
> Softer forms, while the heaving, lurching,
> Tender hours passed in a half-dusk, half-dawn
>   and
> Half-dream, half-real trance. We were the yield-
>   ers,
> Yielding ourselves to everything. It is
> Not for us to scrape the walls of wombs for
> Memories, not for us even to
> Question death, but as child to mother's arms
> We shall give ourselves to the fire or to
> The hungry earth to be slowly eaten,
> Devoured. None will step off his cross
> Or show his wounds to us, no god lost in
> Silence shall begin to speak, no lost love
> Claim us, no, we are not going to be
> Ever redeemed, or made new.

Some names in Indo-Anglian poetry defy easy categorisation. Harindranath Chattopadhyaya, whose first volume of verse appeared in 1918 and was commended by Sri Aurobindo, has retained his poetic fecundity. Among his collections of verse after 1947 are *Spring in Winter* (1956), *Masks and Farewells,* and *Virgins and Vineyards* (1967). Here are poems of love, anger, anxiety and hope. Happily Harindranath does not usually clutter his poetry with his leftist lucubrations, as in his plays. Humayun Kabir, J. Vijayatunga, Manjeri Isvaran and Subho Tagore are some names that will be remembered on account of the distinctive quality of their poetic work.

Keshav Malik's cosmic lyricism is in tune with the Indian mind. *The Lake Surface and other Poems,* (1959), *Rippled Shadow* (1960) and *Poems* (1971) contain most of his poetic output. Poesy is to him an ocean goddess—vast, mysterious, glittering with pearls and precious stones for the bold diver, like-giving for those scorched by the fires of life.

> O no sooner the sea siren strikes,
> The invisible streams stream
> Through the foundations in the bone,
> And song-vines go winding in dream;
> A wave leaps and, slow or swift,

> The measured steps are heard,
> And from somewhere afar a humming
>   bird. . . .

A touch of brightness has been the mark of another remarkable poet, Armando Menezes. But even he cannot avoid frustration at the way independence came to India stained by fratricide:

> Why is your rising, Mother, solemnly cold,
> With the heavens clouded to a murky mood?
> With downcast eyes, and monsters agape for
>   food,
> And angry gnashings in the wintry fold?

The martyrdom of the Mahatma adds a new dimension of bitterness to his poetry:

> Nothing is ours: and the galloping powers
> Of Time eat flower and bud.
> All that I dream shall be an empty theme,
> And my heart's desire shall shrivel in fire,
> And peace shall perish in blood.
> Both creed and state, and love and hate
> Must vanish like dew on flowers.
> And the friend we hail our own shall fail,
> And all things pass as the summer grass:
> Death alone is ours.

Indeed, the trauma of the assassination sent tremors of misery to many an Indo-Anglian poet. Rajendra Varma's 'Gandhi Killing' is a longish poem in three parts. The first is structured like a Greek tragedy with a chorus, and swaying between doubt and hope we come nearer to an understanding of the mystery of avatars. The second part, 'A Lament of the People', is about those who knew him and loved him, and yet failed him at the crucial hour of independence. The third part is a 'dirge'. But there is no room in the end for despair, for the poet races towards a conclusion holding aloft a banner of hope for the future:

> O raise the standard that had dipped it low!
> things all henceforth be vertical, standing dead
>   erect;
> the crooked snake can only eat his tail,
> bent trees only break,
> the Himalayan exaltation, head erect, confirms
>   coldly
> a triumphant upsoaring of pure ascension to-
>   wards the
> infinite's brow.

The Mahatma's end, the ideal of the *Gita,* the wisdom of Sikh scriptures and the crucifiction of Christ were blended in Gopal Singh's *The Man Who Never Died* (1969). This is undoubtedly a nobly conceived poem. Again and again Dr. Gopal Singh's chaste diction glows with striking images. The commonest occurrence is now and then suddenly lit up by the iridescence of thought and feeling:

> Men asked Him:
> 'When we can do not what we want to,
> What shall we do?' And He said;
> 'Pray unto your God
> Which is in the Heaven within you and also
> without'.
> When they asked,
> 'How shall we pray?' He answered:
> 'Does the seed ask: how shall I pray?

It enters into its closet, shuts its door,
and prays in secret as if not praying,
and fasts as if not fasting, till
it grows into a flower, and prays
not with words, but through fragrance'.

Indo-Anglian fiction too has taken bold new strides since 1947. As early as the latter half of the 19th century, Lal Behari Dey, Bankim Chandra, Toru Dutt, Krupabai Sathianadhan and others had begun writing fiction in English. Later came novelists like A. S. P. Ayyar, K. S. Venkataramani and Dhan Gopal Mukherji who were eager to find a wider plank for their interest in history, politics and romance. The independence movement brought the regional intellectuals together and the English language alone provided an easy common medium of communication. There was thus a sudden spurt in Indians writing novels in English. It was also a time of social reform, thanks to the ideas propagated by Mahatma Gandhi; this was the time when R. K. Narayan, Raja Rao and Mulk Raj Anand gained a wide reading public. Mulk Raj Anand wrote a series of novels in the thirties and forties, creating symbol after symbol in characters like Bakha, Munoo and Gangu. This rich creative fire does not, perhaps, burn quite as fiercely in his post-1947 writing, but the creative artist is alive still. *Private Life of an Indian Prince* describes the events in a fairly typical native State during the period immediately before its merger with India; *The Old Woman and the Cow* directly refers to the Partition horrors; *The Road* and *Death of a Hero* make absorbing reading. The latter tells the story of a Kashmiri Muslim who defies the Pakistani invaders and sacrifices his life rather than compromise with the ideal of a patriot.

Anand's most impressive post-independence work is found in the autobiographical series, *Seven Ages of Man.* The first part was published in 1951 as *Seven Summers* and dealt with the childhood of Krishan. In 1968 he published the second part with the title *Morning Face.* Krishan's growth into adolescence in the atmosphere of family relationships, of calf love and genuine attachments, and the birth of the Gandhian Heroic era give the volume an epic quality. Dr. Anand writes some of his best prose when describing the Jallianwallah Bagh atrocity that set aflame the entire nation. Krishan is a rare being caught in a mundane world, a 'divine imbecile, who listened to the music and rhythms and evocations inside me.' If Dr. Anand can continue the series with the same ardour, *Seven Ages of Man* may well become a prose epic of modern India.

R. K. Narayan, already a well-known novelist, achieved an international reputation only after 1947. Each novel of his is a private world. Only in *Waiting for the Mahatma* (1955) does he bring in the Mahatma and his assassination into the central scheme of fictional representation. While reading his other novels—*Mr. Sampath,* (1949), *The Financial Expert* (1952), *The Guide,* (1959), *The Man-Eater of Malgudi* (1961) and *The Vendor of Sweets* (1967)—'we enter an exotic world of half-headed or half-hearted dreamers, artists, financiers, speculators, twisters, adventurers, eccentrics, cranks, cinema stars, *sannyasis'* with the action rarely straying outside Malgudi, the familiar scene of Narayan's novels. The characters are chosen from the common herd, and Narayan carefully portrays the be-

havioural quiddities of the people around him. Though he has not been able to give us a picture of power or a sweeping epic study of the convulsions of independent India, his gifts as a writer in English deserve special commendation within the Indo-Anglian frame. To quote K. R. Srinivasa Iyengar:

> . . . . he wields so difficult and "alien" a language like English with masterful ease, and conveys subtle shades of feeling and thought; unlike Anand, he uses hardly any swearwords at all; he doesn't exploit perversion or sex, and seldom brings in controversial politics. He is a master of comedy who is not unaware of the tragedy of the human situation; he is neither an intolerant critic of Indian ways and modes nor their fanatic defender; he is, on the whole, content to snap Malgudi life's little ironies, knots of satiric circumstance, and tragi-comedies of mischance and misdirection.

In *The Man-Eater of Malgudi* R. K. Narayan tries to read the ancient Indian myth of Bhasmasura Vadha in the story of a heartless modern taxidermist. The novel is a frighteningly perceptive study of an Asuric ego. But in his latest *The Vendor of Sweets,* Narayan has returned to his usual pace of story-telling. Jagan, a thrifty sweet-vendor, his squanderer son and foreign daughter-in-law provide the three sides of the plot's triangle. Jagan's remembrances of things past and his prickly contacts with his Indianised daughter-in-law are brought out with skill and gentle irony. Come to think of it, any private life could be as rich as the sweet vendor's. Narayan's distinctive strength is his English, as noted by William Walsh:

> Mr. Narayan's themes are conveyed in a pure and limpid English which has a strange degree of translucence, and which unaffected by the opacity of a British inheritance is beautifully adapted to communicate a different, an Indian sensibility. Mr. Narayan by serving devotedly a talent of the purest and finest kind, has extended the possibilities of the English language and increased the scope of English fiction. He has blended an Eastern wisdom with a Western method and brought an Indian genius into English art.

However, it is in Raja Rao that we hear the accents of the Indian intellectual's English achieving a life of its own through the fusion of Indian and English traditions. The Indian reader had almost forgotten the novelist who had caused a mild stir in 1938 with the novel *Kanthapura,* a brilliant fictional re-creation of Gandhi's non-co-operation movement. The winding sentences of the novel replete with Indian turns of expression had fully justified the author's foreword wherein he had said:

> It (the English language) is the language of our intellectual make-up—like Sanskrit or Persian was before—but not of our emotional make-up. We are all instinctively bi-lingual, many of us writing in our own language and in English. We cannot write like the English. We should not. We cannot write only as Indians. We have grown to look at the large world as part of us.

After a silence of two decades, Raja Rao came out with

The Serpent and the Rope in 1960. The hero-narrator is Rama, almost a Jean Christophe. He views each experience in sensuous depth. The action moves between India, France and England. But in this novel, the style is verily the soul of the narrative. The hero's speculations flow on, submerging us in a flood of eddying words. It is a sensitive Indian remembering things that have happened to him, the sights that he has seen, and the myths he has absorbed in the course of his life:

> Benares is eternal. There the dead do not die nor the living live. The dead come down to play on the banks of the Ganges, and the living who move about, and even offer rice-balls to the manes, live in the illusion of a vast night and a bright city.

And this paean to womanhood:

> Woman is the earth, air, ether, sound; woman is the microcosm of the mind, the articulations of space, the knowing in knowledge; the woman is fire, movement clear and rapid as the mountain stream; the woman is that which seeks against that which is sought. To Mitra she is Varuna, to Indra she is Agni, to Rama she is Sita, to Krishna she is Radha. Woman is the meaning of the world, the breath, touch, act . . . even when the King is crowned it is the Queen to whom the kingdom comes . . . for even when it is a King that rules, she is the justice, the bender of man in compassion, the confusion of kindness, the sorrowing in the anguish of all. . . .

Mere words? But the novel really demonstrates Raja Rao's sheer mastery over this 'alien' language. Raja Rao's *Cat and Shakespeare* (1966), described by him as 'a metaphysical comedy', makes further extensions in the handling of the English language. The long-windedness of *The Serpent and the Rope* now gives place to the nervous jerkiness of short sentences adding raciness to a piquant story.

The government's linguistic policy of advancing Hindi as the official language of India has certainly not dampened so far the Indian's enthusiasm for English. But hardly a dozen novelists have come up to our expectations. There are single novels like *Kalyani's Husband* (1957) and *Chronicles of Kedaram* (1961) that have touched a deep chord in our consciousness. A few writers like Humayun Kabir, Balachandra Rajan and Khushwant Singh have published a striking novel or two. Sudhin Ghose has presented exotic fantasies in *And Gazelles Leaping* (1949), *Cradle of the Clouds* (1951), *The Vermilion Boat* (1953) and *The Flame of the Forest* (1955). His sensitive handling of English helps the transmission of his visionary moments to the eager reader. Khwaja Ahmed Abbas has many Marxist axes to grind but his genuineness is evident in *Inquilab* (1955) where he has tried to project phases of our independence struggle through the prism of fiction. Manohar Malgonkar's subject is post-independent India with her struggles and sores and triumphs. His *Distant Drum* (1960) views the effect independence had on Indian army life. Malgonkar's satire of the new ruling class is effective because he exercises rigid control over his writing. The same pattern is repeated in the rest of his novels,— *Combat of Shadows,* (1962), *A Bend in the Ganges* (1964)

and *The Princes* (1963)—where the sores of corruption in India are exposed at many levels, in politics, bureaucracy, princely kingdoms and public life. *The Princes* invites meaningful comparison with Anand's novel, *Private Life of an Indian Prince.* In Malgonkar's novel the 'prince' is Abhay, and his private life is made up of his emotional entanglements and a conventional marriage. Abhay's Begwed signs the Instrument of Accession, and Abhay is prince no more. But his eclipse comes to us with a touch of regret, for after all the Congress boss who is to be the new 'prince' is no angel, but almost a Satyr.

The one novelist who has attempted new pastures in each novel and has tried to come to grips with the reality of independent India is Bhabani Bhattacharya. *So Many Hungers* (1947) is about the 1942 Bengal famine. The language hisses out the naked reality:

> Corpses lay by the road, huddled together. Picked to the bones, with eyeless caverns of sockets, bits of skin and flesh rotting on nose and chin and ribs, the skulls pecked open, only the hair uneaten. . . . A family group had sunk into sleep; and beyond the sleep—vultures. . . . Heaven's scavengers. Save for them the air of Bengal would be putrid with the rotting flesh of man. Fellow human beings had ceased to care for the living; how could they care for the dead?

After a brief glance at a domestic situation like an incompatible marriage in *Music for Mohini* (1952), Bhattacharya published *He Who Rides a Tiger* (1954), whose theme is public and individual morality. *A Goddess Named Gold* (1960) is a triumph of symbolistic art. On the surface, it is a childish story with the child-like Meera caught between the business acumen of Seth Samsunderji and the sterling idealism of the wandering minstrel. But the real theme is the cancer of corruption that has begun to spread wide in independent India. The implied warning is that this steep fall in moral standards might endanger our freedom itself in the long run. Independence is not enough, just as a *taveez* is not enough to accomplish alchemy. The wearer of the amulet must be worthy of it too:

> It (freedom) was a touchstone for everyone. To possess this touchstone was not enough, for it could wake to life and work its miracle only when acts of faith were done. . . . Without acts of faith, freedom is a dead pebble tied to the arm with a bit of string, fit only to be cast into the river.

The years immediately before freedom; the coming of freedom; and in *Shadow from Ladakh* (1966) Bhattacharya turns his artistic attention to a major problem of free India: the issue between the Gandhian inheritance and Western materialism. Bhattacharya's narrative is as functionally effective as ever. Bhaskar, a brilliant engineer trained in America, would like to acquire the land adjoining his steel plant, and this involves the taking over of Gandhigram, a community of Gandhians led by Satyajit. Meanwhile the Chinese invasion casts an immense shadow over India. Bhaskar goes ahead with his plans for expanding his steel-plant. This provokes Satyajit to go on a hunger strike. Bhaskar meanwhile falls in love with Satyajit's daughter, Sumita. It is a stalemate, at last resolved by the unilateral withdrawal of the Chinese. But Bhattacharya's question remains. Should we cling to Gandhism, or boldly go the whole hog with modern industrialism, as China and Japan have done? Perhaps it is too early to answer the question. The future alone can tell.

The most significant development for Indo-Anglian fiction in the last twenty-five years has been the emergence of a group of women novelists venturing boldly and successfully into this field. Attia Hosain, Vimala Raina, Shakuntala Shrinagesh and Sita Ratnamal have written novels that shed light on their respective milieu. Santha Rama Rau, who has an excellent pen for travelogue, published *Remember the House* in 1956. The heroine Baba is an autobiographical projection, and the narrative has an authentic ring. Sixteen years had to elapse before the publication of her second novel, *The Adventuress.* The heroine is presented as a typical product of a war-torn age. One must learn to save one's skin! But our sympathies are with her, and her affair with Charles Beaver, a middle-aged American with the Occupation Forces in Japan. Santha's visual style evokes post-war Tokyo, Manila and Shanghai with a rare beauty touched by sadness.

As for Nayantara Sahgal, a young critic recently posed the question: 'Without being uncharitable one could ask, what is it that gives power to her elbow as a novelist if it is not belonging to the Nehru family?' Actually, it *is* an uncharitable thought. There can be no doubt whatsoever about her mastery of the English language. At the same time, her education and life in a great political family have given her language a certain sophistication for dealing with people and affairs. She too brings in a strong autobiographical slant to her novels. *A Time to be Happy* (1958) takes place on the eve of India's independence. *This Time of Morning* (1965) is a scathing portrayal of India's socio-political life after independence. Politicians like Kalyan Sinha, Hari Mohan and Kailash Vrind are juxtaposed with oily diplomats and societal butterflies. There are idealist youngsters like Rakesh and Nita as well. It is not just belonging to the Nehru family but her own capacity for close observation that gives Mrs. Sahgal's style a natural ease, as in this opening paragraph:

> Rakesh stood at one end of the dirty verandah of Palam Airport in the crowd that had just got off the plane, while luggage clattered noisily past him along the moving belt. In India luggage like everything else had to be sturdy to survive. He watched for the new lightweight fibre suitcase that would adapt less readily to rugged handling than the shabby leather boxes and canvas bedding rolls he saw rattling past, lifted off, bumped and banged to the floor. But whatever the condition of their luggage, a lot of people could apparently afford to travel by air. The plane had been full, and the man at the counter had told him all planes travelled with a full load. Sensitive to changes during his absence in foreign parts, every Indian detail held an interest for him.

Storm in Chandigarh (1969), Mrs. Sahgal's third novel, gave equal importance to politics and personal life. The novelist's political background gives her a ring-side seat to watch the animalia in Indian politics with a quizzical eye. At the same time the involvement of Vishal Dubey the bureaucrat in the uneasy marriages of Jit and Mara, and Inder and Saroj, is portrayed convincingly enough. Even more satisfying as a study in feminine psychology is Mrs. Sahgal's latest novel, *The Day in Shadow* (1972). The heroine Simrit is a divorcee and her conflicting emotions are recorded by the novelist with singular ease. The other characters too—some belonging to politics, others to business, but all to the tinsel glitter of India's high society—come out in realistic detail. Mrs. Sahgal has certainly not belied the promise shown in her earlier novels and the autobiographical volumes, *Prison and Chocolate Cake* and *From Fear Set Free.*

Another woman novelist of distinction is Anita Desai. *Cry the Peacock* (1963), which unfolds the tragedy of Maya caught in her own despair, has Proustian undertones. Dr. K. R. Srinivasa Iyengar describes her forte as 'the exploration of sensibility' and this phrase equally fits *Voices in the City* (1965). Calcutta is the city of doom in which the victims are caught as in a Greek tragedy. There is no room for withdrawal or escape. Nirode and Monisha, brother and sister, sensitive creatures both, find no peace in the city. Ghost-like they pace the city of voices till Monisha's suicide ends the tale with a bang. Anita Desai traverses the roads of sensibility again in *Bye-Bye, Blackbird* (1971), a tale of Indian immigrants in England. Dev is a Bengali who has married an English girl, Sarah. His friend Adit too comes to England and joins them. Personalities clash and resolve and clash again. There is no clear-cut remedy for the confrontation between two cultures. However, the novelist's conclusion seems to be that a bird must live for ever in psychic isolation, should it happen to settle in a nest not its own.

And there is, then, Kamala Markandaya. When *Nectar in a Sieve* appeared in 1954, it was hailed as an Indian variation of *The Good Earth.* The heroine, Rukmini, is the long-suffering peasant woman of India. Like millions of her counterparts, she wages an unending struggle against nature, society and industry. Industrialisation drives the peasant away at last, but hope never dies and the peasant returns again. After all, Mother Earth never fails her children!

Kamala Markandaya's second novel *Some Inner Fury* (1957) is about the political turmoil of the 'Quit India' movement. We move here to an entirely different set of characters. Mira the narrator-heroine, sister of an Indian bureaucrat, is in love with an Englishman. But the love is foredoomed. On this side, the family; on the other, the tragic inevitability of sudden violence that is part of Indian politics. Kamala's language is chaste and sensitive, adapting itself to the many changing moods with natural accuracy:

> I cannot think of that evening even now, without a piercing sadness. It was the last time we were all to be together, as a family, in happiness, yet we did not know it. We sat there in amity, warmed by laughter, carefree in a way we were never to be again, and saw no shadow, heard no whisper, to warn us it was the last time. And if we had, what then? We should still have gone our way, moving in orbits we ourselves created,

and could not help creating, because we were what we were. For myself, if I had to choose anew, in full knowledge of what was to come, I still would not wish my course deflected, for though there was pain and sorrow and hatred, there was also love: and the experience of it was too sweet, too surpassing sweet, for me ever to want to choose differently.

In *A Silence of Desire* (1961), Kamala Markandaya explores the inner worlds of the spirit. Faith *versus* scientific truth is an old, old problem. Sarojini relies on the former; her husband Dandekar on the latter. There is the Swamy—is he a saint-healer or the symbol of disharmony? This problem is a familiar one to Indian households, and the creative artist in Kamala has exploited the theme to artistic effect. Kamala's style carries the day in her fourth novel, *Possession* (1963). What is the true basis of art? Valmiki is transferred from the poverty of his village to the posh comforts of occidental life and achieves success as an artist. But he finds true fulfilment only in the loneliness of the cave retreat in his village where he enjoys the ambience of his spiritual guide. Lady Caroline Bell's 'possession' of the artist had been in vain. She could never possess his soul. Or is it that the Western mind reared on materialism can never hope to understand the depth of spirituality in the Indian psyche?

Urban poverty that leads to street violence is the theme of *A Handful of Rice* (1966). Kamala has obviously taken her clue from Bernard Malamud's novel, *The Assistant.* Ravi breaks into tailor Apu's household to get out of an ugly situation. He stays on to become an assistant to Apu and marries the tailor's daughter. Apu dies and Ravi shoulders the responsibility of running the household, which includes his mother-in-law. The daily trials of an impoverished home: the tragedy of the daily struggle for a handful of rice! How long can one struggle against going the way of Fagin? A sick wife and a roomful of children; a constant war of nerves with the parasitic relatives at home; an unspoken battle with his customers; a heart growing numb with misery and frustration. No fight left in them, Ravi and his like will be eternal plodders, suppressing the creaters within leading lives of quiet desperation:

> Sometimes envy of wealth—not displayed, but there—overcame Ravi. The cost of just one of those motor-cars that purred along the Marina, he felt, would keep him and his family over half a lifetime. How, he wondered with a burning curiosity, did anyone ever earn so much? He never would, not if he sewed a dozen shorts in a dozen hours every day of the week for a dozen years! No wonder then that young men like himself felt the itch, as he himself had done, to get into these same cars and drive away—only most of them couldn't have got far, unless they'd had a lesson or two first from a taxi-driver!

Kamala's next novel *The Coffer Dams* (1969) shows further maturity in her art. Like Bhabani Bhattacharya, she too has chosen to probe the problems that industrialisation brings to a tribal environment. The British technicians building a dam across a South Indian river, the Indian engineers employed by the firm, and the labour force drawn from the local tribes are the three discordant forces that come to a clash. The sensitive Helen and the tribal technician, Bashiam, come together as lovers, but misunderstandings pile up among the foreigners, the townsmen and the tribals. Only the aged tribal chief is wise—but he prefers silence. Kamala has a mastery over technical detail, and her language now and then rises to poetic heights in this novel. The criticism has often been levelled against Kamala that she has become too much of an expatriate to be capable of portraying the genuine Indian scene. But a few minor slips need not provoke us to so sweeping a generalisation. The total effect of her novels is the evocation of many-sided India, the village and the city and the adivasi settlement and the artificial township. She is the one post-independence Indo-Anglian novelist who has shown a steady progression in her art, and this is further demonstrated by her latest novel, *The Nowhere Man.*

Many of the Indo-Anglian novelists have also been writing short stories regularly. Collections by Khushwant Singh, Mulk Raj Anand, R. K. Narayan and Bhabani Bhattacharya have achieved considerable popularity. There are other competent writers too like Manoj Das, Manjeri Isvaran, Ruskin Bond, B. Reuben, G. D. Khosla and Rajaji who score by mixing gentle humour with serious intent. Hundreds of short stories are published in Indian periodicals but most of them fade away as soon as read. Nevertheless, some stories linger in our memory: Mulk Raj Anand's 'The Child'; Raja Rao's 'Akkayya'; Manoj Das's 'The Substitute for the Sitar'; B. Reuben's 'The Head Clerk', to name a few. Indian writers of short stories have generally avoided experimentation, and this is perhaps the reason why they have neither achieved astonishing brilliance nor quite plumbed the nadir of unintelligibility.

The one theme that has been powerfully exploited by many of these writers is communal disharmony. From the 1947 Partition Horror to the rape of Bangladesh twenty-five years later, the Indian writer has written scores of stories on the subject. Perhaps, this sore of communal fratricide has given the Indian intellectual a guilt-complex, and he has been trying to get rid of it one way or another. There are stark portrayals by writers from North India, especially Khushwant Singh and Mulk Raj Anand. But even R. K. Narayan hasn't been able to keep away from it. It is not the joy of independence but the guilt of the accompanying holocaust that has brought out the best creative moments of these writers. Narayan's 'Another Community' is an excellent essay in anonymity, and it brings out the helplessness of the individual against mob fury:

> Someone or a body of men killed a body of men a thousand miles away and the result was that they repeated the evil here and wreaked their vengeance on those around. It was an absurd state of affairs. But there it was: a good action in a far off place did not find a corresponding echo, but an evil one did possess that power.

A nameless fear starts gnawing at the vitals of the most innocent, the obscurest common man. His heroism is silenced, his sensitivity is deadened, and his 'saving lie' remains unuttered in spite of his resolution not to 'press the button':

But the button did get pressed. The incident of that alley became known within a couple of hours all over the city. And this uncle and other uncles did press the button; with results that need not be described here. Had he been able to speak again, our friend would have spoken a lie and saved the city: but unfortunately this saving lie was not uttered. His body was found by the police late next afternoon in a ditch in that wretched alley, and identified through the kerosene ration coupon in his breast pocket.

Prema Nandakumar, "English," in Indian Literature Since Independence, edited by K. R. Srinivasa Iyengar, Sahitya Akademi, 1973, pp. 42-70.

On the controversial aspects of Indian writing in English:

What, indeed, could be the aims and objectives of Indo-English creative literature and its authors? One of the answers to this question probably is that a perceptive Indo-English writer seeks primarily avenues for self-expression and, secondarily, aims at projecting India's image to Indians as well as foreigners. The issue is complex and raises many pertinent questions regarding the quality and inherent value of the image (or images) to be projected. What is the kind of image that this Indo-English literature seeks to present or actually does present? Is Indo-English literature original in the true literary sense, or is it derivative in attempting to interpret man the world through the medium of English? Is Indian writing in English inspired by an inwardly felt desire to create great literature or only an impressive establishment? The aura and international fame of Indo-Anglian writers perhaps tend to unduly enhance their importance and value, and make them falsely appear the sole creative interpreters of contemporary Indian scene. "It is better to write literature", says B. Rajan, "than to create an establishment and what this particular establishment has tended to legitimize is a derived and dehydrated idiom, as international and as characterless as aerodromes". Indo-Anglian writing has been harshly criticized precisely on this score: it is like weeds, rootless and alien to the true, native culture. This literature is neither Indian in its natural flowering nor English in its exploration. It is derivative in many ways, linguistically and otherwise, though that this is so is not a valid reason to devalue and denounce it as a hybrid.

Vasant A. Shahane, in "Indo-English Literature: Its Major Concerns and Its Academic Rationale," Alien Voice: Perspectives on Commonwealth Literature, edited by Avadhesh Shirwadkar, Humanities Press, 1982.

Binoo K. John

[In the following essay, John evaluates the status of Indian fiction in English in the 1990s, praising the work of such contemporary authors as Vikram Seth, Amitar Ghosh, Ved Mehta, and V. S. Naipaul.]

The prologue was there for everyone to read. A star burst of writing talent surfaced in the 1980s and captured the imagination of the world of English literature. Not only were Indian writers being published in the West with

heartwarming regularity, but they were setting new standards and getting rave reviews. It has been evident for some time now that India's post-independence, post-queen's-English generation, which does not care too much about split infinitives, is writing with magical plumes.

Their efforts have come to fruition now, and Indian writing in English has reached the rarefied realm where the masters reside. Vikram Seth's new 1,700-page opus, *A Suitable Boy,* has been snatched up by a brash new English publisher, Orion, for a whopping sum that only the likes of Salman Rushdie or popular paper-backers such as Britain's Jeffrey Archer command. Amitav Ghosh's new book, *In an Antique Land,* is expected to be a major publishing event in the West.

Editor-critic Rukun Advani finds a place in the 11th edition of *First Fiction,* an anthology of unpublished short stories that for many years has been considered a launching pad for writers. The publishing firm Faber and Faber has commissioned Rushdie to edit an anthology of Indian short stories that will be published next year, soon after Seth's tour de force is out in February. The Penguin list this year includes 12 first novels by Indian women. This could be an unprecedented and glorious phase for Indian writing.

In the history of a country's literature, such chapters are seldom written. And with most of the writing in a seemingly alien language, the magnitude of the literary renaissance becomes awe-inspiring. English, it seems, has finally become the language in which we Indians will tell our stories to the world. And undoubtedly, some Indian writers are blitzing their way to find their appointed slots among the galaxy of the immortals.

Indian publishers are strutting the hallowed corridors of literature and academia, dangling the names of new finds who can raise many a critical eyebrow. Penguin Books India is leading the pack with its amazing list of nearly 100 books a year, including Seth's, which will first be released in India. All the top-of-the-shelf British publishers now come out with Indian editions, including *Granta* magazine. HarperCollins has opened an editorial office in India. A host of small publishers are daring to come out with bold English titles and coffee-table books. And perhaps an indication of the tightening Indian grip over English literature is the fact that the most coveted job in the world of publishing—president of the U.S.-based Alfred Knopf—is held by an Indian, Sonny Mehta.

"We are no longer bowed down by custom or tradition," says David Davidar, editor of Penguin Books India. "There are no impositions on us anymore. We have extended the boundaries set by previous writers."

Talent obviously cannot bloom in an intellectual wasteland. The new set of formidable Indo-English writers are only building on foundations set very firmly by early Indian writers. From Mulk-Raj Anand and Narayan, beginning in the 1930s, through the 1940s of Ahmed Ali and G. V. Desani, the 1950s of Ruth Jhabvala up to Nirad C. Chaudhuri, Ved Mehta, V. S. Naipaul, and all the rest, these newer writers have had a tradition to fall back on.

We have evidently said "yes" to English, and this renaissance is proof. "English is not anymore for sitters in clubs or for an elite community," says publisher Ravi Dayal. "The writers are truly bilingual and not severed from indigenous traditions." The outpouring of timeless, magical epic stories can be seen as an indication that we have finally snapped the colonial apron strings and have learned to use our own idioms and ideas.

In spite of all this, the literary trail seems to have had its genesis in a bastion of colonial education—particularly Delhi's St. Stephen's College. The "Ghosh Generation," as Advani calls it, was shaped by St. Stephen's.

The new generation of Indian writers is also drawing from the intellectual infrastructure and the long tradition of literary grandeur that the country has had. There is no reason why the post-Ghosh generation—whose members are still in their 30s and have a creative life ahead of them—should not add stories of monumental lives to this tradition. From R. K. Narayan's tales that lead you to little by-lanes inhabited by storytellers and vendors of sweets to Vijayan Malayalam's saga of a 12th-century Egyptian Jew is an incredible gamut of writing for one country's contemporary writers to produce.

Such a golden period naturally invites comparison to the best phase in world literature. Critics have pointed out that during the champagne time in Russian literature, in the last century, there were only 12 classic writers, including Tolstoy and Dostoyevsky. India has around the same number of writers now at the zenith of their powers. *A Suitable Boy* being compared to *War and Peace?*

A book highly rated by a publisher may not stand the test of a classic and could get buried in the sands of time. However, in Seth, Ghosh, and the elite gang, Indian literature has finally found the writers at whose feverish imaginations the world will wonder forever.

> Binoo K. John, *"India's Glorious New Chapter,"* in Indian Express.

INDO-ENGLISH AUTHORS ON THEIR WORK

Balachandra Rajan

[*Rajan is an Indian-born Canadian novelist, educator, and critic. His novels include* The Dark Dancer *and* Too Long in the West. *He has also written and edited studies of the works of John Milton, T. S. Eliot, and other Western authors. In the essay that follows, Rajan discusses the role of the artist in society and defends the choices of Indians writing in English.*]

The word 'identity' has been used lavishly in [the] discussion in contexts which are both cultural and individual. I propose to reserve it for the process of creative self-realization and to refer to the establishing of a collective myth or image by some other term such as nationality. To create an identity is part of the essential business of an artist; to arrive at, or even to contribute towards a declaration of literary nationality, is not necessarily relevant to his concerns an may even infringe on the honesty of those concerns. A sense of nationality can grow out of the discovery of identity and it is important that this should happen frequently, if one is to establish a tradition that is both distinctive and rooted. But while identities may cohere into a nationality, that emerging myth or image should not be used as a frame within which the artist is obliged to discover himself, or by which the value of his discovery is to be judged.

The basic responsibility of an artist is definition, the creation of that unique inevitability which is the work and to which there is no alternative. He may write in the end for an audience but he cannot write as he does merely because an audience exists, with a certain structure of responses and expectations. If the work remakes a collective recognition (and every work remakes what it inherits), it does so because that remaking is part of its living logic, the declaration of its natural right to be. The contract between the writer and his work is an individual, not a social contract. Though social significance may be achieved in the end, it cannot be a requirement of the beginning. This beginning cannot spring from resolutions however carefully drafted, from blueprints however scrupulous, or from inductions from literary performance however cautious and however temperate. The beginning must be where it has always remained—in the creative conscience of the artist and in the struggle for definition which is a condition of that conscience.

What redeems this position from solipsism is the nature of the artist himself. He is a man speaking to other men, more responsible than others, because he is less prepared to compromise with the complexity of his own identity, less willing to surrender the uniqueness of his personal vision to the received formulae of communication. But he is also possessed of the hunger for significance; he is not simply a maker but a maker of meaning; and no act of definition can be enduringly valid for him unless it is also an act of communication, the re-establishing of his identity with others, the rendering of an individual vision without corruption, into a public language.

In newer literatures, the pressures of a literary nationality can be compulsive and the writer writes according to specifications—specifications which can be subtly tempting when the writer himself is committed to them as a citizen. Often these specifications are furnished not by the writer or even the literary critic, but by the sociologist and the cultural anthropologist. Inheritance and adaptation, the theme of this morning's discussion, has a distinctly non-literary resonance; the resonance should remind us that while literature is part of social history, the value of literature is not to be judged by the yield which it offers the social historian. This is the documentary view of literature and one that is understandably popular with the emerging critic in the emerging nation.

More strident than the documentary view is the patriotic, in which the writer becomes the voice of nationhood and the achievement of an Indian writer, for example, is judged by the intensity of his Indianness. What exactly Indianness is, is not clear; those who flourish the term as their exclusive virtue, display in the process very little of the Indian capacity for assimilation or tolerance. In any event what is supposed to be clear is that the Indian who writes in English is *ex hypothesi* un-Indian. He is a product of two cultures and therefore abnormal by the standards of either. His sensibility is mixed and therefore impure. In the dialogue between East and West he can speak for neither participant, though he may have some usefulness when the dialogue breaks down. To these accusations one can only reply that the presence of two cultures in one's mind forms a wider and therefore a saner basis on which to originate the quest for identity and that the discordance between these cultures can be creative as well as merely confusing. Perhaps one can go further and suggest that the man with mixed allegiances is contemporary Everyman and that to shut one's self off from the challenge of the 'non-Indian' betrays not a sense of nationality but an obsession with insularity. The case against the *bona fides* of the writer in English will not bear serious scrutiny; but both its existence and its disconcerting influence help to remind us of the dangers of putting the collective requirement before the creative encounter.

The same logic rules in the diatribes one hears against the use of the English language by Indian writers. The inwardness of Indianness, we are told, cannot be captured by a language essentially foreign; the subtlest and the most vital nuances are accessible only to a living speech with its roots in the soil and in the organic past. This may be so, but those capable of using language with the passionate precision which this argument suggests, must have discovered in the very act of using it that the real requirement is not to provide evidence of a theory however plausible, but to establish one's identity in the language of least compromise. If that language happens to be English the creative choice must be respected and one should judge by results rather than by dismal prophecies of what the result must fail to be. By now the results are sufficient to suggest that certain generalizations should in all honesty be revised. Let me add that language is both a friend and an enemy, as the soil is and as the elements are. The resistance one encounters in it may be a promise of creative strength; it does not necessarily mean that one should turn to a more pliable alternative.

India today is facing radical challenges not merely in its sociological landscape but perhaps even in that immemorial landscape of the heart. The clash is not simply between East and West (a conventional but deceptive stylization) but between the *mores* of a pre-urban civilization and one committed to drastic industrial growth. The question to be answered is whether the Indian tradition with its capacity for assimilation and its unique power of synthesis can come to terms with the new (and the new is the inevitable) without deep erosions in its fundamental character. In creating an image of this challenge there is perhaps a part to be played by the man of mixed sensibility, caught between crossfires, whose own mind is a microcosm of what he seeks to convey.

Yeats's determination to write for his race was mentioned at the beginning of this morning's discussion. That great poet said nearly everything once; in his last poem 'Under Ben Bulben' he seems to me to express his position more fully:

> Many times man lives and dies
> Between his two eternities,
> That of race and that of soul,
> And ancient Ireland knew it all.

Here we approach the philosophy of the mainstream, the conviction that life (and in a higher measure poetry) is the expression both of the traditional and actual, and of the eternal presences which inform them. Yeats spoke early in his criticism of a 'mythology married to rock and hill'. If he is a great poet it is because his work is indissolubly wedded to the hills and the rocks of both the exterior landscape and the interior vision.

> *Balachandra Rajan, "Identity and Nationality," in* Commonwealth Literature: Unity and Diversity in a Common Culture, *edited by John Press, Heinemann, 1965, pp. 106-09.*

R. K. Narayan

[*A novelist, short story writer, essayist, memoirist, travel writer, journalist, critic, and editor, Narayan is widely considered India's foremost author writing in English. Noted for his spare, straightforward writing style, Narayan uses wry, sympathetic humor to examine the universalized conflicts of Malgudi, a fictitious village set in southern India. In his novels, which include* Swami and Friends: A Novel of Malgudi, Mr. Sampath, Waiting for the Mahatma, The Painter of Signs, *and* A Tiger for Malgudi, *Narayan focuses on ordinary characters who seek self-awareness and struggle with ethical dilemmas. In the following essay, Narayan discusses the significance of the English language in India.*]

This paper is in the nature of a personal confession, rather than a learned thesis, on the subject of the English language and my links with it both as a reader and a writer. When I was five years old I was initiated into the mysteries of letters with the appropriate religious ceremonials. After being made to repeat the name of God, I was taught to write the first two letters of the alphabet on corn spread out on a tray, with the forefinger of my right hand held and propelled by the priest. I was made to shape the letters of both the Sanskrit and the Tamil alphabets, Sanskrit because it was the classical language of India, Tamil because it was the language of the province in which I was born and my mother tongue. But in the classroom neither of these two languages was given any importance; they were assigned to the poorest and the most helpless among the teachers, the *pundits* who were treated as a joke by the boys, since they taught only the 'second language', the first being English as ordained by Lord Macaulay when he introduced English education in India. English was important and was taught by the best teacher in the school, if not by the ruling star of the institution, the headmaster himself. The English Primer itself looked differently styled from the other books in the schoolbag with its strong binding and coloured illustrations—those were days when educational material was imported and no one could dream of producing a schoolbook in India. Thus from the Sanskrit alphabet we passed on directly to the first lesson in the glossy primer which began with 'A was an Apple Pie' (or was it just Apple, I don't remember); and went on to explain, 'B bit it' and 'C cut it'. The activities of B and C were understandable, but the opening line itself was mystifying. What was an Apple Pie? From B's and C's zestful application, we could guess that it had to do with the ordinary business of mankind, such as eating. But what was it that was being eaten? Among fruits we were familiar with banana, guava, pomegranate and grape, but not apple (in our part of the country), much less an apple pie. To our eager questioning, the omniscient one, our English teacher, would just state, 'It must be stuff similar to our *idli*, but prepared with apple.' This information was inadequate and one popped up to ask, 'What would it taste like? Sweet or sour?' The teacher's patience now being at an end, he would say, 'Don't be a nuisance, read your lessons,' a peremptory order which we obeyed by reciting like a litany 'A was an Apple Pie'. We were left free to guess, each according to his capacity, at the quality, shape, and details, of the civilization portrayed in our class books. Other subjects were also taught in English. We brooded over arithmetical problems in which John did a piece of work in half the time that Sam took, and when they laboured jointly, when would the work be completed? We also wrestled with bushels of oats and wages paid in pound, shilling and pence, although the characters around us in actual life called themselves Rama and Krishna and handled rupees and annas rather than half-crowns and farthings. Thus we got used to getting along splendidly with unknown quantities in our studies. At a later stage, we read and enjoyed the best of English prose, poetry, and drama, more or less on the same basis, overlooking details in the process of enjoying literature. Chaucer and Ben Jonson, Pope and Dryden, Boswell and Goldsmith, and a hundred others became almost our next-door neighbours. Through books alone we learnt to love the London of English literature. I have a friend, an engineer, who happening to visit West Germany on a technical mission, took off a fortnight in order to go to England and see the literary landmarks. His literary map included not only Keats's house at Hampstead, but also the amphibian world of the Thames bargemen described in the stories of W. W. Jacobs; he tried to follow the trails of Oliver Twist and David Copperfield, and also obtain, if possible, a glimpse of the comfortable world of Soames Forsyte, nor could he overlook the Drones Club mentioned by P. G. Wodehouse. He rounded off the trip with a visit to Stratford-on-Avon and the Lake District, and returned home feeling profoundly happy. Some time ago a more scholarly work appeared about his literary pilgrimage to England by Professor Sadhan Kumar Ghose wherein one will find a methodical account of a devoted scholar's travels in search of literary England past and present.

In our home my father's library was crammed with Carlyle, Ruskin, Walter Pater, and double-column complete works of Wordsworth, Byron, Browning, and Shakespeare. My father enjoyed reading Carlyle and Ruskin, and persuaded me not to miss them. For his sake I read thirty pages of *The French Revolution, Sartor Resartus,* and miscellaneous essays; twenty-five pages of *Marius the*

Epicurean, a hundred pages of Fielding and Thackeray, and skipped through a dozen novels of Sir Walter Scott. We also read many European and Greek classics in English translation. We relied on *The Times Literary Supplement,* the *Bookman, London Mercury, Life and Letters,* and the book pages of the weekly journals, for our knowledge of 'Contemporary' literature. We enjoyed the literary gossip generated in a society dominated by Shaw, Wells, and Chesterton. We were aware of not only what they wrote or were about to write at any given time, but also what they thought of each other and how much they earned in royalties.

For an Indian training in the classics begins early in life. Epics, mythology, and vedic poetry, of Sanskrit origin and of tremendous antiquity, are narrated to everyone in childhood by the mother or the grandmother in a cosy corner of the house when the day's tasks are done and the lamps are lit. Later one reads them all through one's life with a fresh understanding at each stage. Our minds are trained to accept without surprise characters of godly or demoniac proportions with actions and reactions set in limitless worlds and progressing through an incalculable timescale. With the impact of modern literature we began to look at our gods, demons, sages, and kings, not as some remote concoctions but as types and symbols, possessing psychological validity even when seen against the contemporary background. When writing we attempted to compress the range of our observation and subject the particle to an intense scrutiny. Passing, inevitably, through phases of symbolic, didactic, or over-dramatic writing, one arrived at the stage of valuing realism, psychological explorations, and technical virtuosity. The effort was interesting, but one had to differ from one's models in various ways. In an English novel, for instance, the theme of romance is based on a totally different conception of man-woman relationship from ours. We believe that marriages are made in heaven and a bride and groom meet, not by accident or design, but by the decree of fate, the fitness for a match not to be gauged by letting them go through a period of courtship but by a study of their horoscopes; boy and girl meet and love after marriage rather than before. The eternal triangle, such a stand-by for a western writer, is worthless as a theme for an Indian, our social circumstances not providing adequate facilities for the eternal triangle. We, however, seek excitement in our system of living known as the joint-family, in which several members of a family live under the same roof. The strains and stresses of this kind of living on the individual, the general structure of society emerging from it, and the complexities of the caste-system, are inexhaustible subjects for us. And the hold of religion and the conception of the gods ingrained in us must necessarily find a place in any accurate portrayal of life. Nor can we overlook the rural life and its problems, eighty-five out of a hundred Indians being village folk.

English has proved that if a language has flexibility any experience can be communicated through it, even if it has to be paraphrased sometimes rather than conveyed, and even if the factual detail, as in the case of the apple pie, is partially understood. In order not to lose the excellence of this medium a few writers in India took to writing in

English, and produced a literature that was perhaps not first-class; often the writing seemed imitative, halting, inapt, or an awkward translation of a vernacular rhetoric, mode, or idiom; but occasionally it was brilliant. We are still experimentalists. I may straightaway explain what we do not attempt to do. We are not attempting to write Anglo-Saxon English. The English language, through sheer resilience and mobility, is now undergoing a process of Indianization in the same manner as it adopted U.S. citizenship over a century ago, with the difference that it is the major language there but here one of the fifteen listed in the Indian constitution. I cannot say whether this process of transmutation is to be viewed as an enrichment of the English language or a debasement of it. All that I am able to confirm, after nearly thirty years of writing, is that it has served my purpose admirably, of conveying unambiguously the thoughts and acts of a set of personalities, who flourish in a small town located in a corner of South India.

English has been with us for over a century, but it has remained the language of the intelligentsia, less than ten per cent of the population understanding it. In view of this limitation our constitution provides for the changing over of the official language to Hindi in due course. At the same time, special institutes are established where English teachers are trained, and the subject occupies a high place in all universities. I feel, however, that it must reach the market-place and the village green if it has to send down roots. In order to achieve this, the language must be simply taught in a simpler manner, through a basic vocabulary, simplified spelling, and explained and interpreted through the many spoken languages of India. When such a technique of propagation is perfected, we shall see English, whatever its official status, assimilated in the soil of India and growing again from it.

> R. K. Narayan, *"English in India,"* in Commonwealth Literature: Unity and Diversity in a Common Culture, *edited by John Press, Heinemann, 1965, pp. 120-24.*

Problems of the Indian writer in English:

Generally speaking, the language of the Indo-English novels is either a copy of Victorian English or of light fiction of the 20th century. The promising beginnings which can be seen in G. V. Desani's *All About Mr. Hatterr* (1948) and Ved Mehta's *Delinquent Chacha* (1967) remained unnoticed. But it is certainly the use of language that will finally decide the future of the Indo-English language. There is no doubt that the present-day authors do not imitate their English models as much as in the last century, but simple story-telling favoured by the strong oral tradition of their country will not be sufficient to represent the complex reality of India. In comparison, the literature in the Indian languages seems in a better position to produce more satisfactory novels by focussing on a concrete situation in time and space.

Klaus Steinvorth in The Indo-English Novel: The Impact of the West on Literature in a Developing Country, *Franz Steiner, 1975.*

Kamala Markandaya

[*Markandaya is an acclaimed Indian novelist whose works often focus on the clash between traditional Indian lifestyles and the challenges of modernization. Among her best-known works are* Nectar in a Sieve, Some Inner Fury, *and* The Golden Honeycomb. *In the excerpt that follows, originally part of a speech given at a 1975 conference on Commonwealth literature, Markandaya examines some of the difficulties experienced by the Indian writer who chooses to write in English.*]

Let us go back a little, say to the beginning of this century, or even a little earlier. About this time middle class Indian families were beginning to send their sons abroad for education. They did this in the honest and possibly justified belief that it would further their careers. It was a voluntary act, and yet it was fraught with all manner of fears and misgivings. Prayers were said and priests were summoned, and the intensity of emotion was only equalled by the triumph of being able to say 'England-returned' when the hero came back.

To these families 'overseas' implied some very chilling things—things that went beyond the simple misery of separation. It implied that one was cut off from one's culture, and from the ethos of one's clan, and that one's roots were weakened, making the whole persona unstable.

Well, that was yesterday. Today is the jet age. Bombay is a few hours away. There is a temple in Hampstead—or is it Mitcham? There are 147 Indian restaurants in London alone. If you wished you need meet no one except Indians in London. Intercontinental Hiltons bloom, if that is the word, on both sides of the ocean, and what better mark can there be of a shared culture?

But the chill implications of overseas—loss of ethos, culture, roots—all these remain.

Of course all these losses are feasible. I suppose you could, if you tried, disown and cast away most of what made you what you are—people can do anything if they try. Indeed, some people have done it. But it does strike unlikely that the writer would want to discard such basic material, or that, having done so, he can avoid a certain drying-up of his work, an arid quality which can be a precursor of sterility.

So far I have suggested that one's culture and one's ethos and one's roots are fairly hardy and fairly fundamental. So they are. But these near-fundamentals become purely external when set beside that luminous and extraordinary cortex that exists in all of us, a cortex that as it were governs the morality and the sensibilities of creation, and like anything else can be cultivated or neglected.

This cortex has something to do with the brain, and a great deal more to do with the mind, not merely the conscious or limited mind that carries one's own experience of universals like grief or happiness, but that roving and imaginative entity that reaches into and extracts the truth of such universals *whether experienced or not.*

I can put it more simply, actually. I mean being able to feel what the other man feels when he's going through something that you haven't been through. And you can't really do that until you have cut through the culture, and the clothes, and the colour of the skin, and other such comparative externals. One has only to think of the utter blankness of the My Lai participants when their actions were questioned—but then you can find that kind of terrifying incomprehension in every country.

This imaginative process can, I think, be validly compared to living—or dying, for that matter: a process of attrition, a paring away of externals to arrive at a perception of essentials.

So long as we are involved in this process we are involved in universals. And if we are writing about these universals—that is to say books or poetry, as opposed to tourist brochures—we are simply writers, and any qualification, such as 'Commonwealth writer', becomes a shade irrelevant. I say this despite the fact that I think of myself as an Indian writer.

Perhaps, then, I should say that such a qualification, viz., 'Commonwealth writer' *would* be irrelevant in some ideal society yet to be invented. Actually there is in our midst one such innovator, a rugged (as he has to be) visionary by the name of Mr. Gary Davis. He has put forward the daring, if glaringly obvious, proposition, that we are all citizens of one world. The difference between this gentleman and the rest of us is that he is prepared to back his hunch. He has refused to accept any label other than that of world citizen. He has printed his own 'world' passport, which one or two nations are tolerant about, and he has minted, I believe, his own, universal, coins, which absolutely no one, not even his friends, will accept.

His trouble is not that the conception is at fault, but that its implementation is so tricky. And that is the trouble. A world aspect is so cumbersome, so unmanageable, that we have necessarily to break it down into packages. And certainly packages like 'Commonwealth writer' do impose some kind of order on the scene. But when writers take their places in the appropriate package the suspicion arises that they are judged by the standards of that particular package—which may be higher or lower than what prevails elsewhere, that is not the point, but it gives the impression of a special standard.

What I am really doing here is thinking aloud, because I am pretty ambivalent in my thought. But here is D. J. Enright, in a different context, but on roughly similar ground, arguing in similar vein. Here is what he writes: I quote from his classic *Memoirs of a Mendicant Professor:*

> The language of these (non-English) writers is English, and . . . they have entered into competition with the Oxford Book of English Verse and its centuries—just like any other English poet. They will have to decide whether they wish to be judged by absolute, that is literary standards, or by special local standards. The world will urge them to choose the latter, to partake of that new 'subject' . . . called 'Commonwealth literature'.

I do see the dilemma, viz., that Commonwealth literature would be swamped in the general tide if it were *not* singled out for special attention—and the Commonwealth writer would be the loser. So I'm not necessarily complaining. I am only saying that I have noticed a kind of herding instinct in literary editors. They do like to keep like with like. They have these little boxes, and inside you will find a clutch of Caribbean writers, or a batch of Commonwealth writers. Best of all they like keeping the women, bless their hearts and tiny minds, together. Santha Rama Rau, Attia Hosain, Nayantara Sahgal and I have rubbed shoulders for well over a decade.

I have brooded over this, in a state of some curiosity, and explanations do begin to emerge.

In the West, in America and Britain they have a splendid tradition of encouraging the young and emerging artist. You would never guess it to hear them speak—all those snarling references to philistinism, and how there isn't a national theatre in the country worth the name (in fact the national theatre they are building in London will be one of the finest ever built; and most nations can only sigh over what the Kennedy Centre has to offer). Disregarding these national quirks it is possible to see they have this instinct, this inspired policy, of handling the newly-hatched writer as if he were both fragile and precious. So they encourage and they praise. No first novel, no early poem, is so bad that they cannot find something good to say about it. They do not make withering comparisons—comparisons that would petrify the beginner and possibly silence him for good.

And they have extended this endearing habit to the Commonwealth artist. It is rather as if they had come across a tree growing in unlikely places, say in those holes along suburban pavements, and had put up one of those wickerwork baskets around it for protection.

There is a lot to be said for this policy, which has yielded rich dividends, and which is rooted in generosity and a genuine concern for the artist. Indeed I am one of many to have benefited from it, and I am happy to acknowledge my debt. But sometimes I do begin to wonder: Could it be that Professor Enright has a point: and could it be that Commonwealth writing ought, now and then, to come out from behind the wickerwork?

I see now I have come to a part of my notes that is underlined in red, which means it is important. It is this: *in everything I say I speak for myself.* I am not, and never have been, a spokeswoman, or spokesperson if you prefer, for India—an ambassador, as they lightheartedly put it (people who have no notion of the built-in horrors) an 'ambassador for your country'. Nevertheless I do find myself, from time to time, shoved into this heady, but frightful position. This is a situation well known to every Commonwealth writer, overseas or not. It is also what is known as a no-win situation, because you collect whatever opprobrium is going, as ambassadors do, without any of the perks that attach to the office. So I do emphasise that my singular views are precisely that. . . .

I thought I would allow myself a little time to quibble over 'Commonwealth writer overseas' before conceding that the animal does exist. A corollary to that existence is a set of unique—I don't know whether to call it advantages, or perils. There used to be a cliché—before the whole thing went a bit sour, that is to say before the third world took to travelling, and sneaking a look at what the first and second worlds were up to at home—a cliche that travel broadens the mind. It may well do so, although the evidence for it is sketchy: the English who travelled to India seemed to many to have narrower minds than those who stayed at home. But there is no doubt in my mind that the Commonwealth writer abroad is lumbered with double vision. Double vision not in the sense of a flawed vision, but a vision that is slightly enlarged, like an over-active gland, and insists on perceiving two sides to every picture. This is fine for a civil servant. There are even people who prefer these dry civil notes, who like to hear that while on the one hand Indians are rather cruel to their ponies, on the other hand it is a bit near the bone for the British to clamp all those dogs into stocks and force them to smoke, and almost scraping the barrel for the American military to douse a million birds with tergitol and freeze them to death. But it does nothing for the writer, who is obliged to curb his flights of fancy, and yet is not really keen on civil service prose.

The peril, however, is less that the Commonwealth writer overseas will begin to sound like a civil servant, but even more that he won't. In the wholly justified flight away from this ghastly kind of balance, he or she may well overcorrect, producing a lop-sided picture of the mother country, or the host country, which reduces the inhabitants to rage, or has them rolling in the aisles, according to temperament, or perhaps the degree of sophistication. *Pravda* on the subject of Britain, I'm told, is always good for a laugh—the British are very good at laughing at themselves. But *The New Yorker* too, I hear, has raised one or two titters in Delhi.

So here we have the slightly tilted picture as viewed or painted by the man or woman overseas. It is nothing to what can happen when he or she goes home, for there are no shocks like the shocks the homeland can hand out to the returning traveller. For absence has sapped his endurance. It also highlights the horrors. Thin-skinned from his sojourn in the opulent and insulated West he goes from Santa Cruz airport to the Taj Mahal hotel, groaning and flinching every inch of the way. I know, because I have made this journey myself.

And in due course the book appears: one year later in the case of a man, two years later in the case of a woman because, you will remember, she has also had to make some 1500 cups of tea and coffee in the meantime.

The book contains a good deal of what has, quite rightly, offended the writer. It is sprung, at least partly, from guilt, shame, and misery: and it dwells passionately on the defects, failures, dark areas, and areas of filth, muddle, poverty and incompetence of the mother-country and its inhabitants.

Which is fine as far as it goes. It is good, isn't it, to be aware of one's faults? Only way to remedy them, isn't it?

True. But it is somewhat dispiriting for the citizens, who are doing their best, and in the process the dignity of the nation does get a bit mangled.

But perhaps you have to be at a distance to think such thoughts.

More than most the Commonwealth writer overseas has the blessing, or bane, of duality. He, or she, has to steer carefully between justice and criticism, between passion and repression. He, or she, is not helped by being asked bluntly: "What audience do you write for?"

No other kind of writer, not even those charming ladies who produce charming and romantic fairy tales by the bucketful, is so persistently asked: What is your audience?

And the odd thing is that no matter how often one is asked, one is always a bit stunned. It is, isn't it, a little like sacrilege, to ask a serious writer what audience he is writing for? One is not, after all, some kind of catering manager. If there is any certainty in one's life, it is that one is not a catering manager. It is at this high peak of conscious nobility that the twinges begin: sure sign that some kind of truth, usually an awkward truth, is trying to wriggle out.

And the truth is this: no matter how tall the ivory tower in which you dwell, you are still aware that the very fact of writing in English pre-supposes an English-reading audience. English-reading, like three square meals a day, or the lion's share of the world's goodies, is the accepted hallmark of the Westerner. This is the basis of the slightly unnerving statement, which can also sound uncommonly like an indictment, which I have had hurled at me, that I write for a Western or westernised audience.

Where this statement, or accusation, begins to founder is that having an idea of who one's audience is does not necessarily mean that one is writing for it. Because I find there is this curious feature about writing, a kind of regulating mechanism, a built-in justice if you like. The more you strain to write for an audience, the more strained the writing becomes. Once, when my books weren't selling at all, I thought I would write a jolly, cheerful book that a lot of jolly, cheerful people would buy. It turned out so awful I had to scrap it and begin again—after 192 pages. Many writers have had this experience. Most writers are prudent people too, and they soon give up this struggle to write to order, which they suspect will end in bunging up the whole creative process.

There is a paradox here, which would need an analysis of the very nature of ego and communication to resolve. To put it simply, one is aware of an audience, and at the same time that is the last thing one considers when writing. I am not talking about some specialised, or esoteric mode of writing. I am talking about the perfectly ordinary mechanics of ordinary writing, and I believe I know what I'm talking about, because no writer is made to go into it so thoroughly as the Commonwealth writer overseas.

Well, I have had my share of brickbats for having Western readers. In fact like most writers these days I am pleased to hear I have any readers at all, without bothering about their nationality. But I'm also glad to report that I do in fact have my share of Indian readers. At least my Indian publishers tell me so, and I also receive a certain amount of mail, a lot of it from College students. I am rather pleased about this because I have a notion—and it may well be a romantic notion, though romances can be both true and false—that there is a certain strength to be found in, and drawn from, the marketplace.

Indian College students who write to me often ask: How does one become a writer? The answer is one doesn't know. But there are some clues: patience, I suppose: my first published book was the third I had written. And of course luck, one needs a great deal of luck. And being able to sit in a room for hours staring at the wall and apparently doing nothing. Some people believe Latin is basic equipment for those who would write in English. Mr. Khushwant Singh, the distinguished writer and editor, says somewhere that the Indian writer who has not read the Bible has no business to be writing in English. For myself, I think an awareness of history is helpful.

Indeed, the work of many Commonwealth writers, and especially Commonwealth writers overseas, shows a lively awareness of colonial history: an awareness that is sparked by the attitudes they encounter abroad.

Generally speaking, this attitude is one of profound indifference to the Commonwealth. The average person—we are back in the marketplace, the overseas marketplace—is pretty hazy about the history of the Commonwealth, its whys and wherefores. He doesn't want to think about it too much either. But when he does, usually when overseas aid comes up for discussion, some dim memory stirs of what he has learnt from school primers, and he is ready to tell you of the benefits that accrued to empire and colony, which can be summarised as roads, railways, bridges.

But wasn't it, perhaps, a two-way process? You venture to suggest.

Well, yes, we must have got something out of it, mustn't we. But not much, we gave a lot more to the colonies that we ever got out of them.

Nothing drives one back to the history books more quickly than this.

But should a novel have these historical or political subnotes? I can only say that it often seeps through. And when it does it is a fearful struggle between chauvinism, a desire to point up past injustice, and a deep sense of obligation to the country from which one has received so much courtesy and kindness, and the chance to follow one's chosen career, as I have done.

Where I am aware of distance, though—really struck by it—is not in this historical area. The gulf between me and the West really opens when I encounter the assumption, here in the West, that the earth was created for man: an assumption that seems to be used, consciously or unconsciously, to justify almost any kind of assault upon the animal kingdom, and upon the systems of the earth itself.

Whereas I, with my background, happen to believe that everything exists in its own right. I do find I have a way of riding this particular hobbyhorse right into my novels, although I am not aware of it at the time. I don't necessari-

ly approve: novels and sermons are best kept apart. But, as I said, things do have a way of seeping through.

If I could turn now to the English language itself. It has a truly dazzling variety. There is American English and Canadian English, and South African, Australian, West Indian and Indian English, and of course English English with its regional variations. Not only accent and pronunciation, but sometimes usage and idiom show distinct differences. Such diversity must command respect, if only as a manifest of what people can do when they really try.

Some Indians speak Indian English and some Indians speak English-English. I don't only mean accent. Although accents too can vary, and the equivalent of Shaw's Professor Higgins could I daresay spot whether the English-speaking Indian came from Madras, or Trivandrum, or Bombay.

Nor do I mean what is called Hobson-Jobson, sometimes also called Tommy's English, in which Indian words have become incorporated into the English language, for example words like bungalow, jungle, jodhpurs, Blighty, char and so on. I mean the kind of English spoken by the averagely educated Indian as distinct from the highly educated Indian. This kind of English is a bit surprising, and unusual, and takes liberties with grammar and syntax. Some people deplore this sea-change into something rich and strange, on the ground that it does not observe the rules of language: but the language itself gains in zest and immediacy. Some writers capture this beautifully—Patrick White of course, and Shiva Naipaul in his *Fireflies,* and also Nissim Ezekiel, the poet. Here is part of one of his poems:—

> I am standing for peace and non-violence
> My world is fighting fighting
> Why all people of world
> Are not following Mahatma Gandhi
> I am simply not understanding.
> Ancient Indian Wisdom is 100% correct.
> I should even say 200% correct.
> But modern generation is neglecting—
> Too much going for fashion and foreign thing.

One needs a good ear for this, and constant referral back, language being the volatile thing that it is. So far I have generally kept to standard English.

Tied in with this is the use of local words. To indulge or not to indulge is the question. I must confess I am in two minds about this. Sometimes I am a bit of a purist, and feel that Indian words should not be employed simply to give a little local colour. Indeed last year I went so far as to broadcast this view in a programme on the BBC. This year I am not so sure. I am writing a romantic novel, and it seems less forced to use Indian words than their English equivalents—words like *rajkumari, chaprassi, maidan* and so on.

Mulling over this I feel that perhaps the thing to do is to use local words with brio, as the Americans do: that is to say simply to go ahead and use Indian words without italics, or footnotes, or glossaries, or apologies. These devices seem to me to interrupt the natural flow, and to introduce an unfortunate ethnic note. Novels, after all, are not and should not be regarded as ethnic studies.

This is put rather well, I think, by the theatre critic of *The Observer* in his review of *Don's Party*, a play which recently opened in London. I quote:—

> It is probably unfortunate that we still automatically regard Australian plays as ethnic studies.

And he goes on: "The programme glossary is almost too anxiously helpful." Exactly. For 'Australian plays' read 'Indian novels'.

Of course it could be argued that not to explain unfamiliar words is to sacrifice clarity. My American publishers and I have had several arguments on this score. But when I read, say, an American novel there are any number of words I don't know. I have to work for the meaning, and it is a rewarding experience in a way that discovery by footnote could never be. I am inclined to the view that Commonwealth writers, like American writers, should extend this rewarding experience to their readers also. It would carry an added bonus, in that these words could shed their funny plumage, and writers who use them could slide off the ethnic or exotic shelf and enter the mainstream of writing.

There is, of course, a difference between exotic words and exotic content. And despite what I have said I am not arguing against exoticism per se, because I recognise there is a place for it. Many people in both India and the West crave romance and colour. The Indian film industry has perceived this hunger, and there are huge audiences for the sumptuous, escapist films they produce. So why not exotica in books, why not give people all the rajahs, cobras, tigers, lotuses and dancing girls that they ask for? There is no reason not to. After all we have our Indian Jane Austen, and our Indian Macaulay, and our Indian Pearl Buck, so why not an Indian Ouida or Elinor Glyn? Again, no reason. As I say, I am writing a romantic story. But all the same a faint alarm keeps ringing in my mind, because the line between writing a book and a pulp magazine romance is very thin indeed, though both may be equally acceptable. Somehow I feel safer to keep this alarm going.

In an audience like this it is scarcely to be hoped for that contradictions and inconsistencies in what I have said will escape unnoticed. I can only take refuge behind the characteristic reaction of Mahatma Gandhi, when reproached for inconsistency by a pained and exasperated Viceroy. I quote from memory:—

> It is not my concern to be consistent with myself at all times but to be consistent with those aspects of truth as they may present themselves to me from time to time.

Nevertheless there is one belief to which I have remained fairly constant. It is tied in, paradoxically, with the shifting balance of power in the world.

At one time there were the accepted metropolitan areas, in the West, and there were the colonies and later the Commonwealth. On the whole the Commonwealth looked to the metropolis for its standards, and the metropolis, confident of its values, was content that it should. But now there are fewer certainties. A good deal of soul-searching is going on. The Commonwealth has its own theses to put forward, and the metropolis is willing to listen. In this climate I cannot share the gloomy views for Commonwealth literature expressed elsewhere.

> *Kamala Markandaya, "One Pair of Eyes: Some Random Reflections," in* The Commonwealth Writer Overseas: Themes of Exile and Expatriation, *edited by Alastair Niven, M. Didier, 1976, pp. 23-32.*

Mulk Raj Anand

[*Anand is an acclaimed Indian novelist, short story writer, critic, and non-fiction writer. Along with R.K. Narayan and Raja Rao, he is credited with establishing the main themes and philosophical concerns of modern Indo-English literature. Anand's works are typically concerned with Indian social and political dilemmas. Such early fictional works as* Coolie *and* The Untouchable *deal with the cruelties of the caste system and the suffering induced by poverty. Anand's later novels include* The Private Life of an Indian Prince, *and the septet of novels collectively called "The Seven Ages of Man." In the following essay, Anand defends the cultural authenticity of Indian writing in English, and discusses the origins of what he calls "Pigeon-Indian."*]

At the outset, let me state my thesis: I believe that Indian-English writing has come to stay as a literature of India, because it is based on Indian-English language of the most vital character, like Irish English, American English, Welsh English, Australian English or Canadian English. It has the same advantage as those forms of English and similar disadvantages. Of course, the historical accident, which gave rise to this language and literature may have been different from that which produced the other forms of English. In the case of most other forms of English in the British Commonwealth, the natives of Great Britain were primarily involved as the speakers of a tongue which took on the accents the associations, the diction and the accretions of the local atmosphere, as well as some of the 'vulgarizations', which the British first despised but now accept. In India, the original British speakers introduced the English language in the University system for training Babus and other low paid executives to do the dirty work of the routine running of government for them, as the recruitment of the superior British race was not profitable either to the rulers or to their countrymen at home.

Unfortunately, for the British ruling circles in India, some of the Babus themselves were clever enough to learn more English than the inadequate stuff taught in the British-Indian universities; they mastered the alien tongue and used it (it now seems successfully) to make the masters quit India.

Some of the contemptible Babus even went to the sources of English writing, mastered English literature, and have written accomplished prose and verse in this language.

I am inclined to agree with my contemporary, the Indian-English writer, Raja Rao, who has described the process of Indian-English writing, at its most authentic, in the following words:

> One has to convey in a language, that is not one's own the spirit that is one's own. One has to convey the various shades and omissions of a certain thought movement that look maltreated in an alien language. I used the word alien. Yet English is not really an alien language to us. We are all instinctively bilingual, many of us writing in our own language and in English. We cannot write like the English. We should not. We cannot write only as Indians. We have grown to look at the large world as part of us.

That I consider to be cogent justification for Indian-English writing today in the most self-conscious creative writers of this language. I think that those recalcitrants (and there are many more at home than abroad), who do not accept Indian-English writing as an emergent medium for organic expression of the urges of a fairly large part of our people, are barking up the wrong tree. Indian-English writing has come to stay, because some of the finest minds of our country wished to fashion a language for a genuine social purpose, the communication, in a growing language, as vital as was Urdu from the mixture of Persian and Brij Bhasha in Mughal India 300 years ago. Urdu too was at first despised for its novelty in the use of words from a different mother tongue, and then for its verse, and is now being rejected as an alien language, though it grew up in this very land. Indian-English is in a similar position in the eyes of those who wish to 'Indianize' us moderns.

I realize, of course, that, in a situation, where some writers of the Indian-English language have achieved world-wide recognition, because of the extra advantage of communicating, quickly, and with brilliant craftsmanship, with vast audiences in the outside world, they arouse natural antipathies. The writers in the major languages of India feel somewhat surprised that they themselves have not got there. The balance will have to be redressed, because there are major contemporary writers in the national languages of India who must be made known in all parts of our country and abroad. But, those writers of the national languages, who despise Indian-English writing, must be more generous than Chairman Mao and allow 'a hundred flowers to bloom'.

For the Indian-English writers may be the very agents for the translation of the writers in the Indian languages, into at least one medium, English, which can spread the original writings known to wider circles in what is now one of the three universal languages.

I know I am treading on everybody's corns, as I say this. I have ringing in my ears a sharp exchange with the brilliant Urdu poet, Ali Sardar Jafri, which took place in a literary meeting some time ago. In an aside, during the discussion of a political theme, I happened to remark that Indian-English writing is a kind of bridge between our people and the world outside. My friend, who is not given to chauvinism, remarked, 'Yes, it is a bridge on a dry river'. Unfortunately for him, he finds that his own language, Urdu, is being relegated by the Hindi imperialists to the status of a polluted stream which flows in Pakistan, and

I have recently had an occasion to defend the cause of Urdu. I, therefore, offer no apologies for the assertion made above. I have a hunch that Indian-English will last out, in spite of the denigration all round and the deliberate attempts being made to exorcize it from Indian life altogether.

There is irony in the fact that when one of the most eminent Hindi writers asked us to do our creative work in our original mother tongues in a seminar, he himself read his own contribution, not in Hindi but in Indian-English. May I offer the charming effrontery of the talented poetess, Kamala Das, who speaks with some candour on this theme in her poem, 'An Introduction':

> I don't know politics,
> but I know the names,
> Of those in power,
> and can repeat them like,
> Days or weeks, or names of months
> beginning with
> Nehru. I am Indian; very
> brown, born in Malabar.
> I speak three languages
> write in two
> Dream in one. 'Don't
> write in English,' they said,
> 'English is not your mother tongue'.
> why not leave
> me alone,
> Critics, friends, visiting cousins
> Everyone of you, why not let me
> speak in
> Any language I like?
> The language I speak
> becomes mine
> Its distortions, its queernesses
> all mine, mine alone.
> It is half English, half Indian,
> funny perhaps, but it is honest
> It is as human as I am human
> Don't you see?

After these words, the main argument should be declared won.

I would like, however, to differentiate, very loosely, between the higgledy-piggledy spoken English in our country, from the imaginative use of the same language in the hands of the creative writers in Indian English.

I am not doing this arbitrarily, in order to get the rise out of any possible contenders on behalf of purity or impurity. I wish to record the phenomenon and draw attention to those qualities which make for vitality or grace in writing, so that the critics may refrain from attacking the introduction of original metaphor and imagery from our mother tongues into the English language when they single out the clichés and claptrap for snobbish scrutiny.

I would like to define the two kinds of English by entitling the imaginative transformation of Indian-English as 'Pigeon-Indian' and the 'anyhow' speech as 'Pidgin-English', without associating myself in the latter definition, with the British contempt implied in the word 'Pidgin'. I only wish to indicate that, while 'Pigeon-Indian' soars, the 'Pidgin-English' remains in the gutter, where upper-caste discrimination has consigned most people. The two interchange in my opinion. One borrows from the other, because the perversity of human nature takes no notice of British prudery.

Now, let me describe to you the process in which Pigeon-Indian emerges. I hear the echoes of loud voices as I reach the Mall Road in the British-built civil lines anywhere in India. And then the words strike dithyrambically on the tympanum of my ears:

'Hello ji!'

'Thank you ji!'

I see broad smiles and conviviality and good humour. And one young man invites a friend to come and see a favourite star in the film 'Dak Bangalow', the friend says: 'By God; *yaar,* I will come!'

I am transported in my mind to London, just around Christmas time when the bus conductor, relaxing to the gay lights and the buntings and the shopping crowds, accosts me—'Hello—Gandhi! You—Karachi? Bombay? Delhi?'

'Poona!', I say, to strike a cord in his head.

'Oh Poona! Poona! Begad Sir! I am Poonawallah!', he mimics the legendary Colonel Blimp made famous by the cartoonist David Law.

I realize that, wherever Indians meet Indians, or Englishmen meet Indians, and even ex-colonial Englishmen meet ex-colonial Scotsmen, some Indian words in English speech are spoken.

On the first hearing, Indian words in English sound a trifle strange and contemptible, specially, if they are in new recent combinations like 'Helloji!, 'Thank you ji!' or 'By God *yaar!*'. But as most of us in India mix ordinary conversation in our own language with a good sprinkling of English words, we naturally take the words of our language into our exchanges in English freely; and, to most ears, phrases like 'Have you finished your *khana*' (food) or 'Jungli (barbarian), you don't know anything!' become acceptable.

There is a psychological truth behind this kind of synthetic speech. It is this: even when Indians know English grammar and have been used to speaking the alien tongue for a long time, they tend to feel and think in their own mother tongues. And often, the native speech enters into the shell of the sentence in the foreign language through certain indigenous words.

Similarly, those Britishers, who have been to India, remember certain basic local words, which they have heard from their clerks or servants, or in books written by creative writers like Kipling, or the scholars, and they respond to the rhythms of the Indian words, which they have heard and remembered, almost as we all respond to nursery rhymes in any language.

It is only when British critics begin to call Indian-English speech 'Pidgin-English' that the Indian words in English begin to look ludicrous, incongruous and lacking in good taste. The comments in the doggerel verse of Mr. Yule and Mr. Burcell on the problems of Indian words in English are significant:

> In common, here a *chit* serves for business and
>   our wit,
> Banshall's place to lodge our ropes
> And Mango orchards are all *topes*
> *Godown* usurps the warehouse place
> *Compound* dissolves each walled space
> To *dafter, khana, attar, tanks*
> The English language owes no thanks.
> Since office, essence, fish-pond shew
> We need not words so harsh and new
> Much more I could such words expose
> But *Ghats* and *Daks* the list shall close
> Which in plain English is no more
> To wharf and post expressed before.

In spite of this protest against 'Hobson-Jobson' (an English misnomer based on the Indian ejaculation 'Ya Hassan! Ya Hussain!'), there are over 900 Indian words in the *Oxford English Dictionary.* And many more are being added every year. I have myself been considered responsible for adding fifty or more.

There is an invariable phenomenon in the realm of human speech that languages grow up in a miscellaneous manner. They do so through the survival of the fittest and most communicative words, which also have a rhythm about them, even if these words seem somewhat odd, bizarre, and alien to the custodians of pure speech. And no dictate, or law of parliament, or professional sermon can disallow people from using new metaphors and images, or coining new words, or making strange combinations. In fact, many languages are full of alien words, which have, in time, become respectable. The English language is, indeed, by and large, one of these elastic media which may refuse today to translate, transliterate, or interpret, a word from a foreign language, but it took over hundreds of words from Latin, Greek, French as well as the languages of the countries where the British Empire once held sway. And, in spite of the healthy struggle of the creative writers of Great Britain against the clichés and claptrap, there has been a general acceptance of Pidgin-English in English literature.

Now, it would be interesting to ask if the adopted Indian words in English retain the original shades of meaning or have they acquired some new connotations as well?

The answer to this question is complicated by the fact that some of the Indian words, which are now accepted in the *Oxford English Dictionary,* were originally transported by the early Greek and Roman traders and found their way into mediaeval English through Greek and Latin. These words have a singing quality about them: *amber, camphor, ginger, indigo, lac, lilac, musk, opal, sandalwood* and *sugar.* The river Sindhu became Indus, and was, in time, transformed into *India,* from which have come *Indiaman, India rubber, India ink,* and even *Red Indian.* Most of these words have kept close to the original connotations even after they were exported.

As the Portuguese were the first Westerners to trade with India in the mediaeval period, words like *calico,* the cloth made in Calicut, went to Europe from the Malayalam language of South-West India. Some words entered Europe through the French traders, like *cheroot* which derives from the phonetic sound of the Tamil original *shuruttu,* a cigar open at both ends. Other words from the South Indian tongues, which have been only slightly perverted in the borrowing and adorn the English language are: *areca, betel, coir, copra, jaggery, jack,* (a fruit) and *bandicoot* from the original *pandi-kottu,* the name of the pig-rat.

Mulligatawny is the perversion of *mulugu-tani* and means a thick soup on the menu of British restaurants. *Bombay duck* was adopted from the Koli fisherman of Maharashtra from their original *bum mala,* the name of the small dried fish greatly relished by British memsahibs. The English adopted certain useful words from Persian and Hindustani during Mughal rule for the use of John Company, as the trading concern of the East India Company was then called. *Sircar,* the name of a province under the Mughals, which also denoted government, was taken over bodily. *Nawab* became *nabob; durbar,* or the court, came to be used for the British ceremonies like the Delhi Durbar of George V and Queen Mary in 1911.

British scholars used the Sanskrit words of Indian religions and philosophies without corrupting them in order to indicate original meaning. *Yoga* in English is now used for the philosophy of self-realization. *Nirvana* is accepted as the Buddhist ideal. *Karma* denotes good or bad deeds. *Dharma* is understood among British students of Indian thought as religion and has yielded the popular phrase *Dharma bug,* which means prig.

The rank and file Britishers who bought cloth enjoy using the word *Kashmere* for the fine woollen cloth of India. The military officers still order their *Jodhpurs* in Saville Row and the tailors there know that the Sahib is asking to be measured for breeches. The beatniks talk of their *dungarees,* without knowing that the original of this word is *Dongri* in Bombay, where a coarse cloth was used for making overalls for factory workers.

In the nineteenth century, the researches of British orientalists added words from Indian holy books, names of gods and goddesses and other funny but telling perversions. The words *Vedic* and *Vedantist* are derived from *Veda, Brahmanic* from *Brahmin, Mantra* from *mantram, Suttee* from *Sati.* I have seen the word *avatar,* meaning incarnation, being used by English novelists about India. Those who have penetrated deeper into Indian culture, have taken over *amrit*-nectar; *Deva*-god; *guru*-teacher; *granth*-holy book; *stupa*-Buddhist tomb for relics; *vihara*-cave temple; *gopuram*-gateway of South Indian temple; *Krishna, Radha, Shiva, Ganesh, Vishnu* and *Juggernaut,* (perversion of Jagannath, the god of the Puri temple).

The flora and fauna of India were often called by Indian names, because the Latin words were tongue twisters. *Pipal, tulsi, teak, bulbul, cheeta, sambhar, chital, gaur* and *krait* found their way into English usage.

The Burra Sahib's vocabulary was enriched by certain domestic words, because of the absence of the English maid-servants and the necessity of employing an Indian *bera* (bearer). This tolerably efficient shadow of the Sahib, the bearer not knowing the original English for foodstuffs,

forced certain names onto the recalcitrant tongue of the Sahib: *arrack* for *areck,* liquor; *toddi,* palm drink; *punch* for the witches brew of mixed hot rum and lemon; *pillau* for fried rice; *kabab* for skewered meat.

The outdoor sports of the Sahibs brought words like *dhum dhum,* the bullet reminiscent of the mutiny near Calcutta; *dinghy,* small boat, *dhow,* big boat. The environment of the Sahib's bungalow in Civil Lines brought in *Chowkidar,* a necessary personage against would be dacoits, i.e., *dakoos; dhobi*-washerman, *mali*-gardener, *jamadar*-exalted sweeper, *khansama*-cook.

The Sahib's tongue anglicized many things for which there were no English equivalents, because he was essentially conservative by nature. He adopted *maharaja*-king, because the prince, in his finery, was not quite the exalted gentleman in trousers King Edward or King George was. *Goonda*-rogue, is not quite rogue but superior in violence; *mufti* meant the free issue of plain clothes to soldiers and could alone describe the clothes worn in the bazaar, street, by a *sepoy*-soldier. The *gharry*-wheel-carriage, was not quite like the gig, landau or phaeton. *Bandobast* for arrangements was peculiar to India, because nothing could be arranged. *Tamasha* was a spectacle, ranging from the snake-charmer's performance to the dramatic *Raas. Salaam*-salute had to be acknowledged willy nilly, because of the flattery implied at the sight of every man raising his hand to the white man. *Coolie* may have come to the British tongue from *Koli,* the fishing community of the Bombay coast, who began at an early stage to do forced labour.

Even before the British had to quit India, they had, perforce, accepted the vocabulary of the Indian struggle for freedom: *Mahatma*-Saint; *Gandhism, Harijan*-Man of God; *hartal*-strike; *khadi*-home-spun cloth; *Satyagraha*-Gripping of truth; *swadeshi*-home-made; *swaraj*-self-rule.

Since the transfer of power, from British to Indian hands, some other words have entered, through journalism, into the English language. The British 'invented' Pakistan. Subhas Bose introduced the salutation *Jai Hind* through his Indian National Army. The Beatles have familiarized *Maharishi.* Sri Aurobindo's Ashram retreat has become a Mecca for all seekers after escape from the 'technology run mad' of the atomic age.

The researchers Piaget and Kohler have familiarized us with the hypothesis that it is originally the word sound as much as sense which shapes expression. We in India had always considered *vak,* word, to arise from the resonances of the human soul. Children often resort to incoherent perversion of speech for rhythmic alliances. The poet often hovers on the brink of incoherence.

The psychology of Indian-English is rooted in the Indian metabolism. Most Indians, who speak or write English, even when they have been to Oxford or Cambridge or London, tend, naturally, to bring the hangover of the mother tongue, spoken in early childhood, into their expression.

As a people, we talk quickly, walk quickly and make a little go a long way. Unlike the Englishman who talks clearly on the stage, but generally puts the bit in his mouth when conversing, the Indian often gesticulates, moves his facial muscles and is as fluent as an American or an Irishman.

Not only does this general characteristic of dramatic utterance make us a rather loud, even noisy people but the pull of our mother-tongue leads to a heavy sugar-coating of ordinary English words, phrases and sentences; peculiarities which are congenital; exaggerations which can bolster up the sense of humour of the editor of *Punch*.

I am not defending this unconscious use of Indian phraseology. It needs no defence because it is natural. In England itself the Cockney is lord of his own language and says things in his own perverse way, which the so-called gentlemen of the Edwardian and Georgian periods found funny, in bad taste or simply anarchic. I am merely cataloguing the phenomena to remove the impression that the Indian is deliberately violating the English language when he is, as an ex-student of one of our universities where English is generally badly taught, spoken, unknowingly bringing the pressure of his mother's milk to bear on his speech.

Those who know Hindustani know that in our own language in northern India, we are still used to feudal good manners when we ask anyone his name: *'Ap ka isme sherif kya hai?'* So no one should be surprised when a gentleman in an *achkan* in Delhi asks you: 'May I know your good name?' He is only translating the sense of politeness implicit in his own language while asking a personal question. And this figure of speech has assumed common currency through frequent usage. Only our Beatniks say: 'Who the hell are you anyway?' But there are not too many of them yet in our society.

The same applies to pronunciation: George Bernard Shaw has given a classic formulation of the Englishman's accent, in *Pygmalion:* 'An Englishman's way of speaking absolutely classifies him. The moment he talks he makes some other Englishman despise him.' This applies to us, since, apart from other things, we have inherited the class system entire from the English, and added it on to our own intricate, age-old caste system. A man's class or caste can be known in India almost immediately from the moment he opens his mouth. But while, under British rule, the man who could speak with a 'haw-haw' Oxford accent after a brief probation in U.K. to qualify for the Indian Civil Service, was respected as a Sahib, nowadays, the graduation of many erstwhile Babus into the new race of Ministers, Deputy Ministers, Secretaries, Deputy Secretaries and in the new Indian Administrative Service, has made for a reverse snobbery. Even the British establishment seems to respect the speeches of our Parliamentarians, delivered in the same Babu accents which they once despised and catalogued in books like *Honoured Sir by Babuji*.

I do not, therefore, draw a hard-and-fast borderline between what is admissible and what is not admissible in the contemporary Indian-English usage. I feel that the kind of Indian-African-Carribean-American English dialect that has become part of English literature through V. S. Naipaul and other West Indian writers, shows that, if given time and currency, newly coined words of the most telling character will be absorbed into Indian-English literature, provided they communicate nuances

and shades of meaning of different metabolisms, which are not hitherto available in the English language.

Also, the rules of English grammar, whether it is Nesfield or some other, need not apply to creative Indian-English writing, in quite the manner enjoined by the strict grammarians.

I feel that those who presume to do creative writing in the Indian-English language are likely to know enough grammar, before they put pen to paper. The exhortations of the grammarians, therefore, seem fatuous:

> 'Do not break sentences in two.'
> 'Put statements in the positive form.'
> 'Omit needless words.'
> 'Avoid a succession of loose sentences.'
> 'Do not overwrite!'
> 'Use orthodox spelling!'
> 'Do not explain too much!'
> 'Avoid fussy words!'
> 'Do not inject opinion.'
> 'Avoid foreign languages!'
> 'Prefer the standard to the off-beat!'

I must confess that, having broken all these rules myself, and seen my colleagues break them up, I have often felt like asking the prim schoolmaster, with his hair parted in the middle and plastered on his forehead: 'Please, Sir, which is the standard English I should prefer?' He would probably have answered in a strained voice:

'The standard English is standard English, of course, my dear Sir!' This answer would not have satisfied the three Irish writers, George Moore, George Bernard Shaw and James Joyce, who freely broke the rules of English grammar, coined new words and enriched the English language with vivacious prose, each in his own different manner.

The talent of the true imaginative writer is like a flame. It burns away the dead wood of accepted words and shines forth in original images. The style of language, which belongs to him, or her, is the expression of the total personality projected to a vision beyond the routine experienced. The sensitive individual's approach to life, to ordinary things, and to the hitherto unseen phenomena, is the aspiration to awareness of the underlying truth. The writer is possessed of an intensity, which transforms his inner life, and through his realizations, releases the incipient urges, for the flow of sympathy on to the reader. So, he is compelled, if necessary, to break all the rules of the game.

Indeed, if he is not an Englishman, brought up from birth, to hear those early sounds, nursery rhymes and exclamations, which lay the foundation of the mother tongue, he is bound to reflect, from the nourishment of his metabolism, the sounds of his own Indian mother tongue. These sounds, rhythms and cadences form the kinetic flow of the personality. And the kinetic gesture is integral to everyone who has spoken the mother tongue for the first seven years of his life.

It is bound to come through from the biological pressure into any foreign language, which the native may learn to speak afterwards. That is why every English-speaking person, from a particular language group, in our country, is bound to accent his utterance in the alien language with the peculiar pressure of his voice. A Punjabi will always pronounce 'station' with a heavy pressure on the first syllable and the last syllable, *stay-shun*. A person from Uttar Pradesh will add the prefix ē to his pronunciation of the same word 'station' and make it *ēstayshun*. A Tamilian will add *yam* to the plain simple 'em' sound.

I tried to analyse very early in my own writing of the English language, the creative process involved. I found, while writing spontaneously, that I was always translating dialogue from the original Punjabi into English. The way in which my mother said something in the dialect of Central Punjab could not have been expressed in any other way except in an almost literal translation, which might carry over the sound and sense of the original speech. I also found, that I was dreaming or thinking or brooding over two-thirds of the prose narrative in Punjabi, or in Hindustani, and only one-third in the English language. This happened usually while I was writing stories and novels. In the essays, I could control myself and write almost entirely in the English language, as it is written, but I could not make the prose of my essay conversational, in the English spoken sense, in the same way in which my contemporary English writers like George Orwell, Cyril Connolly, or Christopher Isherwood, were making it. My prose in the essay remained Macaulayesque, using the sentence of eighteen to twenty words, as against the contemporary English or American sentence of five, seven or ten words. The rhythm of the prose of the Urdu essays of Altaf Hussain Hali, of Abul Kalam Azad and of Ahmed Shah Bokhari further stilted my writing, because of the dithyrambic echoes which unconsciously came into one's mind from having read their utterances in early youth.

This self-analysis enabled me to consciously introduce translation of Punjabi, Urdu and Hindi words into all my writings, even at the risk of being turned down by English publishers, who naturally thought that the conservative English people would not be able to follow this kind of Indian-English easily to buy my books in large numbers. Later on, however, this kind of Indian-English came to be accepted by the same British publishers because of the contemporary human situation all over the world, which was sought to be understood in the West during the thirties. And, while I used to add glossaries of Indian words with their translations, at the end of my novels, in the first few years, I have not offered these appendices for some years now, because, I feel, the sense of the sentence and the paragraph must bring over the meaning of the prose adequately to communicate the drift of the empathy.

Let me quote here a typical extract from my first novel, *Untouchable,* where the emotional stress is being translated from the felt experience of the Punjabi into the English language:

> 'You know', he began in the impersonal manner with which he always lifted himself from the lousy old man he was to the superior dignity of an aged father, 'You know, when you were a little child, I had a nasty experience too. You were ill with fever and I went to the house of Hakim Baghawan Das, in this very town. I shouted and shouted, but no one heard me. A babu was pass-

ing through the *Dawai Khana* (dispensary) of the Doctor and I said to him:

> 'Babuji, Babuji, God will make you prosperous. Please make my message reach the ears of the Hakimji. I have been shouting, shouting, and have even asked some people to tell the Hakim Sahib that I have a prayer to make to him. My child is suffering from fever. He has been unconscious since last night and I want the Hakimji to give him some medicine.'

> 'Keep away, keep away,' said the babu, 'Don't come riding on at me. Do you want me to have another bath this morning? The Hakim Sahib has to attend to us people who go to offices first, and there are so many of us waiting. You have nothing to do all day. Come another time or wait.'

> 'And with this he walked into the dispensary.'

> 'I remained standing. Whenever anyone passed by I would place my head at their feet and ask them to tell the Hakim. But who would listen to a sweeper? Everyone was concerned about himself.

> 'For an hour I stood like that in a corner, near the heap of litter which I had collected, and I was feeling as if a scorpion was stinging me. That I couldn't buy medicine for my son when I was willing to pay my hard-earned money for it troubled me. I had seen many bottles full of medicine in the house of the Hakimji and I knew that one of those bottles contained the medicine for you, and yet I couldn't get it. My heart was with you and my body was outside the house of the Hakim.'

This attitude of mine was confirmed by Raja Rao, fellow exile writing his novel, *Kanthapura,* at the same time as I was writing *Bakha,* afterwards entitled *Untouchable.*

In his foreword to this novel, he wrote:

> The tempo of Indian life must be infused in our English expression, even as the tempo of Irish or American life has gone into making, of theirs. . . . There must be something in the sun of India, that makes us rush and tumble and run on and our paths are paths interminable. *The Mahābhārata* has 2,14,778 verses and the *Ramayana* 48,000. Puranas there are endless and innumerable.

> We have neither punctuation nor the treacherous 'ats' and 'ons' to bother us. We tell one interminable tale. Episode follows episode and whenever thought stops our breath stops, and we move on to another thought. This was, and still is, the ordinary style of our story-telling.

And as the old woman in *Kanthapura* begins to narrate the story, the reader can almost hear grandma talking: 'Our village—I don't think you ever heard about it—Kanthapura is its name and it is in the province of Kara.'

As the narrative proceeds, the translation from the original Kannada speech becomes audible more and more intimate:

Akkamma had people come to visit them. You know coffee planter Ramayya is the cousin of her sister-in-law. And when he is on his way to Karwar, he sometimes drops in to see them, and even spends the night there. He left his motor on the other side of the river, for the ferry does not ply at night, and he came along. Today he is there and people are all busy trying to see him. For a midday meal he will have vermicelli payasam, and patwari Nanjundia, and his son-in-law are both invited there. The others are coming too. The temple people and the fig-tree-house people, and Dorè, the University Graduate, as they call him. He lost his father and is still young. And his mother died soon after. And as his two sisters had already married and have gone to their mothers-in-law, he was left alone with fifteen acres of wet land and twenty acres of dry land. And he said he would go to the city for higher studies and went to a University. Of course, he never got through the Inter even—but he had city ways, read city books, and even called himself a Gandhi-man. Some two years ago, when he had come back from Poona, he had given up his boots and hat and suit, and had taken to dhoti and khadi and it was said he had even given up his city habits of smoking. Well, so much the better. But to tell you the truth, we never liked him. He had always been such a braggart. He was not like Corner-house Moorthy who had gone through life like a noble cow, quiet, generous, serene, and Brahmanic, a very prince, I tell you. We loved him of course, as you will see. And if only I had not been a daughterless widow, I should have offered him a granddaughter if I had one. . . .

Obviously, here the rhythm in which the narrator talks is derived from the habit of using the mother tongue. And it indicates the search for an authentic style, corresponding to the vision of a bilingual Indian writing in English. This style might correspond to 'the other mind' brought by Gandhi to interpret the truth of the human personality rather than elaborate the illusion of realities in India in the Anglo-Saxon language, for sale to the jaded reading public, in a manner which may be easy and happy to swallow.

I would like to add a quotation from a novel by another writer, who had condemned me for what he calls 'Mulkese'.

The following passage is from Khushwant Singh's novel *Mano Majra,* now called *Train to Pakistan:*

> 'What you say is absolutely right,' he agreed warmly. 'If you want freedom to mean something for you—the peasants and workers—you have to get together and fight. Get the bania Congress government out. Get rid of the princes and the landlords and freedom will mean for you just what you think it should. More land, more buffaloes, no debts.'
>
> 'That is what that fellow told us,' interrupted Meet Singh, 'that fellow . . . , Lambardara what was his name? Comrade something or other. Are you a Comrade, Babu Sahib?'
>
> 'No'.

'I am glad. That comrade did not believe in God. He said when his party came into power they would drain the sacred pool round the temple at Tarun Tarun and plant rice in it. He said it would be more useful.'

'That is foolish talk' protested Iqbal. He wished Meet Singh had remembered the Comrade's name. 'The man should be reported to headquarters and taken to task.'

'If we have no faith in God then we are like animals', said the Muslim gravely. 'All the world respects a religious man. Look at Gandhi! I heard he reads the Koran Sharif and the Unjeel along his Vedas and Shastras. People sing his praise in the four corners of the earth. I have seen a picture in a newspaper of Gandhi's prayer meeting. It showed a lot of white men and women sitting cross-legged. One white girl had her eyes shut. They said she was the Big Lord's daughter. You see, Meet Singh, even the English respect a man of religion.'

'Of course, Chacha. Whatever you say is right to the sixteenth anna of the rupee' agreed Meet Singh, rubbing his belly. Iqbal felt his temper rise. 'They are a race of four-twenties,' he said vehemently. [Section 420 of the Indian Penal Code defines the offence of cheating.] 'Do not believe what they say.'

The reader will find that this narrative also is not in the Queen's English, nor even in the English of the Indian Republic, whatever that may mean, but in the English of the Punjabi-speaking Indian, developing his own style, even as American writers have done.

I hope I have indicated, through these quotations, the creative process behind most of the genuine Indian-English writing, that it is a natural expression of a bilingual talent, nourished mostly on the mother tongue, and seeking communion, beyond communication, on certain levels which had not entered into English literature until the beginning of the twentieth century.

In conclusion, I would like to counter the charge of 'artificiality' of Indian-English writing, which has been frequently made.

One of my correspondents writes:

> I will refrain from saying whether the laurels won and prominence achieved by them abroad are justified or not, as it is a matter of the individual conscience vis-à-vis that of the readers and the literary critics. My only concern is the artificiality of this literature, which presents a thoroughly distorted image of Indian life, culture and traditions and gives the version of India which is unknown to Indians themselves. The native flavour, authenticity of characters and the genuineness of the locales and the modes which one finds coming alive in Phanishwaranath Renu's *Maila Anchal* and Takazi Shiva Shankar Pillay's *Chemmeen* are found nowhere in the works of most of our Indo-Anglian writers. Their writing at best gives the feeling of a cleverly knit story about India by a western writer, on a short hurried trip to this country.

I cannot deny that there is a tendency in Indian-English writing to please the publishers in the West and to win popularity by pandering to Anglo-American predilections about India. In fact, quite a few of the writers judge the success of their Indian-English writing by their sales abroad. But the critic I have quoted, and quite a few of those who complain of the 'artificiality' of Indian-English writing, have not cared to read the felt prose of Aurobindo Ghosh's letters, of Vivekananda's lectures, Nehru's *Autobiography* or the novels of the first few Indian-English writers.

One can accuse them, as one can accuse all pioneers, of mixing metaphors of the mother tongue and of the English they had learned from bad teachers. They have often used regionalisms which, on their first showing, sound strange or awkward (but have only become acceptable and familiar through later currency). They have sometimes overstepped the borderline of the admissible and inadmissible in the usage of the words, tones, and accents of the mother tongue, which only good taste and sensibility can guard against.

There is no doubt that a writer using his mother tongue can, if he is talented, render the atmosphere, communicate the texture of the spoken speech, and reconstruct the illusion of reality more organically. But in literature the rendering of reality is not the only test of criticism. The real tests are different. The first test is in the sincerity of the writer in any language. The second test may be in the degree of sensitiveness, or individual talent, and sheer intensity, by which he, or she, leads others to the renewal of consciousness, or the heightening of it, for the realizations of those areas of awareness which routine life has blunted.

The third test may lie in the transformation of words into prophecy. Because, what is a writer if he is not the fiery voice of the people who, through his own torments, urges and exaltations, by realizing the pains, frustrations and aspirations of others, and by cultivating his incipient powers of expressions, transmutes into art all feeling, all thought, all experience, thus becoming the seer of a new vision in any given situation.

Adib, who often comments on life and letters, has set the tone for this kind of criticism, in a recent essay on Rabindranath Tagore.

Tagore had written:

> Lady of lines,
> These words are not an alien invasion,
> Come to set a limit to your realm,
> They are but some noisy birds
> That for a moment flit across your garden
> While your meaning lies far beyond their chirp-
> ings.

Adib comments:

> I don't know what the lady of lines thinks about the birds. We on our part would like to listen to the chirping of the birds. We have a quick walk in the garden. We don't have to get sentimental about it. We like the man with the masks. We like him even more without any mask. But is everyone in this world ever without a mask? Isn't

it part of the human condition that no one can know what he is! When we honour the prophet, the savant, and the teacher, in Tagore, let us remember that he too was human—all too human. In the years to come it is the all too human in the work of this poet and painter which will appeal to us most!

This fourth criterion of humanness is confirmed by Professor Nihar Ranjan Ray in his recent book, *An Artist in Life,* on Tagore. Professor Ray puts down his *obiter dicta* thus:

> We may compare Tagore's life and art to huge forests, spreading and sprawling, where one can see tiny plants and winding creepers, towering and overshadowing trees. A forest full of sap, colour and beauty, sublime in its intensity. But once we are inside the forest all this majesty disappears: because then we can see only the plants and the creepers and the trees separately.

This approach is also reflected in the critical writing of Professor C. D. Narasimhaiah, one of the most perceptive interpreters of Indian-English writing in India today. In his book, *The Human Idiom,* containing three lectures on Nehru, he writes:

> Creative man, it seems to me, must certainly grapple with things, ideas and problems, though the means he employs vary according to the genius that shapes his tensions—with one it is stone, with another it is clay or canvas, with a third one it may be sounds, or only gesture. Except for words, these media have more or less fallen into the hands of the specialists. . . .

I would dare to say that quite a few Indian-English writers who have lived and worked in heroic disregard of current fashions, categories and definitions, such as Realism, Naturalism, Social-realism or the anti-anti-writingism, express themselves in landscapes of the West and East, when they have been mostly unwanted, but when they are beginning to be analyzed for their worth and accepted as genuine authors of new hitherto undefined styles which don't admit Anglo-Saxon terms of reference altogether.

One day when I was faced with the predicament that I could not publish my Urdu writings in India, because there was no honest publisher I knew of in that language, I asked Bapu Gandhi whether it was wrong for me to write in the English language. The old man said:

> The purpose of writing is to communicate, isn't it? If so, say your say in any language that comes to hand. Only say it quickly. There is no time to lose. . . . And you can come back to your mother tongue when you are able. You are frank to a fault in what you say. I know you will pursue Truth above all in your writings. . . . Be simple and serve the poor. . . . Be honest. . . . Leave Bloomsbury.

I would like to claim for the Indian-English writers the freedom which the prophet of Indian nationalism so liberally conferred on me. I realize that we still do not have the confidence to be ourselves. We submit to many of the arbitrary attitudes of British and American publishers and makers of taste. We tend to be provincialists and overrate the world of professional best-selling writers of the world where fashions come and go. Our world may be full of raw people, of wretchedness beyond wretchedness, of tragic conflicts and breakdowns. But we seek to extend the boundaries of literature beyond pure literature and this is perhaps the very world in which we can bring *karuna* or compassion of our old humanisms to bear on our new humanisms.

Perhaps those of us who write in Indian-English are unconsciously building bridges with those other emergent cultures, beneath the salons, where new writers, as in Australia, Canada, Africa, and other ex-colonies, are bursting out of the bounds laid down by the high priests of western domination. [Is it] possible that we may be able to establish solidarity with the victims of warring civilizations of the West? The new young writers of the West repudiate violence and hatred and contempt and opt out of conscriptions. They seem to shudder in their verse at the hideousness of the world built by those who piled up the instruments of power and money up to saturation point. They are profoundly disturbed and seek creative truth, in the face of genocide, barbarous cruelty on the basis of race and colour and creed, and the vulgar display of luxury based on the profits of armaments. We too question those facile generalizations of contemporary world civilization which may lead to the third world war, to the annihilation of all hope for mankind. We are natural friends. Is it likely then that Indian-English writing may enable us in Shelley's phrase, 'to connect'?

At any rate, I feel that Indian-English writing has come to stay as part of world literature. And this new language has the tang of a rugged rhythm about it, as in a ballad. I would like to suggest dropping the phrase 'Indo-Anglian' in talking about it. I put forward simple Indian-English writing for ordinary use and *Pigeon-Indian* (P-i-g-e-o-n) in metaphor.

I would like to believe that in the best writing in this language, the words soar in the imagination like a pigeon in flight, shrill when they are frightened, nervous and sensitive, often soft and soothing, somewhat heavy-footed, but always compelled by the love of flight.

> *Mulk Raj Anand, "Pigeon-Indian: Some Notes on Indian-English Writing," in* Aspects of Indian Writing in English: Essays in Honour of Professor K. R. Srinivasa Iyengar, *edited by M. K. Naik, The Macmillan Company of India Limited, 1979, pp. 24-44.*

FURTHER READING

Anthologies

Butalia, Urvashi, and Menon, Ritu, eds. *In Other Words: New Writing By Indian Women.* New Delhi: Kali for Women, 1992, 193 p.
    Stories by thirteen contemporary Indian authors. The book includes biographical notes on each of the writers.

Cowasjee, Saros, and Duggal, Kartar Singh, eds. *When the British Left: Stories on the Partitioning of India, 1947.* New Delhi, Arnold Heinemann, 1987, 188 p.
    Sixteen stories set during the violence that followed the 1947 Indian independence. The collection includes Khushwant Singh's "The Riot," and Mulk Raj Anand's "The Parrot in the Cage."

Guptara, Prabhu S., ed. *The Lotus: An Anthology of Contemporary Indian Religious Poetry in English.* Calcutta: Writers Workshop, 1988, 154 p.
    Religious poetry from thirty-two Indian writers, including Kamala Das, Keki N. Daruwalla, P. Lal, Pritish Nandy, and R. Parthasarathy. Biographical notes on the individual poets are included.

Joshi, S. N. *Nascent Warmth: An Anthology of Poems.* New Delhi: Atma Ram and Sons, 1987, 136 p.
    Works by twenty-four authors who participated in a poetry symposium at Shimla, India, in 1985. The volume also includes six critical essays on contemporary Indian poetry in English.

Kumar, Shiv K., ed. *Contemporary Indian Short Stories in English.* New Delhi: Sahitya Akademi, 1991, 241 p.
    Contains stories by Mulk Raj Anand, Keki Daruwalla, Arun Joshi, R. K. Narayan, Raja Rao, and Khushwant Singh.

Mohanty, Niranjan. *Voices: Indian Poetry in English.* Berhampur: Poetry Publications, 1992, 240 p.
    Feautures the work of twenty-five poets, including Nissim Ezekiel. The volume includes a biographical overview of each poet.

Nair, K. R. Ramachandran, ed. *Gathered Grace: An Anthology of Indian Verse in English.* New Delhi: Sterling Publishers, 1991, 180 p.
    Includes poems by early writers such as Henry Derozio, Toru Dutt, and Manmohan Ghose, as well as more recent works by Nissim Ezekiel, Kamala Das, R. Parthasarathy, Keki Daruwalla, Dom Moraes, and Pritish Nandy. This volume also includes a list of books for further reading, indexes of titles and first lines, and notes and commentary on the poems.

Prem, P. C. K. *Contemporary Indian English Poetry from Himachal.* New Delhi: Konark Publishers, 1992, 86 p.
    Includes the work of ten contemporary Indian poets.

Rizvi, Iftikhar Husain, ed. *Contemporary Indian English Love Poetry: An Anthology.* Bareilly: Prakash Book Depot, 1990, 88 p.
    Contains works by thirty-six noted Indo-English poets, including Kamala Das, P. Lal, and Nissim Ezekiel.

Secondary Sources

Amur, G. S. "Forbidden Fruits." *Indian Literature* XXX, No. 6 (November-December 1987): 49-69.
    Reviews recent Indian fiction and poetry in English.

Ariel, Special Issue on Indian Literature in English 14, No. 4 (October 1983): 3-86.
    Includes articles on Salman Rushdie, R. K. Narayan, Raja Rao's *The Serpent and the Rope,* and the poetry of Nissim Ezekiel.

Awasthi, Kamal N., ed. *Contemporary Indian English Fic-*

tion: An Anthology of Essays. Jalandhar: ABS Publications, 1993, 157 p.

 Includes several essays on feminism in the Indian English novel, as well as studies of Anita Desai, Arun Joshi, and Khushwant Singh.

Badal, R. K. *Indo-Anglian Literature: An Outline.* Bareilly: Prakash Book Depot, 1975, 56 p.

 Provides background information and overviews of Indian English poetry, drama, and fiction. Separate chapters are devoted to the work of Anand, Narayan, Raja Rao, and contemporary novelists.

Derrett, M. E. *The Modern Indian Novel in English: A Comparative Approach.* Bruxelles: Editions De l'Institut De Sociologie, 1966, 195 p.

 Explores such topics as theme, form, and style, as well as common backgrounds among writers of the Indian novel in English. The book also includes a chapter on the history of novel written in India's various regional languages.

Gowda, H. H. Anniah, ed. *The Colonial and the Neo-Colonial: Encounters in Commonwealth Literature.* Mysore: University of Mysore, 1983, 243 p.

 Contains articles on the Indian critical tradition and attitudes toward colonialism in the Indian novel in English.

Gupta, G. S. Balarama. *Essays on Indian Writing in English.* Gulbarga: Jiwe Publications, 1975, 85 p.

 Examines the Indian drama in English. Special attention is given to the plays of Harindranath Chattopadhyaya.

Hemenway, Stephen Ignatius. *The Novel of India, Vol. 2: The Indo-Anglian Novel.* Calcutta: Writers Workshop, 1975, 125 p.

 Discusses the pioneers and popularizers of the Indian English novel. The book contains chapters on Narayan, Anand, Bhabani Bhattacharya, and Khushwant Singh, as well as a detailed analysis of Raja Rao's *Kanthapura* and *The Serpent and the Rope.*

Joshi, Vasant. "Contemporary Indian Literature: 1950-1970." *Literature East and West* XV, No. 1 (1971): 38-54.

 Traces the development of the Indian English novel during the 1950s and 1960s.

Kaushik, Asha. *Politics, Aesthetics, and Culture: A Study of the Indo-Anglian Political Novel.* New Delhi: Manohar, 1988, 195 p.

 Analyzes the history and themes of the Indian English political novel.

Krishnaswamy, Shantha. *The Woman in Indian Fiction in English.* New Delhi: Ashish Publishing House, 1984, 369 p.

 Analyzes the treatment of women in the novels of Narayan, Raja Rao, Bhabani Battacharaya, Kamala Markandaya, Anita Desai, and Ruth Prawer Jhabvala.

Kulshrestha, Chirantan, ed. *Contemporary Indian English Verse: An Evaluation.* New Delhi: Arnold Heinemann, 1980, 314 p.

 Includes poetry analysis by M. K. Naik, P. Lal, and K. Ayyappa Paniker. Individual essays focus on the poetry of Nissim Ezekiel, Kamala Das, R. Parthasarathy, and Keki Daruwalla.

Lal, P. *The Concept of an Indian Literature: Six Essays.* Calcutta: Writers Workshop, 1968, 49 p.

 Presents an overview of Indian literature. Individual essays focus on Indian writing in English, Sanskrit drama, and the work of Rabindranath Tagore.

Malhotra, M. L. *Bridges of Literature: 23 Critical Essays in Literature.* Mayur Colony: Ajmer, 1971, 238 p.

 Contains essays on Tagore, Narayan, Manohar Malgonkar, Jawaharlal Nehru, and Anita Desai.

McCutchion, David. *Indian Writing in English.* Calcutta: Writers Workshop, 1969, 120 p.

 An overview of Indian writing in English.

Mehta, P. P. *Indo-Anglian Fiction: An Assessment.* Bareilly: Prakash Book Depot, 1979, 394 p.

 Includes a brief history of the Indian novel in English and a chapter on how novelists treat India's struggle for independence. Mehta also devotes chapters to the works of Anand, Narayan, Raja Rao, Manohar Malgonkar, and Kamala Markandaya.

Melwani, Murli Das. *Themes in Indo-Anglian Literature.* Bareilly: Prakash Book Depot, 1977, 119 p.

 Collection of essays on trends in Indian literature in English.

Modern Fiction Studies, Fiction of the Indian Subcontinent 39, No. 1 (Spring 1993): 1-222.

 Special issue which includes essays on feminism in the Indian English novel as well as analyses of Rushdie's *Midnight's Children* and the works of Narayan and Raja Rao.

Mohan, Ramesh, ed. *Indian Writing in English.* New Delhi: Orient Longman, 1978, 260 p.

 Wide-ranging collection of critical essays. The book includes discussions of style and technique as well as analyses of individual authors.

Naik, M. K. "The Political Novel in Indian Writing in English." *Contributions to Asian Studies* 6 (1975): 6-15.

 Analyzes the political aspects of works by Anand, Raja Rao, Kamala Markandaya, and Khushwant Singh.

———. *Studies in Indian Literature in English.* New Delhi: Sterling Publishers, 1987, 179 p.

 Individual essays comment on the poetry of Keki Daruwalla, Salman Rushdie's *Midnight's Children,* Raja Rao's *The Serpent and the Rope,* G. V. Desani's *All About H. Hatterr,* and the issue of alienation in contemporary Indian English poetry.

Narasimhaiah, C. D. *Moving Frontiers of English Studies in India.* New Delhi: S. Chand and Company, 1977, 109 p.

 Focuses on the history of criticism on Indo-English literature.

Narasimhan, Raji. *Sensibility Under Stress: Aspects of Indo-English Fiction.* New Delhi: Ashajanak Publications, 1976, 144 p.

 Argues that Indian fiction in English has been in decline since Anand, Narayan, and Raja Rao achieved their peak in the 1930s and 40s. The author contends that conventional realism is no longer viable in the Indo-English novel and stresses the need for the "mythic element of sensibility" in creating fiction.

Paniker, K. Ayyappa, ed. *Indian English Literature Since In-*

dependence. New Delhi: The Indian Association for English Studies, 1991, 148 p.

> Concentrates on individual authors, including Kamala Markandaya, Anita Desai, and Salman Rushdie. The book also includes a chapter on humor in the Indo-English essay.

Parthasarathy, R. "Whoring After English Gods." In *Perspectives: A Collection of Essays by the Staff of the SIES College of Arts and Science,* edited by S. P. Bhagwat, pp. 43-60. Bombay: Popular Prakashan, 1970.

> Parthasarathy traces his own evolution as a poet and explores his reasons for continuing to write poetry in English.

Raghavacharyulu, D. V. K., ed. *The Two-Fold Voice: Essays on Indian Writing in English.* Guntur: Navodaya Publishers, 1971, 184 p.

> Anthology of criticism focusing on individual authors and their works. Authors covered include Toru Dutt, Sarojini Naidu, Tagore, Aurobindo Ghose, Nirad C. Chadhuri, Ruth Prawer Jhabvala, Anand, Narayan, and Raja Rao. Attention is also given to the English autobiographies of Mohandas K. Gandhi and Nehru.

Raizada, Harish. *The Lotus and the Rose: Indian Fiction in English (1850-1947).* Aligarh: Aligarh Muslim University Press, 1978, 292 p.

> A survey of Indo-English fiction from the nineteenth and twentieth centuries.

Rao, T. V. Subba. *Indian Writing in English: Is There Any Worth in It?* Madurai: Koodal Publishers, 1976, 46 p.

> Attacks the practice of Indian authors writing in English, calling it a "de-Indianizing" influence.

Sarma, Gobinda Prasad. *Nationalism In Indo-Anglian Fiction.* New Delhi: Sterling Publishers, 1978, 391 p.

> Explores the issue of Indian nationalism as it is treated in Indo-English poetry and prose.

Sharma, K. K., ed. *Indo-English Literature: A Collection of Critical Essays.* Ghaziabad: Vimal Prakashan, 1977, 273 p.

> Contains essays by Indian writers and critics. The works of Anand, Narayan, Raja Rao, Anita Desai, and Bhabani Battacharya are discussed. The book also includes M. K. Naik's "A Defense of Indian Writing in English" and Mulk Raj Anand's "Why I Write?"

Shirwadkar, Meena. *Image of Woman in the Indo-Anglian Novel.* New Delhi: Sterling Publishers, 1979, 169 p.

> Analyzes the portrayal in the Indo-English novel of women's roles in the family and society.

Sinha, R. C. P. *The Indian Autobiographies in English.* New Delhi: S. Chand and Company, 1978, 222 p.

> Details the tradition of the Indian autobiography and discusses the uses of the form by modern politicians and men of letters such as Gandhi and Nehru.

Srivastava, Avadhesh K. *Alien Voice: Perspectives on Commonwealth Literature.* Atlantic Highlands, New Jersey: Humanities Press, 1982, 243 p.

> Includes several articles on Indo-English literature, including Vasant A. Shahane's "Indo-English Literature: Its Major Concerns and Academic Rationale."

Steinvorth, Klaus. *The Indo-English Novel: The Impact of the West on Literature in a Developing Country.* Wiesbaden: Franz Steiner Verlag, 1975, 149 p.

> Examines the Indo-English novel's relationship to Western culture. Steinvorth explores the social and economic background of the novel, its appeal to Western readers, and the issues of Indian life that it addresses.

Suleri, Sara. *The Rhetoric of English India.* Chicago: University of Chicago Press, 1992, 230 p.

> Focuses mainly on the British view of India as represented in the works of authors such as Kipling and E. M. Forster. This book also contains an examination of Rushdie's "deeply Islamic" work, *The Satanic Verses.*

Venugopal, C. V. *The Indian Short Story in English: A Survey.* Bareilly: Prakash Book Depot, 1976, 111 p.

> Discusses the origins, techniques, and major writers of the Indian short story in English.

Verghese, C. Paul. *Essays on Indian Writing in English.* New Delhi: N. V. Publications, 1975, 151 p.

> Explores the major issues and writers of Indo-English literature.

Williams, Haydn Moore. *Studies in Modern Indian Fiction in English.* Calcutta: Writers Workshop, 1973, 94 p.

> Examines the works of Anand and Narayan.

Twentieth-Century
Literary Criticism

Cumulative Indexes
Volumes 1-54

How to Use This Index

The main references

Calvino, Italo
1923-1985.....CLC 5, 8, 11, 22, 33, 39,
73; SSC 3

list all author entries in the following Gale Literary Criticism series:

BLC = *Black Literature Criticism*
CLC = *Contemporary Literary Criticism*
CLR = *Children's Literature Review*
CMLC = *Classical and Medieval Literature Criticism*
DA = *DISCovering Authors*
DC = *Drama Criticism*
HLC = *Hispanic Literature Criticism*
LC = *Literature Criticism from 1400 to 1800*
NCLC = *Nineteenth-Century Literature Criticism*
PC = *Poetry Criticism*
SSC = *Short Story Criticism*
TCLC = *Twentieth-Century Literary Criticism*
WLC = *World Literature Criticism, 1500 to the Present*

The cross-references

See also CANR 23; CA 85-88;
obituary CA 116

list all author entries in the following Gale biographical and literary sources:

AAYA = *Authors & Artists for Young Adults*
AITN = *Authors in the News*
BEST = *Bestsellers*
BW = *Black Writers*
CA = *Contemporary Authors*
CAAS = *Contemporary Authors Autobiography Series*
CABS = *Contemporary Authors Bibliographical Series*
CANR = *Contemporary Authors New Revision Series*
CAP = *Contemporary Authors Permanent Series*
CDALB = *Concise Dictionary of American Literary Biography*
CDBLB = *Concise Dictionary of British Literary Biography*
DLB = *Dictionary of Literary Biography*
DLBD = *Dictionary of Literary Biography Documentary Series*
DLBY = *Dictionary of Literary Biography Yearbook*
HW = *Hispanic Writers*
JRDA = *Junior DISCovering Authors*
MAICYA = *Major Authors and Illustrators for Children and Young Adults*
MTCW = *Major 20th-Century Writers*
SAAS = *Something about the Author Autobiography Series*
SATA = *Something about the Author*
YABC = *Yesterday's Authors of Books for Children*

Literary Criticism Series
Cumulative Author Index

A.
See Arnold, Matthew

A. E. .... **TCLC 3, 10**
See also Russell, George William
See also DLB 19

A. M.
See Megged, Aharon

A. R. P-C
See Galsworthy, John

Abasiyanik, Sait Faik   1906-1954
See Sait Faik
See also CA 123

Abbey, Edward   1927-1989 ...... **CLC 36, 59**
See also CA 45-48; 128; CANR 2, 41

Abbott, Lee K(ittredge)   1947- ...... **CLC 48**
See also CA 124; DLB 130

Abe, Kobo   1924-1993 ..... **CLC 8, 22, 53, 81**
See also CA 65-68; 140; CANR 24; MTCW

Abelard, Peter   c. 1079-c. 1142 ... **CMLC 11**
See also DLB 115

Abell, Kjeld   1901-1961 .... **CLC 15**
See also CA 111

Abish, Walter   1931- .... **CLC 22**
See also CA 101; CANR 37; DLB 130

Abrahams, Peter (Henry)   1919- ..... **CLC 4**
See also BW; CA 57-60; CANR 26;
DLB 117; MTCW

Abrams, M(eyer) H(oward)   1912- ... **CLC 24**
See also CA 57-60; CANR 13, 33; DLB 67

Abse, Dannie   1923- .... **CLC 7, 29**
See also CA 53-56; CAAS 1; CANR 4;
DLB 27

Achebe, (Albert) Chinua(lumogu)
1930- ..... **CLC 1, 3, 5, 7, 11, 26, 51, 75;**
BLC; DA; WLC
See also BW; CA 1-4R; CANR 6, 26;
CLR 20; DLB 117; MAICYA; MTCW;
SATA 38, 40

Acker, Kathy   1948- .... **CLC 45**
See also CA 117; 122

Ackroyd, Peter   1949- .... **CLC 34, 52**
See also CA 123; 127

Acorn, Milton   1923- .... **CLC 15**
See also CA 103; DLB 53

Adamov, Arthur   1908-1970 ...... **CLC 4, 25**
See also CA 17-18; 25-28R; CAP 2; MTCW

Adams, Alice (Boyd)   1926- ... **CLC 6, 13, 46**
See also CA 81-84; CANR 26; DLBY 86;
MTCW

Adams, Douglas (Noel)   1952- ... **CLC 27, 60**
See also AAYA 4; BEST 89:3; CA 106;
CANR 34; DLBY 83; JRDA

Adams, Francis   1862-1893 .... **NCLC 33**

Adams, Henry (Brooks)
1838-1918 .... **TCLC 4, 52; DA**
See also CA 104; 133; DLB 12, 47

Adams, Richard (George)
1920- .... **CLC 4, 5, 18**
See also AITN 1, 2; CA 49-52; CANR 3,
35; CLR 20; JRDA; MAICYA; MTCW;
SATA 7, 69

Adamson, Joy(-Friederike Victoria)
1910-1980 .... **CLC 17**
See also CA 69-72; 93-96; CANR 22;
MTCW; SATA 11, 22

Adcock, Fleur   1934- .... **CLC 41**
See also CA 25-28R; CANR 11, 34;
DLB 40

Addams, Charles (Samuel)
1912-1988 .... **CLC 30**
See also CA 61-64; 126; CANR 12

Addison, Joseph   1672-1719 .... **LC 18**
See also CDBLB 1660-1789; DLB 101

Adler, C(arole) S(chwerdtfeger)
1932- .... **CLC 35**
See also AAYA 4; CA 89-92; CANR 19,
40; JRDA; MAICYA; SAAS 15;
SATA 26, 63

Adler, Renata   1938- .... **CLC 8, 31**
See also CA 49-52; CANR 5, 22; MTCW

Ady, Endre   1877-1919 .... **TCLC 11**
See also CA 107

Aeschylus
525B.C.-456B.C. .... **CMLC 11; DA**

Afton, Effie
See Harper, Frances Ellen Watkins

Agapida, Fray Antonio
See Irving, Washington

Agee, James (Rufus)
1909-1955 .... **TCLC 1, 19**
See also AITN 1; CA 108;
CDALB 1941-1968; DLB 2, 26

Aghill, Gordon
See Silverberg, Robert

Agnon, S(hmuel) Y(osef Halevi)
1888-1970 .... **CLC 4, 8, 14**
See also CA 17-18; 25-28R; CAP 2; MTCW

Aherne, Owen
See Cassill, R(onald) V(erlin)

Ai   1947- .... **CLC 4, 14, 69**
See also CA 85-88; CAAS 13; DLB 120

Aickman, Robert (Fordyce)
1914-1981 .... **CLC 57**
See also CA 5-8R; CANR 3

Aiken, Conrad (Potter)
1889-1973 ... **CLC 1, 3, 5, 10, 52; SSC 9**
See also CA 5-8R; 45-48; CANR 4;
CDALB 1929-1941; DLB 9, 45, 102;
MTCW; SATA 3, 30

Aiken, Joan (Delano)   1924- .... **CLC 35**
See also AAYA 1; CA 9-12R; CANR 4, 23,
34; CLR 1, 19; JRDA; MAICYA;
MTCW; SAAS 1; SATA 2, 30, 73

Ainsworth, William Harrison
1805-1882 .... **NCLC 13**
See also DLB 21; SATA 24

Aitmatov, Chingiz (Torekulovich)
1928- .... **CLC 71**
See also CA 103; CANR 38; MTCW;
SATA 56

Akers, Floyd
See Baum, L(yman) Frank

Akhmadulina, Bella Akhatovna
1937- .... **CLC 53**
See also CA 65-68

Akhmatova, Anna
1888-1966 .... **CLC 11, 25, 64; PC 2**
See also CA 19-20; 25-28R; CANR 35;
CAP 1; MTCW

Aksakov, Sergei Timofeyvich
1791-1859 .... **NCLC 2**

Aksenov, Vassily .... **CLC 22**
See also Aksyonov, Vassily (Pavlovich)

Aksyonov, Vassily (Pavlovich)
1932- .... **CLC 37**
See also Aksenov, Vassily
See also CA 53-56; CANR 12

Akutagawa Ryunosuke
1892-1927 .... **TCLC 16**
See also CA 117

Alain   1868-1951 .... **TCLC 41**

Alain-Fournier .... **TCLC 6**
See also Fournier, Henri Alban
See also DLB 65

Alarcon, Pedro Antonio de
1833-1891 .... **NCLC 1**

Alas (y Urena), Leopoldo (Enrique Garcia)
1852-1901 .... **TCLC 29**
See also CA 113; 131; HW

Albee, Edward (Franklin III)
1928- ...... **CLC 1, 2, 3, 5, 9, 11, 13, 25,**
53; DA; WLC
See also AITN 1; CA 5-8R; CABS 3;
CANR 8; CDALB 1941-1968; DLB 7;
MTCW

Alberti, Rafael   1902- .... **CLC 7**
See also CA 85-88; DLB 108

Alcala-Galiano, Juan Valera y
See Valera y Alcala-Galiano, Juan

Alcott, Amos Bronson   1799-1888 .. **NCLC 1**
See also DLB 1

Alcott, Louisa May
1832-1888 .... **NCLC 6; DA; WLC**
See also CDALB 1865-1917; CLR 1;
DLB 1, 42, 79; JRDA; MAICYA;
YABC 1

Aldanov, M. A.
See Aldanov, Mark (Alexandrovich)

Aldanov, Mark (Alexandrovich)
1886(?)-1957 .... **TCLC 23**
See also CA 118

Antoine, Marc
See Proust, (Valentin-Louis-George-Eugene-) Marcel

Antoninus, Brother
See Everson, William (Oliver)

Antonioni, Michelangelo 1912- ..... **CLC 20**
See also CA 73-76

Antschel, Paul 1920-1970...... **CLC 10, 19**
See also Celan, Paul
See also CA 85-88; CANR 33; MTCW

Anwar, Chairil 1922-1949 .... **TCLC 22**
See also CA 121

Apollinaire, Guillaume .. **TCLC 3, 8, 51; PC 7**
See also Kostrowitzki, Wilhelm Apollinaris de

Appelfeld, Aharon 1932- ...... **CLC 23, 47**
See also CA 112; 133

Apple, Max (Isaac) 1941-........ **CLC 9, 33**
See also CA 81-84; CANR 19; DLB 130

Appleman, Philip (Dean) 1926-..... **CLC 51**
See also CA 13-16R; CAAS 18; CANR 6, 29

Appleton, Lawrence
See Lovecraft, H(oward) P(hillips)

Apteryx
See Eliot, T(homas) S(tearns)

Apuleius, (Lucius Madaurensis)
125(?)-175(?) .... **CMLC 1**

Aquin, Hubert 1929-1977......... **CLC 15**
See also CA 105; DLB 53

Aragon, Louis 1897-1982........ **CLC 3, 22**
See also CA 69-72; 108; CANR 28; DLB 72; MTCW

Arany, Janos 1817-1882........ **NCLC 34**

Arbuthnot, John 1667-1735.......... **LC 1**
See also DLB 101

Archer, Herbert Winslow
See Mencken, H(enry) L(ouis)

Archer, Jeffrey (Howard) 1940- .... **CLC 28**
See also BEST 89:3; CA 77-80; CANR 22

Archer, Jules 1915- .... **CLC 12**
See also CA 9-12R; CANR 6; SAAS 5; SATA 4

Archer, Lee
See Ellison, Harlan

Arden, John 1930- .... **CLC 6, 13, 15**
See also CA 13-16R; CAAS 4; CANR 31; DLB 13; MTCW

Arenas, Reinaldo
1943-1990 .... **CLC 41; HLC**
See also CA 124; 128; 133; HW

Arendt, Hannah 1906-1975 .... **CLC 66**
See also CA 17-20R; 61-64; CANR 26; MTCW

Aretino, Pietro 1492-1556 .... **LC 12**

Arghezi, Tudor.................... **CLC 80**
See also Theodorescu, Ion N.

Arguedas, Jose Maria
1911-1969 .... **CLC 10, 18**
See also CA 89-92; DLB 113; HW

Argueta, Manlio 1936-............ **CLC 31**
See also CA 131; HW

Ariosto, Ludovico 1474-1533........ **LC 6**

Aristides
See Epstein, Joseph

Aristophanes
450B.C.-385B.C.... **CMLC 4; DA; DC 2**

Arlt, Roberto (Godofredo Christophersen)
1900-1942 .... **TCLC 29; HLC**
See also CA 123; 131; HW

Armah, Ayi Kwei 1939- .... **CLC 5, 33; BLC**
See also BW; CA 61-64; CANR 21; DLB 117; MTCW

Armatrading, Joan 1950-.......... **CLC 17**
See also CA 114

Arnette, Robert
See Silverberg, Robert

Arnim, Achim von (Ludwig Joachim von Arnim) 1781-1831 .... **NCLC 5**
See also DLB 90

Arnim, Bettina von 1785-1859.... **NCLC 38**
See also DLB 90

Arnold, Matthew
1822-1888 ..... **NCLC 6, 29; DA; PC 5; WLC**
See also CDBLB 1832-1890; DLB 32, 57

Arnold, Thomas 1795-1842 ...... **NCLC 18**
See also DLB 55

Arnow, Harriette (Louisa) Simpson
1908-1986 .... **CLC 2, 7, 18**
See also CA 9-12R; 118; CANR 14; DLB 6; MTCW; SATA 42, 47

Arp, Hans
See Arp, Jean

Arp, Jean 1887-1966.............. **CLC 5**
See also CA 81-84; 25-28R; CANR 42

Arrabal
See Arrabal, Fernando

Arrabal, Fernando 1932- ... **CLC 2, 9, 18, 58**
See also CA 9-12R; CANR 15

Arrick, Fran..................... **CLC 30**

Artaud, Antonin 1896-1948 ..... **TCLC 3, 36**
See also CA 104

Arthur, Ruth M(abel) 1905-1979.... **CLC 12**
See also CA 9-12R; 85-88; CANR 4; SATA 7, 26

Artsybashev, Mikhail (Petrovich)
1878-1927 .... **TCLC 31**

Arundel, Honor (Morfydd)
1919-1973 .... **CLC 17**
See also CA 21-22; 41-44R; CAP 2; SATA 4, 24

Asch, Sholem 1880-1957 .... **TCLC 3**
See also CA 105

Ash, Shalom
See Asch, Sholem

Ashbery, John (Lawrence)
1927- ...... **CLC 2, 3, 4, 6, 9, 13, 15, 25, 41, 77**
See also CA 5-8R; CANR 9, 37; DLB 5; DLBY 81; MTCW

Ashdown, Clifford
See Freeman, R(ichard) Austin

Ashe, Gordon
See Creasey, John

Ashton-Warner, Sylvia (Constance)
1908-1984 .... **CLC 19**
See also CA 69-72; 112; CANR 29; MTCW

Asimov, Isaac
1920-1992 ...... **CLC 1, 3, 9, 19, 26, 76**
See also BEST 90:2; CA 1-4R; 137; CANR 2, 19, 36; CLR 12; DLB 8; DLBY 92; JRDA; MAICYA; MTCW; SATA 1, 26, 74

Astley, Thea (Beatrice May)
1925- .... **CLC 41**
See also CA 65-68; CANR 11, 43

Aston, James
See White, T(erence) H(anbury)

Asturias, Miguel Angel
1899-1974 .... **CLC 3, 8, 13; HLC**
See also CA 25-28; 49-52; CANR 32; CAP 2; DLB 113; HW; MTCW

Atares, Carlos Saura
See Saura (Atares), Carlos

Atheling, William
See Pound, Ezra (Weston Loomis)

Atheling, William, Jr.
See Blish, James (Benjamin)

Atherton, Gertrude (Franklin Horn)
1857-1948 .... **TCLC 2**
See also CA 104; DLB 9, 78

Atherton, Lucius
See Masters, Edgar Lee

Atkins, Jack
See Harris, Mark

Atticus
See Fleming, Ian (Lancaster)

Atwood, Margaret (Eleanor)
1939- ..... **CLC 2, 3, 4, 8, 13, 15, 25, 44; DA; PC 8; SSC 2; WLC**
See also BEST 89:2; CA 49-52; CANR 3, 24, 33; DLB 53; MTCW; SATA 50

Aubigny, Pierre d'
See Mencken, H(enry) L(ouis)

Aubin, Penelope 1685-1731(?)........ **LC 9**
See also DLB 39

Auchincloss, Louis (Stanton)
1917- .... **CLC 4, 6, 9, 18, 45**
See also CA 1-4R; CANR 6, 29; DLB 2; DLBY 80; MTCW

Auden, W(ystan) H(ugh)
1907-1973 ...... **CLC 1, 2, 3, 4, 6, 9, 11, 14, 43; DA; PC 1; WLC**
See also CA 9-12R; 45-48; CANR 5; CDBLB 1914-1945; DLB 10, 20; MTCW

Audiberti, Jacques 1900-1965 ...... **CLC 38**
See also CA 25-28R

Auel, Jean M(arie) 1936-.......... **CLC 31**
See also AAYA 7; BEST 90:4; CA 103; CANR 21

Auerbach, Erich 1892-1957 .... **TCLC 43**
See also CA 118

Augier, Emile 1820-1889 .... **NCLC 31**

August, John
See De Voto, Bernard (Augustine)

Augustine, St. 354-430 .... **CMLC 6**

Aurelius
See Bourne, Randolph S(illiman)

Austen, Jane
1775-1817 .... **NCLC 1, 13, 19, 33; DA; WLC**
See also CDBLB 1789-1832; DLB 116

Auster, Paul 1947- .... **CLC 47**
See also CA 69-72; CANR 23

Austin, Frank
See Faust, Frederick (Schiller)

Austin, Mary (Hunter)
1868-1934 .... **TCLC 25**
See also CA 109; DLB 9, 78

Autran Dourado, Waldomiro
See Dourado, (Waldomiro Freitas) Autran

Averroes 1126-1198 .... **CMLC 7**
See also DLB 115

Avison, Margaret 1918- .... **CLC 2, 4**
See also CA 17-20R; DLB 53; MTCW

Axton, David
See Koontz, Dean R(ay)

Ayckbourn, Alan
1939- .... **CLC 5, 8, 18, 33, 74**
See also CA 21-24R; CANR 31; DLB 13; MTCW

Aydy, Catherine
See Tennant, Emma (Christina)

Ayme, Marcel (Andre) 1902-1967... **CLC 11**
See also CA 89-92; CLR 25; DLB 72

Ayrton, Michael 1921-1975 .... **CLC 7**
See also CA 5-8R; 61-64; CANR 9, 21

Azorin .... **CLC 11**
See also Martinez Ruiz, Jose

Azuela, Mariano
1873-1952 .... **TCLC 3; HLC**
See also CA 104; 131; HW; MTCW

Baastad, Babbis Friis
See Friis-Baastad, Babbis Ellinor

Bab
See Gilbert, W(illiam) S(chwenck)

Babbis, Eleanor
See Friis-Baastad, Babbis Ellinor

Babel, Isaak (Emmanuilovich)
1894-1941(?) .... **TCLC 2, 13**
See also CA 104

Babits, Mihaly 1883-1941 .... **TCLC 14**
See also CA 114

Babur 1483-1530................. **LC 18**

Bacchelli, Riccardo 1891-1985 ..... **CLC 19**
See also CA 29-32R; 117

Bach, Richard (David) 1936-....... **CLC 14**
See also AITN 1; BEST 89:2; CA 9-12R; CANR 18; MTCW; SATA 13

Bachman, Richard
See King, Stephen (Edwin)

Bachmann, Ingeborg 1926-1973..... **CLC 69**
See also CA 93-96; 45-48; DLB 85

Bacon, Francis 1561-1626 .... **LC 18**
See also CDBLB Before 1660

Bacovia, George................. **TCLC 24**
See also Vasiliu, Gheorghe

Badanes, Jerome 1937-........... **CLC 59**

Bagehot, Walter 1826-1877 ...... **NCLC 10**
See also DLB 55

Bagnold, Enid 1889-1981 .... **CLC 25**
See also CA 5-8R; 103; CANR 5, 40; DLB 13; MAICYA; SATA 1, 25

Bagrjana, Elisaveta
See Belcheva, Elisaveta

Bagryana, Elisaveta
See Belcheva, Elisaveta

Bailey, Paul 1937- .... **CLC 45**
See also CA 21-24R; CANR 16; DLB 14

Baillie, Joanna 1762-1851 .... **NCLC 2**
See also DLB 93

Bainbridge, Beryl (Margaret)
1933- .... **CLC 4, 5, 8, 10, 14, 18, 22, 62**
See also CA 21-24R; CANR 24; DLB 14; MTCW

Baker, Elliott 1922- .... **CLC 8**
See also CA 45-48; CANR 2

Baker, Nicholson 1957- .... **CLC 61**
See also CA 135

Baker, Ray Stannard 1870-1946 ... **TCLC 47**
See also CA 118

Baker, Russell (Wayne) 1925-...... **CLC 31**
See also BEST 89:4; CA 57-60; CANR 11, 41; MTCW

Bakshi, Ralph 1938(?)-........... **CLC 26**
See also CA 112; 138

Bakunin, Mikhail (Alexandrovich)
1814-1876 .... **NCLC 25**

Baldwin, James (Arthur)
1924-1987 ...... **CLC 1, 2, 3, 4, 5, 8, 13, 15, 17, 42, 50, 67; BLC; DA; DC 1; SSC 10; WLC**
See also AAYA 4; BW; CA 1-4R; 124; CABS 1; CANR 3, 24; CDALB 1941-1968; DLB 2, 7, 33; DLBY 87; MTCW; SATA 9, 54

Ballard, J(ames) G(raham)
1930- ...... **CLC 3, 6, 14, 36; SSC 1**
See also AAYA 3; CA 5-8R; CANR 15, 39; DLB 14; MTCW

Balmont, Konstantin (Dmitriyevich)
1867-1943 .... **TCLC 11**
See also CA 109

Balzac, Honore de
1799-1850 .... **NCLC 5, 35; DA; SSC 5; WLC**
See also DLB 119

Bambara, Toni Cade
1939- .... **CLC 19; BLC; DA**
See also AAYA 5; BW; CA 29-32R; CANR 24; DLB 38; MTCW

Bamdad, A.
See Shamlu, Ahmad

Banat, D. R.
See Bradbury, Ray (Douglas)

Bancroft, Laura
See Baum, L(yman) Frank

Banim, John 1798-1842 .... **NCLC 13**
See also DLB 116

Banim, Michael 1796-1874 ...... **NCLC 13**

Banks, Iain
See Banks, Iain M(enzies)

Banks, Iain M(enzies) 1954- ...... **CLC 34**
See also CA 123; 128

Banks, Lynne Reid .... **CLC 23**
See also Reid Banks, Lynne
See also AAYA 6

Banks, Russell 1940- .... **CLC 37, 72**
See also CA 65-68; CAAS 15; CANR 19; DLB 130

Banville, John 1945-............ **CLC 46**
See also CA 117; 128; DLB 14

Banville, Theodore (Faullain) de
1832-1891 .... **NCLC 9**

Baraka, Amiri
1934- .... **CLC 1, 2, 3, 5, 10, 14, 33; BLC; DA; PC 4**
See also Jones, LeRoi
See also BW; CA 21-24R; CABS 3; CANR 27, 38; CDALB 1941-1968; DLB 5, 7, 16, 38; DLBD 8; MTCW

Barbellion, W. N. P.............. **TCLC 24**
See also Cummings, Bruce F(rederick)

Barbera, Jack 1945-............ **CLC 44**
See also CA 110

Barbey d'Aurevilly, Jules Amedee
1808-1889 .... **NCLC 1**
See also DLB 119

Barbusse, Henri 1873-1935 .... **TCLC 5**
See also CA 105; DLB 65

Barclay, Bill
See Moorcock, Michael (John)

Barclay, William Ewert
See Moorcock, Michael (John)

Barea, Arturo 1897-1957 .... **TCLC 14**
See also CA 111

Barfoot, Joan 1946- .... **CLC 18**
See also CA 105

Baring, Maurice 1874-1945 .... **TCLC 8**
See also CA 105; DLB 34

Barker, Clive 1952- .... **CLC 52**
See also AAYA 10; BEST 90:3; CA 121; 129; MTCW

Barker, George Granville
1913-1991 .... **CLC 8, 48**
See also CA 9-12R; 135; CANR 7, 38; DLB 20; MTCW

Barker, Harley Granville
See Granville-Barker, Harley
See also DLB 10

Barker, Howard 1946-............ **CLC 37**
See also CA 102; DLB 13

Barker, Pat 1943-................ **CLC 32**
See also CA 117; 122

Barlow, Joel 1754-1812 .... **NCLC 23**
See also DLB 37

Barnard, Mary (Ethel) 1909-....... **CLC 48**
See also CA 21-22; CAP 2

Barnes, Djuna
1892-1982 ... **CLC 3, 4, 8, 11, 29; SSC 3**
See also CA 9-12R; 107; CANR 16; DLB 4, 9, 45; MTCW

Barnes, Julian 1946-............. **CLC 42**
See also CA 102; CANR 19

Barnes, Peter 1931- .... **CLC 5, 56**
See also CA 65-68; CAAS 12; CANR 33, 34; DLB 13; MTCW

Baroja (y Nessi), Pio
1872-1956 . . . . **TCLC 8; HLC**
See also CA 104

Baron, David
See Pinter, Harold

Baron Corvo
See Rolfe, Frederick (William Serafino
Austin Lewis Mary)

Barondess, Sue K(aufman)
1926-1977 . . . . **CLC 8**
See also Kaufman, Sue
See also CA 1-4R; 69-72; CANR 1

Baron de Teive
See Pessoa, Fernando (Antonio Nogueira)

Barres, Maurice 1862-1923 . . . . . . **TCLC 47**
See also DLB 123

Barreto, Afonso Henrique de Lima
See Lima Barreto, Afonso Henrique de

Barrett, (Roger) Syd 1946- . . . . **CLC 35**
See also Pink Floyd

Barrett, William (Christopher)
1913-1992 . . . . **CLC 27**
See also CA 13-16R; 139; CANR 11

Barrie, J(ames) M(atthew)
1860-1937 . . . . **TCLC 2**
See also CA 104; 136; CDBLB 1890-1914;
CLR 16; DLB 10; MAICYA; YABC 1

Barrington, Michael
See Moorcock, Michael (John)

Barrol, Grady
See Bograd, Larry

Barry, Mike
See Malzberg, Barry N(athaniel)

Barry, Philip 1896-1949. . . . . **TCLC 11**
See also CA 109; DLB 7

Bart, Andre Schwarz
See Schwarz-Bart, Andre

Barth, John (Simmons)
1930- . . . . . . **CLC 1, 2, 3, 5, 7, 9, 10, 14,
27, 51; SSC 10**
See also AITN 1, 2; CA 1-4R; CABS 1;
CANR 5, 23; DLB 2; MTCW

Barthelme, Donald
1931-1989 . . . . . . **CLC 1, 2, 3, 5, 6, 8, 13,
23, 46, 59; SSC 2**
See also CA 21-24R; 129; CANR 20;
DLB 2; DLBY 80, 89; MTCW; SATA 7,
62

Barthelme, Frederick 1943- . . . . **CLC 36**
See also CA 114; 122; DLBY 85

Barthes, Roland (Gerard)
1915-1980 . . . . **CLC 24**
See also CA 130; 97-100; MTCW

Barzun, Jacques (Martin) 1907- . . . . **CLC 51**
See also CA 61-64; CANR 22

Bashevis, Isaac
See Singer, Isaac Bashevis

Bashkirtseff, Marie 1859-1884 . . . **NCLC 27**

Basho
See Matsuo Basho

Bass, Kingsley B., Jr.
See Bullins, Ed

Bass, Rick 1958-. . . . . **CLC 79**
See also CA 126

Bassani, Giorgio 1916-. . . . . **CLC 9**
See also CA 65-68; CANR 33; DLB 128;
MTCW

Bastos, Augusto (Antonio) Roa
See Roa Bastos, Augusto (Antonio)

Bataille, Georges 1897-1962 . . . . **CLC 29**
See also CA 101; 89-92

Bates, H(erbert) E(rnest)
1905-1974 . . . . **CLC 46; SSC 10**
See also CA 93-96; 45-48; CANR 34;
MTCW

Bauchart
See Camus, Albert

Baudelaire, Charles
1821-1867 . . . . . **NCLC 6, 29; DA; PC 1;
WLC**

Baudrillard, Jean 1929- . . . . **CLC 60**

Baum, L(yman) Frank 1856-1919 . . . **TCLC 7**
See also CA 108; 133; CLR 15; DLB 22;
JRDA; MAICYA; MTCW; SATA 18

Baum, Louis F.
See Baum, L(yman) Frank

Baumbach, Jonathan 1933- . . . . . . **CLC 6, 23**
See also CA 13-16R; CAAS 5; CANR 12;
DLBY 80; MTCW

Bausch, Richard (Carl) 1945- . . . . . . **CLC 51**
See also CA 101; CAAS 14; CANR 43;
DLB 130

Baxter, Charles 1947-. . . . . **CLC 45, 78**
See also CA 57-60; CANR 40; DLB 130

Baxter, George Owen
See Faust, Frederick (Schiller)

Baxter, James K(eir) 1926-1972 . . . . **CLC 14**
See also CA 77-80

Baxter, John
See Hunt, E(verette) Howard, Jr.

Bayer, Sylvia
See Glassco, John

Beagle, Peter S(oyer) 1939-. . . . . **CLC 7**
See also CA 9-12R; CANR 4; DLBY 80;
SATA 60

Bean, Normal
See Burroughs, Edgar Rice

Beard, Charles A(ustin)
1874-1948 . . . . **TCLC 15**
See also CA 115; DLB 17; SATA 18

Beardsley, Aubrey 1872-1898 . . . . . **NCLC 6**

Beattie, Ann
1947- . . . . **CLC 8, 13, 18, 40, 63; SSC 11**
See also BEST 90:2; CA 81-84; DLBY 82;
MTCW

Beattie, James 1735-1803 . . . . **NCLC 25**
See also DLB 109

Beauchamp, Kathleen Mansfield 1888-1923
See Mansfield, Katherine
See also CA 104; 134; DA

Beaumarchais, Pierre-Augustin Caron de
1732-1799 . . . . **DC 4**

**Beauvoir, Simone (Lucie Ernestine Marie
Bertrand) de**
1908-1986 . . . . **CLC 1, 2, 4, 8, 14, 31, 44,
50, 71; DA; WLC**
See also CA 9-12R; 118; CANR 28;
DLB 72; DLBY 86; MTCW

Becker, Jurek 1937-. . . . . **CLC 7, 19**
See also CA 85-88; DLB 75

Becker, Walter 1950-. . . . . **CLC 26**

Beckett, Samuel (Barclay)
1906-1989 . . . . . . **CLC 1, 2, 3, 4, 6, 9, 10,
11, 14, 18, 29, 57, 59; DA; WLC**
See also CA 5-8R; 130; CANR 33;
CDBLB 1945-1960; DLB 13, 15;
DLBY 90; MTCW

Beckford, William 1760-1844 . . . . **NCLC 16**
See also DLB 39

Beckman, Gunnel 1910-. . . . . **CLC 26**
See also CA 33-36R; CANR 15; CLR 25;
MAICYA; SAAS 9; SATA 6

Becque, Henri 1837-1899. . . . . **NCLC 3**

Beddoes, Thomas Lovell
1803-1849 . . . . **NCLC 3**
See also DLB 96

Bedford, Donald F.
See Fearing, Kenneth (Flexner)

Beecher, Catharine Esther
1800-1878 . . . . **NCLC 30**
See also DLB 1

Beecher, John 1904-1980. . . . . **CLC 6**
See also AITN 1; CA 5-8R; 105; CANR 8

Beer, Johann 1655-1700. . . . . **LC 5**

Beer, Patricia 1924-. . . . . **CLC 58**
See also CA 61-64; CANR 13; DLB 40

Beerbohm, Henry Maximilian
1872-1956 . . . . **TCLC 1, 24**
See also CA 104; DLB 34, 100

Begiebing, Robert J(ohn) 1946-. . . . . **CLC 70**
See also CA 122; CANR 40

Behan, Brendan
1923-1964 . . . . **CLC 1, 8, 11, 15, 79**
See also CA 73-76; CANR 33;
CDBLB 1945-1960; DLB 13; MTCW

Behn, Aphra
1640(?)-1689 . . . . **LC 1; DA; DC 4; WLC**
See also DLB 39, 80, 131

Behrman, S(amuel) N(athaniel)
1893-1973 . . . . **CLC 40**
See also CA 13-16; 45-48; CAP 1; DLB 7,
44

Belasco, David 1853-1931 . . . . **TCLC 3**
See also CA 104; DLB 7

Belcheva, Elisaveta 1893- . . . . **CLC 10**

Beldone, Phil "Cheech"
See Ellison, Harlan

Beleno
See Azuela, Mariano

Belinski, Vissarion Grigoryevich
1811-1848 . . . . **NCLC 5**

Belitt, Ben 1911-. . . . . **CLC 22**
See also CA 13-16R; CAAS 4; CANR 7;
DLB 5

Bell, James Madison
1826-1902 . . . . **TCLC 43; BLC**
See also BW; CA 122; 124; DLB 50

Bell, Madison (Smartt) 1957- . . . . . . **CLC 41**
See also CA 111; CANR 28

Bell, Marvin (Hartley) 1937-. . . . . **CLC 8, 31**
See also CA 21-24R; CAAS 14; DLB 5;
MTCW

Bonaventura.................... NCLC 35
See also DLB 90

Bond, Edward 1934-...... CLC 4, 6, 13, 23
See also CA 25-28R; CANR 38; DLB 13;
MTCW

Bonham, Frank 1914-1989........ CLC 12
See also AAYA 1; CA 9-12R; CANR 4, 36;
JRDA; MAICYA; SAAS 3; SATA 1, 49,
62

Bonnefoy, Yves 1923-....... CLC 9, 15, 58
See also CA 85-88; CANR 33; MTCW

Bontemps, Arna(ud Wendell)
1902-1973 .... CLC 1, 18; BLC
See also BW; CA 1-4R; 41-44R; CANR 4,
35; CLR 6; DLB 48, 51; JRDA;
MAICYA; MTCW; SATA 2, 24, 44

Booth, Martin 1944-............. CLC 13
See also CA 93-96; CAAS 2

Booth, Philip 1925-.............. CLC 23
See also CA 5-8R; CANR 5; DLBY 82

Booth, Wayne C(layson) 1921- ..... CLC 24
See also CA 1-4R; CAAS 5; CANR 3, 43;
DLB 67

Borchert, Wolfgang 1921-1947 ..... TCLC 5
See also CA 104; DLB 69, 124

Borel, Petrus 1809-1859........ NCLC 41

Borges, Jorge Luis
1899-1986 ... CLC 1, 2, 3, 4, 6, 8, 9, 10,
13, 19, 44, 48; DA; HLC; SSC 4; WLC
See also CA 21-24R; CANR 19, 33;
DLB 113; DLBY 86; HW; MTCW

Borowski, Tadeusz 1922-1951 ...... TCLC 9
See also CA 106

Borrow, George (Henry)
1803-1881 .... NCLC 9
See also DLB 21, 55

Bosman, Herman Charles
1905-1951 .... TCLC 49

Bosschere, Jean de 1878(?)-1953... TCLC 19
See also CA 115

Boswell, James
1740-1795 .... LC 4; DA; WLC
See also CDBLB 1660-1789; DLB 104

Bottoms, David 1949-............. CLC 53
See also CA 105; CANR 22; DLB 120;
DLBY 83

Boucicault, Dion 1820-1890...... NCLC 41

Boucolon, Maryse 1937-
See Conde, Maryse
See also CA 110; CANR 30

Bourget, Paul (Charles Joseph)
1852-1935 .... TCLC 12
See also CA 107; DLB 123

Bourjaily, Vance (Nye) 1922- ... CLC 8, 62
See also CA 1-4R; CAAS 1; CANR 2;
DLB 2

Bourne, Randolph S(illiman)
1886-1918 .... TCLC 16
See also CA 117; DLB 63

Bova, Ben(jamin William) 1932-.... CLC 45
See also CA 5-8R; CAAS 18; CANR 11;
CLR 3; DLBY 81; MAICYA; MTCW;
SATA 6, 68

Bowen, Elizabeth (Dorothea Cole)
1899-1973 ...... CLC 1, 3, 6, 11, 15, 22;
SSC 3
See also CA 17-18; 41-44R; CANR 35;
CAP 2; CDBLB 1945-1960; DLB 15;
MTCW

Bowering, George 1935-........ CLC 15, 47
See also CA 21-24R; CAAS 16; CANR 10;
DLB 53

Bowering, Marilyn R(uthe) 1949-... CLC 32
See also CA 101

Bowers, Edgar 1924- .... CLC 9
See also CA 5-8R; CANR 24; DLB 5

Bowie, David .... CLC 17
See also Jones, David Robert

Bowles, Jane (Sydney)
1917-1973 .... CLC 3, 68
See also CA 19-20; 41-44R; CAP 2

Bowles, Paul (Frederick)
1910- ...... CLC 1, 2, 19, 53; SSC 3
See also CA 1-4R; CAAS 1; CANR 1, 19;
DLB 5, 6; MTCW

Box, Edgar
See Vidal, Gore

Boyd, Nancy
See Millay, Edna St. Vincent

Boyd, William 1952-........ CLC 28, 53, 70
See also CA 114; 120

Boyle, Kay
1902-1992 ..... CLC 1, 5, 19, 58; SSC 5
See also CA 13-16R; 140; CAAS 1;
CANR 29; DLB 4, 9, 48, 86; MTCW

Boyle, Mark
See Kienzle, William X(avier)

Boyle, Patrick 1905-1982.......... CLC 19
See also CA 127

Boyle, T. Coraghessan 1948-.... CLC 36, 55
See also BEST 90:4; CA 120; DLBY 86

Boz
See Dickens, Charles (John Huffam)

Brackenridge, Hugh Henry
1748-1816 .... NCLC 7
See also DLB 11, 37

Bradbury, Edward P.
See Moorcock, Michael (John)

Bradbury, Malcolm (Stanley)
1932- .... CLC 32, 61
See also CA 1-4R; CANR 1, 33; DLB 14;
MTCW

Bradbury, Ray (Douglas)
1920- ... CLC 1, 3, 10, 15, 42; DA; WLC
See also AITN 1, 2; CA 1-4R; CANR 2, 30;
CDALB 1968-1988; DLB 2, 8; MTCW;
SATA 11, 64

Bradford, Gamaliel 1863-1932..... TCLC 36
See also DLB 17

Bradley, David (Henry, Jr.)
1950- .... CLC 23; BLC
See also BW; CA 104; CANR 26; DLB 33

Bradley, John Ed(mund, Jr.)
1958- .... CLC 55
See also CA 139

Bradley, Marion Zimmer 1930-..... CLC 30
See also AAYA 9; CA 57-60; CAAS 10;
CANR 7, 31; DLB 8; MTCW

Bradstreet, Anne 1612(?)-1672 ... LC 4; DA
See also CDALB 1640-1865; DLB 24

Bragg, Melvyn 1939-............. CLC 10
See also BEST 89:3; CA 57-60; CANR 10;
DLB 14

Braine, John (Gerard)
1922-1986 .... CLC 1, 3, 41
See also CA 1-4R; 120; CANR 1, 33;
CDBLB 1945-1960; DLB 15; DLBY 86;
MTCW

Brammer, William 1930(?)-1978 .... CLC 31
See also CA 77-80

Brancati, Vitaliano 1907-1954..... TCLC 12
See also CA 109

Brancato, Robin F(idler) 1936-..... CLC 35
See also AAYA 9; CA 69-72; CANR 11;
CLR 32; JRDA; SAAS 9; SATA 23

Brand, Max
See Faust, Frederick (Schiller)

Brand, Millen 1906-1980.......... CLC 7
See also CA 21-24R; 97-100

Branden, Barbara .... CLC 44

Brandes, Georg (Morris Cohen)
1842-1927 .... TCLC 10
See also CA 105

Brandys, Kazimierz 1916- .... CLC 62

Branley, Franklyn M(ansfield)
1915- .... CLC 21
See also CA 33-36R; CANR 14, 39;
CLR 13; MAICYA; SAAS 16; SATA 4,
68

Brathwaite, Edward (Kamau)
1930- .... CLC 11
See also BW; CA 25-28R; CANR 11, 26;
DLB 125

Brautigan, Richard (Gary)
1935-1984 .... CLC 1, 3, 5, 9, 12, 34, 42
See also CA 53-56; 113; CANR 34; DLB 2,
5; DLBY 80, 84; MTCW; SATA 56

Braverman, Kate 1950- .... CLC 67
See also CA 89-92

Brecht, Bertolt
1898-1956 ...... TCLC 1, 6, 13, 35; DA;
DC 3; WLC
See also CA 104; 133; DLB 56, 124; MTCW

Brecht, Eugen Berthold Friedrich
See Brecht, Bertolt

Bremer, Fredrika 1801-1865 ..... NCLC 11

Brennan, Christopher John
1870-1932 .... TCLC 17
See also CA 117

Brennan, Maeve 1917-............. CLC 5
See also CA 81-84

Brentano, Clemens (Maria)
1778-1842 .... NCLC 1

Brent of Bin Bin
See Franklin, (Stella Maraia Sarah) Miles

Brenton, Howard 1942-........... CLC 31
See also CA 69-72; CANR 33; DLB 13;
MTCW

Breslin, James 1930-
See Breslin, Jimmy
See also CA 73-76; CANR 31; MTCW

Breslin, Jimmy .... **CLC 4, 43**
See also Breslin, James
See also AITN 1

Bresson, Robert 1907- .... **CLC 16**
See also CA 110

Breton, Andre 1896-1966... **CLC 2, 9, 15, 54**
See also CA 19-20; 25-28R; CANR 40;
CAP 2; DLB 65; MTCW

Breytenbach, Breyten 1939(?)- .. **CLC 23, 37**
See also CA 113; 129

Bridgers, Sue Ellen 1942- .... **CLC 26**
See also AAYA 8; CA 65-68; CANR 11,
36; CLR 18; DLB 52; JRDA; MAICYA;
SAAS 1; SATA 22

Bridges, Robert (Seymour)
1844-1930 .... **TCLC 1**
See also CA 104; CDBLB 1890-1914;
DLB 19, 98

Bridie, James .... **TCLC 3**
See also Mavor, Osborne Henry
See also DLB 10

Brin, David 1950- .... **CLC 34**
See also CA 102; CANR 24; SATA 65

Brink, Andre (Philippus)
1935- .... **CLC 18, 36**
See also CA 104; CANR 39; MTCW

Brinsmead, H(esba) F(ay) 1922- .... **CLC 21**
See also CA 21-24R; CANR 10; MAICYA;
SAAS 5; SATA 18

Brittain, Vera (Mary)
1893(?)-1970 .... **CLC 23**
See also CA 13-16; 25-28R; CAP 1; MTCW

Broch, Hermann 1886-1951 ...... **TCLC 20**
See also CA 117; DLB 85, 124

Brock, Rose
See Hansen, Joseph

Brodkey, Harold 1930- .... **CLC 56**
See also CA 111; DLB 130

Brodsky, Iosif Alexandrovich 1940-
See Brodsky, Joseph
See also AITN 1; CA 41-44R; CANR 37;
MTCW

Brodsky, Joseph .... **CLC 4, 6, 13, 36, 50**
See also Brodsky, Iosif Alexandrovich

Brodsky, Michael Mark 1948- ..... **CLC 19**
See also CA 102; CANR 18, 41

Bromell, Henry 1947- .... **CLC 5**
See also CA 53-56; CANR 9

Bromfield, Louis (Brucker)
1896-1956 .... **TCLC 11**
See also CA 107; DLB 4, 9, 86

Broner, E(sther) M(asserman)
1930- .... **CLC 19**
See also CA 17-20R; CANR 8, 25; DLB 28

Bronk, William 1918- .... **CLC 10**
See also CA 89-92; CANR 23

Bronstein, Lev Davidovich
See Trotsky, Leon

Bronte, Anne 1820-1849 .... **NCLC 4**
See also DLB 21

Bronte, Charlotte
1816-1855 ... **NCLC 3, 8, 33; DA; WLC**
See also CDBLB 1832-1890; DLB 21

Bronte, (Jane) Emily
1818-1848 .... **NCLC 16, 35; DA; PC 8;
WLC**
See also CDBLB 1832-1890; DLB 21, 32

Brooke, Frances 1724-1789 .... **LC 6**
See also DLB 39, 99

Brooke, Henry 1703(?)-1783 .... **LC 1**
See also DLB 39

Brooke, Rupert (Chawner)
1887-1915 .... **TCLC 2, 7; DA; WLC**
See also CA 104; 132; CDBLB 1914-1945;
DLB 19; MTCW

Brooke-Haven, P.
See Wodehouse, P(elham) G(renville)

Brooke-Rose, Christine 1926- ...... **CLC 40**
See also CA 13-16R; DLB 14

Brookner, Anita 1928- ..... **CLC 32, 34, 51**
See also CA 114; 120; CANR 37; DLBY 87;
MTCW

Brooks, Cleanth 1906- .... **CLC 24**
See also CA 17-20R; CANR 33, 35;
DLB 63; MTCW

Brooks, George
See Baum, L(yman) Frank

Brooks, Gwendolyn
1917- ...... **CLC 1, 2, 4, 5, 15, 49; BLC;
DA; PC 7; WLC**
See also AITN 1; BW; CA 1-4R; CANR 1,
27; CDALB 1941-1968; CLR 27; DLB 5,
76; MTCW; SATA 6

Brooks, Mel .... **CLC 12**
See also Kaminsky, Melvin
See also DLB 26

Brooks, Peter 1938- .... **CLC 34**
See also CA 45-48; CANR 1

Brooks, Van Wyck 1886-1963 ...... **CLC 29**
See also CA 1-4R; CANR 6; DLB 45, 63,
103

Brophy, Brigid (Antonia)
1929- .... **CLC 6, 11, 29**
See also CA 5-8R; CAAS 4; CANR 25;
DLB 14; MTCW

Brosman, Catharine Savage 1934-.... **CLC 9**
See also CA 61-64; CANR 21

Brother Antoninus
See Everson, William (Oliver)

Broughton, T(homas) Alan 1936- .. **CLC 19**
See also CA 45-48; CANR 2, 23

Broumas, Olga 1949- .... **CLC 10, 73**
See also CA 85-88; CANR 20

Brown, Charles Brockden
1771-1810 .... **NCLC 22**
See also CDALB 1640-1865; DLB 37, 59,
73

Brown, Christy 1932-1981 .... **CLC 63**
See also CA 105; 104; DLB 14

Brown, Claude 1937- .... **CLC 30; BLC**
See also AAYA 7; BW; CA 73-76

Brown, Dee (Alexander) 1908- .. **CLC 18, 47**
See also CA 13-16R; CAAS 6; CANR 11;
DLBY 80; MTCW; SATA 5

Brown, George
See Wertmueller, Lina

Brown, George Douglas
1869-1902 .... **TCLC 28**

Brown, George Mackay 1921-.... **CLC 5, 48**
See also CA 21-24R; CAAS 6; CANR 12,
37; DLB 14, 27; MTCW; SATA 35

Brown, (William) Larry 1951-...... **CLC 73**
See also CA 130; 134

Brown, Moses
See Barrett, William (Christopher)

Brown, Rita Mae 1944- ..... **CLC 18, 43, 79**
See also CA 45-48; CANR 2, 11, 35;
MTCW

Brown, Roderick (Langmere) Haig-
See Haig-Brown, Roderick (Langmere)

Brown, Rosellen 1939- .... **CLC 32**
See also CA 77-80; CAAS 10; CANR 14

Brown, Sterling Allen
1901-1989 .... **CLC 1, 23, 59; BLC**
See also BW; CA 85-88; 127; CANR 26;
DLB 48, 51, 63; MTCW

Brown, Will
See Ainsworth, William Harrison

Brown, William Wells
1813-1884 .... **NCLC 2; BLC; DC 1**
See also DLB 3, 50

Browne, (Clyde) Jackson 1948(?)-... **CLC 21**
See also CA 120

Browning, Elizabeth Barrett
1806-1861 ..... **NCLC 1, 16; DA; PC 6;
WLC**
See also CDBLB 1832-1890; DLB 32

Browning, Robert
1812-1889 .... **NCLC 19; DA; PC 2**
See also CDBLB 1832-1890; DLB 32;
YABC 1

Browning, Tod 1882-1962 .... **CLC 16**
See also CA 141; 117

Bruccoli, Matthew J(oseph) 1931- .. **CLC 34**
See also CA 9-12R; CANR 7; DLB 103

Bruce, Lenny .... **CLC 21**
See also Schneider, Leonard Alfred

Bruin, John
See Brutus, Dennis

Brulls, Christian
See Simenon, Georges (Jacques Christian)

Brunner, John (Kilian Houston)
1934- .... **CLC 8, 10**
See also CA 1-4R; CAAS 8; CANR 2, 37;
MTCW

Brutus, Dennis 1924- .... **CLC 43; BLC**
See also BW; CA 49-52; CAAS 14;
CANR 2, 27, 42; DLB 117

Bryan, C(ourtlandt) D(ixon) B(arnes)
1936- .... **CLC 29**
See also CA 73-76; CANR 13

Bryan, Michael
See Moore, Brian

Bryant, William Cullen
1794-1878 .... **NCLC 6; DA**
See also CDALB 1640-1865; DLB 3, 43, 59

Bryusov, Valery Yakovlevich
1873-1924 .... **TCLC 10**
See also CA 107

Buchan, John 1875-1940 .... **TCLC 41**
See also CA 108; DLB 34, 70; YABC 2

Buchanan, George 1506-1582 .... **LC 4**

Buchheim, Lothar-Guenther 1918- ... **CLC 6**
See also CA 85-88

Buchner, (Karl) Georg
1813-1837 .... **NCLC 26**

Buchwald, Art(hur) 1925-......... **CLC 33**
See also AITN 1; CA 5-8R; CANR 21;
MTCW; SATA 10

Buck, Pearl S(ydenstricker)
1892-1973 .... **CLC 7, 11, 18; DA**
See also AITN 1; CA 1-4R; 41-44R;
CANR 1, 34; DLB 9, 102; MTCW;
SATA 1, 25

Buckler, Ernest 1908-1984........ **CLC 13**
See also CA 11-12; 114; CAP 1; DLB 68;
SATA 47

Buckley, Vincent (Thomas)
1925-1988 .... **CLC 57**
See also CA 101

Buckley, William F(rank), Jr.
1925- .... **CLC 7, 18, 37**
See also AITN 1; CA 1-4R; CANR 1, 24;
DLBY 80; MTCW

Buechner, (Carl) Frederick
1926- .... **CLC 2, 4, 6, 9**
See also CA 13-16R; CANR 11, 39;
DLBY 80; MTCW

Buell, John (Edward) 1927-........ **CLC 10**
See also CA 1-4R; DLB 53

Buero Vallejo, Antonio 1916- ... **CLC 15, 46**
See also CA 106; CANR 24; HW; MTCW

Bufalino, Gesualdo 1920(?)-........ **CLC 74**

Bugayev, Boris Nikolayevich 1880-1934
See Bely, Andrey
See also CA 104

Bukowski, Charles
1920-1994 .... **CLC 2, 5, 9, 41, 82**
See also CA 17-20R; CANR 40; DLB 5,
130; MTCW

Bulgakov, Mikhail (Afanas'evich)
1891-1940 .... **TCLC 2, 16**
See also CA 105

Bulgya, Alexander Alexandrovich
1901-1956 .... **TCLC 53**
See also Fadeyev, Alexander
See also CA 117

Bullins, Ed 1935- .... **CLC 1, 5, 7; BLC**
See also BW; CA 49-52; CAAS 16;
CANR 24; DLB 7, 38; MTCW

Bulwer-Lytton, Edward (George Earle Lytton)
1803-1873 .... **NCLC 1**
See also DLB 21

Bunin, Ivan Alexeyevich
1870-1953 .... **TCLC 6; SSC 5**
See also CA 104

Bunting, Basil 1900-1985.... **CLC 10, 39, 47**
See also CA 53-56; 115; CANR 7; DLB 20

Bunuel, Luis 1900-1983 .. **CLC 16, 80; HLC**
See also CA 101; 110; CANR 32; HW

Bunyan, John 1628-1688 .. **LC 4; DA; WLC**
See also CDBLB 1660-1789; DLB 39

Burford, Eleanor
See Hibbert, Eleanor Alice Burford

Burgess, Anthony
CLC 1, 2, 4, 5, 8, 10, 13, 15, 22, 40, 62,
81
See also Wilson, John (Anthony) Burgess
See also AITN 1; CDBLB 1960 to Present;
DLB 14

Burke, Edmund
1729(?)-1797 .... **LC 7; DA; WLC**
See also DLB 104

Burke, Kenneth (Duva)
1897-1993 .... **CLC 2, 24**
See also CA 5-8R; 143; CANR 39; DLB 45,
63; MTCW

Burke, Leda
See Garnett, David

Burke, Ralph
See Silverberg, Robert

Burney, Fanny 1752-1840 .... **NCLC 12**
See also DLB 39

Burns, Robert
1759-1796 ...... **LC 3; DA; PC 6; WLC**
See also CDBLB 1789-1832; DLB 109

Burns, Tex
See L'Amour, Louis (Dearborn)

Burnshaw, Stanley 1906-..... **CLC 3, 13, 44**
See also CA 9-12R; DLB 48

Burr, Anne 1937- .... **CLC 6**
See also CA 25-28R

Burroughs, Edgar Rice
1875-1950 .... **TCLC 2, 32**
See also CA 104; 132; DLB 8; MTCW;
SATA 41

Burroughs, William S(eward)
1914- .... **CLC 1, 2, 5, 15, 22, 42, 75;**
DA; WLC
See also AITN 2; CA 9-12R; CANR 20;
DLB 2, 8, 16; DLBY 81; MTCW

Burton, Richard F. 1821-1890.... **NCLC 42**
See also DLB 55

Busch, Frederick 1941- ... **CLC 7, 10, 18, 47**
See also CA 33-36R; CAAS 1; DLB 6

Bush, Ronald 1946- .... **CLC 34**
See also CA 136

Bustos, F(rancisco)
See Borges, Jorge Luis

Bustos Domecq, H(onorio)
See Bioy Casares, Adolfo; Borges, Jorge
Luis

Butler, Octavia E(stelle) 1947-..... **CLC 38**
See also BW; CA 73-76; CANR 12, 24, 38;
DLB 33; MTCW

Butler, Robert Olen (Jr.) 1945-..... **CLC 81**
See also CA 112

Butler, Samuel 1612-1680 .... **LC 16**
See also DLB 101, 126

Butler, Samuel
1835-1902 ...... **TCLC 1, 33; DA; WLC**
See also CA 104; CDBLB 1890-1914;
DLB 18, 57

Butler, Walter C.
See Faust, Frederick (Schiller)

Butor, Michel (Marie Francois)
1926- .... **CLC 1, 3, 8, 11, 15**
See also CA 9-12R; CANR 33; DLB 83;
MTCW

Buzo, Alexander (John) 1944-...... **CLC 61**
See also CA 97-100; CANR 17, 39

Buzzati, Dino 1906-1972 .... **CLC 36**
See also CA 33-36R

Byars, Betsy (Cromer) 1928-....... **CLC 35**
See also CA 33-36R; CANR 18, 36; CLR 1,
16; DLB 52; JRDA; MAICYA; MTCW;
SAAS 1; SATA 4, 46

Byatt, A(ntonia) S(usan Drabble)
1936- .... **CLC 19, 65**
See also CA 13-16R; CANR 13, 33;
DLB 14; MTCW

Byrne, David 1952-............... **CLC 26**
See also CA 127

Byrne, John Keyes 1926-......... **CLC 19**
See also Leonard, Hugh
See also CA 102

Byron, George Gordon (Noel)
1788-1824 ...... **NCLC 2, 12; DA; WLC**
See also CDBLB 1789-1832; DLB 96, 110

C.3.3.
See Wilde, Oscar (Fingal O'Flahertie Wills)

Caballero, Fernan 1796-1877..... **NCLC 10**

Cabell, James Branch 1879-1958 ... **TCLC 6**
See also CA 105; DLB 9, 78

Cable, George Washington
1844-1925 .... **TCLC 4; SSC 4**
See also CA 104; DLB 12, 74

Cabral de Melo Neto, Joao 1920-... **CLC 76**

Cabrera Infante, G(uillermo)
1929- .... **CLC 5, 25, 45; HLC**
See also CA 85-88; CANR 29; DLB 113;
HW; MTCW

Cade, Toni
See Bambara, Toni Cade

Cadmus
See Buchan, John

Caedmon fl. 658-680............. **CMLC 7**

Caeiro, Alberto
See Pessoa, Fernando (Antonio Nogueira)

Cage, John (Milton, Jr.) 1912-..... **CLC 41**
See also CA 13-16R; CANR 9

Cain, G.
See Cabrera Infante, G(uillermo)

Cain, Guillermo
See Cabrera Infante, G(uillermo)

Cain, James M(allahan)
1892-1977 .... **CLC 3, 11, 28**
See also AITN 1; CA 17-20R; 73-76;
CANR 8, 34; MTCW

Caine, Mark
See Raphael, Frederic (Michael)

Calasso, Roberto 1941- .... **CLC 81**
See also CA 143

Calderon de la Barca, Pedro
1600-1681 .... **LC 23; DC 3**

Caldwell, Erskine (Preston)
1903-1987 .... **CLC 1, 8, 14, 50, 60**
See also AITN 1; CA 1-4R; 121; CAAS 1;
CANR 2, 33; DLB 9, 86; MTCW

Caldwell, (Janet Miriam) Taylor (Holland)
1900-1985 .... **CLC 2, 28, 39**
See also CA 5-8R; 116; CANR 5

Author Index

Ch'ien Chung-shu 1910-............ **CLC 22**
See also CA 130; MTCW

Child, L. Maria
See Child, Lydia Maria

Child, Lydia Maria 1802-1880 .... **NCLC 6**
See also DLB 1, 74; SATA 67

Child, Mrs.
See Child, Lydia Maria

Child, Philip 1898-1978 .... **CLC 19, 68**
See also CA 13-14; CAP 1; SATA 47

Childress, Alice
1920- .... **CLC 12, 15; BLC; DC 4**
See also AAYA 8; BW; CA 45-48;
CANR 3, 27; CLR 14; DLB 7, 38; JRDA;
MAICYA; MTCW; SATA 7, 48

Chislett, (Margaret) Anne 1943-.... **CLC 34**

Chitty, Thomas Willes 1926-....... **CLC 11**
See also Hinde, Thomas
See also CA 5-8R

Chomette, Rene Lucien 1898-1981 .. **CLC 20**
See also Clair, Rene
See also CA 103

Chopin, Kate .... **TCLC 5, 14; DA; SSC 8**
See also Chopin, Katherine
See also CDALB 1865-1917; DLB 12, 78

Chopin, Katherine 1851-1904
See Chopin, Kate
See also CA 104; 122

Chretien de Troyes
c. 12th cent. - .... **CMLC 10**

Christie
See Ichikawa, Kon

Christie, Agatha (Mary Clarissa)
1890-1976 ...... **CLC 1, 6, 8, 12, 39, 48**
See also AAYA 9; AITN 1, 2; CA 17-20R;
61-64; CANR 10, 37; CDBLB 1914-1945;
DLB 13, 77; MTCW; SATA 36

Christie, (Ann) Philippa
See Pearce, Philippa
See also CA 5-8R; CANR 4

Christine de Pizan 1365(?)-1431(?) .... **LC 9**

Chubb, Elmer
See Masters, Edgar Lee

Chulkov, Mikhail Dmitrievich
1743-1792 .... **LC 2**

Churchill, Caryl 1938-......... **CLC 31, 55**
See also CA 102; CANR 22; DLB 13;
MTCW

Churchill, Charles 1731-1764........ **LC 3**
See also DLB 109

Chute, Carolyn 1947-............. **CLC 39**
See also CA 123

Ciardi, John (Anthony)
1916-1986 .... **CLC 10, 40, 44**
See also CA 5-8R; 118; CAAS 2; CANR 5,
33; CLR 19; DLB 5; DLBY 86;
MAICYA; MTCW; SATA 1, 46, 65

Cicero, Marcus Tullius
106B.C.-43B.C. .... **CMLC 3**

Cimino, Michael 1943-............ **CLC 16**
See also CA 105

Cioran, E(mil) M. 1911-.......... **CLC 64**
See also CA 25-28R

Cisneros, Sandra 1954-...... **CLC 69; HLC**
See also AAYA 9; CA 131; DLB 122; HW

Clair, Rene....................... **CLC 20**
See also Chomette, Rene Lucien

Clampitt, Amy 1920- .... **CLC 32**
See also CA 110; CANR 29; DLB 105

Clancy, Thomas L., Jr. 1947-
See Clancy, Tom
See also CA 125; 131; MTCW

Clancy, Tom..................... **CLC 45**
See also Clancy, Thomas L., Jr.
See also AAYA 9; BEST 89:1, 90:1

Clare, John 1793-1864 .... **NCLC 9**
See also DLB 55, 96

Clarin
See Alas (y Urena), Leopoldo (Enrique
Garcia)

Clark, Al C.
See Goines, Donald

Clark, (Robert) Brian 1932-........ **CLC 29**
See also CA 41-44R

Clark, Eleanor 1913- .... **CLC 5, 19**
See also CA 9-12R; CANR 41; DLB 6

Clark, J. P.
See Clark, John Pepper
See also DLB 117

Clark, John Pepper 1935- .... **CLC 38; BLC**
See also Clark, J. P.
See also BW; CA 65-68; CANR 16

Clark, M. R.
See Clark, Mavis Thorpe

Clark, Mavis Thorpe 1909-........ **CLC 12**
See also CA 57-60; CANR 8, 37; CLR 30;
MAICYA; SAAS 5; SATA 8, 74

Clark, Walter Van Tilburg
1909-1971 .... **CLC 28**
See also CA 9-12R; 33-36R; DLB 9;
SATA 8

Clarke, Arthur C(harles)
1917- ...... **CLC 1, 4, 13, 18, 35; SSC 3**
See also AAYA 4; CA 1-4R; CANR 2, 28;
JRDA; MAICYA; MTCW; SATA 13, 70

Clarke, Austin 1896-1974........ **CLC 6, 9**
See also CA 29-32; 49-52; CAP 2; DLB 10,
20

Clarke, Austin C(hesterfield)
1934- .... **CLC 8, 53; BLC**
See also BW; CA 25-28R; CAAS 16;
CANR 14, 32; DLB 53, 125

Clarke, Gillian 1937-............. **CLC 61**
See also CA 106; DLB 40

Clarke, Marcus (Andrew Hislop)
1846-1881 .... **NCLC 19**

Clarke, Shirley 1925-............. **CLC 16**

Clash, The .... **CLC 30**
See also Headon, (Nicky) Topper; Jones,
Mick; Simonon, Paul; Strummer, Joe

Claudel, Paul (Louis Charles Marie)
1868-1955 .... **TCLC 2, 10**
See also CA 104

Clavell, James (duMaresq)
1925- .... **CLC 6, 25**
See also CA 25-28R; CANR 26; MTCW

Cleaver, (Leroy) Eldridge
1935- .... **CLC 30; BLC**
See also BW; CA 21-24R; CANR 16

Cleese, John (Marwood) 1939- ..... **CLC 21**
See also Monty Python
See also CA 112; 116; CANR 35; MTCW

Cleishbotham, Jebediah
See Scott, Walter

Cleland, John 1710-1789 .... **LC 2**
See also DLB 39

Clemens, Samuel Langhorne 1835-1910
See Twain, Mark
See also CA 104; 135; CDALB 1865-1917;
DA; DLB 11, 12, 23, 64, 74; JRDA;
MAICYA; YABC 2

Cleophil
See Congreve, William

Clerihew, E.
See Bentley, E(dmund) C(lerihew)

Clerk, N. W.
See Lewis, C(live) S(taples)

Cliff, Jimmy..................... **CLC 21**
See also Chambers, James

Clifton, (Thelma) Lucille
1936- .... **CLC 19, 66; BLC**
See also BW; CA 49-52; CANR 2, 24, 42;
CLR 5; DLB 5, 41; MAICYA; MTCW;
SATA 20, 69

Clinton, Dirk
See Silverberg, Robert

Clough, Arthur Hugh 1819-1861.. **NCLC 27**
See also DLB 32

Clutha, Janet Paterson Frame 1924-
See Frame, Janet
See also CA 1-4R; CANR 2, 36; MTCW

Clyne, Terence
See Blatty, William Peter

Cobalt, Martin
See Mayne, William (James Carter)

Coburn, D(onald) L(ee) 1938- ...... **CLC 10**
See also CA 89-92

Cocteau, Jean (Maurice Eugene Clement)
1889-1963 .... **CLC 1, 8, 15, 16, 43; DA;
WLC**
See also CA 25-28; CANR 40; CAP 2;
DLB 65; MTCW

Codrescu, Andrei 1946-........... **CLC 46**
See also CA 33-36R; CANR 13, 34

Coe, Max
See Bourne, Randolph S(illiman)

Coe, Tucker
See Westlake, Donald E(dwin)

Coetzee, J(ohn) M(ichael)
1940- .... **CLC 23, 33, 66**
See also CA 77-80; CANR 41; MTCW

Coffey, Brian
See Koontz, Dean R(ay)

Cohen, Arthur A(llen)
1928-1986 .... **CLC 7, 31**
See also CA 1-4R; 120; CANR 1, 17, 42;
DLB 28

Cohen, Leonard (Norman)
1934- .... **CLC 3, 38**
See also CA 21-24R; CANR 14; DLB 53;
MTCW

Cohen, Matt 1942- .... **CLC 19**
See also CA 61-64; CAAS 18; CANR 40;
DLB 53

Cohen-Solal, Annie 19(?)- .... **CLC 50**

Colegate, Isabel 1931- .... **CLC 36**
See also CA 17-20R; CANR 8, 22; DLB 14;
MTCW

Coleman, Emmett
See Reed, Ishmael

Coleridge, Samuel Taylor
1772-1834 .... **NCLC 9; DA; WLC**
See also CDBLB 1789-1832; DLB 93, 107

Coleridge, Sara 1802-1852....... **NCLC 31**

Coles, Don 1928- .... **CLC 46**
See also CA 115; CANR 38

Colette, (Sidonie-Gabrielle)
1873-1954 ..... **TCLC 1, 5, 16; SSC 10**
See also CA 104; 131; DLB 65; MTCW

Collett, (Jacobine) Camilla (Wergeland)
1813-1895 .... **NCLC 22**

Collier, Christopher 1930- .... **CLC 30**
See also CA 33-36R; CANR 13, 33; JRDA;
MAICYA; SATA 16, 70

Collier, James L(incoln) 1928- ..... **CLC 30**
See also CA 9-12R; CANR 4, 33; JRDA;
MAICYA; SATA 8, 70

Collier, Jeremy 1650-1726.......... **LC 6**

Collins, Hunt
See Hunter, Evan

Collins, Linda 1931- .... **CLC 44**
See also CA 125

Collins, (William) Wilkie
1824-1889 .... **NCLC 1, 18**
See also CDBLB 1832-1890; DLB 18, 70

Collins, William 1721-1759 .... **LC 4**
See also DLB 109

Colman, George
See Glassco, John

Colt, Winchester Remington
See Hubbard, L(afayette) Ron(ald)

Colter, Cyrus 1910- .... **CLC 58**
See also BW; CA 65-68; CANR 10; DLB 33

Colton, James
See Hansen, Joseph

Colum, Padraic 1881-1972........ **CLC 28**
See also CA 73-76; 33-36R; CANR 35;
MAICYA; MTCW; SATA 15

Colvin, James
See Moorcock, Michael (John)

Colwin, Laurie (E.)
1944-1992 .... **CLC 5, 13, 23**
See also CA 89-92; 139; CANR 20;
DLBY 80; MTCW

Comfort, Alex(ander) 1920-........ **CLC 7**
See also CA 1-4R; CANR 1

Comfort, Montgomery
See Campbell, (John) Ramsey

Compton-Burnett, I(vy)
1884(?)-1969 ...... **CLC 1, 3, 10, 15, 34**
See also CA 1-4R; 25-28R; CANR 4;
DLB 36; MTCW

Comstock, Anthony 1844-1915 .... **TCLC 13**
See also CA 110

Conan Doyle, Arthur
See Doyle, Arthur Conan

Conde, Maryse .... **CLC 52**
See also Boucolon, Maryse

Condon, Richard (Thomas)
1915- .... **CLC 4, 6, 8, 10, 45**
See also BEST 90:3; CA 1-4R; CAAS 1;
CANR 2, 23; MTCW

Congreve, William
1670-1729 ... **LC 5, 21; DA; DC 2; WLC**
See also CDBLB 1660-1789; DLB 39, 84

Connell, Evan S(helby), Jr.
1924- .... **CLC 4, 6, 45**
See also AAYA 7; CA 1-4R; CAAS 2;
CANR 2, 39; DLB 2; DLBY 81; MTCW

Connelly, Marc(us Cook)
1890-1980 .... **CLC 7**
See also CA 85-88; 102; CANR 30; DLB 7;
DLBY 80; SATA 25

Connor, Ralph .... **TCLC 31**
See also Gordon, Charles William
See also DLB 92

Conrad, Joseph
1857-1924 ...... **TCLC 1, 6, 13, 25, 43;
DA; SSC 9; WLC**
See also CA 104; 131; CDBLB 1890-1914;
DLB 10, 34, 98; MTCW; SATA 27

Conrad, Robert Arnold
See Hart, Moss

Conroy, Pat 1945-............. **CLC 30, 74**
See also AAYA 8; AITN 1; CA 85-88;
CANR 24; DLB 6; MTCW

Constant (de Rebecque), (Henri) Benjamin
1767-1830 .... **NCLC 6**
See also DLB 119

Conybeare, Charles Augustus
See Eliot, T(homas) S(tearns)

Cook, Michael 1933- .... **CLC 58**
See also CA 93-96; DLB 53

Cook, Robin 1940- .... **CLC 14**
See also BEST 90:2; CA 108; 111;
CANR 41

Cook, Roy
See Silverberg, Robert

Cooke, Elizabeth 1948- .... **CLC 55**
See also CA 129

Cooke, John Esten 1830-1886..... **NCLC 5**
See also DLB 3

Cooke, John Estes
See Baum, L(yman) Frank

Cooke, M. E.
See Creasey, John

Cooke, Margaret
See Creasey, John

Cooney, Ray .... **CLC 62**

Cooper, Henry St. John
See Creasey, John

Cooper, J. California............... **CLC 56**
See also BW; CA 125

Cooper, James Fenimore
1789-1851 .... **NCLC 1, 27**
See also CDALB 1640-1865; DLB 3;
SATA 19

Coover, Robert (Lowell)
1932- ..... **CLC 3, 7, 15, 32, 46; SSC 15**
See also CA 45-48; CANR 3, 37; DLB 2;
DLBY 81; MTCW

Copeland, Stewart (Armstrong)
1952- .... **CLC 26**
See also Police, The

Coppard, A(lfred) E(dgar)
1878-1957 .... **TCLC 5**
See also CA 114; YABC 1

Coppee, Francois 1842-1908 ..... **TCLC 25**

Coppola, Francis Ford 1939-....... **CLC 16**
See also CA 77-80; CANR 40; DLB 44

Corbiere, Tristan 1845-1875 ..... **NCLC 43**

Corcoran, Barbara 1911- .... **CLC 17**
See also CA 21-24R; CAAS 2; CANR 11,
28; DLB 52; JRDA; SATA 3

Cordelier, Maurice
See Giraudoux, (Hippolyte) Jean

Corelli, Marie 1855-1924........ **TCLC 51**
See also Mackay, Mary
See also DLB 34

Corman, Cid...................... **CLC 9**
See also Corman, Sidney
See also CAAS 2; DLB 5

Corman, Sidney 1924-
See Corman, Cid
See also CA 85-88

Cormier, Robert (Edmund)
1925- .... **CLC 12, 30; DA**
See also AAYA 3; CA 1-4R; CANR 5, 23;
CDALB 1968-1988; CLR 12; DLB 52;
JRDA; MAICYA; MTCW; SATA 10, 45

Corn, Alfred 1943-................ **CLC 33**
See also CA 104; DLB 120; DLBY 80

Cornwell, David (John Moore)
1931- .... **CLC 9, 15**
See also le Carre, John
See also CA 5-8R; CANR 13, 33; MTCW

Corrigan, Kevin................... **CLC 55**

Corso, (Nunzio) Gregory 1930-... **CLC 1, 11**
See also CA 5-8R; CANR 41; DLB 5, 16;
MTCW

Cortazar, Julio
1914-1984 ...... **CLC 2, 3, 5, 10, 13, 15,
33, 34; HLC; SSC 7**
See also CA 21-24R; CANR 12, 32;
DLB 113; HW; MTCW

Corwin, Cecil
See Kornbluth, C(yril) M.

Cosic, Dobrica 1921- .... **CLC 14**
See also CA 122; 138

Costain, Thomas B(ertram)
1885-1965 .... **CLC 30**
See also CA 5-8R; 25-28R; DLB 9

Costantini, Humberto
1924(?)-1987 .... **CLC 49**
See also CA 131; 122; HW

Costello, Elvis 1955-............. **CLC 21**

Cotter, Joseph S. Sr.
See Cotter, Joseph Seamon Sr.

Cotter, Joseph Seamon Sr.
1861-1949 .... **TCLC 28; BLC**
See also BW; CA 124; DLB 50

Couch, Arthur Thomas Quiller
　See Quiller-Couch, Arthur Thomas

Coulton, James
　See Hansen, Joseph

Couperus, Louis (Marie Anne)
　1863-1923 . . . . **TCLC 15**
　See also CA 115

Court, Wesli
　See Turco, Lewis (Putnam)

Courtenay, Bryce 1933- . . . . **CLC 59**
　See also CA 138

Courtney, Robert
　See Ellison, Harlan

Cousteau, Jacques-Yves 1910- . . . . . **CLC 30**
　See also CA 65-68; CANR 15; MTCW;
　SATA 38

Coward, Noel (Peirce)
　1899-1973 . . . . **CLC 1, 9, 29, 51**
　See also AITN 1; CA 17-18; 41-44R;
　CANR 35; CAP 2; CDBLB 1914-1945;
　DLB 10; MTCW

Cowley, Malcolm 1898-1989 . . . . **CLC 39**
　See also CA 5-8R; 128; CANR 3; DLB 4,
　48; DLBY 81, 89; MTCW

Cowper, William 1731-1800 . . . . **NCLC 8**
　See also DLB 104, 109

Cox, William Trevor 1928- . . . **CLC 9, 14, 71**
　See also Trevor, William
　See also CA 9-12R; CANR 4, 37; DLB 14;
　MTCW

Cozzens, James Gould
　1903-1978 . . . . **CLC 1, 4, 11**
　See also CA 9-12R; 81-84; CANR 19;
　CDALB 1941-1968; DLB 9; DLBD 2;
　DLBY 84; MTCW

Crabbe, George 1754-1832 . . . . . . **NCLC 26**
　See also DLB 93

Craig, A. A.
　See Anderson, Poul (William)

Craik, Dinah Maria (Mulock)
　1826-1887 . . . . **NCLC 38**
　See also DLB 35; MAICYA; SATA 34

Cram, Ralph Adams 1863-1942 . . . . **TCLC 45**

Crane, (Harold) Hart
　1899-1932 . . . . **TCLC 2, 5; DA; PC 3;
　　　　　　　　　　　　　　　　　　　　　WLC**
　See also CA 104; 127; CDALB 1917-1929;
　DLB 4, 48; MTCW

Crane, R(onald) S(almon)
　1886-1967 . . . . **CLC 27**
　See also CA 85-88; DLB 63

Crane, Stephen (Townley)
　1871-1900 . . . . . . **TCLC 11, 17, 32; DA;
　　　　　　　　　　　　　　　　　　SSC 7; WLC**
　See also CA 109; 140; CDALB 1865-1917;
　DLB 12, 54, 78; YABC 2

Crase, Douglas 1944- . . . . **CLC 58**
　See also CA 106

Crashaw, Richard 1612(?)-1649 . . . . . . **LC 24**
　See also DLB 126

Craven, Margaret 1901-1980 . . . . **CLC 17**
　See also CA 103

Crawford, F(rancis) Marion
　1854-1909 . . . . **TCLC 10**
　See also CA 107; DLB 71

Crawford, Isabella Valancy
　1850-1887 . . . . **NCLC 12**
　See also DLB 92

Crayon, Geoffrey
　See Irving, Washington

Creasey, John 1908-1973 . . . . **CLC 11**
　See also CA 5-8R; 41-44R; CANR 8;
　DLB 77; MTCW

Crebillon, Claude Prosper Jolyot de (fils)
　1707-1777 . . . . **LC 1**

Credo
　See Creasey, John

Creeley, Robert (White)
　1926- . . . . . **CLC 1, 2, 4, 8, 11, 15, 36, 78**
　See also CA 1-4R; CAAS 10; CANR 23, 43;
　DLB 5, 16; MTCW

Crews, Harry (Eugene)
　1935- . . . . **CLC 6, 23, 49**
　See also AITN 1; CA 25-28R; CANR 20;
　DLB 6; MTCW

Crichton, (John) Michael
　1942- . . . . **CLC 2, 6, 54**
　See also AAYA 10; AITN 2; CA 25-28R;
　CANR 13, 40; DLBY 81; JRDA;
　MTCW; SATA 9

Crispin, Edmund . . . . **CLC 22**
　See also Montgomery, (Robert) Bruce
　See also DLB 87

Cristofer, Michael 1945(?)- . . . . **CLC 28**
　See also CA 110; DLB 7

Croce, Benedetto 1866-1952 . . . . . . **TCLC 37**
　See also CA 120

Crockett, David 1786-1836 . . . . **NCLC 8**
　See also DLB 3, 11

Crockett, Davy
　See Crockett, David

Croker, John Wilson 1780-1857 . . **NCLC 10**
　See also DLB 110

Crommelynck, Fernand 1885-1970 . . **CLC 75**
　See also CA 89-92

Cronin, A(rchibald) J(oseph)
　1896-1981 . . . . **CLC 32**
　See also CA 1-4R; 102; CANR 5; SATA 25,
　47

Cross, Amanda
　See Heilbrun, Carolyn G(old)

Crothers, Rachel 1878(?)-1958 . . . . . **TCLC 19**
　See also CA 113; DLB 7

Croves, Hal
　See Traven, B.

Crowfield, Christopher
　See Stowe, Harriet (Elizabeth) Beecher

Crowley, Aleister . . . . **TCLC 7**
　See also Crowley, Edward Alexander

Crowley, Edward Alexander 1875-1947
　See Crowley, Aleister
　See also CA 104

Crowley, John 1942- . . . . **CLC 57**
　See also CA 61-64; CANR 43; DLBY 82;
　SATA 65

Crud
　See Crumb, R(obert)

Crumarums
　See Crumb, R(obert)

Crumb, R(obert) 1943- . . . . **CLC 17**
　See also CA 106

Crumbum
　See Crumb, R(obert)

Crumski
　See Crumb, R(obert)

Crum the Bum
　See Crumb, R(obert)

Crunk
　See Crumb, R(obert)

Crustt
　See Crumb, R(obert)

Cryer, Gretchen (Kiger) 1935- . . . . . . **CLC 21**
　See also CA 114; 123

Csath, Geza 1887-1919 . . . . **TCLC 13**
　See also CA 111

Cudlip, David 1933- . . . . **CLC 34**

Cullen, Countee
　1903-1946 . . . . . . **TCLC 4, 37; BLC; DA**
　See also BW; CA 108; 124;
　CDALB 1917-1929; DLB 4, 48, 51;
　MTCW; SATA 18

Cum, R.
　See Crumb, R(obert)

Cummings, Bruce F(rederick) 1889-1919
　See Barbellion, W. N. P.
　See also CA 123

Cummings, E(dward) E(stlin)
　1894-1962 . . . . . . **CLC 1, 3, 8, 12, 15, 68;
　　　　　　　　　　　　　　　　　　DA; PC 5; WLC 2**
　See also CA 73-76; CANR 31;
　CDALB 1929-1941; DLB 4, 48; MTCW

Cunha, Euclides (Rodrigues Pimenta) da
　1866-1909 . . . . **TCLC 24**
　See also CA 123

Cunningham, E. V.
　See Fast, Howard (Melvin)

Cunningham, J(ames) V(incent)
　1911-1985 . . . . **CLC 3, 31**
　See also CA 1-4R; 115; CANR 1; DLB 5

Cunningham, Julia (Woolfolk)
　1916- . . . . **CLC 12**
　See also CA 9-12R; CANR 4, 19, 36;
　JRDA; MAICYA; SAAS 2; SATA 1, 26

Cunningham, Michael 1952- . . . . **CLC 34**
　See also CA 136

Cunninghame Graham, R(obert) B(ontine)
　1852-1936 . . . . **TCLC 19**
　See also Graham, R(obert) B(ontine)
　Cunninghame
　See also CA 119; DLB 98

Currie, Ellen 19(?)- . . . . **CLC 44**

Curtin, Philip
　See Lowndes, Marie Adelaide (Belloc)

Curtis, Price
　See Ellison, Harlan

Cutrate, Joe
　See Spiegelman, Art

Czaczkes, Shmuel Yosef
　See Agnon, S(hmuel) Y(osef Halevi)

D. P.
　See Wells, H(erbert) G(eorge)

Dabrowska, Maria (Szumska)
1889-1965 . . . . **CLC 15**
See also CA 106

Dabydeen, David 1955- . . . . **CLC 34**
See also BW; CA 125

Dacey, Philip 1939- . . . . **CLC 51**
See also CA 37-40R; CAAS 17; CANR 14,
32; DLB 105

Dagerman, Stig (Halvard)
1923-1954 . . . . **TCLC 17**
See also CA 117

Dahl, Roald 1916-1990. . . . . **CLC 1, 6, 18, 79**
See also CA 1-4R; 133; CANR 6, 32, 37;
CLR 1, 7; JRDA; MAICYA; MTCW;
SATA 1, 26, 73; SATA-Obit 65

Dahlberg, Edward 1900-1977. . . **CLC 1, 7, 14**
See also CA 9-12R; 69-72; CANR 31;
DLB 48; MTCW

Dale, Colin. . . . . **TCLC 18**
See also Lawrence, T(homas) E(dward)

Dale, George E.
See Asimov, Isaac

Daly, Elizabeth 1878-1967. . . . . **CLC 52**
See also CA 23-24; 25-28R; CAP 2

Daly, Maureen 1921- . . . . **CLC 17**
See also AAYA 5; CANR 37; JRDA;
MAICYA; SAAS 1; SATA 2

Daniel, Samuel 1562(?)-1619 . . . . **LC 24**
See also DLB 62

Daniels, Brett
See Adler, Renata

Dannay, Frederic 1905-1982 . . . . **CLC 11**
See also Queen, Ellery
See also CA 1-4R; 107; CANR 1, 39;
MTCW

D'Annunzio, Gabriele
1863-1938 . . . . **TCLC 6, 40**
See also CA 104

d'Antibes, Germain
See Simenon, Georges (Jacques Christian)

Danvers, Dennis 1947- . . . . **CLC 70**

Danziger, Paula 1944- . . . . **CLC 21**
See also AAYA 4; CA 112; 115; CANR 37;
CLR 20; JRDA; MAICYA; SATA 30,
36, 63

Dario, Ruben 1867-1916 . . . . **TCLC 4; HLC**
See also CA 131; HW; MTCW

Darley, George 1795-1846 . . . . **NCLC 2**
See also DLB 96

Daryush, Elizabeth 1887-1977. . . . **CLC 6, 19**
See also CA 49-52; CANR 3; DLB 20

Daudet, (Louis Marie) Alphonse
1840-1897 . . . . **NCLC 1**
See also DLB 123

Daumal, Rene 1908-1944 . . . . **TCLC 14**
See also CA 114

Davenport, Guy (Mattison, Jr.)
1927- . . . . **CLC 6, 14, 38**
See also CA 33-36R; CANR 23; DLB 130

Davidson, Avram 1923-
See Queen, Ellery
See also CA 101; CANR 26; DLB 8

Davidson, Donald (Grady)
1893-1968 . . . . **CLC 2, 13, 19**
See also CA 5-8R; 25-28R; CANR 4;
DLB 45

Davidson, Hugh
See Hamilton, Edmond

Davidson, John 1857-1909. . . . . . . **TCLC 24**
See also CA 118; DLB 19

Davidson, Sara 1943- . . . . **CLC 9**
See also CA 81-84

Davie, Donald (Alfred)
1922- . . . . **CLC 5, 8, 10, 31**
See also CA 1-4R; CAAS 3; CANR 1;
DLB 27; MTCW

Davies, Ray(mond Douglas) 1944- . . **CLC 21**
See also CA 116

Davies, Rhys 1903-1978. . . . . **CLC 23**
See also CA 9-12R; 81-84; CANR 4

Davies, (William) Robertson
1913- . . . . . **CLC 2, 7, 13, 25, 42, 75; DA;**
WLC
See also BEST 89:2; CA 33-36R; CANR 17,
42; DLB 68; MTCW

Davies, W(illiam) H(enry)
1871-1940 . . . . **TCLC 5**
See also CA 104; DLB 19

Davies, Walter C.
See Kornbluth, C(yril) M.

Davis, Angela (Yvonne) 1944- . . . . . . **CLC 77**
See also BW; CA 57-60; CANR 10

Davis, B. Lynch
See Bioy Casares, Adolfo; Borges, Jorge
Luis

Davis, Gordon
See Hunt, E(verette) Howard, Jr.

Davis, Harold Lenoir 1896-1960. . . . **CLC 49**
See also CA 89-92; DLB 9

Davis, Rebecca (Blaine) Harding
1831-1910 . . . . **TCLC 6**
See also CA 104; DLB 74

Davis, Richard Harding
1864-1916 . . . . **TCLC 24**
See also CA 114; DLB 12, 23, 78, 79

Davison, Frank Dalby 1893-1970 . . . **CLC 15**
See also CA 116

Davison, Lawrence H.
See Lawrence, D(avid) H(erbert Richards)

Davison, Peter (Hubert) 1928- . . . . . **CLC 28**
See also CA 9-12R; CAAS 4; CANR 3, 43;
DLB 5

Davys, Mary 1674-1732. . . . . **LC 1**
See also DLB 39

Dawson, Fielding 1930- . . . . **CLC 6**
See also CA 85-88; DLB 130

Dawson, Peter
See Faust, Frederick (Schiller)

Day, Clarence (Shepard, Jr.)
1874-1935 . . . . **TCLC 25**
See also CA 108; DLB 11

Day, Thomas 1748-1789. . . . . **LC 1**
See also DLB 39; YABC 1

Day Lewis, C(ecil)
1904-1972 . . . . **CLC 1, 6, 10**
See also Blake, Nicholas
See also CA 13-16; 33-36R; CANR 34;
CAP 1; DLB 15, 20; MTCW

Dazai, Osamu . . . . **TCLC 11**
See also Tsushima, Shuji

de Andrade, Carlos Drummond
See Drummond de Andrade, Carlos

Deane, Norman
See Creasey, John

de Beauvoir, Simone (Lucie Ernestine Marie
Bertrand)
See Beauvoir, Simone (Lucie Ernestine
Marie Bertrand) de

de Brissac, Malcolm
See Dickinson, Peter (Malcolm)

de Chardin, Pierre Teilhard
See Teilhard de Chardin, (Marie Joseph)
Pierre

Dee, John 1527-1608 . . . . **LC 20**

Deer, Sandra 1940-. . . . . **CLC 45**

De Ferrari, Gabriella . . . . **CLC 65**

Defoe, Daniel
1660(?)-1731 . . . . **LC 1; DA; WLC**
See also CDBLB 1660-1789; DLB 39, 95,
101; JRDA; MAICYA; SATA 22

de Gourmont, Remy
See Gourmont, Remy de

de Hartog, Jan 1914-. . . . . **CLC 19**
See also CA 1-4R; CANR 1

de Hostos, E. M.
See Hostos (y Bonilla), Eugenio Maria de

de Hostos, Eugenio M.
See Hostos (y Bonilla), Eugenio Maria de

Deighton, Len . . . . **CLC 4, 7, 22, 46**
See also Deighton, Leonard Cyril
See also AAYA 6; BEST 89:2;
CDBLB 1960 to Present; DLB 87

Deighton, Leonard Cyril 1929-
See Deighton, Len
See also CA 9-12R; CANR 19, 33; MTCW

Dekker, Thomas 1572(?)-1632. . . . . . . **LC 22**
See also CDBLB Before 1660; DLB 62

de la Mare, Walter (John)
1873-1956 . . **TCLC 4, 53; SSC 14; WLC**
See also CDBLB 1914-1945; CLR 23;
DLB 19; SATA 16

Delaney, Franey
See O'Hara, John (Henry)

Delaney, Shelagh 1939- . . . . **CLC 29**
See also CA 17-20R; CANR 30;
CDBLB 1960 to Present; DLB 13;
MTCW

Delany, Mary (Granville Pendarves)
1700-1788 . . . . **LC 12**

Delany, Samuel R(ay, Jr.)
1942- . . . . **CLC 8, 14, 38; BLC**
See also BW; CA 81-84; CANR 27, 43;
DLB 8, 33; MTCW

De La Ramee, (Marie) Louise 1839-1908
See Ouida
See also SATA 20

de la Roche, Mazo   1879-1961 . . . . . **CLC 14**
See also CA 85-88; CANR 30; DLB 68;
SATA 64

Delbanco, Nicholas (Franklin)
1942- . . . . **CLC 6, 13**
See also CA 17-20R; CAAS 2; CANR 29;
DLB 6

del Castillo, Michel   1933- . . . . **CLC 38**
See also CA 109

Deledda, Grazia (Cosima)
1875(?)-1936 . . . . **TCLC 23**
See also CA 123

Delibes, Miguel . . . . **CLC 8, 18**
See also Delibes Setien, Miguel

Delibes Setien, Miguel   1920-
See Delibes, Miguel
See also CA 45-48; CANR 1, 32; HW;
MTCW

DeLillo, Don
1936- . . . . . **CLC 8, 10, 13, 27, 39, 54, 76**
See also BEST 89:1; CA 81-84; CANR 21;
DLB 6; MTCW

de Lisser, H. G.
See De Lisser, Herbert George
See also DLB 117

De Lisser, Herbert George
1878-1944 . . . . **TCLC 12**
See also de Lisser, H. G.
See also CA 109

Deloria, Vine (Victor), Jr.   1933- . . . . **CLC 21**
See also CA 53-56; CANR 5, 20; MTCW;
SATA 21

Del Vecchio, John M(ichael)
1947- . . . . **CLC 29**
See also CA 110; DLBD 9

de Man, Paul (Adolph Michel)
1919-1983 . . . . **CLC 55**
See also CA 128; 111; DLB 67; MTCW

De Marinis, Rick   1934- . . . . **CLC 54**
See also CA 57-60; CANR 9, 25

Demby, William   1922- . . . . **CLC 53; BLC**
See also BW; CA 81-84; DLB 33

Demijohn, Thom
See Disch, Thomas M(ichael)

de Montherlant, Henry (Milon)
See Montherlant, Henry (Milon) de

de Natale, Francine
See Malzberg, Barry N(athaniel)

Denby, Edwin (Orr)   1903-1983 . . . . . **CLC 48**
See also CA 138; 110

Denis, Julio
See Cortazar, Julio

Denmark, Harrison
See Zelazny, Roger (Joseph)

Dennis, John   1658-1734 . . . . **LC 11**
See also DLB 101

Dennis, Nigel (Forbes)   1912-1989 . . . . **CLC 8**
See also CA 25-28R; 129; DLB 13, 15;
MTCW

De Palma, Brian (Russell)   1940- . . . . **CLC 20**
See also CA 109

De Quincey, Thomas   1785-1859 . . . **NCLC 4**
See also CDBLB 1789-1832; DLB 110

Deren, Eleanora   1908(?)-1961
See Deren, Maya
See also CA 111

Deren, Maya . . . . **CLC 16**
See also Deren, Eleanora

Derleth, August (William)
1909-1971 . . . . **CLC 31**
See also CA 1-4R; 29-32R; CANR 4;
DLB 9; SATA 5

de Routisie, Albert
See Aragon, Louis

Derrida, Jacques   1930- . . . . **CLC 24**
See also CA 124; 127

Derry Down Derry
See Lear, Edward

Dersonnes, Jacques
See Simenon, Georges (Jacques Christian)

Desai, Anita   1937- . . . . **CLC 19, 37**
See also CA 81-84; CANR 33; MTCW;
SATA 63

de Saint-Luc, Jean
See Glassco, John

de Saint Roman, Arnaud
See Aragon, Louis

Descartes, Rene   1596-1650 . . . . **LC 20**

De Sica, Vittorio   1901(?)-1974 . . . . . **CLC 20**
See also CA 117

Desnos, Robert   1900-1945 . . . . **TCLC 22**
See also CA 121

Destouches, Louis-Ferdinand
1894-1961 . . . . **CLC 9, 15**
See also Celine, Louis-Ferdinand
See also CA 85-88; CANR 28; MTCW

Deutsch, Babette   1895-1982 . . . . **CLC 18**
See also CA 1-4R; 108; CANR 4; DLB 45;
SATA 1, 33

Devenant, William   1606-1649 . . . . . . **LC 13**

Devkota, Laxmiprasad
1909-1959 . . . . **TCLC 23**
See also CA 123

De Voto, Bernard (Augustine)
1897-1955 . . . . **TCLC 29**
See also CA 113; DLB 9

De Vries, Peter
1910-1993 . . . . **CLC 1, 2, 3, 7, 10, 28, 46**
See also CA 17-20R; 142; CANR 41;
DLB 6; DLBY 82; MTCW

Dexter, Martin
See Faust, Frederick (Schiller)

Dexter, Pete   1943- . . . . **CLC 34, 55**
See also BEST 89:2; CA 127; 131; MTCW

Diamano, Silmang
See Senghor, Leopold Sedar

Diamond, Neil   1941- . . . . **CLC 30**
See also CA 108

di Bassetto, Corno
See Shaw, George Bernard

Dick, Philip K(indred)
1928-1982 . . . . **CLC 10, 30, 72**
See also CA 49-52; 106; CANR 2, 16;
DLB 8; MTCW

Dickens, Charles (John Huffam)
1812-1870 . . . . . **NCLC 3, 8, 18, 26; DA;
WLC**
See also CDBLB 1832-1890; DLB 21, 55,
70; JRDA; MAICYA; SATA 15

Dickey, James (Lafayette)
1923- . . . . **CLC 1, 2, 4, 7, 10, 15, 47**
See also AITN 1, 2; CA 9-12R; CABS 2;
CANR 10; CDALB 1968-1988; DLB 5;
DLBD 7; DLBY 82; MTCW

Dickey, William   1928- . . . . **CLC 3, 28**
See also CA 9-12R; CANR 24; DLB 5

Dickinson, Charles   1951- . . . . **CLC 49**
See also CA 128

Dickinson, Emily (Elizabeth)
1830-1886 . . **NCLC 21; DA; PC 1; WLC**
See also CDALB 1865-1917; DLB 1;
SATA 29

Dickinson, Peter (Malcolm)
1927- . . . . **CLC 12, 35**
See also AAYA 9; CA 41-44R; CANR 31;
CLR 29; DLB 87; JRDA; MAICYA;
SATA 5, 62

Dickson, Carr
See Carr, John Dickson

Dickson, Carter
See Carr, John Dickson

Didion, Joan   1934- . . . . . **CLC 1, 3, 8, 14, 32**
See also AITN 1; CA 5-8R; CANR 14;
CDALB 1968-1988; DLB 2; DLBY 81,
86; MTCW

Dietrich, Robert
See Hunt, E(verette) Howard, Jr.

Dillard, Annie   1945- . . . . **CLC 9, 60**
See also AAYA 6; CA 49-52; CANR 3, 43;
DLBY 80; MTCW; SATA 10

Dillard, R(ichard) H(enry) W(ilde)
1937- . . . . **CLC 5**
See also CA 21-24R; CAAS 7; CANR 10;
DLB 5

Dillon, Eilis   1920- . . . . **CLC 17**
See also CA 9-12R; CAAS 3; CANR 4, 38;
CLR 26; MAICYA; SATA 2, 74

Dimont, Penelope
See Mortimer, Penelope (Ruth)

Dinesen, Isak . . . . **CLC 10, 29; SSC 7**
See also Blixen, Karen (Christentze
Dinesen)

Ding Ling . . . . **CLC 68**
See also Chiang Pin-chin

Disch, Thomas M(ichael)   1940- . . . **CLC 7, 36**
See also CA 21-24R; CAAS 4; CANR 17,
36; CLR 18; DLB 8; MAICYA; MTCW;
SAAS 15; SATA 54

Disch, Tom
See Disch, Thomas M(ichael)

d'Isly, Georges
See Simenon, Georges (Jacques Christian)

Disraeli, Benjamin   1804-1881 . . **NCLC 2, 39**
See also DLB 21, 55

Ditcum, Steve
See Crumb, R(obert)

Dixon, Paige
See Corcoran, Barbara

Ducharme, Rejean 1941- .... **CLC 74**
See also DLB 60

Duclos, Charles Pinot 1704-1772 ..... **LC 1**

Dudek, Louis 1918- .... **CLC 11, 19**
See also CA 45-48; CAAS 14; CANR 1;
DLB 88

Duerrenmatt, Friedrich
.... **CLC 1, 4, 8, 11, 15, 43**
See also Duerrenmatt, Friedrich
See also DLB 69, 124

Duerrenmatt, Friedrich
1921-1990 ...... **CLC 1, 4, 8, 11, 15, 43**
See also Duerrenmatt, Friedrich
See also CA 17-20R; CANR 33; DLB 69,
124; MTCW

Duffy, Bruce (?)- .... **CLC 50**

Duffy, Maureen 1933- .... **CLC 37**
See also CA 25-28R; CANR 33; DLB 14;
MTCW

Dugan, Alan 1923- .... **CLC 2, 6**
See also CA 81-84; DLB 5

du Gard, Roger Martin
See Martin du Gard, Roger

Duhamel, Georges 1884-1966 .... **CLC 8**
See also CA 81-84; 25-28R; CANR 35;
DLB 65; MTCW

Dujardin, Edouard (Emile Louis)
1861-1949 .... **TCLC 13**
See also CA 109; DLB 123

Dumas, Alexandre (Davy de la Pailleterie)
1802-1870 ...... **NCLC 11; DA; WLC**
See also DLB 119; SATA 18

Dumas, Alexandre
1824-1895 .... **NCLC 9; DC 1**

Dumas, Claudine
See Malzberg, Barry N(athaniel)

Dumas, Henry L. 1934-1968 ..... **CLC 6, 62**
See also BW; CA 85-88; DLB 41

du Maurier, Daphne
1907-1989 .... **CLC 6, 11, 59**
See also CA 5-8R; 128; CANR 6; MTCW;
SATA 27, 60

Dunbar, Paul Laurence
1872-1906 ...... **TCLC 2, 12; BLC; DA;**
PC 5; SSC 8; WLC
See also BW; CA 104; 124;
CDALB 1865-1917; DLB 50, 54, 78;
SATA 34

Dunbar, William 1460(?)-1530(?) .... **LC 20**

Duncan, Lois 1934- .... **CLC 26**
See also AAYA 4; CA 1-4R; CANR 2, 23,
36; CLR 29; JRDA; MAICYA; SAAS 2;
SATA 1, 36, 75

Duncan, Robert (Edward)
1919-1988 .... **CLC 1, 2, 4, 7, 15, 41, 55;**
PC 2
See also CA 9-12R; 124; CANR 28; DLB 5,
16; MTCW

Dunlap, William 1766-1839 .... **NCLC 2**
See also DLB 30, 37, 59

Dunn, Douglas (Eaglesham)
1942- .... **CLC 6, 40**
See also CA 45-48; CANR 2, 33; DLB 40;
MTCW

Dunn, Katherine (Karen) 1945- ..... **CLC 71**
See also CA 33-36R

Dunn, Stephen 1939- .... **CLC 36**
See also CA 33-36R; CANR 12; DLB 105

Dunne, Finley Peter 1867-1936.... **TCLC 28**
See also CA 108; DLB 11, 23

Dunne, John Gregory 1932-........ **CLC 28**
See also CA 25-28R; CANR 14; DLBY 80

Dunsany, Edward John Moreton Drax
Plunkett 1878-1957
See Dunsany, Lord; Lord Dunsany
See also CA 104; DLB 10

Dunsany, Lord.................... TCLC 2
See also Dunsany, Edward John Moreton
Drax Plunkett
See also DLB 77

du Perry, Jean
See Simenon, Georges (Jacques Christian)

Durang, Christopher (Ferdinand)
1949- .... **CLC 27, 38**
See also CA 105

Duras, Marguerite
1914- ...... **CLC 3, 6, 11, 20, 34, 40, 68**
See also CA 25-28R; DLB 83; MTCW

Durban, (Rosa) Pam 1947-........ **CLC 39**
See also CA 123

Durcan, Paul 1944-............ **CLC 43, 70**
See also CA 134

Durrell, Lawrence (George)
1912-1990 .... **CLC 1, 4, 6, 8, 13, 27, 41**
See also CA 9-12R; 132; CANR 40;
CDBLB 1945-1960; DLB 15, 27;
DLBY 90; MTCW

Dutt, Toru 1856-1877.......... **NCLC 29**

Dwight, Timothy 1752-1817...... **NCLC 13**
See also DLB 37

Dworkin, Andrea 1946- .... **CLC 43**
See also CA 77-80; CANR 16, 39; MTCW

Dwyer, Deanna
See Koontz, Dean R(ay)

Dwyer, K. R.
See Koontz, Dean R(ay)

Dylan, Bob 1941- ...... **CLC 3, 4, 6, 12, 77**
See also CA 41-44R; DLB 16

Eagleton, Terence (Francis) 1943-
See Eagleton, Terry
See also CA 57-60; CANR 7, 23; MTCW

Eagleton, Terry .... CLC 63
See also Eagleton, Terence (Francis)

Early, Jack
See Scoppettone, Sandra

East, Michael
See West, Morris L(anglo)

Eastaway, Edward
See Thomas, (Philip) Edward

Eastlake, William (Derry) 1917-..... **CLC 8**
See also CA 5-8R; CAAS 1; CANR 5;
DLB 6

Eberhart, Richard (Ghormley)
1904- .... **CLC 3, 11, 19, 56**
See also CA 1-4R; CANR 2;
CDALB 1941-1968; DLB 48; MTCW

Eberstadt, Fernanda 1960-......... **CLC 39**
See also CA 136

Echegaray (y Eizaguirre), Jose (Maria Waldo)
1832-1916 .... **TCLC 4**
See also CA 104; CANR 32; HW; MTCW

Echeverria, (Jose) Esteban (Antonino)
1805-1851 .... **NCLC 18**

Echo
See Proust, (Valentin-Louis-George-Eugene-)
Marcel

Eckert, Allan W. 1931- .... **CLC 17**
See also CA 13-16R; CANR 14; SATA 27,
29

Eckhart, Meister 1260(?)-1328(?) .. **CMLC 9**
See also DLB 115

Eckmar, F. R.
See de Hartog, Jan

Eco, Umberto 1932-........... **CLC 28, 60**
See also BEST 90:1; CA 77-80; CANR 12,
33; MTCW

Eddison, E(ric) R(ucker)
1882-1945 .... **TCLC 15**
See also CA 109

Edel, (Joseph) Leon 1907-...... **CLC 29, 34**
See also CA 1-4R; CANR 1, 22; DLB 103

Eden, Emily 1797-1869 .... **NCLC 10**

Edgar, David 1948-.............. **CLC 42**
See also CA 57-60; CANR 12; DLB 13;
MTCW

Edgerton, Clyde (Carlyle) 1944- .... **CLC 39**
See also CA 118; 134

Edgeworth, Maria 1767-1849...... **NCLC 1**
See also DLB 116; SATA 21

Edmonds, Paul
See Kuttner, Henry

Edmonds, Walter D(umaux) 1903-.. **CLC 35**
See also CA 5-8R; CANR 2; DLB 9;
MAIC¥A; SAAS 4; SATA 1, 27

Edmondson, Wallace
See Ellison, Harlan

Edson, Russell .... CLC 13
See also CA 33-36R

Edwards, G(erald) B(asil)
1899-1976 .... **CLC 25**
See also CA 110

Edwards, Gus 1939-.............. **CLC 43**
See also CA 108

Edwards, Jonathan 1703-1758.... **LC 7; DA**
See also DLB 24

Efron, Marina Ivanovna Tsvetaeva
See Tsvetaeva (Efron), Marina (Ivanovna)

Ehle, John (Marsden, Jr.) 1925-.... **CLC 27**
See also CA 9-12R

Ehrenbourg, Ilya (Grigoryevich)
See Ehrenburg, Ilya (Grigoryevich)

Ehrenburg, Ilya (Grigoryevich)
1891-1967 .... **CLC 18, 34, 62**
See also CA 102; 25-28R

Ehrenburg, Ilyo (Grigoryevich)
See Ehrenburg, Ilya (Grigoryevich)

Eich, Guenter 1907-1972 .... **CLC 15**
See also CA 111; 93-96; DLB 69, 124

Eichendorff, Joseph Freiherr von
1788-1857 .... **NCLC 8**
See also DLB 90

Evan, Evin
See Faust, Frederick (Schiller)

Evans, Evan
See Faust, Frederick (Schiller)

Evans, Marian
See Eliot, George

Evans, Mary Ann
See Eliot, George

Evarts, Esther
See Benson, Sally

Everett, Percival
See Everett, Percival L.

Everett, Percival L.   1956- .... **CLC 57**
See also CA 129

Everson, R(onald) G(ilmour)
1903- .... **CLC 27**
See also CA 17-20R; DLB 88

Everson, William (Oliver)
1912- .... **CLC 1, 5, 14**
See also CA 9-12R; CANR 20; DLB 5, 16;
MTCW

Evtushenko, Evgenii Aleksandrovich
See Yevtushenko, Yevgeny (Alexandrovich)

Ewart, Gavin (Buchanan)
1916- .... **CLC 13, 46**
See also CA 89-92; CANR 17; DLB 40;
MTCW

Ewers, Hanns Heinz   1871-1943 ... **TCLC 12**
See also CA 109

Ewing, Frederick R.
See Sturgeon, Theodore (Hamilton)

Exley, Frederick (Earl)
1929-1992 .... **CLC 6, 11**
See also AITN 2; CA 81-84; 138; DLBY 81

Eynhardt, Guillermo
See Quiroga, Horacio (Sylvestre)

Ezekiel, Nissim   1924- .... **CLC 61**
See also CA 61-64

Ezekiel, Tish O'Dowd   1943- .... **CLC 34**
See also CA 129

Fadeyev, A.
See Bulgya, Alexander Alexandrovich

Fadeyev, Alexander............... **TCLC 53**
See also Bulgya, Alexander Alexandrovich

Fagen, Donald   1948- .... **CLC 26**

Fainzilberg, Ilya Arnoldovich   1897-1937
See Ilf, Ilya
See also CA 120

Fair, Ronald L.   1932- .... **CLC 18**
See also BW; CA 69-72; CANR 25; DLB 33

Fairbairns, Zoe (Ann)   1948- .... **CLC 32**
See also CA 103; CANR 21

Falco, Gian
See Papini, Giovanni

Falconer, James
See Kirkup, James

Falconer, Kenneth
See Kornbluth, C(yril) M.

Falkland, Samuel
See Heijermans, Herman

Fallaci, Oriana   1930- .... **CLC 11**
See also CA 77-80; CANR 15; MTCW

Faludy, George   1913- .... **CLC 42**
See also CA 21-24R

Faludy, Gyoergy
See Faludy, George

Fanon, Frantz   1925-1961 ..... **CLC 74; BLC**
See also BW; CA 116; 89-92

Fanshawe, Ann .... **LC 11**

Fante, John (Thomas)   1911-1983 ... **CLC 60**
See also CA 69-72; 109; CANR 23;
DLB 130; DLBY 83

Farah, Nuruddin   1945- ...... **CLC 53; BLC**
See also CA 106; DLB 125

Fargue, Leon-Paul   1876(?)-1947 ... **TCLC 11**
See also CA 109

Farigoule, Louis
See Romains, Jules

Farina, Richard   1936(?)-1966 .... **CLC 9**
See also CA 81-84; 25-28R

Farley, Walter (Lorimer)
1915-1989 .... **CLC 17**
See also CA 17-20R; CANR 8, 29; DLB 22;
JRDA; MAICYA; SATA 2, 43

Farmer, Philip Jose   1918- .... **CLC 1, 19**
See also CA 1-4R; CANR 4, 35; DLB 8;
MTCW

Farquhar, George   1677-1707 .... **LC 21**
See also DLB 84

Farrell, J(ames) G(ordon)
1935-1979 .... **CLC 6**
See also CA 73-76; 89-92; CANR 36;
DLB 14; MTCW

Farrell, James T(homas)
1904-1979 .... **CLC 1, 4, 8, 11, 66**
See also CA 5-8R; 89-92; CANR 9; DLB 4,
9, 86; DLBD 2; MTCW

Farren, Richard J.
See Betjeman, John

Farren, Richard M.
See Betjeman, John

Fassbinder, Rainer Werner
1946-1982 .... **CLC 20**
See also CA 93-96; 106; CANR 31

Fast, Howard (Melvin)   1914- ...... **CLC 23**
See also CA 1-4R; CAAS 18; CANR 1, 33;
DLB 9; SATA 7

Faulcon, Robert
See Holdstock, Robert P.

Faulkner, William (Cuthbert)
1897-1962 ..... **CLC 1, 3, 6, 8, 9, 11, 14,
18, 28, 52, 68; DA; SSC 1; WLC**
See also AAYA 7; CA 81-84; CANR 33;
CDALB 1929-1941; DLB 9, 11, 44, 102;
DLBD 2; DLBY 86; MTCW

Fauset, Jessie Redmon
1884(?)-1961 .... **CLC 19, 54; BLC**
See also BW; CA 109; DLB 51

Faust, Frederick (Schiller)
1892-1944(?) .... **TCLC 49**
See also CA 108

Faust, Irvin   1924- .... **CLC 8**
See also CA 33-36R; CANR 28; DLB 2, 28;
DLBY 80

Fawkes, Guy
See Benchley, Robert (Charles)

Fearing, Kenneth (Flexner)
1902-1961 .... **CLC 51**
See also CA 93-96; DLB 9

Fecamps, Elise
See Creasey, John

Federman, Raymond   1928- ...... **CLC 6, 47**
See also CA 17-20R; CAAS 8; CANR 10,
43; DLBY 80

Federspiel, J(uerg) F.   1931- .... **CLC 42**

Feiffer, Jules (Ralph)   1929- .... **CLC 2, 8, 64**
See also AAYA 3; CA 17-20R; CANR 30;
DLB 7, 44; MTCW; SATA 8, 61

Feige, Hermann Albert Otto Maximilian
See Traven, B.

Fei-Kan, Li
See Li Fei-kan

Feinberg, David B.   1956- .... **CLC 59**
See also CA 135

Feinstein, Elaine   1930- .... **CLC 36**
See also CA 69-72; CAAS 1; CANR 31;
DLB 14, 40; MTCW

Feldman, Irving (Mordecai)   1928- .... **CLC 7**
See also CA 1-4R; CANR 1

Fellini, Federico   1920-1993 .... **CLC 16**
See also CA 65-68; 143; CANR 33

Felsen, Henry Gregor   1916- .... **CLC 17**
See also CA 1-4R; CANR 1; SAAS 2;
SATA 1

Fenton, James Martin   1949- .... **CLC 32**
See also CA 102; DLB 40

Ferber, Edna   1887-1968........... **CLC 18**
See also AITN 1; CA 5-8R; 25-28R; DLB 9,
28, 86; MTCW; SATA 7

Ferguson, Helen
See Kavan, Anna

Ferguson, Samuel   1810-1886 ..... **NCLC 33**
See also DLB 32

Ferling, Lawrence
See Ferlinghetti, Lawrence (Monsanto)

Ferlinghetti, Lawrence (Monsanto)
1919(?)- .... **CLC 2, 6, 10, 27; PC 1**
See also CA 5-8R; CANR 3, 41;
CDALB 1941-1968; DLB 5, 16; MTCW

Fernandez, Vicente Garcia Huidobro
See Huidobro Fernandez, Vicente Garcia

Ferrer, Gabriel (Francisco Victor) Miro
See Miro (Ferrer), Gabriel (Francisco
Victor)

Ferrier, Susan (Edmonstone)
1782-1854 .... **NCLC 8**
See also DLB 116

Ferrigno, Robert   1948(?)- .... **CLC 65**
See also CA 140

Feuchtwanger, Lion   1884-1958 ..... **TCLC 3**
See also CA 104; DLB 66

Feydeau, Georges (Leon Jules Marie)
1862-1921 .... **TCLC 22**
See also CA 113

Ficino, Marsilio   1433-1499 .... **LC 12**

Fiedeler, Hans
See Doeblin, Alfred

Fiedler, Leslie A(aron)
1917- .... **CLC 4, 13, 24**
See also CA 9-12R; CANR 7; DLB 28, 67;
MTCW

Field, Andrew 1938- .... **CLC 44**
See also CA 97-100; CANR 25

Field, Eugene 1850-1895 .... **NCLC 3**
See also DLB 23, 42; MAICYA; SATA 16

Field, Gans T.
See Wellman, Manly Wade

Field, Michael .... **TCLC 43**

Field, Peter
See Hobson, Laura Z(ametkin)

Fielding, Henry
1707-1754 .... **LC 1; DA; WLC**
See also CDBLB 1660-1789; DLB 39, 84,
101

Fielding, Sarah 1710-1768 .... **LC 1**
See also DLB 39

Fierstein, Harvey (Forbes) 1954- ... **CLC 33**
See also CA 123; 129

Figes, Eva 1932- .... **CLC 31**
See also CA 53-56; CANR 4; DLB 14

Finch, Robert (Duer Claydon)
1900- .... **CLC 18**
See also CA 57-60; CANR 9, 24; DLB 88

Findley, Timothy 1930- .... **CLC 27**
See also CA 25-28R; CANR 12, 42;
DLB 53

Fink, William
See Mencken, H(enry) L(ouis)

Firbank, Louis 1942-
See Reed, Lou
See also CA 117

Firbank, (Arthur Annesley) Ronald
1886-1926 .... **TCLC 1**
See also CA 104; DLB 36

Fisher, M(ary) F(rances) K(ennedy)
1908-1992 .... **CLC 76**
See also CA 77-80; 138

Fisher, Roy 1930- .... **CLC 25**
See also CA 81-84; CAAS 10; CANR 16;
DLB 40

Fisher, Rudolph
1897-1934 .... **TCLC 11; BLC**
See also BW; CA 107; 124; DLB 51, 102

Fisher, Vardis (Alvero) 1895-1968.... **CLC 7**
See also CA 5-8R; 25-28R; DLB 9

Fiske, Tarleton
See Bloch, Robert (Albert)

Fitch, Clarke
See Sinclair, Upton (Beall)

Fitch, John IV
See Cormier, Robert (Edmund)

Fitgerald, Penelope 1916- .... **CLC 61**

Fitzgerald, Captain Hugh
See Baum, L(yman) Frank

FitzGerald, Edward 1809-1883 .... **NCLC 9**
See also DLB 32

Fitzgerald, F(rancis) Scott (Key)
1896-1940 ..... **TCLC 1, 6, 14, 28; DA;
SSC 6; WLC**
See also AITN 1; CA 110; 123;
CDALB 1917-1929; DLB 4, 9, 86;
DLBD 1; DLBY 81; MTCW

Fitzgerald, Penelope 1916- ...... **CLC 19, 51**
See also CA 85-88; CAAS 10; DLB 14

Fitzgerald, Robert (Stuart)
1910-1985 .... **CLC 39**
See also CA 1-4R; 114; CANR 1; DLBY 80

FitzGerald, Robert D(avid)
1902-1987 .... **CLC 19**
See also CA 17-20R

Fitzgerald, Zelda (Sayre)
1900-1948 .... **TCLC 52**
See also CA 117; 126; DLBY 84

Flanagan, Thomas (James Bonner)
1923- .... **CLC 25, 52**
See also CA 108; DLBY 80; MTCW

Flaubert, Gustave
1821-1880 .... **NCLC 2, 10, 19; DA;
SSC 11; WLC**
See also DLB 119

Flecker, (Herman) James Elroy
1884-1915 .... **TCLC 43**
See also CA 109; DLB 10, 19

Fleming, Ian (Lancaster)
1908-1964 .... **CLC 3, 30**
See also CA 5-8R; CDBLB 1945-1960;
DLB 87; MTCW; SATA 9

Fleming, Thomas (James) 1927- .... **CLC 37**
See also CA 5-8R; CANR 10; SATA 8

Fletcher, John Gould 1886-1950 ... **TCLC 35**
See also CA 107; DLB 4, 45

Fleur, Paul
See Pohl, Frederik

Flooglebuckle, Al
See Spiegelman, Art

Flying Officer X
See Bates, H(erbert) E(rnest)

Fo, Dario 1926- .... **CLC 32**
See also CA 116; 128; MTCW

Fogarty, Jonathan Titulescu Esq.
See Farrell, James T(homas)

Folke, Will
See Bloch, Robert (Albert)

Follett, Ken(neth Martin) 1949- .... **CLC 18**
See also AAYA 6; BEST 89:4; CA 81-84;
CANR 13, 33; DLB 87; DLBY 81;
MTCW

Fontane, Theodor 1819-1898 ..... **NCLC 26**
See also DLB 129

Foote, Horton 1916- .... **CLC 51**
See also CA 73-76; CANR 34; DLB 26

Foote, Shelby 1916- .... **CLC 75**
See also CA 5-8R; CANR 3; DLB 2, 17

Forbes, Esther 1891-1967.......... **CLC 12**
See also CA 13-14; 25-28R; CAP 1;
CLR 27; DLB 22; JRDA; MAICYA;
SATA 2

Forche, Carolyn (Louise) 1950- ..... **CLC 25**
See also CA 109; 117; DLB 5

Ford, Elbur
See Hibbert, Eleanor Alice Burford

Ford, Ford Madox
1873-1939 .... **TCLC 1, 15, 39**
See also CA 104; 132; CDBLB 1914-1945;
DLB 34, 98; MTCW

Ford, John 1895-1973............. **CLC 16**
See also CA 45-48

Ford, Richard 1944- .... **CLC 46**
See also CA 69-72; CANR 11

Ford, Webster
See Masters, Edgar Lee

Foreman, Richard 1937-.......... **CLC 50**
See also CA 65-68; CANR 32

Forester, C(ecil) S(cott)
1899-1966 .... **CLC 35**
See also CA 73-76; 25-28R; SATA 13

Forez
See Mauriac, Francois (Charles)

Forman, James Douglas 1932-...... **CLC 21**
See also CA 9-12R; CANR 4, 19, 42;
JRDA; MAICYA; SATA 8, 70

Fornes, Maria Irene 1930-...... **CLC 39, 61**
See also CA 25-28R; CANR 28; DLB 7;
HW; MTCW

Forrest, Leon 1937- .... **CLC 4**
See also BW; CA 89-92; CAAS 7;
CANR 25; DLB 33

Forster, E(dward) M(organ)
1879-1970 ..... **CLC 1, 2, 3, 4, 9, 10, 13,
15, 22, 45, 77; DA; WLC**
See also AAYA 2; CA 13-14; 25-28R;
CAP 1; CDBLB 1914-1945; DLB 34, 98;
DLBD 10; MTCW; SATA 57

Forster, John 1812-1876 .... **NCLC 11**

Forsyth, Frederick 1938-...... **CLC 2, 5, 36**
See also BEST 89:4; CA 85-88; CANR 38;
DLB 87; MTCW

Forten, Charlotte L. .... **TCLC 16; BLC**
See also Grimke, Charlotte L(ottie) Forten
See also DLB 50

Foscolo, Ugo 1778-1827.......... **NCLC 8**

Fosse, Bob .... **CLC 20**
See also Fosse, Robert Louis

Fosse, Robert Louis 1927-1987
See Fosse, Bob
See also CA 110; 123

Foster, Stephen Collins
1826-1864 .... **NCLC 26**

Foucault, Michel
1926-1984 .... **CLC 31, 34, 69**
See also CA 105; 113; CANR 34; MTCW

Fouque, Friedrich (Heinrich Karl) de la Motte
1777-1843 .... **NCLC 2**
See also DLB 90

Fournier, Henri Alban 1886-1914
See Alain-Fournier
See also CA 104

Fournier, Pierre 1916- .... **CLC 11**
See also Gascar, Pierre
See also CA 89-92; CANR 16, 40

Fowles, John
1926- .... **CLC 1, 2, 3, 4, 6, 9, 10, 15, 33**
See also CA 5-8R; CANR 25; CDBLB 1960
to Present; DLB 14; MTCW; SATA 22

Gallant, Roy A(rthur) 1924- ...... **CLC 17**
See also CA 5-8R; CANR 4, 29; CLR 30;
MAICYA; SATA 4, 68

Gallico, Paul (William) 1897-1976 ... **CLC 2**
See also AITN 1; CA 5-8R; 69-72;
CANR 23; DLB 9; MAICYA; SATA 13

Gallup, Ralph
See Whitemore, Hugh (John)

Galsworthy, John
1867-1933 .... **TCLC 1, 45; DA; WLC 2**
See also CA 104; 141; CDBLB 1890-1914;
DLB 10, 34, 98

Galt, John 1779-1839 .... **NCLC 1**
See also DLB 99, 116

Galvin, James 1951- .... **CLC 38**
See also CA 108; CANR 26

Gamboa, Federico 1864-1939 ..... **TCLC 36**

Gann, Ernest Kellogg 1910-1991 .... **CLC 23**
See also AITN 1; CA 1-4R; 136; CANR 1

Garcia, Cristina 1958- .... **CLC 76**
See also CA 141

Garcia Lorca, Federico
1898-1936 .... **TCLC 1, 7, 49; DA;**
DC 2; HLC; PC 3; WLC
See also CA 104; 131; DLB 108; HW;
MTCW

Garcia Marquez, Gabriel (Jose)
1928- .... **CLC 2, 3, 8, 10, 15, 27, 47, 55;**
DA; HLC; SSC 8; WLC
See also Marquez, Gabriel (Jose) Garcia
See also AAYA 3; BEST 89:1, 90:4;
CA 33-36R; CANR 10, 28; DLB 113;
HW; MTCW

Gard, Janice
See Latham, Jean Lee

Gard, Roger Martin du
See Martin du Gard, Roger

Gardam, Jane 1928- .... **CLC 43**
See also CA 49-52; CANR 2, 18, 33;
CLR 12; DLB 14; MAICYA; MTCW;
SAAS 9; SATA 28, 39, 76

Gardner, Herb .... **CLC 44**

Gardner, John (Champlin), Jr.
1933-1982 ..... **CLC 2, 3, 5, 7, 8, 10, 18,**
28, 34; SSC 7
See also AITN 1; CA 65-68; 107;
CANR 33; DLB 2; DLBY 82; MTCW;
SATA 31, 40

Gardner, John (Edmund) 1926- ..... **CLC 30**
See also CA 103; CANR 15; MTCW

Gardner, Noel
See Kuttner, Henry

Gardons, S. S.
See Snodgrass, W(illiam) D(e Witt)

Garfield, Leon 1921- .... **CLC 12**
See also AAYA 8; CA 17-20R; CANR 38,
41; CLR 21; JRDA; MAICYA; SATA 1,
32, 76

Garland, (Hannibal) Hamlin
1860-1940 .... **TCLC 3**
See also CA 104; DLB 12, 71, 78

Garneau, (Hector de) Saint-Denys
1912-1943 .... **TCLC 13**
See also CA 111; DLB 88

Garner, Alan 1934- .... **CLC 17**
See also CA 73-76; CANR 15; CLR 20;
MAICYA; MTCW; SATA 18, 69

Garner, Hugh 1913-1979 .... **CLC 13**
See also CA 69-72; CANR 31; DLB 68

Garnett, David 1892-1981 .... **CLC 3**
See also CA 5-8R; 103; CANR 17; DLB 34

Garos, Stephanie
See Katz, Steve

Garrett, George (Palmer)
1929- .... **CLC 3, 11, 51**
See also CA 1-4R; CAAS 5; CANR 1, 42;
DLB 2, 5, 130; DLBY 83

Garrick, David 1717-1779 .... **LC 15**
See also DLB 84

Garrigue, Jean 1914-1972 .... **CLC 2, 8**
See also CA 5-8R; 37-40R; CANR 20

Garrison, Frederick
See Sinclair, Upton (Beall)

Garth, Will
See Hamilton, Edmond; Kuttner, Henry

Garvey, Marcus (Moziah, Jr.)
1887-1940 .... **TCLC 41; BLC**
See also BW; CA 120; 124

Gary, Romain .... **CLC 25**
See also Kacew, Romain
See also DLB 83

Gascar, Pierre .... **CLC 11**
See also Fournier, Pierre

Gascoyne, David (Emery) 1916- .... **CLC 45**
See also CA 65-68; CANR 10, 28; DLB 20;
MTCW

Gaskell, Elizabeth Cleghorn
1810-1865 .... **NCLC 5**
See also CDBLB 1832-1890; DLB 21

Gass, William H(oward)
1924- ... **CLC 1, 2, 8, 11, 15, 39; SSC 12**
See also CA 17-20R; CANR 30; DLB 2;
MTCW

Gasset, Jose Ortega y
See Ortega y Gasset, Jose

Gautier, Theophile 1811-1872 ..... **NCLC 1**
See also DLB 119

Gawsworth, John
See Bates, H(erbert) E(rnest)

Gaye, Marvin (Penze) 1939-1984 ... **CLC 26**
See also CA 112

Gebler, Carlo (Ernest) 1954- .... **CLC 39**
See also CA 119; 133

Gee, Maggie (Mary) 1948- .... **CLC 57**
See also CA 130

Gee, Maurice (Gough) 1931- .... **CLC 29**
See also CA 97-100; SATA 46

Gelbart, Larry (Simon) 1923- ... **CLC 21, 61**
See also CA 73-76

Gelber, Jack 1932- .... **CLC 1, 6, 14, 79**
See also CA 1-4R; CANR 2; DLB 7

Gellhorn, Martha Ellis 1908- ... **CLC 14, 60**
See also CA 77-80; DLBY 82

Genet, Jean
1910-1986 ... **CLC 1, 2, 5, 10, 14, 44, 46**
See also CA 13-16R; CANR 18; DLB 72;
DLBY 86; MTCW

Gent, Peter 1942- .... **CLC 29**
See also AITN 1; CA 89-92; DLBY 82

Gentlewoman in New England, A
See Bradstreet, Anne

Gentlewoman in Those Parts, A
See Bradstreet, Anne

George, Jean Craighead 1919- ...... **CLC 35**
See also AAYA 8; CA 5-8R; CANR 25;
CLR 1; DLB 52; JRDA; MAICYA;
SATA 2, 68

George, Stefan (Anton)
1868-1933 .... **TCLC 2, 14**
See also CA 104

Georges, Georges Martin
See Simenon, Georges (Jacques Christian)

Gerhardi, William Alexander
See Gerhardie, William Alexander

Gerhardie, William Alexander
1895-1977 .... **CLC 5**
See also CA 25-28R; 73-76; CANR 18;
DLB 36

Gerstler, Amy 1956- .... **CLC 70**

Gertler, T. .... **CLC 34**
See also CA 116; 121

Ghalib 1797-1869 .... **NCLC 39**

Ghelderode, Michel de
1898-1962 .... **CLC 6, 11**
See also CA 85-88; CANR 40

Ghiselin, Brewster 1903- .... **CLC 23**
See also CA 13-16R; CAAS 10; CANR 13

Ghose, Zulfikar 1935- .... **CLC 42**
See also CA 65-68

Ghosh, Amitav 1956- .... **CLC 44**

Giacosa, Giuseppe 1847-1906 ...... **TCLC 7**
See also CA 104

Gibb, Lee
See Waterhouse, Keith (Spencer)

Gibbon, Lewis Grassic .... **TCLC 4**
See also Mitchell, James Leslie

Gibbons, Kaye 1960- .... **CLC 50**

Gibran, Kahlil 1883-1931 .... **TCLC 1, 9**
See also CA 104

Gibson, William 1914- .... **CLC 23; DA**
See also CA 9-12R; CANR 9, 42; DLB 7;
SATA 66

Gibson, William (Ford) 1948- ... **CLC 39, 63**
See also CA 126; 133

Gide, Andre (Paul Guillaume)
1869-1951 .... **TCLC 5, 12, 36; DA;**
SSC 13; WLC
See also CA 104; 124; DLB 65; MTCW

Gifford, Barry (Colby) 1946- ...... **CLC 34**
See also CA 65-68; CANR 9, 30, 40

Gilbert, W(illiam) S(chwenck)
1836-1911 .... **TCLC 3**
See also CA 104; SATA 36

Gilbreth, Frank B., Jr. 1911- .... **CLC 17**
See also CA 9-12R; SATA 2

Gilchrist, Ellen 1935- .. **CLC 34, 48; SSC 14**
See also CA 113; 116; CANR 41; DLB 130;
MTCW

Giles, Molly 1942- .... **CLC 39**
See also CA 126

Author Index

Gill, Patrick
See Creasey, John

Gilliam, Terry (Vance) 1940- .... **CLC 21**
See also Monty Python
See also CA 108; 113; CANR 35

Gillian, Jerry
See Gilliam, Terry (Vance)

Gilliatt, Penelope (Ann Douglass)
1932-1993 .... **CLC 2, 10, 13, 53**
See also AITN 2; CA 13-16R; 141; DLB 14

Gilman, Charlotte (Anna) Perkins (Stetson)
1860-1935 .... **TCLC 9, 37; SSC 13**
See also CA 106

Gilmour, David 1949- .... **CLC 35**
See also Pink Floyd
See also CA 138

Gilpin, William 1724-1804 .... **NCLC 30**

Gilray, J. D.
See Mencken, H(enry) L(ouis)

Gilroy, Frank D(aniel) 1925- .... **CLC 2**
See also CA 81-84; CANR 32; DLB 7

Ginsberg, Allen
1926- ...... **CLC 1, 2, 3, 4, 6, 13, 36, 69;**
DA; PC 4; WLC 3
See also AITN 1; CA 1-4R; CANR 2, 41;
CDALB 1941-1968; DLB 5, 16; MTCW

Ginzburg, Natalia
1916-1991 .... **CLC 5, 11, 54, 70**
See also CA 85-88; 135; CANR 33; MTCW

Giono, Jean 1895-1970 .... **CLC 4, 11**
See also CA 45-48; 29-32R; CANR 2, 35;
DLB 72; MTCW

Giovanni, Nikki
1943- ...... **CLC 2, 4, 19, 64; BLC; DA**
See also AITN 1; BW; CA 29-32R;
CAAS 6; CANR 18, 41; CLR 6; DLB 5,
41; MAICYA; MTCW; SATA 24

Giovene, Andrea 1904- .... **CLC 7**
See also CA 85-88

Gippius, Zinaida (Nikolayevna) 1869-1945
See Hippius, Zinaida
See also CA 106

Giraudoux, (Hippolyte) Jean
1882-1944 .... **TCLC 2, 7**
See also CA 104; DLB 65

Gironella, Jose Maria 1917- .... **CLC 11**
See also CA 101

Gissing, George (Robert)
1857-1903 .... **TCLC 3, 24, 47**
See also CA 105; DLB 18, 135

Giurlani, Aldo
See Palazzeschi, Aldo

Gladkov, Fyodor (Vasilyevich)
1883-1958 .... **TCLC 27**

Glanville, Brian (Lester) 1931- ...... **CLC 6**
See also CA 5-8R; CAAS 9; CANR 3;
DLB 15; SATA 42

Glasgow, Ellen (Anderson Gholson)
1873(?)-1945 .... **TCLC 2, 7**
See also CA 104; DLB 9, 12

Glassco, John 1909-1981 .... **CLC 9**
See also CA 13-16R; 102; CANR 15;
DLB 68

Glasscock, Amnesia
See Steinbeck, John (Ernst)

Glasser, Ronald J. 1940(?)- .... **CLC 37**

Glassman, Joyce
See Johnson, Joyce

Glendinning, Victoria 1937- .... **CLC 50**
See also CA 120; 127

Glissant, Edouard 1928- .... **CLC 10, 68**

Gloag, Julian 1930- .... **CLC 40**
See also AITN 1; CA 65-68; CANR 10

Gluck, Louise (Elisabeth)
1943- .... **CLC 7, 22, 44, 81**
See also Glueck, Louise
See also CA 33-36R; CANR 40; DLB 5

Glueck, Louise.................. CLC 7, 22
See also Gluck, Louise (Elisabeth)
See also DLB 5

Gobineau, Joseph Arthur (Comte) de
1816-1882 .... **NCLC 17**
See also DLB 123

Godard, Jean-Luc 1930- .... **CLC 20**
See also CA 93-96

Godden, (Margaret) Rumer 1907- ... **CLC 53**
See also AAYA 6; CA 5-8R; CANR 4, 27,
36; CLR 20; MAICYA; SAAS 12;
SATA 3, 36

Godoy Alcayaga, Lucila 1889-1957
See Mistral, Gabriela
See also CA 104; 131; HW; MTCW

Godwin, Gail (Kathleen)
1937- .... **CLC 5, 8, 22, 31, 69**
See also CA 29-32R; CANR 15, 43; DLB 6;
MTCW

Godwin, William 1756-1836 ...... **NCLC 14**
See also CDBLB 1789-1832; DLB 39, 104

Goethe, Johann Wolfgang von
1749-1832 .... **NCLC 4, 22, 34; DA;**
PC 5; WLC 3
See also DLB 94

Gogarty, Oliver St. John
1878-1957 .... **TCLC 15**
See also CA 109; DLB 15, 19

Gogol, Nikolai (Vasilyevich)
1809-1852 .... **NCLC 5, 15, 31; DA;**
DC 1; SSC 4; WLC

Goines, Donald
1937(?)-1974 .... **CLC 80; BLC**
See also AITN 1; BW; CA 124; 114;
DLB 33

Gold, Herbert 1924- .... **CLC 4, 7, 14, 42**
See also CA 9-12R; CANR 17; DLB 2;
DLBY 81

Goldbarth, Albert 1948- .... **CLC 5, 38**
See also CA 53-56; CANR 6, 40; DLB 120

Goldberg, Anatol 1910-1982 .... **CLC 34**
See also CA 131; 117

Goldemberg, Isaac 1945- .... **CLC 52**
See also CA 69-72; CAAS 12; CANR 11,
32; HW

Golden Silver
See Storm, Hyemeyohsts

Golding, William (Gerald)
1911-1993 .... **CLC 1, 2, 3, 8, 10, 17, 27,**
58, 81; DA; WLC
See also AAYA 5; CA 5-8R; 141;
CANR 13, 33; CDBLB 1945-1960;
DLB 15, 100; MTCW

Goldman, Emma 1869-1940 ...... **TCLC 13**
See also CA 110

Goldman, Francisco 1955- .... **CLC 76**

Goldman, William (W.) 1931- .... **CLC 1, 48**
See also CA 9-12R; CANR 29; DLB 44

Goldmann, Lucien 1913-1970 ...... **CLC 24**
See also CA 25-28; CAP 2

Goldoni, Carlo 1707-1793 .... **LC 4**

Goldsberry, Steven 1949- .... **CLC 34**
See also CA 131

Goldsmith, Oliver
1728-1774 .... **LC 2; DA; WLC**
See also CDBLB 1660-1789; DLB 39, 89,
104, 109; SATA 26

Goldsmith, Peter
See Priestley, J(ohn) B(oynton)

Gombrowicz, Witold
1904-1969 .... **CLC 4, 7, 11, 49**
See also CA 19-20; 25-28R; CAP 2

Gomez de la Serna, Ramon
1888-1963 .... **CLC 9**
See also CA 116; HW

Goncharov, Ivan Alexandrovich
1812-1891 .... **NCLC 1**

Goncourt, Edmond (Louis Antoine Huot) de
1822-1896 .... **NCLC 7**
See also DLB 123

Goncourt, Jules (Alfred Huot) de
1830-1870 .... **NCLC 7**
See also DLB 123

Gontier, Fernande 19(?)- .... **CLC 50**

Goodman, Paul 1911-1972 .... **CLC 1, 2, 4, 7**
See also CA 19-20; 37-40R; CANR 34;
CAP 2; DLB 130; MTCW

Gordimer, Nadine
1923- .... **CLC 3, 5, 7, 10, 18, 33, 51, 70;**
DA
See also CA 5-8R; CANR 3, 28; MTCW

Gordon, Adam Lindsay
1833-1870 .... **NCLC 21**

Gordon, Caroline
1895-1981 ...... **CLC 6, 13, 29; SSC 15**
See also CA 11-12; 103; CANR 36; CAP 1;
DLB 4, 9, 102; DLBY 81; MTCW

Gordon, Charles William 1860-1937
See Connor, Ralph
See also CA 109

Gordon, Mary (Catherine)
1949- .... **CLC 13, 22**
See also CA 102; DLB 6; DLBY 81;
MTCW

Gordon, Sol 1923- .... **CLC 26**
See also CA 53-56; CANR 4; SATA 11

Gordone, Charles 1925- .... **CLC 1, 4**
See also BW; CA 93-96; DLB 7; MTCW

Gorenko, Anna Andreevna
See Akhmatova, Anna

Gorky, Maxim.............. TCLC 8; WLC
See also Peshkov, Alexei Maximovich

Goryan, Sirak
See Saroyan, William

Gosse, Edmund (William)
1849-1928 .... **TCLC 28**
See also CA 117; DLB 57

Gotlieb, Phyllis Fay (Bloom)
    1926- . . . . **CLC 18**
    See also CA 13-16R; CANR 7; DLB 88

Gottesman, S. D.
    See Kornbluth, C(yril) M.; Pohl, Frederik

Gottfried von Strassburg
    fl. c. 1210- . . . . **CMLC 10**

Gould, Lois . . . . **CLC 4, 10**
    See also CA 77-80; CANR 29; MTCW

Gourmont, Remy de 1858-1915 . . . . **TCLC 17**
    See also CA 109

Govier, Katherine 1948- . . . . **CLC 51**
    See also CA 101; CANR 18, 40

Goyen, (Charles) William
    1915-1983 . . . . **CLC 5, 8, 14, 40**
    See also AITN 2; CA 5-8R; 110; CANR 6;
    DLB 2; DLBY 83

Goytisolo, Juan
    1931- . . . . **CLC 5, 10, 23; HLC**
    See also CA 85-88; CANR 32; HW; MTCW

Gozzi, (Conte) Carlo 1720-1806 . . **NCLC 23**

Grabbe, Christian Dietrich
    1801-1836 . . . . **NCLC 2**
    See also DLB 133

Grace, Patricia 1937- . . . . **CLC 56**

Gracian y Morales, Baltasar
    1601-1658 . . . . **LC 15**

Gracq, Julien . . . . **CLC 11, 48**
    See also Poirier, Louis
    See also DLB 83

Grade, Chaim 1910-1982 . . . . **CLC 10**
    See also CA 93-96; 107

Graduate of Oxford, A
    See Ruskin, John

Graham, John
    See Phillips, David Graham

Graham, Jorie 1951- . . . . **CLC 48**
    See also CA 111; DLB 120

Graham, R(obert) B(ontine) Cunninghame
    See Cunninghame Graham, R(obert)
    B(ontine)
    See also DLB 98, 135

Graham, Robert
    See Haldeman, Joe (William)

Graham, Tom
    See Lewis, (Harry) Sinclair

Graham, W(illiam) S(ydney)
    1918-1986 . . . . **CLC 29**
    See also CA 73-76; 118; DLB 20

Graham, Winston (Mawdsley)
    1910- . . . . **CLC 23**
    See also CA 49-52; CANR 2, 22; DLB 77

Grant, Skeeter
    See Spiegelman, Art

Granville-Barker, Harley
    1877-1946 . . . . **TCLC 2**
    See also Barker, Harley Granville
    See also CA 104

Grass, Guenter (Wilhelm)
    1927- . . . . . **CLC 1, 2, 4, 6, 11, 15, 22, 32,
                        49; DA; WLC**
    See also CA 13-16R; CANR 20; DLB 75,
    124; MTCW

Gratton, Thomas
    See Hulme, T(homas) E(rnest)

Grau, Shirley Ann
    1929- . . . . **CLC 4, 9; SSC 15**
    See also CA 89-92; CANR 22; DLB 2;
    MTCW

Gravel, Fern
    See Hall, James Norman

Graver, Elizabeth 1964- . . . . **CLC 70**
    See also CA 135

Graves, Richard Perceval 1945- . . . . **CLC 44**
    See also CA 65-68; CANR 9, 26

Graves, Robert (von Ranke)
    1895-1985 . . . . . . **CLC 1, 2, 6, 11, 39, 44,
                        45; PC 6**
    See also CA 5-8R; 117; CANR 5, 36;
    CDBLB 1914-1945; DLB 20, 100;
    DLBY 85; MTCW; SATA 45

Gray, Alasdair 1934- . . . . **CLC 41**
    See also CA 126; MTCW

Gray, Amlin 1946- . . . . **CLC 29**
    See also CA 138

Gray, Francine du Plessix 1930- . . . . **CLC 22**
    See also BEST 90:3; CA 61-64; CAAS 2;
    CANR 11, 33; MTCW

Gray, John (Henry) 1866-1934 . . . . **TCLC 19**
    See also CA 119

Gray, Simon (James Holliday)
    1936- . . . . **CLC 9, 14, 36**
    See also AITN 1; CA 21-24R; CAAS 3;
    CANR 32; DLB 13; MTCW

Gray, Spalding 1941- . . . . **CLC 49**
    See also CA 128

Gray, Thomas
    1716-1771 . . . . . . **LC 4; DA; PC 2; WLC**
    See also CDBLB 1660-1789; DLB 109

Grayson, David
    See Baker, Ray Stannard

Grayson, Richard (A.) 1951- . . . . **CLC 38**
    See also CA 85-88; CANR 14, 31

Greeley, Andrew M(oran) 1928- . . . . **CLC 28**
    See also CA 5-8R; CAAS 7; CANR 7, 43;
    MTCW

Green, Brian
    See Card, Orson Scott

Green, Hannah
    See Greenberg, Joanne (Goldenberg)

Green, Hannah . . . . **CLC 3**
    See also CA 73-76

Green, Henry . . . . **CLC 2, 13**
    See also Yorke, Henry Vincent
    See also DLB 15

Green, Julian (Hartridge) 1900-
    See Green, Julien
    See also CA 21-24R; CANR 33; DLB 4, 72;
    MTCW

Green, Julien . . . . **CLC 3, 11, 77**
    See also Green, Julian (Hartridge)

Green, Paul (Eliot) 1894-1981 . . . . . . **CLC 25**
    See also AITN 1; CA 5-8R; 103; CANR 3;
    DLB 7, 9; DLBY 81

Greenberg, Ivan 1908-1973
    See Rahv, Philip
    See also CA 85-88

Greenberg, Joanne (Goldenberg)
    1932- . . . . **CLC 7, 30**
    See also CA 5-8R; CANR 14, 32; SATA 25

Greenberg, Richard 1959(?)- . . . . **CLC 57**
    See also CA 138

Greene, Bette 1934- . . . . **CLC 30**
    See also AAYA 7; CA 53-56; CANR 4;
    CLR 2; JRDA; MAICYA; SAAS 16;
    SATA 8

Greene, Gael . . . . **CLC 8**
    See also CA 13-16R; CANR 10

Greene, Graham
    1904-1991 . . . . **CLC 1, 3, 6, 9, 14, 18, 27,
                        37, 70, 72; DA; WLC**
    See also AITN 2; CA 13-16R; 133;
    CANR 35; CDBLB 1945-1960; DLB 13,
    15, 77, 100; DLBY 91; MTCW; SATA 20

Greer, Richard
    See Silverberg, Robert

Greer, Richard
    See Silverberg, Robert

Gregor, Arthur 1923- . . . . **CLC 9**
    See also CA 25-28R; CAAS 10; CANR 11;
    SATA 36

Gregor, Lee
    See Pohl, Frederik

Gregory, Isabella Augusta (Persse)
    1852-1932 . . . . **TCLC 1**
    See also CA 104; DLB 10

Gregory, J. Dennis
    See Williams, John A(lfred)

Grendon, Stephen
    See Derleth, August (William)

Grenville, Kate 1950- . . . . **CLC 61**
    See also CA 118

Grenville, Pelham
    See Wodehouse, P(elham) G(renville)

Greve, Felix Paul (Berthold Friedrich)
    1879-1948
    See Grove, Frederick Philip
    See also CA 104; 141

Grey, Zane 1872-1939 . . . . **TCLC 6**
    See also CA 104; 132; DLB 9; MTCW

Grieg, (Johan) Nordahl (Brun)
    1902-1943 . . . . **TCLC 10**
    See also CA 107

Grieve, C(hristopher) M(urray)
    1892-1978 . . . . **CLC 11, 19**
    See also MacDiarmid, Hugh
    See also CA 5-8R; 85-88; CANR 33;
    MTCW

Griffin, Gerald 1803-1840 . . . . **NCLC 7**

Griffin, John Howard 1920-1980 . . . . **CLC 68**
    See also AITN 1; CA 1-4R; 101; CANR 2

Griffin, Peter . . . . **CLC 39**

Griffiths, Trevor 1935- . . . . **CLC 13, 52**
    See also CA 97-100; DLB 13

Grigson, Geoffrey (Edward Harvey)
    1905-1985 . . . . **CLC 7, 39**
    See also CA 25-28R; 118; CANR 20, 33;
    DLB 27; MTCW

Grillparzer, Franz 1791-1872 . . . . . . **NCLC 1**
    See also DLB 133

Grimble, Reverend Charles James
See Eliot, T(homas) S(tearns)

Grimke, Charlotte L(ottie) Forten
1837(?)-1914
See Forten, Charlotte L.
See also BW; CA 117; 124

Grimm, Jacob Ludwig Karl
1785-1863 .... NCLC 3
See also DLB 90; MAICYA; SATA 22

Grimm, Wilhelm Karl 1786-1859 .. NCLC 3
See also DLB 90; MAICYA; SATA 22

Grimmelshausen, Johann Jakob Christoffel
von 1621-1676 .... LC 6

Grindel, Eugene 1895-1952
See Eluard, Paul
See also CA 104

Grossman, David 1954- .... CLC 67
See also CA 138

Grossman, Vasily (Semenovich)
1905-1964 .... CLC 41
See also CA 124; 130; MTCW

Grove, Frederick Philip .... TCLC 4
See also Greve, Felix Paul (Berthold
Friedrich)
See also DLB 92

Grubb
See Crumb, R(obert)

Grumbach, Doris (Isaac)
1918- .... CLC 13, 22, 64
See also CA 5-8R; CAAS 2; CANR 9, 42

Grundtvig, Nicolai Frederik Severin
1783-1872 .... NCLC 1

Grunge
See Crumb, R(obert)

Grunwald, Lisa 1959- .... CLC 44
See also CA 120

Guare, John 1938- .... CLC 8, 14, 29, 67
See also CA 73-76; CANR 21; DLB 7;
MTCW

Gudjonsson, Halldor Kiljan 1902-
See Laxness, Halldor
See also CA 103

Guenter, Erich
See Eich, Guenter

Guest, Barbara 1920- .... CLC 34
See also CA 25-28R; CANR 11; DLB 5

Guest, Judith (Ann) 1936- .... CLC 8, 30
See also AAYA 7; CA 77-80; CANR 15;
MTCW

Guild, Nicholas M. 1944- .... CLC 33
See also CA 93-96

Guillemin, Jacques
See Sartre, Jean-Paul

Guillen, Jorge 1893-1984 .... CLC 11
See also CA 89-92; 112; DLB 108; HW

Guillen (y Batista), Nicolas (Cristobal)
1902-1989 ..... CLC 48, 79; BLC; HLC
See also BW; CA 116; 125; 129; HW

Guillevic, (Eugene) 1907- .... CLC 33
See also CA 93-96

Guillois
See Desnos, Robert

Guiney, Louise Imogen
1861-1920 .... TCLC 41
See also DLB 54

Guiraldes, Ricardo (Guillermo)
1886-1927 .... TCLC 39
See also CA 131; HW; MTCW

Gunn, Bill .... CLC 5
See also Gunn, William Harrison
See also DLB 38

Gunn, Thom(son William)
1929- .... CLC 3, 6, 18, 32, 81
See also CA 17-20R; CANR 9, 33;
CDBLB 1960 to Present; DLB 27;
MTCW

Gunn, William Harrison 1934(?)-1989
See Gunn, Bill
See also AITN 1; BW; CA 13-16R; 128;
CANR 12, 25

Gunnars, Kristjana 1948- .... CLC 69
See also CA 113; DLB 60

Gurganus, Allan 1947- .... CLC 70
See also BEST 90:1; CA 135

Gurney, A(lbert) R(amsdell), Jr.
1930- .... CLC 32, 50, 54
See also CA 77-80; CANR 32

Gurney, Ivor (Bertie) 1890-1937 ... TCLC 33

Gurney, Peter
See Gurney, A(lbert) R(amsdell), Jr.

Gustafson, Ralph (Barker) 1909- .... CLC 36
See also CA 21-24R; CANR 8; DLB 88

Gut, Gom
See Simenon, Georges (Jacques Christian)

Guthrie, A(lfred) B(ertram), Jr.
1901-1991 .... CLC 23
See also CA 57-60; 134; CANR 24; DLB 6;
SATA 62; SATA-Obit 67

Guthrie, Isobel
See Grieve, C(hristopher) M(urray)

Guthrie, Woodrow Wilson 1912-1967
See Guthrie, Woody
See also CA 113; 93-96

Guthrie, Woody .... CLC 35
See also Guthrie, Woodrow Wilson

Guy, Rosa (Cuthbert) 1928- .... CLC 26
See also AAYA 4; BW; CA 17-20R;
CANR 14, 34; CLR 13; DLB 33; JRDA;
MAICYA; SATA 14, 62

Gwendolyn
See Bennett, (Enoch) Arnold

H. D. .... CLC 3, 8, 14, 31, 34, 73; PC 5
See also Doolittle, Hilda

Haavikko, Paavo Juhani
1931- .... CLC 18, 34
See also CA 106

Habbema, Koos
See Heijermans, Herman

Hacker, Marilyn 1942- .... CLC 5, 9, 23, 72
See also CA 77-80; DLB 120

Haggard, H(enry) Rider
1856-1925 .... TCLC 11
See also CA 108; DLB 70; SATA 16

Haig, Fenil
See Ford, Ford Madox

Haig-Brown, Roderick (Langmere)
1908-1976 .... CLC 21
See also CA 5-8R; 69-72; CANR 4, 38;
CLR 31; DLB 88; MAICYA; SATA 12

Hailey, Arthur 1920- .... CLC 5
See also AITN 2; BEST 90:3; CA 1-4R;
CANR 2, 36; DLB 88; DLBY 82; MTCW

Hailey, Elizabeth Forsythe 1938- ... CLC 40
See also CA 93-96; CAAS 1; CANR 15

Haines, John (Meade) 1924- .... CLC 58
See also CA 17-20R; CANR 13, 34; DLB 5

Haldeman, Joe (William) 1943- ..... CLC 61
See also CA 53-56; CANR 6; DLB 8

Haley, Alex(ander Murray Palmer)
1921-1992 .... CLC 8, 12, 76; BLC; DA
See also BW; CA 77-80; 136; DLB 38;
MTCW

Haliburton, Thomas Chandler
1796-1865 .... NCLC 15
See also DLB 11, 99

Hall, Donald (Andrew, Jr.)
1928- .... CLC 1, 13, 37, 59
See also CA 5-8R; CAAS 7; CANR 2;
DLB 5; SATA 23

Hall, Frederic Sauser
See Sauser-Hall, Frederic

Hall, James
See Kuttner, Henry

Hall, James Norman 1887-1951 ... TCLC 23
See also CA 123; SATA 21

Hall, (Marguerite) Radclyffe
1886(?)-1943 .... TCLC 12
See also CA 110

Hall, Rodney 1935- .... CLC 51
See also CA 109

Halliday, Michael
See Creasey, John

Halpern, Daniel 1945- .... CLC 14
See also CA 33-36R

Hamburger, Michael (Peter Leopold)
1924- .... CLC 5, 14
See also CA 5-8R; CAAS 4; CANR 2;
DLB 27

Hamill, Pete 1935- .... CLC 10
See also CA 25-28R; CANR 18

Hamilton, Clive
See Lewis, C(live) S(taples)

Hamilton, Edmond 1904-1977 .... CLC 1
See also CA 1-4R; CANR 3; DLB 8

Hamilton, Eugene (Jacob) Lee
See Lee-Hamilton, Eugene (Jacob)

Hamilton, Franklin
See Silverberg, Robert

Hamilton, Gail
See Corcoran, Barbara

Hamilton, Mollie
See Kaye, M(ary) M(argaret)

Hamilton, (Anthony Walter) Patrick
1904-1962 .... CLC 51
See also CA 113; DLB 10

Hamilton, Virginia 1936- .... CLC 26
See also AAYA 2; BW; CA 25-28R;
CANR 20, 37; CLR 1, 11; DLB 33, 52;
JRDA; MAICYA; MTCW; SATA 4, 56

Hammett, (Samuel) Dashiell
  1894-1961 . . . . CLC 3, 5, 10, 19, 47
  See also AITN 1; CA 81-84; CANR 42;
    CDALB 1929-1941; DLBD 6; MTCW

Hammon, Jupiter
  1711(?)-1800(?) . . . . NCLC 5; BLC
  See also DLB 31, 50

Hammond, Keith
  See Kuttner, Henry

Hamner, Earl (Henry), Jr. 1923- . . . CLC 12
  See also AITN 2; CA 73-76; DLB 6

Hampton, Christopher (James)
  1946- . . . . CLC 4
  See also CA 25-28R; DLB 13; MTCW

Hamsun, Knut . . . . TCLC 2, 14, 49
  See also Pedersen, Knut

Handke, Peter 1942- . . CLC 5, 8, 10, 15, 38
  See also CA 77-80; CANR 33; DLB 85,
    124; MTCW

Hanley, James 1901-1985 . . . CLC 3, 5, 8, 13
  See also CA 73-76; 117; CANR 36; MTCW

Hannah, Barry 1942- . . . . CLC 23, 38
  See also CA 108; 110; CANR 43; DLB 6;
    MTCW

Hannon, Ezra
  See Hunter, Evan

Hansberry, Lorraine (Vivian)
  1930-1965 . . . . . . CLC 17, 62; BLC; DA;
                                                DC 2
  See also BW; CA 109; 25-28R; CABS 3;
    CDALB 1941-1968; DLB 7, 38; MTCW

Hansen, Joseph 1923- . . . . CLC 38
  See also CA 29-32R; CAAS 17; CANR 16

Hansen, Martin A. 1909-1955 . . . . . TCLC 32

Hanson, Kenneth O(stlin) 1922- . . . . CLC 13
  See also CA 53-56; CANR 7

Hardwick, Elizabeth 1916- . . . . CLC 13
  See also CA 5-8R; CANR 3, 32; DLB 6;
    MTCW

Hardy, Thomas
  1840-1928 . . . . . . TCLC 4, 10, 18, 32, 48,
                            53; DA; PC 8; SSC 2; WLC
  See also CA 104; 123; CDBLB 1890-1914;
    DLB 18, 19, 135; MTCW

Hare, David 1947- . . . . CLC 29, 58
  See also CA 97-100; CANR 39; DLB 13;
    MTCW

Harford, Henry
  See Hudson, W(illiam) H(enry)

Hargrave, Leonie
  See Disch, Thomas M(ichael)

Harlan, Louis R(udolph) 1922- . . . . . CLC 34
  See also CA 21-24R; CANR 25

Harling, Robert 1951(?)- . . . . CLC 53

Harmon, William (Ruth) 1938- . . . . . CLC 38
  See also CA 33-36R; CANR 14, 32, 35;
    SATA 65

Harper, F. E. W.
  See Harper, Frances Ellen Watkins

Harper, Frances E. W.
  See Harper, Frances Ellen Watkins

Harper, Frances E. Watkins
  See Harper, Frances Ellen Watkins

Harper, Frances Ellen
  See Harper, Frances Ellen Watkins

Harper, Frances Ellen Watkins
  1825-1911 . . . . TCLC 14; BLC
  See also BW; CA 111; 125; DLB 50

Harper, Michael S(teven) 1938- . . CLC 7, 22
  See also BW; CA 33-36R; CANR 24;
    DLB 41

Harper, Mrs. F. E. W.
  See Harper, Frances Ellen Watkins

Harris, Christie (Lucy) Irwin
  1907- . . . . CLC 12
  See also CA 5-8R; CANR 6; DLB 88;
    JRDA; MAICYA; SAAS 10; SATA 6, 74

Harris, Frank 1856(?)-1931 . . . . . . TCLC 24
  See also CA 109

Harris, George Washington
  1814-1869 . . . . NCLC 23
  See also DLB 3, 11

Harris, Joel Chandler 1848-1908 . . . TCLC 2
  See also CA 104; 137; DLB 11, 23, 42, 78,
    91; MAICYA; YABC 1

Harris, John (Wyndham Parkes Lucas)
  Beynon 1903-1969 . . . . CLC 19
  See also CA 102; 89-92

Harris, MacDonald
  See Heiney, Donald (William)

Harris, Mark 1922- . . . . CLC 19
  See also CA 5-8R; CAAS 3; CANR 2;
    DLB 2; DLBY 80

Harris, (Theodore) Wilson 1921- . . . . CLC 25
  See also BW; CA 65-68; CAAS 16;
    CANR 11, 27; DLB 117; MTCW

Harrison, Elizabeth Cavanna 1909-
  See Cavanna, Betty
  See also CA 9-12R; CANR 6, 27

Harrison, Harry (Max) 1925- . . . . . . CLC 42
  See also CA 1-4R; CANR 5, 21; DLB 8;
    SATA 4

Harrison, James (Thomas)
  1937- . . . . CLC 6, 14, 33, 66
  See also CA 13-16R; CANR 8; DLBY 82

Harrison, Kathryn 1961- . . . . CLC 70

Harrison, Tony 1937- . . . . CLC 43
  See also CA 65-68; DLB 40; MTCW

Harriss, Will(ard Irvin) 1922- . . . . . . CLC 34
  See also CA 111

Harson, Sley
  See Ellison, Harlan

Hart, Ellis
  See Ellison, Harlan

Hart, Josephine 1942(?)- . . . . CLC 70
  See also CA 138

Hart, Moss 1904-1961 . . . . CLC 66
  See also CA 109; 89-92; DLB 7

Harte, (Francis) Bret(t)
  1836(?)-1902 . . . . TCLC 1, 25; DA;
                                        SSC 8; WLC
  See also CA 104; 140; CDALB 1865-1917;
    DLB 12, 64, 74, 79; SATA 26

Hartley, L(eslie) P(oles)
  1895-1972 . . . . CLC 2, 22
  See also CA 45-48; 37-40R; CANR 33;
    DLB 15; MTCW

Hartman, Geoffrey H. 1929- . . . . CLC 27
  See also CA 117; 125; DLB 67

Haruf, Kent 19(?)- . . . . CLC 34

Harwood, Ronald 1934- . . . . CLC 32
  See also CA 1-4R; CANR 4; DLB 13

Hasek, Jaroslav (Matej Frantisek)
  1883-1923 . . . . TCLC 4
  See also CA 104; 129; MTCW

Hass, Robert 1941- . . . . CLC 18, 39
  See also CA 111; CANR 30; DLB 105

Hastings, Hudson
  See Kuttner, Henry

Hastings, Selina. . . . . CLC 44

Hatteras, Amelia
  See Mencken, H(enry) L(ouis)

Hatteras, Owen. . . . . TCLC 18
  See also Mencken, H(enry) L(ouis); Nathan,
    George Jean

Hauptmann, Gerhart (Johann Robert)
  1862-1946 . . . . TCLC 4
  See also CA 104; DLB 66, 118

Havel, Vaclav 1936- . . . . CLC 25, 58, 65
  See also CA 104; CANR 36; MTCW

Haviaras, Stratis. . . . . CLC 33
  See also Chaviaras, Strates

Hawes, Stephen 1475(?)-1523(?) . . . . . LC 17

Hawkes, John (Clendennin Burne, Jr.)
  1925- . . . . . . CLC 1, 2, 3, 4, 7, 9, 14, 15,
                                            27, 49
  See also CA 1-4R; CANR 2; DLB 2, 7;
    DLBY 80; MTCW

Hawking, S. W.
  See Hawking, Stephen W(illiam)

Hawking, Stephen W(illiam)
  1942- . . . . CLC 63
  See also BEST 89:1; CA 126; 129

Hawthorne, Julian 1846-1934 . . . . . TCLC 25

Hawthorne, Nathaniel
  1804-1864 . . . . . . NCLC 39; DA; SSC 3;
                                                WLC
  See also CDALB 1640-1865; DLB 1, 74;
    YABC 2

Haxton, Josephine Ayres 1921- . . . . CLC 73
  See also CA 115; CANR 41

Hayaseca y Eizaguirre, Jorge
  See Echegaray (y Eizaguirre), Jose (Maria
    Waldo)

Hayashi Fumiko 1904-1951 . . . . TCLC 27

Haycraft, Anna
  See Ellis, Alice Thomas
  See also CA 122

Hayden, Robert E(arl)
  1913-1980 . . . . . . CLC 5, 9, 14, 37; BLC;
                                        DA; PC 6
  See also BW; CA 69-72; 97-100; CABS 2;
    CANR 24; CDALB 1941-1968; DLB 5,
    76; MTCW; SATA 19, 26

Hayford, J(oseph) E(phraim) Casely
  See Casely-Hayford, J(oseph) E(phraim)

Hayman, Ronald 1932- . . . . CLC 44
  See also CA 25-28R; CANR 18

Haywood, Eliza (Fowler)
  1693(?)-1756 . . . . LC 1

Hazlitt, William 1778-1830 ...... **NCLC 29**
See also DLB 110

Hazzard, Shirley 1931- .... **CLC 18**
See also CA 9-12R; CANR 4; DLBY 82;
MTCW

Head, Bessie 1937-1986 ... **CLC 25, 67; BLC**
See also BW; CA 29-32R; 119; CANR 25;
DLB 117; MTCW

Headon, (Nicky) Topper 1956(?)- ... **CLC 30**
See also Clash, The

Heaney, Seamus (Justin)
1939- .... **CLC 5, 7, 14, 25, 37, 74**
See also CA 85-88; CANR 25;
CDBLB 1960 to Present; DLB 40;
MTCW

Hearn, (Patricio) Lafcadio (Tessima Carlos)
1850-1904 .... **TCLC 9**
See also CA 105; DLB 12, 78

Hearne, Vicki 1946- .... **CLC 56**
See also CA 139

Hearon, Shelby 1931-............ **CLC 63**
See also AITN 2; CA 25-28R; CANR 18

Heat-Moon, William Least.......... CLC 29
See also Trogdon, William (Lewis)
See also AAYA 9

Hebbel, Friedrich 1813-1863 ..... **NCLC 43**
See also DLB 129

Hebert, Anne 1916- .... **CLC 4, 13, 29**
See also CA 85-88; DLB 68; MTCW

Hecht, Anthony (Evan)
1923- .... **CLC 8, 13, 19**
See also CA 9-12R; CANR 6; DLB 5

Hecht, Ben 1894-1964 .... **CLC 8**
See also CA 85-88; DLB 7, 9, 25, 26, 28, 86

Hedayat, Sadeq 1903-1951....... **TCLC 21**
See also CA 120

Heidegger, Martin 1889-1976 ...... **CLC 24**
See also CA 81-84; 65-68; CANR 34;
MTCW

Heidenstam, (Carl Gustaf) Verner von
1859-1940 .... **TCLC 5**
See also CA 104

Heifner, Jack 1946- .... **CLC 11**
See also CA 105

Heijermans, Herman 1864-1924 ... **TCLC 24**
See also CA 123

Heilbrun, Carolyn G(old) 1926-..... **CLC 25**
See also CA 45-48; CANR 1, 28

Heine, Heinrich 1797-1856 .... **NCLC 4**
See also DLB 90

Heinemann, Larry (Curtiss) 1944- .. **CLC 50**
See also CA 110; CANR 31; DLBD 9

Heiney, Donald (William)
1921-1993 .... **CLC 9**
See also CA 1-4R; 142; CANR 3

Heinlein, Robert A(nson)
1907-1988 ...... **CLC 1, 3, 8, 14, 26, 55**
See also CA 1-4R; 125; CANR 1, 20;
DLB 8; JRDA; MAICYA; MTCW;
SATA 9, 56, 69

Helforth, John
See Doolittle, Hilda

Hellenhofferu, Vojtech Kapristian z
See Hasek, Jaroslav (Matej Frantisek)

Heller, Joseph
1923- .... **CLC 1, 3, 5, 8, 11, 36, 63; DA;**
WLC
See also AITN 1; CA 5-8R; CABS 1;
CANR 8, 42; DLB 2, 28; DLBY 80;
MTCW

Hellman, Lillian (Florence)
1906-1984 ...... **CLC 2, 4, 8, 14, 18, 34,**
44, 52; DC 1
See also AITN 1, 2; CA 13-16R; 112;
CANR 33; DLB 7; DLBY 84; MTCW

Helprin, Mark 1947- ..... **CLC 7, 10, 22, 32**
See also CA 81-84; DLBY 85; MTCW

Helyar, Jane Penelope Josephine 1933-
See Poole, Josephine
See also CA 21-24R; CANR 10, 26

Hemans, Felicia 1793-1835 ...... **NCLC 29**
See also DLB 96

Hemingway, Ernest (Miller)
1899-1961 .... **CLC 1, 3, 6, 8, 10, 13, 19,**
30, 34, 39, 41, 44, 50, 61, 80; DA; SSC 1;
WLC
See also CA 77-80; CANR 34;
CDALB 1917-1929; DLB 4, 9, 102;
DLBD 1; DLBY 81, 87; MTCW

Hempel, Amy 1951- .... **CLC 39**
See also CA 118; 137

Henderson, F. C.
See Mencken, H(enry) L(ouis)

Henderson, Sylvia
See Ashton-Warner, Sylvia (Constance)

Henley, Beth .... **CLC 23**
See also Henley, Elizabeth Becker
See also CABS 3; DLBY 86

Henley, Elizabeth Becker 1952-
See Henley, Beth
See also CA 107; CANR 32; MTCW

Henley, William Ernest
1849-1903 .... **TCLC 8**
See also CA 105; DLB 19

Hennissart, Martha
See Lathen, Emma
See also CA 85-88

Henry, O.......... TCLC 1, 19; SSC 5; WLC
See also Porter, William Sydney

Henry, Patrick 1736-1799 .... **LC 25**

Henryson, Robert 1430(?)-1506(?).... **LC 20**

Henry VIII 1491-1547 .... **LC 10**

Henschke, Alfred
See Klabund

Hentoff, Nat(han Irving) 1925- ..... **CLC 26**
See also AAYA 4; CA 1-4R; CAAS 6;
CANR 5, 25; CLR 1; JRDA; MAICYA;
SATA 27, 42, 69

Heppenstall, (John) Rayner
1911-1981 .... **CLC 10**
See also CA 1-4R; 103; CANR 29

Herbert, Frank (Patrick)
1920-1986 .... **CLC 12, 23, 35, 44**
See also CA 53-56; 118; CANR 5, 43;
DLB 8; MTCW; SATA 9, 37, 47

Herbert, George 1593-1633 .... **LC 24; PC 4**
See also CDBLB Before 1660; DLB 126

Herbert, Zbigniew 1924- .... **CLC 9, 43**
See also CA 89-92; CANR 36; MTCW

Herbst, Josephine (Frey)
1897-1969 .... **CLC 34**
See also CA 5-8R; 25-28R; DLB 9

Hergesheimer, Joseph
1880-1954 .... **TCLC 11**
See also CA 109; DLB 102, 9

Herlihy, James Leo 1927-1993 ...... **CLC 6**
See also CA 1-4R; 143; CANR 2

Hermogenes fl. c. 175- .... **CMLC 6**

Hernandez, Jose 1834-1886...... **NCLC 17**

Herrick, Robert 1591-1674 ..... **LC 13; DA**
See also DLB 126

Herring, Guilles
See Somerville, Edith

Herriot, James 1916- .... **CLC 12**
See also Wight, James Alfred
See also AAYA 1; CANR 40

Herrmann, Dorothy 1941-......... **CLC 44**
See also CA 107

Herrmann, Taffy
See Herrmann, Dorothy

Hersey, John (Richard)
1914-1993 .... **CLC 1, 2, 7, 9, 40, 81**
See also CA 17-20R; 140; CANR 33;
DLB 6; MTCW; SATA 25;
SATA-Obit 76

Herzen, Aleksandr Ivanovich
1812-1870 .... **NCLC 10**

Herzl, Theodor 1860-1904....... **TCLC 36**

Herzog, Werner 1942- .... **CLC 16**
See also CA 89-92

Hesiod c. 8th cent. B.C.- .... **CMLC 5**

Hesse, Hermann
1877-1962 .... **CLC 1, 2, 3, 6, 11, 17, 25,**
69; DA; SSC 9; WLC
See also CA 17-18; CAP 2; DLB 66;
MTCW; SATA 50

Hewes, Cady
See De Voto, Bernard (Augustine)

Heyen, William 1940- .... **CLC 13, 18**
See also CA 33-36R; CAAS 9; DLB 5

Heyerdahl, Thor 1914-............ **CLC 26**
See also CA 5-8R; CANR 5, 22; MTCW;
SATA 2, 52

Heym, Georg (Theodor Franz Arthur)
1887-1912 .... **TCLC 9**
See also CA 106

Heym, Stefan 1913- .... **CLC 41**
See also CA 9-12R; CANR 4; DLB 69

Heyse, Paul (Johann Ludwig von)
1830-1914 .... **TCLC 8**
See also CA 104; DLB 129

Hibbert, Eleanor Alice Burford
1906-1993 .... **CLC 7**
See also BEST 90:4; CA 17-20R; 140;
CANR 9, 28; SATA 2; SATA-Obit 74

Higgins, George V(incent)
1939- .... **CLC 4, 7, 10, 18**
See also CA 77-80; CAAS 5; CANR 17;
DLB 2; DLBY 81; MTCW

Higginson, Thomas Wentworth
1823-1911 .... **TCLC 36**
See also DLB 1, 64

Highet, Helen
See MacInnes, Helen (Clark)

Highsmith, (Mary) Patricia
1921- . . . . **CLC 2, 4, 14, 42**
See also CA 1-4R; CANR 1, 20; MTCW

Highwater, Jamake (Mamake)
1942(?)- . . . . **CLC 12**
See also AAYA 7; CA 65-68; CAAS 7;
CANR 10, 34; CLR 17; DLB 52;
DLBY 85; JRDA; MAICYA; SATA 30,
32, 69

Hijuelos, Oscar 1951- . . . . . . **CLC 65; HLC**
See also BEST 90:1; CA 123; HW

Hikmet, Nazim 1902(?)-1963. . . . . . **CLC 40**
See also CA 141; 93-96

Hildesheimer, Wolfgang
1916-1991 . . . . **CLC 49**
See also CA 101; 135; DLB 69, 124

Hill, Geoffrey (William)
1932- . . . . **CLC 5, 8, 18, 45**
See also CA 81-84; CANR 21;
CDBLB 1960 to Present; DLB 40;
MTCW

Hill, George Roy 1921- . . . . **CLC 26**
See also CA 110; 122

Hill, John
See Koontz, Dean R(ay)

Hill, Susan (Elizabeth) 1942- . . . . **CLC 4**
See also CA 33-36R; CANR 29; DLB 14;
MTCW

Hillerman, Tony 1925-. . . . . **CLC 62**
See also AAYA 6; BEST 89:1; CA 29-32R;
CANR 21, 42; SATA 6

Hillesum, Etty 1914-1943 . . . . **TCLC 49**
See also CA 137

Hilliard, Noel (Harvey) 1929-. . . . . . **CLC 15**
See also CA 9-12R; CANR 7

Hillis, Rick 1956-. . . . . **CLC 66**
See also CA 134

Hilton, James 1900-1954. . . . . **TCLC 21**
See also CA 108; DLB 34, 77; SATA 34

Himes, Chester (Bomar)
1909-1984 . . . . **CLC 2, 4, 7, 18, 58; BLC**
See also BW; CA 25-28R; 114; CANR 22;
DLB 2, 76; MTCW

Hinde, Thomas . . . . **CLC 6, 11**
See also Chitty, Thomas Willes

Hindin, Nathan
See Bloch, Robert (Albert)

Hine, (William) Daryl 1936-. . . . . . . **CLC 15**
See also CA 1-4R; CAAS 15; CANR 1, 20;
DLB 60

Hinkson, Katharine Tynan
See Tynan, Katharine

Hinton, S(usan) E(loise)
1950- . . . . **CLC 30; DA**
See also AAYA 2; CA 81-84; CANR 32;
CLR 3, 23; JRDA; MAICYA; MTCW;
SATA 19, 58

Hippius, Zinaida . . . . **TCLC 9**
See also Gippius, Zinaida (Nikolayevna)

Hiraoka, Kimitake 1925-1970
See Mishima, Yukio
See also CA 97-100; 29-32R; MTCW

Hirsch, E(ric) D(onald), Jr. 1928-. . . **CLC 79**
See also CA 25-28R; CANR 27; DLB 67;
MTCW

Hirsch, Edward 1950- . . . . **CLC 31, 50**
See also CA 104; CANR 20, 42; DLB 120

Hitchcock, Alfred (Joseph)
1899-1980 . . . . **CLC 16**
See also CA 97-100; SATA 24, 27

Hitler, Adolf 1889-1945. . . . . **TCLC 53**
See also CA 117

Hoagland, Edward 1932-. . . . . **CLC 28**
See also CA 1-4R; CANR 2, 31; DLB 6;
SATA 51

Hoban, Russell (Conwell) 1925- . . **CLC 7, 25**
See also CA 5-8R; CANR 23, 37; CLR 3;
DLB 52; MAICYA; MTCW; SATA 1, 40

Hobbs, Perry
See Blackmur, R(ichard) P(almer)

Hobson, Laura Z(ametkin)
1900-1986 . . . . **CLC 7, 25**
See also CA 17-20R; 118; DLB 28;
SATA 52

Hochhuth, Rolf 1931-. . . . . . . **CLC 4, 11, 18**
See also CA 5-8R; CANR 33; DLB 124;
MTCW

Hochman, Sandra 1936-. . . . . **CLC 3, 8**
See also CA 5-8R; DLB 5

Hochwaelder, Fritz 1911-1986. . . . . . **CLC 36**
See also CA 29-32R; 120; CANR 42;
MTCW

Hochwalder, Fritz
See Hochwaelder, Fritz

Hocking, Mary (Eunice) 1921-. . . . . **CLC 13**
See also CA 101; CANR 18, 40

Hodgins, Jack 1938-. . . . . **CLC 23**
See also CA 93-96; DLB 60

Hodgson, William Hope
1877(?)-1918 . . . . **TCLC 13**
See also CA 111; DLB 70

Hoffman, Alice 1952-. . . . . **CLC 51**
See also CA 77-80; CANR 34; MTCW

Hoffman, Daniel (Gerard)
1923-. . . . . **CLC 6, 13, 23**
See also CA 1-4R; CANR 4; DLB 5

Hoffman, Stanley 1944-. . . . . **CLC 5**
See also CA 77-80

Hoffman, William M(oses) 1939- . . . **CLC 40**
See also CA 57-60; CANR 11

Hoffmann, E(rnst) T(heodor) A(madeus)
1776-1822 . . . . **NCLC 2; SSC 13**
See also DLB 90; SATA 27

Hofmann, Gert 1931-. . . . . **CLC 54**
See also CA 128

Hofmannsthal, Hugo von
1874-1929 . . . . **TCLC 11; DC 4**
See also CA 106; DLB 81, 118

Hogan, Linda 1947-. . . . . **CLC 73**
See also CA 120

Hogarth, Charles
See Creasey, John

Hogg, James 1770-1835. . . . . **NCLC 4**
See also DLB 93, 116

Holbach, Paul Henri Thiry Baron
1723-1789 . . . . **LC 14**

Holberg, Ludvig 1684-1754 . . . . **LC 6**

Holden, Ursula 1921-. . . . . **CLC 18**
See also CA 101; CAAS 8; CANR 22

Holderlin, (Johann Christian) Friedrich
1770-1843 . . . . **NCLC 16; PC 4**

Holdstock, Robert
See Holdstock, Robert P.

Holdstock, Robert P. 1948-. . . . . . . **CLC 39**
See also CA 131

Holland, Isabelle 1920- . . . . **CLC 21**
See also CA 21-24R; CANR 10, 25; JRDA;
MAICYA; SATA 8, 70

Holland, Marcus
See Caldwell, (Janet Miriam) Taylor
(Holland)

Hollander, John 1929-. . . . . . **CLC 2, 5, 8, 14**
See also CA 1-4R; CANR 1; DLB 5;
SATA 13

Hollander, Paul
See Silverberg, Robert

Holleran, Andrew 1943(?)-. . . . . **CLC 38**

Hollinghurst, Alan 1954-. . . . . **CLC 55**
See also CA 114

Hollis, Jim
See Summers, Hollis (Spurgeon, Jr.)

Holmes, John
See Souster, (Holmes) Raymond

Holmes, John Clellon 1926-1988. . . . **CLC 56**
See also CA 9-12R; 125; CANR 4; DLB 16

Holmes, Oliver Wendell
1809-1894 . . . . **NCLC 14**
See also CDALB 1640-1865; DLB 1;
SATA 34

Holmes, Raymond
See Souster, (Holmes) Raymond

Holt, Victoria
See Hibbert, Eleanor Alice Burford

Holub, Miroslav 1923-. . . . . **CLC 4**
See also CA 21-24R; CANR 10

Homer c. 8th cent. B.C.-. . . . . **CMLC 1; DA**

Honig, Edwin 1919-. . . . . **CLC 33**
See also CA 5-8R; CAAS 8; CANR 4;
DLB 5

Hood, Hugh (John Blagdon)
1928-. . . . . **CLC 15, 28**
See also CA 49-52; CAAS 17; CANR 1, 33;
DLB 53

Hood, Thomas 1799-1845. . . . . **NCLC 16**
See also DLB 96

Hooker, (Peter) Jeremy 1941-. . . . . . **CLC 43**
See also CA 77-80; CANR 22; DLB 40

Hope, A(lec) D(erwent) 1907-. . . . **CLC 3, 51**
See also CA 21-24R; CANR 33; MTCW

Hope, Brian
See Creasey, John

Hope, Christopher (David Tully)
1944-. . . . . **CLC 52**
See also CA 106; SATA 62

Hopkins, Gerard Manley
1844-1889 . . . . **NCLC 17; DA; WLC**
See also CDBLB 1890-1914; DLB 35, 57

Hopkins, John (Richard) 1931-. . . . . . **CLC 4**
See also CA 85-88

Hopkins, Pauline Elizabeth
1859-1930 . . . . TCLC **28**; BLC
See also CA 141; DLB 50

Hopkinson, Francis   1737-1791 . . . . . . LC **25**
See also DLB 31

Hopley-Woolrich, Cornell George   1903-1968
See Woolrich, Cornell
See also CA 13-14; CAP 1

Horatio
See Proust, (Valentin-Louis-George-Eugene-)
Marcel

Horgan, Paul   1903- . . . . CLC **9, 53**
See also CA 13-16R; CANR 9, 35;
DLB 102; DLBY 85; MTCW; SATA 13

Horn, Peter
See Kuttner, Henry

Hornem, Horace Esq.
See Byron, George Gordon (Noel)

Horovitz, Israel   1939- . . . . CLC **56**
See also CA 33-36R; DLB 7

Horvath, Odon von
See Horvath, Oedoen von
See also DLB 85, 124

Horvath, Oedoen von   1901-1938 . . . TCLC **45**
See also Horvath, Odon von
See also CA 118

Horwitz, Julius   1920-1986 . . . . CLC **14**
See also CA 9-12R; 119; CANR 12

Hospital, Janette Turner   1942- . . . . . CLC **42**
See also CA 108

Hostos, E. M. de
See Hostos (y Bonilla), Eugenio Maria de

Hostos, Eugenio M. de
See Hostos (y Bonilla), Eugenio Maria de

Hostos, Eugenio Maria
See Hostos (y Bonilla), Eugenio Maria de

Hostos (y Bonilla), Eugenio Maria de
1839-1903 . . . . TCLC **24**
See also CA 123; 131; HW

Houdini
See Lovecraft, H(oward) P(hillips)

Hougan, Carolyn   1943- . . . . CLC **34**
See also CA 139

Household, Geoffrey (Edward West)
1900-1988 . . . . CLC **11**
See also CA 77-80; 126; DLB 87; SATA 14,
59

Housman, A(lfred) E(dward)
1859-1936 . . . . . . TCLC **1, 10**; DA; PC **2**
See also CA 104; 125; DLB 19; MTCW

Housman, Laurence   1865-1959 . . . . . TCLC **7**
See also CA 106; DLB 10; SATA 25

Howard, Elizabeth Jane   1923- . . . CLC **7, 29**
See also CA 5-8R; CANR 8

Howard, Maureen   1930- . . . . . CLC **5, 14, 46**
See also CA 53-56; CANR 31; DLBY 83;
MTCW

Howard, Richard   1929- . . . . . . CLC **7, 10, 47**
See also AITN 1; CA 85-88; CANR 25;
DLB 5

Howard, Robert Ervin   1906-1936 . . . TCLC **8**
See also CA 105

Howard, Warren F.
See Pohl, Frederik

Howe, Fanny   1940- . . . . CLC **47**
See also CA 117; SATA 52

Howe, Julia Ward   1819-1910 . . . . . TCLC **21**
See also CA 117; DLB 1

Howe, Susan   1937- . . . . CLC **72**
See also DLB 120

Howe, Tina   1937- . . . . CLC **48**
See also CA 109

Howell, James   1594(?)-1666 . . . . LC **13**

Howells, W. D.
See Howells, William Dean

Howells, William D.
See Howells, William Dean

Howells, William Dean
1837-1920 . . . . TCLC **7, 17, 41**
See also CA 104; 134; CDALB 1865-1917;
DLB 12, 64, 74, 79

Howes, Barbara   1914- . . . . CLC **15**
See also CA 9-12R; CAAS 3; SATA 5

Hrabal, Bohumil   1914- . . . . CLC **13, 67**
See also CA 106; CAAS 12

Hsun, Lu . . . . TCLC **3**
See also Shu-Jen, Chou

Hubbard, L(afayette) Ron(ald)
1911-1986 . . . . CLC **43**
See also CA 77-80; 118; CANR 22

Huch, Ricarda (Octavia)
1864-1947 . . . . TCLC **13**
See also CA 111; DLB 66

Huddle, David   1942- . . . . CLC **49**
See also CA 57-60; DLB 130

Hudson, Jeffrey
See Crichton, (John) Michael

Hudson, W(illiam) H(enry)
1841-1922 . . . . TCLC **29**
See also CA 115; DLB 98; SATA 35

Hueffer, Ford Madox
See Ford, Ford Madox

Hughart, Barry   1934- . . . . CLC **39**
See also CA 137

Hughes, Colin
See Creasey, John

Hughes, David (John)   1930- . . . . CLC **48**
See also CA 116; 129; DLB 14

Hughes, (James) Langston
1902-1967 . . . . . CLC **1, 5, 10, 15, 35, 44**;
BLC; DA; DC **3**; PC **1**; SSC **6**; WLC
See also BW; CA 1-4R; 25-28R; CANR 1,
34; CDALB 1929-1941; CLR 17; DLB 4,
7, 48, 51, 86; JRDA; MAICYA; MTCW;
SATA 4, 33

Hughes, Richard (Arthur Warren)
1900-1976 . . . . CLC **1, 11**
See also CA 5-8R; 65-68; CANR 4;
DLB 15; MTCW; SATA 8, 25

Hughes, Ted
1930- . . . . CLC **2, 4, 9, 14, 37**; PC **7**
See also CA 1-4R; CANR 1, 33; CLR 3;
DLB 40; MAICYA; MTCW; SATA 27,
49

Hugo, Richard F(ranklin)
1923-1982 . . . . CLC **6, 18, 32**
See also CA 49-52; 108; CANR 3; DLB 5

Hugo, Victor (Marie)
1802-1885 . . NCLC **3, 10, 21**; DA; WLC
See also DLB 119; SATA 47

Huidobro, Vicente
See Huidobro Fernandez, Vicente Garcia

Huidobro Fernandez, Vicente Garcia
1893-1948 . . . . TCLC **31**
See also CA 131; HW

Hulme, Keri   1947- . . . . CLC **39**
See also CA 125

Hulme, T(homas) E(rnest)
1883-1917 . . . . TCLC **21**
See also CA 117; DLB 19

Hume, David   1711-1776 . . . . LC **7**
See also DLB 104

Humphrey, William   1924- . . . . CLC **45**
See also CA 77-80; DLB 6

Humphreys, Emyr Owen   1919- . . . . . CLC **47**
See also CA 5-8R; CANR 3, 24; DLB 15

Humphreys, Josephine   1945- . . . . CLC **34, 57**
See also CA 121; 127

Hungerford, Pixie
See Brinsmead, H(esba) F(ay)

Hunt, E(verette) Howard, Jr.
1918- . . . . CLC **3**
See also AITN 1; CA 45-48; CANR 2

Hunt, Kyle
See Creasey, John

Hunt, (James Henry) Leigh
1784-1859 . . . . NCLC **1**

Hunt, Marsha   1946- . . . . CLC **70**
See also CA 143

Hunt, Violet   1866-1942 . . . . TCLC **53**

Hunter, E. Waldo
See Sturgeon, Theodore (Hamilton)

Hunter, Evan   1926- . . . . CLC **11, 31**
See also CA 5-8R; CANR 5, 38; DLBY 82;
MTCW; SATA 25

Hunter, Kristin (Eggleston)   1931- . . . CLC **35**
See also AITN 1; BW; CA 13-16R;
CANR 13; CLR 3; DLB 33; MAICYA;
SAAS 10; SATA 12

Hunter, Mollie   1922- . . . . CLC **21**
See also McIlwraith, Maureen Mollie
Hunter
See also CANR 37; CLR 25; JRDA;
MAICYA; SAAS 7; SATA 54

Hunter, Robert   (?)-1734 . . . . LC **7**

Hurston, Zora Neale
1903-1960 . . . . CLC **7, 30, 61**; BLC; DA;
SSC **4**
See also BW; CA 85-88; DLB 51, 86;
MTCW

Huston, John (Marcellus)
1906-1987 . . . . CLC **20**
See also CA 73-76; 123; CANR 34; DLB 26

Hustvedt, Siri   1955- . . . . CLC **76**
See also CA 137

Hutten, Ulrich von   1488-1523 . . . . LC **16**

Huxley, Aldous (Leonard)
1894-1963 . . . . . CLC **1, 3, 4, 5, 8, 11, 18,
35, 79**; DA; WLC
See also CA 85-88; CDBLB 1914-1945;
DLB 36, 100; MTCW; SATA 63

Jeffers, (John) Robinson
1887-1962 .... **CLC 2, 3, 11, 15, 54; DA; WLC**
See also CA 85-88; CANR 35; CDALB 1917-1929; DLB 45; MTCW

Jefferson, Janet
See Mencken, H(enry) L(ouis)

Jefferson, Thomas 1743-1826 .... **NCLC 11**
See also CDALB 1640-1865; DLB 31

Jeffrey, Francis 1773-1850...... **NCLC 33**
See also DLB 107

Jelakowitch, Ivan
See Heijermans, Herman

Jellicoe, (Patricia) Ann 1927-...... **CLC 27**
See also CA 85-88; DLB 13

Jen, Gish .... **CLC 70**
See also Jen, Lillian

Jen, Lillian 1956(?)-
See Jen, Gish
See also CA 135

Jenkins, (John) Robin 1912-....... **CLC 52**
See also CA 1-4R; CANR 1; DLB 14

Jennings, Elizabeth (Joan)
1926-..................... **CLC 5, 14**
See also CA 61-64; CAAS 5; CANR 8, 39; DLB 27; MTCW; SATA 66

Jennings, Waylon 1937-.......... **CLC 21**

Jensen, Johannes V. 1873-1950.... **TCLC 41**

Jensen, Laura (Linnea) 1948-...... **CLC 37**
See also CA 103

Jerome, Jerome K(lapka)
1859-1927 .... **TCLC 23**
See also CA 119; DLB 10, 34, 135

Jerrold, Douglas William
1803-1857 .... **NCLC 2**

Jewett, (Theodora) Sarah Orne
1849-1909 .... **TCLC 1, 22; SSC 6**
See also CA 108; 127; DLB 12, 74; SATA 15

Jewsbury, Geraldine (Endsor)
1812-1880 .... **NCLC 22**
See also DLB 21

Jhabvala, Ruth Prawer
1927-.................. **CLC 4, 8, 29**
See also CA 1-4R; CANR 2, 29; MTCW

Jiles, Paulette 1943-.......... **CLC 13, 58**
See also CA 101

Jimenez (Mantecon), Juan Ramon
1881-1958 .... **TCLC 4; HLC; PC 7**
See also CA 104; 131; DLB 134; HW; MTCW

Jimenez, Ramon
See Jimenez (Mantecon), Juan Ramon

Jimenez Mantecon, Juan
See Jimenez (Mantecon), Juan Ramon

Joel, Billy .... **CLC 26**
See also Joel, William Martin

Joel, William Martin 1949-
See Joel, Billy
See also CA 108

John of the Cross, St. 1542-1591 .... **LC 18**

Johnson, B(ryan) S(tanley William)
1933-1973 .... **CLC 6, 9**
See also CA 9-12R; 53-56; CANR 9; DLB 14, 40

Johnson, Benj. F. of Boo
See Riley, James Whitcomb

Johnson, Benjamin F. of Boo
See Riley, James Whitcomb

Johnson, Charles (Richard)
1948-............. **CLC 7, 51, 65; BLC**
See also BW; CA 116; CAAS 18; CANR 42; DLB 33

Johnson, Denis 1949-............. **CLC 52**
See also CA 117; 121; DLB 120

Johnson, Diane 1934-........ **CLC 5, 13, 48**
See also CA 41-44R; CANR 17, 40; DLBY 80; MTCW

Johnson, Eyvind (Olof Verner)
1900-1976 .... **CLC 14**
See also CA 73-76; 69-72; CANR 34

Johnson, J. R.
See James, C(yril) L(ionel) R(obert)

Johnson, James Weldon
1871-1938 .... **TCLC 3, 19; BLC**
See also BW; CA 104; 125; CDALB 1917-1929; CLR 32; DLB 51; MTCW; SATA 31

Johnson, Joyce 1935-............. **CLC 58**
See also CA 125; 129

Johnson, Lionel (Pigot)
1867-1902 .... **TCLC 19**
See also CA 117; DLB 19

Johnson, Mel
See Malzberg, Barry N(athaniel)

Johnson, Pamela Hansford
1912-1981 .... **CLC 1, 7, 27**
See also CA 1-4R; 104; CANR 2, 28; DLB 15; MTCW

Johnson, Samuel
1709-1784 ....**LC 15; DA; WLC**
See also CDBLB 1660-1789; DLB 39, 95, 104

Johnson, Uwe
1934-1984 .... **CLC 5, 10, 15, 40**
See also CA 1-4R; 112; CANR 1, 39; DLB 75; MTCW

Johnston, George (Benson) 1913-... **CLC 51**
See also CA 1-4R; CANR 5, 20; DLB 88

Johnston, Jennifer 1930-........... **CLC 7**
See also CA 85-88; DLB 14

Jolley, (Monica) Elizabeth 1923-... **CLC 46**
See also CA 127; CAAS 13

Jones, Arthur Llewellyn 1863-1947
See Machen, Arthur
See also CA 104

Jones, D(ouglas) G(ordon) 1929-.... **CLC 10**
See also CA 29-32R; CANR 13; DLB 53

Jones, David (Michael)
1895-1974 .... **CLC 2, 4, 7, 13, 42**
See also CA 9-12R; 53-56; CANR 28; CDBLB 1945-1960; DLB 20, 100; MTCW

Jones, David Robert 1947-
See Bowie, David
See also CA 103

Jones, Diana Wynne 1934- .... **CLC 26**
See also CA 49-52; CANR 4, 26; CLR 23; JRDA; MAICYA; SAAS 7; SATA 9, 70

Jones, Edward P. 1950-.......... **CLC 76**
See also CA 142

Jones, Gayl 1949-........... **CLC 6, 9; BLC**
See also BW; CA 77-80; CANR 27; DLB 33; MTCW

Jones, James 1921-1977.... **CLC 1, 3, 10, 39**
See also AITN 1, 2; CA 1-4R; 69-72; CANR 6; DLB 2; MTCW

Jones, John J.
See Lovecraft, H(oward) P(hillips)

Jones, LeRoi .... **CLC 1, 2, 3, 5, 10, 14**
See also Baraka, Amiri

Jones, Louis B. .... **CLC 65**
See also CA 141

Jones, Madison (Percy, Jr.) 1925- ... **CLC 4**
See also CA 13-16R; CAAS 11; CANR 7

Jones, Mervyn 1922-.......... **CLC 10, 52**
See also CA 45-48; CAAS 5; CANR 1; MTCW

Jones, Mick 1956(?)-............. **CLC 30**
See also Clash, The

Jones, Nettie (Pearl) 1941-........ **CLC 34**
See also CA 137

Jones, Preston 1936-1979 .... **CLC 10**
See also CA 73-76; 89-92; DLB 7

Jones, Robert F(rancis) 1934-....... **CLC 7**
See also CA 49-52; CANR 2

Jones, Rod 1953- .... **CLC 50**
See also CA 128

Jones, Terence Graham Parry
1942-...................... **CLC 21**
See also Jones, Terry; Monty Python
See also CA 112; 116; CANR 35; SATA 51

Jones, Terry
See Jones, Terence Graham Parry
See also SATA 67

Jones, Thom 1945(?)-............. **CLC 81**

Jong, Erica 1942-........... **CLC 4, 6, 8, 18**
See also AITN 1; BEST 90:2; CA 73-76; CANR 26; DLB 2, 5, 28; MTCW

Jonson, Ben(jamin)
1572(?)-1637 .... **LC 6; DA; DC 4; WLC**
See also CDBLB Before 1660; DLB 62, 121

Jordan, June 1936-.......... **CLC 5, 11, 23**
See also AAYA 2; BW; CA 33-36R; CANR 25; CLR 10; DLB 38; MAICYA; MTCW; SATA 4

Jordan, Pat(rick M.) 1941-........ **CLC 37**
See also CA 33-36R

Jorgensen, Ivar
See Ellison, Harlan

Jorgenson, Ivar
See Silverberg, Robert

Josipovici, Gabriel 1940-........ **CLC 6, 43**
See also CA 37-40R; CAAS 8; DLB 14

Joubert, Joseph 1754-1824 .... **NCLC 9**

Jouve, Pierre Jean 1887-1976...... **CLC 47**
See also CA 65-68

Joyce, James (Augustine Aloysius)
1882-1941 ..... **TCLC 3, 8, 16, 35; DA;**
SSC 3; WLC
See also CA 104; 126; CDBLB 1914-1945;
DLB 10, 19, 36; MTCW

Jozsef, Attila 1905-1937......... **TCLC 22**
See also CA 116

Juana Ines de la Cruz 1651(?)-1695 ... **LC 5**

Judd, Cyril
See Kornbluth, C(yril) M.; Pohl, Frederik

Julian of Norwich 1342(?)-1416(?) .... **LC 6**

Just, Ward (Swift) 1935- .... **CLC 4, 27**
See also CA 25-28R; CANR 32

Justice, Donald (Rodney) 1925- .. **CLC 6, 19**
See also CA 5-8R; CANR 26; DLBY 83

Juvenal c. 55-c. 127 .... **CMLC 8**

Juvenis
See Bourne, Randolph S(illiman)

Kacew, Romain 1914-1980
See Gary, Romain
See also CA 108; 102

Kadare, Ismail 1936- .... **CLC 52**

Kadohata, Cynthia.................. **CLC 59**
See also CA 140

Kafka, Franz
1883-1924 .... **TCLC 2, 6, 13, 29, 47, 53;**
DA; SSC 5; WLC
See also CA 105; 126; DLB 81; MTCW

Kahn, Roger 1927- .... **CLC 30**
See also CA 25-28R; SATA 37

Kain, Saul
See Sassoon, Siegfried (Lorraine)

Kaiser, Georg 1878-1945 .... **TCLC 9**
See also CA 106; DLB 124

Kaletski, Alexander 1946- .... **CLC 39**
See also CA 118; 143

Kalidasa fl. c. 400- .... **CMLC 9**

Kallman, Chester (Simon)
1921-1975 .... **CLC 2**
See also CA 45-48; 53-56; CANR 3

Kaminsky, Melvin 1926-
See Brooks, Mel
See also CA 65-68; CANR 16

Kaminsky, Stuart M(elvin) 1934- ... **CLC 59**
See also CA 73-76; CANR 29

Kane, Paul
See Simon, Paul

Kane, Wilson
See Bloch, Robert (Albert)

Kanin, Garson 1912-.............. **CLC 22**
See also AITN 1; CA 5-8R; CANR 7;
DLB 7

Kaniuk, Yoram 1930-............ **CLC 19**
See also CA 134

Kant, Immanuel 1724-1804 ...... **NCLC 27**
See also DLB 94

Kantor, MacKinlay 1904-1977 ...... **CLC 7**
See also CA 61-64; 73-76; DLB 9, 102

Kaplan, David Michael 1946- ...... **CLC 50**

Kaplan, James 1951- .... **CLC 59**
See also CA 135

Karageorge, Michael
See Anderson, Poul (William)

Karamzin, Nikolai Mikhailovich
1766-1826 .... **NCLC 3**

Karapanou, Margarita 1946-....... **CLC 13**
See also CA 101

Karinthy, Frigyes 1887-1938...... **TCLC 47**

Karl, Frederick R(obert) 1927- ..... **CLC 34**
See also CA 5-8R; CANR 3

Kastel, Warren
See Silverberg, Robert

Kataev, Evgeny Petrovich 1903-1942
See Petrov, Evgeny
See also CA 120

Kataphusin
See Ruskin, John

Katz, Steve 1935- .... **CLC 47**
See also CA 25-28R; CAAS 14; CANR 12;
DLBY 83

Kauffman, Janet 1945-............ **CLC 42**
See also CA 117; CANR 43; DLBY 86

Kaufman, Bob (Garnell)
1925-1986 .... **CLC 49**
See also BW; CA 41-44R; 118; CANR 22;
DLB 16, 41

Kaufman, George S. 1889-1961..... **CLC 38**
See also CA 108; 93-96; DLB 7

Kaufman, Sue .... **CLC 3, 8**
See also Barondess, Sue K(aufman)

Kavafis, Konstantinos Petrou 1863-1933
See Cavafy, C(onstantine) P(eter)
See also CA 104

Kavan, Anna 1901-1968 ...... **CLC 5, 13, 82**
See also CA 5-8R; CANR 6; MTCW

Kavanagh, Dan
See Barnes, Julian

Kavanagh, Patrick (Joseph)
1904-1967 .... **CLC 22**
See also CA 123; 25-28R; DLB 15, 20;
MTCW

Kawabata, Yasunari
1899-1972 .... **CLC 2, 5, 9, 18**
See also CA 93-96; 33-36R

Kaye, M(ary) M(argaret) 1909-..... **CLC 28**
See also CA 89-92; CANR 24; MTCW;
SATA 62

Kaye, Mollie
See Kaye, M(ary) M(argaret)

Kaye-Smith, Sheila 1887-1956..... **TCLC 20**
See also CA 118; DLB 36

Kaymor, Patrice Maguilene
See Senghor, Leopold Sedar

Kazan, Elia 1909-........... **CLC 6, 16, 63**
See also CA 21-24R; CANR 32

Kazantzakis, Nikos
1883(?)-1957 .... **TCLC 2, 5, 33**
See also CA 105; 132; MTCW

Kazin, Alfred 1915- .... **CLC 34, 38**
See also CA 1-4R; CAAS 7; CANR 1;
DLB 67

Keane, Mary Nesta (Skrine) 1904-
See Keane, Molly
See also CA 108; 114

Keane, Molly.................... **CLC 31**
See also Keane, Mary Nesta (Skrine)

Keates, Jonathan 19(?)- .... **CLC 34**

Keaton, Buster 1895-1966 .... **CLC 20**

Keats, John
1795-1821 ... **NCLC 8; DA; PC 1; WLC**
See also CDBLB 1789-1832; DLB 96, 110

Keene, Donald 1922- .... **CLC 34**
See also CA 1-4R; CANR 5

Keillor, Garrison.................. **CLC 40**
See also Keillor, Gary (Edward)
See also AAYA 2; BEST 89:3; DLBY 87;
SATA 58

Keillor, Gary (Edward) 1942-
See Keillor, Garrison
See also CA 111; 117; CANR 36; MTCW

Keith, Michael
See Hubbard, L(afayette) Ron(ald)

Keller, Gottfried 1819-1890....... **NCLC 2**
See also DLB 129

Kellerman, Jonathan 1949- .... **CLC 44**
See also BEST 90:1; CA 106; CANR 29

Kelley, William Melvin 1937-...... **CLC 22**
See also BW; CA 77-80; CANR 27; DLB 33

Kellogg, Marjorie 1922-........... **CLC 2**
See also CA 81-84

Kellow, Kathleen
See Hibbert, Eleanor Alice Burford

Kelly, M(ilton) T(erry) 1947-....... **CLC 55**
See also CA 97-100; CANR 19, 43

Kelman, James 1946-............. **CLC 58**

Kemal, Yashar 1923- .... **CLC 14, 29**
See also CA 89-92

Kemble, Fanny 1809-1893 .... **NCLC 18**
See also DLB 32

Kemelman, Harry 1908-............ **CLC 2**
See also AITN 1; CA 9-12R; CANR 6;
DLB 28

Kempe, Margery 1373(?)-1440(?) ..... **LC 6**

Kempis, Thomas a 1380-1471 .... **LC 11**

Kendall, Henry 1839-1882....... **NCLC 12**

Keneally, Thomas (Michael)
1935- ...... **CLC 5, 8, 10, 14, 19, 27, 43**
See also CA 85-88; CANR 10; MTCW

Kennedy, Adrienne (Lita)
1931- .... **CLC 66; BLC**
See also BW; CA 103; CABS 3; CANR 26;
DLB 38

Kennedy, John Pendleton
1795-1870 .... **NCLC 2**
See also DLB 3

Kennedy, Joseph Charles 1929-...... **CLC 8**
See also Kennedy, X. J.
See also CA 1-4R; CANR 4, 30, 40;
SATA 14

Kennedy, William 1928-... **CLC 6, 28, 34, 53**
See also AAYA 1; CA 85-88; CANR 14,
31; DLBY 85; MTCW; SATA 57

Kennedy, X. J..................... **CLC 42**
See also Kennedy, Joseph Charles
See also CAAS 9; CLR 27; DLB 5

Kent, Kelvin
See Kuttner, Henry

Kenton, Maxwell
See Southern, Terry

Kenyon, Robert O.
See Kuttner, Henry

Kerouac, Jack ..... CLC 1, 2, 3, 5, 14, 29, 61
See also Kerouac, Jean-Louis Lebris de
See also CDALB 1941-1968; DLB 2, 16;
DLBD 3

Kerouac, Jean-Louis Lebris de 1922-1969
See Kerouac, Jack
See also AITN 1; CA 5-8R; 25-28R;
CANR 26; DA; MTCW; WLC

Kerr, Jean 1923-................ CLC 22
See also CA 5-8R; CANR 7

Kerr, M. E. .... CLC 12, 35
See also Meaker, Marijane (Agnes)
See also AAYA 2; CLR 29; SAAS 1

Kerr, Robert .... CLC 55

Kerrigan, (Thomas) Anthony
1918- .... CLC 4, 6
See also CA 49-52; CAAS 11; CANR 4

Kerry, Lois
See Duncan, Lois

Kesey, Ken (Elton)
1935- ..... CLC 1, 3, 6, 11, 46, 64; DA;
WLC
See also CA 1-4R; CANR 22, 38;
CDALB 1968-1988; DLB 2, 16; MTCW;
SATA 66

Kesselring, Joseph (Otto)
1902-1967 .... CLC 45

Kessler, Jascha (Frederick) 1929-.... CLC 4
See also CA 17-20R; CANR 8

Kettelkamp, Larry (Dale) 1933- .... CLC 12
See also CA 29-32R; CANR 16; SAAS 3;
SATA 2

Keyber, Conny
See Fielding, Henry

Keyes, Daniel 1927-.......... CLC 80; DA
See also CA 17-20R; CANR 10, 26;
SATA 37

Khayyam, Omar
1048-1131 .... CMLC 11; PC 8

Kherdian, David 1931-........... CLC 6, 9
See also CA 21-24R; CAAS 2; CANR 39;
CLR 24; JRDA; MAICYA; SATA 16, 74

Khlebnikov, Velimir .... TCLC 20
See also Khlebnikov, Viktor Vladimirovich

Khlebnikov, Viktor Vladimirovich 1885-1922
See Khlebnikov, Velimir
See also CA 117

Khodasevich, Vladislav (Felitsianovich)
1886-1939 .... TCLC 15
See also CA 115

Kielland, Alexander Lange
1849-1906 .... TCLC 5
See also CA 104

Kiely, Benedict 1919-.......... CLC 23, 43
See also CA 1-4R; CANR 2; DLB 15

Kienzle, William X(avier) 1928- .... CLC 25
See also CA 93-96; CAAS 1; CANR 9, 31;
MTCW

Kierkegaard, Soren 1813-1855.... NCLC 34

Killens, John Oliver 1916-1987..... CLC 10
See also BW; CA 77-80; 123; CAAS 2;
CANR 26; DLB 33

Killigrew, Anne 1660-1685.......... LC 4
See also DLB 131

Kim
See Simenon, Georges (Jacques Christian)

Kincaid, Jamaica 1949-... CLC 43, 68; BLC
See also BW; CA 125

King, Francis (Henry) 1923-..... CLC 8, 53
See also CA 1-4R; CANR 1, 33; DLB 15;
MTCW

King, Stephen (Edwin)
1947- .... CLC 12, 26, 37, 61
See also AAYA 1; BEST 90:1; CA 61-64;
CANR 1, 30; DLBY 80; JRDA; MTCW;
SATA 9, 55

King, Steve
See King, Stephen (Edwin)

Kingman, Lee.................... CLC 17
See also Natti, (Mary) Lee
See also SAAS 3; SATA 1, 67

Kingsley, Charles 1819-1875..... NCLC 35
See also DLB 21, 32; YABC 2

Kingsley, Sidney 1906-............ CLC 44
See also CA 85-88; DLB 7

Kingsolver, Barbara 1955-...... CLC 55, 81
See also CA 129; 134

Kingston, Maxine (Ting Ting) Hong
1940- .... CLC 12, 19, 58
See also AAYA 8; CA 69-72; CANR 13,
38; DLBY 80; MTCW; SATA 53

Kinnell, Galway
1927- .... CLC 1, 2, 3, 5, 13, 29
See also CA 9-12R; CANR 10, 34; DLB 5;
DLBY 87; MTCW

Kinsella, Thomas 1928-......... CLC 4, 19
See also CA 17-20R; CANR 15; DLB 27;
MTCW

Kinsella, W(illiam) P(atrick)
1935-................... CLC 27, 43
See also AAYA 7; CA 97-100; CAAS 7;
CANR 21, 35; MTCW

Kipling, (Joseph) Rudyard
1865-1936 ...... TCLC 8, 17; DA; PC 3;
SSC 5; WLC
See also CA 105; 120; CANR 33;
CDBLB 1890-1914; DLB 19, 34;
MAICYA; MTCW; YABC 2

Kirkup, James 1918- .... CLC 1
See also CA 1-4R; CAAS 4; CANR 2;
DLB 27; SATA 12

Kirkwood, James 1930(?)-1989 ...... CLC 9
See also AITN 2; CA 1-4R; 128; CANR 6,
40

Kis, Danilo 1935-1989 .... CLC 57
See also CA 109; 118; 129; MTCW

Kivi, Aleksis 1834-1872 .... NCLC 30

Kizer, Carolyn (Ashley)
1925-................... CLC 15, 39, 80
See also CA 65-68; CAAS 5; CANR 24;
DLB 5

Klabund 1890-1928............. TCLC 44
See also DLB 66

Klappert, Peter 1942-............. CLC 57
See also CA 33-36R; DLB 5

Klein, A(braham) M(oses)
1909-1972 .... CLC 19
See also CA 101; 37-40R; DLB 68

Klein, Norma 1938-1989 .... CLC 30
See also AAYA 2; CA 41-44R; 128;
CANR 15, 37; CLR 2, 19; JRDA;
MAICYA; SAAS 1; SATA 7, 57

Klein, T(heodore) E(ibon) D(onald)
1947- .... CLC 34
See also CA 119

Kleist, Heinrich von
1777-1811 .... NCLC 2, 37
See also DLB 90

Klima, Ivan 1931-................ CLC 56
See also CA 25-28R; CANR 17

Klimentov, Andrei Platonovich 1899-1951
See Platonov, Andrei
See also CA 108

Klinger, Friedrich Maximilian von
1752-1831 .... NCLC 1
See also DLB 94

Klopstock, Friedrich Gottlieb
1724-1803 .... NCLC 11
See also DLB 97

Knebel, Fletcher 1911-1993........ CLC 14
See also AITN 1; CA 1-4R; 140; CAAS 3;
CANR 1, 36; SATA 36; SATA-Obit 75

Knickerbocker, Diedrich
See Irving, Washington

Knight, Etheridge
1931-1991 .... CLC 40; BLC
See also BW; CA 21-24R; 133; CANR 23;
DLB 41

Knight, Sarah Kemble 1666-1727 ..... LC 7
See also DLB 24

Knowles, John
1926- .... CLC 1, 4, 10, 26; DA
See also AAYA 10; CA 17-20R; CANR 40;
CDALB 1968-1988; DLB 6; MTCW;
SATA 8

Knox, Calvin M.
See Silverberg, Robert

Knye, Cassandra
See Disch, Thomas M(ichael)

Koch, C(hristopher) J(ohn) 1932-... CLC 42
See also CA 127

Koch, Christopher
See Koch, C(hristopher) J(ohn)

Koch, Kenneth 1925-......... CLC 5, 8, 44
See also CA 1-4R; CANR 6, 36; DLB 5;
SATA 65

Kochanowski, Jan 1530-1584....... LC 10

Kock, Charles Paul de
1794-1871 .... NCLC 16

Koda Shigeyuki 1867-1947
See Rohan, Koda
See also CA 121

Koestler, Arthur
1905-1983 .... CLC 1, 3, 6, 8, 15, 33
See also CA 1-4R; 109; CANR 1, 33;
CDBLB 1945-1960; DLBY 83; MTCW

Kogawa, Joy Nozomi 1935-........ CLC 78
See also CA 101; CANR 19

Kohout, Pavel 1928-............. CLC 13
See also CA 45-48; CANR 3

Koizumi, Yakumo
See Hearn, (Patricio) Lafcadio (Tessima Carlos)

Kolmar, Gertrud 1894-1943 . . . . . . **TCLC 40**

Konrad, George
See Konrad, Gyoergy

Konrad, Gyoergy 1933- . . . . . . **CLC 4, 10, 73**
See also CA 85-88

Konwicki, Tadeusz 1926- . . . . . **CLC 8, 28, 54**
See also CA 101; CAAS 9; CANR 39;
MTCW

Koontz, Dean R(ay) 1945- . . . . **CLC 78**
See also AAYA 9; BEST 89:3, 90:2;
CA 108; CANR 19, 36; MTCW

Kopit, Arthur (Lee) 1937- . . . . **CLC 1, 18, 33**
See also AITN 1; CA 81-84; CABS 3;
DLB 7; MTCW

Kops, Bernard 1926- . . . . **CLC 4**
See also CA 5-8R; DLB 13

Kornbluth, C(yril) M. 1923-1958 . . . . **TCLC 8**
See also CA 105; DLB 8

Korolenko, V. G.
See Korolenko, Vladimir Galaktionovich

Korolenko, Vladimir
See Korolenko, Vladimir Galaktionovich

Korolenko, Vladimir G.
See Korolenko, Vladimir Galaktionovich

Korolenko, Vladimir Galaktionovich
1853-1921 . . . . **TCLC 22**
See also CA 121

Kosinski, Jerzy (Nikodem)
1933-1991 . . . . **CLC 1, 2, 3, 6, 10, 15, 53, 70**
See also CA 17-20R; 134; CANR 9; DLB 2;
DLBY 82; MTCW

Kostelanetz, Richard (Cory) 1940- . . **CLC 28**
See also CA 13-16R; CAAS 8; CANR 38

Kostrowitzki, Wilhelm Apollinaris de
1880-1918
See Apollinaire, Guillaume
See also CA 104

Kotlowitz, Robert 1924- . . . . **CLC 4**
See also CA 33-36R; CANR 36

Kotzebue, August (Friedrich Ferdinand) von
1761-1819 . . . . **NCLC 25**
See also DLB 94

Kotzwinkle, William 1938- . . **CLC 5, 14, 35**
See also CA 45-48; CANR 3; CLR 6;
MAICYA; SATA 24, 70

Kozol, Jonathan 1936- . . . . **CLC 17**
See also CA 61-64; CANR 16

Kozoll, Michael 1940(?)- . . . . **CLC 35**

Kramer, Kathryn 19(?)- . . . . **CLC 34**

Kramer, Larry 1935- . . . . **CLC 42**
See also CA 124; 126

Krasicki, Ignacy 1735-1801 . . . . **NCLC 8**

Krasinski, Zygmunt 1812-1859 . . . . **NCLC 4**

Kraus, Karl 1874-1936 . . . . **TCLC 5**
See also CA 104; DLB 118

Kreve (Mickevicius), Vincas
1882-1954 . . . . **TCLC 27**

Kristeva, Julia 1941- . . . . **CLC 77**

Kristofferson, Kris 1936- . . . . **CLC 26**
See also CA 104

Krizanc, John 1956- . . . . **CLC 57**

Krleza, Miroslav 1893-1981 . . . . **CLC 8**
See also CA 97-100; 105

Kroetsch, Robert 1927- . . . . . . **CLC 5, 23, 57**
See also CA 17-20R; CANR 8, 38; DLB 53;
MTCW

Kroetz, Franz
See Kroetz, Franz Xaver

Kroetz, Franz Xaver 1946- . . . . **CLC 41**
See also CA 130

Kroker, Arthur 1945- . . . . **CLC 77**

Kropotkin, Peter (Aleksieevich)
1842-1921 . . . . **TCLC 36**
See also CA 119

Krotkov, Yuri 1917- . . . . **CLC 19**
See also CA 102

Krumb
See Crumb, R(obert)

Krumgold, Joseph (Quincy)
1908-1980 . . . . **CLC 12**
See also CA 9-12R; 101; CANR 7;
MAICYA; SATA 1, 23, 48

Krumwitz
See Crumb, R(obert)

Krutch, Joseph Wood 1893-1970 . . . . **CLC 24**
See also CA 1-4R; 25-28R; CANR 4;
DLB 63

Krutzch, Gus
See Eliot, T(homas) S(tearns)

Krylov, Ivan Andreevich
1768(?)-1844 . . . . **NCLC 1**

Kubin, Alfred 1877-1959 . . . . **TCLC 23**
See also CA 112; DLB 81

Kubrick, Stanley 1928- . . . . **CLC 16**
See also CA 81-84; CANR 33; DLB 26

Kumin, Maxine (Winokur)
1925- . . . . **CLC 5, 13, 28**
See also AITN 2; CA 1-4R; CAAS 8;
CANR 1, 21; DLB 5; MTCW; SATA 12

Kundera, Milan
1929- . . . . **CLC 4, 9, 19, 32, 68**
See also AAYA 2; CA 85-88; CANR 19;
MTCW

Kunitz, Stanley (Jasspon)
1905- . . . . **CLC 6, 11, 14**
See also CA 41-44R; CANR 26; DLB 48;
MTCW

Kunze, Reiner 1933- . . . . **CLC 10**
See also CA 93-96; DLB 75

Kuprin, Aleksandr Ivanovich
1870-1938 . . . . **TCLC 5**
See also CA 104

Kureishi, Hanif 1954(?)- . . . . **CLC 64**
See also CA 139

Kurosawa, Akira 1910- . . . . **CLC 16**
See also CA 101

Kushner, Tony 1957(?)- . . . . **CLC 81**

Kuttner, Henry 1915-1958 . . . . **TCLC 10**
See also CA 107; DLB 8

Kuzma, Greg 1944- . . . . **CLC 7**
See also CA 33-36R

Kuzmin, Mikhail 1872(?)-1936 . . . . **TCLC 40**

Kyd, Thomas 1558-1594 . . . . . . **LC 22; DC 3**
See also DLB 62

Kyprianos, Iossif
See Samarakis, Antonis

La Bruyere, Jean de 1645-1696 . . . . . . **LC 17**

Lacan, Jacques (Marie Emile)
1901-1981 . . . . **CLC 75**
See also CA 121; 104

Laclos, Pierre Ambroise Francois Choderlos
de 1741-1803 . . . . **NCLC 4**

Lacolere, Francois
See Aragon, Louis

La Colere, Francois
See Aragon, Louis

La Deshabilleuse
See Simenon, Georges (Jacques Christian)

Lady Gregory
See Gregory, Isabella Augusta (Persse)

Lady of Quality, A
See Bagnold, Enid

La Fayette, Marie (Madelaine Pioche de la
Vergne Comtes 1634-1693 . . . . . . **LC 2**

Lafayette, Rene
See Hubbard, L(afayette) Ron(ald)

Laforgue, Jules 1860-1887 . . . . **NCLC 5**

Lagerkvist, Paer (Fabian)
1891-1974 . . . . **CLC 7, 10, 13, 54**
See also Lagerkvist, Par
See also CA 85-88; 49-52; MTCW

Lagerkvist, Par
See Lagerkvist, Paer (Fabian)
See also SSC 12

Lagerloef, Selma (Ottiliana Lovisa)
1858-1940 . . . . **TCLC 4, 36**
See also Lagerlof, Selma (Ottiliana Lovisa)
See also CA 108; CLR 7; SATA 15

Lagerlof, Selma (Ottiliana Lovisa)
See Lagerloef, Selma (Ottiliana Lovisa)
See also CLR 7; SATA 15

La Guma, (Justin) Alex(ander)
1925-1985 . . . . **CLC 19**
See also BW; CA 49-52; 118; CANR 25;
DLB 117; MTCW

Laidlaw, A. K.
See Grieve, C(hristopher) M(urray)

Lainez, Manuel Mujica
See Mujica Lainez, Manuel
See also HW

Lamartine, Alphonse (Marie Louis Prat) de
1790-1869 . . . . **NCLC 11**

Lamb, Charles
1775-1834 . . . . **NCLC 10; DA; WLC**
See also CDBLB 1789-1832; DLB 93, 107;
SATA 17

Lamb, Lady Caroline 1785-1828 . . **NCLC 38**
See also DLB 116

Lamming, George (William)
1927- . . . . **CLC 2, 4, 66; BLC**
See also BW; CA 85-88; CANR 26;
DLB 125; MTCW

L'Amour, Louis (Dearborn)
1908-1988 . . . . **CLC 25, 55**
See also AITN 2; BEST 89:2; CA 1-4R;
125; CANR 3, 25, 40; DLBY 80; MTCW

Lampedusa, Giuseppe (Tomasi) di . . . **TCLC 13**
See also Tomasi di Lampedusa, Giuseppe

Lampman, Archibald 1861-1899 . . **NCLC 25**
See also DLB 92

Lancaster, Bruce 1896-1963. . . . . . . **CLC 36**
See also CA 9-10; CAP 1; SATA 9

Landau, Mark Alexandrovich
See Aldanov, Mark (Alexandrovich)

Landau-Aldanov, Mark Alexandrovich
See Aldanov, Mark (Alexandrovich)

Landis, John 1950- . . . . **CLC 26**
See also CA 112; 122

Landolfi, Tommaso 1908-1979 . . . **CLC 11, 49**
See also CA 127; 117

Landon, Letitia Elizabeth
1802-1838 . . . . **NCLC 15**
See also DLB 96

Landor, Walter Savage
1775-1864 . . . . **NCLC 14**
See also DLB 93, 107

Landwirth, Heinz 1927-
See Lind, Jakov
See also CA 9-12R; CANR 7

Lane, Patrick 1939- . . . . **CLC 25**
See also CA 97-100; DLB 53

Lang, Andrew 1844-1912 . . . . **TCLC 16**
See also CA 114; 137; DLB 98; MAICYA;
SATA 16

Lang, Fritz 1890-1976 . . . . **CLC 20**
See also CA 77-80; 69-72; CANR 30

Lange, John
See Crichton, (John) Michael

Langer, Elinor 1939- . . . . **CLC 34**
See also CA 121

Langland, William
1330(?)-1400(?) . . . . **LC 19; DA**

Langstaff, Launcelot
See Irving, Washington

Lanier, Sidney 1842-1881 . . . . **NCLC 6**
See also DLB 64; MAICYA; SATA 18

Lanyer, Aemilia 1569-1645 . . . . **LC 10**

Lao Tzu . . . . **CMLC 7**

Lapine, James (Elliot) 1949- . . . . **CLC 39**
See also CA 123; 130

Larbaud, Valery (Nicolas)
1881-1957 . . . . **TCLC 9**
See also CA 106

Lardner, Ring
See Lardner, Ring(gold) W(ilmer)

Lardner, Ring W., Jr.
See Lardner, Ring(gold) W(ilmer)

Lardner, Ring(gold) W(ilmer)
1885-1933 . . . . **TCLC 2, 14**
See also CA 104; 131; CDALB 1917-1929;
DLB 11, 25, 86; MTCW

Laredo, Betty
See Codrescu, Andrei

Larkin, Maia
See Wojciechowska, Maia (Teresa)

Larkin, Philip (Arthur)
1922-1985 . . . . **CLC 3, 5, 8, 9, 13, 18, 33,
39, 64**
See also CA 5-8R; 117; CANR 24;
CDBLB 1960 to Present; DLB 27;
MTCW

Larra (y Sanchez de Castro), Mariano Jose de
1809-1837 . . . . **NCLC 17**

Larsen, Eric 1941- . . . . **CLC 55**
See also CA 132

Larsen, Nella 1891-1964 . . . . . **CLC 37; BLC**
See also BW; CA 125; DLB 51

Larson, Charles R(aymond) 1938- . . . **CLC 31**
See also CA 53-56; CANR 4

Latham, Jean Lee 1902- . . . . **CLC 12**
See also AITN 1; CA 5-8R; CANR 7;
MAICYA; SATA 2, 68

Latham, Mavis
See Clark, Mavis Thorpe

Lathen, Emma . . . . **CLC 2**
See also Hennissart, Martha; Latsis, Mary
J(ane)

Lathrop, Francis
See Leiber, Fritz (Reuter, Jr.)

Latsis, Mary J(ane)
See Lathen, Emma
See also CA 85-88

Lattimore, Richmond (Alexander)
1906-1984 . . . . **CLC 3**
See also CA 1-4R; 112; CANR 1

Laughlin, James 1914- . . . . **CLC 49**
See also CA 21-24R; CANR 9; DLB 48

Laurence, (Jean) Margaret (Wemyss)
1926-1987 . . **CLC 3, 6, 13, 50, 62; SSC 7**
See also CA 5-8R; 121; CANR 33; DLB 53;
MTCW; SATA 50

Laurent, Antoine 1952- . . . . **CLC 50**

Lauscher, Hermann
See Hesse, Hermann

Lautreamont, Comte de
1846-1870 . . . . **NCLC 12; SSC 14**

Laverty, Donald
See Blish, James (Benjamin)

Lavin, Mary 1912- . . . . . . **CLC 4, 18; SSC 4**
See also CA 9-12R; CANR 33; DLB 15;
MTCW

Lavond, Paul Dennis
See Kornbluth, C(yril) M.; Pohl, Frederik

Lawler, Raymond Evenor 1922- . . . . **CLC 58**
See also CA 103

Lawrence, D(avid) H(erbert Richards)
1885-1930 . . . . **TCLC 2, 9, 16, 33, 48;
DA; SSC 4; WLC**
See also CA 104; 121; CDBLB 1914-1945;
DLB 10, 19, 36, 98; MTCW

Lawrence, T(homas) E(dward)
1888-1935 . . . . **TCLC 18**
See also Dale, Colin
See also CA 115

Lawrence of Arabia
See Lawrence, T(homas) E(dward)

Lawson, Henry (Archibald Hertzberg)
1867-1922 . . . . **TCLC 27**
See also CA 120

Lawton, Dennis
See Faust, Frederick (Schiller)

Laxness, Halldor . . . . **CLC 25**
See also Gudjonsson, Halldor Kiljan

Layamon fl. c. 1200- . . . . **CMLC 10**

Laye, Camara 1928-1980 . . . **CLC 4, 38; BLC**
See also BW; CA 85-88; 97-100; CANR 25;
MTCW

Layton, Irving (Peter) 1912- . . . . . **CLC 2, 15**
See also CA 1-4R; CANR 2, 33, 43;
DLB 88; MTCW

Lazarus, Emma 1849-1887 . . . . **NCLC 8**

Lazarus, Felix
See Cable, George Washington

Lazarus, Henry
See Slavitt, David R(ytman)

Lea, Joan
See Neufeld, John (Arthur)

Leacock, Stephen (Butler)
1869-1944 . . . . **TCLC 2**
See also CA 104; 141; DLB 92

Lear, Edward 1812-1888 . . . . **NCLC 3**
See also CLR 1; DLB 32; MAICYA;
SATA 18

Lear, Norman (Milton) 1922- . . . . . . **CLC 12**
See also CA 73-76

Leavis, F(rank) R(aymond)
1895-1978 . . . . **CLC 24**
See also CA 21-24R; 77-80; MTCW

Leavitt, David 1961- . . . . **CLC 34**
See also CA 116; 122; DLB 130

Leblanc, Maurice (Marie Emile)
1864-1941 . . . . **TCLC 49**
See also CA 110

Lebowitz, Fran(ces Ann)
1951(?)- . . . . **CLC 11, 36**
See also CA 81-84; CANR 14; MTCW

le Carre, John . . . . **CLC 3, 5, 9, 15, 28**
See also Cornwell, David (John Moore)
See also BEST 89:4; CDBLB 1960 to
Present; DLB 87

Le Clezio, J(ean) M(arie) G(ustave)
1940- . . . . **CLC 31**
See also CA 116; 128; DLB 83

Leconte de Lisle, Charles-Marie-Rene
1818-1894 . . . . **NCLC 29**

Le Coq, Monsieur
See Simenon, Georges (Jacques Christian)

Leduc, Violette 1907-1972 . . . . **CLC 22**
See also CA 13-14; 33-36R; CAP 1

Ledwidge, Francis 1887(?)-1917 . . . **TCLC 23**
See also CA 123; DLB 20

Lee, Andrea 1953- . . . . **CLC 36; BLC**
See also BW; CA 125

Lee, Andrew
See Auchincloss, Louis (Stanton)

Lee, Don L. . . . . **CLC 2**
See also Madhubuti, Haki R.

Lee, George W(ashington)
1894-1976 . . . . **CLC 52; BLC**
See also BW; CA 125; DLB 51

Lewis, (Harry) Sinclair
    1885-1951 . . . . . **TCLC 4, 13, 23, 39; DA;
        WLC**
    See also CA 104; 133; CDALB 1917-1929;
        DLB 9, 102; DLBD 1; MTCW

Lewis, (Percy) Wyndham
    1884(?)-1957 . . . . **TCLC 2, 9**
    See also CA 104; DLB 15

Lewisohn, Ludwig 1883-1955 . . . . . . **TCLC 19**
    See also CA 107; DLB 4, 9, 28, 102

Lezama Lima, Jose 1910-1976 . . . **CLC 4, 10**
    See also CA 77-80; DLB 113; HW

L'Heureux, John (Clarke) 1934- . . . . **CLC 52**
    See also CA 13-16R; CANR 23

Liddell, C. H.
    See Kuttner, Henry

Lie, Jonas (Lauritz Idemil)
    1833-1908(?) . . . . **TCLC 5**
    See also CA 115

Lieber, Joel 1937-1971 . . . . **CLC 6**
    See also CA 73-76; 29-32R

Lieber, Stanley Martin
    See Lee, Stan

Lieberman, Laurence (James)
    1935- . . . . **CLC 4, 36**
    See also CA 17-20R; CANR 8, 36

Lieksman, Anders
    See Haavikko, Paavo Juhani

Li Fei-kan 1904- . . . . **CLC 18**
    See also CA 105

Lifton, Robert Jay 1926- . . . . **CLC 67**
    See also CA 17-20R; CANR 27; SATA 66

Lightfoot, Gordon 1938- . . . . **CLC 26**
    See also CA 109

Lightman, Alan P. 1948- . . . . **CLC 81**
    See also CA 141

Ligotti, Thomas 1953- . . . . **CLC 44**
    See also CA 123

Liliencron, (Friedrich Adolf Axel) Detlev von
    1844-1909 . . . . **TCLC 18**
    See also CA 117

Lima, Jose Lezama
    See Lezama Lima, Jose

Lima Barreto, Afonso Henrique de
    1881-1922 . . . . **TCLC 23**
    See also CA 117

Limonov, Eduard . . . . **CLC 67**

Lin, Frank
    See Atherton, Gertrude (Franklin Horn)

Lincoln, Abraham 1809-1865 . . . . . **NCLC 18**

Lind, Jakov . . . . **CLC 1, 2, 4, 27, 82**
    See also Landwirth, Heinz
    See also CAAS 4

Lindbergh, Anne (Spencer) Morrow
    1906- . . . . **CLC 82**
    See also CA 17-20R; CANR 16; MTCW;
        SATA 33

Lindsay, David 1878-1945 . . . . **TCLC 15**
    See also CA 113

Lindsay, (Nicholas) Vachel
    1879-1931 . . . . **TCLC 17; DA; WLC**
    See also CA 114; 135; CDALB 1865-1917;
        DLB 54; SATA 40

Linke-Poot
    See Doeblin, Alfred

Linney, Romulus 1930- . . . . **CLC 51**
    See also CA 1-4R; CANR 40

Linton, Eliza Lynn 1822-1898 . . . . **NCLC 41**
    See also DLB 18

Li Po 701-763 . . . . **CMLC 2**

Lipsius, Justus 1547-1606 . . . . **LC 16**

Lipsyte, Robert (Michael)
    1938- . . . . **CLC 21; DA**
    See also AAYA 7; CA 17-20R; CANR 8;
        CLR 23; JRDA; MAICYA; SATA 5, 68

Lish, Gordon (Jay) 1934- . . . . **CLC 45**
    See also CA 113; 117; DLB 130

Lispector, Clarice 1925-1977 . . . . **CLC 43**
    See also CA 139; 116; DLB 113

Littell, Robert 1935(?)- . . . . **CLC 42**
    See also CA 109; 112

Little, Malcolm 1925-1965
    See Malcolm X
    See also BW; CA 125; 111; DA; MTCW

Littlewit, Humphrey Gent.
    See Lovecraft, H(oward) P(hillips)

Litwos
    See Sienkiewicz, Henryk (Adam Alexander
        Pius)

Liu E 1857-1909 . . . . **TCLC 15**
    See also CA 115

Lively, Penelope (Margaret)
    1933- . . . . **CLC 32, 50**
    See also CA 41-44R; CANR 29; CLR 7;
        DLB 14; JRDA; MAICYA; MTCW;
        SATA 7, 60

Livesay, Dorothy (Kathleen)
    1909- . . . . **CLC 4, 15, 79**
    See also AITN 2; CA 25-28R; CAAS 8;
        CANR 36; DLB 68; MTCW

Livy c. 59B.C.-c. 17 . . . . **CMLC 11**

Lizardi, Jose Joaquin Fernandez de
    1776-1827 . . . . **NCLC 30**

Llewellyn, Richard . . . . **CLC 7**
    See also Llewellyn Lloyd, Richard Dafydd
        Vivian
    See also DLB 15

Llewellyn Lloyd, Richard Dafydd Vivian
    1906-1983 . . . . **CLC 80**
    See also Llewellyn, Richard
    See also CA 53-56; 111; CANR 7;
        SATA 11, 37

Llosa, (Jorge) Mario (Pedro) Vargas
    See Vargas Llosa, (Jorge) Mario (Pedro)

Lloyd Webber, Andrew 1948-
    See Webber, Andrew Lloyd
    See also AAYA 1; CA 116; SATA 56

Llull, Ramon c. 1235-c. 1316 . . . . . **CMLC 12**

Locke, Alain (Le Roy)
    1886-1954 . . . . **TCLC 43**
    See also BW; CA 106; 124; DLB 51

Locke, John 1632-1704 . . . . **LC 7**
    See also DLB 101

Locke-Elliott, Sumner
    See Elliott, Sumner Locke

Lockhart, John Gibson
    1794-1854 . . . . **NCLC 6**
    See also DLB 110, 116

Lodge, David (John) 1935- . . . . **CLC 36**
    See also BEST 90:1; CA 17-20R; CANR 19;
        DLB 14; MTCW

Loennbohm, Armas Eino Leopold 1878-1926
    See Leino, Eino
    See also CA 123

Loewinsohn, Ron(ald William)
    1937- . . . . **CLC 52**
    See also CA 25-28R

Logan, Jake
    See Smith, Martin Cruz

Logan, John (Burton) 1923-1987 . . . . . **CLC 5**
    See also CA 77-80; 124; DLB 5

Lo Kuan-chung 1330(?)-1400(?) . . . . . . **LC 12**

Lombard, Nap
    See Johnson, Pamela Hansford

London, Jack . . **TCLC 9, 15, 39; SSC 4; WLC**
    See also London, John Griffith
    See also AITN 2; CDALB 1865-1917;
        DLB 8, 12, 78; SATA 18

London, John Griffith 1876-1916
    See London, Jack
    See also CA 110; 119; DA; JRDA;
        MAICYA; MTCW

Long, Emmett
    See Leonard, Elmore (John, Jr.)

Longbaugh, Harry
    See Goldman, William (W.)

Longfellow, Henry Wadsworth
    1807-1882 . . . . **NCLC 2; DA**
    See also CDALB 1640-1865; DLB 1, 59;
        SATA 19

Longley, Michael 1939- . . . . **CLC 29**
    See also CA 102; DLB 40

Longus fl. c. 2nd cent. - . . . . **CMLC 7**

Longway, A. Hugh
    See Lang, Andrew

Lopate, Phillip 1943- . . . . **CLC 29**
    See also CA 97-100; DLBY 80

Lopez Portillo (y Pacheco), Jose
    1920- . . . . **CLC 46**
    See also CA 129; HW

Lopez y Fuentes, Gregorio
    1897(?)-1966 . . . . **CLC 32**
    See also CA 131; HW

Lorca, Federico Garcia
    See Garcia Lorca, Federico

Lord, Bette Bao 1938- . . . . **CLC 23**
    See also BEST 90:3; CA 107; CANR 41;
        SATA 58

Lord Auch
    See Bataille, Georges

Lord Byron
    See Byron, George Gordon (Noel)

Lord Dunsany . . . . **TCLC 2**
    See also Dunsany, Edward John Moreton
        Drax Plunkett

Lorde, Audre (Geraldine)
    1934-1992 . . . . **CLC 18, 71; BLC**
    See also BW; CA 25-28R; 142; CANR 16,
        26; DLB 41; MTCW

Maclean, Norman (Fitzroy)
      1902-1990 . . . . **CLC 78; SSC 13**
      See also CA 102; 132

MacLeish, Archibald
      1892-1982 . . . . **CLC 3, 8, 14, 68**
      See also CA 9-12R; 106; CANR 33; DLB 4,
      7, 45; DLBY 82; MTCW

MacLennan, (John) Hugh
      1907-1990 . . . . **CLC 2, 14**
      See also CA 5-8R; 142; CANR 33; DLB 68;
      MTCW

MacLeod, Alistair 1936- . . . . **CLC 56**
      See also CA 123; DLB 60

MacNeice, (Frederick) Louis
      1907-1963 . . . . **CLC 1, 4, 10, 53**
      See also CA 85-88; DLB 10, 20; MTCW

MacNeill, Dand
      See Fraser, George MacDonald

Macpherson, (Jean) Jay 1931- . . . . . . **CLC 14**
      See also CA 5-8R; DLB 53

MacShane, Frank 1927- . . . . **CLC 39**
      See also CA 9-12R; CANR 3, 33; DLB 111

Macumber, Mari
      See Sandoz, Mari(e Susette)

Madach, Imre 1823-1864 . . . . **NCLC 19**

Madden, (Jerry) David 1933- . . . . **CLC 5, 15**
      See also CA 1-4R; CAAS 3; CANR 4;
      DLB 6; MTCW

Maddern, Al(an)
      See Ellison, Harlan

Madhubuti, Haki R.
      1942- . . . . **CLC 6, 73; BLC; PC 5**
      See also Lee, Don L.
      See also BW; CA 73-76; CANR 24; DLB 5,
      41; DLBD 8

Madow, Pauline (Reichberg) . . . . **CLC 1**
      See also CA 9-12R

Maepenn, Hugh
      See Kuttner, Henry

Maepenn, K. H.
      See Kuttner, Henry

Maeterlinck, Maurice 1862-1949 . . . **TCLC 3**
      See also CA 104; 136; SATA 66

Maginn, William 1794-1842 . . . . . . **NCLC 8**
      See also DLB 110

Mahapatra, Jayanta 1928- . . . . **CLC 33**
      See also CA 73-76; CAAS 9; CANR 15, 33

Mahfouz, Naguib (Abdel Aziz Al-Sabilgi)
      1911(?)-
      See Mahfuz, Najib
      See also BEST 89:2; CA 128; MTCW

Mahfuz, Najib . . . . **CLC 52, 55**
      See also Mahfouz, Naguib (Abdel Aziz
      Al-Sabilgi)
      See also DLBY 88

Mahon, Derek 1941- . . . . **CLC 27**
      See also CA 113; 128; DLB 40

Mailer, Norman
      1923- . . . . . . **CLC 1, 2, 3, 4, 5, 8, 11, 14,
      28, 39, 74; DA**
      See also AITN 2; CA 9-12R; CABS 1;
      CANR 28; CDALB 1968-1988; DLB 2,
      16, 28; DLBD 3; DLBY 80, 83; MTCW

Maillet, Antonine 1929- . . . . **CLC 54**
      See also CA 115; 120; DLB 60

Mais, Roger 1905-1955 . . . . **TCLC 8**
      See also BW; CA 105; 124; DLB 125;
      MTCW

Maistre, Joseph de 1753-1821 . . . . **NCLC 37**

Maitland, Sara (Louise) 1950- . . . . . . **CLC 49**
      See also CA 69-72; CANR 13

Major, Clarence
      1936- . . . . **CLC 3, 19, 48; BLC**
      See also BW; CA 21-24R; CAAS 6;
      CANR 13, 25; DLB 33

Major, Kevin (Gerald) 1949- . . . . **CLC 26**
      See also CA 97-100; CANR 21, 38;
      CLR 11; DLB 60; JRDA; MAICYA;
      SATA 32

Maki, James
      See Ozu, Yasujiro

Malabaila, Damiano
      See Levi, Primo

Malamud, Bernard
      1914-1986 . . . . . . **CLC 1, 2, 3, 5, 8, 9, 11,
      18, 27, 44, 78; DA; SSC 15; WLC**
      See also CA 5-8R; 118; CABS 1; CANR 28;
      CDALB 1941-1968; DLB 2, 28;
      DLBY 80, 86; MTCW

Malaparte, Curzio 1898-1957 . . . . . **TCLC 52**

Malcolm, Dan
      See Silverberg, Robert

Malcolm X . . . . **CLC 82; BLC**
      See also Little, Malcolm

Malherbe, Francois de 1555-1628 . . . . . **LC 5**

Mallarme, Stephane
      1842-1898 . . . . **NCLC 4, 41; PC 4**

Mallet-Joris, Francoise 1930- . . . . . . **CLC 11**
      See also CA 65-68; CANR 17; DLB 83

Malley, Ern
      See McAuley, James Phillip

Mallowan, Agatha Christie
      See Christie, Agatha (Mary Clarissa)

Maloff, Saul 1922- . . . . **CLC 5**
      See also CA 33-36R

Malone, Louis
      See MacNeice, (Frederick) Louis

Malone, Michael (Christopher)
      1942- . . . . **CLC 43**
      See also CA 77-80; CANR 14, 32

Malory, (Sir) Thomas
      1410(?)-1471(?) . . . . **LC 11; DA**
      See also CDBLB Before 1660; SATA 33, 59

Malouf, (George Joseph) David
      1934- . . . . **CLC 28**
      See also CA 124

Malraux, (Georges-)Andre
      1901-1976 . . . . . . **CLC 1, 4, 9, 13, 15, 57**
      See also CA 21-22; 69-72; CANR 34;
      CAP 2; DLB 72; MTCW

Malzberg, Barry N(athaniel) 1939- . . . **CLC 7**
      See also CA 61-64; CAAS 4; CANR 16;
      DLB 8

Mamet, David (Alan)
      1947- . . . . **CLC 9, 15, 34, 46; DC 4**
      See also AAYA 3; CA 81-84; CABS 3;
      CANR 15, 41; DLB 7; MTCW

Mamoulian, Rouben (Zachary)
      1897-1987 . . . . **CLC 16**
      See also CA 25-28R; 124

Mandelstam, Osip (Emilievich)
      1891(?)-1938(?) . . . . **TCLC 2, 6**
      See also CA 104

Mander, (Mary) Jane 1877-1949 . . . **TCLC 31**

Mandiargues, Andre Pieyre de . . . . . . **CLC 41**
      See also Pieyre de Mandiargues, Andre
      See also DLB 83

Mandrake, Ethel Belle
      See Thurman, Wallace (Henry)

Mangan, James Clarence
      1803-1849 . . . . **NCLC 27**

Maniere, J.-E.
      See Giraudoux, (Hippolyte) Jean

Manley, (Mary) Delariviere
      1672(?)-1724 . . . . **LC 1**
      See also DLB 39, 80

Mann, Abel
      See Creasey, John

Mann, (Luiz) Heinrich 1871-1950 . . . **TCLC 9**
      See also CA 106; DLB 66

Mann, (Paul) Thomas
      1875-1955 . . . . **TCLC 2, 8, 14, 21, 35, 44;
      DA; SSC 5; WLC**
      See also CA 104; 128; DLB 66; MTCW

Manning, David
      See Faust, Frederick (Schiller)

Manning, Frederic 1887(?)-1935 . . . **TCLC 25**
      See also CA 124

Manning, Olivia 1915-1980 . . . . . . **CLC 5, 19**
      See also CA 5-8R; 101; CANR 29; MTCW

Mano, D. Keith 1942- . . . . **CLC 2, 10**
      See also CA 25-28R; CAAS 6; CANR 26;
      DLB 6

Mansfield, Katherine
      . . . . **TCLC 2, 8, 39; SSC 9; WLC**
      See also Beauchamp, Kathleen Mansfield

Manso, Peter 1940- . . . . **CLC 39**
      See also CA 29-32R

Mantecon, Juan Jimenez
      See Jimenez (Mantecon), Juan Ramon

Manton, Peter
      See Creasey, John

Man Without a Spleen, A
      See Chekhov, Anton (Pavlovich)

Manzoni, Alessandro 1785-1873 . . **NCLC 29**

Mapu, Abraham (ben Jekutiel)
      1808-1867 . . . . **NCLC 18**

Mara, Sally
      See Queneau, Raymond

Marat, Jean Paul 1743-1793 . . . . **LC 10**

Marcel, Gabriel Honore
      1889-1973 . . . . **CLC 15**
      See also CA 102; 45-48; MTCW

Marchbanks, Samuel
      See Davies, (William) Robertson

Marchi, Giacomo
      See Bassani, Giorgio

Margulies, Donald . . . . **CLC 76**

Marie de France c. 12th cent. - . . . . . **CMLC 8**

Marie de l'Incarnation 1599-1672 . . . . **LC 10**

Mariner, Scott
See Pohl, Frederik

Marinetti, Filippo Tommaso
1876-1944 .... **TCLC 10**
See also CA 107; DLB 114

Marivaux, Pierre Carlet de Chamblain de
1688-1763 .... **LC 4**

Markandaya, Kamala .... **CLC 8, 38**
See also Taylor, Kamala (Purnaiya)

Markfield, Wallace 1926- .... **CLC 8**
See also CA 69-72; CAAS 3; DLB 2, 28

Markham, Edwin 1852-1940 ..... **TCLC 47**
See also DLB 54

Markham, Robert
See Amis, Kingsley (William)

Marks, J
See Highwater, Jamake (Mamake)

Marks-Highwater, J
See Highwater, Jamake (Mamake)

Markson, David M(errill) 1927- .... **CLC 67**
See also CA 49-52; CANR 1

Marley, Bob................... **CLC 17**
See also Marley, Robert Nesta

Marley, Robert Nesta 1945-1981
See Marley, Bob
See also CA 107; 103

Marlowe, Christopher
1564-1593 ..... **LC 22; DA; DC 1; WLC**
See also CDBLB Before 1660; DLB 62

Marmontel, Jean-Francois
1723-1799 .... **LC 2**

Marquand, John P(hillips)
1893-1960 .... **CLC 2, 10**
See also CA 85-88; DLB 9, 102

Marquez, Gabriel (Jose) Garcia...... **CLC 68**
See also Garcia Marquez, Gabriel (Jose)

Marquis, Don(ald Robert Perry)
1878-1937 .... **TCLC 7**
See also CA 104; DLB 11, 25

Marric, J. J.
See Creasey, John

Marrow, Bernard
See Moore, Brian

Marryat, Frederick 1792-1848 .... **NCLC 3**
See also DLB 21

Marsden, James
See Creasey, John

Marsh, (Edith) Ngaio
1899-1982 .... **CLC 7, 53**
See also CA 9-12R; CANR 6; DLB 77;
MTCW

Marshall, Garry 1934- .... **CLC 17**
See also AAYA 3; CA 111; SATA 60

Marshall, Paule
1929- .... **CLC 27, 72; BLC; SSC 3**
See also BW; CA 77-80; CANR 25;
DLB 33; MTCW

Marsten, Richard
See Hunter, Evan

Martha, Henry
See Harris, Mark

Martin, Ken
See Hubbard, L(afayette) Ron(ald)

Martin, Richard
See Creasey, John

Martin, Steve 1945- .... **CLC 30**
See also CA 97-100; CANR 30; MTCW

Martin, Violet Florence
1862-1915 .... **TCLC 51**

Martin, Webber
See Silverberg, Robert

Martindale, Patrick Victor
See White, Patrick (Victor Martindale)

Martin du Gard, Roger
1881-1958 .... **TCLC 24**
See also CA 118; DLB 65

Martineau, Harriet 1802-1876.... **NCLC 26**
See also DLB 21, 55; YABC 2

Martines, Julia
See O'Faolain, Julia

Martinez, Jacinto Benavente y
See Benavente (y Martinez), Jacinto

Martinez Ruiz, Jose 1873-1967
See Azorin; Ruiz, Jose Martinez
See also CA 93-96; HW

Martinez Sierra, Gregorio
1881-1947 .... **TCLC 6**
See also CA 115

Martinez Sierra, Maria (de la O'LeJarraga)
1874-1974 .... **TCLC 6**
See also CA 115

Martinsen, Martin
See Follett, Ken(neth Martin)

Martinson, Harry (Edmund)
1904-1978 .... **CLC 14**
See also CA 77-80; CANR 34

Marut, Ret
See Traven, B.

Marut, Robert
See Traven, B.

Marvell, Andrew
1621-1678 .... **LC 4; DA; WLC**
See also CDBLB 1660-1789; DLB 131

Marx, Karl (Heinrich)
1818-1883 .... **NCLC 17**
See also DLB 129

Masaoka Shiki................. **TCLC 18**
See also Masaoka Tsunenori

Masaoka Tsunenori 1867-1902
See Masaoka Shiki
See also CA 117

Masefield, John (Edward)
1878-1967 .... **CLC 11, 47**
See also CA 19-20; 25-28R; CANR 33;
CAP 2; CDBLB 1890-1914; DLB 10;
MTCW; SATA 19

Maso, Carole 19(?)- .... **CLC 44**

Mason, Bobbie Ann
1940- .... **CLC 28, 43, 82; SSC 4**
See also AAYA 5; CA 53-56; CANR 11,
31; DLBY 87; MTCW

Mason, Ernst
See Pohl, Frederik

Mason, Lee W.
See Malzberg, Barry N(athaniel)

Mason, Nick 1945- .... **CLC 35**
See also Pink Floyd

Mason, Tally
See Derleth, August (William)

Mass, William
See Gibson, William

Masters, Edgar Lee
1868-1950 ..... **TCLC 2, 25; DA; PC 1**
See also CA 104; 133; CDALB 1865-1917;
DLB 54; MTCW

Masters, Hilary 1928- .... **CLC 48**
See also CA 25-28R; CANR 13

Mastrosimone, William 19(?)- ..... **CLC 36**

Mathe, Albert
See Camus, Albert

Matheson, Richard Burton 1926- ... **CLC 37**
See also CA 97-100; DLB 8, 44

Mathews, Harry 1930-......... **CLC 6, 52**
See also CA 21-24R; CAAS 6; CANR 18,
40

Mathias, Roland (Glyn) 1915-...... **CLC 45**
See also CA 97-100; CANR 19, 41; DLB 27

Matsuo Basho 1644-1694........... **PC 3**

Mattheson, Rodney
See Creasey, John

Matthews, Greg 1949- .... **CLC 45**
See also CA 135

Matthews, William 1942-......... **CLC 40**
See also CA 29-32R; CAAS 18; CANR 12;
DLB 5

Matthias, John (Edward) 1941-...... **CLC 9**
See also CA 33-36R

Matthiessen, Peter
1927- .... **CLC 5, 7, 11, 32, 64**
See also AAYA 6; BEST 90:4; CA 9-12R;
CANR 21; DLB 6; MTCW; SATA 27

Maturin, Charles Robert
1780(?)-1824 .... **NCLC 6**

Matute (Ausejo), Ana Maria
1925- .... **CLC 11**
See also CA 89-92; MTCW

Maugham, W. S.
See Maugham, W(illiam) Somerset

Maugham, W(illiam) Somerset
1874-1965 ...... **CLC 1, 11, 15, 67; DA;
SSC 8; WLC**
See also CA 5-8R; 25-28R; CANR 40;
CDBLB 1914-1945; DLB 10, 36, 77, 100;
MTCW; SATA 54

Maugham, William Somerset
See Maugham, W(illiam) Somerset

Maupassant, (Henri Rene Albert) Guy de
1850-1893 .... **NCLC 1, 42; DA; SSC 1;
WLC**
See also DLB 123

Maurhut, Richard
See Traven, B.

Mauriac, Claude 1914-............. **CLC 9**
See also CA 89-92; DLB 83

Mauriac, Francois (Charles)
1885-1970 .... **CLC 4, 9, 56**
See also CA 25-28; CAP 2; DLB 65;
MTCW

Mavor, Osborne Henry 1888-1951
See Bridie, James
See also CA 104

Maxwell, William (Keepers, Jr.)
     1908- .... **CLC 19**
     See also CA 93-96; DLBY 80

May, Elaine 1932- .... **CLC 16**
     See also CA 124; 142; DLB 44

Mayakovski, Vladimir (Vladimirovich)
     1893-1930 .... **TCLC 4, 18**
     See also CA 104

Mayhew, Henry 1812-1887 ...... **NCLC 31**
     See also DLB 18, 55

Maynard, Joyce 1953- .... **CLC 23**
     See also CA 111; 129

Mayne, William (James Carter)
     1928- .... **CLC 12**
     See also CA 9-12R; CANR 37; CLR 25;
     JRDA; MAICYA; SAAS 11; SATA 6, 68

Mayo, Jim
     See L'Amour, Louis (Dearborn)

Maysles, Albert 1926- .... **CLC 16**
     See also CA 29-32R

Maysles, David 1932- .... **CLC 16**

Mazer, Norma Fox 1931- .... **CLC 26**
     See also AAYA 5; CA 69-72; CANR 12,
     32; CLR 23; JRDA; MAICYA; SAAS 1;
     SATA 24, 67

Mazzini, Guiseppe 1805-1872 .... **NCLC 34**

McAuley, James Phillip
     1917-1976 .... **CLC 45**
     See also CA 97-100

McBain, Ed
     See Hunter, Evan

McBrien, William Augustine
     1930- ....'................. **CLC 44**
     See also CA 107

McCaffrey, Anne (Inez) 1926- ...... **CLC 17**
     See also AAYA 6; AITN 2; BEST 89:2;
     CA 25-28R; CANR 15, 35; DLB 8;
     JRDA; MAICYA; MTCW; SAAS 11;
     SATA 8, 70

McCann, Arthur
     See Campbell, John W(ood, Jr.)

McCann, Edson
     See Pohl, Frederik

McCarthy, Charles, Jr. 1933-
     See McCarthy, Cormac
     See also CANR 42

McCarthy, Cormac .... **CLC 4, 57**
     See also McCarthy, Charles, Jr.
     See also DLB 6

McCarthy, Mary (Therese)
     1912-1989 ... **CLC 1, 3, 5, 14, 24, 39, 59**
     See also CA 5-8R; 129; CANR 16; DLB 2;
     DLBY 81; MTCW

McCartney, (James) Paul
     1942- .... **CLC 12, 35**

McCauley, Stephen (D.) 1955- ..... **CLC 50**
     See also CA 141

McClure, Michael (Thomas)
     1932- .... **CLC 6, 10**
     See also CA 21-24R; CANR 17; DLB 16

McCorkle, Jill (Collins) 1958- ...... **CLC 51**
     See also CA 121; DLBY 87

McCourt, James 1941- .... **CLC 5**
     See also CA 57-60

McCoy, Horace (Stanley)
     1897-1955 .... **TCLC 28**
     See also CA 108; DLB 9

McCrae, John 1872-1918........ **TCLC 12**
     See also CA 109; DLB 92

McCreigh, James
     See Pohl, Frederik

McCullers, (Lula) Carson (Smith)
     1917-1967 .... **CLC 1, 4, 10, 12, 48; DA;
                                          SSC 9; WLC**
     See also CA 5-8R; 25-28R; CABS 1, 3;
     CANR 18; CDALB 1941-1968; DLB 2, 7;
     MTCW; SATA 27

McCulloch, John Tyler
     See Burroughs, Edgar Rice

McCullough, Colleen 1938(?)- ...... **CLC 27**
     See also CA 81-84; CANR 17; MTCW

McElroy, Joseph 1930- .... **CLC 5, 47**
     See also CA 17-20R

McEwan, Ian (Russell) 1948- ... **CLC 13, 66**
     See also BEST 90:4; CA 61-64; CANR 14,
     41; DLB 14; MTCW

McFadden, David 1940-........... **CLC 48**
     See also CA 104; DLB 60

McFarland, Dennis 1950- .... **CLC 65**

McGahern, John 1934-........ **CLC 5, 9, 48**
     See also CA 17-20R; CANR 29; DLB 14;
     MTCW

McGinley, Patrick (Anthony)
     1937- .... **CLC 41**
     See also CA 120; 127

McGinley, Phyllis 1905-1978 ...... **CLC 14**
     See also CA 9-12R; 77-80; CANR 19;
     DLB 11, 48; SATA 2, 24, 44

McGinniss, Joe 1942-............. **CLC 32**
     See also AITN 2; BEST 89:2; CA 25-28R;
     CANR 26

McGivern, Maureen Daly
     See Daly, Maureen

McGrath, Patrick 1950-........... **CLC 55**
     See also CA 136

McGrath, Thomas (Matthew)
     1916-1990 .... **CLC 28, 59**
     See also CA 9-12R; 132; CANR 6, 33;
     MTCW; SATA 41; SATA-Obit 66

McGuane, Thomas (Francis III)
     1939- .... **CLC 3, 7, 18, 45**
     See also AITN 2; CA 49-52; CANR 5, 24;
     DLB 2; DLBY 80; MTCW

McGuckian, Medbh 1950-......... **CLC 48**
     See also CA 143; DLB 40

McHale, Tom 1942(?)-1982....... **CLC 3, 5**
     See also AITN 1; CA 77-80; 106

McIlvanney, William 1936-........ **CLC 42**
     See also CA 25-28R; DLB 14

McIlwraith, Maureen Mollie Hunter
     See Hunter, Mollie
     See also SATA 2

McInerney, Jay 1955- .... **CLC 34**
     See also CA 116; 123

McIntyre, Vonda N(eel) 1948- ..... **CLC 18**
     See also CA 81-84; CANR 17, 34; MTCW

McKay, Claude ..... **TCLC 7, 41; BLC; PC 2**
     See also McKay, Festus Claudius
     See also DLB 4, 45, 51, 117

McKay, Festus Claudius 1889-1948
     See McKay, Claude
     See also BW; CA 104; 124; DA; MTCW;
     WLC

McKuen, Rod 1933-............. **CLC 1, 3**
     See also AITN 1; CA 41-44R; CANR 40

McLoughlin, R. B.
     See Mencken, H(enry) L(ouis)

McLuhan, (Herbert) Marshall
     1911-1980 .... **CLC 37**
     See also CA 9-12R; 102; CANR 12, 34;
     DLB 88; MTCW

McMillan, Terry (L.) 1951-..... **CLC 50, 61**
     See also CA 140

McMurtry, Larry (Jeff)
     1936- .... **CLC 2, 3, 7, 11, 27, 44**
     See also AITN 2; BEST 89:2; CA 5-8R;
     CANR 19, 43; CDALB 1968-1988;
     DLB 2; DLBY 80, 87; MTCW

McNally, T. M. 1961- .... **CLC 82**

McNally, Terrence 1939-...... **CLC 4, 7, 41**
     See also CA 45-48; CANR 2; DLB 7

McNamer, Deirdre 1950-........ **CLC 70**

McNeile, Herman Cyril 1888-1937
     See Sapper
     See also DLB 77

McPhee, John (Angus) 1931- ...... **CLC 36**
     See also BEST 90:1; CA 65-68; CANR 20;
     MTCW

McPherson, James Alan
     1943- .... **CLC 19, 77**
     See also BW; CA 25-28R; CAAS 17;
     CANR 24; DLB 38; MTCW

McPherson, William (Alexander)
     1933- .... **CLC 34**
     See also CA 69-72; CANR 28

McSweeney, Kerry .... **CLC 34**

Mead, Margaret 1901-1978........ **CLC 37**
     See also AITN 1; CA 1-4R; 81-84;
     CANR 4; MTCW; SATA 20

Meaker, Marijane (Agnes) 1927-
     See Kerr, M. E.
     See also CA 107; CANR 37; JRDA;
     MAICYA; MTCW; SATA 20, 61

Medoff, Mark (Howard) 1940- ... **CLC 6, 23**
     See also AITN 1; CA 53-56; CANR 5;
     DLB 7

Meged, Aharon
     See Megged, Aharon

Meged, Aron
     See Megged, Aharon

Megged, Aharon 1920-............. **CLC 9**
     See also CA 49-52; CAAS 13; CANR 1

Mehta, Ved (Parkash) 1934-....... **CLC 37**
     See also CA 1-4R; CANR 2, 23; MTCW

Melanter
     See Blackmore, R(ichard) D(oddridge)

Melikow, Loris
     See Hofmannsthal, Hugo von

Melmoth, Sebastian
     See Wilde, Oscar (Fingal O'Flahertie Wills)

Mitford, Nancy 1904-1973........ **CLC 44**
See also CA 9-12R

Miyamoto, Yuriko 1899-1951 ..... **TCLC 37**

Mo, Timothy (Peter) 1950(?)-...... **CLC 46**
See also CA 117; MTCW

Modarressi, Taghi (M.) 1931-...... **CLC 44**
See also CA 121; 134

Modiano, Patrick (Jean) 1945-..... **CLC 18**
See also CA 85-88; CANR 17, 40; DLB 83

Moerck, Paal
See Roelvaag, O(le) E(dvart)

Mofolo, Thomas (Mokopu)
1875(?)-1948 .... **TCLC 22; BLC**
See also CA 121

Mohr, Nicholasa 1935-...... **CLC 12; HLC**
See also AAYA 8; CA 49-52; CANR 1, 32;
CLR 22; HW; JRDA; SAAS 8; SATA 8

Mojtabai, A(nn) G(race)
1938-................**CLC 5, 9, 15, 29**
See also CA 85-88

Moliere 1622-1673 .... **LC 10; DA; WLC**

Molin, Charles
See Mayne, William (James Carter)

Molnar, Ferenc 1878-1952....... **TCLC 20**
See also CA 109

Momaday, N(avarre) Scott
1934-............... **CLC 2, 19; DA**
See also CA 25-28R; CANR 14, 34;
MTCW; SATA 30, 48

Monette, Paul 1945-............. **CLC 82**
See also CA 139

Monroe, Harriet 1860-1936...... **TCLC 12**
See also CA 109; DLB 54, 91

Monroe, Lyle
See Heinlein, Robert A(nson)

Montagu, Elizabeth 1917-........ **NCLC 7**
See also CA 9-12R

Montagu, Mary (Pierrepont) Wortley
1689-1762 .... **LC 9**
See also DLB 95, 101

Montagu, W. H.
See Coleridge, Samuel Taylor

Montague, John (Patrick)
1929-................... **CLC 13, 46**
See also CA 9-12R; CANR 9; DLB 40;
MTCW

Montaigne, Michel (Eyquem) de
1533-1592 .... **LC 8; DA; WLC**

Montale, Eugenio 1896-1981... **CLC 7, 9, 18**
See also CA 17-20R; 104; CANR 30;
DLB 114; MTCW

Montesquieu, Charles-Louis de Secondat
1689-1755 .... **LC 7**

Montgomery, (Robert) Bruce 1921-1978
See Crispin, Edmund
See also CA 104

Montgomery, L(ucy) M(aud)
1874-1942 .... **TCLC 51**
See also CA 108; 137; CLR 8; DLB 92;
JRDA; MAICYA; YABC 1

Montgomery, Marion H., Jr. 1925-.. **CLC 7**
See also AITN 1; CA 1-4R; CANR 3;
DLB 6

Montgomery, Max
See Davenport, Guy (Mattison, Jr.)

Montherlant, Henry (Milon) de
1896-1972 .... **CLC 8, 19**
See also CA 85-88; 37-40R; DLB 72;
MTCW

Monty Python.................... **CLC 21**
See also Chapman, Graham; Cleese, John
(Marwood); Gilliam, Terry (Vance); Idle,
Eric; Jones, Terence Graham Parry; Palin,
Michael (Edward)
See also AAYA 7

Moodie, Susanna (Strickland)
1803-1885 .... **NCLC 14**
See also DLB 99

Mooney, Edward 1951-........... **CLC 25**
See also CA 130

Mooney, Ted
See Mooney, Edward

Moorcock, Michael (John)
1939-.................**CLC 5, 27, 58**
See also CA 45-48; CAAS 5; CANR 2, 17,
38; DLB 14; MTCW

Moore, Brian
1921-........ **CLC 1, 3, 5, 7, 8, 19, 32**
See also CA 1-4R; CANR 1, 25, 42; MTCW

Moore, Edward
See Muir, Edwin

Moore, George Augustus
1852-1933 .... **TCLC 7**
See also CA 104; DLB 10, 18, 57, 135

Moore, Lorrie .... **CLC 39, 45, 68**
See also Moore, Marie Lorena

Moore, Marianne (Craig)
1887-1972 .... **CLC 1, 2, 4, 8, 10, 13, 19,
47; DA; PC 4**
See also CA 1-4R; 33-36R; CANR 3;
CDALB 1929-1941; DLB 45; DLBD 7;
MTCW; SATA 20

Moore, Marie Lorena 1957-
See Moore, Lorrie
See also CA 116; CANR 39

Moore, Thomas 1779-1852....... **NCLC 6**
See also DLB 96

Morand, Paul 1888-1976 .... **CLC 41**
See also CA 69-72; DLB 65

Morante, Elsa 1918-1985....... **CLC 8, 47**
See also CA 85-88; 117; CANR 35; MTCW

Moravia, Alberto....... **CLC 2, 7, 11, 27, 46**
See also Pincherle, Alberto

More, Hannah 1745-1833 .... **NCLC 27**
See also DLB 107, 109, 116

More, Henry 1614-1687............. **LC 9**
See also DLB 126

More, Sir Thomas 1478-1535 .... **LC 10**

Moreas, Jean.................... **TCLC 18**
See also Papadiamantopoulos, Johannes

Morgan, Berry 1919-............. **CLC 6**
See also CA 49-52; DLB 6

Morgan, Claire
See Highsmith, (Mary) Patricia

Morgan, Edwin (George) 1920-..... **CLC 31**
See also CA 5-8R; CANR 3, 43; DLB 27

Morgan, (George) Frederick
1922-..................... **CLC 23**
See also CA 17-20R; CANR 21

Morgan, Harriet
See Mencken, H(enry) L(ouis)

Morgan, Jane
See Cooper, James Fenimore

Morgan, Janet 1945- .... **CLC 39**
See also CA 65-68

Morgan, Lady 1776(?)-1859...... **NCLC 29**
See also DLB 116

Morgan, Robin 1941-............. **CLC 2**
See also CA 69-72; CANR 29; MTCW

Morgan, Scott
See Kuttner, Henry

Morgan, Seth 1949(?)-1990 .... **CLC 65**
See also CA 132

Morgenstern, Christian
1871-1914 .... **TCLC 8**
See also CA 105

Morgenstern, S.
See Goldman, William (W.)

Moricz, Zsigmond 1879-1942 ..... **TCLC 33**

Morike, Eduard (Friedrich)
1804-1875 .... **NCLC 10**
See also DLB 133

Mori Ogai .... **TCLC 14**
See also Mori Rintaro

Mori Rintaro 1862-1922
See Mori Ogai
See also CA 110

Moritz, Karl Philipp 1756-1793 ...... **LC 2**
See also DLB 94

Morland, Peter Henry
See Faust, Frederick (Schiller)

Morren, Theophil
See Hofmannsthal, Hugo von

Morris, Bill 1952-................ **CLC 76**

Morris, Julian
See West, Morris L(anglo)

Morris, Steveland Judkins 1950(?)-
See Wonder, Stevie
See also CA 111

Morris, William 1834-1896 .... **NCLC 4**
See also CDBLB 1832-1890; DLB 18, 35, 57

Morris, Wright 1910-... **CLC 1, 3, 7, 18, 37**
See also CA 9-12R; CANR 21; DLB 2;
DLBY 81; MTCW

Morrison, Chloe Anthony Wofford
See Morrison, Toni

Morrison, James Douglas 1943-1971
See Morrison, Jim
See also CA 73-76; CANR 40

Morrison, Jim .... **CLC 17**
See also Morrison, James Douglas

Morrison, Toni
1931- .. **CLC 4, 10, 22, 55, 81; BLC; DA**
See also AAYA 1; BW; CA 29-32R;
CANR 27, 42; CDALB 1968-1988;
DLB 6, 33; DLBY 81; MTCW; SATA 57

Morrison, Van 1945- .... **CLC 21**
See also CA 116

Nessi, Pio Baroja y
See Baroja (y Nessi), Pio

Nestroy, Johann 1801-1862 ...... **NCLC 42**
See also DLB 133

Neufeld, John (Arthur) 1938- ...... **CLC 17**
See also CA 25-28R; CANR 11, 37;
MAICYA; SAAS 3; SATA 6

Neville, Emily Cheney 1919- ...... **CLC 12**
See also CA 5-8R; CANR 3, 37; JRDA;
MAICYA; SAAS 2; SATA 1

Newbound, Bernard Slade 1930-
See Slade, Bernard
See also CA 81-84

Newby, P(ercy) H(oward)
1918- .... **CLC 2, 13**
See also CA 5-8R; CANR 32; DLB 15;
MTCW

Newlove, Donald 1928- .... **CLC 6**
See also CA 29-32R; CANR 25

Newlove, John (Herbert) 1938- ..... **CLC 14**
See also CA 21-24R; CANR 9, 25

Newman, Charles 1938- .... **CLC 2, 8**
See also CA 21-24R

Newman, Edwin (Harold) 1919- .... **CLC 14**
See also AITN 1; CA 69-72; CANR 5

Newman, John Henry
1801-1890 .... **NCLC 38**
See also DLB 18, 32, 55

Newton, Suzanne 1936- .... **CLC 35**
See also CA 41-44R; CANR 14; JRDA;
SATA 5

Nexo, Martin Andersen
1869-1954 .... **TCLC 43**

Nezval, Vitezslav 1900-1958 ...... **TCLC 44**
See also CA 123

Ng, Fae Myenne 1957(?)- .... **CLC 81**

Ngema, Mbongeni 1955- .... **CLC 57**
See also CA 143

Ngugi, James T(hiong'o) .... **CLC 3, 7, 13**
See also Ngugi wa Thiong'o

Ngugi wa Thiong'o 1938- ..... **CLC 36; BLC**
See also Ngugi, James T(hiong'o)
See also BW; CA 81-84; CANR 27;
DLB 125; MTCW

Nichol, B(arrie) P(hillip)
1944-1988 .... **CLC 18**
See also CA 53-56; DLB 53; SATA 66

Nichols, John (Treadwell) 1940- .... **CLC 38**
See also CA 9-12R; CAAS 2; CANR 6;
DLBY 82

Nichols, Leigh
See Koontz, Dean R(ay)

Nichols, Peter (Richard)
1927- .... **CLC 5, 36, 65**
See also CA 104; CANR 33; DLB 13;
MTCW

Nicolas, F. R. E.
See Freeling, Nicolas

Niedecker, Lorine 1903-1970.... **CLC 10, 42**
See also CA 25-28; CAP 2; DLB 48

Nietzsche, Friedrich (Wilhelm)
1844-1900 .... **TCLC 10, 18**
See also CA 107; 121; DLB 129

Nievo, Ippolito 1831-1861 .... **NCLC 22**

Nightingale, Anne Redmon 1943-
See Redmon, Anne
See also CA 103

Nik.T.O.
See Annensky, Innokenty Fyodorovich

Nin, Anais
1903-1977 ...... **CLC 1, 4, 8, 11, 14, 60;**
SSC 10
See also AITN 2; CA 13-16R; 69-72;
CANR 22; DLB 2, 4; MTCW

Nissenson, Hugh 1933-.......... **CLC 4, 9**
See also CA 17-20R; CANR 27; DLB 28

Niven, Larry .... **CLC 8**
See also Niven, Laurence Van Cott
See also DLB 8

Niven, Laurence Van Cott 1938-
See Niven, Larry
See also CA 21-24R; CAAS 12; CANR 14;
MTCW

Nixon, Agnes Eckhardt 1927- ...... **CLC 21**
See also CA 110

Nizan, Paul 1905-1940 .... **TCLC 40**
See also DLB 72

Nkosi, Lewis 1936-.......... **CLC 45; BLC**
See also BW; CA 65-68; CANR 27

Nodier, (Jean) Charles (Emmanuel)
1780-1844 .... **NCLC 19**
See also DLB 119

Nolan, Christopher 1965-......... **CLC 58**
See also CA 111

Norden, Charles
See Durrell, Lawrence (George)

Nordhoff, Charles (Bernard)
1887-1947 .... **TCLC 23**
See also CA 108; DLB 9; SATA 23

Norfolk, Lawrence 1963- .... **CLC 76**

Norman, Marsha 1947- .... **CLC 28**
See also CA 105; CABS 3; CANR 41;
DLBY 84

Norris, Benjamin Franklin, Jr.
1870-1902 .... **TCLC 24**
See also Norris, Frank
See also CA 110

Norris, Frank
See Norris, Benjamin Franklin, Jr.
See also CDALB 1865-1917; DLB 12, 71

Norris, Leslie 1921- .... **CLC 14**
See also CA 11-12; CANR 14; CAP 1;
DLB 27

North, Andrew
See Norton, Andre

North, Anthony
See Koontz, Dean R(ay)

North, Captain George
See Stevenson, Robert Louis (Balfour)

North, Milou
See Erdrich, Louise

Northrup, B. A.
See Hubbard, L(afayette) Ron(ald)

North Staffs
See Hulme, T(homas) E(rnest)

Norton, Alice Mary
See Norton, Andre
See also MAICYA; SATA 1, 43

Norton, Andre 1912- .... **CLC 12**
See also Norton, Alice Mary
See also CA 1-4R; CANR 2, 31; DLB 8, 52;
JRDA; MTCW

Norway, Nevil Shute 1899-1960
See Shute, Nevil
See also CA 102; 93-96

Norwid, Cyprian Kamil
1821-1883 .... **NCLC 17**

Nosille, Nabrah
See Ellison, Harlan

Nossack, Hans Erich 1901-1978 ..... **CLC 6**
See also CA 93-96; 85-88; DLB 69

Nosu, Chuji
See Ozu, Yasujiro

Nova, Craig 1945-............. **CLC 7, 31**
See also CA 45-48; CANR 2

Novak, Joseph
See Kosinski, Jerzy (Nikodem)

Novalis 1772-1801 .... **NCLC 13**
See also DLB 90

Nowlan, Alden (Albert) 1933-1983 .. **CLC 15**
See also CA 9-12R; CANR 5; DLB 53

Noyes, Alfred 1880-1958 .... **TCLC 7**
See also CA 104; DLB 20

Nunn, Kem 19(?)- .... **CLC 34**

Nye, Robert 1939- .... **CLC 13, 42**
See also CA 33-36R; CANR 29; DLB 14;
MTCW; SATA 6

Nyro, Laura 1947- .... **CLC 17**

Oates, Joyce Carol
1938- ...... **CLC 1, 2, 3, 6, 9, 11, 15, 19,**
33, 52; DA; SSC 6; WLC
See also AITN 1; BEST 89:2; CA 5-8R;
CANR 25; CDALB 1968-1988; DLB 2, 5,
130; DLBY 81; MTCW

O'Brien, E. G.
See Clarke, Arthur C(harles)

O'Brien, Edna
1936- ... **CLC 3, 5, 8, 13, 36, 65; SSC 10**
See also CA 1-4R; CANR 6, 41;
CDBLB 1960 to Present; DLB 14;
MTCW

O'Brien, Fitz-James 1828-1862... **NCLC 21**
See also DLB 74

O'Brien, Flann........ **CLC 1, 4, 5, 7, 10, 47**
See also O Nuallain, Brian

O'Brien, Richard 1942- .... **CLC 17**
See also CA 124

O'Brien, Tim 1946-.......... **CLC 7, 19, 40**
See also CA 85-88; CANR 40; DLBD 9;
DLBY 80

Obstfelder, Sigbjoern 1866-1900... **TCLC 23**
See also CA 123

O'Casey, Sean
1880-1964 .... **CLC 1, 5, 9, 11, 15**
See also CA 89-92; CDBLB 1914-1945;
DLB 10; MTCW

O'Cathasaigh, Sean
See O'Casey, Sean

Ochs, Phil 1940-1976............. **CLC 17**
See also CA 65-68

Page, Louise 1955-. . . . . **CLC 40**
See also CA 140

Page, P(atricia) K(athleen)
 1916- . . . . **CLC 7, 18**
See also CA 53-56; CANR 4, 22; DLB 68;
MTCW

Paget, Violet 1856-1935
See Lee, Vernon
See also CA 104

Paget-Lowe, Henry
See Lovecraft, H(oward) P(hillips)

Paglia, Camille (Anna) 1947-. . . . . . . **CLC 68**
See also CA 140

Paige, Richard
See Koontz, Dean R(ay)

Pakenham, Antonia
See Fraser, Antonia (Pakenham)

Palamas, Kostes 1859-1943 . . . . **TCLC 5**
See also CA 105

Palazzeschi, Aldo 1885-1974. . . . . . . **CLC 11**
See also CA 89-92; 53-56; DLB 114

Paley, Grace 1922-. . . . **CLC 4, 6, 37; SSC 8**
See also CA 25-28R; CANR 13; DLB 28;
MTCW

Palin, Michael (Edward) 1943-. . . . . **CLC 21**
See also Monty Python
See also CA 107; CANR 35; SATA 67

Palliser, Charles 1947-. . . . . **CLC 65**
See also CA 136

Palma, Ricardo 1833-1919. . . . . . . **TCLC 29**

Pancake, Breece Dexter 1952-1979
See Pancake, Breece D'J
See also CA 123; 109

Pancake, Breece D'J. . . . . **CLC 29**
See also Pancake, Breece Dexter
See also DLB 130

Panko, Rudy
See Gogol, Nikolai (Vasilyevich)

Papadiamantis, Alexandros
 1851-1911 . . . . **TCLC 29**

Papadiamantopoulos, Johannes 1856-1910
See Moreas, Jean
See also CA 117

Papini, Giovanni 1881-1956. . . . . . . **TCLC 22**
See also CA 121

Paracelsus 1493-1541. . . . . **LC 14**

Parasol, Peter
See Stevens, Wallace

Parfenie, Maria
See Codrescu, Andrei

Parini, Jay (Lee) 1948- . . . . **CLC 54**
See also CA 97-100; CAAS 16; CANR 32

Park, Jordan
See Kornbluth, C(yril) M.; Pohl, Frederik

Parker, Bert
See Ellison, Harlan

Parker, Dorothy (Rothschild)
 1893-1967 . . . . **CLC 15, 68; SSC 2**
See also CA 19-20; 25-28R; CAP 2;
DLB 11, 45, 86; MTCW

Parker, Robert B(rown) 1932-. . . . . . **CLC 27**
See also BEST 89:4; CA 49-52; CANR 1,
26; MTCW

Parkes, Lucas
See Harris, John (Wyndham Parkes Lucas)
Beynon

Parkin, Frank 1940-. . . . . **CLC 43**

Parkman, Francis, Jr.
 1823-1893 . . . . **NCLC 12**
See also DLB 1, 30

Parks, Gordon (Alexander Buchanan)
 1912- . . . . **CLC 1, 16; BLC**
See also AITN 2; BW; CA 41-44R;
CANR 26; DLB 33; SATA 8

Parnell, Thomas 1679-1718. . . . . **LC 3**
See also DLB 94

Parra, Nicanor 1914- . . . . **CLC 2; HLC**
See also CA 85-88; CANR 32; HW; MTCW

Parrish, Mary Frances
See Fisher, M(ary) F(rances) K(ennedy)

Parson
See Coleridge, Samuel Taylor

Parson Lot
See Kingsley, Charles

Partridge, Anthony
See Oppenheim, E(dward) Phillips

Pascoli, Giovanni 1855-1912. . . . . . **TCLC 45**

Pasolini, Pier Paolo
 1922-1975 . . . . **CLC 20, 37**
See also CA 93-96; 61-64; DLB 128;
MTCW

Pasquini
See Silone, Ignazio

Pastan, Linda (Olenik) 1932- . . . . . . **CLC 27**
See also CA 61-64; CANR 18, 40; DLB 5

Pasternak, Boris (Leonidovich)
 1890-1960 . . . . . . **CLC 7, 10, 18, 63; DA;
PC 6; WLC**
See also CA 127; 116; MTCW

Patchen, Kenneth 1911-1972. . . **CLC 1, 2, 18**
See also CA 1-4R; 33-36R; CANR 3, 35;
DLB 16, 48; MTCW

Pater, Walter (Horatio)
 1839-1894 . . . . **NCLC 7**
See also CDBLB 1832-1890; DLB 57

Paterson, A(ndrew) B(arton)
 1864-1941 . . . . **TCLC 32**

Paterson, Katherine (Womeldorf)
 1932- . . . . **CLC 12, 30**
See also AAYA 1; CA 21-24R; CANR 28;
CLR 7; DLB 52; JRDA; MAICYA;
MTCW; SATA 13, 53

Patmore, Coventry Kersey Dighton
 1823-1896 . . . . **NCLC 9**
See also DLB 35, 98

Paton, Alan (Stewart)
 1903-1988 . . . . . . **CLC 4, 10, 25, 55; DA;
WLC**
See also CA 13-16; 125; CANR 22; CAP 1;
MTCW; SATA 11, 56

Paton Walsh, Gillian 1937-
See Walsh, Jill Paton
See also CANR 38; JRDA; MAICYA;
SAAS 3; SATA 4, 72

Paulding, James Kirke 1778-1860. . **NCLC 2**
See also DLB 3, 59, 74

Paulin, Thomas Neilson 1949-
See Paulin, Tom
See also CA 123; 128

Paulin, Tom. . . . . **CLC 37**
See also Paulin, Thomas Neilson
See also DLB 40

Paustovsky, Konstantin (Georgievich)
 1892-1968 . . . . **CLC 40**
See also CA 93-96; 25-28R

Pavese, Cesare 1908-1950 . . . . **TCLC 3**
See also CA 104; DLB 128

Pavic, Milorad 1929-. . . . . **CLC 60**
See also CA 136

Payne, Alan
See Jakes, John (William)

Paz, Gil
See Lugones, Leopoldo

Paz, Octavio
 1914- . . . . **CLC 3, 4, 6, 10, 19, 51, 65;
DA; HLC; PC 1; WLC**
See also CA 73-76; CANR 32; DLBY 90;
HW; MTCW

Peacock, Molly 1947-. . . . . **CLC 60**
See also CA 103; DLB 120

Peacock, Thomas Love
 1785-1866 . . . . **NCLC 22**
See also DLB 96, 116

Peake, Mervyn 1911-1968. . . . . . . **CLC 7, 54**
See also CA 5-8R; 25-28R; CANR 3;
DLB 15; MTCW; SATA 23

Pearce, Philippa . . . . **CLC 21**
See also Christie, (Ann) Philippa
See also CLR 9; MAICYA; SATA 1, 67

Pearl, Eric
See Elman, Richard

Pearson, T(homas) R(eid) 1956- . . . . **CLC 39**
See also CA 120; 130

Peck, Dale 1968(?)- . . . . **CLC 81**

Peck, John 1941-. . . . . **CLC 3**
See also CA 49-52; CANR 3

Peck, Richard (Wayne) 1934-. . . . . . . **CLC 21**
See also AAYA 1; CA 85-88; CANR 19,
38; JRDA; MAICYA; SAAS 2; SATA 18,
55

Peck, Robert Newton 1928-. . . . **CLC 17; DA**
See also AAYA 3; CA 81-84; CANR 31;
JRDA; MAICYA; SAAS 1; SATA 21, 62

Peckinpah, (David) Sam(uel)
 1925-1984 . . . . **CLC 20**
See also CA 109; 114

Pedersen, Knut 1859-1952
See Hamsun, Knut
See also CA 104; 119; MTCW

Peeslake, Gaffer
See Durrell, Lawrence (George)

Peguy, Charles Pierre
 1873-1914 . . . . **TCLC 10**
See also CA 107

Pena, Ramon del Valle y
See Valle-Inclan, Ramon (Maria) del

Pendennis, Arthur Esquir
See Thackeray, William Makepeace

Penn, William 1644-1718. . . . . **LC 25**
See also DLB 24

Pepys, Samuel
1633-1703 . . . . **LC 11; DA; WLC**
See also CDBLB 1660-1789; DLB 101

Percy, Walker
1916-1990 . . . . **CLC 2, 3, 6, 8, 14, 18, 47,**
65
See also CA 1-4R; 131; CANR 1, 23;
DLB 2; DLBY 80, 90; MTCW

Perec, Georges 1936-1982 . . . . **CLC 56**
See also CA 141; DLB 83

Pereda (y Sanchez de Porrua), Jose Maria de
1833-1906 . . . . **TCLC 16**
See also CA 117

Pereda y Porrua, Jose Maria de
See Pereda (y Sanchez de Porrua), Jose
Maria de

Peregoy, George Weems
See Mencken, H(enry) L(ouis)

Perelman, S(idney) J(oseph)
1904-1979 . . . **CLC 3, 5, 9, 15, 23, 44, 49**
See also AITN 1, 2; CA 73-76; 89-92;
CANR 18; DLB 11, 44; MTCW

Peret, Benjamin 1899-1959 . . . . **TCLC 20**
See also CA 117

Peretz, Isaac Loeb 1851(?)-1915 . . . **TCLC 16**
See also CA 109

Peretz, Yitzhok Leibush
See Peretz, Isaac Loeb

Perez Galdos, Benito 1843-1920 . . . **TCLC 27**
See also CA 125; HW

Perrault, Charles 1628-1703 . . . . **LC 2**
See also MAICYA; SATA 25

Perry, Brighton
See Sherwood, Robert E(mmet)

Perse, St.-John . . . . **CLC 4, 11, 46**
See also Leger, (Marie-Rene Auguste) Alexis
Saint-Leger

Peseenz, Tulio F.
See Lopez y Fuentes, Gregorio

Pesetsky, Bette 1932- . . . . **CLC 28**
See also CA 133; DLB 130

Peshkov, Alexei Maximovich 1868-1936
See Gorky, Maxim
See also CA 105; 141; DA

Pessoa, Fernando (Antonio Nogueira)
1888-1935 . . . . **TCLC 27; HLC**
See also CA 125

Peterkin, Julia Mood 1880-1961 . . . . **CLC 31**
See also CA 102; DLB 9

Peters, Joan K. 1945- . . . . **CLC 39**

Peters, Robert L(ouis) 1924- . . . . **CLC 7**
See also CA 13-16R; CAAS 8; DLB 105

Petofi, Sandor 1823-1849 . . . . **NCLC 21**

Petrakis, Harry Mark 1923- . . . . **CLC 3**
See also CA 9-12R; CANR 4, 30

Petrarch 1304-1374 . . . . **PC 8**

Petrov, Evgeny . . . . **TCLC 21**
See also Kataev, Evgeny Petrovich

Petry, Ann (Lane) 1908- . . . . . . **CLC 1, 7, 18**
See also BW; CA 5-8R; CAAS 6; CANR 4;
CLR 12; DLB 76; JRDA; MAICYA;
MTCW; SATA 5

Petursson, Halligrimur 1614-1674 . . . . **LC 8**

Philipson, Morris H. 1926- . . . . **CLC 53**
See also CA 1-4R; CANR 4

Phillips, David Graham
1867-1911 . . . . **TCLC 44**
See also CA 108; DLB 9, 12

Phillips, Jack
See Sandburg, Carl (August)

Phillips, Jayne Anne 1952- . . . . . **CLC 15, 33**
See also CA 101; CANR 24; DLBY 80;
MTCW

Phillips, Richard
See Dick, Philip K(indred)

Phillips, Robert (Schaeffer) 1938- . . . **CLC 28**
See also CA 17-20R; CAAS 13; CANR 8;
DLB 105

Phillips, Ward
See Lovecraft, H(oward) P(hillips)

Piccolo, Lucio 1901-1969 . . . . **CLC 13**
See also CA 97-100; DLB 114

Pickthall, Marjorie L(owry) C(hristie)
1883-1922 . . . . **TCLC 21**
See also CA 107; DLB 92

Pico della Mirandola, Giovanni
1463-1494 . . . . **LC 15**

Piercy, Marge
1936- . . . . **CLC 3, 6, 14, 18, 27, 62**
See also CA 21-24R; CAAS 1; CANR 13,
43; DLB 120; MTCW

Piers, Robert
See Anthony, Piers

Pieyre de Mandiargues, Andre 1909-1991
See Mandiargues, Andre Pieyre de
See also CA 103; 136; CANR 22

Pilnyak, Boris . . . . **TCLC 23**
See also Vogau, Boris Andreyevich

Pincherle, Alberto 1907-1990 . . . **CLC 11, 18**
See also Moravia, Alberto
See also CA 25-28R; 132; CANR 33;
MTCW

Pinckney, Darryl 1953- . . . . **CLC 76**
See also CA 143

Pindar 518B.C.-446B.C. . . . . **CMLC 12**

Pineda, Cecile 1942- . . . . **CLC 39**
See also CA 118

Pinero, Arthur Wing 1855-1934 . . . **TCLC 32**
See also CA 110; DLB 10

Pinero, Miguel (Antonio Gomez)
1946-1988 . . . . **CLC 4, 55**
See also CA 61-64; 125; CANR 29; HW

Pinget, Robert 1919- . . . . . . **CLC 7, 13, 37**
See also CA 85-88; DLB 83

Pink Floyd . . . . **CLC 35**
See also Barrett, (Roger) Syd; Gilmour,
David; Mason, Nick; Waters, Roger;
Wright, Rick

Pinkney, Edward 1802-1828 . . . . . **NCLC 31**

Pinkwater, Daniel Manus 1941- . . . . **CLC 35**
See also Pinkwater, Manus
See also AAYA 1; CA 29-32R; CANR 12,
38; CLR 4; JRDA; MAICYA; SAAS 3;
SATA 46

Pinkwater, Manus
See Pinkwater, Daniel Manus
See also SATA 8

Pinsky, Robert 1940- . . . . **CLC 9, 19, 38**
See also CA 29-32R; CAAS 4; DLBY 82

Pinta, Harold
See Pinter, Harold

Pinter, Harold
1930- . . . . . **CLC 1, 3, 6, 9, 11, 15, 27, 58,**
73; DA; WLC
See also CA 5-8R; CANR 33; CDBLB 1960
to Present; DLB 13; MTCW

Pirandello, Luigi
1867-1936 . . . . . . **TCLC 4, 29; DA; WLC**
See also CA 104

Pirsig, Robert M(aynard)
1928- . . . . **CLC 4, 6, 73**
See also CA 53-56; CANR 42; MTCW;
SATA 39

Pisarev, Dmitry Ivanovich
1840-1868 . . . . **NCLC 25**

Pix, Mary (Griffith) 1666-1709 . . . . **LC 8**
See also DLB 80

Pixerecourt, Guilbert de
1773-1844 . . . . **NCLC 39**

Plaidy, Jean
See Hibbert, Eleanor Alice Burford

Planche, James Robinson
1796-1880 . . . . **NCLC 42**

Plant, Robert 1948- . . . . **CLC 12**

Plante, David (Robert)
1940- . . . . **CLC 7, 23, 38**
See also CA 37-40R; CANR 12, 36;
DLBY 83; MTCW

Plath, Sylvia
1932-1963 . . . . . **CLC 1, 2, 3, 5, 9, 11, 14,**
17, 50, 51, 62; DA; PC 1; WLC
See also CA 19-20; CANR 34; CAP 2;
CDALB 1941-1968; DLB 5, 6; MTCW

Plato 428(?)B.C.-348(?)B.C. . . . . **CMLC 8; DA**

Platonov, Andrei . . . . **TCLC 14**
See also Klimentov, Andrei Platonovich

Platt, Kin 1911- . . . . **CLC 26**
See also CA 17-20R; CANR 11; JRDA;
SAAS 17; SATA 21

Plick et Plock
See Simenon, Georges (Jacques Christian)

Plimpton, George (Ames) 1927- . . . . . **CLC 36**
See also AITN 1; CA 21-24R; CANR 32;
MTCW; SATA 10

Plomer, William Charles Franklin
1903-1973 . . . . **CLC 4, 8**
See also CA 21-22; CANR 34; CAP 2;
DLB 20; MTCW; SATA 24

Plowman, Piers
See Kavanagh, Patrick (Joseph)

Plum, J.
See Wodehouse, P(elham) G(renville)

Plumly, Stanley (Ross) 1939- . . . . . . **CLC 33**
See also CA 108; 110; DLB 5

Plumpe, Friedrich Wilhelm
1888-1931 . . . . **TCLC 53**
See also CA 112

Poe, Edgar Allan
1809-1849 . . . . . **NCLC 1, 16; DA; PC 1;**
SSC 1; WLC
See also CDALB 1640-1865; DLB 3, 59, 73,
74; SATA 23

Poet of Titchfield Street, The
See Pound, Ezra (Weston Loomis)

Pohl, Frederik 1919- .... **CLC 18**
See also CA 61-64; CAAS 1; CANR 11, 37;
DLB 8; MTCW; SATA 24

Poirier, Louis 1910-
See Gracq, Julien
See also CA 122; 126

Poitier, Sidney 1927- .... **CLC 26**
See also BW; CA 117

Polanski, Roman 1933- .... **CLC 16**
See also CA 77-80

Poliakoff, Stephen 1952- .... **CLC 38**
See also CA 106; DLB 13

Police, The .... **CLC 26**
See also Copeland, Stewart (Armstrong);
Summers, Andrew James; Sumner,
Gordon Matthew

Pollitt, Katha 1949- .... **CLC 28**
See also CA 120; 122; MTCW

Pollock, (Mary) Sharon 1936- ...... **CLC 50**
See also CA 141; DLB 60

Pomerance, Bernard 1940- .... **CLC 13**
See also CA 101

Ponge, Francis (Jean Gaston Alfred)
1899-1988 .... **CLC 6, 18**
See also CA 85-88; 126; CANR 40

Pontoppidan, Henrik 1857-1943 ... **TCLC 29**

Poole, Josephine .... **CLC 17**
See also Helyar, Jane Penelope Josephine
See also SAAS 2; SATA 5

Popa, Vasko 1922- .... **CLC 19**
See also CA 112

Pope, Alexander
1688-1744 .... **LC 3; DA; WLC**
See also CDBLB 1660-1789; DLB 95, 101

Porter, Connie (Rose) 1959(?)- ..... **CLC 70**
See also CA 142

Porter, Gene(va Grace) Stratton
1863(?)-1924 .... **TCLC 21**
See also CA 112

Porter, Katherine Anne
1890-1980 ...... **CLC 1, 3, 7, 10, 13, 15,
27; DA; SSC 4**
See also AITN 2; CA 1-4R; 101; CANR 1;
DLB 4, 9, 102; DLBY 80; MTCW;
SATA 23, 39

Porter, Peter (Neville Frederick)
1929- .... **CLC 5, 13, 33**
See also CA 85-88; DLB 40

Porter, William Sydney 1862-1910
See Henry, O.
See also CA 104; 131; CDALB 1865-1917;
DA; DLB 12, 78, 79; MTCW; YABC 2

Portillo (y Pacheco), Jose Lopez
See Lopez Portillo (y Pacheco), Jose

Post, Melville Davisson
1869-1930 .... **TCLC 39**
See also CA 110

Potok, Chaim 1929- .... **CLC 2, 7, 14, 26**
See also AITN 1, 2; CA 17-20R; CANR 19,
35; DLB 28; MTCW; SATA 33

Potter, Beatrice
See Webb, (Martha) Beatrice (Potter)
See also MAICYA

Potter, Dennis (Christopher George)
1935- .... **CLC 58**
See also CA 107; CANR 33; MTCW

Pound, Ezra (Weston Loomis)
1885-1972 ...... **CLC 1, 2, 3, 4, 5, 7, 10,
13, 18, 34, 48, 50; DA; PC 4; WLC**
See also CA 5-8R; 37-40R; CANR 40;
CDALB 1917-1929; DLB 4, 45, 63;
MTCW

Povod, Reinaldo 1959- .... **CLC 44**
See also CA 136

Powell, Anthony (Dymoke)
1905- .... **CLC 1, 3, 7, 9, 10, 31**
See also CA 1-4R; CANR 1, 32;
CDBLB 1945-1960; DLB 15; MTCW

Powell, Dawn 1897-1965 .... **CLC 66**
See also CA 5-8R

Powell, Padgett 1952- .... **CLC 34**
See also CA 126

Powers, J(ames) F(arl)
1917- .... **CLC 1, 4, 8, 57; SSC 4**
See also CA 1-4R; CANR 2; DLB 130;
MTCW

Powers, John J(ames) 1945-
See Powers, John R.
See also CA 69-72

Powers, John R. .... **CLC 66**
See also Powers, John J(ames)

Pownall, David 1938- .... **CLC 10**
See also CA 89-92; CAAS 18; DLB 14

Powys, John Cowper
1872-1963 .... **CLC 7, 9, 15, 46**
See also CA 85-88; DLB 15; MTCW

Powys, T(heodore) F(rancis)
1875-1953 .... **TCLC 9**
See also CA 106; DLB 36

Prager, Emily 1952- .... **CLC 56**

Pratt, E(dwin) J(ohn)
1883(?)-1964 .... **CLC 19**
See also CA 141; 93-96; DLB 92

Premchand .... **TCLC 21**
See also Srivastava, Dhanpat Rai

Preussler, Otfried 1923- .... **CLC 17**
See also CA 77-80; SATA 24

Prevert, Jacques (Henri Marie)
1900-1977 .... **CLC 15**
See also CA 77-80; 69-72; CANR 29;
MTCW; SATA 30

Prevost, Abbe (Antoine Francois)
1697-1763 .... **LC 1**

Price, (Edward) Reynolds
1933- .... **CLC 3, 6, 13, 43, 50, 63**
See also CA 1-4R; CANR 1, 37; DLB 2

Price, Richard 1949- .... **CLC 6, 12**
See also CA 49-52; CANR 3; DLBY 81

Prichard, Katharine Susannah
1883-1969 .... **CLC 46**
See also CA 11-12; CANR 33; CAP 1;
MTCW; SATA 66

Priestley, J(ohn) B(oynton)
1894-1984 .... **CLC 2, 5, 9, 34**
See also CA 9-12R; 113; CANR 33;
CDBLB 1914-1945; DLB 10, 34, 77, 100;
DLBY 84; MTCW

Prince 1958(?)- .... **CLC 35**

Prince, F(rank) T(empleton) 1912- .. **CLC 22**
See also CA 101; CANR 43; DLB 20

Prince Kropotkin
See Kropotkin, Peter (Aleksieevich)

Prior, Matthew 1664-1721 .... **LC 4**
See also DLB 95

Pritchard, William H(arrison)
1932- .... **CLC 34**
See also CA 65-68; CANR 23; DLB 111

Pritchett, V(ictor) S(awdon)
1900- .... **CLC 5, 13, 15, 41; SSC 14**
See also CA 61-64; CANR 31; DLB 15;
MTCW

Private 19022
See Manning, Frederic

Probst, Mark 1925- .... **CLC 59**
See also CA 130

Prokosch, Frederic 1908-1989.... **CLC 4, 48**
See also CA 73-76; 128; DLB 48

Prophet, The
See Dreiser, Theodore (Herman Albert)

Prose, Francine 1947- .... **CLC 45**
See also CA 109; 112

Proudhon
See Cunha, Euclides (Rodrigues Pimenta) da

Proulx, E. Annie 1935- .... **CLC 81**

Proust, (Valentin-Louis-George-Eugene-)
Marcel
1871-1922 ... **TCLC 7, 13, 33; DA; WLC**
See also CA 104; 120; DLB 65; MTCW

Prowler, Harley
See Masters, Edgar Lee

Prus, Boleslaw .... **TCLC 48**
See also Glowacki, Aleksander

Pryor, Richard (Franklin Lenox Thomas)
1940- .... **CLC 26**
See also CA 122

Przybyszewski, Stanislaw
1868-1927 .... **TCLC 36**
See also DLB 66

Pteleon
See Grieve, C(hristopher) M(urray)

Puckett, Lute
See Masters, Edgar Lee

Puig, Manuel
1932-1990 ... **CLC 3, 5, 10, 28, 65; HLC**
See also CA 45-48; CANR 2, 32; DLB 113;
HW; MTCW

Purdy, Al(fred Wellington)
1918- .... **CLC 3, 6, 14, 50**
See also CA 81-84; CAAS 17; CANR 42;
DLB 88

Purdy, James (Amos)
1923- .... **CLC 2, 4, 10, 28, 52**
See also CA 33-36R; CAAS 1; CANR 19;
DLB 2; MTCW

Pure, Simon
See Swinnerton, Frank Arthur

Pushkin, Alexander (Sergeyevich)
1799-1837 ...... **NCLC 3, 27; DA; WLC**
See also SATA 61

P'u Sung-ling 1640-1715 .... **LC 3**

Putnam, Arthur Lee
See Alger, Horatio, Jr.

Puzo, Mario 1920- . . . . **CLC 1, 2, 6, 36**
See also CA 65-68; CANR 4, 42; DLB 6;
MTCW

Pym, Barbara (Mary Crampton)
1913-1980 . . . . **CLC 13, 19, 37**
See also CA 13-14; 97-100; CANR 13, 34;
CAP 1; DLB 14; DLBY 87; MTCW

Pynchon, Thomas (Ruggles, Jr.)
1937- . . . . . **CLC 2, 3, 6, 9, 11, 18, 33, 62, 72; DA; SSC 14; WLC**
See also BEST 90:2; CA 17-20R; CANR 22;
DLB 2; MTCW

Q
See Quiller-Couch, Arthur Thomas

Qian Zhongshu
See Ch'ien Chung-shu

Qroll
See Dagerman, Stig (Halvard)

Quarrington, Paul (Lewis) 1953- . . . . **CLC 65**
See also CA 129

Quasimodo, Salvatore 1901-1968 . . . **CLC 10**
See also CA 13-16; 25-28R; CAP 1;
DLB 114; MTCW

Queen, Ellery . . . . **CLC 3, 11**
See also Dannay, Frederic; Davidson,
Avram; Lee, Manfred B(ennington);
Sturgeon, Theodore (Hamilton); Vance,
John Holbrook

Queen, Ellery, Jr.
See Dannay, Frederic; Lee, Manfred
B(ennington)

Queneau, Raymond
1903-1976 . . . . **CLC 2, 5, 10, 42**
See also CA 77-80; 69-72; CANR 32;
DLB 72; MTCW

Quevedo, Francisco de 1580-1645 . . . . **LC 23**

Quiller-Couch, Arthur Thomas
1863-1944 . . . . **TCLC 53**
See also CA 118; DLB 135

Quin, Ann (Marie) 1936-1973 . . . . **CLC 6**
See also CA 9-12R; 45-48; DLB 14

Quinn, Martin
See Smith, Martin Cruz

Quinn, Simon
See Smith, Martin Cruz

Quiroga, Horacio (Sylvestre)
1878-1937 . . . . **TCLC 20; HLC**
See also CA 117; 131; HW; MTCW

Quoirez, Francoise 1935- . . . . **CLC 9**
See also Sagan, Francoise
See also CA 49-52; CANR 6, 39; MTCW

Raabe, Wilhelm 1831-1910 . . . . . . **TCLC 45**
See also DLB 129

Rabe, David (William) 1940- . . . **CLC 4, 8, 33**
See also CA 85-88; CABS 3; DLB 7

Rabelais, Francois
1483-1553 . . . . **LC 5; DA; WLC**

Rabinovitch, Sholem 1859-1916
See Aleichem, Sholom
See also CA 104

Radcliffe, Ann (Ward) 1764-1823 . . **NCLC 6**
See also DLB 39

Radiguet, Raymond 1903-1923 . . . . **TCLC 29**
See also DLB 65

Radnoti, Miklos 1909-1944 . . . . . . **TCLC 16**
See also CA 118

Rado, James 1939- . . . . **CLC 17**
See also CA 105

Radvanyi, Netty 1900-1983
See Seghers, Anna
See also CA 85-88; 110

Raeburn, John (Hay) 1941- . . . . **CLC 34**
See also CA 57-60

Ragni, Gerome 1942-1991 . . . . **CLC 17**
See also CA 105; 134

Rahv, Philip . . . . **CLC 24**
See also Greenberg, Ivan

Raine, Craig 1944- . . . . **CLC 32**
See also CA 108; CANR 29; DLB 40

Raine, Kathleen (Jessie) 1908- . . . **CLC 7, 45**
See also CA 85-88; DLB 20; MTCW

Rainis, Janis 1865-1929 . . . . **TCLC 29**

Rakosi, Carl . . . . **CLC 47**
See also Rawley, Callman
See also CAAS 5

Raleigh, Richard
See Lovecraft, H(oward) P(hillips)

Rallentando, H. P.
See Sayers, Dorothy L(eigh)

Ramal, Walter
See de la Mare, Walter (John)

Ramon, Juan
See Jimenez (Mantecon), Juan Ramon

Ramos, Graciliano 1892-1953 . . . . . **TCLC 32**

Rampersad, Arnold 1941- . . . . **CLC 44**
See also CA 127; 133; DLB 111

Rampling, Anne
See Rice, Anne

Ramuz, Charles-Ferdinand
1878-1947 . . . . **TCLC 33**

Rand, Ayn
1905-1982 . . . . . . **CLC 3, 30, 44, 79; DA; WLC**
See also AAYA 10; CA 13-16R; 105;
CANR 27; MTCW

Randall, Dudley (Felker)
1914- . . . . **CLC 1; BLC**
See also BW; CA 25-28R; CANR 23;
DLB 41

Randall, Robert
See Silverberg, Robert

Ranger, Ken
See Creasey, John

Ransom, John Crowe
1888-1974 . . . . **CLC 2, 4, 5, 11, 24**
See also CA 5-8R; 49-52; CANR 6, 34;
DLB 45, 63; MTCW

Rao, Raja 1909- . . . . **CLC 25, 56**
See also CA 73-76; MTCW

Raphael, Frederic (Michael)
1931- . . . . **CLC 2, 14**
See also CA 1-4R; CANR 1; DLB 14

Ratcliffe, James P.
See Mencken, H(enry) L(ouis)

Rathbone, Julian 1935- . . . . **CLC 41**
See also CA 101; CANR 34

Rattigan, Terence (Mervyn)
1911-1977 . . . . **CLC 7**
See also CA 85-88; 73-76;
CDBLB 1945-1960; DLB 13; MTCW

Ratushinskaya, Irina 1954- . . . . **CLC 54**
See also CA 129

Raven, Simon (Arthur Noel)
1927- . . . . **CLC 14**
See also CA 81-84

Rawley, Callman 1903-
See Rakosi, Carl
See also CA 21-24R; CANR 12, 32

Rawlings, Marjorie Kinnan
1896-1953 . . . . **TCLC 4**
See also CA 104; 137; DLB 9, 22, 102;
JRDA; MAICYA; YABC 1

Ray, Satyajit 1921-1992 . . . . **CLC 16, 76**
See also CA 114; 137

Read, Herbert Edward 1893-1968 . . . . **CLC 4**
See also CA 85-88; 25-28R; DLB 20

Read, Piers Paul 1941- . . . . . . **CLC 4, 10, 25**
See also CA 21-24R; CANR 38; DLB 14;
SATA 21

Reade, Charles 1814-1884 . . . . **NCLC 2**
See also DLB 21

Reade, Hamish
See Gray, Simon (James Holliday)

Reading, Peter 1946- . . . . **CLC 47**
See also CA 103; DLB 40

Reaney, James 1926- . . . . **CLC 13**
See also CA 41-44R; CAAS 15; CANR 42;
DLB 68; SATA 43

Rebreanu, Liviu 1885-1944 . . . . **TCLC 28**

Rechy, John (Francisco)
1934- . . . . **CLC 1, 7, 14, 18; HLC**
See also CA 5-8R; CAAS 4; CANR 6, 32;
DLB 122; DLBY 82; HW

Redcam, Tom 1870-1933 . . . . **TCLC 25**

Reddin, Keith . . . . **CLC 67**

Redgrove, Peter (William)
1932- . . . . **CLC 6, 41**
See also CA 1-4R; CANR 3, 39; DLB 40

Redmon, Anne . . . . **CLC 22**
See also Nightingale, Anne Redmon
See also DLBY 86

Reed, Eliot
See Ambler, Eric

Reed, Ishmael
1938- . . . **CLC 2, 3, 5, 6, 13, 32, 60; BLC**
See also BW; CA 21-24R; CANR 25;
DLB 2, 5, 33; DLBD 8; MTCW

Reed, John (Silas) 1887-1920 . . . . . . **TCLC 9**
See also CA 106

Reed, Lou . . . . **CLC 21**
See also Firbank, Louis

Reeve, Clara 1729-1807 . . . . **NCLC 19**
See also DLB 39

Reid, Christopher (John) 1949- . . . . . **CLC 33**
See also CA 140; DLB 40

Reid, Desmond
See Moorcock, Michael (John)

Reid Banks, Lynne 1929-
　　See Banks, Lynne Reid
　　See also CA 1-4R; CANR 6, 22, 38;
　　　CLR 24; JRDA; MAICYA; SATA 22, 75

Reilly, William K.
　　See Creasey, John

Reiner, Max
　　See Caldwell, (Janet Miriam) Taylor
　　　(Holland)

Reis, Ricardo
　　See Pessoa, Fernando (Antonio Nogueira)

Remarque, Erich Maria
　　1898-1970 . . . . **CLC 21; DA**
　　See also CA 77-80; 29-32R; DLB 56;
　　　MTCW

Remizov, A.
　　See Remizov, Aleksei (Mikhailovich)

Remizov, A. M.
　　See Remizov, Aleksei (Mikhailovich)

Remizov, Aleksei (Mikhailovich)
　　1877-1957 . . . . **TCLC 27**
　　See also CA 125; 133

Renan, Joseph Ernest
　　1823-1892 . . . . **NCLC 26**

Renard, Jules 1864-1910 . . . . **TCLC 17**
　　See also CA 117

Renault, Mary . . . . **CLC 3, 11, 17**
　　See also Challans, Mary
　　See also DLBY 83

Rendell, Ruth (Barbara) 1930- . . **CLC 28, 48**
　　See also Vine, Barbara
　　See also CA 109; CANR 32; DLB 87;
　　　MTCW

Renoir, Jean 1894-1979 . . . . **CLC 20**
　　See also CA 129; 85-88

Resnais, Alain 1922- . . . . **CLC 16**

Reverdy, Pierre 1889-1960 . . . . **CLC 53**
　　See also CA 97-100; 89-92

Rexroth, Kenneth
　　1905-1982 . . . . . . **CLC 1, 2, 6, 11, 22, 49**
　　See also CA 5-8R; 107; CANR 14, 34;
　　　CDALB 1941-1968; DLB 16, 48;
　　　DLBY 82; MTCW

Reyes, Alfonso 1889-1959 . . . . **TCLC 33**
　　See also CA 131; HW

Reyes y Basoalto, Ricardo Eliecer Neftali
　　See Neruda, Pablo

Reymont, Wladyslaw (Stanislaw)
　　1868(?)-1925 . . . . **TCLC 5**
　　See also CA 104

Reynolds, Jonathan 1942- . . . . **CLC 6, 38**
　　See also CA 65-68; CANR 28

Reynolds, Joshua 1723-1792 . . . . **LC 15**
　　See also DLB 104

Reynolds, Michael Shane 1937- . . . . **CLC 44**
　　See also CA 65-68; CANR 9

Reznikoff, Charles 1894-1976 . . . . **CLC 9**
　　See also CA 33-36; 61-64; CAP 2; DLB 28,
　　　45

Rezzori (d'Arezzo), Gregor von
　　1914- . . . . **CLC 25**
　　See also CA 122; 136

Rhine, Richard
　　See Silverstein, Alvin

Rhodes, Eugene Manlove
　　1869-1934 . . . . **TCLC 53**

R'hoone
　　See Balzac, Honore de

Rhys, Jean
　　1890(?)-1979 . . . . **CLC 2, 4, 6, 14, 19, 51**
　　See also CA 25-28R; 85-88; CANR 35;
　　　CDBLB 1945-1960; DLB 36, 117; MTCW

Ribeiro, Darcy 1922- . . . . **CLC 34**
　　See also CA 33-36R

Ribeiro, Joao Ubaldo (Osorio Pimentel)
　　1941- . . . . **CLC 10, 67**
　　See also CA 81-84

Ribman, Ronald (Burt) 1932- . . . . . . **CLC 7**
　　See also CA 21-24R

Ricci, Nino 1959- . . . . **CLC 70**
　　See also CA 137

Rice, Anne 1941- . . . . **CLC 41**
　　See also AAYA 9; BEST 89:2; CA 65-68;
　　　CANR 12, 36

Rice, Elmer (Leopold)
　　1892-1967 . . . . **CLC 7, 49**
　　See also CA 21-22; 25-28R; CAP 2; DLB 4,
　　　7; MTCW

Rice, Tim 1944- . . . . **CLC 21**
　　See also CA 103

Rich, Adrienne (Cecile)
　　1929- . . . . **CLC 3, 6, 7, 11, 18, 36, 73, 76;**
　　　　　　　　　　　　　　　　　　　　　　PC 5
　　See also CA 9-12R; CANR 20; DLB 5, 67;
　　　MTCW

Rich, Barbara
　　See Graves, Robert (von Ranke)

Rich, Robert
　　See Trumbo, Dalton

Richards, David Adams 1950- . . . . . . **CLC 59**
　　See also CA 93-96; DLB 53

Richards, I(vor) A(rmstrong)
　　1893-1979 . . . . **CLC 14, 24**
　　See also CA 41-44R; 89-92; CANR 34;
　　　DLB 27

Richardson, Anne
　　See Roiphe, Anne Richardson

Richardson, Dorothy Miller
　　1873-1957 . . . . **TCLC 3**
　　See also CA 104; DLB 36

Richardson, Ethel Florence (Lindesay)
　　1870-1946
　　See Richardson, Henry Handel
　　See also CA 105

Richardson, Henry Handel . . . . **TCLC 4**
　　See also Richardson, Ethel Florence
　　　(Lindesay)

Richardson, Samuel
　　1689-1761 . . . . **LC 1; DA; WLC**
　　See also CDBLB 1660-1789; DLB 39

Richler, Mordecai
　　1931- . . . . **CLC 3, 5, 9, 13, 18, 46, 70**
　　See also AITN 1; CA 65-68; CANR 31;
　　　CLR 17; DLB 53; MAICYA; MTCW;
　　　SATA 27, 44

Richter, Conrad (Michael)
　　1890-1968 . . . . **CLC 30**
　　See also CA 5-8R; 25-28R; CANR 23;
　　　DLB 9; MTCW; SATA 3

Riddell, J. H. 1832-1906 . . . . **TCLC 40**

Riding, Laura . . . . **CLC 3, 7**
　　See also Jackson, Laura (Riding)

Riefenstahl, Berta Helene Amalia 1902-
　　See Riefenstahl, Leni
　　See also CA 108

Riefenstahl, Leni . . . . **CLC 16**
　　See also Riefenstahl, Berta Helene Amalia

Riffe, Ernest
　　See Bergman, (Ernst) Ingmar

Riley, James Whitcomb
　　1849-1916 . . . . **TCLC 51**
　　See also CA 118; 137; MAICYA; SATA 17

Riley, Tex
　　See Creasey, John

Rilke, Rainer Maria
　　1875-1926 . . . . **TCLC 1, 6, 19; PC 2**
　　See also CA 104; 132; DLB 81; MTCW

Rimbaud, (Jean Nicolas) Arthur
　　1854-1891 . . . . . **NCLC 4, 35; DA; PC 3;**
　　　　　　　　　　　　　　　　　　　　　　WLC

Rinehart, Mary Roberts
　　1876-1958 . . . . **TCLC 52**
　　See also CA 108

Ringmaster, The
　　See Mencken, H(enry) L(ouis)

Ringwood, Gwen(dolyn Margaret) Pharis
　　1910-1984 . . . . **CLC 48**
　　See also CA 112; DLB 88

Rio, Michel 19(?)- . . . . **CLC 43**

Ritsos, Giannes
　　See Ritsos, Yannis

Ritsos, Yannis 1909-1990 . . . . . **CLC 6, 13, 31**
　　See also CA 77-80; 133; CANR 39; MTCW

Ritter, Erika 1948(?)- . . . . **CLC 52**

Rivera, Jose Eustasio 1889-1928 . . . **TCLC 35**
　　See also HW

Rivers, Conrad Kent 1933-1968 . . . . . . **CLC 1**
　　See also BW; CA 85-88; DLB 41

Rivers, Elfrida
　　See Bradley, Marion Zimmer

Riverside, John
　　See Heinlein, Robert A(nson)

Rizal, Jose 1861-1896 . . . . **NCLC 27**

Roa Bastos, Augusto (Antonio)
　　1917- . . . . **CLC 45; HLC**
　　See also CA 131; DLB 113; HW

Robbe-Grillet, Alain
　　1922- . . . . . . **CLC 1, 2, 4, 6, 8, 10, 14, 43**
　　See also CA 9-12R; CANR 33; DLB 83;
　　　MTCW

Robbins, Harold 1916- . . . . **CLC 5**
　　See also CA 73-76; CANR 26; MTCW

Robbins, Thomas Eugene 1936-
　　See Robbins, Tom
　　See also CA 81-84; CANR 29; MTCW

Robbins, Tom . . . . **CLC 9, 32, 64**
　　See also Robbins, Thomas Eugene
　　See also BEST 90:3; DLBY 80

Robbins, Trina 1938- . . . . **CLC 21**
　　See also CA 128

Roberts, Charles G(eorge) D(ouglas)
1860-1943 . . . . TCLC 8
See also CA 105; CLR 33; DLB 92;
SATA 29

Roberts, Kate   1891-1985 . . . . CLC 15
See also CA 107; 116

Roberts, Keith (John Kingston)
1935- . . . . CLC 14
See also CA 25-28R

Roberts, Kenneth (Lewis)
1885-1957 . . . . TCLC 23
See also CA 109; DLB 9

Roberts, Michele (B.)   1949- . . . . CLC 48
See also CA 115

Robertson, Ellis
See Ellison, Harlan; Silverberg, Robert

Robertson, Thomas William
1829-1871 . . . . NCLC 35

Robinson, Edwin Arlington
1869-1935 . . . . TCLC 5; DA; PC 1
See also CA 104; 133; CDALB 1865-1917;
DLB 54; MTCW

Robinson, Henry Crabb
1775-1867 . . . . NCLC 15
See also DLB 107

Robinson, Jill   1936- . . . . CLC 10
See also CA 102

Robinson, Kim Stanley   1952- . . . . . . CLC 34
See also CA 126

Robinson, Lloyd
See Silverberg, Robert

Robinson, Marilynne   1944- . . . . CLC 25
See also CA 116

Robinson, Smokey . . . . CLC 21
See also Robinson, William, Jr.

Robinson, William, Jr.   1940-
See Robinson, Smokey
See also CA 116

Robison, Mary   1949- . . . . CLC 42
See also CA 113; 116; DLB 130

Rod, Edouard   1857-1910 . . . . TCLC 52

Roddenberry, Eugene Wesley   1921-1991
See Roddenberry, Gene
See also CA 110; 135; CANR 37; SATA 45

Roddenberry, Gene . . . . CLC 17
See also Roddenberry, Eugene Wesley
See also AAYA 5; SATA-Obit 69

Rodgers, Mary   1931- . . . . CLC 12
See also CA 49-52; CANR 8; CLR 20;
JRDA; MAICYA; SATA 8

Rodgers, W(illiam) R(obert)
1909-1969 . . . . CLC 7
See also CA 85-88; DLB 20

Rodman, Eric
See Silverberg, Robert

Rodman, Howard   1920(?)-1985 . . . . . CLC 65
See also CA 118

Rodman, Maia
See Wojciechowska, Maia (Teresa)

Rodriguez, Claudio   1934- . . . . CLC 10
See also DLB 134

Roelvaag, O(le) E(dvart)
1876-1931 . . . . TCLC 17
See also CA 117; DLB 9

Roethke, Theodore (Huebner)
1908-1963 . . . . . . CLC 1, 3, 8, 11, 19, 46
See also CA 81-84; CABS 2;
CDALB 1941-1968; DLB 5; MTCW

Rogers, Thomas Hunton   1927- . . . . . CLC 57
See also CA 89-92

Rogers, Will(iam Penn Adair)
1879-1935 . . . . TCLC 8
See also CA 105; DLB 11

Rogin, Gilbert   1929- . . . . CLC 18
See also CA 65-68; CANR 15

Rohan, Koda . . . . TCLC 22
See also Koda Shigeyuki

Rohmer, Eric . . . . CLC 16
See also Scherer, Jean-Marie Maurice

Rohmer, Sax . . . . TCLC 28
See also Ward, Arthur Henry Sarsfield
See also DLB 70

Roiphe, Anne Richardson   1935- . . . CLC 3, 9
See also CA 89-92; DLBY 80

Rojas, Fernando de   1465-1541 . . . . . . LC 23

Rolfe, Frederick (William Serafino Austin
Lewis Mary)   1860-1913 . . . . . . TCLC 12
See also CA 107; DLB 34

Rolland, Romain   1866-1944 . . . . TCLC 23
See also CA 118; DLB 65

Rolvaag, O(le) E(dvart)
See Roelvaag, O(le) E(dvart)

Romain Arnaud, Saint
See Aragon, Louis

Romains, Jules   1885-1972 . . . . CLC 7
See also CA 85-88; CANR 34; DLB 65;
MTCW

Romero, Jose Ruben   1890-1952 . . . TCLC 14
See also CA 114; 131; HW

Ronsard, Pierre de   1524-1585 . . . . LC 6

Rooke, Leon   1934- . . . . CLC 25, 34
See also CA 25-28R; CANR 23

Roper, William   1498-1578 . . . . LC 10

Roquelaure, A. N.
See Rice, Anne

Rosa, Joao Guimaraes   1908-1967 . . . CLC 23
See also CA 89-92; DLB 113

Rosen, Richard (Dean)   1949- . . . . . . CLC 39
See also CA 77-80

Rosenberg, Isaac   1890-1918 . . . . . . TCLC 12
See also CA 107; DLB 20

Rosenblatt, Joe . . . . CLC 15
See also Rosenblatt, Joseph

Rosenblatt, Joseph   1933-
See Rosenblatt, Joe
See also CA 89-92

Rosenfeld, Samuel   1896-1963
See Tzara, Tristan
See also CA 89-92

Rosenthal, M(acha) L(ouis)   1917- . . . CLC 28
See also CA 1-4R; CAAS 6; CANR 4;
DLB 5; SATA 59

Ross, Barnaby
See Dannay, Frederic

Ross, Bernard L.
See Follett, Ken(neth Martin)

Ross, J. H.
See Lawrence, T(homas) E(dward)

Ross, Martin
See Martin, Violet Florence
See also DLB 135

Ross, (James) Sinclair   1908- . . . . CLC 13
See also CA 73-76; DLB 88

Rossetti, Christina (Georgina)
1830-1894 . . . NCLC 2; DA; PC 7; WLC
See also DLB 35; MAICYA; SATA 20

Rossetti, Dante Gabriel
1828-1882 . . . . NCLC 4; DA; WLC
See also CDBLB 1832-1890; DLB 35

Rossner, Judith (Perelman)
1935- . . . . CLC 6, 9, 29
See also AITN 2; BEST 90:3; CA 17-20R;
CANR 18; DLB 6; MTCW

Rostand, Edmond (Eugene Alexis)
1868-1918 . . . . TCLC 6, 37; DA
See also CA 104; 126; MTCW

Roth, Henry   1906- . . . . CLC 2, 6, 11
See also CA 11-12; CANR 38; CAP 1;
DLB 28; MTCW

Roth, Joseph   1894-1939 . . . . TCLC 33
See also DLB 85

Roth, Philip (Milton)
1933- . . . . . . CLC 1, 2, 3, 4, 6, 9, 15, 22,
31, 47, 66; DA; WLC
See also BEST 90:3; CA 1-4R; CANR 1, 22,
36; CDALB 1968-1988; DLB 2, 28;
DLBY 82; MTCW

Rothenberg, Jerome   1931- . . . . CLC 6, 57
See also CA 45-48; CANR 1; DLB 5

Roumain, Jacques (Jean Baptiste)
1907-1944 . . . . TCLC 19; BLC
See also BW; CA 117; 125

Rourke, Constance (Mayfield)
1885-1941 . . . . TCLC 12
See also CA 107; YABC 1

Rousseau, Jean-Baptiste   1671-1741 . . . LC 9

Rousseau, Jean-Jacques
1712-1778 . . . . LC 14; DA; WLC

Roussel, Raymond   1877-1933 . . . . . TCLC 20
See also CA 117

Rovit, Earl (Herbert)   1927- . . . . CLC 7
See also CA 5-8R; CANR 12

Rowe, Nicholas   1674-1718 . . . . LC 8
See also DLB 84

Rowley, Ames Dorrance
See Lovecraft, H(oward) P(hillips)

Rowson, Susanna Haswell
1762(?)-1824 . . . . NCLC 5
See also DLB 37

Roy, Gabrielle   1909-1983 . . . . CLC 10, 14
See also CA 53-56; 110; CANR 5; DLB 68;
MTCW

Rozewicz, Tadeusz   1921- . . . . CLC 9, 23
See also CA 108; CANR 36; MTCW

Ruark, Gibbons   1941- . . . . CLC 3
See also CA 33-36R; CANR 14, 31;
DLB 120

Rubens, Bernice (Ruth)   1923- . . . CLC 19, 31
See also CA 25-28R; CANR 33; DLB 14;
MTCW

Rudkin, (James) David 1936- ...... **CLC 14**
See also CA 89-92; DLB 13

Rudnik, Raphael 1933-............ **CLC 7**
See also CA 29-32R

Ruffian, M.
See Hasek, Jaroslav (Matej Frantisek)

Ruiz, Jose Martinez.............. **CLC 11**
See also Martinez Ruiz, Jose

Rukeyser, Muriel
1913-1980 .... **CLC 6, 10, 15, 27**
See also CA 5-8R; 93-96; CANR 26;
DLB 48; MTCW; SATA 22

Rule, Jane (Vance) 1931- .... **CLC 27**
See also CA 25-28R; CAAS 18; CANR 12;
DLB 60

Rulfo, Juan 1918-1986.... **CLC 8, 80; HLC**
See also CA 85-88; 118; CANR 26;
DLB 113; HW; MTCW

Runeberg, Johan 1804-1877...... **NCLC 41**

Runyon, (Alfred) Damon
1884(?)-1946 .... **TCLC 10**
See also CA 107; DLB 11, 86

Rush, Norman 1933-............. **CLC 44**
See also CA 121; 126

Rushdie, (Ahmed) Salman
1947- .... **CLC 23, 31, 55**
See also BEST 89:3; CA 108; 111;
CANR 33; MTCW

Rushforth, Peter (Scott) 1945- ..... **CLC 19**
See also CA 101

Ruskin, John 1819-1900......... **TCLC 20**
See also CA 114; 129; CDBLB 1832-1890;
DLB 55; SATA 24

Russ, Joanna 1937-.............. **CLC 15**
See also CA 25-28R; CANR 11, 31; DLB 8;
MTCW

Russell, George William 1867-1935
See A. E.
See also CA 104; CDBLB 1890-1914

Russell, (Henry) Ken(neth Alfred)
1927- .... **CLC 16**
See also CA 105

Russell, Willy 1947-.............. **CLC 60**

Rutherford, Mark .... **TCLC 25**
See also White, William Hale
See also DLB 18

Ruyslinck, Ward
See Belser, Reimond Karel Maria de

Ryan, Cornelius (John) 1920-1974 ... **CLC 7**
See also CA 69-72; 53-56; CANR 38

Ryan, Michael 1946- .... **CLC 65**
See also CA 49-52; DLBY 82

Rybakov, Anatoli (Naumovich)
1911- .... **CLC 23, 53**
See also CA 126; 135

Ryder, Jonathan
See Ludlum, Robert

Ryga, George 1932-1987 .... **CLC 14**
See also CA 101; 124; CANR 43; DLB 60

S. S.
See Sassoon, Siegfried (Lorraine)

Saba, Umberto 1883-1957 .... **TCLC 33**
See also DLB 114

Sabatini, Rafael 1875-1950 .... **TCLC 47**

Sabato, Ernesto (R.)
1911- .... **CLC 10, 23; HLC**
See also CA 97-100; CANR 32; HW;
MTCW

Sacastru, Martin
See Bioy Casares, Adolfo

Sacher-Masoch, Leopold von
1836(?)-1895 .... **NCLC 31**

Sachs, Marilyn (Stickle) 1927- ..... **CLC 35**
See also AAYA 2; CA 17-20R; CANR 13;
CLR 2; JRDA; MAICYA; SAAS 2;
SATA 3, 68

Sachs, Nelly 1891-1970 .... **CLC 14**
See also CA 17-18; 25-28R; CAP 2

Sackler, Howard (Oliver)
1929-1982 .... **CLC 14**
See also CA 61-64; 108; CANR 30; DLB 7

Sacks, Oliver (Wolf) 1933- .... **CLC 67**
See also CA 53-56; CANR 28; MTCW

Sade, Donatien Alphonse Francois Comte
1740-1814 .... **NCLC 3**

Sadoff, Ira 1945-.................. **CLC 9**
See also CA 53-56; CANR 5, 21; DLB 120

Saetone
See Camus, Albert

Safire, William 1929-............. **CLC 10**
See also CA 17-20R; CANR 31

Sagan, Carl (Edward) 1934-........ **CLC 30**
See also AAYA 2; CA 25-28R; CANR 11,
36; MTCW; SATA 58

Sagan, Francoise .... **CLC 3, 6, 9, 17, 36**
See also Quoirez, Francoise
See also DLB 83

Sahgal, Nayantara (Pandit) 1927-... **CLC 41**
See also CA 9-12R; CANR 11

Saint, H(arry) F. 1941- .... **CLC 50**
See also CA 127

St. Aubin de Teran, Lisa 1953-
See Teran, Lisa St. Aubin de
See also CA 118; 126

Sainte-Beuve, Charles Augustin
1804-1869 .... **NCLC 5**

**Saint-Exupery, Antoine (Jean Baptiste Marie
Roger) de** 1900-1944 .... **TCLC 2; WLC**
See also CA 108; 132; CLR 10; DLB 72;
MAICYA; MTCW; SATA 20

St. John, David
See Hunt, E(verette) Howard, Jr.

Saint-John Perse
See Leger, (Marie-Rene Auguste) Alexis
Saint-Leger

Saintsbury, George (Edward Bateman)
1845-1933 .... **TCLC 31**
See also DLB 57

Sait Faik .... **TCLC 23**
See also Abasiyanik, Sait Faik

Saki .... **TCLC 3; SSC 12**
See also Munro, H(ector) H(ugh)

Salama, Hannu 1936-............. **CLC 18**

Salamanca, J(ack) R(ichard)
1922- .... **CLC 4, 15**
See also CA 25-28R

Sale, J. Kirkpatrick
See Sale, Kirkpatrick

Sale, Kirkpatrick 1937- .... **CLC 68**
See also CA 13-16R; CANR 10

Salinas (y Serrano), Pedro
1891(?)-1951 .... **TCLC 17**
See also CA 117; DLB 134

Salinger, J(erome) D(avid)
1919- ...... **CLC 1, 3, 8, 12, 55, 56; DA;
SSC 2; WLC**
See also AAYA 2; CA 5-8R; CANR 39;
CDALB 1941-1968; CLR 18; DLB 2, 102;
MAICYA; MTCW; SATA 67

Salisbury, John
See Caute, David

Salter, James 1925- .... **CLC 7, 52, 59**
See also CA 73-76; DLB 130

Saltus, Edgar (Everton)
1855-1921 .... **TCLC 8**
See also CA 105

Saltykov, Mikhail Evgrafovich
1826-1889 .... **NCLC 16**

Samarakis, Antonis 1919- .... **CLC 5**
See also CA 25-28R; CAAS 16; CANR 36

Sanchez, Florencio 1875-1910..... **TCLC 37**
See also HW

Sanchez, Luis Rafael 1936-........ **CLC 23**
See also CA 128; HW

Sanchez, Sonia 1934-........ **CLC 5; BLC**
See also BW; CA 33-36R; CANR 24;
CLR 18; DLB 41; DLBD 8; MAICYA;
MTCW; SATA 22

Sand, George
1804-1876 ...... **NCLC 2, 42; DA; WLC**
See also DLB 119

Sandburg, Carl (August)
1878-1967 .... **CLC 1, 4, 10, 15, 35; DA;
PC 2; WLC**
See also CA 5-8R; 25-28R; CANR 35;
CDALB 1865-1917; DLB 17, 54;
MAICYA; MTCW; SATA 8

Sandburg, Charles
See Sandburg, Carl (August)

Sandburg, Charles A.
See Sandburg, Carl (August)

Sanders, (James) Ed(ward) 1939- ... **CLC 53**
See also CA 13-16R; CANR 13; DLB 16

Sanders, Lawrence 1920-.......... **CLC 41**
See also BEST 89:4; CA 81-84; CANR 33;
MTCW

Sanders, Noah
See Blount, Roy (Alton), Jr.

Sanders, Winston P.
See Anderson, Poul (William)

Sandoz, Mari(e Susette)
1896-1966 .... **CLC 28**
See also CA 1-4R; 25-28R; CANR 17;
DLB 9; MTCW; SATA 5

Saner, Reg(inald Anthony) 1931- .... **CLC 9**
See also CA 65-68

Sannazaro, Jacopo 1456(?)-1530...... **LC 8**

Sansom, William 1912-1976....... **CLC 2, 6**
See also CA 5-8R; 65-68; CANR 42;
MTCW

Santayana, George 1863-1952..... **TCLC 40**
See also CA 115; DLB 54, 71

Scrum, R.
See Crumb, R(obert)

Scudery, Madeleine de 1607-1701..... **LC 2**

Scum
See Crumb, R(obert)

Scumbag, Little Bobby
See Crumb, R(obert)

Seabrook, John
See Hubbard, L(afayette) Ron(ald)

Sealy, I. Allan 1951- .... **CLC 55**

Search, Alexander
See Pessoa, Fernando (Antonio Nogueira)

Sebastian, Lee
See Silverberg, Robert

Sebastian Owl
See Thompson, Hunter S(tockton)

Sebestyen, Ouida 1924- .... **CLC 30**
See also AAYA 8; CA 107; CANR 40;
CLR 17; JRDA; MAICYA; SAAS 10;
SATA 39

Secundus, H. Scriblerus
See Fielding, Henry

Sedges, John
See Buck, Pearl S(ydenstricker)

Sedgwick, Catharine Maria
1789-1867 .... **NCLC 19**
See also DLB 1, 74

Seelye, John 1931- .... **CLC 7**

Seferiades, Giorgos Stylianou 1900-1971
See Seferis, George
See also CA 5-8R; 33-36R; CANR 5, 36;
MTCW

Seferis, George .... **CLC 5, 11**
See also Seferiades, Giorgos Stylianou

Segal, Erich (Wolf) 1937- .... **CLC 3, 10**
See also BEST 89:1; CA 25-28R; CANR 20,
36; DLBY 86; MTCW

Seger, Bob 1945-................ **CLC 35**

Seghers, Anna .... **CLC 7**
See also Radvanyi, Netty
See also DLB 69

Seidel, Frederick (Lewis) 1936-..... **CLC 18**
See also CA 13-16R; CANR 8; DLBY 84

Seifert, Jaroslav 1901-1986..... **CLC 34, 44**
See also CA 127; MTCW

Sei Shonagon c. 966-1017(?) ...... **CMLC 6**

Selby, Hubert, Jr. 1928- ..... **CLC 1, 2, 4, 8**
See also CA 13-16R; CANR 33; DLB 2

Selzer, Richard 1928-............. **CLC 74**
See also CA 65-68; CANR 14

Sembene, Ousmane
See Ousmane, Sembene

Senancour, Etienne Pivert de
1770-1846 .... **NCLC 16**
See also DLB 119

Sender, Ramon (Jose)
1902-1982 .... **CLC 8; HLC**
See also CA 5-8R; 105; CANR 8; HW;
MTCW

Seneca, Lucius Annaeus
4B.C.-65.................... **CMLC 6**

Senghor, Leopold Sedar
1906- .... **CLC 54; BLC**
See also BW; CA 116; 125; MTCW

Serling, (Edward) Rod(man)
1924-1975 .... **CLC 30**
See also AITN 1; CA 65-68; 57-60; DLB 26

Serna, Ramon Gomez de la
See Gomez de la Serna, Ramon

Serpieres
See Guillevic, (Eugene)

Service, Robert
See Service, Robert W(illiam)
See also DLB 92

Service, Robert W(illiam)
1874(?)-1958 ...... **TCLC 15; DA; WLC**
See also Service, Robert
See also CA 115; 140; SATA 20

Seth, Vikram 1952-............... **CLC 43**
See also CA 121; 127; DLB 120

Seton, Cynthia Propper
1926-1982 .... **CLC 27**
See also CA 5-8R; 108; CANR 7

Seton, Ernest (Evan) Thompson
1860-1946 .... **TCLC 31**
See also CA 109; DLB 92; JRDA; SATA 18

Seton-Thompson, Ernest
See Seton, Ernest (Evan) Thompson

Settle, Mary Lee 1918- .... **CLC 19, 61**
See also CA 89-92; CAAS 1; DLB 6

Seuphor, Michel
See Arp, Jean

Sevigne, Marie (de Rabutin-Chantal) Marquise
de 1626-1696 .... **LC 11**

Sexton, Anne (Harvey)
1928-1974 .... **CLC 2, 4, 6, 8, 10, 15, 53;**
DA; PC 2; WLC
See also CA 1-4R; 53-56; CABS 2;
CANR 3, 36; CDALB 1941-1968; DLB 5;
MTCW; SATA 10

Shaara, Michael (Joseph Jr.)
1929-1988 .... **CLC 15**
See also AITN 1; CA 102; DLBY 83

Shackleton, C. C.
See Aldiss, Brian W(ilson)

Shacochis, Bob .... **CLC 39**
See also Shacochis, Robert G.

Shacochis, Robert G. 1951-
See Shacochis, Bob
See also CA 119; 124

Shaffer, Anthony (Joshua) 1926-.... **CLC 19**
See also CA 110; 116; DLB 13

Shaffer, Peter (Levin)
1926- .... **CLC 5, 14, 18, 37, 60**
See also CA 25-28R; CANR 25;
CDBLB 1960 to Present; DLB 13;
MTCW

Shakey, Bernard
See Young, Neil

Shalamov, Varlam (Tikhonovich)
1907(?)-1982 .... **CLC 18**
See also CA 129; 105

Shamlu, Ahmad 1925- .... **CLC 10**

Shammas, Anton 1951-............ **CLC 55**

Shange, Ntozake
1948- .... **CLC 8, 25, 38, 74; BLC; DC 3**
See also AAYA 9; BW; CA 85-88; CABS 3;
CANR 27; DLB 38; MTCW

Shanley, John Patrick 1950-....... **CLC 75**
See also CA 128; 133

Shapcott, Thomas William 1935- ... **CLC 38**
See also CA 69-72

Shapiro, Jane..................... **CLC 76**

Shapiro, Karl (Jay) 1913- .. **CLC 4, 8, 15, 53**
See also CA 1-4R; CAAS 6; CANR 1, 36;
DLB 48; MTCW

Sharp, William 1855-1905 .... **TCLC 39**

Sharpe, Thomas Ridley 1928-
See Sharpe, Tom
See also CA 114; 122

Sharpe, Tom...................... **CLC 36**
See also Sharpe, Thomas Ridley
See also DLB 14

Shaw, Bernard.................... **TCLC 45**
See also Shaw, George Bernard

Shaw, G. Bernard
See Shaw, George Bernard

Shaw, George Bernard
1856-1950 .... **TCLC 3, 9, 21; DA; WLC**
See also Shaw, Bernard
See also CA 104; 128; CDBLB 1914-1945;
DLB 10, 57; MTCW

Shaw, Henry Wheeler
1818-1885 .... **NCLC 15**
See also DLB 11

Shaw, Irwin 1913-1984....... **CLC 7, 23, 34**
See also AITN 1; CA 13-16R; 112;
CANR 21; CDALB 1941-1968; DLB 6,
102; DLBY 84; MTCW

Shaw, Robert 1927-1978 .... **CLC 5**
See also AITN 1; CA 1-4R; 81-84;
CANR 4; DLB 13, 14

Shaw, T. E.
See Lawrence, T(homas) E(dward)

Shawn, Wallace 1943- .... **CLC 41**
See also CA 112

Sheed, Wilfrid (John Joseph)
1930- .... **CLC 2, 4, 10, 53**
See also CA 65-68; CANR 30; DLB 6;
MTCW

Sheldon, Alice Hastings Bradley
1915(?)-1987
See Tiptree, James, Jr.
See also CA 108; 122; CANR 34; MTCW

Sheldon, John
See Bloch, Robert (Albert)

Shelley, Mary Wollstonecraft (Godwin)
1797-1851 .... **NCLC 14; DA; WLC**
See also CDBLB 1789-1832; DLB 110, 116;
SATA 29

Shelley, Percy Bysshe
1792-1822 .... **NCLC 18; DA; WLC**
See also CDBLB 1789-1832; DLB 96, 110

Shepard, Jim 1956-............... **CLC 36**
See also CA 137

Shepard, Lucius 1947- .... **CLC 34**
See also CA 128; 141

Sinyavsky, Andrei (Donatevich)
 1925- . . . . **CLC 8**
 See also CA 85-88

Sirin, V.
 See Nabokov, Vladimir (Vladimirovich)

Sissman, L(ouis) E(dward)
 1928-1976 . . . . **CLC 9, 18**
 See also CA 21-24R; 65-68; CANR 13;
 DLB 5

Sisson, C(harles) H(ubert) 1914- . . . . . **CLC 8**
 See also CA 1-4R; CAAS 3; CANR 3;
 DLB 27

Sitwell, Dame Edith
 1887-1964 . . . . **CLC 2, 9, 67; PC 3**
 See also CA 9-12R; CANR 35;
 CDBLB 1945-1960; DLB 20; MTCW

Sjoewall, Maj 1935- . . . . **CLC 7**
 See also CA 65-68

Sjowall, Maj
 See Sjoewall, Maj

Skelton, Robin 1925- . . . . **CLC 13**
 See also AITN 2; CA 5-8R; CAAS 5;
 CANR 28; DLB 27, 53

Skolimowski, Jerzy 1938- . . . . **CLC 20**
 See also CA 128

Skram, Amalie (Bertha)
 1847-1905 . . . . **TCLC 25**

Skvorecky, Josef (Vaclav)
 1924- . . . . **CLC 15, 39, 69**
 See also CA 61-64; CAAS 1; CANR 10, 34;
 MTCW

Slade, Bernard . . . . **CLC 11, 46**
 See also Newbound, Bernard Slade
 See also CAAS 9; DLB 53

Slaughter, Carolyn 1946- . . . . **CLC 56**
 See also CA 85-88

Slaughter, Frank G(ill) 1908- . . . . . . **CLC 29**
 See also AITN 2; CA 5-8R; CANR 5

Slavitt, David R(ytman) 1935- . . . . **CLC 5, 14**
 See also CA 21-24R; CAAS 3; CANR 41;
 DLB 5, 6

Slesinger, Tess 1905-1945 . . . . **TCLC 10**
 See also CA 107; DLB 102

Slessor, Kenneth 1901-1971 . . . . **CLC 14**
 See also CA 102; 89-92

Slowacki, Juliusz 1809-1849 . . . . . **NCLC 15**

Smart, Christopher 1722-1771 . . . . **LC 3**
 See also DLB 109

Smart, Elizabeth 1913-1986 . . . . **CLC 54**
 See also CA 81-84; 118; DLB 88

Smiley, Jane (Graves) 1949- . . . . **CLC 53, 76**
 See also CA 104; CANR 30

Smith, A(rthur) J(ames) M(arshall)
 1902-1980 . . . . **CLC 15**
 See also CA 1-4R; 102; CANR 4; DLB 88

Smith, Betty (Wehner) 1896-1972 . . . **CLC 19**
 See also CA 5-8R; 33-36R; DLBY 82;
 SATA 6

Smith, Charlotte (Turner)
 1749-1806 . . . . **NCLC 23**
 See also DLB 39, 109

Smith, Clark Ashton 1893-1961 . . . . **CLC 43**
 See also CA 143

Smith, Dave . . . . **CLC 22, 42**
 See also Smith, David (Jeddie)
 See also CAAS 7; DLB 5

Smith, David (Jeddie) 1942-
 See Smith, Dave
 See also CA 49-52; CANR 1

Smith, Florence Margaret
 1902-1971 . . . . **CLC 8**
 See also Smith, Stevie
 See also CA 17-18; 29-32R; CANR 35;
 CAP 2; MTCW

Smith, Iain Crichton 1928- . . . . **CLC 64**
 See also CA 21-24R; DLB 40

Smith, John 1580(?)-1631 . . . . **LC 9**

Smith, Johnston
 See Crane, Stephen (Townley)

Smith, Lee 1944- . . . . **CLC 25, 73**
 See also CA 114; 119; DLBY 83

Smith, Martin
 See Smith, Martin Cruz

Smith, Martin Cruz 1942- . . . . **CLC 25**
 See also BEST 89:4; CA 85-88; CANR 6,
 23, 43

Smith, Mary-Ann Tirone 1944- . . . . . **CLC 39**
 See also CA 118; 136

Smith, Patti 1946- . . . . **CLC 12**
 See also CA 93-96

Smith, Pauline (Urmson)
 1882-1959 . . . . **TCLC 25**

Smith, Rosamond
 See Oates, Joyce Carol

Smith, Sheila Kaye
 See Kaye-Smith, Sheila

Smith, Stevie . . . . **CLC 3, 8, 25, 44**
 See also Smith, Florence Margaret
 See also DLB 20

Smith, Wilbur A(ddison) 1933- . . . . . **CLC 33**
 See also CA 13-16R; CANR 7; MTCW

Smith, William Jay 1918- . . . . **CLC 6**
 See also CA 5-8R; DLB 5; MAICYA;
 SATA 2, 68

Smith, Woodrow Wilson
 See Kuttner, Henry

Smolenskin, Peretz 1842-1885 . . . . **NCLC 30**

Smollett, Tobias (George) 1721-1771 . . **LC 2**
 See also CDBLB 1660-1789; DLB 39, 104

Snodgrass, W(illiam) D(e Witt)
 1926- . . . . **CLC 2, 6, 10, 18, 68**
 See also CA 1-4R; CANR 6, 36; DLB 5;
 MTCW

Snow, C(harles) P(ercy)
 1905-1980 . . . . **CLC 1, 4, 6, 9, 13, 19**
 See also CA 5-8R; 101; CANR 28;
 CDBLB 1945-1960; DLB 15, 77; MTCW

Snow, Frances Compton
 See Adams, Henry (Brooks)

Snyder, Gary (Sherman)
 1930- . . . . **CLC 1, 2, 5, 9, 32**
 See also CA 17-20R; CANR 30; DLB 5, 16

Snyder, Zilpha Keatley 1927- . . . . . . **CLC 17**
 See also CA 9-12R; CANR 38; CLR 31;
 JRDA; MAICYA; SAAS 2; SATA 1, 28,
 75

Soares, Bernardo
 See Pessoa, Fernando (Antonio Nogueira)

Sobh, A.
 See Shamlu, Ahmad

Sobol, Joshua . . . . **CLC 60**

Soderberg, Hjalmar 1869-1941 . . . . **TCLC 39**

Sodergran, Edith (Irene)
 See Soedergran, Edith (Irene)

Soedergran, Edith (Irene)
 1892-1923 . . . . **TCLC 31**

Softly, Edgar
 See Lovecraft, H(oward) P(hillips)

Softly, Edward
 See Lovecraft, H(oward) P(hillips)

Sokolov, Raymond 1941- . . . . **CLC 7**
 See also CA 85-88

Solo, Jay
 See Ellison, Harlan

Sologub, Fyodor . . . . **TCLC 9**
 See also Teternikov, Fyodor Kuzmich

Solomons, Ikey Esquir
 See Thackeray, William Makepeace

Solomos, Dionysios 1798-1857 . . . **NCLC 15**

Solwoska, Mara
 See French, Marilyn

Solzhenitsyn, Aleksandr I(sayevich)
 1918- . . . . . . **CLC 1, 2, 4, 7, 9, 10, 18, 26,
 34, 78; DA; WLC**
 See also AITN 1; CA 69-72; CANR 40;
 MTCW

Somers, Jane
 See Lessing, Doris (May)

Somerville, Edith 1858-1949 . . . . . . **TCLC 51**
 See also DLB 135

Somerville & Ross
 See Martin, Violet Florence; Somerville,
 Edith

Sommer, Scott 1951- . . . . **CLC 25**
 See also CA 106

Sondheim, Stephen (Joshua)
 1930- . . . . **CLC 30, 39**
 See also CA 103

Sontag, Susan 1933- . . . **CLC 1, 2, 10, 13, 31**
 See also CA 17-20R; CANR 25; DLB 2, 67;
 MTCW

Sophocles
 496(?)B.C.-406(?)B.C. . . . . . **CMLC 2; DA;
 DC 1**

Sorel, Julia
 See Drexler, Rosalyn

Sorrentino, Gilbert
 1929- . . . . **CLC 3, 7, 14, 22, 40**
 See also CA 77-80; CANR 14, 33; DLB 5;
 DLBY 80

Soto, Gary 1952- . . . . **CLC 32, 80; HLC**
 See also AAYA 10; CA 119; 125; DLB 82;
 HW; JRDA

Soupault, Philippe 1897-1990 . . . . . . **CLC 68**
 See also CA 116; 131

Souster, (Holmes) Raymond
 1921- . . . . **CLC 5, 14**
 See also CA 13-16R; CAAS 14; CANR 13,
 29; DLB 88; SATA 63

Southern, Terry 1926- .... **CLC 7**
See also CA 1-4R; CANR 1; DLB 2

Southey, Robert 1774-1843 .... **NCLC 8**
See also DLB 93, 107; SATA 54

Southworth, Emma Dorothy Eliza Nevitte
1819-1899 .... **NCLC 26**

Souza, Ernest
See Scott, Evelyn

Soyinka, Wole
1934- .... **CLC 3, 5, 14, 36, 44; BLC;
DA; DC 2; WLC**
See also BW; CA 13-16R; CANR 27, 39;
DLB 125; MTCW

Spackman, W(illiam) M(ode)
1905-1990 .... **CLC 46**
See also CA 81-84; 132

Spacks, Barry 1931- .... **CLC 14**
See also CA 29-32R; CANR 33; DLB 105

Spanidou, Irini 1946- .... **CLC 44**

Spark, Muriel (Sarah)
1918- .... **CLC 2, 3, 5, 8, 13, 18, 40;
SSC 10**
See also CA 5-8R; CANR 12, 36;
CDBLB 1945-1960; DLB 15; MTCW

Spaulding, Douglas
See Bradbury, Ray (Douglas)

Spaulding, Leonard
See Bradbury, Ray (Douglas)

Spence, J. A. D.
See Eliot, T(homas) S(tearns)

Spencer, Elizabeth 1921- .... **CLC 22**
See also CA 13-16R; CANR 32; DLB 6;
MTCW; SATA 14

Spencer, Leonard G.
See Silverberg, Robert

Spencer, Scott 1945- .... **CLC 30**
See also CA 113; DLBY 86

Spender, Stephen (Harold)
1909- .... **CLC 1, 2, 5, 10, 41**
See also CA 9-12R; CANR 31;
CDBLB 1945-1960; DLB 20; MTCW

Spengler, Oswald (Arnold Gottfried)
1880-1936 .... **TCLC 25**
See also CA 118

Spenser, Edmund
1552(?)-1599 .... **LC 5; DA; PC 8; WLC**
See also CDBLB Before 1660

Spicer, Jack 1925-1965 ...... **CLC 8, 18, 72**
See also CA 85-88; DLB 5, 16

Spiegelman, Art 1948- .... **CLC 76**
See also AAYA 10; CA 125; CANR 41

Spielberg, Peter 1929- .... **CLC 6**
See also CA 5-8R; CANR 4; DLBY 81

Spielberg, Steven 1947- .... **CLC 20**
See also AAYA 8; CA 77-80; CANR 32;
SATA 32

Spillane, Frank Morrison 1918-
See Spillane, Mickey
See also CA 25-28R; CANR 28; MTCW;
SATA 66

Spillane, Mickey .... **CLC 3, 13**
See also Spillane, Frank Morrison

Spinoza, Benedictus de 1632-1677 .... **LC 9**

Spinrad, Norman (Richard) 1940-... **CLC 46**
See also CA 37-40R; CANR 20; DLB 8

Spitteler, Carl (Friedrich Georg)
1845-1924 .... **TCLC 12**
See also CA 109; DLB 129

Spivack, Kathleen (Romola Drucker)
1938- .... **CLC 6**
See also CA 49-52

Spoto, Donald 1941- .... **CLC 39**
See also CA 65-68; CANR 11

Springsteen, Bruce (F.) 1949- ...... **CLC 17**
See also CA 111

Spurling, Hilary 1940- .... **CLC 34**
See also CA 104; CANR 25

Squires, (James) Radcliffe
1917-1993 .... **CLC 51**
See also CA 1-4R; 140; CANR 6, 21

Srivastava, Dhanpat Rai 1880(?)-1936
See Premchand
See also CA 118

Stacy, Donald
See Pohl, Frederik

Stael, Germaine de
See Stael-Holstein, Anne Louise Germaine
Necker Baronn
See also DLB 119

Stael-Holstein, Anne Louise Germaine Necker
Baronn 1766-1817 .... **NCLC 3**
See also Stael, Germaine de

Stafford, Jean 1915-1979 ... **CLC 4, 7, 19, 68**
See also CA 1-4R; 85-88; CANR 3; DLB 2;
MTCW; SATA 22

Stafford, William (Edgar)
1914-1993 .... **CLC 4, 7, 29**
See also CA 5-8R; 142; CAAS 3; CANR 5,
22; DLB 5

Staines, Trevor
See Brunner, John (Kilian Houston)

Stairs, Gordon
See Austin, Mary (Hunter)

Stannard, Martin 1947- .... **CLC 44**
See also CA 142

Stanton, Maura 1946- .... **CLC 9**
See also CA 89-92; CANR 15; DLB 120

Stanton, Schuyler
See Baum, L(yman) Frank

Stapledon, (William) Olaf
1886-1950 .... **TCLC 22**
See also CA 111; DLB 15

Starbuck, George (Edwin) 1931-.... **CLC 53**
See also CA 21-24R; CANR 23

Stark, Richard
See Westlake, Donald E(dwin)

Staunton, Schuyler
See Baum, L(yman) Frank

Stead, Christina (Ellen)
1902-1983 .... **CLC 2, 5, 8, 32, 80**
See also CA 13-16R; 109; CANR 33, 40;
MTCW

Stead, William Thomas
1849-1912 .... **TCLC 48**

Steele, Richard 1672-1729 .... **LC 18**
See also CDBLB 1660-1789; DLB 84, 101

Steele, Timothy (Reid) 1948-....... **CLC 45**
See also CA 93-96; CANR 16; DLB 120

Steffens, (Joseph) Lincoln
1866-1936 .... **TCLC 20**
See also CA 117

Stegner, Wallace (Earle)
1909-1993 .... **CLC 9, 49, 81**
See also AITN 1; BEST 90:3; CA 1-4R;
141; CAAS 9; CANR 1, 21; DLB 9;
MTCW

Stein, Gertrude
1874-1946 ...... **TCLC 1, 6, 28, 48; DA;
WLC**
See also CA 104; 132; CDALB 1917-1929;
DLB 4, 54, 86; MTCW

Steinbeck, John (Ernst)
1902-1968 ...... **CLC 1, 5, 9, 13, 21, 34,
45, 75; DA; SSC 11; WLC**
See also CA 1-4R; 25-28R; CANR 1, 35;
CDALB 1929-1941; DLB 7, 9; DLBD 2;
MTCW; SATA 9

Steinem, Gloria 1934-............. **CLC 63**
See also CA 53-56; CANR 28; MTCW

Steiner, George 1929-............. **CLC 24**
See also CA 73-76; CANR 31; DLB 67;
MTCW; SATA 62

Steiner, K. Leslie
See Delany, Samuel R(ay, Jr.)

Steiner, Rudolf 1861-1925........ **TCLC 13**
See also CA 107

Stendhal 1783-1842.... **NCLC 23; DA; WLC**
See also DLB 119

Stephen, Leslie 1832-1904 .... **TCLC 23**
See also CA 123; DLB 57

Stephen, Sir Leslie
See Stephen, Leslie

Stephen, Virginia
See Woolf, (Adeline) Virginia

Stephens, James 1882(?)-1950...... **TCLC 4**
See also CA 104; DLB 19

Stephens, Reed
See Donaldson, Stephen R.

Steptoe, Lydia
See Barnes, Djuna

Sterchi, Beat 1949-............... **CLC 65**

Sterling, Brett
See Bradbury, Ray (Douglas); Hamilton,
Edmond

Sterling, Bruce 1954-............. **CLC 72**
See also CA 119

Sterling, George 1869-1926 .... **TCLC 20**
See also CA 117; DLB 54

Stern, Gerald 1925- .... **CLC 40**
See also CA 81-84; CANR 28; DLB 105

Stern, Richard (Gustave) 1928-... **CLC 4, 39**
See also CA 1-4R; CANR 1, 25; DLBY 87

Sternberg, Josef von 1894-1969..... **CLC 20**
See also CA 81-84

Sterne, Laurence
1713-1768 .... **LC 2; DA; WLC**
See also CDBLB 1660-1789; DLB 39

Sternheim, (William Adolf) Carl
1878-1942 .... **TCLC 8**
See also CA 105; DLB 56, 118

Stevens, Mark 1951- .... **CLC 34**
See also CA 122

Stevens, Wallace
1879-1955 .... **TCLC 3, 12, 45; DA;**
PC 6; WLC
See also CA 104; 124; CDALB 1929-1941;
DLB 54; MTCW

Stevenson, Anne (Katharine)
1933- .... **CLC 7, 33**
See also CA 17-20R; CAAS 9; CANR 9, 33;
DLB 40; MTCW

Stevenson, Robert Louis (Balfour)
1850-1894 .... **NCLC 5, 14; DA;**
SSC 11; WLC
See also CDBLB 1890-1914; CLR 10, 11;
DLB 18, 57; JRDA; MAICYA; YABC 2

Stewart, J(ohn) I(nnes) M(ackintosh)
1906- .... **CLC 7, 14, 32**
See also CA 85-88; CAAS 3; MTCW

Stewart, Mary (Florence Elinor)
1916- .... **CLC 7, 35**
See also CA 1-4R; CANR 1; SATA 12

Stewart, Mary Rainbow
See Stewart, Mary (Florence Elinor)

Stifter, Adalbert 1805-1868 ...... **NCLC 41**
See also DLB 133

Still, James 1906- .... **CLC 49**
See also CA 65-68; CAAS 17; CANR 10,
26; DLB 9; SATA 29

Sting
See Sumner, Gordon Matthew

Stirling, Arthur
See Sinclair, Upton (Beall)

Stitt, Milan 1941- .... **CLC 29**
See also CA 69-72

Stockton, Francis Richard 1834-1902
See Stockton, Frank R.
See also CA 108; 137; MAICYA; SATA 44

Stockton, Frank R. .... **TCLC 47**
See also Stockton, Francis Richard
See also DLB 42, 74; SATA 32

Stoddard, Charles
See Kuttner, Henry

Stoker, Abraham 1847-1912
See Stoker, Bram
See also CA 105; DA; SATA 29

Stoker, Bram .... **TCLC 8; WLC**
See also Stoker, Abraham
See also CDBLB 1890-1914; DLB 36, 70

Stolz, Mary (Slattery) 1920- .... **CLC 12**
See also AAYA 8; AITN 1; CA 5-8R;
CANR 13, 41; JRDA; MAICYA;
SAAS 3; SATA 10, 71

Stone, Irving 1903-1989 .... **CLC 7**
See also AITN 1; CA 1-4R; 129; CAAS 3;
CANR 1, 23; MTCW; SATA 3;
SATA-Obit 64

Stone, Oliver 1946- .... **CLC 73**
See also CA 110

Stone, Robert (Anthony)
1937- .... **CLC 5, 23, 42**
See also CA 85-88; CANR 23; MTCW

Stone, Zachary
See Follett, Ken(neth Martin)

Stoppard, Tom
1937- ...... **CLC 1, 3, 4, 5, 8, 15, 29, 34,**
63; DA; WLC
See also CA 81-84; CANR 39;
CDBLB 1960 to Present; DLB 13;
DLBY 85; MTCW

Storey, David (Malcolm)
1933- .... **CLC 2, 4, 5, 8**
See also CA 81-84; CANR 36; DLB 13, 14;
MTCW

Storm, Hyemeyohsts 1935- .... **CLC 3**
See also CA 81-84

Storm, (Hans) Theodor (Woldsen)
1817-1888 .... **NCLC 1**

Storni, Alfonsina
1892-1938 .... **TCLC 5; HLC**
See also CA 104; 131; HW

Stout, Rex (Todhunter) 1886-1975 ... **CLC 3**
See also AITN 2; CA 61-64

Stow, (Julian) Randolph 1935- .. **CLC 23, 48**
See also CA 13-16R; CANR 33; MTCW

Stowe, Harriet (Elizabeth) Beecher
1811-1896 .... **NCLC 3; DA; WLC**
See also CDALB 1865-1917; DLB 1, 12, 42,
74; JRDA; MAICYA; YABC 1

Strachey, (Giles) Lytton
1880-1932 .... **TCLC 12**
See also CA 110; DLBD 10

Strand, Mark 1934- ...... **CLC 6, 18, 41, 71**
See also CA 21-24R; CANR 40; DLB 5;
SATA 41

Straub, Peter (Francis) 1943- ...... **CLC 28**
See also BEST 89:1; CA 85-88; CANR 28;
DLBY 84; MTCW

Strauss, Botho 1944- .... **CLC 22**
See also DLB 124

Streatfeild, (Mary) Noel
1895(?)-1986 .... **CLC 21**
See also CA 81-84; 120; CANR 31;
CLR 17; MAICYA; SATA 20, 48

Stribling, T(homas) S(igismund)
1881-1965 .... **CLC 23**
See also CA 107; DLB 9

Strindberg, (Johan) August
1849-1912 ...... **TCLC 1, 8, 21, 47; DA;**
WLC
See also CA 104; 135

Stringer, Arthur 1874-1950 .... **TCLC 37**
See also DLB 92

Stringer, David
See Roberts, Keith (John Kingston)

Strugatskii, Arkadii (Natanovich)
1925-1991 .... **CLC 27**
See also CA 106; 135

Strugatskii, Boris (Natanovich)
1933- .... **CLC 27**
See also CA 106

Strummer, Joe 1953(?)- .... **CLC 30**
See also Clash, The

Stuart, Don A.
See Campbell, John W(ood, Jr.)

Stuart, Ian
See MacLean, Alistair (Stuart)

Stuart, Jesse (Hilton)
1906-1984 .... **CLC 1, 8, 11, 14, 34**
See also CA 5-8R; 112; CANR 31; DLB 9,
48, 102; DLBY 84; SATA 2, 36

Sturgeon, Theodore (Hamilton)
1918-1985 .... **CLC 22, 39**
See also Queen, Ellery
See also CA 81-84; 116; CANR 32; DLB 8;
DLBY 85; MTCW

Sturges, Preston 1898-1959 .... **TCLC 48**
See also CA 114; DLB 26

Styron, William
1925- .... **CLC 1, 3, 5, 11, 15, 60**
See also BEST 90:4; CA 5-8R; CANR 6, 33;
CDALB 1968-1988; DLB 2; DLBY 80;
MTCW

Suarez Lynch, B.
See Bioy Casares, Adolfo; Borges, Jorge
Luis

Suarez Lynch, B.
See Borges, Jorge Luis

Su Chien 1884-1918
See Su Man-shu
See also CA 123

Sudermann, Hermann 1857-1928 .. **TCLC 15**
See also CA 107; DLB 118

Sue, Eugene 1804-1857 .... **NCLC 1**
See also DLB 119

Sueskind, Patrick 1949- .... **CLC 44**

Sukenick, Ronald 1932- ..... **CLC 3, 4, 6, 48**
See also CA 25-28R; CAAS 8; CANR 32;
DLBY 81

Suknaski, Andrew 1942- .... **CLC 19**
See also CA 101; DLB 53

Sullivan, Vernon
See Vian, Boris

Sully Prudhomme 1839-1907 ...... **TCLC 31**

Su Man-shu .... **TCLC 24**
See also Su Chien

Summerforest, Ivy B.
See Kirkup, James

Summers, Andrew James 1942- ..... **CLC 26**
See also Police, The

Summers, Andy
See Summers, Andrew James

Summers, Hollis (Spurgeon, Jr.)
1916- .... **CLC 10**
See also CA 5-8R; CANR 3; DLB 6

Summers, (Alphonsus Joseph-Mary Augustus)
Montague 1880-1948 .... **TCLC 16**
See also CA 118

Sumner, Gordon Matthew 1951- .... **CLC 26**
See also Police, The

Surtees, Robert Smith
1803-1864 .... **NCLC 14**
See also DLB 21

Susann, Jacqueline 1921-1974 .... **CLC 3**
See also AITN 1; CA 65-68; 53-56; MTCW

Suskind, Patrick
See Sueskind, Patrick

Sutcliff, Rosemary 1920-1992 ...... **CLC 26**
See also AAYA 10; CA 5-8R; 139;
CANR 37; CLR 1; JRDA; MAICYA;
SATA 6, 44; SATA-Obit 73

Thackeray, William Makepeace
1811-1863 .... **NCLC 5, 14, 22, 43; DA; WLC**
See also CDBLB 1832-1890; DLB 21, 55; SATA 23

Thakura, Ravindranatha
See Tagore, Rabindranath

Tharoor, Shashi 1956- .... **CLC 70**
See also CA 141

Thelwell, Michael Miles 1939- ..... **CLC 22**
See also CA 101

Theobald, Lewis, Jr.
See Lovecraft, H(oward) P(hillips)

Theodorescu, Ion N. 1880-1967
See Arghezi, Tudor
See also CA 116

Theriault, Yves 1915-1983 .... **CLC 79**
See also CA 102; DLB 88

Theroux, Alexander (Louis)
1939- .... **CLC 2, 25**
See also CA 85-88; CANR 20

Theroux, Paul (Edward)
1941- .... **CLC 5, 8, 11, 15, 28, 46**
See also BEST 89:4; CA 33-36R; CANR 20; DLB 2; MTCW; SATA 44

Thesen, Sharon 1946- .... **CLC 56**

Thevenin, Denis
See Duhamel, Georges

Thibault, Jacques Anatole Francois
1844-1924
See France, Anatole
See also CA 106; 127; MTCW

Thiele, Colin (Milton) 1920- .... **CLC 17**
See also CA 29-32R; CANR 12, 28; CLR 27; MAICYA; SAAS 2; SATA 14, 72

Thomas, Audrey (Callahan)
1935- .... **CLC 7, 13, 37**
See also AITN 2; CA 21-24R; CANR 36; DLB 60; MTCW

Thomas, D(onald) M(ichael)
1935- .... **CLC 13, 22, 31**
See also CA 61-64; CAAS 11; CANR 17; CDBLB 1960 to Present; DLB 40; MTCW

Thomas, Dylan (Marlais)
1914-1953 ... **TCLC 1, 8, 45; DA; PC 2; SSC 3; WLC**
See also CA 104; 120; CDBLB 1945-1960; DLB 13, 20; MTCW; SATA 60

Thomas, (Philip) Edward
1878-1917 .... **TCLC 10**
See also CA 106; DLB 19

Thomas, Joyce Carol 1938- .... **CLC 35**
See also BW; CA 113; 116; CLR 19; DLB 33; JRDA; MAICYA; MTCW; SAAS 7; SATA 40

Thomas, Lewis 1913-1993 .... **CLC 35**
See also CA 85-88; 143; CANR 38; MTCW

Thomas, Paul
See Mann, (Paul) Thomas

Thomas, Piri 1928- .... **CLC 17**
See also CA 73-76; HW

Thomas, R(onald) S(tuart)
1913- .... **CLC 6, 13, 48**
See also CA 89-92; CAAS 4; CANR 30; CDBLB 1960 to Present; DLB 27; MTCW

Thomas, Ross (Elmore) 1926- ...... **CLC 39**
See also CA 33-36R; CANR 22

Thompson, Francis Clegg
See Mencken, H(enry) L(ouis)

Thompson, Francis Joseph
1859-1907 .... **TCLC 4**
See also CA 104; CDBLB 1890-1914; DLB 19

Thompson, Hunter S(tockton)
1939- .... **CLC 9, 17, 40**
See also BEST 89:1; CA 17-20R; CANR 23; MTCW

Thompson, James Myers
See Thompson, Jim (Myers)

Thompson, Jim (Myers)
1906-1977(?) .... **CLC 69**
See also CA 140

Thompson, Judith .... **CLC 39**

Thomson, James 1700-1748 .... **LC 16**

Thomson, James 1834-1882 ...... **NCLC 18**

Thoreau, Henry David
1817-1862 ...... **NCLC 7, 21; DA; WLC**
See also CDALB 1640-1865; DLB 1

Thornton, Hall
See Silverberg, Robert

Thurber, James (Grover)
1894-1961 ... **CLC 5, 11, 25; DA; SSC 1**
See also CA 73-76; CANR 17, 39; CDALB 1929-1941; DLB 4, 11, 22, 102; MAICYA; MTCW; SATA 13

Thurman, Wallace (Henry)
1902-1934 .... **TCLC 6; BLC**
See also BW; CA 104; 124; DLB 51

Ticheburn, Cheviot
See Ainsworth, William Harrison

Tieck, (Johann) Ludwig
1773-1853 .... **NCLC 5**
See also DLB 90

Tiger, Derry
See Ellison, Harlan

Tilghman, Christopher 1948(?)- ..... **CLC 65**

Tillinghast, Richard (Williford)
1940- .... **CLC 29**
See also CA 29-32R; CANR 26

Timrod, Henry 1828-1867 .... **NCLC 25**
See also DLB 3

Tindall, Gillian 1938- .... **CLC 7**
See also CA 21-24R; CANR 11

Tiptree, James, Jr. .... **CLC 48, 50**
See also Sheldon, Alice Hastings Bradley
See also DLB 8

Titmarsh, Michael Angelo
See Thackeray, William Makepeace

Tocqueville, Alexis (Charles Henri Maurice Clerel Comte) 1805-1859 ..... **NCLC 7**

Tolkien, J(ohn) R(onald) R(euel)
1892-1973 .... **CLC 1, 2, 3, 8, 12, 38; DA; WLC**
See also AAYA 10; AITN 1; CA 17-18; 45-48; CANR 36; CAP 2; CDBLB 1914-1945; DLB 15; JRDA; MAICYA; MTCW; SATA 2, 24, 32

Toller, Ernst 1893-1939 .... **TCLC 10**
See also CA 107; DLB 124

Tolson, M. B.
See Tolson, Melvin B(eaunorus)

Tolson, Melvin B(eaunorus)
1898(?)-1966 .... **CLC 36; BLC**
See also BW; CA 124; 89-92; DLB 48, 76

Tolstoi, Aleksei Nikolaevich
See Tolstoy, Alexey Nikolaevich

Tolstoy, Alexey Nikolaevich
1882-1945 .... **TCLC 18**
See also CA 107

Tolstoy, Count Leo
See Tolstoy, Leo (Nikolaevich)

Tolstoy, Leo (Nikolaevich)
1828-1910 ..... **TCLC 4, 11, 17, 28, 44; DA; SSC 9; WLC**
See also CA 104; 123; SATA 26

Tomasi di Lampedusa, Giuseppe 1896-1957
See Lampedusa, Giuseppe (Tomasi) di
See also CA 111

Tomlin, Lily...................... **CLC 17**
See also Tomlin, Mary Jean

Tomlin, Mary Jean 1939(?)-
See Tomlin, Lily
See also CA 117

Tomlinson, (Alfred) Charles
1927- .... **CLC 2, 4, 6, 13, 45**
See also CA 5-8R; CANR 33; DLB 40

Tonson, Jacob
See Bennett, (Enoch) Arnold

Toole, John Kennedy
1937-1969 .... **CLC 19, 64**
See also CA 104; DLBY 81

Toomer, Jean
1894-1967 ...... **CLC 1, 4, 13, 22; BLC; PC 7; SSC 1**
See also BW; CA 85-88; CDALB 1917-1929; DLB 45, 51; MTCW

Torley, Luke
See Blish, James (Benjamin)

Tornimparte, Alessandra
See Ginzburg, Natalia

Torre, Raoul della
See Mencken, H(enry) L(ouis)

Torrey, E(dwin) Fuller 1937- .... **CLC 34**
See also CA 119

Torsvan, Ben Traven
See Traven, B.

Torsvan, Benno Traven
See Traven, B.

Torsvan, Berick Traven
See Traven, B.

Torsvan, Berwick Traven
See Traven, B.

Torsvan, Bruno Traven
See Traven, B.

von Daeniken, Erich 1935- .... **CLC 30**
  See also von Daniken, Erich
  See also AITN 1; CA 37-40R; CANR 17

von Daniken, Erich .... **CLC 30**
  See also von Daeniken, Erich

von Heidenstam, (Carl Gustaf) Verner
  See Heidenstam, (Carl Gustaf) Verner von

von Heyse, Paul (Johann Ludwig)
  See Heyse, Paul (Johann Ludwig von)

von Hofmannsthal, Hugo
  See Hofmannsthal, Hugo von

von Horvath, Odon
  See Horvath, Oedoen von

von Horvath, Oedoen
  See Horvath, Oedoen von

von Liliencron, (Friedrich Adolf Axel) Detlev
  See Liliencron, (Friedrich Adolf Axel)
    Detlev von

Vonnegut, Kurt, Jr.
  1922- ...... **CLC 1, 2, 3, 4, 5, 8, 12, 22,**
          40, 60; DA; SSC 8; WLC
  See also AAYA 6; AITN 1; BEST 90:4;
    CA 1-4R; CANR 1, 25;
    CDALB 1968-1988; DLB 2, 8; DLBD 3;
    DLBY 80; MTCW

Von Rachen, Kurt
  See Hubbard, L(afayette) Ron(ald)

von Rezzori (d'Arezzo), Gregor
  See Rezzori (d'Arezzo), Gregor von

von Sternberg, Josef
  See Sternberg, Josef von

Vorster, Gordon 1924- .... **CLC 34**
  See also CA 133

Vosce, Trudie
  See Ozick, Cynthia

Voznesensky, Andrei (Andreievich)
  1933- .... **CLC 1, 15, 57**
  See also CA 89-92; CANR 37; MTCW

Waddington, Miriam 1917- .... **CLC 28**
  See also CA 21-24R; CANR 12, 30;
    DLB 68

Wagman, Fredrica 1937- .... **CLC 7**
  See also CA 97-100

Wagner, Richard 1813-1883. ...... **NCLC 9**
  See also DLB 129

Wagner-Martin, Linda 1936- .... **CLC 50**

Wagoner, David (Russell)
  1926- .... **CLC 3, 5, 15**
  See also CA 1-4R; CAAS 3; CANR 2;
    DLB 5; SATA 14

Wah, Fred(erick James) 1939- ...... **CLC 44**
  See also CA 107; 141; DLB 60

Wahloo, Per 1926-1975 .... **CLC 7**
  See also CA 61-64

Wahloo, Peter
  See Wahloo, Per

Wain, John (Barrington)
  1925- .... **CLC 2, 11, 15, 46**
  See also CA 5-8R; CAAS 4; CANR 23;
    CDBLB 1960 to Present; DLB 15, 27;
    MTCW

Wajda, Andrzej 1926- .... **CLC 16**
  See also CA 102

Wakefield, Dan 1932- .... **CLC 7**
  See also CA 21-24R; CAAS 7

Wakoski, Diane
  1937- .... **CLC 2, 4, 7, 9, 11, 40**
  See also CA 13-16R; CAAS 1; CANR 9;
    DLB 5

Wakoski-Sherbell, Diane
  See Wakoski, Diane

Walcott, Derek (Alton)
  1930- .... **CLC 2, 4, 9, 14, 25, 42, 67, 76;**
                  BLC
  See also BW; CA 89-92; CANR 26;
    DLB 117; DLBY 81; MTCW

Waldman, Anne 1945- .... **CLC 7**
  See also CA 37-40R; CAAS 17; CANR 34;
    DLB 16

Waldo, E. Hunter
  See Sturgeon, Theodore (Hamilton)

Waldo, Edward Hamilton
  See Sturgeon, Theodore (Hamilton)

Walker, Alice (Malsenior)
  1944- .... **CLC 5, 6, 9, 19, 27, 46, 58;**
                  BLC; DA; SSC 5
  See also AAYA 3; BEST 89:4; BW;
    CA 37-40R; CANR 9, 27;
    CDALB 1968-1988; DLB 6, 33; MTCW;
    SATA 31

Walker, David Harry 1911-1992. ... **CLC 14**
  See also CA 1-4R; 137; CANR 1; SATA 8;
    SATA-Obit 71

Walker, Edward Joseph 1934-
  See Walker, Ted
  See also CA 21-24R; CANR 12, 28

Walker, George F. 1947- .... **CLC 44, 61**
  See also CA 103; CANR 21, 43; DLB 60

Walker, Joseph A. 1935- .... **CLC 19**
  See also BW; CA 89-92; CANR 26; DLB 38

Walker, Margaret (Abigail)
  1915- .... **CLC 1, 6; BLC**
  See also BW; CA 73-76; CANR 26;
    DLB 76; MTCW

Walker, Ted .... **CLC 13**
  See also Walker, Edward Joseph
  See also DLB 40

Wallace, David Foster 1962- .... **CLC 50**
  See also CA 132

Wallace, Dexter
  See Masters, Edgar Lee

Wallace, Irving 1916-1990 .... **CLC 7, 13**
  See also AITN 1; CA 1-4R; 132; CAAS 1;
    CANR 1, 27; MTCW

Wallant, Edward Lewis
  1926-1962 .... **CLC 5, 10**
  See also CA 1-4R; CANR 22; DLB 2, 28;
    MTCW

Walpole, Horace 1717-1797. .... **LC 2**
  See also DLB 39, 104

Walpole, Hugh (Seymour)
  1884-1941 .... **TCLC 5**
  See also CA 104; DLB 34

Walser, Martin 1927- .... **CLC 27**
  See also CA 57-60; CANR 8; DLB 75, 124

Walser, Robert 1878-1956 .... **TCLC 18**
  See also CA 118; DLB 66

Walsh, Jill Paton. .... **CLC 35**
  See also Paton Walsh, Gillian
  See also CLR 2; SAAS 3

Walter, Villiam Christian
  See Andersen, Hans Christian

Wambaugh, Joseph (Aloysius, Jr.)
  1937- .... **CLC 3, 18**
  See also AITN 1; BEST 89:3; CA 33-36R;
    CANR 42; DLB 6; DLBY 83; MTCW

Ward, Arthur Henry Sarsfield 1883-1959
  See Rohmer, Sax
  See also CA 108

Ward, Douglas Turner 1930- .... **CLC 19**
  See also BW; CA 81-84; CANR 27; DLB 7,
    38

Ward, Peter
  See Faust, Frederick (Schiller)

Warhol, Andy 1928(?)-1987 .... **CLC 20**
  See also BEST 89:4; CA 89-92; 121;
    CANR 34

Warner, Francis (Robert le Plastrier)
  1937- .... **CLC 14**
  See also CA 53-56; CANR 11

Warner, Marina 1946- .... **CLC 59**
  See also CA 65-68; CANR 21

Warner, Rex (Ernest) 1905-1986.... **CLC 45**
  See also CA 89-92; 119; DLB 15

Warner, Susan (Bogert)
  1819-1885 .... **NCLC 31**
  See also DLB 3, 42

Warner, Sylvia (Constance) Ashton
  See Ashton-Warner, Sylvia (Constance)

Warner, Sylvia Townsend
  1893-1978 .... **CLC 7, 19**
  See also CA 61-64; 77-80; CANR 16;
    DLB 34; MTCW

Warren, Mercy Otis 1728-1814... **NCLC 13**
  See also DLB 31

Warren, Robert Penn
  1905-1989 .... **CLC 1, 4, 6, 8, 10, 13, 18,**
                39, 53, 59; DA; SSC 4; WLC
  See also AITN 1; CA 13-16R; 129;
    CANR 10; CDALB 1968-1988; DLB 2,
    48; DLBY 80, 89; MTCW; SATA 46, 63

Warshofsky, Isaac
  See Singer, Isaac Bashevis

Warton, Thomas 1728-1790 .... **LC 15**
  See also DLB 104, 109

Waruk, Kona
  See Harris, (Theodore) Wilson

Warung, Price 1855-1911 .... **TCLC 45**

Warwick, Jarvis
  See Garner, Hugh

Washington, Alex
  See Harris, Mark

Washington, Booker T(aliaferro)
  1856-1915 .... **TCLC 10; BLC**
  See also BW; CA 114; 125; SATA 28

Washington, George 1732-1799 ...... **LC 25**
  See also DLB 31

Wassermann, (Karl) Jakob
  1873-1934 .... **TCLC 6**
  See also CA 104; DLB 66

Wasserstein, Wendy
   1950- .... **CLC 32, 59; DC 4**
   See also CA 121; 129; CABS 3

Waterhouse, Keith (Spencer)
   1929-........................ **CLC 47**
   See also CA 5-8R; CANR 38; DLB 13, 15;
   MTCW

Waters, Roger 1944-.............. **CLC 35**
   See also Pink Floyd

Watkins, Frances Ellen
   See Harper, Frances Ellen Watkins

Watkins, Gerrold
   See Malzberg, Barry N(athaniel)

Watkins, Paul 1964-.............. **CLC 55**
   See also CA 132

Watkins, Vernon Phillips
   1906-1967 .... **CLC 43**
   See also CA 9-10; 25-28R; CAP 1; DLB 20

Watson, Irving S.
   See Mencken, H(enry) L(ouis)

Watson, John H.
   See Farmer, Philip Jose

Watson, Richard F.
   See Silverberg, Robert

Waugh, Auberon (Alexander) 1939- .. **CLC 7**
   See also CA 45-48; CANR 6, 22; DLB 14

Waugh, Evelyn (Arthur St. John)
   1903-1966 ...... **CLC 1, 3, 8, 13, 19, 27,
   44; DA; WLC**
   See also CA 85-88; 25-28R; CANR 22;
   CDBLB 1914-1945; DLB 15; MTCW

Waugh, Harriet 1944- .... **CLC 6**
   See also CA 85-88; CANR 22

Ways, C. R.
   See Blount, Roy (Alton), Jr.

Waystaff, Simon
   See Swift, Jonathan

Webb, (Martha) Beatrice (Potter)
   1858-1943 .... **TCLC 22**
   See also Potter, Beatrice
   See also CA 117

Webb, Charles (Richard) 1939-...... **CLC 7**
   See also CA 25-28R

Webb, James H(enry), Jr. 1946-.... **CLC 22**
   See also CA 81-84

Webb, Mary (Gladys Meredith)
   1881-1927 .... **TCLC 24**
   See also CA 123; DLB 34

Webb, Mrs. Sidney
   See Webb, (Martha) Beatrice (Potter)

Webb, Phyllis 1927-.............. **CLC 18**
   See also CA 104; CANR 23; DLB 53

Webb, Sidney (James)
   1859-1947 .... **TCLC 22**
   See also CA 117

Webber, Andrew Lloyd............. **CLC 21**
   See also Lloyd Webber, Andrew

Weber, Lenora Mattingly
   1895-1971 .... **CLC 12**
   See also CA 19-20; 29-32R; CAP 1;
   SATA 2, 26

Webster, John 1579(?)-1634(?) .... **DC 2**
   See also CDBLB Before 1660; DA; DLB 58;
   WLC

Webster, Noah 1758-1843 .... **NCLC 30**

Wedekind, (Benjamin) Frank(lin)
   1864-1918 .... **TCLC 7**
   See also CA 104; DLB 118

Weidman, Jerome 1913-............ **CLC 7**
   See also AITN 2; CA 1-4R; CANR 1;
   DLB 28

Weil, Simone (Adolphine)
   1909-1943 .... **TCLC 23**
   See also CA 117

Weinstein, Nathan
   See West, Nathanael

Weinstein, Nathan von Wallenstein
   See West, Nathanael

Weir, Peter (Lindsay) 1944- .... **CLC 20**
   See also CA 113; 123

Weiss, Peter (Ulrich)
   1916-1982 .... **CLC 3, 15, 51**
   See also CA 45-48; 106; CANR 3; DLB 69,
   124

Weiss, Theodore (Russell)
   1916-...................... **CLC 3, 8, 14**
   See also CA 9-12R; CAAS 2; DLB 5

Welch, (Maurice) Denton
   1915-1948 .... **TCLC 22**
   See also CA 121

Welch, James 1940-......... **CLC 6, 14, 52**
   See also CA 85-88; CANR 42

Weldon, Fay
   1933(?)-....... **CLC 6, 9, 11, 19, 36, 59**
   See also CA 21-24R; CANR 16;
   CDBLB 1960 to Present; DLB 14;
   MTCW

Wellek, Rene 1903- .... **CLC 28**
   See also CA 5-8R; CAAS 7; CANR 8;
   DLB 63

Weller, Michael 1942-......... **CLC 10, 53**
   See also CA 85-88

Weller, Paul 1958-.............. **CLC 26**

Wellershoff, Dieter 1925-.......... **CLC 46**
   See also CA 89-92; CANR 16, 37

Welles, (George) Orson
   1915-1985 .... **CLC 20, 80**
   See also CA 93-96; 117

Wellman, Mac 1945- .... **CLC 65**

Wellman, Manly Wade 1903-1986 .. **CLC 49**
   See also CA 1-4R; 118; CANR 6, 16;
   SATA 6, 47

Wells, Carolyn 1869(?)-1942 ...... **TCLC 35**
   See also CA 113; DLB 11

Wells, H(erbert) G(eorge)
   1866-1946 .... **TCLC 6, 12, 19; DA;
   SSC 6; WLC**
   See also CA 110; 121; CDBLB 1914-1945;
   DLB 34, 70; MTCW; SATA 20

Wells, Rosemary 1943-............ **CLC 12**
   See also CA 85-88; CLR 16; MAICYA;
   SAAS 1; SATA 18, 69

Welty, Eudora
   1909- ...... **CLC 1, 2, 5, 14, 22, 33; DA;
   SSC 1; WLC**
   See also CA 9-12R; CABS 1; CANR 32;
   CDALB 1941-1968; DLB 2, 102;
   DLBY 87; MTCW

Wen I-to 1899-1946 .... **TCLC 28**

Wentworth, Robert
   See Hamilton, Edmond

Werfel, Franz (V.) 1890-1945 ...... **TCLC 8**
   See also CA 104; DLB 81, 124

Wergeland, Henrik Arnold
   1808-1845 .... **NCLC 5**

Wersba, Barbara 1932-............ **CLC 30**
   See also AAYA 2; CA 29-32R; CANR 16,
   38; CLR 3; DLB 52; JRDA; MAICYA;
   SAAS 2; SATA 1, 58

Wertmueller, Lina 1928- .... **CLC 16**
   See also CA 97-100; CANR 39

Wescott, Glenway 1901-1987....... **CLC 13**
   See also CA 13-16R; 121; CANR 23;
   DLB 4, 9, 102

Wesker, Arnold 1932- .... **CLC 3, 5, 42**
   See also CA 1-4R; CAAS 7; CANR 1, 33;
   CDBLB 1960 to Present; DLB 13;
   MTCW

Wesley, Richard (Errol) 1945-....... **CLC 7**
   See also BW; CA 57-60; CANR 27; DLB 38

Wessel, Johan Herman 1742-1785 .... **LC 7**

West, Anthony (Panther)
   1914-1987 .... **CLC 50**
   See also CA 45-48; 124; CANR 3, 19;
   DLB 15

West, C. P.
   See Wodehouse, P(elham) G(renville)

West, (Mary) Jessamyn
   1902-1984 .... **CLC 7, 17**
   See also CA 9-12R; 112; CANR 27; DLB 6;
   DLBY 84; MTCW; SATA 37

West, Morris L(anglo) 1916-..... **CLC 6, 33**
   See also CA 5-8R; CANR 24; MTCW

West, Nathanael
   1903-1940 .... **TCLC 1, 14, 44**
   See also CA 104; 125; CDALB 1929-1941;
   DLB 4, 9, 28; MTCW

West, Owen
   See Koontz, Dean R(ay)

West, Paul 1930- .... **CLC 7, 14**
   See also CA 13-16R; CAAS 7; CANR 22;
   DLB 14

West, Rebecca 1892-1983 .. **CLC 7, 9, 31, 50**
   See also CA 5-8R; 109; CANR 19; DLB 36;
   DLBY 83; MTCW

Westall, Robert (Atkinson)
   1929-1993 .... **CLC 17**
   See also CA 69-72; 141; CANR 18;
   CLR 13; JRDA; MAICYA; SAAS 2;
   SATA 23, 69; SATA-Obit 75

Westlake, Donald E(dwin)
   1933-..................... **CLC 7, 33**
   See also CA 17-20R; CAAS 13; CANR 16

Westmacott, Mary
   See Christie, Agatha (Mary Clarissa)

Weston, Allen
   See Norton, Andre

Wetcheek, J. L.
   See Feuchtwanger, Lion

Wetering, Janwillem van de
   See van de Wetering, Janwillem

Wetherell, Elizabeth
   See Warner, Susan (Bogert)

Willingham, Calder (Baynard, Jr.)
1922- .... **CLC 5, 51**
See also CA 5-8R; CANR 3; DLB 2, 44;
MTCW

Willis, Charles
See Clarke, Arthur C(harles)

Willy
See Colette, (Sidonie-Gabrielle)

Willy, Colette
See Colette, (Sidonie-Gabrielle)

Wilson, A(ndrew) N(orman) 1950- .. **CLC 33**
See also CA 112; 122; DLB 14

Wilson, Angus (Frank Johnstone)
1913-1991 .... **CLC 2, 3, 5, 25, 34**
See also CA 5-8R; 134; CANR 21; DLB 15;
MTCW

Wilson, August
1945- .. **CLC 39, 50, 63; BLC; DA; DC 2**
See also BW; CA 115; 122; CANR 42;
MTCW

Wilson, Brian 1942- .... **CLC 12**

Wilson, Colin 1931- .... **CLC 3, 14**
See also CA 1-4R; CAAS 5; CANR 1, 22,
33; DLB 14; MTCW

Wilson, Dirk
See Pohl, Frederik

Wilson, Edmund
1895-1972 .... **CLC 1, 2, 3, 8, 24**
See also CA 1-4R; 37-40R; CANR 1;
DLB 63; MTCW

Wilson, Ethel Davis (Bryant)
1888(?)-1980 .... **CLC 13**
See also CA 102; DLB 68; MTCW

Wilson, John 1785-1854......... **NCLC 5**

Wilson, John (Anthony) Burgess 1917-1993
See Burgess, Anthony
See also CA 1-4R; 143; CANR 2; MTCW

Wilson, Lanford 1937-....... **CLC 7, 14, 36**
See also CA 17-20R; CABS 3; DLB 7

Wilson, Robert M. 1944-........ **CLC 7, 9**
See also CA 49-52; CANR 2, 41; MTCW

Wilson, Robert McLiam 1964- ..... **CLC 59**
See also CA 132

Wilson, Sloan 1920-.............. **CLC 32**
See also CA 1-4R; CANR 1

Wilson, Snoo 1948-............... **CLC 33**
See also CA 69-72

Wilson, William S(mith) 1932- ..... **CLC 49**
See also CA 81-84

Winchilsea, Anne (Kingsmill) Finch Counte
1661-1720 .... **LC 3**

Windham, Basil
See Wodehouse, P(elham) G(renville)

Wingrove, David (John) 1954-...... **CLC 68**
See also CA 133

Winters, Janet Lewis .... **CLC 41**
See also Lewis, Janet
See also DLBY 87

Winters, (Arthur) Yvor
1900-1968 .... **CLC 4, 8, 32**
See also CA 11-12; 25-28R; CAP 1;
DLB 48; MTCW

Winterson, Jeanette 1959-......... **CLC 64**
See also CA 136

Wiseman, Frederick 1930-........ **CLC 20**

Wister, Owen 1860-1938 .... **TCLC 21**
See also CA 108; DLB 9, 78; SATA 62

Witkacy
See Witkiewicz, Stanislaw Ignacy

Witkiewicz, Stanislaw Ignacy
1885-1939 .... **TCLC 8**
See also CA 105

Wittig, Monique 1935(?)-......... **CLC 22**
See also CA 116; 135; DLB 83

Wittlin, Jozef 1896-1976 .... **CLC 25**
See also CA 49-52; 65-68; CANR 3

Wodehouse, P(elham) G(renville)
1881-1975 ... **CLC 1, 2, 5, 10, 22; SSC 2**
See also AITN 2; CA 45-48; 57-60;
CANR 3, 33; CDBLB 1914-1945;
DLB 34; MTCW; SATA 22

Woiwode, L.
See Woiwode, Larry (Alfred)

Woiwode, Larry (Alfred) 1941-... **CLC 6, 10**
See also CA 73-76; CANR 16; DLB 6

Wojciechowska, Maia (Teresa)
1927- .... **CLC 26**
See also AAYA 8; CA 9-12R; CANR 4, 41;
CLR 1; JRDA; MAICYA; SAAS 1;
SATA 1, 28

Wolf, Christa 1929- .... **CLC 14, 29, 58**
See also CA 85-88; DLB 75; MTCW

Wolfe, Gene (Rodman) 1931-....... **CLC 25**
See also CA 57-60; CAAS 9; CANR 6, 32;
DLB 8

Wolfe, George C. 1954-........... **CLC 49**

Wolfe, Thomas (Clayton)
1900-1938 ... **TCLC 4, 13, 29; DA; WLC**
See also CA 104; 132; CDALB 1929-1941;
DLB 9, 102; DLBD 2; DLBY 85; MTCW

Wolfe, Thomas Kennerly, Jr. 1931-
See Wolfe, Tom
See also CA 13-16R; CANR 9, 33; MTCW

Wolfe, Tom .... **CLC 1, 2, 9, 15, 35, 51**
See also Wolfe, Thomas Kennerly, Jr.
See also AAYA 8; AITN 2; BEST 89:1

Wolff, Geoffrey (Ansell) 1937- ..... **CLC 41**
See also CA 29-32R; CANR 29, 43

Wolff, Sonia
See Levitin, Sonia (Wolff)

Wolff, Tobias (Jonathan Ansell)
1945- .... **CLC 39, 64**
See also BEST 90:2; CA 114; 117; DLB 130

Wolfram von Eschenbach
c. 1170-c. 1220 .... **CMLC 5**

Wolitzer, Hilma 1930-........... **CLC 17**
See also CA 65-68; CANR 18, 40; SATA 31

Wollstonecraft, Mary 1759-1797...... **LC 5**
See also CDBLB 1789-1832; DLB 39, 104

Wonder, Stevie .... **CLC 12**
See also Morris, Steveland Judkins

Wong, Jade Snow 1922-........... **CLC 17**
See also CA 109

Woodcott, Keith
See Brunner, John (Kilian Houston)

Woodruff, Robert W.
See Mencken, H(enry) L(ouis)

Woolf, (Adeline) Virginia
1882-1941 ...... **TCLC 1, 5, 20, 43; DA;
SSC 7; WLC**
See also CA 104; 130; CDBLB 1914-1945;
DLB 36, 100; DLBD 10; MTCW

Woollcott, Alexander (Humphreys)
1887-1943 .... **TCLC 5**
See also CA 105; DLB 29

Woolrich, Cornell 1903-1968....... **CLC 77**
See also Hopley-Woolrich, Cornell George

Wordsworth, Dorothy
1771-1855 .... **NCLC 25**
See also DLB 107

Wordsworth, William
1770-1850 .... **NCLC 12, 38; DA; PC 4;
WLC**
See also CDBLB 1789-1832; DLB 93, 107

Wouk, Herman 1915-......... **CLC 1, 9, 38**
See also CA 5-8R; CANR 6, 33; DLBY 82;
MTCW

Wright, Charles (Penzel, Jr.)
1935- .... **CLC 6, 13, 28**
See also CA 29-32R; CAAS 7; CANR 23,
36; DLBY 82; MTCW

Wright, Charles Stevenson
1932- .... **CLC 49; BLC 3**
See also BW; CA 9-12R; CANR 26;
DLB 33

Wright, Jack R.
See Harris, Mark

Wright, James (Arlington)
1927-1980 .... **CLC 3, 5, 10, 28**
See also AITN 2; CA 49-52; 97-100;
CANR 4, 34; DLB 5; MTCW

Wright, Judith (Arandell)
1915- .... **CLC 11, 53**
See also CA 13-16R; CANR 31; MTCW;
SATA 14

Wright, L(aurali) R. 1939-........ **CLC 44**
See also CA 138

Wright, Richard (Nathaniel)
1908-1960 .... **CLC 1, 3, 4, 9, 14, 21, 48,
74; BLC; DA; SSC 2; WLC**
See also AAYA 5; BW; CA 108;
CDALB 1929-1941; DLB 76, 102;
DLBD 2; MTCW

Wright, Richard B(ruce) 1937- ...... **CLC 6**
See also CA 85-88; DLB 53

Wright, Rick 1945-............... **CLC 35**
See also Pink Floyd

Wright, Rowland
See Wells, Carolyn

Wright, Stephen 1946-............ **CLC 33**

Wright, Willard Huntington 1888-1939
See Van Dine, S. S.
See also CA 115

Wright, William 1930-............ **CLC 44**
See also CA 53-56; CANR 7, 23

Wu Ch'eng-en 1500(?)-1582(?)........ **LC 7**

Wu Ching-tzu 1701-1754 .... **LC 2**

Wurlitzer, Rudolph 1938(?)- ... **CLC 2, 4, 15**
See also CA 85-88

Wycherley, William 1641-1715 .... **LC 8, 21**
See also CDBLB 1660-1789; DLB 80

Literary Criticism Series
Cumulative Topic Index

This index lists all topic entries in the Gale Literary Criticism Series *Classical and Medieval Literature Criticism, Contemporary Literary Criticism, Literature Criticism from 1400 to 1800, Nineteenth-Century Literature Criticism,* and *Twentieth-Century Literary Criticism.*

Topic Index

European Romanticism NCLC 36: 149-284
  definitions, 149-77
  origins of the movement, 177-82
  Romantic theory, 182-200
  themes and techniques, 200-23
  Romanticism in Germany, 223-39
  Romanticism in France, 240-61
  Romanticism in Italy, 261-64
  Romanticism in Spain, 264-68
  impact and legacy, 268-82

Existentialism and Literature TCLC 42: 197-268
  overviews and definitions, 198-209
  history and influences, 209-19
  Existentialism critiqued and defended, 220-35
  philosophical and religious perspectives, 235-41
  Existentialist fiction and drama, 241-67

Feminism in the 1990s: Commentary on Works by Naomi Wolf, Susan Faludi, and Camille Paglia CLC 76: 377-415

Feminist Criticism in 1990 CLC 65: 312-60

Fifteenth-Century English Literature LC 17: 248-334
  background, 249-72
  poetry, 272-315
  drama, 315-23
  prose, 323-33

Film and Literature TCLC 38: 97-226
  overviews, 97-119
  film and theater, 119-34
  film and the novel, 134-45
  the art of the screenplay, 145-66
  genre literature/genre film, 167-79
  the writer and the film industry, 179-90
  authors on film adaptations of their works, 190-200
  fiction into film: comparative essays, 200-23

French Enlightenment LC 14: 81-145
  the question of definition, 82-9
  Le siècle des lumières, 89-94
  women and the salons, 94-105
  censorship, 105-15
  the philosophy of reason, 115-31
  influence and legacy, 131-44

French Revolution and English Literature NCLC 40: 96-195
  history and theory 96-123
  romantic poetry 123-50
  the novel 150-81
  drama 181-92
  children's literature 192-95

Futurism, Italian TCLC 42: 269-354
  principles and formative influences, 271-79
  manifestos, 279-88
  literature, 288-303
  theater, 303-19
  art, 320-30
  music, 330-36
  architecture, 336-39
  and politics, 339-46
  reputation and significance, 346-51

Gaelic Revival
  See **Irish Literary Renaissance**

Gates, Henry Louis, Jr., and African-American Literary Criticism CLC 65: 361-405

Gay and Lesbian Literature CLC 76: 416-39

German Exile Literature TCLC 30: 1-58
  the writer and the Nazi state, 1-10
  definition of, 10-14
  life in exile, 14-32
  surveys, 32-50
  Austrian literature in exile, 50-2
  German publishing in the United States, 52-7

German Expressionism TCLC 34: 74-160
  history and major figures, 76-85
  aesthetic theories, 85-109
  drama, 109-26
  poetry, 126-38
  film, 138-42
  painting, 142-47
  music, 147-53
  and politics, 153-58

***Glasnost* and Contemporary Soviet Literature** CLC 59: 355-97

Gothic Novel NCLC 28: 328-402
  development and major works, 328-34
  definitions, 334-50
  themes and techniques, 350-78
  in America, 378-85
  in Scotland, 385-91

influence and legacy, 391-400

Harlem Renaissance TCLC 26: 49-125
  principal issues and figures, 50-67
  the literature and its audience, 67-74
  theme and technique in poetry, fiction, and drama, 74-115
  and American society, 115-21
  achievement and influence, 121-22

Havel, Václav, Playwright and President CLC 65: 406-63

Holocaust, Literature of the TCLC 42: 355-450
  historical overview, 357-61
  critical overview, 361-70
  diaries and memoirs, 370-95
  novels and short stories, 395-425
  poetry, 425-41
  drama, 441-48

Hungarian Literature of the Twentieth Century TCLC 26: 126-88
  surveys of, 126-47
  Nyugat and early twentieth-century literature, 147-56
  mid-century literature, 156-68
  and politics, 168-78
  since the 1956 revolt, 178-87

Indian Literature in English TCLC 54: 308-406
  overview, 309-13
  origins and major figures, 313-25
  the Indo-English novel, 325-55
  Indo-English poetry, 355-67
  Indo-English drama, 367-72
  critical perspectives on Indo-English literature, 372-80
  modern Indo-English literature, 380-89
  Indo-English authors on their work, 389-404

Irish Literary Renaissance TCLC 46: 172-287
  overview, 173-83
  development and major figures, 184-202
  influence of Irish folklore and mythology, 202-22
  Irish poetry, 222-34
  Irish drama and the Abbey Theatre, 234-56
  Irish fiction, 256-86

Irish Nationalism and Literature NCLC 44: 203-273
  the Celtic element in literature, 203-19

TCLC Cumulative Nationality Index

Nationality Index

ISBN 0-8103-2432-6